Lecture Notes in Computer Science 5857

Commenced Publication in 1973
Founding and Former Series Editors:
Gerhard Goos, Juris Hartmanis, and Jan van Leeuwen

Halimah Badioze Zaman   Peter Robinson
Maria Petrou   Patrick Olivier
Heiko Schröder   Timothy K. Shih (Eds.)

Visual Informatics: Bridging Research and Practice

First International Visual Informatics Conference, IVIC 2009
Kuala Lumpur, Malaysia, November 11-13, 2009
Proceedings

 Springer

Volume Editors

Halimah Badioze Zaman
Universiti Kebangsaan Malaysia, Bangi, Malaysia
E-mail: hbz@ftsm.ukm.my

Peter Robinson
University of Cambridge, Cambridge, UK
E-mail: pr10@cam.ac.uk

Maria Petrou
Imperial College, London, UK
E-mail: maria.petrou@imperial.ac.uk

Patrick Olivier
Newcastle University, Newcastle upon Tyne, UK
E-mail: p.l.olivier@ncl.ac.uk

Heiko Schröder
RMIT University, Melbourne, Australia
E-mail: heiko.schroder@rmit.edu.au

Timothy K. Shih
Asia University, Wufeng, Taiwan
E-mail: timothyshih@gmail.com

Library of Congress Control Number: 2009936303

CR Subject Classification (1998): I.4, I.5, I.2.10, I.3.5, I.3.7, I.7.5, F.2.2

LNCS Sublibrary: SL 6 – Image Processing, Computer Vision, Pattern Recognition,
and Graphics

ISSN   0302-9743
ISBN-10   3-642-05035-2 Springer Berlin Heidelberg New York
ISBN-13   978-3-642-05035-0 Springer Berlin Heidelberg New York

springer.com

© Springer-Verlag Berlin Heidelberg 2009
Printed in Germany

Typesetting: Camera-ready by author, data conversion by Scientific Publishing Services, Chennai, India
Printed on acid-free paper   SPIN: 12777617   06/3180   5 4 3 2 1 0

Preface

Visual informatics is a field of interest not just among the information technology and computer science community, but also other related fields such as engineering, medical and health informatics and education starting in the early 1990s. Recently, the field is gaining more attention from researchers and industry. It has become a multi-disciplinary and trans-disciplinary field related to research areas such as computer vision, visualization, information visualization, real-time image processing, medical image processing, image information retrieval, virtual reality, augmented reality, expressive visual mathematics, 3D graphics, multimedia-fusion, visual data mining, visual ontology, as well as services and visual culture. Various efforts has been invested in different research, but operationally, many of these systems are not prominent in the mass market and thus knowledge and research on these phenomena within the mentioned areas need to be shared and disseminated.

It is for this reason that the Visual Informatics Research Group from Universiti Kebangsaan Malaysia (UKM) decided to spearhead this initiative to bring together experts in this very diversified but important research area so that more concerted efforts can be undertaken not just within the visual informatics community in Malaysia but from other parts of the world, namely, Asia, Europe, Oceania, and USA. This first International Visual Informatics Conference (IVIC 2009) was conducted collaboratively, by the visual informatics research community from the various public and private institutions of higher learning in Malaysia, and hosted by UKM. This conference is expected to be undertaken annually. This time the conference was co-sponsored by the Malaysia Information Technology Society (MITS), Malaysia Development Corporation (MDeC), and the Malaysian Research Educational Network (MyREN). The conference was co-chaired by six professors from four different countries (one from the host country, Malaysia; three from the UK; one from Australia and one from Taiwan).

The theme of the symposium," Visual Informatics Synergies : Bridging Research and Practice," reflects the importance of integrating the epistemology and the ontology of the fields involved, in order that all the research undertaken will be applicable for societies all over the world. It also portrayed the shared belief of the organizers that visual informatics is fast becoming an important research area in domains such as computer science, information technology, engineering, medical informatics and education. The visual culture is already taking over a lot of the activities in society and it is expected that very soon even serious reports will be in graphics and visualization especially large datasets in industries. The symposium focused on four key tracks: Visual Technologies and Systems, Virtual Environment, Visualization and Engineering Systems and Visual Culture, Services and Society.

The conference commenced for two days (11 and 12 November 2009) and ended with a one-day workshop (13 November 2009). There were five invited keynote papers and 80 research paper presentations. Presentations were based on topics covered by the four main tracks mentioned earlier. The reviewing of the papers was carried out by reviewers (who were represented by a 70-member Program Committee) composed of experts and researchers from Asia, Europe, USA and Oceania within the four key areas. The rejection rate of the papers was 62%. The reviewing process was managed using an electronic conference management system, OCMS, sponsored by Universiti Utara Malaysia (UUM).

On behalf of the Organizing and Program Committees of IVIC 2009, we thank all authors for their submissions and camera-ready copies of papers, and all participants for their thought-provoking ideas and active participation in the conference. We also thank the Vice Chancellor and the Dean of IT from UKM (the host university), and Vice Chancellors and Deans from all IT faculties of the IHLs for their support in organizing this conference. We also acknowledge the sponsors, members of the Organizing Committees, Program Committee members, support committees and individuals who gave their continuous help and support in making the conference a success. We fervently believe that IVIC will grow from strength to strength and will one day travel to different host countries in Asia, Europe, USA and Oceania. It will continue to provide a stimulating and enriching platform for innovative ideas, to enable the visual informatics community to design and develop systems and services that will transcend cultures, races, beliefs, and religions to create world citizens who are knowledgeable, tolerant, and understanding, in order to create 'one world' that is colorful, harmonious and peaceful for many generations to come.

November 2009

Halimah Badioze Zaman
Peter Robinson
Maria Petrou
Patrick Olivier
Heiko Schröder
Timothy K. Shih

Organization

The first International Visual Informatics Conference (IVIC 2009) was organized by the Visual Informatics Research Group, Universiti Kebangsaan Malaysia, in collaboration with ten local public and private universities in Malaysia, the Malaysian Information Technology Society (MITS), the Multimedia Development Corporation (MDeC), the Malaysian Institute of Microelectronic Systems (MIMOS) and the Malaysian Research Educational Network (MYREN).

Local Executive Committee

General Chair	Halimah Badioze Zaman (UKM)
Deputy Chair	Tengku Mohd Tengku Sembok (UPNM)
Secretary	Azlina Ahmad (UKM)
Assistant Secretary	Wan Fatimah Wan Ahmad (UTP)
Treasurer	Haslina Arshad (UKM)
Assistant Treasurer	Rabiah Abdul Kadir (UPM)
Workshops	Riza Sulaiman (UKM)
	Noor Faezah Mohd Yatim (UKM)

Program Committee

Program Co-chairs
Halimah Badioze Zaman (Universiti Kebangsaan Malaysia)
Peter Robinson (Cambridge University, UK)
Maria Petrou (Imperial College, London, UK)
Patrick Olivier (Newcastle University Upon-Tyne, UK)
Heiko Schroder (RMIT University, Australia
Timothy Shih (Asia University, Taiwan)

Members/Referees

Asia and Oceania	Europe	USA
Heiko Schroder	Maria Petrou	Hshinchun Chen
Jianzhong Li	Andreas Rauber	Edward E. Fox
Li-Zhu Zhou	Andre Ivanov	Carl K. Chang
Jian Zhong Li	James R. Parker	Aditya Mathur
T.H.Tse	Marc Nanard	Dick Simmons
Christopher C. Yang	Rolf Drechler	Eric Wong
Wai Lam	Erich Klink	Paul R. Croll
Sharlini R. Urs	Norbert Fuhr	Vicky Markstein

T.B. Rajashekar

K.S.Raghavan

Ning Zhong

Masatoshi Yoshikawa

Doonkyoo Shin

Hang Bong Kang

Sung Hyung Maeng

Ji-Hun Kang

Mun-Kew Leong

Hwee Hua Pang

Timothy Shih

Yin-Leng Theng

Abdus Sattar Chaudhry

Suliman Hawamdeh

Wee-Keong Ng

Tengku Mohd T. Sembok

Halimah Badioze Zaman

Zailani Mohd Nordin

Lai Jian Ming

Faieza Abdul Aziz

Zainul Abidin

Zaipatimah Ali

Abdul Razak Hamdan

Azizah Jaafar

Nazlia Omar

Fatimah Dato' Ahmad

Zainab Abu Bakar

Azlina Ahmad

Syed Nasir Alsagof

Haslina Arshad

Nor Faezah M. Yatim

M. Iqbal Bin Saripan

Norshariah Abdul Wahab

Choo Wou Onn

Nursuriati Jamil

Riza Sulaiman

Wan Fatimah Wan Ahmad

Dzulkifli Mohamad

Rabiah Abd Kadir

Norshuhada Siratuddin

Thomas Baker

Erich Neuhold

Yannis Ionnidis

Alan Smeaton

Carol Peters

Donatella Castelli

Jonathon Furner

Mike Papazoglau

Kinshuk

Ian Witten

Sergio Velastin

Ingeborg Solvberg

Roy Sterritt

Edie Rasmussen

Jose Borbinha

Peter Kokol

Traugott Koch

Denis L. Baggi

Keith van Rjsbergen

Gibinda Chowdhu

Harold Timbleby

Ann Blandford

Peter Robinson

Patrick Olivier

Micheal H. Hinchey

Josep Torellas

Archan Misra

James Hughes

Joseph Urban

Per-Ake (Paul)Larson

Juan Antonio Carballo

Jie-Wu

Jen-Yao Chung

Reggie Caudill

Bryon Purves

Phillip C-Y Sheu

David A. Bader

Wei Zhao

Anup Kumar

Hanspeter Pfister

Asim Smailagic

Alex Orailoglu

Hong Z. Tan

Narhum Gershon

Local Arrangements Committee

Technical Committee

Head	Halimah Badioze Zaman (UKM)
Members	Azlina Ahmad (UKM)
	Alwin Kumar Rathinam (UM)

Aidanismah Yahya (UKM)
Baharum Baharudin (UTP)
Bahari Belaton (USM)
Choo Wou Onn (UTAR)
Fatimah Dato' Ahmad (UPNM)
Dayang Rohaya Bt Awang Rambli (UTP)
Dzulkifli Mohamad (UTM)
Haslina Arshad (UKM)
Ho Chiung Ching (MMU)
M. Iqbal Bin Saripan (UPM)
Mohd Rawidean Kassim (MIMOS)
Mohd Ridzuan Affandi (MDeC)
Naimah Mohd Hussin (UiTM)
Nasiroh Omar (UiTM)
Nor Faezah Mohd Yatim (UKM)
Nor Laila Md Nor (UiTM)
Norshuhada Shiratuddin (UUM)
Norshahariah Wahab (UPNM)
Nurazzah Abd Rahman (UiTM)
Nursuriati Jamil (UiTM)
Rabiah Abdul Kadir (UPM)
Riza Sulaiman (UKM)
Shahrul Azman Mohd Noah (UKM)
Syamsul Bahrin Zaibon (UUM)
Sim Kok Swee (MMU)
Siti Mariyam Shamsuddin (UTM)
Suhaidi Hassan (UUM)
Syed Nasir Syed Alsagof (UPNM)
Tengku Mohd Tengku Sembok (UPNM)
Wan Fatimah Wan Ahmad (UTP)
Zainal Arif Abdul Rahman (UM)

Publicity Head	Norshuhada Shiratuddin (UUM)
Members	Halimah Badioze Zaman (UKM)
	Azlina Ahmad (UKM)
	Syamsul Bahrin Zaibon (UUM)
	Zainal Arif Abdul Rahman (UM)
	Bahari Belaton (USM)
	Shahruln Azman Mohd Noah (UKM)
	Sim Kok Swee (MMU)
	Nursuriati Jamil (UiTM)
	M. Iqbal Bin Saripan (UPM)
	Dzulkifli Mohamad (UTM)
	Fatimah Dato' Ahmad (UPNM)
	Dayang Rohaya Bt Awang Rambli (UTP)
	Suhaidi Hassan (UUM)
	Choo Wou Onn (UTAR)

Logistic Head	Syed Nasir Alsagof (UPNM)
Members	Riza Sulaiman (UKM)
	Nor Faezah Mohd Yatim (UKM)
	Ho Chiung Ching (MMU)
	Nor Laila Md Nor (UiTM)
	Naimah Mohd Hussin (UiTM)
	Nasiroh Omar (UiTM)
	Nurazzah Abd Rahman (UiTM)
	Nursuriati Jamil (UiTM)
	Norshahariah Wahab (UPNM)
	Choo Wou Onn (UTAR)
Web Portal Head	Riza Sulaiman (UKM)
Members	Halimah Badioze Zaman (UKM)
	Azlina Ahmad (UKM)
	Syamsul Bahrin Zaibon (UUM)
	Norshuhada Shiratuddin (UUM)
	Nurdiyana Mohd Yassin (UKM)
Financial Head	Tengku Mohd Tengku Sembok (UPNM)
Members	Halimah Badioze Zaman (UKM)
	Azlina Ahmad (UKM)
	Wan Fatimah Wan Ahmad (UTP)
	Zainal Arif Abdul Rahman (UM)
	Mohd Ridzuan Affandi (MDeC)
	Mohd Rawidean Kassim (MIMOS)
Food Committee Head	Haslina Arshad (UKM)
Members	Rabiah Abdul Kadir (UPM)
	Norshahariah Wahab (UPNM)
	Nor Faezah Mohd Yatim (UKM)
	Dayang Rohaya Bt Awang Rambli (UTP)

Online Conference Management System (OCMS)

Universiti Utara Malaysia

Sponsoring Institutions

Universiti Kebangsaan Malaysia (UKM)
University Malaya (UM)
University Teknologi PETRONAS (UTP)
Universiti Utara Malaysia (UUM)
Universiti Sains Malaysia (USM)

Universiti Putra Malaysia (UPM)
Universiti Teknologi Malaysia (UTM)
Universiti Teknologi MARA (UiTM)
Universiti Malaysia Sarawak (UNIMAS)
Universiti Pertahanan Nasional Malaysia (UPNM)
Universiti Tunku Abdul Rahman (UTAR)
Multimedia University (MMU)
Malaysian Information Technology Society (MITS)
Multimedia Corporation Malaysia (MDeC)
Malaysian Research Educational Network (MyREN)
Malaysian Institute of Microelectronics (MIMOS)

Table of Contents

Keynotes

Virtual Technologies and Systems

Virtual Environment

Visualization, Engineering and Simulation

Visual Culture, Services and Society

Detecting Emotions from Connected Action Sequences

Daniel Bernhardt and Peter Robinson

Computer Laboratory, University of Cambridge, UK
`firstname.lastname@cl.cam.ac.uk`

Abstract. In this paper we deal with the problem of detecting emotions from the body movements produced by naturally connected action sequences. Although action sequences are one of the most common forms of body motions in everyday scenarios their potential for emotion recognition has not been explored in the past. We show that there are fundamental differences between actions recorded in isolation and in natural sequences and demonstrate a number of techniques which allow us to correctly label action sequences with one of four emotions up to 86% of the time. Our results bring us an important step closer to recognizing emotions from body movements in natural scenarios.

1 Introduction

Inferring emotions from human body motion in natural environments can be very difficult as body movements are virtually unconstrained. This makes it difficult to train emotion recognisers which are robust enough to tolerate this kind of real-world variability while still picking up subtle emotion-communicating cues. In this paper we describe an approach to recognising emotions from natural action sequences. We refer to these sequences as connected actions.

The first contribution of this work is the description of an end-to-end system which is able to detect emotions from connected action sequences. In order to perform emotion recognition effectively, we first need to build a solid understanding about the underlying constraints of human movements. We show that an increased refinement of action models can boost our ability to recognise the emotions communicated through connected actions.

Secondly, we highlight the differences between actions recorded in isolation and as naturally connected sequences. Although obtaining and working with isolated data is often easier, we show that results achieved on isolated data are not necessarily transferable to cases where actions appear in connected sequences. In order to bridge the gap between the two, we describe ways to adapt isolated models to the connected cases. As a result we hope to bring emotion recognition one step closer to naturally-occurring scenarios.

2 Background

Human action and activity recognition has been studied extensively in the past with connection to unusual event detection, crime prevention and the like. In those cases it is

H. Badioze Zaman et al. (Eds.): IVIC 2009, LNCS 5857, pp. 1–11, 2009.

the action itself which is the focus of the recognition effort. Actions, however, can also provide a valuable context for emotion recognition in natural environments. Imagine yourself as a human judge faced with an impoverished video recording of a human subject. The subject you are watching is stretching the right arm backwards and moving it forcefully forwards again. If this subject is involved in a conversation with another person, you might interpret the movement as communicating a hostile stance. If the person, however, was moving a piece of paper this movement can be easily interpreted as a throwing action. Only if the movements were extremely forceful would we be likely to associate the motion itself with an aggressive emotion. This example illustrates that our emotional interpretation of human body motion is based on our understanding of the action which is being performed.

This is the problem pattern recognition algorithms face when classifying emotional content from body movements. Algorithms which have no prior model of movement patterns are likely to register large differences between examples of the same emotion category but in very different actions such as running, walking and knocking. Clearly, this extreme kind of variation will render any attempt to discover the underlying patterns due to emotional changes extremely difficult. In this paper we therefore use explicit models of action patterns to aid emotion classification.

In some cases authors discussing the recognition of emotions from body movements manage to side-step the above problem by only considering one type of action such as knocking [2] or a prescribed arm lowering action [3]. In other cases researchers have focused on stylised body motions. Those are motions which usually arise from laboratory settings where subjects are instructed to act an emotion freely without any constraints. Authors of those studies often find that under those circumstances subjects produce stereotypical expressions [1, 4]. These produce strong patterns which are easier to detect with statistical pattern classification techniques.

In many ways the analysis of connected actions is similar to that of connected speech. Indeed, emotion recognition from speech has been a prominent problem since the early days of affective computing. Many different sets of low level acoustic features have been proposed over the years to capture emotional information in recorded speech. However, one recent study by Lee and Narayanan suggests that major improvements in emotion discrimination can in fact be achieved by making the recognition algorithms aware of higher level lexical and discourse structure [5]. Our work builds on these results by adding structural knowledge about common action patterns to the emotion recognition framework.

Our motion data comes from a motion-captured corpus of actions recorded at the Psychology Department, University of Glasgow [6]. It contains samples of knocking, throwing, lifting and walking actions recorded both in isolation and as naturally connected sequences. 15 male and 15 female untrained subjects were recruited and actions recorded in 4 emotional styles: neutral, happy, angry and sad. For the performance of isolated actions subjects were instructed fairly carefully, e.g. which hands to use for actions and how far to stand from certain props. Connected actions were naturally less constrained.

3 System Overview

Our goal is to classify each of the action sequences in our corpus into one of the four emotion classes. Note that we do not in general know the order of actions that make up a sequence, nor do we know where the action boundaries are. We will present a solution to this segmentation problem in Section 4.2. Currently all our system assumes is that it knows, and has models for, each of the action categories and emotions it could be faced with. We describe in detail how we build those models in Sections 4 & 5.

Importantly, both the action and emotion models are initially trained on isolated samples. In other domains such as speech recognition it is often be- lieved that models need to be trained on data stemming directly from connected samples [8]. Within the scope of this research, our decision to initially base our models on isolated data has a number of advantages:

1. A number of systems that analyse isolated actions have been built and discussed in the past [2, 3].We are building on their insights to derive our action and emotion models.
2. Starting out with isolated models allows us to evaluate their performance for connected actions. We will discuss how isolated models can be adapted to perform better on connected actions. The gained insights are very illuminating in understanding the differences between emotions expressed through isolated and connected actions.

Our recognition framework works as follows. Given a set of action categories $\mathcal{A}$ (e.g. $\mathcal{A}$ = {knocking, throwing, lifting,walking}) and emotion classes $\mathcal{E}$ (e.g. $\mathcal{E}$ = {neutral, happy, angry, sad}), we classify an action sequence $S = (s_1, s_2,...,s_n)$ with $s_i \in \mathcal{A}$ as an emotion $e \in \mathcal{E}$ as follows:

1. Train a set of action models $\Lambda = \{\lambda_a\}$ on samples of isolated actions.

2. Train emotion models $M_{a,\mathcal{E}}$ on isolated samples of action category a and emotion set $\mathcal{E}$.

3. Adapt Λ and $M_{a,\mathcal{E}}$ to the patterns observed in connected actions yielding the adapted models $\hat{\Lambda}$ and $\hat{M}_{a,\mathcal{E}}$

4. Segment S into its component actions $(s_1, s_2,...,s_n)$ using $\hat{\Lambda}$.

5. For each $s_i \in S$, find the most likely emotion class e_i using $\hat{M}_{a,\mathcal{E}}$.

6. Combine $(e_1, e_2,...,e_n)$ into an overall emotion class e for the whole sequence.

Note that we explicitly model the difference of emotional appearance in different actions by training emotion models $M_{a,\mathcal{E}}$ dependent on both emotions and action. This allows us to deal with the cases introduced in our initial example. In the next sections we discuss how we define Λ and $M_{a,\mathcal{E}}$ and how to adapt them to $\hat{\Lambda}$ and $\hat{M}_{a,\mathcal{E}}$ respectively.

4   Action Analysis

In the absence of any context information, isolated actions are defined and identified by the spatio-temporal trajectories of body joints. Formally, we represent an action category a as a set of joints and a description of their movements over time λ_a. We are using Hidden Markov Models (HMMs) to solve the isolated action recognition problem. HMMs have been applied successfully to this kind of temporal pattern recognition problem in the past [8] and we are able to draw on an extensive body of knowledge documenting their use.

HMMs are particularly suitable for modeling temporally evolving systems which produce observable outputs. At each discrete point in time, the system can be in one of a finite number of hidden states. The transitions between states over time are governed by a matrix A of transition probabilities. At every time frame the system outputs an observation vector. The probability of observing a particular output is conditioned only on the current hidden state. Because joint movements exhibit complex trajectories in position and speed we model the system's output as a vector of continuous observation variables, parameterized by the mean and standard deviation of a normal distribution. The observation densities are represented in two matrices O_m and O_s capturing the mean and standard deviation of the observation variables in each state.

4.1   Model Parameters

The essence of an action is its pattern of posture and movement changes over time. We are therefore using the following quantities as our HMM observation variables.
– global body speed
– body-local joint positions
– body-local joint speeds
– body twist (angle between shoulder-shoulder and hip-hip vectors).

These quantities are easy to calculate from the 3D joint position data available directly from the motion capture corpus. Body-local measures are derived by a simple transform placing a coordinate system at the pelvis joint of the subject. This gives us a representation invariant to absolute body position and orientation. The transition matrices for each action model impose a left-to-right structure, thus strictly enforcing a traversal from the first to the last hidden state. The only complication arises for walking motions. They are cyclic in nature and therefore the action model for walking allows a transition from the last back to the first hidden state. The HMM parameters A and (O_m, O_s) are estimated from the isolated action samples using the standard Baum-Welsh algorithm [8]. The number of hidden states for each model was chosen empirically and is in each case less than 10.

4.2   Parsing Connected Actions

We use the isolated action models to build a connected action recogniser. This problem is very similar to connected speech recognition from individual word models [8]. We can therefore make use of the extensive literature available on the subject.

One popular technique developed by Rabiner and Levinson to solve this problem is Level Building (LB) [7]. Given a sequence of observations it uses an efficient Dynamic Programming approach to find the most likely sequence of actions and according segmentation boundaries. This approach is very similar to the Viterbi algorithm which finds the most likely hidden state sequence of a single HMM given an observation sequence. Indeed, LB uses the Viterbi algorithm repeatedly at every level (see Rabiner and Levinson [7] for details). In order to be able to compare the segmentations achieved through LB to some ground truth, we also hand-segmented each of the sequences. We will make use of this manual segmentation in our evaluation in Section 6.

4.3 Isolated and Connected Action Differences

By playing back videos of our motion corpus, we quickly realised that actions did not appear the same in isolation and in connected sequences. Because many constraints were placed on the subjects for the isolated recordings, they tended to appear more controlled and uniform. In the connected case we observe actions blending into each other, making it hard to identify unique transition points between individual actions. Anticipatory effects were particularly strong. For example, isolated knocking actions uniformly started with a succinct arm lift before the knock. When knocking is preceded by a walking action, however, we can observe the arm lift to commence at various points during the walking action and long before the knock itself starts.

We were interested in finding quantitative evidence for the difference in appearance of isolated and connected actions. Here we focus on the amount of variation observed across different subjects and repetitions of the same action. For each action sample, we computed a set of features $\mathcal{F}$ capturing the temporal evolution of each joint as its mean and standard deviation in position, speed, acceleration and jerk. These quantities were shown by Bernhardt and Robinson in [2] to capture the static and dynamic qualities of body motions well. We then compute the sample standard deviations $\sigma_{I,f}$ and $\sigma_{C,f}$ over all isolated and connected action samples respectively. For every feature f, $\sigma_{I,f}$ and $\sigma_{C,f}$ tell us how much f varies across different instances of the same action. Finally, we partition $\mathcal{F}$ into $\mathcal{F}_C$ and $\mathcal{F}_I$ such that

$$f \in \mathcal{F}_C \Leftrightarrow \sigma_{C,f} > \sigma_{I,f} \tag{1}$$

$$f \in \mathcal{F}_I \Leftrightarrow \sigma_{C,f} \leq \sigma_{I,f} \tag{2}$$

That is, $\mathcal{F}_C$ contains the features which show relatively large variation across connected samples while the features in $\mathcal{F}_I$ show larger variation across isolated samples. Figure 1 shows $|\mathcal{F}_C|$ and $|\mathcal{F}_I|$ for every action category. If the isolated and connected cases had similar dynamic characteristics, we would expect each pair of bars to be of roughly the same height. We see, however, that only for lifting actions the variation is relatively similar in both cases. For all other actions, the dynamics differ

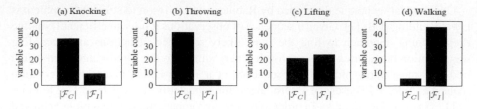

Fig. 1. Difference in variation between isolated and connected actions

substantially between isolated and connected cases. The observed differences in knocking, throwing and walking actions make it necessary to adapt the action models to the connected cases. It is important to note at this point that, although we discussed these dynamic differences in the light of action models, emotion recognition is likely to suffer similarly from these changes in appearance. We will see quantitative evidence for this in Section 6.

4.4 Adapting Action Models

The above differences make it necessary to adapt action models to the appearance of connected actions. We chose to adapt the models statistically using a small set of representative sequences S and an associated set of weak labels $\mathcal{L}$. By weak labels we refer to a sequence of action categories such as "knock, walk, lift, throw" as exhibited by the sequences but without any explicit action boundaries. We can then use a bootstrapping approach to iteratively refine the set of action models Λ as follows:

1. Start with an initial set of models $\hat{\Lambda}^0, i = 0$

2. Segment all sequences in S by LB using $\hat{\Lambda}^i$

3. Retrain a new set of models $\hat{\Lambda}^{i+1}$ using the action samples of sequences which agree with $\mathcal{L}$.

4. If the number of correctly segmented sequences increased $i = i + 1$, goto 2.

To start off the bootstrapping loop we initialise $\hat{\Lambda}^0$ to the isolated action models. Successive iterations then improve the model parameters based on the connected samples which were segmented correctly. For our data, we found that the bootstrapping iterations converge very quickly and we obtain a converged set of models after two iterations. While $\hat{\Lambda}^0$ only segmented 45% of S correctly, $\hat{\Lambda}^2$ improved this to 87%. Subsequent bootstrapping iterations decrease the number of correctly segmented sequences slightly.

5   Emotion Recognition

Our emotion recognition framework is based on Bernhardt and Robinson's framework for classifying isolated knocking motions [2]. We extend their approach by

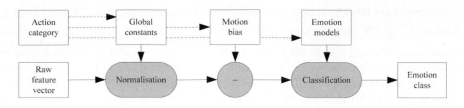

Fig. 2. Emotion recognition pipeline. Grey components denote operations performed on the data components shown in white.

training individual classifiers $M_{a,\mathcal{E}}$ for each supported action category a, thus allowing emotion recognition based on a variety of actions. From each action time series we extract a rich feature vector which captures the static and dynamic information of the action. The features include mean and standard deviations of posture, as well as joint speed, acceleration and jerk [2] calculated over the whole action. We then normalise each feature to ensure similar orders of magnitude for each feature dimension. This aids robust training for pattern recognition algorithms.

As the next step, we then subtract an individual movement bias. This extra normalisation step has been shown to remove a major source of confusion for the classification of emotions [2]. It accounts for the fact that different subjects tend to exhibit different motion idiosyncrasies, thus confounding the subtle dynamic differences between different emotions. The unbiased feature vector is then fed to a Support Vector Machine-based classifier $M_{a,\mathcal{E}}$ which classifies it into one of the emotions in the emotion set $\mathcal{E} = \{$neutral, happy, angry, sad$\}$. This classification pipeline is shown in Figure 2. The inputs shown at the top of the pipeline need to be calculated prior to a classifiction from representative training data. In detail, those are

1. the global normalisation constants calculated per action category
2. the personal motion bias constants calculated per action category and person
3. the emotion classifiers trained for each action category and on all emotion classes.

In order to find a unique emotion label for a sequence S we classify each component action s_i using the classifier $M_{s_i,\mathcal{E}}$. We treat each of the classification results from different component actions as independent evidence towards the overall emotion classification. Therefore, we arrive at a combined emotion class by taking a majority vote. Ties are resolved by assigning one of the candidate classes randomly.

5.1 Adapting Emotion Classifiers

In Section 4.3 we described in detail how the appearance of actions differs when we move from isolated to connected actions. As for our action models, our initial emotion classifiers $M_{a,\mathcal{E}}$ are trained on the appearance of emotions in isolated cases. We may, however, wish to adapt our classifiers to better capture the appearance of emotions in connected actions. A number of adaptation methods are possible, each varying in the associated cost. We will describe each of them here and evaluate their performance in Section 6.

Clearly, the cheapest adaptation method is to simply reuse the isolated emotion models $M_{a,\mathcal{E}}$. We would expect these models still to perform better than random as emotion appearances should not change so extremely as to render the isolated models entirely useless. At the other end of the scale lies a total retraining of the classifiers on connected action data. In essence, we need to recompute all three inputs to the classification pipeline listed in the previous section: global constants, personal bias and emotion classifiers. This is likely to give us the best results. These two extremes represent recalculating either none or all of the three inputs to the pipeline. Apart from these two extremes we explore two intermediate adaptation strategies: recalculating only the first or the first two inputs to the pipeline using the connected data. We call the derived models $\hat{M}^0{}_{a,\mathcal{E}}$, $\hat{M}^1{}_{a,\mathcal{E}}$, $\hat{M}^2{}_{a,\mathcal{E}}$ and $\hat{M}^3{}_{a,\mathcal{E}}$ according to how many inputs are recomputed.

6   Experimental Results

Having discussed approaches to adapt both action and emotion models from isolated to connected data, it is now time to evaluate how much difference these changes actually make on real data. To this end we conducted an experiment using the full set of data in our corpus. At a high level we treated the isolated actions as training data and evaluated our algorithms on the connected action sequences. We had around 4000 isolated action samples and 220 action sequences. The latter all followed the same order: walking, lifting, walking, knocking, walking, throwing. We ignored this knowledge, however, when segmenting the data. The sequence data was also used to adapt the action and emotion models as outlined in Sections 4.4 & 5.1. With a number of adaptation approaches in hand, we asked ourselves the following questions:

1. What recognition rates are achievable with our classification approach?
2. Are there evidence for differences in the expression of emotions through isolated and connected actions?
3. If so, which of the described adaptation schemes provide the best improvements?

To answer these questions our experiment measured the effects of two independent factors: level of adaptation of action models and level of adaptation of emotion classifiers. The dependent variable we measured in each case was the rate of correct emotion classifications for whole sequences. As cases for adapted action models, we considered the segmentations achieved after iterations 0, 1 and 2 of the bootstrapping algorithm presented in Section 4.4. Each of the iterations produced action models of increasing adaptation levels ranging from no adaptation for Λ^0 to good adaptation for Λ^2. As a gold-standard we also considered an ideal set of action models Λ^* which produces the segmentation we had produced manually. As cases for the emotion classifiers we considered $M^0{}_{a,\mathcal{E}}$ to $M^3{}_{a,\mathcal{E}}$. As for the action models, $M^0{}_{a,\mathcal{E}}$ represents no adaptation while $M^3{}_{a,\mathcal{E}}$ represents a gold-standard achieved by totally retraining the emotion models on the connected data. For the last condition we used 10-fold cross validation to prevent training and testing on the same samples.

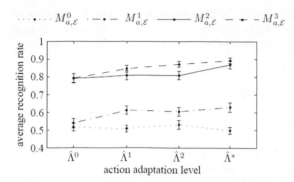

Fig. 3. Recognition rates for various levels of action and emotion model adaptation

Table 1. Average emotion recognition rates for whole action sequences for no adaptation (left) and good adaptation (right). Emotions appear in the order neutral, happy, angry, sad.

0.15	0.06	0.00	0.79	**0.88**	0.03	0.03	0.06
0.07	**0.47**	0.06	0.40	0.12	**0.75**	0.11	0.02
0.01	0.39	**0.47**	0.13	0.00	0.14	**0.86**	0.00
0.00	0.00	0.02	**0.98**	0.24	0.01	0.00	**0.75**
average rate: **0.52**				average rate: **0.81**			

In order to get the most comprehensive picture possible, we decided to adopt a factorial design. By investigating the cases in all possible combinations we get a set of 4×4 classification results. These results are visualised in Figure 3. Each line represents a series of results obtained for different action models Λ and for the same emotion classifier M . Because our voting algorithm resolves ties by making a random choice we also indicate the spread with error bars. As a general trend we observe that the recognition rate increases with the levels of adaptation. In Table 1 we provide the confusion matrices for the pair of unadapted models $(\hat{\Lambda}^0, \hat{M}^0{}_{a,\varepsilon})$ and for the combination of best-adapted models $(\hat{\Lambda}^2, \hat{M}^2{}_{a,\varepsilon})$ short of the gold-standard. The significant increase in recognition rate confirms our initial intuitions.

7 Discussion and Future Work

Our experimental results clearly show that using unadapted models trained on iso-lated data on connected samples produces suboptimal emotion recognition results. This is clear evidence that the appearance of actions change as we move from strictly controlled, isolated samples to more natural, connected sequences. As we have managed to show, this does not only impact the recognition of actions. Emotion recognition performance improves both as we adapt our action models and our emotion models. A change in the appearance of actions therefore degrades emotion recognition in two ways. Firstly, a change in appearance impedes our ability to recognise actions reliably which has a knock-on effect on emotion recognition as we choose the wrong emotion models $\hat{M}_{a,\mathcal{E}}$. Secondly, the change in movement dynamics as we move to connected actions means that our emotion models are simply not representative anymore.

We have shown that our adaptation approaches are effective. As we expected, the recognition rate achieved with unadapted models is significantly better than chance at 52%. This rate can be improved to 81%, however, by using our well- adapted models. Note that for the latter case we did not need to retrain the actual emotion classifiers, but the adaptation stemmed from appropriate preprocessing of the feature vectors. This means that we do not need connected motion sequences labeled by emotion. Using our gold-standard adaptations the sequences can be classified at a rate of 86%. It seems, however, that the adaptation step from $\hat{M}^1_{a,\mathcal{E}}$ to $\hat{M}^2_{a,\mathcal{E}}$ brings the biggest improvement. This suggests that there is no clear pattern with which individuals' behaviour changes when they go from isolated to connected action displays — we simply need to recompute the personal motion bias of connected actions. This highlights once more how important the modelling of individual differences is for the recognition of emotions from body motions — both for isolated [2] and connected actions.

On a larger scale we conclude that data collected under very constrained laboratory conditions is not necessarily representative of data occurring in more natural scenarios. Of course, our connected data was only recorded under laboratory conditions as well and it is therefore likely that truly natural data will show effects beyond of what we observed. Repeating this experiment on data collected in a natural environment will be an interesting goal for future research. Nevertheless we believe that we have taken an important step towards being able to deal with real-world scenarios. It is encouraging to note that although there are changes in appearance, methods previously developed for isolated data are in fact applicable to connected samples if they are adapted appropriately.

References

1. Balomenos, T., Raouzaiou, A., Ioannou, S., Drosopoulos, A.I., Karpouzis, K., Kollias, S.D.: Emotion analysis in man-machine interaction systems. In: Bengio, S., Bourlard, H. (eds.) MLMI 2004. LNCS, vol. 3361, pp. 318–328. Springer, Heidelberg (2005)
2. Bernhardt, D., Robinson, P.: Detecting Affect from Non-stylised Body Motions. In: Paiva, A.C.R., Prada, R., Picard, R.W. (eds.) ACII 2007. LNCS, vol. 4738, pp. 59–70. Springer, Heidelberg (2007)
3. Castellano, G., Villalba, S.D., Camurri, A.: Recognising humanemotions from body movement and gesture dynamics. In: Paiva, A.C.R., Prada, R., Picard, R.W. (eds.) ACII 2007. LNCS, vol. 4738, pp. 71–82. Springer, Heidelberg (2007)
4. Gunes, H., Piccardi, M.: Bi-modal emotion recognition from expressive face and body gestures. Journal of Network and Computer Applications 30(4), 1334–1345 (2007)

5. Lee, C.M., Narayanan, S.S.: Toward detecting emotions in spoken dialogs. IEEE Transactions on Speech and Audio Processing 13(2), 293–303 (2005)
6. Ma, Y., Paterson, H.M., Pollick, F.E.: A motion capture library for the study of identity, gender, and emotion perception from biological motion. Behavior Research Methods 38, 134–141 (2006)
7. Rabiner, L., Levinson, S.: A speaker-independent, syntax-directed, connected word recognition system based on hidden markov models and level building. IEEE Transactions on Acoustics, Speech and Signal Processing 33(3), 561–573 (1985)
8. Rabiner, L.: A tutorial on hidden markov models and selected applications in speech recognition. Proceedings of the IEEE 77(2), 257–286 (1989)

High Performance Computing for Visualisation and Image Analysis

Heiko Schröder

School of Computer Science & Information Technology,
RMIT University, Melbourne, Australia
`heiko@cs.rmit.edu.au`

Abstract. Visualisation of data is an area of increasing importance in a wide range of areas such as complex systems, simulation of large systems, seismic image analysis and medical applications. Image analysis has also increased in importance such as in automatic surveillance. In this presentation I will concentrate on techniques and applications I have been involved with or led. These are 1) The design of the PIPADS machine (Parallel Image Processing and Display System), which was designed to analyse and visualise seismic data as well as remote sensing data. 2) The design of a High Performance fault tolerant parallel computing system for the Singaporean satellite X-Sat, which is a remote sensing satellite equipped with a multi spectral camera. 3) The use of the CO-PACOBANA engine for computer tomography for the Australian Synchrotron, to produce a 10Kx10Kx4K 3D image out of 5K 10Kx4K projections. This engine has the additional particular feature that it is extremely energy efficient – a characteristic of increasing importance.

1 Introduction

High performance computing has evolved in a wide range of different flavours. Most popular in the form of supercomputers, which are typically seen as general purpose computers and the top500 list of supercomputers is based on how fast these computers can execute a range of programs called Linpack, which are mainly routines to solve linear algebra type of problems. The biggest amongst these are now computers with over 200K processors, consuming more than 2MWatt of power. Such machines are unnecessarily powerful to implement algorithms for visualisation and image processing.

Horst Gietl writes: "They are coming from a variety of areas, involving quantum mechanical physics, weather forecasting, climate research, molecular modeling (computing the structures and properties of chemical compounds, biological macromolecules, polymers, and crystals), physical simulations (such as simulation of airplanes in wind tunnels and research into nuclear fusion), cryptanalysis, and improved seismic processing for oil exploration for continued supply. For most of these applications detailed results may only be achieved with systems in the Petaflops range. And hopefully Exascale Systems will be seen first in 2019.

Such machines are unnecessarily powerful to implement algorithms for visualisation and image processing.

H. Badioze Zaman et al. (Eds.): IVIC 2009, LNCS 5857, pp. 12–21, 2009.

Horst Gietl also states: "A serious competitor for the multi-core CPU is represented by graphical processing units (GPUs), which are graphic cards used for scientific computing. There are four basic things about GPUs. They are fast and will get a lot faster. They are cheap, measured on a performance-per-dollar basis. They use less power than CPUs when compared on a performance-per-watt basis. But the fourth thing is their limitations. ... Nevertheless with the Supercomputer »Tsubame« from the institute of Technology in Tokyo we have the first system in the TOP500 list that is running »Tesla«-Graphics-Chip from Nvidia. The system-cluster consists of 170 Tesla-S1070-systems resulting in 170 Teraflops –theoretically. In practice the system reaches 77,48 Teraflops, which means number 29 in the ranking of the TOP500 list (November 2008) ... It is well-known fact that the energy consumption of HPC data centers will double in the next 4 to 5 years, if the current trend continues. A straight forward extrapolation for Exaflops systems shows that they will be somewhere in the range of hundreds of Mega-Watt." [17]

For visualisation and image analysis purposes we do not need a general purpose machine, as the data we are dealing with tends to be short operand integer data. Thus we can design special purpose ALUs (arithmetic logic unit) that cannot deal with floating point numbers and thus are much smaller, faster and much more energy efficient.

In the 1980s many of the special purpose high performance designs were based on the idea of systolic arrays [5, 6, 7]. A typical result of the research related to systolic arrays resulted in the Instruction Systolic Array that we "invented" in 1984, entered the market in 1995 and was finally sold out in 2001 [8]. Some of these ideas also entered the concept of the PIPADS machine that we designed from 1989 to 1994.

The PPU (Parallel Processing Unit) of the X-Sat satellite is a very different concept, as it is based on combining off the shelf micro processors with FPGAs (Field Programmable Gate Array). The FPGAs have as main task to establish the fault tolerance via a flexible connection scheme for the micro processors, all computation is happening in these micro processors (Strong Arm).

The Copacobana engine consists mainly of FPGAs and some additional memory. This allows a very high degree of flexibility in the use of this machine. While the first applications for this machine relate to braking encoded data, the FPGAs can be freely programmed to execute any kind of tasks. In the example of code braking the Copacobana can achieve a reduction of energy consumption of more than 3 orders of magnitude, compared to implemtations on PC clusters.

In the following Chapters I will introduce PIPADS, the X-Sat PPU and Copacobana together with some applications related to visualisation and image analysis.

2 PIPADS for Seismic Analysis and Remote Sensing

The then biggest mining company of Australia BHP co-funded a substantial research project from 1990 to 1994 with CSIRO (Phil Robertson), ADFA (Trevor Hobbs) and ANU (Heiko Schröder). Its predicted performance would have placed it well into the top500 supercomputer list at that time, but a business decision within BHP to totally leave projects that are not directly linked to mining prevented the final fabrication of the corresponding ASIC chips. The machine was designed and tailored towards concept of scan-line image processing [1, 2, 3, 4, 5]. In this paper Phil Robertson states:" A parallel approach to processing and viewing image surfaces is presented. The approach incorporates a parallel SIMD solution to the visibility or hidden-surface, problem for perspective views, visibility maps and shadowing of image surfaces. The algorithm presented belongs to a more general class of techniques based on successive application of one-dimensional scan-line operations, in row and column directions, to appropriate intermediate spatial transformations of images. Data access requirements are regularised and independent of data values, and thus predictable, giving significant advantage on parallel and sequential machines."

The type of visualisation targeted by PIPADS is shown in Figures 1 and 2

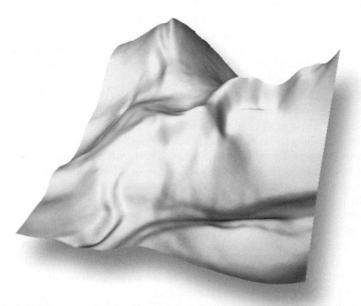

Fig. 1. Seismic visualization: mountains underneath the earth's surface [18]

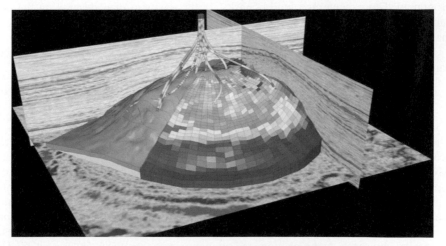

Fig. 2. CoViz 4D, Integrated 2D-3D-4D Visualization [22]

This set of image processing algorithms allowed to do all major algorithms that are needed for visualisation purposes by assigning to each of the 1024 processors of PI-PADS a line of the image (a horizontal or vertical line). To use this suit of routines it was also necessary to transpose images. Thus together with the transpose operation and the routines developed by P. Robertson, we had designed a highly efficient and massively parallel implementation of visualisation tools.

3   A Parallel Processing Unit for the Remote Sensing Satellite X-Sat

The architecture of fault tolerant parallel processing unit (PPU) for the X-Sat satellite [11, 12, 13] is based on research done by the author on fault tolerant arrays from about 1990 to 1994 [9, 10]. For onboard computing devices fault tolerance is essential, as the satellite, once launched can usually not be visited and repaired, while strong radiation tends to damage standard processors, once they are out in space. The kind of damage can be minor, such that only content of registers or other memory is changed (SEU), such can either be taken care of via use of error correcting codes or by a restart (likely with some loss of data). But the damage can be more serious, i.e. a processor cannot be used anymore. To cater for this case the architecture needs the ability to reconfigure itself and restart with a reduced number of processors. We have described a range of options how this can be achieved without doubling or tripling the processor numbers. The architecture we chose for X-Sat is depicted in Figure 3. [draft of the PhD thesis by Sharon Lim Siok Lin, NTU, Singapore]

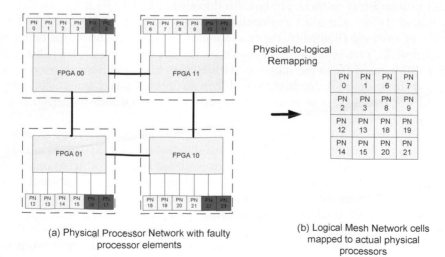

(a) Physical Processor Network with faulty processor elements

(b) Logical Mesh Network cells mapped to actual physical processors

Fig. 3. A practical example of a mapping of a physical processor array to a logical mesh processor array

Fig. 4. Vibration testing X-Sat

X-Sat is a low orbit satellite, that will cycle the earth on a polar orbit within about 90 minutes and it will have contact to its ground station only every few days. While it can potentially take photos permanently, it does not have the capacity to store many of them, nor could it download many while it has contact to the ground station. The exact application of X-Sat is not fixed, it can be used to search for anything (limited by the resolution of the camera), this might be bush fires, oil slicks, certain types of vegetation or settlements, ships, ... But whatever X-Sat will be used for in the course of its life (low orbit satellites survive only a few years in space), it is essential to be able to do onboard image analysis in order to filter out useful parts of images from parts that contain little information of interest.

The PPU has 24 Strong Arm processors, which is an extremely high compute power for a mini satellite (about 100kg), as the standard compute equipment of comparable satellites typically consists of radiation hardened hardware which is orders of magnitude slower and at the same time orders of magnitude more expensive. The COTS approach (components off the shelf) combined with the fault tolerant architecture made it possible to achieve high performance computing on board of the min satellite X-Sat. The major image processing routines to be implemented on X-Sat will be image compression, image analysis and image segmentation, with the later two having the main impact. Figure 5 is an example that gives an indication for the power of the multispectral approach.

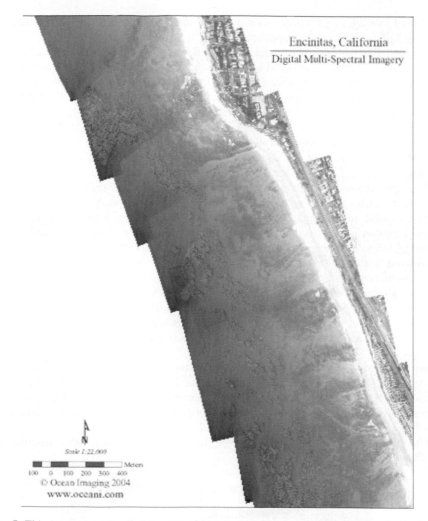

Fig. 5. This is an example of airborne multispectral imagery along the shoreline in Encinitas, CA, in which different bottom substrates are visible [19]

4 COPACOBANA a "Green" and Flexible Special Purpose Architecture

The Copacobana engine is built by the company Sciengines in Germany and was designed by a University research team under leadership of Professor Manfred Schimmler [14, 15, 16]. It consists of 128 FPGAs linked by a fast bus for data I/O. It was designed for algorithms that do not require lots of communication amongst processors. One application in mind was the cracking of code: Copacobana can crack DES encrypted data within about 7 days, while it outperforms a PC by about 4 orders of magnitude it does it with an energy consumption that is reduced by about a factor of 3000. While the Copacobana will consume about 10$ of Energy to crack a single DES encrypted message, a PC cluster would do the same, consuming 30,000$ of energy – about 1/5 of the price of the Copacobana.

"Cryptanalysis of symmetric and asymmetric ciphers is a challenging task due to the enormous amount of involved computations. To tackle this computa- tional complexity, usually the employment of special-purpose hardware is considered as best approach. We have built a massively parallel cluster system (COPACOBANA) based on low-cost FPGAs as a cost-efficient platform primarily targeting cryptanalytical operations with these high computational efforts but low communication and memory requirements. However, some parallel applications in the field of cryptography are too complex for low-cost FPGAs and also require the availability of at least moderate communication and memory facilities. Particularly, this holds true for arithmetic intensive application as well as ones with a highly complex data flow. In this contribution, we describe a novel architecture for a more versatile and reliable COPACO-BANA capable to host advanced cryptographic applications like high-performance digital signature generation according to the Elliptic Curve Digital Signature Algorithm (ECDSA) and integer factorization based on the Elliptic Curve Method (ECM). In addition to that, the new cluster design allows even to run more supercomputing applications beyond the field of cryptography." [24]

Since all the compute power of Copacobana rests within the FPGA, this is a tool that can be used for almost any purpose. Changing the application, i.e. writing new programs, is done via a hardware description language and thus requires people with special skills. To switch between already developed applications can be done within a few seconds.

We have investigated the option to develop the necessary programs for computer tomography, (see Figure 7). Even though this has not been implemented on the Copacobana, preliminary calculations have shown that this will lead to a speedup of corresponding procedures by at least two orders of magnitude, thus significantly speeding up the time for the diagnosis.

The energy consumption might well be the main selling point for a machine like the Copacobana.

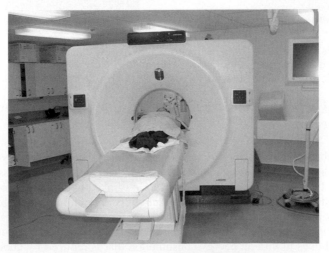

Fig. 6. Computer tomography [20]

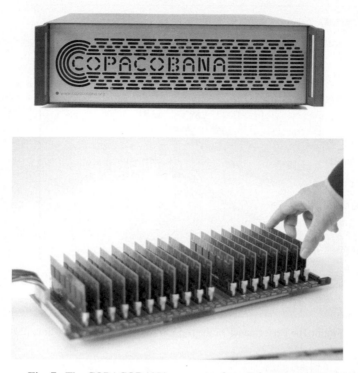

Fig. 7. The COPACOBANA computer from Scienegines [21]

5 Conclusion

There are a range of movements in terms of hardware for visualisation and image analysis. Similarly to what is happening on the supercomputer market, we can expect performance increases at a similar rate as the rate you see in Figure 8, i.e. a performance increase of a factor 10 happens every 4 years (which results of a performance increase of a factor 1000 in just 12 years).

As mentioned above last year a supercomputer has been listed amongst the top500 that is composed of GPU. The company WETA Digital (which produces digital effects for movies like "The Lord of the Rings" trilogy and "King Kong" in New Zealand) has 5 computer clusters in the top500 list, which are based on Intel processors. It can be expected that GPUs do not only become more powerful, mainly through the use of massive parallelism, but possibly also more versatile, so that the separation between CPU and GPU becomes blurred. At this stage (and this has always been the case and might stay this way for a while) it is worth investigating the option of designing special purpose architectures, outperforming off the shelf solutions by at least 2 orders of magnitude and at the same time saving energy in the same order of magnitude – energy saving is likely to become much more important in the near future.

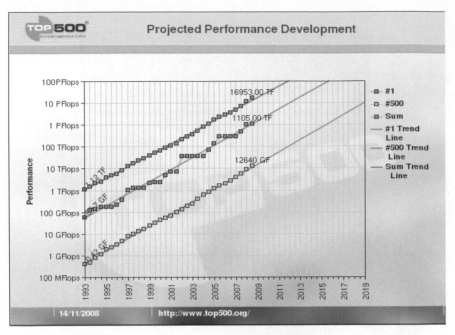

Fig. 8. The performance of the top500 supercomputers over time [23]

References

1. Robertson, P.K.: Parallel algorithms for visualising image surfaces. In: Third International Conference on Image Processing and its Applications, July 18-20, 1989, pp. 472–476 (1989)
2. Spray, A., Schröder, h., Lie, K.T., Plesner, e., Bray, P.D.: PIPADS – a low-cost real-time visualisation tool. In: Parallel Computing – Paradigms and Applications. Thomson Computer Press (1996)
3. Schröder, H., et al.: PIPADS: A Vertically Integrated Parallel Image Processing and Display System. In: 5th Australian Supercomputing Conference, Melbourne (December 1992)
4. Spray, A., Lie, K.T., Schröder, H.: Test Strategies Employed in a Massively Parallel Visualization Engine, PRFTS, Melbourne (December 1993)
5. Spray, A., Schröder, H., Lie, K.T.: A Low-Cost Machine for Real-Time Visualization. In: 5th International Symposium on IC Technology, Singapore (1993)
6. Lenders, P., Schröder, H.: A programmable systolic device for Image Processing — based on Mathematical Morphology. Parallel Computing 13, 337–344 (1990)
7. Sim, L.C., Schroeder, H., Leedham, G.: Major line removal morphological Hough transform on a hybrid system. Journal of Computer and Systems Sciences (2004)
8. Schröder, H.: The Instruction Systolic Array — A Tradeoff between Flexibility and Speed. Computer Systems Science and Engineering 3(2) (April 1988)
9. McDonald, T., Schröder, H.: A simple and Powerfull Mesh Network for Reconfigurable Arrays. The Australian Computer Science Communications 14(1), 589–601 (1992)
10. Kaufmann, M., Schröder, H., Sibeyn, J.: Routing and Sorting on Reconfigurable Meshes. Parallel Processing Letters 5(1), 81–96 (1995)

11. Schröder, H.: On-board fault tolerant parallel computing for small satellites. In: Section Innovative Satellite Architectures: Small Satellite Programs and Their Uses For Communication, Conference on Asian Satellite & Cable TV, also chairperson of the conference, Singapore (February 2001)
12. Schröder, H.: Fault tolerant computing on board of satellites. In: Dynamically Reconfigurable Architectures, Germnay, International conference and Research Center for Computer Science, Schloss Dagstuhl (June 2000)
13. Schröder, H.: On-board fault tolerant parallel computing for small satellites. In: Section Innovative Satellite Architectures: Small Satellite Programs and Their Uses For Communication, Conference on Asian Satellite & Cable TV, also chairperson of the conference. February 2001, Singapore (February 2001)
14. Schmidt, B., Schimmler, M., Schröder, H.: A massively parallel architecture for public-key cryptography. In: International Journal of Computer Research on Cryptographic Hardware and Embedded Systems. Nova Science, NY (2004)
15. Pfeiffer, G., Baumgart, S., Schröder, J., Schimmler, M.: A Massively Parallel Architecture for Bioinformatics. ICCS (1), 994–1003 (2009)
16. Kumar, S., Paar, C., Pelzl, J., Pfeiffer, G., Schimmler, M.: COPACOBANA A Cost-Optimized Special-Purpose Hardware for Code-Breaking. In: FCCM 2006, pp. 311–312 (2006)
17. http://www.top500.org/blog/2009/05/20/top_trends_high_performance_computing
18. http://www.rug.nl/.../oilgas/horizon.jpg
19. http://www.csc.noaa.gov/crs/rs_apps/issues/nearshore.htm
20. http://www.lakesdhb.govt.nz
21. http://www.sciengines.com
22. http://www.dgi.com/coviz/cvpressrelease.html
23. http://www.top500.org/
24. http://www.copacobana.org/docs.html

CCTV Video Analytics: Recent Advances and Limitations

Sergio A. Velastin

Digital Imaging Research Centre,
Faculty of Computing, Information Systems and Mathematics,
Kingston University, Kingston upon Thames, KT1 2EE, United Kingdom
sergio.velastin@ieee.org

Abstract. There has been a significant increase in the number of CCTV cameras in public and private places worldwide. The cost of monitoring these cameras manually and of reviewing recorded video is prohibitive and therefore manual systems tend to be used mainly reactively with only a small fraction of the cameras being monitored at any given time. There is a need to automate at least simple observation tasks through computer vision, a functionality that has become known popularly as "video analytics". The large size of CCTV systems and the requirement of high detection rates and low false alarms are major challenges. This paper illustrates some of the recent efforts reported in the literature, highlighting advances and pointing out important limitations.

Keywords: Closed-circuit television, video analytics, visual surveillance, image processing, security, crowd-monitoring, tracking, object detection.

1 Introduction

The installation of closed circuit television (CCTV) cameras in urban environments is now commonplace and well-known, particularly in the UK. Given the current political climate, other countries are quickly catching up even where traditionally there has been strong public opposition on the grounds of privacy and individual freedom.

It is particularly difficult to have accurate estimates of the number of cameras installed in public places. A study by the UK's CCTV users group [1] estimated that in 2008 there were around 1.5 million CCTV cameras just in city centres, stations, airports and major retail. As resourcing the monitoring of CCTV with human operators is increasingly expensive, there is a tendency to concentrate monitoring on large control rooms, an example of which is shown in Fig. 1. In the UK control rooms with hundreds of cameras for town centre monitoring are not uncommon. Larger systems such as metropolitan railways or airports might have thousands of cameras. In the majority of large CCTV installations, only a small fraction is ever watched. A study [2] conducted for the railways sector in the UK found typical camera to screen ratios of between 1:4 and 1:78, while in [3] it was found that for town centre CCTV these were between 1:4 and 1:30 with ratios of CCTV operators to TV monitors sometimes as high as 1:16. So only a small fraction can be monitored in real-time and in most cases only driven reactively from reports from people on the ground. Post-incident

H. Badioze Zaman et al. (Eds.): IVIC 2009, LNCS 5857, pp. 22–34, 2009.
© Springer-Verlag Berlin Heidelberg 2009

analysis is also a time-consuming operation which requires extensive operator knowledge of the locations of all the cameras. It is more less accepted that a person can only really monitor 1-4 screens at a time [3], so in a typical installation with 100 cameras and 3 people (a typical situation for a UK town or municipality of around 150,000 inhabitants), as little as 3% of screens are likely to being physically watched at any given time. What is important to emphasise is that dramatic incidents such as those related to terrorism are rare and what is sometimes overlooked is the cumulative effect of routine volume crime and disorder. For example in the UK, anti-social behaviour costs taxpayers £3.3 billion a year and a study [4] found 66,000 reports of nuisance and loutish behaviour a day. Fear of crime is also an important factor in making urban life attractive for passengers and staff in public transport networks. For example, figures show that 44% of women and 19% of men feel unsafe waiting at bus stops at night [5].

To appreciate the large size of the data that goes through what are increasingly digital CCTV video systems, consider that a standard PAL camera (720x576 RGB pixels at 25 frames/second) generates 112 GB of data per hour. Even with H.264 compression (a favourite current standard for such systems), a standard 4.7 GB DVD disc would be full in about 5 hours. Current practice in the UK is to store video for around 31 days. For a system of 100 cameras that would require around 15,000 DVDs or about 70 Terabytes. Nevertheless, digital video technology may in principle allow computer-based processing of video images so as to a) label scenes without people or other moving objects as "uninteresting" so that they can be removed or placed in a lower priority set, b) pick up situations that might interest human operators so as to guide them towards what might need their intervention (for prevention, law-enforcement, gathering of evidence, etc.). It is important to highlight here that the driver for automation is not (or should not be) the replacement of people by cheaper systems, but the empowering of human operators so that they get appropriate information in a more timely manner and use their much better powers for situation assessment to quickly put in place measures that can deal with incidents or potential incidents.

Fig. 1. A typical CCTV Control room [from CCTV Image]

The combination of algorithms and systems that can do this, is being referred to as "Video Analytics" or "Video Contents Analysis". Given that as human beings we rely heavily on visual processing, the potential of this technology and its range of applications (security, sports, assisted living, unmanned vehicles, etc.) is enormous but so are the challenges in trying to come anywhere close to natural abilities that have evolved over millions of years. The fundamental problem to solve is that of interpreting the meaning of an image (or a sequence of images) i.e. to transform from pixels to a linguistic entity like a sentence as simple as "intruder detected" or as complicated as "the person wearing a red coat on the right is the same person we saw each day taking photos of strategic buildings in the city". A key problem is that a given picture might have various interpretations depending on context i.e. on information that is not part of the picture itself. In a CCTV monitoring environment, such context is used extensively by human operators and might include operator experience, voice reports received by radio, personal knowledge of known criminals, time of day, place, etc. For example, take the simple photographs shown in Fig. 2. For the picture on the left, one possible interpretation relies on the viewer knowing about the legend of the Loch Ness monster in Scotland, i.e. on having a particular cultural background. It is left to the reader to find out what is the "correct" interpretation of these images.

Fig. 2. Sample photographs to illustrate the importance of context left: Loch Ness monster?, right: crater or hill?)

As we are still not sure on how to include broad knowledge into image interpretation, better results are obtained when the context can be constrained. For example, in a metro station one expects people to circulate (implied context) and not linger (the unusual, to be detected). More generally speaking, in video analytics it is almost assumed that what is important is what is known in the area as "motion", meaning the presence of objects of interest (usually people and/or vehicles), separated from the static scene background (or fixtures). Broadly speaking, therefore, most video analytics systems perform the following (mainly sequential) operations:

1. Extract some key indicators from the images. Such indicators could be the segmentation of moving objects, velocity fields, colour patterns, etc.
2. Tracking these indicators from one image to the next so as to obtain a temporal sequence.

3. Labelling or classifying different types of objects (e.g. vehicular classification) or variations within one class of object (e.g. human poses)
4. Recognition of spatio-temporal patterns usually associated with some basic events (e.g. "person entered from the right") and combination of such events so as to recognise behaviours (e.g. "and then approached another one who had been there for some time").
5. These are then used to raise alarms when a situation of interest is deemed to have happened. Also note that the data at any stage of processing may be stored as metadata linked to the original video to be used for retrieval, typically in an off-line post-event investigation.

For the automatic generation of alarms, there are two major categories of systems:
1. Rule-based: an expert operator programs the system (typically with spatio-temporal rules and appropriate thresholds) so that when a combination of conditions satisfies a certain rule, then an alarm is triggered. These systems are effective in exploiting human knowledge but cannot deal with unexpected situations and setting a variety of thresholds is not a trivial exercise.
2. Learning: in this case the system accumulates typically probability functions to represent what occurs frequently (assumed to be normal and not require human intervention). When an outlier is detected an alarm can be triggered (or the operator asked if such an outlier should be incorporated into the normal population). There is inherent flexibility in this approach, however, training a system can take long times. Furthermore, because incidents tend to be rare, there is a general lack of negative examples with which to improve the robustness of such systems.

2 Examples of Current Capabilities

The EU-funded projects CROMATICA and PRISMATICA [6] (1996-2003) were concerned with investigating and evaluating image processing systems to assist CCTV operators in public transport networks and in particular in metropolitan railways and were perhaps one of the first attempts to test video analytics for pedestrian monitoring in operational conditions. Fig. 3 shows an example where the motion estimation vectors from an MPEG-2 stream have been used (after filtering as seen on the right hand side) to indicate areas of potential interest. The motion field in combination with image luminance is also used to remove the background from the analysis [6]. This simple approach can then be used to detect situations of interest to metro operators such as congestion and stationary people (or abandoned packages). More or less at the same time, many researchers had been investigating two main aspects: detection of objects in varying illumination conditions and tracking of such objects from one frame to another.

Typical of the interest in tracking was the now well-established series of PETS workshops (Performance Evaluation of Tracking Systems, see for example [7]) coordinated by the University of Reading (UK). **Fig. 5** shows an example from the early datasets (2001). PETS, and more recently i-LIDS [8], was crucial to establish a strong culture of thorough evaluation of algorithms in visual surveillance, using public datasets. Yin *et al* [9] describe a set of metrics that is particularly useful to assess

Fig. 3. Left: Raw MPEG-2 motion field, Right: Filtered motion field (motion vectors have been coloured according to predominant directions of motion) [6]

Fig. 4. Using motion fields and foreground analysis to detect congestion (left) and stationary people like the man sitting down (right) [6]

Fig. 5. A scene from early PETS datasets

characteristics of tracking such as track segmentation and id swap. The emphasis on realistic scenarios has been particularly useful to steer work toward working systems. For example, this identified the need to deal with uncontrolled illumination conditions and other artefacts such as camera shake, shadows, waves, leaves on trees moved by the wind, etc. Therefore, many of the current systems rely on segmentation of foreground (pixels of interest, ideally corresponding to moving objects) based on the work by Stauffer and Grimson [10] where pixel intensity is represented by a Gaussian Mixture Model (GMM) on the assumption that most of the time a pixel is background, but affected by illumination changes. A statistically significant change in illumination is indicative of the presence of foreground. Unfortunately, to account for changes in background the method loses objects that become stationary (which effectively disappear). When such objects move on again, they create "ghosts" that may be wrongly identified as separate objects. Yin *et al* have recently [11] suggested a way to deal with this effect. There are also significant problems when dealing with crowded conditions because most of the time pixels correspond to foreground and object detection and separation is particularly challenging. Cucchiara *et al* [12] reviewed and compared existing methods and colour spaces applicable to dealing with shadows. In more recent work, Martel-Brisson and Zaccarin [13] present a method to remove cast shadows using a GMM to separate shadows from foreground and background. The removal of deep shadows is still a problem.

By 2006 there was sufficient work on tracking so as to be summarised in a good review by Yilmaz *et al* [14], where the interested reader can find further details. They categorised the different approaches in terms of:

- Object *detection* (point detectors: Harris, SIFT, etc.; Foreground/Background estimation e.g. through GMM or PCA), segmentation (thresholding, meanshift, graph-cuts, ...) and *representation* (e.g. centroid, blob, silhouettes, articulated shapes, skeletal models and so on).
- Features (colour, edges, optical flow, texture, histograms, ...) and
- Tracking methods (point: MGE, Kalman, MHT (Multiple Hypothesis Tracking which exemplifies the importance of the data association problem, which

can make a "good" tracker fail), particle filters; Kernel: templates and variants such as mean shift, camshift; KLT based on optical-flow; silhouette tracking).

Most of the proposed systems for CCTV monitoring have focused on representing scenes by tracked "blobs" (typically rectangles in 2D or cuboids in 3D). How such blobs are detected and tracked might involve different types of features, learning or heuristics. Nevertheless, it has not been common to look in detail inside the blobs as a means of detecting situations of interest. Such work is normally of interest to researchers in human body motion where one of the primary aims is to estimate human pose (e.g. relative position of human body parts) and then use temporal variation of pose as an indication of human activity and ultimately behaviour. As in PETS and i-LIDS, a database called HumanEva [15] has established itself as a benchmark to compare competing algorithms. A typical application is shown in Fig. 6 from work by Martínez del Rincón *et al* [16]. Computing articulated body parts is complicated, especially when using a single camera. Ragheb *et al* [17] present a method where Fourier descriptors are used to directly capture the spatio-temporal properties of an action as seen by a sequence of silhouettes. In line with current trends, they have made public datasets of both computer-generated [18] and real data [19] of actions seen from many cameras that can be used to test and train algorithms. Related work has been reported by Martinez-Contreras *et al* [20] using self-organising-maps (SOMs) to recognise actions. These efforts are still at a lab stage.

Fig. 6. Locating and tracking lower limbs using a particle filter [16]

Given current security concerns over actions in public places, there has been a growing interest in detecting drop-off and pick-up actions. Indeed this is the topic of one of the i-LIDS tests which, to our knowledge, has not been satisfactorily passed by any commercial system. Damen and Hogg of Leeds University have proposed [21,22] a system to detect bicycles and generate an alarm based on the differences in appearances of the assumed owner rider between drop-off and pickup. An example where a significant difference is detected is shown in Fig. 7.

Fig. 7. Detecting differences between drop-off and pickup [21]

The same team has looked [23] at the problem of detecting people carrying objects (such as backpacks) by matching against templates of normal bodies and detecting protruding regions. An example is shown in Fig. 8. The method was evaluated against the PETS-2006 dataset reaching a precision of 51% and a recall of 55% (still short of practical deployment). If improved, the approach could be used to locate possible candidates to detect drop-off actions indicative of abandoned packages. The PETS-2006 dataset was also used by Lv *et al* [24] to demonstrate the detection of a drop-off (a sample result is shown in Fig. 9).

As mentioned earlier, there are significant challenges when dealing with crowded situations as these complicate foreground/background segmentation and introduce issues of occlusion. In the partially crowded case shown in the left of Fig. 10 (from PETS-2007) we can see some examples of self-occlusion (man on the left), occlusion by other people (the queue) and fixed occluders (environmental fixtures as in the area

Fig. 8. Detecting people carrying objects [23]

Fig. 9. Left: Person detected (labelled "15"), Right: drop off detected [24]

on the right of the picture). The situation shown on the right of Fig. 10 is one where there are little or no visible gaps between people. Given that the human visual system, even in these challenging conditions, can locate and track people relatively easily (given enough time and attention), perhaps a different paradigm is needed, for example one based in shape and appearances irrespective of background. Wu and Nevatia [25] report an algorithm that is trained to locate (even partly occluded) human shapes based on edge chains ("edgelets") used as weak classifiers. Then, Huang *et al* [26] follow this up by proposing a probabilistic framework to deal with occlusions that include the learning of priors related to scene occluders plus a method to handle the usual breaking up of tracks into unconnected smaller tracks (or "tracklets"). Fig. 11 illustrates how results are improved using the method. A disadvantage is the long time it takes for training (days of computing time, even on a 16-node computer cluster).

There is a recent review of the topic of crowd analysis by Zhan *et al* [27]. Researchers have tended to concentrate on what is referred to as "crowd dynamics", meaning extraction and analysis of predominant paths and group motion. One of the exceptions is the work recently reported by Ali and Shah [28]. The method is based on learning priors about sources and sinks (entries and exits), likely direction of motion, obstacles that "repel" flow and on a model of how neighbouring people behave. The authors call these models "floor fields". For the chosen domains (e.g. marathon running) the results are impressive (an example is shown in Fig. 12). The strength

Fig. 10. Examples of crowded situations. Left: PETS-2007 (partially crowded), Right: Heavily crowded (courtesy of Ipsotek Ltd.)

Fig. 11. Refining from tracklets (top) to tracks (bottom), from Huang *et al* [26]

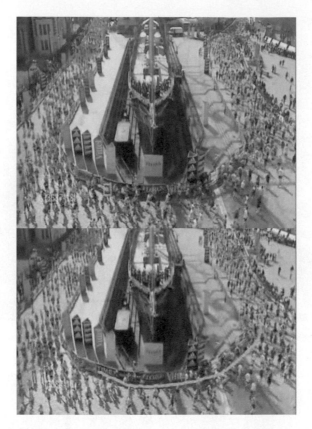

Fig. 12. Left: tracking starts, Right: tracking the same person after many frames [28]

of the algorithm is to be "fit for purpose", consequently it is expected that it might not deal well with unexpected situations (e.g. a person crossing the path of the crowd at 90 degrees or a person walking instead of running or a person moving counterflow).

Finally, real CCTV systems contain many cameras and operators use multiple cameras to follow events. The most tractable problem so far is that of a small number of static cameras (2-5, say) with significant overlaps (so that objects are often seen by more than one camera at once) and with a common ground plane, for example as described by Black *et al* [29]. Makris and Ellis [30] have presented a method to automatically learn the topological and temporal relationships between entry and exit points in different cameras in a network. This is an important spatio-temporal prior used to constraint the search space when tracking people from one camera to another, when there might be many cameras to choose from. An interesting method first proposed by Hu [31] consists in having conventional single-camera trackers from which principal (vertical) axes are computed for each tracked person which are then projected to the common ground plane. For overlapping areas, multiple instances of the same objects are fused on the ground plane to resolve occlusion problems.

3 Conclusions

What has been presented in this paper can only be a small part of what is a vibrant research area. Space restrictions prevents us to go deeper into any of the methods mentioned here and in particular on a presentation of important advances in commercially-available systems which are beginning to see applications for example for sterile zone protection and traffic monitoring. There are still major challenges ahead of which perhaps the most important are robustness to environmental conditions, practical effective calibration procedures (applicable to systems of hundreds and even thousands of cameras), dealing with crowded conditions and being able to handle pan-tilt-zoom (PTZ) cameras.

References

1. CCTV Users Group: How Many Cameras are there? 2008-06-18 (2008),
   http://www.cctvusergroup.com/art.php?art=94
2. Kingston University, Mott MacDonald, Ipsotek Limited: Maximising benefits from CCTV on the railway - Existing Systems, Technical Report, Rail Safety and Standards Board (2003)
3. Dee, H., Velastin, S.A.: How Close are we to Solving the Problem of Automated Visual Surveillance? A Review of Real-World Surveillance. Scientific Progress and Evaluative Mechanisms; Machine Vision and Applications 19(5-6), 329–343 (2008)
4. Whitehead, C.M.E., Stockdale, J.E., Razzu, G.: The Economic and Social Cost of Anti-Social Behaviour: A Review, London School of Economics and Political Science (October 2003), http://www.homeoffice.gov.uk/crimpol/antisocialbehaviour
5. DTLR, based on a report by Crime Concern and Oscar Faber (ref. SP/15 and SP/16) (2002)
6. Velastin, S.A., Boghossian, B.A., Vicencio-Silva, M.A.: A Motion-Based Image Processing System for Detecting Potentially Dangerous Situations in Underground Railway Stations. Transportation Research Part C: Emerging Technologies 14(2), 96–113 (2006)
7. http://www.cvg.rdg.ac.uk/PETS2009/ (accessed 18, August 2009)
8. http://scienceandresearch.homeoffice.gov.uk/hosdb/cctv-imaging-technology/video-based-detection-systems/i-lids/ (Accessed 18, August 2009)
9. Yin, F., Makris, D., Velastin, S.A.: Performance Evaluation of Object Tracking Algorithms. In: 10th IEEE Int. Workshop on Performance Evaluation of Tracking and Surveillance (PETS-2007), Rio de Janeiro, Brazil (2007)
10. Stauffer, C., Grimson, E.: Learning Patterns of Activity Using Real-Time Tracking. IEEE TPAMI 22(8), 747–757 (2000)
11. Yin, Y., Makris, D., Velastin, S.A.: Time Efficient Ghost Removal for Motion Detection in Visual Surveillance Systems. IET Electronics Letters 44(23), 1351–1353 (2008)
12. Cucchiara, R., Grana, C., Piccardi, M., Prati, A.: Detecting Moving Objects, Ghosts, and Shadows in Video Streams. IEEE TPAMI 25/10, 1337–1342 (2003)
13. Martel-Brisson, N., Zaccarin, A.: Learning and Removing Cast Shadows through a Multi-distribution Approach. IEEE TPAMI 29(7), 1133–1146 (2007)
14. Yilmaz, A., Javed, O., Shah, M.: Object Tracking: a Survey, ACM Computing Surveys, 38/4, 13.1–13.45 (2006)

15. Sigal, L., Black, M.J.: HumanEva: Synchronized Video and Motion Capture Dataset for Evaluation of Articulated Motion, Brown University, Tech Rep CS-06-08 (2006)
16. Martinez-del-Rincon, J., Nebel, J.-C., Makris, D., Orrite- Uruñuela, C.: Tracking Human Body Parts Using Particle Filters Constrained by Human Biomechanics. In: British Machine Vision Conference, Leeds (2008)
17. Ragheb, H., Velastin, S.A., Remagnino, P., Ellis, T.: Novel Approach for Fast Action Recognition using Simple Features. In: 8th IEEE Int. Workshop on Visual Surveillance VS 2008, Marseille, France, October 17 (2008)
18. Ragheb, H., Velastin, S.A., Remagnino, P., Ellis, T.: ViHASi: Virtual Human Action Silhouette Data for the Performance Evaluation of Silhouette-Based Action Recognition Methods. In: Workshop on Activity Monitoring by Multi-Camera Surveillance Systems (ACM/IEEE Int'l. Conf. on Distributed Smart Cameras), September 11, Stanford University, California (2008)
19. http://dipersec.king.ac.uk/MuHAVi-MAS/ (2008)
20. Martinez-Contreras, F., Orrite-Uruñuela, C., Herrero-Jaraba, E., Ragheb, H., Velastin, S.A.: Recognizing Human Actions using Silhouette-based HMM. In: 6th IEEE Int. Conference on Advanced Video and Signal Based Surveillance, AVSS, Genoa, Italy, September 2-4 (2009)
21. Damen, D., Hogg, D.: Associating People Dropping off and Picking up Object. In: Proc. British Machine Vision Conference, BMVC (2007)
22. Damen, D., Hogg, D.: Recognizing Linked Events: Searching the Space of Feasible Explanations. In: Computer Vision and Pattern Recognition, CVPR (2009)
23. Damen, D., Hogg, D.C.: Detecting carried objects in short video sequences. In: Forsyth, D., Torr, P., Zisserman, A. (eds.) ECCV 2008, Part III. LNCS, vol. 5304, pp. 154–167. Springer, Heidelberg (2008)
24. Lv, F., Song, X., Wu, B., Kumar Singh, V., Nevatia, R.: Left-Luggage Detection using Bayesian Inference. In: 9th Int Workshop on Performance Evaluation of Tracking and Surveillance, PETS-CVPR 2006 (June 2006)
25. Wu, B., Nevatia, R.: Detection and Tracking of Multiple, Partially Occluded Humans by Bayesian Combination of Edgelet based Part Detectors. Int. J. Computer Vision 75(2), 247–266 (2007)
26. Huang, C., Wu, B., Nevatia, R.: Robust object tracking by hierarchical association of detection responses. In: Forsyth, D., Torr, P., Zisserman, A. (eds.) ECCV 2008, Part II. LNCS, vol. 5303, pp. 788–801. Springer, Heidelberg (2008)
27. Zhan, B., Monekosso, D.N., Remagnino, P., Velastin, S.A., Xu, L.: Crowd Analysis: a Survey. Machine Vision and Applications. Computer Science, 345–357 (2008) ISBN- 978-3-540-88689-1
28. Ali, S., Shah, M.: Floor fields for tracking in high density crowd scenes. In: Forsyth, D., Torr, P., Zisserman, A. (eds.) ECCV 2008, Part II. LNCS, vol. 5303, pp. 1–14. Springer, Heidelberg (2008)
29. Black, J., Ellis, T.: Multi camera image tracking, Image and Vision Computing, vol. 24, pp. 1256–1267. Elsevier, Amsterdam (2006)
30. Makris, D., Ellis, T.: Learning Semantic Scene Models from Observing Activity in Visual Surveillance. IEEE TSMC-B 35(3), 397–408 (2005)
31. Hu, M., Zhou, X., Tan, T., Lou, J., Maybank, S.: Principal Axis-Based Correspondence between Multiple Cameras for People Tracking. IEEE TPAMI 28/4, 663–671 (2006)

Video Forgery and Special Effect Production

Timothy K. Shih[1], Joseph C. Tsai[2], Nick C. Tang[2],
Shih-Ming Chang[2], and Yaurice Y. Lin[2]

[1] Asia University, Taiwan
[2] Tamkang University, Taiwan
timothykshih@gmail.com, kkiceman@gmail.com

*SUMMARY OF KEYNOTE PAPER

Video Forgery is a technique for generating fake video by altering, combining, or creating new video contents. The procedure of producing fake video involves several challenge image and video processing techniques. We discuss these techniques as follows:

The first challenge to alter the behavior of actors (or objects) in the original video involves a precise object tracking technique in stationary and non-stationary videos. Precise object tracking obtains the contour of video object by using color and motion information. The precision of tracking may affect the outcome of altering the obtained object, especially for non-stationary video sequences.

The second issue is related to removing objects from a video, usually, called video inpainting. The key technology of video inpainting in non-station video is to remove object without leaving a "ghost shadow," which is created if the continuity of video frames were not considered in the inpainting procedure. To avoid ghost shadow, motions of objects need to be calculated to produce references for the video inpainting procedure to predict movements.

The third issue in video forgery is to change the behavior of actors. For instance, the outcome of a 100-meter race in the Olympic Game can be falsified. Objects in different layers of a video can be played in different speeds and at different reference points with respect to the original video. In order to obtain a smooth movement of target objects, a motion interpolation mechanism can be used based on reference stick figures (i.e., a structure of human skeleton) and video inpainting mechanism.

The fourth challenge issue is to alter the background video. For instance, special effects in the movie industry usually have fire, smoke, and water, etc. To produce a fake but realistic background, the dynamic motions need to be predicted and reproduced in a realistic way. This step of special effect production can be further enhanced with combining natural scenes, to prepare a background video for inserting actors and objects.

The last interesting issue is to create a video database with a rich set of video clips, classified according to their scenery and video behavior. An efficient retrieval technique needs to be developed along with a friendly authoring tool for video planning. The optimal goal of video planning is to create new video sequences, based on video clips available in a large video database.

H. Badioze Zaman et al. (Eds.): IVIC 2009, LNCS 5857, pp. 35–37, 2009.
© Springer-Verlag Berlin Heidelberg 2009

We demonstrate several examples of special effect productions in the keynote address. Some interesting results are illustrated in the following figures. Video falsifying may create a moral problem. Our intension is to create special effects in movie industry.

Fig. 1. The Left are the original videos and the right are the falsified videos

Fig. 1. (*Continued*)

Segmentation of the Left Ventricle in Myocardial Perfusion SPECT Using Active Shape Model

Wooi-Haw Tan and Rosli Besar

Center for Multimedia Security and Signal Processing, Multimedia University
Persiaran Multimedia, 63100 Cyberjaya, Selangor, Malaysia
{twhaw,rosli}mmu.edu.my

Abstract. In the quantification of myocardial perfusion SPECT (MPS), numerous processes are involved. Automation is desired as it will considerably reduce the laboriousness of the underlying tasks. In this paper, we propose a segmentation scheme for the delineation of left ventricle (LV) using the Active Shape Models. Our scheme will reduce the labour-intensiveness in MPS quantification, while still allowing interactive guidance from the medical experts. The proposed scheme has been applied on clinical MPS tomograms in which it has successfully delineated the LV in 94% of the test data. In addition, it has also shown to be more suitable for LV segmentation than the rivaling Active Contour Model.

Keywords: Image segmentation, deformable models, medical image analysis.

1 Introduction

Myocardial perfusion SPECT (MPS) is a type of functional cardiac imaging, employed to diagnose ischemic heart disease. It reveals the distribution of the radio-pharmaceutical that has been injected into the patient, and therefore the relative blood flow to the different regions of the myocardium. Based on the principle that diseased myocardium receives less blood flow than normal myocardium under the condition of stress, diagnosis is made by comparing the stress images to a set of images obtained at rest [1].

As illustrated in Fig. 1, the quantification of MPS images comprises a variety of processes. This raw data will first undergo some filtering as to suppress the noise and enhance the desired features within the data. The three-dimensional distribution map of the radio tracer is then reconstructed from the raw data by using image reconstruction techniques. As the transaxial images are perpendicular to the long axis of the patient and varies from patient to patient, it is customary to reorient the transaxial images into short-axis images that are perpendicular to the long axis of the left ventricle (LV) [2]. To represent all areas of the myocardium in a single image, the cardiac polar map is generated by sampling and plotting the myocardial circumferential profiles as histogram values against angular location through a polar coordinate transformation with increasing radii [3].

Since the quantification of MPS images involves a series of processes, an interactive and automatic approach is desired as it will reduce the labour-intensiveness of the

H. Badioze Zaman et al. (Eds.): IVIC 2009, LNCS 5857, pp. 38–49, 2009.
© Springer-Verlag Berlin Heidelberg 2009

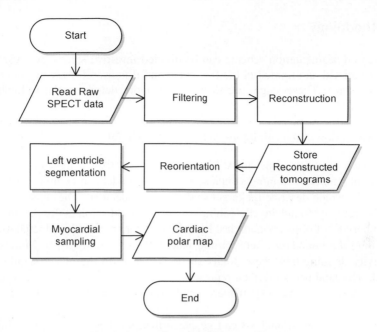

Fig. 1. Process flow in MPS quantification

underlying tasks, while still allowing interactive guidance and intervention from the medical experts. An essential step towards this approach is the segmentation of the LV as successful delineation of the LV would allow reorientation and myocardial sampling to be performed automatically. Nevertheless, the LVs may vary in appearance from one tomogram to another. Due to their inherent deformability, segmentation of LV can be a challenging task.

Several solutions are available for the segmentation of deformable objects. One of these solutions is to employ the Active Shape Models (ASMs), which were originally proposed by Cootes et al [4]. ASMs have gained a widespread popularity as they allow considerable shape variability which are still confined to the objects that they are intended to represent. Since its debut, ASMs have been extensively applied in 2D application. In their pioneering paper, Cootes et al demonstrated the application of ASMs for face recognition [4]. Over the years, ASMs have undergone various modifications. Van Ginneken et al. proposed a segmentation scheme for chest radiographs based on ASMs, which was steered by local features [5]. ASMs were also extended to spatio-temporal domain by Hamarneh et al., in which the extended ASM was applied to echocardiogram of the LV [6].

In this paper, we discuss a segmentation scheme to interactively delineate the LV by making use of the ASMs. This paper is organized as follows. Section 2 describes the underpinning methods in the proposed technique. Section 3 gives the details of the experiment and discusses the results. Finally, the conclusion is drawn in Section 4.

2 Methodology

The proposed segmentation scheme can be divided into two stages. An ASM of the LV is constructed and trained in the first stage and it is used for LV segmentation in the second stage. These stages are discussed in more details in the following sub-sections.

2.1 Construction and Training of Active Shape Model

The first step in constructing an ASM is to build a statistical model of appearance from a set of annotated training samples. Before the model can be built, a suitable set of landmarks which describe the target shape must be decided. The chosen landmarks should be reliably found in all training samples. Good choices for landmarks are points at corners of object boundaries. If such points are not sufficient, equally spaced points along the boundaries between the landmarks can be used [7]. Moreover, the connectivity defining how these points are joined to form the object should also be recorded. The landmarks are then represented as a $2n$-element vector X, where $X = \{(x_1, y_1), (x_2, y_2), \ldots, (x_n, y_n)\}$. If there are S training samples, there will be S such vector.

Before any statistical analysis can be performed on these vectors, it is important that the shapes represented are in the same orientation and scale. This can be achieved by aligning them in the same way with respect to set of axes via scaling, rotating and translating the training shapes so that they correspond to each other as closely as possible. To align two shapes, X_1 and X_2, each centered on the origin, we choose a scale s and rotation θ so as to minimize the sum of square distances between points on shape X_2 and those on the scaled and rotated version of shape X_1, as given in Equation (1). The procedure to align the shapes in a training set has been adopted from [7] and shown in Fig. 2.

$$\left(T_{s,\theta}\left(X_1 \right) - X_2 \right)^2 . \tag{1}$$

Once the shapes are aligned, they form a distribution in the $2n$ dimensional space. By modeling this distribution, new instances similar to those in the original training set can be generated. An efficient approach to model the distribution is the Principal Component Analysis (PCA). PCA computes the main axes of the distribution, allowing one to approximate any of the original points using a model with fewer than $2n$ parameters. The procedure to apply PCA has been adopted from [7] and is depicted in Fig. 3.

After PCA is applied, an instance of the training set X, can be approximated by using:

$$X \approx \overline{X} + \Phi B . \tag{2}$$

where Φ contains t eigenvectors of the covariance matrix and B is a t dimensional vector given by:

$$B = \Phi^T \left(X - \overline{X} \right). \tag{3}$$

The vector B describes a set of parameters of a deformable model. The ith parameter of vector B is denoted as b_i and is known as the ith mode of the model. By varying the values for different modes, variant of shape X can be produced. However, to ensure that the generated shape is similar to those in the training set, b_i should be limited to between $-3\sqrt{\lambda_i}$ and $3\sqrt{\lambda_i}$, where λ_i is the variance of b_i [7]. During the training, we can choose the total number of modes, t, as to explain a given proportion of the variance exhibited in the training set.

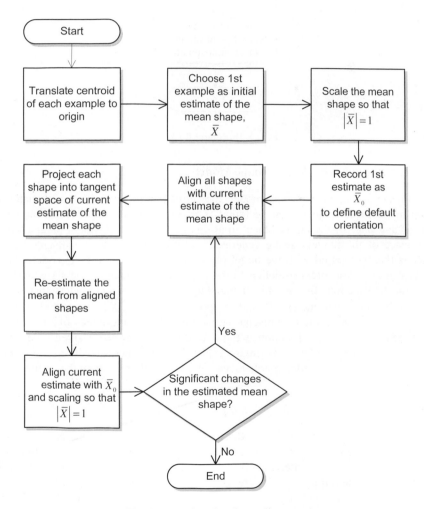

Fig. 2. Procedure for shape alignment

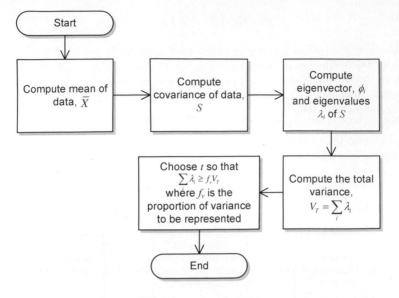

Fig. 3. Procedure for PCA

2.2 Segmentation with Active Shape Model

To delineate an object using the model, the set of parameters which best match the model to the target object must be found. This set of parameters defines the shape, position and pose of the target object in an image. For a set of model parameters, K, an instance of the model can be generated and projected on to the image. This instance is then compared with the target object and a fit function $F(K)$ is determined. The best set of parameters to delineate the object in the image is the set which optimizes the fit function. In the case of the shape models, the parameters that we can vary are the shape parameters, B, and the pose parameters, X_t, Y_t, s and θ. If we assume that the shape model represents boundaries and strong edges of the object, a useful measure for the fit function is the total distance between a given model point and the nearest strong edge in the image [7]. If the model point positions are given in vector X, and the nearest edge points to each model point are Y, then the fit function is given by:

$$F(B, X_t, Y_t, s, \theta) = (Y - X)^2. \tag{4}$$

If there is no a priori knowledge of the location and pose of the target object in an image, finding the parameters that optimize the fit is a challenging task. To overcome this, we allow the user to interactively indicate the approximate location of the target object and its pose through a software tool with graphical user interface (GUI). This would also allow the segmentation to be performed rapidly. Using the GUI, the user guides the operation by first placing and scaling the mean shape model on the image. The model can then be relocated and rotated as to represent the pose of the LV in the image. The segmentation begins once the initial position and pose have been confirmed. To optimize the model fit which is the total distance between model points and nearest strong edges, the edges and their strength should be determined. In this case, the morphological watershed segmentation based on the rainfailing simulation is used [8]. When it is applied on the gradient image, the resulting watershed lines represent the detected edges in the image. A binary image is then created by setting all pixels on the watershed lines to '1' and all others pixels to '0'. When this binary image is multiplied to the gradient image, it would result in an image with the edges and their strength. Next, the model is fitted to the target object via the iterative procedure proposed by Cootes [7], as depicted in Fig. 4.

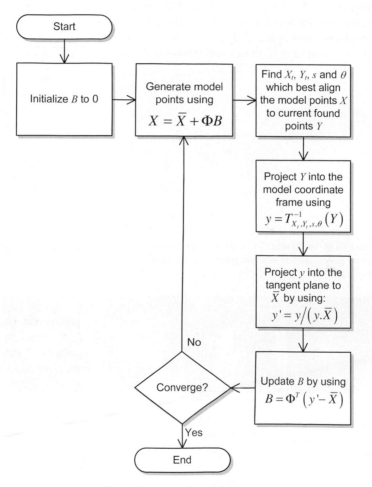

Fig. 4. Procedure for model fitting

3 Experiment Results and Discussions

To evaluate the performance of the proposed technique, an experiment involving 75 sets of clinical MPS tomograms was conducted. These tomograms were smoothed with a two-dimensional Butterworth filter (order=5, cutoff=0.25 Nyquist), as routinely done for MPS studies and reconstructed over 180° (45° RAO to LPO) with ramp filter and filtered backprojection. The mid-ventricular slices from 25 sets of the tomograms were arbitrarily chosen to train the shape model while the remainders (50 sets) were used for performance assessment. The shape model was constructed through manual annotation of the LV. This was done by selecting and placing the landmarks on the LV boundaries. Originally, 16 landmarks were defined for the LV. To outline the LV more precisely, three equal-spaced points between each pair of adjacent landmarks were generated via interpolation to give a total of 64 landmarks. Fig. 5 gives a sample of the landmarks and the order in which they were placed. In order to assist the landmark placement on the LV boundaries, morphological watershed segmentation was applied. Fig. 6 illustrates an example of annotating the LV in a training sample and Fig. 7 shows some annotated LVs from the training set.

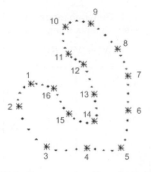

Fig. 5. Example of landmarks: '*' indicates manually selected landmarks, '·' represents equal-spaced points generated via interpolation and the numbers denote the order in which the landmarks are placed

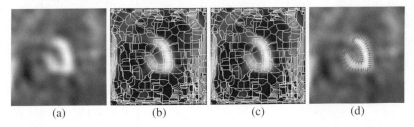

Fig. 6. Annotation of LV: (a) Test image. (b) Watershed lines superimposed on the test image. (c) Annotation of landmarks on the LV boundaries. (d) LV annotated with 64 landmarks.

Fig. 7. Example shapes of annotated LVs from training set

After annotating the images in the training set, the shape alignment illustrated in Fig. 2 were applied. Next, PCA was employed to reduce the dimensionality of the shape vectors from 128 to 15. Even though the resulting shape model only had 15 modes, it could explain 99% of the variance in the landmark positions in the training set. Fig. 8 depicts the effect of varying the first three modes between -3 and 3 times of the standard deviations from the mean value, when all other modes were set to zero.

Mode 1   Mode 2   Mode 3

Fig. 8. Effects of varying the first three modes of the shape model between $\pm 3\sqrt{\lambda_i}$

After the shape model was trained, it was used to interactively delineate the LV in another 50 sets of MPS tomograms. For each set of tomograms, the proposed segmentation technique was applied on the mid-ventricular slice. In each case, a software tool with GUI was used to interactively indicate the approximate position and pose of the LV. The software tool also accepted an additional parameter, *npts*, which is the number of pixels on either side of the model point for which the edge will be evaluated during model fitting. Throughout the experiment, *npts* was set to 1. After the test was conducted, the segmentation results were visually inspected. It was observed that the proposed segmentation scheme had successfully delineated the LV in 47 of the 50 sets of tomograms used in the test. To observe the results, ten of the sample images used in the test are shown in Figure 9 along with the corresponding segmented LVs. The images for which the proposed technique has failed are shown in Fig. 9(h)-(j). Upon close inspection, it was found that the proposed technique failed in these tomograms as the LVs were barely discernable due to severe perfusion defects. Nevertheless, the proposed scheme has achieved a success rate of 94% and this could be improved by having more annotated examples in the training set.

Active Contour Model (ACM) is another popular solution for the segmentation of deformable model [9]. Hence, an experiment was conducted to evaluate the suitability of the proposed technique and ACM in LV segmentation. In the experiment, the gradient vector flow based ACM proposed by Xu and Prince [10] was adopted. In this case, the approximate contour of the LV was interactively specified via a software tool with GUI. ACM was then iteratively applied until a specified number of iterations was reached. After applying ACM on just several test images, we noted that the same set of parameter values could not be applied to different images, even though they were all MPS images. Tuning the parameter values was a tedious task as there were ten adjustable parameters. Fig. 10(c) illustrates the problem with ACM when the same parameter values were applied for three test images. Conversely, the same

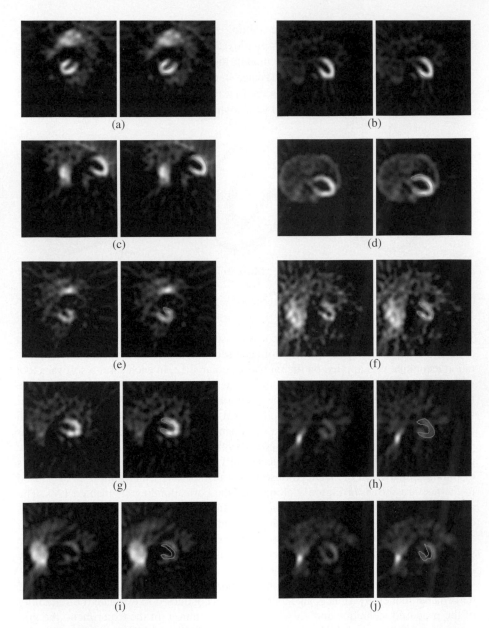

Fig. 9. Results of LV segmentation (left: original, right: segmented LV)

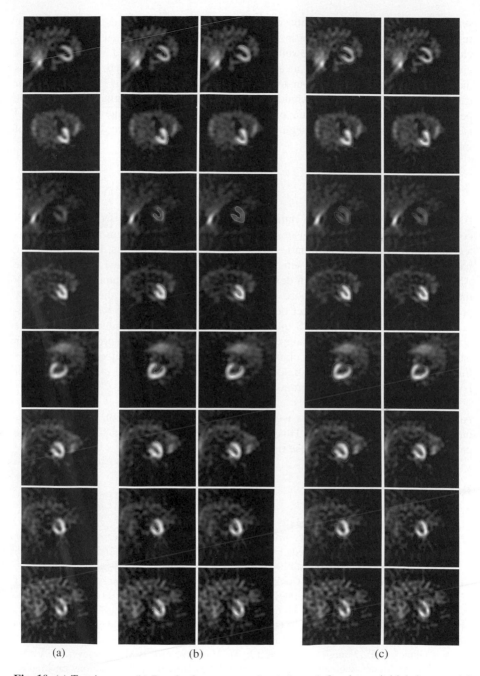

(a)   (b)   (c)

Fig. 10. (a) Test images. (b) Results from proposed technique (left column: initial shape model; right column: segmented LV). (c) Results from gradient vector flow ACM (left column: initial contour; right column: segmented LV).

settings were used with the proposed technique on the test images and satisfactory results were obtained, as shown in Fig. 10(b). From the experiment, it can be concluded that our scheme is more suitable for the segmentation of LV in MPS tomograms. However, this does not mean that it is always more superior than ACM as model training is involved in our technique while ACM does not require any prior training. Thus, the proposed technique is more suitable if the segmentation is to be performed repeatedly for the same object on the same type of images, whereas ACM is more suitable for occasional segmentation of different objects on different types of images

4 Conclusion

As MPS quantification involves numerous processes, automation is desired as it will considerably reduce the laboriousness of the underlying tasks. Segmentation of LV is a critical step towards the automatic processing of MPS tomograms. In this paper, we have proposed a segmentation scheme for the delineation of the LV based on the ASMs. A software tool has been developed to allow the user to interactively specify the approximate position and pose of the LV. Segmentation is then automatically performed to demarcate the exact outline of the LV. This scheme will be able to reduce the laborious tasks in MPS quantification, while allowing interactive guidance and intervention from the medical experts. The performance of the proposed approach has been tested using 50 sets of clinical MPS tomograms with a success rate of 94%. Furthermore, we have also illustrated that the proposed technique is more suited for LV segmentation in MPS tomograms when compared to the ACM.

Acknowledgments. The authors would like to thank Dr. Lee Boon Nang from Department of Nuclear Medicine, Hospital Kuala Lumpur, Malaysia for providing the cardiac SPECT tomograms for use in this work.

References

1. Wikipedia, http://en.wikipedia.org/wiki/SPECT
2. Slomka, P.J., Berman, D.S.: Germano, G.: Quantification of Myocardial Perfusion. In: Germano, G., Berman, D.S. (eds.) Clinical Gated Cardiac SPECT, 2nd edn., pp. 69–91. Blackwell Futura, Massachusett (2006)
3. Van Train, K.F., Garcia, E.V., Cooke, C.D., Areeda, J.S.: Quantitative Analysis of SPECT Myocardial Perfusion. In: DePuey, E.G., Garcia, E.V., Berman, D.S. (eds.) Cardiac SPECT Imaging, 2nd edn., pp. 41–64. Lippincott Williams & Wilkins, Philadelphia (2001)
4. Cootes, T.F., Cooper, D., Taylor, C.J., Graham, J.: Active Shape Models - Their Training and Application. Computer Vision and Image Understanding 61, 38–59 (1995)
5. Van Ginneken, B., Frangi, A.F., Staal, J.J., Ter Haar Romeny, B.M., Viergever, M.A.: Active Shape Model Segmentation With Optimal Features. IEEE Transactions on Medical Imaging 21, 924–933 (2002)
6. Hamarneh, G., Gustavsson, T.: Deformable Spatio-Temporal Shape Models: Extending Active Shape Models to 2D+Time. Image and Vision Computing 22, 461–470 (2004)

7. Cootes, T.F.: An Introduction to Active Shape Models. In: Baldock, R., Graham, J. (eds.), pp. 223–248. Oxford University Press, Oxford (2000)
8. Tan, W.H., Bister, M., Coatrieux, G.: Uncommitted Morphological Merging of Watershed Segments. In: Proc. 2nd IEEE Int. Conf. Information & Communication Technologies: from Theory to Applications, Damascus, pp. 1573–1577 (2006)
9. Kass, M., Witkin, A., Terzopoulos, D.: Snakes: Active Contour Models. In: 1st International Conference on Computer Vision, London, pp. 259–268 (1987)
10. Xu, C.Y., Prince, J.L.: Snakes, Shapes and Gradient Vector Flow. IEEE Transactions on Image Processing 7, 359–369 (1998)

Hierarchical Approach for Fast and Efficient Collision Detection in Urban Simulation

Hamzah Asyrani Sulaiman, Abdullah Bade, Daut Daman, and Norhaida Mohd. Suaib

Department of Computer Graphics and Multimedia,
Faculty of Computer Science and Information System, Universiti Teknologi Malaysia,
81310 Skudai, Johor, Malaysia
themazor@yahoo.com, {abade,daut,nhaida}@utm.my

Abstract. Urban simulation research has become an important research area in computer graphics due to the need to visualize urban environment as realistic as possible. Urban environment consists of elements such as culling, lighting, shadows, collision detection and others that will determine the realism level of simulation. One of the key components that need further consideration is to equip the synthetic world with fast and efficient collision detection approach so that urban simulation can be done realistically. In general, hierarchical approach provides fast and efficient collision detection method in urban simulation. We present a new traversal algorithm of Bounding-Volume Hierarchies (BVH) for collision detection (CD) between static and moving object that can be used in urban simulation. The result from the experiments had shown that the combination of the AABB BVH and optimized traversal algorithm is superior over the previous BVH approaches where less time taken to detect collision between static and moving objects in urban simulation.

Keywords: Hierarchical Approach, Bounding-Volume, Bounding-Volume Hierarchies, Collision Detection, Large-Scale Simulation, Urban Simulation.

1 Introduction

Detecting object interference in 3D application is always challenging problem for researchers to overcome its limitation. Comparing to real world, performing fast and accurate collision detection is never an easy task as each object that contains triangles must be checked for interaction. For example, when a collision occurred between two geometric models that has 1000 triangles each of them, the corresponding system must check every triangle on one object between triangles in another object. Thus it is very expensive just to detect collision between only two objects that has only 1000 triangles. Any applications that have collision detection system must aware of this limitation and find a solution to overcome it. Apart from that, memory management in any 3D application is also must be considered. Furthermore, there are some other criteria and important issues need to be measured when designing a 3D application. For instance, in 3D games, animation and simulation, there are needs to maintain the application runs with suitable frame rates such as 30-60 fps [7, 22, and 28]. To

H. Badioze Zaman et al. (Eds.): IVIC 2009, LNCS 5857, pp. 50–57, 2009.
© Springer-Verlag Berlin Heidelberg 2009

achieve that goal, the applications should put high attention during construction phase through applying some appropriate techniques with some optimization. Instead of that, there is a need to balance between the realism and the complexity of the applications [12, 31].

Theoretically, in order to simulate or designing our 3D application, certain criteria and important issues need to be considered. For instance, in 3D games, animation and simulation, there are needs to maintain the application runs with suitable frame rates such as 30-60 fps [1, 2, and 3]. To achieve that goal, the applications should put high attention during construction phase by undergoing or applying appropriate techniques and minimize memory consumption throughout some optimization. Instead of that, it is necessary to balance between the realism and the complexity of the applications [3, 4].

Countless numbers of researches have been undergoing regarding collision detection algorithms in virtual environments. For urban simulation, it always utilizes a very large number of polygons in order to produce realistic environment setting. Thus, the need to maintain real-time frame rates during running time especially in urban simulation is really demanding. From collision detection perspective, detecting interference between objects in urban simulation is important and not an easy task. Any proposed techniques should be efficient and robust to handle objects interference during running time. Bounding-volume hierarchies' technique has proven to be effective when detecting object interference in urban simulation. Our contribution in this paper is to introduce bounding-volume hierarchies for detecting object interference in urban simulation. We present our tree construction and tree traversal algorithm based on our heuristic to descend our tree hierarchies. It is relatively efficient than previous method for detecting object interference in urban simulation. Our result shows that by using bounding-volume hierarchies, it provides more accurate and fast collision detection method. We believed that the construction and the collision traversal algorithm is the important parameter to detection collision in urban simulation.

2 Related Work

In this section, we will briefly review related work on collision detection and urban simulation. The primary type of collision detection algorithms deals with static rigid bodies in static positions. But many recent studies are concentrated at more difficult situations such as deformable models rather that rigid models. The problems of collision detection in virtual environment have been extensively studied and recent surveys are available in Kockara et al [1] and Lin and Manocha [2]. However, we will limit our discussion to collision detection between rigid bodies in large environment, such as one in urban simulation.

2.1 Hierarchical Approaches

Spatial partitioning or bounding-volume hierarchies are common method for detecting object interference in large-scaled simulation. Both have shown remarkable result when applying them in virtual environment as they create faster and precise collision detection. Common bounding-volume for instance axis-aligned bounding boxes (AABBs) [10, 11], spheres [3, 4, 5, 6, 7, 14], oriented bounding boxes (OBBs) [13], k-DOPs [8, 15], ellipsoid [9] and oriented convex polyhedra [26] have been used to perform collision detection in virtual environment. In order to lower the computational cost of updating the hierarchy trees, it is necessary to use simple bounding-volume such as spheres or AABBs for fast computations.

2.2 Urban Simulation Collision Detection

Collision detection can be distinguished through their design method (how they employ and based). Earlier studies by Cohen et al in 1994 had used exact collision detection for detecting collision between objects in interactive environments [12]. Musse et al. in 1997 developed two methods to detect collision between human crowds [16]. The first method can be achieved by using simple mathematical equations while the second one is using earlier prediction of collision and then change the path through a simple geometric computing. Other researchers such as Loscos et al [17] and Feurtey [18] studied collision detection to determine path motion for human crowd in urban simulation.

Aliaga et al in 1998 had used bounding-volume hierarchy for detecting object interference in massive models [19]. Farenc et al (2002) had developed an Informed Environment city that provided details city information of recognition places and using bounding box for collision detection [20]. Tecchia et al in 2002 used a simple and fast method to detect collision in complex city cramps with human and other 3D models [21]. They used two different approaches to achieve real time collision detection. On one hand, it involves predicting the future or final position of the object. On the other hand, they reallocate the task for detecting collision further from current object position.

Later in 2003, Hamill et al [22] had presented Virtual Dublin urban simulation that can be used as a prototype to test various projects such as crowd and traffic simulation, land design, and disseminated graphics studies. They implemented a Moller Ray-Triangle Intersection Algorithm for detecting collision in urban simulation [23]. Nurminen et al. had suggested a 3D mobile map, called m-LOMA city [24]. The city was designed with special mobile features that can keep the location-based information of the city. In m-LOMA, collision detection had been used to detect intersection between user moving line and the objects of the city.

3 BVH Framework

The framework of bounding-volume hierarchies for detecting collision is conceptual as follows (see figure 1). In urban simulation, all buildings will have BVH constructed from the pre-processing phase. Next, by using top-down approach and binary tree, first we enclosed the building with only one bounding-volume before it can be partitioned into two smaller BVs. Once the splitting procedure of our binary tree has stopped (stopping criterion has been met where we reach the lowest level determine by the user), the collision detection module consists of our traversal algorithm to detect any collision pairs with test object will be conducted. Finally, the program will report any potential nodes that may intersect during the traversal for detecting any collision between building and test object. However for this paper, we only perform experimental on two object only in virtual environment just to show our algorithm performance.

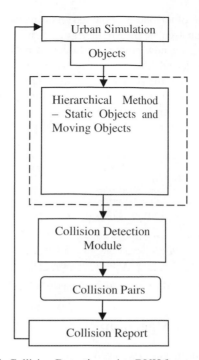

Fig. 1. Collision Detection using BVH framework

4   BVH Creation

Traditionally, a naïve approach to check for any collision is by checking each triangle for intersection with another triangle for each object. However, by checking all the polygons for intersection is quite expensive even in the simulation that has very few objects because collision detection must always checking for intersection, whether it is collided or not. That is why Hubbard et al [4], came out with a concept called broad phase and narrow phase. The main idea of broad phase collision detection is to reduce the computational load by performing only necessary test and prune an unnecessary pair test. Narrow phase intends to perform actual pair test after broad phase confirmed that there is collision. Hence, by using hierarchical method along with bounding-volume, we can localize the areas where the actual collision will be occurred. In our implementation, Sphere and AABB bounding-volume will be used to construct our BVH in urban environment simulation. Both bounding-volumes can efficiently detect object interference faster than other types of bounding-volume because of its simplicity, less memory requirement and easy for testing.

4.1   Building the Binary Tree

In order to build binary tree, we first bound the object with large sphere BV which is become root of our tree. Then, by choosing a splitting point for the BVH, the root tree that covered with sphere is cut into two tight fitted AABB which is either one of them become left tree and the other one become assigned to the right tree. The process of assignment into two sub tree is shown in figure 5 based on our tree construction method. First we assigned a new pointer and declare both right and left as a NULL. Then the algorithm checks whether we really have an empty tree or not. But if we have a tree, then we assigned the AABB to left and right. The algorithm computes the separating axis of parent level in order to become child nodes. The full algorithm for constructing our tree node can be seen in Figure 2. For this tree construction algorithm, we used top-down approach as it is the most preferable approach by most researchers.

```
void CreateBNode(BVHNode *&current,int TreeID)
    if (current == NULL)
            current = new BVHNode (TreeID);
            current->left  = NULL;
            current->right = NULL;
    else
            if (TreeID<TreeDepthTotal)
            CreateBVHNode(current->left,TreeID*2+1);
            CreateBVHNode(current->right,TreeID*2+2);
```

Fig. 2. AABB sub tree assignment to left and right tree

5 Collision Detection Algorithm

We have implemented BVH based on the binary structure. The code was well written in C++ language, using OpenGL library and runs on most Windows XP and Windows Vista operating systems and PC Intel Core 2 Duo, the CPU was a 2.2 Ghz with 2 GB of RAM with frequency of 677 Mhz.

We introduce our traversal algorithm that detects overlap faster than previous well-known traversal algorithm. Our algorithms start by checking the so called mini root without first checking the root of colliding hierarchies eliminating the potential of search for two intersected pairs. Then, we reduce the checking test by simplify the previous algorithm descendant rules by making the tree always traverse left first. Our experiments had shown that by making the tree traverse left first; we can detect many potential of overlapping BV within fewer times. Table 1 below depicts the results obtained by our experiments. In this experiments, we compare performance of Larrson Traversal algorithm (2009) [32], Ericson [30] Traversal algorithm, and generic DFS algorithm.

Table 1. E-Node Traversal Algorithm Performance Comparison. All time in milliseconds.

Algorithm	Number of Overlap				
	10	50	100	150	200
Larrson	4	60	222	334	428
Ericson	4	104	305	490	622
E-Node	6	37	181	301	389
Generic	3	203	413	680	884

From the table, our experiment shows that using E-Node traversal algorithm we could detect collision faster than previous method. At earlier stage, E-Node seems to be little higher as it needs time to detects for all mini roots intersection. However, as it traverses later on, it performs better than any available algorithm such as well knows Larrson algorithm and Ericson algorithm. Figure 3 below depicts the image test between two object using teapot object.

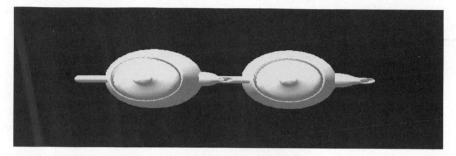

Fig. 3. Teapot intersection testing for Table 1

6 Conclusion and Future Work

We have shown our traversal algorithm that work perfectly in detecting object interference between two objects. It is believed that by using BVH, detecting any object interference becoming faster and efficient (more accurate) compare previous method. According to Somchaipeng et. al.[27], heterogeneous bounding-volume hierarchies is still in limited study thus we believe that it can provides good solution for us to speed up the intersection test using multiple bounding-volume although it may increases the computational cost to be used in urban simulation.

There is lot of future work that needs to be done. BVH will be tested in urban simulation environment where many object must be involved in order to perform collision detection in urban simulation. It also can be used for culling and ray-tracing in urban simulation in order to make urban simulation more realistic and interactive. Linking the gap between fundamental theory of bounding-volume hierarchies and coming up with good algorithms is still an open challenge for researchers and thus creates good opportunities for further research project.

Acknowledgment

We would like express our appreciation to Malaysian Ministry of Science, Technology and Innovation under eScienceFund grant (VOT No. 79237) for financial support of this research.

References

[1] Kockara, S., Halic, T., Iqbal, K., Bayrak, C., Rowe, R.: Collision detection: A survey. In: IEEE International Conference on Systems, Man and Cybernetics, 2007. ISIC 2007, pp. 4046–4051 (2007)

[2] Lin, M.C., Manocha, D.: Collision and Proximity Query. In: Goodman, J.E., O'Rourke, J. (eds.) Handbook of Discrete and Computational Geometry, 2nd edn., ch. 35, pp. 787–807. CRC Press, Boca Raton (2004)

[3] Bradshaw, G., O'sullivan, C.: Adaptive Medial-axis Approximation for Sphere-Tree Construction. ACM Transactions on Graphics 23(1), 1–26 (2004)

[4] Hubbard, P.M.: Collision detection for interactive graphics applications. PhD thesis, Brown University (1995)

[5] Hubbard, P.M.: Approximating polyhedra with spheres for time-critical collision detection. ACM Transactions on Graphics 15(3), 179–210 (1996)

[6] Quinlan, S.: Efficient distance computation between nonconvex object. In: Proceedings of IEEE International Conference on Robotics and Automation, pp. 3324–3329. IEEE Press, Los Alamitos (1994)

[7] Spillmann, J., Becker, M., Teschner, M.: Efficient updates of bounding sphere hierarchies for geometrically deformable models. J. Vis. Comun. Image Represent. 18(2), 101–108 (2007)

[8] Mezger, J., Kimmerle, S., Etzmuss, O.: Hierarchical Techniques in Collision Detection for Cloth Animation. Journal of WSCG 11(2), 322–329 (2003)

[9] Liu, S., Wang, C.C., Hui, K., Jin, X., Zhao, H.: Ellipsoid-tree construction for solid objects. In: Proceedings of the 2007 ACM Symposium on Solid and Physical Modeling, SPM 2007, Beijing, China, pp. 303–30. ACM, New York (2007)

[10] Zhang, X., Kim, Y.J.: Interactive Collision Detection for Deformable Models Using Streaming AABBs. IEEE Transactions on Visualization and Computer Graphics 13(2), 318–329 (2007)

[11] van den Bergen, G.: Efficient collision detection of complex deformable models using AABB trees. Journal of Graphics Tools 4(2), 1–13 (1997)

[12] Cohen, J.D., Manocha, D., Lin, M.C., Ponamgi, M.K.: Interactive and exact collision detection for large-scale environments. Technical Report TR94-005, University of North Carolina at Chapel Hill, Computer Science Department (1994)

[13] Gottschalk, S., Lin, M., Manocha, D.: OBB-Tree: A Hierarchical Structure for Rapid Interference Detection. In: ACM SIGGRAPH, pp. 171–180 (1996)

[14] Benitez, A., del Carmen Ramirez, M., Vallejo, D.: Collision Detection Using Sphere-Tree Construction. In: Proceedings of the15th International Conference on Electronics, Communications and Computer. CONIELECOMP, pp. 286–291 (2005)

[15] Klosowski, M., Held, J., Mitchell, S.B., Zikan, K., Sowizral, H.: Efficient collision detection using bounding-volume hierarchies of k-DOPs. IEEE Trans. Visualizat. Comput. Graph. 4(1), 21–36 (1998)

[16] Musse, S.R., Thalmann, D.: A Model of Human Crowd Behavior: Group Inter-Relationship and Collision Detection Analysis. In: Proc. Workshop Computer Animation and Simulation of Eurographics 1997 (September 1997)

[17] Loscos, C., Marchal, D., Meyer, A.: Intuitive Crowd Behaviour in Dense Urban Environments using Local Laws. In: Proc. Theory and Practice of Computer Graphics 2003. IEEE Computer Society Press, Los Alamitos (2003)

[18] Feurtey, F.: Simulating the Collision Avoidance Behavior of Pedestrians, Master thesis, The University of Tokyo, School of Engeenering (2000)

[19] Aliaga, D., Cohen, J., Wilson, A., Zhang, H., Erikson, C., Hoff, K., Hudson, T., Stuerzlinger, W., Baker, E., Bastos, R., Whitton, M., Brooks, F., Manocha, D.: A Framework for the Real-Time Walkthrough of Massive Models. Technical Report. UMI Order Number: TR98-013., University of North Carolina at Chapel Hill (1998)

[20] Farenc, N., Boulic, R., Thalmann, D.: An Informed Environment Dedicated to the Simulation of Virtual Humans in Urban Context. Computer Graphics Forum 18(3), 309–318 (2000)

[21] Tecchia, F., Chrysanthou, Y.: Real-time Visualisation of Densely Populated Urban Environments: a Simple and Fast Algorithm for Collision Detection. In: Eurographics UK 2000, Swansee (April 2000)

[22] Hamill, J., O'Sullivan, C.: Virtual dublin - a framework for real-time urban simulation. Journal of WSCG 11, 221–225 (2003)

[23] Möller, T., Trumbore, B.: Fast, minimum storage ray-triangle intersection. J. Graph. Tools 2(1), 21–28 (1997)

[24] Nurminen, A.: m-LOMA - a mobile 3D city map. In: Proceedings of the Eleventh international Conference on 3D Web Technology (Web3D 2006), Columbia, Maryland, pp. 7–18. ACM, New York (2006)

[25] Weghorst, H., Hooper, G., Greenberg, D.: Improved computational methods for ray tracing. ACM Transactions on Graphics, 52–69 (1984)

[26] Bade, et al.: Oriented convex polyhedra for collision detection in 3D computer animation. In: Proceedings of the 4th international Conference on Computer Graphics and interactive Techniques in Australasia and Southeast Asia, Kuala Lumpur, Malaysia, November 29 - December 02, 2006, pp. 127–193. ACM, New York (2006)

[27] Somchaipeng, K., Erleben, K., Sporring, J.: A Multi-Scale Singularity Bounding-volume Hierarchy. In: Proceedings of WSCG, pp. 179–186 (2005)

[28] Luiz Gonzaga da, S., Soraia Raupp, M.: Real-time generation of populated virtual cities. In: Proceedings of the ACM symposium on Virtual reality software and technology, ACM, Limassol (2006)

[29] An, N.: Implicit bounding volumes and bounding volume hierarchies, p. 98. Stanford University (2006)

[30] Erikson, C.: Real-Time Collision Detection. Elsevier Inc., Amsterdam (2005)

[31] Xiaoping, L., et al.: Kernel-Based Cellular Automata for Urban Simulation. In: Proceedings of the Third International Conference on Natural Computation, vol. 03, IEEE Computer Society Press, Los Alamitos (2007)

[32] Larrson, T.: PhD Thesis, Adaptive Bounding Volume Hierarchies for Efficient Collision Queries, Mälardalen University (January 2009)

[33] Sulaiman, H.A., Bade, A., Daman, D., Sunar, M.S.: Bounding-volume hierarchies for detecting interference in urban simulation. In: Proc. of Computer Games & Allied Technology in Animation, Multimedia, IPTV & Entertainment, Singapore, pp. 96–102 (April 28-30, 2008)

[34] Sulaiman, H.A., Bade, A., Daman, D., Sunar, M.S.: The framework of bounding-volume hierarchies for detecting interference in urban simulation. In: The 4th International Conference on Information & Communication Technology and Systems, August 5, 2008, pp. 261–266. Institut Teknologi Sepuluh Nopember (ITS), Surabaya (2008)

Generating 3D Visual Expression Using Semantic Simplification Description Based on Logical Representation

Rabiah A.K.[1], T.M.T. Sembok[2], and Halimah B.Z.[3]

[1] Department of Multimedia, Faculty of Computer Science and Information Technology, Universiti Putra Malaysia, 43400, UPM Serdang, Selangor, Malaysia
[2] National Defense University of Malaysia
[3] Universiti Kebangsaan Malaysia
rabiah@fsktm.upm.edu.my, tmts@upnm.edu.my, hbz@ftsm.ukm.my

Abstract. Performance on a question answering system is reflected by the number of correct answers that is produce from a list of alternate choices. However, many answers would appear in documents and passages laden with terms from the query. It becomes more difficult and eventually impossible to make a precise answer to a query. The aim of this study is to determine the keyword of the precise answer to a specific query and illustrate the answer in visual expression. In this paper we propose a method to translate text into visual expression, closest to the correct answer. To achieve a significant illustration capability it is necessary to develop methods of dealing with knowledge base. Firstly, we must consider the real world and the visual expression of key information that can be extracted from the words. The proposed system will analyse and match them using visual semantic simplification description based on logical representation.

Keywords: Visual Expression, Precision Answer Extraction, Question Answering System, Logical Representation.

1 Introduction

Question answering is a central human activity in getting relevant information or a process of any information exchange that involves humans and the data that is not fully structured [1]. When we need information, we ask questions that will help us to obtain it. Question answering processes can impress users and keep them satisfied, improve the domain quality and accelerate the development process. In a question answering system, the first step involves in retrieving answers relevant to the questions. Question answering system has been relatively narrowly focused on the task of searching for and returning the answers of an individual that satisfy a query. However, it usually produces short length answers and many of the answers would appear in documents and passages burdened with terms from the query. It becomes difficult to make a precise answer to a specific query.

Natural language processing technologies lead the possible reformulations of the answers collection, in order to ensure the precise answer. This work presented is an

H. Badioze Zaman et al. (Eds.): IVIC 2009, LNCS 5857, pp. 58–65, 2009.

extension of the previous work found in [2], which is to generate a 3D virtual scene by using semantic simplification description based on logical representation.

In this paper, we will make a brief presentation of our question answering system. Then, we will discuss the problems associated with answer selection, and the strategies that can be used to overcome these problems. Finally, we will describe the solution through investigation of establishing a correspondence between words and visual depictions. This correspondence is not a one-to-one match, but for some semantic domains, it is possible to establish direct correspondence between words and pictorial elements being referenced by those words.

2 Related Work

Theoretical work in question answering is found in Artificial Intelligence (computational linguistic), psychology, linguistics, and philosophy. Thagard (2006) [3] called these interdisciplinary studies as cognitive science. Cognitive science has primarily worked with the computational-representational understanding of the mind: one can understand human thinking by postulating mental representations akin to computational data structures and mental procedures akin to algorithms [3], [4]. Work in these various areas forms the basis for implemented natural language question answering systems. Natural language question answering may be considered the most universal way to provide information access. There are several natural language question answer systems with different purpose such as START (SynTactic Analysis using Reversible Transformations) natural language system, which was developed as an information retrieval system in 1993; ALICE is a chat robot and Deep Read is a reading comprehension prototype system (1999).

Currently, many question answering systems have a growing demand for accurate and cost effective information extraction. Alternatively, to overcome the query deficiencies, automatic extraction algorithm would reduce human interactions in the information extraction. An efficient automatic extraction requires some approaches or algorithm that tries to simulate human thinking, using some expert knowledge. Recently, artificial intelligence has become an efficient tool in human thinking simulation and especially in automatic feature extraction issues [5]. Artificial intelligence can be built using advanced mathematical theories such as fuzzy logic, artificial neural networks and genetic algorithms.

However, this paper focuses on the knowledge issues in translation of semantic logical representation into 3D visual expression for precise answer extraction. Jackendoff in 1987 [6], attempts to establish a correspondence between words and 3D model of objects, but the problem is handled primarily at the single-word level (both nouns and verbs) and does not extend to establishing a correspondence between a sentence/phrase and the complex scene it may evoke.

In the present research, we proposed to generate a virtual scene by using semantic simplification based on logical representation as an input. The representation was based on a semantic approach that it is involved in building up the meaning representation and enforced both syntactic and semantic agreements. On the other hand, this research also exploited additional knowledge in order to understand the text document and produce as its output some descriptions of the information conveyed by the original text. This research evaluated a set of children stories to understand the structure of the story and simplify the complexity of the natural language tasks [2], [7]. In this research too, we are used graphic constraints for simplifying the entire visualization process. All the natural language existed in the stories could generate visual environment from the story descriptions, and can be divided into natural language processing and virtual scene representation tasks [3],[8]. The main challenge of this work was to encapsulate the natural language understanding, incorporate an additional world, and generate appropriate graphical output.

3   Keyword of Answer Extraction

This question answering system comprised two main modules: question analysis and related knowledge base retrieval. The architecture of the system is described as in Figure 1.

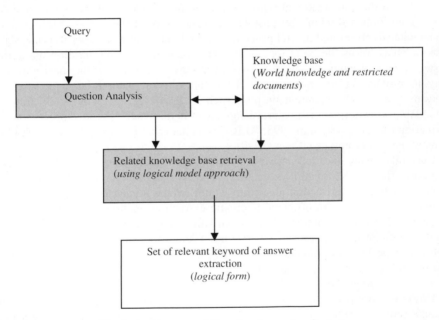

Fig. 1. Architecture of Question Answering System

The question analysis module determined some information about the question such as the key entities to retrieve from the related knowledge. The key entities was then applied to these related knowledge to generate the set of answers. The final module was in charge of filtering the answers from the weighted sentences.

Question Analysis Module: The question analysis module determined some information pertaining to the question by parsing and translating the language into logic form. A lexicon based on WordNet 2.0 was used to categorize them into syntactic and synonym or hypernym words. During question analysis, the system converted the natural language question into a logical query (LQ) representation as has been used for knowledge base extraction. Before creating the logical query representation, this module carried out a syntactic categorization, stop-word removal, lexicon dictionary, phrases and language grammar.

At this stage the system determined whether the question had information and written in the correct rule. When it could not decide the information and rules for the question, it would response with an error message. The information of the question was used for answer finding. For example, the question "Why did Chris write two books of his own?" resulted in the following output:

LQ: ~ cl([two(g46)],[]) # ~ cl([book(g46)],[]) # ~ writes(chris,g46))

Information: objects *(two book)*, events *(write)*

where the first line represented the logical form of the question and the third line represented the question information. Here the information asked about the objects and events, are known as key entities to retrieve the related knowledge base.

Related Knowledge Base Retrieval: The system used knowledge base for answer finding. This module extracted the objects and events that were relevant in response to the questions. This module had two sub modules: Theorem Prover, and Skolem Constant Binding.

Theorem Prover sub module: The focus enabled a theorem prover to keep track of variable bindings as a proof proceeded . For example, when the question asked was in logical form $\exists x P(x)$, then a proof was initiated by adding the clause $\{\sim P(x)\}$ to the knowledge base. When a focus was employed, the clauses $\{\sim P(x), ANSWER(x)\}$ were added instead. The x in the answer $(ANSWER(x))$ would reflect any substitution made to the x in $\sim P(x)$. These focus were returned by the system and sent to the Skolem Constant Binding module before it was displayed to the user.

Skolem Constant Binding sub module: The Skolem Constant Binding sub module took the key entities that were extracted by the theorem prover sub module and then identified the keyword answer literally based on the question infomation. This sub module tied a set of the skolemized clauses containing at least one skolem constant that represented an entity that was bound to other skolemized clauses. A hypothetical answer consisting of a keyword answered literals must be binded to each other in order that the accompanying answer can be considered as a relevant answer.

A relevant answer to a particular question can be generally defined as an answer that implies all clauses to that question. Relevance of the answer has been defined as unifying the skolem constant by the question.

In a rule base consisting solely of skolem constants, the unifying of a single skolem constant to a question would be considered a relevant answer. When rules were added, the experiment became more complicated. When taxonomic relationship was represented in a rule base, a relevant answer can be defined as an interconnection of all clauses that unified and binded the same skolem constants. For example, *g1* is considered as a skolem constant to be unified to a skolemized clause in knowledge base, ~ *end(r(pony & express),g1) :- end(r(pony & express),g1)*. Then *g1* binds to any skolemized clauses consisting the same skolem constant, and tracks all possible skolemized clauses in knowledge base by binding skolem constant exists, *f1*, until all skolem constants binding are complete, *sents(g1,f1); now(g1); mail(g1); new(f1); faster(f1); and way(f1)]*.

4   3D Visual Generation

The main idea of the development of the proposed system is the construction of tools to translate a text description document in natural language input, which is presented from logical form into visual presentation. Text-to-visual presentation conversion has three components in the system shown in Fig. 2, Logical Linguistic Component, Knowledge Base Component and Visual Component. The first component is to analyze the logical form representation, define the thematic rules relations between subject and predicate information in the input file. In the second component, the nouns in the representation files were extracted, and the corresponding images were loaded into the system. Both steps focused on translating the main part of the sentence or text. In the final step, the representation output was used again, and the verb element was extracted from the predicate clause. The step corresponding to this verb was applied to the image retrieved in the second step, and the visual file was thus shown on the screen.

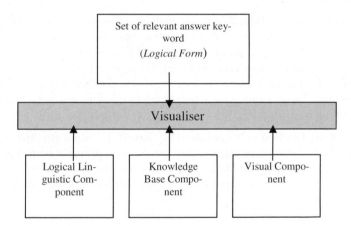

Fig. 2. Architecture of the 3D Visualizer

4.1   Translate Word into Image

The system identifies the noun in the subject phrase that depends on the predicate phrase in the simple sentence translation. When translating sentences, the predicate phrase is the main part of the sentence and is the last part of the sentence, so the system identifies the word in the subject phrase that depends on the last phrase and loads an image corresponding to the noun in the subject phrase. In the text translation, the system first identifies keywords from a subjective piece of text. The system then loads an image corresponding to the keyword. Each keywords-set in the top ten hit pages was compared to that of the target text, then the image that best matches was used.

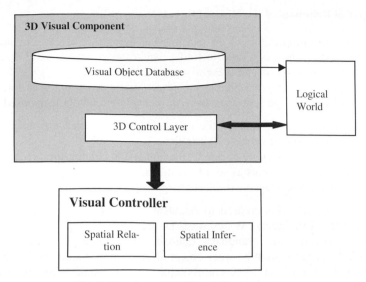

Fig. 3. Structure of 3D Visual Component

5   3D Visualization

The 3D generation stage follows the visual semantic parameterization in visualization process. It specifies and translates the parameterized data into predicate and argument in logical form, called as corresponding objects, and manipulates them by sending events into a visual scene to construct visual expression accordingly. The structure of 3D visual component is as shown in Fig. 3. 3Dimensional visual component consists of two parts; a 3D Control layer, acts as intermediate interface that links to the logical world and a Visual Object Database that stores the 3D models. The second part is Visual controller, consists of a module to handle the attributes of the 3D objects, placement of the objects and determine the final visual representation.

5.1   Changing the Attributes of the Visual Object

Following the visual semantic parameterization in the knowledge base, the output data was specified and translated the modified elements of the visual scene. The Visual Controller contains the methods to handle the following tasks: to create   virtual objects container to store the name of the object for further manipulation. The other one is to access the virtual object attributes and obtain the specific data to enable change of the attributes of the virtual object. Virtual object attributes focused on handling three kinds of descriptive adjectives, i.e. lightness, colour and part of the material.   There are seven parameter elements with their own specified attributes to describe the words respectively. Each attribute provides various methods and additional values, which can be used by the graphic component to set these visual attributes to 3D object. The combination of these elements are sufficient to visualize the materials of a real world in the current stage of development.

5.2 Spatial Relations of the Visual Object

Considering the complexities of the task of visualizing the logical semantic simplification description, there is a need to find a way to restrict the lexicon dictionary and 3D object visualization. In the present work, logical representation had been used as an input source. In addition, object-oriented geometric constraint was introduced into the proposed system. The following were the consideration approach based on [8]:

- Each object was defined by the real value of its spatial attribute through prescribing the detail geometric constraints.
- Logical symbols were regarded as the constraints among the predicate by interpreting these constraints as set of equations.
- Access the numerical constraints among the parameters and calculate the values.

The above approach was created to establish the methods for handling the spatial relations of the virtual scene. We used spatial prepositions to describe spatial relationships with words in natural language. Landau and Jackendoff [8], states that the differences in language system between object identification (nouns) and object localization (spatial preposition) was attributable to the underlying organization of identification and localization channels. In this present work, we concentrated on a rigid object representation. The spatial properties specified the relationship between one object to another object on geometric relations (i.e. above, near). Interpretation of the logical symbol extracts spatial constraint about the object and the preposition phase by accessing the related object. Finally, the extracted qualitative constraints were interpreted as the numerical constraint among the objects. Then, the layout of the virtual scene were constructed.

5.3 Spatial Reasoning

The inference technique was required to address the need for spatial reasoning about rigid objects. In this present research, the integration of the structure with implicit geometric and words constraints was used to handle the spatial reasoning. The spatial inference is to infer the spatial relations directly from the given predicate, which may involve simple or complex object manipulation.

6 Conclusion

In this paper, we proposed a methodology to construct 3D visual expression that is based on relevant keywords of answer extraction. The descriptions were used to define the types of predicate in different constructions. It bridges the gap between words and graphic components. The use of visual constraints to assist in object definitions and spatial construction has also been discussed. However, the construction of 3D Visualizer system is still in progress. For future work, we will revise the predicate visual matching function to take the user's precedent knowledge as a consideration. On the other hand, we will evaluate the appropriateness of the matched images retrieval and scalability of the visual expression and will also conduct experiments to examine how this visualization affects human understanding of the text content in actuality.

References

1. Galitsky, B.: Natural Language Question Answering System, 2nd edn. Advanced Knowledge International Pty Ltd., Adelaide (2003)
2. Rabiah, A.K., Sembok, T.M.T., Halimah, B.Z.: Intelligent Information Extraction using Logical Approach: Skolemize Clauses Binding. In: Proceedings of Knowledge Management International Conference 2008 (KMICe 2008), Langkawi, Malaysia, pp. 251–256 (2008)
3. Computation and the Philosophy of Science (2006),
   `http://cogsci.uwaterloo.ca/Articles/Pages/comp.phil.sci.html`
4. Thagard, P.: Mind: Introduction to Cognitive Science. MIT Press, Cambridge (1996)
5. Mohammadzadeh, A., Valadan Zoej, M.J., Tavakoli, A.: Automatic Main Road Extraction from High Resolution Satelite Imageris by Means of Self-Learning Fuzzy-GA Resolution. Journal of Applied Sciences 3(19), 3431–3438 (2008)
6. Srihari, R.K., Burhans, D.T.: Visual Semantics: Extracting Information from Text Accompanying Pictures (1995)
7. Rabiah, A.K., Sembok, T.M.T., Halimah, B.Z.: Computing Key-word Answer to Hypothetical Queries in the Presence of Skolem Clauses Binding. Journal WSEAS Transaction on Computer 6(93), 514–521 (2007)
8. Zeng, X., Mehdi, Q.H., Gough, N.E.: From Visual Semantic Parameterization to Graphic Visualization (2005)

Optimal Discrete Wavelet Frames Features for Texture-Based Image Retrieval Applications

Mohammad Faizal Ahmad Fauzi

Faculty of Engineering, Multimedia University,
63100 Cyberjaya, Selangor, Malaysia
faizal1@mmu.edu.my

Abstract. In this paper, experiments were conducted to find the optimal configuration for discrete wavelet frames texture feature extraction method for use in real-time content-based image retrieval application. Several parameters of the algorithm such as the wavelet basis, the number of decomposition levels, and the distance metric are evaluated in terms of retrieval performance, and the optimum value for each parameter is suggested. By experimenting on0020the statistical function as well as channel selection, the final DWF configuration is proposed that achieves an average of more than 80% accuracy using the Brodatz texture dataset and about 70% accuracy using the VisTex dataset.

Keywords: Content-based image retrieval, Texture analysis, Discrete wavelet frames.

1 Introduction

Texture analysis is an important and useful area of study in machine vision. Most natural surfaces exhibit texture and a successful vision system must be able to deal with the texture world surrounding it. Texture analysis methods have been utilized in a variety of application domains. In some of the mature domains such as remote sensing, texture has already played a major role, while in other disciplines such as surface inspection, new applications of texture are being found. Some other examples of the fields in which texture plays a major role are medical image analysis, document processing and content-based retrieval.

This paper is particularly concerned with the analysis and development of algorithm for content-based image retrieval (CBIR) applications. Since texture is one of the main features in CBIR (the others being colour and shape), it is important to be able to retrieve images containing texture regions that are visually similar to a query texture. To achieve this, the texture feature extraction algorithm employed must be of very high performance in terms of retrieval accuracy and computational speed. In this experiment, discrete wavelet frames (DWF) technique is chosen as they have been reported to have high classification accuracy while maintaining low computational complexity [1]. Comprehensive experiments were conducted to evaluate and fine tune all parameters associated with the technique. This is followed by experiments with different statistical functions to be used as features as well as optimising channel

H. Badioze Zaman et al. (Eds.): IVIC 2009, LNCS 5857, pp. 66–77, 2009.
© Springer-Verlag Berlin Heidelberg 2009

selection. At the end of the paper, all parameters chosen to provide the optimal result for DWF in content-based retrieval are presented.

This paper is organized as follows. The next section briefly describes the discrete wavelet frames technique, while the subsequent section explains the experimentation and evaluation method. In section 4, the evaluation of the best parameters for use with DWF is presented. Section 5 and 6 discuss improving the performance of the algorithm and evaluation with a colour database respectively. Finally the conclusion is presented in section 7.

2 Discrete Wavelet Frames (DWF)

The discrete wavelet frames [1-5] is nearly identical to the standard wavelet transform [6], except that one upsamples the filters, rather than downsamples the image. While the frame representation is over-complete, and computationally more intensive than PWT, it holds the advantage of being translationally invariant.

Given an image, the DWF decomposes its channel using the same method as the wavelet transform, but without the subsampling process. This results in four filtered images with the same size as the input image. The decomposition is then continued in the LL channels only as in the wavelet transform, but since the image is not subsampled, the filter has to be upsampled by inserting zeros in between its coefficients. The number of channels, hence the number of features for DWF is given by $3 \times l - 1$.

To compute the features, the mean energy of each channel or filtered image are used and are given as:

$$ f = \frac{1}{M \times N} \sum_{i=0}^{m-1} \sum_{j=0}^{n-1} \left| W_k (i, j) \right| \tag{1} $$

where M and N are the number of rows and columns of the channel or filtered images, and W_k is the k-th channel or filtered images.

3 Experimentation and Evaluation Method

In this paper, 3 major experiments are presented. The first two are based on a grey scale database (using Brodatz texture database), and are used to configure the parameters of the chosen method to achieve the optimum performance, as well as improving it using some statistical analysis. The third experiment involved testing the configured method on colour textures (using Vision Texture database).

The Brodatz database [7] contains 112 textures of various kinds, including the many inhomogeneous ones which are not usually included in texture studies. By including the entire Brodatz collection in the database, we allow the potential for confusion and failure that exists when texture algorithms encounter non-texture regions in natural scenes. Each Brodatz texture is scanned at 300 dpi with 256 grey levels, and is 512×512 in resolution. Each 512×512 image was then cut into 16 non-overlapping sub-images of size 128×128. A total of 1792 (112×16) database images are produced from the texture album, where the image classes are defined by the 112 Brodatz textures. Out of the 112 Brodatz textures, 12 texture classes (D013, D042, D043, D044, D045, D058, D059, D061, D069, D090, D091 and D097) however are not used as query because of the inhomogeneity across their children images. The evaluation is therefore based on the remaining 100 homogeneous texture classes, which provide a more meaningful measure of the retrieval performance.

Vision Texture (VisTex) [8] is a collection of texture imagery developed at MIT that is publicly available for evaluating different texture features. It contains 4 components: reference textures, texture scenes, video textures and video orbits which all contain a set of different textures for various experimental purposes. In this paper, the reference textures are used for evaluating the optimized technique on colour textures. There are 167 colour textures in the reference texture components. As in the experiment with the Brodatz textures, all images are cut into 16 non-overlapping 128×128 sub-images, yielding a total of 2672 database images in the VisTex collection.

For both experiment, each textured image in the database is used once as a retrieval prototype and the *precision* and *recall* for the particular query are computed. The average precision and recall over the entire prototypes are plotted for comparison of performance. Based on information retrieval theory, precision is defined as the fraction of images retrieved that are relevant, and recall is defined as the fraction of the relevant image retrieved, and is calculated as below:

$$Precision = \frac{Number\ of\ relevant\ retrieved\ images}{Number\ of\ retrieved\ images} \tag{2}$$

$$Recall = \frac{Number\ of\ retrieved\ relevant\ images}{Number\ of\ relevant\ images} \tag{3}$$

If we set the total number of images retrieved to be the same as the total number of images relevant, in this case 15, then we will have the same measurement for both precision and recall. A 100% precision and recall is achieved if all 15 matches are found within the top 15 retrieved images, R, considered.

4   Determining the Best Parameters for DWF

In this section, a range of wavelet parameters will be tested for the DWF and their effect on the retrieval accuracy will be evaluated. The parameters to be tested include the type of the wavelet basis and the number of decomposition levels used in the computation of the wavelet transform as well as the distance metrics used for the retrieval.

4.1   The Choice of Wavelet Basis

There are many wavelet bases that can be used for computing the wavelet transform and the wavelet frames, making it impractical to evaluate all of them. However, a representative selection of well known bases such as the Daubechies, Haar, Coiflet and Symlet wavelets will be tested. Three different vanishing moments are chosen for each of the Coiflet and Symlet wavelet family, while two and one are chosen from the Daubechies and the Haar wavelet family respectively. The wavelet coefficients for these wavelet families can be obtained from the wavelet literature or from MAT-LAB's wavelet toolbox.

Fig. 1 shows the average precision-recall rate for the nine wavelet bases when retrieving the 100 homogeneous Brodatz texture classes, using 3-level DWF decomposition and normalized Euclidean distance metrics. From the figure, it can be observed that the choice of wavelet basis does not affect the performance of the discrete wavelet frames in texture retrieval significantly, and therefore is not critical. Except for the Haar wavelet, which is the simplest of the wavelet bases, all other wavelet bases give a very similar average precision-recall rate of at least 71%. In terms of speed, there is also not a significance difference between all nine wavelet bases. Nevertheless Daubechies 8-tap wavelet basis is suggested because of its high accuracy and small number of coefficients.

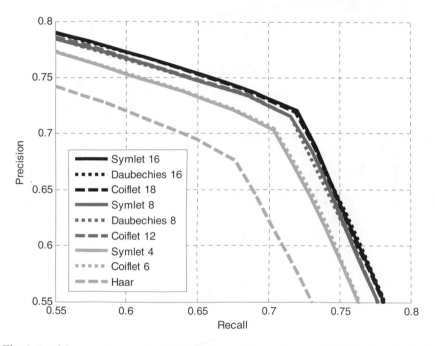

Fig. 1. Precision-recall curve for 9 different wavelet bases (zoomed in for better viewing)

4.2 Number of Decomposition Levels

In this section five different decomposition levels of 1, 2, 3, 4 and 5 are evaluated. This results in 4, 7, 10, 13 and 16 features respectively for the discrete wavelet frames decomposition. Fig. 2 shows the average precision-recall rate of the five levels, using Daubechies 8-tap wavelet basis and normalized Euclidean distance. From the figure, we can conclude that increasing the number of decomposition levels helps in improving the retrieval accuracy of the discrete wavelet frames. The increment in accuracy is quite dramatic from 1 decomposition level to 3 decomposition levels, but only a small increment is observed when the decomposition levels change from 3 levels to 4 and almost no change at all from 4 to 5 levels. Furthermore, the time taken to compute the features also increases quite dramatically when the number of decomposition levels increases.

Table 1 shows the time needed to compute the discrete wavelet frames features for image of various sizes for different number of decomposition levels. From the table, it is clear that by increasing the decomposition levels, the computational load increases almost quadratically. Since the improvement in accuracy over the 3-level decomposition is not very significant, 4- and 5-level decomposition may be deemed unnecessary and we conclude that optimal choice of the decomposition levels for the DWF is therefore the 3-level, with 10 features.

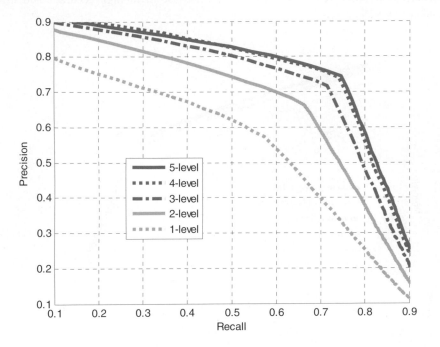

Fig. 2. Precision-recall curve for 5 different decomposition levels

Table 1. Time taken to extract features (in seconds) for 5 different decomposition levels

Decomposition levels	128×128	256×256	512×512
1 (4 features)	0.06	0.17	0.57
2 (7 features)	0.11	0.34	1.19
3 (10 features)	0.19	0.58	2.15
4 (13 features)	0.40	1.14	3.93
5 (16 features)	2.30	5.21	13.38

4.3 Distance Function

The choice of distance measure is an important issue in texture retrieval. The Euclidean distance is the most commonly used distance measure in retrieval applications, but since we are using wavelet coefficients as features, the Euclidean distance might not be the most suitable since the range of the individual features tends to increase dramatically with increasing resolution, i.e. for the lower frequency channels. One alternative way to reduce the domination of the lower frequency components is to normalize each individual features with the standard deviation of the corresponding features.

It is also interesting to observe whether the order in the L_m distance measure contributes to the overall retrieval rate. The Euclidean and the Manhattan distance measures (L_1 and L_2 distance respectively) will be considered. All together, four distance measures will be evaluated which are the Euclidean, Manhattan, normalized Euclidean and normalized Manhattan distance metrics, and are defined as below:

$$\text{Manhattan distance: } \sum_k \left| f^i(k) - f^j(k) \right| \tag{4}$$

$$\text{Euclidean distance: } \sum_k \left(f^i(k) - f^j(k) \right)^2 \tag{5}$$

$$\text{Normalized Manhattan distance: } \sum_k \left| \frac{f^i(k) - f^j(k)}{\sigma(k)} \right| \tag{6}$$

$$\text{Normalized Euclidean distance: } \sum_k \left(\frac{f^i(k) - f^j(k)}{\sigma(k)} \right)^2 \tag{7}$$

where i and j denote two image patterns, $f(k)$ is the k-th component features, and $\sigma(k)$ is the standard deviation of the distribution of features $f(k)$ in the entire database and is used to normalize the individual feature components.

Fig. 3 shows the precision-recall rate of the four different distance measures, using Daubechies 8-tap wavelet and 3-level decomposition. From the figure, both normalized distances give an almost similar performance and are the best among those evaluated. This suggests that the domination of the low frequency components does affect the discrimination ability of the discrete wavelet frames features. When the feature is not normalized, the Manhattan is better than the Euclidean distance. This is probably because the domination of the low frequency features is further amplified by the square element of the Euclidean distance measure. Without the square function, the higher frequency components can still contributes to the discrimination ability of the DWF features.

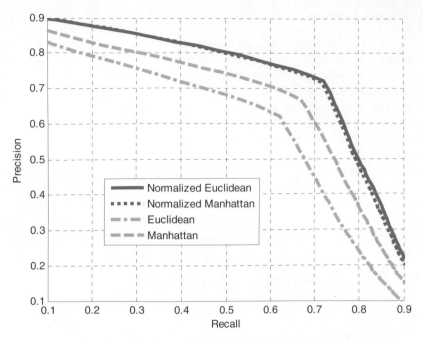

Fig. 3. Precision-recall curve for 4 different distance metrics

5   Improving Retrieval Accuracy

Throughout the last sections, the mean energy of the coefficients in each channel has been used as the channel feature. In this section several other statistical functions will be investigated for their suitability in discriminating textures. First the individual performance of the selected statistical function will be evaluated. This is followed by investigating the best combination of features in order to achieve the best texture retrieval performance. However, in doing so, the speed constraint will always have to be considered in order not to sacrifice the low computational advantage of the discrete wavelet frames while improving the precision-recall rate.

5.1   Individual Functions

Ten individual features are short-listed for evaluation, which are the mean energy, standard deviation of energy, standard deviation of coefficients, maximum value, minimum value, maximum energy, maximum row sum energy, maximum column sum energy, and the number of zero-crossings. Note that the mean of coefficients is not used as they provide no meaningful measure because all the channels except the *low-low* channel of the discrete wavelet frames are zero mean. The experiments are conducted using Daubechies 8-tap wavelet and 3-level decomposition as these parameters are found to give the best results from the previous experiments. As for the normalized metrics, since the Euclidean distance is slightly better than the Manhattan distance, it is chosen as the distance metric.

Fig. 4 shows the performance of the nine functions. From the figure, it is quite clear that the standard deviation of energy feature performs best followed closely by the standard deviation of coefficients. The mean energy and the zero-crossings feature make up the top four ranked statistical features. The performance of the maximum, minimum, maximum energy, maximum absolute row sum and maximum absolute column sum does not fare very well compared to the top four functions. The pair of maximum and minimum values gives a very similar performance, as do the maximum absolute row sum and the maximum absolute column sum. The top four functions, the standard deviation of energy (SDE), the standard deviation of coefficients (SDC), the mean energy (ME) and the zero-crossings (ZC) are chosen for subsequent experiment.

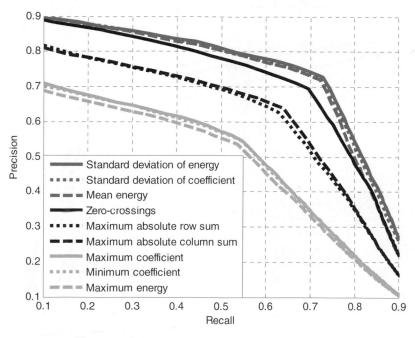

Fig. 4. Precision-recall curve for nine statistical functions

5.2 Combination of Functions

Table 2 summarizes the combination of the functions considered. The first six combinations consist of 20 features while the last two combinations consist of 30 features. Fig. 5 shows the performance of the eight combined functions. The performance of the standard deviation of energy alone is also plotted for comparison. From the graph, almost all combinations of function improve the retrieval accuracy significantly. Combination F_8 for example reaches 81% precision-recall rate for top 15 retrieved images, an increment of almost 9% over the best individual function performance. Overall, the best combination is achieved with F_1, F_7 and F_8 combinations. It is also interesting to note that combining 3 statistical functions does not necessarily have any advantage over the best combination of 2 functions. Therefore we can conclude that for an optimal feature extraction technique using discrete wavelet frames, 20 features are adequate to obtain a very good retrieval performance. In this experiment, specifically it is found that the combination of the standard deviation of energy with the number of zero-crossings is the best possible DWF feature combination.

Table 2. The considered combinations of features

Features	Combinations	Features	Combinations
F_1	SDE + ZC	F_5	ZC+SDC
F_2	SDE + ME	F_6	ME+SDC
F_3	SDE + SDC	F_7	SDE+ZC+ME
F_4	ZC+ME	F_8	SDE+ZC+SDC

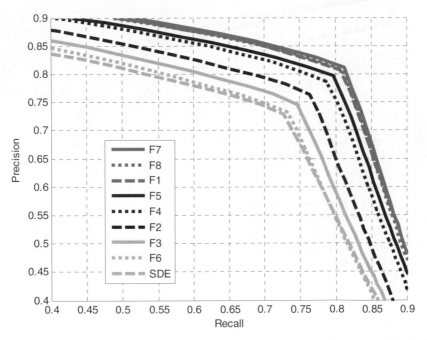

Fig. 5. Precision-recall curve for eight types of functions combination (zoomed in for better viewing)

5.3 Channel Selection

The standard deviation of energy and the zero-crossings feature will be used as texture features for each of the channels of the discrete wavelet frames. For a 3-level decomposition, this results in 20 features for each image. In this section the performance of individual channels is investigated. In other words, we would like to find if using all channels are necessary to obtain the best retrieval result, or whether dropping some channels (hence reducing the number of features) would cause any significant reduction in performance. In certain wavelet papers, the *LL* channels are dropped while some other papers tend to drop the *HH* channels.

The two functions, the standard deviation of energy and the zero-crossings are evaluated separately, followed by combinations of the two as shown in Table 3. It was observed that, on both SDE and ZE functions, the best performance was recorded when all the channels are used. The more channels removed, the poorer the retrieval performance. This is further confirmed in the subsequent experiment, when among all 16 combinations of channel selections, the ones which employ all channels are found to be the best. It is then safer to include all the channels when computing both the standard deviation of energy and the zero-crossings.

Table 3. The considered channel selections

Channel	Combinations
S_1	SDE of all channels
S_2	SDE of only the LH and HL channels
S_3	SDE of all channels except the LL channel
S_4	SDE of all channels except the HH channel
Z_1	ZC of all channels
Z_2	ZC of only the LH and HL channels
Z_3	ZC of all channels except the LL channel
Z_4	ZC of all channels except the HH channel

Channel	Combinations	Channel	Combinations
C_1	$S_1 + Z_1$	C_9	$S_3 + Z_1$
C_2	$S_1 + Z_2$	C_{10}	$S_3 + Z_2$
C_3	$S_1 + Z_3$	C_{11}	$S_3 + Z_3$
C_4	$S_1 + Z_4$	C_{12}	$S_3 + Z_4$
C_5	$S_2 + Z_1$	C_{13}	$S_4 + Z_1$
C_6	$S_2 + Z_2$	C_{14}	$S_4 + Z_2$
C_7	$S_2 + Z_3$	C_{15}	$S_4 + Z_3$
C_8	$S_2 + Z_4$	C_{16}	$S_4 + Z_4$

5.4 The Finalized DWF Texture Method

From all the experiments conducted on the Brodatz database, the best parameters and features to be associated with the discrete wavelet frames can be summarized as:

- 3 levels of decomposition
- Daubechies 8-tap wavelet basis
- normalized Euclidean distance
- SDE + ZC as features
- using all channels

The above constraints resulted in a feature length of 20, and computational speed of 0.19 seconds for an image of size 128×128 on our test platform. The average precision-recall rate for the 100 homogeneous Brodatz texture classes on the entire database is recorded at 80.67% when the top 15 retrieved images are considered.

6 Evaluation on Colour Image Database

The discrete wavelet frames texture method described in the previous section will now be evaluated on the colour image database. To achieve this, the collection from the Vision Texture (VisTex) database will be used. A total of 2672 128×128 database images are produced from the original 167 512×512 images. The images are then converted into gray scale by taking their luminance. Compared to the Brodatz texture database, VisTex database is more challenging because there are more collections of highly inhomogeneous textures in the collection. There are also cases when two or more classes are very similar to one another.

Because of these problems, we have combined several classes that are visually similar as well as removing highly non-homogeneous images for the experiment, reducing the classes from 167 to 142. Details of this reclassification can be obtained in [9]. To obtain the true accuracy of the retrieval, the average precision-recall rate approaches employed in the previous section need to be modified. Because of the reclassification, some classes contain more than 16 children images, hence it is unfair to measure the precision-recall rate at $R=15$ for all classes. In order to observe the retrieval performance of the VisTex database, the following approach is employed. For a texture class of size N, we observe how many of the database images within this class are retrieved within the top $N-1$ retrieved images when one of them is used as query. For example, for a class of size 16, the precision-recall rate is recorded for the top 15, while for class of size 32 and 176, the precision-recall rate is recorded for the top 31 and 175 respectively.

It was observed that the average precision-recall rate for the VisTex database is 68.58%. This is quite a high retrieval rate considering the level of confusion the Vistex database brings. The performance of standard deviation of energy and the zero-crossings individually was also observed, and is recorded to be 56.55% and 53.52% respectively. This further confirms the superiority of the combined features over the individual features for the VisTex database as well.

7 Conclusion

In this paper, experiments were conducted to identify the best parameters to be associated with the DWF for optimal performance, and the combination of Daubechies 8-tap wavelet, 3 levels of decomposition and the normalized Euclidean distance were found to be the most suitable parameters for the DWF. In order to further improve the accuracy, the combination of the standard deviation of energy and the average number of zero-crossings provides the best combination of features. It was also found that dropping one or more wavelet channels in the computation of features reduces the retrieval accuracy of the feature extractor. The enhanced discrete wavelet frames features gave a recall rate of more than 80% for 100 Brodatz texture classes and almost 70% for 142 VisTex textures.

References

1. Unser, M.: Texture classification and segmentation using wavelet frames. IEEE Transactions on Image Processing 4, 1549–1560 (1995)
2. Chen, T., Ma, K.-K., Chen, L.-H.: Discrete wavelet frame representations of color texture features for image query. In: Proceedings of IEEE Second Workshop on Multimedia Signal Processing, pp. 45–50 (1998)
3. Liapis, S., Alvertos, N., Tziritas, G.: Maximum likelihood texture classification and Bayesian texture segmentation using discrete wavelet frames. In: Proceedings of 13th International Conference on Digital Signal Processing, pp. 1107–1110 (1997)
4. Liapis, S., Tziritas, G.: Color and texture image retrieval using chromaticity histograms and wavelet frames. IEEE Transactions on Multimedia 6, 676–686 (2004)
5. Depeursinge, A., Sage, D., Hidki, A., Platon, A., Poletti, P.-A., Unser, M., Muller, H.: Lung Tissue Classification Using Wavelet Frames. In: Proceedings of 29th Annual International Conference of the IEEE Engineering in Medicine and Biology Society, pp. 6259–6262 (2007)
6. Mallat, S.G.: A theory for multiresolution signal decomposition: The wavelet representation. IEEE Transactions on Pattern Analysis and Machine Intelligence 11, 674–693 (1989)
7. Brodatz, P.: Textures: A Photographic Album for Artists and Designers. Dover Publications Inc., New York (1966)
8. Picard, R., et al.: Vision Texture 1.0, MIT Media Laboratory (1995),
   http://www-white.media.mit.edu/vismod/imagery/VisionTexture/
   vistex.html
9. Fauzi, M.F.A.: Content-based image retrieval of museum images. PhD Thesis, University of Southampton (2004)

Design Architecture for IMPlayer as a Tool for Supporting Visual Education Presentation

Rustam Asnawi, Wan Fatimah Bt Wan Ahmad,
and Dayang Rohaya Bt Awang Rambli

Computer and Information Sciences Department
Universiti Teknologi PETRONAS
r_asnawi@yahoo.com, fatimhd@petronas.com.my,
roharam@petronas.com.my

Abstract. Presentation of teaching-learning materials in various visual media forms is immensely necessary and important for educators and students in visual education. Most often these materials which include videos, audios, and images exist in numerous file formats indicating the needs for different types of multimedia applications to run them. Thus, utilizing various combinations of many file formats during a presentation implies the needs to have the necessary media players and be familiar with all of them. This can be very awkward for a presenter especially when switching between players during a presentation. In this paper, an integrated player (IMPlayer) which allows user to run multiple media in a single application is proposed as a solution. Basically, the application provides an interface that allows easy access to various players. The design architecture which supports multiplayer mode and dual-view features is presented. Example uses of the tool to support visual education presentation are also described.

Keywords: visual education, IMPlayer, Dualview, Multimedia Application, Multimedia Player, Multimedia Presentation.

1 Introduction

The visual education has been studied and utilized since World War I and II period. After using of training films and other visual aids during World War II, audiovisual technology gradually developed in sophistication and its use became more widespread in educational establishments [1]. Currently visual education is emerging as a field of education driven by changing practice, contemporary society and technology. Since the educational field is emergent, the nature of visual education is powerfully revealed by attending to the practices, thoughts and ideas [2].

On the other hand, technology provides exciting opportunities for enriching and transforming visual arts teaching, providing educators and students with new tools to access, organize and present information and to enrich lessons through multimedia [3]. The educators and students need specific knowledge for presenting the material of teaching-learning in visual media forms [4]. Visual media forms means the materials must be transformed from such as the simplest hand-drawn chart to video,

H. Badioze Zaman et al. (Eds.): IVIC 2009, LNCS 5857, pp. 78–89, 2009.

Powerpoint© and website presentations. Powerpoint©, as a slide-based presentation, may contain texts, images, graphics and moreover videos materials to make up the presentation. But it implies that its file size will be bigger and need more time to process it [4]. Therefore it is better to separate between powerpoint© file and video files. Hence, in the presentation of visual education the educators and students need some tools to present or to play various visual media forms such as multimedia player applications.

Currently there are many types of multimedia player applications available. Commonly in visual education the educators and students use a different multimedia player to present a different multimedia file type. For instances, when they want to present various multimedia file formats such as for presenting flv, movie in DVD format, SWF, MP4, and VCD or audio in MP3 file they prefer use flv player, DVD player, flash player, MP4 player, Windows Media Player© respectively. For displaying images file they use image viewer such as ACDsee©. Moreover for special task such as video capturing and voice recording, they usually use a special application program.

Indeed this is not a flexible and ineffective presentation task for presenters. They need to present various multimedia file types within a session. They need several players, live video applications and power point© to do the task. Consequently, they need to have experience in various multimedia player applications and it's a high possibility that the teachers would be in confusion in the middle of their presentation.

A design architecture was created to develop an Integrated Multimedia Player (shorted as IMPlayer) to solve those problems. By studying and performing relevant experiments it can prove that IMPlayer can support visual education presentation in flexible ways. IMPlayer is a new concept of multimedia player application that integrates the presentation of multimedia file types (video, audio, animation and e-presentation files). IMPlayer can be operated as video/audio player, image viewer and animation player such as VCD player, DVD player, flv player, mp3 player, jpeg/bmp/gif viewer, and flash player. Also the IMPlayer has ability to utilize dualview feature so the view of IMPlayer's control panel and its output screen is separated into two different monitor [5].

This paper is organized as follow: section one is introduction, and then section 2 is literature review, section 3 describes the system architecture of IMPlayer, section 4 explain the operation modes of IMPlayer for supporting visual education presentation, section 5 the Discussion, and the last section is the conclusion.

2   Literature Review

2.1 Visual Education

The visual education in its broadest sense includes all learning involved which seeing [6]. From [1] visual education is defined as instruction where particular attention is paid to the audio and visual presentation of the material with the goal of improving comprehension and retention. The equipment used for audiovisual presentations are: dioramas, magic lanterns, planetarium, film projectors, slide projectors, opaque projectors (episcopes and epidiascopes), overhead projectors, tape recorders, television, video, camcorders, video projectors, interactive whiteboards, and digital video clips [1].

According to [4], visual education should be proposed as a field of education. The Review of Visual Education's research team has identified four essential attributes of effective Visual Education. These are:

1. Studio-based experience: hands on, embodied practical and cognitive learning through students actively engaging in processes of expressing and communicating visual ideas, applying skills, techniques, processes, conventions and technologies, exploring creativity and innovation for real or authentic audiences and purposes;
2. Working with materials: expressing and communicating ideas with authenticity and exploring creativity and innovation through physically working with a range of materials;
3. Relationships of trust: students and teachers as active co-constructors of learning, promoters of communities of inquiry, working with trust in studio-based mentor/learner relationships;
4. Applied aesthetic understanding: the dynamic individual relationship that each student develops with the arts through active processes of engagement at the intersections of three dimensions:
   a. what they already know, understand, value and can do in visual expression and communication;
   b. their own past experiences of the arts of their own and other times, their own and other cultures and places;
   c. The potential of all experiences and materials available to them.

Over the past 70 - 80 years visual education has had four distinct phases. In the case of the first three, each new phase was in some way a reaction to the one that preceded it. In the case of the fourth, however, the phase has both to look forwards and backwards, to be proactive and not simply reactive to the past; as yet this phase scarcely has defined features [7].

Meanwhile, the goal of visual education is to help students acquire visual reception, cognition and communication, demonstrate devices of visual expression and improve students' vision [8].

There are a number of important factors that contribute to the success of the visual arts education programs. This include the dedication and commitment of the highly skilled and energetic staff, passionate about sharing their enthusiasm with the students. They are recruited to some extent based on their specialist knowledge and skills within the visual arts. For example, there is specialist support for a variety of media including painting, ceramics, photography, video art, graphic design, sculpture, animation, printmaking and textiles [7].

2.2 Multimedia Player Review

Media player is a term typically used to describe computer software for playing back multimedia files. Most software media players support an array of media formats, including both audio and video files. Some media players focus only on audio or video and are known as audio players and video players respectively.

Many media players use libraries. The library is designed to help user organize or catalog the music into categories such as genre, year, rating or other. Good examples of media players that include media libraries are Winamp, Windows Media Player, iTunes, RealPlayer, Amarok and ALLPlayer.

Media Player Classic with media codec provides more services to accommodate more video/audio file types such as flv and mp4. This player has not provided a service to control live streaming video and has not utilized the extended desktop feature [14]. AllPlayer supports and accommodate almost all file types of multimedia: audio, video, image, live video streaming [15]. But this player still has not provided a special service to utilize the extended desktop feature and not support flash files. Beside it the player also has no feature to record a voice or video capturing.

2.3   Extended-Desktop Feature in Windows

Extended desktop feature (or also called as dualview feature) is a standard feature in modern laptop that enable the user to extend the computer's desktop twice of its length, so the computer seemly have two monitor separately [9].

One of the important function of the dualview is its performance to make a difference between LCD projector display and laptop display [9][10]. The LCD display (secondary monitor) can be set as only for screen display from the output of multimedia player and the desktop view or other windows process display are in primary monitor [11]. This can get a benefit, the presenter's private information such as the files and folder list view and any other desktop processing view can be guarded from audience. So this case can improve the convenience and interest of the audience or student [12],[13].

3   The Architecture of IMPlayer

The proposed integrated multimedia player (IMPlayer) presents some solutions to the weakness of today's available multimedia player applications. IMPlayer support almost all video file types and audio file types with the codec already installed before. The IMPlayer can support flash animation (swf), live video streaming and power point files.

3.1   Single Compact Control Panel UI

The IMPlayer uses single compact control panel as its GUI. Shown in Figure 1, all multimedia elements are arranged and controlled in one main window. The IMPlayer's control panel has three tab-pages Main, Flash and Live. The tab-page Main contains three file lists. From left to right, filelist-1 is a list of selected audio video files, filelist-2 is list of selected image files and filelist-3 is list of ppt files. The tab-page Flash contains one file list for take in Flash© animation files (swf). The tab-page Live contains some menu for controlling the live video streaming.

Some terminologies used by IMPlayer are:

a. *Primary monitor device*: the main monitor of computer that has dual-display feature (usually laptop). It is to display window's desktop, window's application program, and also as main area to show the single-compact control panel of IMPlayer.

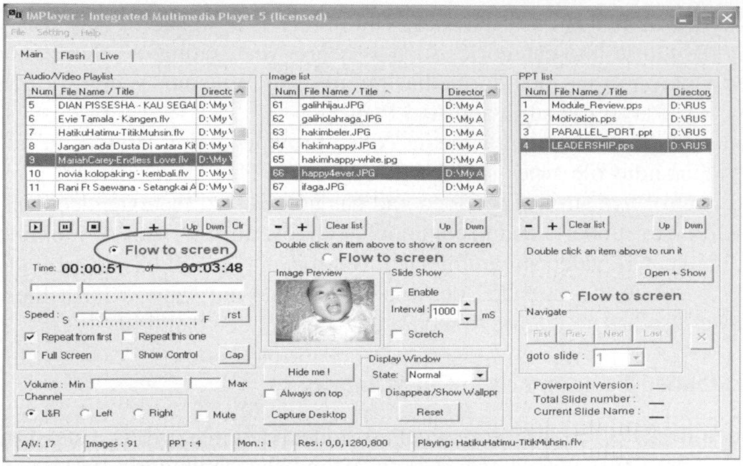

Fig. 1. IMPlayer's user interface

b. *Secondary monitor devices*: it represents a monitor device, TV device, or LCD projector. Secondary monitor is specifically used to display the output of IMPlayer.

c. *Multimedia stream*: is the output from multimedia elements processing. There have five groups of multimedia elements, so there are five streams of multimedia: audio/video stream, image stream, powerpoint stream, flash animation stream and live video stream. A multimedia stream would be displayed to secondary monitor via particular channel.

d. *Channel*: a channel is an "abstract path" for particular multimedia stream. Since there are five multimedia streams so at least five channels are needed.

3.2 The Design Architecture

The overall design architecture of the IMPlayer is depicted in Figure 2. The straight line arrows represent the direction for controlling, managing and or handling any processes. The dashed line arrows describe the direction of the multimedia streams.

Audio controlling routine will control the audio/video file list. If the user selects an audio file in the file list, the system will find the chosen file in particular storage. When the file is read and successfully processed into voice stream then rely the stream to audio/video channel that directly output by sound card. For video controlling routine, when the user select a video file in the file list, the system will read and process the selected file become video and audio streams. Both streams occupy the audio/video channel. The video stream will be output by video adapter into secondary monitor and the audio stream will be output by soundcard.

In the same way, the image controller routine, flash controller routine and PPT controller routine will control the associate file list. When a file in the file list is selected, the system will read and process it to become a particular multimedia stream. If this process is succeeded the multimedia stream will be directed into appropriate channel. Here a channel controller algorithm is used to control which one of the channels is allowed to rely its multimedia stream into secondary monitor.

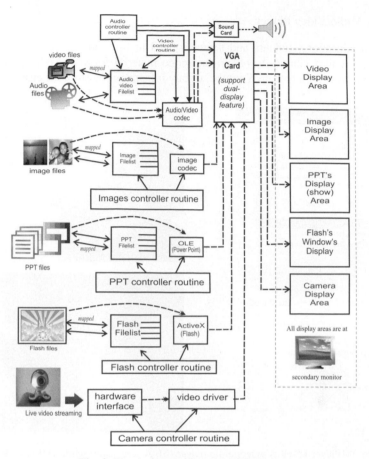

Fig. 2. The design architecture of IMPlayer

The camera controller routine is rather different from other controller. It does not need file list because it directly controls a hardware device such as webcams, CCTVs or others. The Camera controller routine will control the camera properties and features, for examples choosing the appropriate device driver, start or stop preview, start or stop recording, even controlling the display window in secondary monitor.

4   The Operation Modes of IMPlayer for Supporting Visual Education Presentation

As described in section 3, the IMPlayer is to be operated as some mode of multimedia player. In additional, the IMPlayer's user interface offers a flexible way to change among multimedia player types. Therefore this player was proposed as a tool to support some presentation in visual education.

4.1   As Audio/Video Player

In visual education, students and teachers need to use and present some video file types. Today they can easily obtain the video material for visual education, such as download the materials from Youtube, or buy it from online store, or custom made.

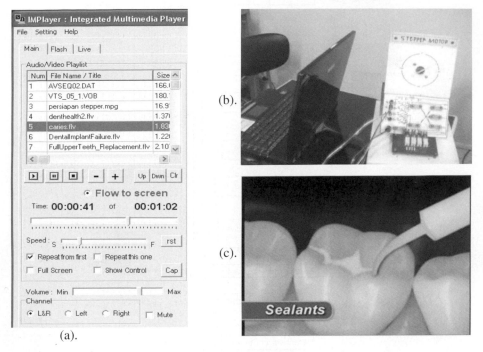

Fig. 3. (a). IMPlayer is set as video/audio player (b). A screenshot while IMPlayer is playing a movie file (c). The screenshot while IMPlayer is playing a flv file.

Youtube is the most popular video resource site that provides many materials for visual education in many areas. The video files from youtube are stored in flv and mp4 file format. In order to play the files the user must have flv or mp4 player. So, the common video files that used by students and teachers are VCD, DVD, avi, and flv.

To set the IMPlayer as Audio/video player only activate the radio button "Flow to screen" under the audio/video filelist. See figure 1 and 3, since the users usually do not play the audio and video file at the same time so the selected audio files and video files are placed into one list. The view of filelist-1 is in primary monitor (Figure 3.(a)). Figure 3(b) depicts the screenshot while playing movie file about PC based interfacing class, in file list is the 3rd file number. Figure 3(c) the screenshot of playing flv file about dental health education, in the file list is the 4th file number. Both fig 3(b) and 3(c) are in secondary monitor.

In this mode, IMPlayer can play many common video and audio files, such as: DVD, VCD, mpeg, mp4, avi, flv, mp3, wav, mid, and wma files (Figure 3.a). If a video file is playing, the video output will occupy the secondary monitor in full screen (Figure 3.b and 3.c) and the audio part output by soundcard (active speaker). And if an audio file is playing, the secondary monitor is in blank with logo. Nevertheless the user can view an image to fulfill the blank screen. At this state the IMPlayer is in multimode player i.e. mp3 player and image viewer.

4.2 As Image Viewer

Picture, image or graphic are other multimedia elements that is important in visual education. By using a camera, a moment in real event can be captured and then stored as a specific image file format in storage device. Then, it becomes materials to support visual education. For an example Figure 4(a) and (b) depict an image about total lunar eclipse. This image can help a teacher to explain about solar eclipse and help the students to understand this knowledge easily and clearly.

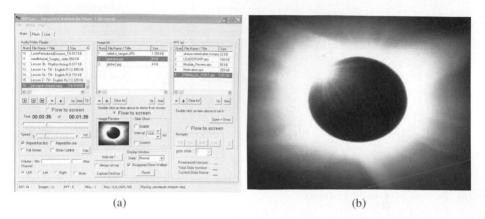

(a)   (b)

Fig. 4. (a). The views of image preview in primary monitor (b). The view of solar eclipse picture in secondary monitor

To set the IMPlayer as an image viewer it only needs to activate the radio button *"Flow to screen"* under the image filelist (This is shown in Figure 4(a)). The image file types that can be shown are bmp, jpg, and gif. There is a feature to show a sequence of images, as image slides. An image preview is used by the user to watch the appearance of the image file in secondary monitor. This mode is the default mode of IMPlayer when start running, so the image that shown on secondary monitor is like a background or wallpaper of secondary monitor.

4.3 As ppt Viewer

This is an additional mode of IMPlayer to make it more flexible to used in educational environments. Setting up the IMPlayer in this mode is by activating the radio button *"Flow to screen"* under the ppt file list. To open and show a ppt file, double click the file or select the file and then click *"Open +Show"* button.

The view of power point is in primary monitor and the show area is in secondary monitor. Presenter uses the power point application to control his or her slides.

4.4 As Flash Player

As known, the Flash© animation can be med to perform interactive visual education. Figure 5 depicts screenshots while playing a Flash© animation file (swf) on Algebra and Social Arithmetic subjects.

To set the IMplayer as a Flash© player, first enter into *tabpage Flash*, then click the play button and activate the radio button *"Flow to screen"* under the file list. The running of a swf file can be controlled by particular menus in the Flash tabpage.

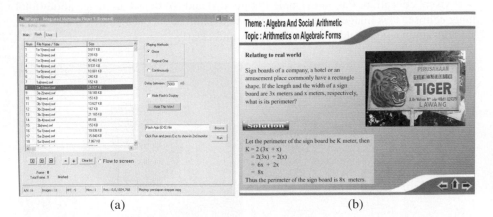

(a)   (b)

Fig. 5. IMPlayer is operated as Flash player (a). The views of Flash player in primary monitor (b). The view of secondary monitor

4.5 As Live Video Previewer and Capturer

The menu controllers of this mode are in tab-page 3 [Live], (see Figure 1). User can select video previewer or capturer. The video previewer is only preview the streaming video without any capturing task. But the video capturer can capture a part or full of the streaming video.

The view of live video streaming can be combined with the view of one of video, image or flash player in secondary monitor. Figure 6 is an example of IMPlayer that used in dentistry area. Assume a lecture in dentistry course teaching about the damage process of a tooth. Figure 6(b) is a screenshot of the live video streaming from a camera in shooting and previewing an array of damage teeth. Figure 6(c) shows live video streaming which combined with Flash© video files (flv) about how carries happen into the teeth that finally create cavities. The educator uses to utility depicted in Figure 6(c) to improve the students' understanding about this subject in visual mode.

IMPlayer can change from one operation mode to the others very easily by activating the radio button under the related file list. IMPlayer can also be operated as more than one mode (multimode player) and only one output mode can be shown in secondary monitor.

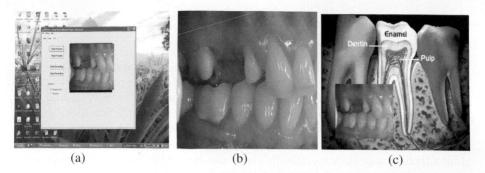

(a)   (b)   (c)

Fig. 6. (a). The view of IMPlayer operating as live video previewer and capturer (b) The view of live video streaming (c) The view of live video streaming joined with the view of video player. Both (b) and (c) are in secondary monitor.

5 Discussion

The multimedia players available today usually have only single file list (media library) for all type of multimedia files. There is no feature to switch quickly when playing each file types. Therefore, it is difficult for user to switch pleasantly between multimedia file types. This style of the user interface does not allow user to play more than one types of multimedia files at same time.

When the user run the conventional multimedia player application sometime the user's view would be an eyesore because the output screen and the control panel (file lists) view are presented in one monitor (same display). There is no multimedia player that specifically designed to utilize dualview feature. With dualview feature the view of output screen and the view of control panel can be separated, for instance the primary monitor for control panel view and the secondary monitor for displaying its output. Another benefit by utilizing the dualview feature is distracting or private information can be hidden from the audience and the available projected area remains unchanged [12]. It can be summarized that the current available multimedia players application only suits for entertain purpose and it is not flexible to support tutoring or teaching learning process.

Since the IMPlayer can be featured with dualview, this player would run in better performance with computer system having a video adapter that supports dualview feature. If it runs in PC with single display video adapter, the view of control panel and its output are in the same display (rather similar with conventional player). Some modern video adapter with dualview feature also featured with TVout port. The TVout port can be connected to TV as secondary monitor instead of LCD projector.

As live video previewer and capturer, the IMPlayer can handle only one video channel. If in the system computer has more than one video channel, it can select among them and only one that can be handled at a time.

Since the IMPlayer can support real time or live video streaming and slide previewer, IMPlayer can be used as multimedia presentation system.

6 Conclusion

This paper discussed the IMPlayer based on the proposed system architecture to high-light a new concept of multimedia player application. This is an integrated multimedia player application that can be operated as Audio player, video player, DVD player, Image viewer, flash© player, ppt viewer, video monitoring, video capturing, and audio recorder. It also support multimode player and dualview feature. Since the materials of presentations usually are stored in various multimedia file formats, by utilizing the IMPlayer the educators and students only use a single application to present it all in a flexible way. As a tool, the IMPlayer can be used to support the presentation of visual education since the materials of visual education are video, audio, image, ppt, flash files and camera.

Acknowledgement

This work is accomplished at Universiti Teknologi PETRONAS and funded in part of graduate assistantship program in Universiti Teknologi PETRONAS. It is a continuation of previous author's work about developing the IMPlayer.

References

1. Audiovisual Education, Online Encyclopedia (2009), http://www.encyclopedia.thefreedictionary.com
2. Dinham, J., Grushka, K., MacCallum, J., Pascoe, R., Wright, P., Brown Neil, C.M.: Visual Education-Repositioning Visual Arts and Design: Educating for Expression and Participation in an Increasingly Visually-Mediated World. The International Journal of Learning 14(6), 77–86 (2009)
3. Renata, P., Carrie, M.: ICT in the secondary visual arts classroom: A study of teachers' values, attitudes and beliefs. Australian Journal of Educational Technology (2008)
4. Dinham, J., Wright, P., Pascoe, R., MacCallum, J., Grushka, K.: Proving and Improving Visual Education: Implication for Teacher Education. In: AARE Conference Fremantle (2007)
5. Asnawi, R.: Development of The Multimedia Player Based on Delphi Components utilizing Extended Desktop Feature. In: The Proceeding of Indonesia National Conference conducted by STTNAS Yogyakarta, Indonesia (2008)
6. Williamson, P.B.: Visual Education for School. American Journal of Public Health (1938)
7. Diana, D.: First We See, The National Review of Visual Education, Australian Government, Department of Education, Employment and Workplace Relation (2008)
8. Erika, P.: Practical Application of Computer Software in Visual Education. Acta Didactica Napocensia 1(2) (2008)
9. Microsoft Help and Support, How to Configure and Use Multiple Monitors in Windows Xp, Microsoft Corp (2004), http://support.microsoft.com/kb/307873
10. Windows Xp Professional Product Documentation, Multiple Monitors Overview, Microsoft Corp. (2004), http://www.microsoft.com
11. Liu, Q., Kimber, D.: Framework for Effective Use of Multiple Display, FX Palo Alto Lab, 3400 Hillview Ave. Bldg. 4, Palo Alto, CA94304 (2004)

12. Turban, G.: Categorization of Educational Presentation Systems. In: Proceedings of the international workshop on Educational multimedia and multimedia education, pp. 5–10 (2007)
13. Turban, G., Muhlhauser, M.: A Framework for the Development of Educational Presentation Systems and its Application. In: Proceedings of the international workshop on Educational multimedia and multimedia education, pp. 115–118 (2007)
14. Free-codecs.com, Media Player Classic 6.4.9.4 (2009),
    http://www.free-codecs.com/download/Media_Player_Classic.htm.
15. Allplayer, ALLPlayer Features (2009),
    http://www.allplayer.org/en/features

Vision-Based Mobile Robot Navigation Using Image Processing and Cell Decomposition

Shahed Shojaeipour, Sallehuddin Mohamed Haris, and Muhammad Ihsan Khairir

Department of Mechanical and Materials Engineering, Universiti Kebangsaan Malaysia, 43600
UKM Bangi, Malaysia
Shojaei@vlsi.eng.ukm.my, salleh@eng.ukm.my,
mihsankk@vlsi.eng.ukm.my

Abstract. In this paper, we present a method to navigate a mobile robot using a webcam. This method determines the shortest path for the robot to transverse to its target location, while avoiding obstacles along the way. The environment is first captured as an image using a webcam. Image processing methods are then performed to identify the existence of obstacles within the environment. Using the Cell Decomposition method, locations with obstacles are identified and the corresponding cells are eliminated. From the remaining cells, the shortest path to the goal is identified. The program is written in MATLAB with the Image Processing toolbox. The proposed method does not make use of any other type of sensor other than the webcam.

Keywords: Mobile robot, Path planning, Cell Decomposition, Image processing, Visual servo.

1 Introduction

Image processing is a form of signal processing where the input signals are images such as photographs or video frames. The output could be a transformed version of the input image or a set of characteristics or parameters related to the image. The computer revolution that has taken place over the last 20 years has led to great advancements in the field of digital image processing. This has in turn, opened up a multitude of applications in various fields, in which the technology could be utilised.

The aim of this paper is to present a method for visual servo control using only visual images from a webcam. Visual servo is the use of image data in closed loop control of a robot. Without doubt, today, the use of vision in robotic applications is rapidly increasing. This is due to the fact that vision based sensors such as webcams are falling in price more rapidly than any other sensor. It is also a richer sensor than traditional ranging devices, particularly since a camera captures much more data simultaneously [1].

Images can be captured by camera, and subsequently, processed using some particular software. Among them, MATLAB, with its Image Processing toolbox, is well suited to perform such tasks. Information obtained from the image processing exercise can then be used to generate motion commands to be sent to the mobile robot.

H. Badioze Zaman et al. (Eds.): IVIC 2009, LNCS 5857, pp. 90–96, 2009.

This sequence is depicted in Fig. 1. Consequently, the robot imitates human vision in 6 stages as follows:

1. Image acquisition
2. Image processing
3. Image analysis and assimilation
4. Image intelligence
5. Control signal reception
6. Motion control of parts of the robot.

Fig. 1. Experimental Setup

The mobile robot motion must be controlled so as to reach its destination without colliding into obstacles. In most cases, the shortest collision-free path would be the best preferred route. The process of determining such a route is known as path planning.

In this paper we consider the Cell Decomposition approach to path planning. This general method requires a complete specification of the environment and is often based on the construction of the mobile robot configuration space (*C*-Space) which reduces the mobile robot to a point. Although a localised method will basically be used, the proposed method can present an alternative approach for guidance of the point, or even joint trajectory planning if complete information about the robot is known [2].

The Cell Decomposition approach divides C $_{free}$ into a set of non overlapping cells as shown in Fig.2. The adjacency relationships between cells are represented by a Connectivity Graph. The graph is then searched for a collision-free path. A solution is obtained by finding the cells that contain the initial and final configurations and then connecting them via a sequence of adjacent cells [3].

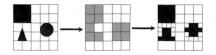

Fig. 2. Cell Decomposition Model

2 Identifying Obstacles

The path to be transverse by the robot must be ensured to be free of obstacles. For this, their existence must be identified and their positions located. This section describes how this could be done.

The image is recorded by a webcam which is installed above the robot. The image is then sent via a USB cable to a PC, to be processed by MATLAB. The experiments were carried out using a computer with 3.60GB free space hard disk and 1GB RAM memory. The algorithm was developed using MATLAB (version 7.6 R2008a).

The image is divided into segments, which become the export databases; usually they are the raw pixels data abstracted from the captured image [4,5 and 6]. The picture could be in JPG or BMP format, in which case, every pixel point uses three numerical values, representing intensity levels of the primary colours: red, green and blue (RGB) to depict its characteristics. Therefore, in such format, computing workload to perform image processing would be very high. Hence, it would be desirable to convert the coloured picture into a greyscale image. [7, 8]

Image processing methods are firstly used to identify the existence of obstacles within the image frame. This is implemented in an eight step MATLAB (with the Image Processing Toolbox) program. The following describes the steps:

- Step 1. Generate input video objects.

  This can be implemented using the command

    Obj = videoinput('adaptorname', device name, 'format');

  Where the adaptor name can be determined using the *'imaqhwinfo'* command, device name is the name given to the device and format refers to the required image format.

- Step 2. Preview the webcam video image.

    Preview('object name');

  where object name is *Obj* in the last command

- Step 3. Set brightness level of image.

    set(obj,' property name' property value);

- Step 4. Capture still image from webcam video.

    getsnapshot(object name);

  The captured image is stored as an array whose elements represent the light level.

- Step 5. Remove the input device from memory.

    delete(object name);

- Step 6. Convert from RGB to greyscale mode.

    I=rgb2ind(I,colorcube(150));

- Step 7. Find edges of objects in the image.

    I=edge(I,'sobel',(graythresh(I).1));*

- Step 8. Remove noise.

    Se90=strel('line',3,90); Se0=strel ('line',3,0); I=imdilate(I,[se90 se0]);
    I=imfill(I,'holes');

A sample implementation of these steps in MATLAB is shown below:

  Input: Take picture using webcam (original image)

```
vid = videoinput('winvideo' , 1,'RGB24_160x120');
preview (vid);
set (vid.source, 'Brightness', 30);
I = getsnapshot(vid);
I = rgb2ind (I,colorcube(150));
PSF = fspecial( 'gaussian',3,3);
I = imfilter(I,PSF,'symmetric' ,'conv');
BW = edge (I, 'sobel', (graythresh(I) * .1));
```

```
se90 = strel('line',3,90);
se0 = strel('line',3,0);
BW1 = imdilate(BW, [se90 se0]);
P = imfill(BW1, 'holes');
P = ~P;
imshow(P);
```

Output: The final is special image

The results of running this program can be seen in Fig. 3, where (A) is the original image, (B)-(F) are the intermediate stages of the image and (G) is the final image.

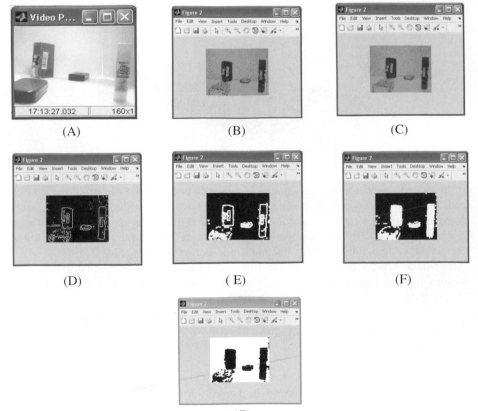

(A)   (B)   (C)

(D)   (E)   (F)

(G)

Fig. 3. A- Original Image, from B to F- intermediate stages of filtering and G- Final image

3 Path Planning

In order to select the shortest path for the robot to transverse, three actions need to be considered: the first is image capture using webcam; the second is to convert the image into a 3D scene, using the Spectral Fractal Dimension (SFD) technique [9, 10]. Previous works have used just two images of the scene for this purpose [11, 12 and 13].

The third action is to use cell decomposition to identify and eliminate paths that are obstructed. The robot would then be able to choose the shortest of the remaining paths. Fig. 4 illustrates the path finding problem, where three paths are being considered. Then,

- Path(1) is not possible (encounter obstacle)
- Path(2) is the shortest distance and possible
- Path(3) is possible but it isn't the shortest path

Obviously, the number of objects and the number of paths would vary, depending on situation. We will focus on using a general program to find the shortest path between the robot and the target.

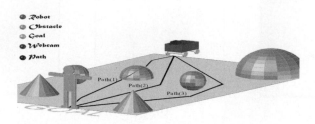

Fig. 4. Analyzed Paths

In order to send the correct control commands to the robot such that the chosen path is followed, the precise position of objects must be measured. Feedback is the comparison of the target and actual positions, and is a natural step in implementing a motion control system. This comparison generates an error signal that may be used to correct the system, thus yielding repeatable and accurate results. [14]

For data transfer to and from the robot, the MATLAB Instrumentation Control toolbox is used. Data transfer may be performed via GPIB, VISA, Serial, TCP/IP or UDP interface.

- In this section the program divides the image matrix obtained from image processing function into many smaller matrices.

```
X=Matrix Y(Section 1,Section 2);
```
    and
```
fX =mean(mean(fX));
```
- If the quantity variables (brightness in the cell) are less than 0.3 they are not considered as obstacles, otherwise (more than 0.3) they are considered obstacles

```
if fX>0.3
    fX=1
else
    fX=0
end
```
- The cells compare with its, so of the right side and left side check

```
Left (or Right) =fX|fY|fZ|fW|fP;
```
- The data of right and left variables are saved in a matrix

```
data = [left right];
```

The following is a sample implementation based on MATLAB.

Input: p = image of the last section (Final image)

```
a=p(11:30,73:88);b=p(31:50,57:72);c=p(51:70,41:56);
d=p(71:90,25:40);e=p(91:110,9:24);
f=p(31:50,89:104);g=p(51:70,105:120);h=p(71:90,121:
136);i=p(91:110,137:152);
fa=mean(mean(a));fb=mean(mean(b));fc=mean(mean(c));
fd=mean(mean(d));fe=mean(mean(e));
ff=mean(mean(fe));fg=mean(mean(g));
fh=mean(mean(h));fi=mean(mean(i));
if fa>.3;  fa=1;  else;  fa=0;end;
if fb>.3;  fb=1;  else;  fb=0;end;
if fc>.3;  fc=1;else;  fc=0;  end;
if fd>.3;fd=1;else;fd=0;end;
if fe>.3;fe=1;else;fe=0;end;
if ff>.3;ff=1;else;ff=0;end;
if fg>.3;fg=1;else;fg=0;end;
if fh>.3;fh=1;else;fh=0;end;
if fi>.3;fi=1;else;fi=0;end;
left=fa|fb|fc|fd|fe;
right=fa|ff|fg|fh|fi;
data=[left right];
```

Output: send data to robot

Running the program will result in the shortest path to the goal being generated. This path is then used to generate the mobile robot motion.

4   Conclusions and Future Work

This paper provides a framework for mobile robot navigation using a robot mounted webcam. Using images captured by the webcam, the location of obstacles are identified. Then, using the Cell Decomposition technique, the shortest path to the target destination is determined. Future work would be to translate the generated optimal path into input commands to the actual robot. The system would also be further developed for situations with moving obstacles and moving targets.

Acknowledgements

This research was supported by the Ministry of Science Technology and Innovation, Malaysia, Grant No. 03-01-02-SF0459.

References

1. Campbell, J., Sukthankar, R., Nourbakhsh, I., Pahwa, A.: A robust visual odometry and precipice detection system using consumer-grade monocular vision. In: Proc. ICRA 2005, Barcelona, Spain (2005)

2. Latombe, J.C.: Robot Motion planning. Kluwer Academic Publishers, London (1982); Robot Arm Kinematics, Dynamic, and Control. Computer 15(12), 62–80 (1991)
3. Hwang, Y.K., Ahuja, N.: Gross motion planning - a survey. ACMComp. Surveys 24(3), 219–291 (1992)
4. Gonzalez, R., wood, R.: Digital Image Processing, 2nd edn. Prentice-Hall Inc., Englewood Cliffs (2002)
5. Jain, A.: Fundamentals of Digital Image Processing. Prentice-Hall Inc., Englewood Cliffs (1989)
6. Duda, R., Hart, P.E., Stork, D.: Pattern Classification, 2nd edn. John Wiley & Sons, Inc., Chichester (2000)
7. Blanchet, G., Charbit, M.: Digital Signal Image Processing Using MATLAB. ISTE Ltd. (2006)
8. Xingqiao, L., Jiao, G., Feng, J., Dean, Z.: Using MATLAB Image Processing to Monitor the ealth of Fish in Aquiculture. In: Proceeding of the 27th Chinese Control Conference, Kunming, Yunnan China, July 16-18 (2008)
9. Akbar, H., Prabuwono, A.S.: Webcam Based System for Press Part Industrial Inspection. IJCSNS International Journal of Computer Science and Network Security 8(10) (October 2008)
10. Modesto, G., Medina, M., Baez-Lopez, D.: Focusing and Defocusing vision system (SIVEDI). In: International Conference on Electronics, Communications and Computers (CONIECOMP 2005). IEEE, Los Alamitos (2005)
11. Jenn, K.T.: Analysis and application of Auto focusing and Three-Dimensional Shape Recovery Techniques based on Image Focus and Defocus. PhD Thesis SUNY in Stony Brook (1997)
12. Nayar, S.K., Watanabe, M., Noguch, M.: Real-time focus range sensor. In: Intl. Conference on Computer Vision, June 1995, pp. 995–100 (1995)
13. Subbarao, M.: Spatial-Domain Convolution/ Disconsolation Transform. Technique Report No.91.07.03,Computer Vision Levorotatory, State University of New York, Stony Brook, NY 11794-2350
14. Aung C.H., Lwin, K. T., Myint, Y.M.: Modeling Motion Control System For Motorized Robot Arm using MATLAB. In: PWASET VOLUME ISSN 2070-3740, August 2008, vol. 32 (2008)

Automated Segmentation and Retrieval System for CT Head Images

Hau-Lee Tong[1], Mohammad Faizal Ahmad Fauzi[2], and Ryoichi Komiya[1]

[1] Faculty of Information Technology
[2] Faculty of Engineering
Multimedia University, Jalan Multimedia, 63100 Cyberjaya, Selangor, Malaysia
{hltong,faizal1,ryoichi.komiya}@mmu.edu.my

Abstract. In this paper, automatic segmentation and retrieval of medical images are presented. For the segmentation, different unsupervised clustering techniques are employed to partition the Computed Tomography (CT) brain images into three regions, which are the abnormalities, cerebrospinal fluids (CSF) and brain matters. The novel segmentation method proposed is a dual level segmentation approach. The first level segmentation, which purpose is to acquire abnormal regions, uses the combination of fuzzy c-means (FCM) and k-means clustering. The second level segmentation performs either the expectation-maximization (EM) technique or the modified FCM with population-diameter independent (PDI) to segment the remaining intracranial area into CSF and brain matters. The system automatically determines which algorithm to be utilized in order to produce optimum results. The retrieval of the medical images is based on keywords such as "no abnormal region", "abnormal region(s) adjacent to the skull" and "abnormal region(s) not adjacent to the skull". Medical data from collaborating hospital are experimented and promising results are observed.

Keywords: Computed tomography, Unsupervised segmentation, Image retrieval.

1 Introduction

With the growing size of medical images, the development of an automatic system in facilitating the processing and analysis of the data has become essential. Image segmentation plays an indispensable role in the study of anatomical structures and medical diagnosis. Segmentation can be performed either semi-automatically [1] or automatically.

Segmentation techniques differ widely depending on the specific application, imaging modality, and some other factors. For instance, the segmentation of brain tissue has different needs from the segmentation of liver. Thus, different techniques have been proposed for the segmentation of brain images such as statistical pattern recognition techniques [2], [3], [4], morphological processing with thresholding [5], [6], clustering algorithm [7],[8] and active contour [9],[10], while some other technqiues have been proposed for liver segmentation such as live wire segmentation, gray level based liver segmentation and so on [11].

H. Badioze Zaman et al. (Eds.): IVIC 2009, LNCS 5857, pp. 97–109, 2009.

General imaging artifacts such as noise and partial volume effects can also have significant consequences on the performance of the segmentation algorithms. On top of these, segmentation of abnormal regions from the image is comparatively difficult as abnormal regions could be too small to form their own clusters. Due to this artifacts for images with abnormalities, the obtained segmentation results [12], [13] are used with rule-based approach to label the abnormal regions such as calcification, hemorrhage and stroke lesion.

In this paper, a new approach for CT head image segmentation is presented and elaborated. The segmentation results are then used in a medical image retrieval system, where the images are retrieved based on the semantics generated from the segmented images.

2   General Overview of the Proposed System

The overall system comprises of three major processes which are pre-processing, abnormal regions segmentation, and CSF and brain matter segmentation, and is summarized in Fig. 1.

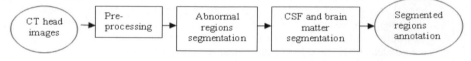

Fig. 1. Flow of the proposed system

The pre-processing is performed in order to prepare the images for the segmentations. The details of the processing are stated in Fig. 2. The process commences with contrast enhancement. This is to improve the visibility of the image especially for the intracranial area. Then the background, the scalp and the skull are removed in order to obtain only the intracranial area. The final step of preprocessing is to refine the contrast of the abnormal regions in order to ease the detection process.

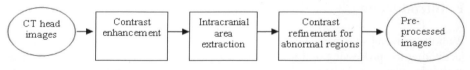

Fig. 2. Flow of pre-processing

For the segmentation of the abnormal regions, pre-processed images will undergo first level segmentation as depicted in Fig. 3.

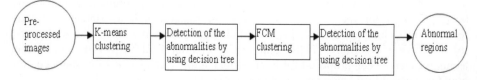

Fig. 3. Flow of abnormalities segmentation

The pre-processed images will experience k-means clustering, followed by FCM segmentation. From the segmented results of k-means segmentation, abnormalities are detected via decision tree. The detected abnormal regions will be excluded from the next detection. Then, FCM segmentation is applied to the pre-processed images and the residual abnormal regions are again detected via decision tree. The two clustering are applied in this particular manner to complement each other. K-means clustering works well for most images. However, for images having blurry abnormal regions, k-means method may experience under-segmentation and cause the abnormal regions to be too small to be detected. FCM clustering, on the other hand, experience over-segmentation for the non-blurry abnormal regions but it works better with the blurry abnormal regions. Therefore, FCM clustering is implemented later to compensate for the drawback of k-means clustering.

In order to acquire the CSF and brain matter, the second level segmentation involving FCM with PDI or EM segmentation is applied as shown in Fig. 4.

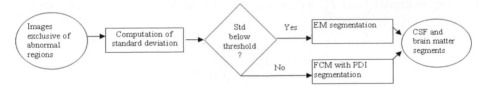

Fig. 4. Flow of CSF and brain matter segmentation

FCM with PDI or EM segmentation will segment the images into CSF and brain matter. The standard deviation is computed for the intracranial area exclusive of the abnormal regions to determine which algorithm should be adopted. The different value of standard deviation actually will affect the results of segmentation. Therefore, in order to obtain the reliable results two different segmentations are needed here. The details will be discussed in later section.

3   Pre-processing

3.1   Contrast Enhancement

The original images are low contrast images. This is because the images are encoded using 12 bits, having pixel values ranging from 0 to 4095. Such a wide dynamic range results in limited contrast for the region of interest as shown in Fig. 6(a). Therefore linear contrast stretching is needed to improve the visibility of the region.

To overcome the low contrast problem, first a histogram is constructed to locate the significant pixel range. The constructed histogram contains several higher and lower peaks as shown in Fig. 5(a). The peaks on the far left are contributed by the background pixels. The peak in the middle, on the other hand is contributed by the soft tissues which offer useful information for image analysis.

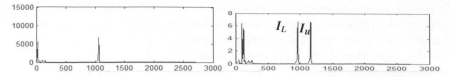

Fig. 5. (a) Histogram of a CT head image (b) Histogram of the absolute first difference

To ease the process of automatically determining the lower and upper limit for contrast stretching, the curve in Fig. 5(a) is smoothened by using convolution operation. From the smoothened curve, the absolute first difference is acquired. The acquired lower and upper limits are denoted by I_L and I_U respectively. From the first difference, the closest peak on the left and right are automatically determined as I_L and I_U respectively as shown in Fig. 5(b).

The obtained I_L and I_U will be utilized in linear contrast stretching algorithm as in equation (1).

$$F(i, j) = I_{\max} \frac{(I(i, j) - I_L)}{(I_U - I_L)} \tag{1}$$

where I_{max}, $I(i,j)$ and $F(i,j)$ denote the maximum intensity in the image, original image and contrast enhanced image respectively. After the contrast stretching, the visibility of the original image is improved and the result is depicted in the Fig. 6(b).

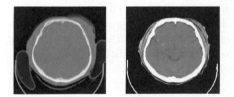

Fig. 6. (a) Original Image (b)Contrast enhanced image

3.2 Intracranial Area Extraction

In order to extract the intracranial area, thresholding technique is applied to the enhanced image in Section 3.1 to transform the image into binary. As a result of the binarization process, only skull and the background are presented in the image as shown in Figure 7(a). The skull can be easily identified as it is always the largest connected component of the brightest regions. The skull is separated from the background by using the connected component analysis to locate the largest connected component.

After acquisition of the largest connected component, the mask of the intracranial area can be obtained by setting the rest of the pixels to zero intensity. Then the intracranial area can be obtained as shown in Fig. 7(b).

3.3 Contrast Refinement for Abnormal Regions

In order to facilitate the process of detection for abnormalities, having good contrast for the abnormal regions is important. Contrast stretching is applied by using the formula in equation (1) to refine the contrast. The only difference is the determination of the lower and upper limits for the contrast stretching. To automatically determine the appropriate lower limit and upper limits, a histogram is constructed for the image from Section 3.2. From the constructed histogram, lower limit, I_L is acquired from the peak position of the histogram. The upper limit, I_U is defined as:

$$I_U = I_L + I_\alpha$$

where I_α is predefined at 400 found from experimental observation. Median filter is then adopted in order to reduce the "salt and pepper" noise. The contrast enhanced result for the original image as in Fig. 6(a) is shown in Fig. 7(c).

Fig. 7. (a) Thresholded image (b) Intracranial area (c) Contrast refined image

4   Abnormal Regions Segmentation

The main objective of the first level segmentation is to obtain segments with purely abnormal regions. Thus, the refined image from Section 3.3 is segmented into two clusters. In theory, two segmented regions with solely normal regions and abnormal regions respectively should be acquired. However, practically the segmentation results usually do not consist of purely abnormal region in a segment. This is caused by the fact that most of the abnormal regions are too small to form their own cluster, causing some bright normal regions to be grouped in the same segment with abnormal regions. Therefore in later section, decision tree is required to distinguish the incorporated normal regions from abnormal regions to form the purely abnormal regions cluster.

In order to obtain the optimized results, four segmentation techniques have been attempted which are Otsu thresholding, k-means clustering, FCM clustering and EM segmentation.

4.1 Background of the Algorithms

All the clustering techniques adopted are unsupervised clustering. Unsupervised clustering can be applied directly on any data as it does not require any training. Otsu method is based on a very simple idea to find the optimum threshold that minimizes the within-class variance to turn the gray level image to a binary image.

K-means clustering is an algorithm to cluster image based on the attributes into k partitions. The main idea is to locate the centroid for each cluster. This algorithm aims to minimize the objective function:

$$J = \sum_{j=1}^{k} \sum_{i=1}^{n} \| x_i^{(j)} - c_j \|^2$$

where $\| x_i^{(j)} - c_j \|^2$ is a squared distance between intensity value of a pixel, $x_i^{(j)}$ and the cluster centre c_j, for n pixels from their respective cluster centre.

FCM on the other hand is a method of clustering which allows one pixel to belong to two or more clusters. It is based on minimization of the objective function defined as:

$$J_m = \sum_{i=1}^{N} \sum_{j=1}^{C} u_{ij}^m \| x_i - c_j \|^2$$

where m is any real number greater than 1, u_{ij} is the degree of membership of x_i in the cluster j, x_i is the intensity value of the ith pixel , and c_j is jth cluster center. The algorithm will iterate to optimize the objective function with the update of membership u_{ij} and the cluster centers c_j. The iteration will terminate when $| \max_{ij} \{| u_{ij}^{(k+1)} - u_{ij}^{(k)} |\} < \varepsilon$, where ε and k denote termination criterion and iteration steps correspondingly.

4.2   Visual Comparison of First Level Segmentation Results

The objective of the first level segmentation is to separate abnormal regions from normal regions. The normal and abnormal regions should not merge together in order to filter out normal regions from abnormal region segment to form purely abnormal region segment. From the obtained results for the respective methods as shown in Fig. 8, Otsu threshold and EM method are not adoptable as the abnormal regions are somehow merged together with the normal region. This caused the subsequent isolation of abnormal regions from normal region to become impossible.

On the other hand, k-means and FCM segmentation generated useful results as the abnormal regions are not merged with the normal regions. This means that the abnormal regions can be distinguished from the normal regions. Therefore, in order to obtain the optimized results only k-means and FCM segmentation are adopted for the first stage segmentation scheme.

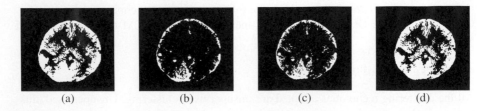

(a)   (b)   (c)   (d)

Fig. 8. Segmented Image obtained by (a) Otsu threshold (b) k-means method (c) FCM method (d) EM method

4.3 Detection and Annotation of Abnormal and Normal Regions

The segmented images obtained from first level segmentation are transformed into binary image. The purpose of the binarization here is to acquire all the connected components for normal and abnormal regions. Then the features are extracted from every connected component as listed in Table 1. The extracted features are used for the classification in order to filter away those normal regions. Based on the CT head image database acquired, we take into consideration a few types of abnormalities which are calcification, hemorrhage, hematoma, lesion and hyperdense lesion. Whereas, other bright regions such as sinus, vessel, midline falx and white brain matter are classified as normal region.

Table 1. Features of the connected component

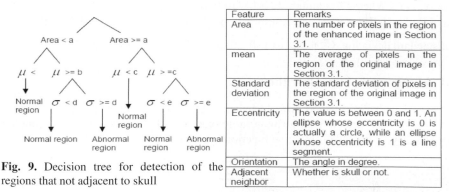

Feature	Remarks
Area	The number of pixels in the region of the enhanced image in Section 3.1.
mean	The average of pixels in the region of the original image in Section 3.1.
Standard deviation	The standard deviation of pixels in the region of the original image in Section 3.1.
Eccentricity	The value is between 0 and 1. An ellipse whose eccentricity is 0 is actually a circle, while an ellipse whose eccentricity is 1 is a line segment.
Orientation	The angle in degree.
Adjacent neighbor	Whether is skull or not.

Fig. 9. Decision tree for detection of the regions that not adjacent to skull

For classification of the normal and abnormal regions, the decision tree is employed as shown in Fig. 9, where μ and σ denote the mean and standard deviation respectively. The major reason of employment of decision tree is due to its flexibility in updating the suitable threshold values and the simplicity of the implementation.

The properties of the abnormal regions adjacent to the skull are different from the abnormal regions that are not adjacent to the skull. Hence, two separate decision trees are established for the detection of the two abnormal regions. As shown in the tree diagram, the area of the regions is categorized into small and large areas. The reason the area is divided into these two types is because for the smaller areas, the intensity is lower than larger areas such as calcification and bleeding. Similarly, for the region adjacent to the skull, a similar decision tree is formed but with two extra features which are orientation and eccentricity. The orientation and eccentricity are to detect the midline falx which is the bright area at top and bottom of the intracranial area. This is to ensure that it will not be misclassified as an abnormal region.

5 CSF and Brain Matter Segmentation

The abnormal regions are excluded from the intracranial area prior to second stage segmentation. The ultimate goal of second stage segmentation is to segment the remaining intracranial area into CSF and brain matter. Two segmentation techniques are considered which are the modified FCM clustering with PDI and the EM segmentation, as shown in Fig. 10. FCM with PDI are considered instead of the conventional FCM as the conventional FCM method has the tendency to form large clusters. This tendency causes the over-segmentation of CSF.

Fig. 10. Decision for segmentation

The decision on which algorithm to use depends on the value of the standard deviation, σ. When σ is higher, FCM with PDI will be executed, otherwise EM will be considered. The details and results will be discussed in Section 6.3. The threshold for standard deviation σ_t is set to 110 based on the segmentation results.

5.1 Background of the Algorithms

The FCM with PDI method aims to balance the contributions of larger and smaller clusters to solve tendency of forming large cluster [14]. The new objective function after modifying the FCM objective function is given as:

$$J_m = \sum_{j=1}^{C} \frac{1}{\rho_j^r} \sum_{i=1}^{N} u_{ij}^m \parallel x_i - c_j \parallel^2$$

where m and r are any real number greater than 1, ρ_j is the normalizer for cluster j, u_{ij} is the degree of membership of x_i in the cluster j, x_i is the intensity value of the ith pixel , and c_j is jth cluster center.

The expectation-maximization (EM) algorithm is a statistical estimation algorithm used for finding maximum likelihood estimates of parameters in probabilistic models, where the model depends on unobserved or missing data. The procedures of EM segmentation basically involve expectation (E) step and maximization (M) step as:

i.   Find the initial values for the maximum likelihood parameters which are means, covariances and mixing weights.

ii. In E step, use the probability density function for a Gaussian distribution to compute the cluster probability for every pixel. The multivariate Gaussian conditional density function is written as:

$$f_i(x|\theta_i) = \frac{1}{(2\pi)^{d/2} |\Sigma_i|^{1/2}} \exp[-\frac{1}{2}(x-\mu_i)^t \Sigma_i^{-1}(x-\mu_i)]$$

where $\theta_i = (\mu_i, \Sigma_i)$, x is a d-dimensional feature vector, μ_i is the mean vector and Σ_i, $|\Sigma_i|$ and Σ_i^{-1} are the d × d covariance matrix, its determinant and inverse respectively.

iii. In M step, use the probability values obtained in E-step to re-compute the means, covariances and mixing weights.
iv.   Repeat E-step in (ii) and M-step in (iii).

The algorithm terminates when the difference between the log likelihood for the previous iteration and current iteration fulfills the tolerance.

6   Experimental Results and Evaluations

The CT head images used in the experiment are provided by the collaborating hospital. The images are in DICOM format with dimension 512 X 512, and the regions in the images have been manually labeled by the radiologists. In total there are 72 images in the dataset, taken from 30 patients, with 149 abnormal regions.

6.1   Visual Inspection of Abnormalities Segmentation Results

In this section, the abnormalities segmentation from Section 4 are evaluated visually. The experiments are conducted to evaluate whether k-means, FCM segmentation or k-means cum FCM segmentation produce better acquisition results. The results obtained from k-means cum FCM segmentation will undergo two separate detections by using the tree decision. The first detection is to detect the abnormal regions from k-means results. The subsequent detection of FCM results is to locate the residual abnormal regions that have not been located in the detection from k-means results.

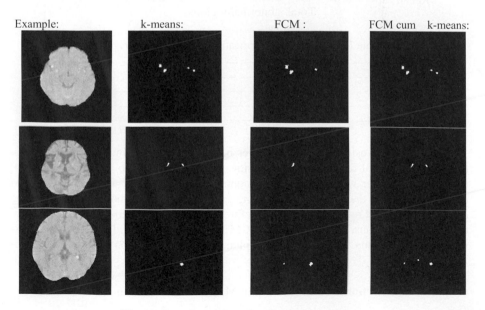

Fig. 11. Experimental results of abnormal regions

The results of the detection of abnormal regions from k-means, FCM and k-means cum FCM method are shown in Fig. 11. From Fig. 11, there is a trade off between FCM and k-means method. K-means clustering works very effectively and efficiently compared to FCM clustering when the images have clear abnormal regions as shown in example 1 and 2. Lesser abnormal regions are being detected from FCM results because FCM clustering has the tendency to form larger cluster. It includes some surrounding noise pixels into the abnormal regions which cause the over-segmentation of the abnormal region. The over-segmentation reduces the average of pixels in the region and makes it being misclassified as normal region.

However, for some images having blurry abnormal regions with intensity too close to the white matter of the brain as in example 3, the abnormal regions obtained from k-means will be relatively too small to be detected. In this case, FCM method is better as it manages to form the proper bigger abnormal regions compared to the k-means method, which makes them more obvious to be detected. As such k-means cum FCM method is better than any individual method as it managed to detect the most abnormal regions.

6.2   Numerical Evaluation of Abnormalities Segmentation Results

For quantitative analysis, the results for the classification accuracy of the abnormal regions are measured in terms of recall. The comparison results for k-means, FCM and FCM cum k-means clustering are depicted in Table 2. In our classification, recall is defined as:

$$\text{Recall} = \frac{\text{Numbers of abnormal regions correctly classified}}{\text{Total abnormal regions}}$$

Table 2. Results of the classification of the abnormal regions

Method	Recall
k-means	83.22%
FCM	77.85%
k-means & FCM	89.26%

The recall rate using k-means is lower because for those abnormal regions misclassified as normal regions; their intensities are very similar to the white matter of the brain even after we have done two contrast enhancements. The recall for FCM clustering is lower than k-means clustering as the number of abnormal regions being detected from FCM results are less. Therefore, in order to compensate the weaknesses of FCM and k-means, the detection of FCM results must succeed the detection of k-means results. In this way they will complement each other to provide optimum segmentation result.

6.3   Visual Inspection of CSF and Brain Matter Segmentation Results

In this section, the segmentation results obtained from EM segmentation are compared to the results obtained from FCM with PDI segmentation. The respective segmented images are shown in Fig. 12. The value of the standard deviation will be higher when the intensity of the CSF is relatively low compared with brain matter. In this scenario, FCM with PDI will produce better results. EM on the other hand will experience the over-segmentation as shown in Example 1. When the standard deviation is lower, FCM with PDI will tend to produce noisy results. However, EM in this case will produce better results as shown in Example 2.

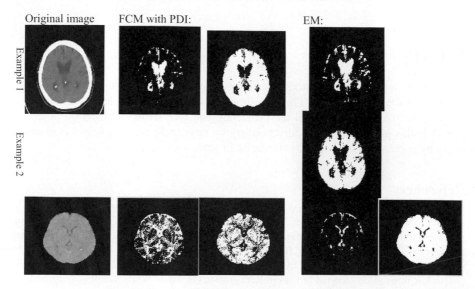

Fig. 12. Results of CSF and brain matter segmentation

6.4 Image Retrieval Results

The retrieval is conducted based on the database mixing both normal and abnormal images. In total, the image database consists of 183 images. The semantic retrieval is executed by the semantic terms which are "no abnormal region", "abnormal region(s) adjacent to the skull" and "abnormal regions not adjacent to the skull". All the semantic terms are annotated by the decision trees and adjacent to neighbor feature as discussed in Section 4.3. The results for respective semantic terms are shown in Table 3. The results of retrieval are evaluated in terms of precision and recall as well. For image retrieval, precision and recall are defined as:

$$Precision = \frac{Numbers\ of\ relevant\ images\ retrieved}{Total\ number\ of\ images\ retrieved} \quad Recall = \frac{Numbers\ of\ relevant\ images\ retrieved}{Total\ numbers\ of\ existing\ relevant\ images}$$

Table 3. Results of the retrieval

Semantic terms	Precision	Recall
no abnormal region	90.90%	97.56%
abnormal region(s) not adjacent to the skull	98.47%	95.56%
abnormal region(s) adjacent to the skull	87.50%	85.71%

For the retrieval by the keywords "no abnormal region", recall is higher than precision is because of the total number of images annotated as normal image is more and reduce the precision value. On the other hand, the precision and recall for keywords "abnormal region(s) adjacent to the skull" are lower than "abnormal region(s) not adjacent to the skull" is due to the challenge in distinguishing the abnormal regions from other bright region such as sagittal sinus and transverse sinus on the boundary of the intracranial area.

7   Conclusion

We have presented a new approach for the automatic segmentation and retrieval system of real CT head images. The experiment results of the CT image segmentation and retrieval have demonstrated the efficiency and effectiveness of the proposed approach in this paper. On top of current query by keywords, plan for future is to enable query by contents as well such as similarity in terms of ventricles.

References

1. Barderaa, A., Boada, I., Feixas, M., Remollo, S., Blasco, G., Silva, Y., Pedraza, S.: Semi-automated method for brain hematoma and edema quantification using computed tomography. Computerized Medical Imaging and Graphics 33(4), 304–311 (2009)
2. Richarda, N., Dojata, M., Garbayvol, C.: Distributed Markovian segmentation: Application to MR brain scans. Journal of Pattern Recognition 40, 3467–3480 (2007)
3. Zhang, Y., Brady, M., Smith, S.: Segmentation of brain MR images through a hidden Markov random field model and the expectation–maximization algorithm. IEEE Transactions Medical Imaging 20, 45–57 (2001)
4. Lee, T.H., Fauzi, M.F.A., Komiya, R.: Segmentation of CT Head Images. In: Conference on Biomedical Engineering and Informatics, pp. 233–237 (2008)
5. Hohne, K.H., Hanson, W.A.: Interactive 3D segmentation of MRI and CT volumes using morphological operations. J. Comp. Assist. Tomogr. 2, 285–294 (1992)
6. Lemieux, L., Hagemann, G., Krakow, K., Woermann, F.G.: Fast, accurate, and reproducible automatic segmentation of the brain in T1-weighted volume MRI data. Magnetic Resonance in Medicine 42, 127–135 (1999)
7. Hu, Q., Qian, G., Aziz, A., Nowinsk, W.L.: Segmentation of brain from computed tomography head images. In: Proceedings of IEEE Engineering in Medicine and Biology 27th Annual conference, September 2005, pp. 3375–3378 (2005)
8. Mohamed, N.A., Ahmed, M.N., Farag, A.: Modified Fuzzy C-Mean in Medical Image Segmentation. In: Acoustics, Speech, and Signal Proceedings, vol. 6, pp. 3429–3432 (1999)
9. Huang, A., Abugharbieh, R., Tam, R., Traboulsee, A.: MRI Brain Extraction with Combined Expectation Maximization and Geodesic Active Contours. In: SP&IT, IEEE International Symposium, August 2006, pp. 107–111 (2006)
10. Maksimovic, R., Stankovic, S., Milovanovic, D.: Computed tomography image analyzer: 3D reconstruction and segmentation applying active contour models – 'snakes'. International Journal of Medical Informatics 58, 29–37 (2000)

11. Campadelli, P., Ouslaghi, E.: Liver segmentation from CT scans: A survey. In: Masulli, F., Mitra, S., Pasi, G. (eds.) WILF 2007. LNCS, vol. 4578, pp. 520–528. Springer, Heidelberg (2007)

12. Cosic, D., Loncaric, S.: Rule-Based Labeling of CT Head Image. In: 6th Conference on Artificial Intelligence in Medicine, pp. 453–456 (1997)

13. Matesin, M., Loncaric, S., Petravic, D.: A rule-based approach to stroke lesion analysis from CT brain images. In: 2nd international symposium on image and signal processing and analysis, June 2001, pp. 219–223 (2001)

14. Shihab, A.I.: Fuzzy Clustering Algorithms and Their Application to Medical Image Analysis. Ph.D. thesis, University of London (2000)

Real-Time Object-Based Video Segmentation Using Colour Segmentation and Connected Component Labeling

Jau U.L. and Teh C.S.

Faculty of Cognitive Science and Human Development,
Universiti Malaysia Sarawak,
94300 Kota Samarahan, Kuching, Sarawak,
Malaysia
lydia_uj@yahoo.com, csteh@fcs.unimas.my

Abstract. In this paper, we described two-scan connected component labeling (CCL) approach on a real-time colour video image segmentation. CCL approach is an act of region labeling and could provides opportunity to find feature of object and establish boundaries of objects which are the common properties needed by many object-based video segmentation applications. We tested the proposed technique in two experimental studies that simulates real-time object-based video segmentation. Our experiments results shown that the proposed technique could perform region labeling in a fast manner. Another advantage of the proposed technique is that it does not provide extra storage to store same label equivalence. This property gives advantage to avoid label equivalence redundancies that always happen in the CCL approach.

Keywords: Connected component labeling (CCL), real-time colour video image, region labeling, object-based video segmentation application.

1 Introduction

Introduced in the year of 1966 by [1], CCL is an approach that labels regions within a binary image. The component of regions is labeled with unique label which was provided by the CCL operation. The CCL approach assigned same label to the same connected component of a region and those in different connected components have different label [2]. CCL is a fundamental step in segmentation of an image objects and regions, or blobs and can be used to establish boundaries of objects, components or regions, count the number of blobs in an image [3] and to find feature of object [4]. In [5], CCL is a fundamental operation in pattern analysis (recognition) and computer (robot) vision and can be found in almost all image-based applications such as fingerprint identification, character recognition, automated inspection, target recognition, face identification, medical image analysis and computer-aided diagnosis. In this study, object-based video segmentation applications refer to the higher-level video image-based applications that require the location and/or feature

H. Badioze Zaman et al. (Eds.): IVIC 2009, LNCS 5857, pp. 110–121, 2009.

of the object in every video frame. The input image for the object-based video segmentation applications is in the form of video sequence and consists of specific scene with objects.

In [4], CCL approach has been demonstrated in a real-time pupil-detection system which is an example of object-based video segmentation application. They described a fast CCL algorithm using a region colouring approach and it compute region attributes such as size, moments and bounding box in a single pass through the image. Their technique shows satisfactorily result in term of time performance, thus was applied in the real-time pupil-detection system. According to [6], time is important factor for real-time application. Because CCL approach could provides opportunity to find feature of object and establish boundaries of objects which are the common properties needed by many object-based video segmentation applications, the aim of this study is to develop a two-scan CCL technique that can be apply in the real-time object-based video segmentation applications.

In this study, the proposed technique is described on real-time colour video image and its time performance is studied in the specified experiments. The experiments results are used to justify the performance of the proposed technique in term of execution time and the applicability of the proposed technique in the real-time object-based video segmentation application. In the following section, previous work on CCL is presented followed by the proposed CCL technique in section 3, experimental studies in section 4, experiments results and discussions in section 5 and conclusion in section 6.

2 Previous Work

In basic, CCL utilize binary image (black and white) as the input image. It also utilize a neighborhood mask as shown in Fig. 1 and a neighborhood function as shown in Fig. 2. The neighborhood mask consist of one object element, $P(i,j)$ and four or eight immediate neighbors. It can be found in a 4 or 8-connectivity type whereby the 4-connectivity mask consist of four immediate neighbors while the 8-connectivity mask consist of eight immediate neighbors. It is used to scan the binary image to assign provisional label to the object pixel (represented by black or white at position (i,j) in the binary image). Assigning provisional label is described in the first pass of the neighborhood function. The first pass assign label which is a provisional label to the object pixel, $P(i,j)$ while the second pass solve label collisions after the first pass.

	P (i,j+1)	
P (i-1,j)	P (i,j)	

P (i-1, j+1)	P (i,j+1)	P (i+1,
P (i-1,j)	P (i,j)	

Fig. 1. Neighborhood mask (Source: Sonka, Hlavac & Boyle, 1999) Left Fig.: 4-connectivity mask Right Fig.: 8-connectivity mask

---

First Pass

- If all the neighbors are background pixels (non-object pixels), assign a new (and as yet) unused label to $P(i,j)$.
- If there is just one neighbor with a non-zero label (object pixel), assign this label to pixel $P(i,j)$.
- If there is more than one non-zero pixel among the neighbors, assign the label of any one to the labeled pixel. If the labels of any of the neighbors differ (label collision), store the label pair as being equivalent in a separate data structure – an equivalence table.

Second Pass

- All of the region pixels were labeled during the first pass, but some regions have pixels with different labels due to label collisions. The whole image is scanned again and pixels are re-labeled using the equivalence table information (for example, with the lowest value in an equivalent class).

Fig. 2. Neighborhood function (Source: [24])

In [1], the CCL operation is an example of two-scan approach. It scans the input image in forward raster sequence and the first scan is used to assign provisional label to object pixels and store label equivalences in separate data structure. The second scan scans the input image again to replace provisional labels with new labels in the equivalence table. In [1], equivalent labels are stored in equivalence table, T as n-tuples of the form $(n_{t1} \dots n_{tk})$ whereby $k = 2$ for the 4-connectivity mask and $k = 4$ for the 8-connectivity mask [7]. After the first scan, the entries of T are sort ascendingly and then T is processed to build another equivalence table, Y by moving the current entry $(n_{t1} \dots n_{tk})$ in T to Y and replacing $n_{t2} \dots n_{tk}$ with n_{t1} in the remaining entries of T. In Y, the first label is the smallest representative of an equivalence class and the remaining labels are elements of the class. In [1], the second scan scans the input image again to compare provisional labels with the labels in Y. Whenever the provisional label is found to be in Y, but not as a first label, replace the provisional label with the corresponding first label. The output of this operation is regions (represented by black or white connected component) are labeled with unique label.

According to [8], the way in which label equivalences are handled shows that it can have a dramatic effect upon the amount of computer processing time. In [5], to label the connected components, the algorithm need to compute the minimal label in the mask corresponding to the pixel, and the same label equivalence may be stored multiple time. A very large memory is then necessary for storing the label equivalences. Hence, the two-scan approach faces challenge against time performance and memory size [9]. [10][11][12] are some of the works to minimize memory storage requirement and execution time for the two-scan approach.

In addition to the above mentioned sequential algorithms, several parallel algorithms have been designed for the parallel machine models such as in [9][13][14]. Other algorithms such as in [15][16][17] were design to label connected component of images in arbitrary dimension that is represented by hierarchical trees. CCL operation too can be performed using one-scan approach based on the contour tracing technique [18][19][20]. In the most recent study, [4] demonstrated single pass CCL operation on an image buffer. In this study, we proposed a two-scan CCL operation on an image buffer. The proposed study then can be used to find feature of object and establish boundaries of objects which are the common properties needed by many object-based video segmentation applications. The following section described the proposed study.

3   Methodology

Fig. 3 depicted the architecture of the proposed system. Input for the system is real-time colour video image where scene as perceived by the censoring device is represented in the form of sequence of image buffer. Colour segmentation is initially performed to identify the location of object of interest via its colour feature and represent the colour feature as object pixel in the image buffer. The output of colour segmentation is used by the proposed CCL as its input image. The output of CCL then is a transformed image buffer consists of regions of interest with unique label. Both colour segmentation and the proposed CCL operation is done on a single image buffer.

The proposed CCL consist of five components: (1) The input image is the image used by the entire operation and the equivalent table is used to store for label equivalences. (2) The image scan is the direction for scanning connected components using the neighborhood mask. (3) The first pass is the process to assign provisional label and storing label equivalences as the image is scanned. (4) The second pass is the process solving label equivalences by replacing provisional label with the new label; and (5) The output image is the resulting image from the entire CCL operation (i.e. from the first pass to the second pass).

Fig. 3. Architecture of the system

3.1   Input Image and Equivalent Table

The input image for the CCL operation is the output from the colour segmentation operation. It is an image buffer namely *imagecopy*; with the size of $N \times M$ pixels (e.g. $N = 320$ and $M = 240$). This image is represented in a binary form in which pixels that are denoted as 1 (i.e. object pixels) represent the position of desired colour feature at coordinate (x,y) while 0 represent the position of undesired colour feature.

The equivalent table also is an image buffer namely *image_test*; with the size of *T x T pixels* (e.g. T = 320). It is used to mark label equivalences during the first pass process. The position of pixel represented by the height and the width is used to represent the labels that were assigned in the first pass process. *image_test* pixels must be initialized as 0 before the scanning begins.

3.2 Image Scan

The direction to scan *imagecopy* is from the top to bottom and left to right with the 8-connectivity mask shown in Fig. 4. *P* is the pixel of interest and *a,b,c,d* are its immediate 8-neighbors respectively. The 8-connectivity mask is used to scan object pixels which are not a border image pixel. This is so that *P* can be analyzed against its immediate neighbors which are at the top row. The idea of scanning the image with the mask is to assign every object pixels in *imagecopy* with the same positive integer label as its 8-neighbors (i.e. *a,b,c,d*) or a new label in the absence of its 8-neighbors. After one image scan (i.e. first pass), object pixels in *imagecopy* are replaced with positive integer labels at their corresponding locations. However, these labels are all a provisional label.

c	b	a
d	P	

Fig. 4. Table 1.8-connectivity mask P is the pixel of interest and a,b,c,d are its immediate 8-neighbors

3.3 First Pass

The first pass requires the new label namely number; is assigned with integer value 2 since object pixels are denoted as 1 in *imagecopy*. As the input image is scanned with the neighborhood mask, whenever *P* is an object pixel; the label of its neighbors is checked. If all of the neighbors has non-object value (i.e. 0), assign the object pixel which denoted as 1 in imagecopy with the new label (i.e. 2). Increase the value of the new label by 1 whenever this case occurred (i.e. all neighbors are 0). If any of the neighbor has an object value, determine the smallest value (but not 0) among the neighbors and assign the smallest label to the object pixel (Fig. 5). Then, mark the value of the object pixel as being equivalent to its neighbor's value (except for 0) as 1 in *image_test* defined earlier (Fig. 6). Continue these processes until all object pixels in the input image has been scanned. The resulting image for imagecopy is all object pixels which are denoted as 1 earlier is being replaced with provisional label from the first pass processes. However each region is being labeled with many different labels due to label collision. Thus second pass is needed to remove the redundant labels.

Fig. 5. Assigning provisional label to object pixel, P based on its neighbor's label

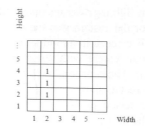

Fig. 6. Marking label equivalences as 1 in the equivalent table Height and width represent the labels that were assigned from the first pass process

3.4 Second Pass

The equivalent table, *image_test* is scanned from direction top to bottom and left to right to find the "mark" which is represented as 1. When found, identify the coordinates of the mark and compare the two coordinates. The highest value is searched in *imagecopy* and when found, replaced it with the smallest value. Then, delete the mark by assigning it as 0 to imply the label equivalent has been solved. The second scan will stop when all marks in *image_test* has been processed. The resulting image for *imagecopy* is all provisional labels are being replaced with the new label from the second pass processes. The *imagecopy* also implies that every region is being labeled with unique label in which same connected component has similar label and those in different connected components has different label.

3.5 Output Image

The output image of the proposed study is *imagecopy* that consist of many integer positive labels. The label represent component of region in which same connected components has similar label and those in different connected components has different label. Thus, every region in the image has a unique label and the labels are in the increasing form from the top to the bottom of the image. However, region label begins with 2 because new label is assigned with integer value 2 earlier. Region's label in the image too appeared not in the numbering order form from the top to the bottom of the image because of label collision.

4   Experimental Studies

Two experiments was conducted to simulate real-time object-based video segmentation application. The system uses a PC camera of resolution 320 x 240 as the censoring device. The computer system was a Windows XP Professional Service Pack 2; with processor of Intel(R) Pentium(R) 4 CPU 2.40GHz and RAM of 1536MB. The software used to program the application was a Microsoft® DirectX® 9.0 software development kit (SDK), with the component that was being used is Microsoft® DirectShow® [21].

Two datasets that involved in the experiments are the simulation of simple and complex scene. The simple scene is a scene in an indoor environment where minimum and different objects exist, and the lighting was uncontrolled (Fig. 7(a)-(d)). For both experiments, object of interest for the system was the red circle on the white paper (Fig. 7(a)-(h)). The complex scene is a scene in an indoor environment where many and different object with similar colour feature with object of interest exist, and the lighting was uncontrolled (Fig. 7(e)-(h)). The censoring device then was set in direction moving towards the static object of interest as shown in Fig. 7.

The proposed technique is tested in the experiments to perform region labeling with the specified datasets. The aim of the experimental studies is to identify the execution time for the proposed technique to label region in the specified datasets. The experiments results are used to justify the performance of the proposed technique in term of execution time and the applicability of the proposed technique in the real-time object-based video segmentation application.

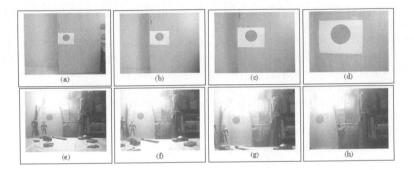

Fig. 7. Four image buffer taken from the video sequence in Experiment 1 and 2 (a) – (d): One image buffer taken from video sequence that is captured by the censoring device which moves towards object of interest in Experiment 1 (e) – (h): One image buffer taken from video sequence that is captured by the censoring device which moves towards object of interest in Experiment 2

4.1 Experiment Procedures

The HSI colour segmentation as in [22] was used to segment object of interest from the dataset background image via the colour feature. Specifically, the red colour feature of the object of interest is represented as object pixel from the colour segmentation process. The object pixels too are used to represent components of regions. The object of interest has no motion but the censoring device was controlled to move towards object of interest from a far distance which distance is represented by object pixel. The C++ time library was used to determine the CPU time in region labeling. This CPU time is used to represent the execution time of the proposed technique in labeling regions in the specified datasets. The time was gained from the beginning of the first pass to the end of the second pass of the proposed technique. Specific function was added in the colour segmentation algorithm to calculate total object pixels in a single image buffer. Specific function too was added in the first pass of the proposed technique to inform the total object pixels that has been processed in a single image buffer. The total object pixels and execution time to perform region labeling was recorded in a text file after the end of the second pass, and used in the experiment results and discussions. The CPU time was used to justify the time performance of the proposed technique in labeling region in single image buffer and also used to justify the applicability of the proposed technique in the real-time object-based video segmentation application which involves simple and complex scene. Following section shows the result from the conducted experiments along with the discussions.

4.2 Experiments Results and Discussions

Results in Fig. 8 consist of the result of colour segmentation, total object pixels and execution time in a single image buffer taken from the video sequence in both experiments. The black and white image refers to the output of colour segmentation, in which the object pixels are represented in white colour while the background pixels are represented in black. The white blobs refer to the regions that have been processed by the proposed technique in the single image buffer. The total object pixels refer to the number of object pixels that was found in the single image buffer by colour segmentation and also the number of object pixels that has been processed by the proposed technique in the single image buffer. The CPU time refers to the execution time for the proposed technique to perform the region labeling in the single image buffer.

The colour segmentation result for both experiments shows that object of interest has successfully been segmented from the background image (Fig. 8 (a)-(g)). This happened because, the colour feature of object of interest has been successfully identified and segmented by the colour segmentation operation. The colour segmentation used in both experiments has the ability to segment image pixels that has HSI colour value that fall within the predefined range. Hence, the colour segmentation used in both experiments can segment region of desired object and region of undesired objects as well (Fig. 8 (a)-(g)). In Fig. 8 (h), the colour segmentation is seen unable to

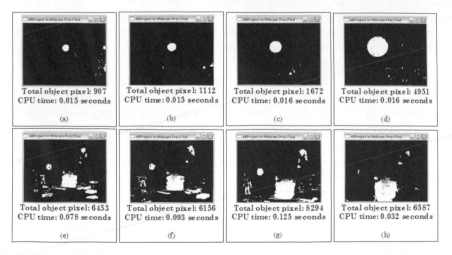

Fig. 8. Results colour segmentation, total object pixels and execution time in the four single image buffer taken from the video sequence in Experiment 1 and 2 (a) - (d): Results from Experiment 1 (e) - (h): Results from Experiment 2

segment object of interest from the background image. This happened because, the colour feature value was not within the predefined range. This is the limitation of the colour segmentation used in this experiment [22].

The total object pixel for each image buffer shown in Fig. 8 (a)-(h) was different for both experiments. This happened because as the censoring device moves towards object of interest, every region appeared appeared bigger and bigger. Region, as described earlier is represented by object pixel from the colour segmentation process. As the region appeared bigger and bigger to the censoring device, the total object pixel for the region also is increased. Hence, the total object pixel in the image buffer (Fig. 8 (a)-(h)) is the sum of total object pixels for every region as perceived by the censoring device. Consequently, from this experiment, the proposed technique has to label every region as perceived by the censoring device. This also means that the proposed technique has to process every object pixels that appeared in the single image buffer. From result in Fig. 8 (a)-(h), the number of total pixel that has been processed by the proposed technique in the single image buffer matches the number of total pixel found by colour segmentation in the single image buffer. Thus, from this experiment result, the proposed technique is able to complete its region labeling task.

From the execution time result represented by the CPU time in Fig. 8 (a)-(h), it shows that the time to label all regions that appeared in the single image buffer was less than 0 second, thus is low. This happened because, the proposed technique uses equivalent table that allows label equivalences are immediately sorted when they appeared in the equivalent table. This technique is different than [1] where the label equivalences are not sorted and they need to sort the label equivalences in the second pass which is not in the case for the proposed technique. In the second pass of the proposed technique, the second pass only need to identify the smallest label between the label equivalents and change the highest label which is a provisional label with the smallest label that has been identified earlier. Time to sort label equivalences was none for the proposed technique. The only time that involved in the second pass of the proposed technique was changing the provisional labels. Thus, from this experiments result, the proposed technique does not take too many times to perform region labeling in a single image buffer.

The equivalent table in the proposed technique also shows another advantage. It allows same label equivalence is marked at the same position. Same label equivalence, as mentioned by [5] could derive multiple times and large memory storage is needed to store all label equivalences. However, from the proposed technique, the equivalent table shows that there is no need to have an extra storage to store same label equivalence. Thus, from this experimental studies, the proposed technique could avoid label equivalence redundancies.

Based on the experiments results, using the proposed technique, region labeling can be done in a short amount of time in a single image buffer that consist of simple and complex scene. The equivalent table used in the proposed technique gives advantage to remove the time to sort label equivalences as in [1]. The equivalent table too gives advantage to remove extra storage to store same label equivalences as same label equivalences always happens as mentioned by [5]. Thus, from this experimental studies, the proposed technique is seen having the opportunity to be applied in the object-based video segmentation application as a method to perform region labeling for both simple and complex scenes. Region labeling, as mentioned earlier, provides opportunity to find feature of object and establish boundaries of objects which are common task for many applications. Following section further demonstrates the applicability of the proposed technique in feature extraction and in establishing the boundaries of objects in another experiment. The experiment results is used to justify the applicability of the proposed technique in the object-based video segmentation applications.

5 Application

Experiment 1 was repeated to identify the performance of the proposed technique in feature extraction and in establishing the boundaries of objects. The dataset however, consist of several datasets examples that was captured in an indoor environment. Any red coloured object was used as the object of interest. Specific function was designed and added to the program to draw the boundaries of the objects. Affine moment invariants as in [23] then was used to extract feature from objects that was bounded by the augmented box. Specifically, the affine moment invariants is used to determine the central of object that is bounded by the augmented box. Fig. 9 shows the results from this experiment. The central of object is represented with the green dot while the boundaries of objects is represented by the augmented box which is in the blue colour. From the results in Fig. 9, it can be seen that the proposed technique indeed could provide opportunity to find feature of object and establish boundaries of the objects. This can be seen when the central and the boundaries of desired objects was found in all dataset examples. Except for some dataset example where the central and the boundaries of some desired object was not found, this happened due to the limitation of colour segmentation as mentioned earlier.

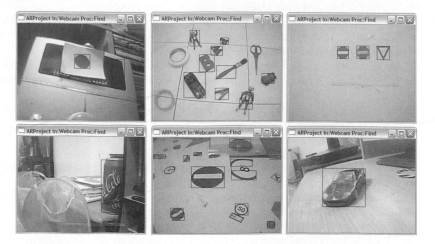

Fig. 9. Application of the proposed technique in different dataset examples

In [4], finding feature of object and establish boundaries of objects are the common properties needed by many object-based video segmentation applications. Based on the results from this experimental study, the proposed technique is applicable in the object-based video segmentation applications. In [6], time is important factor for real-time application. Based on the results from previous experimental studies, the proposed technique able to perform region labeling task in a fast manner. Thus, based on the experiments, the proposed technique is applicable in the real-time object-based video segmentation applications.

6 Conclusion

In this paper, CCL approach is studied for labeling regions in image. A new two-scan CCL operation on an image buffer then has been described and tested in simulation experiments. Based on the experiments results, the proposed technique could perform region labeling task in a fast manner. This is due to the equivalent table used in the proposed technique where it gives advantage to remove the time to sort label equivalences. The equivalent table too gives advantage to remove extra storage to store same label equivalences as same label equivalences always happens.The proposed technique too has been tested for feature extraction and establishing the boundaries of objects in another experiment. From the experiment results, the proposed technique could provide opportunity to find feature of object and establish boundaries of the objects. Consequently, from the conducted experiments, the proposed technique is applicable in the real-time object-based video segmentation applications.

References

1. Rosenfeld, A., Pfaltz, J.L.: Sequential Operations in Digital Picture Processing. Journal of the Association for Computing Machinery 13(4), 471–494 (1966)
2. Yasuaki, I., Koji, N.: Component Labeling for k-Concave Binary Images Using an FPGA. In: IEEE International Symposiun on Parallel and Distributed Processing, IPDPS 2008, Miami, FL, April 14-18, 2008, pp. 1–8 (2008)
3. Jung-Me, P., Carl, G.L., Hui-Chuan, C.: Fast Connected Component Labeling Algorithm Using A Divide and Conquer Technique. In: CATA 2000 Conference on Computers and Their Applications (December 2000), pp. 373–376 (2000)
4. Gabbur, P., Hua, H., Barnard, K.: A fast connected components labeling algorithm and its application to real-time pupil detection (In Press)
5. Lifeng, H., Yuyan, C., Suzuki, K.: A Run-Based Two-Scan Labeling Algorithm. IEEE Transactions on Image Processing 17(5), 749–756 (2008)
6. Bernat, G., Burns, A., Liamosi, A.: Weakly Hard Real-Time Systems. IEEE Transactions on Computers 50(4), 308–321 (2001)
7. Di Stefano, L., Bulgarelli, A.: A Simple and Efficient Connected Components Labeling Algorithm. In: Proceedings International Conference on Image Analysis and Processing, 1999, September 27-29, pp. 322–327 (1999)
8. Ronald, L.: A New Three-Dimensional Connected Components Algorithm. Journal of the Computer Vision, Graphics, and Image Processing 23(2), 207–217 (1983)

9. Ranganathan, N., Mehrotra, R., Subramanian, S.: A high speed systolic architecture for labeling connected components in an image. IEEE Transactions on Systems, Man and Cybernetics 25(3), 415–423 (1995)
10. Haralick, R.M.: Some neighborhood function. In: Onoe, M., Preston, K., Rosenfeld, A. (eds.) Real Time/Parallel Computing Image Analysis. Plenum Press, New York (1981)
11. Lumia, R., Shapiro, L., Zuniga, O.: A new connected components algorithms for virtual memory computers. Journal of the Computer Vision, Graphics and Image Processing 22, 287–300 (1983)
12. Schwartz, J.T., Shahrir, M., Siegel, A.: An efficient algorithm for finding connected components in a binary image. Technical Report 156, Courant Institute, NYU (1985)
13. Cypher, R., Sanz, J.L.C., Snyder, L.: An EREW PRAM algorithm for image component labeling. IEEE Transactions on Pattern Analysis Machine Intelligence 11(3), 258–262 (1989)
14. Ercan, M.F., Fung, Y.-F.: Connected component labeling on a one dimensional DSP array. In: Proceedings of the IEEE Region 10 Conference TENCON 1999, September 15-17, 1999, vol. 2 (2), pp. 1299–1302 (1999)
15. Samet, H., Tamminen, M.: Efficient component labeling of images of arbitrary dimension represented by linear bintrees. IEEE Transactions on Pattern Analysis and Machine Intelligence 10(4), 579–586 (1988)
16. Samet, H.: Connected component labeling using quadtrees. Journal of the ACM 28(3), 487–501 (1981)
17. Dillencourt, M.B., Samet, H., Tamminen, M.: A general approach to connected-component labeling for arbitrary image representations. Journal of the ACM 39(2), 253–280 (1992)
18. Chang, F., Chun-Jen, C.: A Component-Labeling Algorithm Using Contour Tracing Technique. In: Proceedings of the Seventh International Conference on Document Analysis and Recognition (ICDAR 2003), August 3-6, 2003, pp. 741–745 (2003)
19. Chang, F., Chun-Jen, C.: A Linear-Time Component-Labeling Algorithm Using Contour Tracing Technique. Journal of Computer Vision and Image Understanding 93(2), 206–220 (2004)
20. Yapa, R.D., Koichi, H.: A Connected Component Labeling Algorithm for Grayscale Images and Application of the Algorithm on Mammograms. In: Proceedings of the 2007 ACM symposium on Applied computing, Seoul, Korea, March 11-15, 2007, pp. 146–152 (2007)
21. Ng, G.W., Ma, S.-Y., Ritchings, R.T.: An Augmented Reality Training Environment for Computer Accessory Maintenance. In: Proceedings of CE 2004: The 11th ISPE International Conference on Concurrent Engineering: Research and Applications. Tsinghua University Press and Springer Verlag, Beijing (2004)
22. Jau, L.U., Teh, C.S., Ng, G.W.: A comparison of RGB and HSI colour segmentation in real - time video images: A preliminary study on road sign detection. In: Proceedings International Symposium on Information Technology 2008, August 26-29, 2008, vol. 4, pp. 2576–2581. Kuala Lumpur Convention Centre, Malaysia (2008)
23. Flusser, J., Suk, T.: Pattern recognition by affine moment invariants. Journal of Pattern Recognition 26(1), 167–174 (1993)
24. Sonka, M., Hlavac, V., Boyle, R.: Image Processing, Analysis and Machine Vision, 2nd edn. Brooks/Cole Publishing Company, USA (1999)

Automatic Vertebral Fracture Assessment System (AVFAS) for Spinal Pathologies Diagnosis Based on Radiograph X-Ray Images

Aouache Mustapha[1], Aini Hussain[1], Salina Abd Samad[1],
Hamzaini bin Abdul Hamid[2], and Ahmad Kamal Ariffin[3]

[1] Department of Electrical, Electronic & System Engineering
aouache75@hotmail.com, aini@vlsi.eng.ukm.my
[2] Department of Radiology, Faculty of Medicine
hamzaini@mail.hukm.ukm.my
[3] Department of Mechanical
Faculty of Engineering and Built Environment
National University of Malaysia, Bangi 43600, Selangor, Malaysia

Abstract. Nowadays, medical imaging has become a major tool in many clinical trials. This is because the technology enables rapid diagnosis with visualization and quantitative assessment that facilitate health practitioners or professionals. Since the medical and healthcare sector is a vast industry that is very much related to every citizen`s quality of life, the image based medical diagnosis has become one of the important service areas in this sector. As such, a medical diagnostic imaging (MDI) software tool for assessing vertebral fracture is being developed which we have named as AVFAS short for Automatic Vertebral Fracture Assessment System. The developed software system is capable of indexing, detecting and classifying vertebral fractures by measuring the shape and appearance of vertebrae of radiograph x-ray images of the spine. This paper describes the MDI software tool which consists of three main subsystems known as Medical Image Training & Verification System (MITVS), Medical Image and Measurement & Decision System (MIMDS) and Medical Image Registration System (MIRS) in term of its functionality, performance, ongoing research and outstanding technical issues.

Keywords: spine x-ray pathologies, image processing, ASM model, B-spline, AVFAS, MIMDS, MITVS, MIRS.

1 Introduction

The role of medical imaging in diagnostic features is innumerable and computer assisted imaging is now the challenging work of many researchers. Medical images play important role to detect functional information of the body part for diagnosis, medical research and education [1]. Modern standards such as Digital imaging and communication (DICOM) [2] and picture archival and communication systems (PACS) [3], enable easy storage and transportation of these images and thus, increase interoperability. Medical images of diverse modalities such as computerized tomography (CT), magnetic resonance image (MRI), positron emission tomography (PET), and signal

H. Badioze Zaman et al. (Eds.): IVIC 2009, LNCS 5857, pp. 122–135, 2009.

photon emission computed tomography (SPECT) ultrasound, microscope pathology and histology images are generally complex in nature and require extensive image processing techniques for computer aided diagnosis [4]-[5]. Due to this reason, in most instances physicians or radiologists examine images in the conventional ways based on their individual experiences and knowledge and such practice is exhaustive to the physicians or radiologists. Therefore, there is an urgent need to automate this process. An ideal scenario would be where medical images generated by an imaging station can be automatically compared with the existing images stored in a data base. Then possible abnormalities can be identified and suggested by the system. With such capabilities, role of medical imaging would expand and the focus could shift from image generation and acquisition to more effective post processing, organization and interpretation. To approach this kind of automation two main technologies, namely image retrieval and image registration need to be addressed and integrated in a computer assisted diagnostic environment. Image retrieval in the field of medical domain has been one of the most exciting and fastest growing research areas over the last decade [4], [5].

2 Objectives of the Research

Pathologies found on the spine x-ray images that are of interest to the medical researchers are generally expressed along the vertebral boundary. These pathologies include anterior osteophytes (AO), intervertebral disc degeneration and resulting disc space narrowing, subluxation and spondylolisthesis. However, the work presented in this paper will only focus on anterior osteophytes (AOs). The AOs or Osteoporosis is a tricky bones disease in which one may not even know that they have it until they break a bone. When this occurs it means that the disease is already well advanced [6].Therefore, the long-term goal of this work is to develop a computer-aided system for screening and classifying radiograph x-ray images of the spine presence with/without bone fractures. To do so, we have to the followings:

- Acquire and annotate a large database of spine images (cervical /lumbar).
- Develop algorithms that automatically locate and measure all the vertebrae in the image.
- Develop new techniques for classifying and matching vertebrae.
- Produce a user-friendly software tool that can be used by regular clinicians.
- Develop a fully automatic mode for use in large-scale clinical trials and epidemiological studies.

3 Current AVFAS Design Prototype System

The AVFAS prototype software is implemented in MATLAB version 7. Fig. 1 shows the design of the main interface of AVFAS prototype screening system (MIMDS, MIRS and MITVS) whereas Fig. 2 shows the block diagram of AVFAS system component.

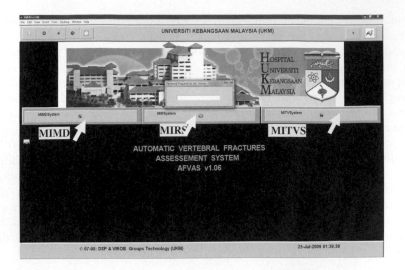

Fig. 1. Design of the Main interface of AVFAS System

In this current system the user manipulates the main GUI tools to select either one of the three sub- system interfaces. 1-Medical Image Measurement & Decision System (MIMDS), 2- Medical Image Training & Verification System (MITVS), 3- Medical Image Registration System (MIRS). The MITVS system performs the following functions:

- Image pre-preprocessing comprising the region-of-interest (ROI)-localization, and ROI enhancement.
- Modeling process where models extracted from the vertebral boundary shape determination based on active shape modeling (ASM) and B-spline enhancement in terms of list of points selected are built and trained.
- Shape boundary analysis based on extracted features and morphometric measurements
- Build and train classifier models to detect and classify various AOs classes based on the medical classification and grading schemes provided
- Build models for shape query and retrieval based on matching and similarity techniques.
- Establish database reference according to the medical expert observation using Microsoft access database

The MIMDS system tasks are listed as follow:

- Image pre-preprocessing task as before which involves ROI-localization and ROI enhancement
- Evaluating the locate accuracy of the shape models extracted automatically from the modeling stage
- Detecting and diagnosing the pathologies founded based on their classification schemes provided by the medical expert
- Perform matching and similarity between a query shape and those stored in database

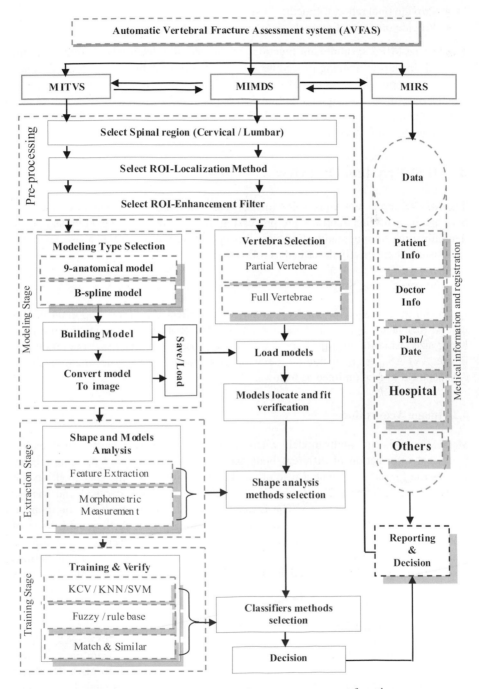

Fig. 2. Block diagram of AVFAS system component function

- Provide final report for medical use.
- Provide other function such (zooming in and out, image viewer etc)

Finally, the MIRS system main function is to record all related information about the medical diagnostic imaging procedure. The information includes the image database source, its coordinate system and its origin, the anatomy, region of the anatomy, etc Details of patient medical data and physician planning, date and timing etc. are also part of the information stored in the MIRS. A unique object identifier is used to archive and store information of segmented objects produce during diagnosis.

4   MITVS System Overview

The MITVS inputs are x-ray spine images (cervical/lumbar) selected from the database and its main functions are, pre-processing stage, modeling stage, boundary shape determination, training and testing classifier system, reporting and database reference establishment are briefly described as follows.

4.1   Pre-processing Stage

In general the quality of computer segmentation is affected by three important factors that is, first factor is region of interest (ROI), the second is image quality, the third image size/resolution in spine x–ray images, pre-processing stage plays important role in the AVFAS system including x-ray images acquisition, ROI-localization, ROI-enhancement and be outlined as follows.

4.2   Image Acquisition

Medical images are multi-modal, where each modality reveals anatomical and/or functional information of different body parts and has its own set of requirements such as file format, size, spatial resolution, dimensionality, and image acquisition and production techniques [12],[13]. In this work, more than 500 cervical and lumbar spine image were selected from The Lister Hill Center for Biomedical Communications, an intramural research and development division of the U.S. National Library of Medicine (NLM), who maintains a digital archive of 17,000 cervical and lumbar spine images collected from the second National Health and Nutrition Examinations Survey (NHANES II) conducted by the U.S National Center for Health Statistics (NCHS) [7].

4.3   Region Localization

Initially, a manual technique is being developed to select the ROI from the x-ray images. Using the mouse, two separate landmarks points are chosen to mark the object position within the region of interest. Automatically, the system responds by returning a display of those two landmarks points associated with the x-ray ROI images desired.

4.4 ROI-Enhancement

The image quality resulting from the ROI selection in spine x-ray image is poor with ambiguous vertebral boundaries, making a reliable segmentation a challenging task. In order to detect the presence of the vertebrae and obtain a good detection, it is necessary to enhance the localized region. Various enhancement techniques such adaptive histogram-based equalization, adaptive gamma value and adaptive contrast enhancement were implemented and evaluated based on the threshold approach and visual inspection. The cervical vertebrae C1, C2 and C7 are basically left out and not considered because these structures are often not visible on the radiograph and hence it is difficult to characterize them. However, lumbar vertebrae of (L1/L2/L3/L4/L5) can be clearly observed. Pre-processing steps for both (cervical/lumbar) spine x-ray images are shown in Fig.3

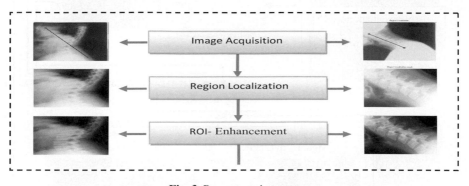

Fig. 3. Pre-processing steps

5   Boundary Shape Determination

Shape is an important characteristic for describing pertinent pathologies in various types of medical image and it is a particular challenge regarding vertebra boundary segmentation in spine x-ray images. It was realized that the shape representation method would need to serve the dual purpose of providing a rich description of the vertebra shape while being acceptable to the end user community consisting of medical professionals. ASM model [8] has been used to obtaining a boundary shape determination of a shape vertebra in terms of a list of points, two schemes list points were used at this stage. A 9-anatomical points shape (9-APS) assigned by an expert that is indicative of the pathology found to be consistent and reliable in detecting the image collection, where B- spline technique for smoothing have been implemented successfully to accurately and robustly locate vertebrae in lateral spinal x ray images based on the 9-anatomical pseudo points shape (9-APPS) which is constructed of 27 pseudo points on the vertebrae between the selected 9-anatomical points.

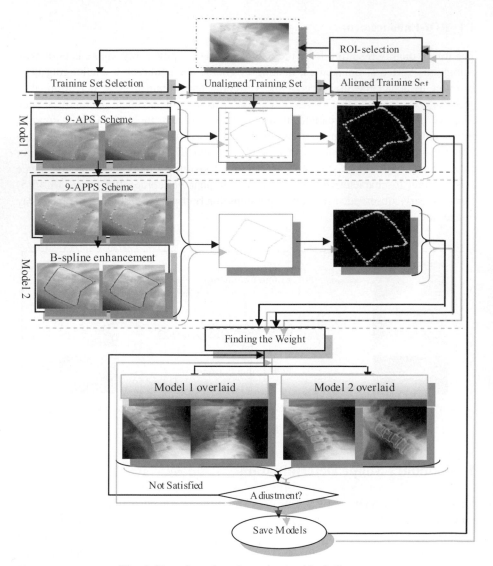

Fig. 4. Shape boundary determination block diagram

The vertebrae boundary points are extracted as (x, y) coordinates in the image space. These are then presented in a suitable form for archiving, indexing, classification, similarity and matching .The segmentation results from the ASM technique based on the two schemes indicated that include the template and segmentation object are stored with unique object identifier. Each stored object records the information about the vertebrae and the images. Fig.4 below shows the block diagram of the shape boundary determination which consists of the Training Stage, Finding the Weight and 3-Verifying Stage) using active shape model associated with B-spline algorithm.

6 Boundary Shape Analysis

At this stage, three schemes of boundary shape analysis are being implemented. The first scheme is the shape analysis based feature vector extraction where the second is the shape analysis based on morphometric measurement including angles and intra-bone ratio measurement. The third and last scheme is the matching and similarity analysis. The index resulted from this analysis is then used as input for the classifier systems. The aforementioned schemes outlined are briefly described below.

6.1 Analysis Based Feature Vector Extraction

The system provide three techniques based feature vector as input for the classification system where the feature vectors output size invariant base on the each technique applied.

- Feature vector based eigenvector extracted from the ASM model with variant size   where size of (18 x1) features based on 9-anatomical points shape and size of (100x1) features based on 9-anatomical pseudo points shape enhanced using b-spline for each unique vertebra .
- Feature vector based Gabor wavelets filter bank extracted of size (150x150) from convolution of each vertebra shape with suitable selection of mask size (7x7) and frequency level between 10 to15 for both shape boundary determination methods
- Feature vector based Gray Level Co-Occurrence Matrix
- Feature vector based Orientation Histogram

6.2 Analysis Based Morphometric Measurement

In order to distinguish between normal and abnormal vertebrae effectively and efficiently, an analysis based on morphometric measurements was determined through experiments. This analysis involves two types of measurements, namely angle measurements and intra-bone ratio measurements. The angle based measurements comprise three angles measurements from a shape that can be used to distinguish AOs are selected and it's called Horizontal angle ($H\Theta$), vertical angle ($V\Theta$) and corner angle ($C\Theta$). The second measurement which is the intra-bone ratio of the anterior, medial and posterior height form vertebra shape are then computed to produce distinguish index of AOs classes.

6.3 Analysis Based Matching and Similarity

Shape matching is an important component in shape retrieval, recognition and classification, alignment and registration, and approximation and simplification. This analysis treats various aspects that are needed to solve shape matching problems. It involves choosing the precise problem, selecting the properties of the similarity measure that are needed for the problem, choosing the specific similarity measure, and constructing the algorithm to compute the similarity.

6.4   Classifier and Matching Models

The classifier system implemented for the MITV system based on shape analysis techniques where,

- K-fold cross validation (*KCV*), K-nearest neighbor (*KNN*) and Support vector machine (SVM) for classification based feature vector extraction.
- Fuzzy logic and rule-base models for classification and evaluation based morphometric measurement analysis.
- Minimum average correlation energy (MACE) filter and K-mean clustering for matching and similarity.

Main MITVS Subsystem screening design and functions is as shown below in Fig. 5

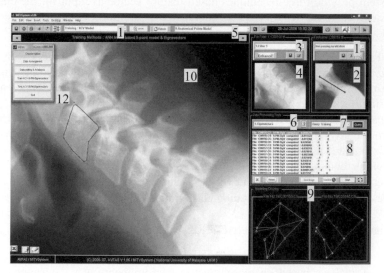

Fig. 5. Main MITVS screen interface system[1]

7   MIMDS System Overview

Currently, this sub-system is a semi-automated system and access to the subsystem is via the graphical interface that allows the users to load medical images organized as field of rational database that can be measured, processed and classified. The system function-modules are briefly described and the MIMDS screen interface system is shown in Fig.6.

7.1   Pre-Processing Stage

The pre-processing stage methods in MIMDS system are identical to those in the MITVS system which have been previously discussed.

---

[1] MITVS sub-system screening & validation tools description on table 1 (Appendix).

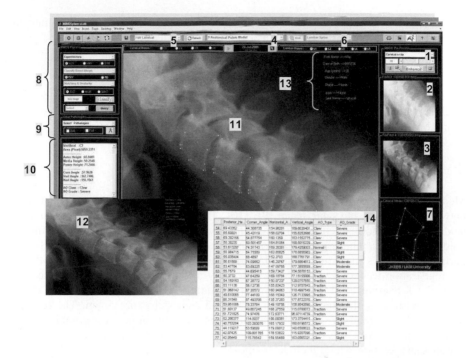

Fig. 6. Main MIMDS Screen interface system[2]

7.2 The AO Classes and Grading Scheme

In order to evaluate the system performance, it is necessary to provide the interpretation of these shapes a priori. There are two common classification schemes for the AOs. One is the Macnab classification [14], [15], [16] where the data set adopt two osteophytes type (claw and traction) indexed from (0-2), in which index 0 reflects normal vertebra whilst index 2 reflects claw. In most cases, claw often possesses a triangular shape and is curved at the tips. A class 2 reflects a traction that consists of spur that protrudes horizontally with moderate thickness and does not curve at the tips. The second classification is the severity grading system [17] where three severity levels are defined namely as slight, moderate and severe. The grades ranging from 1 to 3 is used for assessing the severity level of the AOs. Grade 1 reflects slight i.e. no narrowing or the angle by the osteophyte from the expected normal face of the vertebra is less than 15^0. Grade 2, on the other hand, reflects moderate severity. This represents the middle narrowing or can also be interpreted as the condition where the angle by the osteophyte from the expected normal anterior face of the vertebra is between 15^0 to 45^0. Finally, grade 3 reflects severe condition with sharp narrowing or when the angle by the osteophyte from the expected normal anterior face of the vertebra is equal or greater than 45^0. By combining the two classification schemes mentioned above, six categories of pathology can be established to assist the radiologist in vertebrae trusting. Radiologist can use the grade assignment examples for the vertebral

---

[2] MIMDS system screening & validation tools description on table 2 (Appendix).

fractures from the Online Digital Atlas Version 2.0 developed by the Communications Engineering Branch of the National Library of Medicine [7].

7.3 Decision and Reporting

Data set consisting of 276 vertebrae spine of both cervical and lumbar images were used as test dataset. The performance of the developed software system is very encouraging and promising since it can classify and match them correctly.

8 MIRS System Overview

Medical image registration can be defined as an establishment of correspondences between image and physical space [9], [10]. This kind of correspondence has been studied and practiced, such as in monitoring changes of a pathological object, images guided surgery, combining information from multiple imaging modalities and comparing individual's anatomies to standard. However, to achieve realistic application of the registration technology, there are still many technical barriers to overcome [10], [11]. Brief overviews of the approaches including related requirements to render proper registration, the main research focus and approaches are given. The registration system is currently a semi-automated process and it is done via a graphical interface that allows two types of data: patient archive data such as name, sex, age etc and feature classification which includes pathology on the basis of shape, labelling of the

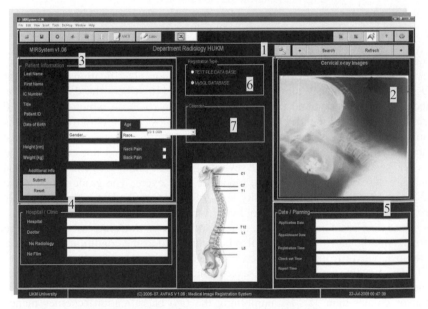

Fig. 7. Main MIRS screen interface system[3]

---

[3] MIRS system screening & validation tools description on table 3 (Appendix).

segmented structure by proper anatomical name, and classification of the segmented and measurement labelled structures into groups corresponding to high level semantic features of interest.

9 Conclusion

This paper presents the progress of an on-going research effort in medical image retrieval and indexing. The work also points out some promising research directions which are to develop combined system architecture for automatic and efficient diagnosis in a hospital or clinical environment. The need for an accurate and practical image based diagnosis system is growing rapidly as more healthcare professionals utilize image guided diagnosis in their daily activities and research. Although to build an enterprise class system that is reliable and robust is a complex task; the benefits it would bring to the heath community are unimaginable.

References

1. Tagare, H.D., Jafe, C., Duncan, J.: Medical image databases: A content based re-trieval approach. Journal of the American Medical Informatics Association 4(3), 184–198 (1997)
2. Bidgood Jr, W.D., Horii, S.C., Prior, F.W., Van Syckle, D.E.: Understanding and Using DICOM, the data Interchange Standard for Biomedical Imaging. J. Am. Med. Inform Assoc. 4(3), 199–212 (1997)
3. Lehmann, T.M., Gould, M.O., Thies, C., Fischer, B., Keysers, M., Kohnen, D., Schubert, H., Wein, B.B.: Content- Based Image Retrieval In Medical Applications For Picture Archiving And Communication Systems. In: SPIE Proceedings of Medical Imaging, San Diego, California, USA, vol. 5033 (2003)
4. Müller, H., Michoux, N., Bandon, D., Geissbuhler, A.: A Review of Content-based Image Retrieval Applications Clinical Benefits And Future Directions. International Journal of Medical Informatics 73, 1–23 (2004)
5. Robb, R.A. (ed.): Biomedical Imaging, Visualization and Analysis. Wiley-Liss, Chichester (1999)
6. Spine universe website, http://www.spineuniverse.com/article/osteoporosis-4040.html
7. National Library of Medicine, http://archive.nlm.nih.gov/
8. Cootes, T.F., Taylor, C.J.: Slatislica Models of Appearance for Computer Vision, of Manchester, Wolfson Image Analysis Unit, and Biomedical Engineering, University of, MI2 9PT. U.K., Tech. Rep (February 2001)
9. Hawkes, D.: Registration Methodolgy – Introduction. In: Hajnal, J., Hawkes, D., Hill, D. (eds.) Medical Image Registration, ch. 2 (2000)
10. Maintz, J.B.A., Viergever, M.A. (eds.): A Survey of Medical Image Registration, Medical Image Analysis (1998)
11. Hajnal, J.V., Hill, D.L., Hawkes, D.J.: A View Of The Future. In: Hajnal, J., Hawkes, D., Hill, D. (eds.) Medical Image Registration, ch. 16 (2000)
12. Wong, S.T.C., Tjandra, D.: A Digital Library for Biomedical Imaging on the Internet. IEEE Communications Magazine 37(1), 84–91 (1999)
13. Robb, R.A.: Biomedical Imaging Visualization and Analysis. Wiley-Liss, Chichester (1999)

14. Heggeness, M., Doherty, B.: Morphologic study of lumbar vertebral osteophytes. Southern Medical Journal 91(2), 187–189 (1998)
15. Pate, D., Goobar, J., Resnick, D., Haghighi, P., Sartoris, D., Pathria, M.: Traction osteophytes of the lumbar spine: Radiographic-pathologic correlation. Radiology 166(3), 843–846 (1988)
16. Macnab, I.: The traction spur: An indicator of segmental instability. Journal of Bone and Joint Surgery 53(4), 663–670 (1971)
17. Shou, J., Antani, S., Long, L.R., Thoma, G.: Evaluating partial shape queries for pathology-based retrieval of vertebra. In: Proc. of the 8th World Multi-conference on Systemic, Cybernetics and Informatics, July 18-21, vol. 12, pp. 155–160 (2004)

Appendix

Table 1. MITVS system screening and salidation sools

Index	Description
1	ROI-localization method selection
2	ROI-localization resulting display
3	ROI-Enhancement and filtering method selection
4	ROI- Enhancement resulting display
5	Shape boundary determination method selection
6	Shape analysis methods selection
7	Shape matching and similarity methods selection
8	Processing stages display and screening
9	Models measurement and verification display
10	Main screen for x-ray shape boundary determination and verification
11	Training different classifier system
12	Testing and validation different classifier system

Table 2. MIMDS system screening and salidation sools

Index	Description
1	Pre-processing stage toolbar (ROI-selection, ROI-enhancement)
2	Image Acquisition display
3	ROI-enhancement display
4	Shape boundary determination selection method
5	Cervical bones selection (full spine /partial)
6	Lumbar bones selection (full spine/ partial)
7	Select model overlaid evaluation
8	Classification & matching techniques toolbar
9	Select other pathologies (DSN/subluxation / spondylolisthesis)
10	Classification, matching an measurement report for unique vertebra
11	Main screening shows model overlaid verification using model 1
12	Main screening shows model overlaid verification using model 2

Table 3. MIRS system screening and salidation sools

Index	Description
1	Image viewer toolbar
2	Image viewer display
3	Patient information key in
4	Hospital and clinic information key in
5	Date and planning key in
6	Registration type
7	Calendar

Quasi-Gaussian DCT Filter for Speckle Reduction of Ultrasound Images

Slamet Riyadi[1], Mohd. Marzuki Mustafa[1], Aini Hussain[1], Oteh Maskon[2], and Ika Faizura Mohd. Noh[2]

[1] Department of Electrical, Electronic and Systems Engineering
Faculty of Engineering and Built Environment, Universiti Kebangsaan Malaysia, Bangi
43600 {riyadi,marzuki,aini}@eng.ukm.my
[2] Universiti Kebangsaan Malaysia Medical Center, Kuala Lumpur 56000 Malaysia
auajwad@yahoo.com, azuzayz@yahoo.ie

Abstract. In recent time, ultrasound imaging is a popular modality for various medical applications. The presence of speckle noise affects difficulties on features extraction and quantitative measurement of ultrasound images. This paper proposes a new method to suppress the speckle noise while attempting to preserve the image content using combination of Gaussian filter and discrete cosine transform (DCT) approach. The proposed method, called quasi-Gaussian DCT (QGDCT) filter, is a quasi Gaussian filter in which its coefficients are derived from a selected 2-dimensional cosine basis function. The Gaussian approach is used to suppress speckle noise whereas the selected DCT approach is intended to preserve the image content. The filter will be implemented on the synthetic speckle images and the clinical echocardiograph ultrasound images. To evaluate the effectiveness of the filter, several quantitative measurements such as mean square error, peak signal to noise ration, speckle suppression index and speckle statistical analysis, are computed and analyzed. In comparison with established filters, results obtained confirmed the effectiveness of QGDCT filter in suppressing speckle noise and preserving the image content.

Keywords: Gaussian, DCT, speckle, ultrasound image, echocardiography.

1 Introduction

Ultrasound imaging is an essential tool and has been proven effective for many medical applications mainly because of its portability, non-invasiveness and radiation free attributes. Additionally, it affords a real-time imaging at low cost imaging modality. Over the years, this imaging method has been an active research area in which ultrasound data acquisition, processing and interpretation are amongst the topics studied. A major constraint with the ultrasound method is the issue of speckle noise. The presence of speckle noise further adds difficulties to the tasks of features extraction and quantitative measurement of ultrasound image. Consequently, it makes harder for physician to analyze and interpret images as well as for the computer assisted diagnosis system.

Generally speaking, speckle reduction can be performed during ultrasound data acquisition stage and image processing stage. In the image processing stage, a number

H. Badioze Zaman et al. (Eds.): IVIC 2009, LNCS 5857, pp. 136–147, 2009.
© Springer-Verlag Berlin Heidelberg 2009

of speckle reduction methods have been proposed and developed. Lee defined and verified a statistical noise model and then introduced a multiplicative noise-smoothing algorithm for speckle appearing in synthetic aperture radar [1]. Frost et al proposed a multiplicative noise model that leads to an adaptive digital filtering technique [2]. This method used locally estimated parameter to provide minimum mean of square error inside a homogeneous area of an image. Meanwhile other filter methods are not derived from speckle noise model. They can be spatial domain such as mean, median, geometric and morphological filter [3]. Transformation based filters were proposed using wavelet decomposition method [4]. In this technique, the image is decomposed into wavelet coefficients and then an optimum threshold value is applied to suppress the speckle. The end result image is obtained by using inverse wavelet transform. Even though, each technique has reported its own successful filter model, the issue still remains and has opened a wide range of filter development due to the complexity of speckle phenomenon.

In this paper, we propose a new method to suppress speckle noise while preserving the image objects using the combination approach of Gaussian filter and discrete cosine transform (DCT). On its own, these two techniques are very popular low pass filtering technique and video compression method, respectively. The proposed method, which we called quasi-Gaussian DCT (QGDCT) filter, is a quasi Gaussian filter. Its coefficients are derived from a selected 2-dimensional cosine basis function and the Gaussian approach is used to suppress the speckle noise whilst the selected DCT approach is use to preserve the image object. The paper is outlined as such. Section 2 describes the speckle ultrasound image model followed by Section 3 that describes the methodology for filter development. Results are presented and discussed in Section 4 and conclusion is given in Section 5.

2 Speckle Ultrasound Image Model

Although, ultrasound imaging research is not a new area, an accurate modeling of speckle noise is still an active investigation subject as it involves complex analytical model. The acquisition of ultrasound image introduces a special noise as known as speckle. The speckle noise has a logarithmic compressed Rayleigh distribution [5]. The observed ultrasound image, u_O, can be modeled as an original image, u, with signal-dependent noise as equation [6]

$$u_0 = u + \sqrt{un}$$ (1)

where n is a zero-mean Gaussian variable with standard deviation σ_n.

3 Methodology

3.1 Gaussian Filter

Gaussian filter is a filter that gives no overshoot to a step function input while minimizing the rise and fall time of the bell function as shown in Fig. 1(a). The characteristic of the kernel follows the Gaussian function

$$f(x)=ae^{-\frac{(x-b)^2}{2c^2}} \tag{2}$$

where a is the height of the curve peak, b is the position of the centre of the peak and c controls the width of the bell.

Gaussian filters are widely applied in image processing tasks where two dimensional (2D) Gaussian functions are used for Gaussian smoothing. The idea of Gaussian smoothing is to convolve the image with a Gaussian kernel. Since the image is represented by the number of pixels, the discrete Gaussian kernel should be approximated prior to convolution. Theoretically, the Gaussian function has an infinite distribution which results in a large convolution kernel. However, in practice, the kernel is effectively zero for more than about three standard deviations from the mean. Fig. 1(b) shows an example of an approximation of Gaussian kernel for a 2D data.

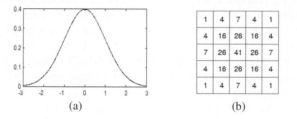

(a)   (b)

Fig. 1. (a) Bell function of Gaussian, (b) Discrete approximation of a Gaussian kernel

3.2 Discrete Cosine Transform (DCT)

In the last decade, DCT technique has been widely used as a standard in the video coding compression. A DCT represents signal in term of a sum of cosine function oscillating at different frequencies. According to [8][9], the one dimensional (1D) cosine function can be expressed

$$C(u) = \alpha(u) \sum_{x=0}^{N-1} f(x) \cos \left[\frac{\pi(2x+1)u}{2N} \right] \tag{3}$$

where u=0, 1, 2, …, N-1 and

$$\alpha(u) = \begin{cases} \sqrt{\dfrac{1}{N}}, & u = 0 \\ \sqrt{\dfrac{2}{N}}, & u \neq 0 \end{cases}$$

The first coefficient (u=0) is a constant DC value whereas the other coefficients (u=1, 2, …, N-1) give waveforms with progressive frequency as shown in Fig. 2.

For image processing purpose, a 2D-DCT is a direct extension of the 1D-DCT given by the following equation [10]

$$C(u,v) = \alpha(u)\alpha(v) \sum_{x=0}^{N-1}\sum_{y=0}^{N-1} f(x,y) \cos \left[\frac{\pi(2x+1)u}{2N} \right] \cos \left[\frac{\pi(2y+1)v}{2N} \right] \tag{4}$$

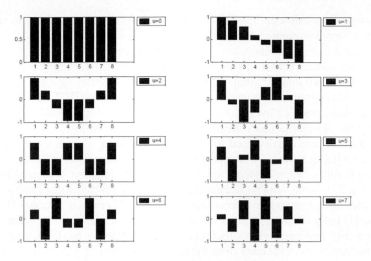

Fig. 2. 1D cosine basis function with N=8

The 2D basis function is obtained by multiplying the horizontal and vertical set of 1D basis of the same function. Fig. 3 shows the 2D basis function with N=8. Similarly with 1D basis, the top left function is the constant basis and the others increase the function progressively in the both horizontal and vertical direction.

Fig. 3. 2D cosine basis function (N=8)

3.3 Quasi-Gaussian DCT Based Filter

The estimation of optical flow field using global regularization technique is quite simple and straight forward. Assumptions are taken to simplify the computation and often do not agree with the real movement. Due to its limitation, the computed optical flow vectors have errors both in direction and magnitude. Instead of the improvement in the optical flow estimation itself, in this paper we introduce a filter to smoothen optical flow vector computed before.

The main drawback of Gaussian filtering is uniform blurring on the image region caused by the natural kernel of Gaussian. On the other hand, the DCT function was proven as a standard image coding technique which means that the DCT has a powerful function to represent an image. Our basic idea is to use the DCT function to create a new Gaussian kernel, called quasi-Gaussian DCT based filter (QGDCT).

Using the 2D cosine basis function (N=8) as shown in Fig. 3, only 36 selected top-left functions are usually used for JPEG compression. To use these functions to create the QGDCT kernel are inappropriate since it requires large computing time. According to our previous observation, the down-right function, indicated by the red circle in Fig. 3, is more suitable since it represents the high frequency function.

In order to understand how to create the QGDCT kernel, it is easier if one considers the 1D basis function (N=8) with u=7 as shown in Fig. 4(a). This function consists of positive and negative coefficients. A quasi-Gaussian model is created by removing the negative coefficients from the function as show in Fig. 4(b). It can be seen that the model is similar to the natural discrete Gaussian kernel without even term coefficients. Likewise, the 2D QGDCT kernel can be obtained using similar steps applied on the down-right function of 2D DCT basis.

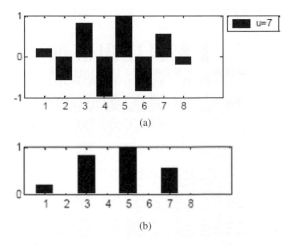

Fig. 4. (a) Selected 1D DCT function, (b) a quasi-Gaussian model

3.4 Filter Performance Evaluation

In general, there are two types of filter evaluation, that are, 1) via visual interpretation of the filtered images and 2) via evaluating quantitative performances. The former, involving visual evaluation, investigates both the filter capability to suppress speckle noise and to preserve the image details. It is an easy and efficient way and probably, provides the best assessment method for filter performance [7]. The latter which involves some quantitative performances evaluation has its drawbacks [11][12].

Depending on the performances measure, the filter has limited capability to perform both speckle suppression and preserve the image details, simultaneously. For instance, using a specific performance measure a filter may be able to reduce speckle noise but may not be able to preserve the image details effectively, and vice versa.

1. Mean Square Error (MSE)

Mean square error (MSE) parameter evaluates the pixel-by-pixel difference between the noisy (X) and filtered image using equation

$$MSE = \frac{\sum_{i=1}^{M}\sum_{j=1}^{N}\left[X(i,j) - P(i,j)\right]^2}{MN} \tag{5}$$

where M and N are the width and height of the image. This parameter shows the smoothing capability of filter. The lower MSE value indicates a better performance of filter to reduce the speckle.

2. Peak Signal to Noise Ratio (PSNR)

Peak signal to noise ratio (PSNR) also measures the capability of filter to reduce the speckle noise. The definition of PSNR is given by

$$PSNR = 10\log\left[\frac{255}{MSE}\right] \tag{6}$$

The filtered image tends to have a higher PSNR that indicates a better performance of speckle noise reduction.

3. Speckle Suppression Index (SSI)

Speckle strength is commonly measured by the coefficient of variance. Speckle suppression index (SSI) is defined as the ratio of the coefficient of variance of the filtered image and the noisy image, which is formulated as

$$SSI = \frac{\sum_{i=1}^{M}\sum_{j=1}^{N}\left[X(i,j) - u_X\right]^2}{\sum_{i=1}^{M}\sum_{j=1}^{N}\left[P(i,j) - u_P\right]^2} \tag{7}$$

where μ_x and μ_p are mean of noisy and filtered image respectively. A filtered image should have less variance or smaller SSI value because the speckle noise is suppressed [12].

4. Speckle Image Statistical Analysis

As the ultrasound image is multiplicative in nature, the amplitude of speckle can be represented by the ratio of noisy to filtered image [12]. It is defined as

$$Sp = \frac{\sum_{i=1}^{M}\sum_{j=1}^{N} X(i,j)}{\sum_{i=1}^{M}\sum_{j=1}^{N} P(i,j)} \tag{8}$$

where Sp is speckle image. For ideal filter, the speckle image has normal distribution with a mean value 1.0. This is the reason why the mean of speckle image is suitable to be used in assessing the ability of filter to retain the original image content. In other words, for best performance, the mean of speckle image must be retained closed to 1.0.

4 Result and Discussion

4.1 Application to Synthetic Speckle Images

The proposed QG-DCT filter technique has been applied on a grayscale image *eight.tif* of size (242x208) that has been contaminated with synthetically generated speckle noise of 0.04 noise variance. The filter performance is evaluated at different filter size of (3x3), (5x5) and (7x7) as shown in Fig. 5. Evaluating via visual appearances, we found that the proposed filter was able to suppress the speckle noise using any filter size. The filter also succeeded to improve the PSNR from 62.422 dB to 83.204 dB when filter of size (3x3) is used. Analyzing in term of the filter size, filter size (3x3) performed the best noise reduction which is indicated by the higher PSNR value.

Fig. 6 (a), (b), (c) and (d) depict the end results of filter implementation using Mean, Median, Frost and QGDCT, respectively. The QGDCT filtered image as shown in Fig. 6 (d) outperforms the other three with its most suppressed background. In term of PSNR, the QGDCT filter improves the ratio to 83.204 dB whereas mean filter 77.753 dB, median filter 68.077 dB and Frost filter 71.978 dB. Consequently, through visual evaluation, it can be confirmed that the QGDCT filter outperforms the other filters and can effectively suppress speckle noise.

Eventhough visual evaluation is an easy and efficient assessment method, its results can be biased and vary depending on the expert who performs the assessment. Therefore, four quantitative criteria, including mean square error (MSE), peak signal to noise ratio (PSNR), speckle suppression index (SSI) and speckle image statistical analysis (SISA), are computed for the analysis of each filtered image. Various window size are also tested to study the effect of filter size on the performance.

Fig. 7 and Fig. 8 depict the quantitative measurement of MSE and PSNR of the filtered images. The QGDCT filter performed significant improvement of noise reduction as compared to others since the MSE value of the QGDCT filter is the lowest and the PSNR is the highest. As aforementioned, the best filter shall have the lowest MSE and highest PSNR. Variation of filter size does not affect the performance of the proposed filter. The ability of filter to reduce speckle noise is also evaluated by SSI measurement as shown in Fig. 9. This figure agrees with the previous fact that the QGDCT filter suppresses speckle noise better than others since the SSI value is the lowest at every filter size. The ability of filter to preserve the image content is evaluated by the SISA measurement as shown in Fig. 10. Eventhough the SISA values for the other filters are closer to 1.0 compared to QGDCT, the SISA of QGDCT filter is still within the acceptable range and this means that the QGDCT filter is still able to retain the image content.

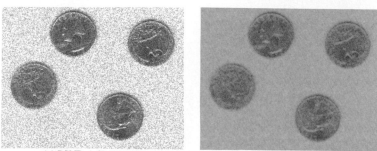

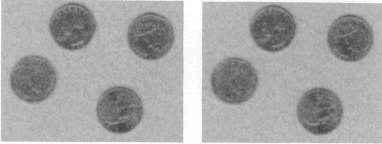

(a) PSNR = 62.422 dB

(b) PSNR = 83.204 dB

(c) PSNR = 82.923 dB

(d) PSNR = 83.045 dB

Fig. 5. (a) Speckle noisy image at noise variance 0.04, (b), (c) and (d) Filtered image by the QGDCT filter at different filter size

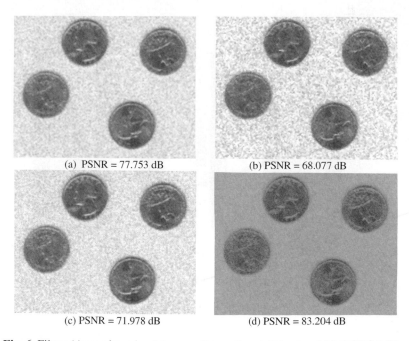

(a) PSNR = 77.753 dB

(b) PSNR = 68.077 dB

(c) PSNR = 71.978 dB

(d) PSNR = 83.204 dB

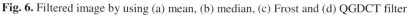

Fig. 6. Filtered image by using (a) mean, (b) median, (c) Frost and (d) QGDCT filter

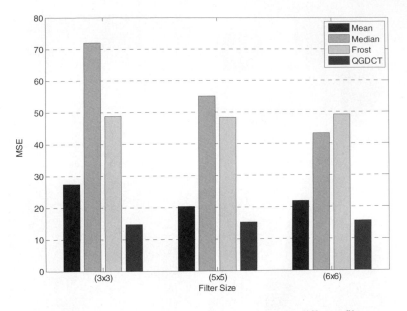

Fig. 7. Mean square error (MSE) for filtered images by different filter

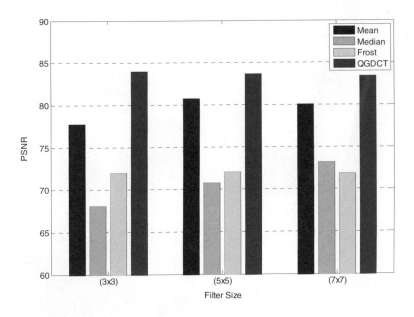

Fig. 8. Peak signal to noise ratio (PSNR) for filtered images by different filter

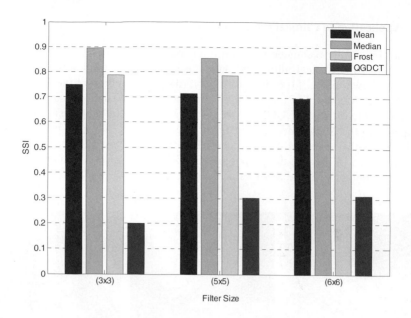

Fig. 9. Speckle suppression index (SSI) for filtered images by different filter

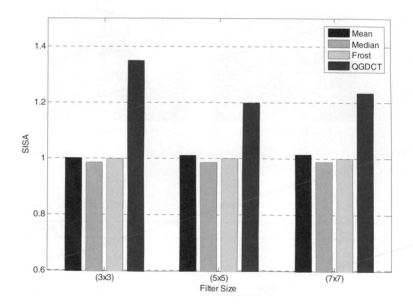

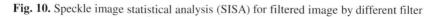

Fig. 10. Speckle image statistical analysis (SISA) for filtered image by different filter

4.2 Application to Clinical Ultrasound Images

The proposed filter technique was also implemented on real clinical ultrasound data. A sample of the clinical ultrasound data consisting of the original echocardiograph image is shown in Fig. 11(a). Fig. 11(b), (c), (d) and (e) represent the filtered images of the Mean, Median, Frost and QGDCT, respectively. Visually, it can be concluded that the filtered image of QGDCT yields the best speckle suppression result when compared to the Mean, Median and Frost filters. This is indicated in Table 1 since QGDCT has the lowest MSE, the highest PSNR and the lowest SSI values. In addition, as shown in Fig. 11, the proposed QGDCT filter is also effective in preserving the image content since the SISA value is closed to 1.0.

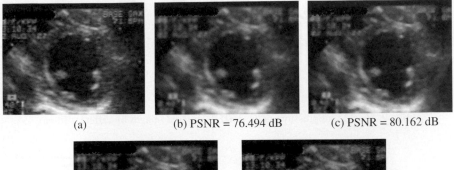

| (a) | (b) PSNR = 76.494 dB | (c) PSNR = 80.162 dB |

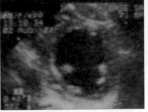
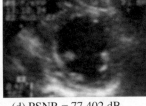

(d) PSNR = 77.402 dB   (e) PSNR = 85.926 dB

Fig. 11. (a) Original echocardiography image, (b) to (e) filtered image window size (3x3) for Mean, Median, Frost and QGDCT filter

Table 1. Quantitative measurement of echocardiography filtered image

Filter	MSE	PSNR	SSI	SISA
Mean	30.9727	76.494	0.8674	1.0113
Median	21.4629	80.162	0.9064	1.0338
Frost	28.2850	77.402	0.9054	0.9946
QGDCT	12.0604	85.926	0.7698	0.9802

5 Conclusion

This paper has afforded a new filtering method to suppress speckle noise and at the same time, preserve the image content of ultrasound images. From the results, the so-called QGDCT filter has been proven effective basing on the qualitative assessment through visualization of the filtered image and quantitative measures of the MSE, PSNR, SSI and SISA. In conclusion, a new filter that can suppress speckle noise and simultaneously preserve the image content has been successfully developed and tested using image data that has been synthetically corrupted with speckle noise and real field data comprising the clinical echocardiograph ultrasound images.

Acknowledgement

The authors would like to acknowledge Universiti Kebangsaan Malaysia (Project code UKM-GUP-TKP-08-24-080) for the financial support awarded for this research.

References

1. Lee, J.-S.: Speckle Suppression and Analysis for Synthetic Aperture Radar Images. Optical Engineering 25(5), 636–643 (1986)
2. Frost, V.S., Stiles, J.A., Shanmugan, K.S., Holtzman, J.C.: A Model for Radar Images and Its Application to Adaptive Digital Filtering of Multiplicative Noise. IEEE Transactions on Pattern Analysis and Machine Intelligence 4(2), 157–166 (1982)
3. Grimmins, T.R.: Geometric Filter for Reducing Speckle. Opt. Eng. 25(4), 652–654 (1986)
4. Donoho, D.L.: De-noising by Soft-thresholding. IEEE Trans. Inform Theory 41, 613–627 (1995)
5. Dutt, V., Greenleaf, J.: Adaptive Speckle Reduction Filter for Log Compressed B-scan Images. IEEE Trans. Med. Imaging 15(6), 802–813 (1996)
6. Krissian, K., Vosburgh, K., Kikinis, R., Westin, C.F.: Anisotropic Diffusion of Ultrasound Constrained by Speckle Noise Model. Tech. report. Harvard Med. School (2004)
7. Raouf, A., Lichtenegger, J.: Integrated Use of SAR and Optical Data for Coastal Zone Management. In: ERS Satellite Radar Imagery: Proceedings of the Third ERS Symposium, ESA SP-1204 (1997)
8. Petland, A., Horowitz, B.: Recovery of Non-rigid Motion and Structure. IEEE Transaction on Pattern Analysis and Machine Intelligent 13, 730–742 (1991)
9. Khayam, S.A.: The Discrete Cosine Transform: A Theory and Application.Tutorial of the Dept. of Electric & Computer Engineering, Michigan State University (2003)
10. Richardson, I.E.G.: H.264 and MPEG-4 Video Compression: Video Coding for Next-generation Multimedia. John Willey & Sons, West Sussex (2003)
11. Lee, J.S., Jurkevich, I., Dewaele, P., Wambacq, P., Oosterlinck, A.: Speckle Filtering of Synthetic Aperture Radar Images: A Review. Remote Sensing Review 8, 313–340 (1994)
12. Qiu, F., Berglund, J., Jensen, J.R., Thakkar, P., Ren, D.: Speckle noise reduction in SAR imagery using a local adaptive median filter. GIScience and Remote Sensing 41(3), 244–266 (2004)

Additional Cues Derived from Three Dimensional Image Processing to Aid Customised Reconstruction for Medical Applications

Tan Su Tung[1], Alwin Kumar Rathinam[1], Yuwaraj Kumar[1],
and Zainal Ariff Abdul Rahman[1,2]

[1] Virtual Reality Centre, University of Malaya, Kuala Lumpur, Malaysia
[2] Professor (Head), Department of Maxillofacial Surgery,
University Malaya Medical Centre, Kuala Lumpur, Malaysia
{tanst,alwin,yuwaraj,zainalr}@um.edu.my,
umvrc.research@gmail.com

Abstract. Three dimensional (3D) image processing and visualisation methods were applied in craniomaxillofacial surgery for preoperative surgical procedures and surgery planning. Each patient differed in their formation of cranium and facial bones, hence requiring customised reconstruction to identify the defect area and to plan procedural steps. This paper explores the processing and visualisation of patients' data into 3D form, constructed from flat two dimensional (2D) Computed Tomography (CT) images. Depth perception has been useful to identify certain regions of Interest (ROI) elusive in 2D CT slices. We have noted that the 3D models have exemplified the depth perception with the provision of additional cues of perspective, motion, texture and steropsis. This has led to the improvement of treatment design and implementation for patients in this study.

Keywords: 3D stereo visualisation, virtual reality, 3D modelling, medical image processing, VRC-UM.

1 Introduction

The enhancement in medical related technologies has lead to the increased usage of medical imaging as a diagnostic tool with elevated applications in medical surgery. The ability to view patients internally before the operation has vast advantages in surgery planning and diagnostics. There are various methods to obtain medical images for diagnostic purposes which include X-rays, ultrasounds, fluoroscopy, endoscopy, electroencephalogram (EEG), electrocardiogram (ECG), tissue-doppler, MRI and Computed Tomography (CT) imaging which is a commonly used method.

CT images have been used in diagnostic procedures, preoperative and surgery planning since the 1970's [1]. The American College of Radiology(ACR) and the National Electrical Manufacturers Association (NEMA) have recognised the need of standardising methods of transfer for images and relevant information between various devices by manufacturers, therefore they formed a joint committee in 1983. As an outcome of this committee, DICOM was structured as a standard for multi-part medical image

H. Badioze Zaman et al. (Eds.): IVIC 2009, LNCS 5857, pp. 148–155, 2009.

documents [1], [2]. Most medical images are printed out on paper or film which is in two dimensional (2D) form. Recently these images were able to be transferred and analyzed with ease digitally but still retained in a 2D form [1].

1.1 Drawbacks of 2D

2D slices have been known to emulate certain drawbacks for example, the inability to view the human anatomy in actual perception. This is so, as the actual human anatomy is in 3D. There is also a lack of feel of the 2D medical image because of its flat representation of human body parts. Various attempts have been made to bridge this gap [3].

3D visualisation methods have been long been in popularity in computer graphics with the focus areas in games development [4] and in most animation [5]. Recently, 3D applications have started to gain popularity in medical usage [12].

The application of the 3D images have been known to be an advantage in visualisation compared to 2D as it is able to provide additional information known as cues. Depth is one of the most important cue as it creates the perception that the object viewed is almost real [12], [19].

1.2 Virtual Reality (VR)

Despite the visually compelling nature of earlier computer graphics, viewers still found it difficult to precisely judge object sizes, exocentric distances between different scene points, and egocentric distances from the observation point to points in the scene [18]. VR is a relatively newer approach that communicates shape and other spatial information to the viewer with the objective of creating perception that the object is real in existence [7], [20].

Maximisation of virtual reality viewing can be achieved when the viewer is able to view two separate images corrected for both eyes; this method of binocular disparity has been termed as stereopsis [7], [9]. This added realism in VR elevates human judgement and provides additional information compared to information extracted from a 2D data set.

2 Related Work

Goodman et al. (1995) employed a 3D reconstruction technique for the evaluation of hepatic injuries in a series of eight trauma patients [13]. Compared to the conventional CT, the imaging provided by 3D reconstruction allowed hepatic CT scans data to be interpreted with greater ease and accuracy.

3D visualisation of the human eyes, blood vessels and the heart have been reconstructed by Flack et al. (2007) from 2D medical scan data [12]. The 3D organs were animated and presented with colour, form and light. Aspin et al. (2008) presented a real-time visualisation application that could visually present the medical data, with sufficient clarity and details which enabled the viewer to comprehend and determine the particular tissues and pathologies [14]. The system was developed using QT as the Graphical User Interface (GUI) with Open Graphics Library (OpenGL) and Open Scene Graph (OSG) widget for the presentation in the 3D volumetric form.

Tong et al. (2007) proposed a Computer-aided Diagnosis Algorithm Platform (CADAP), which included medical image 3D visualization, image enhancement, image segmentation, region of interest (ROI) detection, feature extract and classification algorithm by reusing the key algorithm of Computer Aided Design (CAD) system [15]. The Visualization ToolKit (VTK) and Insight Segmentation and Registration Toolkit (ITK) were utilised to develop and process the 3D medical images.

Lim et al (2008) proposed a 3D visualisation for medical applications using marching cubes algorithm for the surface rendering technique and OpenGL to create 3D representations of the obtained meshes [16]. The effects of lighting, vertex normal shading and transparency were applied in the study. The software program produced was able to perform rotation, zooming and moving operation using mouse and keyboard as input devices.

Carvalho et al.(2008) proposed a cartographic-oriented model to visualise and analyse medical data relative to the human body [17]. The prototype produced could read JPEG and DICOM format file to create 3D visualizations.

3 Methodology

Six patients admitted to the Department of Neurosurgery and the Department of Oral and Maxillofacial Surgery in UMMC (University Malaya Medical Center) were studied. Three male and three female patients' data, aged between 25 to 60 with various cranium defects due to trauma were used in the study for surgery planning and preoperative procedures.

Preoperative CT scans with the accuracy of 1.5 mm to 3.0 mm were performed in all patients studied. The DICOM images produced from the CT scans were then group into one or more series of images. A series of DICOM images collected in this process consisted of 200 to 300 slices in DICOM format files.

DICOM Files were then loaded into a segmentation software developed in house using the open source ITK (Insight Toolkit) library. The ITK libraries are specialised in providing application programmers interface (API) for the segmentation and registration of 3D medical image data [11]. The greyscale DICOM images were then segmented using thresholding where bones and soft tissues were divided based on the brightness of the monochrome pixels. ROI of the skull such as frontal, parietal, temporal, occipital and mandible bones were selected using region growing method. The 3D visuals of the selected regions were then constructed using triangulation and saved in triangulated meshes format file.

To construct the virtual reality model of the data, the triangulated meshes were then converted into point cloud format of 3D coordinates of the three points of each triangle saved in sequence. The point cloud was then rendered and displayed at a 3D stereoscopic system using OpenGL. The 3D stereoscopic system utilised 2 circular polarization filters on two CRT projectors positioned at an angle to rear project onto a non polarising screen. Figure 3.0 illustrates a user utilising the system by wearing a pair of circular polarized glasses which filters the images for both left and right eyes.

As a result, the left and right eye will see two separate images that create a depth perception to the viewer.

Stereo effect was also generated on a single screen applying the anaglyph method. The 3D models were displayed using two different filtered colored images for the left and the right eyes as illustrated in Figure 5. A pair of anaglyph spectacles with cyan and red plastic filters was used to view these anaglyph models. This anaglyph method was carried out to illustrate the point that expensive high end equipments are not always required to generate 3D stereo effects.

4   Results

Additional cues using 3D techniques have provided sturdier visualisation of the patients' skull. The following are some of the 2D and 3D visualization techniques collected in this study.

4.1   CT Scan -2D Data

Figure 1 below illustrates the original transaxial CT scans of one patient, which only allows 2D visual of the defect area using one plane (transverse). This provides limited information to the surgeons who require comprehensive visuals of the defect area. Multiple slices of the 2D scan are then stacked up vertically and extracted using methods described earlier into a 3D form. This drawback has motivated us to analyse various forms of 3D images in order to view additional cues that are obtainable from the data presented as follows.

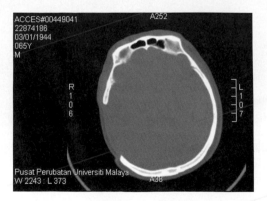

Fig. 1. Transaxial CT scan of a patient's skull

4.2   Texture (Shading)

Figure 2 illustrates the differences between a point clouds and shading done on triangulated point mesh. Point cloud view does not provide depth perception as strong as the triangulated mesh with shading and lighting as shown on the right.

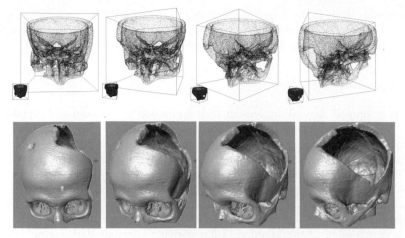

Fig. 4. Multiple screen shots of rotating 3D and point clouds skull models

4.5 Anaglyph

Anaglyph model of the skull was visualised based on the concept that two images of the same skull drawn in red and cyan and was rotated and superimposed on top of

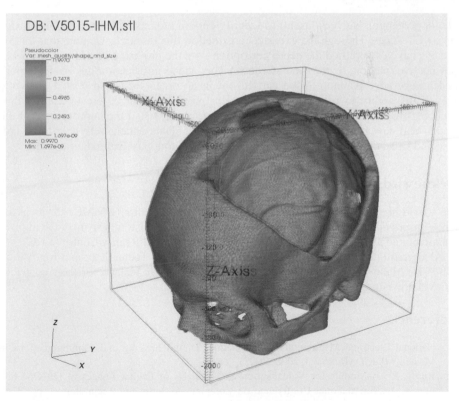

Fig. 5. Anaglyph model of a patient's skull

each other resulting in the image as illustrated in the figure 5 below which requires a pair of anaglyph spectacles to be viewed in 3D stereo. The viewer can enhance the stereo effect by panning the head to the left and right.

5 Discussion

Patients examined showed variants in their formation of cranium and facial bones, therefore customised reconstruction of the medical images is required. This specialised medical image processing was required by surgeons in order to provide as much as information as needed to give a more accurate and rapid diagnosis and well organised surgery planning. This is based on our qualitative analysis of the six patients used in this study, we have noted that a better customised medical implant and planning was achieved due to the realm of 3D information with the assistance of additional cues derived from 3D image processing.

The visualisation of the 3D models has assisted surgeons with pre-operative in-depth visuals of the defected area. During the operation, this may prevent misoriented placement of the implants. On the other hand, medical implants that suit every patient can be customised, and the preoperative design of the surgery can be visualised.

6 Conclusion

Depth perception has been useful to identify certain regions of Interest (ROI) elusive in 2D CT slices. Through the experience gained in this research, we note that the 3D models have exemplified the depth perception with the provision of additional cues of perspective, motion, texture and steropsis. This added information has made surgery and preoperative planning to be carried out in an organised manner as it gives the viewer the ability to rotate and visualise the virtual patient before operating, thus reducing surgery time. These visualizations have also assisted the improvement of the design and development of customised medical implants which were able to be created and fitted onto the 3D stereo models virtually before physical manufacturing.

Acknowledgement

We would like to thank the Universiti Malaya Medical Centre (UMMC) for its assistance in providing data and surgeries conducted using customised medical implant manufactured using our skills and services from the Virtual Reality Centre (VRC).

Also gratitude is extended to the Ministry of Science, Technology and Innovation (MOSTI) Malaysia and the management of University of Malaya for their contribution via provision of research grants.

References

1. National Electrical Manufacturers Association: Digital Imaging and Communications in Medicine (DICOM), PS 3.1-2008 (2008)
2. Rusev, R.: A Module for Visualisation and Analysis of Digital Images in DICOM File Format. In: International Conference on Computer Systems and Technologies, pp. 314–319 (2003)

3. Tomazevic, D., Likar, B., Pernus, F.: Gradient-based registration of 3D MR and 2D X-ray images. In: International Congress Series, Computer Assisted Radiology and Surgery, vol. 1230, pp. 338–345. Elsevier Science, Amsterdam (2001)

4. Chehimi, F., Coulton, P., Edwards, R.: Evolution of 3D mobile games development. Personal and Ubiquitous Computing 12(1), 19–25 (2008)

5. Lasseter, J.: Principles of traditional animation applied to 3D computer animation. ACM SIGGRAPH Computer Graphics 21(4), 35–44 (1987)

6. Cavazza, M., Simo, A.: A virtual patient based on qualitative simulation. In: The 8th international conference on Intelligent user interfaces, Miami, Florida, pp. 19–25 (2003)

7. Hu, H.H., Gooch, A.A., Thompson, W.B., Smits, B.E., Rieser, J.J., Shirley, P.: Visual cues for imminent object contact in realistic virtual environment. In: Conference on Visualization 2000, pp. 179–185. IEEE Computer Society Press, Los Alamitos (2000)

8. Cumming, B.G., DeAngelis, G.C.: The physiology of stereopsis. Annual Review of Neuroscience 24, 203–238 (2001)

9. Ware, C., Franck, G.: Evaluating stereo and motion cues for visualizing information nets in three dimensions. ACM Transactions on Graphics (TOG) 15(2), 121–140 (1996)

10. Lo, C.H., Chalmers, A.: Stereo vision for computer graphics: the effect that stereo vision has on human judgments of visual realism. In: 19th spring conference on Computer graphics, pp. 109–117. ACM, New York (2003)

11. Yoo, T.S., Ackerman, M.J., Lorensen, W.E., Schroeder, W., Chalana, V., Aylward, S., Metaxas, D., Whitaker, R.: Engineering and algorithm design for an image processing Api: a technical report on ITK–the Insight Toolkit. In: Studies in health technology and informatics, pp. 586–592. IOS Press, Amsterdam (2002)

12. Flack, S.R., McGhee, J.B.: 3-D computer visualisation and animation in clinical care. In: International Conference on Computer Graphics and Interactive Techniques, article no. 1. ACM, New York (2007)

13. Goodman, D.A., Agarwal, N., Tiruchelvam, V., Rhoads, J.E., Tabb, D.R.: 3D CT reconstruction in the surgical management of hepatic injuries. Annals of The Royal College of Surgeons of England 77, 7–11 (1995)

14. Aspin, R., Smith, M., Hutchinson, C., Funk, L.: MediVol: An initial study into real-time, interactive 3D visualization of soft tissue pathologies. In: 12th IEEE/ACM International Symposium on Distributed Simulation and Real-Time Application, pp. 103–110 (2008)

15. Tong, J., Dazhe, Z., Wei, L.: Research and Implementation of a Computer-aided Diagnosis Algorithm Platform. In: 2nd IEEE Conference on Industrial Electronics and Applications, ICIEA, pp. 2135–2139 (2007)

16. Lim, D.W.L., Ibrahim, H., Umi, K.N.: Development of Virtual Reality System for Medical Application Using OpenGL. In: IEEE Conference on Innovative Technologies in Intelligent System and Industrial Applications, pp. 44–48 (2008)

17. Carvalho, E., Marcos, A., Santos, M.Y., Mendes, J.E.: A Prototype for Cartographic Human Body Analysis. In: Computer Graphics and Applications, pp. 16–21. IEEE Computer Society Press, Los Alamitos (2008)

18. Loomis, J.M., Knapp, J.M.: Visual perception of egocentric distance in real and virtual environments. In: Hettinger, L.J., Haas, M.W. (eds.) Virtual and Adaptive Environments, Erlbaum, Mahwah (1999) (in press)

19. Young, M.J., Landy, M.S., Maloney, L.T.: A Perturbation Analysis of Depth Perception from Combinations of Texture and Motion Cues. Vision Research 33(18), 2685–2696 (1993)

20. Deering, M.F.: Explorations of Display Interfaces for Virtual Reality. In: IEEE Virtual Reality Annual International Symposium 1993, Seattle, WA, pp. 144–147 (1993)

A New Approach of Skull Fracture Detection in CT Brain Images

Wan Mimi Diyana Wan Zaki[1], Mohammad Faizal Ahmad Fauzi[2], and Rosli Besar[3]

[1] Faculty of Engineering and Built Environment, Universiti Kebangsaan Malaysia,
43600 Bangi, Selangor, Malaysia
wmdiyana@vlsi.eng.ukm.my
[2] Faculty of Engineering, Multimedia University,
63100 Cyberjaya, Malaysia
[3] Faculty of Engineering and Technology, Multimedia University,
75450 Melaka, Malaysia
{faizal1,rosli}@mmu.edu.my

Abstract. This work demonstrates a new automated approach to segment skull from 2D-CT brain image to detect any fracture case. The key steps in the proposed approach include image normalization, centroid identification, multi-level global segmentation and skull skeletonization. Feature vectors such as location and fracture size are then extracted to represent fracture cases. Twenty eight encephalic fracture images are queried from a database of 3032 normal and fractured CT brain images to evaluate the usefulness of the skull segmentation as well as the extracted feature vectors in content-based medical image retrieval system (CBMIR). Retrieval performance of Normalized Euclidean and Normalized Manhattan distance metrics show almost perfect average recall-precision plots that portray the suitability of this approach to the CBMIR of fracture cases.

Keywords: Skull fracture, multi-level segmentation, skeletonization, CT brain images, CBMIR.

1 Introduction

Computed Tomography (CT) combines sophisticated x-ray and computer technology that has become a valuable diagnostic tool and its uses has been widely and rapidly increasing. CT images can show a combination of bones, soft tissues and blood vessels. Compared to MRI, CT scan has widespread availability, ease of access, optimal detection of calcification and hemorrhage, and excellent bony details. It is also valuable in patients who cannot have MRI due to metal implanted in their heads. CT scanning of head does however have few drawbacks such as radiation burden on the patient, low tissue contrast and artifact due to beam hardening and spiral-off centre [1]. Nevertheless, in spite of these limitations, CT continues to be one of diagnostic tools of head pathology.

From CT brain images, various structures of the brain can be examined to look for masses, strokes, areas of bleeding, or blood vessel abnormalities as well as skull. A CT scans of the brain identify skull fractures in about two thirds of head injury

H. Badioze Zaman et al. (Eds.): IVIC 2009, LNCS 5857, pp. 156–167, 2009.

patients [2]. A severe impact or blow results in fracture of the skull which later may be accompanied by injury to the brain. Broken fragments of skull can bruise the brain or damage blood vessels. If the fracture occurs over a major blood vessel, significant bleeding can occur within the skull, so head injury patients with skull fracture have many more intracranial hematomas than those without fractures [3, 4]. These facts provide the motivation for this work. This paper proposes a new approach to automatically detect skull fractures and extract their features, for use in content-based retrieval of head fracture cases in CT images. Besides, this work provides an alternative way to search for cases with serious hematomas due to head injury; by retrieving images with fracture skull.

1.1 Related Work

The challenges associated with CT brain segmentation to detect abnormalities such as intracranial hemorrhage (ICH) [5, 6], tumor [7], edema [8, 9], hematoma and calcifications [10] have given rise to many different approaches. However, there are relatively sparse works devoted to detection of skull fractures in CT brain images. Shao H. and Zhao H. in Ref. [11] worked on the CT brain segmentation for the sake of automatic diagnosis of the fracture skull. In their work, the region growing method whose seeds and growing criterions had been chosen using k-means before diagnosis rules based on information entropy were applied to the head images. The method proved to give high recognition rate, although its complexity and performance can be further simplified and improved respectively. James D. et al. [12] proposed a technique to automatically quantify the shape of the skull cavity in CT brain axial slices. The algorithms were able to extract the shape of the inner edge of the skull, later to be represented by a radius function. Their algorithm showed that the extracted shape could be precisely quantified by the harmonic analysis using the Fourier Transform of the radius function.

Vongkornvoravej P. et al. [13] had constructed a model of human head, based on computerized 3-dimensional database. They estimated an appropriate thresholding value for skull using principle of probability and statistic describing gray scale level distribution of CT images before segmenting the skull using the a priori knowledge-based thresholding method. Then, a voxel-based model was constructed by creating a database containing a spatial data of the 3D skull model. The work had been developed to study the effect of electromagnetic waves to human, in which head is the nearest organ. In another work, Shapiro L.G. et al. [14] had implemented a prototype system for shape-based image retrieval of skull imaging for craniofacial medicine. Their proposed system supported retrieval based on their shape similarity to a query image using four extracted shape descriptors of numeric and symbolic features.

2 Proposed Skull Segmentation

Skull segmentation in medical images is an important step toward complete segmentation of the tissue in the human head. It is a significant step in the application of content-based medical image retrieval. There are three important steps which are image normalization, multi-level global segmentation and skull skeletonization.

2.1 Pre-processing: Image Normalization

Image normalization is necessary before skull segmentation and feature extraction can be carried out. This process may overcome any inconsistency of grey level values in the medical image database. This problem results in different segmented regions within the same intensity level. It is mainly caused by inconsistent measurement parameters used during the scanning procedures. During this preprocessing process, the original CT brain image is normalized by mapping the values of its intensity image to range of values such that the image is saturated at new minimum, t_{new_min} and new maximum, t_{new_max} intensities of the original image. Fig 1 displays a histogram of the original CT brain image and the corresponding new range of its intensity values.

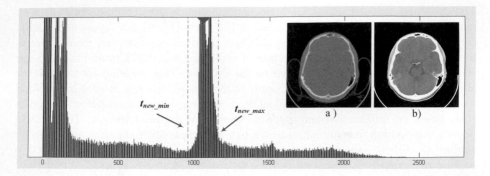

Fig. 1. Intensity histogram of p86_009.dcm slice. a) Original image of CT brain images; b) The same image after normalization process.

Identification of centroid. Centroid is defined as the center of the segmented skull and can be used to present location information of the CT brain images. It is important to accurately identify the centroid since it will be the main reference point for feature extraction. Calculation of location of quadrants and fracture's angles highly depends on the accuracy of the centroid. Due to that reason, identification of centroid should be robust and reliable. Shao H. and Zhao H. had used moment calculation to identify center of mass for symmetry calculation. In this work, we have applied a simpler approach but reliable (shown in Figure 2) to identify the centroid, as below.

A portion of program code used to calculate centroid, adapted from Fahad N. Abasi (2004) Matlab File Exchange.

```
=START
Read the gray scale image;
Set the matrix with each pixel to its x coordinate;
Set the matrix with each pixel to its y coordinate;
Compute the area;
Calculate x-coordinate of the centroid ;
Calculate y-coordinate of the centroid ;
STOP
```

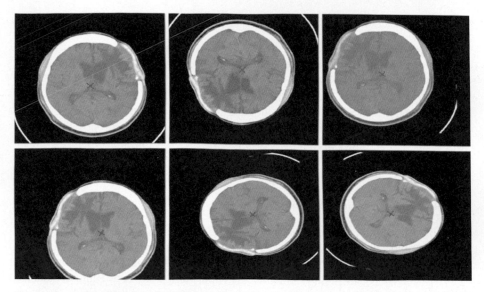

Fig. 2. Results of centroid (red crosses) identification tested on an encephalic slice in various orientations

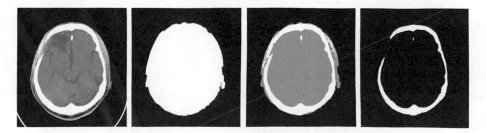

Fig. 3. Global segmentation results. From left to right: Normalized image of an original brain CT scan; Segmented region of interest (scalp, skull and intracranial); Segmented regions of scalp, skull and intracranial after multi-level segmentation; binary region of segmented skull.

2.2 Skull Extraction: Multi-level Global Segmentation Method

Global segmentation employs the Fuzzy C-Mean (FCM) clustering to firstly extract the background from the original CT head images followed by extraction of skull or region of interests (ROIs) from the head. This multi-level FCM has shown to success-fully extract the ROIs from the CT head images. Fig. 3 illustrates results of step by step processes in the global segmentation.

One major drawback of this multi-level FCM method is the longer execution time. This is due to the fact that it involves iterative optimization of minimization of the objective function, $J_m = \sum_{i=1}^{N} \sum_{j=1}^{C} u_{ij}^m \parallel x_i - c_j \parallel^2$, $1 \leq m < \infty$ with updated mem-bership, u_{ij} and cluster center, c_j [15]. m is any real number greater than 1, N is the number of cluster, C is the number of measured data, u_{ij} is the degree of membership of x_i in the cluster j, x_i is the i th of d -dimension measured data, c_j is the d - dimension center of the cluster, and $\| * \|$ is any norm expressing the similarity between any measured data and the center.

Using Matlab 7.0 as the software tool and Intel Core™ 2 Duo processor 2.26GHz CPU and 2GB DDR3 as the testing platform, performance of the proposed approach has shown to mostly depend on the execution time of multi-level FCM in the global segmentation. However, it is still tolerable and not a crucial issue as accurate segmentation is deemed more important as this stage.

2.3 Skull Skeletonization: Thinning process

The process of computing skeletons is called skeletonization. Skeletons are geometric shape-descriptor and they are centered within the shape, and capture the topology and geometry of the shape in a compact manner. The idea of skeletonization was introduced by Blum in 1967 for the purpose of biological application. Known as Blum or standard skeletons, they have then been adopted by computer science fields such as

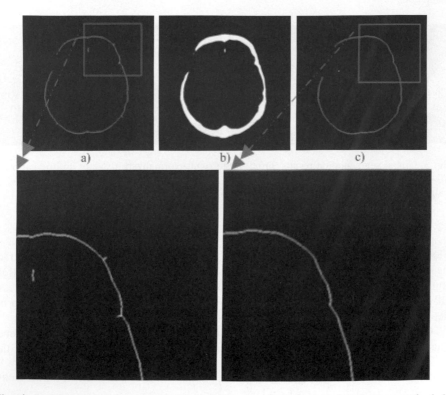

Fig. 4. A CT brain skull skeletonization: a) Results of standard skeletonization method, b) Binary segmented skull region, c) Results of the curve skeletonization

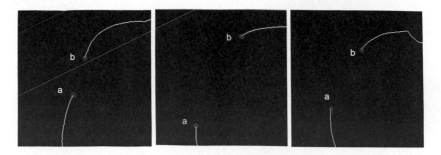

Fig. 5. B Endpoints detection of skull fractures

computer-aided design, visualization and medical analysis [16, 17]. Denise et al. had proposed a new approach to compute skeletons as shape descriptor that is robust to boundary noise. His work has been applied to detect the presence of broken skull or fracture. In the shape matching and retrieval, the curve skeleton can be applied for thinning method so that matching shape can be more accurate.

The skull skeleton is generated from the binary skull image segmented from the CT brain images. Generating the skull skeleton is an important step for feature extraction process. Performances of the skeletonization using standard skeleton and the selected curve skeleton are shown in Fig 4. The curve skeleton proved to be more robust to noise in which is very useful to identify any endpoints for fracture cases. Besides, the curve skeleton is also smoother without false junction points. The most challenging part of this thinning process is to get reliable skeleton so that important features such as endpoints and junction points can be accurately extracted. Fig 5 portrays few examples of endpoints detection of skull skeleton for the fracture cases.

3   Fracture Feature Representation

From the skull skeleton of CT brain images, features characterizing fracture are extracted. A significant feature vector reduces the amount of irrelevant information and produce robust skull descriptors for the retrieval task. In this experimental work, the features are selected based on their ability to separate fracture from normal or non-broken skulls. Flowchart in Fig 6 shows the step-by-step procedure of feature representation.

Prior to the feature extraction, coordinates on the Cartesian's axes of the 2D- brain image should be firstly allocated. The main reference point on the Cartesian's axes is the centroid. Fig 7 illustrates how the centroid is positioned on the axes and four quadrants are assigned. Based on these, the following features are identified to form the fracture feature vector.

1) **Quadrant identification**: Fracture location is identified by comparing the quadrant assignment on the Cartesian coordinates and the skeleton coordinates of the two endpoints, (x_a, y_a) and (x_b, y_b).

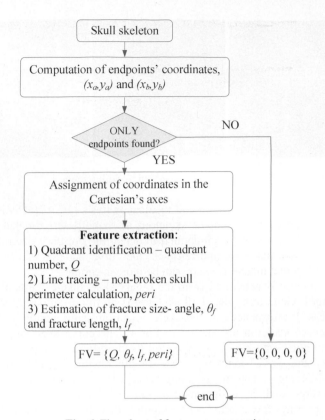

Fig. 6. Flowchart of feature representation

2) ***Line tracing of non-broken skull***: Skull skeleton is formed by one-pixel thinned medial line. Thus, the length of non-broken skull is simply equivalent to the total number of white pixels that formed the skeleton.

3) ***Estimation of fracture size***: Knowing both coordinates of the endpoints, A and B as well as the coordinates of the centroid, O computation of the fracture angle, θ_f and the fracture length, l_f are quite straightforward. Let u and v are two vectors formed by line OA and OB in the Cartesian coordinates, and θ_f is the angle between them, then the dot product, denoted by $u \cdot v$ is defined as $u.v = |u\|v|\cos\theta_f$. Thus, θ_f can be calculated as $\theta_f = \cos^{-1}\left[\dfrac{u \cdot v}{|u\|v|}\right]$. Using a simple equation manipulation, an estimation of fracture length is derived from Eq. 1.

$$l_f = \left[\frac{\theta_f}{360° - \theta_f}\right]\left(l_{non\_broken}\right) \tag{1}$$

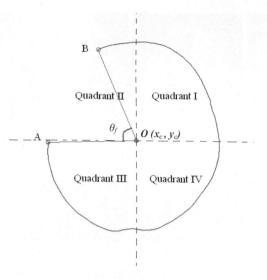

Fig. 7. Fracture features representation

Feature vector for fracture cases are constructed by combinations of 4 main statistical components which is $f = \{Q, \theta_f, l_f, peri\}$.

4 Experimental Results and Discussion

The database used in our experiment consists of 3032 CT brain images from various slices of 100 patients in Putrajaya Hospital, Malaysia. From the 3032, 28 original encephalic images of CT brain of one patient are used as target images in the experiments. The target images are fracture cases; hence those images are used as queries for the retrieval experiment. The evaluation is based on the ability of algorithm to detect the skull fracture, later use to locate its fracture and identify its size. One major problem in this work is the lack of fracture CT brain images. Thus, for evaluation purposes, we have manipulated the 28 original encephalic CT slices by flipping them rightwards, downwards as well as rightwards followed by the downwards. These result another 3 classes of encephalic CT slices. Some of them are illustrated in Figure 8 together with their corresponding fracture skull detected by our proposed algorithm. The algorithm has successfully detected only two endpoints as well as no junction points that represent the existence of fracture in the skull. On another hand, there is no endpoint (for encephalic slices) or more than 2 endpoints (for nasal cavity slices) detected in the skull skeletons for normal CT brain images. Figure 9 portrays two examples of the skull detection results that led to the feature vector representation for normal cases as $FV = \{0,0,0,0\}$.

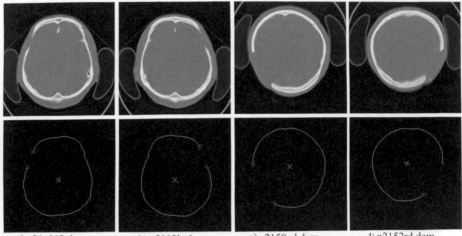

a) p21_012.dcm   b) p2113lr.dcm   c) p2150ud.dcm   d) p2152rd.dcm

Fig. 8. (Top row) Examples of original encephalic slices of an original CT fracture brain images, followed by generated images; Class 1 (flipped rightwards), Class 2 (flipped downwards) and Class 3 (flipped rightwards then downwards). (Bottom row) Their corresponding skull skeletons are plotted with the centroid (red crosses) and the two endpoints (blue crosses)

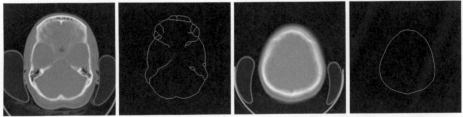

a) A normal slice of nasal cavity region   b) A normal slice of encephalic region

Fig. 9. The results of skull skeletonization after the skull are segmented from the original CT brain images

Table 1. Some features extracted from fracture cases

Class	Query image	Quadrant number	Non-broken skull perimeter, $peri(pixels)$	Fracture angle, $\theta_f (°)$	Fracture length, $l_f (pixels)$
1	p21_012.dcm	2	931	24.3	67.4
1	p21_024.dcm	2	769	61.9	159.7
2	p2113lr.dcm	1	916	29.4	81.5
2	p2118lr.dcm	1	812	23.6	57.0
3	p2140ud.dcm	3	934	23.7	65.7
3	p2150ud.dcm	3	786	69.1	177.0
4	p2143rd.dcm	4	872	45.6	126.5
4	p2152rd.dcm	4	771	61.54	158.98

Table 2. Percentage of average recognition rate for different distance metrics

Distance metric	Number of retrieved images considered=28
	Recall rate
Euclidean	91.33
Manhattan	90.43
Mahalanobis	88.39
Normalized Euclidean	95.15
Normalized Manhattan	96.30

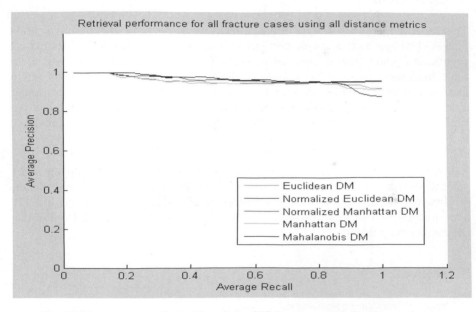

Fig. 10. The average recall-precision plots of 28 fracture encephalic CT scan images

Possible combination of location and size features are chosen as feature vectors to demonstrate their usefulness in a simple CBMIR system. Size and position are among the important features used by human doctors to classify potential abnormal presents in the CT brain images [6]. Table 1 shows the capability of our algorithm to extract all the four features.

The usefulness of this approach has been measured based on the ability of the extracted feature vectors to retrieve the fracture cases from a database consisting of 3004 normal and 28 original fracture cases. Table 2 shows the average recognition rate of the Euclidean, Manhattan, Normalized Euclidean, Normalized Manhattan and Mahalanobis distance metrics. Recognition rate sometimes known as recall is also used individually to measure the progress of retrieve rate against the number of retrieved images. The performance of the proposed approach using the five distance metrics are presented in an average recall-average precision plot, as in Figure 10. Recall and precision are calculated as:

$$Recall = \frac{Number\_relevant\_that\_are\_retrieved}{Total\_number\_relevant} \tag{2}$$

$$Precision = \frac{Number\_retrieved\_that\_are\_relevant}{Total\_number\_retrieved} \tag{3}$$

From our observation, both the normalized distances give a quite similar performance and are the best among the evaluated. Besides, their precision-recall plots are almost straight lines which reflect good retrieval performances.

5   Conclusion

This paper proposes a new approach to effectively detect skull fracture in CT brain images. This approach is simple and fast as well as reliable to automatically extract significant features from the segmented skull. The continual refinement of the algorithm from previous work has introduced the feature vectors that represent fracture location and its size, which are useful for the medical image retrieval to find similar cases for training and diagnosis purposes. This approach proves to have a bright potential to be integrated in the application of medical image diagnosis in providing second opinions to doctors or radiologists.

Acknowledgments. The authors are grateful to the MOSTI for their support under grant number 01-02-01-SF0014 (the eScienceFund Project), and to our collaborator, the Imaging Department of Hospital Putrajaya, Malaysia, which provides the CT brain images used in this work. Besides, we also would like to thank Dr. Fatimah Othman for her guidance.

References

1. National Brain Tumor Foundation,
   http://www.braintumor.org/diagnosisfaq
2. Neurosurgery Department, NNI,
   http://www.neurosurgery.com.sg/index.php?id=69
3. Zaki, W., Mimi Diyana, W., Faizal Ahmad Fauzi, M., Besar, R.: Automated Method of Fracture Detection in CT Brain Images. In: 3rd IEEE International Conference on Intelligent System and Knowledge Engineering, pp. 1156–1160 (2008)
4. Liu, R., Tan, C.L., Leong, T.: Hemorrhage slices detection in brain CT images. In: Proc ICPR, pp. 1–4 (2008)
5. Loncaric, S., Cosic, D., Dhawan, A.P.: Hierarchical Segmentation of CT Head Images. In: IEEE Eng. in Medicine and Biology Society, pp. 736–737 (1996)
6. Tianxia, G., Ruizhe, L., Chew, L.T., Neda, F., Cheng, K.L., Boon, C.P., et al.: Classification of CT brain images of head trauma. In: Rajapakse, J.C., Schmidt, B., Volkert, L.G. (eds.) PRIB 2007. LNCS (LNBI), vol. 4774, pp. 401–408. Springer, Heidelberg (2007)
7. Mancas, M., Gosselin, B.: Towards an Automatic Tumor Segmentation Using Iterative Watershed. In: Proceedings of the Medical Imaging Conference of the International Society for Optical Imaging, pp. 1598–1608 (2004)

8. Loncaric, S., Kovacevic, D., Cosic, D.: Fuzzy Expert System for Edema Segmentation. In: 9th IEEE Mediterranean Electrotechnical Conference, pp. 1476–1479 (1998)
9. Cosic, D., Loncaric, S.: Two Methods for ICH Segmentation. In: 11th International Symposium on Biomedical Engineering, pp. 63–66 (1996)
10. Matestin, M., Loncaric, S., Petravic, D.: A Rule-Based Approach to Stroke Lesion Analysis from CT Brain Images. In: 2nd International Symposium on Image and Signal Processing and Analysis, pp. 219–222 (2001)
11. Shao, H., Zhao, H.: Automatic Analysis of the Skull Based on Image Content. In: 3rd International Symposium on Multispectral Image Processing and Pattern Recognition, pp. 741–746 (2003)
12. Devenish, J., Linggard, R., Michalak, K., Parker, K., Emelyanova, I., Cala, L., Attikiouzel, Y., Hicks, N., Robbins, P., Mastaglia, F.: Quantifying Skull Shape. In: 7th IEEE International Control Automation, Robotics and Vision, pp. 530–535 (2002)
13. Vongkornvoravej, P., Roongruangsorakarn, S., Chaisaowong, K.: Segmentation of Medical Images from Computed Tomography to Create a 3-Dimensional Model of Human Skull. In: Special Session of the 3th International Conference on Computer Graphics, Animation and Multimedia (2007)
14. Shapiro, L.G., Atmosukarto, I., Cho, H., Lin, H.J., Ruiz-Correa, S., Yuen, J.: Case-Based Reasoning on Images and Signal: Similarity-Based retrieval for Biomedical Applications. SCI, vol. 73, pp. 355–387. Springer, Heidelberg (2008)
15. Image Processing Toolbox User's Guide. Matlab Image Processing Toolbox User Guide's Version 5.2 (R2006a)
16. Reniers, D.: Skeletonization and Segmentation of Binary Voxel Shape. PhD thesis, Eindhoven University of Technology, Netherlands (2008)
17. Malandain, G., Fernadez-Vidal, S.: Euclidean Skeleton. J. Image and Vision Computing 16, 317–327 (1998)

Application of Information Visualization Techniques in Representing Patients' Temporal Personal History Data

Shahrul Azman Noah[1], Suraya Yaakob[1], and Suzana Shahar[2]

[1] Faculty of Information Science & Technology, Universiti Kebangsaan Malaysia 43600 UKM
Bangi Selangor, Malaysia
{samn,suraya}@ftsm.ukm.my
[2] Faculty of Allied Health Sciences, Universiti Kebangsaan Malaysia 43600 UKM Bangi
Selangor, Malaysia
suzanas@medic.ukm.my

Abstract. The anthropometries and nutrients records of patients are usually vast in quantity, complex and exhibit temporal features. Therefore, the information acceptance among users will become blur and give cognitive burden if such data is not displayed using effective techniques. The aim of this study is to apply, use and evaluate Information Visualization (IV) techniques for displaying the Personal History Data (PHD) of patients for dietitians during counseling sessions. Since PHD values change consistently with the counseling session, our implementation mainly focused on quantitative temporal data such as Body Mass Index (BMI), blood pressure and blood glucose readings. This data is mapped into orientation circle type of visual representation, whereas data about medicinal and supplement intake are mapped into timeline segment which is based on the thickness of lines as well as the colors. A usability testing has been conducted among dietitians at Faculty of Allied Health Sciences, UKM. The result of the testing has shown that the use of visual representations capable of summarising complex data which ease the dietitian task of checking the PHD.

Keywords: information visualization, health information system, temporal data.

1 Introduction

The anthropometries and nutrients records of patients are usually vast in quality, complex and exhibit temporal features. Therefore the information acceptance among users can become vague and give cognitive burden if such data is not displayed using effective techniques. As a result the needs to understand and extract knowledge from stored data are increasingly becoming important [1]. In this sense, the properties of visual representation should be manipulated accordingly in order to leverage the problems of data overload and complexity. Visualization is seen as one of the best alternatives to represent data that was dominantly represented with text and numeric. The Information Visualization (IV) discipline is therefore been actively researched as early as 1996. IV produces (interactive) visual representations of abstract data to reinforce human cognition; thus enabling the viewer to gain knowledge about the internal structure of the data and causal relationships in it. Plaisant [2] stated that the

H. Badioze Zaman et al. (Eds.): IVIC 2009, LNCS 5857, pp. 168–179, 2009.

application of IV capable of giving meaning to data, reduced information loss, point to styles and patterns of data and visualize relations among data.

Suggesting and planning healthy dietary menus for patients is an important but complicated tasks which mainly performed by dietitians through consultation with patients. During the consultation session, the dietitian needs to go through the overall patient's Personal History Data (PHD) in order to obtain summaries of the patient's background and conditions. In certain situation, the dietitian needs to obtain detail information of certain information before any menu suggestions can be put forward. A number of information system to assist dietitians has been proposed. DietPal [3] is one of these which was developed at the Universiti Kebangsaan Malaysia (UKM) and tested at the Hospital of UKM. Although, DietPal has the capacity of assisting dietitians in managing and suggesting suitable dietary menus for patients based on standard procedures, dietitians are still struggling to view effectively required information which requires opening different menus and windows to make such information visible. According to Moore [4], the huge number of interfaces is one of the main problem in health information system. This paper proposed to apply, use and evaluate IV mechanisms for displaying the anthropometry and nutrients intakes in PHD, in such a way that the problem of information overload and cognitive burden can be reduced.

2   Background and Related Research

IV is about visual representations of the semantics, or meaning, of information. The main of IV is to reduce the complexity of understanding among users on some complex data [5]. It can be considered as the process of transforming data, information and knowledge into visual by making use of humans' natural capabilities [6]. The applications of IV are numerous and cross many disciplines. For temporal data a number of systems have been implemented such as Lifelines, PRIMA MMVIS, and LifeStream.

Temporal data has been used in many domains particularly in the domains of healthcare, marketing and flight management and scheduling. Lifelines use the timeline visual representation that is dynamic and interactive. Its dynamic feature enable immediate changes based on the changes of data and its interactive feature allow users to acquire further details of certain information. LifeStreams [7] represents data as time orientation file flows. Documents are sorted sequentially according to time series which eventually creating a flow of records. As a result the selection of documents will be much easier. PRIMA [8] on the other hand uses aggregation technique. Information containing similar chronology will be placed under the same cluster and each cluster is represented dynamic horizontal line. From our review, *timeline* is favored by many researchers working with temporal data.

2.1   Applications of IV in Health Information System

Health Information System (HIS) deals with the resources, devices, and methods required to optimize the acquisition, storage, retrieval, and use of information in health and biomedicine. IV, by providing interactive visual representations of data and information aims to deepen exploration of the "information space", support optimal use of data and information - and help avoid overload. Chittaro [9] summarizes some of the goals of IV technologies for healthcare which includes:

- To allow "users to explore available data at various levels of abstraction"
- To give "users a greater sense of engagement with data"
- To give "users a deeper understanding of data"
- To encourage "the discovery of details and relations which would be difficult to notice otherwise"
- To support "the recognition of relevant patterns by exploiting the visual recognition capabilities of users."

One example the use IV technique in healthcare is LifeLines [2]. LifeLines provides a general visualization environment for personal histories. A one screen overview of the record using timelines provides direct access to the data. For a patient record, medical problems, hospitalization and medications can be represented as horizontal lines, while icons represent discrete events such as physician consultations, progress notes or tests. Line color and thickness can illustrate relationships or significance. Rescaling tools and filters allow users to focus on part of the information, revealing more details. Timelines, icons and lines are three techniques for visualizing health data in LifeLines.

2.2 Dietary Menu Planning System

Dietary menu planning is a complicated and tedious process that researchers have tried to automate since 1960s. A number of systems have been developed of which the focus is mainly to assist healthy individuals calculate their calorie intake and to help monitor the selection of menus based upon a prespecified calorie value. Although these prove to be helpful in some ways, they are not suitable for monitoring, planning, and managing patients' dietary needs and requirements. DietPal [3] is one of the systems meant to fill the gap by providing assistance for dietitian in planning and managing healthy dietary menu for patients. DietPal, however, has its limitation particularly in terms of too many information need to accessed from different interfaces and traditional representations of data. As mentioned earlier, dietitians need to view a number of information during the consultation session and a single visual representation of such information could reduce the cognitive burden among dietitians. Fig. 1 shows the interface for accessing different data of each patient in the web-version of DietPal.

To our knowledge, research or applications focusing on visualizing information for assisting in dietary menu planning and suggestion is currently not in existence. In this paper, we therefore embark on the suitability of using IV techniques in visualizing information related to this activity. We used the DietPal system as our reference of requirement specification among dietitians. The following section will provide discussion on the visual design process and then follows by a brief overview of the implemented system. We then conclude with conclusions and future research work.

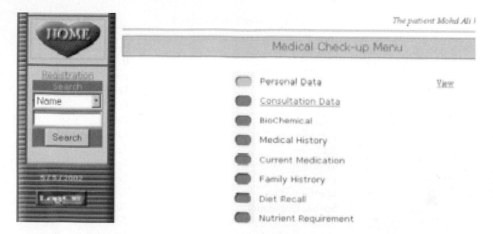

Fig. 1. Interface of DietPal

3   Visual Design Process

The visual design process includes five important phases: visual mapping; representation for information structure; overall overview strategy; navigational strategy; and interaction strategy.

3.1   Visual Mapping and Representation for Information Structure

The visual mapping is the process of transforming PHD to visual representation. It is part of the visual pipeline proposed by Card et al. [10] as illustrated in Fig. 2, that is a computational process for transforming information into visual representation that can interact with users.

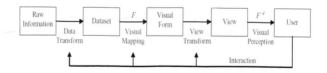

Fig. 2. Visualization pipeline

In the case of our study, we have identified the information used by dietitians during consultations process which are patient's personal data, medical history; biochemical data, dietary history and anthropometry data. It is, however beyond the scope of this work to visualize all the data. We therefore limit the data to be included as illustrated in Table 1 together with its corresponding visual mapping.

All the PHD proposed to be visualized in Table 1 will be examined in detail in order to identify the suitable visual features. The selection of which attributes to be visualized is based upon consultation with dietitians. Therefore, the quality of each attributes will first be identified either as quantitative, ordinal or nominal. Then the visual feature is chosen for each attributes based on its effectiveness and preciseness in representing the data quality. These are shown in Table 2.

Table 1. Personal History Data

Personal History Data (PHD) Types	Attributes	Proposed Representations
Personal Data	Name	Text
	Age	Text
	Race	Text
	Gender	Text
	Employment	Text
	Address	Text
	Telephone Number	Text
	Income	Text
	Marital Status	Text
	Spouse Occupation	Text
	Spouse Income	Text
	Number of Children	Text
	Living with who	Text
Anthorpometry Data	BMI Values	Visual
	Height	Text
	Weight	Text
	BMI Classification	Visual
Glucose Test	RBS Reading	Text
	FBS Reading	Text
	Glucose Level Classification	Visual
Full Blood Picture	Pressure Reading	Text
	Pressure Level Classification	Visual
Blood Pressure	Sistol/Diastol Readings	Text
	Blood Pressure Classification	Visual
Medicinal Intake Record	Type of Medicine	Text
	Amount of Intake	Visual
Supplement Intake Record	Type of Supplement Taken	Text
	Amount of Supplement Taken	Visual
Dietary Record	All dietary record	Visual and text

Once the visual representation has been achieved, the next process it the allocation of visual representation into space and vertical time of users' view. There are four types of information structure to be considered: tabular; space and temporal; trees and network; and text and documentations. In this study, the space and temporal structure will be the focused. Temporal data is divided into two: temporal dimension and temporal structure. Temporal dimension is the space or locations for the overall process of visual coding whereas temporal structure is the date values under study and mapped into visual presentation. The visual presentation produced from the temporal

Table 2. Visual features for PHD

Personal History Data (PHD) Types	Attributes	Data Quality	Visual Feature
Anthorpometry Data	BMI Values	Quantitative	Label - text
	Height	Quantitative	Label - text
	Weight	Quantitative	Label - text
	BMI Classification	Nominal	Orientation-Angle / Size-Sector
Glucose Test	RBS Reading	Quantitative	Label - text
	FBS Reading	Quantitative	Label - text
	Glucose Level Classification	Nominal	Orientation-Angle / Size-Sector
Full Blood Picture	Pressure Reading	Quantitative	Label - text
	Pressure Level Classification	Nominal	Orientation-Angle / Size-Sector
Blood Pressure	Sistol/Diastol Readings	Quantitative	Label - text
	Blood Pressure Classification	Nominal	Orientation-Angle / Size-Sector
Medicinal Intake Record	Type of Medicine	Nominal	Line-Segment
	Amount of Intake	Quantitative	Size-Thickness
	Level of Intake	Quantitative	Colour
Supplement Intake Record	Type of Supplement Taken	Nominal	Line-Segment
	Amount of Supplement Taken	Quantitative	Size-Thickness
	Level of Intake	Quantitative	Colour
Dietary Record	All dietary record	Nominal and Quantitative	Dot – Simple Representation

structure will be allocated in the temporal dimension. In this study the specific temporal visualization process is based from the work of Daasi et al. [11] as illustrated in Fig. 3. The first step involves identifying temporal values to be visualized and then transforming the values into analytical abstractions.

In the case of our study the circle orientation, timeline and simple icon used to represent PHD will be placed in the temporal space. Temporal value identified is time and PHD is divided into two time categories: linear and periodic. The linear category involves data such as anthropometry, blood pressure, glucose level, biochemical and dietary records. Each data values will be assigned a single timestamped such as '01/05/2009'. The periodic category involves data such as intake of medicine and

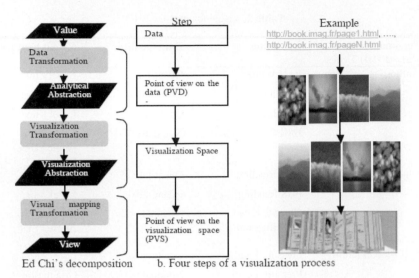

Ed Chi's decomposition   b. Four steps of a visualization process

Fig. 3. Information visualization data state reference model.

supplement intake, and each values will be assigned a periodic timestamped such as '*05/05/2009 to 08/07/2009*'. The analytical abstraction will then divided the time unit into smaller units. In our case, time is divided into granular and multi-granular whereby granular is in year unit and multi-granular is decomposed into semester and month. Fig. 4 illustrates an example of analytical abstraction.

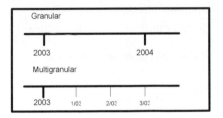

Fig. 4. Decomposition of temporal values in analytical abstraction

These analytical abstractions are then transformed into visualization abstracts. The process will result in the creation of temporal space and dimensions. We represent time as a single temporal space with one dimension. All the related PHD are uploaded into the temporal space. The granular and multi-granular are located at *x*-axis whereas data values are located at *y*-axis as illustrated in Fig. 5.

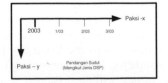

Fig. 5. The *x* and *y* axis of temporal space

The last step is to place the analytical abstractions into the temporal space for user's presentation. Timeline is chosen in this study because it is the best method to represent temporal information. Fig. 6 shows an example timeline representation for anthropometry data.

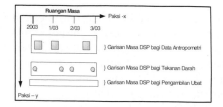

Fig. 6. Timelines for anthropometry data

3.2 Overview Strategy

Overview strategy is one of the interactive mechanism in IV for summarizing the PHD of each patient. In our implementation, all the PHD can be viewed into one screen and the data is represented in a compact visual representation. We used the tabular fisheye view technique for arranging all the interfaces into one canvas and the canvas can be distributed into columns and rows. Fig. 7 shows the implementation of the overview strategy.

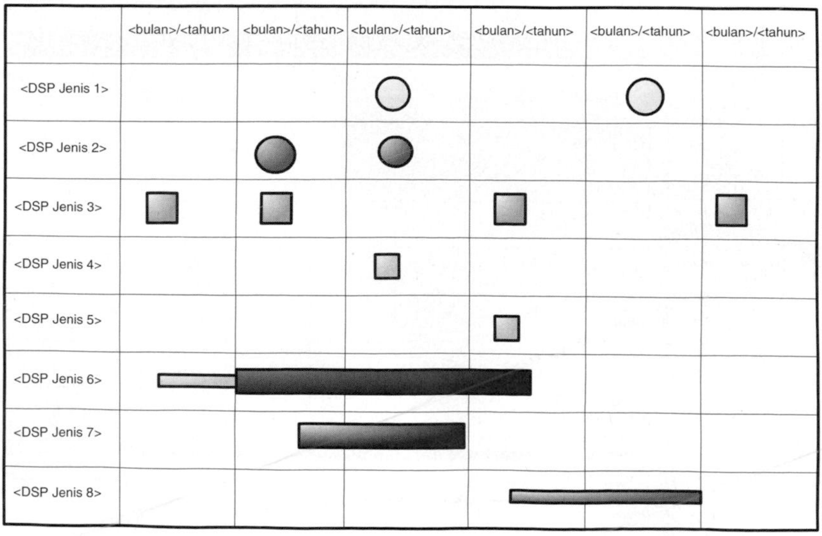

	<bulan>/<tahun>	<bulan>/<tahun>	<bulan>/<tahun>	<bulan>/<tahun>	<bulan>/<tahun>	<bulan>/<tahun>
<DSP Jenis 1>			◯		◯	
<DSP Jenis 2>		●	●			
<DSP Jenis 3>	▣	▣		▣		▣
<DSP Jenis 4>			▢			
<DSP Jenis 5>				▢		
<DSP Jenis 6>	▬▬▬▬					
<DSP Jenis 7>		▬▬▬				
<DSP Jenis 8>				▬▬▬		

Fig. 7. Allocation of all PHD in one interface for the overall overview strategy

3.3 Navigational and Interaction Strategy

Navigational strategy is meant to support navigation of the overall overview strategy for viewing the details of the required item. There are quite a number of method available such as *zoom and pan*, *overview and details*, and *focus and context*. In our implementation the *zooming* technique is used which allow users to *zoom in* or *zoom our* with a single mouse click with a scale of 0.25 to 1.00.

4 DietVis

The implementation of the aforementioned design is called DietVis. As mentioned earlier DietVis is meant for dietitians during consultation with patients. DietVis is integrated with the existing DietPal system which is a system for managing and planning healthy dietary menu for patients. DietVis was developed using Java and utilized the packages provided by Piccolo [12]. The main interface of DietVis is as illustrated in Fig. 8. As can be seen the interface is divided into three main spaces: personal data space, caption space and PHD space. For significant reason, we focused our discussion on the PHD space only.

The PHD space is clearly the most important space it occupies the majority of the DietVis interface. This is where all the health and dietary records of a specific patient is visually mapped. As can be seen in Fig. 8 the space is divided into column and row where the time and PHD data are represented respectively. The circle orientation, icons and timelines are the three visual representations occupying this space. The circle representation is meant to visually indicate the various category of nominal values such as the glucose level and BMI classification. Each colored and occupying sector indicate different classification from low to high risk factor. For example the Fig. 9 shows different classifications of BMI: slim, ideal, pre-obesity and obesity.

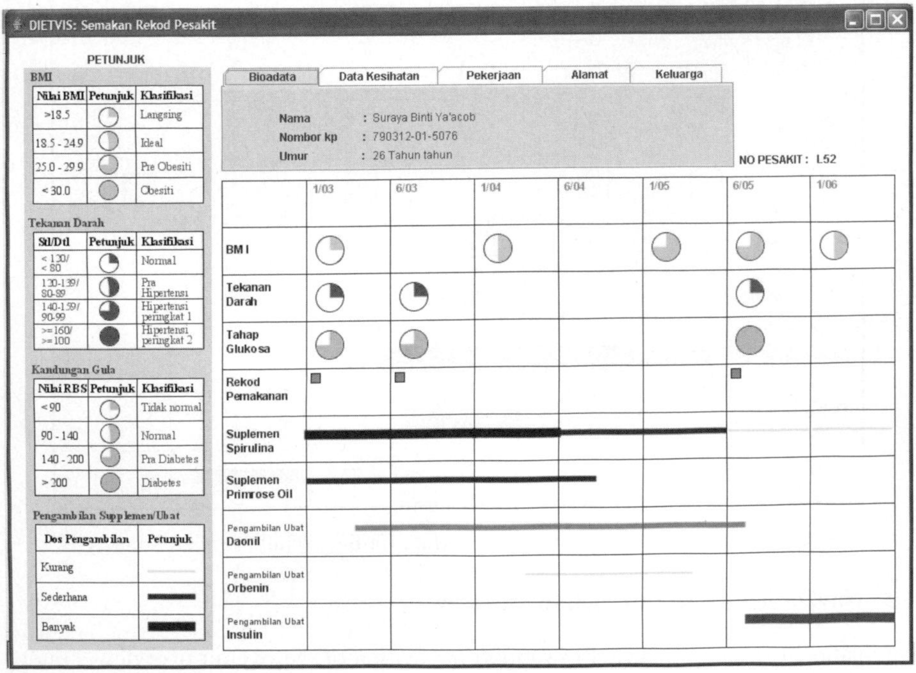

Fig. 8. Main interface of DietVis

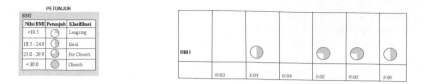

Fig. 9. Different classification of BMI based on the circle orientation

Before zoom-in   After zoom-in

Fig. 10. Example of zoom-in feature for glucose level data

Tekanan Darah						
Tahap Glukosa						
Rekod Pemakanan						
Suplemen Spirulina						

Tarikh Konsultasi: 2/2/2003
Perkara Pengambilan Saranan
Jenis Diet   -   LPr,HFi
Bil Hdgn   7 hdgn   6 hdgn
CHO   221.2   249.8
Protein   56.6   62.9
Fat   93.4   73.7
Fiber   5.6   19.56
Na   1172   1294
Kalori   1950   1922.81
(kcal)

Fig. 11. Icon representation for patient's dietary record

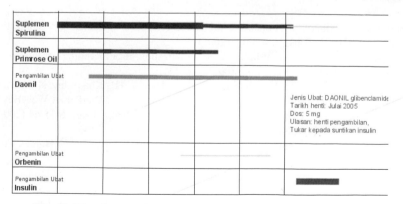

Suplemen Spirulina						
Suplemen Primrose Oil						
Pengambilan Ubat Daonil						
Pengambilan Ubat Orbenin						
Pengambilan Ubat Insulin						

Jenis Ubat: DAONIL glibenclamide
Tarikh henti: Julai 2005
Dos: 5 mg
Ulasan: henti pengambilan,
Tukar kepada suntikan insulin

Fig. 12. Timeline representation for medicine and supplement intake

From one glance, a dietitian will be able to know the BMI classification of each patient from the occupying space of the circle.

It is beyond the scope of this paper to discuss DietVis in great detail. However some of the important features of DietVis is briefly illustrated. Fig. 10 shows the *zoom in* and *zoom out* features of DietVis. Fig. 11 and 12 on the other hand show the visual representation of the patient's dietary record and timeline for medicine and supplement intake.

5   Conclusion

This paper described the application of IV in dietary menu planning and management. We have conducted a usability testing among dietitians using the framework proposed by [13] consisting of five elements: limitations, cognitive complexity, spatial organization, information coding and state transition. The usability testing has been conducted among eight dietitians and an average score of more than 80% for all criteria except spatial organization. The low score for spatial organization is due to the limitation of the system to provide instant actual date for each data.

Our on-going research work among others is to improve the spatial organization of the system in terms object location and spatial orientation. Spatial organization is related to the overall layout of a visual representation, which comprises analyzing how easy it is to locate an information element in the display and to be aware of the overall distribution of information elements in the representation. Locating an information element can be hard if some objects are occluded by others, and if the layout does not follow a "logical" organization depending on some characteristics of the data elements. So, degree of object occlusion and logical order are characteristics to be measured in the visual representation. The spatial orientation, which contributes for the user being aware of the distribution of information elements, is dependent on the display of the reference context while showing a specific element in detail.

References

1. North, C.: Handbook of Human Factors and Ergonomics: Information Visualization, 3rd edn. John Wiley & Sons, New York (2005)
2. Plaisant, C.: The challenge of information visualization. In: Proceedings of the Conference in Advanced Visual Interfaces, pp. 109–116 (2004)
3. Noah, S.A., Abdullah, S.N., Shahar, S., Abdul-Hamid, H., Khairudin, N., Yusoff, M., Ghazali, R., Mohd-Yusoff, N., Shafii, N.S., Abdul-Manaf, Z.: DietPal: A Web-Based Dietary Menu-Generating and Management System. J. Med. Internet Res. 6(1), e4 (2004)
4. Moore, M.: Top ten problems on health systems (March 1999)
5. Schneiderman, B.: Designing the User Interface: Strategies for Effective Human Computer Interaction. Addison-Wesley, Maryland (1998)
6. Gershon, N., Eick, S.G., Card, S.: Information visualization. ACM Interactions 5(2), 9–15 (1998)
7. Freeman, E., Gelernter, D.: Lifestreams: A Storage Model for Personal Data. ACM SIGMOD Bulletin (1996)

8. Gresh, D.L., Rabenhorst, D.A., Shabo, A., Slavin, S.: PRIMA: A case study using IV techniques for patient record analysis. In: IEEE Visualization, pp. 509–512 (2002)
9. Chittaro, L.: Information visualization and its application to medicine. In: Procd. AI in Medicine, vol. 22, pp. 259–262
10. Card, S.K., Mackinlay, J.D., Schneiderman, B.: Readings in Information Visualization: Using Vision to Think. Morgan Freeman, San Francisco (1999)
11. Daasi, S., Nigay, L., Fauvet, M.C.: Visualization process of temporal data. In: 15th International Conference on Database and Expert System Application, pp. 914–924 (2004)
12. Bederson, B.B., Grosjean, J., Meyer, J.: Toolkit design for interactive structured graphics. IEEE Transactions on Software Engineering 30(8), 535–546 (2004)
13. Freitas, C., Luzzardi, P., Cava, R., Winckler, M., Pimenta, M.S., Nedel, L.P.: On evaluating information visualization techniques. In: IEEE Proc. of Advance Visual Interfaces, pp. 373–374 (2002)

Development of Total Knee Replacement Digital Templating Software

Siti Fairuz Yusof[1], Riza Sulaiman[1], Lee Thian Seng[1], Abdul Yazid Mohd. Kassim[2], Suhail Abdullah[2], Shahril Yusof[2], Masbah Omar[2], and Hamzaini Abdul Hamid[3]

[1] Department of Industrial Computing,
Faculty of Information Science and Technology, UKM
[2] Department of Orthopaedic & Traumatology,
Faculty of Medicine, UKM
[3] Department of Radiology,
Faculty of Medicine, UKM
rs@ftsm.ukm.my

Abstract. In this study, by taking full advantage of digital X-ray and computer technology, we have developed a semi-automated procedure to template knee implants, by making use of digital templating method. Using this approach, a software system called OrthoKnee™ has been designed and developed. The system is to be utilities as a study in the Department of Orthopaedic and Traumatology in medical faculty, UKM (FPUKM). OrthoKnee™ templating process employs uses a technique similar to those used by many surgeons, using acetate templates over X-ray films. Using template technique makes it easy to template various implant from every Implant manufacturers who have with a comprehensive database of templates. The templating functionality includes, template (knee) and manufactures templates (Smith & Nephew; and Zimmer). From an image of patient x-ray OrthoKnee™ templates help in quickly and easily reads to the approximate template size needed. The visual templating features then allow us quickly review multiple template sizes against the X-ray and thus obtain the nearly precise view of the implant size required. The system can assist by templating on one patient image and will generate reports that can accompany patient notes. The software system was implemented in Visual basic 6.0 Pro using the object-oriented techniques to manage the graphics and objects. The approaches for image scaling will be discussed. Several of measurement in orthopedic diagnosis process have been studied and added in this software as measurement tools features using mathematic theorem and equations. The study compared the results of the semi-automated (using digital templating) method to the conventional method to demonstrate the accuracy of the system.

Keywords: Digital templating, digital X-ray.

1 Introduction

According to Kakeda et al. [1]; Dahab et al. [2]; Wolf et al. [3]; Shrout et al. [4]; Seeberger et al. [5], digitalized image with integrated computer system has become an

H. Badioze Zaman et al. (Eds.): IVIC 2009, LNCS 5857, pp. 180–190, 2009.
© Springer-Verlag Berlin Heidelberg 2009

important tool in medicines assisting diagnosis, surgeries, and therapy. Orthopedic surgery, the branch of medicine that deals with the musculoskeletal system, its repair, disease diagnosis and implantation, is no exception.

Conventionally, X-ray films have played an important role in executing a successful orthopedic surgery. The common applications of X-ray films include the preoperative determination or estimation of implant size, placement location and postoperative outcomes analysis. Over the last few years, the importance of preoperative implant templating has significantly increased because planning for surgery is now a mandatory and prudent part of the procedure for joint replacements. In addition, the current trend for minimal invasive surgery makes sizing at the operational table more difficult and places increased reliance on accurate pre-operative implant templating.

Conventional methodology of implant templating requires the surgeons to manually lay printed acetates templates of prosthesis of various sizes over X-ray film. Once the optimal size and position has been established, the acetate is fixed in position with tape and used for visual reference during the operation.

This conventional approach demands time and labor by highly trained orthopedic surgeons or technicians, and can easily lead to greater levels of intra- and inter-observer variability. Any errors generated from templating may increase the complexity of the operation as well as potentially comprise the success of the operation.

This study is to design a semi-automated templating using digital templating method that which can determine the size of knee implant to provide and improved conventional orthopedic templating method. This process involves matching the size and shape of an implant to the anatomical size.

2   Background and Reviews

2.1   Anatomy of Knee Joint

The knee joint consist of the distal femur, proximal tibia, proximal fibula and patella (Fig.1 shows the knee joint). The articulate surfaces of these bony structures are covered by hyaline cartilage and are arranged into three distinct compartments; medial compartment, lateral compartment, and patella femoral compartment [6]. Degerative Arthritis can involve a single compartment (unicomparmental) or all three compartments (tricompartmental), each to a different extent.

The alignment of the knee joint can be divided into two axes; mechanical and anatomic axes. Mechanical is defined by a line extending from the center of femur head to the center of Tibial Plafond and extending to the ankle joint. The normal mechanical axis distributes 60% of the load to medial compartment and 40% to the lateral compartment. If the mechanical axis is misalignment due to disease or trauma, thus shifting the load disproportionately to one compartment lead to progressive degeneration. Anatomic axis is the angle created at the tibiofemoral joint by the intersection of line drawn parallel to the femoral and tibia intramedullary canal. The femoral axis 5 to 7 degrees of valgus and tibia axis parallel to the mechanical axis and perpendicular to the articular surface.

Q angle is the angle formed by intersection of line parallel to the pull of the quadriceps tendon with a line parallel to the pull of the patellar tendon. The angle is about

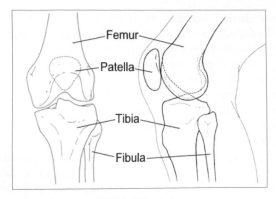

Fig. 1. Knee joint

20 degrees. The Q angle must be restored during knee arthroplasty by appropriate component rotation, medialization of the patella and soft tissue balancing.

2.2 Total Knee Replacement (TKR)

Total knee replacement (TKR), also referred to as total knee arthroplasty (TKA), and continues to be a highly successful procedure, resulting in good pain relief and functional improvement. This surgical procedure is for disease such as osteoarthritis and rheumatoid arthritis of knee joint where damaged surfaces of a knee joint are removed and replaced with artificial surfaces. However, patient selection remains the key to surgical success. The population that demonstrates the best functional results is the older, less active group of patients in whom conservative medical management has failed. Overall, patient selection criteria for primary TKA should include pain, severe arthritis on radiographs, and inability to perform the activities of daily living.

2.3 Radiography

Radiography, or x-ray as it is most commonly known, is the oldest and most frequently used form of medical imaging. They are used to produce diagnostic images of

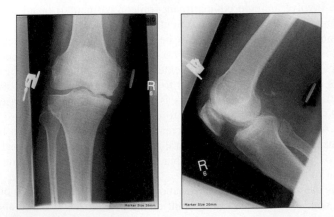

Fig. 2. AP radiograph (left) and lateral radiograph (right) of the knee

the human body on film or are converted to digital data and displayed on a computer screen. X-ray imaging is the fastest and easiest way for a physician to view the damage knee joint with osteophytes formation, reduced joint space, subchondral cyst and sclerotic joint lines (Fig. 2).

2.4 Implants

During the total replacement of the knee: the lower ends (condyles) of the femur, the top surface of the tibia, and the back surface of the patella are replaced. Components are designed so that metal always articulates against plastic, which provides smooth movement and results in minimal wear.

2.4.1 Femoral Component
The metal femoral component curves around the end of the thighbone and has an interior groove so the kneecap can move up and down smoothly against the bone as the knee bends and straightens. Usually, one large piece is used to resurface the end of the bone. If only one side of the femur is damaged, a smaller piece may be used to resurface just that part of the bone. Some designs, called posterior stabilized, have an internal post with a center cam. This works with a corresponding tibial component to prevent the femur from sliding forward too far on the tibia when the knee is flexed.

2.4.2 Tibial Component
The tibial component is a flat metal platform with a polyethylene cushion. The cushion may have either a flat surface (cruciate-retaining) or a raised surface with a center cam (posterior-stabilized).

2.4.3 Patellar Component
The patellar component is a dome-shaped piece of polyethylene that duplicates the shape of the patella (Fig. 3).

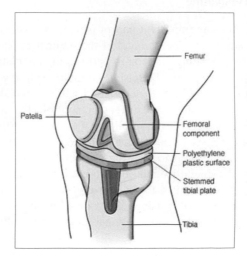

Fig. 3. Total knee implant.

2.5 Template

Template in this study refers to, an outline used to trace bones in order to standardize its form. Surgeons use templates of implants to measure against a patient's x-rays to select the best size and best design for the patient's anatomy and surgical needs. Templates were collected from the manufacturer for each prosthetic design. Normally templates are generated at a magnification of, 115% (for Zimmer) and 117% (for Smith & Nephew) to allow for average magnification on radiographs. The templates provided by the implant manufacturer, were superimposed on the AP and lateral view of the radiographs to determine the sizes of tibial and femoral components. Fig. 4, show the implant templates provided by the manufacturer.

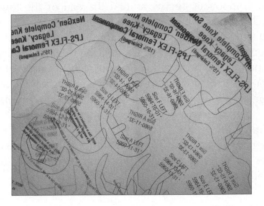

Fig. 4. Implant templates

2.6 Preoperative Templating

Preoperative templating is an important part of patient assessment whereby the operating surgeon will gain an idea beforehand of the optimal implant size. The normal practice will be for the operating surgeon to perform the templating excercese. Then with the results, will make the final decision on table regarding the implanted size. Templating at this stage would give an accurate idea of the implant size to the operating surgeon and also allow stock and inventory control. The use of the templates applied to radiographs before operation allows the surgeon to determine the most appropriate size of prosthesis to be used. For conventional templating, it is highly dependent on the technique used to take the preoperative radiographs of the bones. Any factor that alters the magnification or rotation of the image would affect the accuracy of templating. Conventional templating involves assessment of the size of a joint (three-dimensional object) by using radiographs (two-dimensional views) in two different planes. Fig. 5, Illustrates conventional templating of the X-rays in order to plan the operation.

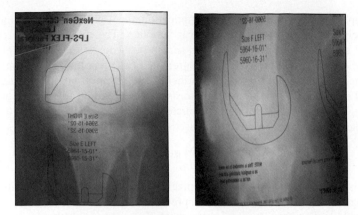

Fig. 5. Conventional preoperative templating for AP radiograph (left); and lateral radiograph (right) of the knee

2.7 Digital Templating

In preoperative templating planning scenario, digital templating utilize the digital images, manipulate it and provide measurement tools, as well as prosthetic templates for orthopedic surgery. Digital preoperative planning enables the surgeon to select from a library of templates and electronically overlay them on an image, automatically scaled for radiographic magnification. The surgeon can then perform the necessary measurements to the templating and do the stepwise preoperative planning process in a digital environment.

3 Method

The following procedures were used to select an optimal implant on digitized X-ray image:

3.1 Image Scaling

In conventional templating, the operating surgeon has to deal with two different magnification scales. The first is on the x-ray film and the second on the various acetate images representing implants at some magnification. Based on the imaging environment and the anatomical location, the X-ray film is generated either in compressed or magnified mode. The conversion of the X-ray image on the film to the actual size of the anatomy is indispensable preprocessing for digital templating. The scaling factor (magnification / compression) on the X-ray film is obtained either by placing a scale marker on the side of the anatomical joint when taking X-ray image or using the scale on the X-ray plate. The magnification scale on the series of acetate images are usually defined by manufacture. Usually these two magnification scales are not identical. In the traditional method, surgeons do this adjustment manually, which is both time-consuming and labor-intensive. In the developed digitized templating method, by executing this procedure in automated way, the system addresses these limitations. After resolving the scaling conversion, the image is digitized and displayed on the system application. With the aid of the application, the user then stepwise method and interactively measuring to find an optimal template. The digital system requires an additional scale translation to convert on screen pixel density measurement to actual size of templates. Pixel density is a measurement of the resolution of a computer display, related to the size of the display in inches and the total number of pixels in the horizontal and vertical directions. This measurement is often referred to as dots per inch, though that measurement more accurately refers to the resolution of a computer printer. The conversion tasks were expressed in the following formula;

$$M_{mm} = * M_{pixel} / I_{resolution} \qquad (1)$$
$$= C / S$$

Where C is the coefficient to transform pixel magnitude to millimeter units, and S is the scaling factor to transform any compressed/magnified X-ray image to original dimension. $I_{resolution}$ is the image resolution of X-ray, M_{pixel} is the measurements in pixel on image, and M_{mm} is the "true" measurements in millimeter. This magnitude conversion is applied to both the horizontal and vertical dimensions.

3.2 Templating

The library of templates has unique templates for each and every implant model store in the system application. The implant templates were created using CAD model. Fig. 6, shows an example of the implant template created using CAD software (Autocad 2002). However to apply these templates into system application, the image format from CAD (.dwg file) must be converted to .gif file format.

In case there were more than one best matching sizes, a situation that may arise when the algorithm generated size lies between two closest templates, the user must take the stepwise approach to choose a size based on the user's experiences and judgment. Once the user chooses the desired size of the implant, the template of the best matching implant size was superimposed on top of the X-ray image. The system

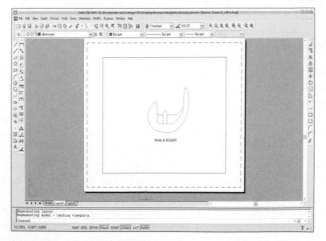

Fig. 6. Femoral (CAD model)

then allows the user to manipulate the position of the template interactively to further confirm the match. The manipulation includes rotation and shift in two dimensions of the template on top of the digitized X-ray. Four measurements were taken: femoral anterior-posterior (AP), and femoral lateral, tibial AP, and tibial lateral.

3.3 Supporting System

The developed system allows information related to X-rays image including patient identification, X-ray details, and implant templates to be stored in a database for the ease of retrieval. Illustrations of implant templates created in CAD application were reformatted as sets of graphics interchange format (.gif file) using a supporting software program. Information on implant including manufacturer suppliers and sizes was also stored in a database. Surgeons can save the information as a report for future use.

3.4 Measurement Features

Several types of measurements in the orthopedic diagnosis process have been studied and were added in this application software as a measurement tools features using mathematic theorem and equations, e.g. line, diameter etc. The measurement using Theorem Pythagoras to find the length applied. The basic formula of this theorem;

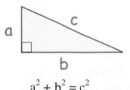

$$a^2 + b^2 = c^2 \tag{2}$$

So, the square of a (a^2) plus the square of b (b^2) is equal to the square of c (c^2). If we know the lengths of two sides of a right angled triangle, a and b, then Pythagoras' Theorem allows us to find the length of the third side, c. This basic concept applied to the system to find length of two points, z, using two coordinates, x_1,y_1 (first point) and x_2,y_2, (second point) where;

$$(x_2 - x_1)^2 + (y_2 - y_1)^2 = z^2 \tag{3}$$

4 Experiment

In order to investigate the accuracy and efficiency of the developed system, an experiment was conducted using the assistance from an experienced surgeon for (Stephens, 1997) the traditional approach to determine implant. The results by traditional approach were compared to the results produced by our semi-automated application. The same technician also performed templating using the semi-automated system. The experiment recorded implant size to be used and time taken by both methods. Orthoknee^{TM} software was developed based on algorithms using Visual Basic 6.0 Pro, were discussed earlier and executed on a PC that a 1.6 GHz computing speed with 516MB main memory at least. Randomly selected X-rays of unidentified patients were used for templating for both techniques. Digital X-rays were obtained,

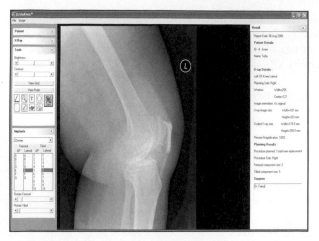

Fig. 7. Digital templating using OrthoKnee application

provided by the Department of Orthopedic and Traumatology in medical faculty, UKM (FPUKM). The graphical user interface for Orthoknee^{TM} was developed (fig. 7), allows user easily visualize and manipulate the template over the X-ray image to get the optimal size.

5   Discussion

The decision support system showed promising results where the selected implant using this method was within acceptable range to results from traditional method. With the further studies on pixel density, this gave lack of human errors and variances. In addition, compared to traditional templating method, it also saves time and labor of highly trained person. Other supporting features such as multi-level viewing allow surgeon to accurately identify reference points for size determination.

However, further tests are needed on usability, inter- and intra- variance with larger sample population including multiple users and digitized images. As another investigation, mapping methods in template matching to enhance automatically detection were investigated. It should be pointed out that the quality of X-rays is important for accurate optimal matching. Although the current approach is in semi-automatic way, it could be extended to automated technique by employing more sophisticated noise removal and image analysis algorithms.

Finally, the developed method can be applicable to other body joints such as hip, shoulder and elbow with small modification, which will be another task in the future.

6   Conclusion

This paper has presented a semi-automatic, decision support method of determining an implant by making use of digital templating algorithm. Compared to traditional templating method, it not only saves time and labor of highly trained person, but also reduces human errors and possibly inter- and intra variances especially in image scaling issues. Overall, this method can become effective tools helping surgeons in surgery planning and decision making processes.

Acknowledgement. The authors wish to thank Universiti Kebangsaan Malaysia (UKM) and the Ministry of Higher Education, Malaysia for providing the Fundamental Research Grant (No.: UKM-TT-02-FRGS0009-2006) that helped to carry out the research as discussed in this paper.

References

[1] Kakeda, S., Moriya, J., Sato, H., Aoki, T., Watanabe, H., Nakata, H., Oda, N., Katsuragawa, S., Yamamoto, K., Doi, K.: Improved Detection of Lung Nodules on Chest Radiographs Using a Commercial Computer-Aided Diagnosis System. AJR Am. J. Roentgenol, 505–510 (2004)

[2] Dahab, G.M., Kheriza, M.M., El-Beltagi, H.M., Fouda, A.M., El-Din, O.A.: Digital quantification of fibrosis in liver biopsy sections: Description of a new method by Photoshop software. J. Gastroenterol Hepatol, 78–85 (2004)

[3] Wolf, G., Nicoletti, R., Schultes, G., Schwarz, T., Schaffler, G., Aigner, R.M.: Preoperative image fusion of fluoro-2-deoxy-D-glucose-positron emission tomography and computed tomography data sets in oral maxillofacial carcinoma: potential clinical value. J. Comput. Assist. Tomogr., 889–895 (2003)

[4] Shrout, M.K., Jett, S., Mailhot, J.M., Potter, B.J., Borke, J.L., Hildebolt, C.F.: Digital image analysis of cadaver mandibular trabecular bone patterns. J. Periodonto, 1342–1347 (2003)

[5] Seeberger, T.M., Matsumoto, Y., Alizadeh, A., Fitzgerald, P.G., Clark, J.I.: Digital image capture and quantification of subtle lens opacities in rodents. J. Biomed. Opt., 116–120 (2004)

[6] Gray, H., Goss, C.M.: Anatomy of The Human Body. Lea & Febiger, Michigan (1973)

[7] Goshtasby, A.A.: 2-D and 3-D Image Registration for Medical, Remote Sensing and Industrial Applications. Wiley, United States (2005)

[8] Arora, J.: The Role of Pre-operative Templating in Primary Total Knee Replacement. Knee Surg. Sports Traumatol Arthosc., 187–189 (2004)

[9] Heal, J., Blewitt, N.: Kinemax Total Knee Arthroplastly: Trial by Template. J. Arthroplastly, 90–94 (2002)

[10] Lewis, J., Hossain, M., Mustafa, A., Sinha, A.: Comparison of Digital and Plain Radiography Preoperative Templating in Total Knee Arthroplastly. Eur. J. Orthop. Surg. Traumatol, 1–4 (2008)

[11] Bono, J.V.: Digital Templating in Total Hip Arthroplastly. J. Bone Joint Surg. Br., 118–122 (2004)

[12] Radermacher, K.: Computer Assisted Orthopaedic Surgery With Image Based Individual Templates. Clin. Orthop., pp. 28–38.

[13] Conn, K.S., Clarke, M.T., Hallet, J.P.: A Simple Guide to Determine the Magnification of Radiographs and to Improve the Accuracy of Preoperative Templating. J. Bone Joint Surg. Br., 269–272 (2002)

[14] Aslam, N., Steven, L., Nagarajah, K., Pasapula, C., Akmal, M.: Reliability of Preoperative Templating in Total Knee Arthroplastly. Acta Orthop. Belg., 560–564 (2004)

[15] Orthoview, Meridian Technique Ltd, http://www.orthoview.com

[16] Eggli, S., Pisan, M., Muller, M.E.: The Value of Preoperative Planning for Total Hip Ar-
     throplastly. J. Bone Joint Surg. Br., 382–390 (1998)
[17] Chauhan, S.K., Scott, R.G., Breidahl, W., Beaver, R.J.: Computer-assisted Knee Arthro-
     plastly versus a Conventional Jig-based Technique: A Randomised, Prospective Trial. J.
     Bone Joint Surg. Br., 372–377 (2004)
[18] White, S.P., Shardlow, D.L.: Effect of Introduction of Digital Radiographic Techniques
     on Pre-operative Templating in Orthopaedic Practice. Ann. R. Coll. Surg. Engl., 53–54
     (2005)
[19] Stephens, R.: Visual Basic Graphics Programming. In: Hands on Applications and Ad-
     vanced Color Developmen, 2nd edn., Wiley, New York (2000)
[20] Stephens, R.: Visual Basic Graphics Programming. Wiley, New York (1997)
[21] Bothra, V., Lemon, G., Lang, D., Ali, A.: Reliability of Templating in Estimating the Size
     of Uni-condylar Knee Arthroplastly. J. Arthroplastly 780 (2003)
[22] Howcroft, D.W.J., Fehily, M.J., Peck, C., Fox, A., Dillon, B., Johnson, D.S.: The Role of
     Preoperative Templating in Total Knee Arthroplastly: Comparison of Three Prostheses.
     The knee, 427–429 (2006)

Inter-frame Enhancement of Ultrasound Images Using Optical Flow

Balza Achmad, Mohd. Marzuki Mustafa, and Aini Hussain

Department of Electrical, Electronic and Systems Engineering,
Universiti Kebangsaan Malaysia
43600 UKM Bangi, Selangor Darul Ehsan, Malaysia
balzach@ugm.ac.id, marzuki@vlsi.eng.ukm.my, aini@vlsi.eng.ukm.my

Abstract. Ultrasound imaging, also known as ultrasound scanning or sonography, is a very popular medical test that helps medical doctors diagnose and treat medical conditions of their patients. However, one common problem that persists is that ultrasound images suffer from speckle noise that degrades their quality. In this paper we present an enhancement technique for ultrasound images by making use of three consecutive frames extracted from an ultrasound video. The technique uses the optical flow algorithm to reconstruct an intermediate frame based on the preceding and the following frames. The reconstructed image is then utilized to enhance the middle frame by mean of fusion. Based on the test, the best result is achieved using Lukas-Kanade optical flow and average operator.

Keywords: Optical flow, inter-frame enhancement, speckle noise, ultrasound image.

1 Introduction

Various imaging instruments have been developed to facilitate medical doctors in making diagnosis for their patients' health conditions, such as Ultrasound, CT-Scan, MRI and X-ray machines. Among those instruments, ultrasound machine is considered as the cheapest, non invasive and the most acceptable to patients, hence this machine is very popular throughout the world. Ultrasound imaging involves the use of high-frequency sound waves on selected part of the body to produce pictures of the inside of the body. Unlike in x-rays machine, ultrasound exams do not use ionizing radiation and as such, it is a safer method. Additionally, since the procedure is done in real-time, the structure and the movement of the body's internal organs, as well as blood flowing through blood vessels can be observed.

Despite of the abovementioned advantages, ultrasound machine has a major disadvantage in that the generated image contains speckle noise. The noise is due to the nature of interaction of ultrasound waves and patients organs. As a result, doctors often find it hard to analyze ultrasound image since the details of the imaged organs are not clear. Therefore, the generated images need to be enhanced prior to the analysis.

Many techniques have been developed in order to enhance the quality of ultrasound image, such as Speckle Reduction Imaging (SRI) method (Liasis et al., 2008),

H. Badioze Zaman et al. (Eds.): IVIC 2009, LNCS 5857, pp. 191–201, 2009.

wavelet-based method (Rallabandi, 2008), morphological fuzzy filter (Filho et al, 2004), and anisotropic diffusion filter (Munteanu et al., 2008). Those techniques are based on a single image. Ultrasound machine, however, generates a sequence of images which are usually stored as a video.

Some researchers develop enhancement techniques utilizing multiple images from the video. Evans et al. (1996) proposed speckle reduction using biased motion-adaptive temporal filtering. Grau and Noble (2006) proposed motion-guided anisotropic filtering, which apply anisotropic diffusion technique simultaneously on several time-based images. Coleshill et al. (2007) developed a technique that enhanced general image sequence by eliminating part in the frame that suffered from abnormal lighting. Jung et al. (1999) proposed an enhancement technique based on convex projection of inter-frame coded images.

In this paper, we propose an enhancement technique for ultrasound images by making use of three consecutive frames extracted from an ultrasound video. The proposed technique utilizes the optical flow algorithm to enhance the middle frame based on the preceding and the following frames. Optical flow itself has been used by some researchers, for instance, to increase the frame rate of ultrasound videos (Nam et al, 2006). Zhao (2004) used optical flow to repair missing blocks in general video.

2   The Proposed Technique

The proposed technique consists of four main steps namely, frame extraction, optical flow, frame reconstruction and frame fusion as shown in Fig. 1. The main idea behind this technique is to provide a second image to the image being enhanced and then, by combining the two images the speckle noise contained in the image can be reduced.

2.1   Frame Extraction

Firstly, three consecutive frames are extracted from an ultrasound video which we identified as Previous frame, Current frame and Next frame. Current frame is the frame that will be enhanced by making use of the other two frames.

2.2   Optical Flow

An optical flow algorithm is then applied to the Previous frame and Next frame. The output of this operation is motion vectors representing the movement of each pixel in the Previous frame to its position in Next frame. For example, in Fig. 2, pixel P in Previous frame moved by a vector $\vec{V}$ to pixel P'' in Next frame. In this paper we have considered two optical flow techniques, i.e. Lukas-Kanade and Horn-Schunck techniques.

Basically, an optical flow algorithm is based on image constraint equation representing the movement of a voxel in an image at position (x, y, t) with intensity $I(x, y, t)$ to another position in another image at position $(x+dx, y+dy, t+dt)$. The intensity of the voxel is preserved as given in Equation (1).

$$I(x+dx, y+dy, t+dt) = I(x, y, t) \ . \tag{1}$$

For small movement, the expansion of Taylor series of $I(x, y, t)$ leads to Equation (2).

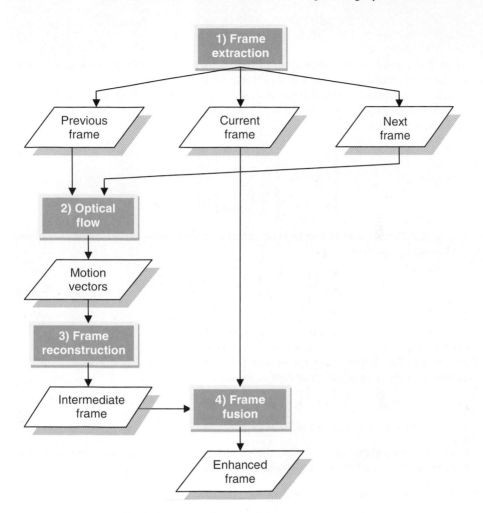

Fig. 1. Schematic diagram of the proposed method

Fig. 2. Motion vector representing the movement of a pixel in Previous frame

$$I_x V_x + I_y V_y = -I_t .$$
(2)

where I_x, I_y, and I_t are the derivatives of the image at position (x, y, t) while V_x and V_y are the velocity of $I(x, y, t)$ for x and y direction, respectively.

The Lukas-Kanade optical flow method assumes that the flow is constant within certain small window. Therefore a set of equations based on the above equation can be derived as follows.

$$\begin{bmatrix} I_{x1} & I_{y1} \\ I_{x2} & I_{y2} \\ \vdots & \vdots \\ I_{xn} & I_{yn} \end{bmatrix} \begin{bmatrix} V_x \\ V_y \end{bmatrix} = \begin{bmatrix} -I_{t1} \\ -I_{t2} \\ \vdots \\ -I_{tn} \end{bmatrix} .$$
(3)

The optical flow V_x and V_y can then be calculated using least square method, yielding the following equation.

$$\begin{bmatrix} V_x \\ V_y \end{bmatrix} = \begin{bmatrix} \sum I_{xi}^2 & \sum I_{xi} I_{yi} \\ \sum I_{xi} I_{yi} & \sum I_{yi}^2 \end{bmatrix}^{-1} \begin{bmatrix} -\sum I_{xi} I_{ti} \\ -\sum I_{yi} I_{ti} \end{bmatrix} .$$
(4)

Alternatively, the Horn-Schunck optical flow method assumes that the flow is smooth over the whole image, hence it can be formulated as a global energy that needs to be minimized. The derivation of the optical flow energy function using Euler-Lagrange equations leads to an equation system as follows

$$\left(I_x^2 + \alpha^2\right)u + I_x I_y v = \alpha^2 \bar{u} - I_x I_t$$
$$I_x I_y u + \left(I_y^2 + \alpha^2\right)v = \alpha^2 \bar{v} - I_y I_t$$
(5)

where α is a regularization constant that determine the smoothness of the flow. This equation system can be solved by mean of the Jacobian iteration.

2.3 Frame Reconstruction

Utilizing Previous frame and the optical flow motion vectors, an intermediate frame between Previous frame and Next frame can be reconstructed. Considering that the movement of the imaged object is relatively small, the position of certain pixel in Intermediate frame (P' in Fig. 3) can be assumed located halfway from its original position in Previous frame (P) to its position in Next frame (P"). Hence, position P' can be determined using vector $\vec{w}$ as given in Equation (6).

$$\vec{W} = \frac{\vec{V}}{2} .$$
(6)

The pixel P is then mapped to Intermediate frame by copying its intensity in Previous frame to position P' in the Intermediate frame using Equation (7).

$$I_{Intermediate}(P') = I_{Previous}(P) .$$
(7)

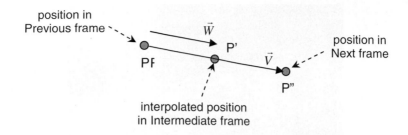

Fig. 3. Interpolated position of any pixel in Intermediate frame

where $I_{Intermediate}(P')$ is the image intensity at position P' in the Intermediate frame; $I_{Previous}(P)$ is the image intensity at position P in the Previous frame.

By mapping all pixels from Previous frame using the motion vectors resulted from the optical flow, the Intermediate frame can thus be reconstructed.

2.4 Frame Fusion

The reconstructed intermediate frame then acts as a second frame to the Current frame. By providing more frames, the speckle noise can be reduced. Therefore, the last step combines the reconstructed Intermediate frame and Current frame using certain fusion operator. The result is the enhanced version of Current frame. In this paper, we use mean and maximum operator as given in Equation (8) and (9).

$$I_{Enhanced}(P') = \frac{I_{Current}(P') + I_{Intermediate}(P')}{2} . \qquad (8)$$

$$I_{Enhanced}(P') = \max(I_{Current}(P') + I_{Intermediate}(P') . \qquad (9)$$

3 Result and Discussion

We tested the proposed technique using a recording of cardiac ultrasound video gathered from the Hospital Universiti Kebangsaan Malaysia, Kuala Lumpur, Malaysia. Following, we provide a sample of the test results. Fig.4 shows three consecutive frames extracted from the ultrasound video for short axis view (SAX) of heart, comprising (a) Previous, (b) Current, and (c) Next frames. As mentioned above, Current frame is the frame that will be enhanced using this technique.

The reconstructed intermediate frames by applying Lukas-Kanade and Horn-Schunck optical flow algorithms are given in Fig. 5. The mapping technique used nearest neighbor interpolation. Both images contains crack-like pattern due to the change of shape of the imaged object. However, the frame resulted from Lukas-Kanade optical flow (Fig. 5a) appears to be more solid compare to that from Horn-Schunck optical flow (Fig. 5b).

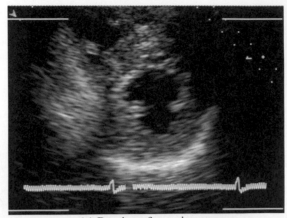

(a) Previous frame image

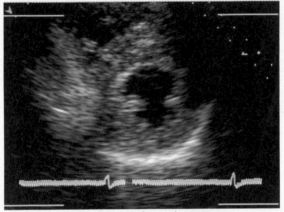

(b) Current frame image

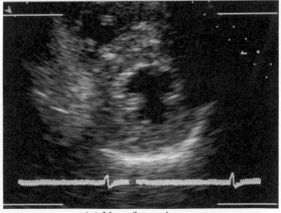

(c) Next frame image

Fig. 4. Frames extracted from a cardiac ultrasound video

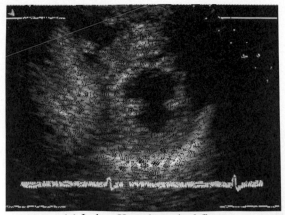

(a) Lukas-Kanade optical flow

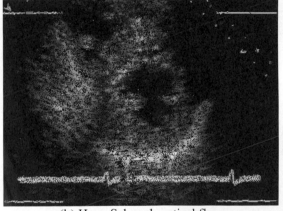
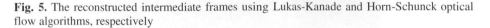

(b) Horn-Schunck optical flow

Fig. 5. The reconstructed intermediate frames using Lukas-Kanade and Horn-Schunck optical flow algorithms, respectively

The reconstructed intermediate frames are then combined with the Current frame yielding enhanced frames. Fig. 6 shows the enhanced frames resulted from the reconstructed intermediate frames in Fig. 5 using average as well as maximum operators.

Visually, all the enhanced frames look clearer than the original frame (Current frame). However, the maximum operator generated frames (those shown in Fig. 6c and 6d) are brighter than the average operator (as shown in Fig. 6a and 6b). This is because the maximum operator holds higher intensity value during fusion process, which represent whiter pixel. In addition, Lukas-Kanade optical flow produced frames (shown in Fig. 6a and 6c) those are cleaner than Horn-Schunck optical flow. It is obvious that the enhanced frame using Horn-Schunck optical flow and maximum operator (Fig. 6d) contains white spots.

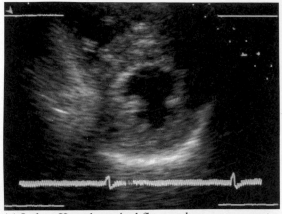

(a) Lukas-Kanade optical flow and average operator

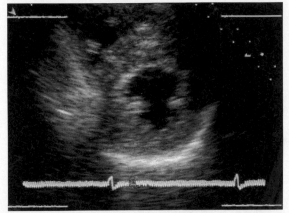

(b) Horn-Schunck optical flow and average operator

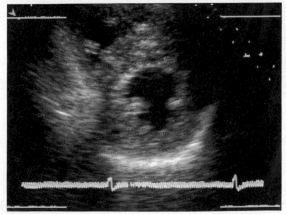

(c) Lukas-Kanade optical flow and maximum operator

Fig. 6. The enhanced frames using both optical flow algorithm and different fusion operators

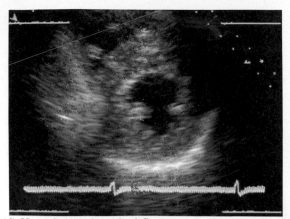

(d) Horn-Schunck optical flow and maximum operator

Fig. 6. (*Continued*)

To show the effect of the technique in reducing speckle noise, we present intensity profile of a line in the image. The line is as shown in Fig. 7. The Lukas-Kanade optical flow and average operator intensity profile as shown in Fig. 8a relatively perform best compare to the others in reducing speckle noise. The maximum operator elevates the intensity of darker pixels.

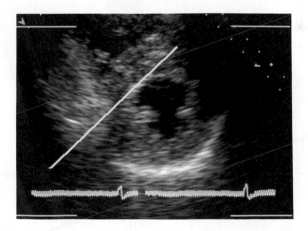

Fig. 7. A line drawn in the Current frame for intensity profiling

(a) Original frame

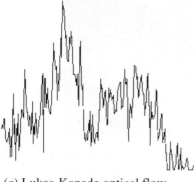

| (a) Lukas-Kanade optical flow | (b) Horn-Schunck optical flow |
| and average operator | and average operator |

(c) Lukas-Kanade optical flow
and maximum operator

(d) Horn-Schunck optical flow
and maximum operator

Fig. 8. Intensity profile of the original and enhanced frames using both optical flow algorithm and different fusion operators

4 Conclusion

In this paper we afforded an enhancement technique for ultrasound images making use of three consecutive frames extracted from an ultrasound video. The technique uses optical flow algorithm to reconstruct an intermediate frame based on the preceding and the following frames. The reconstructed image is then utilized to enhance the middle frame by mean of image fusion. Based on the test, the best result is achieved using Lukas-Kanade optical flow and average operator.

Acknowledgement

The authors wish to acknowledge Universiti Kebangsaan Malaysia for the financial support of this research through research grant contract number UKM-GUP-TKP-08-24-080.

References

Evans, A.N., Nixon, M.S.: Biased Motion-Adaptive Temporal Filtering for Speckle Reduction in Echoradiography. IEEE Transactions on Medical Imaging 15(1), 39–50 (1996)

Munteanu, C., Morales, F.C., Fernández, J.G., Rosa, A., Déniz, L.G.: Enhancing Obstetric and Gynecology Ultrasound Images by Adaptation of the Speckle Reducing Anisotropic Diffusion Filter. Artificial Intelligence in Medicine 43, 223–242 (2008)

Filho, E.D.S., Yoshizawa, M., Iwamoto, T., Tanaka, A., Saijo, Y.: Morphological Fuzzy Filter for Enhancement of Intravascular Ultrasound Images. In: SICE Annual Conference in Sapporo, Japan (2004)

Coleshill, J.E., Ferworn, A., Stacey, D.: Image Enhancement using Frame Extraction Through Time. In: 2007 International Conference on Systems, Computing Sciences and Software Engineering (CISSE), pp. 131–135 (2007)

Liasis, N., Klonaris, C., Katsargyris, A., Georgopoulos, S., Labropoulos, S., Tsigris, C., Giannopoulos, A., Bastounis, E.: The Use of Speckle Reduction Imaging (SRI) Ultrasound, in the Characterization of Carotid Artery Plaques. European Journal of Radiology 65, 427–433 (2008)

Nam, T.J., Park, R.H., Yun, J.H.: Optical Flow Based Frame Interpolation of Ultrasound Images. In: 2006 International Conference on Image Analysis and Recognition (ICIAR), pp. 792–803 (2006)

Jung, S.C., Woo, H.B., Paik, J.K., Choi, W.: Enhancement of Inter-Frame Coded Images Based on Convex Projection. In: 1999 IEEE TENCON, pp. 1275–1278 (1999)

Grau, V., Noble, J.A.: Motion-Guided Anisotropic Filtering of Ultrasound Sequences. ISBI, 209–212 (2006)

Rallabandi, V.P.S.: Enhancement of Ultrasound Images using Stochastic Resonance-Based Wavelet Transform. Computerized Medical Imaging and Graphics 32, 316–320 (2008)

Zhao, W.Y.: Motion-Based Spatial-Temporal Image Repairing. In: 2004 International Conference on Image Processing (ICIP), pp. 291–294 (2004)

Segmentation of Sinus Images for Grading of Severity of Sinusitis

Lila Iznita Izhar, Vijanth Sagayan Asirvadam, and San Nien Lee

Intelligent Imaging Technology Group, Electrical and Electronic Engineering Programme
Universiti Teknologi PETRONAS, Bandar Sri Iskandar, 31750 Tronoh, Perak, Malaysia
lilaiznita@petronas.com.my, vijanth_sagayan@petronas.com.my,
leesannien@gmail.com

Abstract. Sinusitis is commonly diagnosed with techniques such as endoscopy, ultrasound, X-ray, Computed Tomography (CT) scan and Magnetic Resonance Imaging (MRI). Out of these techniques, imaging techniques are less invasive while being able to show blockage of sinus cavities. This project attempts to develop a computerize system by developing algorithm for the segmentation of sinus images for the detection of sinusitis. The sinus images were firstly undergo noise removal process by median filtering followed by Contrast Limited Adapted Histogram Equalisation (CLAHE) for image enhancement. Multilevel thresholding algorithm were then applied to segment the enhanced images into meaningful regions for the detection and diagnosis of severity of sinusitis. The multilevel thresholding algorithms based on Otsu method were able to extract three distinct and important features namely bone region, hollow and mucous areas from the images. Simulations were performed on images of healthy sinuses and sinuses with sinusitis. The developed algorithms are found to be able to differentiate and evaluate healthy sinuses and sinuses with sinusitis effectively.

Keywords: sinusitis, CT scan, CLAHE, multilevel thresholding, region growing.

1 Introduction

Sinusitis is the inflammation or infection of the sinus cavities behind the nose, caused by bacteria, viruses, fungi and allergies. Sinus cavities are the moist, hollow spaces in the bones of the skull. There are four pairs of sinuses in the skull, namely the frontal sinuses, the maxillary sinuses, the ethmoid sinuses and the sphenoid sinuses. When inflamed or infected, the mucosal lining in the sinuses produce more mucous than usual, building up the pressure inside the sinuses, thus causing pain. Besides that, it is estimated 1% or 2% of adults have lost their sense of smell and taste due to sinusitis [1]. The estimated prevalence rate of sinusitis in Malaysia is approximately 12.80% [2]. This means that around 3 million Malaysians are suffering from sinusitis at any one time. Sharing similar symptoms as common cold, sinusitis is found difficult to diagnose, resulting in unnecessary antibiotic treatment [3]. Sinusitis is treated with medications or surgery for severe cases.

H. Badioze Zaman et al. (Eds.): IVIC 2009, LNCS 5857, pp. 202–212, 2009.
© Springer-Verlag Berlin Heidelberg 2009

Imaging techniques are popular in detecting sinusitis as they are less intrusive. Current imaging techniques used to detect sinusitis are the X-ray, CT scan and MRI scan. Images taken with these imaging techniques have to be interpreted by doctors manually and this gives room for inconsistency or in some cases, inaccuracy. The variability in the interpretations is caused by different levels of experience [4]. Variability may be particularly high in the case of paranasal sinuses due to their complex anatomy [4]. Image segmentation is important as the results of segmentation are used for diagnosis and surgical planning. At present, manual segmentation and semi-automatic segmentations are used. However, these methods are not useful for everyday surgical workflow because they take too much time [5]. Manual and semi-automatic segmentations may still give room for variations in the results. Therefore, looking at the errors that may be caused by manual interpretations and segmentations of images, fully automatic and reproducible segmentation algorithms are needed for the segmentation of paranasal sinuses and nasal cavity.

This study uses CT scan sinus images as input data. CT scan is more commonly used to visualise sinusitis as doctors find CT scan images more helpful [2]. CT scan sits in the middle of the operating cost range in between X-ray and MRI and is commonly available in state hospitals and district hospitals with resident radiologists [6]. CT scan images are greyscale images with depth of 8 bits, representing intensity level range from 0 to 255. Simulations were performed on CT scan sinus images of healthy sinuses and sinuses with sinusitis as shown in Fig. 1.

This paper presents the development of an algorithm to segment sinuses for grading of severity of sinusitis based on CT scan sinus images.

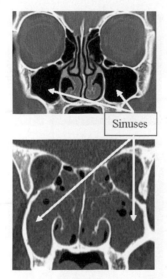

Fig. 1. (a) Image of healthy sinuses. (b) Image of sinuses with sinusitis. Notice that the healthy sinuses are entirely black, indicating the absence of mucous while the sinuses with sinusitis are grey, indicating the presence of mucous.

2   Image Enhancement

2.1   Noise Reduction

Median filtering is commonly used to reduce noise in the images. Median filters are spatial filters where the median of the points encompassed in a filter window is chosen as the center value of that filter window. Median filter of sized 3 by 3 is applied to the sinus images as it is found to be most suitable to reduce noise as well as preserving edges in the images. The median filtered images are shown in Fig. 2.

2.2   Contrast Enhancement

Image contrast enhancement is then performed using the Contrast Limited Adaptive Histogram Equalization (CLAHE) method on the median filtered images. CLAHE divides the median filtered images into regions. It is a window based enhancement method that has been chosen to improve the contrast of the sinus adaptively. The CLAHE has divided the image into non-overlapping contextual regions of size 8 by 8.

Histogram equalization is then carried out on the histograms of each individual region. This process evens out the distribution of grey level values, making the hidden features of the image more visible [7]. CLAHE managed to distribute the pixels more evenly across the entire intensity level range, smoothened the histograms of the images. Fig. 3 shows the resultant image of CLAHE while Fig. 4 shows the smoothened image histogram of the image with healthy sinuses by CLAHE.

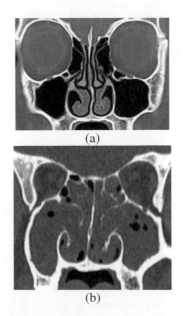

(a)

(b)

Fig. 2. Results of median filtering. (a) Image of healthy sinuses. (b) Image of sinuses with sinusitis.

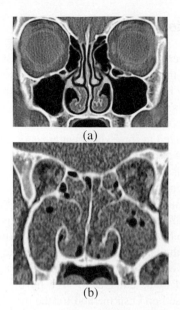

(a)

(b)

Fig. 3. Results of CLAHE. (a) Image of healthy sinuses. (b) Image of sinuses with sinusitis.

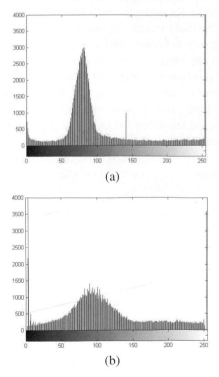

(a)

(b)

Fig. 4. Histogram of image with healthy sinuses is smoothened after image enhancement resulting in better contrast. (a) Original histogram. (b) Smoothened histogram.

3 Image Segmentation

The sinus images have very distinct intensity level clusters for the three different regions; the bone region, the mucous areas and the hollow areas of the sinuses, as shown in Fig.5. The image histogram in Fig. 5 shows the pixels distribution across the grey levels. The grey levels are represented with 8 bits, therefore, the grey level intensities start with 0 (black) up to 255 (white). As can be seen in the image histogram in Fig. 5, the pixels are clustered at three different areas of grey level. The image histogram shows three hills and two valleys. The first hill starting from black indicates the hollow area, the second hill at grey indicates the mucous area and the third hill ending with white indicates the bone area.

The purpose of the segmentation in sinus mages is to partition the images into the three distinct regions. Multilevel thresholding algorithm is used to achieve this. The algorithm searches for two threshold values, T_1 and T_2, from the image histogram. T_1 is obtained by calculating the value in between the first and the second clusters and T_2 from another one in between the second and third clusters. Fig. 6 shows the two threshold values that need to be calculated. We have applied an algorithm of the multilevel thresholding based on Otsu method for the threshold calculation in the later stage of our work. Both the initial and the improved algorithm of the multilevel thresholding share similar working steps. The algorithms firstly searches for three hill peaks, P1, P2 and P3. After obtaining the peaks, the algorithm then perform calculations in search of two threshold values, T1 and T2; one in between the first and second clusters and another one in between the second and third clusters. The thresholds partition the image into the three regions. The pixels located before the T1 will be converted into black pixels having values of 0, the pixels found between T1 and T2 will be converted into grey pixels having values of 127 and the pixels located after T2 will be converted into white pixels having values of 255. The difference in the improved algorithm is that the threshold values are now determined based on the Otsu method for each histogram cluster.

The initial algorithm used for multilevel thresholding in this work searches for three peaks from the image histogram and then takes the median intensity value between two peaks as a threshold value. The pseudo-codes are shown below:

1. Search for three peaks from histogram, P_1, P_2 and P_3.
2. Determine the grey level at each peak, G_1, G_2 and G_3.
3. Calculate thresholds, T_1 and T_2.

$$T_n = \frac{G_n + G_{n+1}}{2}$$

4. Segment image into three regions using the calculated thresholds.
   Grey level $< T_1$ => black (0)
   $T_1 <$ Grey level $< T_2$ => grey (127)
   Grey level $> T_2$ => white (255)

In order to improve the accuracy of image segmentation by the multilevel thresholding based on median value, the algorithm used in the later stage of our work searches for three peaks from the image histogram and then calculated the threshold values using Otsu method. The pseudo-codes are shown below:

1.   Search for three peaks from histogram, P_1, P_2 and P_3.
2.   Select three initial thresholds.
3.   Calculate the average grey level in each region, G_1, G_2 and G_3.

$$G_n = \frac{\sum(I \times \text{no. of pixels at I})}{\text{total number of pixels in region}}$$

where I is intensity levels present in region
4.   Calculate thresholds, T_1 and T_2.

$$T_n = \frac{G_n + G_{n+1}}{2}$$

5.   Segment image into three regions using the calculated thresholds.
Grey level $< T_1$ => black (0)
$T_1 <$ Grey level $< T_2$ => grey (127)
Grey level $> T_2$ => white (255)

The segmentation algorithms developed in this study were successful in segmenting the images into the three regions; the bone region, the mucous areas and the hollow areas of the sinuses. Only three intensity levels are present in the segmented image; 0 (black) for the hollow areas, 127 (grey) for the mucous areas and 255 (white) for the bone areas. The improved algorithm segmented the images with less artifacts and less disjointed areas, hence giving a more accurate representation of the different regions in the images. Figure 16 shows the segmentation results of healthy sinuses while Figure 17 shows the segmentation results of sinuses with sinusitis.

In Fig. 7 it can be seen that the improved multilevel thresholding was able to elimi-nates / reduce false segmentation of bone regions with intensity level of 255 (white) in the sinuses region. In Fig. 8, we can also see that more bone regions were seg-mented by using the improved algorithm. The segmentation algorithms developed in this study were successful in segmenting the images into the three distinct regions; the bone region, the mucous areas and the hollow areas of the sinuses.

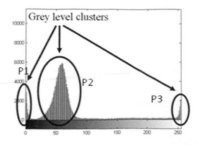

Fig. 5. Typical histogram of input images showing the three grey level clusters. The first cluster consists of very dark pixels, indicating the hollow area of the sinuses. The second cluster is in the middle of the intensity range, indicating the mucous areas. The third cluster is at the white end of the intensity level, indicating the bone region.

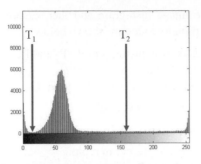

Fig. 6. T_1 and T_2 are the threshold values to be calculated.

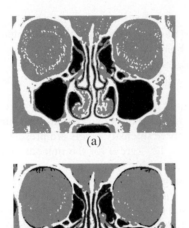

(a)

(b)

Fig. 7. Results of segmentation for healthy sinuses based on multilevel thresholding. (a) Image segmented using the initial algorithm. (b) Image segmented using the improved algorithm.

Comparing the results for the healthy sinuses and the sinuses affected with sinusitis, there are more black areas in the image of healthy sinuses. The image of sinuses of sinusitis contains more grey areas, indicating presence of mucous in the sinuses and therefore sinusitis. The segmentation algorithms were able to differentiate between healthy sinuses and sinuses with sinusitis.

4   Grading of Sinusitis

In order to grade the severity of sinusitis, a morphology reconstruction process is performed based on seed based region growing (SRG). Region growing technique is a well-known technique to extract foregrounds from a noisy background effectively [7].

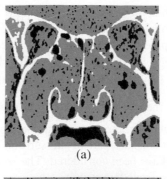

(a)

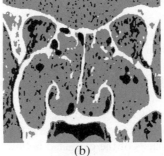

(b)

Fig. 8. Results of segmentation for sinuses with sinusitis based on multilevel thresholding. (a) Image segmented using the initial algorithm. (b) Image segmented using the improved algorithm.

In this process, the initial seeds are placed on the mucous areas and the hollow areas of the sinuses. The first is to obtain the total area of the sinuses affected by sinusitis and the latter is to obtain the total area of the sinuses not affected by sinusitis. The area of sinuses affected by sinusitis (by the presence of mucous) obtained will then be divided by the total area of the sinuses to evaluate the severity factor of sinuses area that is affected by sinusitis as shown in Eq. 1. The further this severity factor is from 1, the more affected the sinuses are with sinusitis. Extracting the mucous areas and the hollow areas ensures that diagnosis can be performed on sinuses of different sizes, making this method robust.

$$\text{severity} = \frac{\text{total area of mucous area}}{\text{total area of sinuses}} \tag{1}$$

where

total area of sinuses = total area of mucous areas + total area of hollow areas .

   The homogeneity criterion used in the SRG is defined as the difference between the intensity of the candidate pixel and the intensity of pre-merged region. The intensity difference is called the pixel tolerance value. To obtain this value, the maximum and the minimum intensity levels of pixels in the region of interest are investigated and the difference between these two values is calculated. SRG are carried out with tolerance value of 20 which is found to be able to include as much the region of interest without expanding or growing other parts.

In SRG, the initial seed-pixels (size of 1 pixel by 1 pixel each) are chosen manually among neighbouring pixels of the region to be extracted. In SRG process as shown in Eq. 2, if the difference in intensity between a seed-pixel, $S_{x,y}$ and the neigbouring pixels, $I_{x,y}$ is smaller than the tolerance value, T_val at a particular point, the seed pixel is considered to be intensity homogeneous to the region of interest and is part of the region. Otherwise, it is consider part of the surrounding. The process continues recursively until all pixels have been considered. The resultant image consists of the seed-grown region and the surrounding region.

$$\left| S_{x,y} - I_{x,y} \right| \leq T\_val \tag{2}$$

The grading was performed on both image of healthy sinuses and sinuses with sinusitis. Figures 9 and 10 show the results of the SRG for both healthy sinuses and sinuses with sinusitis respectively. Both of the input images come with diagnosis by medical experts. In Fig. 9, it can be seen that a healthy sinus is free from mucous. Therefore, in the segmented regions of hollow in Fig. 9(a), the total area of healthy sinuses are actually being extracted. The severity factor in this case is 0 as there are no mucous areas in the sinuses. The resultant images of the extracted hollow and mucous areas of a sinus that was diagnosed as having sinusitis by medical experts are shown in Fig. 10. In this case, it can be seen that, the segmented mucous area is found larger than

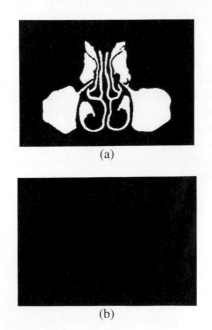

(a)

(b)

Fig. 9. Extracted areas from image of healthy sinuses. (a) Extracted hollow areas. (b) Resultant image showing the absent of mucous areas.

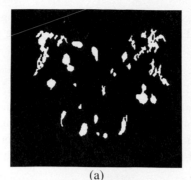

(a)

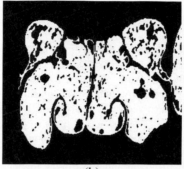

(b)

Fig. 10. Extracted areas from image of healthy sinuses. (a) Extracted hollow areas. (b) Extracted mucous areas.

that of the hollow area. The calculated severity factor in this case is 0.88. This shows that the developed algorithm is able to evaluate the sinuses to be heavily affected with sinusitis. The calculations matched the diagnosis of both the healthy sinuses and the sinuses with sinusitis. Besides the calculated severity factor, the binary output images of this process show very clearly the mucous and hollow areas of the sinuses.

5 Discussion and Conclusion

This study has shown promising possibility of using image segmentation techniques for the grading of severity for sinusitis. The sinus images are firstly smoothened by median filtering of sized 3 by 3. This is then followed by contrast enhancement using CLAHE. CLAHE is able to evenly enhance the three constituent regions in sinuses namely the bone, hollow and mucous. When the quality of the sinus images are much improved, segmentation based on multilevel thresholding is performed to extract the three constituent regions. The three important regions in the images are effectively separated by the segmentation algorithms. The segmented images are then used to evaluate the severity of the sinusitis cases by extracting the mucous areas and the hollow areas in the images. The results of severity percentage obtained show the high potential of the developed method in evaluating and grading the severity of sinusitis.

Acknowledgement

First and foremost, the authors are grateful to Dr. Balanchandran Appoo, Klinik Pakar Otorinolaringologi, Hospital Sungai Buloh, Selangor, Malaysia, for consenting to collaborate in this project. The authors are also thankful for the valuable discussions with the staff members at Klinik Pakar Otorinolaringologi and the data obtained from Hospital Sungai Buloh.

References

1. eHealthMD. What is Endoscopic Sinus Surgery? (2002 -2005),
   http://www.ehealthmd.com/library/endosinus/ESS_whatis.html
   (Retrieved August 14, 2008)
2. Editors of CureResearch. Statistics by Country for Sinusitis (2000 – 2007),
   http://www.cureresearch.com/s/sinusitis/stats-country.htm
   (Retrieved August 14, 2008)
3. Persson, L., Kristensson, E., Simonsson, L., Andersson, M., Svanberg, K., Svanberg, S.: Human Sinus Studies using Monte Carlo Simulations and Diode Laser Gas Absorption Spectroscopy. Institute of Electrical and Electronics Engineer (IEEE), 0-7803-9774-6/06/ (2006)
4. German Medical Science (GMS) Publishing House. Analysis of Manual Segmentation in Medical Image Processing (May 4, 2008),
   http://www.egms.de/de/meetings/hnod2008/08hnod453.shtml
   (Retrieved August 14, 2008)
5. Tingelhoff, K., Moral, A.I., Kunkel, M.E., Rilk, M., Wagner, I., Eichhorn, K.W.G., Wahl, F.M., Bootz, F.: Comparison between Manual and Semi-Automatic Segmentation of Nasal Cavity and Paranasal Sinuses from CT Images. Institute of Electrical and Electronics Engineers (IEEE), 1-4244-0788-5/07/, 5505 – 5508 (2007)
6. Joo, B.S., Sathyamoorthy, P., Subramani, V., Fauziah, H., Bakri, R., Onn, L.T.: Ministry of Health. In: Economic Evaluation of Ministry of Health Diagnostic Imaging Services, Clinical Research Center Publication, Kuala Lumpur (2002)
7. Ahmad Fadzil, M.H., Lila Iznita, I., Venkatachalam, P.A., Karunakar, T.V.N.: Extraction and reconstruction of retinal vasculature. Journal of Medical Engineering Technology 31, 435–442 (2007)

A Proposed Biologically Inspired Model for Object Recognition

Hamada R.H. Al-Absi and Azween B. Abdullah

Department of Computer & Information Sciences
Universiti Teknologi PETRONAS
Bandar Seri Iskandar, 31750 Tronoh, Perak , Malaysia
Hamada.it@gmail.com, azweenabdullah@petronas.com.my

Abstract. Object recognition has attracted the attention of many researchers as it is considered as one of the most important problems in computer vision. Two main approaches have been utilized to develop object recognition solutions i.e. machine and biological vision. Many algorithms have been developed in machine vision. Recently, Biology has inspired computer scientist to map the features of the human and primate's visual systems into computational models. Some of these models are based on the feed-forward mechanism of information processing in cortex; however, the performance of these models has been affected by the increase of clutter in the scene. Another mechanism of information processing in cortex is called the feedback. This mechanism has also been mapped into computational models. However, the results were also not satisfying. In this paper an object recognition model based on the integration of the feed-forward and feedback functions in the visual cortex is proposed.

Keywords: Object recognition, Bio-Inspired systems, Feed-forward model, Feedback model, Human Visual System.

1 Introduction

Object recognition has been one of the topics that caught many researchers' attention for the past three decades. Many researchers have developed algorithms that have the ability to recognize objects such as faces, cars, and cars' number plate and so forth. Object recognition has many applications in life, it has been used to recognize diseases such as cancer [21], and it is also being used in recognizing faces for the purpose of access control [1]. All these algorithms [1, 20, and 21] were developed using machine vision.

Recently, researchers have utilized biology to build object recognition systems; this is referred to as biologically inspired systems. In this methodology, researchers would study a natural living system and design its corresponding computational systems [6] that will help in solving complex problems.

Many methodologies have been developed to achieve object recognition with different sizes, scales, transformations and so on. Moreover, object recognition is a challenging task especially in partially occluded scenes and cluttered backgrounds.

H. Badioze Zaman et al. (Eds.): IVIC 2009, LNCS 5857, pp. 213–222, 2009.

However, neither of these algorithms is able to beat the human visual system that has an amazing ability for recognizing all types of objects regardless of their size, scale, rotations and etc. Although some researchers have already developed models such as the models in [2, 3] of object recognition based on the primates' visual system, however, the results obtained are still unsatisfactory especially for partially occluded objects or when the amount of clutter increases in the scene.

In this paper, a biologically inspired model based on the human visual system is proposed in order to build an object recognition system that is capable of recognizing partially occluded objects and objects in cluttered scenes.

1.1 Human Visual System

In this section, we discuss the human visual cortex, its parts and their functions in recognizing objects. Figure 1 shows the visual route from the eye to the visual cortex.

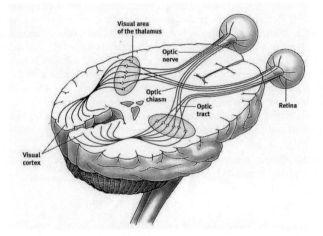

Fig. 1. Visual path from the eye to the visual cortex [6]

The visual cortex refers to the primary visual cortex (striate cortex) or area V1, and the extra striate cortical areas (V2, V3, V4 and IT) (Figure 2). The primary visual cortex or area V1 receives the input information from the lateral geniculate nucleus (LGN) and then pass those information on to two primary pathways, the dorsal pathway which is called the "where" path way, and the ventral pathway which is called the "what" pathway. The dorsal pathway is associated with motion and location, while the ventral pathway is associated with object recognition and categorization. Figure 2 shows the areas in the ventral stream "what pathway", their organization in the brain and the connection between them which is in feed-forward and backward.

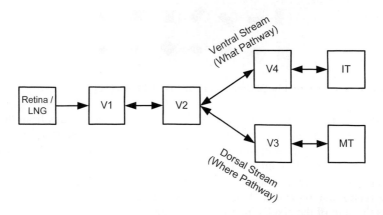

Fig. 2. The organization of the ventral Stream of visual cortex

The visual cortex areas in the ventral stream (what pathway) that is associated with object recognition are [7]:

- *Area V1:* Consists of selective spatiotemporal filters, which process the spatial frequency, orientation, motion, direction, speed, and other features.
- *Area V2:* function is similar to V1; however V2 neurons' responses are adjusted by more complex properties such as the orientation of false contours.
- *Area V4:* Part of the ventral stream. V4 is adjusted for orientation, spatial frequency, color and object features of intermediate complexity.
- *Inferior Temporal Cortex (IT):* an area in the brain that is responsible on object representation in both human and monkey [8].

2   Background

Achieving accurate results in object recognition systems has been a problem for both computer vision and biological vision. Although there are so many techniques that have been developed, yet, both computer vision and biological vision are still looking into building systems that can produce better results of object recognition. In this section computer vision, biological vision and different algorithms / techniques that have been developed to achieve object recognition are discussed.

2.1   Computer Vision

The main aim of computer vision is developing an intelligent application that can perceive the world around us. Many algorithms have been developed that can achieve object recognition such as principle component analysis (PCA) that was proven to perform well in recognizing objects such as faces [10].

In computer vision, a system will start by extracting features from the input image. This will help the classifier to decide on whether or not the intended object is in the scene. Many feature extraction algorithm are available such as Haar-Like feature extraction algorithm [11] and Gabor filters [12].

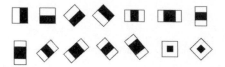

Fig. 3. Common Haar-Like features [11]

Haar-like features is one of the algorithms used to extract features from the image or input video (frames). These features use the change in contrast values between neighboring rectangular groups of pixels rather than using the intensity values of the pixel. Figure 3 shows the common Haar features.

The simple rectangular features of the image can be calculated by using an intermediate representation called "Integral Image" [11]. This integral image is an array contains the sum of the pixel's intensity values located to the left of a pixel and above the pixel at location (x, y) [13]. If we assume that A[x,y] is the original image and AI[x,y] is the integral image then:

$$AI[x, y] = \sum_{x' \le x, y' \le y} A(x', y') \tag{1}$$

Where AI[x,y] is the integral image while A(x',y') is the original image. The computed feature value is then used as an input to a simple decision tree classifier that usually has two nodes that can be represented as 1 or 0 (where 1 representing the existence of the object and 0 for the absence of the object). In fact, all features can be calculated in a fast constant time for any size for two auxiliary images [12].

Another set of features that are used to extract features are called Gabor filter [13]. This filter extracts features of different orientations and scales (Figure 4). This filter has been used for edge detection and it was proved to be sufficient in extraction features [12].

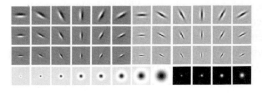

Fig. 4. Gabor filter [13]

2.2 Biological Vision

Biological vision is another technique that has recently been a topic of interest for many researchers. This discipline looks into the way the human or primate visual system works and maps it into a computational system. Human visual system outperforms any state-of-the-art systems in computer vision. Therefore, researchers have been studying the way the information is being processed in the visual system and tried to develop computational models.

Most researchers have studied the monkey's brain and mapped its visual system functionalities into computational models; that is because the anatomy of the monkey's brain is similar to the human's brain [18].

Feed-forward models of object recognition have been proven to be robust. They follow the feed-forward manner of information processing in visual cortex. Hubel and Wisiel [2] were the first to discover how the visual system works in cats in 1962.

In 1999, Riesenhuber and Poggio [14,15] developed what is called as "the standard model of object recognition" based on Hubel and Wisiel theory of simple cells to complex cells at the visual system. The model belongs to the feed-forward family that consists of hierarchical layers. Each layer has S units and C units. S units perform template matching of size and orientation. The outcome of the S unit is grouped and used as an input to C units that perform the MAX operation.

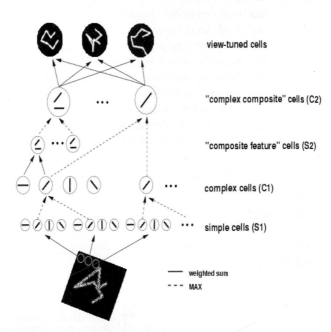

Fig. 5. Model of object recognition based on the feed-forward mechanism [14]

The simulation of the model has shown that the essential properties are robust. The results of the experiments on the model proved that it can be an extended model of the natural model proposed by Hubel and Wisiel. The model extracts features from the object, then runs a classifier on them. The results obtained from the system have been compared with other systems, and it shows that this feature provides consistently better results than other systems [3].

Serre et al [3, 16] proposed a framework that introduces a set of features to ensure the robustness of object recognition; the proposed system is inspired by the standard model of object recognition (Figure 5).

Another model, yet not different from the models in [3, 15, 16] has been proposed by Serre et al [9]. It is also based on the standard model of object recognition and is part of the feed-forward family of models inspired by the visual cortex. Unlike the models proposed in [3, 16], this model has more than 2 layers of the S and C cells which perform the same tasks as explained in [3, 16].

Models that are based on the feed-forward model of visual system have provided some good results. However, these results are only obtained when recognizing objects in scenes that have little amount of clutter and zero occlusion during the first glimpse. We human sometimes cannot recognize objects in the first glimpse in clear scenes, and therefore, if there was clutter in the scene, it will be hard for us to recognize all objects. Hence, feed-forward mechanism of object recognition is not the best solution since it cannot handle all situations, even in [17] it was mentioned that the perform-ance of the feed-forward model dropped from 90% to 74% when the amount of clutter increased in the scenes that were used for testing.

Another process that has been discovered in neuroscience is the feedback process in the visual system. In fact, both feed-forward and feedback are two processes that complement each other to help human and primates to recognize objects [23]. Visual attention is associated with feedback, where it is a function that enables us to focus our attention on a region then explore and recognize the objects in that region. Simi-larly, the biologically inspired models in [22] and [23] are recognizing or categorizing objects using the same mechanism and the results were good as well.

Although the current models that are depending on feedback process are quiet good, however, neuroscience evidence shows the importance of recognizing objects by integrating both feed-forward and backward processes in order to get a better result and mimic the ability of the human and primates visual systems.

3   Bio-inspired Model

We present a model of object recognition (Figure 6) that integrates certain functions of the feed-forward and feedback mechanisms in the human visual system. The model

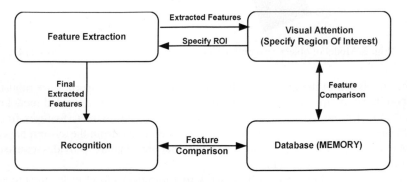

Fig. 6. The Proposed Bio-Inspired Model of Object Recognition

maps the functions of the feed-forward mechanism in the human visual system such as feature extraction that is the first step that the brain does to recognize objects. It also maps some function of the feedback mechanism such as the visual attention method that helps in focusing attention at certain regions in a scene which improves the accuracy and therefore assists in recognizing the intended object(s). Moreover, the model maps the memory of the human that uses previous knowledge to recognize objects.

3.1 Feature Extraction (FE) Component

Feature extraction in the human visual system is being done in areas V1 & V2 and it is part of the feed-forward mechanism. In our model, FE will extract features of all objects in the input image / video sequence and send them to the visual attention component to specify the region of interest (ROI). After that, the ROI will be sent to the feature extraction again – feedback mechanism - for another round of feature extraction at the specified region. The final extracted features will be sent to the recognition components. Figure 7 shows the feature extraction process.

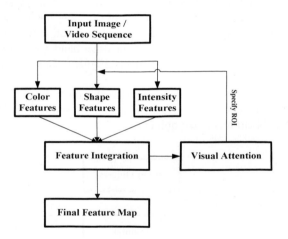

Fig. 7. Feature Extraction process

3.2 Visual Attention (VA) Component

In the human visual system, visual attention is part of the feedback mechanism that provides the lower areas in the visual system with infrormations from the higher level areas in order to produce an accurate visual results.

In our model, the visual attention component's role is to specify the region of interest that contains the intended object(s). First, VA will get the features form the FE components and send them to the database. Based on the feedback of the database, the VA should be able to specify the ROI and send it to the FE component for further processing. Figure 8 shows the Visual attention process.

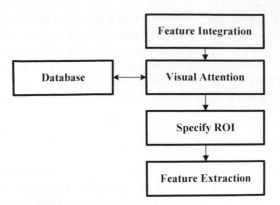

Fig. 8. Visual Attention process

3.3 Database (DB) Component

When the visual attention sends the extracted features to the database, a comparison between the stored data and the incoming data from the VA will take place. The result of the comparison will determine whether or not the input image contains any objects that are similar to those stored in the database. After that, it will send a feedback to VA that will help in specifying the ROI. On the other hand, the DB will be utilized by the recognition component to recognize objects. Figure 9 shows the process of storing object's information in the database.

The database in this model is mapped from the function of the human memory which is storing the objects' information. The memory sends a feedback to the visual system to make it able to recognize objects.

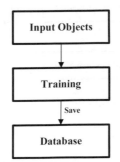

Fig. 9. Storing Objects in the Database

3.4 Object Recognition Component

The final extracted features by FE will be sent to the recognition component. The recognition component will use the data stored in the database to compare them with the input features from the FE components, and recognize the objects according to their availability in the database. The connection between the object recognition

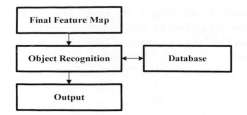

Fig. 10. Object Recognition process

component and the database is in feed-forward and feeback as well. Figure 10 shows the final stage of object recognition in the model.

4 Conclusion

In this paper, we presented a model of object recognition based on the functions of the feed-forward and feedback mechanisms in the human visual systems. Previous models have shown some good results; however, those models showed a decrease in their performance under certain conditions such as increasing in the amount of clutter. Our model integrates the function of feed-forward and feedback with the objective to possibly obtain an accurate result under different visual situations just as our visual system.

References

[1] Paliy, I., Sachenko, A., Koval, V., Kurylyak, Y.: Approach to Face Recognition Using Neural Networks. In: Inst. of Comput. Inf. Technol., Ternopil Acad. of Nat. Econ., Ternopil.; This paper appears in: Intelligent Data Acquisition and Advanced Computing Systems: Technology and Applications, 2005. IDAACS 2005. IEEE, Los Alamitos (2005)
[2] Hubel, D., Wiesel, T.: Receptive fields, binocular interaction and functional architecture in the cat's visual cortex. J. Physiol. (Lond.) 160, 106–154 (1962)
[3] Serre, T., Wolf, L., Poggio, T.: Object Recognition with Features Inspired by Visual Cortex. In: Proceedings of IEEE Computer Society Conference on Computer Vision and Pattern Recognition (CVPR). IEEE Computer Society Press, San Diego (2005)
[4] Serre, T., Wolf, L., Bileschi, S., Riesenhuber, M., Poggio, T.: Robust Object Recognition with Cortex-Like Mechanisms. IEEE Transactions on Pattern Analysis and Machine Intelligence 29(3) (2007)
[5] Peerasathein, T., Woo, M., Gaborski, R.S.: Biologically Inspired Object Categorization in Cluttered Scenes. In: 36th IEEE Applied Imagery Pattern Recognition Workshop, AIPR (2007)
[6] http://www.rhsmpsychology.com
[7] http://www.experiencefestival.com/visual_cortex
[8] http://www.scholarpedia.org
[9] Serre, T., Oliva, A., Poggio, T.: A Feedforward Architecture Accounts for Rapid Categorization. In: Proceedings of the National Academy of Sciences (PNAS), vol. 104(15), pp. 6424–6429 (2007)

[10] Aravind, I., Chandra, C., Guruprasad, M., Sarathi Dev, P., Samuel, R.D.S.: Numerical approaches in principal component analysis for face recognition using eigenimages. In: IEEE International Conference on Industrial Technology, IEEE ICIT 2002 (2002)

[11] Ian Wilson, P., Fernandez, J.: Facial Feature Detection Using Haar Classiffiers. Journal of Computing Sciences in Colleges 21(4) (2006)

[12] Ji, Y., Chang, K.H., Hung., C.-c.: Efficient edge detection and object segmentation using Gabor filters. In: ACM Southeast Regional Conference, pp. 454–459 (2004)

[13] Lienhart, R., Kuranov, A., Pisarevsky, V.: Empirical analysis of detection cascades of boosted classifiers for rapid object detection. In: Michaelis, B., Krell, G. (eds.) DAGM 2003, vol. 2781, pp. 297–304. Springer, Heidelberg (2003)

[14] Riesenhuber, M., Poggio, T.: Hierarchical models of object recognition in cortex. nature. Neuroscience 2(11) (November 1999)

[15] Riesenhuber, M., Poggio, T.: Models of object recognition. Nature neuroscience supplement 3 (November 2000)

[16] Serre, T., Wolf, L., Poggio, T.: A New Biologically Motivated Framework for Robust Object Recognition. CBCL Paper #243/AI Memo #2004-026, Massachusetts Institute of Technology, Cambridge, MA (November 2004)

[17] Kreiman, G., Serre, T., Poggio, T.: On the limits of feed-forward processing in visual object recognition. VSS (May 2007),
http://www.cosyne.org/c/images/6/65/Cosyne-poster-I-52.pdf

[18] Tanaka, K.: Mechanisms of visual object recognition: monkey and human studies. Curr. Opin. Neurobiol. 7, 523–529 (1997)

[19] Bryliuk, D., Starovoitov, V.: Access Control by Face Recognition Using Neural Networks (2000), http://neuroface.narod.ru

[20] Zheng, L., He, X.: Number Plate Recognition Based on Support Vector Machines. In: IEEE International Conference on Video and Signal Based Surveillance, AVSS 2006, p. 13 (2006)

[21] Liu, J., Ma, W.: An effective recognition method of breast cancer based on PCA and SVM algorithm. In: Zhang, D. (ed.) ICMB 2008. LNCS, vol. 4901, pp. 57–64. Springer, Heidelberg (2007)

[22] Siagian, C., Itti, L.: Rapid Biologically-Inspired Scene Classification Using Features Shared with Visual Attention. IEEE Transactions on Pattern Analysis and Machine Intelligence 29(2), 300–312 (2007)

[23] Kim, S., Jang, G.-J., Lee, W.-H., Kweon, I.S.: How human visual systems recognize objects - a novel computational model. In: Proceedings of the 17th International Conference on Pattern Recognition (2004)

Visualization of the Newly Designed Jig and Fixture for Computer-Assisted Knee Replacement Surgery

Intan Syaherra Ramli[1], Haslina Arshad[1], Abu Bakar Sulong[2],
Nor Hamdan Mohd. Yahaya[3], and Che Hassan Che Haron[2]

[1] Department of Industrial Computing, Faculty of Information Science and Technology,
Universiti Kebangsaan Malaysia, Bangi, Selangor
syaherraintan@yahoo.com
[2] Department of Mechanical and Materials Engineering
Faculty of Engineering and Built Environment,
Universiti Kebangsaan Malaysia, Bangi, Selangor
[3] Department of Orthopaedic &Traumatology
Faculty of Medicine
Universiti Kebangsaan Malaysia, Bangi, Selangor

Abstract. Surgical training systems based on virtual reality (VR) are highly desired as they offer a cost effective and efficient alternative compared to traditional training methods. Traditional surgical training methods require cadavers or plastic models which are costly. Cadavers cannot be used repeatedly and training with plastic models cannot provide the realistic experience. This paper describes a visualization to show the use of newly design jig and fixture for computer-assisted knee replacement surgery. Orthopedic surgeons found it difficult to align the existing jig with the computer-assisted device during the operation and it is time consuming to place it at the right position. A newly design jig and fixture has been proposed to solve this problem. Visualization is needed to show the surgeons on how it will be used in the computer-assisted knee replacement surgery. Virtual models used in this visualization are constructed from the actual equipment and real human dataset.

Keywords: Virtual Reality, Jig, Fixture, Virtual Surgery.

1 Introduction

Virtual reality techniques have long been applied in the field of medical, especially for virtual training surgery. The techniques have been applied in various types of surgery such as orthopedics, otolaryngology, gastroenterology, gynecology and abdominal surgeries. A lot of research have been done to improve the medical image techniques and to provide a better visualization for training purpose. Computed tomography (CT), magnetic resonance imaging (MRI) and ultrasound (US) are common medical imaging modalities. Currently, most of the methods for surgical training use animals, cadavers and plastic models which are costly. Apart from that, traditional surgery training methods which use the cadavers cannot be repeated, animal's body cannot represent the real human body and plastic models are not realistic enough. Surgical visualization can be used in medical education and training to reduce cost, to

H. Badioze Zaman et al. (Eds.): IVIC 2009, LNCS 5857, pp. 223–231, 2009.

provide experience with greater variety of pathologies and complications, and possible to repeat and replay training procedures [1]. Therefore, the visualization is needed to allow the repetitive session in order to improve the understanding about the surgery procedure. Total knee replacement surgery is not new as it has been practiced worldwide for 40 years. Knee surgery will remove the damage portion of femur (tight bone) and tibia (lower leg bone). After reshaping the bone, they will replace it with the implant metal. As it is commonly practiced for many years, most surgeons will study the problem with the patient's knee first before the operation. Then, they will start to mark and achieve proper alignment based on their experience. During the operation, they will use the jig (guiding blocks) to determine where the best position to remove unnecessary bone is for the implant. As a result, by using the manual method the bone cutting is not precise and natural bone cannot be replaced.

In order to improve this, a new method which is computer–assisted surgery has been implemented. It uses infrared cameras, images and advanced tracking devices to achieve precise alignment for knee replacement surgery. Computer-assisted device will combine the digital image of the femur and tibia with an implant specific software package. The computer hardware will track the precise position of the patient's knee and the jig at all time by using the sensor that is attached to the jig. Basically, the computer will capture the position of the patient's knee and jig. Then, computer device will analyze the data and provide the information to the surgeon where the precise cut should be made. Besides jig, there are a few more equipments that will be used in the knee replacement surgery. There are bone saw, drill, mallet, scalpel, implant metal and cement to attach the implant metal with the patient's bone.

2 Related Work

A great deal of research effort has been directed toward developing virtual reality surgery training in recent years. Studies on how to enhance the quality of visualization and 3D imaging for medical purpose have been done rapidly for many types of surgery. Various techniques have been applied to produce a quality 3D image and real effect of visualization and simulation.

Due to cost effectiveness and more efficient method compared to traditional methods, a virtual-reality training system for knee arthroscopic surgery was developed [2]. The system simulates soft tissue deformation with topological change in real-time using finite-element analysis and offers realistic tactile feedback using a tailor-made force feedback hardware. The system presented mesh generation, real-time soft tissue deformation, cutting, and collision detection. Two types of meshes are generated in the virtual-reality training system for knee arthroscopic surgery. They modeled the non-deformable organs such as bone by using the surface meshes. For deformable organs such as muscle and ligament they generated the tetrahedral meshes. In this research, they also provide realistic haptic rendering while real-time performance is achieved. For software architecture, they used OpenGL and C++.

The complexity of the procedure and high level of costs for surgical training (caused by traditional training methods like anatomical studies and surgical training on human cadavers) were the decisive reasons to develop a virtual training system in endoscopic sinus surgery [1], [3], [4], [5]. In this research, they generated the virtual model based on MRI dataset of real patient. The dataset was then segmented in VE-SUV (segmentation software for medical image dataset). Then for polygonal modeling they used KisMo, a modeling software for deformable object for polygonal modeling. KISMET (simulation software) is used to simulate the system and is connected with force feedback device IO-Master. The system was tested by 10 inexperienced surgeons. Virtual training system for surgery makes the inexperienced surgeons better prepared for the real operation [3], [6], [7].

The learning practice of minimally invasive surgery (MIS) makes unique demands on surgical training programs and that inspired the researcher to develop a virtual reality simulation for operating room [8]. The focus for this research is proficiency-based training as paradigm shift in surgical skill training. The results show that VR is more likely to be successful if it is systematically integrated into a well-thought-out education and training program. Validated performance metrics should be relevant to the surgical task being trained in the VR training program. They also stressed that VR is only a training tool that must be thoughtfully introduced into a surgical training curriculum to improve surgical technical skills.

Gibson et.al [9] and McCarthy [10] applied real-time techniques in the knee arthroscopic surgery system. The focus mostly relies on the high–end workstation for real-time visualization. Imaging technologies have been used for orthopedic visualization and simulation [11] for orthopedics training of the upper limb region. Tissue identification was performed on the CVH (Chinese Visible Human) volume data. Volume-rendered visualization algorithm is used to perform translation and rotational transformation on the volume data set.

Three techniques have been presented in simulating arthroscopic knee surgery [12]. The techniques are volumetric object representation, real-time volume rendering and haptic feedback. The advantages of using volumetric object, representation are, the data organization is the same as the acquired data, since no surface extraction or other data reformatting is required, errors introduced by fitting surfaces or geometric primitives to the scanned image can be avoided and volumetric object can incorporate detailed information about the internal anatomical or physiological structure of organs and tissue.

3   Design of New Jig and Fixture

This research is a collaboration between Hospital Universiti Kebangsaan Malaysia (HUKM), Faculty of Engineering and Faculty of Information Science and Technology. The real procedure of knee replacement surgery with computer- assisted has been observed at HUKM. During the operation, the surgeon faced many problems to align and match the current jig with the precise alignment as shown in the computer-assisted device. The process to position the jig at the right angle will take a lot of time. Most of the time, the surgeon will need an assistance from other surgeon to place the jig at the patient's knee. This happened especially at the time they wanted to fix the jig at the correct position with the pin and screw. During that time, they have to readjust and realign the jig position several times. This procedure is very tedious and therefore a new jig and fixture has been designed by researchers from Faculty of Engineering, Universiti Kebangsaan Malaysia (UKM) which consists of jig (guiding

block), base and arm as shown in Fig. 1. An "arm" was designed to support the jig
and base, so the structure becomes more stable and will allow the surgeon to control
the jig movement. This will make it easier to match the jig with the precise alignment
as shown in the computer-assisted device.

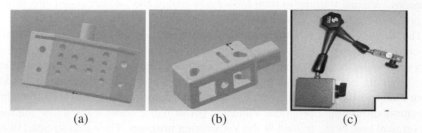

(a)   (b)   (c)

Fig. 1. Shows the fixture (base (b) and arm (c)) that will be used to support the newly jig (a)

A group of engineering researchers have developed the 3D model for jig and fixture.
It's included the guiding block, base and arm. The existing jig and fixture was used as
the basis in developing the new design. The design was produced in 3D by using the 3D
software (Solidworks 2007) as in Fig 2. In order to produce a virtual process on how to
position the jig, it still has to involve other components like bone, pin and the bone saw.
In this situation, Solidworks will be used to create the components.

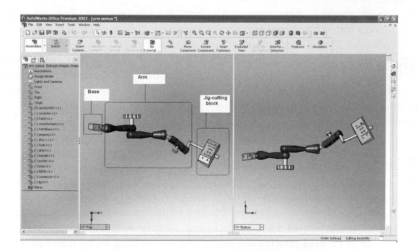

Fig. 2. 3D model of jig components

Bone is the most critical component to be modeled. Therefore, in this research,
segmentation on a series of magnetic resonance imaging (MRI) image was made and
a volume in which the bone part was tagged was obtained. Through this method, the
image processing will extract the areas with specific information. After that, the
surface mesh is created from the series of 3-D contours using Catia V5 (refer Fig. 3)
and will convert the surface mesh to solid.

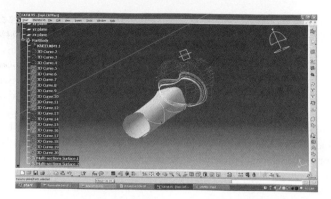

Fig. 3. Bone development process using Catia V5

4 Visualization of Jig and Fixture in the Knee Replacement Surgery

The newly design of jig has not been tested to any of the patient's yet. Therefore visualization is needed to show how the new jig will be applied in the knee surgery procedure. Apart from that, the visualization will also include the computer-assisted interface. A real time technique will be applied to show the topological change of jig movement at user interface with the data as shown in the computer- assisted surgery interface. Real time is referred to a simulation that proceeded at a rate that matched the real process it was simulating.

The software that will be used to visualize the 3D models image is SolidWorks and Virtools. Virtools is widely used in VR application. In this research, a real-time technique will be used to show the topological change between the jig movement and the readings shown in the computer assisted-interface. Kinematic equation will be used to determine the movement of jig at each point of DOF (degree of freedom) and synchronize it with the value stated in computer-assisted interface. The development process of the visualization is as shown in Fig. 4.

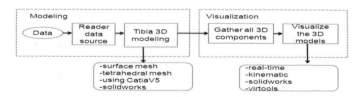

Fig. 4. Development process of the visualization

The visualization will show the users two interfaces which are user interface and computer-assisted interface. User interface will show the users on how to assemble the new jig and base with the new arm. It will prompt a caption to place the jig at the tibia part and place the base. It will also allow the users to use the cursor to control the movement of arm and match it at tibia. Once the position is in place with the precise alignment shown in the computer-assisted interface, user can use the cursor to lock the jig movement. Basically, user needs to adjust the actual plane (blue) which represent the jig and match it with the planned resection plane (yellow). This is as the real process on how the surgeon found the best angle of jig position using computer-assisted device before they proceed with the bone cutting. There are two movements that can be made by the user to adjust the jig (refer Fig. 5). Firstly, part A of arm will allow the users to move the jig block up and down (180 degrees). Once the user confirmed the position, they can lock the A nut. For part B of the arm, it will allow the user to move the jig from left to the right (180 degrees) and lock the B nut once the reading is precise. After that, the visualization will show how the pin is placed inside the jig to avoid the jig from moving around and proceed with the bone cutting.

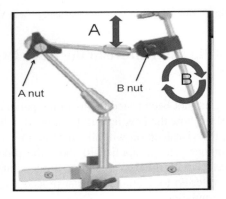

Fig. 5. The movement of jig and fixture

For the computer-assisted surgery interface, it will show the current structure of patient's tibia and the correct alignment that should be made by the jig (cutting block) for tibia cutting procedure. The real data of patient's knee is provided by surgeons from HUKM and it will be set as default in this system. The value of the resection high, resection low and varus have been set as default in this system. However, the value of post slope will depend on the position of the jig at tibia. The value of the post slope shown in computer-assisted interface will change accordingly with the movement of the jig. The actual plane (blue) will represent the jig and the default value for the post slope is 6.0 degree. This value will decrease as the actual plane (blue) move towards the planned resection plane (yellow). Fig. 7 shows the relation between the movements of the actual plane (blue) with the value of the post slope in the computer-assisted surgery interface. The position of jig is placed correctly on the tibia once the post slope state the value of 0 or 0.5 degree. The example of the output is as shown in Fig. 6.

After the system was successfully developed, a group of surgeon will do a testing on the system. They will visualize the assembly process and they will also try to position the newly design jig at the patient's tibia as in the real operation. After that, the doctors will be evaluated based on their understanding on how the newly designed jig will be used.

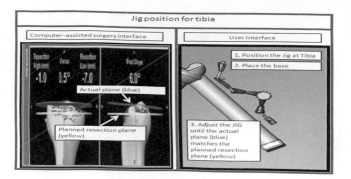

Fig. 6. Example of the output

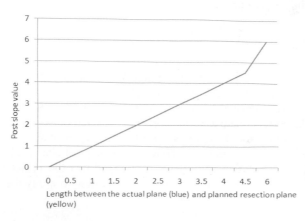

Fig. 7. Relation between the length of actual plane and planned resection plane

Figure 7 shows the relation between the length of actual plane and planned resection plane with the post slope value. It shows that when the length between the actual plane and planned resection plane decrease, the post slope value will also decrease. This may lead to the accuracy of the jig placement at the tibia part at user interface.

Fig. 8. Surgery using Current Jig

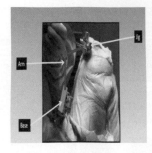

Fig. 9. Surgery using new designed jig with arm

The illustrations of the knee surgery using the existing and newly designed jig and fixture are as shown in Fig.8 and Fig. 9 respectively.

5 Conclusion

A visualization of the newly designed jig and fixture for computer-assisted knee re-placement surgery was developed to show the surgeon on how it will be applied in bone cutting procedure during the surgery. It will also involve user interaction to position the jig at the correct place as in the computer-assisted device. Bone (tibia) will be generated using surface mesh to produce a better quality of image. The real-time and kinematic technique will be applied to show the topological changes between the user interface and computer-assisted interface. It is hoped that the visualization can help the surgeon and inexperienced doctor to understand how to apply the new design of jig and fixture in the knee replacement surgery.

References

1. Slack, R., Bates, G.: Functional Endoscopic Sinus Surgery. Am. FamPhys. 58(3), 707–718 (1998)
2. Pheng-Ann, H., Chun-Yiu, C., Tien-Tsin, W., et al.: A Virtual-Training System for Knee Antroscopic Surgery. IEE transactions on information technology in biomedicine 2(8), 217–227 (2004)
3. Pöhnecka, A., Nowatiusb, T., Trantakisa, C., Cakmakc, C., Maassc, H., Kühnapfelc, U., Dietz, A., Strauha, G.: A Virtual Training System in Endoscopic Sinus Surgery. International Congress Series 1281 3(184), 527–530 (2005)
4. Hilbert, M., Muller, M., Strutz, J.: Developement of a surgical Simulator for Interventions of the Paranasal Sinuses, Techniquel principles and initial prototype. Laryngorhinootologie 77(3), 153–156 (1998)
5. Edmond Jr., et al.: ENT Endoscopic Surgical Training Simulator. Stud. Health Technol. (39), 518–528 (1997)
6. Weghorst, E., et al.: Validation of the Madigan ESS Simulator. Stud. Health Technol. (50), 399–405 (1998)
7. Rudman, T., et al.: Functional Endoscopic Sinus Surgery Training Simulator. Laryngoscope (108), 1643–1647 (1998)

8. Gallagher, A., et al.: Virtual Reality Simulation for the Operating Room, Proficiency-Based Training as a Paradigm Shift in Surgical Skill Training. Annals of surgery 241(2), 364–372 (2005)
9. Gibson, S., Samosky, J., Mor, A., Fyock, C., Grimson, E., Kanade, T., Kikinis, R., Lauer, H., Mckenzie, N., Nakajima, S., Ohkami, H., Osborne, R., Sawada, A.: Simulating Arthroscopic Knee Surgery using Volumetric Object Representation, Real Time Volume Rendering and Haptic Feedback. In: Proceedings CVRmed-MRCAS, pp. 369–378 (1997)
10. McCarthy, D., Hollands, R.: A Commercially Viable Virtual Reality Knee Arthroscopy Training System. In: Proc. Medicine Meets Virtual Reality, pp. 302–308 (1998)
11. Peng Ann, H.: Imaging Technologies for Orthopaedic Visualization and Simulation. Department of Computer Science and Engineering and Shun Hing Institute of Advanced Engineering, The Chinese University of Hong Kong, Shatin, N.T., Hong Kong, China. pp. 52–63
12. Sarah, G., et al.: Simulating Arthroseopic Knee Surgery Using Volumetric Object Representations, Real-Time Volume Rendering and Haptic Feedback, MERL, 201Broadway, Cambridge, USA MassachusettsInstitut Technology, Cambridge, USA, Carnegie Mellon University, Pittsburgh, USA Brigham and Women's Hospital, Boston, USA Mitsubishi Electric Corporation, Hyogo, Japan, pp. 370–378

The Determination of the Number of Suspicious Clustered Micro Calcifications on ROI of Mammogram Images

Ting Shyue Siong, Nor Ashidi Mat Isa, Zailani Mohd. Nordin,
and Umi Kalthum Ngah

School of Electrical and Electronic Engineering,
Universiti Sains Malaysia,
Seri Ampangan, 14300 Nibong Tebal,
Pulau Pinang, Malaysia
stanleysiong@hotmail.com, ashidi@eng.usm.my,
zailani_mohd_nordin@hotmail.com, umi@eng.usm.my

Abstract. Micro calcifications (MCCs) appear as a small cluster of white spots on mammographic images. Numerous researches have been conducted on this abnormality. However, most of the methods focus on MCCs detection without further processing of the original mammogram image. The purpose of this paper is to detect and determine the number of suspicious MCCs on the mammogram image. In the MCCs detection, the system allows the manipulation of mammogram image by using digital image processing techniques. An automated segmentation cluster of suspicious MCCs is done based on the region of interest (ROI). For MCCs detection and determination, this paper proposes the use of Contrast-Limited Adaptive Histogram Equalization (CLAHE), Morphological Tophat filtering, Sobel edge detection and Morphological operation. The number of MCCs from the ROI mammogram image is determined by using the process of morphological structuring. As a result, the approach has been successfully tested on a number of samples and returns an accurate detection of MCCs on the ROIs of the mammogram image.

Keywords: Mammogram image, Micro calcification, Filtering, Edge detection, segmentation.

1 Introduction

Breast cancer is one of the common causes of death all over the world. According to the latest statistics, it is also the most frequent type of cancer reported among Malaysia women. Based on a report by National Cancer Registry of Malaysia in 2003 [1], 31.0% of newly diagnosed female cases of cancer for women in Malaysia was attributed to breast cancer. The disease is prevalent regardless of ethnic group and occurs in patients as young as the age of 15 [1].

Experts have pointed out that early diagnosis is an important approach for prognosis [2]. The benefits of early diagnosis are far more significant than any treatment methods.

H. Badioze Zaman et al. (Eds.): IVIC 2009, LNCS 5857, pp. 232–242, 2009.

Striving for the finding of detection and diagnosis method as early as possible will be a fundamental strategy in improving curative effect of breast cancer for the future.

Mammography is a radiological screening technique which can be used to detect the early signs of breast cancer [3]. By using low doses of X-rays, mammography is capable of detecting the presence of MCCs. Since abnormalities of MCCs might be a tiny part of a whole mammogram and camouflaged by dense breast tissue, the interpretation of mammogram is delicate [4]. In mammographic images, different tissues correspond to different gray level intensity [5]. So, one could distinguish among background, fat, parenchyma tissues, and masses based on intensity level which generally increases in the same order.

It is sometime difficult to detect true positive MCCs. As an effort to improve the accuracy of mammography interpretation, computer aided diagnosis (CAD) has been proposed. This measure has been proven to work but the recall rate (i.e. patients need to undergo another mammogram screening) is higher [6]. Here, the computer functions as a second reader to improve a radiologist's decision making in mammography interpretation. However, due to the complexity of mammograms, the similarity between normal dense tissues and the great variations of masses, the CAD methods usually generate high rate of false positives with the difficult cases missed remained undetected. This will greatly degrade the efficacy of CAD in improving screening mammography. Therefore, a system which is developed for this purpose should focus on computerized analysis and detection of MCCs to enhance the effect of CAD detection.

In the recent past, many approaches have been proposed for the automatic detection of clusters of MCCs, based on wavelets, Gaussian filtering, artificial neural networks, texture analysis, mathematical morphology and fuzzy logic [3].

This paper focuses on two main objectives. First, ROI will be processed on mammogram images to obtain automatic detection of suspicious MCCs, and secondly to calculate the number of suspicious MCCs. The detail of the methodology used is presented in section 2.

2 Methodology

This section will discuss the approaches for segmentation clusters of MCCs. The mammogram images used in this study were taken from Hospital Universiti Sains Malaysia, Kubang Kerian, Kelantan.

Fig. 1 shows an overview of the process of determining the number of MCCs based on the mammogram images. Preprocessing in the form of image enhancement is extracted to increase the subtle signs of MCCs. Contrast enhancement of mammogram image is a delicate process in which it may significantly increase the amplitude of background noise leading to false detections. The morphological top-hat transformation is then applied to the transformed image for enhancing detail clusters of MCCs from the background region of breast. Subsequently, the enhanced image undergoes Sobel edge detection to segment the enhanced borders from the background image. Finally, the number of MCCs will be calculated.

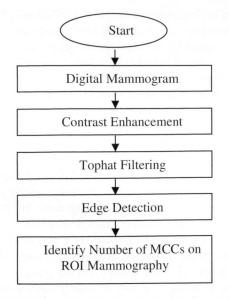

Fig. 1. Brief Overview of Determination Number of MCCs

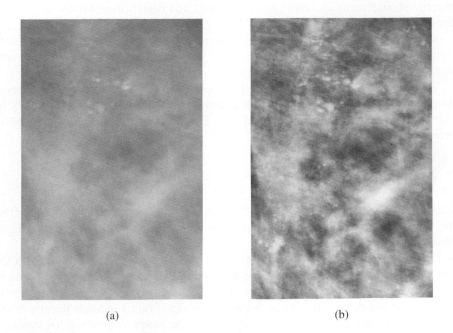

      (a)   (b)

Fig. 2. ROIs of digital mammograms containing MCCs. (a) Original image (b) Image enhanced by CLAHE.

2.1 Contrast Enhancement

In this section, adaptive histogram equalization (adapthisteq) is used to enhance the contrast of the gray scale image by transforming the values using contrast-limited adaptive histogram equalization (CLAHE) [7]. Adaptive histogram equalization maximizes the contrast throughout an image by adaptively enhancing the contrast of each pixel relative to its local neighbourhood. This process produces improved contrast for all levels of contrast (small and large) in the original image. For adaptive histogram equalization to enhance local contrast, a histogram is calculated for small regional areas of pixels, producing local histogram.

CLAHE of the simple piecewise linear function is a contrast-stretching transformation. Low contrast images may result from poor illumination or lack of dynamic range in the imaging. The idea of contrast stretching is to increase the dynamic range of the gray levels in the image being processed [8].

Fig. 2 shows the contrast enhancement technique applied on the original ROI of the mammogram image. A sample of an original mammographic image containing clusters of low contrast MCCs is shown in fig. 2(a), and the contrast enhanced image after applying the technique of CLAHE algorithm is shown in Fig. 2(b). The ROI image with the bright region becomes brighter and the black region becomes darker.

2.2 Tophat Filtering

Tophat filtering involves morphological gray scale opening of the input image. The isolation of gray-value objects that are convex can be accomplished with Tophat filtering [9]. This transformation which uses a cylindrical or parallelepiped structuring

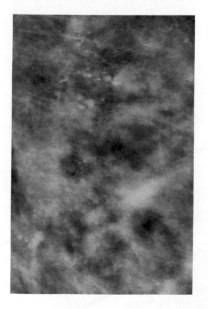

Fig. 3. Image enhanced by Tophat filtering

.lement function with a flat top, is very useful for enhancing details in the presence of shading. Tophat filtering can also be used to correct the illumination and make the result more easily visible when the background is dark.

Fig. 3 shows the resultant image after being applied with the Tophat filtering technique on the image shown in fig. 2 (b). The subtle signs of MCCs within the dense tissue is visually enhanced from the background region of breast tissues.

2.3 Sobel Edge Detection

The Sobel gradient operator is used to distinguish the MCCs from the ROI mammogram images. Normally, the gradient operator is a combination of two masks [10]. One mask represents the x-direction while the other represents the y-direction. Each mask is convolved with the image and the greater of the two, the average of the two, or the square-root of the two is then taken as the result. This represents the orthogonal components of the magnitude of the gradient vector.

This method involves the calculation of the gradient of each pixel in the image. This is to detect the direction in which there is a bigger change in the pixel intensity. This technique defines whether the pixel belongs to an image's border or an image's homogeneous region based on a defined threshold. The Sobel operator is an edge detection operator, so the summary of all the elements in the template will be 0.

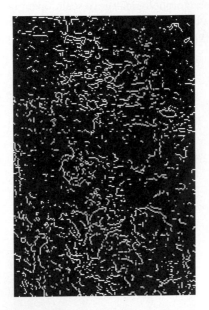

Fig. 4. Edge detection by Sobel gradient operator

Fig. 4 shows the resultant image after applying the technique of Sobel gradient operator to the image shown in figure 3. The effect of applying edge detection is to capture the edges in a closed contour fashion. Secondly, it is used to extract MCCs clusters accurately by obtaining much more hidden information which may not be detected by the naked eye and gives information of closed loop edge which may be of considerable use in image processing techniques involved later on.

2.4 Morphological Operation

Morphological operation is used to remove unwanted noise from the background region of ROI image after the Sobel edge detection. The Sobel binary output image is subjected to the morphological shrink. It removes pixels objects without holes, shrinking them to a point while objects with holes shrink to a connected ring halfway between each hole and the outer boundary. Finally, morphological function 'Clean' is applied to remove isolated pixels (individual 1's that are surrounded by 0's).

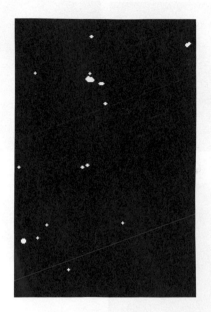

Fig. 5. Segmentation Clusters of MCCs

Fig. 5 shows the resultant image of MCCs clusters after the morphological operation is applied to the image shown in figure 4. The effect is to completely remove the structures surrounding the groups of MCCs and extracts the exact edges of the clusters of MCCs.

3   Results and Discussions

The system has been developed to display the clusters of MCCs clearly by the segmentation techniques based on Sobel edge detection to the ROI mammogram image. In order to obtain an accurate result of extracting precise edges in efforts to increase the diagnosis rate of breast cancer, the proposed techniques have been applied to the ROI of several mammogram images.

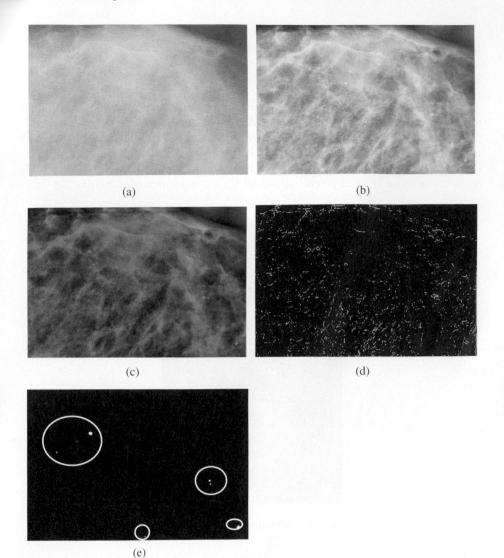

Fig. 6. The results for ROI mammogram image containing clusters of MCCs (a) Original image (b) Image enhanced by CLAHE (c) Image enhanced by Tophat filtering (d) Edge detection by Sobel gradient operator (e) Segmentation clusters of MCCs

Fig. 6, Fig. 7 and Fig. 8 show the results obtained after applying the techniques of digital image processing on the clusters of MCCs on ROI mammogram images. For each of the images in Figs. 6, 7, and 8, image (a) shows an original ROI mammogram image containing clusters of MCCs, image (b) shows the contrast enhancement after applying the technique of CLAHE, image (c) shows the background enhancement after applying the technique of morphological Tophat filtering, image (d) shows an edge detection after applying the Sobel gradient operator, and image (e) shows the segmentation clusters of MCCs.

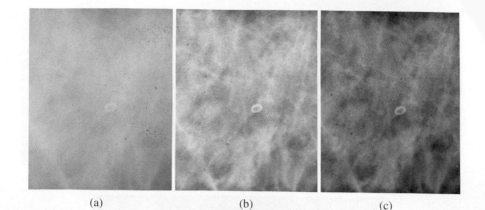

(a)   (b)   (c)

(d)   (e)

Fig. 7. The results for ROI mammogram image containing clusters of MCCs (a) Original image (b) Image enhanced by CLAHE (c) Image enhanced by Tophat filtering (d) Edge detection by Sobel gradient operator (e) Segmentation clusters of MCCs

From Fig. 6 (e), the number of suspicious MCCs detected on ROI mammogram image is six. Two of them are on the top left region, three of them are on the bottom right, and the rest is on the bottom centre of ROI mammogram image. From Fig. 7 (e), the number of suspicious MCCs detected on ROI mammogram image is two. The cluster of MCCs can be clearly observed in the centre and the bottom right of the ROI mammogram image. From Fig. 8 (e), there are one hundred and six numbers of the MCCs detected on the ROI mammogram image. The clusters of MCCs which can be clearly observed are accommodated at the centre of the sample image.

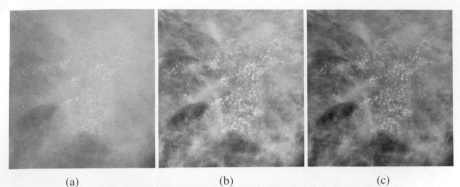

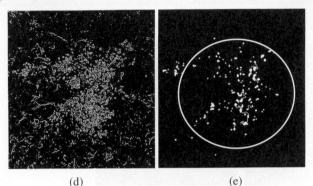

Fig. 8. The results for ROI mammogram image containing clusters of MCCs (a) Original image (b) Image enhanced by CLAHE (c) Image enhanced by Tophat filtering (d) Edge detection by Sobel gradient operator (e) Segmentation clusters of MCCs

Table 1. Number of MCCs detected on ROI mammogram images

	Number of MCCs
Figure 6	6
Figure 7	2
Figure 8	106

Table 1 shows the results of automatic detection and determination tests executed on the ROI mammogram images.

The sample image shows that MCCs residing in different regions within the breast tissue would require digital image preprocessing. By using the approach proposed by the use of CLAHE, Morphological Tophat filtering, the detection clusters of MCCs can be easily observed from the ROI mammogram images. This approach can be combined with other existing contrast enhancement, denoising techniques, edge detection techniques and morphological operation techniques, making them reliable to the MCCs detection and determination. The advantage of the prop. method is that it enabled the automatic detection and segmentation process to ident. the number of MCCs in the ROI of mammogram images. Our results show that quantitative analysis of mammography provides an objective way to detect and segment ROI of mammogram images for the presence of MCCs.

4 Conclusions

The system developed is designed for the automatic detection and determination of the number of MCCs on ROI mammogram image. The mammogram image comprises of contrast enhancement and segmentation based on the Sobel edge detection. The Sobel edge detector allows for obtaining closed edges of MCCs. The results show that quantitative analysis of mammography provides a way of extracting the edges of objects in image data. The proposed algorithm is fully automated for the detection of MCCs clusters. The system can serve as an aid to detect breast cancer in the early stage and greatly assists the radiologists to identify clusters of MCCs on ROI mammography, thereby saving time for the health care providers.

Acknowledgement

This project is partially supported by Fundamental Research Grant Scheme (FRGS) entitled 'Investigation of Mammogram Image Characteristics for Medical Imaging Application' and Research University (RU) Grant USM entitled 'Imaging'.

References

1. Lim, G.C.C., Yahaya, H.: Second Report of the National Cancer Registry - Cancer Incidence in Malaysia. National Cancer Registry (2003), http://www.acrm.org.my/publications.htm (Retrieved January 5, 2008)
2. Ma, Y., Wang, Z., Jeffrey Zheng, Z., Lu, L., Wang, G., Li, P., Ma, T.X., Xie, Y.F.: Extracting Micro-calcification Clusters on Mammograms for Early Breast Cancer Detection. In: IEEE International Conference on Information Acquisition, pp. 499–504 (2006)
3. D'Elia, C., Marrocco, C., Molinara, M., Poggi, G., Scarpa, O., Tortorella, F.: Detection of Microcalcifications Clusters in Mammograms through TS-MRF Segmentation and SVM-based Classification. In: IEEE International Conference on Pattern Recognition (2004)
4. Wu, Z.Q., Jiang, J., Peng, Y.H.: Effective Features Based on Normal Linear Structures for Detecting Microcalcifications in Mammograms. IEEE, Los Alamitos (2008)
5. Tabar, L., Dean, P.B.: Teaching Atlas of Mammography. Georg Thieme Verlag, New York (1985)
6. Gilbert, F.J., Astley, S.M., Gillan, M.G.C., Agbaje, O.F., Wallis, M.G., James, J., Boggis, C.R.M., Duffy, S.W.: Single Reading with Computer-Aided Detection for Screening Mammography. New England Journal of Medicine 359, 1675–1684 (2008)

ıo, E.D., Cole, E.B., Hemminger, B.M.: Image Processing Algorithms for Digital ammography: A Pictorial Essay, Imaging & Therapeutic Technology, pp. 1479–1592 (2000)

. Gonzalez, R.C., Woods, R.E.: Digital Image Processing, 2nd edn. Prentice Hall, New Jersey (2002)

9. Bhattacharya, M., Das, A.: Fuzzy Logic Based Segmentation of Microcalcification in Breast Using Digital Mammograms Considering Multiresolution. In: International Machine Vision and Image Processing Conference, pp. 98–105 (2007)

10. Li, K.Y., Dong, Z.: A Novel Method of Detecting Calcifications from Mammogram Images Based on Wavelet and Sobel Detector. In: IEEE International Conference on Mechatronics and Automation, pp. 1503–1508 (2006)

Assessment of Ulcer Wounds Size Using 3D Skin Surface Imaging

Ahmad Fadzil M. Hani[1], Nejood M. Eltegani[1], Suraiya H. Hussein[2], Adawiyah Jamil[2], and Priya Gill[2]

[1] Dept. of Electrical and Electronic Engineering,
Universiti Teknologi PETRONAS, 31750 Tronoh, Perak, Malaysia
[2] Department of Dermatology, Hospital Kuala Lumpur
Jalan Pahang, 50586 Kuala Lumpur, Malaysia

Abstract. In this work 3D surface scans of wounds are used to obtain several measurement including wound top area, true surface area (rue area), depth, and volume for the purpose of assessing the progress of ulcer wounds throughout treatment. KONICA MINOLTA 910 laser scanner is used to obtain the surface scans. The algorithm for estimating top area and true surface area from surface scan can reduce the inaccuracy that might result when using manual method. Two methods for solid construction and volume computation were considered; namely mid-point projection and convex hull approximation (Delaunay tetrahedralization). The performance of convex hull approximation method for volume estimation is improved by performing surface subdivision prior to the approximation. The performance of these algorithms on different patterns of simulated wound models is presented. Furthermore the algorithms are tested in two molded wounds printed using rapid prototyping (RP) technique.

Keywords: Ulcer wounds, surface scan, solid reconstruction, convex hull approximation, mid-point projection, Delaunay tetrahedralization, rapid prototyping.

1 Introduction

Ulcer wound refers to open wound or sore in which certain conditions present that impede healing. In some ulcer cases, wounds can take up to two years to heal. Non healing wounds can cause economical and psychological distress for patients. Identifying appropriate treatment regime will reduce healing time. The effectiveness of a treatment regime can be estimated by measuring changes in the ulcer wound.

Wound follow-up indicates whether the wound is healing or not and describes the different tissues covering the wound. Quantitative measurement (top area, true surface area, depth and volume) can indicate objectively the progression/regression of the wound. For both top area and true surface area the outer boundary of the wound is traced in a plastic and the number of squares inside is counted as shown in Figure 1(a) and Figure 1(b). The different is for true surface area, the acetate sheet should be placed into the wound (touching the wound bed directly). Inaccuracy in estimating area can happen when the wound boundary includes partial squares. Digitizing the

H. Badioze Zaman et al. (Eds.): IVIC 2009, LNCS 5857, pp. 243–253, 2009.
© Springer-Verlag Berlin Heidelberg 2009

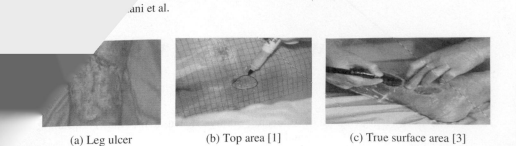

(a) Leg ulcer   (b) Top area [1]   (c) True surface area [3]

Fig. 1. Leg ulcer and boundary tracing

traced wound and computing the area using the computer can solve this overestimation problem [1, 7].

Another measurement is depth; one way of measuring the depth is by using moistened cotton tip applicator placed into the depth of the wound and marking the healthy skin level [7]. Current methods of determining ulcer wound volume are based on filling the wound with measured amount of saline or with alginate paste [9].

Noninvasive techniques for obtaining 3D surface scans for determining different measurements for wounds are being introduced to the medical field. In addition to the advantage of being non-invasive, data is kept in databases for follow up and historical purposes. Techniques that can provide depth measurement and surface profile include photogrammetry [3, 5, 10], structured light [14], and laser scanning [16].

It is important to note that the representation of geometric models is the main factor in choosing the appropriate volume computation method [13]. In the case of ulcer wound, boundary representation is in a form of a triangular mesh. Reconstructing a solid from wound surface is the first step in computing volume.

Projecting surface faces to a plane aligned to points at the top boundary of the wound can be used to reconstruct solid out of surface scan and compute volume of wound as shown in Figure 2(a) [2]. Another method is to interpolate the missing skin surface on top of the wound using the information from the skin surrounding the wound and stitch the scanned and interpolated surface for solid reconstruction as shown in Figure 2(b). It is easier to reconstruct accurately over a small wound area

(a)Projecting surface faces to a plane [2]   (b) Interpolation and Stitching surfaces [14]

Fig. 2. Constructing solids out of wounds scan

while for larger wounds the reconstruction become increasingly more inaccurate. For large wounds the increase in distance between control points reduce the efficiency of surface interpolation; in addition slight displacement on the interpolated surface will lead to higher error in volume computation [14].

Additional methods for constructing solids from surface without a complete boundary representation are convex hull approximation and projecting a surface to a reference point [11]. Enclosing the surface in a smallest convex hull polyhedron will give an estimation of the object size [4]. Solid model from surfaces can also be generated by either projecting meshed surface faces to a reference point [11] or introducing more points on the solid surface. Different locations of reference points result in a variety of solids; the mid-point at the top of the surface is suggested here for constructing solid out of wound surface.

Difficulties can arise when dealing with leg ulcers: (a) in some cases the ulcer might surround the circumference of a part of a leg; the healthy skin around the wound will not be complete (b) when dealing with leg ulcers, leg swollen and existence of scales will lead to errors in constructing the missing skin surface. Wounds located on different sites of the body should be treated differently based on the limp shape.

Generally, the current available techniques suffer from limitations such as inability to measure large wounds, generating reproducible results and dealing with different pattern of ulcer wounds in different body parts.

The objective of this research is to develop computer algorithms to measure ulcer wound size using 3D surface imaging. The wounds of interest are the wound located at the leg. The algorithms should construct wound models and compute volume without getting affected by irregularities on wound surface and to model leg curvature.

2 Methodology

In this study, 10 patients from Hospital Kuala Lumpur are involved in providing 22 3D laser scanned surface images of ulcers at the legs. Prior to applying the appropriate volume computation, leg ulcer wounds images of patients are analyzed. Parameters that describe the wounds are developed based on real ulcer wounds surface images for solid wound modeling. Wounds models representing possible ulcer wounds developed on AutoCAD software are used to investigate performance of volume computation techniques. The following sections provide a detailed description on how the computation is performed on real and modeled wound images.

2.1 Scanning and Preprocessing

Figure 3 illustrates the different steps taken prior to volume computation using Rapidform software [8].

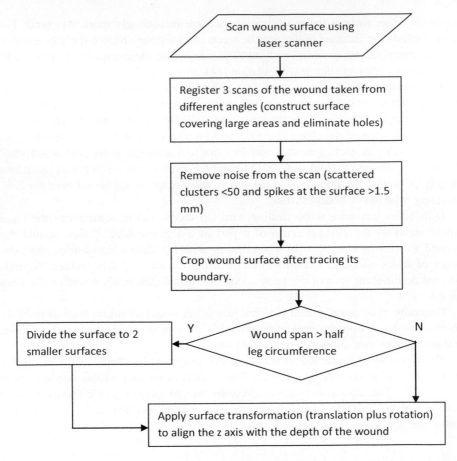

Fig. 3. Surface acquisition and preprocessing steps

2.2 Wound Modeling

After careful examination of leg ulcer wounds it is found that real wounds can be modeled by three wound attributes with descriptors for the shape of wound edges and wound boundary, and for the curvature of wound base as depicted in Figure 4.

(a) Cross section view   (b) top view

Fig. 4. Schematic figures illustrating the geometrical attributes of ulcer wounds

Table 1 lists the descriptors of each wound attribute that it can take based on the analysis of real ulcer wounds. Several solid models are simulated based on different combinations of these geometrical attributes.

Table 1. Wound attributes and their descriptors

Attribute	Descriptors	Schematic
Wound edge - raised sides of the wound	Slope shape	
	Chopped	
	Punched out	
Wound base - bottom part of the wound	Homogeneous depth	
	Depressed	
	Elevated base	
Boundary - shape obtained by tracing around the wound surface	Regular	
	Irregular	

The above ulcer models which can be obtained from filling a wound surface have been modeled using AutoCAD and their volumes determined by the software (reference volume).

2.3   Measuring Wound Area, Surface Area, and Depth

The outer boundary of the wound can be obtained from the triangular mesh and it is defined as all the edges which belong to only one triangle [12]. All the internal edges are shared by exactly two triangles. The top area of the wound is calculated as the area of the polygon created by extracting the wound boundary after projecting it to the XY plane (z=0). Figure 5 (a) displays a surface and Figure 5(b) shows its corresponding boundary polygon.

Average depth can be calculated by dividing wound volume by wound area. While surface true area is obtained by summing the areas of all the triangles composing the meshed surface.

(a) Meshed surface   (b) Boundary edges

Fig. 5. Extracting surface boundary

Overestimation in obtaining top area and true surface area measurement can be solved by replacing the manual method grid counting and work in the scanned or digitized wound surface. Using computer algorithm will result to smaller error since the surface can be divided to small elements unlike the manual method.

2.4 Constructing Solids from Surfaces

In order to calculate the volume of a cavity or wound; a solid can be constructed by filling in the cavity covered by a surface.

2.4.1 Creating Solid by Adding More Points (Mid-Point)

Here, a solid is reconstructed by connecting all the triangular faces to a mid-point creating many tetrahedra as shown in Figure 6(b). The volume of the cavity or wound is computed by summing up the volume of the individual tetrahedra. The mid-point is calculated from a number of points in the boundary of the wound.

2.4.2 Convex Hull Approximation (Delaunay Tetrahedralization)

A convex hull or 3D model can be obtained by performing tetrahedralization. A tetrahedralization of V is a set T of tetrahedra in 3D whose vertices collectively are V, whose interiors do not intersect each other, and whose union is the convex hull of V. A Convex Hull, CH(V) is the smallest polyhedron in which all elements of V on or in its interior [15, 4]. Figure 6(c) displays convex hull of Figure 6(a).

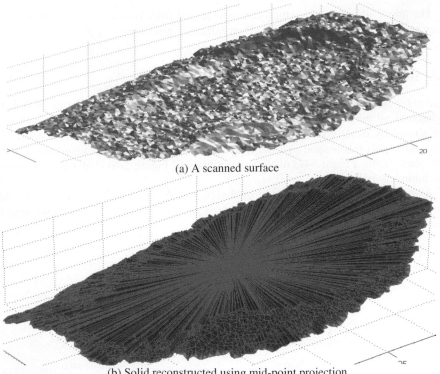

(a) A scanned surface

(b) Solid reconstructed using mid-point projection

Fig. 6. Solid reconstruction for skin surface

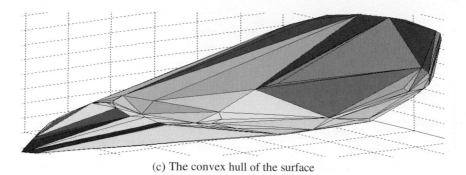

(c) The convex hull of the surface

Fig. 6. (*Continued*)

2.5 Surface Subdivision

The shape of the leg can be simulated by a tabulated surface .In order to construct the wound solid as a tabulated surface, the wound surface can be subdivided along the leg length (creating equal distance parts) and constructing convex hull shapes (Delaunay tetrahedralization) from the divisions has been used for solid reconstruction as in Figure 7(b) and 7(c).

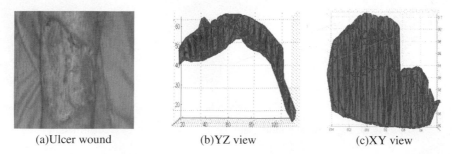

(a)Ulcer wound   (b)YZ view   (c)XY view

Fig. 7. Wound solid model reconstruction

3 Results and Analysis

Figure 8 shows the percentage error in volume computation using midpoint, convex hull, and convex hull with 2, 5, 10 and 20 surface divisions in the wound models compared to the reference volume of the wound models described in section 2.2.

Excluding models with elevated base, volume computation error ranges from (0 - 6.5%) for midpoint method, while convex hull (Delaunay tetrahedralization) preceded by 20 surface divisions the errors ranges from (0 - 7%).

When using surface subdivision prior to convex hull approximation, it is clearly seen that errors in volume computation are reduced significantly with the increase in surface subdivisions. Surface subdivision gives more accurate results in volume

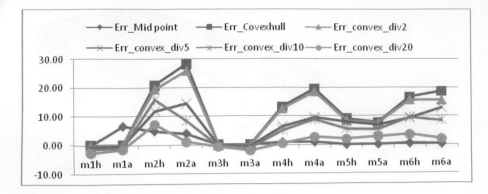

Fig. 8. Results of Volume computation using mid-point, convex hull with 2,5,10 and 20 subdivisions

computation and reduces errors which occur due to irregular boundaries. With the increase in surface subdivision, the shape of the reconstructed surface for irregular shape models will be closer to the original model as shown in Figure 9.

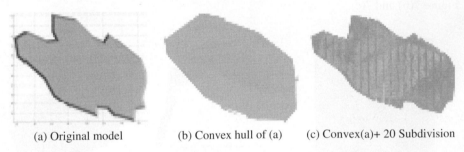

(a) Original model   (b) Convex hull of (a)   (c) Convex(a)+ 20 Subdivision

Fig. 9. Top view of a model and the model after surface reconstruction

Both algorithms produce overestimation when measuring the volume for models with elevated base. The convex hull approximation overestimates the volume as a result of wrapping any irregularity in the shape inside the nearest convex object. In the case of mid-point projection method, overestimation happens due to inclusion of virtual volume from faces which are not visible to the mid-point. Table 2 presents a cross section of two of the models and their percentage error produced by the two algorithms.

The elevation at the base is normally due to limb curvature (global) and/or irregularity at the base (local). In case of midpoint projection method, for elevated base models, the error increase with the decrease in distance between the base and the midpoint (higher error for shallow wounds). From observation elevation at the base from local curvature is not as high as the elevation from global curvature. Midpoint projection is not affected by local curvature but significantly affected by global curvature.

In the case of global curvature the reconstructed model using convex hull preceded by surface division can simulate the leg curvature as can be seen in Figure 7. Local curvature will still produce overestimation in volume computation.

Table 2. The percentage error when computing volume for elevated base models

Model #	Model Cross Section	Err_midpoint	Err_convexhull
m3b		19.7	39.8
m5b		0.4	24.8

3.1   Comparions of the Results Using Molded Wounds

Rapid Prototyping (RP) technique is used to compare the algorithms performance of the different measurements against the measurement obtained using the invasive-methods. Two wound models were printed from two surface scans using layers of

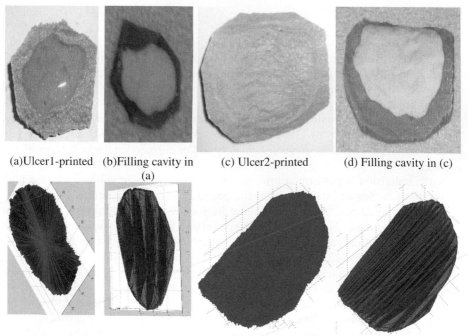

(a)Ulcer1-printed   (b)Filling cavity in   (c) Ulcer2-printed   (d) Filling cavity in (c)
                         (a)

(e)Mid-point   (f)Convex hull with (g)Mid-point projection of   (h)Convex hull with
projection of ulcer 1 division of ulcer 1   ulcer 2   division of ulcer 2

Fig. 10. Ulcer wounds printed using RP and the reconstructed models

Table 3. Comparison between the results using different methods

Ulcer/Method	Top Area (mm²)	True Surface area (mm²)	Depth	Volume I (mm³)	Volume II (mm³)
Ulcer1 / invasive	412	568		Saline	Alginate paste
				950	1000
Ulcer1 / noninvasive	314	632	3	Mid - point	Convex hull
				929	927
Ulcer2 / invasive	2952	3472		Saline	Alginate paste
				-	10000
Ulcer2 / noninvasive	1795	3144	5.5 − 5.1	Mid - point	Convex hull
				9803	9227

wax fused together and build up a solid model. Figure 10 displays the two molded wounds and it reconstructed models using two algorithms, and Table 3 presents the measurement obtained from the surface scans and the molded surfaces.

The percentage differences in the results between invasive and noninvasive methods are {(23.8%) (39%)} for top area, {(11.2%) (9.4%)} for true surface area, and {(7.3%, 2.2%), (7.7%, 2%)} for volume measurements.

4   Conclusion

For volume computation mid-point projection and convex hull approximation (Delaunay tetrahedralization) methods can compute volume of leg ulcer without getting affected by irregularities in the healthy skin around the wound. Only the edge and base information are used for solid reconstruction.

For convex hull approximation low errors is produced in case of regular boundary models excluding the elevated base models. Overestimation in volume for convex hull method can either be due to irregular boundary and/or elevation at the base (both global and local).

Surface division is performed prior to convex hull approximation so that the high curvature of the leg and irregularity at the boundary can be represented using a number of linear segments. With the increase in Surface division error due to irregular boundary is reduced. No effect of surface division on regular boundary models. In the case of global curvature the reconstructed model using convex hull preceded by surface division simulate the leg curvature.

Midpoint projection outperforms convex hull approximation for all the models excluding models with elevated base. Midpoint projection can construct solids for wound surfaces with local curvature while for surfaces with high global curvature the error is high. Midpoint method is not suitable for shallow and very large wounds.

From the results using invasive and noninvasive methods in the printed scans, invasive methods for estimating top area and volume produced quantities which are higher than the quantities obtained by noninvasive methods. While surface area (true surface area) measurement using noninvasive method could be higher than when using the invasive methods (acetate sheet) since this methods will not closely follow the fine surface changes.

References

[1] Ahn, C., Salcido, R.M.: Advances in Wound Photography and Assessment Methods. Advances in Skin & Wound Care 21(2), 85–93 (2008)

[2] Albouy, B., Lucas, Y., Treuillet, S.: 3D Modeling from Uncalibrated Color Images3D Modeling from Uncalibrated Color Images for a Complete Wound Assessment Tool. In: Conference of the IEEE EMBS

[3] Baranoski, S., Ayello, E.A.: Wound Care Essentials: Practice Principles, 2nd edn. Lippincott Williams & Wilkins (August 1, 2007)

[4] Barber, C.B., Dobkin, D.P., Huhdanpaa, H.T.: The Quickhull algorithm for convex hulls. ACM Trans. on Mathematical Software 22(4), 469–483 (1996), http://www.qhull.org

[5] Boersma, S.M., Van den Heuvel, F.A., Cohen, A.F., Scholtens, R.E.M.: Photogrammetric wound measurement with a three-camera vision system. In: Int. Archives of Photogrammetry and Remote Sensing, Amsterdam, vol. XXXIII (2000)

[6] Callieri, M., Cignoni, P., Pingi, P., Scopigno, R., Coluccia, M., Gaggio, G., Romanelli, M.N.: Derma: Monitoring the evolution of skin lesions with a 3D system. In: Proc. Vision, Modeling, and Visualization Conf., Munich, pp. 167–174 (2003)

[7] Dealey, C.: The Care of Wounds A Guide for Nurses, 2nd edn. Blackwell Science Ltd, Malden (1999)

[8] INUS Technology. Rapidform2006 Tutorial (December 15, 2005)

[9] Langemo, D., Anderson, J., Hanson, D., Hunter, S., Thompson, P.: Measuring Wound Length, Width, and Area: Which Technique? Advances in Skin and Wound Care January 21(1) (2008)

[10] Malian, A., Azizi, A., Heuvel van den, F.A.: MEDPHOS: A New Photogrammetric System for Medical Measurements. In: Proceedings of ISPRS Congress, Istanbul, Turkey, vol. XXXV, pp. 311–316 (2004)

[11] Ohanian, O.J.: Mass Properties Calculation and Fuel Analysis in the Conceptual Design of Uninhabited Air Vehicles (2003)

[12] Persson, P.-O., Strang, G.: A Simple Mesh Generator in MATLAB. SIAM Review 46(2), 329–345 (2004)

[13] Pflipsen, B.: Volume Computation - a comparison of total station versus laser scanner and different software; Universsity Of Gavle (2006)

[14] Plassmann, P., Jones, B.F., Ring, E.F.J.: A structured light system or measuring wounds: Photogrammetric Record, vol. 15(86), pp. 197–203 (1995)

[15] Shewchuck, J.R.: Lecture Notes on Delaunay Mesh Generation. University of California at Berkeley (1999)

[16] 3D Digitizing KONICA MINOLTA 3D Laserscanner Applications in medical science, http://www.konicaminolta-3d.com

[17] Zhang, X., Morris, J., Klette, R.: CITR, Volume Measurement Using a Laser Scanner, Computer Science Department The University of Auckland, Private Bag 92019, Auckland

[18] Lee, Y.T., Requicha, A.A.G.: Algorithms for Computing the Volume and other Integral Properties of Solids, Part I and Part II. Comm. ACM 25(9), 635–641 (1982)

Enhanced Lips Detection and Tracking System

M.H. Sadaghiani, Kah Phooi Seng, Siew Wen Chin, and Li-Minn Ang

School of Electrical and Electronic Engineering,
The University of Nottingham Malaysia Campus,
Jalan Broga, Semenyih, 43500 Selangor, Malaysia
{kecx82mhd,Jasmine.Seng}@nottingham.edu.my

Abstract. In this paper, an adjustable processing window based on lips-skin ratio is proposed to enhance the lips detection and tracking algorithm presented in [1]. The algorithm suggested in [1] is only working well if the tracked subject is moving horizontally with the same lips size. The fixed small window is failed to be used to capture the whole lips region which gradually increased when the subject moves towards the detection device. In this paper, a lips-skin ratio is keep tracked to ensure that in every small window, the entire lips region is properly encircled which a certain skin region. If the obtained ratio is greater than the threshold, means the lips region has exited the window; the size of window is hence adjusted till it satisfies the threshold value. The proposed approach is adapted into [1] and the simulation results have manifested an improvement of the overall watershed lips segmentation and detection system.

Keywords: Watershed, Lips detection and tracking, lips-skin ratio, audio-visual speech recognition, H_∞ filtering.

1 Introduction

Automatic lips detection and tracking system has become a research trend recent years since it possesses the potential of wide spread employment. In many applications such as audio-visual speech recognition (AVSR) [1, 2], the lips detection and tracking process is a crucial preprocessing step, where it is the key to obtain the most representative information from the visual modality. In addition, it is as well implicated in the intelligent human computer information (IHCI), and human expression recognition [3].

There are various approaches for the lips detection published in the past [4]-[6]. Zhang et al. [5] proposed a lips detection technique using red exclusion and Fisher transform. The red exclusion approach is applied to enhance the lips image and separated from the skin image through a thresholding process. Furthermore, the lips detection in the normalized RGB colour scheme is presented by Jamal et al. [6]. The lips detection is performed on the skin pixels after segmenting the normalized image into skin and non-skin regions using the histogram thresholding. As to increase the discrimination between the lips and skin, Eveno et al. [4] presented a new colour mixture and chromatic transformation for a better lips segmentation.

H. Badioze Zaman et al. (Eds.): IVIC 2009, LNCS 5857, pp. 254–265, 2009.
© Springer-Verlag Berlin Heidelberg 2009

Regarding to the presented lips detection algorithms as mentioned above, it is noticed that most of the proposed approaches required a prerequisite face localization process at the early stage [7, 8]. In paper [1], an automatic watershed lips detection system is presented to bypass the preliminary face localization process. For an input image, the watershed lips detection is first applied and the successfully obtained lips region is then sent to the H_∞ lips tracking system to estimate the lips location on the successive input image. For the subsequent image, the watershed and segmentation and lips detection process is only focused on the fixed small window size around the predicted lips location. If the prediction of the lips position is incorrect, a full image processing would restart again.

Nevertheless, the algorithm proposed by [1] is only working fine if the subject is moving horizontally, which means the size of the lips to be detected must always kept approximately equivalent. In the circumstances where the subject moving forward to the detection device, the gradually increased lips size would not be able to fully fitted into the fixed small window for the subsequent watershed segmentation and detection. The exited lips region will cause the failure of the detection process and will yield the full image screening again. Besides, even if the lips detection is able to be working on the fixed small window where only a small portion of lips region exceeded, some of the important information from the detected lips would be missing for further analysis such as visual speech recognition process.

Dealing with the aforementioned problem, an adjustable processing window is proposed and adapted into [1] to improve the robustness of the overall lips detection and tracking approach. The overview of the proposed enhancement is illustrated in Fig. 1. Firstly, the watershed lips detection and verification is applied on the full size input image. In this paper, instead of using the symmetry detection for the lips verification as in [1], skin cluster boundary which is able to deal with the face rotation matter is applied. The detected lips with its centre point is passed to the H_∞ lips tracking system to estimated the lips location at the succeeding image. For the incoming frame, the small window set around the predicted location is first adjusted according to the proposed lips-skin ratio as depicted in the red-dotted box in Fig. 1.

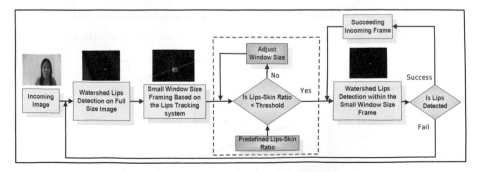

Fig. 1. The overview of the lips detection and tracking system

After obtaining an optimum window size where the lips region is properly encircled with a certain amount of skin region, the watershed lips detection would only be working within the finely adjusted small window size image. If the lips position is estimated wrongly and the lips is failed to be detected, the full size screening would be going through again.

2   The Lips Segmentation and Detection System

Watershed transform is applied for the lips segmentation as it possesses the characteristic of closed boundary segmentation. An incoming grayscale image is observed as a topographic surface in the watershed algorithm. Every pixel is placed at a certain altitude according to the gray level. Black is treated as the minimum altitude while white is the maximum altitude. The other pixels are allocated to a particular altitude between these two extremes. With the watershed transform, the image is split into a set of catchment basins which formed by its own regional minimum. According to the steepest descending path, every pixel would fall into only one of the aforementioned catchment basins. The labeling number for each pixel to a specific catchment basin would be the outcomes of the watershed transform [8].

The overall watershed lips segmentation and detection is illustrated in Fig.2. As shown in Fig.2, the image is first sent for pre-processing before going into the watershed transform directly to deal with the watershed over-segmentation matter as

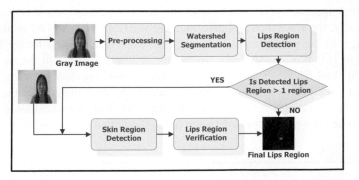

Fig. 2. The overall watershed lips segmentation and detection system

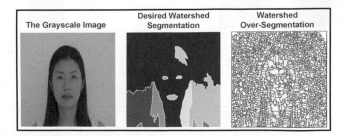

Fig. 3. (a)The grayscale image (b) The desired segmented regions (c) The over-segmentation problem

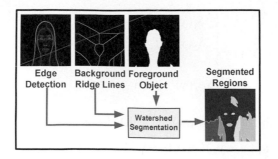

Fig. 4. The watershed segmented regions with pre-processing

illustrated in Fig. 3. The pre-processing (shown in Fig. 4) includes edge detection using Sobel filtering, obtaining the foreground object and the background ridge line. The desired watershed segmented region with the pre-processing is depicted in Fig.4.

Subsequently, the watershed segmented regions are passed to the lips detection process to obtain the final lips region. The lips detection system is built with the cubic spline interpolant (CSI) lips colour modeling. The Asian Face Database (AFD) [uni-9] is used to generate the lips colour model. 6 sets of 6x6 dimensions lips area are cropped from each of the subject, the total amount of 642 sets lips data is first converted from RGB into the YCbCr colour space and plotted onto a Cb-Cr graph as illustrated in Fig. 5(a). Only the heavily plotted pixels are categorized as the lips colour cluster. The final lips colour cluster after the morphological closing process is depicted as in Fig. 5(b). Consequently, the cluster is encircled by the cubic spline interpolant boundary as equated in (1)-(2). The generated boundary as shown in Fig. 5(b) is saved for further lips detection process, where the watershed segmented region which falls within the boundary is detected as the lips region.

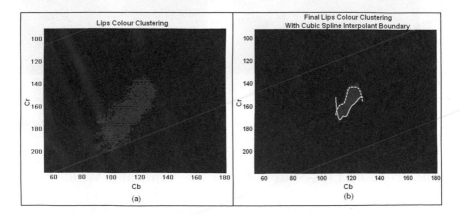

Fig. 5. (a) Initial lips colour cluster (b) final lips colour cluster encircled with the cubic spline interpolant boundary

$$S(y) = \begin{cases} S_1(y) & if \quad x_1 \le x \le x_2 \\ S_2(y) & if \quad x_2 \le x \le x_3 \\ \vdots \\ S_{k-1}(y) & if \quad x_{k-1} \le x \le x_k \end{cases} \tag{1}$$

Where S_n is the third degree polynomial which denoted as:

$$S_n(y) = a_n(y - y_n)^3 + b_n(y - y_n)^2 + c_n(y - y_n) + d_n \tag{2}$$

For $n=1, 2, 3 \dots k-1$.

After the aforementioned lips detection process, if more than one region is detected as the lips, a further verification process is triggered to obtain the final lips region. Instead of using the symmetry detection as suggested in [1], the skin cluster boundary is used for the verification. The detected region which also situated within the predefined skin cluster boundary would only be verified as the final detected lips region. The skin cluster boundary is defined using the similar methodology as the lips cluster boundary. 20x20 dimension skin areas is collected from each subjects in the AFD and the skin cluster which plotted in Cb-Cr graph is as in Fig. 6(a). The skin boundary for verification process is then generated and depicted in Fig. 6(b).

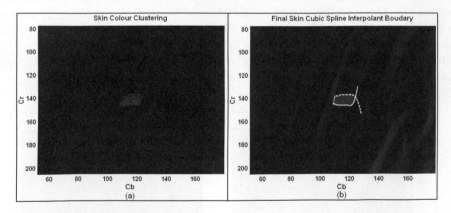

Fig. 6. (a) Initial skin colour cluster (b) final skin colour cluster encircled with the cubic spline interpolant boundary

3   The Proposed Lips-Skin Ratio for the Adjustable Window

Instead of continuously applying the aforementioned watershed segmentation and detection on the lips region throughout the full size image of the entire video flow, as proposed in [1], the successfully detected lips region on the current image would be then sent to the H_∞ lips tracking system to predict the lips location on the subsequent incoming

video frame. It is claimed that the computational time of the overall image processing would be reduced since the watershed segmentation and detection process would only be focused within the fixed small window size area around the predicted point.

However, the proposed system in [1] would only be working fine in the situation where the subjects moving in the horizontal direction, in the other words, the size of the tracked lips is always approximately similar. The algorithm is failed when the subject moving towards the detection device as depicted in Fig. 7, which means the lips region is increased and it might be exit the fixed small window area. The watershed segmentation on the exited lips region is failed and the full size image screening would be going through again. Furthermore, even if the watershed segmentation and detection is able to work on some of the exited lips region, the final obtained lips region might not be the desired output, since some of the lips information would be missing. Regarding to the aforementioned issue, an adjustable window instead of fixed size window is presented in this section.

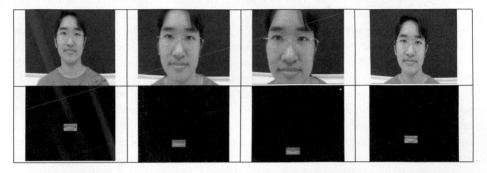

Fig. 7. (a) The problem of the lips detection with the fixed small window from [1]

3.1 Adjustable Window

Lip tracking via a rectangular window which corresponds to location of lip defines overall ROI and in a sequence of images as dynamic tracking method plays central role. After defining such a window in first image it should be able to adapt itself to lip's area automatically. In [1] (New Lips Detection and Tracking System), if person moves forward, ROI window would not be able to change its size to cover whole lip and system faces to missing some data. By detecting the center of lip and set a constant value for ROI still this problem arises. For reducing this problem a new method base on colour space distribution could be able to solve this problem. This method can be used by applying it to all of colour spaces such as RGB, HSV, YCbCr, etc. For example to mask image (Fig. 8(a)) that consists of binary values and is known as bit map as well as RGB colour space it is possible to apply this method. In details because most of the time the ROI contains skin around the mouth, by knowing the fact that skin colour and lip colour have different colour characteristics, it can be assume that in the default window each is set manually, always ratio of lip's colour to skin's colour is constant and can be seen as percentage of these to area. Here, this method is described for system that uses RGB colour space comparison method to narrow down image till finding ROI.

3.2 RGB Approach

For preparing a window size which is able to cover possible lip shapes, system should be trained by different lip images and for more accuracy images should be as more as possible. The result is a ROI with constant average value of skin colour as well as lip colour in desired rectangular window. In the case of RGB region of interest, needed values can be calculated by averaging each colour plans separately for selected lip colour and similarly for skin around the data-base. By dividing averaged lip colour plans correspond to averaged skin colour plans $(R_L/R_S, G_L/G_S, B_L/B_S)$, system can decides if ROI has cover entire lip or has not. R_L, G_L, B_L, R_S, G_S and B_S are integers and calculating by meaning over each plan. It should be mentioned that ratio of skin extracts from data-base but for more convenience it could be defined by another data-base which is completely dedicated to lip or skin colour. To make it more clearly, subscript L represents lip's colour space and S stands for skin colour space. The values save as a global threshold of lip colour to skin colour. This ratio defines to which extend the ROI should capture lip and its sour ended area. Then by comparing the approximated ROI window on the next image base on central point, to these values correctness of this approximation measures. Default window size for first image should be come into account because averaging of colour directly depends to it. In general two facts are vital to process algorithm, first is the averages of R, G and B colour plans for lip (Fig. 9) and skin (Fig. 10) colour and second is the number of pixels which these two categories occupy in the ROI and we can say *number_of_lip_colour_pixels + number_of_skin_colour_pixels = total_number_of_ pixels_in_ROI*. The reason for averaging is to detect and distinguish between lip colour or skin colour, then allocate each pixel to appropriate category So it is possible to average the ratio of lip colour to skin colour and keep it as a measure of later ROI's size. As a shortcut it is possible to detect and count number of skin colour and subtract it from total number of pixels in ROI, so number of skin colour obtains.

If *IMAGE $_{(i+1)}$* > $(R_L/R_S, G_L/G_S, B_L/B_S)$ it means lip area is bigger than skin and adapting is needed. So if there was any mismatch between the ratio of lip colour to skin colour, ROI window can use another algorithm to increase ROI size till it

Fig. 8. (a) Reference window.(b) Mask image.

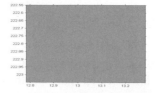

Fig. 9. Average lip colour   **Fig. 10.** Average skin colour

satisfies threshold value and ROI captures correct area. In first step of this algorithm number of pixels correspond to lip colour as well as skin colour calculates, then the ratio of each one compares to entire size of ROI window and for next picture base on previous ROI window. After these two steps these values compare to threshold value which is prepared from data-base.

In this paper, the threshold values based on ROI with size of *256 × 256* is suggested as *(R_L/R_S, G_L/G_S, B_L/B_S)= (1.064, 1.254, 1.061)*.

In Fig. 11, some ROI windows are represented which all have same window size. It is obvious that when target face moves forward window cannot adapt itself to capture complete shape of lip, and purposed algorithm in [1] suffers from this limitation. But if Adaptive lip tracking employs it is possible to train system to expand the rectangular window for example by a constant value and examine ROI again to make sure that this value is sufficient to other next step of lip processing. Worst case happens when ROI detects a region which does not have any lip colour component and [1] recommends less likely detection that does not have lip pixels.

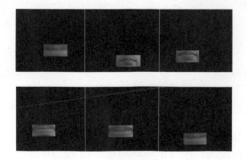

Fig. 11. Detected lips by ROI

4   The H_∞ Lips Tracking System

A linear, discrete-time state and measurement equation is mathematically represented as:

$$\text{State equation} \qquad : \ x_{n+1} = Ax_n + Bu_n + w_n \tag{3}$$

$$\text{Measurement equation} \ : \ y_n = Cx_n + v_n \tag{4}$$

where x is the system state while A is known as the transition matrix which brings the state value x_n from time n to $n+1$; B is the matrix that connects the input vector, u with the state variables and the process noise is represented by w_n; Besides, y is known as the measured output; C is the observation model which maps the true state space to the observed space and the measurement noise is known as v_n.

At a particular time step, the system information is represented by the state vector in (3) and the system changes is described with respect to the function of time. Regarding the aforementioned linear system, an accurate estimation of the next incoming position is needed if we desired to track the target or the lips region. Instead of using the Kalman filtering as the tracking tool, the H_∞ filtering which does not required to deal with the process and measurement noise covariance is applied. By using the H_∞ filtering as the tracking tool, there would be no assumption for the system uncertainties due to the reason that H_∞ filtering possesses a characteristic of considering the worst case estimation error.

In this paper, the center position of the targeted lips in the respective horizontal and vertical position would be used as the state vector for the lips tracking system. The updating rule for the H_∞ filtering is mathematically represented as below:

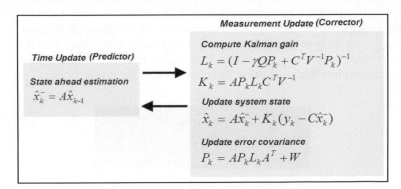

Fig. 12. The flow of H_∞ filtering algorithm

Q, W, and V are the weighting matrices for the estimation error, process noise and measurement noise respectively. The robustness of H_∞ filtering will only preserved if the value of γ is chosen where all the value of the eigenvalue P is less than one.

5 Simulations and Analysis

5.1 Simulation Results on the Lips Detection and Verification Process

The AFD is used to evaluate the lips detection and verification system. Fig. 13(b) and 14(b) show some of the watershed segmentation results. Furthermore, the predefined CSI lips colour boundary is applied to analyze the segmented regions. The segmented region which falls within the CSI lips colour boundary is obtained as the final lips region as depicted in Fig. 13(c) and 14(d). However, if there is more than one region to be

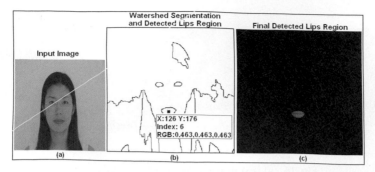

Fig. 13. (a) The incoming image (b) watershed segmentation and detection (c) final detected lips

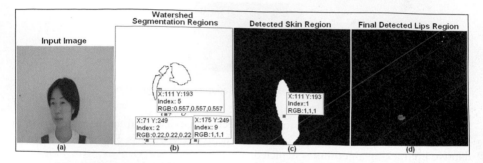

Fig. 14. (a) The incoming image (b) watershed segmentation and detection (c) skin boundary verification (d) final detected lips

detected, a further verification process using the skin colour boundary is triggered. The segmented region which as well drops into the skin colour cluster would only be known as the final lips region. The output of the verification is illustrated in Fig. 14(c).

5.2 Simulation Results on the Proposed Adjustable Processing Window

Some in-house prepared video sequences are used to analyze the lips segmentation and detection process for the algorithm proposed in [1] and our proposed approach. In Fig. 15, (a) is input image similar to Fig. 14(a) and after applying watershed algorithm and finding central point of mouth in Fig. 15(b), ROI window detects lip area in image.

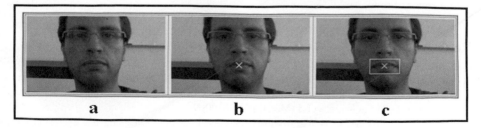

Fig. 15. Ideal lip tracking. (a) input image, (b) central point, (b) ROI window.

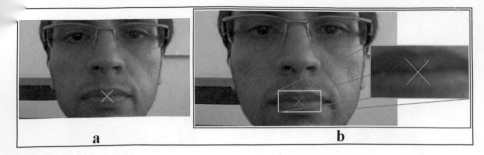

Fig. 16. (a) next image, (b) lip tracking with fixed size

Fig. 17. Result after applying adaptive ROI algorithm

In Fig. 16(a), face, moved toward detection device, and as result shows in Fig. 15(b), ROI window did not cover mouth properly. And in Fig. 17, outcome of daptive lip tracking algorithm is depicted.

6 Conclusion

Since there are a vast amount of research and effort bust the visual part of a speech recognition system, for improving the accuracy and avoiding of unnecessary processes, an enhanced method for lip detection and tracking system is introduced. After segmenting and detecting an area which is more likely contains lip's information in the first image in dynamic approach, a window base on the central point of lip creates that should have ability to find similar part on the rest of video sequences. Proposed method, suggests an adaptive ROI window which after finding the central point of lip, regardless to the movement of face toward the external detection device can determine a portion of lip and some desired skin which allows system to extract suitable information. Results show its practical efficiency in the application of dynamic visual recognizer systems.

References

1. Chin, S.W., Seng, K.P., Ang, L.-M., Lim, K.H.: New Lips Detection and Tracking System. In: Proceedings of the International MultiConference of Engineers and Computer Scientists, IMECS 2009, Hong Kong, vol. I (March 18 - 20, 2009)
2. Lewis, T.W., Powers, D.M.W.: Audio-visual speech recognition using red exclusion and neural networks. Journal of Research and Prac. In Info. Tech. 35(1), 41–63 (2003)

3. Kaucic, R., Dalton, B., Blake, A.: Real-time lip tracking for audio-visual speech recog. applications. In: Proc. Ofthe 4th Euro. Conf. on Comp. Vis., vol. 2, pp. 376–387. Spring Heidelberg (1996)
4. Zhang, X., Broun, C.C., Mersereau, R.M., Clements, M.A.: Automatic speech reading with applications to human-computer interfaces. Eurasip Journal on Applied Signal Processing 2002(11), 1228–1247
5. Zhang, J.-M., Wang, L.-M., Niu, D.-J., Zhan, Y.-Z.: Research and implementation of a real time approach to lip detection in video sequence. In: Int. Conf. on Machine Learning and Cybernetics, IEEE, Los Alamitos (2003)
6. Dargham, J.A., Chekima, A.: Lips detection in the normalized RGB color scheme. In: 2nd ICTTA 2006, Inf. And Comm.Tech., IEEE, Los Alamitos (2006)
7. Wark, T., Sridharan, S.: A syntactic approach to automatic lip feature extraction for speaker identification. In: Proc. of the, IEEEInt conf. on Acoustic, Speech, and Signal Processing (1998)
8. Yeong, L.S., Ang, L.-M., Seng, K.P.: Closed boundary face detection in grayscale images using watershed segmentation and DSFPN. In: Int. Sym. On Intelligent Signal Processing and Comm. Sys., IEEE, Los Alamitos (2008)

Time-Space-Activity Conflict Detection Using 4D Visualization in Multi-storied Construction Project

Mohammed E. Haque and Muzibur Rahman

Texas A&M University, Department of Construction Science,
College of Architecture, College Station, TX 77845, USA
mhaque@tamu.edu

Abstract. This study investigated whether a 4D model can help project participants of construction sites to detect possible errors in construction process.
Identifying problems in work sequence and elements are possible when necessary measures are implemented to rectify the problems in advance using a 4D
model. The common problem associated with a construction project is a time-
space conflict which may lead to project delays and cost overrun. Construction
space management and activity sequencing are important aspects for timely
project completion within an estimated budget. This research explored the effective use of 4D visualization that could help overcome timespace problems.
In order to fulfill this research goal, a 4D model was developed that incorporated spatial requirements along a chronological schedule of events. The model
produced logical evidence that a 4D model could effectively be usedin a construction site to detect time-space conflicts.

Keywords: 4D Model, Construction Project Management, Time-Space Conflict.

1 Introduction

Construction operations range from relatively simple to the most complex. They involve multiple pieces of equipment, labor trades, and materials that can interact in
complex ways. Traditional methods used to design them prove ineffective in many
cases where simulation modeling and visualization can be of substantial help [1].

Bar charts and network diagrams are typical means to represent and communicate
construction schedules. Individuals having different background and being unfamiliar
with these techniques find it difficult to evaluate and communicate the schedules [2].
Visual 4D planning and scheduling technique that combines 3D Computer Aided Design (CAD) models with construction activities (time) has proven benefits over the
traditional tools [3]. In 4D models, project participants can effectively visualize and
analyze problems regarding sequential, spatial, and temporal aspects of construction
schedules. Therefore, more robust schedules can be generated and hence reduce re-
works and improve productivity.

Effective planning and scheduling of construction operations is critical for the success of any construction project, irrespective of its magnitude. Simulation modeling is

H. Badioze Zaman et al. (Eds.): IVIC 2009, LNCS 5857, pp. 266–278, 2009.

a valuable construction management tool that is well suited to the analysis of construction processes, the majority of which are resource driven. Simulation allows construction planners and analysts to experiment with and evaluate different scenarios during the planning phase [1].

Subject to increasing pressure for time to market, general contractors must increase the amount of work done per time unit by increasing the resources utilized by activities, and by scheduling more activities concurrently. Both of these strategies increase the demand for space per time unit. Since space is limited at many construction sites, an increase in space per unit time can result in time-space conflicts, in which an activity's space requirements interfere with another activity's space requirements, or with work-in-place [4].

Time-space conflicts have three characteristics that differentiate them from design conflicts: (1) they have temporal aspects, i.e., they occur only during certain periods of times, (2) they exist in different forms, and (3) they create different types of problems on site. Therefore, the challenges in time-space conflict analysis involve the detection of spatial conflicts in x, y, z, and time dimensions, the categorization of the conflicts detected, and the prioritization of the conflicts categorized [4].

4D construction planning is an effective way to show the construction process with chronological order which makes the virtual model easy to understand, analyze and plan for the sequence of activities. 4D models help designers, owners, and contractors to visualize the quality of plans and identify potential problems during project planning. The use of 4D and similar applications will cost money, but the potential savings are several times the cost of implementing them through preventing delay during the construction. Advanced techniques cost more, but offer greater return if properly applied. Time–cost trade-off considerations mean that delays on a large project can easily cause additional costs, therefore if work can be carefully monitored and managed beforehand so that it may proceed without extra cost, the final result would satisfy the client.

The activity level intricacy makes the whole construction process quite complicated and difficult for planners. The lack of tools for activity level visualization of construction projects presents problems to planners when considering the future implications of their decisions [5]. In the architecture, engineering and construction industries, computer visualization usage can cover the whole lifecycle of a product from presentation of initial concepts to the final stages of production and can also extend to maintenance issues [5]. Extensive research has been conducted in recent past on the use of 4D Model in construction industry. Many Contractors also started to use 4D model to improve the construction delivery. Different experiments were conducted and the results demonstrate that 4D visualization and virtual models increase ability to analyze the schedule for potential conflicts. The recent works on 4D visualization have been categorized as per their intended applications.

4D model helps to detect the inconsistencies in the level of detailing opened ended activities and impossible schedule sequence of a project. This also helps to predict potential time space conflicts and accessibility problems. Automating schedule data preparation and 4D model generations in the design stages of a project can expedite 4D model development and use. Users need to be able to generate 4D model at multiple levels of detail, generate and evaluate alternative scenarios rapidly [6].

The use of 4D models and their associated database on site results in an average of 5% savings in cost growth, 4% savings in schedule growth and 65% savings in rework. Use of these tools, by the project management personnel, pre project planning, design, procurement and material management, construction, start-up and commissioning phases of a project can result in unanticipated savings [7]. There are many benefits that we expected to gain from utilizing the 4D construction model or BIM. 4D visualization of construction process helps planners and practitioners a better understanding of the construction schedule and helps detect any logical errors[8].

2   Research Objectives and Methodology

The purpose of this study was to develop a 4D model with construction activities linked with their schedule and construction space requirements, and simulate the 4D model to detect whether there is any conflict among the activities, time schedule and construction space requirements. This model can be used to detect any conflict during design phases as well as during construction phases. Figure 1 shows the steps that were used to construct a 4D model. The following paragraphs describe in detail the model development methodology.

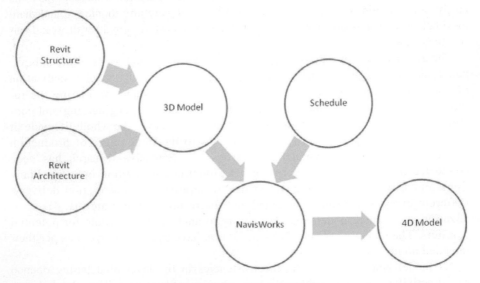

Fig. 1. Steps of creating 4D Model

2.1   Developing a 4D Model

Creating a 3D model: A 3D model of an Academic Building was created using object based modeling software like, Autodesk Revit. The amount of details required in the 3D model depends on the level of detail of construction schedule intended. Based on the contract drawings of the building, a 3D model was created. Figure 2 is an image of the 3D model.

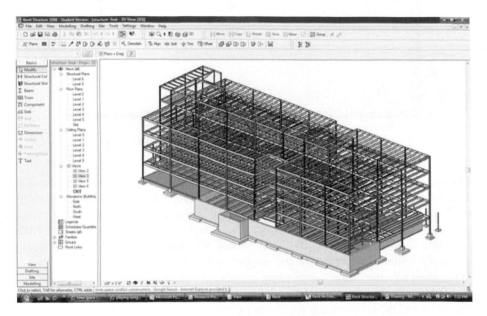

Fig. 2. 3D Model using Revit Structure

Preparing a Work Breakdown Structure (WBS): WBS is a top-down structure that defines the desired end result of a project and is made up of related elements often called tasks and subtasks. Creating a WBS is a key to prepare a constructible schedule. Each level of WBS is assigned with an alphanumeric code that represents the task position within the hierarchical structure. These WBS codes act as a bridge to link 3D models, schedules and space requirements for activities.

Developing a Construction Schedule: A series of activities was added at the lowest level of the WBS hierarchy and was logically linked following the construction process. The schedule information of each activity like duration, predecessors, successors, space requirements, and other information were added in the activity database. Two main methodologies were followed in scheduling of the construction work – (1) Activity based scheduling, and (2) Location based scheduling. The activity-based schedules follow the CPM (Critical Path Method), which can be prepared using MS Project or Primavera, and the location-based schedules follow the line of balance method, which can be prepared using Constructor 2007. In this project, the schedule was done by using MS Project (Figure 3).

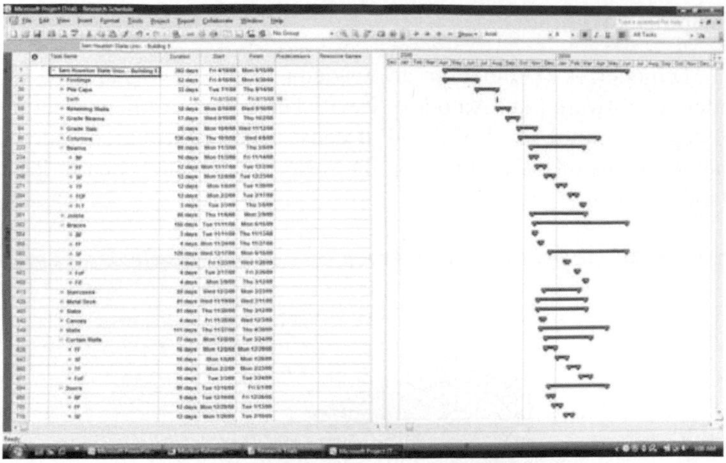

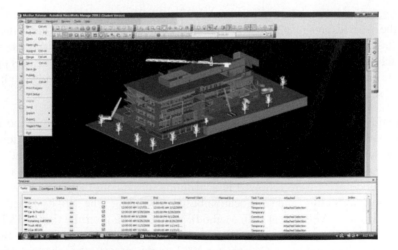

Fig. 3. Developing schedule using MS Project

Integrating 3D Model and Construction Schedule: Once the 3D model and the construction schedule were prepared, they were to be integrated in a common environment to get a 4D model. Each 3D component of the model was linked to the related activity in the schedule. This linking was facilitated the WBS codes in the schedule and component names in the 3D model. Some 4D modeling software automatically detect the related 3D component and respective activity provided there is consistency in the nomenclature of the components in both 3D model and the construction schedule. Latest 4D visualization packages like Jetstream V5 from Navisworks provide a link to import the construction schedules from the latest scheduling packages like MS Project. Figure 4 shows the integrated model.

Fig. 4. Navisworks to incorporate 3D Model and Schedule

2.2 Time-Space Conflict Detection

Creating 3D space required for activities of different tasks: After preparing the 3D model, a volume of space requirement to complete a specific task was developed in Revit Structure. Each volume was identified by different color codes in Navisworks. Each work space requirement and construction activity/task was linked with the schedule. Figure 5 shows the required activity space for corresponding task.

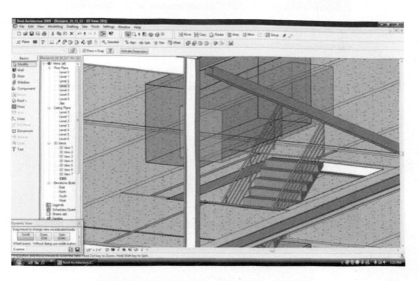

Fig. 5. Required space to complete specific task

Running Simulation: During simulation one can see if there is any conflict between activity with time and spaces requirements or not. If the required areas for two adjacent activities overlapped each other, there will be no conflict when they are scheduled in different time zone (Figure 6). But if the parallel activities occurred in same time zone, there will be conflict (Figure 7). Figure 6-A is showing the required 3D space for an activity indicated by Yellow color when active. When activity is done; that space color turns to neutral transparent color (Figure 6-B). New activity is started indicated by Purple color (Figure 6-C); but no conflict as the adjacent job is completed earlier.

Figure 7-A shows the same type of simulation in different location. 3D volume showing required space for an activity indicated by Yellow color when active. New activity is started indicated by Purple color before finishing the earlier job – showing conflict (Figure 7-B). Figure 7-C shows the next step; earlier work is completed when the second work is still active.

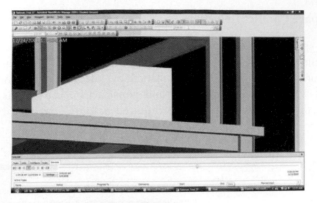

Fig. 6-A

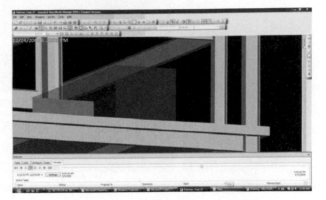

Fig. 6-B

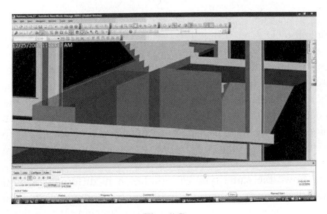

Fig. 6-C

Fig. 6. Activity sequence showing no conflict

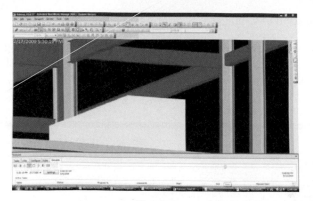

Fig. 7-A

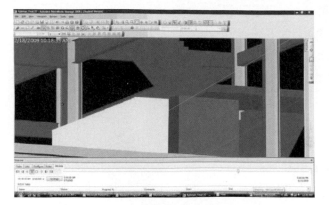

Fig. 7-B

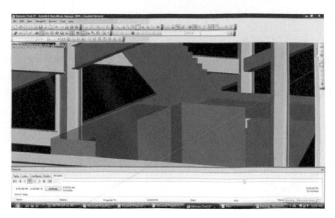

Fig. 7-C

Fig. 7. Activity sequence showing conflict

2.3 Incorporation of Changes

After conflicts were identified, the corrections were made by reviewing the workflow. Adjustment in activities was done by bringing changes in schedule. Figure 8 shows the changes to be made in schedule.

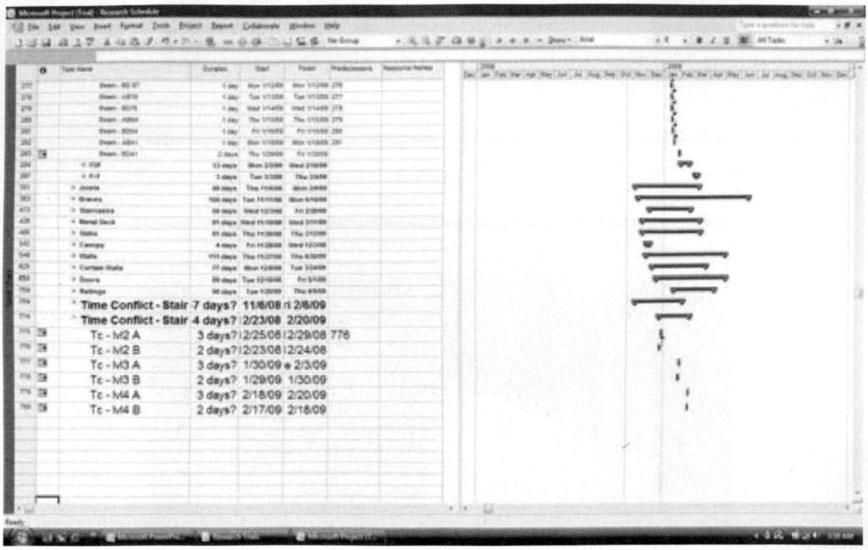

Fig. 8. Changes in schedule to revise work-flow

2.4 Resolving One Clash May Create Other Clash

To avoid time-space clash between two adjacent activities, activity duration of one task can be modified by bringing changes in schedule. Hence one specific conflict can be resolved; but may create another conflict with other activities. A study was conducted to see the after effect of changes in schedule. The following are the steps of the study:

A new space was defined for equipment; and the required area was assumed as 25 SFT (5'X5'). After running simulation, there was no conflict among adjacent activities. Figure 9 shows the simulation. The activity-A is shown in Yellow color (Figure 9A), activity for equipment is shown in Green color (Figure 9-B), and activity-B is shown in Purple color (Figure 9-C).

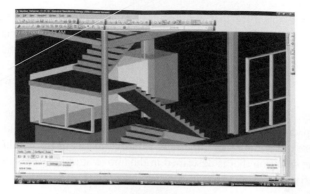

Fig. 9-A

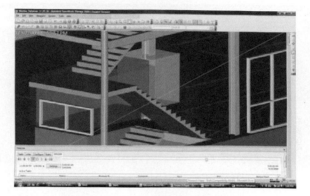

Fig. 9-B

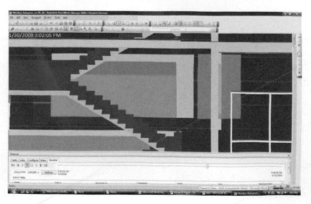

Fig. 9-C

Fig. 9. Simulation showing 3 different activities

If the required space for that equipment changes from 25 to 100 SFT (10'X10'), one can see the after effect from simulation (Figure 10). Figure 10-A is showing conflict; the overlapping between Activity-A and equipment space. After revising the schedule for equipment activity, there is no conflict with Activity-A (Figure 10-B). But new schedule for Equipment activity created a new conflict with Activity-B (Figure 10-C).

In this study, it was shown that changing schedule is not always the solution to resolve Time-Space conflict. In some cases, schedule adjustment could help to avoid clash. But there are some other situations where adjustment in schedule might bring new clash. The situation that is described in the above study requires the management to take alternative measures to avoid conflicts.

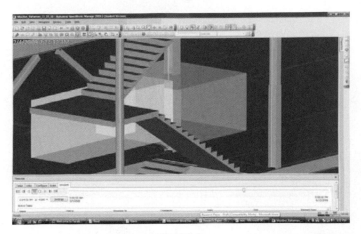

Fig. 10-A

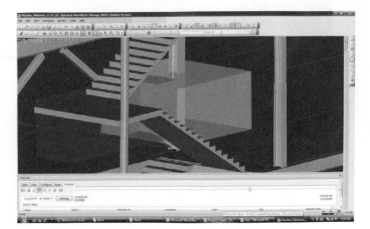

Fig. 10-B

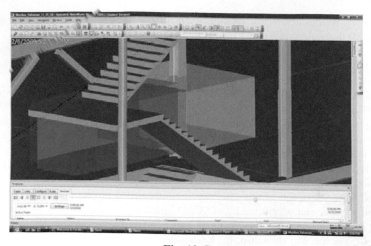

Fig. 10-C

Fig. 10. Simulation showing the after-effect of schedule changes

3 Conclusion/Future Research

Construction space management and scheduling of sequenced activities are important aspects for timely completion of a project within estimated budget. This research explored the effective use of 4D visualization in order to detect time-spaceactivity conflict in pre-construction and during construction. A 3D model of a multistoried building was developed, and each construction activity was linked to schedule and construction space requirements. Various color codes were used for activity and space requirement. The activities and space requirement colors were changed once the task activities were completed. During 4D simulation, these color codes help to detect if there is any conflict between activities and construction space requirements. The model produced the logical evidence that a 4D model could be effectively used in a construction site to detect time-space conflicts. In addition, the 4D model could be integrated into the academic classes to give students a better 4D visualization of time-space-activity conflict detection. However, the model is limited to preliminary planning as it lacks an established relationship with databases and / or servers. Further study should be conducted to discern the methodology for linking SQL servers for integrating different data to parameter cost information such as resource costs, activity completion costs, lost-time accident costs, rework costs, etc. These features could be incorporated into Microsoft Visual Basic to better database information for a more predictive project management model.

References

1. Kamat, V.R., Martinez, J.C.: 3D Visualization of Construction Processes and Products. In: Proceedings of CIT2000 - The CIB-W78, IABSE, EG-SEA-AI International Conference on Construction Information Technology, Reykjavik, Iceland, pp. 506–512 (2000)

McKinney, K., Fischer, M.: Generating, Evaluating and Visualizing Construction Schedules with CAD tools. Automation in Construction 7(6), 433–447 (1998)

3. Akbas, R.: 4D Modeling and Product Model Transformations in Experience Music Project (1998), http://www.stanford.edu/group/4D/4D-home.html (Paper retrieved on November 20, 2005)

4. Akinci, B., Fischer, M., Levitt, R., Carlson, B.: Formalization and Automation of Time-Space Conflict Analysis. J. of Computing in Civil Engineering 6(2), 124–135 (2002)

5. Haque, M.E., Mishra, R.: 5D Virtual Constructions: Designer/Constructor's Perspective. In: Proceedings of the 10th International Conference on Computer and Information Technology (ICCIT 2007), Dhaka, Bangladesh, December 27-29 (2007)

6. Koo, B., Fischer, M.: Feasibility Study of 4D CAD in Commercial Construction. J. Construction Engineering and Management. 126(4), 251–260 (2000)

7. Griffis, F.H., Sturts, C.S.: Fully integrated and automated project process (FIAPP) for the project manager and executive. In: 4D CAD and Visualization in construction: Developments and Applications, pp. 55–73 (2003)

8. Kam, C., Fischer, M., Hanninen, R., Karjalainen, A., Laitinen, J.: The product model and fourth dimension project. ITcon, Vol. 8, Special issue IFC – Product models for the AEC arena (2003), http://www.itcon.org/cgi-bin/works/Show?2003_12

Haptic Texture Rendering Based on Visual Texture Information: A Study to Achieve Realistic Haptic Texture Rendering

Waskito Adi and Suziah Sulaiman

Universiti Teknologi PETRONAS,
Bandar Seri Iskandar, 31750 Tronoh, Perak, Malaysia
waskito@gmail.com, suziah@petronas.com.my

Abstract. Haptic texture rendering has recently received a lot of attention among the haptic community. By adding haptic textures onto an object could enhance its realism. The objective of this paper is to propose a rendering method that could improve such realism. We examine haptic rendering techniques that involve sine waves and Fourier series, and identify any problems that may occur. We argue that haptic texture rendering can employ 2D texture images data to generate the haptic texture, and suggest that wavelet transformations could be used to filter the texture information and generate haptic texture surfaces. Thus, a rendering method based on an image's visual information is proposed. The advantages of this method include the dynamic and instant haptic texture rendering based on the object's visual information extracted from the visual texture.

Keywords: Haptic texture rendering, haptic texture, visual texture, wavelet texture.

1 Introduction

Haptic refers to sensing manipulation through touch. The term haptic is used for studies on active touch of real objects. Haptics can be divided into: (i) human haptics (ii) machine haptics and (iii) computer haptics. Computer haptics involves algorithms and associated with generating and rendering the touch and feel of virtual objects. This area has a close relation with computer graphics and virtual reality.

Computer haptics is growing rapidly; resulting in the emerging of multiple disciplines such as medical, biomedics, neuroscience psychophysics, robot design and control, mathematical modeling and simulation converge to support computer haptics. There are various applications that have emerged and span many areas of human needs such as medical trainers and rehabilitation. In medical application, haptic is integrated into the system to simulate palpation and surgery.

In computer haptics, topics on texture rendering have received an increasing attention [1]. The goal of texture rendering is to create a more realistic virtual object. Such an object if rendered without textures usually feels plain and smooth. By involving haptic texture in rendering objects one can enhance the virtual objects' realism. For example, a cubic object could be perceived as a brick or a foamy box depending on

H. Badioze Zaman et al. (Eds.): IVIC 2009, LNCS 5857, pp. 279–287, 2009.

ow we render the object's texture. When the object is rendered using a rough and stiff surface, it could become a brick, otherwise if rendered using a smooth and soft texture, the object becomes a foamy box.

Developing haptic texture rendering techniques requires a lot of effort. In [2], Miguel developed a texture rendering algorithm and conducted an experiment involving texture interaction between objects. During the haptic rendering process there are several problems that occur. The most common problem in haptic texture rendering is that sometimes the texture becomes unstable. This relates to the complex nature of the haptic rendering and how human deals with the factors contributing to perceptual artifacts. This paper addresses the problem by attempting to improve the haptic texture rendering in order to achieve a richer and a more realistic haptic texture.

This paper is organized as follows: The next section describes the existing research pertaining to texture rendering. Section 3 presents the haptic rendering techniques to be used in our experiments. In Section 4 we explain how the series of experiments have been conducted. Section 5 presents the findings and analysis from the experiments and finally in the last section we conclude and describe our future work.

2 Related Work

Texture is the smallest independent quantity in an object. The simplest and conventional way to create a realistic object is by employing sine waves to generate the texture surfaces [1][3]. Figure 1 illustrates the texture rendering model using sine waves. In [1], Choi and Tan employ sine waves to render the texture surface in order to analyze the stability during haptic texture rendering. Wall in [3] takes a different approach by employing Fourier series to generate haptic texture surface. Sawtooth and square waves have also been used as rendering techniques to produce surface texture [4]. In a medical application such as a dental simulation [5], it is essential to simulate plaques on the virtual tooth. To simulate such textures, sawtooth wave has been employed. To enrich the type of textures stochastic process can be used [4] [6].

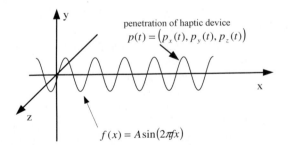

penetration of haptic device
$$p(t) = \left(p_x(t), p_y(t), p_z(t) \right)$$

$$f(x) = A\sin(2\pi f x)$$

Fig. 1. Illustration of the texture rendering method and models employed sine wave

Nowadays, most of the research work conducted on textures in general involve the image and signal processing. When dealing with textures in a haptic domain, image and signal processing is indirectly involved because the characteristics of both textures are quite similar. There are many algorithms in image processing that could be used to generate or reconstruct texture. In [7], Yong and colleagues employ wavelet transform to interpolate and generate the missing pattern in the texture images. In other research [8], Gallagher introduces a new idea of using wavelet decomposition as a basis for nonparametric texture synthesis. The results show an order of magnitude improvement in computational speed and a better approximation of the dominant scale in the synthesized texture.

The closest work to our research is haptic texture rendering based on image processing [6]. Wu in [6] introduces a novel method to render haptic forces based on the visual information obtained from texture images. He employs Fourier transform to reduce the instability during rendering process. He also applies Gaussian kernel on the texture images to interpolate and reduce noise during the process.

3 Techniques for Rendering Haptic Surfaces

When working with textures, the algorithm to process and analyze those textures needs to be dealt with as well. Most of the research on texture analysis involves image processing that employs spectral and spatial analysis. The most common method to analyze texture is using transformation, such as Fourier series, wavelet transform and Gabor filter. Texture can be generated or reconstructed by extracting the information from the actual texture. In image processing field [7] and [8], the researchers employ wavelet decomposition and wavelet reconstruction to reconstruct the texture. To generate a more sophisticated and complex texture, more texture sample is required.

As highlighted in Section 2, the simplest way to generate haptic texture is by using sine waves. The technique involves adjusting the parameters that are the amplitude and frequency. A sine wave to generate surfaces texture is denoted as:

$$f(x) = A\sin(2\pi f x) \tag{1}$$

From equation 1, the texture rendering using sine wave is illustrated in Figure 1. In order to achieve a more realistic texture, Wall [3] employed Fourier series to generate the surfaces of the objects. Fourier series can be denoted as:

$$f(x) = \frac{a_0}{2} \sum_{n=1}^{N} \left[a_n \cos(nx) + b_n \sin(nx) \right] \tag{2}$$

where:

$$a_n = \frac{1}{\pi} \int_{-\pi}^{\pi} f(t)\cos(nt)dt, \qquad n \geq 0 \tag{3}$$

$$b_n = \frac{1}{\pi} \int_{-\pi}^{\pi} f(t)\sin(nt)dt, \qquad n \geq 1 \tag{4}$$

decomposing the texture information, Fourier transform is employed. Fourier transform and Fourier series is denoted as below:

$$F(w) = \int_{-\infty}^{\infty} f(x)e^{-2\pi i \omega x} \partial x \tag{5}$$

The inverse of Fourier transform, which allows going from spectrum to the signal is as follows:

$$f(x) = \int_{-\infty}^{\infty} F(x)e^{2\pi i \omega x} \partial \omega \tag{6}$$

With Fourier transform, it is possible to analyze and extract information using frequency spectrum from signals or images. In this process the texture images can be decomposed into combination of sine and cosine waves (equation 3). Except for Fourier transform, it is also possible to employ wavelet transform to render texture surfaces. Unlike Fourier transform which uses sine and cosine waves as a basis of transformation, wavelet transform uses small transient wave to transform and analyze the signal. Wavelet transform can also be used to reconstruct images or waves like Fourier series.

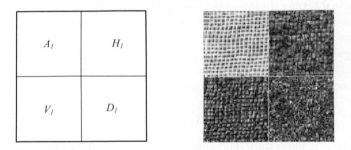

Fig. 2. Texture decomposition using wavelet db-8

To analyze a reconstruct texture or signal, wavelet decomposition or wavelet packet is used. In analyzing a 2D signal, it is common to use a 2D wavelet packet (2-WPT) or 2D wavelet decomposition (2D-WDT). The difference between a 2D-WPT and 2D-WDT is the way how it decomposes the signal. In 2D-WPT, it will recursively decompose signal, including the approximation and detailed signal. On the other hand 2D-WDT decomposes only the approximation coefficient (Figure 2). The 2D-WPT can be denoted as:

$$A_1 = C_{4k,(i,j)}^{p+1} = \sum_m \sum_n h(m)h(n)C_{k,(m+2i,n+2j)}^{p} \tag{7}$$

$$H_1 = C_{4k+1,(i,j)}^{p+1} = \sum_m \sum_n h(m)h(n)C_{k,(m+2i,n+2j)}^{p} \tag{8}$$

$$V_1 = C^{p+1}_{4k+2,(i,j)} = \sum_m \sum_n h(m)h(n)C^p_{k,(m+2i,n+2j)} \tag{9}$$

$$D_1 = C^{p+1}_{4k+3,(i,j)} = \sum_m \sum_n h(m)h(n)C^p_{k,(m+2i,n+2j)} \tag{10}$$

4 Methodology

The techniques used for creating haptic texture surfaces are the sine waves, Fourier series and wavelet transform. Each technique was used in three separate experiments. The overall objective of these experiments is to investigate for a more realistic and richer haptic texture rendering. Phantom Omni haptic device is used in all experiments to generate and feel the force feedback. The research method involves examining each technique in terms of its haptic stability and advantages offered.

4.1 Artificial Haptic Texture

The first experiment involves generating haptic feedback using sine wave. To render the surface using sine wave, we read the position of the haptic device stylus. By employing equation 1 and read the x and z point in the haptic device, we generated the texture surface.

Referring to equation 1, the sine wave equation becomes:

$$y = f(x) = A\left(\sin(2\pi f x) + \sin(2\pi f z)\right) \tag{11}$$

By adjusting the frequency and the amplitude of the formula, we can generate different kind of texture surface. This method is quite simple and effective to render a simple haptic texture. However, for rendering a more sophisticated texture, it is quite difficult because it only has two adjustable parameter, amplitude and frequency.

In the second experiment, we employ the Fourier series in order to generate the artificial textures. The method of this rendering is quite similar to the sine wave. This method read stylus position and then calculates texture amplitude value. Using the Fourier series we generated the square and sawtooth waves to obtain the texture surface.

4.2 Visual Texture to Haptic Texture

For the third experiment, we propose a haptic rendering algorithm that employs wavelet transform and visual information from the actual visual texture to create the haptic surface. The steps involved to perform the algorithm are as follows:

1. The original images for image sampling and pre processing were taken using a digital camera. There were 46 types of different clothes images were used. To obtain the texture contour, we transform the color image into grayscale image.

2. Gaussian filter was employed to eliminate the noise in the image. This filter is a low pass filter that will remove the high frequency signal. The function is to smooth the edge of the image.
3. Rather than filtering the image, the next process is to transform the image by using the wavelet transform. This results in obtaining the coefficient and texture information. By using the right subband, we reconstruct the texture and use the data as haptic rendering data.

Since texture heights map are acquired. The haptic texture is generated through binding the texture height map to virtual surface or virtual clothes. Schematic representation of the haptic texture is shown in Figure 3.

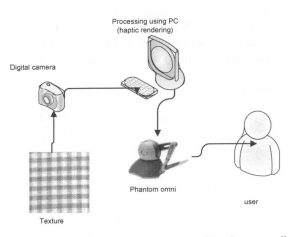

Fig. 3. Illustration of schematic representation of haptic texture display

The force generated while virtual stylus contacting the virtual surface texture is modeled as resultant force of texture force F_t and friction force F_f. The texture force is calculated as follows:

$$F_t = kd(x, y) \tag{12}$$

k is a constant factor that adjust the height of the map texture. $d(x,y)$ is the texture map, where x and y is the coordinate position in the texture height map. During the haptic rendering, the texture will be generated based on the texture map (equation 10).The friction force for the surface can be modeled as :

$$F_f = k_l \Delta hn \tag{13}$$

The result of the rendering in 3D plane by using texture visual information is presented in Figure 4.

k_l is the friction coefficient which is different for several texture process. Since the friction and texture forces have been obtained, the force for rendering process can be denoted as:

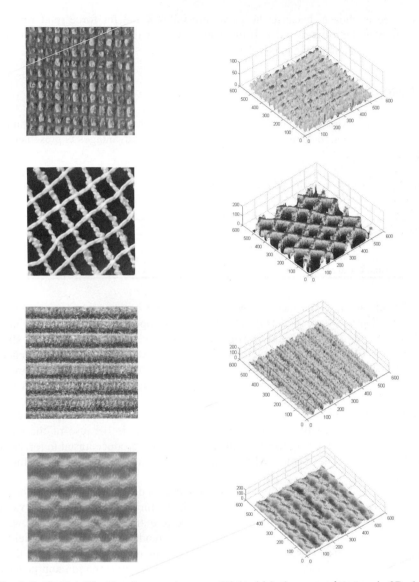

Fig. 4. (Left side): The visual texture images; (Right side): the mapped texture in 3D plane

$$F_c = F_t + F_f \tag{14}$$

During the test, we manage to normalize the texture map height. The maximum of the texture map is normalized into 1. This means that the value of the haptic texture is between 0 and 1.

$$0 < F_c < 0.8$$

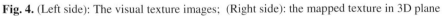

This range is chosen, because the maximum index value for force rendering using phantom is in the range 0 and 1. If the value is greater that 1 it will produce unstable forces and will damage the haptic device [9].

5 Results and Discussion

From the three experiments conducted, a table of summary that identify the potential of each rendering algorithm in terms of its stability and advantages is presented. This is shown in Table 1.

Table 1. The stability and advantages of rendering using sine wave, Fourier series and texture visual images

Rendering algorithm	Stability	Advantage
Sine wave	Stable	Simple and stable
Fourier series	Not stable	Flexible
Visual texture	Not stable	More realistic

The result of the experiment shows that sine wave can produce haptic rendering surface for haptic texture rendering. This finding is supported by [1] and [3] who have used the technique. Using sine wave for haptic rendering is simple and slightly straight forward. This method is suitable for simple texture because it only generates sine wave with different frequency and different amplitude for different texture type. The stability of this rendering technique is good because it only deals with simple wave and data.

Based on the Fourier series, we generated the square and sawtooth waves. The problems appear when the square wave was used. This is because of the extreme value changes. When the stylus swept the texture, it will produce unstable forces. This rendering algorithm has been used by Wall to render and manipulate the texture surfaces [3].

In the last experiment, we employed the texture rendering algorithm based on the visual information of the texture and wavelet. The texture image provides the value of the haptic texture. In order to eliminate noise and to extract the edge feature, we employ wavelet and Gaussian filter. During the haptic rendering we map the pixel value with the haptic texture surface. The advantages of this rendering method are the texture can be rendered instantly based on the texture visual information and provides a more realistic haptic texture. The problem encountered with this technique is that the rendering is not quite stable.

6 Conclusion and Future Work

Haptic texture can be generated using sine wave, Fourier series and combination of visual texture and wavelet transform. The experimental study indicates that the combination of visual texture and wavelet transform provides a more realistic texture. From this technique, the height map of the texture is obtained based on the visual texture and wavelet transform. The texture friction and surface is transformed from image data with no specialized 3D geometrical scanning device used. However, the problem that arises in this experiment when we employed wavelet and texture images is the stability issue during haptic rendering. For future work, we need to improve the technique and test the effectiveness of the proposed method in order to overcome the instability issue.

References

1. Choi, S., Tan, H.Z.: An Analysis of Perceptual Instability during Haptic Texture Rendering. In: 10th Symposium on Haptic Interfaces for Virtual Environment and Teleoperator Systems, p. 129. IEEE Computer Society, Washington (2002)
2. Otaduy, M.A., Jain, N., Sud, A., Lin, M.C.: Haptic Display of Interaction between Textured Models. In: VIS 2004 – 15th IEEE Visualization Conference, Austin, TX, pp. 297–304 (2004)
3. Wall, S.: An Investigation of Temporal and Spatial Limitation of Haptic Interfaces. PhD Thesis, Department of Cybernetics, University of Reading (2004)
4. Campion, G., Gosline, A.H.C., Hayward, V.: Passive Viscous Haptic Textures. In: Symposium on Haptic interfaces for Virtual Environment and Teleoperator Systems, pp. 379–380 (2008)
5. Somrang, N., Chotikakamthorn, N.: Interactive Haptic Simulation of Dental Plaque Removal. In: International Symposium on Communication and Information Technology, pp. 319–322 (2006)
6. Wu, J., Song, A., Zou, C.: A Novel Haptic Texture Display Based on Image Processing. In: IEEE International Conference on Robotics and Biomimetics, pp. 1315–1320 (2007)
7. Choi, Y., Koo, J.-K., Lee, N.Y.: Image Reconstruction using the Wavelet Transform for Positron Emission Tomography. IEEE Transaction on Medical Imaging 20(11), 1188–1193 (2001)
8. Gallagher, C., Kokaram, A.: Nonparametric Wavelet Based Texture Synthesis. IEEE International Conference on Image Processing, 11-462-5 (2005)
9. OpenHaptic API Reference Manual, SensAble Technologies, Inc., USA (2005)

Multi-tiered S-SOA, Parameter-Driven New Islamic Syariah Products of Holistic Islamic Banking System (HiCORE): Virtual Banking Environment

B.Z. Halimah[1], A. Azlina[1], T.M. Sembok[1], I. Sufian[1], Sharul Azman M.N.[1],
A.B. Azuraliza[1], A. O. Zulaiha[1], O. Nazlia[1], A. Salwani[1], A. Sanep[1],
M.T. Hailani[1], M.Z. Zaher[1], J. Azizah, M.Y. Nor Faezah[1], W.O. Choo[1],
Chew Abdullah[2], and B. Sopian[2]

[1] Faculty of Information Science and Technology
Universiti Kebangsaan Malaysia, 43600 Bangi, Selangor
[2] Fuziq Software Sdn Bhd
hbz@ftsm.ukm.my

Abstract. The Holistic Islamic Banking System (HiCORE), a banking system suitable for virtual banking environment, created based on university-industry collaboration initiative between Universiti Kebangsaan Malaysia (UKM) and Fuziq Software Sdn Bhd. HiCORE was modeled on a multi-tiered Simple - Services Oriented Architecture (S-SOA), using the parameter-based semantic approach. HiCORE's existence is timely as the financial world is looking for a new approach to creating banking and financial products that are interest free or based on the Islamic Syariah principles and jurisprudence. An interest free banking system has currently caught the interest of bankers and financiers all over the world. HiCORE's Parameter-based module houses the Customer-information file (CIF), Deposit and Financing components. The Parameter based module represents the third tier of the multi-tiered Simple SOA approach. This paper highlights the multi-tiered parameter-driven approach to the creation of new Islamiic products based on the 'dalil' (Quran), 'syarat' (rules) and 'rukun' (procedures) as required by the syariah principles and jurisprudence reflected by the semantic ontology embedded in the parameter module of the system.

Keywords: Virtual banking environment, multi-tiered S-SOA architecture, parameter-driven approach, semantic ontology, Syariah ontology.

1 Introduction

Islamic banks like conventional banks, are to be profitable organizations. Their aim is to gain profit but based on the Islamic rules, laws and traditions, they are not allowed to deal with interest (riba') or to engage in any trade or business prohibited by Islam (gharar). Whilst conventional banking is believed to have begun in the middle of the twelfth century, Islamic banking first emerged only in the late seventies and earl

H. Badioze Zaman et al. (Eds.): IVIC 2009, LNCS 5857, pp. 288–301, 2009.

eighties, although the history of Islamic banking activities can be traced back to the birth of Islam. Thus, although Islamic banking only emerged as a new reality in the international financial scene since the 1970s, its philosophies and principles are not new. In fact, Islamic banking principles have been outlined more than 1,400 years ago in the Holy Qur'an and the Sunnah of the Prophet Muhammad (p.b.u.h.) [1]. The emergence of the Islamic banking is evident of the revival of Islam and the desire of Muslims to live all aspects of their lives in accordance with the teachings of Islam.

Islamic banking and finance has become an alternative approach to banking and finance system throughout the world not just for the Muslim customers but the other customers as well [3]; [4]; [11]. This approach offers new opportunities for institutions and vendors to service a previously unexplored customer segment. The growing demands of the world's 1.3 billion Muslims for Syariah-compliant products and services has led to greater standardization of the Islamic Banking and Finance regulations [1]; [2];[11]; [12]. Financial institutions all over the world have now created a range of products to address this new market demand, although there are still many significant operational challenges to overcome [5]; [6]; [7]; [8]; This has offered many new opportunities for technology and services firms. A group of researchers in Universiti Kebangsaan Malaysia (from three faculties: Computer Science and Information Technology; Economics and Business and Islamic Studies) in collaboration with a software company called Fuziq Software Sdn. Bhd. embarked on a research developing a Holistic Islamic Banking System, HiCORE.

2   Problem Statement

The main problem with the current scenario in Islamic banking is that the systems available in the market have various limitations. In other words, there is currently no one totally holistic Islamic Banking System, that covers both deposits and financing that is based on the syariah principles. What is available today in the banks both in Malaysia and overseas are what one would term as 'Islamic windows' [11]. Most of the systems available too, does not allow the possibility of creating new Islamic products easily [11]; [12]. Some of the systems such as MISYS Banking System, IPBS and PTC Banking System are all either partly or not at all Syariah compliant. Due to the fact that HiCORE is designed based on the parameter-based semantic approach, new products can be easily created. HiCORE makes it possible for banks to generate new Islamic products based on current and future Syariah principles.

3   Overall Design of HiCORE

In order to overcome the problems faced by the banking system in implementing Islamic banking in Malaysia and the other countries practicing Islamic banking, a solution in the form of a simple SOA (Services Oriented Architecture) parameter-based semantic approach . The main objectives of this research were as follows:

a. To conduct a comprehensive literature review on the domains involved in the development of the Holistic Islamic Banking System (HiCORE)
b. To determine and document the Systems Requirement Specifications (SRS) of HiCORE
c. To design and develop a simple SOA architecture model for the Holistic Islamic Banking System (HiCORE)
d. To design and develop a parameter-based HiCORE system
e. To develop a middleware called Enterprise Application Integrator (EAI) that can link legacy and current systems already available in Banks with HiCORE.

The overall design of the system was conceptualised on a multi-tiered simple Services Oriented Architecture (SOA) model as can be observed in Figure 1.

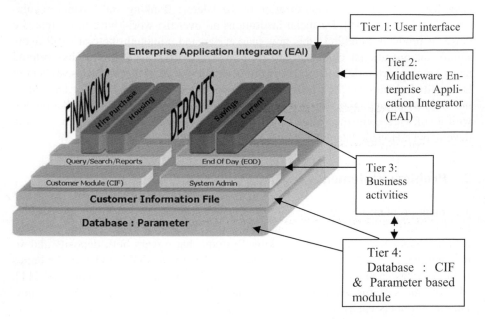

Fig. 1. Multi-tiered Conceptual Model of HiCORE for Virtual Banking

Generally, SOA uses the "find-bind-execute" paradigm [13] through which service providers register their services, and service consumers find the services they desire. Although HiCORE was modeled on the SOA, not all attributes of SOA was implemented in the system. The researchers applied what is known as the S-SOA or Simple SOA. The S-SOA however, still maintained the "find-bind-execute" paradigm which involved basic entities as follows:

i.   Service Consumer : To execute a service, a service consumer needs to locate one from the registry, bind to the service and execute the service

ii. Web services was used in implementing this S-SOA-Based architecture. The services are not invoked directly by client applications. Instead, client applications invoke services indirectly via the EAI subsystem which acts as a service proxy. The subsystem, on behalf of the client applications, does the calling of the web services, passing the required parameters and reading the returned results. This approach, thus, decouples services from the client applications. One advantage of this is that the extra layer of indirection can be leveraged to implement useful features, such as logging for data mining purposes and process coordination.

iii. The services deployed within HiCORE are defined based on the basic hierarchical service structure which can generally be divided into two general categories, namely, banking-related services and non-banking-related services. Non-banking-related services refer to services that are not directly related to banking processes and operations. An example of such services are those at the "HiCORE system level" which are related to the functioning of HiCORE itself. The other category, i.e. banking-related services, can be subdivided further to two subcategories. The first of which refers to basic banking services encompassing basic banking operations such as cash withdrawal and creation of new customers. The other subcategory groups services are related to Islamic Banking.

The multi-tiered model of HiCORE can be categorised simply as follows:

Tier 1: is the user interface of the system HiCORE. The interface was designed based on the cognitivist-intuitive model. The user interface is user friendly and helps users to intuitively choose the right icons or button to start their cognitive process of conducting their banking businesses or operations.

Tier 2: is the existence of the middleware known as the Enterprise Application Integrator (EAI) which has the functionality of linking legacy systems to HiCORE. In other words, EAI also functions as a service proxy on behalf of client applications calling of the web services, passing the required parameters and reading the returned results.

Tier 3: involves all the operations and business activities of Deposit and Financing. It is at this tier that components of the operations such as openings of current and saving accounts and hire purchase and housing loans are conducted. The tier also houses components on queries, end-of the-day and system admin.

Tier 4: involves the data warehouse component that houses the CIF and the parameter modules. This is the novelty of this system. The parameter-driven approach adopted in this data warehouse allows the creation of current and new Islamic products based on the Syariah principles and jurisprudence.

Details on the parameter-driven approach adopted in the creation of new Islamic Syariah products are explained below.

4   Conceptualisation of Parameter - Driven Module

The parameter - driven module of HiCORE as mentioned earlier is housed in the 4th Tier of the system, i.e. in the Data Warehouse of HiCORE and its architecture is as hown in Figure 2.

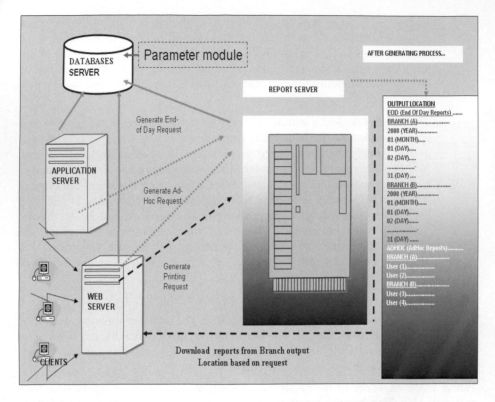

Fig. 2. The architecture of the data warehouse of HiCORE

Specifically, a parameter-driven module is one that utilises parameters to define certain characteristics of the module. The module is expected to produce different results when variables within the parameter set are changed. Everything else being equal (i.e using the same set of programs), the module will be able to process different types of deposit and financing products, deliver the correct results to the users. One of the challenges in designing a parameterised module in an Islamic Banking System is the definition of processing rules for both Deposit and Financing products. These rules must be guided by the Syariah principles and jurisprudence. This can be observed from the features of the Parameter-Driven module as indicated in Figure 3.

When creating Deposit and Financing products in HiCORE, it is required to specify what type of Syariah principles the product will adopt. For example, it is highly plausible to create a new Al-Wadiah Savings Account strictly based on Wadiah Yad Dhamanah, Mudharabah or Qard principles or its combination. This can be observed in Figure 3. In is anticipated, since Islam is a religion of all times,

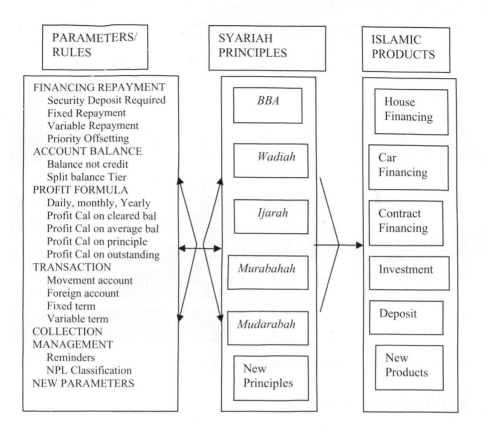

Fig. 3. Features of the Parameter-Driven Module of HiCORE

new Syariah principles may be necessary to create due to changes in social, economic and political climate in the future. The parameter-driven module will be able to allow this.

In order to allow the creation of new Islamic products based on the Syariah laws and jurisprudence, semantic technology needed to be applied to the engine, so that the parameters or rules can be applied to the right Syariah principles for the right Islamic products required. This was done by creating semantic ontology based on financial syariah ontology. The first step is creating the mapping of rules, syariah principles and possible new products as can be observed in Figure 4.

The next step is to create the financial Syariah ontology. An example of the financial Syariah Ontology is as shown in Figure 5. This ontology created was then embedded in the engine of the parameter module in order to allow the creation of new Islamic products based on Syariah principles.

	Syariah Principle		Al-Wadiah	Qard al-hassan	Mudharabah	Musyarakah	Murabahah	Bai Bithaman Ajil	Bai Al-Istisna	Bai' Al Salam	Bai' al inah	Bay Ad-Dayn	Bay Al-Istijrar	AITAB	Ijarah	Ijarah Wal Iqtina	Ijarah Thumma al-Hibah
	Agreed by both parties																
Capital	Cash		√	√	√	√											
	Goods/commercial value	Mixed				√											
		Not nessesary equal				√											
	Eligible for selling and buying																
	Own by leasor														√	√	√	√
Profit	Distribution Ratio	Mutual Agreement			√	– √	√										
		Capital Contribution				√ –											
	Predetermined				√	√	√	√									
Hibah	Hibah-from Bank		√														
	Hibah-from Customer				√												
Ujrah														√			
Diskaun												√	√				
Effort	Distribution	Investor			√ + √												

Fig. 4. Mapping of Rules, Syariah Principles and Possible New products

5 Parameter Module

The Parameter module for new product creation can be accessed through the main page of the system as can be observed in Figure 6. As can be seen from the print screen of the system, HiCORE has eight modules as follows:

    i.   Islamic Banking Concept module
    ii.   Branch Delivery System module
    iii. CIF module
    iv. Report Module
    v.   Blotter
    vi. Deposit
    vii. Financing
   viii. Parameter module

As mentioned earlier, the Parameter Module allows users to create new products based on the syariah principles. The module has various functionalities that allows users to not only create new products but update, delete and make inquiry or search for the right or required Syariah principles.

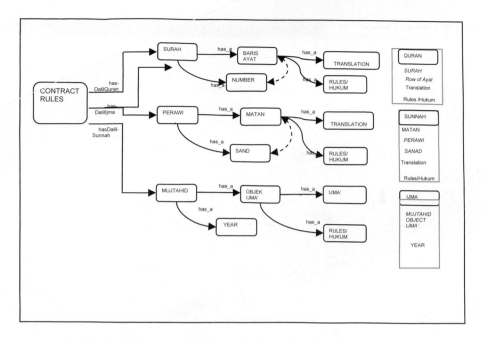

Fig. 5. An Example of the Semantic Ontology Created for HiCORE

Table 1. Access Navigation for Parameter Module

Screen Mode	Access Buttons Provided / Replaced	Remarks
New	Save and Cancel buttons,	**Save** button will be enabled only when the Main Field is keyed in.
Update	Update and Cancel buttons	If current record is not Active Update is not Allowed. **Update** button will be enabled when there are changes in the input fields.
Delete	OK and Cancel buttons	If current record is not Active Delete is not Allowed.
Inquiry	Search and Cancel buttons.	Both buttons are enabled.

The 'New', 'Update', 'Delete' and 'Inquiry' option buttons or functionalities are enabled depending on the user access right option as shown in Table 1.

The flow of the Parameter module and its Sub modules as well as its functionalities is shown in Figure 7. For example if an Inquiry on a Syariah principle *Murabahah* is made : users will access the Syariah Principle Code Description sub module and search for *Murabahah* . The system will allow the user to view the

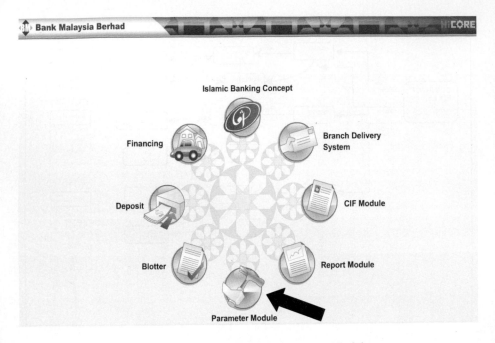

Fig. 6. Main page of HiCORE: Parameter Module

Dalil or Source (Verses of Quran in Arabic and English); show the Rukun → (the procedures); and the Syarat → (the rules); the A/C Characteristic (Show the rules) . So it is if users want to create new Islamic products, they can search for the right principles to be adopted. The correct principles selected can then be saved, updated, edited and confirmed. Should the user wants to delete the record, it is also possible.

The novelty of this system as can be observed from the flow is that there is no Islamic banking system available anywhere in the world that allows users to create new products through parameter-driven approach and also allows users to check on the source of the principle from a *Dalil*, the *Rukun* and the *Syarat* . This not only educates the bank officers involved in handling the Islamic products but also the customers who wants to know about the Islamic products offered. Both banks and clients will be more confident with the products involved. Figures 8-12 shows print screens of the Parameter module and its functionalities.

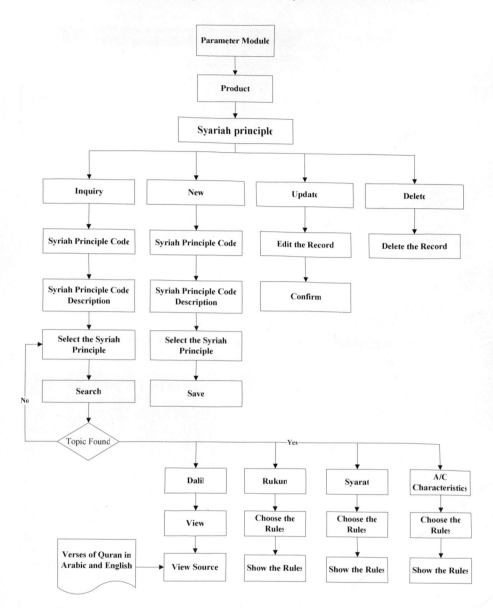

Fig. 7. Flow of the sub module on the creation of new Islamic Syariah products

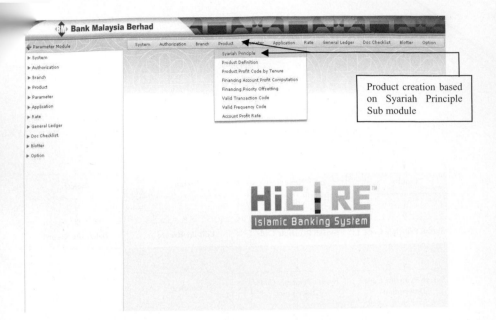

Fig. 8. Parameter module: Creation of Product through Syariah Principle

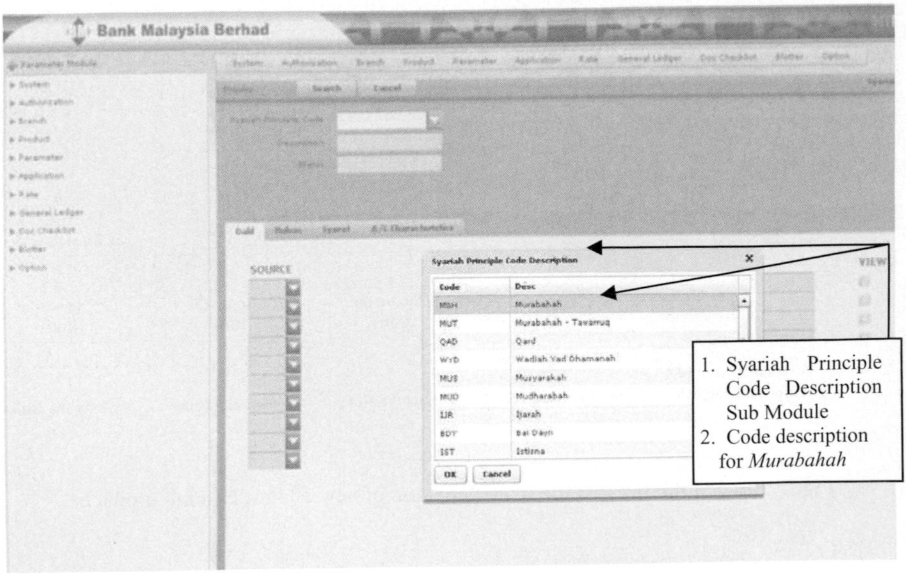

Fig. 9. Parameter module: Syariah Principle Code Description for product *Murabahah*

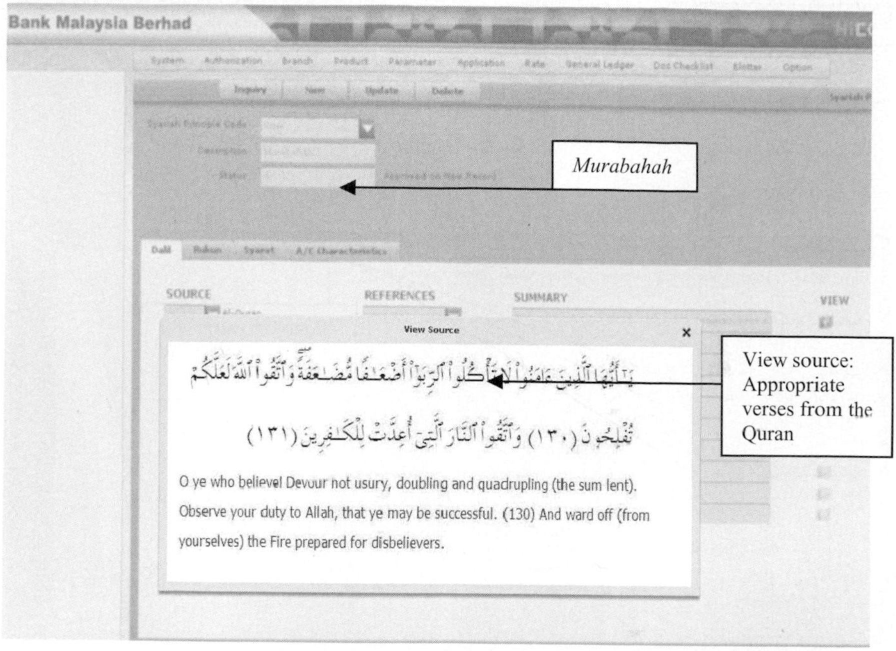

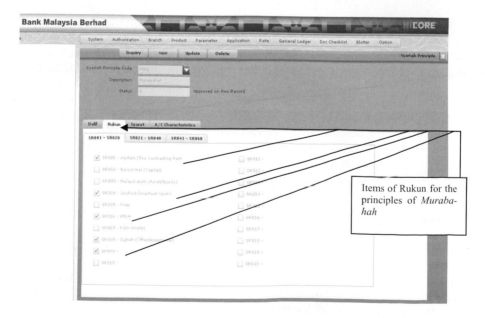

Fig. 10. Paramnetr Module: View Source shows related verses from the Quran

Fig. 11. Parameter Module: View *Rukun* (Rules of Syariah Principles)

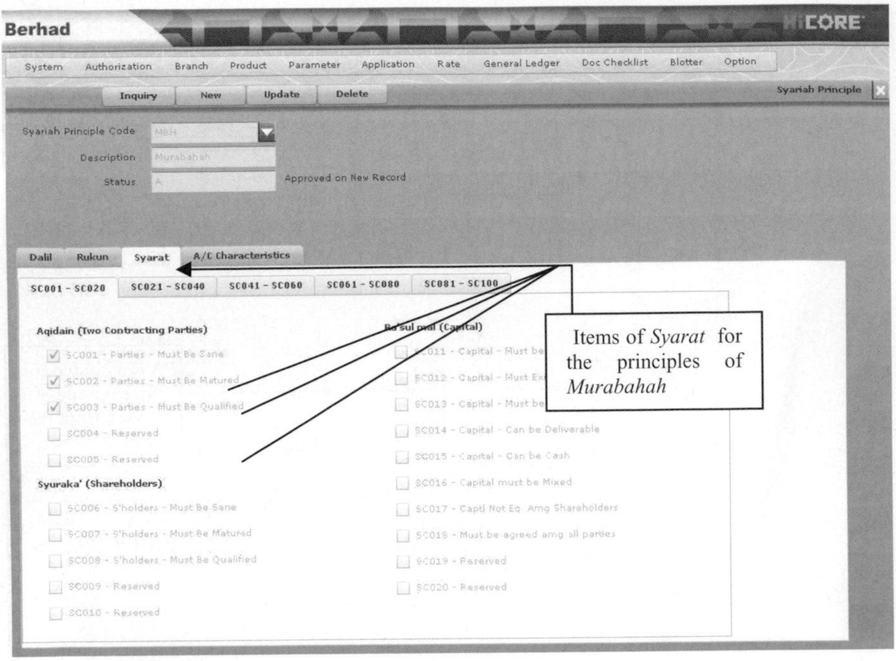

Fig. 12. Parameter Module: View *Syarat* (Rules of Syariah Principles)

6 Conclusion

The Multi-Tiered Simple Services Oriented Architecture (S-SOA) approach with its middleware, the Enterprise Application Integrator (EAI), allows HiCORE to be inter-operable irrespective of any platforms used by Banks. This also means that any legacy systems of Banks can be easily linked to this system. The system is modular, so banks need not adopt the whole system of HiCORE. Banks can choose the modules and add to their current available system. The Parameter module of HiCORE is a novelty of the system. There is no systems currently known that allows the creation of new Islamic products based on the Syariah principles using a semantic ontology embedded in the engine of the system.

References

[1] Lee, M.P., Detta, I.J.: Islamic Banking and Finance Law. Pearson Malaysia Sdn Bhd, Petaling Jaya (2007)
[2] El-Hawary, D.: Regulating Islamic Financial Institutions. World Bank, New York (2004)
[3] Saleh, N.A.: Unlawful gain and legitimate profit in Islamic Law: Riba, Ghahar, and Islamic Banking. Cambridge University Press, Cambridge (1986)
[4] El-Hawary, D.: Regulating Islamic Finanacial Institutions. World Bank, New York (2004)

[5] Grais, W., El-Hawary, D.: Islamic Financial Services and Microfinance. World Bank, New York (2005)

[6] Uzair, M.: Interest Free Banking. Nice Printing Press, New Delhi (2000)

[7] Wilson, R.: The contribution of Muhammed Baqir al-Sadr to Contemporary Islamic Economic Thought. Journal of Islamic Studies 9(1), 46–59 (1998)

[8] Wison, R.: Islamic Financial Markets. Routledge, London (1990)

[9] Wade, I.: Islamic Finanace in the Global Economy. Edinburgh University Press, Edinburgh (2000)

[10] Chapra, M.U.: The need for new economic system. Review of Islamic Economics 1(1), 93–103 (1991)

[11] Malaysia, Prime Minister's Department, Industrialisation from an Islamic Perspective. Isnstitute of Islamic Understanding. Kuala Lumpur: EPU, Prime Minister's Department (1993)

[12] Hisham, K.B., Safar, M.S., Rohani, M.: Assessing production effeciency of Islamic Banks and Conventional Bank Islamic Windows in Malaysia. In: MPRA Paper. University of Munich, Germany (2008)

[13] Mahmoud, Q.H.: Service-Oriented-Architecture (SOA) and Web Services. Sun Microsystems Inc., New York (2005)

Tangible Interaction in Learning Astronomy through Augmented Reality Book-Based Educational Tool

Aw Kien Sin and Halimah Badioze Zaman

Faculty of Information Science and Technology
Universiti Kebangsaan Malaysia, 43600 Bangi, Selangor
awkiensin@yahoo.com, hbz@ftsm.ukm.my

Abstract. Live Solar System (LSS) is an Augmented Reality book-based educational tool. Augmented Reality (AR) has its own potential in the education field, because it can provide a seamless interaction between real and virtual objects. LSS applied the Tangible Augmented Reality approach in designing its user interface and interaction. Tangible Augmented Reality is an interface which combines the Tangible User Interface and Augmented Reality Interface. They are naturally complement each other. This paper highlights the tangible interaction in LSS. LSS adopts the 'cube' as the common physical object input device. Thus, LSS does not use the traditional computer input devices such as the mouse or keyboard. To give users a better exploration experience, Visual Information Seeking Mantra principle was applied in the design of LSS. Hence, LSS gives users an effective interactive-intuitive horizontal surface learning environment.

Keywords: Tangible Augmented Reality, Tangible User Interface, Augmented Reality, virtual environment, tangible interaction.

1 Introduction

Augmented Reality (AR) superimposes virtual objects in the real environment by registering in 3D and giving real time interactivity to users [1][2]. In 1965, Ivan Sutherland created the first AR by building the first Head-Mounted-Displays (HMD) which can display a simple wireframe cube overlaid on the real world [3]. In 1990, the term AR was coined by Boeing in a project, with the intention of helping their workers assemble cables into aircraft [4]. AR is a variation of Virtual Reality (VR) [1], therefore, both have the same fundamental elements, namely virtual objects, real-time response and visual equipment [5]. However, they are different in a few aspects. AR only superimposes virtual objects on the real objects, where the real environment can still be seen by users, as showed in Figure 1. In VR, the real environment is totally replaced with the virtual environment. Hence, VR will limit user activities within a room area because users cannot see the obstructs around them. Whereas, outdoor activities can be carried out by using AR, because the real environment still exists in AR [6]. VR and AR both have a remarkable requirement differences in the depth of immersion [7]. The main objective of VR is a totally immersive artificial environment, which requires high level of realism of virtual environment, but that is not a necessary goal in AR [5].

H. Badioze Zaman et al. (Eds.): IVIC 2009, LNCS 5857, pp. 302–313, 2009.

Fig. 1. Example of Augmented Reality in LSS. Unlike VR, user can see the real environment.

For the rest of the paper, we will first review the role of AR in education, and Tangible Augmented Reality as user interface in Section 2.0. Section 3.0 describes the implementation process of LSS such as the system work flow and the applied interaction techniques, and section 4.0 concludes the paper.

2 AR and Augmented Virtuality

2.1 AR in Education

A Reality-Virtuality Continuum was proposed by Milgram & Kishino [7] to explain the relationship between real and virtual environment. According to the continuum (Figure 2), real environment is located on the left end side of the continuum and the virtual environment on the other hand, is located on the right side. AR and augmented virtuality (AV) are located in between them. In the continuum, AR position is closer to the real environment, and this means that there is a higher proportion of real environment in AR. Whereas, AV is closer to the virtual environment because of its higher proportion of virtual environment. Mixed Reality however, is a domain which contains all these elements mentioned between the real and virtual environment.

In recent years, a number of AR applications have been widely applied in various domains, such as military, entertainment, medical and education. In storytelling, MagicBook [8] allows users to read the book and see the virtual objects through handheld displays (HHD). Without using any AR displays, users still can read the text on the book, look at the pictures and flip the pages. Augmented Chemistry [9] is an example of the implementation of AR in science learning. It is a workbench consisting of a table and a rear-projection screen. Augmented Chemistry has helped users to understand the molecules or atoms structure by showing the structure in 3-Dimension. Users still uses booklets, gripper and cube to interact with these molecules and atoms models. In children's education, 'The Book of Colours' [10] uses AR to explain the basic theory and concepts of colours through Head-Mounted-Displays (HMD). The children can interact and observe the visual feedback from 3-Dimension virtual character. AR is not only applied in formal education, but it is also applied in informal

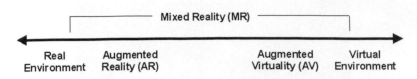

Fig. 2. Reality-Virtuality Continuum (Source: Milgram & Kishino, 1994)

education. Orlando Science Center in US had used AR to show sea creatures. Visitors can navigate a Rover through the ocean environment, to explore reptiles and fishes in DinoDigs exhibition hall [11].

AR is able to enrich educational benefits by supporting seamless interaction with both the real and virtual environment, using tangible interface metaphor for object manipulation, and offers smooth transition between reality and virtuality [12]. Shelton and Hedley [13] explored the used of AR in teaching undergraduates on earth-sun relationship in terms of axial tilt and solstices, and found that AR is useful in teaching subjects where students cannot possibly experience it first hand in the real world. Besides, AR can clearly show spatial concepts, temporal concepts and contextual relationships between real and virtual objects, and all these factors enable AR to be a powerful educational tool [14].

2.2 Tangible Augmented Reality

Tangible User Interface (TUI), was introduced by Ishii & Ulmer in 1997. They defined TUI as augmenting the real physical world by coupling digital information to everyday physical object [15]. TUI provides a physical interaction by turning physical object into input and output device for computer interface [16]. Physical interaction is able to provide direct, manipulability and intuitive understanding to users [17]. For instance, it is very natural for humans to pick up, rotate and place a physical object. Hence, when physical objects are used as input or output device, users are not required to learn much about the way of manipulating these physical objects. TUI gives an intuitive and seamless interaction with digital and physical objects, because TUI do not require any special purpose input devices [18]. Fitzmaurice & Buxton [19] and Patten & Ishii [20] in their respective research, showed that TUI is an outperformed standard mouse and keyboard-based-interface [21].

However, TUI has limitation in dynamically change an object's physical properties [22]. Thus, the physical object needs to be chosen carefully to avoid any spatial gap. Humans deduce the inherent functionality of objects from their physical qualities such as shape, weight, size and colour [23], so physical objects can offer a clear spatial mapping to their functions. Spatial gap will exist when the chosen object does not match with the desired functionality in a computer interface.

The previous sections had discussed on user interaction with virtual content through HMD, HHD or projection screen in AR interface. Interaction gap will exist when users use the special-purpose input device in AR interaction, because this will result in two different interfaces (virtual and physical workspace) [18].

TUI offers a seamless interaction, but consists of a spatial gap. Whilst AR interface supports spatially seamless workspace, it has the interaction gap. Due to the complimentary nature of AR and TUI, Billinghurt et. al. [24] proposes a new interface known as Tangible Augmented Reality (TAR). TAR is an interface which combines Tangible User Interface (TUI) with Augmented Reality Interface. With TAR, each object is registered as a physical object, and users interact with the virtual objects by manipulating the corresponding tangible objects [24].

Tangible Augmented Street Map (TASM) is a cube designed using the TAR concept tiled with a street map in cartographic visualization [25]. The digital graphic of the street map is superimposed on the cube. By rotating the cube (up, down, left, right), users can access the map in 4 different directions (north, south, east, west). Tangible Augmented Reality Modeling (TARM) system is a modeling system which provides users with the natural way to create 3D models [26]. By applying TAR, users can create models by manipulating the physical block. Users can also use a real pen to draw a curve or surfaces directly on the models. Immersive Authoring of Tangible Augmented Reality (iaTAR) is another authoring system which allows users to develop and test their AR application concurrently [27]. iaTAR has few interactions built for users to use in their development. Users can build their AR application via interaction to create or destroy a virtual object, browsing a component, or modify object's properties by connecting it with inspector pad and keypad. The involved physical objects are in reality, papers and a cube printed with marker. Besides, Ulbricht & Schmalsticg [28] had built a TAR Tabletop Game. During the game, users are sitting or standing around the glass table, and shooting the opponent's 3D virtual balloons by 3D virtual catapult. Users conduct the game by moving the cardboard with a marker on it. Augmented Chemistry [9] is not only a learning science AR application as discussed in the previous section, but it is also a TAR application. Booklet, Gripper with button and cube with markers are the interaction physical objects. In story telling, children can use both hands to unfold the Magic Cube [29] and explore the contents of the "Noah's Ark" story. There are many examples to show that TAR is already applied in various fields. Hence, TAR is able to offer intuitive and tangible interaction to users.

3 Implementation of LSS

3.1 Live Solar System (LSS)

Live Solar System (LSS) is an AR based educational tool to help student learn about astronomy. Therefore, various multimedia elements like video, graphic, text and 3D objects were included in LSS to achieve the intended purpose. Figure 3 shows that LSS consists of both the physical world as well as the digital world. Its implementation involves the use of a webcam to capture the real world view and then send for the marker detection process. Associated digital contents such as the 3D objects will be loaded after ID of the marker is determined. Then, the captured real world view will be combined with the digital contents and sent out to the users either through the HMD or monitor. In LSS, the cube was used as the input device.

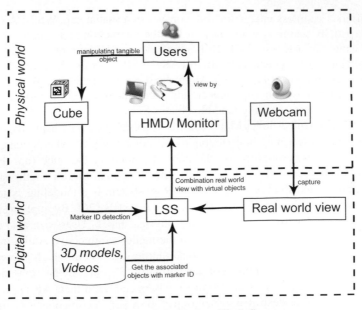

Fig. 3. Live Solar System Work flow

LSS allows students to explore freely in the AR solar system, so that they can understand in a more concrete manner the eight planets in our solar system. Besides, they can also learn about the characteristics of the planets for example, the sun as well as its phenomena, through the combination of physical and digital learning materials. To provide a better exploration experience to users, the Visual Information Seeking Mantra principle was used as a guide in designing LSS. The Visual Information Seeking Mantra, which adopts *"Overview first, zoom and filter, then details on demand"* describes how data should be presented on screen so that it is most effective for users to understand [34]. In LSS, users will have an overview of the solar system through observation. Then, they can zoom and filter down to one of the planets by selecting their planet of interest. Users can acquire more information about the selected planet by performing some interaction related to 'detail on demand'. This process will be discussed in detail in section 3.2.

Based on LSS, the mouse and keyboard devices were not involved during the interactions. This is due to the fact that LSS applied the TAR concept. This means that LSS offers an intuitive-tangible interaction to users. Cubes were chosen as the physical object which will be used during these interactions. Cube was chosen as it is one of the familiar physical objects in our daily lives, and all of us know how to manipulate a cube. Sheridan et. al. [35] had studied about the cube affordance to humans and the ways humans manipulate a cube. Actions like 'place', 'pick up', 'throw', 'squeeze', 'press', 'rotate' and 'hold' are usually performed by humans. Thus, some of the selected natural behaviors of humans will be used in the LSS interaction (Figure 4). Figure 5 shows the cubes and some printed markers used in LSS. These cubes were specifically designed in 3x3x3 cm, so that they are small enough to hold in users' hands, and easy for them to manipulates the cubes.

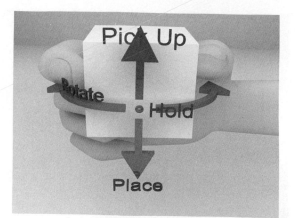

Fig. 4. Interaction techniques uses familiar actions usually performed by humans on a cube

Fig. 5. LSS cubes used as physical input objects

3.2 Interaction Techniques in LSS

Figure 4 shows a few interaction techniques used in LSS. These techniques represent the natural and intuitive actions usually performed by humans in their daily lives when handling physical objects. Thus, users need not learn new interaction techniques when using LSS.

When using LSS for the first time, users can observe the solar system (Figure 6). They can observe the surface and size of each planet, the revolution speed on each planet's orbit and the rotation speed of each planet on their own axis. Besides, users can change the current mode (normal mode) to temperature mode or gravity mode. To do so, they just need to hold and rotate the "menu cube" in their hand (Figure 7). The menu cube designed has 3 different unique markers printed on it, and each of them represents normal, temperature and gravity mode. The planet's surface will change when users change the normal mode to other modes by rotating the menu cube. Meanwhile, the text in 3D form will be shown on the screen to notify users which mode they are currently viewing. In these modes, users can compare the different temperatures and gravity forces of each planet with the help of the scale provided.

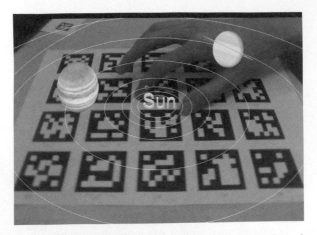

Fig. 6. Observing specific planet's surface, size, revolution and rotation speed

Fig. 7. Changing mode by rotating the menu cube in hand

By manipulating the 'pointer cube', users can pick any interested planet to have a closer and better view of the planet (Figure 8). A pointer cube with a marker will be superimposed by a computer generated red pointer on it. To pick a planet from the solar system, users only need to hold the cube and approach the interested planet. Once the red pointer touches the selected planet, the planet will be copied on the cube. Collision detection method is used to determine which planet is selected by users. The pseudo code used for this method is as indicated below:

```
IF collisionDectection==True && 3D object on cubeMarker
==3D pointer object
        READ collision object
        copy and rename collision object
        set scale on copied new object
```

```
    hide the 3D pointer object from cubeMarker
    load the new copied object on cubeMarker
END IF
```

After having a planet on the cube, users can view the other side of the selected planet by rotating the cube. This is because the planet will rotate according to the performed actions. And similar actions are normally conducted in users' daily lives. For instance, when shopping, they are used to rotating a package of some sort to know the contents of the package or to know the expired date of the package.

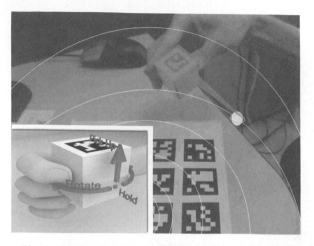

Fig. 8. Picking planet by manipulating the 'pointer cube'

LSS allow users to know more about the planets in the solar system. First, users can select the interested planet with the 'pointer cube'. They can then, place the cube on an 'information center'. This information center is a paper printed with a marker and 'I' icon (Figure 11). Approximation method is used to detect the distance between the information center's marker and the pointer cube's marker. Once the distance is close enough, the information of the selected planet, such as diameter, mass, average temperature, gravity, total days of rotation and evolution, will be shown on the HMD or monitor (Figure 9). To help users get the appropriate distance, an area was drawn on the information center's paper. Thus, users just need to place the cube on the designated area to perform the desired action (Figure 10). 'Trash bin' is another paper printed with a marker with a trash bin icon. Its function is to allow users to delete the selected planet, so that they can then select other planets (Figure 11). The way that it functions is similar to the information center. Both uses the approximation method. The pseudo code for this method is indicated below:

```
WHILE CubeMarker==True && TrashBinMarker==True
          IF cubemarker 3D object != 3D pointer object
            READ CubeMarker position
            READ TrashBinMarker position
```

```
OMPUTE Distance between CubeMarker and TrashBinMarker
           IF Distance < DeleteDistance
              delete 3D object from CubeMarker
              load 3D Pointer object on CubeMarker
           END IF
        END IF
END WHILE
```

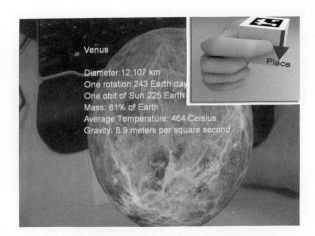

Fig. 9. Placing cube on the designated area to show details of selected planet

Fig. 10. Delete selected planet from cube

Fig. 11. 'Trash bin' and 'Information center' in LSS

Video is one of the multimedia elements used in LSS to show the phenomena of the sun. The metaphor of 'on and off the television and monitor' in daily lives was applied in LSS video interaction approach. Figure 12 shows the way users play and stop the video in LSS. Users can press the 'play' button to start the video, and at the same time the 'play' button will automatically change to 'stop' button. Users can repeat the same action to stop the video, and the 'stop' button will change back to 'play' button. Simple occlusion method is used to determine whether the marker is occluded by the finger or not. The following shows the pseudo code of the method mentioned:

```
Initialise PressCount to zero
WHILE MovieMarker==True && ButtonMarker==True
         IF ButtonMarker==False
             add one to PressCount
             IF Press mod 2==0
               Start playing movie
               change play icon to stop icon
             ELSE
               Stop playing movie
               change stop icon to play icon
         END IF
END WHILE
```

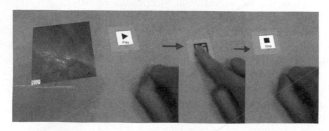

Fig. 12. Techniques to 'play' and 'stop' video in LSS

Conclusion

Augmented Reality is overlaid with virtual objects on real objects offers a new interactive approach that can be conducted between users and the computer. The characteristics of an AR allows it to be a new approach in teaching and learning. The combination of AR interface and TUI provides a seamless interaction to users. Many research has been conducted to help learning in various subject matter domains. In this research, the Live Solar System (LLS) is an AR book-based educational tool with the purpose of helping students learn astronomy. LSS applied the TAR approach in designing which allows users to have a natural and intuitive interaction with the system. This new approach gives a new and more engaging learning experience process for learners. The visual information seeking mantra approach embedded in the system, allows users to have an overview of the whole solar system, then select an interested planet among the eight planets with the 'pointer cube', and then obtain details of the selected planet by placing it on the 'information center'. By manipulating the cube using natural processes such as rotating, picking up, placing and holding, users are able to have effective interaction during exploration of the LSS. Thus, the traditional computer input devices are no longer needed with the introduction of LSS.

References

1. Azuma, R.: A Survey of Augmented Reality. Teleoperators and Virtual Environments 6(4), 355–385 (1997)
2. Azuma, R., Baillot, Y., Behringer, R., Feiner, S., Julier, S., MacIntyre, B.: Recent Advance in Augmenteed Reality. IEEE Computer Graphics and Application (2001)
3. Sutherland, I.: The Ultimate Display. In: Interational Federation of Information Processing, vol. 2, pp. 506–508 (1965)
4. Barfield, W., Caudell, T.: Fundamentals of Wearable Computers and Augmented Reality, pp. 447–468. Lawrence Erlbaum Associates, Mahwah (2001)
5. Jong, S.P.: Augmented Reality Introduction. In: Slaid. Deparment of Computer Science and Engineering, University Incheon (2005)
6. Jung, Y.M., Jong, S.C.: The Virtuality and Reality of Augmented Reality. Journal of Multimedia 2(1), 32–37 (2007)
7. Milgram, P., Takemura, H., Utsumi, A., Kishino, F.: Augmented Reality: A class of displays on the reality-virtuality continuum. Proceedings of Telemanipulator and Telepresence Technologies (1994)
8. Billinghurst, M., Kato, H., Poupyrev, I.: The MagicBook: Moving Seamlessly between Reality and Virtuality. IEEE Computer Graphics and Applications 21(3), 6–8 (2001)
9. Fjeld, M., Voegtli, B.M.: Augmented Chemistry: An Interactive Educational Workbench. In: Proceedings of the 1st international Symposium on Mixed and Augmented Reality, vol. 259. IEEE Computer Society, Los Alamitos (2002)
10. Ucelli, G., Conti, G., Amicis, R.D., Servidio, R.: Learning Using Augmented Reality Technology: Multiple Means of Interaction for Teaching Children the Theory of Colours. In: Maybury, M., Stock, O., Wahlster, W. (eds.) INTETAIN 2005. LNCS (LNAI), vol. 3814, pp. 193–202. Springer, Heidelberg (2005)
11. Hughes, C.E., Smith, E., Stapleton, C., Hughes, D.E.: Proceedings of KSCE (2004), http://www.mcl.ucf.edu/research/seacreatures/KSCE04HughesEtAl.pdf
12. Billinghurst, M.: Augmented Reality in Education, http://www.newhorizons.org/strategies/technology/ billinghurst.htm

13. Shelton, B., Hedly, N.: Using augmented reality for teaching earth-sun relationships to dergraduate geography students. In: The 1st IEEE international augmented reality tool workshop, Darmstadt, Germany (2002)
14. Woods, E., Billinghurst, M., Aldridge, G., Garrie, B.: Augmenting the Science Centre and Museum Experience. In: Proceedings of the 2nd international conference on Computer graphics and interactive techniques in Australasia and South East Asia, pp. 230–236 (2004)
15. Isii, H., Ulemr, B.: Tangible Bits: Towards Seamless Interfaces between People, Bit, and Atoms. In: Conference on Human Factors in Computing Systems, CHI 1997, pp. 234–241 (1997)
16. Kim, M.J., Maher, M.L.: Comparison of Designers Using A Tangible User Interface and A Graphical User Interface and the Impact on Spatial Cognition. In: Proceedings of International Workshop on Human Behaviour in Designing, pp. 81–94 (2005)
17. Wang, Q., Li, C., Huang, X., Tang, M.: Tangible Interface: Integration of real and virtual. In: 7th International Conference on Computer Supported Cooperative Work in Design, pp. 408–412 (2002)
18. Poupyrev, I., Tan, D.S., Billinghurst, M., Kato, H., Regenbrecht, H., Tetsutani, N.: Developing a Generic Augmented-Reality Interface. Computer 35(3), 44–50 (2002)
19. Fitzmaurice, G., Buxton, W.: An Empirical Evaluation of Graspable User Interfaces: towards specialized, space-multiplexed input. In: Proceedings of the ACM Conference on Human Factors in Computing Systems (CHI 1997), pp. 43–50 (1997)
20. Patten, J., Ishii, H.: A Comparision of Spatial Organization Strategies in Graphical and Tangible User Interface. In: Proceedings of Designing Augmented Reality Environments, pp. 41–50 (2000)
21. Hoven, E.V.D., Frens, J., Aliakseyeu, D., Martens, J.B., Overbeeke, K., Peters, P.: Design research & Tangible Interaction. In: 1st International conference on tangible Embedded interaction, TEI 2007, pp. 109–115 (2007)
22. Billing, M.: Crossing the chasm. In: Proceedings of International Conference on Augmented Tele-Existence (ICAT 2001) (2001), http://www.hitl.washington.edu/publications/r-2002-62/r-2002-62.pdf
23. Sharlin, E., Waston, B., Kitamura, Y., Kishino, F., Itoh, Y.: On tangible user interface, human and spatiality. Personal ubiquitous Computer 8(5), 338–346 (2004)
24. Billinghurst, M., Kato, H., Poupyrev, I.: Collaboration with tangible augmented reality interfaces. In: HCI International 2001, pp. 234–241 (2001)
25. Moore, A.: A Tangible Augmented Reality Interface to Tiled Street Maps and its Usability Testing. In: Progress in Spatial Data Handling, pp. 511–528. Springer, Heidelberg (2006)
26. Park, J.Y., Lee, J.W.: Tangible Augmented Reality. In: Rauterberg, M. (ed.) ICEC 2004. LNCS, vol. 3166, pp. 254–259. Springer, Heidelberg (2004)
27. Lee, G.A., Nelles, C., Billinghurst, M., Kim, G.J.: Immersive Authoring of Tangible Augmented Reality Applications. In: Proceedings of the 3rd IEEE/ACM international Symposium on Mixed and Augmented Reality, pp. 172–181 (2004)
28. Ulbricht, C., Schmalstieg, D.: Tangible Augmented Reality for Computer Games. In: Proceedings of the Third IASTED International Conference on Visualization, Imaging and Image Processing 2003, pp. 950–954 (2003)
29. Zhou, Z., Cheok, A.D., Li, Y., Kato, H.: Magic cubes for social and physical family entertainment. In: CHI 2005 Extended Abstracts on Human Factors in Computing Systems, pp. 1156–1157 (2005)
30. Sheridan, J.G., Short, B.W., Laerhoven, V.K., Villar, N., Kortuem, G.: Exploring cube affordances: towards a classification of non-verbal dynamics of physical interfaces for wearable computing. Eurowearable. pp. 113-118 (2003)
31. Shneiderman, B.: The eyes have it: A task by data type taxonomy of information visualizations. In: Proceeding IEEE Visual Languages 1996, pp. 336–343 (1996)

Using Wavelet Extraction for Haptic Texture Classification

Waskito Adi and Suziah Sulaiman

Universiti Teknologi PETRONAS, Computer Science Department, Bandar Seri Iskandar,
31750 Tronoh, Perak, Malaysia
waskito@gmail.com, suziah@petronas.com.my

Abstract. While visual texture classification is a widely-research topic in image analysis, little is known on its counterpart i.e. the haptic (touch) texture. This paper examines the visual texture classification in order to investigate how well it could be used for haptic texture search engine. In classifying the visual textures, feature extraction for a given image involving wavelet decomposition is used to obtain the transformation coefficients. Feature vectors are formed using energy signature from each wavelet sub-band coefficient. We conducted an experiment to investigate the extent in which wavelet decomposition could be used in haptic texture search engine. The experimental result, based on different testing data, shows that feature extraction using wavelet decomposition achieve accuracy rate more than 96%. This demonstrates that wavelet decomposition and energy signature is effective in extracting information from a visual texture. Based on this finding, we discuss on the suitability of wavelet decomposition for haptic texture searching, in terms of extracting information from image and haptic information.

Keywords: Texture recognition, supervised learning, machine learning, haptic texture search engine, wavelet decomposition.

1 Introduction

Lately, computer vision has become one of the most popular research subjects. Computer vision contributes in various fields that include medical, engineering, and robotics. One of the most interesting topics in computer vision is texture recognition. Being the smallest entity, textures could be used as a parameter to recognize a particular object. There are many different types of applications involving texture analysis, including medical imaging, industrial inspection, remote sensing, document segmentation, and computer based image retrieval [1].

Feature extraction plays an important role in a classification process. The effectiveness of such classification relies greatly on the choice of this feature. In this case, a suitable extraction algorithm influences the process end result. Parallel to computer vision, computer haptic is also another area which is gaining its popularity among researchers. Computer haptic enable user to touch and interact with the virtual objects. Similar to computer vision, haptic texture is a growing research topics and its application has been noted in medical field, arts, and textile, to name a few.

H. Badioze Zaman et al. (Eds.): IVIC 2009, LNCS 5857, pp. 314–325, 2009.
© Springer-Verlag Berlin Heidelberg 2009

Even though computer vision and computer haptic are among the favorite to, late, no attempt has been made to integrate both texture classifications into the s system such as a search engine. Current practices have seen visual and haptic textur been dealt with separately; and the trend is that visual aspect has been the dominant topics of the two texture types. The absence of such integration may hinder one from getting a complete set of surface information of a particular object. This is because visual textures could inform us on the macro-geometric information while haptic textures on the micro-geometric details [15]. The lacking in combining both visual and haptic textures needs addressing.

In this paper, we attempt to address the issue of lacking the effort in integrating visual and haptic textures. We propose a way to analyze and classify haptic textures based on an approach used from computer vision. The focus of our work here is on visual textures and examines how such result could inform haptic texture classifications. This involves conducting an experiment to test the visual texture classification and feature extraction performance. In the classification process, supervised learning has been used as a testing method.

The outline of this paper is organized as follows: in section 2, we review some related works pertaining to visual and haptic textures analysis. This is followed by section 3 in which we describe the method involved in our experiment that include wavelet transformation, and statistical classification. In section 4, we present our scheme in extracting texture information, and also how the experiments were conducted. Finally, in section 5 we analyze the experimental results and discuss the findings.

2 Related Works

2.1 On Visual Textures

Visual texture analysis has been studied over the past three decades. Most of the early research focused on the analysis of the first or second order statistics of textures and stochastic model such as Gaussian Markov random fields and auto regression [2].

Recently, the development of texture classification and analysis has been using frequency and spatial analysis, such as Fourier transform, Gabor filter, and Wavelet transform. Since a texture image is in 2D representation, measuring its characteristics could be done by employing a 2D transformation or filtering. For example, to extract texture information, a 2D Fourier transform can be employed. Azencott et al [3] define a distance between textures for texture classification from texture features based on windowed Fourier filters. In the research, Fourier transformation is used as a method to extract information from textures.

In employing a more advanced technique, Fountain [4] has conducted an experiment using Gabor filter for texture extraction. Also, in [7], Miaohong conducted an experiment using Gabor filter to extract features at different orientation from hyperspectral images. In that particular research, it is said that accuracy of the classification is over 90%. Using a different technique, Shankar conducted an experiment [5] by using wavelet transform to extract information from finger print. Similarly, Chi-Man Pun [6] has also conducted an experiment using wavelet to extract information from

. It is reported in his research that wavelet gives a better result than Gabor In this particular case, although Gabor filter is a multi-resolution filter, wavelet .sform still outperforms.

2.2 On Haptic Textures

Texture is the smallest independent quantity in an object. Research works that involve texture are mostly conducted in image and signal processing. When including texture in haptics field, mage and signal processing algorithm will be involved. To create a realistic object the simplest way is by employing sine wave to generate the texture surfaces. In [16] Seungmoon Choi and Hong Z. Tan employ sine wave to render the texture surface in order to analyze the stability during haptic texture rendering.

In order to simulate the surface of haptic texture, there are some algorithms that can be used [16][17]. The simplest one is using sine wave. By adjusting amplitude and frequency of the sine wave the texture of surfaces could be obtained. In [14] Wall develops a haptic texture rendering technique using Fourier series. The basic idea of this rendering technique is similar with rendering using sine wave because Fourier series using sine wave as basis to create new wave. In order to create realistic texture for haptic rendering, Juan Wu introducing new rendering method based on image processing [17].

3 Methodology

3.1 Equating Haptic Texture to Visual Texture

To obtain a texture sensation, a simple technique such as sinusoidal waves could be used to render the force feedback. Different texture pattern or profile is obtained by adjusting frequency, and amplitude of the sine waves which could result in different haptic sensation. For example, Wall [14] conducted an experiment that simulates texture surface by employing Fourier series to achieve different types of haptic texture surface.

The texture profile used in haptic rendering and its 2D image counterpart share a similar characteristic. When rendering a property of an object, such as its haptic texture using sinusoidal waves, the (haptic) surface will have surface properties similar to (visual) sine waves, but in 3D plane. However, when these haptic properties are plotted onto a 2D plane they will appear similar to 2D images. Fig. 1 shows a 2D representation of sine and square haptic waves (Fig 1.1 & 1.2) and the actual visual images (Fig 1.3 & 1.4).

Comparing the images of the four images in Fig. 1, it could be assumed that haptic texture images generated using both sine square waves have similar patterns with those non artificial visual textures (Fig. 1.3 & 1.4). Based on the similarity of their appearances on a 2D plane, we could claim that computer vision (CV) algorithm could also be employed to extract information from haptic rendering data.

Fig 1.1. sine wave (haptic) texture   Fig 1.2. square wave (haptic) texture

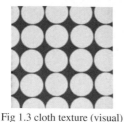

Fig 1.3 cloth texture (visual)   Fig 1.4 cloth texture (visual)

Fig. 1. Image visualization from haptic texture

3.2 Equating Haptic Texture to Visual Texture

Transformation is one of the most powerful tools to analyze signal information. With transformation, signal can be analyze and manipulated. The most common method to analyze signal is by using Fourier transform. Fourier transforms use sine wave as basis of the transformation, by using Fourier transform assumption, it can be inferred that every signal is constructed by sine waves superposition. Fourier transform is denoted as:

$$F(w) = \int_{-\infty}^{\infty} f(x)e^{-2\pi i \omega x}\partial x \qquad (1)$$

The inverse of Fourier transform, which allows going from spectrum to the signal is:

$$f(x) = \int_{-\infty}^{\infty} F(x)e^{2\pi i \omega x}\partial \omega \qquad (2)$$

Consider a square wave, (Fig. 2), $f(x)$ of length $2L$. The range $[0, 2L]$, could be written:

$$f(x) = 2\left[H\left(\frac{x}{L}\right) - H\left(\frac{x}{L} - 1\right) \right] - 1 \qquad (3)$$

By using Fourier transform, information of square signal can be retrieved. In this case, square signal can be decomposed into different sine wave frequency and amplitude. Referring to the Fourier transform, if a square wave equation is transformed, it will produce a Fourier series shown follows:

$$f(x) = \frac{4}{\pi} \int_{n=1,3,5,...}^{\infty} \frac{1}{n}\sin\left(\frac{n\pi x}{L}\right) \tag{4}$$

Unlike Fourier series that uses sine wave, wavelet is a transformation that uses transient signal as its basis. In other word wavelet transform is better than Fourier for analyzing transient signal. Wavelet transform of $f(x)$ is denoted as:

$$W_\psi f(a,b) = \int_R \psi_{a,b}(x)f(x)\partial x \tag{5}$$

Consider a signal shown in (Fig. 2), in wavelet analysis.

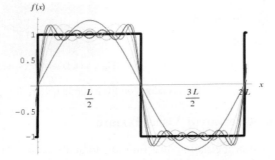

Fig. 2. Decomposition of square wave using Fourier Transform

The signal can be decomposed into different small basis transient signal. Otherwise if Fourier transform is employed, the signal will be decomposed into different amplitude and frequency of sine wave.

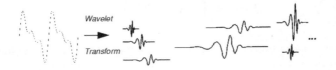

Fig. 3. Illustration of 1-D wavelet transforms. Unlike Fourier transform that used sine wave as basis, wavelet transform use small transient signal to transform or decompose the source signal.

Wavelet multiresolution analysis has been used as texture characterization. It provides spatial or frequency information of an image. There are two method extractions in wavelet multiresolution: (i) wavelet decomposition (ii) wavelet packet decomposition.

In our experiment we use 2D wavelet decomposition to extract texture images. The decomposition offer results for image analysis. Although it not as rich as 2D wavelet packet (2D-WPT), it is adequate to do analysis to an image with 2D wavelet decomposition. In 2D wavelet decomposition transform (2D-WDT), an image x is split into an approximation and three detail image (Fig. 3). 2D-WDT can be described as a pair of filter L and H [9], H is low pass filter, and L is high pass filter. The 2D-WDT of a discrete N x M image can be recursively defined as:

$$A_1 = C_{4k,(i,j)}^{p+1} = \sum_m \sum_n h(m)h(n)C_{k,(m+2i,n+2j)}^p \tag{6}$$

$$H_1 = C_{4k+1,(i,j)}^{p+1} = \sum_m \sum_n h(m)h(n)C_{k,(m+2i,n+2j)}^p \tag{7}$$

$$V_1 = C_{4k+2,(i,j)}^{p+1} = \sum_m \sum_n h(m)h(n)C_{k,(m+2i,n+2j)}^p \tag{8}$$

$$D_1 = C_{4k+3,(i,j)}^{p+1} = \sum_m \sum_n h(m)h(n)C_{k,(m+2i,n+2j)}^p \tag{9}$$

A1 is approximation coefficient, H1 is horizontal detail, V1 is vertical detail, and D1 is diagonal detail, illustrated in (Fig. 4). In practice, the image x only has finite number of pixels, for boundary handling different technique such as symmetric, periodic could be used. The difference between 2D-WDT and 2D-WPT is in the extraction process. In 2D-WDT only approximation coefficient will be transformed whereas in 2D-WPT all of the coefficient will be recursively transformed. In the proposed method, an image is decomposed into 4-levels. 4-level decomposition results 3n+1 sub-band, it means that decomposition results 13 sub-band.

In general transformation processes compress information from data. In wavelet transform, if the basis signal for transformation has correlation with transformed signal it will produce homogenous transformed coefficient. Referring to those characteristics, characteristics of each sub-band can be used as information to form feature vector. In order to form a feature vector, f=(x1, x2, x3,. . ., xn), the energy or characteristic each sub-band of images have been calculated using formula (Table 1).

Table 1. Energy Calculation Formula

Energy Type	Formula
Norm 2	$e_1 = \dfrac{1}{NM} \sum\limits_{m=1}^{M} \sum\limits_{n=1}^{N} \left| C_{M,N} \right|$
Norm 1	$e_2 = \dfrac{1}{NM} \sum\limits_{m=1}^{M} \sum\limits_{n=1}^{N} \left| C_{M,N} \right|$
Standard Deviation	$e_3 = \sqrt{\dfrac{1}{NM} \sum\limits_{m=1}^{M} \sum\limits_{n=1}^{N} C_{M,N}}$
Average Residual	$e_4 = \dfrac{1}{NM} \sum\limits_{M} \sum\limits_{N} C_{M,N}$
Entropy	$e_5 = \dfrac{1}{NM} \sum\limits_{M} \sum\limits_{N} C_{M,N}$

It is a common issue that data stored in feature vector have redundancy. To reduce redundancy form the feature vector, PCA (Principle Component analysis) algorithm should be employed [7][12][1]. With PCA algorithm, classification process could be more effective and efficient

3.3   Pattern Recognition a Statistical Approach

In our research, we will employ the supervised learning to classify the texture. In our study, in order to test the classification performance, we employ linear, quadratic and mahalanobis classifiers. Bayesian rule has been used as a fundamental concept for the entire classifiers. Bayesian rule is denoted as:

$$P(\omega_j \mid x) = \frac{p(x \mid \omega_j)P(\omega_j)}{p(x)} \tag{10}$$

Let say there are two classes of data ω_1 and ω_2, $P(\omega_j)$ is prior probability and $p(x)$ is probability density function (PDF). Referring to the maximum likelihood theorem, by maximizing the conditional probabilities $P(\omega_j|x)$ decision of the class could be obtained. In this case if $P(\omega_1|x) > P(\omega_2|x)$ the data will belong to class ω_1, otherwise if ω_2 data belong to ω_2. Referring to Bayesian rule, if it assumes PDF is a normal distribution or Gaussian, linear, quadratic and mahalamobis classifier could be obtained. Quadratic, linear and mahalanobis could be denoted as:

Quadratic classifier:

$$\max \left| -\frac{1}{2}(x-\mu_j)^T \Sigma_j^{-1}(x-\mu_j) + \ln P(\varpi_j) - \ln |\Sigma_j| \right| \tag{11}$$

Linear Classifier:

$$\max \left| -\frac{1}{2}(x-\mu_j)^T \Sigma_j^{-1}(x-\mu_j) + \ln P(\varpi_j) \right| \tag{12}$$

Mahalanobis Classifier:

$$\max \left| -(x-\mu_j)^T \Sigma_j^{-1}(x-\mu_j) \right| \tag{13}$$

To obtain the data classes (refer to equation 11, 12, 13), there is a need to maximize the conditional probability. In equations 11 and 12, all data are calculated based on the relative distance between the data and data distribution, and also using prior probability of the class as weight parameter. In mahalanobis classifier algorithm, (equation 13), it calculates relative distance between data and the data distribution.

4   Proposed Framework and Experiment

To this end, we have claimed that computer haptic texture classification could replicate similar technique from computer vision. In the previous section, we have described how wavelet and its feature extraction could be a potential candidate to address this situation. Fig. 4 presents a proposed framework for a system that can adopt both visual and haptic search. The framework combines both visual and haptic texture extractions and classifications.

The visual information [1] as shown in Fig. 4 consists of the texture image data; this information is passed to the extraction process [2]. The process involves the wavelet decomposition (using db-8) to get the characteristics from each image. At this stage the energy calculation formula will be used. The feature vector f is formed as a result of this process.

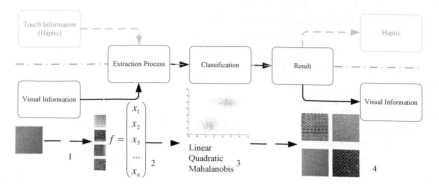

Fig. 4. Proposed Framework involving the extraction and classification processes

In the classification stage [3], we employ the linear, quadratic and mahalanobis classifiers to examine the most suitable classifier in terms of its performance. Using the chosen classifier, the system will suggest some possible matching results [4].

4.1 Experiment

The effectiveness of wavelet decomposition for texture analysis and classification has been tested in an experiment, using 76 samples of texture images. The texture set consists of natural, artificial, and semi natural textures. The objectives of the experiments are:

- To determine the texture classification performance for each classifier
- To identify the most effective and efficient variable to be used in a classification process.

During the performance test, we use three different types of classifiers. We employ linear, quadratic, and mahalanobis classifiers. Daubechies wavelet family has been employed as algorithm to extract the textures. Table 2 shows 16 tap of daubechies wavelet transform filter coefficient.

Table 2. 16 Tap of Daubechies-8 Wavelet Transform Filter Coefficient

h(0)	0.0385	h(8)	-0.0123
h(1)	0.2212	h(9)	-0.0312
h(2)	0.4777	h(10)	0.0099
h(3)	0.4139	h(11)	0.0062
h(4)	-0.0112	h(12)	-0.0034
h(5)	-0.2008	h(13)	-0.0003
h(6)	0.0003	h(14)	0.0005
h(7)	0.0910	h(15)	-0.0001

The textures have been decomposed into 4-level. It means that decomposition processes results in 13 coefficient sub-band. To conduct the experiment we prepare a learning sample and testing data sets. We create a random 512x512 pixel image from the texture image. For each 512x512 pixel image we partition this image into 4

.65x265 without overlapping each other. We generate 100 random images 128x128 from each 256x256 images. In other words, for each sample we have 400 samples. We use 200 samples for learning process and the other 200 samples for testing.

To test the performance of the classification, we conduct three experiments with different feature vectors and different classification methods. We employed the linear, quadratic, and mahalanobis classifiers in the experiments, consecutively. For the first experiment, we use the entire feature of vector element, meaning that all the extracted information was used. The second experiment was to test the effect of the element number with classification process. We start by using 1 feature vector element up to the entire elements. In the third experiment, we use only one type of energy calculation algorithm.

5 Findings and Analysis

As described earlier, in the experiment we have used the three classifiers to measure the accuracy of classification performance. In each classification process we measure the error rate of each method. The classification testing involves:

1) Measuring the number of feature vector element versus error rate
2) Measuring the effect using different type of feature vector
3) Comparing the classification method
4) Finding the optimum number of feature vector element

The first experiment was conducted by measuring the error rate for each feature vector that have different element. Since we have Level-4 wavelet decomposition, it means that we have 13 different sub-bands. For each sub-band we calculate the energy using the formula in (Table 1), which means we have 65 different values to form a feature vector. In this experiment we form a feature vector started using 1 element to 65 elements, f(x¬1) to f(x1, x1, x1,. . ., x65). In this test, quadratic classifier gives the most accurate results when compared with linear and mahalanobis classifiers. The classification results are summarized in Figure 5 and Table 3.

We carried out a second experiment similar to the first but for this time we only use one type of energy to form the feature vector. This means that the feature vector

Table 3. 16 Tap of Daubechies-8 Wavelet Transform Filter Coefficient

Energy	Norm1	Norm2	Std dev	Ave. residual	Entropy
1	0.8661	0.8656	0.8584	0.9212	0.8666
2	0.6899	0.8379	0.7063	0.5719	0.6389
3	0.4606	0.8200	0.5540	0.3503	0.5241
4	0.3198	0.7755	0.5337	0.2409	0.4041
5	0.3068	0.7460	0.3248	0.2226	0.3936
6	0.1672	0.7065	0.1607	0.1461	0.2459
7	0.1072	0.6691	0.1057	0.1022	0.1727
8	0.0917	0.6361	0.0744	0.0605	0.1594
9	0.0527	0.6205	0.0610	0.0311	0.1113
10	0.0348	0.6057	0.0562	0.0228	0.0840
11	0.0210	0.5903	0.0327	0.0179	0.0683
12	0.0126	0.5580	0.0199	0.0140	0.0524
13	0.0068	0.5432	0.1066	0.0119	0.0411

only formed from norm1, norm2, standard deviation, average residual and ene (Table 3). The experimental results show that the best performance was achieved w average residual energy calculation. In this experiment quadratic classifier has been employed and overall error rate is 1.19%. This suggests that average residual is more effective than other energy calculation method.

From the experimental result, it shows that the number of element of feature vector, and the number of energy used are affecting the accuracy of classification process. Using the data of the experiment, optimization of the classification system could be done by reducing the element of the feature vector. In Figure 5.1, it is indicated that the optimum number element is 20. The visual representation shows that the error rate starts to convergence when the number of feature vector element is 20. This means that if we add more elements in, more energy will be used. This does not show any significant improvement to Figure 5.1.

The experiment has resulted in the quadratic classifier being the most accurate method. Error rate for quadratic classifier is 0.18%. This result shows that feature extraction using wavelet is suitable for texture classification. Based on the second experiment it shows that the most effective and efficient energy calculation algorithm is using the average residual, (Figure 5.2). Overall error rate for 13 number of energy, i.e. element of the feature vector, is 1.19%. Overall accuracy is about 98%. From this result we can suggest that wavelet feature extraction should be suitable for haptic texture searching that deals not only with visual representation, but also the touch sensation.

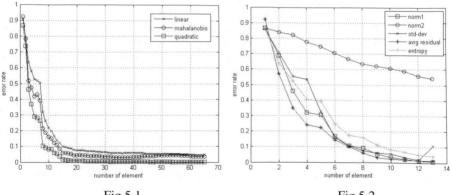

Fig 5.1   Fig 5.2

Fig 5. Classification Accuracy experiment by using different type of energy. In this particular experiment, quadratic classifier has been employed. In this experiment, average residual gives most effective feature vector element for classification. 1). error propagation for quadratic, linear and mahalanobis classifier. 2). Propagation error for quadratic classifier for each type of energy.

6   Conclusion and Future Work

In this paper, we have addressed the problem in haptic searching method and proposed a framework that integrates both visual and haptic in a texture search engine.

...aimed that techniques in computer vision could be replicated for computer hap-
...We predicted that wavelet decomposition could be the best candidate. In justify-
...g our claim, we reviewed the standard 2D wavelet decomposition. Then we defined
an algorithm to extract the texture. The feature extraction involves wavelet transform
and five different energy measurements. The construction of feature vector is done
using different techniques. Firstly, we used the entire energy from entire sub-band;
secondly, we used only one type of energy for entire sub-band.

The several series of experiment an experiment to find out the suitable method for
extraction and searching process show that quadratic classifier outperforms two other
classification methods. Also, based on the experiment, average residual is the most
effective and efficient energy measurements method, beside norm 2. The overall error
rate for average residual energy calculation in quadratic classification was 1.19%.

Since haptic rendering data and 2D images have similarity, based on this experiment, we can conclude that 2D wavelet decomposition and wavelet energy signature
could be employed in haptic data extraction. With this experiment results we could
suggest that this method could be suitable for our proposed haptic texture searching.
Future work will include implementation of this method in our haptic texture search
engine.

References

1. Datta, R.: Image Retrieval: Ideas, Influences, and Trends of New Age. ACM Computing surveys 40(2),Article 5 (April 2008)
2. Conners, R.W., Harlow, C.A.: A Theoretical Comparison of Texture Algorithms. IEEE Trans. Pattern Analysis and Machine Intelligence 2, 204–222 (1980)
3. Azencott, R.: Texture classification using windowed Fourier filters. IEEE Trans. Pattern Analysis and Machine Intelligence 19, 148–153 (1997)
4. Fountain, S.R.: Rotation invariant texture features from Gabor filters. In: Chin, R., Pong, T.-C. (eds.) ACCV 1998. LNCS, vol. 1352. Springer, Heidelberg (1997)
5. Nikam, S.B., Agarwal, S.,: Wavelet energy signature and GLCM features-based finger-print anti-spoofing. In: International Conference on Wavelet Analysis and Pattern Recognition, ICWAPR 2008 (2008)
6. Pun, C.: Log-Polar Wavelet Energy Signatures for Rotation and Scale Invariant Texture Classification. IEEE Transactions on Pattern Analysis and Machine Intelligence 25(5) (May 2003)
7. Shi, M.,: Hyperspectral Texture Recognition Using a Multiscale Opponent Representation. IEEE Transaction on Geoscience and Remote Sensing 41(5) (May 2003)
8. Yektaii, M., Bhattacharya, P.: Cumulative global distance for dimension reduction in handwritten digits database. In: Qiu, G., Leung, C., Xue, X.-Y., Laurini, R. (eds.) VISUAL 2007. LNCS, vol. 4781, pp. 216–222. Springer, Heidelberg (2007)
9. Mallat, S.: A theory for Multiresolution Signal Decomposition: The Wavelet Representation. IEEE Trans. on Pattern Analysis and Machine Inteligence 11(7), 674–693 (1989)
10. Daubechies, I.: Orthonormal Bases of Compactly Supported Wavelets. Comm. Pure and Applied Math. 41, 909–996 (1988)
11. Cédric, V.: Generalized Daubechies Wavelet Families. IEEE Transactions on Signal Processing 55(9) (September 2007)

12. Farrell Michael, D.: On The Impact of PCA Dimmension Reduction for Hyperspect
    tection of Difficult Targets IEEE Transaction on Geoscience and Remote Sensing
    ters 2(2) (April 2005)
13. Hadsell, R., Chopra, S., LeCun, Y.: Dimensionality Reduction by Learning an nvarian.
    Mapping. In: IEEE Conf. Comp. Vision and Pattern Recog., pp. 1735–1742. IEEE Com-
    puter Society Press, Los Alamitos (2006)
14. Wall, S.. An Investigation of Temporal and Spatial Limitation of Haptic Interfaces. Uni-
    versity of Glasgow (2004)
15. Klatzky, R.L., Lederman, S.J., Touch, I.A.F., Healy, R.W. (eds.): Experimental Psychol-
    ogy. In: Weiner, I.B. (ed.) Handbook of Psychology, vol. 4, Wiley, New York (2004)
16. Seungmoon, C., Tan, H.Z.: An Analysis of Perceptual Instability During Haptic Texture
    Rendering. In: 10th Symposium on Haptic Interfaces for Virtual Environment and Teleop-
    erator Systems (2002)
17. Wu, J., Song, A., Zou, C.: A Novel Haptic Texture Display Based on Image Processing.
    In: IEEE International Conference on Robotics and Biomimetics (December 2007)

Mixed Reality Book: A Visualization Tool

Rasimah Che Mohd. Yusoff and Halimah Badioze Zaman

Universiti Kebangsaan Malaysia
43600 Bangi, Selangor
rasimah@ic.utm.my, hbz@ftsm.ukm.my

Abstract. Mixed Reality (MR) is one of the newest technologies explored in education, promises the potential to promote teaching and learning and making learners' experience more "engaging". In this paper, we describe the importance of science research education, related research for augmented book, learning principles to promote learning using mixed reality book technology and the potential use of mixed reality book technology in understanding science research. We also explain a model of a mixed reality book's affordances work with other factors in shaping a meaningful learning process.

Keywords: science research education, mixed reality book.

1 Introduction

This Virtual Environment (VE) can be defined as a 3D data set describing an environment based upon real world or abstract objects and data [1]. The term virtual environment also refers to a Virtual Reality (VR) which use of computer graphics systems in combination with various display and interface devices to provide the effect of immersion in the interactive 3D computer-generated environment. VE used specifically for educational purposes can be refer as Virtual Learning Environment (VLE) [2]. Augmented Reality (AR) or Mixed Reality (MR) is a technology can be used to create the sensation that virtual objects are present in the real world. To achieve the effect, software combines VR elements with real world [3]. A VLE created using VR or Mixed Reality (MR) technology not only provides rich learning patterns and teaching contents, but also helps to improve learners' ability of analyzing problems and exploring new concepts The range of words that users can explore and experience in a VE is unlimited, ranging from factual to fantasy, set in the past, present or future [4]. In [5], Kirkley et al considers the MR technology in education as the next generation blended learning environment that is realistic, authentic, engaging and extremely fun. These technologies are now maturing, and they enable even more complex and authentic interactions not only with regard to physical and cognitive fidelity but the ability to embed learning and training experiences into the real world (instead of the other way around). These capabilities provide exciting opportunities for designing innovative learning environments that can hopefully make learning more fun, interactive, effective, relevant and powerful. Mixed reality book which used the mixed reality technology on real books has the potential to promote learning. In this paper, we

H. Badioze Zaman et al. (Eds.): IVIC 2009, LNCS 5857, pp. 326–336, 2009.

describe the design of Mixed Reality book as a potential tool to promote understanding on tissue engineering science research for Biomedical students.

2 Related Works

In this section, we describe the importance of science research education, related research for augmented book, learning principles to promote learning using mixed reality book technology and the potential use of mixed reality book technology to promote understanding on science research education.

2.1 Science Research Education

Science research highly contribute to social and economical benefits to a nation. For example, Malaysia's BioValley (a biotech-based research and development/R&D and industry cluster) uses biotechnology as an economic growth vehicle towards the national dream of developed nation status by the year 2020. Human resources play a crucial roles in ensuring the successfulness of the program and graduates from universities are among the resources that can contribute to the cause [6]. Hence, it is important to promote understanding of the students on scientific research and to identify the potential technology that can be used to help them in understanding research.

Several approaches have been made in order to encourage young people's interest in science such as astronomy, biotechnology, genetic and tissue engineering. The Malaysian High Schools Biotechnology Awareness Program is meant to provide basic exposure and awareness towards biotechnology among students and teachers. The program conducted road shows that consisted of a series of talks, lectures, discussions and three different hands-on sub-sessions which are games, wet-lab hands-on and multimedia self exploration.

The Biotechnology Outreach Education Center (BOEC) in Iowa, provides exposure to teachers, students and general public on the world of biotechnology. Among the activities involved are hands-on activities such as extracting DNA, DNA fingerprinting, PCR and GMO testing; broadcast on television; workshops that train Iowa teachers to implement the technologies and principles of biotechnology; and discussion of ethical issues. In addition, the center also has a Virtual Reality Center that allows students to rapidly determine optimal conditions for fermentation.

A Project Step in USA, gives exposure on tissue engineering research. Students in grade 10 and 11 investigate how the knowledge, skills and interests learned in science classes apply to the careers students plan to pursue. In relation to that, Pittsburg Tissue Engineering (PTEI) arranges several activities to give exposure on tissue engineering such as the hands-on summer camp. This camp involves classroom activities and experiments to help them learn about the field of tissue engineering and its remarkable promise for treating disease and injury. Students also work in laboratories of scientists at Pittsburgh's leading research centers. Besides that, PTEI is also partnering with the Carnegie Science Center and the University of Pittsburgh Learning Research and Development Center to create a 1,200 square-foot exhibit on tissue engineering concepts. The exhibit will designed at a middle-school curriculum level but will also have a broader appeal and application to high school classes, elementary school students and family groups.

2.2 Augmented Books

Electronic book can be an electronic version of a traditional text (online interactive book and electronic book readers) or traditional book with electronic features (audio book and multimedia CD ROM book). Marshall et al. [7] have shown that users still love the physicality of a real book because it offers a broad range of advantages, such as: transportability, flexibility, robustness, etc. However, the traditional textbooks, novels, magazines, and any form of print publication suffer from two weaknesses - inability to directly portray three-dimensional (3D) objects, and the inability to convey time evolving information in a dynamic way such as showing motion [8].

These factors support research into another future for books : digitally augmenting and enhancing real books. This combines the advantages of physical books with new interaction possibilities offered by digital media. One type of visually enhanced books is the use of Augmented Reality (AR) or known as AR book [9]. AR book is an interactive paper implementing some form of physical-to-digital links where physical artefacts particularly paper documents become augmented with digital information. Table 1 shows a few examples of augmented book projects using AR technology.

Table 1. Examples of augmented book using AR technology

Project	Description
MagicBook [10]	An early attempt to explore how to use a physical object to smoothly transport users between reality and virtuality. One or more users can work with a book in three different ways controlled by buttons: access printed information only, overlay and augment the physical content with 3D models or switch from the physical information to a completely virtual computer generated environment.
AR Volcano [11]	An exhibit using six page AR book that teaches about volcanoes. Use interactive slider to control everything from volcano formation and the movement of tectonic plates to the eruption of Mount St Helens.
Virtual Pop-Up Book [12]	Picture storybook that combined 2D printed page with 3D images.

Figure 1 shows the classification of the augmented book based on their physicality which parallels the Continuum of Object Meaning for tangible interface and the reality-virtuality continuum [9]. Based on these motivations, mixed reality book which digitally augmenting and enhancing real books has the potential to promote understanding on scientific research.

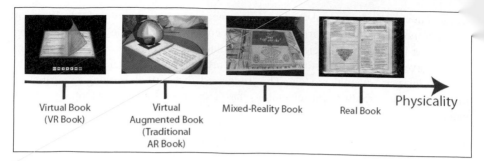

Fig. 1. The Physically Continuum

2.3 Learning Principles

Developing any medium of effective materials that facilitate learning requires an understanding and appreciation of the principles underlying how people learn. One of the related basic principle of learning is social constructivist approach which emphasized that learning occurs through sensory experiences and interaction with the environment. This statement was supported by traditional sensory stimulation theory has as its basic premise that effective learning occurs when the senses are stimulated. Laird quotes research found that the vast majority of knowledge held by adults is learned through seeing (75%), hearing (13%) and the other senses - touch, smell and taste (12%) [13]. By stimulating the senses, especially the visual sense, learning can be enhanced. However, this theory says that if multi-senses are stimulated, greater learning takes place. Stimulation through the senses is achieved through a greater variety of colours, volume levels, strong statements, facts presented visually, use of a variety of techniques and media.

Most students having difficulties in their studies because of the factors associated with their development of appropriate mental models. To master the abstract science concepts, learners should be able to build generic and runnable mental models which often incorporate invisible factors. Unfortunately, learners have trouble identifying important factors or imagining new perspectives. They also lack of real-life analogies upon which to build their mental models [14]. As a result, most learners—including many science majors—have difficulty understanding science concepts and models at the qualitative level, let alone the problems that occur with quantitative formulation. These misconceptions, based on a lifetime of experience, are very difficult to remediate with instructionist pedagogical strategies. Substantial research indicates that traditional lectures and laboratory sessions are not adequate for teaching difficult science concepts.

Often the mental models do not adequately explain the phenomena and need to be explicitly changed through appropriate instruction to more strongly represent the phenomena. In [15], Sopiah also added that the methods of instruction in physics, biology and science should emphasize the development of scientific reasoning skills, as these skills are required for conceptual understanding. Dede [14] mentioned a few methods to help learners master complex scientific concept : attract learners to engage in the learning activity, using meaningful representations, using multiple mapping of information and additionally learning-by-doing. A method suggested to help arners develop good mental models is to provide *conceptual models* [16]. Whereas a mental model exists in a learner's mind, conceptual models are devices presented by teachers or instructional materials. Computer diagram, animations, and video presentations have all been suggested as means of providing conceptual models that help develop learners' mental models. This suggested that virtual learning environment that incorporates multimedia technology has great potential for developing mental models [17].

2.4 Virtual Environment and Conceptual Understanding

One goal of science education is the conceptual understanding. There are many definitions for conceptual understanding. In [18], Nazli defined conceptual understanding as correct mental model, while in [15], Sopiah in her study defined conceptual understanding as the degree to which a student's explanation of the concept corresponds to the scientifically accepted explanation. In [2], Mayer referred understanding as a students' ability to creatively use presented information to solve problem transfer.

A number of educational projects using VR or MR technology that promote conceptual understanding have been developed for the teaching of science subjects. The users ranging from pre-school to tertiary education that have been applied in formal and informal educational settings with a goal to apply and evaluate the potential of VR or MR as a medium for educating students. Examples AR or MR application for tertiary education to learn the spatial relationship of the sun and earth [19], chemistry education [20] and structural molecular biology[21] . There are MR applications for informal education or semi-formal learning such as educational exhibits for use in science centres, museums and libraries[22].

AR and MR have several features that aid conceptual understanding :

- As a new technology, MR draws people's attention. Drawing students' attention is an important factor in instruction [23].
- Can be used to create a constructivist environment to enhance learning [14]. In [20], Chen used AR as an alternative way to view the chemistry world and allowed students to interact with the system and discover knowledge by themselves.
- Increase reliance on sensory information which allow users to interact with the system by using their body, especially hands, and provides 'sensorimotor feedback' [24].
- Create visual images and spatial cues which users can obtain a sense of spatial feeling. Main advantage of virtual objects is that they can be animated, respond to the users actions and are not constrained by the costs and practical or physical limitations of real objects [22].
- Provides a first-person experience.
- A tool which requires users to interact and think carefully since users have to concentrate on the AR system and focus on virtual objects which require them to pay more attention to think about what happens next. And thus make them think more deliberately [25].

3 Mixed Reality Tissue Engineering Book

Mixed Reality Tissue Engineering Book (MRTE Book) is a real book that use AR technology and   integrated the multimedia elements with content. In this section, we describe a learning environment model for MRTE Book's affordances work with other factors in shaping a meaningful learning, the content, software and hardware for developing MRTE Book.

3.1 Model of Learning Environment

One of the main problems with virtual reality or mixed reality as a learning tool is that there are hardly any theories or models upon which to found and justify the application development [26]. Figure 2 shows a model that describes how we believe a MRTE Book's affordances work with other factors in shaping a meaningful learning environment which was adapted from VR learning [26] and meaningful learning process [27].

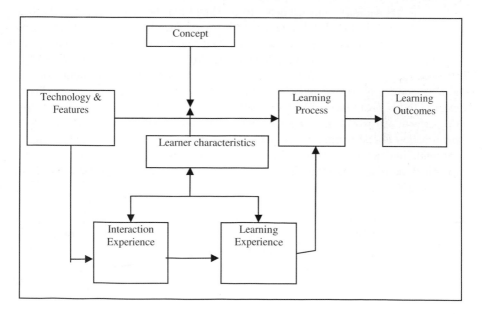

Fig. 2. Model of Learning Environment MRTE Book

Concept
Tissue engineering concepts involves with three-dimensional, invisible, temporal and few observable real-life metaphors. To give the basic exposure of tissue engineering concepts, this MRTE Book prototype will consist of four modules : *The Natural World, The Science of Tissue Engineering, Glossary* and *Mind Test.*

The Natural World - This module will first introduce the concept of tissue engineering by exposing to the innate ability of lower life forms (starfish arm and lizard tails) to regenerate lost parts and limited ability in human. This module also will give basic introduction to cells and tissues.

The Science of Tissue Engineering – This module will introduce the basic concept of tissue engineering, the needs for tissue engineering, and the basic process of tissue engineering.

Glossary – This module will give more detail explanation on Cells, Tissue, Tissue Growth, Scaffolding etc.

Mind Test – Consist of printed set of questions to reflect students understanding.

Technology & Features
In [24], the characteristics of AR and MR are: combines real and virtual; interactive in real time and registered in 3-D. So MR technology support 3-D representation and multisensory cues. The goal of this MRTE Book is as a visualization technology that will explain the in-vivo and in-vitro process to support the learning experience on understanding Tissue Engineering concept [24]. This can be achieve by adding virtual visual and auditory enhancements to a printed real book which have the basic background [25]. MRTE Book might help learners since learners be able to interact with complex and invisible phenomena and concepts through familiar cognitive and physical means to better understand the content. MRTE Book' s features are likely to influence the learning as it can enhances a user's perception of and interaction with the real world. The virtual objects display information that the user cannot directly detect with his own senses. The information conveyed by the virtual objects helps a user perform real-world tasks. Besides that, the unique capabilities of MR include the amplification of real world environments, the ability of team members to talk face-to-face while interacting simultaneously in the virtual environment, and the capacity to promote kinesthetic learning through physical movement through sensory spatial contexts [26].

Learner characteristics
Learner characteristics refer to the pre-existing knowledge and capabilities that learner brings to the learning situation. For this research, the target group will focus on novices rather than experts, that is on third and fourth year Biomedical students who lack of prerequisite knowledge and capabilities for the subject domain [28]. According to Mayer in [2], less skilled students are most likely to benefit from direct instruction for the to-be-learned material, whereas more skilled students are likely to easily understand the concepts.   They also have enough computer skills and gaming experience which can motivate them to use the MRTE Book prototype.

Interaction experience
Interaction experience refer to how easily the user can interact with the system. For visualization and tracking, this prototype is using marker that use a handheld camera manipulated by the user and a computer screen behind the book. User can interact with the system by flipping the book page, moving marker and using real artifacts that normally used in the laboratory.

Learning experience

In order, for the learners to be motivated and engage, this MRTE Book will enhance of visual representations with multisensory cues. So MRTE Book will emphasize on audio-visual experience which involving temporal and contextual conceptualisation. These characteristics can help users to feel presence and enjoy during learning process.

Learning process

Learning processes refer to the way in which students encode to-be-learned material. This will affected by how the instruction is design and the information processing inside the participants memory. MRTE which use semi-formal learning will integrate the constructivist learning model namely Needham Instructional Constructivist Model which integrate five interrelated processes jointly lead to students' integrated understanding : orientation, generating the idea, structuring the idea, application of the idea and reflection. This constructivist learning cycle activity sequences will promote learners' understanding by trigger their cognitive conflict through assimilation, accommodation and disequilibrium.

Learning outcomes

The learning outcome refers to the knowledge that the students acquires as a result of the learning processes. This semi-formal learning intends to promote learners' understanding on tissue engineering concept.

3.2 Content

This MRTE Book will be printed with 2D background scene. The computer will generate virtual content either 3D static models, 3D dynamic models, ambient sound (music, background) and spatial sound (sound depending on the user action and location).

3.3 Hardware and Software

For the development the minimum hardware requirements are :
- Pentium 4
- Monitor
- Graphics card
- Web cam

Related software are:
- Virtools with integrated ARToolKitPlus
- Related software for creating and editing 3D image (3D Studio Max), Adobe Premiere

ARToolKitPlus generated from ARToolKit applications which allow virtual imagery to be superimposed over live video of the real world. By using fiducial marker which is black squares used as tracking markers. The ARToolKitPlus tracking works as follows:

- The camera captures video of the real world and sends it to the computer.
- Software on the computer searches through each video frame for any square shapes.
- If a square is found, the software uses some mathematics to calculate the position of the camera relative to the black square.
- Once the position of the camera is known a computer graphics model is drawn from that same position.
- This model is drawn on top of the video of the real world and so appears stuck on the square marker.

Figure 3 shows the basic of tracking in MRTE Book.

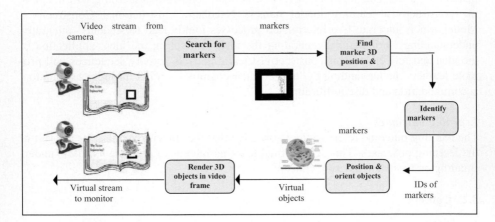

Fig. 3. Tracking In MRTE Book

4   Conclusion and Future Works

In this paper we have discussed the potential of mixed reality book as a visualization tool to promote understanding on science research particularly Tissue Engineering. We also describe a model that of a MRTE Book's affordances work with other factors in shaping a meaningful learning, the content, software and hardware required for developing MRTE Book.

References

1. Vince, J.: Virtual Reality System. Addison-Wesley, Reading (1995)
2. Mayer, R.E.: The Cambridge Handbook of Multimedia Learning. Cambridge University Press, Cambridge (2005)
3. Cawood, S., Fiala, M.: Augmented Reality: A Practical Guide. The Pragmatic Programmers (2007)
4. Zhigeng Pana, A.D.C., Yanga, H., Zhua, J., Shia, J.: Virtual reality and mixed reality for virtual learning environments. Computers & Graphics 30(2006), 20–28 (2006)

5. Kirkley, S.E., Kirkley, J.R.: Creating Next Generation Blended Learning Environments Using Mixed Reality, Video Games and Simulations. Tech.Trends 49(3), 42–53 (2005)
6. Firdaus-Raih, M., Senafi, S., Murad, A.M., Sidik, N.M.: A nationwide biotechnology outreach and awareness program for Malaysian high schools. Electronic Journal of Biotechnology 8(1) (2005)
7. Marshall, C.C.: Reading and Interactivity in the Digital Library: Creating an experience that transcends paper. In: Proceedings of CLIR/Kanazawa Institute of Technology Roundtable (2005)
8. Craig, A., McGrath, R.E.: Augmenting Science Texts with Inexpensive Interactive 3D Illustrations (2007)
9. Grasset, R., Duenser, A., Billinghurst, M.: The Design of a Mixed-Reality Book: Is It Still a Real Book? (2008)
10. Billinghurst, M., Kato, H., Poupyrev, I.: The MagicBook— Moving Seamlessly between Reality and Virtuality. IEEE Computers & Graphics Application 21(3), 6–8 (2001)
11. Woods, E., Billinghurst, M.: Graham Aldridge. AR Volcano (2004)
12. Taketa, N., Hayashi, K., Kato, H., Noshida, S.: Virtual pop-up book based on augmented reality. In: Smith, M.J., Salvendy, G. (eds.) HCII 2007. LNCS, vol. 4558, pp. 475–484. Springer, Heidelberg (2007)
13. Laird, D.: Approaches To Training and development. Addison Wesley, Reading (1985)
14. Chris Dede, M.S., Bowen Loftin, R.: Using Virtual Reality Technology to Convey Abstract Scientific Concepts. In: Learning the Sciences of the 21st Century: Research, Design, and Implementing Advanced Technology Learning Environments (1997)
15. Moi, S.N., Abdullah, S.: The Effects of Inquiry-based Computer Simulation with Cooperative Learning on Scientific Thinking and Conceptual Understanding of Gas Laws Among Form Four Students in Malaysian Smart Schools. PhD Dissertation, Universiti Sains Malaysia (2005)
16. Hagmann, S., Mayer, R.E., Nenniger, P.: Using structural theory to make a work-processing manual more understandable. Leaning and Instructions 8(1), 19–35 (1998)
17. Alessi, S.M., Trollip, S.R.: Multimedia For Learning, Methods and Development. Ally & Bacon (2001)
18. Yahya, N.: Development and Evaluation of a Web-Based Learning System To Support Re-Conceptualization: Basic Electric Circuits. PhD Dissertation, Universiti Teknologi Malaysia (2003)
19. Shelton, B.E.: How Augmented Reality Helps Students Learn Dynamic Spatial Relationships. Ph.D Dissertation, College of Education, University Washington, USA (2003)
20. Chen, Y.-C.: A study of comparing the use of augmented reality and physical models in chemistry education. In: VRCIA 2006, Hong Kong, June 14–17 (2006)
21. Gillet, A., Olson, A.: Tangible Augmented Interfaces for Structural Molecular Biology. In: ISMAR 2005 (2005)
22. Woods, E., Billinghurst, M., Aldridge, G., Garrie, B.: Augmenting the Science Centre and Museum Experience. In: Proceedings: 2nd International Conference on Computer Graphics and Interactive Techniques, Singapore, pp. 230–236 (2004)
23. Gagne, R.M., Briggs, L.J., Wager, W.W.: Principles of Instructional Design. Harcourt Brace Jovanovich College Publishers (1992)
24. Hanson, K., Shelton, B.E.: Design and Development of Virtual Reality: Analysis of Challenges Faced by Educators. Educational Technology & Society 11(1), 118–131 (2008)

25. Schank, P., Kozma, R.: Learning chemistry through the use of representation-based knowledge building environment. Journal of Computers In Mathematics and Science Teaching 21(3), 253–279 (2002)
26. Salzman, M.C., Dede, C., Bowen Loftin, R., Chen, J.: The Design and Evalution of Virtual Reality-based Learning Environments. In: Presence: Teleoperators and Virtual Environments (special issue on education) (1995)
27. Mayer, R.E.: Models For Understanding. Review of Educational Research 59(1), 43–64 (1989)
28. Yusoff, R.C.M., Zaman, H.B.: Mixed Reality Technology To Promote Understanding on Tissue Engineering Concept. In: International Conference on Educational Research and Practice, Putrajaya Malaysia (2009)

Usability Evaluation of Multimedia Courseware (MEL-SindD)

Rahmah Lob Yussof and Halimah Badioze Zaman

Jabatan Sains Maklumat, Fakulti Teknologi dan Sains Maklumat,
Universiti Kebangsaan Malaysia,
43600 Bangi, Selangor Darul Ehsan, Malaysia

Abstract. Constructive evaluations on any software are needed to ensure the effectiveness and usability of the software. This assesment on the multimedia courseware is part of the researcher's study towards the development and usability of the early reading software for students with Down Syndrome (MEL-SindD). This paper will discuss the usability assesment of this courseware, the methods used for the evaluation as well as suitable approaches that can be deployed to evaluate the courseware effectiveness to disabled children.

Keywords: Usability, Courseware, Syndrome Down.

1 Introduction

The research on the development and usability of the MEL-SindD focuses on the creation of an effective courseware targeted to improve early reading amongst children with Down Syndrome (DS). Such children differ from normal children in numerous dimensions such as cognitive processing, language acquisitions, physical ability as well as personal and social characteristics. Compared to normal children, DS children also have lower motivation levels and will generally require more time to complete a task.

Computer-based technology can positively impact students with learning disabilities both in primary and secondary schools [1] and [2]. Multimedia softwares combining audio, graphics, animation, texts and video will help to improve motivation and strengthen learning. [3]. A number of independent research also discovered positive shift in behaviors of students with learning disabilities when technology is made part of the learning process [4] and [5]. Nevertheless, to ensure the effectivenes any courseware that is developed, an objective usability assessment mus conducted.

This paper will discuss the evaluation on how MEL-SindD impact the me of children with DS when they are at the early stage of learning how to evaluation is done to observe the results on the effectiveness of MEL involves a sample population of 11 DS students and 3 teachers from schools for children with learning disabilities as well as the pa students.

ᵣe Zaman et al. (Eds.): IVIC 2009, LNCS 5857, pp. 337–343, 2009.
⸗rlag Berlin Heidelberg 2009

2   Software Usability Evaluation

Human computer interaction (HCI) research covers all aspects of human factors and performance improvements to hardware and software. [6] defines HCI as "the study of the relationships which exist between human users and the computer systems they use in the performance of their various tasks" (p. 1). The goal of HCI is to improve and optimize the interaction between humans and technology. This requires an understanding of environment, human restrictions and constraints, task, performance requirements, technology, and other components that influence this interaction. Improvements to systems are measured through evaluation and testing. Usability evaluation practices are an integral part of the HCI life cycle.

This usability assessment can be used in many ways. The evaluation is done to obtain quantitative and qualitative data which can help to produce empirical results which can tested statistically. The evaluation can also be used to improve the interface of any softwares before these programs are marketed since it can help to identify anomalies and mistakes within the softwares [7]. According to [8], evaluating the usability of a courseware differs from evaluating a commercial software because the results of studying the courseware are obtained from understanding the materials delivered and not from merely the activities of using the product. As such, the evaluation must be done to consider not only the inter-face of the courseware but also the effective learning of students.

Probably the best known definition of usability is by [9]: Usability is a quality attribute that assesses how easy user interfaces are to use. Usability by Nielsen is defined by five quality characteristics: learnability, efficiency, memorability, errors and satisfaction. However, the definition of usability from International Standards Organization(ISO) 9241-11 is and important standards related to usability. (ISO) 9241-11 defines usability as *"the extent to which a product can be used by specified users to achieve specified goals with effectiveness, efficiency and satisfaction in context of use or particular environments"* [10]. The ISO 9241-11 is defined usability by three characteristics: effectiveness, efficiency and satisfaction. This standard is becoming the main reference in usability. In addition, it is largely recognized in literature, the ISO 9241-11 definition of usability is used in recent Common Industry Format (CIF) for usability testing.

The usability characteristics that are measured during usability evaluation are common across most usability evaluation methods (UEM). To date, many methods that allow systematic ways of evaluating usability in software have been developed. By integrating these methods into the various stages within the life cycle of software design and development, the usability of the software could be assured. Table 1 shows the summary of usability evaluation methods. Researchers and practitioners must make tradeoffs when selecting a usability evaluation method in a particular development situation. Typical issues to be considered include the nature of the study, the timing of the study with reference to the design life cycle of the product, the costs and the availability of test subjects and experts [11].

Table 1. Summary of Usability evaluation methods

Evaluation Methods	Explanation
Heuristic	It involves usability expert evaluator. Assessment is done based on a checklist or pre-prepared questionnaire
Cognitive Walkthrough	A task-oriented method. Testing is done based on a checklist which has been prepared. Emphasizes on cognitive issues, such as learnability, by analyzing the mental processes required by the user
Pluralistic Walkthrough	An extension of cognitive walkthrough. Users, developers, and usability experts go through the interface and discuss on the elements concern.
Observation	The evaluator will assess how users interacts with the computers and the softwares in questions. The evaluator will note interactions which can represent success, failure, happiness, and dissatisfaction displayed by users
Questionnaires	A questionnaire was used to obtain information pertaining to the user such as competency levels, previous experiences using computers and softwares, interests, opinions and any specific needs.
Think Aloud	It involves having an end user continuously thinking out loud while using the software. By verbalizing their thoughts, the users enable the evaluator to understand how they view the software, which makes it easier to identify the end user misconceptions.
Interview	Meetings between the evaluator and users were arranged and interviews were conducted to obtain information relating to the needs, methods that can be used, opinion as well as responses towards the courseware.

3 Study Environment and Methods

An extensive evaluation was done involving one student with DS. The courseware was developed after taking into account the needs and problems faced by this particular student. The testing of the usability was done to obtain feedback on the user-friendliness and effectiveness of the courseware. Further extensive evaluations were done involving 11 additional students with SD from Sekolah Rendah Kebangsaan Koperasi Polis, Kuala Lumpur. All students have mild intellectual disability, and have limited reading skills.

MEL-SindD was developed as a teaching and learning aid targeted to help motivate students with DS to learn how to master reading skills. To succeed in this goal, the courseware needs to be designed with ease-of-use functionality that can be accessed by the user.

The learning environment consists of a courseware called MEL-SindD, a computer notebook, a webcam camera and a microphone. MEL-SindD consists of four modules and each module contains sub-modules. The study was conducted in the students' everyday environment.

3.1 Data Collection

The procedure for data gathering and usability assessment is based on observation, interview, and performing an expert evaluation of the courseware. The usability testing procedures for the courseware can be divided into a number of phases as indicated in Table 2.

Data collections were done over several months, in pre stage that is before the development phase and during the usability evaluation. The data collection process started by interviewing paediatrician and teachers of DS students. This is followed by creating a social relationship with the students, identifying the learning needs of these individuals as well as understanding issues through conversations with parents. Medical specialists, teachers and parents were interviewed as informants on the background of the students and the research.

In Phase 1, data collection was done iteratively with the subjects of this research during the development of the courseware. Testing was done to objective of knowing the suitability levels of the courseware based on the learning problems faced by SD students. During the testing, improvements on the courseware were done continuously until all the needs of these students can be addressed. The usability testing covers a number of usability characteristics which can benefit SD students. In Phase II, the usability assessment is further strengthened by involving 11 students. Data gathering in Phase III was conducted by the researcher will specialist teachers and parents of the selected DS students. All questions were asked based on an interview schedule that was prepared beforehand.

Table 2. Phases of data collection and evaluation methods

Stages	Activities	Usability Evaluation Method
Pre I, II, and III	Data gathering during initial analysis stage involving (I) peadiatricians, teachers and students with DS who are involved under the study (II)The researcher associates with SD students inorder to built trust between the students and the researcher. (III). Identify the needs of the students involved	Interview, observation, informal walkthrough, cognitive walkthrough
I	Involves testing done iteratively on test-subject students	Observation, informal walkthrough
II	Assesment was done on the 11 students selected to undergo the observation as test subjects	Observation, informal walkthrough,
III	Data gathering were done with teachers and parents of the selected DS students.	Interview, Expert evaluations

4 Usability Evaluation Methods in This Study

Usability evaluation of the MEL-SindD courseware was done through usability evaluation methods such as observation, interview, informal walkthrough, cognitive walkthrough and expert evaluation. The different methods of data collection revealed different aspects of how the courseware support the learning of Down Syndrome students.

4.1 Observational

During observations the researcher observes courseware use in the user's environment. The goal is to observe without disturbing the user in their work environment. Observation is really the simplest of all usability methods since it involves visiting one or more users and the doing as little as possible in order not to interfere with their work. Of course, the observer can take notes (unobtrusively), and it may even be possible to use videotaping in some environments [11].

In this study, observation involves visiting users in their school. Testing with DS students was carried out based on visual observations since these students were unable to respond to the written questionnaire given. The researcher directed the students on how to use the courseware and later the students were given the opportunity to explore the courseware by themselves. The researcher was always on hand to give assistance whenever needed. A checklist on the user-friendliness of the courseware was used when the researcher made her observations.

Observations were also carried out using video and screen recordings. Video recordings are needed to observe behaviors [12] of DS students during the entire usage sessions of the MEL-SindD courseware. Every behavior and body language were recorded. Screen recordings were done suing screen recording softwares and this allowed the researcher to observe the interactions between the DS students with the MEL-SindD courseware. The screen recordings can be used as supportive data to complement the video recordings [12].

4.2 Interview

Interviewing is a good method for qualitative data collection. Interviews with paediatrician was done to obtain feedback on the views on DS. Interviews with teachers were conducted to know more on the teaching and learning scenarios involving DS students as well as the developments and problems faced by such students in school.

This approach was also adopted with the DS students who were selected as test subjects to this research. Even interviewing a student with learning disabilities such as SD requires special consideration from researcher. Simple, short and clear questions are necessary to provoke answers from the students. Sometimes the answer has to be waited for, and the interviewer must be patient. The researcher needs to know the participant's characteristics to interpret the reasons for delays in answering. It is important to keep the interview in a slow pace.

4.3 Informal Walkthrough

Walkthrough methods are based on cognitive theory [13]. An informal walkthrough is a method where the moderator does not prepare detailed test tasks in advance but lets the participant explore the system in the user own pace and order. This method is applicable to find out how intuitive and easy to navigate the system. To support this method, a checklist of the functionality is derived.

In this research, the informal walkthrough was used to collect information from the users. The students have been exposed to the courseware several times and the informal walkthrough was started by asking the students, one at a time, to show the researcher how they used the courseware. For example, "what would you like to show to me?", "what do you do with it?". Based on these questions, the students demonstrated how they used some of the button to do the navigation. A checklist of functionality is also prepared.

4.4 Cognitive Walkthrough

The main focus of the cognitive walkthrough is to identify ease of use, ease of learning and usability problem. This method is a task-oriented method by which the researcher with the help of usability expert explores the courseware functionality: that is cognitive walkthrough simulates step-by-step user behaviour for a given task. cognitive walkthrough emphasizes cognitive issues, such as learnability, by analyzing the mental processes required by the user. This can be achieved during the design by making the repertory of available actions salient.

In this research the cognitive walkthrough help the researcher to effective identify problems arising from interaction with the courseware, and to help to define users' goals.

4.5 Expert Evaluation

This method of evaluation also called as heuristic evaluation. Heuristic evaluation involves having a small set of evaluators examine the interface and judge its compliance set with recognized usability principles or interface design guidelines [11]. According to Nielsen, the procedure for conducting heuristic evaluation involves individual and private evaluation of the interface by individuals. Nielsen suggests that the researcher should go through the interface at least twice.

In this study, the experts in interface design and experts in learning contents was used to evaluate the courseware at the last phase of usability evaluation. During the actual evaluation, the expert goes through the interface several times, inspects the various interactive elements, and compares them with a checklist. Once all the evaluations are completed, the results are aggregated and shared.

5   Conclusion

This paper puts forward some explanation on the usability assessments of MEL-SindD courseware which is currently being developed by the researcher. The evaluation was done using methods explained in Table 2. As such, this study also provide additional complementary findings.

The evaluation was conducted after taking into account various assessment tools to seek the effectiveness of the courseware and uncover usability problems for the perspective of the user. The evaluation was done on the users on a one-to-one basis.

The study also revealed the special nature of working with users with learning disabilities. The researcher has to pay extra attention to obtain trust amongst the users, and getting to know them before the evaluation session.

References

1. Forgrave, K.E.: Assistive technology: Empowering students with learning disabilities. The Clearing House 75(3), 122–127 (2002)
2. Judge, S.L.: Computer applications in programs for young children with disabilities: current status and future directions. Journal of Special Education Technology 16(1), 29–40 (2001)
3. M.A.Z.M. Zakaria, N. Saman.: Pembangunan dan penilaian perisian berbantukan komputer bertajuk "promosi" menggunakan elemen motivasi ARCS. Fakulti Pendidikan, UTM (2005)
4. Howard, W., Ellis, H., Rasmussen, K.: From the arcade to the classroom: Capitalizingbof students' sensory rich media preferences in discipline-based learning. College Student Journal 38(3), 431–440 (2004)
5. Lebedine-Manzoni, M.: To what students attribute their academic success and unsuccess. Education 124(4), 699–708 (2004)
6. Faulkner, C.: The essence of human-computer interaction. Prentice Hall, London (1998)
7. Shneiderman, B.: Designing the user interface strategies for effective human-computer interaction, 3rd edn. Addison-Wesley, Reading (1998)
8. Mayes, J.T., Fowler, C.J.: Learning technology and usability: A framework for understanding courseware. Interacting with Computers 11, 485–497 (1999)
9. Nielsen, J.: Usability 101: Introduction to usability. Jakob Nielsen's Alertbox (2003), http://www.useit.com/alertbox/20030825.html
10. Jokela, T., Livari, N., Matero, J., Karukka, M.: The standard of user-centered design and the standard definition of usability: Analyzing ISO 13407 against ISO 9241-11
11. Nielsen, J.: Usability engineering. AP Professional, Cambridge (1993)
12. Ismail, M.: Perisian Kursus Multimedia (BACA) untuk pembelajaran Bahasa Melayu peringkat Pra sekolah menggunakan pendekatan Vygotsky. Tesis Dr. Fal. Universiti Kebangsaan Malaysia. Bangi (2009)
13. Rieman, J., Franzke, M., Redmiles, D.: Usability evaluation with cognitive walkthrough. In: CHI 1995 Conference proceeding: Human factors in computing systems, pp. 387–388. ACM Press, New York (1995)

Development of an Augmented Reality Rare Book and Manuscript for Special Library Collection (AR Rare-BM)

Behrang Parhizkar and Halimah Badioze Zaman

Department of Information Science, Faculty of Information Science and Technology,
University Kebangsaan Malaysia, 43600 Bangi, Selangor
haniukm@yahoo.com, hbz@ftsm.ukm.my

Abstract. This research aims to study the development of augmented reality of rare books or manuscripts of special collections in the libraries. Augmented reality has the ability to enhance users' perception of and interaction with the real world. Libraries has to ensure that this special collection is well handled as these rare books and manuscripts are priceless as they represent the inheritance of each nation. The use of augmented reality will be able to model these valuable manuscripts and rare books and appear as augmented reality to ensure that the collection can be better maintained. Users will be able to open the augmented rare book, and flip the pages, as well as read the contents of the rare books and manuscripts using the peripheral equipment such as the HMD or the Marker. The AR Rare-BM developed is modeled as an augmented reality that allows users to put the augmented rare book on his palm or table and manipulate it while reading. Users can also leave a bookmark in the AR Rare-BM after reading so that they can read their favourite sections again at a later date.

Keywords: Augmented reality, Virtual environment, Rare books and manuscripts, Tangible User Interface.

1 Introduction

In the last decade, a new domain study in Computer Science and Information Technology has occurred, called augmented reality. Augmented Reality is a variation of Virtual Reality which allows users to see the real world, with virtual objects superimposed upon or composited with the real world [1]. Therefore, augmented reality supplements reality, rather than completely replaces it. The field of augmented reality has been acknowledged as one of the most promising area in knowledge and computer graphics. Currently, many innovative applications have been implemented and highlighted on the importance of augmented reality in the daily lives of mankind. It is a technology that creates a view of the real scene by incorporating computer-generated virtual objects, including those with full three-dimensional properties, into the scene [2]. Figure 1 shows how users can interact with the real world with the virtual objects composited with the real world.

H. Badioze Zaman et al. (Eds.): IVIC 2009, LNCS 5857, pp. 344–355, 2009.
© Springer-Verlag Berlin Heidelberg 2009

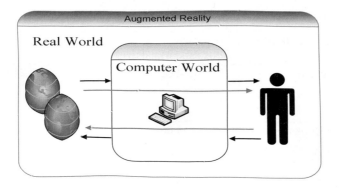

Fig. 1. Augmented Reality

In this paper, the authors discuss how rare books and manuscripts were modeled in order that users (namely, researchers) in various fields researching in libraries can use priceless old rare books and manuscripts in their study, by flipping the pages and read the contents through the augmented reality books instead of the real books and manuscripts. In addition, users can also search through augmented rare books and bookmark the specific pages to be referred to at a later date. The bookmarked pages can be saved in the data base and can be printed out based on the particular pages required. This rare book and manuscript augmented reality system is called Augmented Rare Book and Manuscript (AR Rare-BM).

1.1 Problem Statement

Rare books and manuscripts in every library are among the most valuable and priceless collections, because they represent the heritage of the nation. On the other hand, due to the fact that these books are used as references for various fields of study, there are normally, numerous requests by researchers and students. Therefore, the more the number of requests by researchers and students, the greater the tendency and the eventuality for these books and manuscripts to get spoilt and damaged.Table1 shows the total number of rare books and manuscript and requests by researchers and students in 2007 at the Special Collection of National Library Malaysia (*Nadir Koleksi Perpustakaan Negara Malaysia*) and Special Collection of Universiti Kebangsaan Malaysia (*Nadir Koleksi Perpustakaan Tun Seri Lanang*).

Interview sessions conducted with librarians from the special collections of both Negara Library of Malaysia and Tun Sri Lanang Library, Universiti Kebangsaan Malaysia indicated that one of the most important requests often made by researchers was to have the permission to access the special collection respectively. The rare books and manuscripts are not only old and rare but very valuable for both the libraries. For both these libraries, users may sometimes not be allowed to borrow or access certain special items. This is because the rare books and manuscripts are hand written in materials that are sensitive and can be easily damaged and tarnished. Due to the fact that these documents are rare and valuable they must be kept in safety for generations to come, the researchers need special permission to access these books. Moreover, researchers are not allowed to take out rare books or manuscript for further

.ble 1. Total number of rare books and manuscripts in UKM and NLM

	Type of Collection	Total No. of Rare Books and Manuscripts	Number of requests for use
	Manuscripts	4,267	4,214
2.	Rare Books	3,067	690
	Total	**7,443**	**4,904**

Table 2. Problems faced by Librarians from NLM and UKM

Name of Library	Similar problems faced by NLM & TSL (UKM)
1. Special Collection National Library of Malaysia 2. Special Collection of Tun Sri Lanang. UKM	• Long process to obtain permission to use the special collections from both Libraries. • Manuscripts and rare books are easily damaged and tarnished, thus use has to be limited. • Rare books and manuscripts need special care and environment. • Users are given limited time to use the rare books and manuscripts. • Users are not allowed to photocopy any page from the manuscripts and rare books.

reading and researching. This means that they have very limited time to keep those books. In addition, they are not allowed to photocopy any page of the rare books or manuscripts. In order to overcome these problems as well as those shown in Table 2, this research applied the augmented reality technology to provide the solution. Figure 5 shows how a rare book was modelled in to the 3D objects. This has made it inconvenient for many researchers.

In addition, the library staff interviewed also mentioned that they constantly received complaints from researchers on the rules applied to the use of rare book collections in both the libraries. The existence of stringent rules and regulations on the use of rare and old books as well as manuscripts collections, made it difficult for researchers to make important references to valuable knowledge such as History, Economics, Geography and Medicine. It was with this problem in mind, that this research was conducted. This research involves the design and development of augmented reality technology on rare books and manuscript to help libraries overcome the problem faced by their users to access rare books and manuscripts for research purposes. Among the objectives of this study is to model the rare books and manuscripts using augmented reality technology as well as the use of special equipment such as the HMD and Marker, to enable users to browse the rare books and manuscripts while they are walking in the real library without actually handling the real books and manuscripts. With this technology, they will be able to open the augmented rare books and manuscripts, flip and control their pages, and read their contents using HMD or marker. This means that users can experience a virtual object in the real world and at the same time, have the opportunity to open the rare books which are placed on the table or in their palms, and enjoy reading the contents of the books. Users can also use the bookmark functionality of the AR Rare BM on particular pages and save it in their own accounts. This means that they can print out the bookmarked pages at a later time. Users can also search through the augmented pages by typing the page number in the portable device.

2 Related Work

Since the first augmented reality interface was developed by Southerland in 1960's [4], various applications and research have been accomplished in the field of augmented reality. Research on Augmented Reality and its applications are more popular and advanced today. The development of this technology has helped researchers innovate and improve the technology of Augmented Reality to meet the life style and needs of societies throughout the world. The marker-based augmented reality technology particularly, has been used in various applications domains such as business, education, architecture, military, science, medicine and entertainment. The research discussed in this paper incorporates the use of various elements such as tracking, user interface and display techniques. Tracking technique is one of the fundamental enabling technologies for augmented reality[5];[6].There are various tracking techniques applied in augmented reality such as sensor-based tracking system, hybrid tracking techniques and vision-based tracking [7].

AR Rare BM applied the vision-based tracking technique. The advantage of this technique is that registration can be very accurate, and there is no delay between the motions of real and virtual scene elements [8]. In contrast, marker-based methods are not scalable to handle large scale navigation which may be required in an outdoor environment [9]; [10];[11];[12]. AR Rare-BM improved the accuracy of the tracking, by using the ARToolkit markers or ARTag markers for a small scale environment. Zhang conducted an interesting comparative study on various types of visual markers [13]; [14]; [15];[16] that can be applied in Augmented Reality applications.

The apprehension that constantly affects researchers in this field is creating appropriate interaction techniques and user interface for augmented reality applications which allow end users to interact with the virtual content in a perceptive way. Among all the techniques which were applied and proposed by researchers in last decade, three of them are the most appropriate for user interface. These techniques are tangible augmented reality, collaborative augmented reality and hybrid augmented reality interface. In AR Rare-BM system, we concentrate on tangible augmented reality interface. Tangible augmented reality interface combines the enhanced display possibilities of augmented reality with the intuitive manipulation and interaction of physical objects or Tangible User Interface [18]. Tangible augmented reality interfaces are those in which each virtual object is registered to a physical object and the users interact with virtual objects by manipulating the corresponding tangible objects. In the Tangible Augmented Reality approach, the physical objects and interactions are equally as important as the virtual imagery and provide a very intuitive way to interact with the augmented reality interface [19];[20]; [21]; [22];[23]; [24]. A study conducted on the combination of physical and tangible qualities of a real map with the possibilities of dynamic and selective visualisation of digital media [24] was conducted in 2005. Another related study is one on the universal media book which applied a mixed reality interface for accessing information that combined projected information and a physical book that acted as the display surface. The pages of the book were not marked with fiducials marker, to enable the user to experience interacting data using tactile or visual simulation in a natural way [25]. Hand gesture recognition is one of the most natural ways to interact with an augmented reality environment[26];[27][28]; [29];[30];[31;[32];[33].

One way to create a new type of visually enhanced books is the use of augmented reality. For example, is the magic book [34]. The magic book explores how interfaces can be developed that allows for seamless transition between physical, augmented and immersive reality in a collaborative setting. The magic book is a normal book that allows users to turn pages, look at pictures, and read text in the book without any additional technology. The basic concept of the augmented instructions (book) is closely related to the MagicBook, proposed as a traditional AR interface that uses a real book to seamlessly transfer users from reality to virtuality. In this research, handheld PC was applied instead of HMD. Based on the current research, the use of HMD was found to be a better choice because it does not require using the hands. However, it has a limitation in that it is difficult to read the document due to low resolution. The use of a tablet can capture writing on a paper notebook and the use of the PDA in addition, can act as an "interaction lens" or window between the physical and electronic documents. Our approach is document-centered, with a software architecture based on layers of physical and electronic information [35].

Various study has been conducted on augmented books, virtual books and 3D books [36]; [37]. These books however, lacked features for accessing large format books, such as an index or table of contents. These limitations parallel the limitations confronted by other attempts to simulate books. Large books have generally been implemented in 2D, with suggestive 3D features like page turning of tabs [39]. For example, Flip Viewer is a 2D based simulated book product with animated page turning that holds collections of objects such as photographs [38]. For visual augmented books, different projects have explored the application of the Magic Book and the memory book concept in different areas such as cultural heritage [39]. Recently, a group of researchers have proposed the integration of a physical controller in an augmented reality books[41]. The research concentrated on how to design and develop applications for educational purposes with the use of the ARToolkit and the domain applied was medicine for children called *My Inside the body Book* (MIBB). The book used 3D objects on pictures illustrated in the book[42].

3 Methodology

In order to overcome the problems faced by the libraries on the handling of their rare books and manuscript collections, a solution in the form of augmented reality rare book and manuscript for special collections in the library called AR Rare-BM was designed using the Iterative-Simulative Participatory Software Development Life Cycle Methodology (ISP- SDLC), where the librarians and researchers were part of the active collaborators of the research in the design and development process. This research provides a solution in the form of an augmented reality rare book to be used in the special collection of libraries. The main contributions were as follows:

i) Developed a suitable methodology for the development of an augmented reality rare book object to be used in special collections of libraries which was based on the Iterative-Simulative Software Development Life Cycle model for Augmented Reality (I-SSDLC-AR).

ii) Designed a suitable model for the development of augmented reality of rare books and manuscripts in library special collections, applying augmented reality techniques, based on Sperling's cognitive theory on haptic interaction approach.

iii) Developed a prototype of an augmented reality book based on the fiducial marker and Head Mounted Display (HMD) called Augmented Reality Rare Books and Manuscripts System (AR Rare-BM).

iv)Designed a system which allows bookmarks be done on augmented pages of the rare book and also allows searching in the augmented pages.

v) Test results on the strengths and weaknesses of the augmented reality rare book and manuscripts system (AR-Rare -BM).

This research delt with the rare books and manuscripts of the special collections of the National Library of Malaysia (NLM). The rare books and manuscripts were modeled to 3D objects using augmented reality techniques. The 3D modeled objects were assigned to the fiducial marker which is pasted on the books as well as the bookshelves in the national library. With the use of the HMD, the augmented reality rare books in special collections of NLM could be browsed and read. Two main options were designed for the users: i) users could walk through the bookshelves of rare books and manuscripts in the library and ii) users can open, flip and read the contents of the pages from the bookshelves. The users used the HMD to track the 3D objects on the markers. As figure 3 shows, the marker which was pasted on a bookshelf, contains the category and list of rare books with their titles. Users used the HMD and walked along the bookshelves and at the same time, track the information in the book. In the second option, users read the contents of the augmented rare books placed on the table. The users were able to also see all descriptions of the book such as the title, introduction and full text of the books by using HMD. The users needed to register as members before they could access to read the augmented rare books and manuscripts. Users could also bookmark particular pages of interest whilst reading the contents. The bookmarked pages could be saved in the portable memory. This also meant that users could print out pages that they wanted to. Moreover, users could search specific pages of each book based on the page number. This also made it easy for users to explore the pages. Figure 3 shows the flow chart of the augmented rare book and manuscript system (AR Rare-BM).

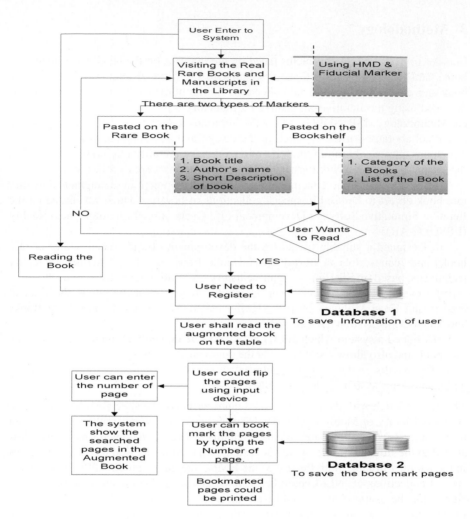

Fig. 3. The flowchart of AR Rare-BM system

4 Implementation

The rare books as shown in Fig 4 belongs to the Special Collection in the National Library of Malaysia *(Nadir Koleksi Perpustakaan Negara Malaysia)*. To demonstrate the effectiveness of the proposed approaches, several procedures were conducted as indicated in Fig 3.The selected rare books were divided into two modules. The first module involved scanning the pages of rare books or manuscript. The scanned pages were saved as image files and were edited by Photoshop. The files were then converted to text files. The second module of implementation stage delt with modelling the rare books to 3D objects. The modelled objects had to be textured and rendered according to the purpose of the research. Texturing and rendering were accomplished using the software called 3D Max. Then, the two modules were combined at this

Fig. 4. Example of the Original Rare Book from NLM

stage. The text format of the scanned pages were then attached to the modelled pages which were designed in 3D Max. The next stage is importing to the ARToolkit whereby, the 3D modelled objects were assigned to the markers. These markers were pasted on the bookshelves as well as the rare books. Finally, the markers on the book shelves and rare book were tracked by the HMD worn by the users. Figure 4 shows an example of the original rare book from NLM.

Based on the figure below, the book at the top was assigned the marker which was pasted on the book. This makes it possible for users to manipulate the book while walking along the bookshelves. This also meant that users could see the title of the book and the name of the authors, as well as a brief description of the book. The book at the bottom shows the complete modeled rare books with its full contents.

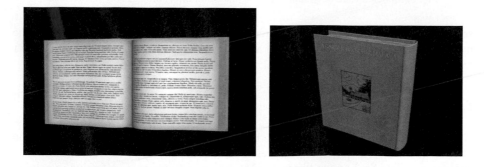

Figure 5 shows 3D book modeled on the table or on the palm of the hand.Thus, users could read the contents of the rare books without causing any harm or damage to the original priceless books of knowledge. In addition, users could also

Fig. 5. Modeled Rare book that could be placed on the Table or Palm of the Hand

search pages of the rare books by entering the number of the particular page on the portable computer device. They could also bookmark the pages of interest for further reading at another time.

5 Conclusion

Augmented reality technology for rare books and manuscripts in a special collection of libraries such as national libraries (eg. National Library of Malaysia) or university libraries (eg. Tun Sri Lanang libary, UKM), has been found to be effective in helping the respective libraries overcame handling and borrowing services problems. Various other domains such as education, training, medicine, and interactive entertainment too can benefit from augmented reality technology. In this research, augmented reality was used to model rare books and manuscripts from the National Library of Malaysia to help overcome problems of both librarians and researchers. Based on this research, user of the NLM (namely researchers), were able open the rare book, flip its pages, as well as read the contents of the 'book' using peripheral equipment such as the HMD or Marker. The AR rare book and manuscript system (AR Rare-BM) developed was designed and modeled as an augmented reality book, which allow users to place the 'rare book' on the table or in the palm of his/her hands to manipulate it. The system was designed and developed using the Iterative-Simulative Participatory Software Development Life Cycle Methodology (ISP- SDLC) in order to create suitable specifications to meet the needs of the users.

References

1. Azuma, R.T.: A Survey of Augmented Reality. Presence: Teleoperators and Virtual Environments 6(4), 355–358 (1997)
2. Vallino, J.R.: Interactive Augmented Reality. Degree Doctor of Philosophy. University of Rochester, New York (1998)
3. Milgram, P., Takemura, H., et al.: Augmented Reality: A Class of Displays on the Reality-Virutality Continuum. In: Das, H. (ed.) SPIE Proceedings: Telemanipulator and Telepresence Technologies, vol. 2351, pp. 282–292. SPIE, San Jose (1994)
4. Southerland, I.: The ultimate display. In: IFIP 1965, pp. 506–508 (1965)
5. Azuma, R.T., Baillot, Y., Behringer, R., Feiner, S., Julier, S., MacIntyre, B.: Recent advances in augmented reality. IEEE Computer Graphics & Applications 21, 34–47 (2001)
6. Kato, H., Billinghurst, M.: Marker Tracking and HMD calibration for a video based augmented reality conferencing system. In: IWAR 1999, pp. 85–94 (1999)
7. Zhou, F., Duh, H.B.L., Billinghurst, M.: IEEE International Symposium on Mixed and Augmented Reality, Cambridge, UK, September 15–18 (2008)
8. Park, B.J., Neumann, U.: Vision-based pose computation: robust and accurate augmented reality tracking. In: IWAR 1999, pp. 3–12 (1999)
9. Pressigout, M., Marchand, E.: Hybrid tracking algorithms for planer and non-planer structure subjects to illumination changes. In: ISMAR 2006, pp. 52–55 (2006)
10. Pressigout, M., Marchand, E.: Model-free augmented reality by virtual visual servoin. In: ICPR 2004, Cambridge, vol. 2, pp. 887–891 (2004)
11. Simon, G., Berger, M.: Pose estimation for planer structures. IEEE Computer Graphics and Application 22(6), 46–53 (2005)
12. Haag, M., Nagel, H.H.: Combination of edge element and optical flow estimates for 3D model based vehicle tracking in traffic image sequences. Int. J. of Computer Vision 35(3), 295–319 (1999)
13. Zhang, X., Nava, N.: Tracking and pose estimation for computer assisted localization in industrial environments. In: IEEE Workshop on Application of Computer Vision, pp. 214–221 (2000)
14. Reiners, D., Stricker, D., Klinker, G., Muller, S.: Augmented reality for construction tasks: Doorlock assembly. In: Proc. IEEE International Workshop on Augmented Reality, New York (1999)
15. Neumann, U., You, S., Cho, Y., Lee, J., Park, J.: Augmented reality tracking in natural environments. In: Otha, Y., Tamura, H. (eds.) Mixed Reality: merging real and virtual worlds, pp. 101–130. Ohmsha, Ltd, Tokyo

16. Navab, N., Cubillo, E., Bascle, B., Lockau, J., Kamsties, K.D., Neuberger, M.: CyliCon: a software platform for the creation and update of virtual factories. In: Proc. of the 7th IEEE International Contefence on Emerging technologies and factory Automation, Barcelona, Spain, pp. 459–463 (1999)
17. Zhang, X., Nava, N.: Tracking and pose estimation for computer assisted localization in industrial environments. In: IEEE Workshop on Application of Computer Vision, pp. 214–221 (2000)
18. Billinghurst, M., Kato, H., Poupyrev, I.: Magic Book: Transitioning between reality and virtuality. IEEE Computer Graphics Applications 21(3), 6–8 (2001)
19. Fitzmaurice, G., Boxton, W.: An empirical evaluation of graspable user interfaces: toward specialized, space-multiplexed input. In: Proceeding of the ACM Conference on Human Factors in Computing System (CHI 1997), pp. 43–50. ACM, New York (1997)
20. Ishii, H., Ullmer, B.: Tangible bits: towards seamless interface between people, bits and atoms. In: ACM CHI 1997, pp. 234–241 (1997)
21. Gibson, J.: The theory of affordances. In: Shaw, R.E., Bransford, J. (eds.) Perceiving, Action, and Knowing. Lawrence Erlbaum Associates, Hillsdale (1997)
22. Norman, D.: The design of everyday things. Double day Business, New York (1998)
23. Kato, H., Billinghurst, M., Poupyerv, I.: Tangible Augmented Reality for human Computer Interaction. In: Proceedings of Nicograph, Nagoya, Japan (2001)
24. Reitmayr, G., Eade, E., Drummond, T.W.: Localisation and interaction for augmented maps. In: ISMAR 2005, pp. 120–129 (2005)
25. Gupta, S., Jaynes, C.O.: The universal media book: tracking and augmenting moving surfaces with projected information. In: ISMAR 2006, pp. 177–180 (2006)
26. Malik, S., McDonald, C.: G, Roth. 2002. Tracking for interactive pattern-based augmented reality. In: ISMAR 2002, pp. 117–126 (2002)
27. Dorfmuller, K., Schmalstieg, D.: Finger tracking for interaction in augmented environments. In: ISAR 2001, pp. 55–64 (2001)
28. Gorbet, M., Orth, M., Ishii, H.: Triangles: tangible interface for manipulation and exploration of digital information topography. In: CHI 1998, pp. 49–56 (1998)
29. Singer, B., Hindus, D., Stifelman, L., Whutel, S.: Tangible Progress: less is more in some wire audio spaces. In: CHI 1999, pp. 104–111 (1999)
30. Benko, H., Ishak, E.W., Feiner, S.: Collaborative mixed reality visualization of an archaeological excavation. In: Proceeding of the third IEEE and ACM International Symposium and Augmented Reality (ISMAR 2004), pp. 132–140 (2004)
31. Wang, H.: Distributed augmented reality for visualization collaborative construction tasks. A Thesis in the Department of Computer science and Software Engineering, Concordia University, Montreal, Quebec, Canada (2008)
32. Bimber, O., Frohlich, B.: Occlusion shadows: using projected light to generate realistic occlusion effects for view-dependent optical see-through displays. In: ISMAR 2002, pp. 186–193 (2002)
33. Kiyokawa, K.: An introduction to head mounted displays for augmented reality. In: Haller, M., Billinghurst, M., Thomas, B.H. (eds.) Emerging Technologies of Augmented Reality Interfaces and Design, pp. 43–63. Idea Group, Hershey (2007)
34. Asai, N., Kobayashi, H., Kondo, T.: Augmented Instructions: A fusion of augmented reality and printed learning materials. In: Proceeding of the 5th IEEE International Conference on Advanced Learning Technologies (ICALt 2005) (2005)
35. Mackay, W., Pothier, G., Letondal, C., Boegh, K., Sorenses, H.E.: The missing link: augmenting biology laboratory notebooks. In: UIST 2002, pp. 41–50. ACM, New York (2002)

36. Singer, B.: Fundamental concepts for interactive paper and cross media information space. PhD Thesis, Swiss Federal Institute of Technology Zurich (2005)
37. Card, S., Hong, L., Mackinlay, J.D., Chi, E.H.: 3Book: A scalable 3D virtual book. In: CHI 2004, pp. 1095–1098. ACM, New York (2004)
38. E-Book System (2004), http://www.flipviewer.com
39. Walczak, K., Wojciechowski, R.: Dynamic creation of interactive mixed reality presentations. In: VRST 2005, pp. 167–176. ACM, New York (2005)
40. Juan, M.C., Rey, B., Prez, D., Tomas, D., Alca, M.: The memory book. In: ACE 2005, pp. 379–380. ACM, New York (2005)
41. Nischelwitzer, A., Lenz, F.J., Searle, G., Holzinger, A.: Some aspects of the development of low-cost augmented reality; earning environments as examples for future interfaces in technology enhanced learning. In: Universal Access in Human-Computer Interaction. Application and services (2007)
42. Taketa, N., Hayash, K., Kato, H., Nishida, S.: Virtual pop-up book based on augmented reality. HCI, 475–484 (2007)

Virtual Visualisation Laboratory for Science and Mathematics Content (Vlab-SMC) with Special Reference to Teaching and Learning of Chemistry

Halimah Badioze Zaman[1], Norashiken Bakar[2], Azlina Ahmad[1], Riza Sulaiman[1], Haslina Arshad[1], and Nor Faezah Mohd. Yatim[1]

[1] Faculty of Information Science and Technology
Universiti Kebangsaan Malaysia, 43600 Bangi, Selangor
hbz@ftsm.ukm.my
[2] Faculty of Computer Science
University of Technology, Malacca
norasiken@kutkm.edu.my

Abstract. Research on the teaching of science and mathematics in schools and universities have shown that available teaching models are not effective in instilling the understanding of scientific and mathematics concepts, and the right scientific and mathematics skills required for learners to become good future scientists (mathematicians included). The extensive development of new technologies has a marked influence on education, by facilitating the design of new learning and teaching materials, that can improve the attitude of learners towards Science and Mathematics and the plausibility of advanced interactive, personalised learning process. The usefulness of the computer in Science and Mathematics education; as an interactive communication medium that permits access to all types of information (texts, images, different types of data such as sound, graphics and perhaps haptics like smell and touch); as an instrument for problem solving through simulations of scientific and mathematics phenomenon and experiments; as well as measuring and monitoring scientific laboratory experiments. This paper will highlight on the design and development of the virtual Visualisation Laboratory for Science & Mathematics Content (VLab-SMC) based on the Cognitivist-Constructivist-Contextual development life cycle model as well as the Instructional Design (ID) model, in order to achieve its objectives in teaching and learning. However, this paper with only highlight one of the virtual labs within VLab-SMC that is, the Virtual Lab for teaching Chemistry (VLab-Chem). The development life cycle involves the educational media to be used, measurement of content, and the authoring and programming involved; whilst the ID model involves the application of the cognitivist, constructivist and contextual theories in the modeling of the modules of VLab-SMC generally and Vlab-Chem specifically, using concepts such as 'learning by doing', contextual learning, experimental simulations 3D and real-time animations to create a virtual laboratory based on a real laboratory. Initial preliminary study shows positive indicators of VLab-Chem for the teaching and learning of Chemistry on the topic of 'Salts and Acids'.

H. Badioze Zaman et al. (Eds.): IVIC 2009, LNCS 5857, pp. 356–370, 2009.
© Springer-Verlag Berlin Heidelberg 2009

Keywords: Virtual laboratory, Visualization laboratory, Chemistry Teaching and Learning, Virtual Learning.

1 Introduction

Like in many other emerging developed country, the need for excellent higher education in Malaysia called for an "education revolution" to ensure that the citizens of Malaysia can face the challenges ahead on par with citizens of developed nations. With this in mind, the Government set up a committee to study, review and make recommendations pertaining to higher education in Malaysia. In a report entitled " Towards Excellence", one hundred and thirty eight (138) recommendations were formulated to achieve world class status and to make the country a regional centre of excellence [14].These recommendations can be grouped under five categories as follows: i). Excellence in Teaching and Learning.

ii). Excellence in Research and Development.

iii). Excellence in the capability of institutions of higher education to make contributions to the economy and society.

iv). Excellence in the capacity of institutions of higher learning to fulfill their core functions.

v). Excellence in initiating the democratization of education by ensuring access and participation of all Malaysians irrespective of race, religion or socio-economic status.

This paper shall discuss the research carried out based on three categories: excellence in teaching and learning ,excellence in research and development and excellence in democratizing of education through the use of the technology as an enabler and in this case, the virtual environment technology. The use of computer graphics technology enables one to create a remarkable variety of digital images and when given the right environment and conditions, can effectively enrich learning [4]. Real-time computer graphics are an essential component of multi-sensory environment of Virtual Reality (VR). Virtual Reality has been used in learning environments using various devices such as head-mounted audio-visual display, 6-D position sensors, and tactile interface device, in order to inhabit the computer-generated environments, to enable students to see, hear and touch virtual objects. VR allows one to meet real people in virtual worlds, one can tele-exist in real places all over the world and beyond and one can superimpose virtual displays onto the physical world. However, this research will only discuss the preliminary study in using a Virtual Laboratory for Chemistry (Vlab-Chem) which is one component of the Virtual Visualisation Laboratory for Science and Mathematics Content (VLab-CMS). VLab-Chem was tested amongst form 4 and Form 5 students. This lab can eventually be used in higher institutions of learning.

2   Conceptual Framework of VLab-CMS

In order to achieve excellence in the Teaching and Learning in both schools and Higher Institutions of learning and to achieve excellence in democratization of education, this study was conducted to achieve the objectives as follows:

i.   To design and develop a suitable research framework for the study on Virtual Visualisation Laboratory for Science and Mathematics Content (Vlab-CMS).
ii. To design and develop a suitable methodology for the development of a Virtual Visualisation Laboratory for teaching and learning of the Science and Mathematics.
iii. To design and develop a suitable Instructional Design (ID) model and modules for the Virtual Visualisation laboratory for Science and Mathematics Content adopting the Cognitivist-Constructivist theories and the contextual approach.
iv. Develop the prototype of one of the component of the Virtual Visualisation Laboratory for teaching and learning of Chemistry (VLab-Chem) for the topic Salts and Acids.
v.   Evaluate the prototype (VLab-Chem) for its effectiveness in order to ascertain its strengths and weaknesses .

It would be interesting to observe the results of the research as to whether 'learning by doing' through virtual environment really enhance learners' understanding of the sciences or vice versa and whether learning through a new technology and media such as the VLab-CMS provide a better understanding of scientific and Mathematics concepts to be taught. Besides, the results of this research is important for curriculum developers and policy makers to ensure that the teaching and learning of science and mathematics through new technologies and new media is taken into consideration in order to practice democratisation of education for the citizens irrespective of their race, religion and socio-economic status. The results of the study would also help policy makers in ensuring that Malaysia does not lag behind other nations in terms of changes taking place in education and technology in the current virtual-driven culture.

New technology needs thoughtful introduction in the teaching and learning process. Technology generally, and virtual reality technology specifically, by itself cannot improve teaching and learning. Even the most promising of education innovations, needs skilful application to be effective. However, there is clearly the potential that virtual learning environments can be powerful educational experiences for both lecturers and learners. Virtual environment provides a testbed for exploring the very foundations of teaching and learning. Knowledge is generally taught to students on the assumptions that they will learn on how the world works and what is valuable. The pedagogical approaches adopted are normally based on the understanding of the role of the mind in learning. Educators are re-examining, the philosophical foundations of education by comparing the implications of Cognitivism-Objectivism with that of Cognitivism-Constructivism. Both represent alternative conception to learning and thinking. The former, assumes that the role of mental activities to represent the

real world and that the role of teaching and learning is to help learners learn abo
world and replicate its contents and structure in their thinking. The latter on the o.
hand, claims that learners construct their own reality through interpreting perceptu.
experiences and that reality is in the mind of the knower rather than the object of the
learners' knowing. Constructivists rather than prescribing learning outcomes, focus on
tools and environments, helping learners interpret the multiple perspectives of the
world in creating their own knowledge [6].

Learning as stated by [12] has to be conducted and constructed by learners themselves in order to achieve the best results. The teaching and learning process that allows learners to be active in the learning process [1], will also make learning more
meaningful [10]. Research on virtual laboratory in the sciences, has been carried out
due to the fact that current conventional methods were found to be ineffective [2];
[8], because results of some experiments when not conducted properly cannot be
proved easily in the real world and thus, students were not able to see the expected
actual outcomes; then some scientific experiments are dangerous due to some
chemical reactions and using this methodology allows students to carry out the experiments as many times as they want without causing dangerous outcomes [8]. The
concept 'learning by doing' based on cognitivism-constructivism, and contextual
approach also allows students to be active in their learning process and makes them
self-reliant.

The cognitivism-constructivism theories adopted in the design and modeling of
the VLab-CMS and the prototype, VLab-Chem, ensures that students refer to the
thinking process whilst in the process of learning, create a cognitive structure in
their memory, use all their experience in learning, store all these experience in their
memory until they want to use it again , in order to help them in the learning process [1]; [13]; and finally construct their own answers based on their 'hands-on' experimental experiences through interaction with the virtual environment. Although
students can be working in pairs or groups, each may have differing observations
and inferences. Mistakes can be traced and students can learn to correct their mistakes at their own pace. Through the Cognitivist-constructivist approach adopted in
the VLab-CMS and the prototype, Vlab-Chem also means, that students are given
the chance to form their own opinions at the end of the experience and thus formal-
ise their own knowledge based on their previous background knowledge and the
new knowledge acquired [10]; [8].

Incorporating the Cognitivist-Constructivist approach in Vlab-CMS and the prototype Vlab-Chem, also helps students can integrate their previous experience with the
new experience and knowledge, through activities that should be in the context
deemed necessary and presented in various different perspectives [6]; [9] ; [5].Thus,
the reason for incorporating the Contextual approach in the design and modeling of
the VLab-CMS.

Research by [11], found that teaching and learning based on the contextual approach can help teachers and lecturers explain content based on real life situations
and thus helps to motivate students to relate knowledge gained with the real lifetime
experience. Research by [4], conducted based on a case study adopting the Contextual approach in the teaching and learning process, found that students were able to

concepts learned with real lifetime knowledge much better than those adopt-
...e conventional approach. [7], also found that students learn more successfully,
 terms of gaining knowledge and able to enhance their academic achievement
through the use of this approach. This is due to the fact that the contextual approach
focuses on a practical approach to enhance students' experiences through using materials used in real life experiments, and experiencing 'hands-on' based on real life
experiments through a virtual environment. For the prototype, VLab-Chem used for
the Chemistry content,, this approach was also incorporated through the use of videos (what is expected to be called in the future 'virties' or 'virdeos' just like 'e' being used for everything Internet based, such as e-learning or e-commerce would be
termed vir-learning and vir-trade respectively), to relate experiments that will be
conducted by students with real lifetime related industry research [10] ;[8] through
the virtual environment created.

Based on the literature review conducted and all the concepts discussed above, a
conceptual framework of the Virtual Visualisation Laboratory for the teaching and

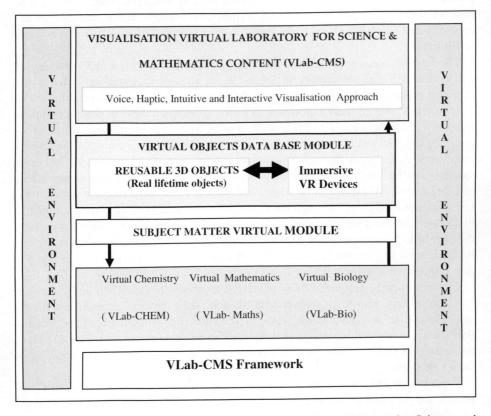

Fig. 1. Conceptual Framework of the   Virtual Visualisation Laboratory for Science and
Mathematics Content (VLab-CMS)

learning of Science and Mathematics Content (Vlab-CMS) with the component of prototype Vlab-Chem, was designed as depicted in Figure 1. From the diagram, it ca be observed that the research and development process was conducted in three phases namely: Analysis and Design, Development and Implementation and Evaluation. The Analysis and Design phase, involves the early analysis relating to problems of teaching and learning of sciences and mathematics (although in this paper, the case study chosen is on one of its component, the virtual chemistry lab, Vlab-Chem for the teacing of chemistry); ascertaining the systems requirement specifications (SRS); design and modeling of the Virtual laboratory concept; internalising and adopting various related teaching and learning theories suitable for teaching of chemistry using new technology and finally designing and developing the Instructional Design model for the specific subject matter (in this case, Chemistry through VLab-Chem) which encompasses one of the Virtual Visualisation Laboratory for Content (Vlab-CMS). The Development and Implementation phase, involves the development of storyboards and implementation of 2D and 3D graphics and animation programming for the Virtual Laboratory for the teaching and learning of Chemistry (VLab-Chem), specifically on the topic of Salts and Acids The Evaluation phase on the other hand, involves the testing of VLab-CMS to see the effectiveness of the virtual visualisation lab in supporting teaching and learning through the virtual laboratory for content concept, and specifically the effectiveness of VLab-Chem for the teaching and learning of Chemistry, particularly on the topic of Salts and Acids. The whole concept can be easily transferred to mobile applications like PDAs and mobile phones through the use of mobile and wearable technologies [7] in this virtual driven culture, so that learners can learn wherever they are through their regular appliances that are wearable or constantly carried with them.

3 Methodology

For the purpose of this paper, the methodology of the research is conducted in two parts: firstly, the methodology for the development of the Virtual Visualisation Laboratory for Science and Mathematics Content (VLab-CMS), which incorporates the component of the virtual laboratory for the teaching of Chemistry (VLab-Chem); and secondly, the methodology for conducting evaluation or testing of the prototype, VLab-Chem. The former will be discussed in this section, whilst the latter will be discussed later in the section on evaluation.

The methodology adopted for the development of VLab-CMS, which also incorporates the VLab-Chem component, was based on the accepted standards of Systems Development Life Cycle (SDLC) and Instructional Design model of Dick and Carey. The actual model architectured for this research was based on the *model Kitar Hayat Kognitivis-Konstruktivis-Konteksual* (KHK³) or Cognitivist-Constructivist-Contextual Life Cycle model. This model encompasses three layers (L1-L3) as can be observed in Figure 2.

epresents the intra inner layer of the model which involves the standard systems elopment entities such as Analysis & Design; Development & Implementation; nd Evaluation. The Analysis and Design phase, involves ascertaining the problems and SRS of the system; and designing the ID model of the system. The Development and Implementation phase involves the development of storyboards and implementation of suitable programming for the Virtual Visualisation Laboratory for Content (VLab-CMS) and its components, VLab-Chem.,VLab-Maths and VLab-Bio (for this paper only the Vlab-Chem will be discussed) as well as evaluation for its strengths and weaknesses. The whole phases in the intra inner layer was carried out iteratively in order to achieve excellence.

L2: represents the inner layer of the model. This layer is the result of the output obtained from L1.The inner layer comprises of entities such as ascertaining the problem-based learning outcomes as well the teaching and learning outcomes to be set by the teachers or the lecturers or already being developed by the syllabus and curriculum creators. Apart from that, this inner layer also involves the design of learning and teaching strategies based on sound theories and approaches in relation to Cognitivism,

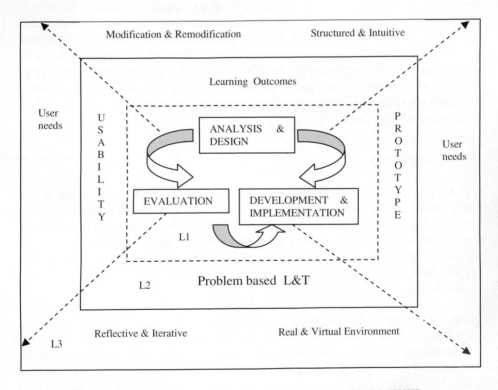

Fig. 2. Cognitivist-Constructivist-Contextual Life Cycle Model (KHK³)

Constructivism and Contextualism. This layer also involves the design of the Instructional Design (ID) model suitable for the architecture of the virtual visualization laboratory for content (VLab-CMS) and the prototype VLab-Chem. Based on the model, this layer also deals with entities such as the appropriate design and development of the storyboards for the specific prototypes; the appropriate virtual reality objects, programming that could be used to develop the prototype to suit the content to be delivered and the targeted user needs. Finally, the inner layer of the KHK³ encompass the entity of usability testing, comprising also of conducting pre and post testing of the prototype to determine its weaknesses for modification and remodification purposes so as to achieve excellence in research and development of the laboratory in the virtual environment.

L3: represents the final or outer layer of the model. This layer is the result of the output obtained from L2.This layer involves the entities such as structured and intuitive (which represents cognitivism-contructivism-contextualism approach in terms of knowledge representation); real and virtual environment in terms of the objects (graphics and animations) to be included in the content; reflective and iterative as well as modification and remodification in terms of design and development respectively, to ensure quality assurance and quality control of the whole research and the specific design and development of the prototypes.

4   Design of Prototype: VLab Chem

The architecture of the prototype, Vlab-Chem were designed based on 2 Dimensional and 3 Dimentional Graphics for virtual environment, divided into three sections as indicated below:

i. Section 1 (Architecture 1): Main Hall- A1 encompasses the main hall and is confronted by learners when they first enter VLab-Chem. The main hall consists of a main door through which users can enter in order to go through the other rooms (*vir-rooms*) in the virtual lab.

ii. Section 2 (Architecture 2): Store Room-A2 encompasses two sub sections namely:

   a. Store- scientific equipments which contain all the required equipment that will be used by the students during the practical experiment sessions based on the topic chosen. This sub section was also equipped with 2D and 3D graphics, images, voice and information on the equipment and apparatus stored in the store room.

   b. Store- scientific materials including all the materials that will be used in the experiments. This sub section too was equipped with 2D and 3D graphics, images, voice and information on the scientific materials stored in the store room.

iii. Section 3 (Architecture 3):Example of Experimental Labs on CHEMISTRY - A3 encompasses two sub sections as follows:

a.   SA3.1: Acid and Base Experimental Lab where all experiments carried out on the topic of Acids and Base will be presented in the form of lectures, videos, animations, 2D and 3D graphics, text and audio.

b.   SA3.2: Salt Experimental Lab where all experiments conducted on the topic of Salt will be presented in an interactive mode. User can choose any chemical substance and apparatus that they want to use in the experiment to be carried out. Experiments can be observed as real life experiments.

Figures 3 -6 show the experimental modules of VLab-Chem

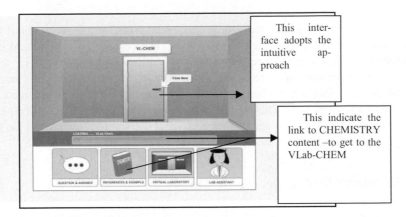

Fig. 3. The Main Hall of VLab-Chem

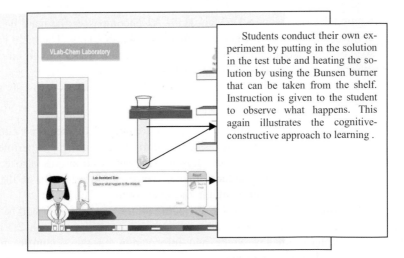

Fig. 4. Experiment conducted in the virtual lab for Chemistry (VLab-Chem)

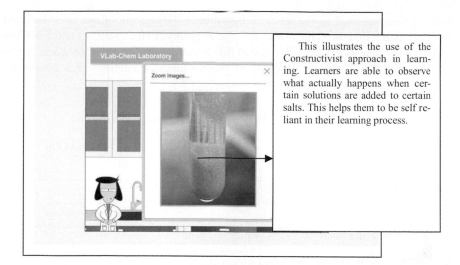

This illustrates the use of the Constructivist approach in learning. Learners are able to observe what actually happens when certain solutions are added to certain salts. This helps them to be self reliant in their learning process.

Fig. 5. Results of the Experiment conducted in VLab for Chemistry (VLab-CHEM)

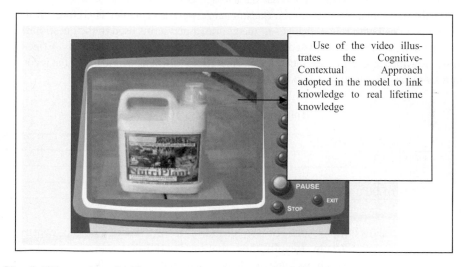

Use of the video illustrates the Cognitive-Contextual Approach adopted in the model to link knowledge to real lifetime knowledge

Fig. 6. Video on how fertilizers are made using certain salts in the factory that can be seen in VLab-CHEM

5 Evaluation of Prototype: Vlab-Chem

The evaluation of the prototype, VLab-Chem was conducted using the quasi-experimental approach based on the constructs: effectivesness, learnablity, user interface and user satisfaction. For this preliminary evaluation, the sample of the research consists of 30 students from a secondary school in Malacca, a state in central Malaysia; and 6 Chemistry teachers from 6 schools around Malacca. A questionnaire was used as the research instrument. The questionnaire was designed and developed based on three constructs: Learnability, Effectiveness, and User satisfaction. The questionnaire was tested for reliability using the Cronbach Alpha value as shown in Table 1. Analysis of the preliminary findings was conducted based on the mean score analysis.

Table 1. Reliabilty test on the Research Instrument (Questionnaire)

CATEGORY	CRONBACH ALPHA VALUE
Learnability	0.813
Effectiveness	0.744
User Interface	0.759
User satisfaction	0.731
Cronbach Alpha Average Result	**0.762**

The reliability test results show that the average Cronbach Alpha value is higher than 0.7. This means that all items in the questionnaire were acceptable. Therefore, all items were maintained with minor changes in the grammar and terms used in the questionnaire. The mean analysis level was used to measure the four contructs: Learnability, Effectiveness, User Interface, and User satisfaction. According to Kotschevar (2004), the recorded min score can be categorised into three levels as shown in the Table 2.

Table 2. Mean Analysis Level

MEAN LEVEL	EXPLANATION
1.00 to 2.39	Low
2.40 to 3.79	Average
3.80 to 5.00	High

Table 3 shows the results of the usability testing based on the construct: learnability of VLab-Chem. Results show that the overall min average is 4.11. This means that the virtual lab is 'easy to learn' and thus can be used easily by the students. The highest min score is obtained form the item CA3 with a mean score of 4.21. Based on the item, students indicate that they can handle the virtual lab successfully from beginning to the end. The lowest min score is obtained from the item CA1 with a mean score of 4.00. This score still indicates a high score. This means that the virtual lab is easy to use. Item CA2 also indicates a high score with the mean score of 4.11; indicating that the vitual lab can be easily used without any problems.

Table 3. Mean Score of the Construct:Learnability (in descending order) (n=30 students)

ITEM NO	STATEMENT	MEAN
CA3	System can be used without much help of the instructor from beginning to end of the program	4.21
CA2	It can be used easily without any problems	4.11
CA1	The virtual lab is easy to use and handle	4.00
	Overall Mean Average	**4.11**

Table 4 shows the results of the usability testing based on the construct: effectiveness of virtual lab, Vlab-C based on the content of Chemistry (VLab-CHEM). Generally, the overall mean average score is 4.17. This can be construde that the virtual lab is effective in the learning process of students on the subject of Chemistry, particularly on the topic: Acid, Base and Salts. Item CB1 shows the highest mean score with 4.37. This shows that learning through the virtual lab adopting the contextual approach, makes it easier for students to understand chemistry concepts and chemical formulations as compared to the conventional method. The lowest mean score is obtained from item CB2 with 4.05 which is still high based on the mean analysis level. Item CB3 shows a mean score of 4.15, which is the second highest.This means that the exploratory and the 'learning by doing' approach adopted in the virtual lab, makes learning more interesting and meaningful as compared to the conventional method. The students are able to explore during the navigation process and carrying their own experiments makes them understand and retain the new knowledge better. Item CB4 item is the third highest score with 4.10, shows learning chemistry through the simulated experiments and 'hands-on' approach on the topic Acid, Base and Salts is made easy through the use of the virtual lab.

Table 4. Mean Score of the Construct: Effectiveness (in descending order) (n=30 students)

ITEM NO	STATEMENT	MEAN
CB1	Easier to understand chemistry concepts and chemical formulations through the use of various everyday contexts taught through the virtual lab as compared to conventional method	4.37
CB3	Exploratory and learning by doing approach used in the activities make learning chemistry more interesting and meaningful	4.15
CB4	Learning chemistry by conducting experiments through simulations in the virtual lab makes learning on Acid, Base and Salts more easily understood and meaningful	4.10
CB2	Understanding the different experiments required to be conducted for different salts using different solutions is made easy through the use of the virtual lab	4.05
	Overall Mean Average	**4.17**

Table 5 shows the results of the evaluation based on the construct: User Satisfaction of the VLab for the content of chemistry (VLab-Chem). Overall results shows that the mean average score is 4.32. This indicate that the virtual lab developed based on the cognitivist-constructivist-contextual approach helps learning and satisfies user needs.

Table 5. Mean Score of the Construct: User Satisfaction in descending order (n=30 students)

ITEM NO	STATEMENT	MEAN
CD1	Virtual lab help learners in their learning process and satisfies user needs	4.58
CD7	Satisfied that virtual lab enhances learners' scientific skills	4.47
CD2	Satisfied that virtual lab enhances overall learning of Chemistry and is suitable with target users	4.42
CD3	Satisfied that the virtual lab help to improve the learning ability of learners	4.32
CD6	Satisfied that the virtual lab enhances the learning and thinking skills of learners	4.32
CD5	Satisfied that learning outcomes are achieved	4.11
CD4	Satisfied that the virtual lab can be used just as effectively by users who do not have any computer skills	4.05
	Overall Mean Average	**4.32**

The highest mean score is obtained from item DC1 with 4.58. This means that learners are satisfied that the virtual lab enhances their scientific skills. The lowest mean score is obtained from item CD4 with 4.05. This score is still high based on the mean analysis level. This means that users are satisfied that the virtual lab can be used just as effectively by users who do not have any computer skills. There are two items that received the same score of 4.32,i.e. items CD3 and CD6. This means that the virtual lab helps improve learning ability of learners and enhances not just their learning but also their thinking skills respectively. Item CD7 has a mean score of 4.42, which indicates that the users are satisfied that the virtual lab help them in enhancing their scientific skills. Item CD5 obtained a mean score of 4.11, which indicate that the learning outcomes of the program are achieved.

Teachers' perception on the effectiveness of VLab-Chem was also measured. Results show that generally, teachers' perception on the virtual lab is positive. Based on Table 6, it can be observed that the overall mean average score of the items included in the questionnaire is 4.23. This indicate that the virtual lab helps students retain knowledge in their short-term and long-term memory on the topic: Acid, Base and Salt. Results also indicate that students were able to produce more interesting experimental reports as compared to conventional method used. Item DA2 obtained the highest mean score of 4.50, which indicate that the electronic reports produced by the students are more interesting, and attracive as they are filled with appropriate experimental diagrams and that the reports are easier to edit and print. The lowest mean score of 4.00 was obtained from item DA3, which is still high based mean analysis level, which indicate that electronic report writing help students to think and be more focused when writing the experimental inferences. Item DA5 item obtained the second highest with a mean score of 4.33, which indicate that that students are able to retain knowledge in their short-term memory and long-term memory based on the topic taught. Items DA1 and DA4 share the same mean score of 4.17,which indicate that students understand the topic taught better; and the 'hands-on' experimental approach gives students the confident to write their reports and to apply the concepts learned in their report writing.

Table 6. Teacher's Perception based on Construc :Effectiveness of the Electronic Report Writing module in descending order (n=6 teachers)

ITEM NO	STATEMENT	MEAN
DA2	Electronic report produced is more interesting, attractive filled with suitable experimental diagrams. Reports also easier to edit and can be printed by the system	4.50
DA5	Reports produced after using Vlab-Chem indicate that students are able to retain knowledge in their short-term memory and long-term memory based on the topic taught	4.33
DA1	Results of experimental tasks conducted by students in-dicate that they understand the topic taught better	4.17
DA3	Vlab-Chem help students to think and be more focused on writing the experimental inferences.	4.00
	Overall Mean Average	4.23

6 Conclusion

The information era and the knowledge economy era is here to stay and along with it is the advancement of Information and Communications Technologies (ICTs) and multimedia, moving just as fast to virtual and holographic technology. The technologies will continue to improve further and nations have to grow with all these advancements. Excellence in teaching and learning cannot be achieved through technology alone.Teachers and lecturers are still the main mover for excellence. The preliminary research carried out and discussed in this paper shows that virtual laboratory in itssimplest form based on the cognitivist-constructivist-contextual approach has potential in enhancing students' short-term memory and long-term memory; make learning more 'hands-on'; allows learners to construct their own new knowledge and be self reliant in their learning process; and able to link new knowledge learned based on their previous knowledge and experience as well as linking new knowledge with real lifetime industry experience. Preliminary evaluation of VLab-CMS based on its prototype component, VLab-Chem also indicate the virtual labs has the potential in enhancing the teaching and learning of scientific subjects, specifically Chemistry.

References

1. Alessi, S.M., Trollip, R.: Computer Based Instruction: Methods and Development. Ed. Ke-3. Prentice Hall, New Jersey (2001)
2. Aris, B., Shariffudin, R.S., Subramaniam, M.: Reka Bentuk Perisian Multimedia. Penerbit Universiti Teknologi Malaysia, Johor (2002)
3. Clark, R.: Reconsidering research on learning from media. Review of Educational Research 53(4), 445–459 (1983)
4. Hardy, T.C.: Contextual Teachin. In: Science. Citing Internet sources (2003), http://www.kennesaw.edu/english/ContextualLearning/2003/Bartow/TeraHardy.pdf (accessed January 25, 2006)
5. Harun, J., Aris, B., Tasir, Z.: Pembangunan Perisian Multimedia Satu Pendekatan Sistematik. Venton Publishing, Kuala Lumpur (2001)
6. Jonassen, D.: Objectivism vs Constructivism: Do we need a new philosophical paradigm? University of Colorado, Colorado (1990)
7. Ketter, C.T., Arnold, J.: Implementing Contextual Teaching and Learning: Case Study of Nancy, A High School Science Novice Teacher. Internet sources (2003), http://www.coe.uga.edu/ctl/casestudy/Arnold.pdf (accessed February 20, 2006)
8. Bakar, N., Zaman, H.B.: Development and Design of 3D Virtual Laboratory for Chemistry Subject based on Constructivism-Cognitivism-Contextual Approach. In: Abdul-Rahman, A., Zlatanova, S., Coors, V. (eds.) Innvations in 3D Geo Information Systems. Lecture Notes in Geoinformation and Cartography. Springer, Heidelberg (2006)
9. Oliver, K.M.: Methods for Developing Constructivist Learning on The Web. Educational Technology 40(6), 5–18 (2000)
10. Abdullah, R.B.: Pembangunan Dan Keberkesanan Pakej Multimedia Kemahiran Berfikir Bagi Mata Pelajaran Kimia. Ph.D.diss., Universiti Kebangsaan Malaysia (2004)
11. Scars, S.J.: What Is Contextual Teaching And Learning? Internet sources (1999), http://www.contextual.org/ (accessed December 15, 2005)
12. Shapiro, B.: What Children Bring To Light: A Constructivist Perspective on Children Learning In Science. Teachers College Press, New York (1994)
13. Simonson, M., Thomson, A.: Educational Computing Foundations. Merill Publishing Company, Ohio (1990)
14. TARCASA (Tunku Abdul Rahman College Academic Staff Association). In: 31st Annual General Meeting. KL Main Campus, TAR College, Kuala Lumpur (2006)

Augmented Reality as a Remedial Paradigm for Negative Numbers: Content Aspect

Elango Periasamy and Halimah Badioze Zaman

Fakulti Teknologi Sains Maklumat, Universiti Kebangsaan Malaysia, Bangi, Selangor
hbz@ftsm.ukm.my, surensutha@yahoo.com

Abstract. Augmented reality as a strategy to help students visualize the subtraction process of Negative Numbers involved during problem solving. Technology can help students learn subtraction process of Negative Numbers only if it is designed appropriately in content for its specific purpose. This paper will discuss the study to identify the suitable content as the aspect in instructional model for developing AR as a Remedial Paradigm for Negative Numbers subtraction operation that involved single and double digit integers. Researcher used library search and survey methodology through document search, questionnaire and interview methods. The respondent of this study were 124 students aged 14 years old and five mathematics teachers from two secondary schools in Sepang district. The finding shows types of mistakes made by the students for each type of items tested. Thus, a suitable content that researcher can use in AR remedial strategy was identified.

Keywords: Augmented Reality, Mathematics Education.

1 Introduction

Augmented Reality (AR) technology is not new, it's potential in education is just beginning to be explored [1]. AR can help to assist a student to explore the information at their own pace (helping construct knowledge framework), and can also enable critical analysis to assist in challenging this framework, which indicates that AR has considerable educational potential [2]. In conjunction, researcher believe that in AR despite of the exciting possibilities of the new media, educational content creation for an interactive system is at least as difficult as authoring good textbooks and will require a substantial amount of time and work [3,4]. It is explained by [2] as the current state of technology is such that creating new content is still quite difficult, requiring specialist in software and skills. But according to [5], technology can help people learn only when it is designed well for the subject domain in both content and the representation itself. This paper will discuss the study carried out in the process of identify the suitable content as the aspect in instructional model for developing AR as a Remedial Paradigm for Negative Numbers.

H. Badioze Zaman et al. (Eds.): IVIC 2009, LNCS 5857, pp. 371–381, 2009.
© Springer-Verlag Berlin Heidelberg 2009

2 Related Works

Fisher used the SNARC (for spatial-numerical association of response codes) effect to examine whether negative numbers become associated with the left side of space as a result of experience with them [6]. He presented fourteen students (age range: 20-38 years) with pairs of digits and asked them to press the button near the smaller (or larger) number. The response times in two critical conditions were compared: the A+N- condition and the A-N+ condition (Table 1). The notation here indicates whether the left-right ordering of the digits' absolute magnitudes was congruent (A+) or incongruent (A-) with the left-right orientation of the mental number line, and whether the left-right ordering of the digits' numerical magnitudes was congruent (N+) or incongruent (N-) with the left-right orientation of the mental number line. It is predicted that the comparison speed will be faster in the A-N+ condition than in the A+N- condition if students have a mature mental number line extending to both left and right from zero. On the other hand, if students' mental number line is immature and contains only positive entries, the response time should be faster in the A+N- condition. The researcher found that his participants have a mature mental number line, on which negative numbers are associated with the left side of the space, indicating a numerical continuum from $-\infty$ (left) to $+\infty$ (right). Then, [7] used Fisher's experiment [6] as a basis with the same set of digit pairs in the two critical conditions (the A+N- condition and the A-N+ condition) in their research. The research was carried out with a respondent who often made errors in executing the integer calculating (her answer to 2 - 5 was 3). Findings implied that the respondent mental number line was a numerical continuum from 0 (left) to $+\infty$ (right) and not from $-\infty$ (left) to $+\infty$ (right). This shows the important of selecting the appropriate content for its specific purpose can help researcher learn more about its investigation.

According to [4], Construct3D is a three-dimensional geometric construction tool specifically designed for mathematics and geometry education. It is based on the

Table 1. Number pairs used for calculation and comparison

Condition	1st digit	2nd digit	Addition	Subtraction	Condition	1st digit	2nd digit	Addition	Subtraction
A+N+	4	9			A+N-	-4	-9		
	2	8				-3	-8		
	0	7				-2	-7		
	-2	6				-1	-6		
	3	5				0	-5		
	1	4				1	-4		
	-1	3				2	-3		
A- N+	-9	-4			A-N-	9	4		
	-8	-3				8	2		
	-7	-2				7	0		
	-6	-1				6	-2		
	-5	0				5	3		
	-4	1				4	1		
	-3	2				3	-1		

mobile collaborative augmented reality system "*Studierstube*." They describe that the efforts in developing a system for the improvement of spatial abilities and maximization of transfer of learning. In order to support various teacher-student interaction scenarios they implemented flexible methods for context and user dependent rendering of parts of the construction. Together with hybrid hardware setups they allow the use of Construct3D in classrooms now days and provide a test bed for future evaluations. Means of application and integration in mathematics and geometry education in high school, as well as in university, level are being discussed. Anecdotal evidence supports their claim that Construct3D is easy to learn, encourages experimentation with geometric constructions, and improves spatial skills. But, they believe that a lot of work remains to be done. In particular, a comprehensive evaluation of the practical value of an education tool such as theirs will require the development of substantial educational content that is put to real use in classroom. Furthermore, they say that we are currently at the stage where we have working tools available, but now need to apply them to real educational work. For the beginning, they plan to create tutorials for vector algebra, conic sections and Boolean operations. They believe that despite of the exciting possibilities of the new media, educational content creation for an interactive system is at least as difficult as authoring good textbooks and will require a substantial amount of time and work.

The purpose of [5] study was to investigate how students interact with AR and physical models and evaluate their perceptions regarding these two representations in learning pertaining to amino acids. The results show that some students liked to manipulate AR by rotating the markers to see the different orientations of the virtual objects. However, some students preferred to interact with physical models in order to get a feeling of physical contact. Their interactions with AR demonstrated that they tended to treat AR as real objects. Based on the findings, some AR design issues are elicited and the possibility to use AR in the chemistry classroom is discussed. The other design issue of using AR in chemistry education is to identify which chemical concepts are appropriate to incorporate AR to facilitate students' understanding. AR is a visualization tool which can convey either static virtual objects or dynamic animation at the same time. However, technology is not a panacea to all conceptual representation. Instructional designers should be cautious in determining how to integrate AR into the curriculum properly. Concluded that technology can help people learn only when it is designed well for the subject domain in both content and the representation itself.

We are currently at the stage where we have working tools available, but now we need to apply them to real educational work [4]. Thus, one of the aspects that researcher needs to focus is the content of AR strategy integration in education. So that the engaging process of AR based strategy will be more meaningful and able to help students in their learning process.

3   AR Content Creation Approach

The researcher carried out three steps in the process of identifying the suitable content as the aspect in instructional model for developing AR as a Remedial Paradigm for Negative Numbers. The first step (Step 1) is to investigate students' problem in

Negative Numbers through library search methodology. Then, followed by the second step (Step 2) is to investigate types of students' problem identified in Step 1, where researcher used survey methodology through creating instrument to test students and interview Mathematics teachers. And the final step (Step 3) is to identify the suitable content for AR mode remedial help. These three steps are further illustrated below.

3.1 Step 1: Investigate Students' Problem in Negative Numbers

An early analysis was carried out to identify the needs of developing a remedial technology. The needs analysis is important to identify the research problem, aim of study, objectives and specification needs of remedial technology. The researcher conducted a document search of Lower Secondary Examination (PMR) report from the Malaysian examination Board in order to identify the problem among students. Students are unable to master the skills and understanding the abstract concepts that involves negative number operation in fraction, transformation and algebra [8]. But in the 2002 PMR examination, 47% showed clear weaknesses in operation involving negative number such as (-17+14), (-17+22+8), (-17-14) and (-17+30) [9]. Naylor, M. [10] explains that negative numbers extend our number line and greatly simplify our calculations, but sometimes students struggle with the concepts. So, this reveals that students are also having difficulties solving negative number addition and subtraction operation involving single and double digit integers.

3.2 Step 2: Investigate Types of Student Problem in Previous Step

An initial study carried out by the researcher involved two secondary schools from the district of Sepang, Selangor. The initial study is to report and discuss the result of the test conducted for the respondent to investigate the existence of the above mentioned problem. The questionnaire for this initial study was created by the researchers. The questionnaires divided into two sections. The first section consists of demography data to understand the respondent profile. An example of item is "Sex: Male/Female". The second section consists of 24 items and only one correct answer for each item. An example of item is "-5-2=". Face validity was done with five Mathematics teachers from five schools in the district of Sepang. They have been teaching Negative Number topic for at least five years. A pilot test was carried out with a subject of 35 school students aged 14 years old from a secondary school in the district of Sepang. The calculation of reliability coefficient using Kuder-Richardson formula is used for dichotomy question with right wrong answer such as the objective questions [11]. The Kuder-Richardson (KR20) reliability estimation value of this instrument is 0.919544. The reliability is calculated using the KR20 formula [12] with Microsoft Office Excel 2007. According to [12] when the test format has only one correct answer, KR20 is algebraically equivalent to Cronbach alpha. Therefore, in this case the KR20 reliability estimation value of this pilot test is equivalent to Cronbach alpha coefficient.

Initial Study Respondent Profile

With reference to Table 2, the initial analysis of respondent profile shows that 124 respondents were involved. They were 53 boys and 71 girls. The number of respondent achieved grade A is 26 (20.97%), grade B 58 (46.77%) and grade C 40(32.26%) for their Primary School Evaluation Examination (UPSR) in mathematics subject. The histogram in figure 1 illustrates the UPSR grade with percentage of respondent with respect to table 2. The histogram in figure 1, illustrates the level of respondent achieving grade A, B and C and they are approximately normally distributed.

Table 2. Respondent Profile

Boy			
Girl		53(42.74 %)	
		71(57.26%)	
UPSR Mathematics Grade	A	B	C
	26	58	40
	(20.97%)	(46.77%)	(32.26%)

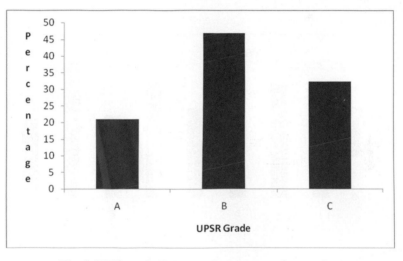

Fig. 1. UPSR grade (A,B,C) and percentage of respondent

Initial Study Finding

Table 3, shows the initial analysis of item 1 to item 8 which involves subtraction operation of two single digit integers. The result interpreted as follows: 77 (62.10%) respondents answered wrongly item 7 is the highest, 66 (53.23%) respondents answered wrongly item 5 is the second highest, 65 (52.42%) respondents answered wrongly item 2 is the third highest, 62 (50.00%) respondents answered wrongly item 3 is forth highest, 51 (41.13%) respondents answered wrongly item 4 is the fifth highest, 47 (37.90%) respondents answered wrongly item 6 sixth highest, 45 (36.29%) respondents answered wrongly item 8 is seventh highest and 6 (4.84%) respondents answered wrongly item 1 is the lowest. The histogram in figure 2 illustrates that the item number and percentage of wrong answers given by the respondents with respect to table 3.

Table 3. Subtraction Operation of Two Single Digit integers

No	Item	Number of wrong answers
1.	5 - 2 =	6 (4.84%)
2.	-5 - 2 =	65 (52.42%)
3.	-5 - (-2) =	62 (50.00%)
4.	5 - (-2) =	51 (41.13%)
5.	-2 - 5 =	66 (53.23%)
	2 - 5 =	47 (37.90%)
6.	-2 - (-5) =	77 (62.10%)
7.	2 - (-5) =	45 (36.29%)

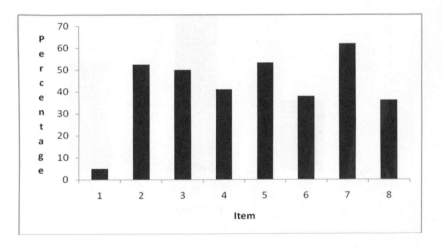

Fig. 2. Item (1 to 8) and percentage of wrong answers given by respondent

With reference to Table 4, the initial analysis of shows that 77 (62.10%) respondents answered wrongly item 13, 75 (60.48%) respondents answered wrongly item 10, 74 (59.68%) respondents answered wrongly item 15, 72 (58.06%) respondents answered wrongly item 11, 58 (46.77%) respondents answered wrongly item 16, 54 (43.55%) respondents answered wrongly item 12, 52 (41.94%) respondents answered wrongly item 14 and 15 (12.10%) respondents answered wrongly item 9. The histogram in figure 3 illustrates that the item number and percentage of wrong answers given by respondents with respect to table 4.

Table 4. Subtraction Operation of Single Digit with Double digit integers

No	Item	Number of wrong answers
9.	13 - 8 =	15 (12.10%)
10.	-13 - 8 =	75 (60.48%)
11.	-13 - (-8) =	72 (58.06%)
12.	13 - (-8) =	54 (43.55%)
13.	-8 - 13 =	77 (62.10%)
14.	8 - 13 =	52 (41.94%)
15.	-8 - (-13) =	74 (59.68%)
16.	8 - (-13) =	58 (46.77%)

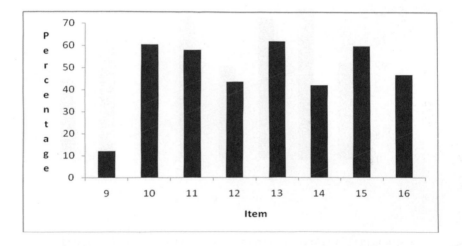

Fig. 3. Item (9 to 16) and percentage of wrong answers given by respondent

With reference to Table 5, the initial analysis of shows that 79 (63.71%) respondents answered wrongly item 18, 75 (60.48%) respondents answered wrongly item 21, 74 (59.68%) respondents answered wrongly item 19, 66 (53.23%) respondents answered wrongly item 23, 51 (41.13%) respondents answered wrongly item 17, 49 (39.52%) respondents answered wrongly item 20, 42 (33.87%) respondents answered wrongly item 24 and 18 (14.52%) respondents answered wrongly item 22. The histogram in figure 4 illustrates the item number and percentage of wrong answers given by respondents with respect to table 5.

Table 5. Subtraction Operation of Two Double Digit Integers

No	Item	Number of wrong answers
17.	16 - 23 =	51 (41.13%)
18.	-16 - 23 =	79 (63.71%)
19.	-16 - (-23) =	74 (59.68%)
20.	16 - (-23) =	49 (39.52%)
21.	-23 - 16 =	75 (60.48%)
22.	23 - 16 =	18 (14.52%)
23.	-23 - (-16) =	66 (53.23%)
24.	23 - (-16) =	42 (33.87%)

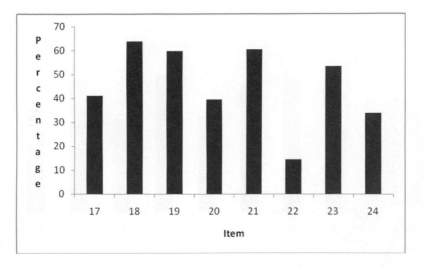

Fig 4. Item (17 to 24) and percentage of wrong answers given by respondent

Summary

Table 6 shows the initial study result is summarised based on number of respondent with wrong answer interval. Item 7,13,10,18 and 21 received the highest number of respondent unable to get correct answer. Followed by item 5, 2, 3, 15, 11, 16, 12, 19 and 23 received 50 to 74 respondents unable to get correct answer. Item 4, 6, 8, 14, 17, 20 and 24 received 25 to 49 respondents unable to get correct answer. Finally, item 1, 9 and 22 received below 24 respondents unable to get correct answer. Thus, all the items were considered suitable content as the aspect in instructional model for developing AR as a Remedial Paradigm for Negative Numbers subtraction operation involving single and double digit.

Table 6. Number of students with wrong answer interval

Number of respondent wrong answers Interval	Item
Above 75	7,13,10,18 and 21
50 to 74	5, 2, 3, 15, 11, 16, 12, 19 and 23
25 to 49	4, 6, 8, 14, 17, 20 and 24
Below 24	1, 9 and 22

3.3   Step 3: Identifying the Suitable Content for AR Mode Remedial Paradigm

Table 7, shows the suitable content as the aspect in instructional model for developing AR as a Remedial Paradigm for Negative Numbers subtraction operation involving single and double digit. The instrument was identified through SOLO taxonomy [13] and not discussed in this paper.

Table 7. Content for AR Mode Subtraction operation in Negative Numbers Remedial Paradigm involving single and double digit integers

Number	Item	Number	Item
1.	$5 - 2 =$	13.	$-8 - 13 =$
2.	$-5 - 2 =$	14.	$8 - 13 =$
3.	$-5 - (-2) =$	15.	$-8 - (-13) =$
4.	$5 - (-2) =$	16.	$8 - (-13) =$
5.	$-2 - 5 =$	17.	$16 - 23 =$
6.	$2 - 5 =$	18.	$-16 - 23 =$
7.	$-2 - (-5) =$	19.	$-16 - (-23) =$
8.	$2 - (-5) =$	20.	$16 - (-23) =$
9.	$13 - 8 =$	21.	$-23 - 16 =$
10.	$-13 - 8 =$	22.	$23 - 16 =$
11.	$-13 - (-8) =$	23.	$-23 - (-16) =$
12.	$13 - (-8) =$	24.	$23 - (-16) =$

4   Discussions

The finding of the early study is supported by report released for Lower Secondary Mathematics Examination [9]. This is because, the diverse contexts such as take away, comparison, and completion give rise to subtraction problems, thus students must pay attention to the different roles that the numbers take, which reflects the fact that subtraction is not commutative [14]. Research by [7] suggests that cognitive task analysis and assessment of the mental representation of numbers can provide a foundation for effective teaching of integer addition and subtraction. Thus, we hope AR as a strategy to help students visualize the subtraction process of Negative Numbers involved during problem solving. Nevertheless, [5] said that technology can help people learn only when it is designed well for the subject domain in both content and the representation itself. With that, this content shows its appropriateness as content for developing AR as a Remedial Paradigm for Negative Numbers.

5 Conclusions

In the process of developing Construct3D, regular visits by teachers, students, colleagues and friends who evaluated the system and gave feedback on its quality helped to constantly improve the application and adopt it to the students' needs [3]. This Mathematical content identification process is an important aspect of feedback to improve AR remedial strategy with respect to students needs. Thus, in the process of identifying suitable content for remedial work in Mathematics, researchers would like to suggest the following steps as a guide. Step 1: Investigate student problem in Mathematics. Researcher can use library search. Step 2: Investigate types of students' problem in previous step: Researcher can use an instrument to test students and interview Mathematics teachers. Step 3: Identifying the suitable content for AR mode remedial paradigm. These steps are known as part of early analysis of this study is to identify the suitable content as the aspect in instructional model for developing AR Remedial Paradigm for Negative Numbers subtraction operation.

6 Future Works

The future works in development of remedial paradigm for Negative Numbers in an AR mode is to identify appropriate technique that will help students visualize the problem solving steps for the content as the aspect in instructional design model and evaluate it.

References

[1] Billinghurst, M.: Augmented Reality in Education, New Horizons for Learning (2002), http://www.newhorizons.org/strategies/technology/billinghurst.htm

[2] Woods, E., Billinghurst, M., Looser, J., Aldridge, G., Brown, D., Garrie, B., Nelles, C.: Augmenting the science centre and museum experience. In: Spencer, S.N. (ed.) Proceedings of the 2nd international Conference on Computer Graphics and interactive Techniques in Australasia and South East Asia, GRAPHITE 2004, Singapore, June 15 - 18, 2004, pp. 230–236. ACM, New York (2004)

[3] Kaufmann, H.: Construct3D: an augmented reality application for mathematics and geometry education. In: Proceedings of the Tenth ACM international Conference on Multimedia, MULTIMEDIA 2002, Juan-les-Pins, France, December 01 - 06, 2002, pp. 656–657. ACM, New York (2002)

[4] Kaufmann, H., Schmalstieg, D.: Mathematics and geometry education with collabora. augmented reality. In: ACM SIGGRAPH 2002 Conference Abstracts and Application. SIGGRAPH 2002, San Antonio, Texas, July 21 - 26, 2002, pp. 37–41. ACM, New York (2002)

[5] Chen, Y.: A study of comparing the use of augmented reality and physical models in chemistry education. In: Proceedings of the 2006 ACM international Conference on Virtual Reality Continuum and Its Applications, VRCIA 2006, Hong Kong, China, pp. 369–372. ACM, New York (2006)

[6] Fisher, M.H.: Cognitive Representations of Negative Numbers. Psychological Science 14, 278–282 (2003)

[7] Terao, A., Sawaki, R., Hasegawa, M., Murohashi, H.: Improving Skills of Addition and Subtraction Involving Negative Numbers Based on Cognitive Task Analysis and Assessment of Mental Representations of Negative Numbers: A Case Study of a Seventh-Grade Student (2005),
http://www.cogsci.rpi.edu/CSJarchive/Proceedings/2005/docs/p2172.pdf

[8] Lembaga Peperiksaan Malaysia. In: Laporan Prestasi PMR 1993. Kementerian Pendidikan Malaysia, Kuala Lumpur (1993)

[9] Lembaga Peperiksaan Malaysia. In: Laporan Prestasi PMR 2002. Kementerian Pendidikan Malaysia, Kuala Lumpur (2002)

[10] Naylor, M.: Accentuate the Negative. Teaching Pre K - 8 36(4), 34, 36 (2006)

[11] Baba, A.: Statistik Penyeludikan dalam Pendidikan dan Sains Sosial. Penerbit Universiti Kebangsaan Malaysia, UKM Bangi (1999)

[12] Mervis, L., Spagnolo, J.: Assessment Book: A Guide for Developing Assessment programs in Illinois Schools (1995),
http://www.gower.k12.il.us/Staff/ASSESS/index.htm#assessment

[13] Atherton, J.S.: Learning and Teaching; SOLO taxonomy (2005),
http://www.learningandteaching.info/learning/solo.htm

[14] Flores, A.: Subtraction of Positive and Negative Numbers: The Difference and Completion Approaches with Chips. Mathematics Teaching in the Middle School 14(1), 21 (2008)

Collaborative Augmented Reality: Multi-user Interaction in Urban Simulation

Ajune Wanis Ismail and Mohd. Shahrizal Sunar

Department of Computer Graphic and Multimedia,
Faculty of Computer Science and Information System
Universiti Teknologi Malaysia
81310 Skudai Johor, Malaysia
ajunewanis@ymail.com,
shah@fsksm.utm.my

Abstract. Augmented reality (AR) environment allows user or multi-user to interact with 2D and 3D data. AR simply can provide a collaborative interactive AR environment for urban simulation, where users can interact naturally and intuitively. AR collaboration approach can be effectively used to develop face to face interfaces. This is because AR provides seamless interaction between real and virtual environments, the ability to enhance reality, the presence of spatial cues for face-to-face and remote collaboration, support of a tangible interface metaphor, the ability to transition smoothly between reality and virtuality. The fusion between real and virtual world, existed in AR environment, achieves higher interactivity as a key features of collaborative AR. Collaborative AR approach allows multi-user to simultaneously share a real world surrounding them and a virtual world. The features of collaboration in AR environment will be identified. The key for the proposed technique of precise registration between both worlds and multi-user are important for the collaborations using AR environment. Common problems in AR environment and issues in collaborative AR will be discussed. This paper will give an overview for collaborative AR framework employed in urban simulation and the multi-user interaction on how to share these virtual spaces with other users in collaboration. The work will also cover numerous systems in different cases of collaborative AR environments for multi-user interaction.

Keywords: Augmented Reality, Multi-User Interaction, Collaborative, Urban Simulation.

1 Introduction

Augmented reality (AR) environments are defined by Milgram and Kishino [1] as those in which real world and virtual world objects are presented together on a single display. The AR applications have shown that AR interfaces can enable a person to interact with the real world in ways never before possible [2]. A comprehensive survey of AR is found in [3].

Architectural of urban simulation for urban planning and design process has always caught up with highly cooperative tasks. Individual phases within a project often

H. Badioze Zaman et al. (Eds.): IVIC 2009, LNCS 5857, pp. 382–391, 2009.

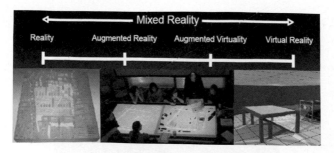

Fig. 1. A concept of Mixed Reality introduced by Milgram and Kishino

change between close cooperative situations, for instance, during design and review meetings, and individual work carried out by the users or third parties. Real collaboration is often limited to the very early design sketches. From an architect's point of view it would be desirable to have an additional support tool allowing enhancing the cooperation in a way that supports real collaboration within meetings. As a result, this would in turn allow for much faster design and review cycles.

Traditionally urban design is perceived, communicated and created using physical and digital media. However, these realms are handled as separate entities, which hinder collaboration, understanding and communication. Collaborative AR systems can integrate these tasks into one media type and allow a different conversation with complex issues. Human Computer Interfaces and Tangible User Interfaces play a key role in AR. They allow the combination with both the real and virtual component of an urban design project.

A collaborative AR system supporting for urban simulation is an environment and tools to support the collaboration between the experts involved in these particular meetings [4]. AR collaboration and multi-users for urban simulation are reflected by the use of intuitive interaction mechanisms, which allow even untrained users to benefit from the enhancements provided by the AR environment. Additionally, a few current AR systems for urban simulation exist with tools such as CAD systems and simulation programs that already used by the people involved. They were integrated to provide a rather seamless transition between their individual daily work and the collaborative work at the round table meetings. However, in developing AR environment for urban simulation, a few common problems might be encountered.

Therefore, in this paper we are focusing in two problems, there are registrations and user collaboration. The main challenge in AR applications for urban simulation is to ensure, that the displayed information is aligned with the user's view of the surrounding world, because the human visual system is very sensitive to misalignment. This alignment is often referred to as registration. Related to registration is the problem of calibrating a head-worn display and dealing with slight shifts of the HMD relative to the eye which result in noticeable misalignment. The collaboration between users in virtual spaces in AR environment for urban simulation has been an important research topic in the past few years.

The research will also cover numerous systems of collaborative AR environments for multi-user. There have been a number of previous works can be found in this research. Studierstube [5] is an environment for collaboration AR which uses HMD

Fig. 2. The Augmented Round Table

displays to project artificial 3D objects into the real world. The Augmented Round Table as shown in figure 2, as mentioned in [6], is providing a new interface for collaborative design and review for architecture and urban planning. The interface relies on unobtrusive input mechanisms and natural and intuitive user interactions. It focuses on providing an intuitive environment, which supports natural interaction with virtual objects while sustaining accessible collaboration and interaction mechanisms.

As stated in [7] the MagicMeeting system limits direct user communication due to the use of video augmentation. In [8], Grasset et. al. proposed MARE system that uses wired tracking devices and non-commodity hardware. The Luminous Table highlighted in [9] that attempts to tackle this issue by integrating multiple forms of physical and digital representations. 2D drawings, 3D physical models, and digital simulation are overlaid into a single information space in order to support the urban design process. In [10], ARTHUR allows user directly access to geometrical data and provides a tabletop immersive environment. Seichter [11] claimed in his research that one of the most important purposes of collaborative AR environment is to promote social interaction among multi-user located in the same physical space.

2   Collaborative Augmented Reality Environment

In face-to-face collaboration, people use speech, gesture, gaze and non-verbal cues to attempt to communicate in the clearest possible fashion [12, 13]. Real objects are also more than just a source of information; they are also the constituents of the collaborative activity, create reference frames for communication and alter the dynamics of interaction, especially in multi-user settings.

2.1   Features of Collaborative AR Environment

The multi-user AR environment developed allows multiple users to share a virtual space projected into their common working environment [6]. As stated in [13, 14], features of collaborative AR environment as below:

Virtuality. The potential of objects can be viewed and examined, either are not reachable or do not exist in the physical spaces can be carried out in AR environment.

Augmentation. Real objects that do exist in real world can be augmented annotations. As a result, it allows a smooth fusion between real objects an properties in propose processes.

Multi-user. The situations where multi-user gather together in a room to discu design, or perform other types of cooperative work or collaboration. Higher interac tivity among multi-user effectively interacts with themselves using normal sense of human interactions, like verbal and gestures are now simply possible in an augmented reality setup.

Independence. Each user has the option to move freely and independently of the other users. Each user may freely control his own independent viewpoint. However, not only is observation independent, interaction can also be performed independently without interrupting any action that performed by other users.

Individuality. In general models and objects are shared among users means all users can observe the same coherent model, consistent in sense of visibility. The displayed objects can also be different for each observer, as required by the application's needs and the individual's option.

2.2 Issues in Collaborative Augmented Reality

Registration. Registration is common issue in AR. As already mentioned in section 1, registration error is misalignment that the displayed information is aligned with the user's view of the surrounding world, because the human visual system is very sensitive to misalignment [25, 28]. As stated in Azuma [2] and Grasset [8], they classified the possible alignment errors in two categories:

- **Static error.** The misalignment the user can perceive when he is not moving and remain static. Static error is due to various causes: position error, noise, numerical error, and any possible causes since AR system is very sensitive to their misalign-ment. *Calibration* is compensating all those error sources which are the process to accurately compute these static transformation matrices for each group.
- **Dynamic error.** The misalignment the user can perceive when he is moving around in the environment. Dynamic error is due to the time lag between the ob-jects or user's movement and visual feedback.

Interaction with real object. As classified by Grasset and friends research [8], they also have highlighted the issues in interacting with real objects in AR environment. The issues mentioned in their paper are:

- **Occlusion compatibility.** It happens between virtual and real object which is parts of virtual objects behind by real objects should not be displayed.
- **Law of physics.** It happens between the two world which is virtual object laid on top of real object should remain in line view.
- **Manipulation sensitivity.** The awareness on the AR system which is it must be updated after a real object is moved in the shared space.
- **User calibration.** An ideal calibration method is able to separate user-specific parameters (eye position) from parameters that are constant for a given HMD or

ensor setup, minimizing the number of data points necessary for user-
e calibration.

Collaborative AR Environment for Multi-user

The section before we have discussed on features of collaborative AR environment
that have a force on overcoming major issues with collaborative AR. Here describes
the previous collaborative AR environments that have already developed and proposed by group of AR researcher that focusing on AR collaboration for multi-user. As
shown in Table I, the comparative studies on previous works of AR projects, focusing
on collaborative AR environment for multi-user.

Table 1. AR collaboration environment for multi-users

AR System	System Overview
ARTHUR	It allows designers a direct access to geometrical data and provides a tabletop immersive environment. By using optical augmentation and wireless computer–vision based trackers to allow for a natural 3D collaboration. However, it attempts to integrate manipulation techniques of CAD directly through spatial 2D menus and does not provide an estimate of this approach. [10]
The Luminous Table	It attempts to tackle this issue by integrating multiple forms of physical and digital representations. 2D drawings, 3D physical models, and digital simulation are overlaid into a single information space in order to support the urban design process. [9]
The Augmented Round Table	It provides a new interface for collaborative design and review for architecture and urban planning. Focus on providing an intuitive environment, which supports natural interaction with virtual objects while sustaining accessible collaboration and interaction mechanisms. [6]
Urban Sketcher	A mix of multi-modal input devices enhances collaborative interaction in real-time, while visual feedback is given to multi-users on a projected live video augmentation from urban sketcher. Sketching, modifying the scene on site. [23]
Magic Meeting	A Collaborative Tangible Augmented Reality System. Supports product review meetings by augmenting a real meeting location. Instead of real mock-ups, virtual 3D models are used, which may be loaded into the environment from usual desktop applications or from PDAs.[7]

4   Multi-user Interaction in Collaborative AR Environmen.

AR can create an augmented workspace which multi-user may access a shared
populated by virtual objects, while remaining grounded in the real world [23]. One
the most important purposes of collaborative AR environment is to promote socie
interaction among multi-user located in the same physical space [24]. This is powerful
for urban studies and planning purposes when multi-user are collocated and can use
natural means of communication such as speech or gestures.

AR Collaboration technique can be effectively used to develop fundamentally different interfaces for face-to-face and remote collaboration. This is because AR provides seamless interaction between real and virtual environments, the ability to enhance reality, the presence of spatial cues for face-to-face and remote collaboration,
support of a tangible interface metaphor, the ability to transition smoothly between
reality and virtuality [25, 26]. In this paper we have addressed a several problems
occur in collaborative AR environment for urban simulation. Then we have focused
the highlighted issues on multi-users in collaborative AR in order to design and construct the collaborative AR technique for urban simulation. We want to bring collaborative AR for multi-users into the urban simulation and provide new effective approach in urban simulation and to enhance collaboration shared physical urban workspace in planning and design process.

AR collaboration and multi-user for urban simulation are reflected by the use of intuitive interaction mechanisms, which allow even untrained users to benefit from the
enhancements provided by the AR environment. However, in this paper we have
discussed two problems in collaborative AR; there are registrations and multi-user
collaboration [25].

The main challenge in applying AR for urban simulation is to ensure, that the displayed information is aligned with the user's view of the surrounding world, because
the human visual system is very sensitive to misalignment. This alignment is often
referred to as registration. Related to registration is the problem of calibrating a head-
worn display and dealing with slight shifts of the HMD relative to the eye which
result in noticeable misalignment. One of the most relevant technical issues in developing AR applications is solving the registration problem: registration means aligning

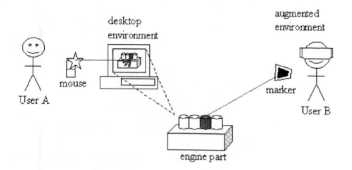

Fig. 3. Two user interact with different devices in different environment

.nformation with the real world so that it appears to be a part of the real
.ent. This registration must occur in real time; otherwise the user will experi-
. unacceptable lag of the visualization when he moves. Another issue will
is how to share these virtual spaces with other users in collaboration. AR envi-
.ment allows multiple participants or multi-user to interact with 2D and 3D data.
.R simply can provide a collaborative interactive AR environment for urban simulation, where users can interact naturally and intuitively. In addition, the collaborative
AR makes multi-user in urban simulation to share simultaneously a real world and
virtual world.

4.1 Collaborative AR Environment for Urban Simulation Framework

In collaboration, people use speech, gesture, gaze and non-verbal cues to attempt to
communicate in the clearest possible fashion. Interactions can be divided into two
groups: user-object interactions and user-user interactions. User-user interactions deal
with communication between users, such as chat. Firstly there is a need to construct
the framework of the collaborative AR environment. All the display technologies that
suitable for AR environment should be setting up. Marker in augmented reality is
assigned as base marker and also can be used as interaction tools which we can assign
action for each single marker. The base marker is a set of marker used to station the
virtual object [23, 24].

Setting up collaborative AR workbench. Once we got a few users interact among
them in AR environment with user-object interaction and user-user interaction, we
referred this kind of environment as collaborative AR environment. The framework
for collaborative AR environment is setting up as illustrated in figure 4.

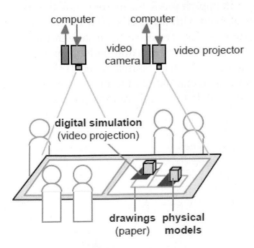

Fig. 4. Collaborative AR environment framework

Marker. We may treat each of these markers as a single marker. Each of these markers can be assigned with an action. We may use the pattern type provided with AR-
ToolKit library is shown in figure 5. However we customise the patterns so that it
meets your preferences.

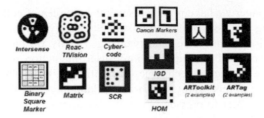

Fig. 5. Sample of marker pattern

Shared communication cues. Shared communication cues in the space between them as shown in figure 6 below. These cues include gaze, gesture, and nonverbal behaviors.

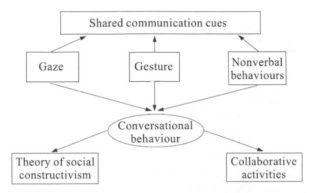

Fig. 6. Structure of shared communication cues

5   Conclusion

In this paper we proposed a framework to employ a multi-user interaction technique in collaborative AR for urban simulation. On the first section of this paper, we have described about AR environment and AR for urban simulation. Next section we identified the collaborative AR environment. We found common features in AR collaborative environment. In this paper also we described the major issues in AR collaboration system. This paper has summarised the previous collaborative AR environments that have already developed and proposed by group of AR researcher that focusing on AR collaboration for multi-user. Users experience with these interfaces have shown that they facilitate collaboration in a natural manner, enabling people to use normal gestures and non-verbal behavior in face-to-face collaboration, and to have access to their conventional tools and workplace by both face-to-face and remote collaboration.

AR techniques can be effectively used to develop fundamentally different interfaces for face-to-face and remote collaboration. This is because AR provides seamless interaction between real and virtual environments, the ability to enhance reality, the presence of spatial cues for face-to-face and remote collaboration, support of a tangible interface metaphor, the ability to transition smoothly between reality and virtuality. In this paper we have provided several examples of collaborative AR environment in gaming and also comparative studies on previous works of collaborative AR environment for urban studies and planning. Finally we have focused the highlighted the framework and technique for multi-user interaction. Then final section has discussed about the interaction technique for multi-user in collaborative AR environment. The challenge of this survey is to bring collaborative AR for multi-user into the urban simulation in order to provide new effective approach in urban simulation and to enhance collaboration shared physical urban workspace. As conclusion, we hope that this research is useful for AR urban simulation and also brings benefit to the computer graphics community especially in AR emerging technologies.

Acknowledgments. We would like express our appreciation to Universiti Teknologi Malaysia (UTM) and Malaysian Ministry of Science, Technology and Innovation (MOSTI) for providing financial support of this research through eScienceFund (01-01-06-SF0472) grant scheme.

References

1. Milgram, P., Kishino, F.: A taxonomy of Mixed Reality visual displays. IEICE Transactions on Information Systems E77-D, 12 (1994)
2. Azuma, R.: A Survey of Augmented Reality. PRESENCE: Teleoperators and Virtual Environments 6(4), 355–385 (1997)
3. Azuma, R., Baillot, Y., Behringer, R., Feiner, S., Julier, S., Blair, M.: Recent advances in augmented reality. IEEE Computer Graphics and Applications, 20–38 (2001)
4. Fuhrmann, A., Loffelmann, H., Schmalstieg, D.: Collaborative Augmented Reality: Exploring Dynamical Systems. In: Proc. Visualization 1997, pp. 459–462 (1997)
5. Schmalstieg, D., Fuhrmann, A., Szalavari, Z., Gervautz, M.: Studierstube - An Environment for Collaboration in Augmented Reality. In: CVE 1996 Workshop Proceedings, Nottingham, Great Britain, September 19-20 (1996)
6. Broll, W., Stoerring, M., Mottram, C.: The Augmented Round Table – a new Interface to Urban Planning and Architectural Design. In: Rauterberg, M., et al. (eds.) Human-Computer Interaction, INTERACT 2003, (c) IFIP, pp. 1103–1104. IOS Press, Amsterdam (2003)
7. Regenbrecht, H., Wagner, M., Baratoff, G.: MagicMeeting: A Collaborative Tangible Augmented Reality System. Virtual Reality 6(3), 151–166 (2004)
8. Grasset, R., Gascuel, J.D.: MARE: Multiuser Augmented Reality Environment on table setup. In: SIGGRAPH, Conference Abstracts and Applications, Computer Graphics Annual Conference Series (2002)
9. Ishii, H., Ben-Joseph, E., Underkoffler, J., Yeung, L., Chak, D., Kanji, Z., Piper, B.: Augmented Urban Planning Workbench: Overlaying Drawings, Physical Models and Digital Simulation. In: Proceedings of the IEEE/ACM International Symposium on Mixed and Augmented Reality ISMAR 2002, pp. 203–211. IEEE Computer Society, Los Alamitos (2002)
10. Broll, W., Lindt, I., Ohlenburg, J., Wittk, M., Yuan, C., Novotny, T., Fatah, S., Mottramy, C., Strothmann, A.: ARTHUR: A Collaborative Augmented Environment for Architectural Design and Urban Planning. Journal of Virtual Reality and Broadcasting 1(1), 1 (2004)
11. Seichter, H.: Augmented Reality And Tangibilit in Urban design. In: Dong, A., Vande Moere, A., Gero, J.S. (eds.) CAADFutures 2007, pp. 3–16. Springer, Heidelberg (2007)

12. Billinghurst, M., Kato, H., Poupyrev, I.: The Magic-Book – Moving Seaml[ ] Reality and Virtuality. IEEE Computer Graphics and Applications 21(3), 272–[ ]

13. Wanis, A., Sunar, M.S.: Multi-user Interaction in Collaborative Augmented R[ ] Urban Simulation. In: The International Conference on Graphic and Image Pro[ ] 2009 (ICGIP 2009), Kota Kinabalu Sabah, Malaysia, November 13-15 (2009)

14. Wanis, A., Sunar, M.S.: An Overview on Collaborative Augmented Reality Environme[ ] Potentials in Urban Planning. In: 5th International Conference on Information & Communication Technology and Systems (ICTS 2009), Surabaya Indonesia, August 4 (2009)

15. Fish, R.S., Kraut, R.E., Root, R.W., Rice, R.: Evaluating Video as a Technology for Informal Communication. Bellcore Technical Memorandum (1991)

16. Gaver, W.: The Affordances of Media Spaces for Collaboration. In: Proc. CSCW 1992, Toronto, Canada, October 31-November 4, pp. 17–24. ACM Press, New York (1992)

17. Cheok, A.D., Yang, X., Zhou, Z.Y., Billinghurst, M., Kato, H.: Touch-Space: Mixed Reality Game Space Based on Ubiquitous, Tangible, and Social Computing. Personal and Ubiquitous Computing 6(2), 430–442 (2002)

18. Ohshima, T., Sato, K., Yamamoto, H., Tamura, H.: AR2Hockey: A case study of collaborative augmented reality. In: Proceedings of VRAIS 1998, pp. 268–295. IEEE Press, Los Alamitos (1998)

19. Thomas, B.H., Close, B., Donoghue, J., Bondi, P., Morris, M., Wayne, P.: ARQuake: An Outdoor/Indoor Augmented Reality First Person Application. In: Proceedings of the Fourth International Symposium on Wearable Computers (ISWC 2000), Atlanta USA (2000)

20. Szalavári, Z., Gervautz, M.: The Personal Interaction Panel – A Two-Handed Interface for Augmented Reality. In: Computer Graphics Forum Proceedings of EUROGRAPHICS 1997, September 1997, vol. 16(3), pp. 335–346 (1997)

21. Wagner, D., Pintaric, T., Ledermann, F., Schmalstieg, D.: Towards Massively Multi-User Augmented Reality on Handheld Devices. Vienna University of Technology (2005)

22. Ajune, W., Zakiah, N.: Augmented Reality and applications. In: Shahrizal, M., Najib, M. (eds.) Advances in Computer Graphic & Virtual Environment, pp. 87–105. Universiti Teknologi Malaysia (2008)

23. Schmalstieg, D., Sareika, M.: Urban Sketcher: Mixing Realities in the Urban Planning and Design Process. In: Proceedings of 6th IEEE and ACM International Symposium on Mixed and Augmented Reality, pp. 27–30 (2007)

24. Seichter, H.: Augmented Reality And Tangibility In Urban Design. In: Dong, A., Vande Moere, A., Gero, J.S. (eds.) CAADFutures 2007, pp. 3–16. Springer, Heidelberg (2007)

25. Wanis, A., Sunar, M.S.: Survey on Collaborative AR for Multi-user in Urban Studies and Planning. In: Edutainment 2009. Lecture Note in Computer Science, vol. 5670. Springer, Heidelberg (2009)

26. Wanis, A., Sunar, M.S.: Survey on Collaborative AR for Multi-user in Urban Simulation. In: 5th Postgraduate Annual Research Seminar 2009 (PARS 2009), Universiti Teknologi Malaysia, Johor (2009)

27. Sato, K., Ban, Y., Chihara, K.: MR Aided Engineering: Inspection Support Systems Integrating Virtual Instruments and Process Control. In: Tamura, H., Ohta, Y. (eds.) Mixed Reality Merging Real and Virtual Worlds, Springer, Heidelberg (1999), ISBN 3-540-65623-5

28. Noh, Z., Wanis, A., Sunar, M.S.: Exploring the potential of using Augmented Reality Approach in Cultural Heritage System. In: 2nd International Conference on Advanced Computer Theory and Engineering (ICACTE 2009), Cairo, Egypt, September 25-27 (2009)

~ET: An Educational Virtual Environment for the ~aching of Road Safety Skills to School Students

Kee Man Chuah, Chwen Jen Chen, and Chee Siong Teh

Faculty of Cognitive Sciences and Human Development,
Universiti Malaysia Sarawak,
94300 Kota Samarahan, Malaysia
chuahkeeman@gmail.com,
{cjchen,csteh}@fcs.unimas.my

Abstract. Virtual reality (VR) has been prevalently used as a tool to help students learn and to simulate situations that are too hazardous to practice in real life. The present study aims to explore the capability of VR to achieve these two purposes and demonstrate a novel application of the result, using VR to help school students learn about road safety skills, which are impractical to be carried out in real-life situations. This paper describes the system design of the VR-based learning environment known as Virtual Simulated Traffics for Road Safety Education (ViSTREET) and its various features. An overview of the technical procedures for its development is also included. Ultimately, this paper highlights the potential use of VR in addressing the learning problem concerning road safety education programme in Malaysia.

Keywords: virtual reality, educational virtual environments, road safety education, instructional technology.

1 Introduction

The utilisation of computer simulations in enhancing teaching and learning has become popular in recent years largely due to technological advancements in three-dimensional (3D) graphic processing and declining costs of computer peripherals. Virtual reality (VR) is a more recent technology that is used for computer simulations. VR enables users to interact with three-dimensional data, creating a potentially powerful interface to both static and dynamic information [1]. Studies conducted by various researchers [2, 3, 4, 5] further reveal that VR offers a large number of possibilities in instructions due to its capabilities, which are absent in other tools. The key capability is that VR helps learners to experience and visualise directly some physical properties of objects and events that are unavailable or unfeasible in the real world due to distance, time, cost, or safety reasons. In light of this, VR is regarded as a potential instructional tool to provide simulated training and skills teaching in dangerous or logistically impossible circumstances such as roads with heavy traffics, house on fire or coal mine. VR is thus increasingly eminent in prevention training as well as emergency or disaster management [6].

H. Badioze Zaman et al. (Eds.): IVIC 2009, LNCS 5857, pp. 392–403, 2009.
© Springer-Verlag Berlin Heidelberg 2009

One area of concern in which VR can provide a plausible solution is
education that is often confined to the use of verbal teaching and printed ma.
impractical to be carried out on real roads [7]. The present work aims to exp.
potential of VR in addressing these issues pertaining to the current implementati
road safety education in Malaysia. Based on the meticulous review of materials u.
for the teaching of road safety skills in the classroom and prior related studies, a VR
based learning environment known as Virtual Simulated Traffics for Road Safety
Education (ViSTREET) is designed and developed. ViSTREET aims to complement
the current road safety curriculum in Malaysian schools by providing authentic road
safety practices to school students aged 12 to 14. In particular, ViSTREET teaches
students on crucial pedestrian skills such as detecting dangerous situations, gap timing
and safe place finding [8] by 'placing' them in life-like simulated traffic conditions
within the learning environment. This paper explains the system design of the ViS-
TREET learning environment as well as the technical procedures for developing the
learning environment.

2   Road Safety Education in Malaysia

Malaysia is among the countries that has consistently recorded a large number of road
traffic accidents in proportion to its population annually over the last three decades
[9]. A closer look at the statistics on fatalities due to road accidents in Malaysia shows
that pedestrians are among the top three high-risk groups, after motorcyclists and
motorists [10]. In addition to that, studies conducted by Road Safety Department of
Malaysia and Malaysian Institute of Road Safety Research (MIROS) reveal that a
majority of pedestrian casualties involve children and young teenagers aged 9 to 14
[9]. Therefore, under the Malaysian Road Safety Plan (2006-2010), the Road Safety
Department in collaboration with Ministry of Education has initiated a road safety
education programme targeting school students. The programme is being introduced
into primary and secondary schools in stages, starting with Year One in 2008. It will
be fully implemented in all schools by 2011 and at all school levels [11]. The programme has its emphasis on teaching pedestrian safety skills to school students by
using training materials like posters, multimedia, video and pamphlets. Teachers are
also told to use roads within the school compound to provide students necessary practical training.

Real-world practical training in pedestrian skills is known to be highly effective at
improving the performance of children as young as 8 years of age. The ideal context
for practical training would seem to be at the roadside and there is no doubt that roadside training can be highly effective [8]. When conducted at the roadside, however,
this training can be time-consuming, labour intensive, dangerous and subject to dis-
ruption from poor weather and a lack of traffic situations of the types required. In
addition, the teaching of pedestrian safety skills using printed materials such as pamphlets or posters (refer to Fig. 1 for an example) has its limitation in the sense that
learners cannot visualise the traffic scenarios in a more concrete manner. On the other
hand, the use of multimedia application in teaching road safety skills is mainly focused on factual drills without road simulations that allow active participation of the
students. In general, these applications present traffic situations with the use of static

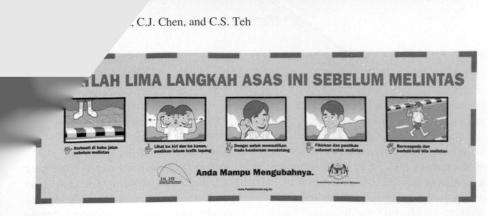

Fig. 1. Poster Showing Road Crossing Tips as provided by Road Safety Department of Malaysia

or animated graphics and ask students to memorise key safety skills by identifying the correct actions. While this can be useful to highlight salient safety facts, it does not train crucial road safety skills in an authentic manner. As such, VR-based learning environment offers a way round these difficulties. The VR capabilities of allowing three-dimensional visualisation of problem as well as guided exploration make it well-suited to be used as an instructional tool to address the aforementioned learning problems.

3 VR for Educational and Training Purposes

A typical definition of the term VR is an image produced by a computer that surrounds that person looking at it and seems almost real. Here, the word reality refers to the external physical world and when it exists virtually, the reality suggests something can be explored by our senses, and yet does not physically exist [12]. There is a general acceptance that VR is about creating acceptable substitutes for real objects or environments, and is not really about constructing imaginary worlds that are indistinguishable from the real world [13]. VR-based environments have two principal variants: immersive and non-immersive VR. The present study focuses on non-immersive VR, which is also commonly known as desktop VR. Desktop VR displays 3D graphical virtual world on a standard computer screen and allows user responses via generic input devices such as keyboard and computer mouse. Desktop VR is chosen mainly due to the much lower cost that it incurs as compared to immersive VR. Despite its lower cost, desktop VR is equally powerful in creating life-like virtual environments for user to explore.

According to Burdea and Coiffet [12], VR is capable of affording constructivist learning due to its ability to mediate world exploration and construction, its mapping of a user to any character he or she chooses and the provision of shared virtual worlds. Through its interactive environment, repetition and one-to-one experimentation, VR can help improve knowledge retention and this makes it appropriate for educational and training purposes. In the case of this study, a virtual environment can be used to simulate a real situation that is too dangerous, complex, or expensive to train in. There is potential for increasing safety standards, improving efficiency, and reducing overall training costs.

A particular advantage over traditional teaching and training technologies, such as books and video, is that the learner is active and can improve skills and understanding through practice. For example, Smith and Ericson [6] developed a VR-based learning environment to teach fire safety to school children. Students were able to identify home fire hazards and then practised escaping from a simulated fire in the virtual environment. Their studies also found out that students were more engaged by the learning environment without comprising skills acquisition. Kizil and Joy [14] on the other hand, developed a system to help prepare miners for dangerous situation that could not be addressed through traditional training methods. In terms of road safety education, the use of VR technology is slowly gaining momentum though still very limited. One rare example would be the learning system developed by Tolmie et al. [8]. The system provides simulation training by using a game-like scenario. Learners are asked to navigate through several town settings via an avatar or character. The activities in the virtual environment were mainly about making decisions on when or how to cross the street. When a decision was made, the computer demonstrated the consequences of that decision. However, this system lacks depth in terms of the environment details as it uses mainly plain comic-like graphics and it does not offer first-person point of view, which could be vital in influencing learner's judgment. Hence, it is the intention of this study to address these by creating a more life-like VR learning environment for the teaching of road safety skills.

4   ViSTREET System Design

As mentioned, ViSTREET is a desktop VR-based learning environment for teaching school children pedestrian road safety skills. Based on the input gathered from pertinent literature, the VR-based learning environment focuses on three broad and related areas of pedestrian skills as suggested by Tolmie et al. [8]:

i.   Safe-place finding – perception of the dangers posed by aspects of road layouts.
ii.   Roadside search – awareness of potential and actually vehicle movements and the implication for road crossing.
iii. Gap-timing – co-ordinating road crossing with vehicle movements

Opinions from researchers at MIROS on these skills were also obtained as to check on their relevance towards the road safety curriculum used in Malaysian schools. In general, each skill is addressed by a distinct module consist of VR-based scenarios, which share the same town settings.

4.1   Instructional Design

In ensuring that ViSTREET is able to achieve the intended goal of delivering road safety instructions in a more authentic manner, special attention were given to the selection of the guiding instructional design model. A more recent instructional design model or theoretical framework that specifically addresses instructional issues in VR-based learning environment, known as VRID [15] was chosen. This theoretical framework provided guidance on the methods for facilitating learning as well as provided assistance in deciding the design of ViSTREET.   The framework comprises

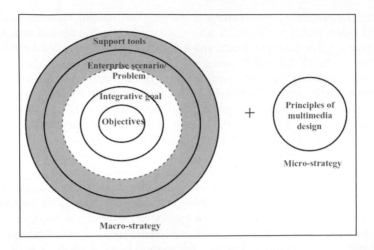

Fig. 2. Theoretical framework for designing a desktop VR-based learning environment [15]

macro-strategy and micro-strategy (see Fig. 2). The macro-strategy combines the concept of integrative goals proposed by Gagné and Merrill [16] and the model of designing constructivist learning environment proposed by Jonassen [17] The micro-strategy, on the other hand, is based on the cognitive theory of multimedia derived by Mayer [18] which is used to guide the design of the instructional message.

Macro Strategy. Goals that are to be achieved from learning are presumed to be the starting point of the instructional design process. Thus, the VRID model starts with identifying the instructional goal which is a combination of several individual objectives that are to be integrated into a comprehensive purposeful activity known as enterprise. This is the concept of integrative goal proposed by Gagné & Merill (1990). These individual objectives may fall in the category of verbal information, labels, intellectual skills, or cognitive strategies. In the case of the ViSTREET learning environment, based on the three broad areas of pedestrian skills identified, the types of learning and the corresponding learning objectives (refer to Table 1) were formulated. In addition, the integrative goals for this learning environment are identified as the learner's capabilities to interpret the basic skills of safe walking on various traffics scenarios (for example, crossing a busy street and walking to the park safely).

The instructional designer then needs to design instruction that enables the learners to acquire the capability of achieving this integrated outcome, which is called the enterprise scenario. As mentioned by Chen et al. [15], the enterprise scenario is similar to the problem posed in a constructivist learning environment. The VRID model stresses on the importance of posing an appropriate problem which includes three integrated components: the problem context, problem presentation, and problem manipulation. The incorporation of these components in the ViSTREET learning environment is depicted in Table 2.

Table 1. Types of Learning and Corresponding Learning Objectives for ViSTREET Learning Environment

Types of Learning	Learning Objectives
Labels	• State the name of various traffic signs • State the name of various line markings • State the various types of roads (two-way, double lane and single lane).
Verbal Information	• Describe the meaning of various traffic signs • Describe the meaning of line markings (e.g. zebra crossing)
Intellectual Skills	• Differentiate the use of various traffic signs • Differentiate the use of various line markings • Identify the basic rules when crossing the road • Identify the basic rules when walking on busy streets • Identify the safe zone for road crossing
Cognitive Strategies	• Reflect on the consequences of not following the right pedestrian road safety skills. • Reflect on the actions taken when exploring the virtual road scenario

Table 2. The Description of Enterprise Scenario in the Learning Environment

Enterprise Scenario Component	Descriptions
Problem Context	• Constructivist learning environment must describe in the problem statement all of the contextual factors that surround a problem to enable the learners to understand the problem. In ViSTREET, the learning goal is presented to the learners when they begin exploring the environment.
Problem Representation	• Constructivist learning environment must provide an interesting, appealing and engaging problem representation that is able to perturb the learner. In ViSTREET, a story-based problem is presented to the learner together with the virtual environments. This helps the learner to build a mental representation of the problem. Based on the given story line, the learner needs to complete several tasks, fulfilling each objective.
Problem Manipulation Space	• Constructivist learning environment must allow active manipulation space for a problem. Learners must manipulate something and obtain feedback as how their manipulations affect the environment. In ViSTREET, the virtual traffic scenarios serve as the problem manipulation space that allows the leaner to navigate through the world in a "walking mode" using input devices such as a mouse or keyboard. The "waking mode" in the virtual environment is similar to the movement in the real world, allowing a better representation of the problem.

In addition, constructivists believe that individual's knowledge is a function of one prior's experiences, mental constructs, and beliefs that are used to interpret events and objects. Therefore, the instructional design has to provide various supports that may assist the learners to construct their knowledge and engage in meaningful learning in the learning environment. These support tools include related cases, information resources, cognitive tools, conversation and collaboration tools, and social or contextual support.

Related cases refer to a set of related experiences or knowledge that the learner can refer to. This is mainly because skills or knowledge learned in a particular context are easily repeated by learners as long as they are in a similar context. In the ViSTREET learning environment, the various traffic simulations provide real-life representations that the learners could easily relate to. For instance, the learning environment is based upon a three-dimensional simulation of a small town, complete with buildings, roads, traffic signs, and vehicle movements, which allow the learners to explore the various consequences of their action such as crossing the road. This allows them to learn the safety skills better as opposed to learning it through text or static image presentation.

Information resources refer to the rich sources of information that help learners to construct their mental models and comprehend the problems. In the ViSTREET learning environment, hyperlinks to related resources (for example, traffic signs explanation, road safety tips, and description of traffic scenarios) are given. These resources are easily accessible via the menu provided together with the learning environment. Thus, the learner is free to access these resources while trying to solve the given problem.

Cognitive tools are tools that can scaffold the learners' ability to perform the task. Conversation and collaboration tools allow learners to communicate, collaborate and share ideas. Social or contextual support stresses on the importance of considering contextual factors, such as physical, organizational, and cultural aspects of the environment. In the ViSTREET learning environment, cognitive tools are provided. The virtual simulated traffics act as a visualisation tool where learners can visualise a dynamic three-dimensional representation of the problem. Apart from that, the learning environment also provides screenshots of physically impossible viewpoints of the traffic scenarios. These include a plan view map that offer bird's eye view of various parts of the scenarios and a tracer icon that shows the position of the learner on the plan view map in real-time.

Another important component stressed by the VRID model is instructional activities. There are three types of instructional activities: modelling, coaching and scaffolding.

Modelling. In the ViSTREET learning environment, both behavioural modelling and cognitive modelling are incorporated. Behavioural modelling is provided by virtual characters in the learning environment that practises good pedestrian safety skills. Cognitive modelling in the learning environment, on the other hand, promotes reflection of such behaviour in the form of text-based narrative.

Coaching. In terms of coaching, the learning environment provides it using feedback messages. These messages appear as the learner is exploring the virtual scenarios, and can guide the learner as he or she is learning the intended skill. These feedback messages are presented in a more appealing manner in order to highlight them to the leaner.

Scaffolding. As for scaffolding, the learning environment splits the learning problem into four sub-problems. The four sub-problems are linked to provide scaffold for the learner's performance in approaching the learning problem. Such scaffolding is known as strategic scaffolding. In addition, the learning environment also provides learners with a help link that scaffolds the learner's abilities to perform navigational task in the virtual environment, which could impede their learning. This type of scaffolding is known as procedural scaffolding [15]. Another type of scaffolding is known as conceptual scaffolding, in which in the learning environment various hints that guide the learner to available resources are given to assist them in solving the given task.

Micro Strategy. To complement the macro-strategy, Mayer's [18] principles of multimedia design is used as the micro-strategy to guide the design of instructional message in the learning environment for a more effective learning. The five principles of multimedia adopted are multimedia principle, spatial contiguity principle, coherence principle, modality principle and redundancy principle. In line with the multimedia principle, the content in the learning environment is presented using both words and pictures. Images or pictures are labelled accordingly rather than solely depending on texts. In terms of spatial contiguity principle, the texts used to describe the learning problem in the learning environment are presented near to a given snapshot (e.g. picture of the destination they are required to go). This is one example of enhancing spatial contiguity. As for coherence principle, guiding content in the learning environment is made clear and simple without overloaded texts, sounds or pictures. The remaining principles are applied when deemed necessary as the ViSTREET learning environment only uses ample amount of narration.

4.2 Development of Learning Environment

The development of ViSTREET is based on the integration of Virtual Reality Modelling Language (VRML) and Hypertext Markup Language (HTML). These are selected due to its feasibility to be widely used without the need to expensive software. In ViSTREET, each skill to be taught is presented in one specific scenario. The combination of virtual road scenarios formed the complete learning environment. The learning environment was then integrated onto the web interface to allow better visualisation and flexibility in adding other useful web-based components. Fig. 3 shows the steps involved in developing one single virtual road scenarios. These steps are occasionally repeated to form the full learning environment.

Select a Skill Focus. As mentioned in the earlier chapter, the VR-based learning environment for the present study was developed based on the suggestions given by the subject matter expert. Prior to developing the scenarios, a skill focus was selected. This is to help form the focus on the types of scenarios to be identified.

Identify a Scenario. After the skill focus was selected, a specific scenario was identified with the assistance of the subject matter expert. The scenario was then divided into several sub-scenarios to provide proper scaffolding for the learner. Example of this scenario is walking to the school for co-curricular activity when learner's father was unavailable to fetch him or her there.

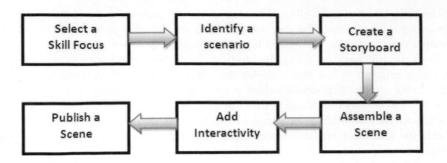

Fig. 3. Steps for developing a virtual road scenario for the learning environment

Create a Storyboard. Based on the identified scenario, a storyboard was created. The storyboard include sketches of two-dimensional plan on grid paper, scripts for instructional events as well as sketches of relevant objects like characters, buildings and plans.

Assemble a Scene. Following the storyboard, the virtual road scenario was assembled using the ParallelGraphics' Internet Scene Assembler (ISA) version 2.0, a three-dimensional VRML authoring tool with the help of Internet Space Builder software (a VRML object builder) To begin, a new scene in ISA was created. The newly created scene was blank and contains no background or any landscape on it. In order to set the environment, a pre-build scene developed using ISA, was imported and used as the core environment. The scene contains the basic landscape of a town setting with roads. The background of the scene was then changed to a more realistic sky look inserting the image via the Background tool object. Using the pre-build environment, related objects such as buildings, roads and plants were added to the scene for the specific scenario. ISA allows great integration with ISB objects. As such, all objects were created in ISB and saved in the ISB format before being added or imported to ISA. A two-dimensional plan view available in ISA also permits the moving and repositioning of objects. Fig. 4 shows some of the features available in ISA that are used to create and add virtual objects.

Add Interactivity. Each object in ISA contains fields that hold the values of its parameters. These parameters can be changed to create animation and interaction. The way to change a field is to send an event to that field by means of a mechanism through which this event can be programmed to cause changes in other object. In ISA, this is known as route, which is the connection between an object generating an event and an object receiving the event. ISA allows object animation by changing the position, orientation and size of any object in the scene. Other properties such as colour, transparency, intensity can also be animated. To add further interactivity, several Javascript functions (using the JSFunction object in ISA) such as pop-up alert, sound control and fading effects are added

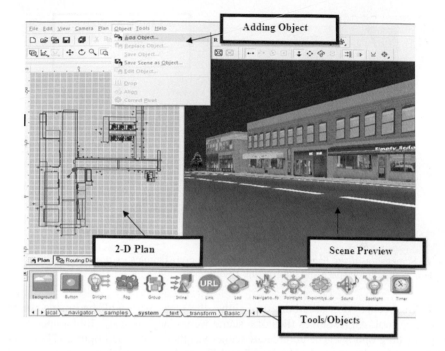

Fig. 4. Features available in creating and adding objects within ISA

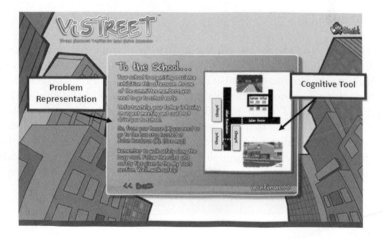

Fig. 5. Screenshot of the learning environment showing examples of cognitive tools and problem representation

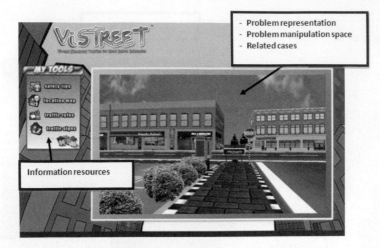

Fig. 6. Screenshot of the learning environment showing examples of problem representation, problem manipulation space and information resources

Publish a Scene. After all editing was done, the scene was published using the ISA publishing tool. All resources files of a scene were placed in a sub-folder specified in the publishing options. The completed scene was then embedded onto a HTML page together with its interface design. Fig. 5 and Fig. 6 show screenshots of the completed ViSTREET learning environment.

5   Conclusions

This paper has presented the use of VR as a tool to enhance the teaching of road safety skills to school students in Malaysia. The design and development of the ViS-TREET learning environment are also described. Demonstrating correct behaviour in a classroom setting does not necessarily translate to real-world situations. VR applications such as ViSTREET show potential for providing the means for teaching and training of road safety skills in a safe and authentic environment. They allow students to experience a more realistic virtual ''on-site'' experiences for high-risk safety training, which cannot be achieved through lectures or regular video presentation. Thus, the present study demonstrates a significant step towards improving road safety education for school students.

References

1. Louka, M.N., Balducelli, C.: Virtual Reality Tools for Emergency Operation Support and Training. In: Proceedings of TIEMS (The International Emergency Management Society), Oslo (2001)
2. Dickey, M.D.: Teaching in 3D: Pedagogical Affordances and Constraints of 3D Virtual Worlds for Synchronous Distance Education. Distance Education 24, 105–121 (2007)

3. Hamada, M.: An Example of Virtual Environment and Web-based Application in Learning. International Journal of Virtual Reality 7(3), 1–8 (2008)
4. Pantelidis, V.: Designing virtual environments for instructions: Concept and Considerations. VR in the Schools 2(4), 6–10 (1997)
5. Roussou, M.: Learning by doing and learning through play: an exploration of interactivity in virtual environments for children. ACM Computers in Entertainment 2(1), 1–23 (2004)
6. Smith, S., Ericson, E.: Using immersive game-based virtual reality to teach fire-safety skills to children. Virtual Reality 13, 87–99 (2009)
7. Ampofo-Boateng, K., Thomson, J.A.: Child pedestrian accidents: A case for preventative medicine. Health Education Research: Theory and Practice 5, 265–274 (1990)
8. Tolmie, A., Thomson, J., Foot, H., McLaren, B.: Child development and the aims of road safety education. Department of Transport, Road Safety Report (1) (1996)
9. Mustafa, N.M.: Overview of Current Road Safety Situation in Malaysia (2006),
   http://www.unescap.org/ttdw/roadsafety/Reports2006/
   Malaysia_RSpaper.pdf
10. Moe, H.: Road Traffic Injuries among Patients Who Attended The Accident and Emergency Unit of the University of Malaya Medical Centre, Kuala Lumpur. JUMMEC 11(1), 22–26 (2008)
11. Road Safety Education portal, http://www.pkjr.org.my
12. Burdea, G.C., Coiffet, P.: Virtual reality technology, 2nd edn. Wiley & Sons, New Jersey (2003)
13. Vince, J.: Essential virtual reality fast: How to understand the techniques and potential of virtual reality. Springer, New York (1998)
14. Kizil, M.S., Joy, J.: What can virtual reality do for safety? St University of Queensland, Lucia (2001)
15. Chen, C.J., Toh, S.C., Wan, M.F.: The theoretical framework for designing desktop virtual reality based learning environments. Journal of Interactive Learning Research 15(2), 147–167 (2004)
16. Gagne, R.M., Briggs, L.J., Wager, W.W.: Principles of instructional design, 4th edn. Harcourt Brace Jovanovich Publishers, Texas (1992)
17. Jonassen, D.H.: Designing constructivist learning environments. In: Reigeluth, C.M. (ed.) Instructional-design theories and models: A new paradigm of instructional theory, 2nd edn., pp. 215–239. Lawrence Erlbaum Associates, New Jersey (1999)
18. Mayer, R.E.: Multimedia learning. Cambridge University Press, Cambridge (2002)

Designing 3 Dimensional Virtual Reality Using Panoramic Image

Wan Norazlinawati Wan Abd Arif[1], Wan Fatimah Wan Ahmad[1],
Shahrina Md. Nordin[2], Azrai Abdullah[2], and Subarna Sivapalan[2]

[1] Department of Computer and Information Sciences,
Universiti Teknologi of PETRONAS
Bandar Seri Iskandar, 31750 Tronoh, Perak, Malaysia
Tel.: +605 368 8000; Fax: +605 365 4075
wnorazlinawati@gmail.com, fatimhd@petronas.com.my
[2] Department of Management and Humanities,
Universiti Teknologi of PETRONAS
Bandar Seri Iskandar, 31750 Tronoh, Perak, Malaysia
Tel.: +605 368 8000; Fax: +605 365 4075
{shahrina_mnordin,azraia,subarna_s}@petronas.com.my

Abstract. The high demand to improve the quality of the presentation in the knowledge sharing field is to compete with rapidly growing technology. The needs for development of technology based learning and training lead to an idea to develop an Oil and Gas Plant Virtual Environment (OGPVE) for the benefit of our future. Panoramic Virtual Reality learning based environment is essential in order to help educators overcome the limitations in traditional technical writing lesson. Virtual reality will help users to understand better by providing the simulations of real-world and hard to reach environment with high degree of realistic experience and interactivity. Thus, in order to create a courseware which will achieve the objective, accurate images of intended scenarios must be acquired. The panorama shows the OGPVE and helps to generate ideas to users on what they have learnt. This paper discusses part of the development in panoramic virtual reality. The important phases for developing successful panoramic image are image acquisition and image stitching or mosaicing. In this paper, the combination of wide field-of-view (FOV) and close up image used in this panoramic development are also discussed.

Keywords: image acquisition, image stitching, oil and gas plant virtual environment panorama, technical writing, and virtual reality.

1 Introduction

Education is one of the most important aspects which needs to be continuously improved parallel to the development of the nation. This is to ensure that the future generation is well-prepared to be competent in the new technologies. Among the courses undertaken by undergraduates, technical writing is one of the most important subjects that technical or engineering students need to learn during their study. In this particular subject, the students learn how to write proper reports such as technical report,

H. Badioze Zaman et al. (Eds.): IVIC 2009, LNCS 5857, pp. 404–414, 2009.
© Springer-Verlag Berlin Heidelberg 2009

resume, memo, memorandum, and proposal. These types of report writing include technical jargon to ensure that the objective of the reports will be achieved.

Based on the challenges in teaching and learning, students nowadays require help in their study to ensure that they can absorb the subject since there are things which they will learn without even knowing concretely what exactly they are or there are things which they do not have the chance to see them by themselves. Thus, Virtual Reality (VR) technology can be used to help students overcome certain limitation. This technology will not only enhance the quality of presentation but also the quality of the graduates. It also improves productivity and help in visualising conceptual, innovative, and creative ideas [1].

VR is defined as an experience where users are provided with an option to be in control of the system as they navigate the immersive virtual world [2]. By adapting VR in education technology, developer shares many advantages such as it allows a sense of being there (the place itself) while navigating the system where users are able to control and interact with the objects or environment projected [1]. Panoramic images are one of the VR presentations. The images could be used to solve some of the problems which arise in traditional learning since the technology will provide interactive panoramic environment with rich sense of presence [3].

Collaborative learning is where an integration of sets of intellectual learning collaboration between students or between students and teacher. Together with panoramic VR technology, collaborative learning can be effectively achieved [4].

These technologies will help in reducing the burden of conducting manual classes with the students and reduce time taken for the preparations. [5] [6] stated that immersive Panoramic VR has the strength to overcome the limitations which both students and educators usually face in traditional learning:

1) VR does not have any limitation in the number of users who can interact with the developed environment at the same time.
2) There is no limitation in what kind of environment or object that the system can create. Almost any size or shape of object can be created with the technology.
3) Developer of the system could help educator in simplifying the presentation thus the simulation helps to present situation which is not possible to be experienced directly.
4) VR simulation helps to present the location which is hard to reach thus, audiences have a chance to get to know the environment directly.

The four elements mentioned above therefore indicate the needs and the reasons why VR should be adapted in the teaching and training of technical writing.

In a typical classroom, students are given lectures based on the traditional learning method. Technical writing requires students to write technical reports with precise information. In order for them to be capable of writing especially in critical writing, they first need to identify the exact problem but it is impossible for them to visit the oil and gas plant themselves because of safety reasons.

Panoramic VR helps user's interactivity in many multimedia applications since it increases the perceived level of reality including in its educational applications. In most application of this type, wide field-of-view (FOV) is needed to immerse user into the virtual environment or reconstructed environment of the application. A wide FOV feature is necessary in many applications [7]. The view must be 360° FOV. The objective of this paper is thus to discuss the designing of a courseware using panoramic stitching images.

2 Related Work

Virtual reality environment is not new. It has been agreed that the uniqueness of VR would contribute in enhancing the quality of education today. The ability to simulate even small molecules and atom would help to solve chemicals study problems. The unique capabilities of this area help such application deliver the content better and increase the feeling of curiosity amongst the learners in learning activities.

One of the most unique and main characteristics of VR learning environment is its ability to direct experience through the immersion and semi-immersion experiential learning if compared to learning based on third-person's knowledge or from the text book.

As the first-person knowledge sharing, users have a chance to take control over their activity. This will help the users in making them feel in control of their own action and without realizing it, virtual learning environment also teaches them to take responsibilities for user's action.

Zengo Sayu [8] is an application which uses an element of immersion and interaction of virtual environment. The system adopted a unique aspect of sound and gesture recognition to interact with the users. The combination supports the view of [9].

Collaborative Virtual Interactive Simulations (C-Visions) is a network based on a collaborative learning environment, which offers simulations and also provides text based communication or voice chat [10]. Via the chance of interacting directly with the object prepared in the system it allows users to be actively involved in the learning process.

VR system currently moving toward to industrial field as it helps in employee safety training in mining industry [1] and for medical industry [11][12]. VR simulations have been applied in health and safety training as this technology is able to produce similar environment image of the target area and provide examples of dangerous action that should not be done by the miner. As for medical industry application, the system provide training via VR technology as these application is now shows increasing results in medical training. These two applications represent similar advantages of using VR technology such as application is always ready for the training purpose and this will helps in reducing the training cost, time and risk of conducting actual training.

There are three categories in existing VR system either geometry-based, image-based and hybrid-based [7]. The proposed application is under the category of image-based systems. Image-based VR is described as one of the alternatives of traditional VR. It has the advantage of presenting the presence of panorama with image calibration [13]. Image based application such as [1] [11] [12] applied actual images taken from the focus environment or images as a reference. These will advantage the user since they already look at the situation.

Image-based VR application for this proposed application required special photography, i.e. fisheye photography [14]. Fisheye lens that has being use to take full eye pictures in order to get wide field of view image. This image attained will soon stitch and the result of using this type of image is it will be high quality images.

3   Image Based System

The Panoramic VR requires 360 ° images which can be obtained by using a single camera and special lenses. For this proposed courseware, the image is obtained by using fisheye lens in order to produce drum type fisheye images. This type of image is the most efficient way to stitch high quality panoramas. When using this type of photo to create panoramic images, the resulting depiction of the scene has an almost infinite depth of field due the unique properties of the lenses [14]. Unlike most real-time 3D computer graphics, the image obtained from this lens shows sharp details on objects both close to the viewer and far away.

Fig. 1 (a) shows the example of total 360° images from the lens must look. The image also can be 180 ° in all direction. This type of this image has needed features which have good images in order to give good view of target area. Fig. 1 (b) shows an indoor top image of oil and gas industrial plant fisheye image which can be used to develop this courseware. It is one of the examples of top (T) image which needed for overall stitching. Fig. 1 (c) shows a potential floor image of oil and gas industrial factory fisheye image which can be used to create outdoor panoramic environment.

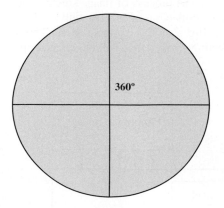

Fig. 1. (a) The view of an image of 360° angle

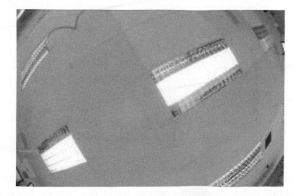

Fig. 1. (b) Indoor top image

Fig. 1. (c) Floor image

4   Panoramic Image Mosaicing

Image or photo stitching combines multiple images with overlapping fields of view to produce panoramic image. The process of image stitching or mosaicing is also known as the task of combining a collection of images with small FOV to obtain an image of larger FOV [7][15][16]. Fig. 2 is the example of an image stitching hierarchy. The process starts with selecting images that will be stitched up until the final panoramic image is produced.

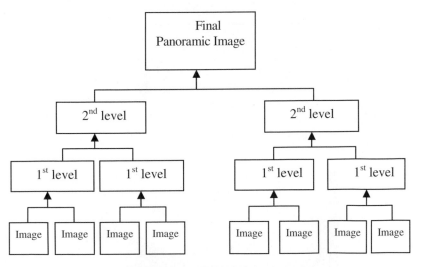

Fig. 2. Image stitching hierarchy

Fig. 3 shows steps which have to be followed in images mosaicing construction [17][18].

The process starts with acquiring images of the proposed location or scenarios. This involves taking pictures using specific tools or camera since this application needs fisheye images.

All these images are further warped with the other images that have neighboring points that enable the pictures to be stitched together and produce cubic panoramic images. Image alignment and stitching [19] start with building the correspondence between each image pair by estimating a homography. Stitching will use the result of image alignment to create image stitching [20]. From another research, image stitching applications vary in the way they handle motion, image alignment and blending [21].

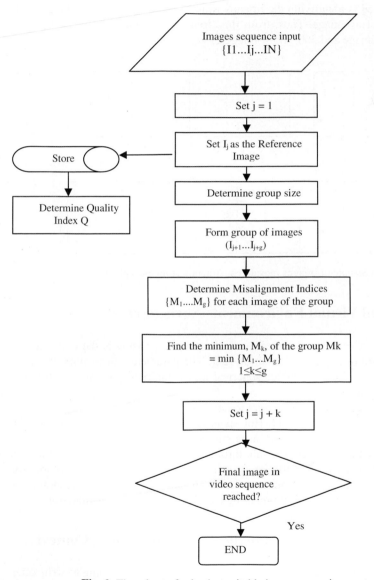

Fig. 3. Flowchart of selecting suitable images mosaic construction

For this project, images of the proposed scenarios are taken. There are two categories of photograph which were taken - indoors and outdoors. Minimal problems can be expected from indoor images due to lack of appropriate lighting that needs further image reconstruction or editing. But the outdoor images need more attention since it also involves the weather and the surrounding.

Fig. 4 shows a sample of images mosaic construction from multiple images. By using the software, it helps render the image directly. The software notifies the matching points and matches it following the sequence.

The method used is identifying the images which have the closest matching points with the neighbouring image. Thus, from this, four images will be stitched together with the top 360° image and 360 ° floor images.

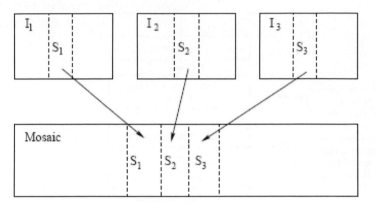

Fig. 4. Sample of images mosaic construction from multiple images

5   Image-Based Virtual Environments Navigation

From the scene representation point of view, the panoramic view is the collection of all light rays toward one specified position [22]. The parameters determine the range of viewing directions. For the cubic, spherical and cylindrical panoramas, different viewing direction ranges are used.

This courseware will also enable users to navigate from their starting point to other place according to their own needs. Hot spots are created to identify regions of a panoramic image for interactions, such as navigation or activating actions.

This courseware enables users to walk through around the application. The idea is to give users an idea of what exactly happens in the plant. Few links are prepared for users to further explore the environment. This will help the user's understanding of the process or activities involved in preparing a technical report in real situation.

6   Matching the Environment to the Technical Writing Context

OGPVE is purposely designed for directing users to what they are going to write after they learn the different types of reports [4]. The VR system provides users with panoramic view of the plant. The objective of this system is to give an idea of how the actual plant looks like.

Stitching of images will be collaborated with proposed framework to be published as a courseware. This courseware will also provide users an option to get involved as part of the staff in the Oil and Gas Plant (OGP). This will help them to enhance the sense of belonging to the environment.

At the beginning of the lesson, user will be introduced to the type of technical writing. Next step is where the user will go through the virtual environment. During this step, the user will experience collaborative virtual walkthrough and they will performed assign task where they need to discuss with the group member. This is where communication involved and users generate their own idea by discussing among themselves [4]. Then, user need to write report based from the data gathered. This phase require user to make use the information and experience they already gone through.

Fig. 5 shows the sample of one of the outdoor design of OGPVE after stitching process has been done. The panorama can be viewed using full screen Flash, Quick-Time and Java players for immersive view. This panoramic uses the stitched four images, one top image and one floor image.

Fig. 6 and 7 show the sample of basic navigation of panoramic view. Several options will be given where users can navigate via their mouse or by clicking the button prepared on the screen. This panoramic view then will be linked to other images where users can view the tools or devices located in this plant. With this application, users are able to identify which devices failed and from there they can write the report. The idea is to bring users to the virtual location in order to help them 'feel' as if they are in the real environment.

Fig. 5. Outdoor OGPVE

Fig. 6. Sample of basic navigation of OGPVE

Fig. 7. Top view of OGPVE

7   Conclusion and Future Work

This courseware described in the paper is needed for students' usage since it is difficult for them to enter any oil and gas plant because of safety reasons. Many VR advantages have been highlighted in this paper. Educators must work harder to find a way to implement Panoramic VR in knowledge sharing and share the positive outcome of adapting collaborative learning. Hence, there are some elements which might differ if VR is to be implemented in other subjects. Technical writing course needs students to be actively involved throughout the process. Different situation might need different type of writing. By adapting collaborative learning, users collaborate with each other using cognitive and constructive theories in order to be familiar with different situation. For future work, developers can also come up with an option of communicating via simple text message during the walkthrough. The messaging will further enhance collaborative learning. The panoramic VR can further enhance to other VR applications which will enable users to sense the heat and smell around the environment.

References

1. Wyk, E.V., Villiers, R.D.: Virtual Reality Training Applications for the Mining Industry. In: Proc. of Afrigraph 2009, pp. 53–64 (2009)
2. Yuan, X., Chee, Y.S.: Embodied Tour Guide in an Interactive Virtual Art Gallery. In: Proc. of the International Conference on Cyberworlds 2003, pp. 432–439 (2009)
3. Hoeben, A., Stappers, P.J.: Taking Clues From The World Outside: Navigating Interactive Panoramas. Journal of Personal and Ubiquitous Computing 10(2.3), 122–127 (2006)
4. Wong, L.K., Chee, Y.S.: iHASBS: Collaborative Learning in a Networked, Immersive Simulation Environment. In: Proc. of the Tenth International Conference on Virtual Systems and Multimedia, pp. 1243–1252 (2004)
5. Norazlinawati, W., Arif, W.A., Fatimah, W., Ahmad, W., Nordin, S.M.: Development of a Framework for Technical Writing Courseware Using 3-Dimensional Virtual Reality. In: National Postgraduate Conf., Tronoh, Malaysia (2009)
6. Davis, N., Rose, R.: Professional Development for Virtual Schooling and Online Learning, North America Council for Online Learning, http://www.nacol.org/docs/NACOL_PDforVSandOlnLrng.pdf (retrieve August 15, 2008)
7. Gredler, M.E.: Learning, and Instruction: Theory into Practice, 5th edn. Pearson Education, Upper Saddle River (2005)
8. Tong, W.K., Wong, T.T., Heng, P.A.: A System for Real-Time Panorama Generation and Display in Tele-Immersive Applications. IEEE Transactions on Multimedia 7(2), 280–292 (2005)
9. Rose, H., Billinghurst, M.: Zengo Sayu: An Immersive Educational Environment for Learning Japanese. In: (Technical Report), Seattle: University of Washington, Human Interface Laboratory of the Washington Technology Centre (1996)
10. Nordin, S.M., Sulaiman, S., Rambli, D.R.A., Ahmad, W.F.W., Mahmood, A.K.: A Conceptual Framework for Teaching Technical Writing Using 3D Virtual Reality Technology. In: The International Symposium on Information Technology, Malaysia, pp. 1321–1327 (2008)
11. Tzovaras, D., Moustakas, K., Nikolakis, G., Strintzis, M.G.: Interactive Mixed Reality White Cane Simulation for the Training of the Blind and the Visually Impaired. In: Pers Ubiquit Computing, pp. 51–58 (2009)
12. Lehmann, K.S., Ritz, J.R., Maass, H., Cakmak, H.K., Kuehnapfel, U.G., Germer, C.T., Bretthauer, G., Buhr, H.J.: A Prospective Randomized Study to Test the Transfer of Basic Psychomotor Skills From Virtual Reality to Physical Reality in a Comparable Training Setting. Annals of Surgery 241(3), 442–449 (2005)

13. Haque, S., Srinivasan, S.: A Meta-Analysis of the Training Effectiveness of Virtual Reality Surgical Simulators. IEEE Trans. on Information Technology in Biomedicine 10(1), 51–58 (2006)
14. Snavely, N., Seitz, S.M., Szeliski, R.: Modeling the World from Internet Photo Collections. Int. Journal of Computer Vision 80, 189–210 (2008)
15. Hoeben, A., Stoppers, P.J.: Taking Clues from the world outside: Navigating Interactive Panoramas. In: Journal of Personal and Ubiquitous Computing, vol. 1 (2-3), pp.122-127 (2006)
16. Greenhill, S., Venkatesh, S.: Virtual Observers in a Mobile Surveillance System. Journal of Multimedia, 579–588 (2006)
17. Peleg, S., Ben-Ezra, M.: Stereo Panorama with a Single Camera. Computer Vision and Pattern Recognition. In: IEEE Computer Society Conference, vol. (1) (1999)
18. Sun, X., Foote, J., Kimber, D., Manjunath, B.S.: Region of Interest Extraction and Virtual Camera Control Based on Panoramic Video Capturing. IEEE Transaction on Multimedia 7(5), 981–990 (2005)
19. Liu, F., Hu, Y.H., Gleicher, M.L.: Discovering Panoramas in Web Videos. Journal of Multimedia ACM, 329–338 (2008)
20. Greenhill, S., Venkatesh, S.: Virtual Observers in a Mobile Surveillance System. In: Proc. of Multimedia, pp. 579–588 (2006)
21. Liu, P., Sun, X., Georganas, N.D., Dubois, E.: Augmented Reality: A Novel Approach for Navigating in Panorama-based Virtual. In: Proc. of HAVE, pp. 13–18 (2003)
22. Kabisch, E., Kuester, F., Penny, S.: Sonic Panoramas: Experiments with Interactive Landscape Image Signification. In: Proc. of International Comprehensive Anatomical Terminology, pp. 156–163 (2005)

Design Framework for Sketch Based Technique in 3D Navigation of Cluttered Virtual Environment

Nordiana Sairuni, Dayang Rohaya Awang Rambli, and Nordin Zakaria

Universiti Teknologi PETRONAS, Bandar Seri Iskandar, 31750 Tronoh,
Perak, Malaysia
dian1712@gmail.com, {roharam,nordinzakaria}@petronas.com.my

Abstract. Most virtual environments encompass more space than can be viewed from a single vantage point. To obtain different views of the scene efficiently necessitates users to be able to navigate effectively within these environments. Current virtual environment (VE) systems employ a number of techniques for navigation such as walking on a plane, or flying through space and locomotion. In fact, a 3D world is only as useful as the user's ability to get around and interact with the information within it. This paper proposes a design framework for constructing sketch-based technique for navigation in 3D cluttered virtual environment. Previous and related works in integrating cluttered virtual environment with sketching technique were discussed. The development stages that have been encountered throughout this research are also being discussed for future guidelines. Implementation and relevance of this technique in potential application areas are highlighted.

Keywords: Virtual environment, Sketching technique, Navigation.

1 Introduction

Navigation in virtual environment plays a significant task in Virtual Reality and Computer Animation. Navigation or movement is a fundamental component either in real world or virtual world. In virtual 3D scene, users can observe and investigate 3D objects from different angles of view by means of navigation to get more useful information [1]. Such virtual environment is more useful when user can interact with the environment and objects within it. Navigation was originally defined as the process of moving through an environment. Darken R. and Sibert J. L. [2] extends this definition of navigation as the process of determining and traveling a path through an environment. The definition then extends to follow reference from aids and cues for successful navigation in virtual environments. Benyon and Höök [3] also categorize navigation activities to be either goal-oriented (how to find a way to reach a known destination), or explorative (just interested to have a look around and find out what's there), or aiming at object identification (finding categories and clusters of objects spread across the environment, finding interesting configurations of objects, finding information about the objects). It is useful to add that these categories, though equally difference [4], may become connected during navigation, for instance, exploration may invoke goal-oriented search activities, but the opposite direction is feasible as well.

H. Badioze Zaman et al. (Eds.): IVIC 2009, LNCS 5857, pp. 415–426, 2009.
© Springer-Verlag Berlin Heidelberg 2009

Navigation in virtual environment can be classified into two main categories; on understanding the cognitive principles behind navigation and on developing navigation techniques for specific tasks and applications [5]. The later will be the focus issue of our research. Navigation technique is needed to explore within virtual environment and move freely between objects in the space. A crucial aspect of interacting with a Virtual Environment (VE) is represented by navigation that can be informally defined as the process whereby people determine where they are, where everything else is, and how to get to particular objects or places [6]. Insufficient navigation support provided by user interfaces of VEs causes people to become disoriented and get lost. Navigation problems become even more critical in large-scale VEs [7]. In this case, users cannot learn the structure of the environment from a single point of view but they are forced to navigate extensively and to integrate information deriving from different points of view. This task can be very complex since perception in VEs is different from perception in the physical world, due to the absence of much sensorial stimuli. The aim of navigation aids research is to prevent disorientation problems as much as possible and to keep navigation (which is rarely the primary goal when interacting with a VE but is typically necessary to achieve that goal) as simple as possible, while preserving the elements of exploration and discovery [8].

In this paper, we propose the use of sketch based technique for intuitive and efficient navigation in a complex environment. This work is an extension to the navigation technique introduced by Igarashi and colleagues [9]. We want to integrate path planning algorithm in control loop of 3D interaction to compute collision-free movement to the targeted goal configuration. This path will then be followed by the camera viewpoint. Besides investigating sketch-based technique in terms of ease navigation task, this research work also explored application of collision-free motion and path planning algorithm.

The remainder of this paper is organized as follows. In Section 2, we provide a review of previous works on sketch-based technique in various applications. The following subsection will explain about sketching technique for navigation. Design framework for sketch-based technique development will be discussed in Section 3. System Architecture and Data flow for sketch-based technique in order to navigate cluttered virtual environment also being described. Section 4 explains implementation issues during development process. We conclude the paper in Section 5 with discussion on benefits and potential application area of the technique arise during system developing and some lines of future research direction.

2 Sketch-Based Technique for Navigation in VE

Systems that employ sketch-based input have been the focus of much research [10]. Most of the sketching technique is use widely for modeling objects onto the sketching application interface but the goal still the same which is attempting to create an experience similar to drawing lines or curve with pencil and paper. One such approach is by Do [10], presents Sketch-3D which is a pen-based interface that recognizes simple geometric shapes in a two-dimensional view. User needs to draw lines and circle in a simple "cocktail napkin" sketch to indicate the placement of walls and columns with the purpose of creating architectural space. User also allowed selecting different colors for the element drawn and the 3D world is created accordingly. Another approach that takes input strokes sketch by the user using a mouse or tablet was presented by Cherlin et al [11] which is the work applied sketch-based system for the interactive modeling of a variety of free-form 3D objects using just a few strokes. This technique was inspired by the traditional shape sketching methods of spiral, scribble and bending.

Turner et al. [12] developed software named Stilton which demonstrates the direct input to computer of a hand drawn perspective sketch to create a virtual environment. They start with a photograph of a real environment or an existing Virtual Reality Modeling Language (VRML) model, and then use a mouse or pen pad to sketch line drawings onto the scene. Sketchpad+ by [13] allows users to draw strokes with a pen on a large tilted digital design table and generate 3D sketches by projecting them onto user defined grids in 3D. The positioning and orientation of these grids are specified using typical 3D manipulation operations such as rotation and translation. This system also allows the strokes to be interpreted as boundaries which enclose surfaces.

A very basic approach to sketch animation path in navigating through virtual environment was presented by Igarashi et al. [9]. The advantage of sketch-based interface has been studied in [14] for collaboration and this research work also navigates through environment by looking around the virtual world due to mouse event. In [9], his work presented a simple interaction technique for a walkthrough in which the user draws the intended path directly on the screen, and the avatar automatically moves along the path. Similar approach has been use as bottom line for this research technique where user can sketch lines on the screen in order to make a path and automatically allows user to traverse the environment. The intention to employ sketch-based technique is to let user freely traverse in the environment where user are allowed to decide their own route by just sketching a stroke on the screen, in order to navigate through environment. This can ease user move in the VE without adhering to the generated path by system.

Sketch-based navigation is conceptually a higher level navigation technique, as relieves the user from controlling the motion task and even can assist in wayfinding [15]. Only few approaches seem to target at sketch-based navigation in 3D VEs [15] as presented in next subsections.

2.1   Sketch Based Route Planning with Mobile Devices in Immersive VE

Knodel S. et al. [16] proposed a research whereby a mobile device (PDA, Tablet PC) presents a World-in Miniature (WIM) which user can interact with. This work allowed user to travel in distributed environment in two stage process. User draws preferred navigation path directly onto touch sensitive mobile device whereas the data present in WIM form during the first stage. Afterwards, the sketched input results in a smooth camera animation path through the virtual environment which is presented on large screen as shown in Figure 1 below.

User can observe the environment by rotating the camera performing simple pen strokes moving along the path, similar to a trackball rotation. In contrast, our system allows the user to predefine the orientation during the animation by pointing at elements, drawing lines at regions of interest or circle whole areas of interest.

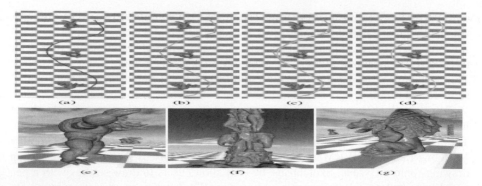

Fig. 1. (a) Sketched input stroke (b) sampled control points and control hull (c) control hull and generated B-Spline (d) resulting BSpline Animation Path (e), (f) and (g) show three example views of the resulting animation [16]

2.2 Harold: A World Made of Drawings

Harold is an idea to create 3D scene from 2D input and introduces new concepts to make an interactive system for creating 3D worlds [17]. The interface model in Harold allows all objects to be created simply by drawing them with a 2D input device. Most of the 3D objects in Harold are collections of planar strokes that are reoriented in a view-dependent way as the camera moves through the world. Virtual worlds created in Harold are rendered with a stroke-based system so that a world will maintain a hand-drawn appearance as the user navigates through it. As shown in Figure 2 below, a stroke drawn will represent as camera path to perform motion task.

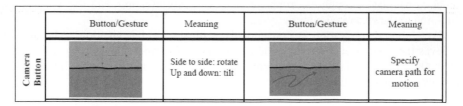

	Button/Gesture	Meaning	Button/Gesture	Meaning
Camera Button		Side to side: rotate Up and down: tilt		Specify camera path for motion

Fig. 2. Path drawn represent as camera path [17]

To move the camera, the user draws a stroke on the ground with the camera button depressed. This path is displayed as a red line, and the red dots are a click. The user then clicks on a point on the world. The camera moves along the drawn path at a constant speed (5 meters per second) and ends up looking at the point where the user clicked. A click on the sky while the camera is traveling along a path cancels the current path.

2.3 Sketch Based Navigation in 3D VE

Hagedorn B. et al. [15] present a novel method for specifying and controlling navigation in 3D VE based on sketching navigation commands. This approach [15] is similar with ours when its employ sketch-based navigation intention on top of the perspective projection of the 3D scene. However, our approach is different when it comes to sketching interpretation whereby this work interprets these sketches regarding their geometry, spatial context and temporal context. For the sketch interpretation stage, this work considers sketch geometry (curves and points), spatial context which are virtual location where the sketch is aligned or associated, and temporal context are about sketch composition, command history and drawing speed. This approach also fall more to Motion-oriented Navigation while ours are tend to be Task-oriented Navigation.

Fig. 3. Example of a sketch-based navigation command[15]

As illustrated in Figure 3 above, sketch-based navigation command act as a preview of how the system interprets the sketches, which path to induce navigation and allow the users to verify whether their navigation intention has been correctly recognized. The resulting visual cues integrated in the 3D scene shown on left of the figure. The path arrow on right figure symbolizes the camera movement and the target arrow points to the selected building. This approach is similar to our research concept to integrate sketches with environment.

2.4   Navidget for Easy 3D Camera Positioning from 2D Inputs

Navidget derives from the Point-of-Interest (POI) technique was introduced by Martin Hachet et al. [18], where the user selects the endpoint of a trajectory in order to automatically fly to a corresponding location. This technique is also known as the "go to" function for a wide range of 3D viewers [18]. This work uses circle-shaped gesture to let the user control where to look at and define their target destination. Circling is very intuitive metaphor as the user directly draws what he or she would like to see.

Fig. 4. Pointing at the target may result senseless view (left). Circling will move the camera to an appropriate view (right) [18].

As illustrated in Figure 4, sketching a circle onto the screen will move the camera to the appropriate view. After a release event, the camera moves towards the center of the circle. The viewing direction at destination is automatically computed in existing POI techniques. Generally, the camera looks at the target point with a viewing direction that is aligned with the normal of the related face, or with a pre-defined oblique view and focusing in small area.

2.5 An Approach towards Semantic Based Navigation in 3D City Models on Mobile Devices

This work proposes a novel solution for accessing virtual 3D city models on mobile devices [19]. The user controls the navigation within the virtual 3D city model by navigation command sketches drawn directly on the view-plane of the mobile client. The sketches are sent to the server, which reprocess the sketches onto the 3D scene accordance to the sketches to scene objects, interpret these sketches in terms of navigation commands, and send the resulting video-encoded image stream to the mobile client. That is, the mobile client enables users to specify and retrieve step-by-step created video sequences that correspond to their navigation intentions.

Fig. 5. (Left) User sketches a point on a junction and draw circle-like gesture as secand input. (Center) In resulting animation, the camera will narrow down to the marked junction. (Right) and then performs a turn-around [19].

As illustrated in Figure 5, the sketch-based navigation commands within their spatial and temporal context provide such mechanisms. For example, drawing a single, straight path along a street object indicates, "walk along the street". Circle-like (close or nearly closed) paths drawn on the terrain surface indicates "look around" using a drawn point as camera position. A path drawn along a street with a final indicated u-turn indicates, "Walk along to the end of the street, turn around, and walk back".

2.6 Path Drawing for 3D Walkthrough

One interesting feature of Igarashi's technique [9] is that it employed user-steered navigation in which user doesn't need spatial or cognitive knowledge when navigating in such environment. Due to the simplicity of this technique, many research works are based on this technique. User-steered technique allows user to navigate in the environment independently and give the user opportunity to choose their route or path while moving independently. This allows user to interact directly by sketching 2D strokes using a cursor from mouse interaction and user indicates with a mouse which route he wants to travel. In [9], his work as illustrated in Figure 6 below, presented a simple interaction technique for a walkthrough in which the user draws the intended path directly on the screen, and the avatar automatically moves along the path. Our approach is based on this technique where user can sketch lines on the screen in order to make a path and automatically allows user to traverse the environment.

Igarashi et al. [9] developed an intuitive interaction approach for specifying navigation command where the user draws the intended navigation path as a curve on the view plane. This path is mapped to the 3D scene and determines the 3D path for the avatar to move. This way, the user can specify not only the goal position, but also the route and the camera direction at the goal with a single stroke. The idea behind this technique is that the user can draw easily (freehand drawing) a path directly into the environment and the camera will follow.

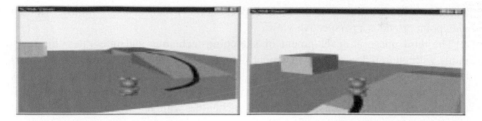

Fig. 6. (Left) User draws desired path directly on the screen (Right) then avatar and camera move along the projected path [9]

User interacts with such an environment by sketching on a screen. This allows the user to interact directly by sketching 2D strokes using mouse. With the given input the system calculates the path drawn and the camera will follow. Indirectly, user controls the camera motion presented on the screen. These gesture-based techniques, where the user can control the system by way of simple 2D gestures inspired our work

A limitation of path drawing is that it cannot be directly applied to completely free 3D movements (not constrained to a walking surface) and has been employ in simple VE. Another limitation is that the avatar must be present on the screen in order for a path to be drawn at the avatar's feet, but this problem may not be so serious because path drawing can naturally coexist with flying and driving in real applications.

3   The Design Framework

This section presents an explanation of our system design and describes details of our sketch-based technique development process. The system's interface combines sketching and rendering process whereas the scene is a representation of real world into virtual environment. This research adopts virtual environment technology to develop the world. Virtual area has been developed as a case study of this research as depicted in Figure 7. Firstly, the entire design of the virtual world is drawn on the paper. Next, the coordinate and data of every object are determined and stored in text file. Finally, these data are loaded using OpenGL library and Java programming to

Fig. 7. An example of sketching technique

build the virtual environment. A virtual environment is one layer and has plane floor.Users are allowed to immediate inspect the environment using mouse. Camera viewpoint provides a perspective view.

The third phase is development of sketching technique and integrates this technique with cluttered virtual environment. There have been a number of "direct interaction" 3D construction systems built in recent years, but in many of these systems "direct interaction" still means drawing with a 2D mouse over a monoscopic 3D image projection. Integrating sketch-based technique with an environment needs an environment to apply interface that allow sketching process.

The performance of interaction techniques can be quantified by running them through the various parts of a testbed. Testbed evaluations are distinguished from other types of formal experiments because they combine multiple tasks, multiple independent variables, and multiple response measures to obtain a more complete picture of the performance characteristics of an interaction technique [20].

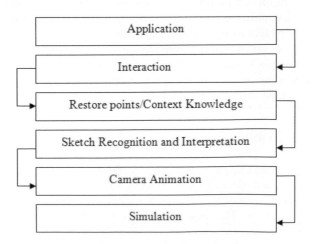

Fig. 8. Data Flow

Data flow for this system as shown in Figure 8, is described as follows.

(1)   The system provides a graphic user interface running on regular desktop PC's. Users will manually navigating in the virtual environment.

(2)   Specifying location of interest onto the plane and starting to generate customized tour when user presses "A" on keyboard.

(3)   Passing the path drawn to the Sketch Recognition and Interpretation module. Each path drawn basically is a line whereas line is an object which only has two points in 3D space [21].

(4)   The drawing is buffered as a set of 2-Dimension (2D) line segments, which are later, projected into the 3-Dimensional (3D) environment. Segments of points will be passing to Camera animation module to generate motion simulation.

(5)   Passing the motion of the tour path and the camera to the virtual environment and simulate navigation process.

The animation stops when the system has finished traversing all desired locations.

3.1 Design Flow of Sketch-Based Navigation

Processing sketch-based navigation commands will be operated once user finishes drawing a path and pressing "A" from keyboard. Additionally, sketch-based navigation technique processing comprises sketch recognition, sketch interpretation and camera animation will be explained in the next subsection.

3.1.1 Interpreting Navigation Sketches

For interpretation of navigation sketches, our technique takes into account the sketch geometry (lines and curves) and spatial context (the virtual location to which the sketch aligned or associated). By simply inputting a sketch onto 3D virtual display, a series of points (nodes) from the line drawn correspond to the ground plane and come up with the coordinates of the vertexes. Then, navigation system will store the coordinate and vertexes for moving process later.

3.1.2 Mapping Navigation Commands to Camera Orientation

Based on determined navigation intention, the camera animation is planned. By default the camera is oriented along the animation path; therefore user can observe the environment at their interest. For each sketch drawn, the system features a handler to record and derive paths and orientation from projected sketches and gestures. The navigation handlers generate camera setting from starting point, intermediate points and end point of camera path which are integrating altogether for creating the animation.

Basic concept applied in our approach is user draw a line which is represent as start point and target point for both ends respectively. The algorithm of navigation command sequence is shown in Figure 9. Then, check the value of the point on the line one by one. If the point checked, is an obstacle point or colliding with object in the environment, the system will find the boundary points then read the boundary route to find the local basic path, add the local path into the path linked list. The basic path can meet the demand of collision-free, but it is not yet the optimal path. We perform an algorithm where three ways of collision response will take place. The navigation

```
1.0      Start
         1.1      Output ←  an interface with an environment + consist with two different
                           mode: "Edit" mode and "Navigation" mode.
2.0      if ("Edit" mode)
                  2.1      Draw/sketch a line onto the screen
                  2.2      Input ←  a path to be use as navigation technique later.
         else ("Navigation" mode)
                  2.3      Navigation process start
3.0      if (start point !=      target point)
                  3.1      do{
                  3.2      Begin (mode of collision response)
                           3.2.1      for (mode "A")
                                      Output ←  avoid obstacle by proceed the movement to the left
                           3.2.2      for (mode "B")
                                      Output ←  avoid obstacle by proceed the movement to the right
                           3.2.3      for (mode "C")
                                      Output ←  avoid obstacle by proceed the movement over the object
                           }
                  3.3      while   (path collide with object || faces obstacle)
4.0      else (target point)
                  break.
5.0      Output ←  navigation process. movement along the path from start point to target point.
6.0      End
```

Fig. 9. Sketch-based navigation technique algorithm

process will then follow optimized path and change moving decision if it detects a future collision. If the point is non-obstacle point, check the next point, and if the point checked is target point (last point), the algorithm will stop.

3.1.3   Navigation Visualization and Local Walk

Once the path has been found and the nodes restored, the path will be rendered for the user and also provide an automatic navigation function along the path. After user finish sketching and press a button in order to start navigation process, the interface will display camera movement which scene will change based on the configuration.

4   Implementation Issue

Dealing with cluttered virtual environment is a time consuming. Navigation in virtual environment becomes more crucial when dealing with large scale virtual worlds. Virtual environments can be evaluated by means of different techniques, including formal tests, empirical approaches, informal observation, etc. For navigation in cluttered virtual environment, the proposed evaluation was conducted in a very informal way, through asking the opinion of participants of the research group of the authors, and of other people that could be a user of the system. The evaluation referred mainly to usability aspects.

This technique was inspired by the concept of path planning algorithm which user can decide the route to take in order to precede the navigation process till the target point. The idea that applied here is user can decide their route to proceed after colliding with object by continue the path whether to the left, right or over the object. This algorithm will only apply and activate when collision occurs.

5   Conclusion

In this paper, we propose to apply sketch based technique for navigation in complex environment. Most of the earlier work in this area has either been limited to local navigation modes based on driving, flying, or real-walking, or has dealt with relatively small environments. The development of the prototype is still currently in progress. We employ sketch-based technique for navigation in cluttered virtual environment. Mouse input devices will be use to interact with the prototype as well as to navigate virtual world and to sketch the navigation path. A suitable adaptive collision approximation technique will be selected in order to generate a more realistic navigation process.

The proposed technique is developed to provide the user a different navigation experience and it is expected to ease the navigation process especially for complex environment. For future work, following the completion of the prototype, we plan to conduct a user study to evaluate the effectiveness of this technique.

References

1. Jansenn-Osmann, P.: Using desktop virtual environment to investigate the role of landmarks. Computer in human behavior 18, 427–436 (2002)
2. Darken, R.P., Sibert, J.L.: Wayfinding Strategies and behaviors in large virtual world. In: Proceedings of Computer Human Interaction 1996, pp. 142–149. ACM Press, New York (1996)
3. Benyon, D., Hook, K.: Navigation in Information Spaces: Supporting the individual. In: Human Computer Interaction: Interact 1997, pp. 39–46. Chapman and Hall, Boca Raton (1997)
4. Darken, R.P., Sibert, J.L.: A Toolset for navigation in virtual environment. In: Proceedings of UIST 1993, pp. 157–165. ACM Press, Atlanta (1993)
5. Salomon, B., Garber, M., Lin, M.C., Manocha, D.: Interactive Navigation in Complex Environment Using Path Planning. In: SI3D 2003: Proceedings of the 2003 Symposium on Interactive 3D Graphics, pp. 41–50. ACM Press, New York (2003)
6. Susanne, J., Furnas, G.W.: Navigation in Electronic Worlds. SIGCHI Bulletin 29(4), 44–49 (1997)
7. Weatherford, D.L.: Representing and Manipulating Spatial Information from Different Environments: Models to Neighborhoods. In: Cohen, R. (ed.) The development of spatial cognition, vol. 8, pp. 41–70. Lawrence Erlbaum Associates, New Jersey (1985)
8. Chittaro, L., Burigat, S.: 3D Location-pointing as a Navigation Aid in Virtual Environments. In: Proceedings of the working conference on Advanced Visual Interfaces, Gallipoli, Italy, pp. 267–274 (2004)
9. Igarashi, T., Kadobayashi, R., Mase, K., Tanaka, H.: Path Drawing for 3D Walkthrough. In: Proceedings of User Interface Software and Technology 1998, vol. 15, pp. 173–174. ACM Press, New York (1998)
10. Do, Y.E.L.: Sketch that scene for me: Creating virtual world by freehand drawing. In: Proceedings of 18th Conference on Education in Computer Aided Architectural Design, Europe, pp. 265–268 (2000)
11. Cherlin, J.J., Samavati, F., Sousa, M.C., Jorge, J.A.: Sketch Based Modeling with Few Strokes. In: Proceedings of 21th Spring Conference on Computer Graphics, Budmerice, Slovakia, pp. 137–145 (2005)
12. Turner, A., Chapman, D., Penn, A.: Sketching a Virtual Environment: Modeling Using Line-Drawing Interpretation. In: ACM Proceedings of VRST 1999-Virtual Reality Software and Technology, London, United Kingdom (1999)

13. Piccolotto, M.A.: Sketchpad+ Architectural Modeling through Perspective Sketching on a Pen-based Display. Master's thesis, Cornell University (1998)
14. Sin, J.E., Choy, C.Y., Lim, B.S.: A Study on Sketch Input Technique by Surface of 3D Object for Collaboration. In: International Conference on Hybrid Information Technology, ICHIT 2006 (2006)
15. Hagedorn, B., Döllner, J.: Sketch-based navigation in 3D virtual environments. In: Butz, A., Fisher, B., Krüger, A., Olivier, P., Christie, M. (eds.) SG 2008. LNCS, vol. 5166, pp. 239–246. Springer, Heidelberg (2008)
16. Knodel, S., Hachet, M., Guitton, P.: Sketch-based Route Planning with Mobile Devices in Immersive Virtual Environments. In: Proceedings of INRIA (KHG 2007) (2007)
17. Cohen, M., John, F.H., Robert, C.Z.: HAROLD: A World made of drawings. In: Proceedings of the 1st International Symposium on Non- Photorealistic Animation and Rendering, Annecy, France, pp. 83–90 (2000)
18. Hachet, M., Decle, F., Knodel, S., Guitton, P.: Navidget: for easy 3D camera positioning from 2D inputs. In: IEEE User Symposium on 3D User Interfaces, pp. 83–89 (2008)
19. Dollner, J., Hagedorn, B., Schmidt, S.: An approach towards semantic-based navigation in 3D City Models on Mobile Devices. In: Proceedings of the 3rd Symposium on Location based Services and Telecartography, pp. 357–368 (2007)
20. Kessler, G.D., Bowman, D.A., Hodges, L.F.: The Simple Virtual Environment Library: An Extensible Framework for Building VE Applications. Presence: Teleoperators and Virtual Environments 9(2), 187–208 (2000)
21. Kavakli, M., Jayarathna, D.: Virtual Hand: An Interface for Interactive Sketching in Virtual Reality appears in Computational Intelligence for Modeling, Control and Automation, Vienna, pp. 613–618 (2005)

Applying Virtual Rehearsal Principle in Developing a Persuasive Multimedia Learning Environment (PMLE)

Wan Ahmad Jaafar and Sobihatun Nur

Centre for Instructional Technology and Multimedia,
Universiti Sains Malaysia,
11800 Penang, Malaysia
wajwy@usm.my, sobihatun@uum.edu.my

Abstract. This paper is outlining the potential use of virtual environment in persuading through computer simulation. The main focus of the paper is to apply an attempt of how virtual rehearsal principle can be designed into educational material using CD ROM based multimedia application to persuade as well as to reduce children dental anxiety particularly in Malaysian children context. This paper divided in three stages. Firstly, we provide a conceptual background of virtual rehearsal principle and how the principle has been applied in designing the information interfaces and presentation of a persuasive multimedia learning environment (PMLE). Secondly, the research design was administered to measure the effects of the PMLE in reducing children dental anxiety. Primary school children age between seven and nine years old are selected as respondents. Thirdly, the result of the study has revealed the feedback from children regarding baseline test and children dental anxiety test. The results on presenting this PMLE to primary school children show how it was able to reduce children dental anxiety and could let the children have a "mentally-prepared" condition for dental visit in the future.

Keywords: virtual rehearsal principle, persuasive multimedia learning environment (PMLE), persuade, children dental anxiety.

1   Introduction

Technology innovators have only begun to explore the persuasive possibility of computer simulated experiences. This is perhaps the most promising new path for computers as persuasive technologies. Computer simulations can create experiences that mimic experiences in the real world, or create hypothetical worlds that are experienced as "real". One category of simulation that is relevant to persuasive multimedia in this study is simulated environments. The principle of virtual rehearsal providing a motivating simulated environment in which to rehearse a behavior can enable people to change their attitudes or behavior in the real world.

Simulated environments can persuade through creating situations that reward and motivate people for a target behavior; allow users to practice a target behavior; control exposure to new or frightening situations; and facilitate role-playing and adopting another person's perspective. The health and fitness industry is among the leaders in

H. Badioze Zaman et al. (Eds.): IVIC 2009, LNCS 5857, pp. 427–435, 2009.

using environment simulations to motivate and influence people (Fogg, 2003). These technologies leverage the fact that our environment plays a key role in shaping our behaviors and thoughts.

A difference between simulated environment and virtual reality is due to the unneeded preparation of real-time gadgets such as real-time computer graphics, body tracking devices, visual displays, and other sensory input devices to immerse a participant in a computer-generated virtual environment. This simulated environment allows virtual rehearsal in practicing target behaviour in the minimum requirements for example using only 2D (two-dimension) or 3D (three-dimension) cartoon animation and it maybe result in reduced the cost and time spent in developing and consuming the application.

2 Principle of Virtual Rehearsal

Fogg's (2003) principle of virtual rehearsal providing a motivating simulated environment in which to rehearse a behavior can enable people to change their attitudes or behavior in the real world. In this multimedia learning environment, provides an authentic context that reflects the way the knowledge will be used in real-life, that preserves the full context of the situation without fragmentation and decomposition that invites exploration and allows for the natural complexity of the real world (Herrington and Oliver, 1995). Jonassen (1999) points out that with authentic context will engage learners and represent meaningful challenge to them. The implications of this for the design of interactive multimedia are not simply that suitable examples from real-world situations are used to illustrate the point being made. The context must be all-embracing, to provide the purpose and motivation for the use of the program, and to provide a sustained and complex learning environment that can be explored at length.

3 Applying the Principle of Virtual Rehearsal

The simulated environment within the multimedia learning environment attempted to replicate situations that create children dental anxiety feeling. There are three simulated environment situations which are in the house, in the dental waiting room and in the dental setting room. The main character called "Gg" described the experience of a child being informed about dental check up a day before dental appointment in the house, experience of a child being attended to dental clinic in a waiting room and experience of a child undergoing dental treatment. This multimedia learning environment provide a safe 'place' to explore good behaviors of attending dental appointment with new perspectives. And unlike real environments, multimedia learning environments are controllable where users can start or stop the experience at any time, and when they return for additional multimedia learning experience, they can pick up where they left off. For example, in Figure 1 showed the main screen of the persuasive multimedia learning environment (PMLE).

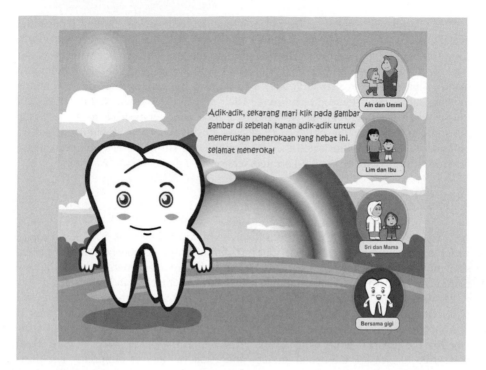

Fig. 1. Main screen of the persuasive multimedia learning environment

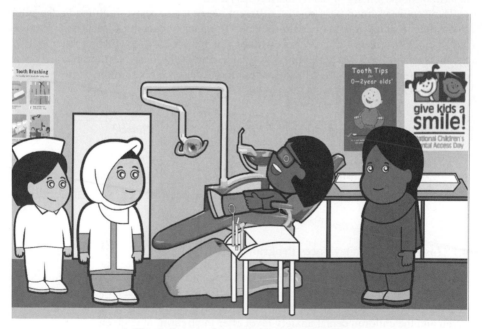

Fig. 2. Screen of the simulated dental setting

This multimedia learning environment attempted to persuade children reduce their dental anxiety through creating situations that motivate them for a target behavior as shown in the prototype. It also allowed users to practice a target behavior by imitating how the animated children character behaves in the multimedia learning environment. This prototype also facilitates role-playing by playing the role of children mothers, nurse, dentist and the children. The role-playing is attempted to let the anxious children adopting another person's in a good new perspective so that the role-playing can influence the children to behave positively when attending dental appointment. Figure 2 illustrated the simulated dental sitting in 2D environment and provided role-playing in a voice-narrated version.

4   Research Design

An experimental research design has been used to evaluate the PMLE prototype, which assess children dental anxiety before and after the demonstration of a persuasive multimedia learning environment. This study excluded control groups because there is no standard benchmark appointed by Ministry of Health in Malaysia.

This study involved random assignment of the intact groups to treatment with specific criteria, rather than assignment of individuals. The sample of this study must be a group of students that have a feeling on dental anxiety. Therefore, to make sure whether the group is equivalent, the baseline test in the phase 1 (see Figure 3) has been used to measure the dental anxiety understanding among children. The measurement instrument will be Smiley Faces Program which will be given and analyzed in term of homogeneity of dental anxiety level.

The treatment group performed a different set of a persuasive multimedia learning environment which was intended to develop their understanding of dentistry particularly dental treatment. Figure 3 illustrates the research design in this study. This research design involves three phases. Phase one is the baseline test, phase two is exploration and the use of PMLE as a treatment, and the phase three is the children dental anxiety (CDA) test.

Treatment group	Phase 1 $O_{1=}$ Baseline test (using SFP instrument)	Phase 2 $Y_{1=}$ PMLE (treatment)	Phase 3 $O_{2=}$ Children dental anxiety (CDA) test (using SFP instrument)

Fig. 3. Research design

4.1   Instrument: Smiley Faces Program (SFP)

The instrument that has been used in the experiment is a Smiley Faces Program (SFP) instrument which is used in the baseline test and the children dental anxiety test. SFP is used to measure both the baseline of children dental anxiety before the treatment is given and the children dental anxiety level after the treatment is given.

According to Buchanan (2005), the SFP is a dental anxiety measurement for children which consisting five dimensions of children dental anxiety. The SFP instrument is attached in Appendix A. All five dimensions are the major causal factors of children dental anxiety. Figure 4 illustrates the dimensions in the SFP.

1. Going to the dentist tomorrow
2. Sitting in the waiting room
3. About to have a tooth drilled
4. About to have tooth taken out
5. About to have an injection

Fig. 4. Dental anxiety dimensions in SFP

The measurement scale for SFP is using a set of five faces represents the feeling of children's response towards the dimensions of dental anxiety. The five dimensions included in the SFP score ranges from 1 to 5. Hence, the minimum score possible is 1 and the maximum is 5 which higher scores indicate higher anxiety.

4.2 Characteristics of Sample

Two to three intact classes were chosen from each of five different primary schools. A total of Year 1 to 3 school students participated in this experiment. The 120 learners (children) who had dental anxiety feeling were randomly divided into a group on their intact classes. The group was assigned to the PMLE as a treatment in reducing the children dental anxiety.

5 Results of the Study

Overall, PMLE had significant positive effect on reducing children dental anxiety. This was evidence by the statistical results that PMLE obtained significantly higher mean score for the baseline test which means the children used to have the dental anxiety feeling. In relation to the children dental anxiety scores (CDA), PMLE obtained significantly lower mean score for the CDA test which means the children is successful in reducing their dental anxiety level as well as achieved the intended result of this study as illustrated in Figure 5. This result proves that the PMLE is perhaps should be an alternative solution in reducing children dental anxiety, particularly in Malaysia context.

This result is based on the hypothesis test which defined that there will be no significant difference in scores of each children dental anxiety dimension between the two presentation modes. Detailed result of the hypothesis is discussed in the following section.

5.1 Paired Samples T-Test

In testing the hypothesis, paired samples T-test is used. Table 1 is indicated that there is a mean difference in scores of each children dental anxiety dimension between the

PMLE. In non-text version, the mean scores on the CDA test for each dental anxiety dimension was lower than the mean score on the Baseline test for each dental anxiety dimension. For example, the mean score on p2a (M=2.2000) was lower than the mean score p1a (M=4.0583). Meaning that, there is a reduction in a children dental anxiety. Figure 5 illustrated the reduction scores based from the mean scores difference in scores of each children dental anxiety dimension using PMLE as a treatment.

In this analysis, the confidence interval used is 95% or 0.05. If there will be no significant difference in scores of each children dental anxiety dimension between the two presentation modes, probability that will be derived a difference from a sample is at least 0.000. As from the paired sample test result in Table 1, significant value for

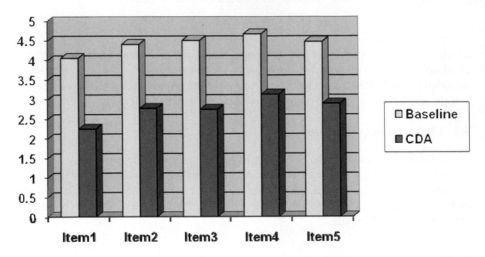

Fig. 5. The reduction scores based from the mean scores difference in scores of each children dental anxiety dimension

Table 1. Paired Samples T-Test Statistics of Children Dental Anxiety Test

PMLE Treatment		Mean	N	Std. Deviation	Std. Error Mean	Sig. value
Pair 1	P1a	4.0583	120	1.03140	.09415	0.0000
	p2a	2.2500	120	1.38570	.12650	0.0000
Pair 2	P1b	4.4083	120	.66731	.06092	0.0000
	p2b	2.7750	120	1.44631	.13203	0.0000
Pair 3	p1c	4.5083	120	.50203	.04583	0.0000
	p2c	2.7500	120	1.56780	.14312	0.0000
Pair 4	p1d	4.6723	119	.56911	.05217	0.0000
	p2d	3.1345	119	1.59939	.14662	0.0000
Pair 5	p1e	4.4746	118	.72456	.06670	0.0000
	p2e	2.9153	118	1.71756	.15811	0.0000

each dental anxiety dimension is 0.000. This value shown the probability for this phenomenon to be happened is small which is lower than 0.025 or 25% (two-tailed). Table 2 below is summarize the result of the hypothesis of this study.

Table 2. Summary of the effects of PMLE in reducing children dental anxiety

Presentation Modes	Children dental anxiety dimension		Results
	P1 (Baseline test)	P2 (Children dental anxiety test)	
Text version	a. Going to the dentist tomorrow b. Sitting in the waiting room c. About to have a tooth drilled d. About to have tooth taken out e. About to have an injection	a. Going to the dentist tomorrow b. Sitting in the waiting room c. About to have a tooth drilled d. About to have tooth taken out e. About to have an injection	Significant Significant Significant Significant Significant

6   Implications of the Study

There are three major implications of this study as elaborated below.

6.1   Digital Persuader: Feasible Design Strategies: Persuasive Design Principles

The successful design strategy and development of PMLE using virtual rehearsal principle provides evidence on the feasibility of employing the virtual rehearsal principle to guide the design of PMLE (Sobihatun Nur and Wan Jaafar, 2009a and Sobihatun Nur and Wan Jaafar, 2009b). Such theoretical design framework can also be generalized and be used to guide the design processes of other persuasive multimedia based learning environments and will be particularly appropriate for learning environments that employ the multimedia and persuasive elements.

Figure 6 illustrated the effects of a simulation of PMLE just before and after the exploration and using the prototype in reducing children dental anxiety. The figure shown the intended result of the study and has been achieved in the exact result of the study.

6.2   PMLE: Alternative Learning Environment in Reducing Children Dental Anxiety

The finding from this research performed significant result in reducing children dental anxiety. From the practical aspect, this study showed that PMLE is an effective digital persuader as well as learning aids to reduce children dental anxiety. This studies also shown that the PMLE strategy should be used in school setting where students can

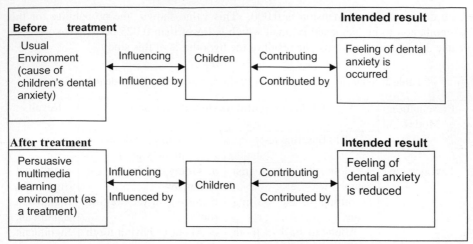

Fig. 6. Achievable intended result of the PMLE experiment

play with PMLE while waiting for dental treatment in school. PMLE also should be used as teaching and learning aids in health education subject.

This study has been successfully implemented and experimented in school and the result has proven that PMLE should be a self-mechanism in helping children to reduce their dental anxiety. Other than school, PMLE also has been implemented by paediatric dentist in one of the general hospital in Malaysia. The dentist has introduced the patient (children) to PMLE before attending dental check up. From observation, the particular dentist found that children would be easy and effective to be persuaded using PMLE in gaining their confidence and cooperation to have a dental check up as well as dental treatment. Hence, the dentist realized that the PMLE is also efficient as they can reduce their time spent in persuading the children to build up their confidence.

6.3   Value to Education and Society

The finding from this research performed significant result in reducing children dental anxiety. Social learning has been embedded in the PMLE as a persuasive technology in building up child confidence to dental visit (Sobihatun Nur, A.S. and Wan Jaafar, W. Y., 2009c). Therefore, this study might be used to educate our society, especially children to have a self confidence so that they can confidently communicate and give cooperation in the society.

7   Recommendations for Future Investigations

This study has opened up several interesting issues that warranted further research. First, in the effort to further refine and/or revise the design and development framework (both theoretical design framework and instructional development model), more design and development of various types of persuasive technology integrated with multimedia learning environment based on the proposed framework are needed. This will lead to the generation of a more robust and comprehensive design and development framework for persuasive multimedia-based learning environment especially in educational purposes.

8 Summary and Conclusion

The design and development of the PMLE based on the example of an application of a virtual rehearsal principle formed a feasible application of a persuasive technology that empirically contributed to the children in educating them to feel confident and creating their readiness to dental visit. The finding of the study shown, PMLE can be used as an alternative dental anxiety treatment because it has been empirically proven in educating, persuading also motivating the children to control their dentally anxious feeling. This finding is hoped to be a motivation for technology people, parents, teachers and public to bring up this persuasive technology potential in Malaysian society.

References

1. Buchanan, H.: Development of a computerized dental anxiety scale for children: validation and reliability. British Dental Journal 199, 359–362 (2005)
2. Fogg, B.J., Lee, E., Marshall, J.: In: Dillard, J.P., Pfau, M. (eds.) The Persuasion Handbook: Developments in Theory and Practice. SAGE Publications, Thousand Oaks (2002)
3. Fogg, B.J.: Persuasive technology: Using computers to change what we think and do. Morgan Kaufmann Publishers, San Francisco (2003)
4. Herrington, J., Oliver, R.: Critical Characteristics of Situated Learning: Implications for the Instructional Design of Multimedia (1995),
   http://www.ascilite.org.au/conferences/melbourne95/smtu/
   papers/herrington.pdf
5. Jonassen, D.: Designing Constructivist Learning Environment. In: Reigeluth, C. (ed.) Instructional Design Theories and Models: A new Paradigm of Instructional Theories, vol. II, pp. 215–239. Lawrence Erlbaum Associates, Mahwah (1999)
6. Sobihatun Nur, A.S., Wan Ahmad Jaafar, W.Y.: A Persuasive Multimedia Learning Environment (PMLE): Design Strategies for Reducing Children Dental Anxiety. DESIGN: Principles and Practices: And International Journal 3 (2009a)
7. Sobihatun Nur, A.S., Wan Ahmad Jaafar, W.Y.: Teknologi Pemujukan: Inovasi Dan Kreativiti Dalam ICT Dalam Mendidik Kanak-Kanak Mengurangkan Rasa Risau Terhadap Rawatan Pergigian. In: Prosiding Seminar Kebangsaan ICT Dalam Pendidikan, Ipoh. (2009b) (in Malay)
8. Sobihatun Nur, A.S., Wan Ahmad Jaafar, W.Y.: Embedded Social Learning in a Persuasive Technology: Building up Child Confidence to Dental Treatment. In: International Conference on Science in Society. Cambridge University, Cambridge (2009c)

Visualization of Positive and Monotone Data by Rational Quadratic Spline

Samsul Ariffin Abdul Karim[1,*] and Malik Zawwar Hussain[2]

[1] Fundamental and Applied Sciences Department,
Universiti Teknologi Petronas, Bandar Seri Iskandar,
31750 Tronoh, Perak Darul Ridzuan, Malaysia
samsul_ariffin@petronas.com.my
[2] Department of Mathematics, University of Punjab,
Lahore, Pakistan
malikzawwar@math.pu.edu.pk

Abstract. A curve interpolation scheme based on piecewise rational quadratic spline is discussed. To preserve the shape of the data, the constraints are made on the free parameters r_i, in the description of rational quadratic interpolant. We examine the positivity and/or monotonicity preserving of this rational quadratic interpolant to a given data set. The method easy to used and require less computational steps. The degree of smoothness attained is C^1. Some numerical results will be presented.

Keywords: Visualization, Interpolation, Positivity, Monotonicity, Shape Preserving.

1 Introduction

Scientific visualization provides a means of understanding various physical phenomena, from limited or incomplete information. The data that are known represent only a sample and may not be sufficient to let one visualize the entire entity. As such one uses interpolation to construct an empirical model which matches the data samples and approximates the unknown entity at intermediate locations. The properties that are most often used to quantify "shape" are convexity, monotonicity (for non-parametric data) and positivity. It is the last two of these that is of interest in our work, namely if the sampled data are monotonic and/or positive, then the interpolating curve (or surface) should be monotonic and/or positive everywhere. Ordinary spline interpolating scheme is not much desired for "shaped" data, due to the occurrence of unwanted oscillations which may completely destroy the data features. Thus, the need for shape preserving interpolation technique is unavoidable. Specific problems on shape preserving interpolation have been considered by a number of authors, for instance [5] and [6] discussed interpolation of monotonic data using C^1 piecewise cubic polynomials. An alternative to the use of polynomials, in order to interpolate monotonic data and positive data, is the application of piecewise rational splines

---

Corresponding author.

adioze Zaman et al. (Eds.): IVIC 2009, LNCS 5857, pp. 436–447, 2009.
inger-Verlag Berlin Heidelberg 2009

which is also called tension methods. For more details, ones can be referred the references in [1-18] and papers cited therein. In this paper, we will focus on preserving positivity and/or monotonicity data by using rational interpolant type quadratic/quadratic (quadratic numerator and quadratic denominator). numerical comparison with the established method from [15] and [16] will be presented.

2 Rational Quadratic Function

Suppose $(x_i, f_i), i = 1,...,n$ are a given set of data points, where $x_1 < x_2 < ... < x_n$. $h_i = x_{i+1} - x_i$, $\Delta_i = \dfrac{(f_{i+1} - f_i)}{h_i}$ and a local variable θ is defined by $\theta = \dfrac{(x - x_i)}{h_i}$ so that we have $0 \le \theta \le 1$.

For $x \in [x_i, x_{i+1}], i = 1, 2,..., n-1$, we define

$$s(x) = s(x_i + h_i \theta) \equiv S_i(\theta) = \frac{P_i(\theta)}{Q_i(\theta)}, \tag{1}$$

where

$$P_i(\theta) = f_i(1-\theta)^2 + (r_i f_i + h_i d_i)\theta(1-\theta) + f_{i+1}\theta^2$$

$$Q_i(\theta) = 1 + (r_i - 2)\theta(1-\theta),$$

Here the parameter d_i which is the slope of the curve will be determined by the data which we will discuss later in Section 5. The shape parameter r_i defined in the interval $[x_i, x_{i+1}]$ is free to be utilized. When $r_i = 2$, $q_i(\theta) = 1$, the rational curve reduces to a polynomial quadratic. To make the rational interpolant (1) be C^1 in $[x_1, x_n]$, we need to impose the following interpolatory properties:

$$S(x_i) = f_i, \quad S(x_{i+1}) = f_{i+1}, \\ S^{(1)}(x_i) = d_i, \quad S^{(1)}(x_{i+1}) = d_{i+1}, \tag{2}$$

By differentiate (1) w.r.t to x, we obtain

$$S^{(1)}(x) = \frac{\sum_{j=0}^{2} A_{j,i}(1-\theta)^{2-j}\theta^j}{\left[1 + (r_i - 2)\theta(1-\theta)\right]^2}, \tag{3}$$

where

$$A_{0,i} = d_i,$$
$$A_{1,i} = 2\Delta_i,$$
$$A_{2,i} = r_i \Delta_i - d_i.$$

Now $S(x)$ will preserve the first order continuity if and only if $S^{(1)}(x_{i+1}) = d_{i+1}$. By using basic algebraic manipulation, we have the following:

$$r_i = \frac{d_i + d_{i+1}}{\Delta_i} \tag{4}$$

Proposition 1. The rational quadratic interpolant (1) will preserves C^1-continuity if condition (4) is satisfied.

Remark 1. From the definition of rational interpolant (1) we have the following shape analysis observation

i) When $r_i = 2$, the rational interpolant (1) reduces to the standard quadratic polynomial. Which is in general it is not shape preserving.

ii) When $r_i \rightarrow 0$, the rational interpolant (1) can be rewriting as

$$S_i(x) = \frac{f_i(1-\theta)^2 + h_i d_i(1-\theta)\theta + f_{i+1}\theta^2}{1 - 2(1-\theta)\theta}, \tag{5}$$

In this case, the curve gets loosed.

iii) When $r_i \rightarrow \infty$, $S_i(x) = f_i$,

iv) In this paper, we restrict the condition on shape parameter such that $r_i > -2$, in order to ensures a strictly positive for denominator in the rational spline (1). This is our first constraint on the shape parameter, r_i.

3 Positive Rational Quadratic Interpolation

The rational quadratic spline method, described in the previous section, has some deficiencies as far as positivity preserving issue is concerned. For example, the rational quadratic function in Section 2 does not always preserve the shape of positive data (see Fig. 1 and Fig. 3). It is required to assign appropriate values to the shape parameter, namely r_i so that the rational interpolant will preserved the shape of the data. For simplicity of presentation, let us assume positive set of data:

$(x_i, f_i), i = 1, 2, ..., n$ with $x_1 < x_2 < ... < x_n$ and $f_i > 0, i = 1, 2, ..., n$ we want to construct a positive interpolant $S(x)$ in the whole interval $[x_1, x_n]$, that is $S(x_i) = f_i$ such that

$$S(x_i) > 0, x_1 \leq x \leq x_n$$

As $r_i > -2$ guarantees positive denominator $Q_i(\theta)$, so initial conditions on r_i are

$$r_i > -2, \quad i = 1, 2, ..., n-1. \tag{6}$$

Now the positivity of $S(x)$ depends on the positivity of the quadratic polynomial $P_i(\theta)$. Thus the problem reduces to the determination of appropriate values of r_i for which polynomial $P_i(\theta)$ is positive. Now, according to the Bezier theory of polynomials [14], $P_i(\theta) > 0$ if and only if

$$r_i > \frac{-h_i d_i}{f_i}, \tag{7}$$

Hence $S(x) > 0$, if and only if

$$r_i > Max\left\{-2, \frac{-h_i d_i}{f_i}\right\} \tag{8}$$

We can be rearranged (8) as:

$$r_i = l_i + Max\left\{-2, \frac{-h_i d_i}{f_i}\right\}, \quad l_i > 0 \tag{9}$$

Proposition 2. Given a strictly positive data, the rational quadratic interpolant (1) preserves positivity if and only if (8) is satisfied.

Remark 2. In [10], in order to preserves the positivity data, the authors state the shape parameter r_i must satisfy the following inequality

$$r_i = e_i + Max\left\{-2, 2\sqrt{\frac{f_{i+1}}{f_i}} - \frac{h_i d_i}{f_i}\right\}, \quad e_i > 0 \tag{10}$$

It is interesting to note that, this constraints for the shape parameters will be produce same interpolating curves for the same value of r_i. Easily we may obtained the relationship between $l_i > 0$ and $e_i > 0$ as follow

$$l_i = e_i - 2\sqrt{\frac{f_{i+1}}{f_i}}$$

Therefore we have a unique representation for rational quadratic interpolant for both paper namely [9] and [10].

4 Monotone Rational Quadratic Interpolation

In this section, we will examine the monotonicity preserving property of the rational interpolant to a given data set. For simplicity of presentation, let us assume monotonic increasing set of data such that $f_1 \le f_2 \le ... \le f_n$ or equivalently

$$\Delta_i \ge 0, i = 1, 2, ..., n - 1. \tag{11}$$

(In a similar idea, one can derived the condition for monotonic decreasing data).
   We choose the derivative value d_i such that

$$d_i \ge 0, i = 1, 2, ..., n. \tag{12}$$

Now, $S(x)$ is monotonic if and only if

$$S^{(1)}(x) > 0 \tag{13}$$

for all $x \in [x_1, x_n]$. For $x \in [x_i, x_{i+1}]$, $S^{(1)}(x)$ are given by (3), thus we have the following conditions:

$$A_{j,i} > 0, \quad j = 0,1,2. \tag{14}$$

If $\Delta_i > 0$ (strict inequality) then the following are sufficient conditions for (14):

Since $A_{0,i} > 0, A_{1,i} > 0$,

$$A_{2,i} > 0,$$

$$r_i \Delta_i - d_i > 0, \tag{15}$$

$$r_i > \frac{d_i}{\Delta_i} \tag{16}$$

Proposition 3. Given conditions (11) on the derivatives parameters, (16) is the sufficient conditions for interpolant (1) to be monotonic increasing.

(16) can be rearranged as the follow:

$$r_i = m_i + \frac{d_i}{\Delta_i}, \ m_i > 0 \tag{17}$$

Proposition 4. The sufficient conditions for the interpolant (1) to be positive as well as monotonic are

$$r_i = \kappa_i + Max\left\{-2, \frac{-h_i d_i}{f_i}, \frac{d_i}{\Delta_i}\right\}, \quad \kappa_i > 0 \tag{18}$$

5 Computation and Demonstration

In most applications, the derivatives parameters d_i are not given and hence must be determined either from the data $(x_i, f_i), i = 1, 2, ..., n$ or by some other mean method. In this paper, we use the arithmetic mean method (three-point different approximation). The detail as follows:

$$d_1 = \begin{cases} 0, & \text{if} \quad \Delta_1 = 0 \quad \text{or} \quad \text{sign}(d_1^*) \neq \text{sign}(\Delta_1) \\ d_1^* & \text{o.w} \end{cases}$$

$$d_1^* = \Delta_1 + (\Delta_1 - \Delta_2)\left(\frac{h_1}{h_1 + h_2}\right) \tag{19}$$

$$d_n = \begin{cases} 0, & \text{if} \quad \Delta_{n-1} = 0 \quad \text{or} \quad \text{sign}\left(d_n^*\right) \neq \text{sign}\left(\Delta_{n-1}\right) \\ d_n^* & \text{o.w} \end{cases}$$

$$d_n^* = \Delta_{n-1} + \left(\Delta_{n-1} - \Delta_{n-2}\right)\left(\frac{h_{n-1}}{h_{n-1} + h_{n-2}}\right) \tag{20}$$

For $i = 2,3,...,n-1$, d_i are given by

$$d_i = \begin{cases} 0 & \text{if} \quad \Delta_{i-1} = 0 \quad \text{or} \quad \Delta_i = 0 \\ \dfrac{h_{i-1}\Delta_i + h_i\Delta_{i-1}}{h_{i-1} + h_i} & \text{o.w} \end{cases} \tag{21}$$

For detail on determination of derivative parameters, please refer to [3] and [14]. An algorithm for generating the interpolating monotone and/or positive curve is given below.

Algorithm 1

1. Input the number of data points, n
2. Input data points $\left\{x_i\right\}_{i=1}^n$ and $\left\{f_i\right\}_{i=1}^n$
3. Initialize the end point conditions d_1 and d_n by using (19) and (20)
4. For $i = 1,...,n-1$
   - (a) Define h_i and Δ_i
   - (b) Calculate d_i by using (21)
   - (c) Set $r_i = 2$ to generate a default curve
5. For $i = 1,...,n-1$

   modify r_i interactively by using (9) for positivity, (17) for monotonic and (18) for positive and monotonic preserving (The parameter l_i, m_i and κ_i are free to utilized).

6. For $i = 1,...,n-1$ generate the piecewise interpolating curve by (1) for each r_i from step (5) above.

To demonstrate the rational quadratic interpolant are capable to preserves the positive and/or monotonic data, we implement the Algorithm 1 by choosing three different data set taken from [15], [16] and [17] respectively.

Table 1. Data set from [17]

i	1	2	3	4	5	6
x_i	2	3	7	8	13	14
y_i	10	2	3	7	3	10

Table 2. Data set from [16]

i	1	2	3	4	5
x_i	0	2	3	9	11
y_i	0.5	1.5	7	9	13

Table 3. Data set from [15]

i	1	2	3	4	5
x_i	0	6	10	29.5	30
y_i	0.01	15	15	25	30

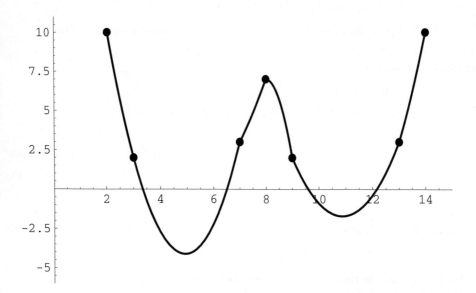

Fig. 1. Default curves to the data in Table 1 (when $r_i = 2$)

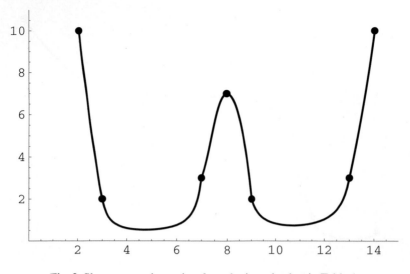

Fig. 2. Shape preserving rational quadratic to the data in Table 1

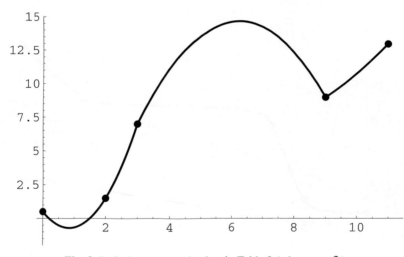

Fig. 3. Default curves to the data in Table 2 (when $r_i = 2$)

We can see from Fig. 1 and Fig. 3, the standard quadratic polynomial (when $r_i = 2$) are unable to preserve the positivity of the data in Table 1 and Table 2 respectively. By using the result in Proposition 2 we obtained visual pleasing curve that preserve the positivity features from the data as we can see clearly from Fig. 2 and Fig. 4. From Fig. 4 we can see that the interpolating curve only preserve positivity but not preserve the monotonicity on interval [0,2].

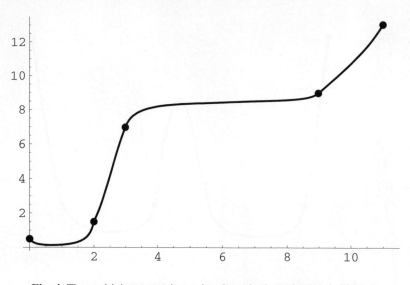

Fig. 4. The positivity preserving rational quadratic to the data in Table 2

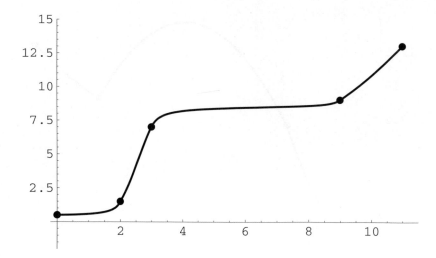

Fig. 5. The shape preserving spline for the positivity and monotonicity data in Table 2

The data in Table 2 are also monotone. By using the result in Proposition 4, we obtained the resulting curve preserve positivity and the monotonicity of the data as we can see clearly in Fig. 5. Fig. 6 show the shape preserving spline using [16] for the data set in Table 2. Fig. 7 show the shape preserving rational quadratic spline for data from Table 3 and Fig. 8 show the shape preserving spline by using [15]. We conclude that, by using the proposed scheme, we still obtain very visual pleasing result and it requires less computations and easy to be implemented. Furthermore from the numerical results, the schemes are comparable with the results from [15] and [16].

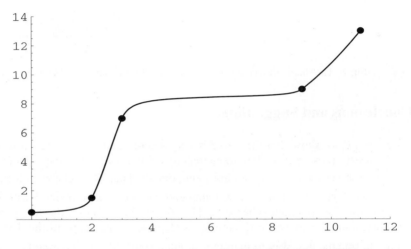

Fig. 6. The shape preserving spline using [16] for the data in Table 2

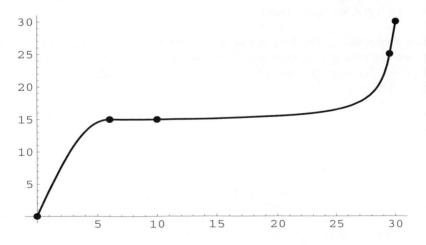

Fig. 7. The shape preserving rational quadratic spline for the data in Table 3

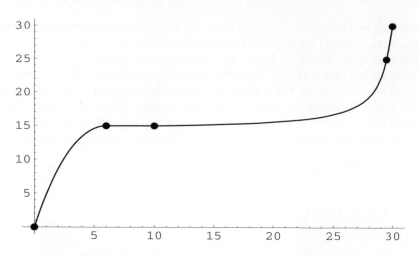

Fig. 8. The shape preserving spline using [15] for the data in Table 3

6 Conclusions and Suggestions

Numerical examples show that the curve is very smooth and keeps inherent features of the given data (positivity and/or monotonicity). By utilized the shape parameters r_i, we can preserves the positivity and/or monotonicity data. This scheme is local and simple to used together require a few computational steps as compared with other shape preserving interpolation scheme i.e.,[15,16,17]. Furthermore, the free parameters are turned into the constrained parameters to preserve the shape of the data. It is interesting to find the best way to maintain simultaneously the C^1 continuity together with preserving the positivity and monotonicity simultaneously. The authors are keen to discuss it in a subsequent paper.

Acknowledgements. The first author would like to thank to Universiti Teknologi Petronas for providing support and the computing facilities for this research to be carried out. We would like thank the anonymous referee for valuable suggestions that improved this paper.

References

1. Butt, S., Brodlie, K.W.: Preserving positivity using piecewise cubic interpolation. Computer Graphics 17(1), 55–64 (1993)
2. Delbourgo, R., Gregory, J.A.: Shape Preserving piecewise rational interpolation. SIAM J. Stat. Comput. 6, 967–976 (1985a)
3. Delbourgo, R., Gregory, J.A.: The Determination of Derivative Parameters for a Monotonic Rational Quadratic Interpolant. IMA J. of Numerical Analysis 5, 397–406 (1985b)
4. Duan, Q., Djidjeli, K., Price, W.G., Twizell, E.H.: Constrained control and approximation properties of a rational interpolating curve. Information Sciences 152, 181–194 (2003)

5. Fritsch, F.N., Butland, J.: A method for constructing local monotone piecewise cubic interpolants. SIAM J. Sci. and Statist. Comput. 5, 300–304 (1984)
6. Fritsch, F.N., Carlson, R.E.: Monotone piecewise cubic interpolation. SIAM J. Numer. Anal. 17, 238–246 (1980)
7. Goodman, T.N.T.: Shape preserving interpolation by curves. In: Levesley, J., Anderson, I.J., Mason, J.C. (eds.) Algorithms for Approximation IV, pp. 24–35. University of Huddersfield Proceedings, Huddersfield (2002)
8. Gregory, J.A.: Shape preserving spline interpolation. CAD 18(1), 53–57 (1986)
9. Hussain, M.Z., Ayub, N., Irshad, M.: Visualization of 2D data by rational quadratic functions. Journal of Information and Computing Science 2(1), 17–26 (2007)
10. Hussain, M.Z., Ali, J.M.: Visualizing positive data by rational quadratic curve. In: 12th Simposium Kebangsaan Sains Matematik (2004)
11. Kvasov, B.I.: Methods of shape-preserving spline approximation. World Scientific, Singapore (2000)
12. McAllister, D.F., Roulier, J.A.: An algorithm for computing a shape preserving osculatory quadratic spline. ACM Trans. Math. Software 7, 331–347 (1981)
13. Passow, E., Roulier, J.A.: Monotone and convex spline interpolation. SIAM J. Numer. Anal. 14, 904–909 (1977)
14. Sarfraz, M.: Visualization of positive and convex data by a rational cubic spline interpolation. Information Sciences 146, 239–254 (2002)
15. Sarfraz, M.: A rational cubic spline for the visualization of monotonic data: an alternate approach. Computers & Graphics 27, 107–121 (2003)
16. Sarfraz, M., Butt, S., Hussain, M.Z.: Visualization of shaped data by a rational cubic spline interpolation. Computer Graphics 25, 833–845 (2001)
17. Sarfraz, M., Hussain, M.Z., Chaudhry, F.S.: Shape preserving cubic spline for data visualization. Computer Graphics and CAD/CAM 01, 185–193 (2005)
18. Schmidt, J.W., Heß, W.: Positivity interpolation with rational quadratic splines. Computing 38, 261-267 (1987)

Thickness Characterization of 3D Skin Surface Images Using Reference Line Construction Approach

M.H. Ahmad Fadzil[1] , Hurriyatul Fitriyah[1], Esa Prakasa[1], Hermawan Nugroho[1],
S.H. Hussein[2], and Azura Mohd. Affandi[2]

[1] Department Electrical and Electronics Engineering
Universiti Teknologi PETRONAS, Perak Darul Ridzuan 31750, Malaysia
fadzmo@petronas.com.my, hfitriyah@gmail.com,
esa.prakasa@informatika.lipi.go.id, dewa132@yahoo.com
[2] Department of Dermatology
Hospital Kuala Lumpur, Jalan Pahang, 50568, Kuala Lumpur, Malaysia
suraiya.hussein@gmail.com, azura@yahoo.co.uk

Abstract. Irregular elevation is commonly formed in skin surface during dermatological diseases. Thickness is one of the parameters to assess the severity. In this research, the thickness is defined as the elevation of lesion surface from its constructed reference line which is generated by smoothing the lesion surface using moving average filter. This method is applied in dermatological disease which caused by disorder cell growth. In the clinical trial, Dermatologist classifies the thickness severity into 4 classes. The classes are divided by its thickness appearance. Dermatologist assesses 40 3D images of skin lesion taken from 16 patients. The quantitative and objective measurement of the lesions performed in this research has characterized the thickness range of each class as well as met the doctor's thickness classification.

Keywords: Thickness Characterization, 3D Skin Surface Image, Reference Line Construction.

1 Introduction

In various dermatological cases, the disorder affects skin surfaces and builds up elevation compare to the surrounding healthy skin. Clinical cases such as Acne, keratosis, dermatofibroma, psoriasis, and rosacea, experience the situation. Measuring the thickness is one of the ways to determine the disorder severity. During assessment, dermatologist runs finger through the patient skin lesion to assess the severity.

In this research, the algorithm is applied in measuring the thickness of Psoriasis. This is a chronic inflammatory skin disease which is caused by genetic fault where immune system is mistakenly triggered. Hence skin cells grow faster and thicker than the normal. This disease may occur on the entire body, especially elbows, knees, scalp, lower back, face, palms, and soles. Epidemiological studies around the world reports the prevalence of psoriasis ranges from 0.05 to 11.8 % [1].

Related research has been developed to measure and score the thickness of psoriasis lesion by taking histopathological image using Olympus BX50 microscope [2]. Image

H. Badioze Zaman et al. (Eds.): IVIC 2009, LNCS 5857, pp. 448–454, 2009.

is transferred to computer with a Panasonic GP-KR222 camera and converted to BMP files. Pathpic image analysis software is used to examine the image and perform the measurement. Epidermal thickness is determined by measuring the distance between the top and the bottom of the rete.

Another research uses ultrasound technology to measure the skin thickness [3]. In psoriasis, ultrasound with 15MHz frequency which applied in the lesion has able to quantify the thickness in percentage compare to the normal [4].

This research objective is to develop a computer vision system to characterize the thickness of psoriasis classes. The digital imaging technology used is 3D scanner which produces 3D skin surface image. The psoriasis images of each class are shown in Figure 1.

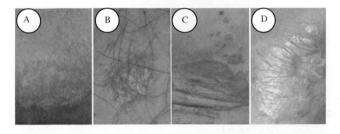

Fig. 1. Skins with Psoriasis Lesion and its Class, Assigned by Dermatologist

The Psoriasis is classed into 4 according to its severity. Dermatologist used the standard description as in Table 1 to assign each psoriasis lesion into its class.

Table 1. Psoriasis Thickness Classes Description

Class	Elevation
A	Slight plaque elevation
B	Moderate elevation
C	Marked elevation
D	Very marked elevation

2 Method

2.1 Data Acquisition

The skin-with-psoriasis images are taken from 16 male patients, age varies from 21 to 60 years old. The clinical trial is conducted with Dermatological Unit of General Hospital Kuala Lumpur, Malaysia. The dermatologist assesses the lesion thickness by running through their finger and assigns each lesion into 4 classes. The dermatologist is asked to conduct the assessment twice to ensure the consistency. In this paper, 40 images are tested, each 10 images for every class.

The skin images are taken using Konica Minolta Non-Contact 3D Digitizer VIVID 910. Using laser triangulation as basic principle, the object is scanned by a plane of laser light coming from the source aperture [5]. The plane of light is swept across the

field of view by a mirror, rotated by a precise galvanometer. The laser light is reflected from the surface of the scanned object. Each scan line is observed by a single
frame, captured by CCD camera. The contour of the surface is derived from the shape
of the image of each reflected scan line. The image is acquired using middle lens,
focal length distance f = 14 mm. It captures 198 to 823 mm in X direction, 148 to 618
mm in Y, and 70 to 800 mm in Z. The accuracy is up to 0.10 mm to the reference
plane. The example of skin image with psoriasis captured by 3D scanner is shown in
Figure 2.

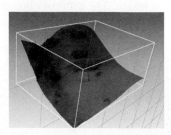

Fig. 2. 3D Image of Skin with Psoriasis Lesion taken using 3D Scanner

The Psoriasis lesion is taken perpendicular to normal direction of 3D scanner to assure that height information in the lesion is taken solely. Zero reference is at the lens
position; hence the height of skin recorded is negative.

2.2 Image Pre-processing

3D image taken consists of lesion and normal skin. Hence, a cropping method needs
to be performed since only the lesion surface is needed in the algorithm. The image
captured from 3D scanner is in MDL extension file. The lesion surface cropped is
then converted to STL file extension since only height value is occupied, omits the
color information. From STL file extension, related point of cloud is determined using
Matlab function. The function fits the 3D STL file surface to   uniform grid data point
using triangle-based linear interpolation. This image pre-processing step is shown in
Figure 3.

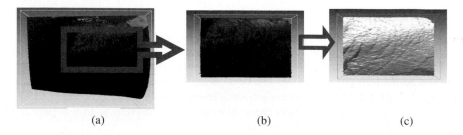

(a)   (b)   (c)

Fig. 3. Image Pre-processing Step (a) Skin (normal skin + Psoriasis lesion) 3D Images, MDL
file (b) Cropped Skin (Psoriasis lesion only) 3D Images, MDL file (c) MDL file of Cropped
Skin Converted to STL (height values only)

2.3 Reference Line Construction

Thickness is determined as the subtraction between image surface and its base. In data acquisition, 3D scanner only captured the height information of lesion. Hence, a base is created only by utilizing the surface height. The base constructed is not the actual base of lesion. The base in here is a reference surface as the approach to resemble the lesion base. In flat and horizontal lesion surface, a base can be easily created as a flat surface that is connected from edges to edges. But it should be remembered that the 3D images are taken from non flat skin. They are located at elbow, chest, back, finger, and other curvy body area hence the straight-line method can not be applied.

Based on the nxn uniform grid data points from 40 patients, the lesion surface is acknowledged to be curvy and rough. To create smooth surface, a filter should be applied to the lesion surface. In this research, surface is smoothed line per line each in horizontal and vertical line to seek the smoothest reference line. This line profiling is illustrated in Figure 4.

Since lesion surface acts like random noise to the normal skin, a moving average filter is used. This filter is commonly used since its simplicity to reduce random noise [6]. A moving average filter smoothes data by replacing each data point with the average of the neighboring data points defined within the length size [7]. The length size should be an odd number. The moving average equation with length size can be written as in Equation 1.

$$Z_s(i) = \frac{1}{2L+1}\sum_{k=-L}^{L} Z(i+k) \tag{1}$$

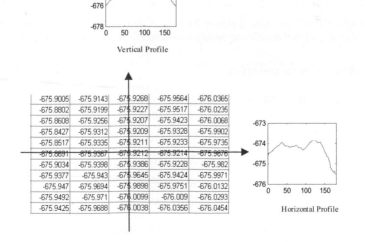

Fig. 4. Line Profiling, Horizontally and Vertically

$Z(i)$ is the original value from the data, $Z_s(i)$ is the smoothed value. Equation 1 is applied to one-dimensional computation, and L as the length sizes are varied from several data points.

Length size of the moving average filter affects smoothness of lesion profile. The more the length size, the smoother and flatter of a profile with noise are. Beside a smooth profile, base as a resemblance of normal skin beneath the lesion surface has to be constructed as low as the normal skin itself. The information of normal skin is able to be obtained from the lesion edges. Moving average filter is also used in this research since it edges values are included in every data points averaging. This will bring the noisy profile to as low as the edges, as expected. The effects of different filter's length size from vertical profile in Figure 4 are shown in Figure 5. The length size in the simulation varies from 31 to 111.

To meet the reference line construction objective which is smooth and low as edges, 91 length size is chosen based on simulation result in Figure 5. An nxn uniform grid data point surface has n numbers of reference lines in horizontal direction and n numbers of reference lines in vertical direction.

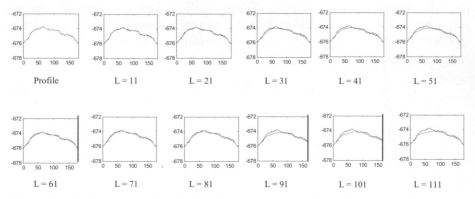

Fig. 5. Profile Smoothing using Various Moving Average Filter's Length Size (L). Surface profile is blue line while smoothed reference line is red line.

2.4 Thickness Characterization

After constructing reference line, elevations can be measured as the distance between lesion profile and reference line as shown in Equation 2.

$$Elevation = Z_{lesion} - Z_{reference} \qquad (2)$$

An approach to construct reference line using moving average filter can bring $Z_{reference}$ higher than Z_{lesion}, thus makes elevation at several points can be negative. This value is omitted from the next calculation since elevation from convex surface such as psoriasis lesion has to be positive.

Every nxn lesion grid data points have nxn number of values from horizontal profiling as well as nxn number of values from vertical profiling. The thickness is then determined by averaging all of the elevations.

In this research, median is used as the representative value of thickness average as shown in Equation 3. Since compare to mean, which is easily affected by outlier and left-right skewness in the distribution, median is more stable [8]. Outlier and skewness happens in image which has noise from hair or skin ripple such in knee and elbow, as well as the smoothing approach effects. Median is the value of sample which divides the total number of sample into two equal sizes.

$$Thickness = median(elevations) \qquad (3)$$

The thickness result is not the measure of lesion thickness, but it is the value or index to characterize the subjective assessment of each score conducted by dermatologist.

3   Result and Discussion

The algorithm is applied to 40 lesion images captured from 16 Psoriasis patients, 10 images to each class. The thickness value or index is shown as histogram in Figure 6.

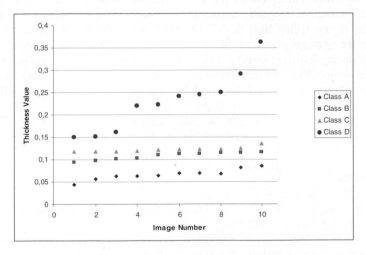

Fig. 6. Thickness Value in each Class

From Figure 6, the thickness range of each class can be arranged as in Table 2.

Table 2. Thickness Classes Range

Class	Thickness	
	Minimum	Maximum
A	0.04491	0.08727
B	0.09274	0.11557
C	0.11731	0.13489
D	0.13698	0.36325

From Table 2 it can be inferred that the thickness value characterized by the proposed method is able to follow the dermatologist's characterization. The dermatologist is the expert knowledge in psoriasis skin assessment.

Table 2 also shows the differentiate value between classes. Hereafter, the new skin with Psoriasis lesion images taken using 3D scanner can be assigned objectively to the class. Thickness value or index between class ranges can be assigned to the nearest neighbor class. For the example is thickness value of 0.11600 is assigned to the class B, since 0.11600 is closer to maximum value or index of class B (0.1157) compare to minimum value or index of class C (0.11731).

4   Conclusion

An algorithm to characterize the thickness of lesion skin has been developed through this research. Thickness is determined as the median of the total lesion elevation in the skin image. Elevation is determined by subtracting the lesion profile with the lesion reference line. The reference line is constructed using moving average of related lesion profile, each horizontally and vertically profiled. The reference line is then utilized as the reconstructed base or normal skin beneath the lesion surface. Median is chosen as the average parameter of all elevations measured as it is robust to outlier and stable during left-right skewed distribution. Classification into 4 classes is applied during the clinical trials by dermatologist. From the characterization, thickness range from every class is determined. The result has met the dermatologist's classification.

Acknowledgment. This research is collaboration between Universiti Teknologi Petronas (UTP) and Dermatology Unit, General Hospital Kuala Lumpur, Malaysia.

References

1. Neimann, A.L., Porter, S.B., Gelfand, J.M.: The Epidemiology of Psoriasis. Expert Review of Dermatology 1(1), 63–75 (2006)
2. Alper, M., et al.: Measurement of epidermal thickness in a patient with psoriasis by computer-supported image analysis. Journal of Medical and Biological Research 37, 111–117 (2004)
3. Alexander, H., Miller, D.L.: Determining Skin Thickness with Pulsed Ultra Sound. The Journal of Investigative Dermatology 72, 17–19 (1979)
4. Serup, J.: Non-invasive quantification of psoriasis plaques–measurement of skin thickness with 15 MHz pulsed ultrasound. Journal of Clinical and Experimental Dermatology 9(5), 502–508 (2006)
5. Konica Minolta Vivid 910 Non Contact 3D Digitizer Manual Handbook, Japan (2001)
6. Smith, S.W.: The Scientist and Engineer's Guide to Digital Signal Processing. California Technical Publisher, USA (1997)
7. Moving Average Filter, Matlab Documentation
8. Bowers, D.: Statistics from Scratch: An Introduction for Health Care Professional. Wiley, USA (1996)

An Approach to Derive Parametric L-System Using Genetic Algorithm

Humera Farooq, M. Nordin Zakaria, Mohd. Fadzil Hassan, and Suziah Sulaiman

Department of Computer and Information Sciences,
Universiti Teknnologi PETRONAS
Bandar Seri Iskandar, 31750 Tronoh, Perak, Malaysia
humera_farooq@utp.edu.my,
{nordinzakaria,mfadzil_hassan,suziah}@petronas.com.my

Abstract. In computer graphics, L-System is widely used to model artificial plants structures and fractals. The Genetic Algorithm (GA) is the most popular form of Evolutionary Algorithms. This paper examines a method for automatic plant modeling which is based on an integration of GA and Parametric L-System using appropriate fitness function. The approach is specifically based on the implementation of two layered GA to derive the rewriting rules of Parametric L-System. The higher level of GA deals with the evolution of symbols and lower level deals with the evolution of numerical parameters. Initial results derived from the approach are very promising, which shows that complicated branching structures can be easily derived by the multilayered architecture of GA.

Keywords: Evolutionary Algorithm, Computer Graphics, Genetic Algorithm, Parametric L-System, Visualization.

1 Introduction

L-System provides a powerful method to represent the modeling of branching structures in 3D environment. L-System works in the same way as the Chomsky Grammar, but there is a major difference in the method of application between the two approaches. The rules of L-System are applied in parallel [1], replacing all characters in one step while in Chomsky grammar, the rules are applied in a sequence; one character is replaced in each step. Initially the L-systems rules are used to represent cell division in multi-cellular organism [2] and hence, its parallelism mimics that in nature. These rules work recursively to model complex plant and tree structures. Nowadays, L-System is widely used to generate natural looking scenes, fractals, medical images and branching structures.

In branching structures there are different functional modules (flower, leaves, and buds) which are arranged and correspond together to make-up a plant. Each module of the plant has sub modules and these sub modules has layers of sub modules. By increasing the levels of modules, plant structure becomes more complicated. The

H. Badioze Zaman et al. (Eds.): IVIC 2009, LNCS 5857, pp. 455–466, 2009.

natural patterns applied by nature for these branching structures can be translated into mathematical equations using L-system, and GA is used to derive the L-system. In the presented work, 2 layers GA is introduced, in which the 1st layer will work on symbols of L-System and in 2_{nd} layers GA are concerned on how the parameter will be evolved. In other words, the symbols and parameters of the L-System were directly mapped as chromosomes in GA in layered architecture. We select the Deterministic Parametric L-System because in Parametric L-System each symbol has its own associated parameters. These parameters can be used during the interpretation of the produced string whereas in simple deterministic L-System, every branch, angle, thickness is controlled by the global parameters.

In our proposed methodology both populations run independently in top to bottom layered architecture.GA then is used get the optimized solutions for both symbols and numerical parameters. We also introduced special mutation operator and scaling values to achieve this goal.

2 Background

Genetic Algorithm invented by John Holland in 1960's is widely used to solve the optimization problems in various fields of science. GA was introduced by Holland [3], and they have gained massive popularity because of its effectiveness in solving difficult optimization problems. Direct search method and robustness quality makes this algorithm more favorable compared to other techniques. The main theme of the paper is the use of L-System to represent a complex structure and on the GA to derive the optimal L-System.

The L-System and GA are well addressed in literature. Many research studies have been carried out on this topic. Previous work, such as [4], deals only with the symbols of deterministic L-System evolved using GA, however there approach is well addressed on the repair mechanism and to prevent the synthetically incorrect results. The System developed by [5] consists of evolving parameters of Parametric L-System, Timed and Stochastic L-System and redraw them in 3-D space. They worked in modeling of complex branching structures of same phenotype. A database of images of Parametric DOL-System is created by [6] by applying several image processing algorithm techniques on images. They described the structure of human retina with combine evolutionary operators , in which GA is used to derive symbols and evolution strategies is used to evolved numerical parameters. An interactive model is developed by [7] using Parametric DOL-System and GA is used to evolved parameters. In [8] Parametric 0L-system is used to draw branching structures. The parameters works in the form of tag functions and GA evolved these tag functions. A parallel evolution approach is adopted by [9]. The symbols and numerical parameters of Parametric DOL-System are evolved by evolutionary algorithms, in which symbols are optimized by GA and parameters by using evolution strategies. The idea behind their research is to run two parallel populations so that they can exchange best individual with each other.

2.1 Parametric L-System

The idea behind Parametric L-System is to use parallel rewriting with parametric words instead of strings of symbols [10]. The alphabet is denoted by Σ, and the set of parameters is the set of real numbers R. A module with letter a $\in \Sigma$ and parameters (p1, p2 …….pn) $\in$ R is denoted by a (p1, p2 ….pn).The real-valued actual parameters appearing in words have a counterpart with formal parameters which may be used in the specification of L-system productions.

Let $\prod$ be the set of formal parameters. The combination of formal parameters and numeric constant using arithmetic operators (+, -, *, /), the logical operators (&&, ! , ||) , the relational operators (>, <, >=, <= , =) and parenthesis (()) will make a complete set of $\prod$ having all constructed logical and arithmetic expressions. These are noted as C ($\prod$) and E ($\prod$). A Parametric L-system is an ordered quadruplet G = (Σ, $\prod$, α, p t), where,

- Σ is the *alphabet* of the system
- $\prod$ is the set of formal parameters
- α .$\in$ (Σ x R*) + is a nonempty word called axioms.
- p $\subseteq$ (Σ x $\prod$) x C ($\prod$) x (Σ x $\in$($\prod$))* is a finite set of productions.

A production rule takes the following form:

Predecessor | Condition → successor

In applying the production rules specified in the L-System, the predecessor will be recursively expanded and replaced with the relevant successors. Consider the following example:

Axiom: F (α)
Rule 01: F -> F (α_1) [-(θ_1) F(α_2)] F(α_3) [+(θ_2) F(α_4)] … F (α_n) [+(θ_n) F(α_n)]

There is one module F in axiom and the parameter α respectively. It consists of one production rule that rewrite the occurrence of F with the precise successor modules. In Fig 01, a tree is generated with Parametric L-System after 05 iterations, using the following rules:

Axiom: ! (1) F (200) / (15) A
Rule 01:   A -> !(width) F(50) [-(rot) F(150) A] /(Ang01)
           F (150) [& (rot) F (50) A] / (Ang02) [&(rot) F(50) A]

Rule 02:   !(w) -> !(w*width)

Constants: Ang01 = 435.74, Ang02 = 832.63,
             rot   = 20.95 , width = 1.932

Fig. 1. Tree generated after 05 iterations

2.2 Turtle Interpretation

The L-System rules can be easily visualized using a turtle interpretation. The turtle graphics are used to build a geometrical interpretation of L-System strings. These turtle interpretation can be extended to 3-D space.

Table 1. Turtle Symbols used to draw in 3-D space

Symbols	Direction	Orientation
F(s)	Move forward a step of length s	Draw a line
F(s)	Move forward a step of length s	No draw line
+, -	Turn left and right	Matrix $R_U(\delta)$
&, ^	Pitch down and up	Matrix $R_L(\delta)$
\, /	Roll left and right	Matrix R_H
|	Turning around	Matrix $R_U(180°)$
[,]	Push and pop current state of from stack.	Use for Branching
!(w)	Set line width to w	Increase width

The current orientation of turtle in space is represented by 3 vectors: H, L, U, indicating turtle's heading, the direction to the left, and, the direction to the right. The symbols used to control this orientation are described in Table 1.

3 Genetic Algorithm for Parametric L-System

The essential components of GA are based on genetic operators, in which a crossover operator is used to crossover some parts of genes for reproducing 2 new solutions and a mutation operator to randomly mutate a part of solution depends on probability ratio , and a well defined fitness function to determine how well a proposed solution matches the problem. In the present paper Parametric L-System evolved using GA, so two types of chromosomes we need to encode into GA, the symbols of Parametric L-System and the parametric values. In this way two layer GA will be evolved. The individual of GA based on string (symbolic values) and parameters as real coded values.

The symbols of L-System are used directly as a gene and these symbols are represented as strings encoding in GA. The parameters of Parametric L-System are encoded as real values into the GA. Since real values are involved, some special operators are used to get optimizer solution.

3.1 GA Operators

These chromosomes or individuals are used to create an initial population. Initially population of individual is created randomly. By using a suitable fitness function and the GA operators, the next generation is created and this process continues until an optimal solution is obtained. Three operators used by GA are selection, crossover and mutation. Since real values are involved, some special operators are used to get optimizer solution. In the heart of GA is the fitness function, with an appropriate fitness function the optimized solution can be achieved easily.

Fitness Function. To evaluate the fitness of an individual the L-string generated by GA is compared with the target array. Let an input array be denoted by α, the set of numbers are obtained as $\alpha = (\alpha 1, \alpha 2 \ldots\ldots\ldots \alpha n)$ and Target array is obtained by β, the set of numbers obtained as $\beta = (\beta 1, \beta 2 \ldots\ldots \beta n)$, The fitness of an individual is based on the difference of distance between two strings, smaller the distance, more chance to be selected, thus indicates the higher fitness of an individual. For evolving the symbols, the fitness calculated by the following formula:

$$f = \sum_{i=1}^{i=n} (I_i - T_i)^2$$

(1)

Where I is the input string and T is the target string and f is the fitness function. Here $(I - T)$ is the distance between input and target characters of a string. Thus, this evaluation function shows a fitness (f) measures to each individual which indicated its suitability to be selected.

For real values the square of difference of two arrays is calculated. This proceeds in the following manner.

$$df = \sum_{i=0}^{n} (I_i - T_i)^2$$

(2)

Where I is the input array and T is the target array and df is the square difference between two arrays. Fitness depends as follows:

$$f = \sqrt{df}$$

(3)

Thus (f) will be the fitness value of the current evolving individual. This evaluation functions analyze fitness measures to each individual indicating its suitability to be selected.

Selection. Roulette Wheel Selection is used to select parents for next generation. Based on the normalized fitness, each member will be added into matting pool for certain number of times. The higher the fitness, the more entries it has into the matting pool, thus more the chance to be selected as a parent .The lower the fitness, the less entries it has into the matting pool, thus the less chance to be selected as parent. Roulette Wheel Selection works in the following manner:

1) Calculate the total fitness for the population.

$$F = \sum_{k=1}^{pop\_size} f(i_k)$$

(4)

2) Calculate selection probability p_k for each chromosome v_k.

$$p_k = \frac{f(i_k)}{F}$$

(5)

3) Calculate cumulative probability q_k for each chromosome v_k.

$$q_k = \sum_{j=1}^{k} p_j$$

(6)

Where k = 1, 2........., pop_size and it processed in this way:

1. Generate a random number r from the range [0, 1].

2. If $r \le q_1$, then select the first chromosome v_1; else, select the k_{th} chromosome v_k ($2 \le k \le$ pop_size) such that $q_{k-1} < r \le q_k$.

Crossover. One Point Crossover is used, in which a randomly cut- point is selected according to the some probability rate *(pc)* and genetic part of parent is exchanged. Not all the chromosomes undergo for the crossover, for example if the crossover rate is 0.25 then only 25% of chromosomes of the population undergo for the crossover. It works as follow:

1. Select two Parents.

2. One cut-point (r_c) selected by random generator.

3. If $r_c < p_c$ then it undergo for crossover.

Mutation. Mutation alters one or more genes with probability equal to the mutation rate p_m. If p_m is 0.01 then only 1% of the genes in the population will mutated. Every gene has equal chance to be mutated. However some especial techniques needed to handle the real encoding values. The procedure is as follows:

1. Randomly generate the values (r_m).

2. If $r_m < p_m$ than mutation value (v_m) will be equal
3. $r_m * s_v$, where s_v is a scale value.

4. And the array (T_i) will become

$$T_i = \sum_{i=0}^{n} (v_m - s_v / 2 \tag{6}$$

Where i = (0 .....n), n is the length of T_i, which is the input array of population.

   After completing the process of selection, crossover and mutation, the next population can be evaluated. Thus the one generation of GA depends on the selection, recombination, mutation and evaluation.

3.2 Evolution Process

As it was mentioned above, the symbols and parameters will be evolved using two layers of GA. The evolved symbols and parameters are send back to draw in 3-D environment using Parametric L-System. This integration will be based on some especial criteria i.e. The individuals having higher fitness value will be selected or a median fitness will calculate for the selection. In our multilayered architecture, we have chosen most fitted individuals (best fitness) from upper layered GA (evolving symbols) and the individuals having higher fitness from bottom layered GA (evolving numerical parameters) and integrated these individuals as the rules of parametric L-System and visualize them in 3-D space as shown in Fig. 2.

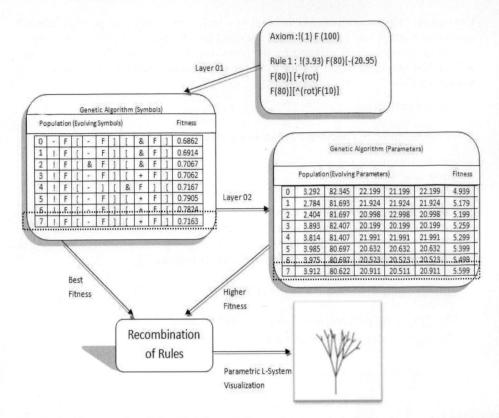

Fig. 2. Architecture of evolving Multilayered GA evolving symbols in first layer and parameters in second layer

To prevent the synthetically incorrect results, repair mechanism is applied on each individual at the time of production of a new child. For example two direction symbols cannot come together. In the same way push '[' and pop ']' should be arranged properly. The idea for repair mechanism is adopted from [5]. After recombination of the optimized individuals from both GA, they visualized in 3D environment.

4   Results and Discussion

In order to draw the branching structures in 3-D environment, symbols and parameters have to be optimized. In the first step, the symbols are fed as input string (chromosome) to the upper layer and the parameters are evolved in the lower layer of the GA respectively. During the evolution process, different GA parameters, selection methods and optimized fitness calculations are tested, and their impact on the algorithm efficiency is analyzed.

Fig. 3. Case 1Optimized Solution for first demonstrated branching structure,
Symbols =! F [-F] [&F] F [-F] [^F] [&F],
Parameters = 5.92, 75.00, 45.93, 45.95, 45.95, 45.98

Table 2. Operators and parameters used by GA

GA	Symbols	Parameters
Population Size	150	150
No. of Genes	No Fixed Length	6
No of Generations	137	1000
Crossover Rate	0.2	0.5
Mutation Rate	0.1	0.05
Mutation scale	Null	1.5

Fig. 3. Displays a branching structure for Case 1 with one production rule and one iteration step. All the angles are controlled with constants variables. Table 2 lists all the operators and parameters used for the figure. The best individual is selected based on the best average fitness, value which identified the fittest individual of the population. Following are the rules for Parametric L-System:

Axioms: $! (1) F (100)$

Rule 1 :   F -> !(width) F(75) [-(rot) F(75)] [&(rot)
F(75)] F(100) [-(rot) F(75)]   [^(rot) F(50)]
[&(rot) F(50)]

Iteration: 01
Constants: rot   = 45.95, width = 5.93

The population run consists of 150 individuals having different numbers of generations for the symbols, whereas for the parameters, we found that after 800 generations the same individuals are running, so the GA is stopped at 1000 generations. A different branching structure Case 2 is demonstrated in Fig. 4. With a single iteration, having different parameters associated with symbols. All the operators and parameters are the same for the GA as shown in Table 2, except that optimized solution for symbols are obtained 91 generations. The best individual is selected based on the best average fitness; value identified the fittest individual of the population. The axiom and rule applied for Case 2 are given as follows:

Axioms: ! (1) F(200)

Rule1:   F -> !(2.932) F(75.32) [-(45.95) F(75.32)]
           [&(25.95) F(75.32)] F(75.32) [+(35.95)
           F(75.32)] [^(15.95) F(75.32)]

Fig. 4. Case 2 Optimized Solution for second demonstrated branching structure
Symbols =   ! F [-F] [&F] F [+F] [^F]
Parameters = 2.93, 75.30, 35.96, 45.91, 25.94, 15.92

Fig. 5. Shows the performing for the Case 1 and Case 2. Case 1(a) and Case 2 (a) show the graph for evolving parameters of 1000 generations with the average fitness of 0.690662 and 0.51238173 respectively. The Graph for Case 1(b) and Case 2 (b) shows the evolution of symbols of generation 137 with average fitness of 0.7715941, and of generation 91 with average fitness of 0.792281 respectively.

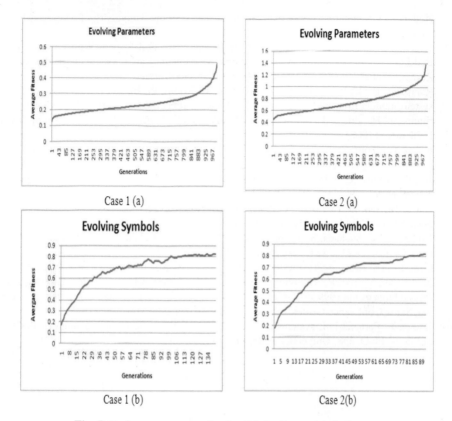

Fig. 5. Performance curves for the GA for Parametric L-System

5 Conclusion

We have demonstrated the feasibility of using a GA to automate the derivation of L-system specifications for complex branching structures. This paper also examined the effective use of Parametric L-System to generate the branching structure. This powerful and versatile ability of Parametric L-System appeals to the developers to build up animation based on natural evolution. Our system in its present state is able to manipulate 3- D branching structures. The future works includes the Visual representation of genomes to see the actual work going inside of GA search space and some improvements on the visualization of branching structures in 3-space with different phenotypes.

References

1. Prusinkiewicz, P., Lindenmayer, A.: The Algorithmic Beauty of Plants. Springer, Heidelberg (1990)
2. Lindenmayer, A.: Mathematical models for cellular interaction in development, Parts I and II. Journal of Theoretical Biology 18, 280–315 (1968)

3. Holland, J.: Adaptation in Natural and Artificial Systems. University of Michigan Press, Ann Arbor (1975)
4. Noser, H., Wellauer, W., Stucki, P.: Rule-Based Animation System With GAs As Test-Bed For Generic Evolutionary Applications, Multimedia Laboratory of the University of Zurich, Winterthurerstrasse 190, CH-8057 Zurich, Switzerland
5. Runqiang, B., Chen, P., Burrage, K., Hanan, J., Room, P., Belward, J.: Derivation of L-system models from measurements of biological branching structures using genetic algorithms. In: Hendtlass, T., Ali, M. (eds.) IEA/AIE 2002. LNCS, vol. 2358, p. 514. Springer, Heidelberg (2002)
6. Kokai, G., Toth, Z., Vanvi, R.: Modeling Blood Vessels of the Eye with Parametric L-Systems Using Evolutionary Algorithms. In: Horn, W., Shahar, Y., Lindberg, G., Andreassen, S., Wyatt, J.C. (eds.) AIMDM 1999. LNCS (LNAI), vol. 1620, pp. 433–442. Springer, Heidelberg (1999)
7. Curry, R.: On the Evolution of Parametric L-Systems, Technical Report, Dept. of Computer Science, and University of Calgary (2000)
8. Yodthong, R., Suchada, S., Chidchanok, L., Prabhas, C., Tadahiro, F., Norishige, C.: Modeling Leaf Shapes Using L-systems and GAs,
   http://www.cp.eng.chula.ac.th/~piak/paper/2002/nico2002.pdf
9. K´okai, G., V´anyi, R.: Evolving Artificial Trees Described by Parametric L-systems. In: Proceedings of the 1999 IEEE Canadian Conference on Electrical and Computer Engineering, Shaw Conference Center, Edmonton, Alberta, Canada, May 9-12 (1999)
10. Hanan, J.: Parametric L-systems and Their Application to the Modeling and Visualization of Plants. Ph.D. diss, University of Regina (1992)

Recyclable Waste Paper Sorting Using Template Matching

Mohammad Osiur Rahman, Aini Hussain, Edgar Scavino, M.A. Hannan,
and Hassan Basri

Faculty of Engineering & Built Environment, Universiti Kebangsaan Malaysia, Malaysia
osiur_rahman@yahoo.com, aini@eng.ukm.my, scavino@eng.ukm.my,
eehannan@eng.ukm.my, drhb@eng.ukm.my

Abstract. This paper explores the application of image processing techniques in recyclable waste paper sorting. In recycling, waste papers are segregated into various grades as they are subjected to different recycling processes. Highly sorted paper streams will facilitate high quality end products, and save processing chemicals and energy. Since 1932 to 2009, different mechanical and optical paper sorting methods have been developed to fill the demand of paper sorting. Still, in many countries including Malaysia, waste papers are sorted into different grades using manual sorting system. Due to inadequate throughput and some major drawbacks of mechanical paper sorting systems, the popularity of optical paper sorting systems is increased. Automated paper sorting systems offer significant advantages over human inspection in terms of fatigue, throughput, speed, and accuracy. This research attempts to develop a smart vision sensing system that able to separate the different grades of paper using Template Matching. For constructing template database, the RGB components of the pixel values are used to construct RGBString for template images. Finally, paper object grade is identified based on the maximum occurrence of a specific template image in the search image. The outcomes from the experiment in classification for White Paper, Old Newsprint Paper and Old Corrugated Cardboard are 96%, 92% and 96%, respectively. The remarkable achievement obtained with the method is the accurate identification and dynamic sorting of all grades of papers using simple image processing techniques.

Keywords: Waste Paper Sorting, Grades of Paper, and Template matching.

1 Introduction

The primary challenge in the recycling of paper is to obtain raw material with the highest purity. In recycling, waste papers are segregated into various grades as they are subjected to different recycling processes. Highly sorted paper streams will facilitate high quality end product, and save processing chemicals and energy. Grade refers to the quality of a paper or pulp [1]. Since 1932 to 2009, different mechanical and optical paper sorting methods have been developed to fill the demand of paper sorting. Still, in many countries including Malaysia, waste papers are sorted into different grades using manual sorting system. Due to inadequate throughput and some major

H. Badioze Zaman et al. (Eds.): IVIC 2009, LNCS 5857, pp. 467–478, 2009.

drawbacks of mechanical paper sorting systems, the popularity of optical paper sorting systems is increased. The waste paper sorting systems are classified into Manual and Automated Systems. Automated paper sorting systems offer significant advantages over manual paper sorting systems in terms of fatigue, throughput, speed, and accuracy.

Faibish et al. [2] proposed an automated paper recycling system where ultrasounds are used to separate different grades of papers. However, due to contact manipulation and sensing, the system is too slow (80 ms/sub-frame) for industrial applications.Ramasubramanian et al. [3] developed lignin sensor that works well for separating newsprint samples from others. But the lignin sensors are influenced by sensor distance from the sample and color. Hottenstein et al. [4] proposed a sensor-based sorting approach in which a brightness sensor (reflected light intensity at 457 nm) is used to sort papers primarily into three categories, namely, white papers containing optical brighteners, white papers without optical brighteners, and other types of paper. Venditti et al. [5] developed a stiffness sensor that is used to sort recovered paper into paperboard and others. However, it cannot distinguish between a stack of newsprint versus a single paperboard. Sandberg [6] patented a sorting device to separate paper objects from contaminants. The sensor-based sorting method by Bialski et al [7] and Grubbs et al. [8] have not been successful mainly due to the absence of reliable sensing systems to distinguish between grades. In 2002, Khalfan et al. [9] introduced an optical paper sorting method using diffuse reflectance to identify a sheet of paper as either white or non-white. Their proposed paper sorting system segregated papers into white and ground wood paper according to the amount of lignin content. Eixelberger et al. [10] proposed optical paper sorting method to separate waste paper into two classes based on the radiation reflected from the surface of the papers. Bruner et al [11] proposed one optical paper sorting method to separate waste papers into bright white paper and others based on amount the fluorescence present on the surface of paper objects. Doak et al. [12] proposed an optical paper sorting method to separate different grades of paper based upon at least one characteristics of color, glossiness and the presence of printed matter. Gschweitl et al. [13] developed paper sorting method using visible light, ultraviolet light, x-rays and / or infrared light to illuminate the paper for sorting. They utilized mechanical pickers thus indicating that the system would operate at relatively low speeds.

The implementation of the previous methods, while being a step forward in the large-volume automated sorting technology, is still complex, expensive and sometimes offers limited reliability. All the systems segregate only two types of papers at one time. Moreover, no image processing or intelligence techniques are used to extract features or characteistics from the paper objects.

MO Rahman et al [14] developed an electronic image based waste paper sorting technique. The technique focused on the four points in the periphery of the paper object and then features are extracted surrounding those four points. Since the method didn't consider texture information of the entire paper objects, it may provide misleading information regarding paper grade. Thus, the main goal of this study is the development of a smart vision sensing system that will be able to separate the different grades of paper using template matching [15]. In this proposed system, RGB color components of the entire paper object are considered to create RGBString for N-cells of search image, which leads to overcome the major drawback of the previous electronic image based waste paper sorting technique. Moreover, the algorithm provides robust result because of filtering the unexpected and misleading color regions of the paper object during feature extraction process.

The remainder of this paper is organized as follows: Section 2 briefly describes the proposed Template Matching Based Waste Paper Grade Identification System. Section 3 discuses the experimental results and section 4 draws the concluding remarks.

2 Template Matching Based Waste Paper Grade Identification System

Figure 1 illustrates the basic block diagram of the recyclable waste paper grade identification system using Template Matching. The proposed system operates in two phases, i.e. enrollment and identification. Both phases have some common components. The enrollment phase consists of image acquisition, preprocessing, feature extraction, RGBString construction for template images and creation of the reference database. The identification phase consists of image acquisition, preprocessing, feature extraction, RGBString construction for N-cells, matching, and decision. In the subsection 2.1 to 2.4, it will be discussed all the processes of both enrollment and identification phases.

2.1 Image Acquisition

In this proposed system, 320×240 RGB images are taken from inspection zone on the conveyor belt using a commercially available Webcam. In webcam properties setting, the brightness, contrast and saturation are adjusted at 50%, 50% and 100% of their respective scales. In the experiment, it is observed that the performance of the vision system is extremely influenced by the lighting arrangement. After necessary calibration, front lighting-directional-darkfield illumination [15] is selected for this experiment. The conveyor belt speed is 14 feet per minute. The real time scanning process produces two types of signals namely presence of object (PObj) and absence of object (AObj). The system always performs scanning operation to detect the presence of object. The system captures the images from the inspection zone based on two signals. If AObj signal is detected after the signal PObj, then the system captures the image of paper object from the inspection zone. This technique separates individual paper object from the sequence of paper objects.

2.2 Preprocessing

The first step in the preprocessing block is to take the image from inspection zone after trimming unnecessary boundary portion of the image. After that, the background noise is eliminated from the image using combined operation of threshold and morphological operation erosion [15] with 3×3 minimum convolution filter.

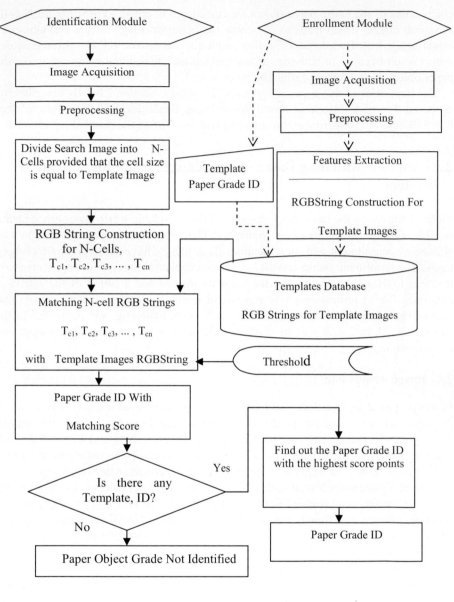

Fig. 1. Block Diagram of the Paper Grade Identification System Using Template Matching

2.3   RGB String for Template and Search Image

The paper object image consists of three components red, green and blue. For gray scale value, standard grayscale transformation is obtained from the original RGB image components. The four components 'R' (red), 'G' (green), 'B' (blue) and 'Y' (gray) are considered for the paper images. 'Y' is taken for gray component to avoid the conflict with green 'G'. The basic strategies followed in the construction of RGB string is that the color component take first place in the RGBString, which component value is the maximum out of red, green and blue component values, then second and third. Finally fourth color position is reserved gray component. The repetition of the color component depends on the value of the color component since the ranges of the color component values are different for various types of paper grades shown in [14].

For template construction, the system generated RGBString for template image after getting the value of template width, TW and template height, TH for template image and information regarding the interested region of the preprocessed image. The Search image is divided into N-cells shown in Figure 2. The cell size must be equal to the template image. The RGB strings for N-cells are obtained using the RGBStringForSearchImage, RGBString and ColorRepeat procedures. The unnecessary cells are filtered during calculating RGB string.

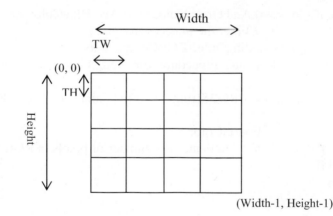

Fig. 2. Template Image and Search Image

Procedure: RGBStringForSearch Image

MCOL   =   Width/ TW   ' MCOL stands for Number of Columns

NROW =   Height / TH   'NROW stands for Number of Rows

NCELL =   MCOL × NROW   ' NCELL stands for number of Cells in Search Image

For I = 1   To   MCOL

    For   J= 1   To   NROW

      StartCellWidth = (I-1) × TW

      EndCellWidth = (I × TW)-1

```
        StartCellHeight = (J-1) × TH
        EndCellHeight = (I × TH) –1
        Call RGBString (StartCellWidth, EndCellWidth, StartCellHeight,
EndCellHeight)
        Save the RGBString
     Next J
  Next I
```

Procedure: RGBString

```
    For  m = StartCellWidth     To     EndCellWidth
      For        n= StartCellHeight        To      EndCellHeight
          pointRGB = ImagePoint(m, n)
          RedColor = pointRGB Mod 256
          GreenColor = ((pointRGB And &HFF00FF00) / 256&)
          BlueColor = (pointRGB And &HFF0000) / (256& * 256&)
          GrayColor = (RedColor + GreenColor + BlueColor) / 3

        If RedColor <> 0 And GreenColor <> 0 And BlueColor <> 0 Then
                    //Filter the unnecessary pixels
            SortingDescendingOrder(RGBComponents)
          Call  ColorRepeat()  procedure  for  Red,  Green,  Blue  and  Gray
Color Values
            RGBString    =    RGBString   +   FirstColor   +   SecondColor   +
ThirdColor +
                    FourthColor + "."
                    // "." Indicates the number of pixels in RGB-Strings
        End If
      Next n
    Next m
```

Procedure: ColorRepeat (ColorValue As Integer)

ColorRepeat procedure take the Color Values of Red, Green, Blue, and Gray level value and return the integer number for repeating the "R", "G", "B" and "Y" in the RGB string for each pixel value.

```
    If  ColorValue <=63 Then
          ColorRepeat = 1
    Else
        If   ColorValue >=64 and ColorValue  <=184 Then
              ColorRepeat = 2
        Else
            If   ColorValue >=185 and ColorValue  <=229 Then
              ColorRepeat = 3
```

Else

0   ColorRepeat = 4

        End If
     End If
End If

2.4 Matching and Decision

The matching process is implemented by string matching algorithm. In this process, RGB strings of N-cells are compared with all the template RGB strings. For each Template RGBString, after matching with RGBString of one cell of the search image, the matching score between template RGBString and Cell RGBString compared with threshold value; if the matching score crosses the threshold level then the respective template gets one point. The matching scores value 92% is considered as the threshold value. In this way, the maximum occurrence of a specific template in the search image will achieve the highest points. Finally, the template ID with the highest points is identified as the candidate paper object grade ID. The variable cn stands for the maximum number of cells in search image and c1 stands for 1. The variable tm stands for the maximum number of templates and t1 is for the starting value of template and t1 value is 1.

Pseudocode: Matching Process

```
For I = t1  to tm                // I stands for Template Image
    For J = c1  To cn      //J stands for Cell Images of Search Image
        Compare    RGBString of Template T[I] with RGBString of Cell Im-
age T[J]
        If   the matching score >= threshold Then
                OccurrenceOfTemplateImage    [I]    =    OccurrenceOfTem-
plateImage [I] +1
            End IF
        Next J
    Next I
```

Pseudocode: Decision Process

```
Max = OccurrenceOfTemplateImage [1]  // Max temporary variable
PaperGrade = 1     //Paper grade for  the candidate paper objects
 t2= 2               // t2 stands for 2nd Template Image
tm = Number  of  Template  Images
For I = t2 to tm            // I stands for Template Image
    IF OccurrenceOfTemplateImage [I] > Max Then
        Max = OccurrenceOfTemplateImage [I]
        PaperGrade = I
    End If
```

Next I
    Print PaperGrade   //PaperGrade finally return the Paper grade ID of the
Search Image

3   Experimental Results and Discussion

In this section a relative comparison is made based on the outcomes of this proposed
method for Old Corrugated Cardboard (OCC), Old News Paper (ONP) and White Paper (WP). The three types of waste papers- WP, ONP and OCC had taken in this experiment because of their dominating role in waste papers. One hundred paper samples per grade are considered in this experiment. Figure 3 illustrated the ONP images
in both original and preprocessed forms. The Figure 3(a) is represented the original
ONP image with background noises and Figure 3(b) is represented the preprocessed
ONP image without background noise.

(a)

(b)

Fig. 3. Original and Preprocessed Paper Image: (a) Old Newsprint Paper With Background
Noise, and (b) Preprocessed ONP image after removing background noise

Table 1. Some Example of RGB-String Units For Single Pixel

Sl. No.	RGBString for Single Pixel
1.	RGBY
2.	RRGGBBYY
3.	RRRGGGBBBYYY
4.	RRRRGGGGBBBBYYYY
5.	RBGY
6.	RRBBGGYY
7.	RRRBBBGGGYYY
8.	RRRRBBBBGGGGYYYY
9.	BRGY
10.	BBRRGGYY
11.	BBBRRRGGGYYY
12.	BBBBRRRRGGGGYYYY
13.	BGRY
14.	BBGGRRYY
15.	BBBGGGRRRYYY
16.	BBBBGGGGRRRRYYYY
17.	GRBY
18.	GGRRBBYY
19.	GGGRRRBBBYYY
20.	GGGGRRRRBBBBYYYY
21.	GBRY
22.	GGBBRRYY
23.	GGGBBBRRRYYY
24	GGGGBBBBRRRRYYYY

The paper object image consists of collection of pixels and the pixels color consists of red, green and blue components. The hybridization of red, green and blue components produces millions of colors (24 bits (3 bytes) yields 16,777,216 colors). From the experimental and industrial observations, the basic colors of WP, ONP and OCC are fully distinctive. But in printing subtractive colors- cyan, magenta, yellow, and

Table 2. Identification success rate for Different Template size

Method	Template Size Width × Height	Template Image	Name of the Paper Grade	Correct Identification Rate
Template Matching	5 × 5		WP	96%
			ONP	92%
			OCC	96%
	10 × 10		WP	86%
			ONP	82%
			OCC	84%
	20 × 20		WP	78%
			ONP	72%
			OCC	76%

black are used, which are based on reflective light. As a result of different combination of printed colors, the recyclable waste papers have diversity in color configurations. Due to different color combination, it is difficult to segregate different types of paper objects. In this experiment, different template images are created for different grade of papers. Even different template images are created for same paper grade with different template sizes. The performance of this experiment is greatly influenced by template size. If the template size is decreased then the success rate of paper grade recognition is increased. But the computational time is increased due to the number of cells in search image. The template image data is the multiple or polymer of any one of the RGBString units from table 1. The repetition of the RGBString units in template RGBString is depended on the number of pixels (or size) of the template image.

In experiment, it has been found that the WP template consists of multiple of BBBBRRRRGGGGYYYY RGBString unit (serial no 12) or BBBBGGGGRRRRYYYY (serial no 16), the ONP template consists of multiple of RRRGGGBBBYYY RGBString unit (serial no 3) or RRRBBBGGGYYY (serial no 7) and the OCC template consists of multiple of RRGGBBYY RGBString unit (serial no 2) or RRBBGGYY (serial no 6). Moreover, the repetition of "R", "G", "B" and "Y' color components in the RGBString for the pixel value is significantly influenced by the lighting arrangement. Thus, in order to achieve the best performance from this method, it should to maintain the lighting consistency in both enrollment and identification phases of this system.   The success rates of the paper grade identification process for different template sizes are shown in Table 2. The correct identification rate is calculated based on the percentage of the number of paper objects are classified into their respective paper grades. When the template size is 5 × 5 then the achieved classification rates for WP, ONP, and OCC are 96%, 92% and 96%, respectively.

4 Conclusion

The main emphasis of this work is on the development of a new method for automated paper sorting system. In the experiment, it is observed that the performance of the vision system is extremely influenced by the lighting arrangement and template size. The method described here mainly transforms the pixels value to RGB strings, comparison of RGB-strings among template images and N-cells of search image, apply matching score and threshold value to identify the grade of the paper object. From the review, it was noted that five sensors namely ultrasonic, lignin, gloss, stiffness and color sensors are used in paper sorting systems. Ultrasonic sensors are slow, which make them unsuitable for industry use. Lignin sensor can only be used to separate the newsprint papers from others and its performance is strictly color dependent. Stiffness sensor is typically used for separating cardboard from others paper grades where as gloss sensor is used for the separation of glossy paper from others. Color sensor, on the other hand, measures the radiation of the paper surface and commonly used to identify white papers.   Thus, the most important point addressed in the proposed method is that the method, which uses computer vision, can be easily implement for sorting multiple grades of papers. The remarkable achievement obtained from the proposed method is the result of identification for three major paper grades -WP, ONP and OCC just using simple image processing techniques. The further works can be carried out for all grades of papers and the work may also be extended to other solid wastes sorting like plastic, metal, glass and so on.

Acknowledgements

The project is sponsored by the Ministry of Science, Technology and Innovation of Malaysia under E-science Project 01-01-02-SF0011 and Universiti Kebangsaan Malaysia under the GUP grant of UKM-GUP-KRIB-6 / 2008.

References

[1] Paper Grades, http://www.paperonweb.com/ppmanf.htm
[2] Faibish, S., Bacakoglu, H., Goldenberg, A.A.: An Eye-Hand System for Automated Paper Recycling. In: Proceedings of the IEEE International Conference on Robotics and Automation, Albuquerque, New Mexico, pp. 9–14 (1997)

[3] Ramasubramanian, M.K., Venditti, R.A., Ammineni, C.M., Mallapragada, M.: Optical Sensor for Noncontact Measurement of Lignin Content in High-Speed Moving Paper Surfaces. IEEE Sensors Journal 5(5), 1132–1139 (2005)

[4] Hottenstein, F.A., Kenny, G.R., Friberg, T., Jackson, M.: High-Speed automated optical sorting of recovered paper. In: Proc. TAPPI Recycling Symposium, Atlanta, GA, vol. 1, pp. 149–158 (2000)

[5] Venditti, R.A., Ramasubramanian, M.K., Kalyan, C.K.: A Noncontact Sensor for the Identification of Paper and Board Samples on a High Speed Sorting Conveyor. Appita Journal: Journal of the Technical Association of the Australian and New Zealand Pulp and Paper Industry 60(5), 366–371 (2007)

[6] Sandberg, N.H.: Sorting Device For Waste Paper. US Patent No. 1,847,265 (1932)

[7] Bialski, A., Gentile, C., Sepall, O.: Paper sorting apparatus. US Patent No. 4, 236, 676 (1980)

[8] Grubbs, M., Kenny, G.R., Gaddis, P.G.: Paper Sorting System. US Patent No.6, 250, 472 (2001)

[9] Khalfan, Z., Greenspan, S.: Optical Paper Sorting Method Device and Apparatus. US Patent No. 7,081,594 (2006)

[10] Eixelberger, R., Friedl, P., Gschweitl, K.: Method and Apparatus for Sorting Waste Paper of Different Grades and Conditions. US Patent No. 6, 506, 991 (2003)

[11] Bruner, R.S., Morgan, D.R., Kenny, G.R., Gaddis, P.G., Lee, D., Roggow, J.M.: System and Method for Sensing White Paper. US Patent No. 6, 570, 653 (2003)

[12] Doak, A.G., Roe, M.G., Kenny, G.R.: Multi-Grade Object sorting system and method. US Patent No.7173709 (2007)

[13] Gschweitl, Heinz, K.: Method for sorting waste paper. European Patent, EP0873797 (1998)

[14] Rahman, M.O., Hannan, M.A., Scavino, E., Hussain, A., Basri, H.: An Efficient Paper Grade Identification Method for Automatic Recyclable Waste Paper Sorting. European Journal of Scientific Research 25(1), 96–103 (2009)

[15] Pham, D.T., Alcock, R.J.: Image Acquisition and Enhancement, Segmentation, Feature Extraction and Selection, and Classification. In: Smart Inspection System -Techniques and Applications of Intelligent Vision, ch. 2,3,4,5, pp. 38–47, 55–59, 84, 99–102, 115–116, 133–134. Academic Press, Great Britain (2003)

Noise Detection Fuzzy (NDF) Filter for Removing Salt and Pepper Noise

H.S. Kam and W.H. Tan

Multimedia University,
Selangor, Malaysia
{hskam,twhaw}@mmu.edu.my

Abstract. In this paper, we propose a Noise Detection Fuzzy (NDF) filter, to achieve improved filtering performance in terms of effectiveness in removing salt-and-pepper noise while preserving image details. It operates in a moving window where the update value of the central pixel is a function of the median of the pixels in the window. The proposed NDF filter consists of three sequential stages. Firstly, a noise-detection scheme is developed to classify each pixel to be uncorrupted pixel, or otherwise. Secondly, if a pixel is suspected to be noise, it is not used for determining the update value of other pixels. Thus we can prevent noise pixels from distorting the "correct" update value. Thirdly, the fuzzy filter part will then adaptively assign weights to the recorded pixel values to produce the central pixel update value. Experimental results show that our NDF filter outperforms other standard median based techniques.

Keywords: Adaptive median filter, fuzzy weighted median filter, image enhancement, impulse noise detection, nonlinear filter.

1 Introduction

Noise removal is an important pre-processing step followed by other tasks such as object recognition, edge detection, feature extraction and pattern recognition. Generally, linear averaging filters have the ability to remove additive Gaussian noise, but are ineffective against impulse noises. Edges and image details also get blurred due to linear filtering. Conversely, edge-preserving filters will retain the edges and line structures but tend to amplify noise. Different methods have been proposed in literature to address this issue. The most effective approaches are nonlinear and adaptive in nature [1-2]. Depending on the noise type, we are required to apply the optimum choice of filters to obtain the best output for a particular pixel.

There are several methods which use fuzzy selection filters for smoothing. The adaptive filter proposed by Taguchi and Meguro [3] for the removal of mixed noise combines the outputs of five classical operators depending upon the values of three local features. The operators are midpoint filter, mean filter, median filter, identity filter, and a small-window median filter. A robust image enhancement technique was proposed by Choi and Krishnapuram [4] in order to remove impulse noise, smooth out non-impulse noise and preserve edges and other salient structures. There are three

H. Badioze Zaman et al. (Eds.): IVIC 2009, LNCS 5857, pp. 479–486, 2009.
© Springer-Verlag Berlin Heidelberg 2009

different fuzzy filters, one for each task. Their outputs are combined depending on the value of a local feature, which evaluates the gray-level and spatial differences between the central pixel and its neighbours.

This paper is organized as follows. Section 2 describes the noise detection scheme. Section 3 discusses the subsequent treatment of the pixels based on their detected characteristics and section 4 describes the Fuzzy weighted filter. These three sections establish the fundamental principles and structure of the proposed NDF filter. Section 5 presents a summary of implementation procedures and test results. The conclusion is drawn in Section 6.

2   Noise Detection

Impulse noise pixels are outliers as they are very different from their neighbours. The filter for reduction of impulse noise works by first detecting the outlier neighbours then performing noise filtering. This reduces the chances for impulse noise corrupted neighbours to contribute to the update value for the centre pixel. We can detect the outlier neighbours by using a parameter β [4]. The parameter β is a scale parameter which can be determined on the basis of variations in pixel intensity values in a given spatial window and can reflect the variance of the grey level differences between a centre pixel $x(i,j)$ and its neighbouring pixels $x(m,n)$. One of the formulas proposed for this scale estimate is the mean of $(x(i, j) - x(m, n))^2$ in the neighbourhood, i.e.

$$\beta_{x(i,j)} = \frac{1}{N-1} \sum_{x(m,n) \in A} \left(|x(i, j) - x(m, n)| \right) \tag{1}$$

where A is the set of N-1 neighbouring pixels.

The proposed method uses a 3x3 window ($N = 9$), where outlier detection is performed on the centre pixel's neighbours by considering their β. If β of a pixel is small, it is similar to its neighbours and is not an outlier. Conversely, if β is larger than a certain threshold, it is dissimilar to its neighbours and is more likely an outlier. Through experiment, the threshold value was set as 90.

3   Median of Neighbours

If the β of a neighbour pixel is above a certain threshold, it is considered an outlier and the median of its neighbours is taken in its place. Therefore, not only does this filter consider the neighbourhood around the centre pixel, but also the neighbourhood surrounding each neighbour pixel for more accurate noise removal. Fig. 1 shows the two neighbourhoods of pixels.

Fig. 1. Neighbourhood of pixels

The pseudocode for the procedure is shown below:

```
Pseudocode: At each pixel,

For index = 1 to number of neighbours

        If β of neighbour <threshold

                temp(index) = neighbour intensity       /* keep 'clean' neighbours */

        Else

                /* Take median of the neighbour's neighbours in its place */

                temp(index) = median (neighbour's neighbours)

        End

End
```

If β of a neighbour is less than *threshold*, it is assumed to be non impulse noise and is stored. Otherwise, the median value of its neighbours is stored instead because the median is the approximation of the 'noiseless' neighbour pixel. After going through all the N-1 neighbours, the median value $median_x(i,j)$ from the N-1 stored values is taken. This median of the non-outlier neighbours can be considered a good estimate of the noiseless centre pixel.

4 Fuzzy Weight Assignment

The difference between this $median_x(i,j)$ and the centre pixel $x(i,j)$ is the basis for assigning memberships. The membership degree is a measure of the noisiness of the centre pixel. If the difference is large, the centre pixel is likely an impulse and a large membership degree is assigned for maximum correction. If the difference is small, the centre pixel is not impulse noise and a small or zero membership degree is assigned to retain the original value to prevent loss of detail. The membership degree of the centre pixel $x(i,j)$ is:

$$s(i, j) = \cfrac{1}{1 + \exp\left(\cfrac{t(i, j) \times \left(\left| median_x(i, j) - x(i, j) \right| - a(i, j) \right)}{L - 1} \right)} \qquad (2)$$

where a and t are the sigmoid parameters, median$_x(i,j)$ is the median value from the N-1 stored values from the window surrounding pixel $x(i,j)$ and range $L = 255$.

The membership degree is used as the weight to multiply the difference i.e. median$_x(i,j) - x(i,j)$ later on.

This membership function is a sigmoid function. It is a smooth, monotonic/squashing function that maps real values into a bounded interval. It is a transfer function and has been used in fuzzy logic as an intensification function and in image contrast stretching [5]. The sigmoid function depends on two parameters a and t as given by:

$$s(d) \quad = \frac{1}{1 + e^{-t(d-a)}} \tag{3}$$

where t and a adjust the shape of μ. Specifically, t controls the steepness or slope of μ and a controls the crossover point along the y axis at which inflection occurs. Plot of a sigmoid curve is shown in Fig. 2.

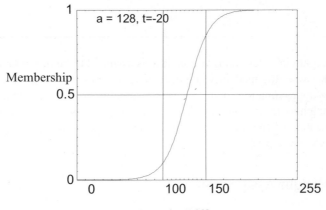

Fig. 2. Example of a Sigmoid curve with a = 128 and t = -20

In the proposed method, the sigmoid parameters t and a are designed to be continuously varying from pixel to pixel so that the filter is adaptive to the local neighbourhood characteristics. To adaptively assign the values for t and a, a compatibility measure was used. Pixels that are corrupted with impulse noise have lower compatibility with their neighbours. Total Compatibility (TC) is a formulation to measure compatibility. Shown below is the calculation for TC which is modified from [4]. It is able to distinguish edges more distinctly than the original formula because more neighbourhood information is used to calculate TC.

Compatibility of a pixel with its neighbours,

$$\mu_{x(i,j)} = \exp\left(-\frac{\left(|x(i,j) - x(m,n)|\right)}{\beta_{x(m,n)}}\right), x(m,n) \in A \qquad (4)$$

where A is the set of 8 neighbours in a 3x3 window and $x(i,j)$ is the pixel in question and $x(m,n)$ is its neighbour.

Total Compatibility of a centre pixel is given as:

$$\mu_{TC} = \frac{\displaystyle\sum_{x(m,n) \in A} \mu(m,n)}{\displaystyle\sum_{x(m,n) \in A} w(m,n)} \qquad (5)$$

where A is the set of N-1 neighbouring pixels and $w(m,n) = 1$ for small window sizes.

The sigmoid parameters t a006Ed a vary according to TC as follows:

$$t(i,j) = t_1 \times TC(i,j) + t_2 \qquad (6)$$

$$a(i,j) = a_1 \times TC(i,j) + a_2 \qquad (7)$$

The constants t_1, t_2, a_1, a_2 determine the range of a and t. In order to remove impulse noise, t should be a negative number. The absolute magnitude of t determines the steepness. The higher the magnitude, the steeper it is. In this filter we have made t proportional to TC. The higher the TC membership (meaning that the central pixel is less likely to be impulse noise), the less steep the sigmoid, so as not to change the centre pixel drastically. Through experiment, the values of $t_1 = 50$, $t_2 = -70$ were chosen so that the range of t is from -70 to -20 for $0 < TC < 1$.

Parameter a is made proportional to TC based on the rationale that if TC is low, (indicating that the centre pixel might be impulse noise) then a is set higher to let only high differences affect the central pixel, for maximum correction. If the TC of a centre pixel is high, then its not impulse noise, so the original pixel should be retained as far as possible. Therefore there is a minimum value for a to prevent unnecessary smoothing. Through experiment, the values of $a_1 = 40$, $a_2 = 40$ were chosen so that the range of a is from 40 to 80 for $0 < TC < 1$.

Finally, to update the value of the centre pixel we calculate:

Correction term, $c(i,j) = s(i,j) \times (x(i,j) - median_x(i,j))$ \qquad (8)

Update value for the central pixel, $y(i,j) = x(i,j) - c(i,j)$ \qquad (9)

The filter can be run progressively (more than once) by taking the output to be the input to the filter again. Often, this can improve the result. However, too many iterations can blur the image to the point of losing detail.

5   Performance Evaluation

For filter performance evaluation, the house image was corrupted with salt-and-pepper noise at density 10%. The noise was generated by a Matlab subroutine. The proposed filter was run progressively three times and the result was compared with 5 other existing filtering techniques:

1.   Median filter [6-7]. Window size - Three sizes (3 x 3, 5 x 5 and 7 x 7) were tested. As the 3x3 window gave the best result, it was chosen for comparison.
2.   Adaptive median filter [8]. Maximum window size, *Smax* = 7
3.   Technique for Image Restoration [9].Parameters $a = 80$; $b = 40$; $c = 0.1$. c was set to a low value to minimize blurring. The parameter values were set for removing impulse noise.
4.   Hybrid median filter [10]
5.   Relaxed median filter [11]. Window size lower limit = 3, Upper limit = 5.

Shown below are the results of filtering by the various filters.

Fig. 3. The (a) original and (b) noisy images. The results on the house image by the (c) proposed filter, (d) Restoration technique, (e) Hybrid median filter, (f) Relaxed median sieve, (g) Adaptive median filter and (h) median filter.

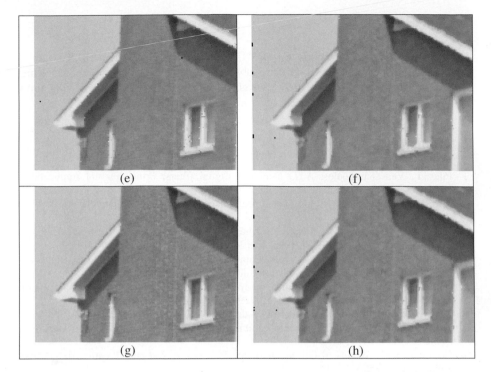

Fig. 3. (*Continued*)

All the above methods manage to remove the impulse spikes. However, the proposed filter retains the fine detail such as the brick patterns better. The edges are sharper as well. For quantitative comparison, we have used the root-mean-square error (RMSE), Peak signal-to noise Ratio (PSNR) and Mean Structural Similarity index (MSSIM) [12]. A higher MSSIM would indicate higher structural similarity between the filtered image and the original uncorrupted image, which is desirable. As can be seen, the proposed filter performs better than all the other filtering techniques in the various measures.

Table 1. Summary of results

Measure	Proposed Filter	Restoration Technique	Adaptive Median	Median filter	Hybrid Median	Relaxed Median
RMSE	2.371849	2.902679	3.53799	5.899725	5.373653	5.750791
MSSIM	0.981763	0.957143	0.940804	0.867061	0.923483	0.869527
PSNR	40.62906	38.84164	37.15567	32.71417	33.52541	32.93625

6 Conclusion

In this paper, a Noise Detection Fuzzy (NDF) Filter is described. It incorporates a noise detection scheme, followed by the subsequent treatment of each pixel according to its classification and finally fuzzy weighted filtering. Experimental results show that our method performs better than other median-based filters.

References

1. Pitas, I., Venetsanopoulos, A.N.: Nonlinear digital filters: Principles and Applications. Kluwer Academic Publishers, Dordrecht (1990)
2. Mitra, S.K., Sicuranza, G. (eds.): Nonlinear Image Processing. Academic Press, London (2000)
3. Taguchi, A., Meguro, M.: Adaptive L-filters based on fuzzy rules. In: Proc. IEEE Int. Symp. Circuits Systems, ISCAS 1995, Seattle, WA, April 15, pp. 961–964 (1995)
4. Choi, Y.S., Krishnapuram, R.: A robust approach to image enhancement based on fuzzy logic. IEEE Trans. Image Processing 6(6), 808–825 (1997)
5. Hanmandlu, M., Jha, D.: An optimal fuzzy system for color image enhancement. IEEE Transactions on Image Processing 15(10), 2956–2966 (2006)
6. Tukey, J.W.: Exploratory Data Analysis. Addison-Wesley, Menlo Park (1971)
7. Tukey, J.W.: Nonlinear (nonsuperposable) methods for smoothing data. Congr. Res. EASCON, 673 (1974)
8. Gonzalez, R.C., Woods, R.E.: Digital Image Processing, 2nd edn. Prentice Hall, Upper Saddle River (2002)
9. Russo, F.: A technique for image restoration based on recursive processing and error correction. In: Proceedings of the 17th IEEE Instrumentation and Measurement Technology Conference (IMTC 2000), vol. 3, pp. 1232–1236 (2000)
10. Nieminen, A., Heinonen, P., Neuvo, Y.: A new class of detail-preserving filters for image processing. IEEE Trans. Pattern Anal. Mach. Intell. 9(1), 74–90 (1987)
11. ben Hamza, A., Luque-Escamilla, P.L., Aroza, J.M., Roldan, R.R.: Removing noise and preserving details with relaxed median filters. Journal of Mathematical Imaging and Vision 11(2), 161–177 (1999)
12. Wang, Z., Bovik, A.C., Sheikh, H.R., Simoncelli, E.P.: Image quality assessment: From error visibility to structural similarity. IEEE Transactions on Image Processing 13(4), 600–612 (2004)

Handwriting Recognition Algorithm in Different Languages: Survey

Hamid Mirvaziri [*], Mohammad Masood Javidi, and Najme Mansouri

Department of Computer Science, University of Kerman Iran
h.vaziri@gmail.com, javidi@mail.uk.ac.ir
najme.mansouri@gmail.com

Abstract. In this paper several handwriting recognition algorithms have been evaluated with respect to the size of database, language and recognition rate. These algorithms apply supervised, unsupervised and sometimes combination of those classifiers. In number of those cases some suggestions are given about classifier and size of database to improve recognition rate.

Keywords: Handwriting Recognition, Neural Network, Genetic Algorithm, Fuzzy membership function.

1 Introduction

Handwriting recognition like other intelligent systems provides some application in hand phones, robots and other devices for identification and verification purposes. For example it can be used for crime tracking or in a touchpad handwriting recognition system. The history of handwriting recognition turns back to 1914 when Goldberg tried to recognize handwriting numerals to control machine in real time processes. Active area research in handwriting includes online recognition, offline recognition, signature verification, postal- active interpretation and bank-check processing and in this paper some of online handwriting recognition algorithms have been evaluated in terms of accuracy, methodology and the size of database. Online handwriting recognition engages in text conversion that is written on any kind of digitizer after sensing and converting that kind of data to digital. It can be recognized and separated to letters which are usable with any kind of text–processing application [1]. Challenging problems in online hand writing recognition are different character sizes, different writing styles and duplicate pixels produced by hesitation in writing or interpolated non-adjacent pixels caused by fast writing. Although there are many techniques for feature extraction ([2], [3], [4]–[8]) these techniques will not be investigated in this paper. Different handwriting recognition algorithms will be compared and their critical issue will be discussed. The Best handwriting recognition algorithms with a high degree of accuracy are introduced, considering low error rate for separation and classification of letters. Good accuracy depends on field isolation,

---

[*] Hamid Mirvaziri, Department of Electrical, Electronics and System, Faculty of Engineering, National University of Malaysia (UKM), Bangi, 43600 Malaysia.

H. Badioze Zaman et al. (Eds.): IVIC 2009, LNCS 5857, pp. 487–497, 2009.

segmentation, recombining segments, evolving characters, and dictionary–based correction. There are many methodologies in handwriting recognition such as Neural and Fuzzy methodologies, Genetic Algorithm, Dynamic Time Warping and etc.

2   Algorithms

In the following handwriting recognition algorithms there are varieties of databases differ in language, size and writer.

2.1   DTW and HMM Combination (CSDTW): [9]

Bahlmann and Burkhardt developed the cluster generative Statistical Dynamic Time Warping (CSDTW), which based on DTW (Dynamic Time Warping) and HMM (Hidden Morkov Model). CSDTW is a solution to combine clustering and statistical sequence modelling. Cluster analysis and statistical classification takes place in the same feature space and they have employed a closely related distance measure. One of the properties of CSDTW can be raising recognition rate in accordance with classifier size. Viterbi training is used to learn in HMM but instead of maximizing the probability density function the path optimize variant

$$L*(R^{IK}) = \sum_{x \in C^{IK}} LnP(x, \phi_{x,R}^* \mid R^{IK})$$

has been maximized that provides estimation of model parameters in an iteration of two basic steps. Step one computes Viterbi alignment $\phi_{x,R^{IK}}^*$ for $x \in C^{IK}$ and in step two an ML (Maximum Likelihood) parameters re-estimation of μ_j^{ik} and $\sum_j^{ik}$ was performed based on all sample points that have been aligned to j in step one. The experiments of this method are based on section 1a, 1b and 1c (digits, upper and lower case characters respectively) of the UNIPEN [10] Train – R01/V07 database and 67% of database was used for training set and 33% for testing set. 2.9% error rate has been achieved for 1a, 7.2% for 1b and 9.3% for 1c. Comparing CSDTW with MLP (Multilayer Perceptron) and HMM shows that the error rate was decreased 0.1% and 0.3% respectively in 1a (digits) database and it was decreased 0.4% comparing with DAG – SUM – GDTW [11]. In 1b the error rate of CSDTW was decreased 5.1% and 4.8% comparing with MLP and HMM respectively for 1c (lower case) database.

2.2   Discriminative Learning Quadratic Discriminant Function (DLQDF): [12]

Liu proposed another new algorithm based on discriminative learning for optimization parameters of MQDF (Modified Quadratic Discriminant Function) to improve the classification accuracy that was recommended by Kimura et al. [13]. They conducted their experiment into digit and numeral string recognition and they used DLQDF (Discriminative learning Quadratic Discriminant function) that adheres to the Gaussian density assumption and optimizes the parameters under MCE (Minimum Classification Error) criterion and due to their findings, recognition performance of DLQDF is competitive with neural classifiers, MLP and PC (Polynomial Classifier).

They also changed MQDF into MQDF2 that its parameters have deviated from ML estimation. In the database chosen from NIST special database 19 (SD19), 600 writer's handwritings were used for training and 400 writer's handwriting was used for testing [14]. The total numbers of training data-set and testing data-set are 66214 and 45398 respectively. After splitting and merging digit images they generated 16000 non-character samples for training and 1000 samples for testing. Numeral string images were extracted from the HSF pages of 300 writers and among them 4 pages with faded ink were excluded. They also tested the numeral string recognition performance on 3-digit and 6-digit string images. Some samples were excluded that mismatch the ground truth labels from the 1480 3-digit and 1480 6-digit images and because of this reason, they had 1471 3-digit samples and the same number of 6-digit samples in testing. The accuracy of MQDF2 with no sample rejection was 94.51%for 3-digit string images and for DLQDF was between 95.73% to 96.48% rate for 6-digit string images. It was 93.75% for MQDF2 and between 95.45% and 95.48% for DLQDF with no sample rejection.

Table 1. Recognition rate, Languages and objects in different algorithms

Algorithm	Training set	Testing set	Level	Language	Recognition rate
DLGDF	66214	45398	3-digit string	English	96.48
			6-digit string		95.58
Associative memory	4896	2448	Character	Arabic	94.56
CTC and ML	3298424	24255242	Word	English	79.6
BPN	2000	1000	Character	English	87
PCGM	704650	506848	Character	Chinese	97.89
Template	839	839	Word	Arabic	92.3
SADFUNN	Optical data 3823	1797	Digit	English	94.99
	Pen-based 7494	3498	Digit	English	94.6
	combined two database				98.3
Genetic Algorithm and visual encoding	500	300	Word	Arabic	97
A hierarchical approach	10800	127	Character	Bangle	80.58
Fuzzy	5000	60089	Digit	English	88.72
MCE	96563	9832	Character	English	91.7
CSDTW	67% of UNIPEN Train-R01/V07	67% of UNIPEN Train-R01/V07	Digit	English	97.1,
			Upper case		92.8 and
			Lower case		90.7

2.3 Associative Memory: [15]

Another method for handwriting recognition proposed in 2005 by Mezghani et al. and in this method Kohonen network was used for training in addition with pruning and filtering to improve the classification strength. This network can be used where the designer need a memory for classification. The statistics of features based on histograms of tangents and tangent differences is investigated at regularly spaced points along the character signal. They combined Kohonen network with the multilayer perceptron. Large numerals printed characters pruning was used since dead nodes were caused part of the error rate and filtering was used to remove outlier nodes that caused distortion. The database that has been used contains 432 samples of each character written by 18 writers. The training set contains 4896 samples and 2448 samples in the testing set. Recognition rate for this database was between 94.07% and 94.60% depending on the Euclidian distance, Hellinger distance or Kullback-Leibler divergence. The last classifier had fewer training iteration than the others and demonstrated that Kohonen network that was used has better recognition rate at least 0.53%. They also suggested that Kohonen network training can be improved with different distance measures. They have also recommended using genetic algorithm (GA), kernel principle component analysis (PCA) or minimum entropy principle for better character representation.

2.4   Connectionist Temporal Classification and Language Model (CTC and LM): [16]

Graves et al. applied a recurrent neural network (RNN) to online handwriting recognition. The RNN architecture is bidirectional Long Short-Term Memory [17], was chosen for its ability to process data with long time dependencies. They combined CTC network (connectionist temporal classification) and LM (language model). CTC is an objective function designed for sequence labelling with RNNs but it does not require pre-segmented training data to transform the network outputs into labelling. CTC directly map input sequences to the conditional probabilities for network training. This training employed gradient descent by differentiating OCTC with respect to outputs and then utilized backpropagation through time to differentiate weights with respect to the network. This training is similar to forward-backward algorithm in HMM model. IAM – On DB consists of pen trajectories collected from 221 different writers using a 'smart white board' [18]. IAM – On DB was divided into a training set, two validation sets, and a testing set, containing respectively 5364, 1438, 1518 and 3859 written lines taken from 775, 192, 216 and 544 from. The datasets contained a total of 3298424, 885964, 1036803 and 24255242 pen coordinates respectively. In their experiment, each line was used as a separate sequence. A dictionary consisting of 2000 most frequently occurring words in the LOB corpus was used for decoding, a long with a bigram language model optimized on the training and validation set [19]. 5.6% of the words in the test set were not in the dictionary. They got 20.4% word error rate with pre-processed input made a decline at least 5.4% in the rate comparing with HMM model.

2.5   Backpropagation Neural Network Online Handwriting Recognition (BPN): [20]

This method utilized from backpropagation neural network (BPN) as a classifier. Backpropagation or propagation of error is a method of inductive learning that propagates the errors backward. It allows quick convergence on local minimum and it necessarily should be used in multilayer perceptron. They concentrated on sub-character primitive feature extraction technique that did not utilize resizing of characters. Direction encoding was used to shorten the characteristics of characters and they combined them to create a global feature vector. The database had 2000 characters collected from 40 subjects using tablet Summa Sketch III. The script classifier may require training on different surfaces because the writing styles may vary considerably on those surfaces. In the way of comparing and study of behaviour of different recognition model, 26 upper case English alphabets considered and about 1000 more handwriting sample were used for testing purposes.

Performance of this algorithm is up to 87%. The recognition rate gradually decrease by applying tough thresholds but this makes the system more reliable by tempting less false recognition.

2.6 Minimum Classification Error: [21]

Biem described another method for handwriting recognition based on HMM with MCE training and he demonstrated in his paper that MCE criterion achieved more than 30 percent character error rate reduction compare to maximum likelihood-based system for word recognition. After separating a word to sequence, the model of each word computes discriminate function and this function helps the algorithm to quantify the membership degree of the incoming sample where this quantity have a logarithmic relation with probability of the corresponding composite HMMs of input sequence. The Viterbi algorithm was used in order to compute the maximum quantity of HMM. Database created by the author involved 92 characters resulted into 404 allographs. This data were divided into two sets 94563 examples written by 157 writers used for training and the remaining 9832 written by 17 writers for testing. The author implements another experiment for word recognition and the database used for testing had 1157 freely written words taken from sentences written by 75 writers with one sentences per person by his own styles. For word training based on ML and MCE method 52210 words were used written by 100 writers in their proper writing style. He illustrated that as lexicon size has increased from 5k to 10k, the error rate has decreased between %3 and %5. Using character model, MCE has improved the performance of baseline ML system from 83.9% to 88%, using allograph model, MCE improved this rate from 87.9% to 90.9% when trained at the allograph level, and to 91.7% when trained at the character level. In word level two MCE training schemes has been used; a Lexicon Driven MCE training and a Lexicon Agnostic MCE training. Lexicon Driven MCE training achieved 9.75% relative word error reduction from the ML estimated system with 5k (no pruning) dictionary and 6.19% relative reduction in word error rate with 10k dictionary and Lexicon Agnostic MCE training achieved 17.48% relative word error rate reduction with 5k dictionary (no pruning) and 12.5% relative reduction in word error rate with 10k dictionary (with beam based pruning).

2.7 Precision Constrained Gaussian Model (PCGM): [22]

In 2008 another work was presented in pattern recognition for Chinese handwriting characters by Wang and Huo. In their work they employed PCG (precision constrained Gaussian) model and on that model they extended the ML transformation to EMLLT (extended maximum likelihood linear transformation) that is used for modelling each inverse covariance matrix by basis expansion, where expansion coefficients are character-dependent. In Nakayosi as a Japanese character database about 1.7 million character samples from 163 writers exist and kuchibue database contains about 1.4 million character samples from 120 writers [23]. About 92%

samples were utilized from the Nakayosi database in training phase and 76% samples from the kuchibue in testing phase, while the remaining samples from both databases were used for development set. There are 704650 samples in the training set, 229398 in development set and 506848 in testing set respectively. PCGM got 97.89% recognition accuracy rate by using 2.82 MB memory; proper memory for this kind of recognizer.

2.8   Template Matching: [24]

Sternby et al. proposed a novel algorithm in the application of template matching scheme for connected Arabic script recognition [24]. In their work the dual–graph has been employed [25]. Segmentation graph is first constructed from template database and this graph contains the distance for matching a certain prototype and second graph as a recognition graph to produce the final recognition candidate. A database consisted of 40 people's inputting words from 66 Arabic words (totally 1578 samples). 839 word samples and 27 writers were used to train. Recognition rate was 92.3% in testing phase when the dictionary size was 66 words and the testing database was chosen through trained database. This accuracy rate was about 92% in the same dictionary size when the database was out of the trained database.

2.9   Combination of Adaptive Function Neural Network (ADFUNN) and On-Line Snap – Drift Learning

Kang and Brown recommended the combination of two methods to get better recognition system; adaptive function neural network (ADFUNN) and unsupervised single layer snap-drift [26]. Snap-drift is efficient in extracting distinct features from the complex cursive-letter, and single layer ADFUNN solves linear inseparable problems without hidden neurons. They utilized 250 samples per person collected from 44 people who were randomly divided into two sets 30 forms for training and 14 for writer independent testing that is a collected dataset by Alpaydin et al. [27, 28]. Optical dataset recommended by NIST were used [29] .There was 3823 training patterns and 1797 writer-independent testing patterns. They had also used pen-based dataset generated by WACOM PL-100V pressure sensitive tablet with an integrated LCD display and a cordless stylus. There are 7494 training patterns and 3498 writer-independent testing patterns in this database. By Combining the two dataset they got 98.3% accuracy on the writer independent testing data. Their K-NN classifier comparing with MLP (multilayer perceptron) has high generalization ability and it is easy and fast to train and implement. They called their method SADFUNN (snap-drift Adaptive Function neural network).

2.10   Genetic Algorithm and Visual Encoding: [30]

Another work that has been introduced by Kherallah et al. was based on combination of visual encoding, beta-elliptical model and GA for Arabic words recognition .A heuristic method employed for visual codes extraction. A new approach based on visual indices similarity is developed to calculate the evaluation function and they optimized the times cooling of their system to give the final output (proposed words). Fitness function comes out by comparison between two handwriting words (tested word and randomly selected word) from initial population and was measured by paralleling and comparing their different bits. They collected 500 words written by different writer. 200 words were used as data prototypes for the selection of the initial population of the GA and the others were used for testing their system. They repeated same experiment for 30 times; the average of measured recognition rate was about 97%.

2.11   A Hierarchical Approach for Bangla Character

This algorithm was based on MLP classifier and word image segmentation on Matra hierarchy to recognize individual word segment and finally identifies the constituent character of the word image through intelligent recognition decision of associated word segments [31]. Major problem to improve the character recognition rate was weakness of zone boundary detection algorithms and various classifiers. The MLPs designed to work as the first pass classifiers with 3 folds of training sets, each trained for 10000 iterations of BP algorithm and for the second pass, each trained for 2000 iterations of BP algorithm. Two following database sources were used in these algorithms: CVPR unit of ISI and CMATER database. The sizes of two databases are 1800 samples and 1200 samples respectively. Upper zone and lower zone character segment are collected from character images written on box formatted data sheet to form this databases then scaled to 32*32 pixel size after forming with minimum bounding box so that the Character Digit Modified (CDM) classifier consisted of 2160 samples of three categories including basic character, digit and modified shapes. The average recognition rate on Bangla samples is 80.58%, compared to average recognition of the first pass classifiers improved by 2.28%. Basu et al. suggested classifier combination to improve the lower accuracy. They recommended arranging dictionary matching to improve recognition rate and word level recognition.

2.12   Simplified Structural Classification Using Fuzzy Method: [32]

Jou and Lee proposed a new methodology on simplified structural classification by using Fuzzy memberships. They extract five kinds of primitive segment for each image then a fuzzy membership function is used to estimate the likelihood being close to two vertical boundaries of the image and finally tree-like classifier applied to classify the numerals on fuzzy memberships. They used handwritten numerals from National Institute of Standards and Technology (NIST) special database 19, which collected 810000 handwriting characters of 3600 people enclosed in forms. Each character was scanned in 300 dpi resolutions to obtain a 128*128 bitmap image. The number of handwritten numeral in it was 60089. Handwritten numerals in NIST are recognized by their system with the accuracy rate of 88.72%.

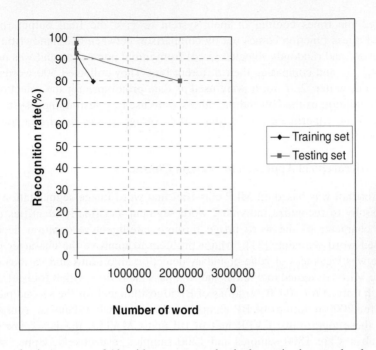

Fig. 1. Accuracy of Algorithms on test and train dataset in character level

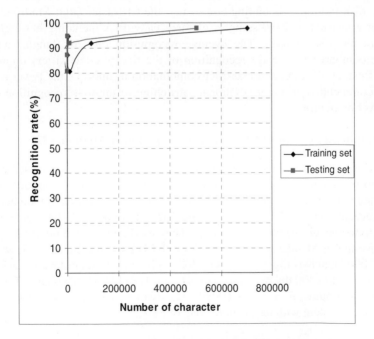

Fig. 2. Accuracies of Algorithms on test and train dataset in word level

3 Conclusion

A great number of algorithms about handwriting recognition have been evaluated in this paper. Normally it is difficult to compare them to each other because of different aims, different databases and different languages. Most of authors have seemed more concerned with new algorithms rather than improving existing one. It has not been possible to conduct an exhaustive review and comparison in this paper and also we are aware of a number of other algorithms that could have been included if space were unlimited. We have compared the algorithms mention above with respect to size of database and   recognition rate that may help readers in comparing other algorithms that are not evaluated in this paper. In terms of recognition rate and accuracy SAD-FUNN was the best algorithm with 98.3% recognition rate following by PCGM algorithm that its recognition rate is about 97.89% and the third one was CSDTW with 97.1% recognition rate. Table 1 attempts to compare the main features of interest in different algorithms that was mentioned in this paper. It was shown that in character recognition at the beginning recognition rate is increased dramatically corresponding with the size of database but in bigger databases need better classifier to have that growth like the one was designed in Wang and Huo algorithm. It seems that there is an optimum point for the size of database as illustrated in Fig.1 and as it is demonestrated in Fig.2 character recognition decrease when the size of database is grown unconcern with methodology and technique. Level of recognition is classified in Table.1 to indicate the type of objects for classification. It should be emphasised that for word recognition, supervised classifier (MLP for example) can not provide high recognition rate alone but supervised and unsupervised classifier combination (GA and fuzzy) can provide better recognition rate.

References

1. Goldberg, Eli, H.: "Controller", United States Patent 1,117,184 (November 17, 1914)
2. Chakraborty, Chakraborty, G.: A new feature extraction technique for online recognition of handwritten alphanumeric characters. Information Sciences 148, 55–70 (2002)
3. Sanchez, G., Gago Gonzalez, J.A., Dimitriadis, Y.A., Cano Izquierdo, J.M., Lopez Coronado, J.: Experimental study of a novel neuro-fuzzy system for online handwritten UNIPEN digit recognition. Pattern Recognition Lett. 19, 357–364 (1998)
4. Hammandlu, Murali Mohan, K.R., Chakraborty, S., Goyal, S., Choudhury, D.R.: Unconstrained handwritten character recognition based on fuzzy logic. Pattern Recognition 36, 603–623 (2003)
5. Jaeger, Manke, S., Reichert, J., Waibel, A.: Online recognition: the NPen++ recognizer. Int. J. Doc. Anal. Recognition 3, 169–180 (2001)
6. Parizeau, Lemieux, A., Gagne, C.: Character recognition experiments using unipen data proceedings. In: 6th Int. Conf. on Doc. Anal. and Recognition, paper 481 (2001)
7. Ping, Lihui, C.: A novel feature extraction method and hybrid tree classification for handwritten numeral recognition. Pattern Recognition Lett. 23, 45–56 (2002)
8. Trier, D., Jain, A.K., Taxt, T.: Feature extraction methods for character recognition - A Survey. Pattern Recognition 29, 641–662 (1996)

9. Bahlamann, Burkhardt, H.: The writer independent online handwriting recognition system frog on hand and cluster generative statistical dynamic time warping. IEEE Trans. Pattern Anal. Mach. Intell. 26, 299–310 (2004)

10. Guyon, Schomaker, L.R.B., Plamondon, R., Liberman, M., Janet, S.: UNIPEN project of on-line data exchange and recognizer benchmarks. In: Proc. 12th Int'l Conf. Pattern Recognition, pp. 29–33 (1994), http://www.unipen.Org/

11. Bahlmann, Haasdonk, B., Burkhardt, H.: Online handwriting recognition with support vector machines—A Kernel Approach. In: Proc. Eighth Int'l Workshop Frontiers in Handwriting Recognition, pp. 49–54 (2002)

12. Lue, Sako, H., Fujisawa, H.: Discriminative learning quadratic discriminant function for handwriting recognition. IEEE Transactions on Neural Networks 15, 430–443 (2004)

13. Kimura, Takashina, K., Tsuruoka, S., Miyake, Y.: Modified quadratic discriminant functions and the application to Chinese character recognition. IEEE Trans. Pattern Anal. Mach. Intell. 9, 149–153 (1987)

14. Grother, J.: NIST special database 19: Hand printed forms and characters database. Tech. Rep. (1995)

15. Mezghani, Mitiche, A., Cheriet, M.: A new representation of shape and its use for high performance in online Arabic character recognition by an associative memory. Int. J. Doc. Anal. 7, 201–210 (2005)

16. Graves, Fernandez, S., Liwicki, M., Bunke, H., Schmidhuber, J.: Unconstrained online handwriting recognition with recurrent neural networks (2006)

17. Graves, Schmidhuber, J.: Framewise phoneme classification with bidirectional LSTM and other neural network architectures. Neural Networks 18, 602–610 (2005)

18. Liwicki, Bunke, H.: IAM-OnDB - an on-line English sentence database acquired from handwritten text on a whiteboard. In: Proc. 8th Int. Conf. on Doc. Anal. and Recognition, pp. 956–961 (2005)

19. Liwicki, Graves, A., Fern´andez, S., Bunke, H., Schmidhuber, J.: A novel approach to on-line handwriting recognition based on bidirectional long short-term memory networks. In: Proc. 9th Int. Conf. on Doc. Anal. and Recognition, Brazil (2007)

20. Zafar, F., Mohamad, D., Anwar, M.M.: Recognition of online isolated handwritten characters by backpropagation neural nets using sub-character primitive features, pp. 157–162 (2006)

21. Biem: Minimum classification error training for online handwriting recognition. IEEE Trans. Pattern Anal. Mach. Intell. 28, 1041–1051 (2006)

22. Wang, Huo, Q.: Modeling inverse covariance matrices by expansion of tied basis matrices for online handwritten Chinese character recognition. Pattern Recognition 41, 1–7 (2008)

23. Nakagawa, Matsumoto, K.: Collection of on-line handwritten Japanese character pattern databases and their analysis. Int. J. Doc. Anal. Recognition 7, 69–81 (2004)

24. Sternby, Morwing, J., Andersson, J., Friberg, C.: Online Arabic handwriting recognition with templates. Pattern Recognition 41, 1–9 (2008)

25. Sternby, Friberg, C.: The recognition graph—language independent adaptable online cursive script recognition. In: Proc. of the Eighth Int. Conf. on Doc. Anal. and Recognition, pp. 14–18 (2005)

26. Kang, P.-B.D.: A modal learning adaptive function neural network appliedto handwritten digit recognition. Information Sciences 178, 3802–3812 (2008)

27. Alimoglu, Alpaydin, E.: Combining multiple representations for pen-based handwritten digit recognition. Turkish Journal of Electrical Engineering and Computer Sciences 9, 1–12 (2001)

28. Alpaydin, Kaynak, C., Alimoglu, F.: Cascading multiple classifiers and representations for optical and pen-based handwritten digit recognition. In: The 7th International Workshop in Frontiers in Handwriting Recognition (IWFHR 2000), Amsterdam, The Netherlands (2000)
29. Garris, D.: NIST form-based handprint recognition system. National Institute of Standard and Technology Interagency Reports, NISTIRs 5469 (1991)
30. Kherallah, Bouri, F., Alimi, A.M.: Online Arabic handwriting recognition system based on visual encoding and genetic algorithm. Engineering Application of Artificial Intelligence 22, 153–170 (2009)
31. Basu, Das, N., Sarkar, R., Kundu, M., Nasipuri, M., Basu, D.K.: A hierarchical approach to recognition of handwritten Bangla characters. Pattern Recognition 42, 1467–1484 (2009)
32. Jou, Lee, H.: Handwritten numeral recognition based on simplified structural classification and fuzzy memberships. Expert Systems with Applications 36, 1–6 (2009)

United Zernike Invariants for Character Images

Norsharina Abu Bakar and Siti Mariyam Shamsuddin

Soft Computing Research Group,
K-Economy Research Alliance
Universiti Teknologi Malaysia, Skudai, Johor
norsharina85@gmail.com, mariyam@utm.my

Abstract. Feature extraction is one of the major components in traditional pattern recognition. There are many methods for extracting the features, either structural approach or global approach. In this paper, we present integrated formulation of Zernike Moments and United Moment Invariant for extracting the character images accordingly. The extraction values are validated by measuring the Inter-class and intra-class analysis to illustrate the effectiveness of the proposed solution. The results yield that the proposed method are feasible and better for extracting the images for both inter-class and intra-class analysis.

Keywords: Pattern Recognition, Feature Extraction, Granular Mining, Zernike Moment Invariant, United Moment Invariant, Intra-class, and Inter-class.

1 Introduction

Nowadays, there are many techniques have been produced in Pattern Recognition for extracting the features either structurally or globally, such as Moment Functions (MF). Previous studies on moment functions, particularly on Geometrical Moments have illustrated some drawbacks [3][4]. MFs that are widely used in pattern recognition include Zernike Moment Invariant [5]; Affine Moment Invariant [9], Aspect Moment Invariant [8], and etc (refer to table 1).

Table 1. Moment Functions

Year	Researcher	Technique
1962	Hu	Geometric Moment Invariant
1980	Teague	Zernike Moment Invariant
1980	Teague	Legendre Moment Invariant
1992	Flusser and Suk	Affine Moment Invariant
1993	Chen	Improve Moment Invariant
1994	Feng And Keane	Aspect Moment Invariant
2000	S. M. Shamsuddin	Higher Order Centralized Scale – Invariant
2001	R.Mukundan	Tchebichef Moment Invariant
2003	Yinan	United Moment Invariant
2003	Yap	Krawtchouk Moment Invariant

H. Badioze Zaman et al. (Eds.): IVIC 2009, LNCS 5857, pp. 498–509, 2009.
© Springer-Verlag Berlin Heidelberg 2009

Due these weaknesses, other techniques are emerging by integrating the formulation of MF with other types of moment Invariant as illustrated in Table 2. All the said techniques were proposed for unequally scaling with its basis is from Geometric Moment Invariant [2][7].

Table 2. Related Studies on Integration Formulation of Moment Invariants

Reseachers	*Techniques*
Shamsuddin (2000)	An Integration between High Order Moment and Aspect Moment Invariant
A.K Muda(2007)	An integration of United Moment Invariant and Higher Order Centralized Scale - Invariant
A.K Muda(2008)	An integration of Aspect Moment Invariant and United Moment Invariant
Rela Puteri Pamungkas & Shamsuddin.(2009)	An integration of Weighted Moment Invariant and Aspect Moment Invariant

This paper presents an integration formulation of Zernike Moment with United Moment Invariant for characters recognition. The remainder of this paper is organized as follows: Section II describes the drawbacks of Geometric Moment Invariants in pattern recognition; Section III provides an algorithm of integration between Zernike Moments with United Moment Invariant; Section IV presents the research methodology of the study. Section V introduces the concept of inter-class and intra-class, experimental results and analysis of the proposed approach. Finally, Section VI gives the conclusion of the study.

2   Drawbacks of Geometric Moment Invariant

The emergence of other moment functions was inspired due to the drawbacks of Geometric Moment Invariants as proposed by Hu [1] (refer to Table 3). Ding had found that GMI was loose scale invariance in discrete condition [6]. Due to this weakness, Hongtao [11] proposed new technique of moment invariant in discrete condition, and followed by Botao Wong [12] on Relative moments. In 1993, Chen proposed Improved Moment Invariant based on boundary condition [4].

However, in 1992, Flusser [9] found another drawback of Hu's Moments that which was reliant and incomplete. Hu's Moments is invariant only under basic transformation: translation, rotation and scaling. Therefore, Flusser [9] proposed a new technique that which is invariant under general affined transformations.

Besides that, Wong (1994) found that Hu's moments could only be applied on a small subset of moment invariants, and cannot be found on a complete set of Moment Invariants. Consequently, he improved the third-order moment and fourth-order moment of Geometric Moment invariants in recognition rate for Characters recognition.

Table 3. Drawbacks of geometrical moment invariant

YEAR	RESEARCHER	PROBLEMS
1992	Ding	Loose scale invariance in discrete condition
1992	Flusser	reliant and incomplete
1993	Chen	Improve boundary condition
1994	Wong	only be applied on a small subset of moment invariants
2001	Ivar	data with a position far away from the center of coordinate
2003	Yinan	Improve region,boundary and discrete condition
1993-2007	Raveendran *et.al* (1993), Feng(1994), Raveendran *et.al* (1995), Palaniappan *et.al* (2000), Yinan et.al (2003), Shamsuddin (2000) and Muda (2007),	Unequally scaling data by Hu(1962) $$\eta_{pq} = \frac{\mu_{pq}}{\mu_{pq}^{\frac{p+q+2}{2}}} \cdot$$

Ivar (2001) found that Hu's Moment have some problems with the data which is a position far away from the centre of coordinate. It is because Hu's Moment cannot recognize the data which is concentrated near the centre-of-mass effectively. Therefore, the data will be neglected so that the data is closed to the centre moment. Consequently, Rela & Siti Mariyam[10]proposed a new integration techniques called Weighted Aspect Moment Invariant.

In 2003, Yinan[3] found that Hu's Moments are valuable based on regions .Hence, he came up with a new technique to assure that translation, scaling and rotation can be discretely kept invariant into region and boundary condition.

In addition, there are many researchers found that the drawbacks of Geometric Moment Invariant is came from the unequally scaling data. The improvement of unequally scaling data based on normalization centre moment was beginning from 1993 until 2003. Many formulations on normalization of central moment can be found accordingly such as Raveendran *et.al* (1993), Feng (1994), Raveendran *et.al* (1995), Palaniappan *et.al* (2000), Yinan et.al (2003). Furthermore, many integration techniques were also proposed by other researchers to reduce the drawbacks of Geometric Moment Invariant such as Higher Order Centralized Scale (Shamsuddin *et.a l*, 2000), Higher Order United Scaled (A.K Muda *et. al*, 2007) and Aspect United Moment Invariant (A.K Muda *et. al*, 2008).

3 Zernike United Representation

Zernike Moment Invariant was produced by Teague in 1980[5]. This technique was proposed to enhance the conventional Geometric Invariants for rotation purposed. Figure 1 illustrates the design and implementation of Zernike United representation. It is observed that Zernike and United were derived from the geometrical function.

Therefore, in this study, an integration formulation between Zernike Moment Invariant and United Moment Invariant will be derived to obtain effectiveness results for intra-class and inter-class analysis in the terms of rotation, region, discrete and boundary condition. The algorithm to execute the proposed method is described below.

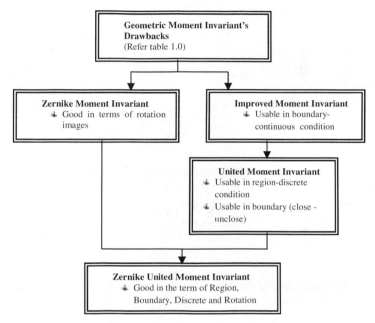

Fig. 1. Design and Implementation of Zernike United Moment Invariant

The integration algorithm of ZMI and UMI is given as:

1. The image data will be read and processed. Geometric Moment Invariant will generate as[1]:

$$m_{pq} = \sum_{x=0}^{N} \sum_{y=0}^{M} f(x, y)$$

(1)

For

$$p, q = 0,1,2,....$$

With

$$f(x, y)$$

And shows the level for the gray background of the image which will be set as 0 whereas 1 is set on the object. It will be diminished to

$$m_{pq} = \sum_{i=1}^{L} x_i^p y^q \tag{2}$$

L as a guide to the number of pixels that have the object

2. Then, the image centered as shown below:

$$(\bar{X}, \bar{Y})$$

With

$$\bar{x} = \frac{m_{10}}{m_{00}} \, , \bar{y} = \frac{m_{01}}{m_{00}} \tag{3}$$

Set the image centered invariant computed on the shift

$$\mu_{pq} = \sum_{x} \sum_{y} (x - \bar{x})^p (y - \bar{y})^q f(x, y) \tag{4}$$

3. The definition of scaling equation normal (5), discrete (6) and boundary (7) as given below:

$$\eta_{pq} = \frac{\mu_{pq}}{(\mu_{00})^{\frac{p+q+2}{2}}} \tag{5}$$

$$\eta'_{pq} = \rho^{p+q} \eta_{pq} = \frac{\rho^{p+q}}{(\mu_{00})^{\frac{p+q+2}{2}}} \mu_{pq} \tag{6}$$

$$\eta''_{pq} = \frac{\mu_{pq}}{(\mu_{00})^{p+q+1}} \tag{7}$$

4. The eight formulas for United Moment Invariants (UMI) are presented as:

$$\theta_1 = \sqrt{\phi_2}/\phi_1 \qquad \theta_2 = \phi_6/\phi_1\phi_4$$
$$\theta_3 = \sqrt{\phi_5}/\phi_4 \qquad \theta_4 = \phi_5/\phi_3\phi_4$$
$$\theta_5 = \phi_1\phi_6/\phi_2\phi_3 \qquad \theta_6 = (\phi_1 + \sqrt{\phi_2})\phi_3/\phi_6$$
$$\theta_7 = \phi_1\phi_5/\phi_3\phi_6 \qquad \theta_8 = (\phi_3 + \phi_4)/\sqrt{\phi_5}$$

$$(8)$$

5. However, in this integration, the ϕ values are substituted by Zernike's moments as shown below.

$$ZM_1 = \frac{3}{\pi}[2(\eta_{20} + \eta_{02} - 1)]$$

$$ZM_2 = \frac{9}{\pi^2}\left[(\eta_{20} - \eta_{02})^2 + 4\eta_{11}^2\right]$$

$$ZM_3 = \frac{16}{\pi^2}\left[(\eta_{03} - 3\eta_{21})^2 + (\eta_{30} - 3\eta_{12}{}^2)\right]$$

$$ZM_4 = \frac{144}{\pi^2}\left[(\eta_{03} - 3\eta_{21})^2 + (\eta_{30} + \eta_{12})^2\right]$$

$$ZM_5 = \frac{13824}{\pi^4}\left\{ \begin{array}{l}(\eta_{03} - \eta 3\eta_{21})(\eta_{03} + \eta_{21})\left[(\eta_{03} + \eta_{21})^2 - 3(\eta_{30} + \eta_{12})^2\right] \\ -(\eta_{30} - 3\eta_{12})(\eta_{30} + \eta_{12})\left[(\eta_{30} + \eta_{12})^2 - 3(\eta_{03} + \eta_{21})^2\right] \end{array} \right\}$$

$$ZM_6 = \frac{864}{\pi^3}\left\{ \begin{array}{l}(\eta_{02} - \eta_{20})\left[(\eta_{30} + \eta_{12})^2 - (\eta_{03} + \eta_{21})^2\right] \\ + 4\eta_{11}(\eta_{03} + \eta_{21})(\eta_{30} + \eta_{12}) \end{array} \right\}$$

$$(9)$$

4 Experimental Research Design

In this study, character images will be used. These character images are scanned with 300 dpi (dot per inch) and 150 dpi resolutions (refer to Figure 2).

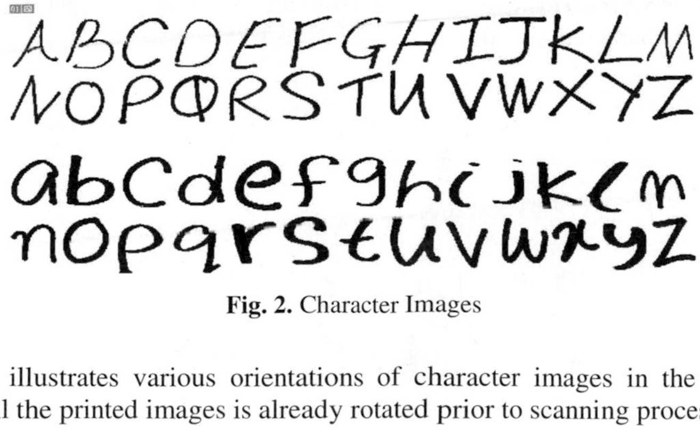

Fig. 2. Character Images

Figure 3 illustrates various orientations of character images in the same class. Basically, all the printed images is already rotated prior to scanning process.

Fig. 3. Character Images(Orientation)

5   Result and Analysis

In this section, we describe the invarianceness of the proposed integrated formulations by presenting the validation in terms of intra-class and inter-class concept. In our study, the invarianceness is defined as the best result for the intra-class and inter-class analysis in terms of shape and rotation. The process that defines the similar images with the small value of Mean Absolute Error (MAE) is called intra-class concept. However, inter-class is the process that defines the high value of MAE with the different images. The MAE is given as:

$$MAE = \frac{1}{n}\sum_{i=1}^{n}\left|(x_i - r_i)\right|,$$

where n is number of image, x_i is the current image and r_i is the reference image. In our study, the first image is the reference image.

5.1   Intra-class Analysis

In this research, characters of uppercase and lowercase have been used in this research. From Figure 4, Zernike Moment Invariant gives the higher value of MAE for the all lowercase characters.

Table 3 shows the MAE of the lowercase characters. As shown in Table 4, Zernike United Moment Invariants give small MAE values for the bold characters (a,e,m,n,o,s,u,w,x,y,z). However, United Moment Invariant gives the small value of MAE for other characters (b,c,d,f,g,h,I,j,k,l,p,q,r,s,t,v).

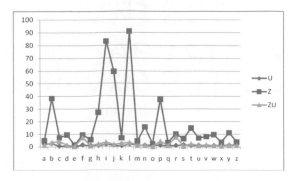

Fig. 4. Intra-class anylisis result for lowercase characters

Table 4. MAE of Lowercase Characters

	U	Z	ZU
a	2.121303	4.899467	1.264206
b	2.532234	38.36238	3.383113
c	0.466142	7.241842	4.187599
d	0.933289	9.500966	1.277886
e	0.539864	1.437383	0.329964
f	1.356021	9.485567	7.32424
g	0.863246	5.449352	0.626108
h	0.680351	27.21004	1.974887
i	1.664244	83.31634	3.436587
j	0.975384	59.52517	1.629552
k	0.590778	6.980908	2.625261
l	2.049863	90.99872	3.329608
m	1.406635	4.494424	1.212053
n	1.29662	15.86073	1.237367
o	1.575373	2.449911	0.269019
p	1.275066	37.64254	4.575979
q	1.039522	3.506299	1.093572
r	1.105685	10.21371	7.962292
s	1.642202	6.458625	0.516307
t	0.929813	14.90048	2.31271
u	1.102647	6.941306	0.910839
v	0.652563	8.034618	1.421965
w	0.967629	9.635414	0.920255
x	1.123817	3.569825	0.536638
y	1.150224	11.13917	0.969381
z	1.616942	3.920627	1.102686

Table 5. MAE of Uppercase Characters

	U	Z	ZU
A	2.814686	45.16599	1.929047
B	1.407917	24.95112	1.032693
C	1.105832	21.97463	0.98932
D	0.704838	16.97781	1.225409
E	0.374994	35.24637	19.98226
F	1.239719	8.755773	4.491405
G	1.515726	19.89788	1.404531
H	2.628187	12.76827	0.936871
I	1.491554	30.27587	2.335628
J	0.255395	2.167779	1.020834
K	1.716915	8.666278	1.964969
L	1.221332	33.57352	9.655203
M	0.966486	21.99051	1.169756
N	2.715259	20.15975	1.721595
O	1.429697	23.86374	1.528476
P	1.685112	13.9396	1.884636
Q	2.160555	2.533339	0.809534
R	0.88277	2.431493	2.005768
S	1.677413	6.757688	1.131169
T	1.281098	18.98232	0.642375
U	0.783356	4.185653	0.997532
V	0.843589	49.48092	2.949426
W	0.972933	6.006607	2.705254
X	1.509192	6.264912	0.76327
Y	1.193231	40.70955	1.166322
Z	1.402532	14.9044	1.249249

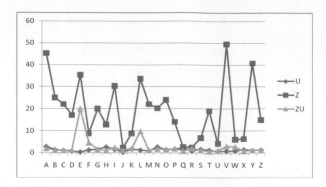

Fig. 5. The graph of intra-class anylisis result for uppercase characters

5.2   Inter-class Analysis

The images that have the similarity of shape have been used in the interclass analysis. Hence, we have prepared 4 testing images:

- "a" and "d"
- "b" and "p"
- "m" and "n"
- "l" and "i"

From Table 6, we found that Zernike Moment Invariant gives higher value of MAE for all characters except for "b" and "p". This is due to Zernike United Moment Invariants give higher MAE values for these characters ("b" and "p.) as shown in Figure 6. Therefore, Zernike Moment Invariants are good for interclass analysis of the characters compared to other techniques.

In conclusion, the above experiments have proven that Zernike United Moment Invariants are good for identifying the characters that have similarity in shape and orientation such as 'a' and 'e' or 'u' and 'n'.

Table 6. MAE of Inter-Class for Characters

	U	ZU	Z
a,d	2.41546	0.273454	10.72511
b,p	0.910757	7.924332	4.226392
m,n	1.226273	0.943614	23.30394
l,i	0.659015	3.674756	56.44773

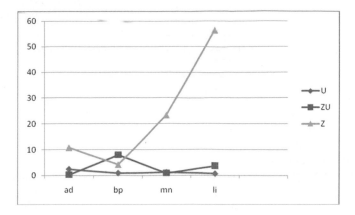

Fig. 6. The graph of inter-class anylisis result for lowercase characters

6 Conclusion

Table 7 provides the summary of the experiments conducted in this study. In this study, we can draw the conclusion that Zernike United Moment Invariants and United Moment Invariants, both are good for intra-class analysis of character images based on the shape and orientation conditions. However, Zernike Moment Invariant is good for the inter-class analysis of characters.

Table 7. Summary of the Experiments

Technique	Invarianceness	Result	Images
The proposed *Integrated*	Intra-class	Better	Uppercase:(A,B,C,G,H,N,Q,S,T,X,Y,Z) Lowercase: (a,e,m,n,o,s,u,w,x,y,z)
Formulation *(Zernike United* *Moment* *Invariant)*	Inter-class	Good	Comparison between "b" and "p"
Zernike	Intra-class	Bad	All Characters images
Moment *Invariant*	Inter-class	Better	• Comparison between "a" and "d" • Comparison between "l" and "i" • Comparison between "m" and "n"
United Moment *Invariant*	Intra-class	Better	Uppercase:(D,E,I,J,K,L,M,O,P,R,U,V,W) Lowercase:(b,c,d,f,g,h,I,j,k,l,p,q,r,s,t,v)
	Inter-class	Bad	All Characters images

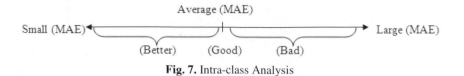

Fig. 7. Intra-class Analysis

The definition of the intra-class analysis is presented in figure 7. It defines that:

Better   : the techniques have a small value of MAE compare other techniques.
Good   : the techniques have a similar value of MAE compare other techniques.
Bad   : the techniques have a large value of MAE compare other techniques.

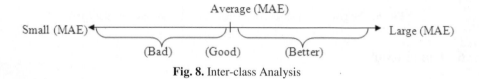

Fig. 8. Inter-class Analysis

In addition, figure 8 shows the definition of the inter-class analysis of this study. It defines that:

Better   : the techniques have a large value of MAE compare other techniques.
Good   : the techniques have a similar value of MAE compare other techniques.
Bad   : the techniques have a small value of MAE compare other techniques.

Acknowledgments. Authors would like to thank Research Management Centre (RMC) Universiti Teknologi Malaysia, for the research activities, and *Soft Computing Research Group* (SCRG) for the support in making this study a success.

References

1. Hu, M.-K.: Visual pattern recognition by moment invariants. Information Theory, IRE Transactions on 8(2), 179–187 (1962)
2. Muda, A.K., Shamsuddin, S.M., et al.: Invariancenes of higher order united scaled invariants. Advances in Computer Science and Engineering 1(2), 105–118 (2007)
3. Sun, Y., Liu, W., et al.: United moment invariants for shape discrimination. In: Proceedings IEEE International Conference on Robotics, Intelligent Systems and Signal Processing (2003)
4. Chen, C.-C.: Improved Moment Invariant for Shape Discrimination. Patter Recognition 26, 683–686 (1993)
5. Teague, M.R.: Image analysis via the general theory of moments. J. Opt. Soc. Am. 70(8), 920 (1980)
6. Ding, M., Chang, J., Peng, J.: Research on Moment Invariant Algorithm. Journal of Data Acquisition & Processing 7(1), 1–9 (1992)

7. Shamsuddin, S.M., Sulaiman, M.N., Darus, M.: Invarianceness of Higher Order Central-ised Scaled-invariants Undergo Basic Transformations. International Journal of Computer Mathematics 79, 39–48 (2002)
8. Feng, P., Keane, M.: A new set of moment invariant for Handwritten Numeral Recogni-tion. In:IEEE Intern. Conf. on Image Processsing, pp. 154–158 (1994)
9. Flusser, J., Suk, T.: Pattern Recognition By Affine Moment Invariant. Institute of Theory And Automation 26, 167–172 (1991)
10. Pamungkas, R.P., Shamsuddin, S.M.: Weighted Aspect Moment Invariant in Pattern Rec-ognition. LNCS, vol. 5593, pp. 806–818. Springer, Heidelberg (2009)
11. Lv, H., Zhou, J.: Research on Discrete Moment Invariant Algorithm. Journal of Data Ac-quisition & Processing 8(2), 151–155 (1993)
12. Wang, B., Sun, J., Cai, A.: Relative Moments and their Application to Geometric Shape Recognition. Journal of Image and Graphics 6(3), 296–300 (2002)

Using Animation in Active Learning Tool to Detect Possible Attacks in Cryptographic Protocols

Mabroka Ali Mayouf and Zarina Shukur

Faculty of Technology and Information Science,
University Kebangsaan Malaysia, Selangor, Malaysia

Abstract. Interactive Visualization tools for active learning of generic cryptographic protocols are very few. Although these tools provide the possibility to engage the learner by asking him to describe a cryptographic protocol using a simple visual metaphor to represent the abstraction of the concepts being visualized, the problem is that some cryptographic operations are not visualized or animated and hidden from the learner's perspective such as encryption/decryption actions. Other operations are not supported by these tools such as timestamp and freshness. So, it's difficult to cover all possible attack that the intruder might employ with such operations are missing. The purpose of this research is to provide an interactive visualization tool for teaching undergraduate students security protocols concepts especially key distribution, multiple operations such as encryption/decryption and signed/unsigned operations, and possible protocol attacks. By designing a high quality graphical user interface and simple visual metaphor, learners will be able to specify the protocols and consider the possible attack at each step of protocol demonstration.

Keywords: visual metaphor, active learning, animation, cryptographic protocols, possible attacks.

1 Introduction

The Theory of Multiple Intelligences [1] implies that teaching with visual and other techniques can make learning more effective. Visualization together with animation has been used in many areas of computer science education such as distributed algorithms, computer networks, computer architecture, and information security systems [2], [3], [4], [5], [6], [7], [8], [9]. Many computing educators agree that visualization technology positively impact learning [10]. The effectiveness of visualizations as an educational tool has been debated in the literature with mixed results [10]. Looking specifically at algorithm visualizations, Saraiya, et. al., attempted to identify key features of successful visualizations [6].

Many concepts which are related to cryptography are explained by using visual metaphors. Metaphor involves the presentation of a new idea (target) in terms of a more familiar one (source) [11], [12]. Metaphors differ from analogies in that an analogy is functionally identical where as a metaphor is only partially similar to the target [13]. Critical to the power of metaphor is that the convocation of source and

H. Badioze Zaman et al. (Eds.): IVIC 2009, LNCS 5857, pp. 510–520, 2009.

target ideas must involve some transformation; hence users do actively construct the relationships that comprise the metaphor during interaction with the system [14].

Regarding of the common use of visual metaphors, there are a few tools that can be used as aids in teaching and understanding generic cryptographic protocols and possible attack. In this research, we propose for a software tool that provides an interactive visualization for helping students to understand cryptographic protocols concepts especially key distribution, encryption/decryption and signed/unsigned operations, and possible attacks.

2 Related Works

Many animated visualization tools has been developed in computer science education. There is a widespread belief among computer educators that visualization technology can improve the effectiveness of learning [10]. Although tools for illustrating computer networking and security protocols concepts exist [15], [16], [17] users are not able to add or modify these tools in order to consider different concepts or protocols. There are a few systems that are able to generate the visual representation of a target protocol on-the-fly. A literature of some related visualization tools together with comparisons between them are available in our paper [18].

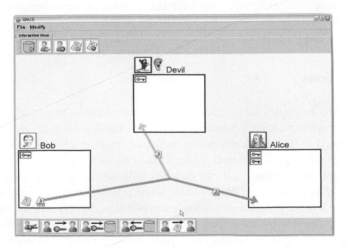

Fig. 1. GRACE Tool View

One of the most related works to this research is GRACE [19] which is an interactive Java-based system for the visualization of cryptographic protocols. It presents the user with a graphical window displaying a scenario where several virtual parties coexist. Each party has his own visual "desktop" containing resources like documents and cryptographic keys with associated operations. Each party can perform a set of operations related to communication, documents and cryptographic operations. The tool view is described in fig. 1.

The tool can be used by teachers to quickly and easily assemble a straightforward visual description of a cryptographic protocol. It's also can be used by students with at least some basic knowledge of a cryptographic protocol, So, for example, it would be possible for a student to execute an RSA-based secure communication scheme and verify that, if the steps of the protocol are executed in the correct order. In fact,

GRACE dose not cover some cryptographic protocols operations such as time-stamp and freshness so it's difficult to consider most possible attack to the given protocol. Besides, it does not support multiple operations such as multiple encryption/decryption and signed/unsigned operations. It also requires some initial programming effort if the protocol to be visualized and/or the cryptographic techniques it uses are not already supported by the tool.

3   Cryptographic Protocols Problems

The security of cryptographic protocol depends on the types of attacks over it. The worst-case assumption is that a penetrator can not only listen to arbitrary messages, but can also modify or delete them, and introduce his own fabricated messages [20]. The intruder is assumed to be a legal user of the network and is assumed to know the protocol format and all public information. With all of these capabilities, it is difficult to cover and understand all the tactics the intruder might employ, and defend against them in a protocol. By animation of protocol specifications it's possible to guess most tactics the intruder might behave after each step of protocol demonstration. It's possible for the Students to pretend to be an intruder in order to understand the protocol vulnerabilities and try to modify the protocol to defend well.

4   Motivations

There are many examples of visualization techniques used to help students to understand cryptographic protocols. Some of these applications tend to be very effective as they are tailored to the visualization of a particular cryptographic protocol. However, this may turns out to be a drawback as the visualizations they perform cannot be customized to meet user's needs, nor can they be easily adapted to visualize other protocols. Beside, the existing tools did not cover some cryptographic operations and hided them from the learner perspective such as encryption/decryption actions. Other operations are not supported by these tools such as timestamp and freshness. So, it's difficult to cover all possible attack that the intruder might employ if these operations are missing.

All these motivate us to develop an interactive visualization tool for teaching undergraduate students security protocols concepts especially key distribution, multiple operations such as encryption/decryption and signed/unsigned operations, and possible protocol attacks.

5   Design Approach

Current approaches to avoiding protocol failure either attempt to construct possible attacks, using algebraic properties of the algorithms in the protocols, or attempt construct proofs, using specialized logics based on a notion of "belief" , that protocol participants can confidently reach desire conclusions [21]. Animation technique can be used for constructing possible attacks by animating the protocol specifications. In our proposed tool, protocols are specified using high graphical user interface and simple visual metaphors. The tool provides visual metaphor for each component of protocol specifications (principals and messages). It's also provided with a built-in support for protocol components involved in the execution of cryptographic protocols and that can be used to create multiple scenarios. The students will be able to read through the animation specifications to understand the potential behaviors of the protocol specifications. They also will be able to detect possible attacks by checking every possible scenario defined in the specifications involving attacker actions. The following sections explain our design approach in more details.

5.1 Active Leaning

Active learning has been described as involving students in the classroom in activities other than listening that are meaningful and make them think about what they are doing [22]. Such activities can cover a wide variety of techniques from simple classroom dialoging to complex role-playing [23]. By adapting visualizations and animations techniques in our proposed tool, student will be able to build a certain protocol and construct possible attacks by using simple metaphors to make them engage in the learning process and gain knowledge about the impact of their actions.

5.2 Protocol Demonstration

In our previous work, we have specified protocols using NLPS approach [24]. From our experience, it's better for protocol specifications to be defined using graphical user interface GUI choices rather than keyboard input to minimize errors keyboard input. For this reason, we redesign our tool in such away to be simpler, robust, and prevent user from incorrect input by specifying protocols using high graphical user interface and visual metaphors. Further information on NLPS and our previous prototype are provided in [24].

In order to demonstrate protocols, enlisted are the aid of several actors (Table 1). Alice and Bob are the first two. They will perform all general protocols. As a rule, Alice will initiate all protocols and Bob will respond. If the protocol requires a third or fourth person, Carol and Dave will perform those roles. Other actors will play specialized roles as needed.

Our tool presents the user with a graphical user interface displaying a scenario where several actors communicate with each other in order to exchange messages among them. Each actor has his own visual panel containing resources like cryptographic keys, timestamp, and nonce with associated operations. Moreover, each actor can perform a set of operations related to communication, messages and cryptographic operations. The user of the visualization can use the GUI of the system to "instruct" one of the actors to perform certain operations.

Table 1. Protocol actors

Name	Explanation	Visual form
Alice	First participant in all protocols	
Bob	Second participant in all protocols	
Carol	Third participant in the three- and four party of protocols	
Dave	Fourth participant in the four party of protocols	
Mallory (Intruder)	Malicious active attacker (someone is stealing your message and making change to it)	
Trent	Trusted arbitrator (it might be a server, in this research protocols will be called a Key Distribution Center KDC)	

For each actor, user can generate a certain type of keys according to the stated protocols. Each actor has a unique color associated with his/her keys except for the secret key which is always black. Keys are given different design in order to distinguish between each them as illustrated in table 2.

Table 2. Keys Description

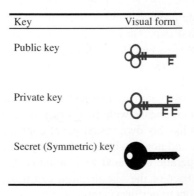

Key	Visual form
Public key	
Private key	
Secret (Symmetric) key	

5.3 Constructing Attacks over Protocols

Our tool will allow the user to construct possible attack that has in mind or to detect a new one. After the user specified the protocol in a number of scenes, the intruder actor "Intruder" is added. After each scene, the intruder section shows the possible knowledge that he could get from the sent or received message between the sender and receiver. Intruder will be able to construct and send malicious messages from this knowledge. The user can also decide whether the message is received by the intruder or not to make an explicit way for the intruder to build his knowledge.

5.4 An Example Interaction

Below is a demonstration of a run through a brief scenario using Diffe-Hellman protocol. This protocol allows two or more actors to exchange a secret key over a public communication channel without sharing any prior secrets. It consists of the following steps:

1. Alice generates a random number Na. the value of Na is assumed to be Alice's private key. Alice then computes G^{Na} where G is a number known by every actor. The value of G^{Na} is assumed to be the public key of Alice and is sent to Bob.
2. Bob generates a random number Nb. the value of Nb is assumed to be Bob's private key. Bob also computes G^{Nb}. The value of G^{Nb} is assumed to be the public key of Bob and is sent to Alice.
3. Alice compounds her private key Na with Bob's public key G^{Nb} and produces a secret key $K=((G^{Nb})^{Na})$ and Bob also do the same. He compounds her private key Nb with Alice's public key G^{Na} in such that $k=((G^{Na})^{Nb})$.
4. Both of them consider K as a symmetric key shared between each other and they exchange messages encrypted with this key.

Protocol Visualization. In order to visualize the Diffe-Hellman protocol, first, the user has to select the two actors that will run the key agreement protocol (mostly Alice and Bob). Then, the user will be prompted to input the two natural numbers to be used as private keys by the two actors. Finally, actors can exchange their own public keys with each other to get a copy of the public key of any other actor and combine it with his/her own private key. The combination of the two keys will result in the generation of a new secret key. Once generated, the new symmetric key can be used by the actor to encrypt a message and send it to another actor. The animated scenes progressively demonstrate the idea of the considered protocol is shown in Fig. 2.

Constructing Attacks over Protocols. Diffie-Hellman protocol is well-known to suffer from a man in the middle attack. The intruder can read every message over the network. So, every message is sent, first of all, to the intruder before being transmitted to the expected actor. In our tool, after the user specified the protocol in a number of scenes, the intruder actor "Intruder" is added. After each scene, the intruder section shows the possible knowledge that he could get from the sent or received message between the sender and receiver. Protocol demonstration by adding the intruder actor will be as follow:

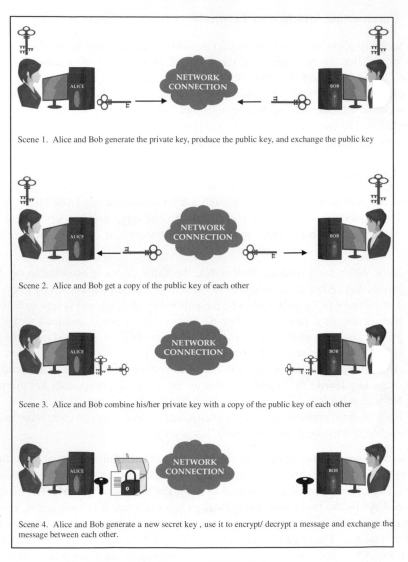

Fig. 2. The animated scenes of Diffie-Hellman protocol

1. Alice generates a random number Na. the value of Na is assumed to be Alice's private key. Alice computes G^{Na} where G is a number known by every actor. The value of G^{Na} is assumed to be the public key of Alice and is sent to Bob. At this moment, the intruder pretends to be Bob. He receives the message from Alice and generates a random number Ni. The value of Ni is assumed to be Intruder's private key. Intruder also computes G^{Ni}. The value of G^{Ni} is assumed to be the public key of Intruder and is sent to Bob.

2. Bob receives the intruder's public key and he thought it's from Alice. He generates a random number Nb. the value of Nb is assumed to be Bob's private key.

He computes G^{Nb}. The value of G^{Nb} is assumed to be the public key of Bob and is sent to Alice. Again, the intruder receives Bob's message and sends his public key G^{Ni} to Alice.

3. Alice compounds her private key Na with Intruder's public key G^{Ni} and produces a secret key shared with the intruder Kia and Bob also do the same. He compounds his private key Nb with Intruder's public key G^{Ni} and produces a secret key shared with the Intruder Kib. The intruder also establishes two keys: Kia and Kib.

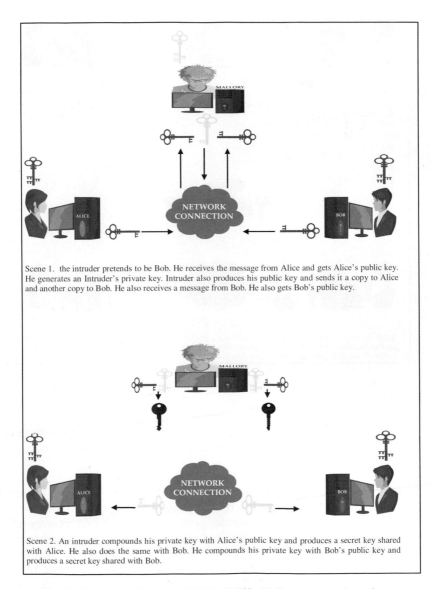

Scene 1. the intruder pretends to be Bob. He receives the message from Alice and gets Alice's public key. He generates an Intruder's private key. Intruder also produces his public key and sends it a copy to Alice and another copy to Bob. He also receives a message from Bob. He also gets Bob's public key.

Scene 2. An intruder compounds his private key with Alice's public key and produces a secret key shared with Alice. He also does the same with Bob. He compounds his private key with Bob's public key and produces a secret key shared with Bob.

Fig. 3. The animated scenes (1 & 2) of Diffie-Hellman protocol attack

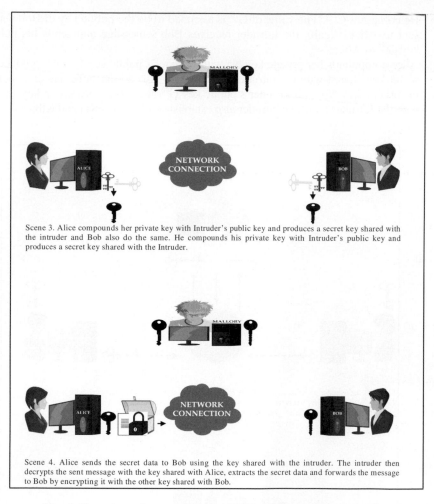

Scene 3. Alice compounds her private key with Intruder's public key and produces a secret key shared with the intruder and Bob also do the same. He compounds his private key with Intruder's public key and produces a secret key shared with the Intruder.

Scene 4. Alice sends the secret data to Bob using the key shared with the intruder. The intruder then decrypts the sent message with the key shared with Alice, extracts the secret data and forwards the message to Bob by encrypting it with the other key shared with Bob.

Fig. 4. The animated scenes (3 & 4) of Diffie-Hellman protocol attack

4. Finally, Alice sends the secret data to Bob using the key Kia shared with the intruder. The intruder then extracts the secret data and forwards it to Bob with the other key.

Protocol Visualization. The visualization of intruder part is similar to the previous visualization which was described in fig. 2 except of adding the Intruder (that is the Mallory actor) to the scenes. The intruder pretends to be Bob and receives the message from Alice. Once again, he pretends to be Alice and receives another message from Bob. The intruder sends his public key to both Alice and Bob. Then, Alice compounds her private key with Intruder's public key and produces a secret key shared with the intruder and Bob also do the same. He compounds his private key with Intruder's public key and produces a secret key shared with the Intruder. The intruder also establishes two secret keys. Alice sends the secret data to Bob using the key shared with the intruder. The intruder then extracts the secret data and forwards it to Bob with the other key. The animated scenes progressively demonstrate the protocol attack is shown in Fig. 3 and 4.

6 Discussion

The scenario is a concept used by several research communities in several different ways. Regarding to cryptographic protocol specifications, a scenario is hereby defined as a series of scenes or events. So, it is possible to consider the protocol as a series of scenes and each scene involve two or more actors and one message passing. Each scene is animated and run consequently. Therefore, an animation of protocol specifications using scenario-based approach certainly has the capability of improving the readability and understandability of protocol behavior and cryptographic protocol concepts.

7 Conclusions

The purpose of this paper is to propose an interactive visualization tool for teaching undergraduate students about security protocols concepts especially key distribution, multiple operations such as encryption/decryption and signed/unsigned operations, and possible protocol attacks. Timestamp and freshness operations are also described using high quality graphical user interface. The possibility of using animation for detecting possible attacks in cryptographic protocol is the most important objective to be improved in our tool design. We believe that such kind of tool can really enhance the understandability of cryptographic protocol operations and provide the possibility of detecting attacks using animation technique.

References

1. Gardner, H.E.: Frames of Mind: The Theory of Multiple Intelligences. Back Books, Inc., New York (1985)
2. Holliday, M.A.: Animation of computer networking concepts. Journal on Educational Resources in Computing (JERIC) 3 (2003)
3. Null, L., Rao, K.: CAMERA: Introducing Memory Concepts via visualization. ACM SIG-CSE Bulletin 37, 96–100 (2005)
4. Shene, C.-K.: ThreadMentor - A system for teaching multithreaded programming. ACM SIGCSE Bulletin 34, 229 (2002)
5. Kerren, A., Stasko, J.T.: Algorithm animation. In: Diehl, S. (ed.) Dagstuhl Seminar 2001. LNCS, vol. 2269, pp. 1–15. Springer, Heidelberg (2002)
6. Saraiya, P., et al.: Effective features of algorithm visualizations. ACM SIGCSE Bulletin 36, 382–386 (2004)
7. Schweitzer, D.: Designing interactive visualization tools for the graphics classroom. ACM SIGCSE Bulletin 24, 299–303 (1992)
8. Schweitzer, D., et al.: GRASP: a visualization tool for teaching security protocols. In: The Tenth Colloquium for Information Systems Security Education (2006)

9. Schweitzer, D., Baird, L.: The design and use of interactive visualization applets for teaching ciphers. In: Proceedings of the 7th IEEE Workshop on Information Assurance (2006)

10. Naps, T.L., et al.: Exploring the role of visualization and engagement in computer science education. ACM SIGCSE Bulletin 35, 131–152 (2003)

11. Carroll, J.M., Mack, R.L.: Metaphor, computing systems, and active learning. International Journal of Human-Computer Studies 51, 385–403 (1999)

12. Ortony, A.: Metaphor and Thought, 2nd edn. Cambridge University Press, Cambridge (1993)

13. Wozny, L.A.: The application of metaphor, analogy, and conceptual models in computer systems. Interacting with Computers 1, 273–283 (1989)

14. Alty, J.L., et al.: A framework for engineering metaphor at the user interface. Interacting with Computers 13, 301–322 (2000)

15. Baxley, T., et al.: LAN Attacker: A Visual Education Tool. In: Information Security Curriculum Development Conference, pp. 118–123. ACM Press, New York (2006)

16. Yuan, X., et al.: An animated learning tool for Kerberos authentication architecture. Journal of Computing Sciences in Colleges, the twelfth annual CCSC Northeastern Conference 22, 147–155 (2007)

17. Yuan, X., et al.: An Animated Simulator for Packet Sniffer. In: Proceedings of WECS7 - The Seventh Workshop on Education in Computer Security (2006)

18. Mayouf, M.A., Shukur, Z.: Features of a visualization tool for specification and analysis of security protocol. In: International Symposium on Information Technology, ITSim 2008, pp. 1–5 (2008)

19. Cattaneo, G., Santis, A.D., Petrillo, U.F.: Visualization of cryptographic protocols with GRACE. Journal of Visual Languages and Computing 19, 258–290 (2008)

20. Millen, J.K., Clark, S.C., Freedman, S.B.: The Interrogator: Protocol Secuity Analysis. IEEE Transactions on Software Engineering, SE 13, 274–288 (1987)

21. Brackin, S.H.: An Interface Specification Language For Automatically Analyzing Cryptographic Protocols. In: Proceedings of the 1997 Symposium on Network and Distributed System Security. IEEE Computer Society Press, Washington (1997)

22. Bonwell, C., Eison, J.: Active Learning: Creating Excitement in the Classroom. ASHE-ERIC Higher Education Report 1 (1991)

23. Schweitzer, D., Brown, W.: Interactive visualization for the active learning classroom. ACM SIGCSE Bulletin 39, 208–212 (2007)

24. Mayouf, M.A., Shukur, Z.: Animation of Natural Language Specifications of Authentication Protocol. Journal of Computer Science 4, 503–508 (2008)

Secure Minutiae-Based Fingerprint Templates Using Random Triangle Hashing

Zhe Jin[1], Andrew Beng Jin Teoh[2], Thian Song Ong[1], and Connie Tee[1]

[1] Faculty of Information Science & Technology
Multimedia University, Jalan Ayer Keroh Lama,
75450 Malacca, Malaysia
{jin.zhe,tsong,tee.connie}@mmu.edu.my
[2] School of Electrical and Electronic Engineering
Yonsei University, College of Engineering
262 Seongsanno, Seodaemun-gu, Seoul 120-749, Korea
bjteoh@yonsei.ac.kr

Abstract. Due to privacy concern on the widespread use of biometric authentication systems, biometric template protection has gained great attention in the biometric research recently. It is a challenging task to design a biometric template protection scheme which is anonymous, revocable and noninvertible while maintaining acceptable performance. Many methods have been proposed to resolve this problem, and cancelable biometrics is one of them. In this paper, we propose a scheme coined as Random Triangle Hashing which follows the concept of cancelable biometrics in the fingerprint domain. In this method, realignment of fingerprints is not required as all the minutiae are translated into a pre-defined 2 dimensional space based on a reference minutia. After that, the proposed Random Triangle hashing method is used to enforce the one-way property (non-invertibility) of the biometric template. The proposed method is resistant to minor translation error and rotation distortion. Finally, the hash vectors are converted into bit-strings to be stored in the database. The proposed method is evaluated using the public database FVC2004 DB1. An EER of less than 1% is achieved by using the proposed method.

Keywords: cancelable biometrics, fingerprint minutiae, template protection, random triangle hashing.

1 Introduction

Biometrics has become an attractive alternative to personal authentication over the traditional password-based authentication due to its ability to discriminate users based on biological or behavioral traits. However, the biometric authentication system imposes many inherent risks, which can lead to security breaches and privacy threats when they are underestimated. One of the main concerns for biometric security is the possible reveal of the user's private information due to the strong binding between the biometric template and the user's identity. Another concern is associated with the security of the template which cannot be reproduced or replaced when compromised.

H. Badioze Zaman et al. (Eds.): IVIC 2009, LNCS 5857, pp. 521–531, 2009.
© Springer-Verlag Berlin Heidelberg 2009

In literature, cancellable biometrics [1] and biometric cryptosystem [2] are the two major approaches for template protection. Cancellable biometrics applies an irreversible transform onto the biometric template to ensure the security and privacy of the actual biometric template. Hence, the actual biometric data is never stored in the user database but only its irreversible representation. On the other hand, biometric cryptosystem encompasses the design of template protection method by incorporating biometric authentication into cryptographic bounds, thus enabling the use of biometrics to derive an encrypted template for more stringent template security.

Theoretically, a template protection scheme must fulfill the following requirements:

1) Revocability. A new template can be reissued provided that the generation of the new template does not affect the performance of the existing system.

2) Non-invertibility. It must be impossible or computationally hard to obtain the original biometric template from the transformed or encrypted template and helper data.

3) Performance. The recognition performance, in terms of False Rejection Rate (FRR) or False Acceptance Rate (FAR) should not be poorer than the performance of using the original biometric data.

This paper presents a key-specific transformation technique for fingerprints without pre-alignment on the registration point of the fingerprint image. Our scheme involves minutiae translation, Random Triangle Hashing and bit-string conversion. The proposed technique makes it computationally hard to invert the transformed template without presenting the unique personal key. Besides, in the case that the transformed template is compromised; a new one can be regenerated by simply assigning a different key to the biometric template.

1.1 Related Work

Current biometrics researchers divided their work into two categories: biometric cryptosystems and cancelable biometrics.

Biometric cryptosystems is based on a cryptographic primitive by means of associating the biometric data with cryptographic keys [2]. Clancy et al. [3] and Uludag et al [4] proposed their methods based on fuzzy vault scheme. In their methods, the minutiae positions were used to encode and decode the secret (S). But there is an assumption that fingerprints used for locking and unlocking the vault are pre-aligned. Yang et al. [5] proposed a way of determining a reliable reference point based on the similarity indices of minutiae pairs by using several enrolled fingerprints. Based on this reference point, each minutia was represented by a polar coordinate and then used as locking and unlocking sets in the fuzzy vault scheme. Recently, Chung et al [6] proposed an automatic fingerprint alignment approach that used geometric hash tables.

For cancelable biometrics, the main idea is to store an irreversibly transformed version of the biometric template which provides a high privacy level by allowing multiple templates to be associated with the dame biometric data [7]. Ratha et al [1] described three transformation methods, Cartesian, polar and functional transformation. The Cartesian and polar transformation methods divided a fingerprint into sub-blocks and then scrambled those sub-blocks. In the functional transformation,

transformation was based on a Gaussian function. However, all the three methods required alignment before transformation. Teoh et al. [8] use an external confidential token to protect biometric templates; however, it will be vulnerable since the external token is easy to be lost, stolen or compromised. Farooq et al. [9] generated a bit-string from fingerprint minutiae representation based on minutiae triplets. The invariant features: the length of three sides, the three angles between the sides and minutiae orientations and the height of the triangles are extracted then quantized and hashed into bit-string (2^{24} bits). But this method required calculating all the possible triple invariant features which results additional computation costs. Shi et al [10] proposed a template protection scheme call Biomapping that integrate the feature extraction, noninvertible transform and anonymous query as a whole. But the latency for recognition and the size of the secure template are the concern in practices.

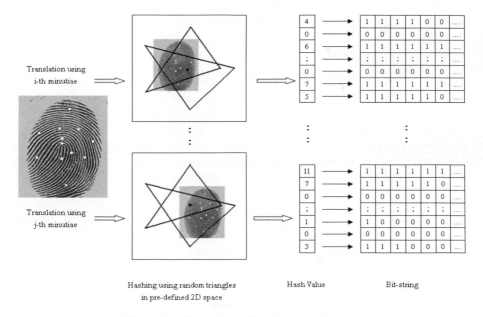

Fig. 1. Overall transformation of proposed scheme

2 Proposed Scheme

In this section, we describe a transformation scheme which can generate revocable bit-strings from a set of minutiae points. Fig. 1 shows the overall process flow of the proposed method. Most of the fingerprint researchers reported in the literature rely on a reliable registration point (core), but the location of this registration point is not always feasible in practices [1] [8] [11] [12]. Hence, in our proposed method, a reference minutia is chosen from the minutiae set, and the remaining minutiae are translated based on the selected reference minutiae. The application of this transformation technique is based on the fact that rotation and translation invariance can be achieved by using the same reference minutiae. After that, we calculate the number of minutiae that is confined in the random regions (triangles) to produce short hash vectors. A categorization based on the minutiae orientation is conducted in order to obtain more information for authentication. Finally, a binary histogram (bit-string) is generated from the short hash vectors. This bi-string is the final representation of the fingerprint template.

2.1 Rotation and Translation of Minutiae

Suppose that $M_i = [x_i, y_i, \theta_i]$ depicts the i-th minutiae, where x_i, y_i and θ_i ([0, 2π]) represent the Cartesian coordinates and the orientation of the minutiae. One of the minutiae is selected as the reference minutiae $M_r = [x_r, y_r, \theta_r]$. The rest of the minutiae are rotated and translated based on this reference minutiae. The transformed minutiae $M_i^t = [x_i^t, y_i^t, \theta_i^t]$ can be obtained as follow:

$$\begin{bmatrix} x_i^t \\ y_i^t \\ \theta_i^t \end{bmatrix} = \begin{bmatrix} \cos\theta_r & -\sin\theta_r & 0 \\ \sin\theta_r & \cos\theta_r & 0 \\ 0 & 0 & 1 \end{bmatrix} \times \begin{bmatrix} x_i - x_r \\ -(y_i - y_r) \\ \theta_i - \theta_r \end{bmatrix} + \begin{bmatrix} W \\ H \\ 0 \end{bmatrix} \tag{1}$$

where W and H represent the width and height of the pre-defined 2D space. In this paper, W and H are set to be double the size of the input fingerprint image. This is to ensure that the reference minutia is located in the center region of the pre-defined 2D space. Fig. 2 demonstrates the 2D space schematically.

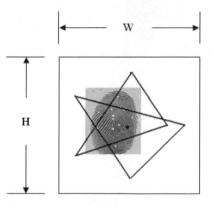

Fig. 2. Pre-defined 2D space

2.2 Random Triangle Hashing

The principle of Random Triangle Hashing is used to construct a hash string by counting the number of minutiae contained in random regions. In this research, triangle is used as the region shape due to its simplicity of implementation as it contains fewer vertexes as compared to other polygonal shapes. After that, the minutiae contained in each triangle will be used to generate the template for verification.

a)   Secret Key. Each subject is assigned a unique secret key. This secret key is the source of randomness used for determining the random triangles [13]. In other words, the secret key is a set of random number that indicates the location of the three vertexes that form the random triangles. Therefore, each subject has a unique template based on the different secret keys assigned to him/her. In the case when the template is compromised, a new key can be assigned to the subject to replace the old one.

b)   Hashing. Random Triangle Hashing counts the number of minutiae contained in the random region. It can be described as the transformation function which maps the minutiae representation into decimal vector. It can be described as the following function:

$$f : X \rightarrow Z^n \tag{2}$$

where $X = \{ X, Y, \theta \}$ and X_i, Y_i and θ_i represent the position and the orientation of a minutia and Z^n is an n-dimensional integer vector in which each element denotes the number of minutiae that can be found in a random triangle. Fig. 3 illustrates the conversion from minutiae representation into an integer vector. The number of random triangles formed, n is determined experimentally.

Random Triangle Hashing is based on the rational that the configuration of the minutiae on human finger is unique and can be used to distinguish each other. Besides, the key based hashing methodology with randomized triangle produces short hash strings that cannot be used to reconstruct the original fingerprint without knowledge of the secret key [13].

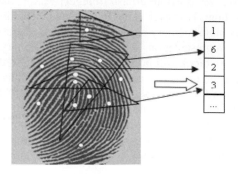

Fig. 3. Conversion from minutiae representation into integer vector

We conducted a minutiae orientation based blocking mechanism by using the minutiae orientation information. We blocked/divided the minutiae orientation into fixed-sized ranges, and count the number of minutiae points falling in a specific range. For example, let say there are five minutiae contain in the random triangle shown in Fig. 4. We take the orientation of each minutia and count the number of minutiae falling in the pre-defined orientation range. From the figure, we find that among the five minutiae, one of them falls in the range $[0,60)$, one in $[120,180)$, two in $[240,300)$, and one in $[300,360)$. These numbers form the building block for bit string generation in the next procedure. Note that the orientation range without any corresponding minutiae count is set to zero. We repeat the same process for the remaining triangles. The fixed-length (6 digits) vectors generated from each triangle are concatenated to form the hash vector used to construct the final feature representation in bit-string format.

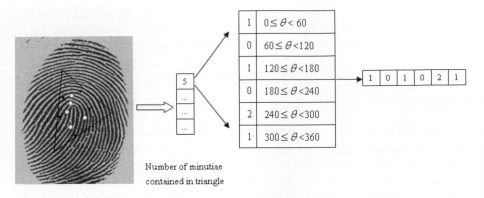

Number of minutiae
contained in triangle

Fig. 4. Blocking of minutiae orientation detail

2.3 Bit String Generation

In the previous section, we generate a hash (integer) vector that is acquired through Random Triangle Hashing. However using integer representation for template is not secure and it occupies more memory space in the database. Our solution is to convert the integer into binary representation. To do this, a fixed binary block is first initialized to zeros. This binary block will be set to ones according to the integer in the hash vector. For example, if the integer in a hash block is 5, its binary counterpart will be 1111100000. By repeating this process for the remaining hash blocks, all the integers in the hash vector will be converted into binary representation. We call this process as Bit-Block Coding. The length resultant binary block is d x n x m, where d refers to the number of hash blocks for each triangle, n denotes the total number of triangles formed, and m is the number of bits used to represent the binary counterpart of each hash block.

2.4 Calculating the Dissimilarity Score

In a perfect environment, the two 1 dimension bit strings generated based on the same reference minutiae will be the same. However, we have no information to locate the corresponding minutiae used for alignment in the enrolled template and query template. Therefore, we need to compare all the 1 dimensional bit-strings between the enrolled and query sets to determine the closest pair. The dissimilarity score between the enrolled bit-strings (B) and query bit-strings ($\overline{B}$) are calculated as follows:

$$Score(i, j) = \frac{\sum_{k=1}^{d}\left(B_{j,k} \oplus \overline{B_{i,k}}\right)}{L} \tag{3}$$

where $\oplus$ represents the XOR operation, $B_{j,k}$ and $\overline{B}_{i,k}$ denote the k-th bit in B_j and $\overline{B}_i$, L represents the length of B_j and $\overline{B}_i$. Fig. 5 shows the comparisons between the query and enrolled bit-strings. A matrix $Score(i, j)$ is used to store the dissimilarity scores. Next we calculate the mean of the minimum distance for each column in $Score(i, j)$ and denote it as MeanCol, and compute the mean of the minimum distance of each row in $Score(i, j)$ and signify it as MeanRow. We choose the minimum MeanCol and MeanRow as the final score.

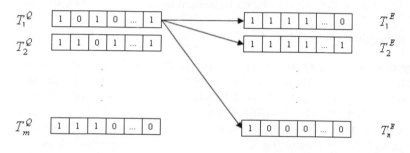

Fig. 5. Comparison between the query and the enrolled template

3   Experimental Analysis

The database, FVC2004 DB1 [14] that is available on the public domain is used for our test. It consists of 100 different users and each user has 8 fingerprint images. The minutiae features X, Y coordinates and orientation are obtained by using the trial version of VeriFinger Standard SDK [15]. We performed two sets of experiments, namely genuine test and impostor test. For the test on the genuine set, we compared the enroll fingerprint and the query fingerprint among the *same* user. For the test on imposters, the scores of imposter are generated by comparing the enroll fingerprint and the query fingerprint from the *different* users. We used false acceptance rate (FAR), false reject rat (FRR) and equal error rate (EER) to evaluate the proposed algorithm while the genuine and imposter distribution in section 3.3 illustrate the performance of the proposed algorithm graphically.

3.1 Number of Random Triangles Determination

Theoretically, we will achieve better result when more random triangles are used. But in practice, we have to strike a balance between accuracy and computational requirements. Table 1 lists the performance by using different amount of random triangles.

Table 1. Equal Error Rate (EER) of different number of random triangles

Number of Random Triangles	EER
10 Random Triangles	2.81%
15 Random Triangles	0.32%
20 Random Triangles	0.20%

We observe from Table 1, that the EER drops with the increase of random triangles. The reason for this is that when more random triangle is used, more information could be extracted so that the feature became more discriminative. But in real-time scenario, computational performance should also be considered. In this case, we select parameter of 20 random triangles to be used in our subsequent experiments.

3.2 Revocability

In the case of lost secret key where the key or the transformed template is compromised, we should be able to cancel the template and key and assign the individual a new key and hence template [**Error! Reference source not found.**]. In order to test this statement, we generated n different keys for each individual, and used these keys to generate n binary templates. These binary templates are different from each other, even though they represent the same individual. In this experiment, we achieve an EER of less than 1%. This does not only vindicate the claim of revocability, it also solves the problem of cross-matching in databases [9]. Fig.6 shows the sample results obtained using different keys.

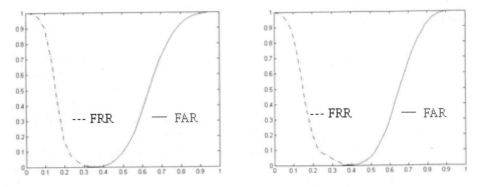

Fig. 6. Sample results (EER) obtained using different keys

3.3 Verification

In this experiment, we assume that the secrete keys are never lost, and each individual is assigned a unique key that is stored in the database. Based on the secrete keys, the enrolled binary template and test binary vector are generated and the scores for verification were calculated using Formula 3. By using these scores, we plot the genuine and imposter distribution as shown in Fig. 7. An EER (equal error rate) of less than 1% was achieved on public database FVC2004 DB1 [14].

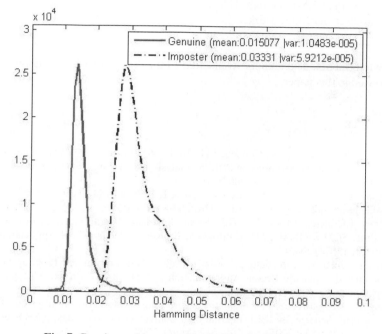

Fig. 7. Genuine and imposter distribution for FVC2004 DB1

3.4 Security of Proposed Method

When we assume that a template is revealed, the adversary has to further reconstruct the corresponding hash vector. However, the template revealed is only randomized version of the original data. Assume the number of random triangles is 20 and bit block is 240 bits, then the total length of the template will be 4800 bits. This makes it computational difficulty to invert the original hash vector. In case the hash vector has been reconstructed, the adversary will also have no clue to determine the exact location of each minutia since we just count the number of minutiae contained in the random triangle.

4 Conclusion

We have presented a new scheme for one-way biometric transformation that uses randomized triangles to compute fingerprint hashes. In the template protection domain, our method fulfills three requirements, namely performance in terms of False Rejection Rate (FRR) and False Acceptance Rate (FAR), non-invertibility and revocability. Another advantage of our method is that pre-alignment of fingerprint is not required. Our further work would emphasis on a scenario wherein secret key is utilized by an adversary to gain access to the system, coined as stolen-token scenario. In the current work, EER more than 10% is reported for stolen-token case. We will look into this issue in our future work.

Acknowledgments. The authors would like to thank Chulhan Lee in contribution of data set used in this paper.

References

1. Ratha, N.K., Chikkerur, S., Connell, J.H., Bolle, R.M.: Generating Cancelable Fingerprint Templates. IEEE Transactions on Pattern Analysis and Machine Intelligence, Special Issue on Biometrics 29(4), 561–572 (2007)
2. Uludag, U., Pankanti, S., Prabhakar, S., Anil, K.J.: Biometric Cryptosystems: Issues and Challenges. Proceedings of the IEEE 92(6), 948–960 (2004)
3. Clancy, T.C., Kiyavash, N., Lin, D.J.: Secure Smartcard-based Fingerprint Authentication. In: Proc. SCM SIGMM 2993 Multimedia, Biometrics Methods and Applications Workshop, pp. 45–52 (2003)
4. Uludag, U., Pankanti, S., Jain, A.: Fuzzy Vault for Fingerprints. In: Proc. of Audio- and Video-based Biometric Person Authentication (AVBPA), Rye Brook, NY, pp. 310–319 (July 2005)
5. Yang, S., Verbauwhede, I.: Automatic Secure Fingerprint Verification System Based on Fuzzy Vault Scheme. In: IEEE International Conference on Acoustics, Speech, and Signal Processing (ICASSP 2005), pp. 609–612 (March 2005)
6. Chung, Y., Moon, D., Lee, S., Jung, S., Kim, T., Ahn, D.: Automatic Alignment of Fingerprint Features for Fuzzy Fingerprint Vault, Information Security and Cryptology. In: Feng, D., Lin, D., Yung, M. (eds.) CISC 2005, vol. 3822, pp. 358–369. Springer, Heidelberg (2005)
7. Ratha, N., Connell, J., Bolle, R.: Enhancing security and privacy in biometrics-based authentication systems. IBM Systems Journal 40(3), 614–634 (2001)
8. Teoh, A.B.J., Goh, A., Ngo, D.C.L.: Random Multispace Quantization as an Analytic Mechanism for BioHashing of Biometric and Random Identity Inputs. IEEE Transactions on PAMI 28(12), 1892–1901 (2006)
9. Farooq, F., Bolle, R., Ruud, M., Jea, T., Ratha, N.: Anonymous and Revocable Fingerprint Recognition. In: Computer Vision and Pattern Recognition, CVPR 2007, June 17-22, pp. 1–7 (2007)
10. Shi, J.Y., You, Z.Y., Gu, M., Lam, K.Y.: Biomapping Privacy Trustworthy Biometrics Using Noninvertible and Discriminable Constructions. In: IEEE International Conference on Pattern Recognition, ICPR 2008 (2008)
11. Teoh, A., Ngo, D., Goh, A.: Biohashing: two factor authentication featuring fingerprint data and tokenised random number. Pattern Recognition 37(11), 2245–2255 (2004)

12. Ratha, N., Connell, J., Bolle, R., Chikkerur, S.: Cancelable Biometrics: A Case Study in Fingerprints. In: Proc. ICPR 2006, vol. 4, pp. 370–373 (2006)
13. Jakubowski, M.H., Venkatesan, R.: Randomized Radon Transforms for Biometric Authentication via Fingerprint Hashing. In: Proceedings of the 2007 ACM workshop on Digital Rights Management (2007)
14. Third International Fingerprint Verification Competition (2004),
    http://bias.csr.unibo.it/fvc2004/
15. Neurotechnologija, Inc. VeriFinger (2006),
    http://www.neurotechnology.com/verifinger.html

Combinatorial Color Space Models for Skin Detection in Sub-continental Human Images

Shah Mostafa Khaled, Md. Saiful Islam, Md. Golam Rabbani,
Mirza Rehenuma Tabassum, Alim Ul Gias, Md. Mostafa Kamal,
Hossain Muhammad Muctadir, Asif Khan Shakir, Asif Imran, and Saiful Islam

Institute of Information Technology, University of Dhaka, Dhaka-1000, Bangladesh
Department of Statistics, Biostatistics and Informatics, University of Dhaka, Dhaka-1000,
Bangladesh
khaled@univdhaka.edu

Abstract. Among different color models HSV, HLS, YIQ, YCbCr, YUV, etc. have been most popular for skin detection. Most of the research done in the field of skin detection has been trained and tested on human images of African, Mongolian and Anglo-Saxon ethnic origins, skin colors of Indian sub-continentals have not been focused separately. Combinatorial algorithms, without affecting asymptotic complexity can be developed using the skin detection concepts of these color models for boosting detection performance. In this paper a comparative study of different combinatorial skin detection algorithms have been made. For training and testing 200 images (skin and non skin) containing pictures of sub-continental male and females have been used to measure the performance of the combinatorial approaches, and considerable development in success rate with True Positive of 99.5% and True Negative of 93.3% have been observed.

Keywords: image processing, color space model, color segmentation, skin detection.

1 Introduction

Computer vision is one out of many areas that wants to understand the process of human functionality and copy that process with intention to complement human life with intelligent machines. For better human–computer interaction it is necessary for the machine to see people. Automatic skin detection has been intensively studied for human-related recognition systems. Human skin color has been used and proved to be an effective feature in many applications from human face detection to content prediction to motion tracking. The main challenge in skin detection is to make the recognition robust to the large variations in appearance of skin that may occur, like in color and shape, effects of occultation, intensity, color, location of light source, etc. Imaging noise can appear as speckles of skin like color, and many other objects like wood, cooper and some clothes are often confused as skin.

In general human skin is characterized by a combination of red and melanin (yellow, brown) and there is somewhat a range of hue for skin and saturation that

H. Badioze Zaman et al. (Eds.): IVIC 2009, LNCS 5857, pp. 532–542, 2009.

represent skin-like pixels. More deeply colored skins are with more melanin, the saturation is more when the skin is yellowish [1]. The main goal of skin detection and classification is to build a decision rule that discriminate between skin and non-skin pixels. Identifying skin color pixels involves finding a range of values for which most skin pixels would fall in a given color space. The target is to achieve a high detection rate and low false positive rate, that is, skin pixels must be detected in maximum and the amount of non-skin pixels classified as skin should be minimized.

Among different skin detection research that have been published, the well-known statistical color models to estimate skin density in chrominance space are the single Gaussian model [4, 5, 6], histograms [2, 3], and others. The histogram model based on local approximation is simple and fast but becomes effective only when training data is sufficiently large to be dense. Moreover, it requires additional memory to keep the histograms. A single Gaussian model, although is simple and fast, it however does not adequately represent the variance of the skin distribution where illumination condition varies.

Most works done in the area of skin detection have been concentrated on detecting skins of European, Black or East Asian ethnicities, whereas less focus have been concentrated to detect Indian-like skins. This paper makes a comparative study of three algorithms that use three different color models for statistical skin detection. For training and testing of algorithms used in this study, 200 skin and non skin images of people from Indian sub-continent some of which have been captured locally and others collected randomly from the Internet have been used. The prime focus of experimentation is to find out image properties that are best suited for searching Indian skin in images with cluttered background. This research also focus on some combinatorial algorithms that consider parameters from different color models for boosting and confirmation of performance, and compares the performance of combinatorial approaches to skin detection to that of approaches that use single color model.

The paper is organized as follows: section 2 covers the relevant works on skin detection, section 3 describes the approaches used, section 4 describes the experimental setup and makes an analysis of performance of given algorithms and section 5 makes the concluding remarks.

2   Related Works

Human skin color has been used to identify and differentiate the skin. This has been proven as useful methods applicable in face recognition, identification of nude and pornographic images [7, 2] and also such image processing tasks have been used extensively by intelligence agencies [8].

A number of image processing models have been applied for skin detection. The major paradigms included heuristic and recognizing patterns which were used to obtain accurate results. Among various types of skin detection methods, the ones that make use of the skin color as a tool for the detection of skin is considered to be the most effective [9]. Human skins have a characteristic color and it was a commonly accepted idea driven by logic to design a method based on skin color identification. The problem arose with the provision of different varieties of human skin found in different parts of the world. A number of published researches included various skin models and detection techniques [9, 10, 11], however, none came up with complete accuracy.

There have been many problematic issues in the domain of skin detection. The choice of color space, the model of precise skin color distribution, and the way of mechanizing color segmentation research for the detection of human skin. Most researches have been focused on pixel based skin recognition, classifying each pixel either as skin or non skin. Each pixel is considered to be an individual unit [11]. Pixel-base skin recognition is considered to be one of the finest models that under normal conditions give high level of accuracy at the detection phase of the process. Due to its high applicability and efficiency, some color models are used extensively in the arena of skin detection. These models make use of pixel based skin recognition using a model such as RGB [12]. The RGB model makes use of the three colors red, green and blue to identify the chrominance. Then using an efficient model the necessary range is used and applied to a selected photo to determine the presence of skin. Skin color varies depending on ethnicity and region, therefore additional work must to address the issue.

There is another model called the region based method. This method was applied by [13, 14, 15]. In this method the researchers considered the spatial method of skin pixels, and took them into account during the detection phase with the target of maximizing efficiency. As a contradiction to the fact that different people have different types of skin colors, it is found that the major difference does not lie in their chrominance; rather it is determined by intensity to a large extent. The simplest color models useful for intensity invariant skin detection are HSV [16], YUV [17] or YIQ [18]. The HSV model is an effective mechanism to determine human skin based on hue and saturation. Other efficient models are YUV and YIQ which follow the same brand of modeling using the RGB color space.

Fig. 2.1(a) depicts the color cluster of hue for Indian sub-continental skin. This has been found by plotting the hue values of a number of randomly chosen human skin images. Fig. 2.1(b) and 2.1(c) shows the Indian sub-continental skin color clusters using YUV and YIQ color models.

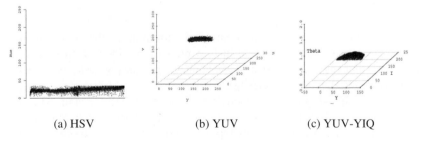

(a) HSV   (b) YUV   (c) YUV-YIQ

Fig. 2.1. Indian sub-continental skin color cluster in different color models

This paper mainly focuses on the use of YUV, YIQ and HSV models to determine skin. It also focuses on the effectiveness of the models and their combinations for confirmation and maximization with respect to Indian sub-continental skin.

3 Color Models for Skin Detection

The skin color detection significantly depends on the chosen color model. The RGB color space is default in many image formats. Color space transformation can be applied to reduce the overlap between skin and non-skin pixels and will thereby aid skin pixel classification and achieve high accuracy in varying illumination conditions.

3.1 The HSV Color Space

Hue-saturation based color spaces were introduced when there was a need for the user to specify color properties numerically. *Hue* defines the dominant color (such as red, green, purple and yellow) of an area; *saturation* measures the colorfulness of an area in proportion to its brightness. The "intensity", "lightness" or "value" is related to the color luminance [19]. Hue can be used as a decision parameter to detect human skin. Algorithm 3.1 presents the HSV color model based skin detection procedure.

Algorithm 3.1: SkinHSV( )
Input Parameters
      Image: Input Image
      T_1 and T_2: Thresholds, discussed in Section 4
Input Parameters
      Image: Image with skin pixels detected
Procedure
1.   Read the image header, BMPhead
2.   **for** i = 1 to BMPhead.height
3.   **for** j = 1 to BMPhead.width
4.   Read pixel Color
5. $mx = \max(Color \cdot R, \quad Color \cdot G, \quad Color \cdot B)$
6. $mn = \min(Color \cdot R, \quad Color \cdot G, \quad Color \cdot B)$
7. $\partial = mx - mn$
8.   If ($mx = Color \cdot R$) then
9. $h = (Color \cdot G - Color \cdot B)/\delta$
10.   Else If ($mx = Color \cdot G$) then
11. $h = 2 + (Color \cdot B - Color \cdot R)/\delta$
12.   Else
13. $h = 4 + (Color \cdot R - Color \cdot G)/\delta$
14.   End if
15. $h = h \times 60$
16.   If(h<0) then
17. $h = h + 360$
18.   End if
19.   if($T_1 \le h \le T_2$) then
20.   detect pixel as skin
21.   end if
22.   end
23. end

3.2 The YUV Color Space

YUV is the color space used in the PAL system of television broadcasting which is the standard in most of Europe and some other places. The RGB values are transformed into YUV values using the formulation given below:

$$\begin{bmatrix} Y \\ U \\ V \end{bmatrix} = \begin{bmatrix} 16 \\ 128 \\ 128 \end{bmatrix} + \begin{bmatrix} 0.257 & 0.504 & 0.098 \\ -0.148 & -0.291 & 0.439 \\ 0.439 & -0.368 & -0.071 \end{bmatrix} \begin{bmatrix} R \\ G \\ B \end{bmatrix}$$

The chromaticity information is encoded in the U and V components [20]. Hue and saturation are gotten by the following transformation.

$$ch = \sqrt{|U|^2 + |V|^2} \quad \text{and} \quad \theta = \tan^{-1}\left(|V|/|U|\right)$$

θ represents hue, which is defined as the angle of vector in YUV color space. Ch represents saturation, which is defined as the mode of U and V [20]. Algorithm 3.2 presents the YUV color model based skin detection procedure.

```
Algorithm 3.2: SkinYUV( )
    Input Parameters
        Image: Input Image
        T₁ and T₂: Thresholds, discussed in Section 4
    Input Parameters
        Image: Image with skin pixels detected
    Procedure
1.   Read the image header, BMPhead
2.   for i = 1 to BMPhead.height
3.     for j = 1 to BMPhead.width
4.       Read pixel Color
5.         y = 0.257×Color·R + 0.504×Color·G + 0.098×Color·B + 16
6.         u = −0.148×Color·R − 0.291×Color·G + 0.439×Color·B + 128
7.         v = 0.439×Color·R − 0.368×Color·G − 0.071×Color·B + 128
8.         If ( T₁ ≤ y ≤ T₂ & T₃ ≤ u ≤ T₄ & T₅ ≤ v ≤ T₆ ) then
9.           detect pixel as skin
10.          end if
11.    end
12.  end
```

3.3 The YIQ Color Space

Like YUV color space, YIQ is the color primary system adopted by NTSC for color TV broadcasting. Conversion from RGB to YIQ may be accomplished using the color matrix:

$$\begin{bmatrix} Y \\ I \\ Q \end{bmatrix} = \begin{bmatrix} 0.299 & 0.587 & 0.114 \\ 0.596 & -0.274 & -0.322 \\ 0.211 & -0.523 & 0.312 \end{bmatrix} \begin{bmatrix} R \\ G \\ B \end{bmatrix}$$

I is the red-orange axis, Q is roughly orthogonal to I. The less I value means the less blue-green and the more yellow [20]. Through some experiments, we find that the combination of *YUV* and *YIQ* color space is more robust than each other. Algorithm 3.3 presents the YUV and YIQ color model based skin detection procedure.

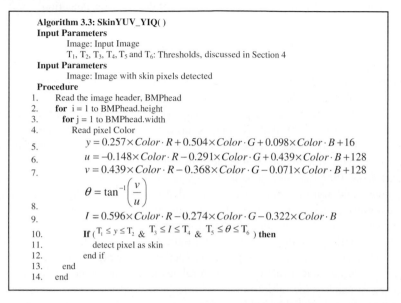

Algorithm 3.3: SkinYUV_YIQ( )
Input Parameters
        Image: Input Image
        T_1, T_2, T_3, T_4, T_5 and T_6: Thresholds, discussed in Section 4
Input Parameters
        Image: Image with skin pixels detected
Procedure
1.   Read the image header, BMPhead
2.   **for** i = 1 to BMPhead.height
3.   **for** j = 1 to BMPhead.width
4.   Read pixel Color
5. $y = 0.257 \times Color \cdot R + 0.504 \times Color \cdot G + 0.098 \times Color \cdot B + 16$
6. $u = -0.148 \times Color \cdot R - 0.291 \times Color \cdot G + 0.439 \times Color \cdot B + 128$
7. $v = 0.439 \times Color \cdot R - 0.368 \times Color \cdot G - 0.071 \times Color \cdot B + 128$
8. $\theta = \tan^{-1}\left(\dfrac{v}{u}\right)$
9. $I = 0.596 \times Color \cdot R - 0.274 \times Color \cdot G - 0.322 \times Color \cdot B$
10.   **If** ($T_1 \le y \le T_2$ & $T_3 \le I \le T_4$ & $T_5 \le \theta \le T_6$) **then**
11.   detect pixel as skin
12.   end if
13.   end
14. end

3.4 Combinatorial Approach

Each color model discussed above has different success rates in skin pixel detection. Table 4.1, 4.2 and 4.3 indicates that one color model is suitable for identifying skin pixels while another is appropriate for filtering out non-skin pixels. One has less false positives than others while another has more false negatives. It is possible to combine multiple color models to enhance the true positives and true negatives as well as diminish the false positives and false negatives. The model that we have used in our experimentation is shown in Fig. 3.1.

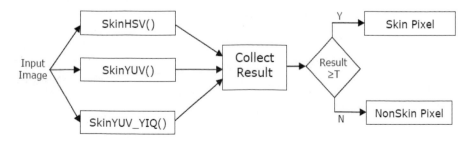

Fig. 3.1. Combinatorial approach of skin pixel detection

The input image is fed to algorithms with different color models (algorithms can be executed in parallel to reduce detection time) and their results are collected. The accumulated results are then checked against threshold and detected as skin and non-skin pixels. We believe combinatorial approach will perform better than executing each model standalone and will thereby enhance the confidence of the detection.

4 Experimental Setup and Performance Analysis

The comparative study presented in this paper measures the human images of Indian sub-continental region. It considered 200 color images for training and testing of given algorithms and evaluates performance. There were 60 images where all the image area was covered by skin, 70 images did not have any skin and the other 70 had both human skin and other objects. A total of 120 images were used in the training phase of the experimentation, while the other 80 was used to test the performance. The data acquisition has been done in two ways. A digital camera was used to capture some human and non-human images, while other images for testing and training have been randomly collected from the Internet. The images used for training and testing were under different lighting and illumination conditions.

The first challenge in the study is to find out effective range for thresholds of decision parameters (as discussed in previous section) on which the detection of skin depends. Different statistical tools of central tendency and standard deviation have been used to reach some initial ranges of threshold used for skin recognition. Algorithms with these initial thresholds were trained on a collection of test images. The range of these thresholds was heuristically modified to optimize the value range and get better detection rate. Table 4.1, 4.2, 4.3 provides instances such threshold optimization with respect to false positives, true positives, true negatives and false negatives.

Table 4.1. Threshold optimization for detection based on HSV color model

Range	True Positive	True Negative	False Positive	False Negative
2<h<45	95.4	81.8	18.2	4.6
4<h<40	93.2	83.6	16.4	6.8
5<h<35	91.1	88.1	11.9	8.9
10<h<30	84.8	90.2	9.8	15.2

Table 4.2. Threshold optimization for detection based on YUV color model

Range	True Positive	True Negative	False Positive	False Negative
75<y<185 & 105<u<150 & 100<v<180	92.2	81.2	18.8	12.8
70<y<175 & 95<u<145 & 95<v<170	91.4	84.4	15.6	8.6
65<y<170 & 85<u<140 & 85<v<160	88.3	88.4	11.6	11.7
60<y<160 & 80<u<135 & 75<v<150	86.8	91.3	8.7	13.2

Fig. 4.1 shows the example outputs of skin like region segmentation of different test images with different color model based algorithms. It can be observed that all the algorithms were able to detect the majority of the skin area in the images.

Table 4.3. Threshold optimization for detection based on YUV-YIQ color model

Range	True Positive	True Negative	False Positive	False Negative
75<y<190 &10<I<122 & -60< θ <170	96.8	75.5	24.5	3.2
75<y<185 &15<I<112 & -54< θ <160	94.5	77.3	22.7	5.5
70<y<175 & 20 <I<102 & -48< θ <150	91.2	81.5	18.5	8.8
65<y<170 & 25<I<102 & -42< θ <140	89.3	85.7	14.3	10.7

As can be observed from the figure, there are some areas of non skin images detected as skin by the algorithms, these are False Positives. There are, however, some skin areas in some images that could not be rightly detected as skin by the given algorithms, these are False Negatives. The graphs in Fig. 4.2- 4.5 present the performance of the discussed algorithms on randomly chosen 20 images.

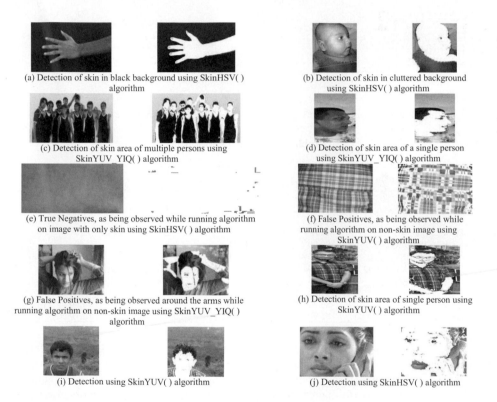

(a) Detection of skin in black background using SkinHSV( ) algorithm

(b) Detection of skin in cluttered background using SkinHSV( ) algorithm

(c) Detection of skin area of multiple persons using SkinYUV_YIQ( ) algorithm

(d) Detection of skin area of a single person using SkinYUV_YIQ( ) algorithm

(e) True Negatives, as being observed while running algorithm on image with only skin using SkinHSV( ) algorithm

(f) False Positives, as being observed while running algorithm on non-skin image using SkinYUV( ) algorithm

(g) False Positives, as being observed around the arms while running algorithm on non-skin image using SkinYUV_YIQ( ) algorithm

(h) Detection of skin area of single person using SkinYUV( ) algorithm

(i) Detection using SkinYUV( ) algorithm

(j) Detection using SkinHSV( ) algorithm

Fig. 4.1. Example of skin detection

Table 4.4 Summarizes the performance of given algorithms tested on 80 images with optimized thresholds with respect to success parameters – true positive, true negative, false positive, false negative.

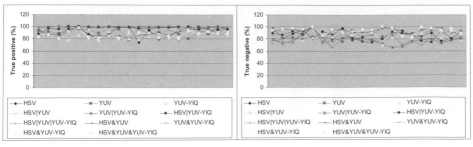

Fig. 4.2. True positives   **Fig. 4.3.** True negatives

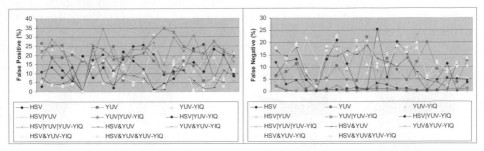

Fig. 4.4. False positives   **Fig. 4.5.** False negatives

Table 4.4. Average Performance

Algorithm	True Positive(%)	True Negative(%)	False Positive(%)	False Negative(%)
HSV	91.10	88.10	11.90	8.90
YUV	91.40	84.40	15.60	8.60
YUV & YIQ	91.20	81.50	18.50	8.80
HSV | YUV	98.80	78.95	21.05	1.20
YUV | YUV-YIQ	99.40	78.00	22.00	0.60
YUV-YIQ | HSV	97.60	85.10	14.90	2.40
HSV | YUV | YUV-YIQ	99.50	78.90	21.10	0.50
HSV & YUV	88.58	93.20	06.80	11.42
YUV & YUV-YIQ	89.06	89.90	10.10	10.94
YUV-YIQ & HSV	86.20	91.60	08.40	13.80
HSV& YUV & YUV-YIQ	86.90	93.29	06.70	13.10

From the above table, considering the outcome on experimentation on different skin detection algorithms, trained using 120 images and tested on 80 separate images, we see that combinatorial approaches to Indian sub-continental skin recognition showed the better performance. It is evident from Table 4.4 that combinatorial approaches are suitable to meet diversified application specific requirements. For example, combinatorial approach (HSV & YUV) has very low false positive and relatively lower true positive, hence is better suitable for applications where careful detection of skin pixels is more required. On the contrary, combinatorial approach (HSV | YUV), although has good true positive, it has greater false positive and is suitable for applications that need to detect maximum of skin pixels.

5 Conclusion

This paper presents a study for accurate skin-color detection. In the first step, three algorithms based on HSV, YUV and YIQ color models have been tested for detecting skin pixels. Combinatorial skin detection algorithms have been developed using the detection parameters like hue, Y, U, V, θ, etc. to boost the performance of detection. In comparison with traditional methods based on unique color models, the experimental results indicate that the combinatorial methods achieve a significantly lower false-positive and false-negative rates for skin detection. Another observation of this research is to cluster the skin color for Indian sub-continental human images under different lighting conditions. One of the directions that future research might take is to develop better heuristic ways to integrate multi-cues, including color, texture, spatial and shape, into an even more powerful classifier for the skin detection task.

References

1. Rossotti, H.: Colour: Why the World isn't Grey. Princeton University Press, Princeton (1983)
2. Jones, M.J., Rehg, J.M.: Statistical Color Models with Application to Skin Detection. In: CVPR (1999)
3. Wu, H., Chen, Q., Yachida, M.: Face Detection from Color Images Using a Fuzzy Pattern Matching Method. IEEE Trans. Pattern Analysis and Machine Intelligence (1999)
4. Yang, J., Lu, W., Waibel, A.: Skin-Color Modeling and Adaptation. In: Proc. of ACCV (1998)
5. Menser, B., Muller, F.: Face Detection in Color Images using Principal Component Analysis. In: Proc. of Image Processing and its Applications (1999)
6. Fan, L., Sung, K.K.: Face Detection and Pose Alignment Using Colour, Shape and Texture Information. In: Proc. of Visual Surveillance (2000)
7. Fleck, M., Forsyth, D.A., Bregler, C.: Finding Naked People. In: Buxton, B.F., Cipolla, R. (eds.) ECCV 1996. LNCS, vol. 1065, pp. 592–602. Springer, Heidelberg (1996)
8. Ahlberg, J.: A System for Face Localization and Facial Feature Extraction. Technical Report, LiTH-ISY-R-2172, Linkoping University (1999)
9. Zarit, B.D., Super, B.J., Quek, F.K.H.: Comparison of Five Color Models in Skin Pixel Classification. In: ICCV 1999 Int'l Workshop on recognition, analysis and tracking of faces and gestures in real-time systems, pp. 58–63 (1999)
10. Terrillon, J.C., Shirazi, M.N., Fukamachi, H., Akamatsu, S.: Comparative Performance of Different Skin Chrominance Models and Chrominance Spaces for the Automatic Detection of Human Faces in Color Images. In: Proc. of Intl. Conf. on Face and Gesture Recognition, pp. 54–61 (2000)
11. Brand, J., Mason, J.: A Comparative Assessment of three Approaches to Pixel Level Human Skin-Detection. In: Proc. of Intl. Conf. on Pattern Recognition, vol. 1, pp. 1056–1059 (2000)
12. Albiol, A., Torres, L., Delp, E.J.: Optimum Color Spaces for Skin Detection. In: Proc. of Intl. Conf. on Image Processing, vol. 1, pp. 122–124 (2001)
13. Kruppa, H., Bauer, M.A., Schiele, B.: Skin Patch Detection in Real-World Images. In: Van Gool, L. (ed.) DAGM 2002, vol. 2449, pp. 109–117. Springer, Heidelberg (2002)

14. Yang, M., Ahuja, N.: Gaussian Mixture Model for Human Skin Color and its Application in Image and Video Databases. In: Proc. SPIE: Conf. on Storage and Retrieval for Image and Video Databases (SPIE 1999), vol. 3656, pp. 458–466 (1999)
15. Gomez, G., Morales, E.F.: Automatic Feature Construction and a Simple Rule Induction Algorithm for Skin Detection. In: Proc. of ICML Workshop on Machine Learning in Computer Vision, pp. 31–38 (2002)
16. Lee, J.Y., Yoo, S.I.: An Elliptical Boundary Model for Skin Color Detection. In: Proc. of Intl. Conf. on Imaging Science, Systems, and Technology (2002)
17. Chai, D., Bouzerdoum, A.: A Bayesian Approach to Skin Color Classification in YCbCr Color Space. In: Proc. of IEEE Region Ten Conf. (TENCON 2000), vol. 2, pp. 421–424 (2000)
18. Martinkauppi, B., Soriano, M.: Basis Functions of the Color Signals of Skin under Different Illuminants. In: 3rd Intl. Conf. on Multi-spectral Color Science, pp. 21–24 (2001)
19. Vezhnevets, V., Sazonov, V., Andreeva, A.: A Survey on Pixel-Based Skin Color Detection Techniques. GRAPHICO 2003, 85–92 (2003)
20. Bourke, P.: Converting Between RGB and CMY, YIQ, YUV (1994), http://local.wasp.uwa.edu.au/~pbourke/texture_colour/convert/ (Last accessed on 23.07.2009)

Visualization of JPEG Metadata

Kamaruddin Malik Mohamad and Mustafa Mat Deris

Faculty of Information Technology and Multimedia,
Universiti Tun Hussein Onn Malaysia (UTHM),
86400 Parit Raja, Batu Pahat, Johor, Malaysia
{malik,mmustafa}@uthm.edu.my

Abstract. There are a lot of information embedded in JPEG image than just graphics. Visualization of its metadata would benefit digital forensic investigator to view embedded data including corrupted image where no graphics can be displayed in order to assist in evidence collection for cases such as child pornography or steganography. There are already available tools such as metadata readers, editors and extraction tools but mostly focusing on visualizing attribute information of JPEG Exif. However, none have been done to visualize metadata by consolidating markers summary, header structure, Huffman table and quantization table in a single program. In this paper, metadata visualization is done by developing a program that able to summarize all existing markers, header structure, Huffman table and quantization table in JPEG. The result shows that visualization of metadata helps viewing the hidden information within JPEG more easily.

Keywords: JPEG Metadata, Metadata Viewer, Digital Forensics.

1 Introduction

The International Organization for Standardization (ISO) started to look into ways to use high resolution graphics and pictures in computers in 1983[1]. Joint Photographic Experts Group (JPEG) was formed by the International Telegraph and Telephone Consultative Committee three years later to develop a standard procedure for encoding grayscale and color images. JPEG finally come out with guideline which is referred to ITU-T T.81 [2]. In 1992, JPEG File Interchange Format (JFIF) [3] is introduced with introduction of some metadata in the non entropy coded segment [4]. This is a de-facto file format, used for sharing in different applications and in the Internet [5]. JPEG Exchangeable Image File Format (Exif) was introduced by Japan Electronic Industry Development Association (JEIDA) in 1996, to be used for digital cameras [6, 7, 8]. Exif 2.2, a newer version of Exif was introduced by the Japan Electronics and Information Technology Industries Association (JEITA), which is formerly known as JEIDA.

There are four distinct modes of encoding processes namely, sequential DCT based (also known as baseline JPEG), progressive DCT-based, lossless, and hierchical [2]. Implementations are not required to provide all of these.

H. Badioze Zaman et al. (Eds.): IVIC 2009, LNCS 5857, pp. 543–550, 2009.
© Springer-Verlag Berlin Heidelberg 2009

There are two alternatives of entropy coding namely Huffman coding and arithmetic coding. Patented arithmetic coding produces slightly better compression but slower than patent-free Huffman coding. Huffman coding is more widely used for JPEG image compression. No default values for Huffman tables (DHT) are specified, so that applications may choose tables appropriate for their own environments. However, default tables are defined for the arithmetic coding. Baseline JPEG uses Huffman coding, while the extended DCT-based and lossless processes may use either Huffman or arithmetic coding.

JPEG file are segmented by a special two-byte codes called markers. Most markers are start of marker segments containing a related group of parameters (e.g. DHT, quantization table (DQT), start-of-frame (SOF), define-arithmetic-coding (DAC), start-of-scan (SOS), define-number-of-line (DNL), define-restart-interval (DRI), define-hierarchical-progression (DHP), expand-reference-component (ERC), application segment (APP), reserved for JPEG extensions (JPG), comment (COM)); and some markers are stand alone (e.g. start-of-image (SOI), end-of-image (EOI), restart-interval-termination (RST)). All these markers are assigned two-byte codes, 0xFF byte followed by a byte which is not equal to 0x00 or 0xFF.

JFIF file must have "JFIF\0" identifier, without it maybe it is another type of JPEG files e.g. JPEG Exif [7] which is a commonly used format for digital camera that can be identified by a SOI and "Exif\0" identifier.

Formally, the Exif and JFIF standards are incompatible. This is because both specify that their particular application segment (APP0 for JFIF, APP1 for Exif) must be the first in the image file. In practice, many programs and digital cameras produce files with both application segments included. This will not affect the image decoding for most decoders, but poorly designed JFIF or Exif parsers may not recognize the file properly.

In this paper, a program is developed to enable visualization of JPEG metadata to include summary of markers, header structure, Huffman and quantization table. Thus, the software can be helpful to digital forensic investigator to compare photo obtained from the computer at the crime scene against the evidence photo. Furthermore, corrupted image can be reconstructed by refering to the evidence photo. Finally, the metadata is much easier to be viewed and understood as opposed to view it through hex editor.

The rest of the paper is organized as follows. Section 2 describes related works, section 3 discussed about the experiments done, section 4 discussed about the result and discussion and finally section 5 concludes this paper.

2 Related Works

There are mainly two types of software available in the Internet, the image viewer and the metadata viewer. In this paper, we are focusing on visualizing the metadata hidden in JPEG image. Most JPEG metadata viewers concentrate on visualizing the metadata content of JPEG Exif files only. An open-source Linux-based Exif metadata viewer program called jhead, allows the retrieval of Exif headers from JPEG Exif files [6]. The sample output from jhead is illustrated in Figure 1. The Windows-based Exif Image Viewer [9] output is displayed in Figure 2. More Exif metadata viewer software can be found at [10]. There are also metadata readers, editors and extraction s available.

These softwares mainly focuses on visualizing typical selected Exif attributes information such as camera make, model, date and time, focal, exposure time, aperture as illustrated in Figure 1 and 2. However, we develop a more detailed program to visualize all available JPEG markers into summary, headers, Huffman tables and quantization tables.

```
File name: logo.jpg
File size: 800000 bytes
File date: 2009:01:01 09:09:09
Camera make: EASTMAN KODAK COMPANY
Camera model: KODAK LS443 ZOOM DIGITAL CAMERA
Date/Time: 2008:12:31 10:10:10
Resolution: 2448 x 1632
Flashed used: No
Focal length: 21.2mm
Exposure time: 0.011 s (1/90)
Aperture: f/4.7
Exposure: program (auto)
Jpeg process: baseline
```

Fig. 1. Typical jhead output

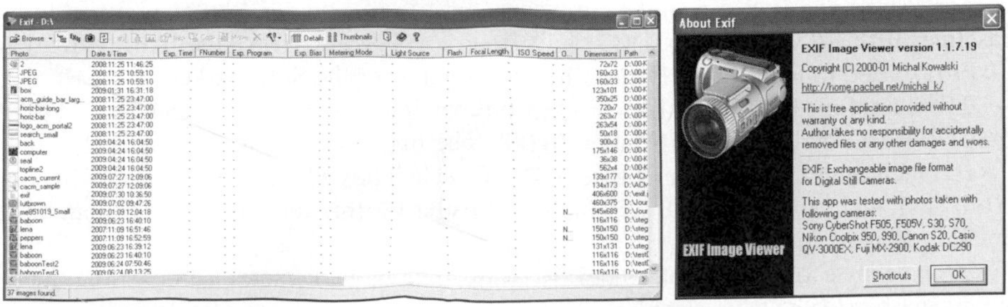

Fig. 2. Exif Image Viewer [9]

Table 1. Metadata readers, editors and extraction tools [10]

SOFTWARE	OPERATING SYSTEM
BR's EXIFextracter (freeware)	Windows
DateTree	Macintosh
EXIF Image Viewer and EXIF InfoTip (freeware)	Windows
Exif Reader (freeware)	Windows
EXIF Tag Parsing Library for Developers	
EXIF-O-Matic	Windows/ Macintosh /Linux
Exifer	Windows
EXIFread, EXIFren, and JPEGget	Windows
EXIFutils	Windows/ Macintosh /Linux
FotoTagger	Windows
Full Image Info	Windows
Ignore EXIF Color Space Plug-in for Photoshop	Macintosh
Ignore EXIF Color Space Utilities for Photoshop	Windows
iTag - Photo Tagging Software	Windows

Table 1.(*continued*)

Jhead	Windows/ Macintosh /Linux
Microsoft Photo Info	Windows
Namexif	Windows
Simple EXIF Viewer	Macintosh OS X
xMeta - Metadata Export from Photoshop	Macintosh

3 Experimentation

All valid two-byte markers found will be displayed on to the screen with its marker's name, its hex value and offset from the beginning of file. Stuffed byte (0x00 following 0xFF) and consecutive 0xFF will be skipped.

In this paper, the JPEG file will be visualized in few ways. It will be displayed as a summarized version by displaying all markers found in the file, specific JFIF metadata, specific Exif metadata, Huffman tables, quantization tables, and header. In this experiment, many JPEG files are used including "baboon" (baboon.jpg) and "lena" (lena.jpg). In this experiment, only results on baboon image will be discussed. Nevertheless, the result obtained could represent the general result for other JPEG images.

A summary of "baboon.jpg" is illustrated in Figure 4. A comprehensive list of markers are displayed including SOI, APP0, DQT, start-of-frame (SOF), DHT, start-of-scan (SOS) and EOI. From the summary, the file of size 4473 bytes is found to be baseline JFIF file with two DQT and four DHT. Moreover, the APP0 marker (0xFFE0) used to identify JFIF file is located right after the SOI marker.

There are four Huffman tables used in baboon.jpg. Figure 5 illustrates the detail of first DHT DC table used with index 0x00. The first DHT segment size is 27 bytes (0x1B) including DHT length (2 bytes), DHT table index (1 byte), Huffman-bit-codes (16 bytes), and variable length DHT table (8 bytes for this table only). Huffman table detail is tabulate in Table 2.

A single byte of DHT table index is comprises of two values namely four most-significant-bit (MSB) table class (tc) and four least-significant-bit (LSB) destination identifier (th). tc of value 0x0 denotes AC table and value 0x1 denotes DC table. Thus, there are altogether two DHT DC tables (0x00, 0x01) and two DHT AC tables (0x10, 0x11).

Fig. 3. Some of the test files used in this experiment; baboon and lena

Fig. 4. A summary of baboon.jpg

Fig. 5. First Huffman table details in baboon.jpg

Fig. 6. Header details in baboon.jpg

Table 2. Detail of first Huffman table in baboon.jpg

Huffman-bit-code size (in bits)	Number of codes	Huffman-bit-code values
2	2	0x04, 0x05
3	3	0x00, 0x03, 0x06
4	1	0x02
5	1	0x01
6	1	0x07

The detail header for baboon.jpg is illustrated in Figure 6. The APP0 marker value is 0xFFE0 identifying JFIF file. Followed by size of header of 16 bytes (or 0x10 from 'header size' to 'thumbnail height'). JFIF identifier take up another 5 bytes ("JFIF" string terminated by a NULL ('0x00') or '0x4A 0x46 0x49 0x46 0x00'). Other values in the header including density unit (1 byte), x density (1 byte), y density (1 unit), thumbnail width (1 byte) and finally thumbnail height (1 byte).

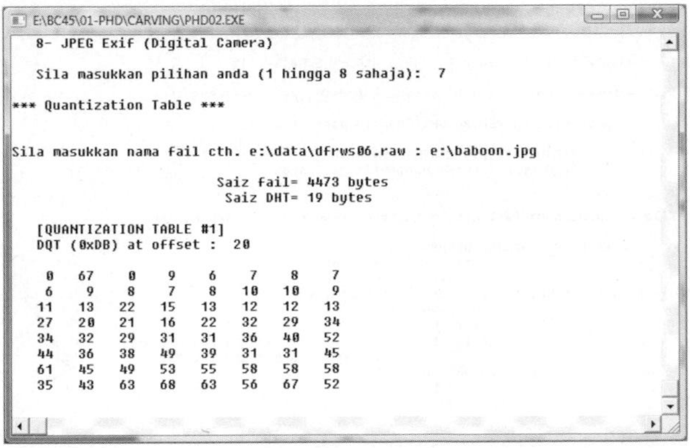

Fig. 7. First quantization table in baboon.jpg

There are two quantization tables in baboon.jpg. The first quantization table is illustrated in Figure 7. The quantization table is an 8x8 matrix with 64 values.

4   Result and Discussion

There are many standalone (e.g. SOI, EOI, RST) or start of segment two-byte markers (e.g. DHT, DQT, SOF, DAC, SOS, DNL, DRI, DHP, ERC, APP, JPG, COM). These markers are important information in digital forensic investigations. In this paper, these markers are visualized in many ways. First, all available markers are summarized with their offset address (refer to Figure 4). Secondly, information can be displayed by segment basis e.g. header (refer to Figure 5), DHT (refer to Figure 6), DQT (refer to Figure 7).

From the summary, digital forensic investigator can check similarity of the photo found in the computer at the crime scene with the evidence photo by looking at these markers and their offsets, comparison of Huffman and quantization tables. Two

Fingerprint Classification Based on Analysis of Singularities and Image Quality

Fadzilah Ahmad and Dzulkifli Mohamad

Department of Computer Graphics & Multimedia,
Universiti Teknologi Malaysia, Skudai, Johor
fadzilah.fa@gmail.com, dzulkifli@utm.my

Abstract. One of the open issues in fingerprint classification is the lack of robustness when dealing with image-quality degradation. Poor-quality images effect on spurious and missing important features for classification, thus degrading the overall performance for distinguish fingerprint classes. In this work, we review existing approaches that have been applied in fingerprint classification which concerning on image quality problems. We have also presents an approach for classifying a fingerprint by analysis of singularities features and improvement on image quality. The main objective of this study is to provide the reader with some insights into the strength and importance of the quality images for fingerprint classification system. In particular, it discusses the fingerprint singularities features that are useful for distinguishing fingerprint classes and reviews the methods of classification that have been applied based on these features.

Keywords: Fingerprint Classification, Image Quality, Singularities.

1 Introduction

Automatic fingerprint recognition has become widely used in both personal identification tools and biometric applications. Despite the technology in this area has been present for a few hundred years, the accurate and reliable automatic fingerprint recognition is still a challenging research problem. As an example, fingerprint identification is still computationally demanding especially for a large database. The accuracy of identification process is dropping down while the size of database is growing up and the processing speed of Automatic Fingerprint Identification Process (AFIS) also decreases if it involves a large fingerprint database. A fingerprint has to be compared with all the fingerprint templates stores in the database, which is the identification process, may take higher response time.

In a large scale of fingerprint identification systems, some methods of classifying a fingerprint images were developed to reduce the complexity of database searching. The classification of fingerprints is computationally demanding [1] and has attracted a significant amount of interest in the scientific community due to its importance and difficulty. According to [2] a central problem in designing such a classification scheme is to decide what features should be used to classify fingerprints and how categories are defined based on these features.

H. Badioze Zaman et al. (Eds.): IVIC 2009, LNCS 5857, pp. 551–560, 2009.

The aim of this paper is to discuss a variety of classification techniques that have been used by many researchers and provide the reader with some insights into the strengths and importance of the quality fingerprint images for classification. Then, we propose an approach for fingerprint classification that based on extracting the singularities features of fingerprint images. The proposed approach includes the enhancement process in the pre-processing stage to provide good quality input fingerprint images. A problem that has become one of the recent critical issues in fingerprint classification is related to the presence of noise in fingerprint images. It is important task in fingerprint classification systems to recover the original ridge patterns, and therefore pre-processing steps are required to enhance the fingerprint image.

Our ideas will give better insights on how we can improve the quality of fingerprint images in pre-processing step. The proposed work is to attempt the problem with poor quality and the presence of noise in fingerprint images. The system must be design to be robust when dealing with the quality of fingerprint images and it will give better performance in fingerprint classification system. The rest of the paper is organized as follows. In Section 2 the related works by researchers will be analyzed that concern with quality image for fingerprint classification. Section 3 discusses quality image problems that influence the classification performance. Section 4 elaborated about the singularities of fingerprint image. In Section 5, we present the framework and concept of proposed method. Section 6 will be a discussion for this research and ends up with a conclusion.

2   Related Works

As we know, fingerprint classification method requiring the information from the entire fingerprint images and it may be too restrictive for many applications. One of the problems that have become recent critical issue in classifying a fingerprint is relies on the quality of fingerprint image. Since the quality of a fingerprint image cannot be correctly measured, therefore it depends heavily to the clarity of the ridge structure in the fingerprint image. In our study, we proposed an approach of classification which takes into consideration the quality of fingerprint image.

Based on the above mentioned problem, a number of approaches have been developed by researchers in different ways. According to [3] the structural and statistical methods can be used for classification which is this methods suffer from sensitivity to noise that usually appears in fingerprint images. The global features of fingerprint image such as cores and deltas might be missing due to noise and as a result it would lead to erroneous classification. To avoid misclassification and improve the accuracy of fingerprint classification, Wafaa M.S., and Fatma Abou-Chadi [4] adopted a pre-processing stage using inverse filtering as a method to enhance the fingerprint image.

In Byoq-Ho Cho et al. [5], the proposed classification method is based on the curvature and the orientation of core. The algorithm uses an efficient enhancing method of fingerprint image to get the high-quality directional image. The proposed method achieve 92.3% classification accuracy and false classified for several fingerprints due to the additional delta that caused by the noise and low quality of input image due to the same reason. Alberto et al., [6] stated that the main drawback of the classification approach based on singularities is the influence of spurious singularities that may originate from the presence of written words, lines, noisy or low quality image. Those unwanted singular points may cause classification errors in fingerprint images.

Karu and Jain [2], eliminate the noise in fingerprint images by dividing the vectors in the reduced directional image according to their distance to the center of the image to alleviate the above problem. Alberto et al. [6] take a different approach that applies a masking step on the directional image that allows ignoring pixels in the background of the image area. Overall successful percentage for classification that has been achieved is 78%. The proposed method still obtains some errors mainly motivated by poor quality impressions of fingerprint images.

Based on Qinzhi Zhang et al., [7], poor quality of fingerprint image due to noise such as that caused by scars, breaks, too oily or too dry, or having a partial image is one of the factor that make fingerprint images hard to classify according to their classes. The proposed method still has misclassification between the arch and some loops as they have very similar ridge patterns. According to them, by applying a good enhancement method on fingerprint images, the classification performance can be improved. Zhi Han and Chang Ping [8] also addressed the image quality issue in their research. The authors stated that the low quality fingerprint image cause error in their classification system because of incorrect reference point location.

In order to overcome the quality issue in classification performance, Sen Wang et al., [9] use some steps to preprocess the input fingerprint images which are as followed: (i) normalization process; (ii) smoothing and histogram equalization process. The authors stated that due to the many noises in original fingerprint image, the features extracted for classification cannot be accurate. Therefore, the accuracy of proposed algorithm is low because of some fingerprint images have missing delta point. The classification process is heavily depends on the quality of the fingerprint image. A noisy image will generate a lot of spurious singular points and tend to fail fingerprint classification [10].

According to Jayant et al., [11], the input image quality adversely affects the performance of the classification algorithm. When the quality of the input fingerprint images is poor, the performance of the algorithm degrades rapidly. Poor quality image and existing of noise in fingerprint image make it difficult to get the correct number and position of the singularities which are widely used in current structural classification methods [8]. Jun Li et al., [12] uses a model-based method to reconstruct the orientation near the candidate point for classification.

The fingerprint images that acquired from the sensor will usually contain noise in the background region. If the entire image is used the orientation model generated will be affected by noise and reduce the classification performance. Jun Li et al., [13] cropped the input image in order to reduce the noise in background region. However, care must be taken such that the cropped image will contain necessary information for classification process. The proposed method has an error in classification that effect from poor quality images with significant noise.

According to Neil and Adnan [14], the best feature for classifying fingerprint is based on fingerprint singularities due to their high stability, rotation and scale-invariant. However, the presence of noise in fingerprint images will make the singular points difficult to detect. Based on this related issue, the next section will discuss on the problem of fingerprint classification when dealing with poor quality input fingerprint images.

3   Quality Image Problems

Quality of the fingerprint image is an important factor in the performance of fingerprint classification algorithms. A good quality fingerprint image (see Figure 1(a)) has high contrast between ridges and valleys. While a poor quality image (see Figure 1(b) and (c)) is low contrast, noisy, broken, or smudgy, that causes spurious and missing importance information for identification process. There are several reasons that may degrade the quality of fingerprint image:

1.   The ridges are broken by presence of cuts, creases, or bruises on the surface of finger tip.

2.   Excessively wet or dry skin conditions lead to fragmented ridges.

3.   Sweaty fingerprints lead to bridging between successive ridges.

4.   Uncooperative attitude of subjects, damaged and unclean scanner devices.

5.   Low quality fingers. Might be from elderly people or manual worker.

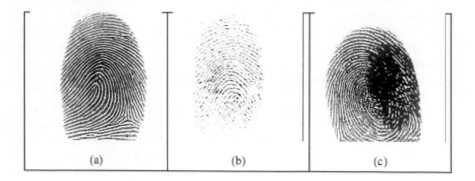

Fig. 1. (a) A good quality fingerprint image; (b) a poor quality fingerprint caused by extremely dry skin; (c) a noisy fingerprint image

The challenges faced in implementation of classification systems that deal with poor quality image are as followed:

(a)   a significant number of spurious minutiae may be created, thus reducing its discriminating power;

(b)   loss of singular points (core and delta) and therefore, a classification algorithm that used of these singularities is prone to failure;

(c)   the elasticity of human skin and humidity can cause distortions.

In order to increase the robustness and accuracy performance of fingerprint classification algorithm, an enhancement process is necessary which can improve the clarity of ridge structures. Considering to image quality issue, our main research focus is on how to handle the quality of fingerprint image that affect the performance of fingerprint classification system.

4   Singularities

Singular regions, known as core and delta are the most important global feature which is not only used for fingerprint pattern classification [2, 15], but also as the reference points in the some fingerprint matching [16, 17, 9]. The core point is defined as the top most point on the innermost upward recurving ridge [18] and delta point is defined as the point of bifurcation(in a delta-like region) on a ridge splitting in two branches which extend to encompass the complete pattern area [18]. Though the core and delta points of fingerprint images are not always necessary to be present, it still appear as unique landmarks in fingerprint images that can be used as reference points for classification process [19]. Fig. 2 shows an example of core and delta points.

Most automatic fingerprint classification problems, classify the fingerprints by using the number and the positions of the singularities. Although the singularities provide very efficient fingerprint class clues, methods that rely on the fingerprint singular points only may not be very successful. This is due to the lack of availability of such information and the difficulty in extracting the reference points information from the noisy fingerprint images.

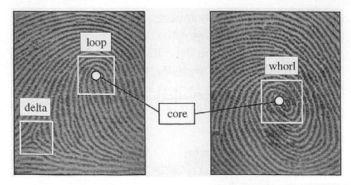

Fig. 2. Singular regions: core and delta points

Generally, accurate and efficient singular points detection considerably affects the overall fingerprint identification system. A various method of core point detection has been examined starting with Kawagoe and Tojo from 1984. Since then, there are many new approaches introduced. Most of the approaches proposed by the researchers for the singularities detection operate on the fingerprint ridge orientation image. The orientation field determined from the input of fingerprint images may not be very accurate and the extracted ridges may contain many artifacts. Therefore, the orientation estimation cannot be directly used for fingerprint classification. Over the last thirty years, at least four major approaches have been proposed by the researchers for automatic fingerprint classification system. They are the model-based, structure-based, frequency-based and syntactic approached [20].

4.1 Singular Points Detection

Generally, most of the approaches proposed by the researchers for the singularity detection operate on the ridge orientation image. In order to locate the position of singular points accurately, we should compute the reliable orientation field of finger-print images and make full use of this property. However, to improve the reliability of orientation field image is still a challenging task because of the noise or poor quality of fingerprint image. Poincare index (PC) method may lead with this problem as it is ease to be affected by the noise of orientation field image and may detect the false singularities In view of the matter, an interesting implementation of Following are the overall steps for the PC technique as described by [2][22]:

1. Let $\theta(i, j)$ be the orientation field and estimate the orientation by using the least square estimation algorithm as mentioned in [20] [9].
2. Initialize a label image A which is used to indicate the core point. For each pixel in $\theta(i, j)$ compute Poincare index, PI (x, y) as defined in the [9] [22].

$$Poincare(x, y) = \frac{1}{2\pi} \sum_{k=0}^{N-1} \Delta(k)$$

Where

$$\Delta(k) = \begin{cases} \delta(k) & if |\delta(k)| < \dfrac{\pi}{2} \\ \pi + \delta(k) & if \delta(k) \leq -\dfrac{\pi}{2} \\ \pi - \delta(k) & otherwise \end{cases}$$

and

$$\delta(k) = \theta(x_{(k+1) \bmod N}, y_{(k+1) \bmod N}) - \theta(x_k, y_k)$$

3. As mentioned in [23] the core point object should yield the Poincare Index between 0.40-0.51. If it comes then we label the corresponding A (i, j) with 1 else we label it with 2. If the Poincare index is -0.5 then such a block is the delta block.

4. Then, we calculated the center of that object. The largest regions and the center of the block with the value of one are considered to be a core point. However, it is enabling to make average calculation if there is more than one block with those values.

5.   The center location will gives us the core point location. But, first found core point may be slightly error. To overcome this problem, core point tuning is being performed on that false regions area as described in [14].

5   Proposed Method

This section outlines the proposed framework of fingerprint classification system based on analysis of singularities and enhanced fingerprint image. Most of the decisions are inspired from findings of previous research that has been done by various researchers. The proposed and concept of this framework can be divided into three phase:

1.   Pre-processing phase

2.   Feature extraction phase

3.   Application phase

In the pre-processing phase, the input image is grabbing through image acquisition process and the enhancement process will be applied to that image. The ridge enhancement process is needed to improve the clarity structure of ridges and valleys while preserve the identity of the fingerprint image. In order to perform this we will make use of algorithm implemented by Chikkerur et al., [21]. This algorithm has been proved can reduce space requirements compared to more popular Fourier domain based filtering techniques. In addition, this algorithm makes full use information of entire fingerprint image including local ridge orientation and local frequency in which required for classification purposes.

Meanwhile, the goal of feature extraction phase is to estimate the orientation field of fingerprint image and extract the global information from the input data that is useful for distinguishing fingerprint classes. The global features include the ridge orientation map and singular points locations. Singularities can be classified into cores and deltas which play an important role in fingerprint pattern classification. The accuracy of singularity extraction basically depends on the quality images. Therefore, in order to improve the classification performance we need to enhance the image during pre-processing phase.

In particular, the existing methods which have been implemented by other researcher that is Poincare Index method will be used to extract the singularities features. Then, the effectiveness of the algorithm will be analyzed. As to improve the performance of singularities extraction and classification accuracy, we need to enhance the existing algorithm into precise way. The results of Poincare Index method cannot be directly used to obtain core and delta point locations and it may need some post-processing steps.

The existence and location of these singularities will be further assessed using the classifier. It is well known in general pattern recognition that all classifiers have its own strengths and weaknesses. Hidden Markov Model (HMM), Neural Network (NN) and Support Vector Machine (SVM) are an example of existing classifier that can be used in application phase. Consequently, the effectiveness of the proposed method will be evaluated from the success rate of fingerprint classification that

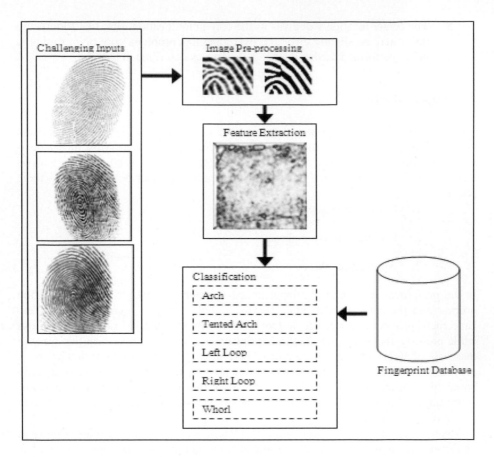

Fig. 3. Overview of proposed method

produced by the classifier. Figure 3 shows the overview of the proposed method that consists of three phases.

6   Discussion and Conclusion

From our study, we found that there are various techniques and features that have been used for classifying a fingerprint image. However, as claimed by [14] there are still open research opportunities in this field that related to the performance of a system that rejects such a high percentage of its input. Some algorithms reject an input image for various reasons. For example, fingerprints can be rejected during pre-processing phase when the image is slightly in poor condition.

Poor quality image is one of the most crucial issues in distinguishing fingerprint classes. This means that more attention should be given in the image pre-processing phase in order to solve this problem as well. An enhancement process is required to increase the accuracy of orientation estimation and get the better results for extracting singularities features. The process of singularities detection must be accurate due to their influences in the performance of classification system.

The implementation and refinements of existing techniques to this research must be considered and cannot be applied directly. Considering to the importance of the problem and the need for performance improvements, we tend to study fingerprint classification algorithms. Apart from that, there are many research opportunities for advancements and innovations in this field.

Acknowledgments. Authors would like to thank Research Management Centre (RMC) Universiti Teknologi Malaysia, for the research activities, and providing financial support under Vot.No. 79270.

References

1. Lee, H.C., Gaensslen, R.E.: Advances in Fingerprint Technology. Elsevier, New York (1991)
2. Hong, L., Jain, A.K.: Classification of Fingerprint Images. In: Proceedings of 11th Scandividian Conference on Image Analyss (1999)
3. Chong, M.M.S., Ngee, T.H., Jun, L., Gay, R.K.L.: Geometric Framework for Fingerprint Image Classification. Pattern Recognition 30(9), 1475–1488 (1997)
4. Shalash, W.M., Abou-Chadi, F.: A Fingerprint Classification Technique Using Multilayer SOM. In: 17th National Radio Science Conference (2000)
5. Cho, B.-H., Kim, J.-S., Bae, J.-H., Bae, I.-G., Yoo, K.-Y.: Core-Based Fingerprint Image Classification. In: 15th International Conference on Pattern Recognition, ICPR 2000, vol. 2, p. 2859 (2000)
6. Bartesaghi, A., Fernández, A., Gómez, A.: Performance Evaluation of an Automatic Fingerprint Classification Algorithm Adapted to a Vucetich Based Classification System. In: Bigun, J., Smeraldi, F. (eds.) AVBPA 2001. LNCS, vol. 2091, pp. 259–265. Springer, Heidelberg (2001)
7. Zhang, Q., Huang, K., Yan, H.: 'Fingerprint Classification Based on Extraction and Analysis of Singularities and Pseudoridges'. In: Pan-Sydney Area Workshop Visual Information Processing (VIP2001), Sydney, Australia, vol. 11 (2001)
8. Han, Z., Liu, C. P.: Fingerprint classification based on statistical features and singular point information. In: Li, S.Z., Sun, Z., Tan, T., Pankanti, S., Chollet, G., Zhang, D. (eds.) IWBRS 2005. LNCS, vol. 3781, pp. 119–126. Springer, Heidelberg (2005)
9. Wang, S., Zhang, W.W., Wang, Y.S.: Fingerprint Classification by Directional Fields. In: Proceedings of the Fourth IEEE InternationalConference on Multimodal Interfaces, ICMI 2002(2002)
10. Leong, C.E.: Fingerprint classification: a BI-resolution approach to singular point extraction. Master's thesis, Universiti Teknologi Malaysia (2004)
11. Kulkarni, J.V., Jayadevan, R., Mali, S.N., Abhyankar, H.K., Holambe, R.S.: A New Approach for Fingerprint Classification based on Minutiae Distribution. International Journal of Computer Science 1(4) (2006)
12. Li, J., Yau, W.-Y., Wang, H.: Singular Points Detection Using Interactive Mechanism in Fingerprint Images. In: ICARCV (2006)
13. Li, J., Yau, W.-Y., Wang, H.: Combining Singular Points and Orientation Image Information for Fingerprint Classification. Pattern Recognition 41(1), 353–366 (2008)

14. Yager, N., Amin, A.: Fingerprint classification: a review. Pattern Analysis & Applications 7(1), 77–93 (2004)
15. Qinzhi, Z., Hong, Y.: Fingerprint Classification Based on Extraction and Analysis of Singularities and Pseudo Ridges. Pattern Recognition 37, 2233–2243 (2004)
16. Chan, K.C., Moon, Y.S., Cheng, P.S.: Fast Fingerprint Verification Using Subregions of Fingerprint Images. IEEE Transactions on Circuits and Systems for Video Technology 14, 95–101 (2004)
17. Jain, A.K., Prabhakar, S., Hong, L., Pankati, S.: Filterbank-Based Fingerprint Mathcing. IEEE Transactions on Image Processing 9(5), 846–859 (2005)
18. Srinivasan, V.S., Murthy, N.N.: Detection of Singular Points in Fingerprint Images. Pattern Recognition 25(2), 139–153 (1992)
19. Cho, B.H., Kim, J.S., Bae, J.H., Bae, I.G., Yoo, K.Y.: Core-Based Fingerprint Image Classification. In: Proceedings of the 15th IEEE International Conference on Pattern Recognition, pp. 863–866 (2000)
20. Maltoni, D., Maio, D., Jain, A.K., Prabhakar, S.: Handbook of Fingerprint Recognition. Springer, Heidelberg (2003)
21. Chikkerur, S.S.: Online Fingerprint Verification System. State University of New York, Buffalo: Master Thesis (2005)
22. Wang, S., Wang, Y.: Fingerprint Enhancement in the Singular Point Area. IEEE Signal Processing Letters 11(1) (2004)
23. Kawagoe, M., Tojo, A.: Fingerprint Pattern Classification. Pattern Recognition 17(3), 295–303 (1984)

An Algorithm for Treating Uncertainties in the Visualization of Pipeline Sensors' Datasets

A. Folorunso Olufemi, Mohd. Shahrizal Sunar, and Sarudin Kari

Department of Graphics & Multimedia,
Faculty of Computer Science and Information Systems,
Universiti Teknologi Malaysia, 81310, Skudai, Johor
oafolorunso2@siswa.utm.my, shah@fsksm.utm.my,
aukauk@itc.utm.my

Abstract. Researchers have seen visualization as a tool in presenting data based on available datasets. Its usage is however undermined by its inability to acknowledge the associated uncertainties in real world measurements. Visualization results are said to be "too generous", providing us with visual assumptions that though, may not be too far from reality, but the associated inaccuracies could become significant when dealing with life dependant datasets. Uncertainty reality is now becoming a significant research interest. In most cases accuracy is a neglected issue. Two wrong assumptions are believed; the first is that the data visualized is accurate, and the second is that the visualization process is exempt from errors. The objectives of this paper are to present the implications of inaccuracies and propose a treatment algorithm for the visualizations of pipeline sensors' datasets. The paper also features attributes that gives a user an idea of sensors' datasets inaccuracies.

Keywords: Uncertainty Visualisation, Nuggets, Pipeline-Sensors, Signal Dataspace, LDS.

1 Introduction

The unreliabilities and uncertainties of sensors' datasets have been widely studied. Work from ETH Zurich recognizes the poor behavior of the technology [4] other sensor-based applications have encountered similar issues with regards to 'dirty' sensor datasets [5]. These projects, however, either do not address cleaning or incorporate cleaning logic directly into the application.

Sensors measures physical quantity and convert it into a signal which can be read by an observer or by an instrument. For example, a mercury thermometer converts the measured temperature into expansion and contraction of a liquid which can be read on a calibrated glass tube. A thermocouple converts temperature to an output voltage which can be read by a voltmeter. For accuracy, all sensors need to be calibrated against known standards. For most leakage detection systems (LDSs), data cleaning is treated separately from any secondary application or devices using it such as the Supervisory Control and Data Acquisition (SCADA) system, the

H. Badioze Zaman et al. (Eds.): IVIC 2009, LNCS 5857, pp. 561–572, 2009.

converters and the display devises. This old data cleaning process tends to restrict their application on a small set of well-defined tasks, which includes but not limited to transformations, matching, and duplicate elimination [7]. Added to this include the AJAX tool [10] which was an extensible, declarative means of specifying cleaning operations in a data warehouse. These techniques focus on offline cleaning for use in data warehouses. In real-time, the nature of pipeline-bound applications or the LDSs, however, preclude such techniques. More fundamentally, the nature of the errors in sensors' datasets is not easily corrected by traditional cleaning, such technology typically does not utilize the temporal or spatial aspects of datasets. Errors emanating from the sensors or the initial reading devices are often regarded as primary errors.

Sensors are used in everyday objects such as touch-sensitive elevator buttons and lamps which dim or brighten by touching the base. There are also innumerable applications for sensors of which most people are never aware. Applications include cars, machines, aerospace, medicine, manufacturing, pipelining and robotics. A sensor's sensitivity indicates how much the sensor's output changes when the measured quantity changes. For instance, if the mercury in a thermometer moves 1 cm when the temperature changes by 1°C, the sensitivity is 1cm/°C. Sensors that measure very small changes must have very high sensitivities. Sensors also have an impact on what they measure; for instance, a room temperature thermometer inserted into a hot cup of liquid cools the liquid while the liquid heats the thermometer. Sensors need to be designed to have a small effect on what is measured; making the sensor smaller often improves this and may introduce other advantages. Technological progress allows more and more sensors to be manufactured on a microscopic scale as micro-sensors. In most cases, a micro-sensor reaches a significantly higher speed and sensitivity compared with macroscopic approaches. A good sensor must therefore be sensitive to the measured property, insensitive to any other property and does not influence the measured property.

Most sensors used in pipelining are expected to satisfy the above rules, however, due to variation of designs and implementations, most of these sensors do not meet all these requirements, hence they become a source of error themselves. Ideal sensors are designed to be linear. The output signal of such a sensor is linearly proportional to the value of the measured property. The sensitivity is then defined as the ratio between output signal and measured property. For example, if a sensor measures temperature and has a voltage output, the sensitivity is a constant with the unit [V/K]; this sensor is linear because the ratio is constant at all points of the measurement.

2   Previous Efforts for Treating Sensors' Errors

Many manufacturers and designers of sensors have developed techniques for cleaning and correction of error for wireless sensor datasets an example is found in [13,14]. Some systems uses models of sensor datasets to accurately and efficiently answer wireless sensor network queries with defined confidence intervals [11]. For example, TinyDB provides a declarative means of acquiring data from a sensor network. Application Level Events, (ALE) defines an interface for building middleware for some applications; ALE defines concepts similar to what is described as temporal and spatial data granules. The Context Toolkit (CT) advocates an architectural approach to hiding the details of sensor devices [9]. Visual data mining VDM incorporates the users in data extraction process [2]. There is also the regression method which was applied to sensor networks for inference purposes by [8]-an approach that usually involves building and maintaining complex models. Other work such as [6] advocated an infrastructural approach to sensor data access and management, but does not directly addressed data cleaning. Several systems provide mechanisms for interacting with wireless sensor networks see [6, 12]. In the context of pipeline sensors' datasets, data cleaning is as an important step for data management especially for prediction and localization purposes.

3 Assumptions

Correctness or otherwise of sensors' datasets is subjective, so we have assumed that the sensors have no manufacturer or hardware errors. We have also assumed that the users have equal level of competence to reading and understanding the various display signals produced by these sensors and that the sensors signals could be gracefully approximated to a parabola. Lastly, any inconsistencies with respect to the aforementioned are totally ignored or are approximated as calibration errors.

4 Procedures

We observed that an improvement on the novel analysis guided exploration system called the Nugget Management System NMS proposed by [3] could be used to deal with intrinsic data patterns hidden in such large industrial life dependant datasets represented on display devises. NMS has been proved to solve problems of inaccurate discoveries and also guide users' exploration by making use of a well defined extracted nugget pool. Our extension is tailored to admit multiple users because of the nature of the datasets and its applications. Our algorithm extends the nugget extraction procedure to encompass multiple queries from multiple users with the isolation and separate treatment of the missingness or uncertainties in the display devise errors.

We have modified the contour sequence approach for handling the displays of these sensors' datasets. Our algorithmic procedure frames and initializes the entire display into fixed size contiguous square unit containing a predefined set of pixels. The size of each square put at [0.5] units, halve of the proposed method by [15]. We notice that with such reduction, the display devise error is further reduced by **25** percent which is a good improvement when it has to do with life sensitive datasets of this sort. Each signal is tested to fit into one or more of these fixed size squares. A scan of the entire datasets is done beginning from any of the predefined square units; the result is then subjected to the UTa below:

4.1 Proposed Uncertainty Treatment Algorithm (UTa)

The UTa algorithm frames the entire display of the sensor signal into a set of predefined square units of dimension [0.5] containing finite number of pixels. The entire signal dataspace is then scanned beginning from any of the predefined squares. The signal, during normal operation is approximated into parabola and the scanned pixels of each square are checked for intersections with the signal functional definition. A frame is excluded if it contains no single intersection of the path of signal j and its functional definition and thus not part of the computational time calculations (CoT). Any excluded frame is then removed from the total number of frames within the initial boundaries and the focus frames are reduced accordingly. The overall benefit of this is the reduction in the computational time (CoT) required by the display devises to present the visualized signals.

```
begin:-
      select a predefined square unit from set x_i...x_n
      with dim n [0.5];
          procedure scan pixels((1,2,3,4,…n ∈ x_i);
              for pixel 1 ≤ n ≤ ∞ , n ∈ I;
                  read pixels coordinates;

                          determine fitness of each
                          pixel into the predefined
                          square x_i;

                          initialize k=0;

                  /* k being a counter*/

                          while x_i ≠ φ;

                  /* i.e square not empty*/

                          k=k+1;
```

```
                /* k now contains the numbers of pixels in x_i*/
                              while end;
                    end for;
              end procedure;

                  initialize n=1;

                  initialize p=1;

              /* n, p being counters*/

signal j of y_i pass through x_i if (

          begin:-
                    for:  i ∈ x_i ≤  k+1;
                          there exist :    j ∈ y_i  ≤   k+1;


    Such that the coordinates of x_i and y_i are equal;

                              do until k= k+n;

                        /* n being natural*/

                                    /*select  nth  order
                                    pass  for  each  pixel
                                    within    each    prede-
                                    fined    square    units
                                    and  repeat until  all
                                    pixels scanned;*/
                          ….

    { avoid outliers and redundancies at this stage}

                          ….
                              end do;

                      increment p & n;

        begin  procedure  check  for  emptiness  of
        square();

              begin:-
                    while x_1, … x_n  ≠empty;

                                    set focus= focus of
                                    current  datasets  and
                                    decrement counter p;

                          if focus >1 for any x;
                    set loose focus =true;
                              end if;
                      while end;
              end;
```

```
                    begin :-

                    direct mapping:

                    Set procedure Mapping =true;
                        do;

                        ….

                        mapping;

(i.e. Initializing a call function into 1-1 mapping);
                        ….
                            end do;
                end;

        end;

            end procedure;

end;
```

4.2   UTa-Explained

The UTa algorithm is implemented in multi-pass processes. A single pass begins with the *procedure scan pixels()* which scans the entire pixels of a predefined *square x_i of [0.5] unit* the coordinates of each pixel is then checked for inclusion within the frame or the predefined square. A counter k is then initialed and made to contain the total numbers of pixels in the frame. Two other counters are initialed n & p to 1 (this is to avoid zero elements recorded for each frame); the first is to count the number of traversed positions and steps along the signal path and the other is to count the number of frames already traversed.

The set of coordinated of points of path of the signal j of y_i (where y_i is the approximated underlining function defining j – which we have approximated to a parabola in the example explained below) are then checked against the stored previously scanned elements x_i of the predefined frames ensuring that emptiness is avoided as much as possible. For each non empty of x_i, the points of intersections of j and any pixel of x_i proves that j passes through x_i, n number of times. The selection of the nth order pass for each pixel of x_i within the predefined square units is repeated until all pixels of x_i are scanned. A major challenge is to isolate and deal with the outliers and exceptional data patterns within the entire scan; UTa gracefully deals with this situation by simply avoiding them by redirecting its focal point. set loose focus is set true if any of these exemptions occur and the algorithm simply proceed into direct mapping (1-1) (i.e. coordinates induced mapping) .

A frame is excluded if it contains no single trace of the path of signal j and thus not part of the computational time calculations (CoT). Any excluded frame is then removed from the total number of frames within the initial boundaries and the focus frames are reduced accordingly. The overall benefit of this is the reduction in the computational time (CoT) required by the display devises to present the visualized signals.

Typical reading extracted from a sensor -Velocity Volume Vane Thermo Ane-mometer manufactured by KOREC DIRECT® is as presented in the table below. In this illustration, the sensor employed is determined to measure changes in volume flow velocity over time. The displayed result is the data captured by the sensor in 1 second measured in approximately 360 equal time intervals. (120 readings contains no entries for either of the measured variables and were not displayed). A Quantum –Time Slice is included only if it contains at least one entry for the measured variables.

Table 1. Showing typical reading extracted from a sensor-Velocity Volume Vane Thermo Anemometer

*Source- NNPC, Nigeria

	Quantum- Time slice No.	FLOW VELOCITY (M/S)	VOLUME FLOW RATE (M³/H)	TEMPERATURE (⁰C)
1	07	12.002302	0.0055546	19.302978
2	11	12.002302	0.0055544	19.302990
3	23	–	–	19.302990
4	24	12.003421	–	–
5	35	12.004523	0.0055546	19.302978
6	36	12.005620	0.0055544	18.999996
7	47	–	–	18.999996
8	49	12.002302	–	–
9	50	12.002302	–	19.302978
10	51	–	–	18.999996
11	52	12.004523	0.0055546	18.999996
12	60	12.003421	0.0055544	18.999996
13	63	12.005620	–	–
14	66	–	–	19.302978
15	67	12.005620	–	18.999996
16	69	12.004623	0.0055731	–
17	71	–	0.0055231	19.302978
18	72	12.004561	0.0055546	19.302999
19	77	12.004523	0.0055544	–
20	78	–	–	19.302300
21	79	12.002302	0.0055546	19.302978
22	82	–	0.0055544	19.302999
23	100	12.004523	–	–
24	101	–	–	19.000034
25	102	12.003421	–	19.302999
26	120	12.004523	0.0055546	19.342979
27	121	–	0.0055544	18.999996

Table 1. (*Continued*)

	Quantum- Time slice No.	FLOW VELOCITY (M/S)	VOLUME FLOW RATE (M³/H)	TEMPERATURE (°C)
28	123	12.005620	-	18.999996
29	129	-	-	18.999985
30	130	-	-	19.003487
31	133	-	-	19.342978
32	135	12.004523	-	18.999996
33	140	12.003421	0.0055546	-
34	160	-	0.0055544	19.302300
35	166	12.002302	-	19.302999
36	167	12.002302	-	-
37	169	12.002391	0.0055546	19.003258
38	170	12.005620	0.0055544	18.999996
39	188	12.004449	0.0500000	-
40	189	12.004523	0.0055468	26.000010
41	190	-	-	19.422978
42	191	12.009888	0.0056768	-
43	201	-	-	09.302300
44	202	12.004523	0.0055231	19.302999
45	220	12.005620	0.0055241	-
46	222	12.002302	-	19.542978
47	225	12.002302	0.0055631	18.999996
48	240	12.002302	0.0054231	
49	245	12.004523	0.0054237	19.302999
50	246	12.005620	0.0055546	19.302300
51	287	13.000000	0.0055544	19.002978
52	288	12.003421	-	19.003487
53	300	12.004523	0.0055546	19.003458
54	302	12.005620	0.0055544	19.003478
55	307	12.004623	-	19.003468
56	322	12.002302	-	19.002978
57	333	12.002302	0.0055231	19.302300
58	340	12.002302	-	19.302999
59	351	12.005521	0.0055546	19.345979
60	358	12.003420	0.0055544	19.003768
	REPORTED	*9.01961162*	*0.0037917*	*15.284743*

The dashes represent instances of missed or un-captured readings. The sensor merely reported the average of each of the captured measured variables which we believe may not be the best for this kind of life dependant application. The dataset for the flow velocity is captured as *9.01961162* representing the mean of the class ignoring the missing entries. This attitude of most sensors may lead to greater problems as illustrated below. **Fig.1.** (a) shows the reading with missing data counted as part of dataset or approximated to null, while **Fig.1.**(b) shows same dataset dealing

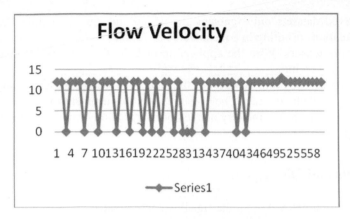

Fig. 1 (a). Showing captured dataset for the flow velocity

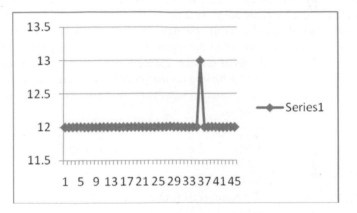

Fig. 1 (b). Showing captured dataset for the flow velocity with observed datasets only(note the visibity of outliers singular at 36)

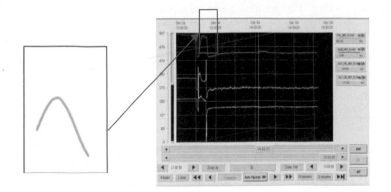

Fig. 2. Showing display of Flow against Time values during a leak trial and our interested region *curled from REL Instrumentation Ltd. (UK)(2001) report on ATMOS$_{PIPE}$

with observed datasets only ignoring the 45 missing quantum time slices in the mean calculations resulting in a mean value of *12.0261488* closer to the actual readings from the sensors. With the application of UTa, the outliers are dealt with by simply ignoring them.

Under normal operating conditions, the signal is or could be gracefully approximated into a parabola; the **Fig.2**. below shows the flow against time before and during a leak trial. Our interest is majorly on the normal situation or normal operating conditions as indicated below.

5   Results and Discussion

In the illustration below Fig.3., the signal is approximated to a hyperbola, the predefined squares are **28** within the boundaries and the number in focus is set to **16**. With the algorithm this is reduced to **13** thereby reducing the uncertainty drastically by **10.7**percent (Table 2.), saving about **19.2** percent computational time (CoT) by reducing its computational index (CI) in one pass, but since this is a sort of alternating function; the resultant saving could be approximated to halve of this i.e **9.6**percent. With this, we could bring errors of sensors' datasets displays closer to its minimum by implementing the algorithm step by step on the predefined square units on the display devices. Irrespective of their orientation however, we could also isolate outliers more easily in any disorganized display.

$$CI= \frac{\text{Number of frames in focus}}{\text{Total available frames within boundaries}} \tag{1}$$

$$CoT= CI*\text{Number of frames within boundaries} \tag{2}$$

Decreasing the frame size further amazingly attracted a lesser precision of the uncertainty visualisation. The algorithm excludes frames that is completely unaffected by the signal under processing. The greatest gains however are noticed at the vertices of the approximated parabola. The observation is measured in milliseconds and the overall effect on the entire signal dataspace could be estimated and presented to the user alongside the 'actual' visualisation.

Table 2. Showing the summary of the result obtained

N=28	CI	CoT(ms)	FOCUS (FRAMES)	% CoT	%CoT-Gain/Loss %
BEFORE	1.0000	28	16	57.14	0
AFTER	0.4643	13	13	46.43	10.71 **+**

SAMPLE SIGNAL

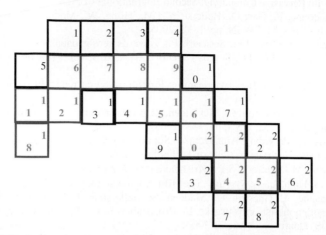

Fig. 3. Showing sample signal and the predefined 28 frames

6 Future Work

The future direction of this work is on the possibility of applying both the NMS and the algorithm to further improve the depiction of certainty of the sensors' datasets visualisation as well as providing new methods for saving operational and hazards costs in pipelining. Dealing with the abnormal situations especially during a leak, outliers and exceptional data patterns would also be major considerations of our next researches.

Acknowledgements

Thanks to Mr.Olubunmi Owoso, the rector of Yaba College of Technology, Nigeria, for the assistance through Study Leave Approval for the main author, the Nigerian National Petroleum Corporation (NNPC) for providing the needed data, and the Ministry of Science, Technology & Innovation, Malaysia for the release of financial support for this research through eScienceFund (01-01-06-SF0472) grant scheme.

References

1. McCormick, B., DeFanti, T., Brown, M.: Visualization in scientific computing. Computer Graphics 21(6), 1–14 (1987)
2. Keim, D.A.: Information visualisation and visual data mining. IEEE Trans. on Visualisation and Comp. Graphics 7(1), 100–107 (2002)
3. Yang, D., Rundensteiner, E.A., Ward, M.O.: Analysis Guided Visual Exploration of Multivariate Data. In: Proceedings of IEEE Symposium on Visual Analytics Science and Technology, Sacramento, CA, USA, October-November 2007, pp. 83–90 (2007)

4. Floerkemeier, C., Lampe, M.: Issues with RFID usage in ubiquitous computing applications. In: Pervasive Computing: Second International Conference, PERVASIVE (2004)
5. Buonadonna, P., Gay, D., Hellerstein, J.M., Hong, W., Madden, S.: TASK: Sensor Network in a Box. In: EWSN, pp. 1–12 (2005)
6. Bonnet, P., Gehrke, J.E., Seshadri, P.: Towards sensor database systems. In: Tan, K.-L., Franklin, M.J., Lui, J.C.-S. (eds.) MDM 2001. LNCS, vol. 1987, pp. 3–14. Springer, Heidelberg (2000)
7. Erhard, R., Do, H.-H.: Data cleaning: Problems and current approaches. IEEE Data Eng. Bull. 23(4), 1–11 (2000)
8. Paskin, M.A., Guestrin, C., McFadden, J.: A robust architecture for distributed inference in sensor networks. In: IPSN, pp. 1–8 (2005)
9. Dey, A.K.: Providing Architectural Support for Building Context-Aware Applications. Ph.D. thesis, Georgia Institute of Technology (2000)
10. Franklin, M.J., Jeffery, S.R., Krishnamurthy, S., Reiss, F., Rizvi, S.: Design Considerations for High Fan-In Systems: The HiFi Approach. In: CIDR (2005)
11. Deshpande, A., Guestrin, C., Madden, S., Hellerstein, J., Hong, W.: Model-Driven Data Acquisition in Sensor Networks. In: Proceedings of Conference on Very Large Data Bases (VLDB) Conference (August 2004)
12. Madden, S., Franklin, M.J., Hellerstein, J.M., Hong, W.: The Design of an Acquisitional Query Processor For Sensor Networks. In: Association for Computing Machinery ACM - SIGMOD 2003 (2003)
13. Elnahrawy, E., Nath, B.: Cleaning and querying noisy sensors. In: Proceedings of the 2nd Association for Computing Machinery international conference on Wireless sensors network and applications, San Diego, CA, USA, September 2003, p. 19 (2003)
14. Fishkin, K.P., Jiang, B., Philipose, M., Roy, S.: I Sense a Disturbance in the Force: Unobtrusive Detection of Interactions with RFID-tagged Objects. In: Ubicomp, IRS-TR-04-013 Intel Research Seattle tech memorandum, June 2004, pp.1–17 (2004)
15. Lopes, A.M.: Accuracy in Scientific Visualisation, Ph.D thesis, University of Leeds, United Kingdom. pp. 10, 37–61 (1999)
16. Floerkemeier, C., Lampe, M.: Issues with RFID usage in ubiquitous computing applications. In: Ferscha, A., Mattern, F. (eds.) PERVASIVE 2004. LNCS, vol. 3001, pp. 188–193. Springer, Heidelberg (2004)
17. Brusey, J., Floerkemeier, C., Harrison, M.G., Fletcher, M.: Reasoning about uncertainty in location identification with RFID. In: 18th International Joint Conference on Artificial Intelligence (IJCAI 2003): Workshop on Reasoning with Uncertainty in Robotics, Acapulco, Mexico, August 9-10, 2003, pp. 9–10 (2003)

Event Based Simulator for Parallel Computing over the Wide Area Network for Real Time Visualization

Elankovan Sundararajan[1], Aaron Harwood[2], Ramamohanarao Kotagiri[2], and Anton Satria Prabuwono[1]

[1] Department of Industrial Computing, Faculty of Information Sciences and Technology, Universiti Kebangsaan Malaysia, 43600 BANGI UKM, Selangor, Malaysia
[2] Department of Computer Science and Software Engineering, Faculty of Engineering, University of Melbourne, 111 Barry Street, Carlton, Victoria, 3010 Australia
{elan,antonsatria}@ftsm.ukm.my,
{aaron,rao}@csse.unimelb.edu.au.

Abstract. As the computational requirement of applications in computational science continues to grow tremendously, the use of computational resources distributed across the Wide Area Network (WAN) becomes advantageous. However, not all applications can be executed over the WAN due to communication overhead that can drastically slowdown the computation. In this paper, we introduce an event based simulator to investigate the performance of parallel algorithms executed over the WAN. The event based simulator known as SIMPAR (SIMulator for PARallel computation), simulates the actual computations and communications involved in parallel computation over the WAN using time stamps. Visualization of real time applications require steady stream of processed data flow for visualization purposes. Hence, SIMPAR may prove to be a valuable tool to investigate types of applications and computing resource requirements to provide uninterrupted flow of processed data for real time visualization purposes. The results obtained from the simulation show concurrence with the expected performance using the L-BSP model.

Keywords: Parallel computing, Simulation, WAN.

Introduction

The computational requirement of applications in computational science continues to grow tremendously [6], such that High Performance Computing (HPC) resources available locally in a single domain can often become insufficient to solve them in the required time. At the same time, the independent advances in computer network technology have increased the effectiveness of distributed computing [6]. Thus, the use of resources distributed geographically apart becomes advantageous.

However, the complexity involved in developing parallel applications effectively on these resources is prohibitively large. This is due to: *(i)* the use of Wide Area Network (WAN) for communication between participating nodes, which contributes to

H. Badioze Zaman et al. (Eds.): IVIC 2009, LNCS 5857, pp. 573–584, 2009.

the volatility in communication delay, *(ii)* the probability of at least one node failing becomes high when a large number of nodes are used, *(iii)* the slowest computing node determines the overall performance of the application when significant communication is required between computing nodes, *(iv)* a single link failure between any pair of computing nodes will result in the failure of the whole parallel computation and *(v)* unreliability that arises due to sharing of these distributed resources with many other users. User usage patterns too affect the available computing power and adversely affect performance of parallel computations. With so many factors affecting the performance of parallel computations over the WAN, visualization softwares may not receive smooth flow of data for real time visualization purposes. Thus, a simulator can be useful to investigate the types of parallel applications that can be effectively executed over the WAN with acceptable performance for visualization. In this paper, we present a simulator that we developed for this purpose.

Background

The extent to which a system can be called High Performance Computing (HPC) architecture is in general ambiguous and dynamic now, because the contemporary HPC architecture and the notion of HPC can be liberally extended to cover collections of resources that are combined to solve a single problem. It is also clear that, in general problems are migrating from classical HPC architectures towards the contemporary computational grid [6] (or at least that the use of the Internet is becoming prevalent in order to tie more computing resources together), either explicitly by direct programming efforts or implicitly through virtualization. There are two main categories of these contemporary architectures, one that ties together a collection of very powerful supercomputers and clusters over the WAN and the other uses a collection of a very large number of PCs donated by home PC users. The later is more popularly called volunteer computing or public resource computing [7].

A well known example of computing that falls in the second category is Berkeley Open Infrastructure for Network Computing (BOINC) [7]. BOINC provides scientists with easy to create and operate public-resource computing projects. Many projects such as SETI@home [9], Folding@home [10], and ClimatePrediction.net [11] are based on BOINC [7]. These projects have attracted millions of participants who donate their home PCs. In 2003, SETI@home was running on 1 million computers, with a potential processing power of 60 TeraFLOPS Other desktop computing research project includes XtremWeb [12] and SZTAKI Desktop Grids [13]. Entropia Inc and the United Devices are among several companies that provide Desktop Grid solutions for enterprises. Applications executed in these projects do not involve significant communication between computing nodes and use the master-slave paradigm for computations. Parallel computation requiring message passing between computing nodes is currently lacking on grids because it is challenging implement.

Challenges in Developing Parallel Applications in General

When developing application software for HPC, parallel application developers must emphasize both ends of architecture, namely the memory hierarchy and the interprocessor communication as the data size grows. This is due to the cost of fetching data that is far from the processing unit. It is not a big issue for small data sets that can fit into local memory, but contributes significantly to the performance of applications that use large data sets. Furthermore, the rate of data access is not as fast as the rate of computation performed by the processors due to bandwidth limitations for both the inter-processor and processor-memory data transfer. It is also interesting to note that, all of the parallel computing models that are used to assist in developing efficient parallel applications consider data movement costs in a system under consideration, as accurately as possible. Thus, real time systems that use distributed computing such as volunteer computing for computation must consider data movement aspects for good visualization experience.

Challenges on a Wide Area Network
Traditionally, HPC had been performed on a single dedicated supercomputer built for solving computationally intensive problems. The traditional parallel computing assumptions are that: *(i)* a system will be with no failures, *(ii)* a single homogeneous architecture *(iii)* with minimal security features, *(iv)* consistency in the state of application components, *(v)* availability of global information, and *(vi)* simple resource sharing policies. In a highly distributed environment, these assumptions are not applicable and makes staging parallel computations on WAN a formidable task. Large amounts of empirical trace data is available for determining characteristics of a WAN such as usage patterns, loss-rate measurements, bandwidth, and latency [14, 15, 16]. However, an effective approach to analyze this information and to find optimal or suboptimal outcome is difficult due to the dynamic nature of the computational resources and the WAN. Consequently, simulation tools such as SIMPAR can be valuable to investigate achievable performance of parallel computation over the WAN for real time visualizations purposes.

Communication Delay
As the size of computational grids continues to grow, to become what we call very large scale grids (VLSG), the number of WAN connections between islands of clusters and other HPC centers grows rapidly to the number of nodes. These WAN connections put limits on the granularity of parallel applications that could otherwise benefit from the available computing power, i.e. computation to communication ratio needs to be significantly large in order for the communication complexity to not dominate the run-time. Embarrassingly parallel, data parallel and parametric problems that do not require significant message passing can be efficiently parallelized but problems that require significant communication present major challenges. Combined with the pathological behavior of the WAN, execution of these types of parallel processes is difficult and requires critical attention. Here, SIMPAR can assist in identifying types of applications that can provide good speedup for uninterrupted flow of processed data for real time visualization softwares.

Simulator for Parallel Computation over the WAN

A simulator called SIMPAR (SIMulation of PARallel Computation over WAN) was developed to investigate the performance of parallel algorithms over the WAN.

SIMPAR allows simulation of discrete events that occurs in a parallel computation, where each of the processor involved in the computation produces events that are stored in an event queue. The events waiting to be processed in the event queue are then processed in time stamp order. SIMPAR is a tool that can be used for performance prediction of parallel algorithms over the WAN. The simulation results obtained from this simulator will provide significant insight into the achievable performance of parallel algorithms.

Discrete Event Simulation

Discrete event simulation involves two fundamental concepts: the concepts of simulation objects and events. Simulation objects maintain a set of local variables that describe their state while the events "act" on simulation objects to possibly change their state and/or to schedule future events for potentially any other object in the simulation. A set of time-tagged pending events must be maintained by the simulation machinery [4]. A way of maintaining this set is to keep events sorted by time using a Red Black tree [5]. The earliest time-tagged event is popped out of the list and processed. If that event generates new events, then these are inserted back into the list preserving the sorted nature of the list.

Events Produced by the Computing Nodes

There are five types of events produced by the "computing nodes" involved in the simulation. These are WORKDONE, SENDPACKET, RECEIVEPACKET, TRANSMITPACKET, and RETRY events. A global variable, CurrentTime is used to keep track of the time taken for completing the parallel computation. A WORKDONE event is transmitted when a work given to a processor is completed. For example, if a work requires t seconds to complete, the sum of t and CurrentTime is the time the WORKDONE event will happen. The SENDPACKET event occurs when a processor sends a packet to another processor. Whereas the TRANSMITPACKET event occur when a packet is transmitted from a sending processor to the receiving processor. The RECEIVEPACKET event happens when a processor receives the packet sent by the sending processor. RETRY event is posted to the event queue each time a processor sends a data packet. This is to ensure the data packet is resent again (after timeout period) in case the data packet is lost. If the packet is sent successfully all the retry event posted for the packet will be ignored.

The Event Queue

Events are posted by different computing nodes into the event queue and are kept in a sorted order. The events are queued (sorted) according to their time-stamp value using the Red-Black (RB) tree algorithm. We use RB tree algorithm because it does search, insert and delete in $O(log(N))$ time, where N is the number of elements in the queue. With RB tree algorithm a newly inserted event will be placed in a position such that the event queue is always in sorted order. The head of the queue will always be an event that is to happen first and the tail of the queue will be an event that is to occur last at any point of time.

Network Description

Communication between computing nodes are performed using UDP data packets and acknowledgment packets for reliability. The events SENDPACKET, RE-CEIVEPACKET, TRANSMITPACKET and RETRY are posted during any one communication. In our simulation, we take the cost of sending data packet from a computing node to the nearest router to be the ratio of packet size and upload bandwidth. The transmission cost from that router to the router that is close to the receiving node is obtained from the random value generated by DS^2 [3]. The cost of receiving a data packet from the nearest router to the receiving computing node is the ratio of packet size and download bandwidth. To reflect the unpredictable nature of WAN, we use random values with the ratio as shown in Table. 1 for upload and download bandwidth. The probability of packet loss can be provided by the user (as a command line parameter) or can be automatically selected from the empirical results (average packet loss that depends on the packet size) obtained from PlanetLab [8].

Table 1. Ratio of upload and download bandwidth and floating point operations used for computing nodes in SIMPAR

	50%	20%	10%
Upload (kbits)	64	128	256
Download (kbits)	256	512	1500
MFLOPS	500	1000	2000

Computation

The time required for computation is taken as the ratio of number of instructions required and the average number of FLOPS that can be performed by the processors. Table 1. Shows the ratio of random values we used in the simulation for processor speed in MFLOPS.

Development of SIMPAR

SIMPAR was developed using C programming language. We present in this section details on the data types and data structures used in the simulator.

Data Types and Data Structures
Data types that are unique to SIMPAR are:

```
typedef unsigned short HostID; (for Host identification)
typedef unsigned int QueueSize; (to track size of Queue)
typedef unsigned char Communication; (takes value 1 if
communication exists between two node else 0)
```

typedef unsigned int BandWidth; (for upload and download bandwidth)

typedef unsigned int NumOfFLOPS; (to keep information on processors FLOPS)

typedef unsigned short RoundNum; (for keeping track of number of rounds)

typedef unsigned short NumOfPack; (for keeping track of number of packets received, sent or required)

typedef unsigned int PackSize; (Size of packets)

typedef unsigned int NumOfRetries; (To track the number of retries)

typedef unsigned char PacketType; (Type of packet: data or acknowledgment

Data structure for packets
This data structure holds information on the packet that are transmitted. The packets can be either data packets or an acknowledgement packet. The packet data structure has information on the size of packet, round number, packet source (ID of the packet sending node) and packet destination (ID of the receiving node).

```
enum packet Type {DataType, AckType};

typedef struct{

  PacketType packetType;

  PackSize size; (packet size in bytes)

  RoundNum round;

  HostID source;

  HostID dest;

}Packet;
```

Data structure for events
The Event data structure keeps information of the type of event and information about the packet sent by the host.

```
enum event type {WORKDONE, SENDPACKET, RECEIVEPACKET, RE-
TRY, TRANSMITPACKET};

typedef struct{
        EventType eventType;
        float eventTime;
```

```
            HostID host;

            Packet packet;

}Event;
```

Data structure for hosts

The HOST data structure represents each computing nodes involved in the simulation. Every host keeps information on the current round, number of acknowledgment and data packets received, number of retries due to packet losses, a queue each for incoming packets and outgoing packets, the number of packets received, the required number of packets and Boolean variable to determine if the host is waiting to receive a packet.

```
typedef struct{

            RoundNum roundNum;

            NumOfPack **acksRecv;

            NumOfPack **packetsRecv;

            NumOfRetries **retries;

            PacketQueue inQueue;

            PacketQueue outQueue;

            NumOfPack *numPacketsRecv;

            NumOfPack reqPackets;

            Uchar waiting;

}HOST;
```

Cost of Communication on WAN

For each computing nodes we provide two queues (unlimited size) for incoming packet and outgoing packet and an event queue to post different events for computation and communication. Fig. 1 shows the overall picture of the cost associated with packet movements from the source to the destination. A data packet ($k=1$) is injected into the nearest router at a cost of $\frac{c(n)}{n}\alpha$. Here, α, represents the throughput of data from the computing node to the router or vice-versa. The data packet then goes through the Internet taking approximately half of the average round-trip time between computing nodes, which is represented as $\frac{\beta}{2}$. It then reaches the final router before being sent to the destination node with a cost of $\frac{c(n)}{n}\alpha$.

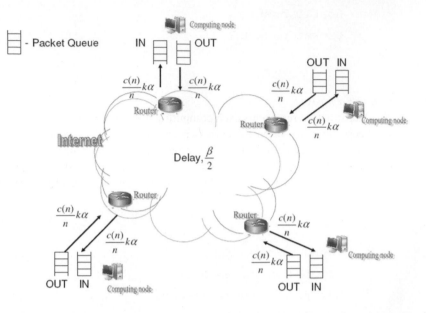

Fig. 1. Cost of communication for packet movement from sender to the receiver, where k is the number of packet copies used

Thus, the total cost for data packet to move from the sending node to the receiving node is $2\frac{c(n)}{n}\alpha+\frac{\beta}{2}$. Assuming the typical acknowledgment packet size of 40 bytes, the cost of injecting this packet into the Internet can be assumed to be negligible. However, the cost of delay, β, is still significant. Thus the total cost of sending data packet and receiving acknowledgment packet is $\tau=2\frac{c(n)}{n}\alpha+\beta$. We take 2τ as the timeout period in our calculation. As the size of node, packet size and communication complexity changes, the timeout period changes accordingly. The timeout period is important because it provides a balance between congestion control and performance of computation.

Simulation Results

In this section we provide simulation results to compare our model for different communications $c(n)$. In the simulation, we divide bandwidth into upload and download bandwidth for each computing nodes. Usually, the bandwidth of a normal desktop computer varies depending on many factors. In the L-BSP model we have used the average bandwidth for upload and download. We obtained two sets of simulation results, one without randomness and the other with randomness for bandwidth and FLOPs.

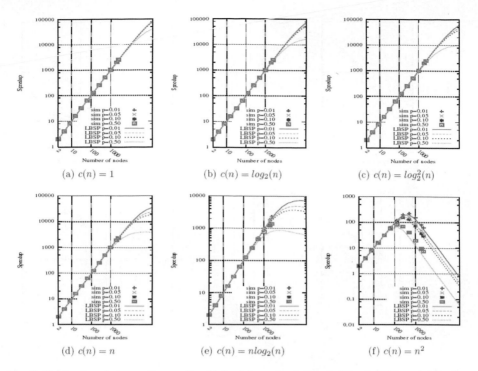

Fig. 2. Comparison between the results obtained from simulation and the L-BSP model for the first set (without randomness)

The first set of simulation runs, refer Fig. 2, shows that without randomness for the bandwidth and number of FLOPs for all nodes, the L-BSP model provides accurate results for different communication types. We observe that, for low communication between computing nodes (such as when $c(n) = 1$, $log_2(n)$, $log_2^2(n)$), the results from simulation and L-BSP [1,2,6] show similar results. Some variation are seen for computation with significant communication between computing nodes. These variations are due to the time-out cost of 2τ used in the L-BSP mode. In the simulation, communications may have completed before the end of time-out time (i.e. the speedup achieved is higher). Thus, L-BSP model produces lower speedup compared to what is achieved in simulations. The L-BSP model also shows that for parallel computation that requires all-to-all communication (i.e. $c(n)=n^2$), the maximum speedup achievable is limited. The simulation results that we obtained concur with this observation.

In the second set of simulation, refer Fig. 3, SIMPAR uses random upload and download bandwidth, and random FLOPs with the ratio as given in Table.1. The delay (i.e. the time spent on the Internet) is predicted using the DS^2 [3]. We use random values to approximate the real time behavior of communication and computation when parallel program is executed over the Internet. For this set of simulation, the L-BSP model takes the average of the values in Table.1 and the average delay is obtained from DS^2.

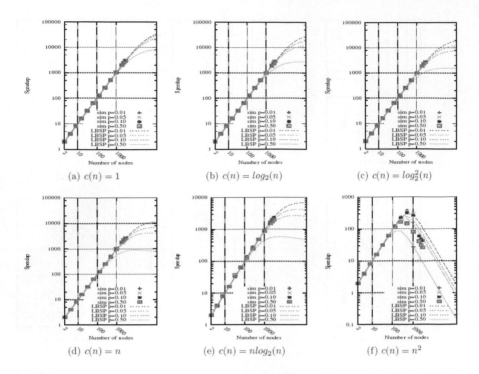

Fig. 3. Comparison between the results obtained from simulation and the L-BSP model for the second set (with randomness)

The results for the second set indicate that, when randomness is introduced for the bandwidth and floating point operations, the results show some variations for computation with significant communication. This can be clearly observed when packet loss probability is $p \geq 0.5$, and for higher communication complexity such as $c(n) = nlog_2(n)$ and $c(n) = n^2$. This is due to the number of simulation runs that is not large enough. Also, inconsistency between L-BSP model and simulation is contributed by the average values used in the L-BSP model. If the number of simulation runs are large enough, the values obtained from the simulation will concur with the predicted values of L-BSP model.

The result obtained from SIMPAR depicts the possible performance of parallel computation with different types of communication. SIMPAR can be extended further to consider more factors that contribute to performance of parallel application over the WAN and to different types of application for real time visualization.

SIMPAR and Visualization

Visual Informatics involves visualization of and interaction with very large data sets, including both text and numeric data, e.g. in chemical and molecular structures, and genome sequences. Visual informatics softwares (such as Logical Images' VisualDx) provide real time visual decision support for such things as diagnosis of disease [17].

Some of these visualization softwares use very large real-time data that must be processed before any visualization can be performed. The processing of these data usually requires immense computing power. As described in section 2, volunteer computing provides a means to harness a huge pool of computing resources for processing real time data. Here, SIMPAR may prove to be a valuable tool to understand the types of parallel applications and computing resources requirements (e.g. number of processors, memory and bandwidth requirements, etc) such that real time data can be processed on time for visualization purposes.

Conclusions

In this work, we developed a simulator called SIMPAR. The simulator is used to simulate the achievable performance of different types of communications when parallel computation is performed over the WAN. SIMPAR can be easily extended to simulate different types of parallel applications. The insights provided by the simulator can be used in determining types of parallel applications (for real time visualization) that will be suitable to be computed over the WAN. The results obtained from our initial work are accurate for the first set (without randomness) when compared with the L-BSP model. The second set (with randomness) however shows some variance. This we believe is due to the number of simulation runs. If more simulation runs are performed, the results will concur with the L-BSP model which predicts the average performance. In future work, we will include more factors into the SIMPAR such as random failures, fault tolerance, check pointing and other factors that impacts performance of parallel computations over the WAN (Internet).

References

1. Sundararajan, E., Harwood, A., Ramamohanarao, K.: Lossy Bulk Synchronous Parallel Processing Model for Very Large Scale Grids. Journal of Parallel and Distributed Computing (September 2008) (submitted)
2. Sundararajan, E., Harwood, A., Ramamohanarao, K.: Incorporating Fault Tolerance with Replication on Very Large Scale Grids. In: Eighth International Conference on Parallel and Distributed Computing, Applications and Technologies, PDCAT 2007, Adelaide, Australia, pp. 319–328. IEEE Computer Society Press, Los Alamitos (2007)
3. Internet Delay Space Synthesizer, http://www.cs.rice.edu/~bozhang/ds2/
4. Steinman, J.S.: Discrete-event simulation and the event horizon. SIGSIM Simulation, Digest 24(1), 39–49 (1994)
5. Cormen, T.H., Leiserson, C.E., Rivest, R.L., Stein, C.: Introduction to Algorithms, 2nd edn. MIT Press and McGraw-Hill (2001)
6. Sundararajan, E.: The Lossy Bulk Synchronous Processing model for Wide Area Network Parallel Processing, PhD Thesis, University of Melbourne (2008)
7. Anderson, D.P.: Public computing: Reconnecting people to science. In: Proceedings of the Conference on Shared Knowledge and the Web, Residencia de Estudiantes, Madrid, Spain (November 2003)
8. PlanetLab: An Open Platform for developing, deploying, and accessing planetary-scale services, http://www.planet-lab.org/

9. Anderson, D.P., Cobb, J., Korpela, E., Lebofsky, M., Werthimer, D.: Seti@home: an experiment in public-resource computing. ACM Communication 45(11), 56–61 (2002)
10. Folding@Home Distributed Computing, http://folding.stanford.edu/
11. ClimatePrediction. Net gateway, http://climateprediction.net/
12. Fedak, G., Germain, C., Neri, V., Cappello, F.: XtremWeb: A Generic Global Computing System. In: CCGRID 2001: Proceedings of the 1st International Symposium on Cluster Computing and the Grid, Washington, DC, USA, p. 582. IEEE Computer Society Press, Los Alamitos (2001)
13. Kacsuk, P., Podhorszki, N., Kiss, T.: Scalable desktop grid system. Technical Report TR-0006, Institute on System Architecture, CoreGRID - Network of Excellence (May 2005)
14. CoMon-A Monitoring Infrastucture for PlanetLab,
    http://comon.cs.princeton.edu/
15. PlanetLab - All Sites Ping, http://ping.ececs.uc.edu/ping/
16. Scalable Sensing Service: PlanetLab Data,
    http://networking.hpl.hp.com/scube/pl/
17. Jörgensen, C., Fleischmann, K., Fast, K., Eberstein, A.V., Jörgensen, P.: Panel: Towards a Research Agenda for Visual Informatics. In: ASIST 2005, Westin Charlotte, Charlotte, North Carolina, October 28 - November 2 (2005)

Adaptive-Neuro Fuzzy Inference System for Human Posture Classification Using a Simplified Shock Graph

S. Shahbudin[1], A. Hussain[1], Ahmed El-Shafie[1], N.M.Tahir[2], and S.A. Samad[1]

[1] Department of Electrical, Electronics & Systems Engineering,
Faculty of Engineering, Universiti Kebangsaan Malaysia,
Bangi, Selangor Darul Ehsan, Malaysia
shaqay@vlsi.eng.ukm.my, aini@vlsi.eng.ukm.my
[2] Department of Computer,
Faculty of Electrical Engineering
Technology University of Mara,
Shah Alam, Selangor Darul Ehsan, Malaysia

Abstract. In this paper, a neuro-fuzzy technique known as the Adaptive-Neuro Fuzzy Inference System (ANFIS) has been used to highlight the application of ANFIS to perform human posture classification task using the new simplified shock graph (SSG) representation. Basically, a shock graph is a shape abstraction that decomposed a shape into a set of hierarchically organized primitive parts. The shock graph that represents the silhouette of an object in terms of a set of qualitatively defined parts and organized in a hierarchical, directed acyclic graph is used as a powerful representation of human shape in our work. The SSG feature provides a compact, unique and simple way of representing human shape and has been tested with several classifiers. As such, in this paper we intend to test its efficacy with another classifier, that is, the ANFIS classifier system. The result showed that the proposed ANFIS model can be used in classifying various human postures.

Keywords: Adaptive-Neuro Fuzzy Inference System (ANFIS), simplified shock graph (SSG), Artificial Neural Network (ANN).

1 Introduction

ANFIS is a well-known neural fuzzy controller with fuzzy inference capability. ANFIS can generate better training performance with smaller root mean square error (RMSE) which determines the error between computed output and target. ANFIS learns the features in the data set and adjusts the system parameters according to a given error criterion [1],[2]. Successful implementations of neuro-fuzzy network in human body classification and gesture posture recognition [6],[7] have been reported. Data analysis using fuzzy inference system has also been studied [8],[9]. In this work, we intend to evaluate the effectiveness of ANFIS to perform human posture classification using a new set of feature vectors as introduced in [3] which is termed as Simplified Shock Graph (SSG). The SSG feature set is based on the Blum's Medial Axis. In essence, a shock graph is a generic representation of a 2-D shape, where structural

H. Badioze Zaman et al. (Eds.): IVIC 2009, LNCS 5857, pp. 585–595, 2009.

descriptions are derived from the shocks (singularities) of a curve evolution process, acting on bounding contours. In this work, we afford a framework for the classification of human postures based on their silhouettes using shock graph representation. Basically, the aim of this paper is to highlight the application of AN-FIS to perform human posture classification using the new simplified shock graph (SSG) representation. Additionally, we also like to show that SSG has the potential to be a unique feature vectors for use in human posture classification or interpretation and for shape classification, in general. Accordingly, the ANFIS classifier is chosen as a mechanism to prove the SSG efficacy. The detail explanation of SSG is described in following section.

All in all, this paper is outlined as such, the description of SSG is presented in Section 2 followed by explanation of the ANFIS method given in Section 3. In section 4, the results are presented and discussed. Finally, section 5 concludes the findings.

2   Simplified Shock Graph

As revealed in [3], the shock graph of a shape is the medial axis, the locus of centers of circles which are at least bitangent to the boundary, endowed with dynamic and geometric information. Shock graphs are a richer descriptor of shape than the boundary by itself. Shock graphs encode information about the interior of the shape by pairing shape boundary segments [10]. The shock graph has emerged as a powerful, generic shape description possessing these properties, and is based on a labeling partitioning of the skeleton points (shocks) making up the MAT of a shape. A shock graph is a shape abstraction which decomposes a shape into a set of hierarchically organized primitive parts [11],[12]. Shock graph is an image transform and a thinning algorithm, which requires an already segmented image. Intuitively, the result of this process yields the

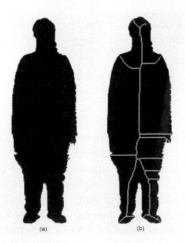

Fig. 1. Sample of shock graph extraction: (a) original segmented image and (b) its shock graph. [3]

skeleton of an object, encoding in it additional information. For example, when the algorithm processes an image as shown in Fig. 1(a), a shock graph as in Fig. 1(b) is produced, where the black color serves as an indication of the shape of the input object meanwhile the white 'skeletal' line is the shock graph itself.

The novel used of shock graph for classification was proposed in [3] and the work also produced a new algorithm, which yields the simplified shock graph (SSG). How the SSG produced using the pruning process is explained briefly as follows: after the detection of all four end points of the skeleton shape, the pruning process is initiated on every remaining end point detected and progresses inwards until it reaches the medial axis of the skeleton. As such, our pruning strategy aims to produce a simple shock graph comprising of only two intersection nodes and four end nodes. This simpler looking shock graph is what we term an SSG. The two intersection nodes lie within the boundary of the shape, and the end nodes lie on the boundary itself. Nevertheless, if both feet are not positioned at the same level, the third and fourth end points will be detected from the lower foot. [3]

Next, a set of body parameter consisting three measurements are extracted from the SSG and used as feature vectors. As explained in [3], the feature vectors are the distances d_1, d_2, and d_3 as illustrated in Figure 2.

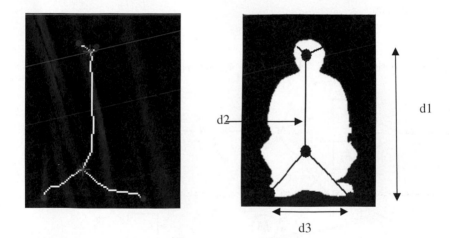

Fig. 2. Sample of SSG and the posture non-standing anterior (non-standing front) showing the three extracted feature vectors shock graph

Parameter d_1 covers the length from the upper intersection node to either of the lower end nodes, d_2 represents the distance between the upper and lower intersection nodes and d_3 is the horizontal distance between the two lower end nodes. The four subsets that represent the posture positions are non-standing front (NF) as a class one, represent non-standing sideway (NS) for class two, class three represent standing front (SF) and standing sideway (SS) constitute as class four.

3 ANFIS

3.1 Architecture of ANFIS

Adaptive-Network-Based fuzzy interface system [1], which is referred to as ANFIS, is a class of adaptive networks that is functionally equivalent to the fuzzy interface systems. Its architecture combines a fuzzy system and a neural network system. The ANFIS is a fuzzy Sugeno model put in the framework of adaptive systems to facilitate learning and adaptation [1][2]. In general, Sugeno-type systems can be used to model any inference system in which the output membership functions are either linear or constant.

As an example, consider the ANFIS architecture with two fuzzy if–then rules based on a first-order Sugeno model:

Rule 1 : If (x isA$_1$) and (y is B$_1$) then (f1 = p$_1$x + q$_1$y + r$_1$)
Rule 2 : If (x isA$_2$) and (y is B$_2$) then (f2 = p$_2$x + q$_2$y + r$_2$)

where x and y are the inputs, A$_i$ and B$_i$ are the fuzzy sets, f$_i$ are the outputs within the fuzzy region specified by the fuzzy rule, p$_i$, q$_i$ and r$_i$ are the design parameters that are determined during the training process. The ANFIS architecture to implement these two rules is as shown in Figure 3. This architecture contains five layers, two inputs and one output.

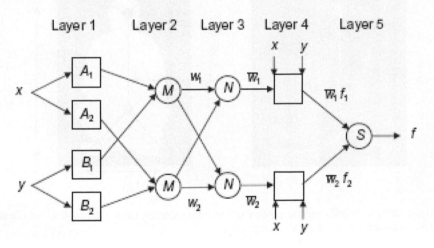

Fig. 3. ANFIS architecture for two-input, two-rule first-order Sugeno model

In layer 1, the output of each node is

$$O_{1,i} = \mu_{A_i}(x) \qquad for\ i = 1,2$$

(1)

$$O_{1,i} = \mu_{B_{i-2}}(y) \qquad for\ i = 3,4$$

(2)

So, the $O_{1,i}(x)$ is essentially the membership grade for x and y. The membership functions could be anything but for illustration purposes the bell shaped function will be used is given by:

$$\mu_A(x) = \frac{1}{1 + \left|\frac{x - c_i}{a_i}\right|^{2b_i}} \tag{3}$$

where a_i, b_i, c_i are parameters to be learnt. These are the premise parameters. In layer 2, every node in this layer is fixed. This is where the t-norm is used to 'AND' the membership grades - for example the product:

$$O_{2,i} = w_i = \mu_{A_i}(x)\mu_{B_i}(y), \quad i = 1,2 \tag{4}$$

Layer 3 contains fixed nodes that calculate the ratio of the firing strengths of the rules:

$$O_{3,i} = \overline{w}_i = \frac{w_i}{w_1 + w_2} \tag{5}$$

The nodes in layer 4 are adaptive and perform the consequent of the rules:

$$O_{4,i} = \overline{w}_i f_i = \overline{w}_i(p_i x + q_i y + r_i) \tag{6}$$

The parameters in layer 4 (p_i, q_i, r_i) are to be determined and are referred to as the consequent parameters. The last layer, layer five, is a single node that computes the overall output as illustrate in equation (7)

$$O_{5,i} = \sum_i \overline{w}_i f_i = \frac{\sum_i w_i f_i}{\sum_i w_i} \tag{7}$$

3.2 Learning Parameter in ANFIS

The aim of ANFIS is to optimize the parameter of the fuzzy inference system by applying a learning algorithm using input–output data sets. Parameter optimization is done in a way such that the error measure between the target and the actual output is minimized. The task of the learning algorithm for this architecture is to tune all the modifiable parameters, namely $\{a_i, b_i, c_i\}$ and $\{p_i, q_i, r_i\}$, to make the ANFIS output match the training data. When the premise parameters a_i, b_i and c_i of the membership function are fixed, the output of the ANFIS model can be written as:

$$f = \frac{w_1}{w_1 + w_2} f_1 + \frac{w_1}{w_1 + w_2} f_2 \tag{8}$$

Substituting Eq. (4) into Eq. (7) yield:

$$f = \overline{w_1} f_1 + \overline{w_2} f_2 \qquad (9)$$

Substituting the fuzzy if-then rules into Eq. (8), it becomes:

$$f = \overline{w_1}(p_1 x + q_1 y + r_1) + \overline{w_2}(p_2 x + q_2 y + r_2) \qquad (10)$$

After rearrangement, the output can be expressed as:

$$f = (\overline{w_1} x) p_1 + (\overline{w_1} y) q_1 + (\overline{w_1}) r_1 + (\overline{w_2} x) p_2 + (\overline{w_2} y) q_2 + (\overline{w_2}) r_2 \qquad (11)$$

or
$$f = \begin{bmatrix} \overline{w_1} x & \overline{w_1} y & \overline{w_1} & \overline{w_2} x & \overline{w_2} y & \overline{w_2} \end{bmatrix} \begin{bmatrix} p_1 \\ q_1 \\ r_1 \\ p_2 \\ q_2 \\ r_2 \end{bmatrix} \qquad (12)$$

When input-output training pattern exit, the vector $[p_1, q_1, r_1, p_2, q_2, r_2]^T$, which consists of the consequence parameters, can be solved using a regression technique.

During the learning process of ANFIS, these premise parameters in the fuzzy layer and the consequent parameters in the de-fuzzy layer are tuned until the desired response of the fuzzy inference system (FIS) is achieved.

In this paper, hybrid learning algorithm is employed to determine the optimum values of the FIS parameters of Sugeno-type. It applies a combination of the least - squares method and the back-propagation gradient descent method for training FIS membership function parameters to emulate a given training data set. It means that, in the forward pass of the hybrid learning algorithm, functional signals go forward till layer 4 and the consequent parameters are identified by the least squares estimation. In the backward pass, the error propagates backward and the premise parameters are updated by the gradient descent.

In this work, a Pentium IV, 3.0 GHz computer with 768 MB RAM was used to execute the FIS function of GENFIS1 in Matlab 7. The execution generates a single-output Sugeno-type FIS using a grid partition on the data with specific number of membership functions per input, type of input and output membership functions. Details of ANFIS classifier can be found in [1][2].

4 Results

By applying the K-fold cross-validation method, a total of 400 images of various human postures were divided equally into four subsets (i.e. K=4) where each subset contains 100 postures. In this study, 300 vectors (75 vectors from each class) were used for training and the 100 vectors (25 vectors from each class) were used for testing. The cross-validation process is then repeated K times (the folds), with each of the K sub-samples used exactly once as the validation data. Since the ANFIS classifier only generates one single output, four ANFIS classifiers were trained with the hybrid learning algorithm. The trained classifiers are later employed for the classification of four classes of human postures. Specifically in this study, the three feature vectors extracted from SSG are applied as input in which parameter d_1 is assigned as input 1, input 2 represented by parameter d_2 and parameter d_3 as input 3. The four classes that represent the posture positions which are class one to class four were assigned as binary target values of (0,0,0,1), (0,0,1,0), (0,1,0,0) and (1,0,0,0) respectively.

In ANFIS, the training data was used to train (or tune) a fuzzy model, whereas the testing set was used to determine when training should be terminated. After training, 100 testing data were used to validate the accuracy and the effectiveness of the trained ANFIS model for classification of four human postures. ANFIS posture interpretation and classification results were displayed by a distribution performance between prediction output and desired output and confusion matrix. In a confusion matrix, each cell contains the raw number of exemplars classified for the corresponding combination of desired and actual network outputs.

In ANFIS, several parameters need to be set up before training. After several simulations for obtaining minimum error, we set the number of membership functions to three in which each membership function has a bell-shaped. The membership function of each input parameter is then divided into three regions, namely, small, medium and large. The step size is the length of each gradient transition in the parameter space. Thus, in this study, the initial step size value is set to 0, step size decrease rate set equal to 0.9 and the step increase rate is set to 1.1. The number of iteration (epoch number) which is equal to 100 epochs was chosen. Meanwhile the hybrid of learning

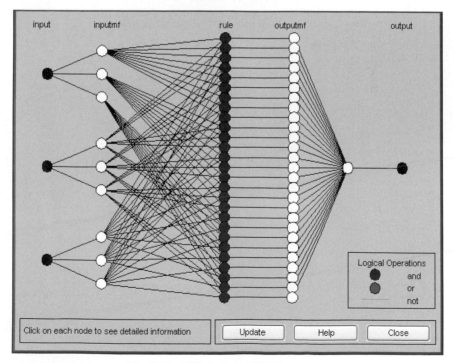

Fig. 4. The 27-rule base ANFIS structure

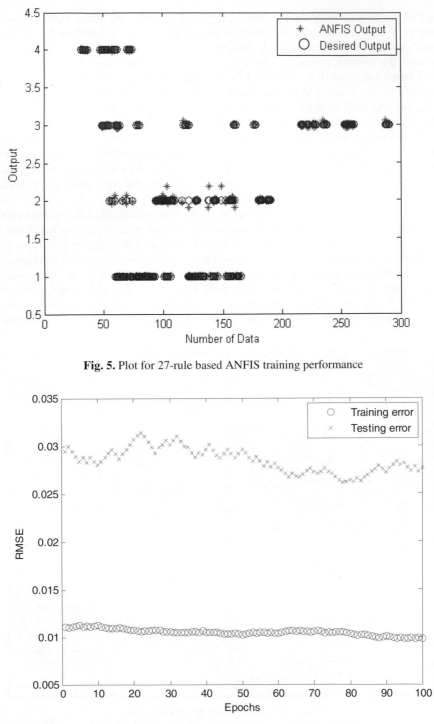

Fig. 5. Plot for 27-rule based ANFIS training performance

Fig. 6. Training and Testing RMSE curves of the ANFIS

is employed and the output type is set up to as a linear type. This experiment uses three inputs that generate 27 rules nodes for the FIS structure. The 27-rule ANFIS structure is shown in Figure 4.

Figure 5 shows the plot for the 27 rule-based ANFIS training performance in classifying the 300 human posture data. Since ANFIS implementation in Matlab only supports a single output, the results can only be visualized and depicted using the simple sequential plot. As shown in Figure 4, the red '*' symbol represents the computed output from the ANFIS structure where as the blue colored 'O' symbol denotes the desired target (actual output). It can be seen that the result depicts that ANFIS output are strictly tied to the desired output.

In addition, the root mean square error (RMSE) for both training and testing of the ANFIS are compared and shown in Figure 6. It can be seen from the graph, the final convergence values for both training error and testing error are 0.0097 and 0.026 respectively.

For the purpose of comparison, we have included the ANN model and applied it to perform the same task using the same feature sets. Basing on the training and testing error convergence, it can be summarized that ANFIS final convergence error is smaller than the ANN whereas for training, reverse is true. Results are tabulated in Table 1.

Table 1. Comparison of Error Rate

Classifier	Epoch Number	Training Error	Testing Error
ANFIS	100	0.0097	0.0261
ANN	100	0.0035	0.0435

From Table 1, during the training process, the ANN has the lowest root means square error (RMSE) compared to the ANFIS method. This implies that the ANN classifier is the better learning method in which it recorded the lowest training error of 0.0035 compared to ANFIS which recorded 0.0097. However, in the testing stage where 100 data comprising the three feature vectors extracted from the SSG were used, the ANFIS model recorded a lower error compared to the ANN classifier. For the task to recognize and classify the four different human poses, the ANFIS model outperformed the ANN classifier in term of the convergence error. The testing RMSE for both ANFIS and ANN are 0.0261 and 0.046, respectively.

Table 2 represents the confusion matrix and the average classification accuracy of each classifier. As tabulated in table 2, the total classification accuracies for the ANFIS and ANN classifiers are 99% and 94% respectively. These results suggest that ANFIS is a better classifier than ANN and confirmed the effectiveness of SSG for shape representation. Specifically, SSG is found to be a suitable 2-D representation for representing human pose based on the silhouette.

Table 2. Confusion Matrix

Desired Output	Predicted Output ANFIS				Predicted Output ANN			
	NF	NS	SF	SS	NF	NS	SF	SS
NF	25	0	0	0	20	4	0	1
NS	0	24	1	0	0	24	1	0
SF	0	0	25	0	0	0	25	0
SS	0	0	0	25	0	0	0	25
Average Accuracy Rate (%)	99				94			

5 Conclusions

In conclusion, this work further confirmed the effectiveness of SSG as feature vectors for human posture interpretation or classification problems. All being considered it can be generalized that the SSG feature set has great potential and can be used in any shape or object classification problems. Furthermore, a new application of ANFIS employing feature extracted of SSG in classifying human postures is presented. The results demonstrated that the proposed ANFIS model can be used in classifying various human postures by taking into consideration the misclassification rates.

References

1. Jang, J.-S.R.: ANFIS: Adaptive-Network-based Fuzzy Inference Systems. IEEE Transactions on Systems, Man, and Cybernetics 23(3), 665–685 (1993)
2. Jang, J.-S.R., Sun, C.-T., Mizutani, E.: Neuro-Fuzzy and Soft Computing: A Computational Approach to Learning and Machine Intelligence. Prentice Hall, US (1997)
3. Tahir, N.M., Hussain, A., Samad, S.A., Husain, H.: Shock Graph Representation and Modelling of Posture. ETRI Journal 29(4) (2007)
4. Shahbudin, S., Hussain, A., Tahir, N.M., Samad, S.A.: Multi-class Support Vector Machine for Human Posture Classification Using a Simplified Shock Graph. In: 2008 International Symposium on Information Theory and its Applications (2008)
5. Tahir, N.M., Hussain, A.: Human Shape Analysis Using Artificial Neural Network. In: Proc. of ICOM 2005, Kuala Lumpur (2005)
6. Lin, C.-J., Wang, J.-G., Lee, C.-Y.: Pattern recognition using neural- fuzzy networks based on improved particle swam optimization. Expert systems with application 36(3), 5402–5410 (2009)
7. Bailador, G., Guadarrama, S.: Robust Gesture Recognition using a Prediction-Error-Classification Approach. In: IEEE International Fuzzy Systems Conference, FUZZ-IEEE 2007, pp. 1–7 (2007)

8. Data Analysis using Fuzzy Inference System,
    `http://www3.ntu.edu.sg/home/aswduch/Teaching/Assign2/`
    `ZhaoGuopeng.pdf`
9. Virant-Klun, I., Virant, J.: Fuzzy logic alternative for analysis in the biomedical sciences.
    Comput. Biomed. Res. 32, 305–321 (1999)
10. Siddiqi, K., Kimia, B.B.: A Shock Grammar for Recognition. In: Proc. of the IEEE Conf.
    Computer Vision and Pattern Recognition, San Francisco, June 1996, pp. 507–513 (1996)
11. Belongie, S., Malik, J., Puzicha, J.: Matching Shapes. In: Proc. of IEEE Int'l. Conf. Com-
    puter Vision, pp. 454–461 (2001)
12. Sidiqqi, K., Shokoufandeh, A., Dickinson, S.J., Zucker, S.W.: Shock Graphs and Shape
    Matching. Int'l J. of Computer Vision 35(1), 13–32 (1999)
13. Sebastian, T.B., Klein, P.N., Kimia, B.B.: Recognition of Shapes by Editing Their Shock
    Graphs. IEEE Transactions on Pattern Analysis and Machine Intelligence 26(5), 550–571
    (2004)
14. Klein, P.N., Sebastian, T.B., Kimia, B.B.: Shape matching using edit- distance: an imple-
    mentation. In: Symposium on Discrete Algorithms in Proceedings of the twelfth annual
    ACM-SIAM symposium on Discrete algorithms, pp. 781–790 (2001)
15. Klein, P.N., Tirthapura, S., Sharvit, D., Kimia, B.B.: A tree-edit distance algorithm for
    comparing simple, closed shapes. In: Symposium on Discrete Algorithms in Proceedings
    of the twelfth annual ACM-SIAM symposium on Discrete algorithms, pp. 696–704 (2000)
16. Xu, W., Li, L., Zou, S.: Detection and Classification of Microcalcifications Based on DWT
    and ANFIS. In: The 1st International Conference on Bioinformatics and Biomedical Engi-
    neering, 2007. ICBBE 2007, July 6-8, pp. 547–550 (2007)
17. Übeyli, E.D.: Adaptive Neuro-Fuzzy Inference Systems for Automatic Detection of Breast
    Cancer. Journal of Medical System 18, 157–174 (2008)

Extraction and Classification of Human Gait Features

Hu Ng[1], Wooi-Haw Tan[2], Hau-Lee Tong[1], Junaidi Abdullah[1],
and Ryoichi Komiya[3]

[1] Faculty of Information Technology, Multimedia University, Persiaran Multimedia,
63100 Cyberjaya, Selangor Malaysia
[2] Faculty of Engineering, Multimedia University, Persiaran Multimedia, 63100 Cyberjaya,
Selangor Malaysia
[3] Department of Mechatronic and BioMedical Engineering, Faculty of Engineering and Science,
Universiti Tunku Abdul Rahman, Jalan Genting Kelang, Setapak 53300 Kuala Lumpur
{nghu,twhaw,hltong,junaidi}@mmu.edu.my, ryoichi@utar.edu.my

Abstract. In this paper, a new approach is proposed for extracting human gait features from a walking human based on the silhouette images. The approach consists of six stages: clearing the background noise of image by morphological opening; measuring of the width and height of the human silhouette; dividing the enhanced human silhouette into six body segments based on anatomical knowledge; applying morphological skeleton to obtain the body skeleton; applying Hough transform to obtain the joint angles from the body segment skeletons; and measuring the distance between the bottom of right leg and left leg from the body segment skeletons. The angles of joints, step-size together with the height and width of the human silhouette are collected and used for gait analysis. The experimental results have demonstrated that the proposed system is feasible and achieved satisfactory results.

Keywords: Human identification, Gait analysis, Fuzzy k-nearest neighbour.

1 Introduction

Personal identification or verification schemes are widely used in systems that require determination of the identity of an individual before granting the permission to access or use the services. Human identification based on biometrics refers to the automatic recognition of the individuals based on their physical and/or behavioural characteristics such as face, fingerprint, gait and spoken voice. Biometrics are getting important and widely acceptable nowadays because they are really personal / unique that one will not lose or forget it over time.

Gait is unique, as every individual has his/her own walking pattern. Human walking is a complex locomotive action which involves synchronized motions of body parts, joints and the interaction among them [1]. Gait is a new motion based biometric technology, which offers the ability to identify people at a distance when other biometrics are obscured. Furthermore, there is no point of contact with any feature capturing device and is henceforth unobtrusive.

H. Badioze Zaman et al. (Eds.): IVIC 2009, LNCS 5857, pp. 596–606, 2009.
© Springer-Verlag Berlin Heidelberg 2009

Basically, gait analysis can be divided into two major categories, namely model-based method and model-free method. Model-based method generally models the human body structure or motion and extracts features to match them to the model components. The extraction process involves a combination of information on the human shape and dynamics of human gait. This implies that the gait dynamics are extracted directly by determining joint positions from model components, rather than inferring dynamics from other measures, thus, reducing the effect of background noise (such as movement of other objects). For instance, Johnson used activity-specific static body parameters for gait recognition without directly analyzing gait dynamics [2]. Cunado used thigh joint trajectories as the gait features [3]. The advantages of this method are the ability to derive gait signatures directly from model parameters and free from the effect of different clothing or viewpoint. However, it is time consuming and the computational cost is high due to the complex matching and searching process.

On the other hand, model-free method normally distinguishes the entire human body motion using a concise representation without considering the underlying structure. The advantages of this method are low computational cost and less time consuming. For instance, BenAbdelkader proposed an eigengait method using image self-similarity plots [4]. Collins established a method based on template matching of body silhouettes in key frames during a human's walking cycle [5]. Philips characterized the spatial-temporal distribution generated by gait motion in its continuum [6].

This paper presents the unique concept of extracting the human gait features of walking human from consecutive silhouette images. First, the height and width of the human subject are determined. Next, each human silhouette image is enhanced and divided into six body segments to construct the two-dimension (2D) skeleton of the body model. Then, Hough transform technique is applied to obtain the joint angle for each body segment. The distance between the bottoms of both lower legs can also be obtained from the body segment skeletons. This concept of joint angle calculation is found faster in process and less complicated than the model-based method like linear regression approach by Yoo [7] and temporal accumulation approach by Wagg [8].

2   Overview of the System

First, morphological opening is applied to reduce background noise on the raw human silhouette images. The width and height of each human silhouette are then measured. Next, each of the enhanced human silhouettes is divided into six body segments based on the anatomical knowledge [10]. Morphological skeleton is later applied to obtain the skeleton of each body segment. The joint angles are obtained after applying Hough transform on the skeletons. Step-size, which is the distance between the bottoms of both legs are also measured from the skeletons of the lower legs. The dimension of the human silhouette, step-size and six joint angles from body segments – head and neck, torso, right hip and thigh, right lower leg, left hip and thigh, and left lower leg are then used as the gait features for classification. Fig. 1 summarizes the process flow of the proposed system.

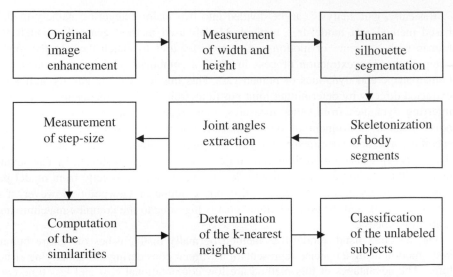

Fig. 1. Flow chart of the proposed system

2.1 Original Image Enhancement

The acquired original raw human silhouette images are obtained from the small subject gait database, University of Southampton [9]. They used static cameras to capture eleven subjects walking along the indoor track in four different angles. Video data was first preprocessed using Gaussian averaging filter for noise suppression, followed by Sobel edge detection and background subtraction technique to create the human silhouette images.

Due to poor lighting condition during the video shooting, shadow was found especially near to the feet. It appeared as part of the subject body in the binary human silhouette image as shown in Fig. 2. The present of the artefact affects the gait feature extraction and the measurement of joint angles. This problem can be reduced by applying morphological opening with a 7×7 diamond shape structuring element, as denoted by

$$A \circ B = (A \ominus B) \oplus B) . \tag{1}$$

where A is the image and B is the structuring element. The opening first performs erosion operation and followed by dilation operation. Fig. 2 shows the result of applying morphological opening on a human silhouette image.

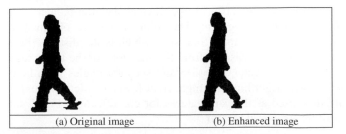

(a) Original image	(b) Enhanced image

Fig. 2. Original and enhanced image after morphological opening

2.2 Measurement of Width and Height

The width and height of the subject during the walking sequences are measured from the bounding box of the enhanced human silhouette, as shown in Fig. 3. These two features will be used for gait analysis in the later stage.

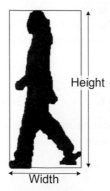

Fig. 3. The width and height of a human silhouette

2.3 Dividing Human Silhouette

At this stage, the enhanced human silhouette is divided into six body segments based on the anatomical knowledge [10]. First, the centroid of the subject is determined by calculating the centre of mass of the human silhouette. The area above the centroid is considered as the upper body – head, neck and torso. The area below the centroid is considered as the lower body – hips, legs and feet.

Next, one third of the upper body is divided as the head and neck. The remaining two thirds of the upper body are classified as the torso. The lower body is divided into two portions – (i) hips and thighs (ii) lower legs and feet with the ratio one to two. Again, the centroid coordinate is used to divide the two portions into the final four segments – (i) right hip and thigh (ii) lower right leg and foot (iii) left hip and thigh and (iv) lower left leg and foot.

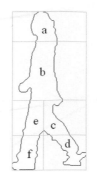

Fig. 4. Six body segments

Fig. 4 shows the six segments of the body, where "a" represent head and neck, "b" represents torso, "c" represents right hip and thigh, "d" represents lower right leg and foot, "e" represents left hip and thigh and "f" represents lower left leg and foot.

2.4 Skeletonization of Body Segments

To better represent each body segment, morphological skeleton is used to construct the skeleton for each of the body segments. Skeletonization involves consecutive erosions and opening operations on the image until the set difference between the two operations is zero.

<u>Erosion</u>   <u>Opening</u>   <u>Set differences</u>

$$A \ominus kB \qquad (A \ominus kB) \circ B \qquad (A \ominus kB) - ((A \ominus kB)) \circ B \qquad (2)$$

where A is an image, B is the structuring element and k is from zero to infinity. Fig. 5. shows the skeleton of the body segments.

Fig. 5. Skeleton on a torso segment

2.5 Joint Angles Extraction

To extract the joint angle for each body segment, Hough transform is applied on the skeleton. Hough transforms maps pixels in the image space to the straight line

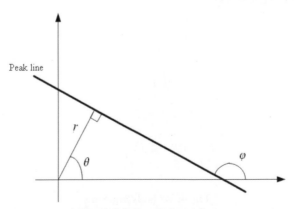

Fig. 6. Joint angle formation

through a parameter space. The skeleton in each body segment, which is the longest line, is indicated by the highest intensity point in the parameter space. Fig. 6 shows the joint angle formation from the most probable straight line detected via Hough transform, where ϕ is the joint angle calculated using

$$90° + \theta = \phi \ . \tag{3}$$

2.6 Measurement of Step-Size

To obtain the step-size of each walking sequence, the Euclidian distance between the bottom ends of lower right leg and lower left leg are measured.

Fig. 7 shows all the gait features extracted from a human silhouette, where Angle 7 is the thigh angle, calculated as

$$\text{Angle 7} = \text{Angle 6} - \text{Angle 4} \ . \tag{4}$$

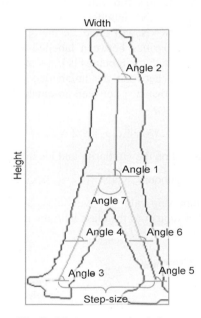

Fig. 7. All the extracted gait features

3 Classification Technique

For the classification, the supervised fuzzy K-Nearest Neighbour (KNN) algorithm is applied, as there is sufficient data to be used for training and testing. Basically, KNN is a classifier to distinguish the different subjects based on the nearest training data in the feature space. In other words, subjects are classified according to the majority of nearest neighbours.

In extension to KNN, J.M. Keller [11] has integrated the fuzzy relation with the KNN. According to the Keller's concept, the unlabeled subject's membership function of class i is given by Equation (5).

$$u_i(\bar{x}) = \frac{\sum\limits_{x \in KNN} u_i(x) \left(\dfrac{1}{\| \bar{x} - x \|^{\frac{2}{m-1}}} \right)}{\sum\limits_{x \in KNN} \left(\dfrac{1}{\| \bar{x} - x \|^{\frac{2}{m-1}}} \right)} . \tag{5}$$

where $\bar{x}$, x and $U_i(x)$ represent the unlabelled subjects, labelled subjects and x's membership of class i respectively. Equation (5) will compute the membership value of unlabeled subject by the membership value of labelled subject and distance between the unlabelled subject and KNN labelled subjects.

Through the fuzziness, the KNN will annotate the appropriate class to the unlabelled subject by sum of similarities between labelled subjects. The algorithm involved in the identification of the human beings is implemented as follows:

Step 1: Compute the distance between the unlabelled subject, and all labelled or training subjects. The distance between an unlabelled subject x_i and labelled subject, x_j is defined as:

$$D(x_i, x_j) = \| x_i, x_j \| - 2 . \tag{6}$$

Step 2: Sort the objects based on the similarity and identify the k-nearest neighbours.

$$\text{k-nearest neighbours, KNN} = \{x_1, x_2, \ldots, x_k\} . \tag{7}$$

Step 3: Compute the membership value for every class using Equation (5).
Step 4: Classify unlabelled subject to the class with the maximum membership value as shown in Fig. 8.

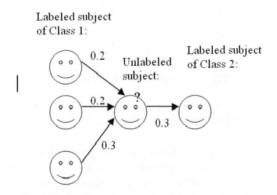

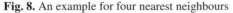

Fig. 8. An example for four nearest neighbours

From Fig. 8, the values on the lines denote the similarities between unlabelled and labelled subjects. The sum of membership values for Class 1, $m_1=0.7$ and for Class 2, $m_2=0.3$. Since m_1 is more than m_2, so the unlabelled subject is classified as Class 1.

4 Experimental Results and Discussion

The experiment was carried out for nine subjects with three different conditions, which are walking with normal speed, walking in own shoes and walking in boots. The major objective was to identify the degree of accuracy for fuzzy KNN technique by using the different values of k. For each subject, there were approximately twenty sets of walking data in normal track (walking parallel to the static camera).

In order to obtain the optimized results, five features were adopted for the classification. First, maximum thigh angle, θ^{max} was determined from all the thigh angles collected during a walking sequence. When θ^{max} was located, the corresponding values for the step-size, S and width, w and height, h are determined as well. From the graph plotted, it can be observed that the width for each subject changes in a sinusoidal patter over time, as shown in Fig. 9. Therefore, the last employed feature is the average of the maximum width, A^P.

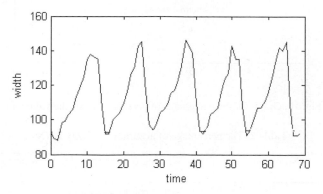

Fig. 9. Graph of width versus time

All the features were channelled into the classification process and the distance of similarity between unlabelled object, x_i and labelled object, x_j was defined by Equation (8).

$$D(x_i, x_j) = (\theta_i^{max} - \theta_j^{max})^2 + (w_i - w_j)^2 + (h_i - h_j)^2 + (S_i - S_j)^2 + (A_i^p - A_j^p)^2 . \qquad (8)$$

The adopted algorithm was supervised fuzzy KNN, which requires training and testing. For the training part, a minimum of eight set of walking data were used for each subject. The residual data were used for the testing. The allocation of the training and testing data for each condition is shown in Table 1.

Table 1. Allocation of the data for each condition

	Testing data set	Training data set
Normal speed	106	78
Wearing own shoes	101	79
Wearing boots	100	74

Different values of k nearest neighbours were adopted for the classification, where k = 3, 4, 5, 6, 7 and 8. Since the minimum of the training data is eight, the maximum value of k was set to eight. The results obtained are depicted in Fig. 10 and Table 2.

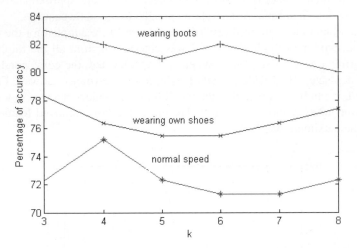

Fig. 10. Graph for the percentage of accuracy versus the value of k

Table 2. The percentage of accuracy for fuzzy KNN

k	Normal speed (%)	Wearing own shoes (%)	Wearing boots (%)
3	78.3	72.3	83
4	76.4	75.2	82
5	75.5	72.3	81
6	75.5	71.3	82
7	76.4	71.3	81
8	77.4	72.3	80

From Table 2, it can be concluded that the changes of value k do not have a significant impact on the accuracy of the classification. However, when k = 3, results were slightly better on others. More satisfactory classification results might be obtained if more features are employed.

In addition to evaluation for each condition, classification results for each subject were evaluated as well. This was to determine which unlabelled subjects were well identified and vice versa for all the conditions. Since k = 3 provided the best result for all three conditions, the experiment was carried out using k = 3 for subject evaluation.

The obtained results for respective subject are shown in Table 3. From Table 3, subject 1 produces the most satisfactory classification results for all three conditions. This was contributed by the adopted features for subject 1 which was highly distinctive from other subjects. Furthermore, there were not many variations between training and testing data for subject 1. In other words, subject 1 was well recognizable under these three conditions. For the rest of the subjects, the accuracy of the classification was highly depending on the conditions. For instance, under normal speed the accuracy for subject 8 only achieved an accuracy of 36.4%. This was due to the large number of misclassifications of subject 8 to other subjects.

Table 3. The percentage of the classification results for three conditions when k = 3

	Normal speed (%)	Wearing own shoes (%)	Wearing boots (%)
Subject 1	100	81.8	100
Subject 2	81.8	58.3	90.9
Subject 3	92.3	70	81.8
Subject 4	80	37.5	81.8
Subject 5	100	53.8	90.9
Subject 6	100	90.9	45.5
Subject 7	57.1	85.7	85.7
Subject 8	36.4	80	91.7
Subject 9	50	83.3	90

5 Conclusion

We have described a new approach for extracting the gait features from enhanced human silhouette image. The gait features is extracted from human silhouette by determining the skeleton from body segment. The joint angles are obtained after applying Hough transform on the skeleton. In the future, more gait features will be extracted and applied in order to achieve higher accuracy of classification.

Acknowledgment

The authors would like to thank Prof Mark Nixon, School of Electronics and Computer Science, University of Southampton, United Kingdoms for providing the database for use in this work.

References

1. BenAbdelkader, C., Culter, R., Nanda, H., Davis, L.: EigenGait: Motion-based Recognition of People Using Image Self-similarity. In: Proceeding of International Conference Audio and Video-Based Person Authentication, pp. 284–294 (2001)
2. Bobick, A., Johnson, A.: Gait Recognition Using Static, Activity-specific Parameters. In: Proceeding IEEE Computer Vision and Pattern Recognition, pp. 423–430 (2001)

3. Cunado, D., Nixon, M., Carter, J.: Automatic Extraction and Description of Human Gait Models for Recognition Purposes. Computer and Vision Image Understanding 90, 1–41 (2003)
4. BenAbdelkader, C., Cutler, R., Davis, L.: Motion-based Recognition of People in Eigengait Space. In: Proceedings of Fifth IEEE International Conference, pp. 267–272 (2002)
5. Collin, R., Gross, R., Shi, J.: Silhouette-based Human Identification from Body Shape and Gait. In: Proceedings of Fifth IEEE International Conference, pp. 366–371 (2002)
6. Phillips, P.J., Sarkar, S., Robledo, I., Grother, P., Bowyer, K.: The Gait Identification Challenge Problem: Dataset and Baseline Algorithm. In: Proceedings of 16th International Conference Pattern Recognition, pp. 385–389 (2002)
7. Yoo, J.H., Nixon, M.S., Harris, C.J.: Extracting Human Gait Signatures by Body Segment Properties. In: Fifth IEEE Southwest Symposium on Image Analysis and Interpretation, pp. 35–39 (2002)
8. Wagg, D.K., Nixon, M.S.: On Automated Model-based Extraction and Analysis of Gait. In: Proceedings of 6th IEEE International Conference on Automatic face and Gesture Recognition, pp. 11–16 (2004)
9. Shutler, J.D., Grant, M.G., Nixon, M.S., Carter, J.N.: On a Large Sequence-based Human Gait Database. In: Proceedings of 4th International Conference on Recent Advances in Soft Computing, pp. 66–71 (2002)
10. Dempster, W.T., Gaughran, G.R.L.: Properties of Body Segments Based on Size and Weight. American Journal of Anatomy 120, 33–54 (1967)
11. Keller, J., Gray, M., Givens, J.: A Fuzzy K-Nearest Neighbour Algorithm. IEEE Trans. Systems, Man, Cybern. 15, 580–585 (1985)

Salt and Pepper Noise Removal from Document Images

Hasan S.M. Al-Khaffaf, Abdullah Zawawi Talib, and Rosalina Abdul

Salam School of Computer Sciences, Universiti Sains Malaysia, 11800 USM Penang, Malaysia
{hasan,azht,rosalina}@cs.usm.my

Abstract. In this paper a noise removal algorithm is proposed by adding a procedure to enhance noise removal to a third party algorithm as a post processing step. The procedure (TAMD) has been proposed to enhance salt and pepper noise removal. TAMD analyzes thin line blobs before deciding to retain or remove them. It has been successfully applied previously in two noise removal algorithms by integrating their algorithm logic with the procedure. In this paper, a noise removal algorithm is proposed by utilizing it as a post processing step. The performance of the proposed noise removal algorithm is compared to many other algorithms including state of the art methods such as median and center weighted median. Real scanned images of mechanical engineering drawings corrupted by 20% salt and pepper noise are used in the experiment. Objective performance evaluation (PSNR and DRDM) has shown that our proposed noise removal algorithm is better than other studied algorithms.

Keywords: Noise Removal, Salt and Pepper, Mechanical Engineering Drawings, Line Drawings.

1 Introduction

Salt and pepper noise removal in natural images has been tackled extensively in image processing literature. Many filters including state of the art filters like Standard Median (SM), center weighted median (CWM), and tri-state median (TSM) have been proposed [1][2]. However, new methods for detecting and removing noise are still being published with the aim of removing more noise or reducing the side effect of changing clean image parts [3][4][5]. This is also partially true in binary document images where many methods are proposed to remove salt and pepper noise from document images. These methods are usually oriented to OCR applications [6][7][8] while other methods are focused on document images that contain graphics and text [9].

A procedure (named TAMD) for enhancing salt and pepper noise removal from binary images of engineering drawings has been proposed previously [10][11]. The purpose of this procedure is to track and analyze thin graphical elements and to decide whether to retain or remove these elements. This procedure can be integrated with other noise removal methods in order to enhance its noise removal capability. The utilization of this procedure leads to processed images with their weak features being retained and edges of the graphical elements being cleaned. Previously, two methods were proposed for removing noise from mechanical engineering drawings [10][11] by integrating TAMD into the algorithm logic of two third party noise removal methods. In

H. Badioze Zaman et al. (Eds.): IVIC 2009, LNCS 5857, pp. 607–618, 2009.

this paper we propose a new algorithm by performing TAMD as a post processing step after a third party algorithm. The performance of the propose noise removal algorithm is then compared to other methods including off the shelf methods such as SM and CWM. Real scanned images of mechanical engineering drawing are used in the experiment. The images are corrupted by 20% uniform salt and pepper noise. Two objective performance evaluation methods (PSNR and DRDM) are used as the criteria to judge the quality of the processed images.

The rest of this paper is organized as follows. Section 2 reviews noise removal algorithms in document images. Section 3 presents a short description of TAMD procedure. The proposed noise removal algorithm is then presented in Section 4. Experiment setup is presented in Sections 5. Section 6 presents objective performance evaluation methods used in the experiment. Experimental results and discussion are presented in Section 7. The paper ends with a section on conclusions.

2   Related Work

SM is a non linear filter that can remove salt and pepper noise from images. It has good capability of removing impulsive noise, but it has the disadvantage of removing fine details and sharp corners in the image [1]. The median of the set of values that include the neighboring pixels as well as the core (center) pixel of a $k*k$ window is used as the new value of the window center. k is an odd number that represents the width and the height of the moving window. If $X_{(i,j)}$ is the pixel to be processed then the new value is given by:

$$Y_{(i,j)} = \text{median } \{X_{(i-s,j-t)} \mid (s, t) \in W\} \tag{1}$$

where $Y_{(i,j)}$ is the new output value. W is the window and its coordinates is defined relative to the center. If a 3 * 3 window is used, W is given by:

$$W = \{(s, t) \mid -1 \le s \le +1, -1 \le t \le +1\} \tag{2}$$

CWM is an extension of the SM filter proposed by [1] with the aim of setting better trade off between removing impulsive noise and keeping the fine details intact. CWM gives more weight to the core pixel than to the neighboring pixels. Therefore it can control the behavior of the cleaning by setting a suitable weight for the center.

Dilation and erosion are two morphological operators used for removing noise [12][13]. In dilation the border of the graphical objects is grown by adding another layer of ON pixel to it. In erosion, the graphical elements are shrunk by removing one layer of ON pixels from its boundary. Closing operator (dilation followed by erosion) is used to remove salt noise while opening (erosion followed by dilation) removes pepper noise. Removing of salt-and-pepper noise by these filters requires a sequence of opening-closing operations. The disadvantages of using opening operator and closing operator are the removal of thin lines and the joining of too close objects respectively.

kFill algorithm is an iterative filter designed to remove salt-and-pepper noise from binary images [7][6]. The $k*k$ window is moved in a raster scan manner over the image and the core of the window is set to ON or OFF depending on three variables.

Another salt and pepper noise removal algorithm based on kFill proposed by Chinnasarn et al. enhances the performance (i.e. removing more noise) of kFill algorithm [8]. In this paper it is called Enhanced kFill. The equation originally proposed in kFill is also used in this method, however some other rules are modified in order to be able to remove noise spots smaller than windows' core size. Its disadvantages are: (i) with small value of k (3 for example) the algorithm only shortens one-pixel-wide blobs connected to graphical elements without removing it while it also shortens one-pixel-wide graphical elements, (ii) with larger value of k (4 and above) some graphical elements are extensively eroded.

In a more recent study by Simard and Malvar, a noise removal algorithm based on activity detection (hence called Activity Detector) was proposed [9]. The algorithm can remove salt-and-pepper noise in electronic documents that contain texts, dithered patterns, and graphics. First, all Connected Components (CCs) are computed with their bounding boxes (in our implementation we use the method proposed by [14] to compute CCs). Each CC bounding box is expanded and will participate in the calculation of activity map by the value of one for each of its pixels. Next the CCs are classified into three sets depending on their activity measure and number of pixels. The first set includes CCs near text areas or dithered areas. The second set includes only CCs in dithered areas. The rest of the CCs belong to the third set which includes areas of graphical elements. Finally the salt-and-pepper noise is performed by removing selected CCs that follow prescribed rules. The disadvantage of this method is the inability of removing noise connected to graphical elements. Since the removal of noise is implemented by removing the whole CC, it cannot remove such noise as it is considered part of that CC. In this paper we attempt to improve this method by integrating it with a procedure (called TAMD) as a post processing step.

3   TrackAndMayDel Procedure (TAMD)

To overcome some of the weaknesses in noise removal algorithms, a procedure TAMD has been previously proposed to help in getting better choices before changing the values of the pixels [11][10]. The idea is to perform further investigation before changing of end points. TAMD starts performing when an end point is detected. The purpose of this procedure is to check whether the already detected end point is part of thin line or part of small spurious branch connected to a graphical element. The TAMD procedure gives the algorithms the ability to check pixels outside the $3*3$ window. This widens the area of the image viewed by the algorithms without the need of using a larger window size (which is costly in term of processing time).

The procedure has two parts. The first is a tracking part where the branch is tracked starting from its end point and the tracked pixels are recorded. Tracking will stop when either an end point or branch point is reached; or the number of tracked points exceeds a predefined threshold (LT). The second is when the procedure will remove the already tracked branch if it is shorter than or equal to LT; and it is either connected to thick element or it is a separate object.

We have previously proposed two algorithms for salt and pepper noise removal from document images [11][10]. In the algorithms TAMD is integrated with third party algorithm logic. However, in this work we attempt another alternative which involves performing TAMD as a post processing step. A flowchart, mathematical foundation, examples, and algorithmic description of TAMD can be found in Al-Khaffaf et al. [11].

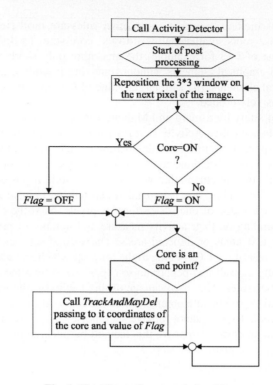

Fig. 1. Flowchart of proposed algorithm

4   Proposed Noise Removal Algorithm

The proposed algorithm consists of two stages: noise removal stage which is based
on Activity Detector noise removal method and a post processing stage by means of
TAMD. This is different from our previous work where TAMD was integrated into
the algorithms logics of other third party methods [11][10]. The activity detector
part is as described in Section 2. The activity detector part removes most of the
noise except those that are connected to the boundary of graphical elements. Then
the image is further processed by TAMD which yields the final image. The flowchart of the algorithm is shown in Figure 1. The post processing step involves one
full raster scan of the image. A 3*3 sliding window will move from top to bottom
and from left to right across the image. The center pixel of the window will be investigated whether to be candidate for ON fill (if it is currently OFF) or for OFF fill
(if it is currently ON). If there is only one neighbors of the center pixel with the
same intensity as the core pixel, a thin line is detected and further processing by
means of TAMD is to be performed. TAMD will analyze the thin line and decide
whether to retain it or remove it.

5   Experiment Setup

Seven noise removal algorithms (the proposed algorithm and the six algorithms reviewed in Sect. 2) are implemented in C++ using Visual Studio 7.0. The experiment is performed on Pentium 4 PC running Windows XP.

Different real scanned images of mechanical engineering drawings are used in the experiment. A compressed file with many images used in International Workshop on Graphics Recognition GREC'03 contest on arc segmentation i is obtained[11]. The images contain straight lines and circular arcs with no text. The lines also have different line widths ranging from one pixel to three pixels. The four images (1.tif, 2.tif, 3.tif, 4.tif) are generated by scanning four drawings into grey level images and then thresholded using moderate value [15]. Image 2 100.tif and 3 100.tif are similar to images 2.tif and 3.tif respectively. The threshold used to convert these two images from grey to binary is small and thus creating degraded images with many thin and disconnected lines. The two degraded images 2 100.tif and 3 100.tif are included for completeness. Each test image is corrupted by uniform salt-and-pepper noise at 20% noise level.

The algorithms have parameters such as window size. To keep the size of the experiment within a manageable size, the test in this paper is limited to 3 * 3 window sizes for all algorithms. The weights for CWM are selected as 3 and 5. CWM 5 is proven to retain one-pixel-wide lines [1]. For Activity Detector, the default values (chosen for strong noise removal) suggested by Simard and Malvar are used [9]. Window size of 3 * 3 is used throughout the proposed noise removal algorithm and also for TAMD. If the information inside the window is not sufficient to decide the new value of the pixel under investigation, TAMD is to collect more information by studying the pixels adjacent to the pixel under investigation. In other words, bigger window size is less crucial under this proposed algorithm because it is taken care by TAMD. When no sufficient information is available to decide the value for a pixel p, TAMD can move the 3 * 3 window around the neighborhood of p to search for more clues in order to decide the proper value for it. The threshold LT will decide how far TAMD can go away from p during clue collection. In the experiment we do not determine the suitable values of LT directly. Instead we perform empirical experiment by varying LT values between 2 and 12. The size of the window used to calculate DRD is taken to be 5 * 5.

6   Distortion Measurement

Human Visual System (HVS) can be used to judge the quality of processed images. However, HVS lacks the accuracy of the objective methods. It also should not be used when the processed image is meant for further processing by a computer rather than visualized directly by human such as the case of graphics recognition applications where the cleaned image is to be further processed by raster to vector conversion methods. For this reason, two objective performance evaluation methods are to be used in this work. For completeness, subjective performance evaluation is also to be

---

[1] http://www.cs.cityu.edu.hk/~liuwy/ArcContest/ArcSegContest.htm

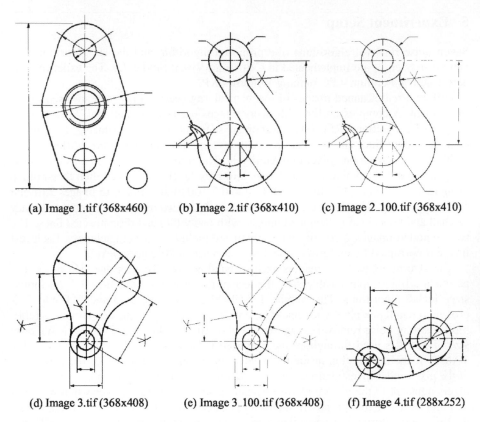

(a) Image 1.tif (368x460)   (b) Image 2.tif (368x410)   (c) Image 2_100.tif (368x410)

(d) Image 3.tif (368x408)   (e) Image 3_100.tif (368x408)   (f) Image 4.tif (288x252)

Fig. 2. Test images used in our experiments

used. The PSNR is the traditional criteria used for evaluating image processing algorithms [16][13]. The calculation of this term is based on the amount of changed pixels between the original and the processed image. For a source image $S_{(i,j)}$ and processed image $Y_{(i,j)}$ which is measured in *dB* is given below:

$$PSNR = 20.\log_{10}(\frac{Max}{\sqrt{MSE}}) \tag{3}$$

where Max is the maximum possible intensity. For one bit per pixel images $Max = 1$. The Mean Square Error (MSE) is given below:

$$MSE = \frac{1}{MN}\sum_{i-1}^{M}\sum_{j=1}^{N}(S_{(i,j)} - Y_{(i,j)})^2 \tag{4}$$

The above criteria are applicable to both binary and grey level images.

An objective measure for distortion in document images was proposed by Haiping et al. [16][17]. This method which is called Distance Reciprocal Distortion Measurement (DRDM) is developed specially for document images where graphical elements are separated from the background by clear edges. It takes advantage of human visual system, that is, the change of a pixel is more visible when the focus of vision is on its neighbor. The sensitivity of vision to flipping of the pixel is increased when the two pixels are close to each other. This measure is based on creating a weighted matrix with weights computed as the reciprocal distance from each pixel to the center pixel within a small neighborhood of $m * m$ window size. The DRD of the processed image $g(x, y)$ is given as follows:

$$DRD = \frac{\sum_{k=1}^{S} DRD_k}{NUBN} \qquad (5)$$

where $NUBN$ is the number of nonempty area in the image and DRD_k is the weighted sum of the pixels in the block B_k. It is taken as the number of nonuniform blocks of 8 * 8 pixels in f(x, y).

7 Experimental Results and Discussion

In this experiment, the proposed algorithm will be compared to third party algorithms. Well known methods (SM and CWM) are used in this experiment. The results of this experiment are presented in the context of PSNR and DRDM measures. Figure 3 shows the performance (in PSNR) of the proposed algorithm compared to other studied algorithms on 20% noise levels. The figure also shows the performance of the proposed algorithm with different values of LT ranging from 2 to 12. Figure 4 shows the performance (in DRDM) of the proposed algorithm compared to other studied algorithms on 20% noise levels. The figure also shows the performance of the proposed algorithm with different values of LT ranging from 2 to 12.

Figure 5 shows the result of applying different noise removal algorithms on one of the test images namely 2.tif. Only partial parts of the images are shown. The image is corrupted by 20% salt-and-pepper noise before applying the different noise removal algorithms. The method used to add the noise is described in Al-Khaffaf et al. [18].

Getting clean images (hence high values of PSNR) when removing noise from binary documents involves two factors i.e. removing the actual noise and retaining image detail. The former can be further expressed in two terms i.e. removing noise in the foreground/background and removing the noise that is attached to the graphical elements. Noise removal algorithms have different ability in balancing between the two factors. The two factors should be taken into consideration when designing a noise removal algorithm as well as when discussing the results of different noise removal algorithms. The discussion on the performance of our algorithm compared to other algorithms is presented next.

Now let's consider the case of the four images corrupted by 20% salt and pepper noise level in more detail. From Figure 3, we can note the following: Our proposed algorithm shows the best performance in all of the test images compared to the other six algorithms. CWM 3 is the second best performer. It can remove most of background noise and noise attached to the graphical elements (Fig. 5(h)). Activity Detector is the third best performer. It removes most of the background noise. However, its performance is suffered due to its inability to remove noise attached to the graphical elements

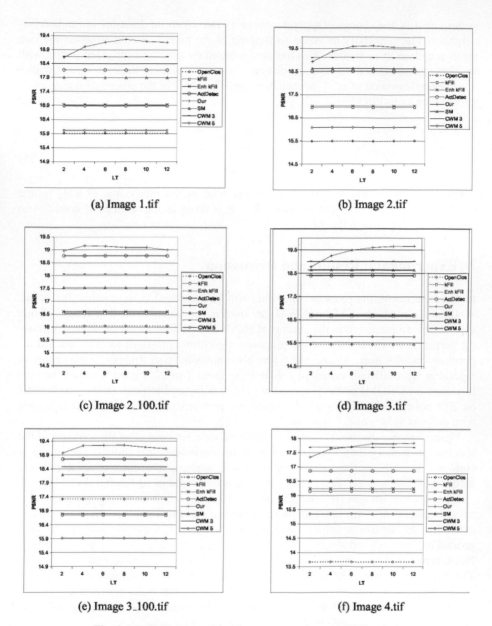

Fig. 3. PSNR for many algorithms on many images (20% noise)

(Fig. 5(f)). SM removes most of the background noise, but it also degrades the image fine detail. kFill and Enhanced kFill have moderate performance. These two filters leaves many noise speckles in the background ((c) and (d) of Fig. 5). Although CWM 5 can retain thin lines, it also skips a lot of noise in the image background (Fig. 5(i)). Opening-closing has the lowest performance. It removes all background noise, but it also distort almost all the lines in the image creating many disconnected lines (Fig. 5(j)).

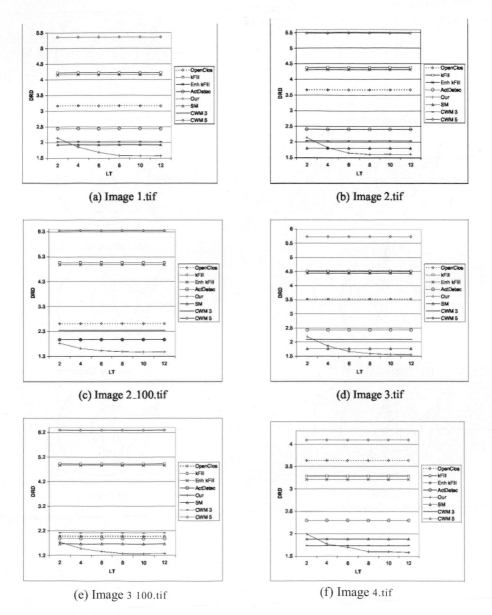

(a) Image 1.tif

(b) Image 2.tif

(c) Image 2_100.tif

(d) Image 3.tif

(e) Image 3 100.tif

(f) Image 4.tif

Fig. 4. DRD for many algorithms on many images (20% noise)

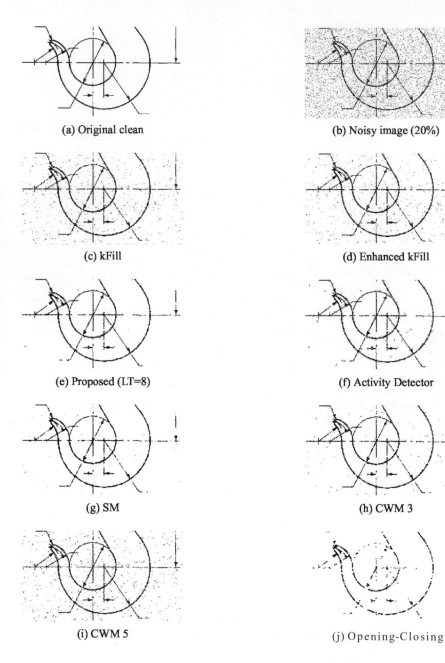

(a) Original clean

(b) Noisy image (20%)

(c) kFill

(d) Enhanced kFill

(e) Proposed (LT=8)

(f) Activity Detector

(g) SM

(h) CWM 3

(i) CWM 5

(j) Opening-Closing

Fig. 5. Image 2.tif cleaned by different algorithms

The DRD is computed between the original clean image and the filtered image. Low value of DRD indicates less distortion, hence visually better-quality images. It is shown from the DRD values of Figure 4 that our method produces better quality images compared to other methods for most of the images (the four scanned images and the two degraded ones) corrupted by 20% noise level. Low values of DRD occur when LT is more than 6, which is also consistent with all test images.

It can be seen from Fig. 5 that the methods that retain thin lines while removing most of the noise are the proposed method and Activity Detector method as shown in (e) and (f) of Fig. 5, respectively. However, the overall performance of our algorithm in PSNR is better than Activity Detector (Fig. 3). Fig. 5(f) contains more noise compared to Fig. 5(e). Most of the noise is attached to the contour of the graphical elements and it is visible if careful comparison between Fig. 5(a) and Fig. 5(f) is carried out. PSNR is sensitive to change of pixels value (even if such change is small and difficult to be observed by human visual system), hence Fig. 5(f) gets lower value of PSNR compared to the proposed noise removal method shown in Fig. 5(e). SM removes most of image noise. However, it also harms image detail which leads to a drop in PSNR value. SM also gets higher DRD value compared to our proposed method for the same previous reason.

8 Conclusions

In this paper, a noise removal algorithm is proposed. A procedure named TAMD that has been proposed previously to analyze thin lines before deciding to remove or retain it is also utilized in this work. This procedure could be integrated with other third party methods or performed as a post processing step following Activity Detector. Unlike the previous work, the proposed noise removal algorithm created by performing TAMD after Activity Detector. The proposed algorithm has the ability to produce a processed image with clean background and clean graphical edges. Simulation results on real scanned images of mechanical engineering drawings corrupted by 20% uniform salt and pepper noise is also shown. Analysis of the results based on two objective performance evaluation methods (PSNR and DRDM) show that the proposed algorithm has better performance compared to six other algorithms.

Acknowledgment

The first author would like to thank USM for its support through USM fellowship.

References

1. Ko, S.J., Lee, Y.H.: Center weighted median filters and their applications to image enhancement. IEEE Transactions on Circuits and Systems 38(9), 984–993 (1991)
2. Chen, T., Ma, K.K., Chen, L.H.: Tristate median filter for image denoising. IEEE Transactions on Image Processing 8(12), 1834–1838 (1999)
3. Windyga, P.S.: Fast impulsive noise removal. IEEE Transactions on Image Processing 10(1), 173–179 (2001)

 4. Aizenberg, I., Butakoff, C.: Effective impulse detector based on rank-order criteria. IEEE Signal Processing Letters 11(3), 363–366 (2004)
 5. Awad, A.S., Man, H.: High performance detection filter for impulse noise removal in images. Electronics Letters 44(3), 192–194 (2008)
 6. Story, G.A., O'Gorman, L., Fox, D., Schaper, L.L., Jagadish, H.V.: The rightpages image-based electronic library for alerting and browsing. Computer 25(9), 17–26 (1992)
 7. O'Gorman, L.: Image and document processing techniques for the rightpages electronic library system. In: Proc. 11th IAPR International Conference on Pattern Recognition. Conference B: Pattern Recognition Methodology and Systems, The Hague, pp. 260–263 (1992)
 8. Chinnasarn, K., Rangsanseri, Y., Thitimajshima, P.: Removing salt-and-pepper noise in text/graphics images. In: The 1998 IEEE Asia-Pacific Conference on Circuits and Systems, Chiangmai, pp. 459–462 (1998)
 9. Simard, P.Y., Malvar, H.S.: An efficient binary image activity detector based on connected components. In: Proc. IEEE International Conference on Acoustics, Speech, and Signal Processing, vol. 3, pp. 229–233 (2004)
10. Al-Khaffaf, H.S.M., Talib, A.Z., Salam, R.A.: Removing salt-and-pepper noise from binary images of engineering drawings. In: 19th International Conference on Pattern Recognition, Tampa, Florida, USA, vol. 1-6, pp. 1271–1274 (2008)
11. Al-Khaffaf, H.S.M., Talib, A.Z., Salam, R.A.: Enhancing salt-and-pepper noise removal in binary images of engineering drawing. IEICE Transactions on Information and Systems E92-D(4), 689–704 (2009)
12. Pratt, W.K.: Digital Image Processing: PIKS Inside, 3rd edn. John Wiley & Sons, Inc., Chichester (2001)
13. Bovik, A., Gibson, J.D.: Handbook of Image and Video Processing. Academic Press Series in Communications, Networking, and Multimedia. Academic Press, London (2000)
14. Di Stefano, L., Bulgarelli, A.: A simple and efficient connected components labeling algorithm. In: Proc. International Conference on Image Analysis and Processing, Venice, pp. 322–327 (1999)
15. Liu, W.: Report of the arc segmentation contest. In: Lladós, J., Kwon, Y.-B. (eds.) GREC 2003. LNCS, vol. 3088, pp. 363–366. Springer, Heidelberg (2004)
16. Haiping, L., Kot, A.C., Shi, Y.Q.: Distance-reciprocal distortion measure for binary document images. IEEE Signal Processing Letters 11(2), 228–231 (2004)
17. Haiping, L., Jian, W., Kot, A.C., Shi, Y.Q.: An objective distortion measure for binary document images based on human visual perception. In: Proceedings of 16th International Conference Pattern Recognition, vol. 4, pp. 239–242 (2002)
18. Al-Khaffaf, H.S.M., Talib, A.Z., Abdul Salam, R.: A study on the effects of noise level, cleaning method, and vectorization software on the quality of vector data. In: Liu, W., Lladós, J., Ogier, J.-M. (eds.) GREC 2007. LNCS, vol. 5046, pp. 299–309. Springer, Heidelberg (2008)

Color Image Magnification: Geometrical Pattern Classification Approach

Tien Fui Yong[1], Wou Onn Choo[1], and Hui Meian Kok[2]

[1] Department of Knowledge Science, Faculty of Science, Engineering and Technology
[2] Department of Advertising, Faculty of Arts and Social Science
Universiti Tunku Abdul Rahman, Malaysia
{yongtf,choowo,kokhm}@utar.edu.my

Abstract. In an era where technology keeps advancing, it is vital that high-resolution images are available to produce high-quality displayed images and fine-quality prints. The problem is that it is quite impossible to produce high-resolution images with acceptable clarity even with the latest digital cameras. Therefore, there is a need to enlarge the original images using an effective and efficient algorithm. The main contribution of this paper is to produce an enlarge color image with high visual quality, up to four times the original size of 100x100 pixels image. In the *classification phase*, the basic idea is to separate the interpolation region in the form of geometrical shape. Then, in the *intensity determination phase*, the interpolator assigns a proper color intensity value to the undefined pixel inside the interpolation region. This paper will discuss about problem statement, literature review, research methodology, research outcome, initial results, and finally, the conclusion.

Keywords: Image Interpolation, Anti-aliasing, Edge Detection, Resolution, Magnification.

1 Introduction

The rapid advancement of technology has made available huge amount of digital images to users from all walks of life. Digital cameras and video-camcorders are becoming common gadgets that users can now take as many digital images. The Internet, on the other hand, enables multimedia content sharing amongst surfers. In an era where technology keeps advancing, it is vital that high-resolution images are available to produce high-quality displayed images and fine-quality prints. The problem is that it is quite impossible to produce high-resolution images with acceptable clarity even with the latest digital cameras. Therefore, there is a need to enlarge the original images using an effective and efficient algorithm. The main contribution of this paper is to produce an enlarge color image with high visual quality, of up to four times the original size of 100x100 pixels image.

In order to perform the interpolation process, there are generally two phases involved. In the *classification phase*, the basic idea is to separate the interpolation

H. Badioze Zaman et al. (Eds.): IVIC 2009, LNCS 5857, pp. 619–626, 2009.
© Springer-Verlag Berlin Heidelberg 2009

region in the form of geometrical shape, which will eventually smoothen the curvy and non-linear edges (See Fig. 1). Then, in the *intensity determination phase*, the interpolator assigns a proper color to the undefined pixel inside the interpolation region. It does not assign the value based on a weighted average model, which would generally cause aliasing effect. What it does is that it performs pixels analysis in the neighboring 5x5 matrix to determine the proper color with its intensity value then calculated a weighted average formula similar to the one used in bicubic interpolation technique. What is different in the proposed method is for the intensity value to be computed from the same 5x5 matrix, however, excluding those intensity value from other color groups within the interpolation region being analyzed. By doing this, the proposed technique is expected to produce a much clearer interpolated image when enlarged as it will reduce jaggies and aliasing effects, and that colors of objects in the image do not blend in with other colors in the background.

2   Problem Statement

In an era where technology keeps advancing, high-quality display and printing services are the most required even to the most novice computer users. Thus, it is vital that high-resolution cameras, crystal clear display monitors, fine-quality printers, sharp scanners, and high-resolution images are available to produce high-quality displayed images and fine-quality prints. This is particularly crucial for photo studios, advertising, and desktop publishing. The problem is that it is quite impossible to produce high-resolution images with acceptable clarity even with the latest digital cameras in the market. Therefore, there is a need to enlarge the original images using an effective and efficient algorithm to process the images.

3   Literature Review

Image processing is not a new field of study. It has probably started back in 1970s when personal computers are first commercialized. A large number of interpolation techniques for magnifying images have been proposed. A typical weakness in most interpolation techniques is that they all seem to focus much attention on smoothing edges in the zoomed images but not preserving the original content such as color intensity of pixels. Most of the modern techniques have aliasing effect (blurring) on the transformed image, which generally cause the entire image to appear blurry. A possible solution would require a type of non-linear interpolation for maintaining the sharpness, clarity and smoothness of the new enlarged image.

The simplest technique to enlarge images is the pixel replication [2]. Unfortunately, the resulting images have jagged edges commonly known as jaggies in image processing. The method simply makes the pixels larger without smoothing the edges, which increase the visibility of jaggies. The color of the enlarged pixels is obtained from original pixel. Visually, it will result in blocking artifacts.

Better techniques apply bilinear or bicubic interpolation. Bilinear interpolation determines the intensity value of a new pixel by calculating a weighted average of the four pixels in the closest 2x2 neighboring pixels in the original image [2]. The averaging creates anti-aliasing effect and therefore produces relatively smoother edges with minimum jaggies. Bicubic interpolation works similar to bilinear, however, it calculates the weighted average of its closest 16 pixels in the 4x4 cubic surrounding the original pixel to determine the intensity value of the enlarged pixels [1], [4]. The latter method produces much smoother edges than the former one. However, both techniques do well in smoothing edges but a limitation is that they do not preserve the clarity and color details of the original image, causing the interpolated image appear blurry.

Freeman *et al.* [3] and Hertzmann *et al.* [4] proposed methods that have capability to learn the transformation between high and low resolution images from a set of related training data, carefully chosen for the purpose of recognizing sample patterns. The strength of these approaches is that fine details can be preserved in the zoomed image, provided that the input image is in the same class of image as the training data. The disadvantages of these approaches are that they incur high computational cost in training the system and that they will fail completely if the training data does not match the input image.

Johan *et al.* [5] proposed a progressive refinement approach for image magnification to preserve the color details and sharpen images without generating distinct artifacts. The optimization method used by them sometimes produces jaggies. Also, it still contains aliasing effect.

Sajjad *et al.* [6] proposed an image enlargement that takes into account information about the edges and smoothness of the image. It determines a threshold, classifies a geometrical shape and then uses the threshold to assign suitable intensity values to the undefined pixels in the expanded image. The advantage of the approach is that it can produce high-level of smoothness in edges, but the method still does not provide any solution to the problem of making clearer images. Neither can the method be used to magnify color images.

4 Research Methodology

To ensure the research project is well managed and smooth development work, it is proposed to combine project management techniques and phased development methodology for the entire research project. Since project initiation process has been carried out during the preparation of this proposal, the whole project is now divided into four major processes: planning, executing, monitoring and controlling.

In the planning process, much of the attentions are focused on selecting reference materials such as books, selecting tools, software and hardware for the creation of prototypes and experimentation, cost estimation and budgeting, and most importantly application for internal and external research funds.

Then, in executing process, a majority of the time is spent on reviewing literatures, define the scope of the research, collecting data, learning related software packages, performing series of experimentations to compare several related image interpolation techniques.

The phased development methodology is a type of rapid application development chosen to be used to develop prototypes to test the hypotheses. The results will be useful when writing and reporting an academic finding. The phased development methodology can be divided into four major phases: planning, analysis, design and implementation, in which the last three phases are repeated several times to produce different versions of the system, until the final version is achieved. This method is particularly useful in condition where requirements are unclear, unfamiliar technology, it involves complexity, and with schedule visibility. Next, monitoring and controlling process plays a vital role in ensuring work is done on time, to the expected level of research quality and at the right cost. The four phases are summarized below:

Table 1. Phases in the Phased Development Methodology

Phases in the Phased Development Methodology	Things to Perform
Planning	Selecting data (images), image interpolation techniques and software for the development of prototypes.
Analysis	Study the image interpolation techniques to learn how they work, how they are measured, and what are their strengths and weaknesses.
Design	Design a prototype system using tools such as UML diagrams and image viewing/editing software packages.
Implementation	Perform programming works using the selected programming language. Perform unit testing, integration testing and system testing to achieve best result.

5   Research Outcome and Contributions

Relevant information is collected during magnification process and the proposed technique will be able to select both the color value and the pattern to fill the interpolated region. Thus, it preserves not only the visual sharpness but also the clarity of the original image in general despite its generally costly processing. The focus of the proposed technique is aimed at producing high quality interpolation of color images. The research outcomes, through quantitative analysis of the proposed technique, are expected to cover some of the weaknesses of other techniques up to some extent with respect to quality and possibly efficiency.

The research is expected to produce a prototype system named *Pattern Interpolation System (PAINTERS)* to evaluate the effectiveness and efficiency of the proposed method. *PAINTERS* will have some important features to load multiple image files, select magnification factors from 2 to 4 times, save images in color or grayscale format, and several other basic image editing functionalities such as cropping, zooming, brightness and contrast controls, as well as hue and saturation settings.

Besides having basic image editing capabilities, *PAINTERS* can be used to support not just graphic designing but also as an image viewer where the selected files can be magnified to fit display screen when the images are smaller than the computer screen resolution settings. Some popular image viewers, such as that of Windows Picture and Fax Viewer, do not magnify image until the zoom button is pressed and the enlarged image would appear blurry due to the aliasing effect produced by other traditional interpolation techniques. *PAINTERS* is specially designed to make image viewing easier and appear larger on screen regardless of the image's resolution size. Images larger than quarter the screen's resolution will appear full-screen, while smaller ones will be projected up to four times its original size, depending on user's preferences. Smaller image contents are saved in computer servers, but larger images can be produced when required, thus saving the server storage space significantly.

In addition, *PAINTERS* also offer other benefits to home or mobile closed-circuit television (CCTV) users in such a way that it has feature to display simultaneously two or more separate images, one of which or all may be screenshots from a CCTV footage obtained from the proprietor software that comes along with the CCTV system. The images can be viewed, edited, cropped, magnified, and then printed out to be used as evidence in event a house is break in by thieves. The proposed method is likely to produce a clearer magnification that is likely to help police investigation.

Next, it is probably a good idea to incorporate the proposed technique with digital imaging systems, such as mobile phone's cameras in particular. Most of the latest mobile phone's cameras do not have the capability and capacity to capture and store larger image contents. The manufacturers of these products may use the proposed technique to form an alternative to promote their products without having to spend huge amount of money to research into new technology to produce gadgets with higher and higher resolutions, commonly known as mega pixels. The proposed method may be a vital solution to the memory-hungry technology used in most new cameras today. However, the only hiccup when using the magnification technique in cameras is that captured images will have to be magnified in the background as photo shooting is taking place due to the high processing power the proposed method requires. Images, when captured, will have to be stored in an image queue for magnification on the fly. Despite the limitation, it remains as an appropriate option to reduce the production cost of the cameras.

6   Initial Result

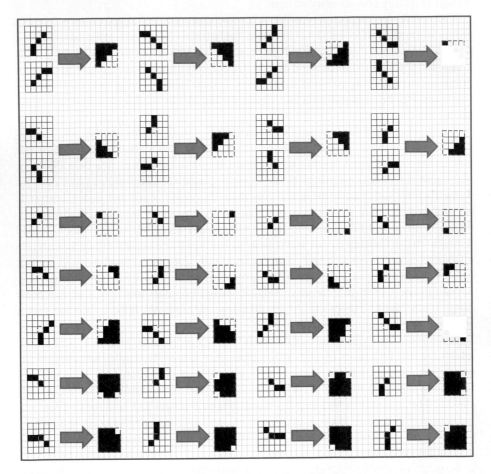

Fig. 1. This figure shows how a 5x5 pixel matrix from the original image separates the interpolation region in the form of geometrical shape. These are only partial representation of the whole proposed model.

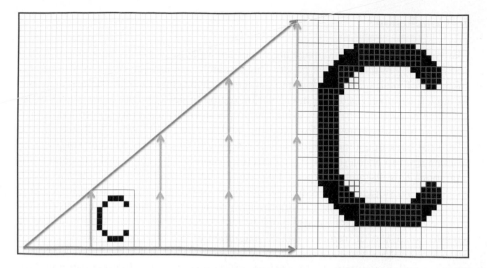

Fig. 2. This figure shows a 4 times magnification of original 10x8 pixels image into 40x32 pixels image with edge smoothing based on geometrical pattern classification

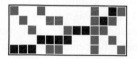

Fig. 3. This figure shows part of the original image with a size of 5x13 pixels

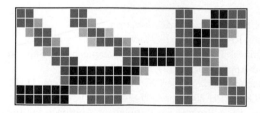

Fig. 4. This figure shows a 2 times magnification of part of the original image using the common weighted average models. Notice the aliasing effect at the edges.

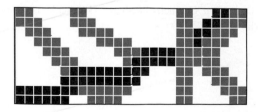

Fig. 5. This figure shows a 2 times magnification of part of the original image using the proposed model. Notice the anti-aliasing effect at the edges and the smoothing of curvy edges.

7 Conclusion

Clarity and sharpness of an image are important aspects for good image magnification and is the key in this research paper. This research explored the effective use of classification of interpolation region into geometric shapes and intensity determination of the undefined pixel inside the interpolation region to detect edges of an object within an image and recolor the edges using the proper intensity and color to produce a visually clear magnified image. However, the model is limited to work well with images where the background and object colors are widely distinctive. Further study should be conducted to enable better edge detection technique be employed to enhance this limitation. This research is expected to provide direct benefits to areas such as graphics designing, storage space reduction of image contents especially for mobile phone and digital camera users, and online image production for Internet users. It also can provide indirect benefits to many home or mobile CCTV users in situation where the recorded snapshots of intruders can be magnified to facilitate police investigations or being streamed to home owner's mobile phone as animated clips taken from their home surveillance system. Unlike before, office servers or the Internet can now keep smaller digital image contents for more effective storage management. For example, a typical 100GB hard disk space can hold approximately 70,000 pieces of 1.5MB image file size. With image interpolation technique, the same server can now store more than 200,000 pictures of 50KB each; a significantly improved storage management by nearly 300%. Whatever the reasons are, there is a continuous need for better image interpolation techniques to benefit the general society from all walks of life.

References

1. Adobe Photoshop, http://www.adobe.com
2. Digital Photography Review, http://www.dpreview.com
3. Freeman, W.T., Jones, T.R., Pasztor, F.C.: Example based Super-resolution. IEEE Computer Graphics and Applications 22(2), 56–65 (2002)
4. Hertzmann, A., Jacobs, C.E., Oliver, N., Curless, B., Salem, D.H.: Image Analogies. In: Proceedings of SIGGRAPH 2001, pp. 327–340 (2001)
5. Johan, H., Nishita, T.: A Progressive Refinement Approach for Image Magnification. In: Proceedings of the 12th Pacific Conference on Computer Graphics and Applications (PG 2004), pp. 1550–4085. IEEE Computer Society Press, Los Alamitos (2004)
6. Sajjad, M., Khattak., N., Jafri, N.: Image Magnification using Adaptive Interpolation by Pixel Level Data-Dependent Geometrical Shapes. International Journal of Computer Science and Engineering, 118–127 (2007)

Lifting Scheme DWT Implementation in a Wireless Vision Sensor Network

Jia Jan Ong, L.-M. Ang, and K.P. Seng

The University of Nottingham Malaysia
Jalan Broga, 43500 Semenyih, Selangor, Malaysia
{keyx9ojj,kezklma,kezkps}@nottingham.edu.my

Abstract. This paper presents the practical implementation of a Wireless Visual Sensor Network (WVSN) with DWT processing on the visual nodes. WVSN consists of visual nodes that capture video and transmit to the base-station without processing. Limitation of network bandwidth restrains the implementation of real time video streaming from remote visual nodes through wireless communication. Three layers of DWT filters are implemented to process the captured image from the camera. With having all the wavelet coefficients produced, it is possible just to transmit the low frequency band coefficients and obtain an approximate image at the base-station. This will reduce the amount of power required in transmission. When necessary, transmitting all the wavelet coefficients will produce the full detail of image, which is similar to the image captured at the visual nodes. The visual node combines the CMOS camera, Xilinx Spartan-3L FPGA and wireless ZigBee® network that uses the Ember EM250 chip.

Keywords: Wireless Visual Sensor Network (WVSN), Wireless Sensor Network (WSN), Discrete Wavelet Transform (DWT).

1 Introduction

The existence of camera-based network for security purposes has been around for many years. However, the surveillance camera operates independently that sends out video streams to a central processing server [10]. Usually, the video is analyzed by a human operator at the central processing server. With huge advancement in the image sensor technology, low-powered image sensors have appeared in a number of consumer products. Since the sensor consumes very little amount of power, it is then being implemented onto the wireless sensor networks (WSN). Tiny visual sensor nodes which replace the sensors used in the WSN to give wireless visual sensor networks (WVSN). As the image sensor capturing capability is kept on improving, large amount of data is generated by the camera-nodes. However, there is a limit in the network bandwidth which takes a large amount of time to transfer the video stream. The usage of camera-nodes in real-time applications is much more impossible. Compression is needed and less amount of video stream data to be transmitted across the network. Less detail of the data is received but real-time video streaming is possible to achieve. Besides, amount of power required to transmit the compressed video is

H. Badioze Zaman et al. (Eds.): IVIC 2009, LNCS 5857, pp. 627–635, 2009.

significantly less than the power needed to transmit the original image. Less amount of power is required in transmitting the compressed video data, which allows longer operating hours. DWT is one of the best candidates in performing the compression compares to other methods. Since DWT is considered to be lossless image compression, transferring all the wavelet coefficients will allow a full detail video stream to be obtained.

The following section discusses the overview of system implemented on wireless visual sensor nodes. Section 3 explains the lifting scheme discrete wavelet transform that is implemented onto the visual node. Section 4 compares a few different DWT filters and the best filter to be implemented. Section 5 discusses the device used for transmitting data through wireless. Section 6 will describe on the base-station implementation and how the data are received. Section 7 shows the results of the implemented system. Section 8 concludes the paper.

2 System Overview

The implemented DWT wireless visual sensor network consists of a CMOS camera, frame buffer (memory), Xilinx Spartan-3L, Telegesis ZigBee® wireless module (ETRX2-PA) and a computer. Frames of images are captured by the camera which is stored into a memory buffer. It is then processed once a full image of size 64x64 is captured from the camera. The image is filtered with 3 DWT modules that produce LL3, LH3, HL3, HH3, LH2, HL2, HH2, LH1, HL1, HH1 wavelet coefficients. Once all the coefficients are stored into the memory buffer, these coefficients will be transmitted to a computer through Telegesis ETRX2-PA modules. With all the coefficients received at the computer, inverse wavelet transform is performed onto these coefficients that will produce image that is similar to the one captured by the camera. From Figure 1, the wavelet coefficients are transferred from the memory buffer through RS232, ZigBee® wireless link and then RS232 to the computer. The hardware used

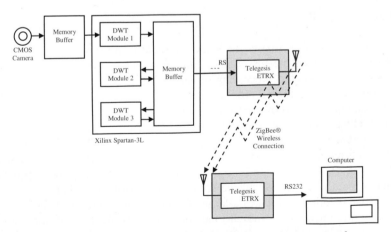

Fig. 1. Whole system overview of DWT on wireless sensor network

for these implementations is Celoxica RC10, which consists of an OmniVision OV9650 CMOS camera, Xilinx Spartan-3L FPGA chip and RS232 communication port.

This implementation imitates the wireless visual sensor node that has local processing such that less amount of data are needed to be transmitted through the network [10]. With basic information that are transmitted to the base-station, the base-station will then process and determine whether the detail image is required. The CMOS camera, Xilinx Spartan-3L and Telegesis ETRX2 ZigBee® module constitute the wireless visual sensor node. Whereas for the base-station, it comprises a Telegesis ZigBee® module and a computer, which processes the received wavelet coefficients back into an image.

3   Lifting Scheme Discrete Wavelet Transform

Initially, there are two types of wavelet transform which are continuous wavelet transform (CWT) and discrete wavelet transform (DWT). CWT requires enormous computational power to perform wavelet analysis. As for DWT, it is to implement wavelet transform into an iterated digital filter bank [1]. Lifting scheme wavelet transform was then introduced by Wim Sweldens [2]. It is an alternative method to perform the DWT computational. This scheme requires less operation to compute the wavelet transform compared to the conventional DWT filter bank scheme. The scheme also allows the use of integer wavelet transform. The wavelet transform filter that maps integers to integers [3,4] which provides the opportunity to be used for designing image compressions systems. This allows the wavelet transform to be implemented directly, without the use of any auxiliary memory [5].

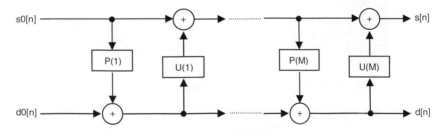

Fig. 2. The wavelet transform with lifting scheme filter bank

In Figure 2, image pixels are split into odd, d0[n] and even, s0[n] samples. The predict, P which is a dual lifting step that consists of applying a lowpass filter [3] to s0[n] and subtracting the result from d0[n] [4]. The update, U is the lifting step that does the opposite of predict where d [n] is passed through a highpass filter and subtract the result from s0[n]. With s0[n] and d0[n] going through several dual and primal lifting steps, the s0[n] would become the low pass coefficients, s[n] and d0[n] would be the high pass coefficients, d[n]. Different types of wavelet filters would have different arrangements of the lifting scheme filter bank.

4 Implemented Wavelet Filters

Five different wavelet filters were compared in simulations using Matlab before implemented onto actual hardware. The filters that were compared are Haar, 2/6, 5/3, 6/2 and 9/7. Comparison is done by performing 5 levels filtering on five different images in size of 256x256 pixels – Lena1.tif, Bird.tif, Bridge.tif, Camera.tif and Slope.tif.

By comparing the PSNR of the compressed wavelet coefficients, it is found that the 5/3 wavelet filter provides an average performance with simpler complexity of the architecture of filter. With referring to [4,6,7,8], a generalized architecture for the mentioned filters is shown in Figure 3. From Table 1a and 1b, the coefficients correspond to each filters are different when used on the generalized architecture.

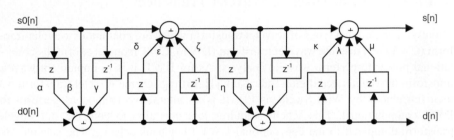

Fig. 3. The generalized wavelet filter architecture

Table 1a. Coefficient applied on generalized architecture (part 1)

Filter	α	β	γ	δ	ε	ζ
Haar	0	1	0	0	1/2	0
2/6	0	1	0	0	1/2	0
6/2	0	-1	0	-1/16	1/2	1/16
5/3	0	-1/2	-1/2	1/4	1/4	0
9/7	0	-203/128	-203/128	-217/4096	-217/4096	0

Table 1b. Coefficient applied on generalized architecture (part 2)

Filter	η	θ	ι	κ	λ	μ
Haar	0	0	0	0	0	0
2/6	-1/4	0	-1/4	0	0	0
6/2	0	0	0	0	0	0
5/3	0	0	0	0	0	0
9/7	0	113/128	113/128	1817/4096	1817/4096	0

Video captured by a camera can be considered as having a number of images captured in one second. Therefore, video could be filtered using wavelet transform filters, where each frame of video is processed. As the image pixels will be filtered, two filters 5/3 wavelet filters will be used for each level of filtering. In Figure 4, it shows the whole DWT module architecture consists of one row module wavelet filter and one column module wavelet filter.

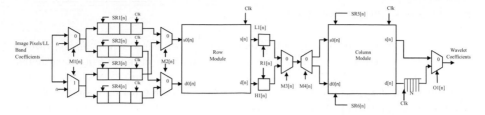

Fig. 4. Whole DWT module architecture

The architecture of the 5/3 row and column wavelet filters [9] are both implemented onto the hardware, which is shown in Figure 5 and Figure 6 respectively. These two filters will constitute in one level of filtering the images. For better compression of the image, 3 levels of filtering are performed on the images. This requires a total of six filters that consists of 3 row filters and 3 column filters. Each levels of the filtering that is performed by a module that consists of row and column wavelet filters.

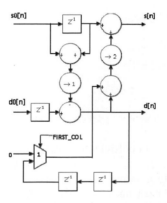

Fig. 5. Architecture of the 5/3 row module wavelet filter

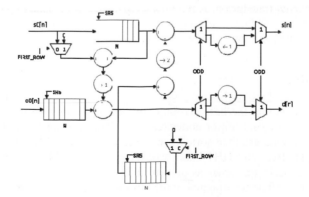

Fig. 6. Architecture of the 5/3 column module wavelet filter

5   Wireless Sensor Network

Typically, a wireless sensor network (WSN) consists of a few sensor nodes, from a few ten to thousands of nodes that have the same function in monitoring a particular region to obtain data [11]. Wireless sensor network usually consists of a data acquisition network and a data distribution network, which is monitored and controlled by a management centre [12]. As for wireless vision sensor network (WVSN), it consists of many vision nodes, network modes and a base-station. A vision node is the end point of the network that is responsible for capturing visual data. The captured data is then sent to the base-station through another visual nodes or network modes. However, the implementation here is done using the Telegesis ETRX2-PA ZigBee® modules. The ETRX2-PA module uses the Ember EM250 single chip ZigBee® which is in the IEEE802.15.4 standard. The module operates at a frequency of 2.4GHz with a throughput of 20kbps data transmitting to another module. There is some embedded system that uses ZigBee® device. This device is made in a simple, low power and low cost wireless communication technology [11].

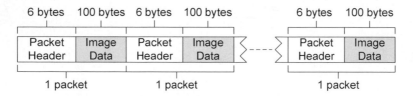

Fig. 7. Transmission of wavelet coefficients through ETRX2=PA

In order to have the wavelet coefficients to be transmitted wireless, two Telegesis ETRX2-PA modules were use. One is used on the visual sensor nodes (camera) with another one on the base-station (computer). The wavelet coefficients are sent in packets to the base-station. For each packets of data transmitted, it consists of a packet header and then followed by the image data. Figure 7 shows that the packet header takes up 6 bytes and 100 bytes of data is sent in each packet. In order to have all the wavelet coefficients transferred, it requires 43 packets to be sent to the base-station. Though the amount of data to be sent is 4291 bytes for each frame, the last packet which will have the last 9 bytes of empty data sent from the sensor node.

6   Base-Station

For this implementation, the base-station (computer) will receive the wavelet coefficients sent from the visual sensor nodes (camera). The wavelet coefficients sent from the visual sensor node are then sorted according to the LL3, LH3, HL3, HH3, LH2, HL2, HH2, LH1, HL1 and HH1 band wavelet coefficients. The arrangement of the coefficients is done in the order as shown in Figure 8. With having the third level filtered wavelet coefficients arranged at the top most let side. Then this is followed by the second level and first level filtered wavelet coefficients.

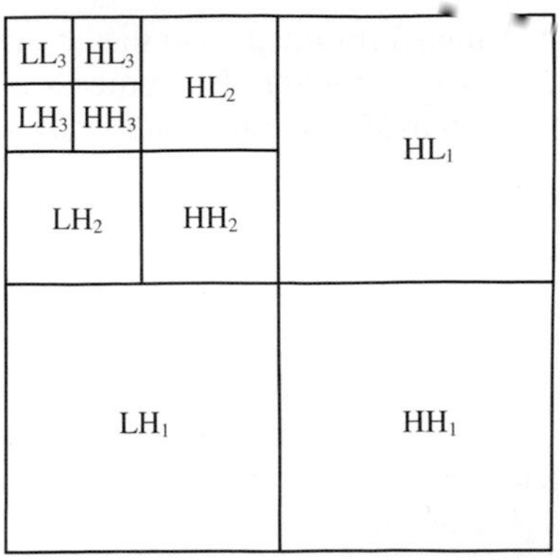

LL₃	HL₃	HL₂	HL₁
LH₃	HH₃		
LH₂		HH₂	
LH₁			HH₁

Fig. 8. Arrangement of wavelet coefficients received

Written Matlab function was used to receive the data through the Telegesis ETRX2-PA module. The Matlab function will detect a packet header which has "RAW:" character for each packet of data transmitted from the visual sensor node. Then it will be followed by 100 bytes of data – wavelet coefficients, sent from the visual sensor node. After receiving 100 bytes of data (wavelet coefficients), the base-station will receive a new packet of data that contains the following 100 wavelet coefficients. The process of detecting the packet header is performed for 43 times in which all the wavelet coefficients have transferred to the base-station. With receiving a total of 4300 bytes of data from the visual sensor nod, only the first 4291 data are the wavelet coefficients produced from the filters. The wavelet coefficients received will be arranged to the respective bands and levels of filtering. Inverse wavelet transform is performed onto the wavelet coefficients to produce image that is similar to the captured from the CMOS

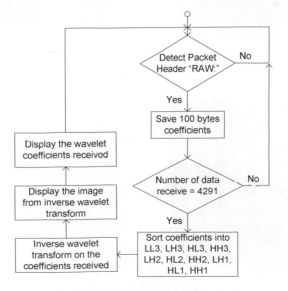

Fig. 9. Matlab data receiving flowchart

camera. An inverse wavelet transform image and the arranged wavelet coefficients are displayed out on the screen of the monitor. This process is repeatedly performed. The whole process flowchart written in Matlab function is shown in Figure 9.

7   System Implementation

The implemented system consists of a visual sensor node and a base-station. An Om-niVision OV-9650 CMOS camera, 3 modules of DWT filters in Xilinx Spartan-3L and Telegesis ETRX2-PA ZigBee® module that will transmit the wavelet coefficients out. The wavelet coefficients are transferred from Celoxica RC10 to the ZigBee® module through RS232 port available. As for the base-station, it is made up of a Telegesis ETRX2-PA ZigBee® module and a computer. The computer will store each frame of received wavelet coefficients from visual node. Then performs inverse wavelet transform onto each frame of wavelet coefficients received to give the similar image captured at the camera. The hardware setup for both visual node and base-station are shown in Figure 10.

Camera node (visual node).   Receiving node (base-station).

Fig. 10. Hardware used for implementations

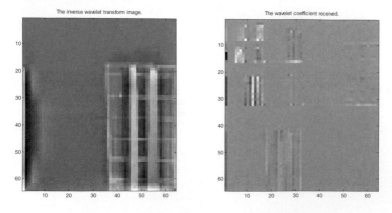

Fig. 11. Display the inverse transform of image and wavelet coefficients

Written Matlab function was used to detect the packet header and receive the data from the Telegesis ZigBee® module. The wavelet coefficients were also sorted accordingly as shown in Figure 8. Both the wavelet coefficients and inverse transformed image are then displayed on the monitor. Figure 11 shows the 64x64 image captured by the camera that is filtered and transferred through wireless network to computer.

8 Conclusion

Three layers of DWT filters can be implemented onto the visual sensor node that processes each frame of video. Only image of size 64x64 is able to be implemented onto the Celoxica RC10. The reason is that the amount of block RAMs available are insufficient to filter an image of size 160x120. Therefore, hardware with large amount of block RAMs to store the image and wavelet coefficients is needed. As for the transmitting of data, improvement can be made by including a start header and stop header for each packet of data sent. This will make sure that correct data are transferred and received at base-station.

References

1. Valens, C.: A Really Friendly Guide to Wavelets (1999)
2. Sweldens, W.: The Lifting Scheme: A Construction of Second Generation Wavelets (May 1995)
3. Gnavi, S., Penna, B.: Wavelet Kernels on a DSP: A Comparison Between Lifting and Filter Banks for Image Coding. Eurasip Journal on Applied Signal Processing 9, 981–989 (2002)
4. Calderbank, R., Daubechies, I., Sweldens, W.: Wavelets Transforms that Map Integers to Integers. Applied and Computational Harmonic Analysis 5, 332–369 (1998)
5. Strang, G., Nguyen, T.: Wavelets and Filter Banks. Wellesley-Cambridge Press, Wellesley (1997)
6. Adams, M.D.: Reversible Integer-to-Integer Wavelet Transforms for Image Compression: Performance Evaluation and Analysis. In: Natural Sciences and Engineering Research Council of Canada, and Image Power Inc. (December 12, 1999)
7. Lee, S.-W., Lim, S.-C.: VLSI Design of a Wavelet Processing Core. IEEE Transactions on Circuits and Systems for Video Technology 16(11) (November 2006)
8. Daubechies, I., Sweldens, W.: Factoring Wavelet Transforms into Lifting Steps. The Journal of Fourier Analysis and Applications 4(3) (1998)
9. Ang, L.M., Yeong, L.S., Seng, K.P.: A Low Complexity Interleaved Image Wavelet Transform Architecture for a Visual Sensor Node. In: International Conference Computational Intelligence of Security (2006)
10. Soro, S., Heinzelman, W.: A Survey of Visual Sensor Networks. Advances in Multimedia 2009, Article ID 640386, 21 pages (2009)
11. Yick, J., Mukherjee, B., Ghosal, D.: Wireless sensor network survey. Computer Networks 52(12), 2292–2330 (2008)
12. Lewis, F.L.: Smart Environments: Technology, Protocols and Applications. John Wiley, New York (2004)

Illumination Compensation for Document Images Using Local-Global Block Analysis

Mohd. Hafrizal Azmi, M. Iqbal Saripan, Raja Syamsul Azmir, and Raja Abdullah

Department of Computer & Communication Systems Engineering,
Faculty of Engineering, Universiti Putra Malaysia
43400, UPM Serdang, Selangor, Malaysia

Abstract. This paper presents the illumination compensation technique for document images using local-global block analysis. Imbalance illumination will affect the performance of classification and segmentation process because the darker regions conceal the information of the image. This method will split the image into non-overlapped blocks, and utilize the information within the local and global area of the image. The output images were binarized with simple global thresholding technique and the result shows that the output image is comparable in quality with the existed method. A comparative result will be presented with other document binarization methods.

Keywords: Illumination compensation, local-global block analysis, OCR.

1 Introduction

Document image analysis becomes very important nowadays since we are dealing with documents in almost every aspect in our life. With the rapid development of technology, people are starts to convert from using the traditional way in documentation to the new modern techniques. This includes the applications of image processing technique to enhance the image of cheque deposit and recognize the characters and numbers written on it. The modern techniques are mostly applied to the digital images because it is easier to be processed for specific purposes. That is why we can see that people are starting to employ the digital document instead of the traditional way. Since documents are being digitalized, efficient methods to manage them are required. There are two categories of document image analysis; one is textual processing while the other is graphical processing [1]. Textual processing focuses on the text components of the document while the later deals with non-textual figures in the document including the line and symbols [1]. The details about this concept can be read in [1] since it is out of this paper's direction.

Optical Character Recognition (OCR) is an important component in textual processing for document image analysis. The past decade has seen many algorithms were introduced either to enhance the existed method or implementing the new techniques. Despite its active developments, there are still no such algorithms that can perform perfectly for every condition [3]. There are limitations for different cases and researchers are concentrating on developing algorithm that could adapt for most conditions while still maintain the quality of output image and consider other important factors such as the time consumption.

H. Badioze Zaman et al. (Eds.): IVIC 2009, LNCS 5857, pp. 636–644, 2009.

The main problem that occurs before we proceed with the recognition process is the non-uniform illumination. Unless we can ensure that the capturing process will be held in a controlled environment with a very bright and balance lighting effect which is so troublesome, the variable illumination will cause some regions in the captured image looks darker or brighter. This situation will affect the process to distinguish the background and the foreground text which will leads to false segmentation and classification. In the field of OCR, the wrongly interpretation of the foreground text and background can leads to the out-of-shape character image. Besides, it will become worse if the algorithm will segment the wrong character which will give wrong information.

There are many algorithms introduced to solve the imbalance illumination occurs in document images including adaptive thresholding [5] and polynomial surface smoothing [4]. We have introduced one method for illumination compensation in [2] that will utilize the information within local area and global area of an image. But it focused on texture images. In texture image, there is assumption that the surface of an image could have many rapid changes of intensity which demonstrate the existence of texture information. For document image, we can say that the foreground text plays a role similar to the texture information. Based on this assumption, we believed that local-global block analysis method could be used for imbalance illumination correction for document image. This paper will focus on implementation of the local-global block analysis method for document images to observe the effectiveness of the method for future use in OCR. The results will be presented in a form of binary image comparative to other illumination compensation method for document images.

2 Related Work

There are many techniques that have been introduced to solve the variable illumination in OCR. The most popular approach is the adaptive thresholding which will divide the image into smaller windows and set the unique threshold value for each window. Niblack has proposed this kind of technique [6] and Sauvola made some improvements to the algorithm by imposing a new assumption that stated that the text pixels have near 0 grey values and non-text pixels have near 255 grey values [7]. Based on our literature on both works, it can be said that Sauvola's work performs better than Niblack's, but problem occurs when the assumption made is not agreed [5]. As for example, if the document images are captured within very low illumination with low contrast, the different value of the text and non-text pixels are insufficient for the algorithm to perform effectively.

Christian [8] has also proposed a technique to overcome the weakness of Sauvola's method which will normalize the contrast and the mean gray value to determine the threshold value. But Meng-Ling Feng in [5] has proved that his work outperforms Christian's method in an image which is affected by large variations of illumination.Meng-Ling Feng has proposed contrast adaptive binarization method which improved Christian's work to adapt the algorithm with large variation of illumination and low contrast problem. The technique suggested considering two types of windows which are primary and secondary. The primary local window is the area of interest while the secondary local window will provide extra information to be considered, but will not cover the whole image. The contrast adaptive binarization seems to be the best among other adaptive thresholding method introduced before in terms of adaption to the uneven illumination, low contrast image and less-noise occurrence.

3 Proposed method

3.1 Local-Global Block Analysis

Digital images can be described as a form of a set of square pixels that contain an intensity value of the image. Even though every pixel contains their own unique information, the neighborhoods of the pixels do correlate to each other. It means that any modifications that need to be made to any pixel should not ignore their adjacent pixels. There are also techniques that will put together a set of pixels into blocks and process the image based on the information of pixels within the block. Local-global block analysis method uses this approach to compensate the variable illumination in the document images. This method will utilize the information of groups of pixels and normalize it to the information of the image.

If we split the image into several blocks that are not overlapped to each other, we can define the region covered within block is known as local while region that covers the whole image is known as global. We can see in Figure 1 that a digital image, $f(x, y)$ with a size of $M \times N$, are divided into blocks of $f(a, b)$. $M_b \times N_b$ represents the local region and also the size of the block, while $M \times N$ represents the global

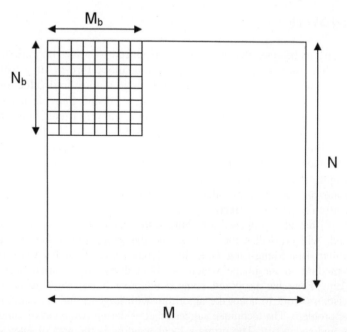

Fig. 1. Local and global area of a digital image

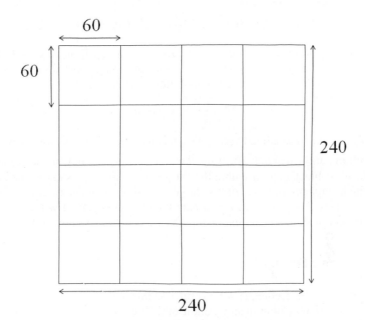

Fig. 2. Diagram of image sized 240×240 splitted into 16 blocks of 60×60 block size

region which is actually area covered by the whole image. At the beginning of this technique, the local mean values of each block are calculated. Let say the size of the image is 240×240 pixels, and we would like to configure the block size to 60×60 pixels, the total blocks present in the image is 4×4 and if each block has unique local mean value, it means that there are 100 different local mean values which each value represent each block. For better understanding, refer to Figure 2, which shows the diagram of image split into blocks.

In order to calculate the local mean value of each local region, we need to know every pixel intensity value that exists within the block area. Then, a simple operation to find mean value will be performed. The expression is shown in equation 1:

$$\mu_{local}(a,b) = \left(\sum_{x=a \times M_a}^{M_a-1} \sum_{y=b \times N_b}^{N_b-1} f(x,y)\right) \Big/ (M_a \times N_b) \qquad (1)$$

where $\mu_{local}(a,b)$ is the local mean of the local blocks, $(M_b \times N_b)$ is the size of the local blocks and (a,b) is the index number of the blocks. The global mean value is actually the average value of intensity of the image which can be determined by this equation:

$$\mu_{global} = \sum_{x=0}^{M} \sum_{y=0}^{N} f(x,y) \Big/ M \times N \qquad (2)$$

where μ_{global} is the global mean of an image, $f(x,y)$. After we compute the global and local mean values, we need to find the residual value for each pixel and their local mean. The expression is as follow:

$$\Delta(x, y) = f(x, y) - \mu_{local}(x(a), y(b)) \tag{3}$$

The residual values are finally will be normalized to the position of global mean by a simple expression shown by equation 4. The output image will display the residual values which are normalized to the value of global mean.

$$\hat{f}(x, y) = \Delta(x, y) + \mu_{global} \tag{4}$$

where $\hat{f}(x, y)$ is the normalized value. This technique will successfully solve the non-uniform illumination without affecting the foreground text but in the same time, it will produce the block pattern within the image. This situation is known as blockiness effect, which happens because of the large variation of intensity values across the block boundaries. The solution to eliminate the blockiness effect will not be covered in this paper but it should be an interesting issue to be discussed in the future.

4   Results and Discussion

We have applied the technique to several document images captured using digital camera under different illumination conditions. The size of image to be processed is fixed to 240×240 pixels and the block size vary between different images, based on which will give the best results. As for the results presented in this paper, the details about the block size and the threshold value are shown in Table 1. Notice that the threshold value for contrast adaptive binarization method is not included since the value was determined by the algorithm itself.

Table 1. Configuration details

Sample image	Contrast adaptive binarization	Local-global block analysis	
	Secondary window size	Block size	Threshold
1	24	24	73
2	16	30	95
3	30	24	104

Figure 3 shows the intensity value along the selected row in the sample image. It includes intensity information from the original image and the output image of local-global analysis. Horizontal axis represents the position of pixels along the same row while the vertical axis represents the amplitude of intensity for each pixel. Each line represents different images as stated in the legend of the graph.

If we examine the trend of the graph, we can see that the original image has higher intensity value at the left region compared to the right region. It shows that the right side of the image is darker than the left side and this situation clarify the non-uniform illumination existence in the image. On the darker region, the intensity of the background could be the same as the text pixels on the brighter area. Whenever we set the threshold value for simple global thresholding technique, there will be background

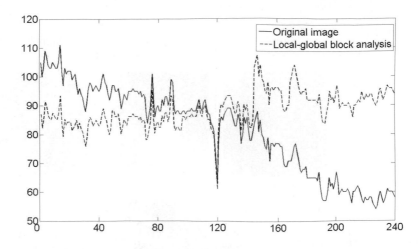

Fig. 3. Intensity values along the same horizontal line across the sample image

area in the image that is interpreted as the text pixels, so that will be displayed as black after binarization. This is why we cannot simply apply the simple global thresholding method to the image that suffered from imbalance illumination.

Using the local-global block analysis technique, the distribution of the intensities of the image is normalized and the illumination is better compared to the original image. We can see that every pixel is now lying near to the global mean value. Furthermore, later in the explanation will prove that this technique seems to successfully keep the information of the image, which is in this case, the foreground text information.

Table 2 shows the output images of local-global block technique comparative to the simple global thresholding and contrast adaptive binarization. Each output image were binarized except for the contrast adaptive since the algorithm has already includes binarization. The threshold value was set manually as shown in Table 1 and the value has been applied to every methods excluding contrast adaptive.

As we can see, the simple global thresholding technique is not applicable for image suffered with uneven illumination because the darker area in the image will become black since the area is interpreted as a foreground text. From this observation, we can simply say that simple global thresholding failed to distinguih the text and non-text pixels. Contrast adaptive works well to adapt to uneven illumination but it has problem to deal with a document image that has small size of texts. Whenever we applied the algorithm to a small text document image, at certain area, the binarized character will be displayed as it connected to other character. This could leads to the the complexity of classification process.

If we refer to the output images of local-global block analysis method, it can b said that the method capables to perform well in correcting the non-unifo illumination in document images without sweeping away the shape of the text wh is a very important characteristic for OCR. But, before the images have

Table 2. Output images

Sample/method	Sample 1	Sample 2	Sample 3
(a) Original image			
(b) Simple global thresholding			
(c) Contrast adaptive binarization			
(d) Local-global block analysis			
Binarization of (d)			

binarized, we can notice that there are block pattern visible in certain area of the image. This is called blockiness effect. It happens because there are rapid changes of intensity value across the block boundary due to the difference value of local mean for different blocks. After binarization, the output images of local-global analysis display the text as clear as shown by contrast adaptive for large text document image. From this observation, we can say that the blockiness effect will not significantly affect the performance of this method after binarization. For small text document image, binarized image of local-global method outperform the contrast adaptive. The algorithm manages to display the text pixels and maintain the shape of the characters. However, we can see some noise occurrence within the binarized iamge of local-global analysis method. But, since it has not significantly affect the text pixels, further procedure to remove the noise should not be too hard.

To maintain the optimal performance of this method for document images, we have made some assumption and limitations that need to be consider. First, the illumination intensity changes should not be too significant. If it does happen, the text information within the local area will be affected. Thus for image that suffered with a very significant changes of illumination within a local region, the performance of this method will decreased accordingly. To adapt to this assumption, the configuration of block size must be small, but cannot be too small because it will sweep away the shape of the texts that need to be kept. Second, as explained, the block size is vary depends on the condition of the image and the threshold value is set manually for each sample image. For an automatic real-time system, this could be very inefficient since every case needs the new configuration for the block and the threshold value. Therefore, this algorithm requires some modifications to suit with the automatic real-time OCR system.

5   Conclusion

We have presented the implementation of local-global block analysis method to compensate the variable illumination in document images by normalizing the local mean value to the global mean value of the image. The binarized output images are comparable in quality to the images applied with contrast adaptive. Furthermore, for document image that suffered low contrast and consist of small size text, this method outperform the contrast adaptive method. However, the configuration of block size that depend on the condition of the image and the threshold value that have to be set manually should be improvise to be more competent for automatic system in OCR area.

We also noticed that before binarization procedure, there is a block pattern visible in the image after we applied the local-global analysis. This is known as blockiness effect. But after binarization, it is shown that the blockiness effect does not h significant effect to the quality of the final output images. So we could simply ig that effect for this purpose. However, it is an interesting issue to be discussed l the future.

References

1. Kasturi, R., O'Gorman, L., Govindaraju, V.: Document Image Analysis: A Primer. Sadhana 27, Part 1, 3–22 (2002)
2. Saripan, M.I., Azmi, M.H., Raja Abdullah, R.S.A., Anuar, L.H.: Illumination Compensation in Pig Skin Texture Using Local-global Block Analysis. Journal of Modern Applied Science 3(2), 89–93 (2009)
3. de Mello, C.A.B., Lins, R.D.: A Comparative Study on OCR Tools. In: Vision Interface 1999, Trois-Rivieres, Canada, pp. 224–232 (1999)
4. Lu, S., Tan, C.L.: Binarization of Badly Illuminated Document Images through Shading Estimation and Compensation. In: ICDAR, pp. 312–316 (2007)
5. Feng, M.-L., Tan, Y.-P.: Contrast adaptive binarization of low quality document images. IEICE Electronic Express 1(16), 501–506 (2004)
6. Niblack, W.: An Introdution to Digital Image Processing, pp. 115–116. Prentice Hall, Englewood Cliffs (1986)
7. Sauvola, J., Pietikainen, M.: Adaptive Document Image Binarization. Pattern Recognition 33, 225–235 (2000)
8. Wolf, C., Jolion, J.-M.: Extraction and Recognition of Artificial Text in Multimedia Documents. Pattern Analysis Applications 6(4), 309–326 (2004)

Automatic Image Annotation Using Color K-Means Clustering

Nursuriati Jamil and Siti 'Aisyah Sa'adan

Faculty of Computer & Mathematical Sciences, Universiti Teknologi MARA
40450 Shah Alam, Selangor, Malaysia
liza@tmsk.uitm.edu.my, aisyah.sadan@gmail.com

Abstract. Automatic image annotation is a process of modeling a human in assigning words to images based on visual observations. It is essential as manual annotation is time consuming especially for large databases and there is no standard captioning procedure because it is based on human perception. This paper discusses implementation of automatic image annotation using K-means clustering algorithm to annotate the colors with the appropriate words by using predefined colors. Experiments are conducted to identify the number of centroids, distance measures and initialization mode for the best clustering results. A prototype of an automatic image annotation is developed and then tested using thirty-five beach scenery photographs. Results showed that annotating image using evenly-spaced initialization mode and 100 centroids measured using City-Block distance function managed to achieve a commendable 75% precision rate.

Keywords: Automatic image annotation, K-means clustering, RGB model, initialization mode, cluster number.

1 Introduction

Automatic image annotation is defined indirectly as the process by which a computer system automatically assigns words in the form of captioning to a digital image [14]. Commonly, automatic image annotation is used in image retrieval systems to organize and locate images of interest from a database. Annotation-based image retrieval is perceived as better than content-based image retrieval (CBIR) because it allows user to compose queries freely using their natural language [4]. Furthermore, CBIR system matches images based on the low-level visual similarities. Thus, it has some limitations due to missing semantic information [8].

Clustering algorithms are commonly used in classifying low-level features of images prior to annotation. [1] defined clustering as the process of organizing ob... into groups whose members are similar in some way. A cluster is therefore a col... of objects that are similar between them and are dissimilar to objects belo... other clusters. Several popular clustering algorithms include K-Means, E... Maximization (EM) and Discreet Distribution (D2) clustering [7] algorithm... clustering relies on hard assignment of information to a given set of p...

H. Badioze Zaman et al. (Eds.): IVIC 2009, LNCS 5857, pp. 645–652, 2009.
© Springer-Verlag Berlin Heidelberg 2009

known as cluster centers or the *K* centroids [13]. At every step of the algorithm, each data value is assigned to the nearest centroid based on some similarity parameter that is calculated using distance measurement. Then, the centroids are then recalculated based on these hard assignments. With each successive pass, a data value can change the centroid where it belongs to, thus altering the values of the centroid at every pass. K-Means clustering has been used extensively to facilitate in classifications of low-level features in image retrieval systems [3][14][11][7][9]. The EM algorithm employed in [13] [14], on the other hand relies on soft assignment of data given set of centroids. Every data value is associated with every centroid through system of weight based on strongly the data value should be associated with the particular centroid. In general, K-Means clustering works better than EM algorithm and is fairly simple to implement for image segmentation using color as the feature parameter [13].

In this paper, implementation of K-Means clustering algorithm is experimented to automatically annotate beach scenery photographs using their RGB color features. The purpose of the study is to investigate the suitable number of centroids, distance measures and initialization mode in an attempt to achieve the best clustering performance.

2   K-Means Clustering

The K-Means is a very popular algorithm and one of the best for implementing the clustering process [12]. It has a time complexity that is dominated by the product of the number of patterns, the number of centroids, and the number of iterations. For an image, K-Means clustering may be implemented as follows:

i)   Place *K* points into the space represented by the pixels that are being clustered. These points represent initial cluster centroids *(K)*, also known as initialization point.
ii)   Assign each pixel to the cluster that has the closest centroid (obtain by measuring distance).
iii)   When all pixels have been assigned, recalculate the positions of the *K* centroids.
iv)   Repeat Steps 2 and 3 until the centroids no longer move.

Factors that may affect performance of K-Means algorithm are the initialization mode, distance measures and the number of centroids used during clustering process. Initialization mode is important in order to have accurate RGB representation for the centroids at the starting point of the clustering. Each pixel in the image is then assign to its proper cluster based on its similarity by using a distance measure. This will influence the shape of the clusters, as some elements may be close or further away to ̱ne another according to the distance calculated [10]. Thus, the distance measurement ̱d is also vital to ensure every pixel is assigned to its centroid precisely. Common ̱nce functions used in clustering are Euclidean distance, City Block distance, ̱wski distance and Canberra distance. Number of centroids, *K* chosen in the ̱ng process must also be taken into consideration too. According to [13], the ̱f the centroids used in the segmentation has a very large effect on the output. ̱centroids used in the color setup, more possible colors are available to show ̱put.

3   Materials and Methods

As mentioned previously, this paper discusses the implementation of an automatic annotation prototype that will annotate beach photographs using eight predefined words: sky, sea, beach, cloud, tree, hill, grass and rock. Fig. 1 demonstrates the diagram of the annotation process.

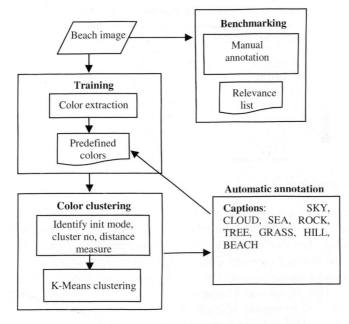

Fig. 1. Automatic annotation processes

3.1   Data Collection

Ten natural beach scenery photographs are downloaded from [5][6] as these images have been classified into their proper categories for benchmarking purpose. These images are chosen from a total of 3,360 photograph images to be used as training images. For testing purposes, thirty-five photograph images are collected randomly from search engine Yahoo! and Google. The criteria of the test images are that they are beach scenery photographs and they must have at least one of the eight beach elements, which are sky, sea, beach, cloud, tree, hill, grass and rock.

3.2   Manual Image Annotation

All thirty-five testing images are manually annotated using visual inspection of three people. They are given a selected list of words taken from Oxford Fajar dictionary [2] that describe beach scenery and they manually annotated the test images based on the given words. Results of these manual annotations are then used as benchmarking of the proposed prototype.

3.3 Color Feature Extraction

Color features using RGB model of the eight beach elements mentioned earlier are extracted from the training images. These predefined color features are later used during the testing phase for annotating the test images. Table 1 shows the RGB average color values for all the beach elements.

Table 1. Predefined colors of the beach elements

Beach element	Average RGB values
Sky	88, 122, 170
Sea	58, 97, 123
Beach	187, 174, 147
Grass	59, 69, 30
Hill	43, 88, 75
Tree	72, 79, 36
Rock	76, 67, 69
Cloud	190, 189, 199

3.4 Color Clustering

Two experiments are conducted to determine the initialization mode, distance function and number of clusters in an effort to achieve the highest performance of K-Means algorithm. The first experiment is to discover the best combination of initialization mode and distance measure. The initialization modes that are tested are evenly-spaced mode and max-data mode; and the distance measurements that are involved are Euclidean, City Block and Canberra. Objective of the second experiment is to identify the appropriate number of centroids *(K)* to be implemented in automatic annotation prototype. These centroids contain the RGB values to be compared later with predefined color of beach elements. The numbers of centroids to be tested are 8K, 30K, 50K and 100K.

   To evaluate the performance of the clustering algorithm, Recall and Precision measures are computed [14], where *numCorrect* is the number of correctly retrieved words from output caption, *numRetrieved* is the total number of retrieved words from the caption and *numExist* is the actual number of retrieved words for the caption.

$$\mathrm{Re}call = \frac{numCorrect}{num\,\mathrm{Re}\,trieved} \tag{1}$$

$$\mathrm{Pr}ecision = \frac{numCorrect}{numExist} \tag{2}$$

3.5 Development of Automatic Annotation Prototype

Based on the experiment results, a prototype of an automatic annotation system was developed using Java programming language. The software development tools used are BlueJ version 2.1.2 with Java Development Kit of version jdk1.6.0_05, Java Runtime Environment of version jre1.6.0_07, Java Advance Imaging Development Kit version jai-1_1_3-lib-windows-i586-jdk and Java Advance Imaging Runtime Environment version jai-1_1_3-lib-windows-i586-jre. The prototype is then tested and evaluated using thirty-five photographs of beach scenery.

4 Results and Discussions

Table 2 shows results of the first experiment to determine the combination of initialization mode and distance measure in achieving the best performance of clustering. Overall, evenly-spaced initialization mode performed better compared to max-data mode. It can be also seen that the highest average precision rate of 88% is accomplished by using evenly-spaced initialization mode and City Block distance measure. Even though recall rate of this combination is slightly lower than Canberra measure, we perceived precision rate as a better judgment of clustering performance.

Table 2. Performance of different combinations of initialization modes and distance measures

Initialization Mode	Precision			Recall		
	Euclidian	CityBlock	Canberra	Euclidian	CityBlock	Canberra
Evenly-spaced	0.80	0.88	0.83	0.40	0.40	0.46
Max-data	0.82	0.87	0.88	0.34	0.32	0.37

The experiment result of comparing the number of centroids is recorded in Table 3. From the table, it is shown that 8K and 100K have equal precision rate of 88% in annotating the images. Therefore, we include the recall rate of 40% in order to conclude that the highest performance was achieved when the highest number of centroids of 100 is used. It is also interesting to note that when using 30 and 50 centroids, the precision rates are in fact lower than when utilizing only 8 centroids.

After all the techniques and distance measure are determined, the prototype was developed and tested with the 35 testing images. Fig. 2 illustrates an output of one of the annotated image. Recall and precision rates of the tested images are demonstrated in Table 4 showing and average precision rate of 75% and recall rate of 50%.

Table 3. Performance of different number of centroids

average	Number of Centroids (K)			
	8	30	50	100
Precision	0.88	0.87	0.87	0.88
Recall	0.32	0.34	0.38	0.40

Table 4. Recall and Precision Rates of the Prototype

Image	Precision	Recall
beach001.jpg	0.5	0.25
beach002.jpg	0.67	0.4
beach003.jpg	0.4	0.5
beach004.jpg	1	0.33
beach005.jpg	1	0.4
beach006.jpg	0.5	0.2
beach007.jpg	1	0.4
beach008.jpg	1	0.4
beach009.jpg	1	0.5
beach010.jpg	0.57	1
beach011.jpg	1	0.2
beach012.jpg	1	0.4
beach013.jpg	0.5	1
beach014.jpg	0.8	0.8
beach015.jpg	1	0.4
beach016.jpg	1	0.2
beach017.jpg	1	0.4
beach018.jpg	0.5	0.2
beach019.jpg	0.67	0.5
beach020.jpg	0.5	0.25
beach021.jpg	1	0.67
beach022.jpg	1	0.33
beach023.jpg	0.67	1
beach024.jpg	0.57	1
beach025.jpg	1	0.4
beach026.jpg	0.5	0.25
beach027.jpg	1	0.25
beach028.jpg	1	0.4
beach029.jpg	0.5	0.4
beach030.jpg	0.5	1
beach031.jpg	0.67	1
beach032.jpg	0.2	0.33
beach033.jpg	0.33	0.35
beach034.jpg	0.63	1
beach035.jpg	1	0.25
Average	**0.75**	**0.50**

Table 5 illustrated the result of the percentage of each beach element correctly retrieved. From the table, it is shown that SKY and CLOUD have the highest retrieval rate at 77% and 70%, respectively. This is due to the fact that SKY has similar color to CLOUD. In other words, when there is SKY, there is possibility of CLOUD to annotated. However, ROCK has 0% of correctly retrieved rate. The main reason of the little occurrence of ROCK in all the tested images.

Caption: SEA ; GRASS ; HILL ; TREE ; ROCK

Fig. 2. An image automatically annotated with 5 words related to beach scenery

Table 5. Percentage of beach elements correctly retrieved

Beach Element	Manual Annotation	Automatic Annotation	Correctly Retrieved
SKY	35	27	**77.14**
SEA	28	11	**39.29**
BEACH	33	13	**39.39**
GRASS	6	2	**33.33**
HILL	8	1	**12.50**
TREE	21	7	**33.33**
ROCK	4	0	**0.00**
CLOUD	20	14	**70.00**

5 Conclusion

From the experimental results, it shows that the prototype is best implemented using evenly spaced values for initialization mode with City Block distance for distance measure in K-Means clustering. Even though the training data is very small, due to lack of free image database, the prototype achieved a commendable precision rate of 75 %. This shows that K-Means algorithm is robust enough to be utilized in clustering low-level features of an image for annotation purposes. Our study is an initial work of automatic image annotation. There are several constraints and limitations that shou̵ be overcome with further research.

Future work to improve the accuracy of the system can take many directions example, this prototype needs to be tested with other color model that is mo₁ with human vision such as HSV color model. More training images shou̵ quired to increase the accuracy of the feature extractions. Finally, mo̵ should be extracted from the image to imply more meaning when annot̵ is performed.

References

1. A Tutorial on Clustering Algorithm,
   `http://home.dei.polimi.it/matteucc/Clustering/tutorial_html/index.html`
2. Hawkins, J.M.: Kamus Dwibahasa Oxford Fajar: Melayu Inggeris, 4th edn. Fajar Bakti, Selangor (2004)
3. Çavuş, Ö., Aksoy, S.: Semantic Scene Classification for Image Annotation and Retrieval. In: da Vitoria Lobo, N., et al. (eds.) IAPR 2008. LNCS, vol. 5342, pp. 402–410. Springer, Heidelberg (2008)
4. Inoue, M.: On the Need for Annotation-Based Image Retrieval. In: Workshop of Information Retrieval in Context, pp. 44–46 (2004)
5. James Wang Research Group, `http://wang.ist.psu.edu/~jwang/test1.zip`
6. Jia Li Research Group,
   `http://www.stat.psu.edu/~jiali/li_photograph.tar`
7. Li, J., Wang, J.Z.: Real-Time Computerized Annotation of Pictures. In: ACM Multimedia Conference, pp. 911–920 (2006)
8. Pan, J.Y., Yang, H.J., Duygulu, P., Faloutsos, C.: Automatic Image Captioning. In: IEEE International Conference on Multimedia and Expo., pp. 1987–1990 (2004)
9. Sayar, A., Yarman-Vural, F.T.: Image Annotation by Semi-Supervised Constrained by SIFT Orientation Information. In: 23rd International Symposium on Computer and Information Sciences, pp. 1–4 (2008)
10. Similarity Measurements, `http://people.revoledu.com/kardi/tutorial/Similarity/index.html`
11. Srikanth, M., Varner, J., Bowden, M., Moldovan, D.: Exploiting Ontologies for Automatic Image Annotation. In: 28th International ACM SIGIR Conference on Research and Development in information Retrieval, pp. 552–558 (2005)
12. Vrahatis, M.N., Boutsinas, B., Alevizos, P., Pavlides, G.: The New k-Windows Algorithm for Improving the K-Means Clustering Algorithm. J. Complexity 18(1), 375–391 (2002)
13. Vutsinas, C.: Image Segmentation: K-Means and EM Algorithms,
    `http://www.ces.clemson.edu/~stb/ece847/fall2007/projects/kmeans_em.doc`
14. Wang, L., Liu, L., Khan, L.: Automatic Image Annotation and Retrieval using Subspace Clustering Algorithm. In: 2nd ACM International Workshop on Multimedia Databases, pp. 100–108 (2004)
15. Li, W., Sun, M.: Automatic Image Annotation Based on WordNet and Hierarchical Ensembles. In: Gelbukh, A. (ed.) CICLing 2006. LNCS, vol. 3878, pp. 417–428. Springer, Heidelberg (2006)

Image Compression Using Stitching with Harris Corner Detector and SPIHT Coding

Wai Chong Chia, Li-Minn Ang, and Kah Phooi Seng

The University of Nottingham in Malaysia Campus,
School of Electrical and Electronic Engineering,
Jalan Broga, 43500, Semenyih, Selangor Darul Ehsan, Malaysia
{keyx7cwc,kezklma,kezkps}@nottingham.edu.my

Abstract. An image compression technique that uses the Harris corner detector and SPIHT coding to encode images from two cameras with overlapping field of view is proposed in this paper. Firstly, the Harris corner detector is used to extract the feature points in the two images separately. Secondly, the feature points are matched and the homography that relates the two images is estimated using RANSAC. Finally, the two images are stitched together and the SPIHT coding is used to compress the stitched image. Since the resolution of the stitched image is not always fixed and difficult to be predetermined, the tree structure that is adopted by the SPIHT coding is slightly modified to resolve the problem. Generally, this technique can also be viewed as an alternative solution for joint sources image compression. The simulation results show that the file size can be reduced by approximately 14.25-25.49% depending on the amount of the overlapping region.

Keywords: Image compression, Image stitching, Harris corner detector, SPIHT.

1 Introduction

Since the field of view of a camera is smaller than human eye, it increases the need in using multiple cameras to capture the scene or object from different angle or position, when additional information is required. However, observing the information from two cameras or above separately can be tedious and might not help the user in gaining a better vision on the complete environment. Due to this reason, some methods have been developed to stitch multiple images together. As shown in Fig. 1, it can be seen that the stitched image can give a better vision on the scene as compared to the images captured by two different cameras separately. In addition, this can also to improve the trackability of an object, since the user can observe the object the complete environment.

Although a similar effect can be achieved using cameras that equip wide-angle or fish-eye lens, the images taken under this condition will c tion [1]. Moreover, the resolution of these images is also lower than t age, since the resolution of a camera is always fixed. However, the f

oze Zaman et al. (Eds.): IVIC 2009, LNCS 5857, pp. 653–663, 2009.
Verlag Berlin Heidelberg 2009

Camera 1   Camera 2

Stitching

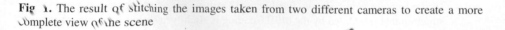

Stitched Image

Fig 1. The result of stitching the images taken from two different cameras to create a more complete view of the scene

stitched image also results in larger file size. Therefore, coding is necessary to perform the compression before the image is transmitted.

Generally, the technique which stitches multiple images together and followed by coding on the stitched image can also be viewed as an alternative solution for joint sources compression. In this case, the overlapping region between images captured by different cameras with overlapping field of view is first exploited in the encoder to remove the redundancy of the two images before any coding is performed. This can help to overcome the problem in conventional coding which can only remove the redundancy within the image itself, and lead to further reduce in bandwidth usage and power consumption, when compared to transmitting the two images separately. It has been proven that the power consumption in transmitting data is much higher than in processing data [2]. Hence, it is a critical issue for mobile devices which is battery-powered.

The technique described above appears to be one of the methods which can practically resolve the problem in joint sources compression, other than methods based on Slepian-Wolf (SW) [3] or Wyner-Ziv (WZ) [4] theorems. Those methods based on SW or WZ theorems do not require the information of the multiple images to be in the encoder. In this case, the redundancy will be computed and estimated side information generated in the decoder. This reduces the overall complexity encoder by shifting the computation burden to a centralized decoder which with a powerful processor. However, the performance of these methods is by the accuracy of the side information and overlapping region. It is the side information to be estimated accurately to achieve a good

are BlueJ version 2.1.2 with Java Development Kit of version jdk1.6.0_05, Java Runtime Environment of version jre1.6.0_07, Java Advance Imaging Development Kit version jai-1_1_3-lib-windows-i586-jdk and Java Advance Imaging Runtime Environment version jai-1_1_3-lib-windows-i586-jre. The prototype is then tested and evaluated using thirty-five photographs of beach scenery.

4   Results and Discussions

Table 2 shows results of the first experiment to determine the combination of initialization mode and distance measure in achieving the best performance of clustering. Overall, evenly-spaced initialization mode performed better compared to max-data mode. It can be also seen that the highest average precision rate of 88% is accomplished by using evenly-spaced initialization mode and City Block distance measure. Even though recall rate of this combination is slightly lower than Canberra measure, we perceived precision rate as a better judgment of clustering performance.

Table 2. Performance of different combinations of initialization modes and distance measures

Initialization Mode	Precision			Recall		
	Euclidian	CityBlock	Canberra	Euclidian	CityBlock	Canberra
Evenly-spaced	0.80	0.88	0.83	0.40	0.40	0.46
Max-data	0.82	0.87	0.88	0.34	0.32	0.37

The experiment result of comparing the number of centroids is recorded in Table 3. From the table, it is shown that 8K and 100K have equal precision rate of 88% in annotating the images. Therefore, we include the recall rate of 40% in order to conclude that the highest performance was achieved when the highest number of centroids of 100 is used. It is also interesting to note that when using 30 and 50 centroids, the precision rates are in fact lower than when utilizing only 8 centroids.

After all the techniques and distance measure are determined, the prototype was developed and tested with the 35 testing images. Fig. 2 illustrates an output of one of the annotated image. Recall and precision rates of the tested images are demonstrated in Table 4 showing and average precision rate of 75% and recall rate of 50%.

Table 3. Performance of different number of centroids

Average	Number of Centroids (K)			
	8	30	50	100
Precision	0.88	0.87	0.87	0.88
Recall	0.32	0.34	0.38	0.40

Table 4. Recall and Precision Rates of the Prototype

Image	Precision	Recall
beach001.jpg	0.5	0.25
beach002.jpg	0.67	0.4
beach003.jpg	0.4	0.5
beach004.jpg	1	0.33
beach005.jpg	1	0.4
beach006.jpg	0.5	0.2
beach007.jpg	1	0.4
beach008.jpg	1	0.4
beach009.jpg	1	0.5
beach010.jpg	0.57	1
beach011.jpg	1	0.2
beach012.jpg	1	0.4
beach013.jpg	0.5	1
beach014.jpg	0.8	0.8
beach015.jpg	1	0.4
beach016.jpg	1	0.2
beach017.jpg	1	0.4
beach018.jpg	0.5	0.2
beach019.jpg	0.67	0.5
beach020.jpg	0.5	0.25
beach021.jpg	1	0.67
beach022.jpg	1	0.33
beach023.jpg	0.67	1
beach024.jpg	0.57	1
beach025.jpg	1	0.4
beach026.jpg	0.5	0.25
beach027.jpg	1	0.25
beach028.jpg	1	0.4
beach029.jpg	0.5	0.4
beach030.jpg	0.5	1
beach031.jpg	0.67	1
beach032.jpg	0.2	0.33
beach033.jpg	0.33	0.35
beach034.jpg	0.63	1
beach035.jpg	1	0.25
Average	**0.75**	**0.50**

Table 5 illustrated the result of the percentage of each beach element correctly retrieved. From the table, it is shown that SKY and CLOUD have the highest retrieval rate at 77% and 70%, respectively. This is due to the fact that SKY has similar color with CLOUD. In other words, when there is SKY, there is possibility of CLOUD to be annotated. However, ROCK has 0% of correctly retrieved rate. The main reason of this is the little occurrence of ROCK in all the tested images.

Image Compression Using Stitching with Harris Corner Detector and SPIHT Coding

Wai Chong Chia, Li-Minn Ang, and Kah Phooi Seng

The University of Nottingham in Malaysia Campus,
School of Electrical and Electronic Engineering,
Jalan Broga, 43500, Semenyih, Selangor Darul Ehsan, Malaysia
{keyx7cwc,kezklma,kezkps}@nottingham.edu.my

Abstract. An image compression technique that uses the Harris corner detector and SPIHT coding to encode images from two cameras with overlapping field of view is proposed in this paper. Firstly, the Harris corner detector is used to extract the feature points in the two images separately. Secondly, the feature points are matched and the homography that relates the two images is estimated using RANSAC. Finally, the two images are stitched together and the SPIHT coding is used to compress the stitched image. Since the resolution of the stitched image is not always fixed and difficult to be predetermined, the tree structure that is adopted by the SPIHT coding is slightly modified to resolve the problem. Generally, this technique can also be viewed as an alternative solution for joint sources image compression. The simulation results show that the file size can be reduced by approximately 14.25-25.49% depending on the amount of the overlapping region.

Keywords: Image compression, Image stitching, Harris corner detector, SPIHT.

1 Introduction

Since the field of view of a camera is smaller than human eye, it increases the need in using multiple cameras to capture the scene or object from different angle or position, when additional information is required. However, observing the information from two cameras or above separately can be tedious and might not help the user in gaining a better vision on the complete environment. Due to this reason, some methods have been developed to stitch multiple images together. As shown in Fig. 1, it can be seen that the stitched image can give a better vision on the scene as compared to the two images captured by two different cameras separately. In addition, this can also helps to improve the trackability of an object, since the user can observe the object under the complete environment.

Although a similar effect can be achieved using cameras that equipped with a wide-angle or fish-eye lens, the images taken under this condition will contain distortion [1]. Moreover, the resolution of these images is also lower than the stitched image, since the resolution of a camera is always fixed. However, the high resolution of

H. Badioze Zaman et al. (Eds.): IVIC 2009, LNCS 5857, pp. 653–663, 2009.

Fig. 1. The result of stitching the images taken from two different cameras to create a more complete view of the scene

stitched image also results in larger file size. Therefore, coding is necessary to perform the compression before the image is transmitted.

Generally, the technique which stitches multiple images together and followed by coding on the stitched image can also be viewed as an alternative solution for joint sources compression. In this case, the overlapping region between images captured by different cameras with overlapping field of view is first exploited in the encoder to remove the redundancy of the two images before any coding is performed. This can help to overcome the problem in conventional coding which can only remove the redundancy within the image itself, and lead to further reduce in bandwidth usage and power consumption, when compared to transmitting the two images separately. It has been proven that the power consumption in transmitting data is much higher than in processing data [2]. Hence, it is a critical issue for mobile devices which is battery-powered.

The technique described above appears to be one of the methods which can practically resolve the problem in joint sources compression, other than methods based on the Slepian-Wolf (SW) [3] or Wyner-Ziv (WZ) [4] theorems. Those methods based on SW or WZ theorems do not require the information of the multiple images to be shared in the encoder. In this case, the redundancy will be computed and estimated from the side information generated in the decoder. This reduces the overall complexity of the encoder by shifting the computation burden to a centralized decoder which is equipped with a powerful processor. However, the performance of these methods is strongly affected by the accuracy of the side information and overlapping region. It is necessary for the side information to be estimated accurately to achieve a good performance, and this is one of the main reasons that lead to the huge difference in performance for practical implementations [5].

Due to the reasons stated above, the image compression technique that uses the Harris corner detector [6] to first determine the feature points in two images, followed by stitching and SPIHT [7] coding is proposed. In this case, the feature points in the two images are first extracted and matched. The homography which relates the two images is then computed to stitch the two images together under the same perspective. Finally, the stitched image generated is compressed by using the SPIHT coding. The tree structure of the SPIHT coding adopted in this paper is also slightly modified to overcome the problem where the resolution of the stitched image is not always fixed and difficult to be predetermined.

This paper is organized as follows. Firstly, the basic of Harris corner detector and SPIHT is briefly explained in Section 2 and Section 3 respectively. Then, the proposed technique and the changes in tree structure of the SPIHT coding will be explained in Section 4. This is followed by the simulation results that are presented in Section 5, and conclusion on the proposed technique in Section 6.

2   Harris Corner Detector

The Harris corner detector is used to detect the corner that appears in an image. It is a fast and simple detector. Moreover, it is invariant to noise, changes in illumination and rotation. In other words, the detector will be able to detect the same feature points in the same image, although there are changes in illumination and rotation. Fig. 2 shown an example on feature points (square box) extracted out using the Harris corner detector. The complete algorithm of the Harris corner detector can be found in [6].

Fig. 2. The feature points (square box) that were extracted using the Harris corner detector

3   SPIHT

Before the SPIHT algorithm is applied, the Discrete Wavelet Transform (DWT) is first performed to decompose an image into different frequency subbands. The number of subbands created is determined by the level of decomposition of DWT. By using the correlation that exists in different frequency subbands, a Spatial Orientation Tree (SOT) structure as shown in Fig. 3 is constructed. It can be seen that a node in the tree is either connected to four offspring or no offspring (leaves). The root of the tree is located in the lowest frequency subband which is situated at the top left corner. Due to the need in forming a group of 2 x 2 adjacent pixels, the row and column of the lowest frequency subband have to be even numbers.

Once the transformation is completed, the SPIHT algorithm will be used to encode the coefficients. The SPIHT algorithm uses the zerotree coding method which is based on the observation that when the root of the tree is insignificant, it is very likely that its descendents are also insignificant. In this case, it is possible to encode the entire tree with a single symbol to achieve compression. The details of the SPIHT algorithm can be obtained in [7].

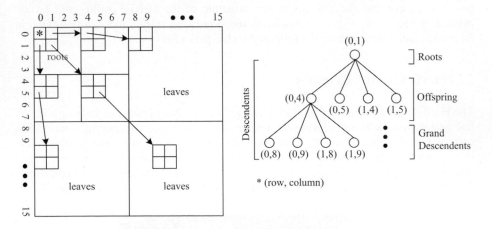

Fig. 3. The roots-offspring relationship of the SPIHT tree structure

4   Proposed Technique

Generally, the proposed technique can be divided into six steps as shown in the block diagram illustrated in Fig. 4. The details for the important steps are explained in detail in the following subsections.

4.1   Feature Extraction

As mentioned earlier, the feature points in the two images will be extracted using the Harris corner detector. However, the feature points in the two images cannot be matched directly, since the output is just a set of coordinates that indicates the positions of the feature points. Hence, extra information is required to "describe" the uniqueness of each feature point. This can be done by taking into consideration the characteristics of neighboring pixels, and generate a "description" for each feature point by using the keypoint descriptor.

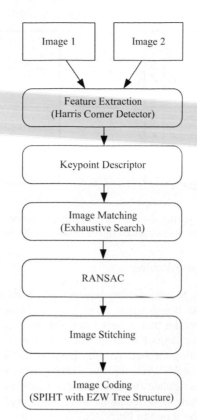

Fig. 4. The block diagram of the proposed technique

4.2 Keypoint Descriptor and Image Matching

The descriptor that is adopted in our proposed technique is the one used by Lowe in the SIFT detector [8]. In this case, the magnitude and orientation of the feature point are first determined using the local gradient. This will help to improve the accuracy in finding the matched point when there is a rotation. Then, magnitudes and orientations for the neighboring pixels were also computed and summed together as shown in Fig. 5.

The sum of magnitudes and orientations will serves as the "description" for the feature point when perform the matching. It should be noted that the illustration only uses an 8 x 8 array as an example. In actual implementation, a 16 x 16 array which is categorized into 16 regions in the form of 4 x 4 array is adopted. This descriptor is slightly simplified to work with the Harris corner detector that is different from SIFT which can be considered as a multi-scale detector. After the "description" is generated, the matching of feature points between the two images can be carried out.

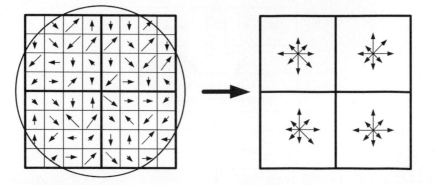

Fig. 5. An example of computing the sum of magnitude and orientation of the neighboring pixels in an 8 x 8 array, which is categorized into 4 regions in the form 2 x 2 array

4.3   RANSAC and Image Stitching

The task for RANSAC is to estimate the homography parameters that are related to the transformation of the two images. Based on the matched feature points, the RANSAC will define a model that is best fitted for them. Then, it will try to determine the inliers and outliers from the set of feature points. Only the best fitted model will be adopted in generating the homography parameters. By using the homography parameters estimated by RANSAC, the two images can now be stitched together. These parameters will manipulate the pixels in both images to perform the transformation and determine their new locations after stitching. More details about the RANSAC algorithm can be found in [9].

4.4   Image Coding

When the SPIHT coding is adopted to encode the stitched image, the row and column of the lowest frequency subband have to be kept in even numbers. This will reduce the elasticity of the SPIHT coding in handling images with different resolution. Since the overlapping region between the images might change from time to time, the resolution of the stitched image is not fixed and difficult to be predetermined. Due to the use of DWT, it is sometimes necessary to extend the resolution of the stitched image by using zero padding. Therefore, it is better to modify the SPIHT coding so that it can process images in different resolution with as little padding as possible, since padding will increase the requirement in dynamic memory and affect the coding efficiency.

The SPIHT coding is modified in such a way that the SOT structure is replaced with another tree structure shown in Fig. 6. Since this tree structure is used by another well-known image compression technique called the EZW [10] coding, it will be denoted as the EZW tree structure in the remaining part of the paper. It can be seen that the EZW tree structure does not required to keep the roots in a group of 2 x 2 adjacent pixels. Hence, the row and column of the lowest frequency subband can be in odd or even numbers.

On the other hand, the SPIHT algorithm is also modified to accommodate the changes in the number of offspring that are connected to a node. It is also important to

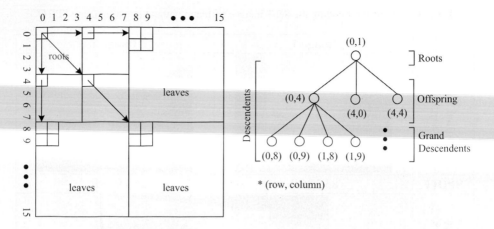

Fig. 6. The roots-offspring relationship of the EZW tree structure

note that although the performance of SPIHT is better than EZW, the improvement is mainly contributed by the SPIHT algorithm and not the changes in tree structure. From our observation, the difference in using the SOT and EZW tree structure together with SPIHT algorithm is almost negligible when the level of decomposition for DWT is more than or equal to five.

5 Simulation Results and Discussions

The performance of the proposed technique is evaluated by comparing the file size of the images with and without using stitching. In the simulation, the CDF 9/7-tap filter [11] is used to perform the DWT. It should be noted that zero padding will be used to extend the boundary of the stitched images, so that six levels of decomposition for DWT can be applied to the original and stitched image. On the other hand, the parameters adopted for the Harris corner detector and RANSAC are remain the same for the entire simulation. This also helps to find out the parameters that will work for most of the situations. In this case, the scale constant, k for Harris corner detector is 0.04, whereas the distant threshold, t and maximum iterations for RANSAC are 3 and 500 respectively.

Four sets of images in gray-scale are tested with the proposed technique, and all the resulting images with their respective file size are summarized in Table 1 to Table 4. These four sets of images are used to evaluate the proposed technique in stitching images that are mainly form by an object (car), scene, words, and human respectively. The amount of extension used for padding is also stated in the tables. From the simulation results, it can be seen that the amount of data to be transmitted for stitched image is 14.25-25.49% lower than the total amount of data for transmitting the two images separately. More importantly, it can be seen that the stitched image can give a better vision on the complete environment.

Table 1. The result for coding the Set 1 images with and without stitching using SPIHT

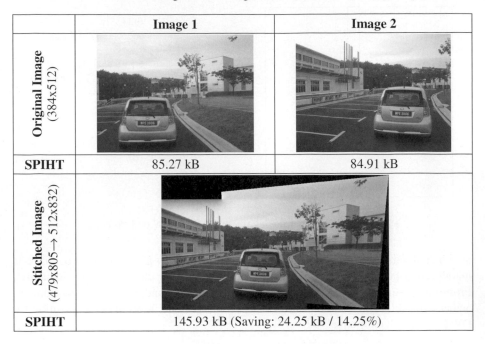

	Image 1	Image 2
Original Image (384x512)		
SPIHT	85.27 kB	84.91 kB
Stitched Image (479x805 → 512x832)		
SPIHT	145.93 kB (Saving: 24.25 kB / 14.25%)	

Table 2. The result for coding the Set 2 images with and without stitching using SPIHT

	Image 1	Image 2
Original Image (384x512)		
SPIHT	74.32 kB	71.80 kB
Stitched Image (407x718 → 448x768)		
SPIHT	108.88 kB (Saving: 37.24 kB / 25.49%)	

Table 3. The result for coding the Set 3 images with and without stitching using SPIHT

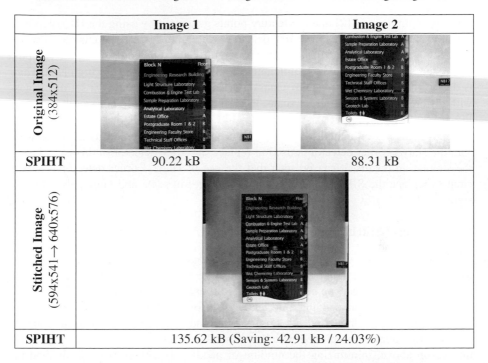

	Image 1	Image 2
Original Image (384x512)		
SPIHT	90.22 kB	88.31 kB
Stitched Image (594x541→ 640x576)		
SPIHT	135.62 kB (Saving: 42.91 kB / 24.03%)	

Table 4. The result for coding the Set 4 images with and without stitching using SPIHT

	Image 1	Image 2
Original Image (384x512)		
SPIHT	59.36 kB	68.59 kB
Stitched Image (485x739→ 512x768)		
SPIHT	100.72 kB (Saving: 27.23 kB / 21.28%)	

5.1   Robustness of Harris Corner Detector and SIFT Detector

It has been proven in [12] that the feature points generated by using the Harris corner detector is not as robust as the SIFT detector, when there is a large change in scale and view point. Although SIFT detector is one of the best detectors [13], the computation and memory required to implement the SIFT detector are very high [14]. This is due to the use of Difference of Gaussian (DoG) when computing a set of images with different sigma at different scale. Even though the effect is not significant in a PC, it is different when comes to the implementation in FPGA or ASIC. Indirectly, the high computation may also result in higher power consumption. Due to this reason, the Harris corner detector is used to replace the SIFT detector in this case. From the simulation results, it can be seen that the use of Harris corner detector is sufficient to replace the SIFT detector when the changes in scale and view point are not significant.

5.2   Padding of Stitched Image

Although padding should be avoided whenever possible, it is sometimes easier than implementing an additional algorithm to resolve the problem. For example, tree pruning is a method that can be used to discard those additional numbers of trees that were created due to the padding, and lead to improve in performance. However, the gain is almost negligible from our observation, and it is also required to determine the trees that need to be pruned which will result in increase of complexity. Due to the reason above, minimizing the amount of padding is a more feasible method to resolve the problem. The advantage of replacing the SOT structure of SPIHT is that less padding is required for the EZW tree structure. For example, the original resolution of the stitched image in Set 1 is 479 x 805. Since the row and column of the lowest frequency subband must be an integer number, the resolution is extended to 512 x 832. In the same case where the SOT structure is used, the resolution will be extended to 512 x 896.

6   Conclusions

It has been shown that the proposed technique can be an alternative solution for joint sources compression. The file size can be reduced by 14.25-25.49% after stitching the two images together before any coding is applied. Moreover, stitching the images together can also provide a more complete view of the scene. This can also help to improve the trackability of an object that will be moving across different cameras. For future works, method that can be used to overcome the abrupt changes in illumination as shown in Table 3 and Table 4 after stitching will be considered. In addition, the shape-adaptive DWT can be used to replace the conventional DWT for better performance. Furthermore, it is also important to seek for the possibility in further reducing the computational complexity or improving the robustness of the detector, so that a complete system can be created and implemented into devices with lower processing power.

References

1. Bhosle, U., Chaudhuri, S., Roy, S.D.: A Fast Method for Image Mosaicing using Geometric Hashing. IETE Journal of Research, 317–324 (2002)
2. Wu, M., Chen, C.W.: Collaborative Image Coding and Transmission over Wireless Sensor Networks. EURASIP Journal on Advances in Signal Processing (2007)
3. Slepian, D., Wolf, J.K.: Noiseless Coding of Correlated Information Sources. IEEE Transactions on Information Theory, 471–490 (1973)
4. Wyner, D., Ziv, J.: The Rate-Distortion Function for Source Coding with Side Information at the Decoder. IEEE Transactions on Information Theory, 1–10 (1976)
5. Guo, X., Lu, Y., Wu, F., Zhao, D., Gao, W.: Wyner-Ziv-Based Multiview Video Coding. IEEE Transactions on Circuits and Systems for Video Technology, 713–724 (2008)
6. Harris, C., Stephens, M.J.: A Combined Corner and Edge Detector. In: Proceedings of the 4th Alvey Vision Conference, pp. 147–152 (1988)
7. Said, A., Pearlman, W.A.: A New, Fast, and Efficient Image Codec based on Set Partitioning in Hierarchical Trees. IEEE Transactions on Circuits and Systems for Video Technology, 243–250 (1996)
8. Lowe, D.: Distinctive Image Features from Scale-Invariant Keypoints. International Journal of Computer Vision, 91–100 (2004)
9. Dirchler, M., Bolles, R.: Random Sample Consensus: A Paradigm for Model Fitting with Application to Image Analysis and Automated Catography. Communication of the ACM, 381–395 (1982)
10. Shapiro, J.M.: Embedded Image Coding using Zerotrees of Wavelet Coefficients. IEEE Transactions on Signal Processing, 3445–3462 (1993)
11. Antonini, M., Barlaud, M., Mathiew, P.: Image Coding using Wavelet Transform. IEEE Transactions on Image Processing, 205–220 (1992)
12. Schmid, C., Mohr, R., Bauckhage, C.: Evaluation of Interest Point Detectors. International Journal of Computer Vision, 151–172 (2000)
13. Mikolajczyk, K., Schmid, C.: A Performance Evaluation of Local Descriptors. IEEE Transactions on Pattern Analysis and Machine Intelligence, 1615–1630 (2005)
14. Bonato, V., Marques, E., Constantinides, G.A.: A Parallel Hardware Architecture for Scale and Rotation Invariant Feature Detection. IEEE Transactions on Circuits and Systems for Video Technology, 1–11 (2008)

SMARViz: Soft Maximal Association Rules Visualization

Tutut Herawan[1,2], Iwan Tri Riyadi Yanto[1,2], and Mustafa Mat Deris[2]

[1] CIRNOV, Universitas Ahmad Dahlan, Yogyakarta, Indonesia
[2] FTMM, Universiti Tun Hussein Onn Malaysia, Johor, Malaysia
tutut81@uad.ac.id, iwan015@gmail.com, mmustafa@uthm.edu.my

Abstract. Maximal association rule is one of the popular data mining techniques. However, no current research has found that allow for the visualization of the captured maximal rules. In this paper, *SMARViz* (*Soft Maximal Association Rules Visualization*), an approach for visualizing soft maximal association rules is proposed. The proposed approach contains four main steps, including discovering, visualizing maximal supported sets, capturing and finally visualizing the maximal rules under soft set theory.

Keywords: Data mining; Maximal association rules; Soft set theory; Visualization.

1 Introduction

Maximal association rule is firstly introduced by Feldman *et al.* [1]. While regular association rules [2] are based on the notion of frequent itemsets which appears in many records, maximal association rules are based on frequent maximal itemsets which appears maximally in many records [3]. Every maximal association rule is also regular association, with perhaps different support and confidence. Maximal association rules have been studied by many authors. Bi *et al.* [4] and Guan *et al.* [3,5] proposed the same approach for discovering maximal association rules using rough set theory [6] based on quality of approximation [7,8]. Later, Amir *et al.* [9] refined the definition of maximal association rule. Currently, we have proposed the idea of soft maximal association rule [10]. The idea is inspired from the fact that every rough set can be considered as a soft set [11]. We have shown that by using soft set theory, the maximal rules captured are equivalent. Association rules visualization has been a growing area of research in recent years. In general, association rules visualization's objective is to display data in a manner that facilitates user interpretation. Many authors have developed several visualization techniques to support the analyses of association rules. Wong *et al.* [12] used 3D method on visualizing association rules for text mining. Bruzzese and Buono [13] presented a visual strategy to analyze huge rules by exploiting graph-based technique and parallel coordinates to visualize the results of association rules mining algorithms. Ceglar *et al.* [14] presented a review of current hierarchical and association visualization techniques and introduces a novel technique for visualizing hierarchical association rules. Kopanakis *et al.* [15] developed 3-Dimensional visual data mining technique for the representation and mining of classification outcomes and association rules. Lopes *et al.* [16] presented a framework for

H. Badioze Zaman et al. (Eds.): IVIC 2009, LNCS 5857, pp. 664–674, 2009.

visual text mining to support exploration of both general structure and relevant topics within a textual document collection. The proposed approach starts by building visualization from the text data set. On top of that, a novel technique is presented that generates and filters association rules to detect and display topics from a group of documents. Leung *et al.* [17-19], develop a visualizer technique for frequent pattern mining. The methods for visualizing association rules already mentioned above have concentrated only on visualizing the regular association rules. In this paper, *SMARViz (Soft Maximal Association Rules Visualization)*, a technique for visualizing maximal association rules under soft set theory is proposed. The proposed approach contains four main steps. Firstly, we propose a technique for discovering maximal supported set under soft set theory. The technique is based on co-occurrence of items in each transaction. Secondly, we present a visualization of the maximal supported sets. The visualization is based on three bar dimensional plots. Thirdly, we capture the maximal association rules based on the maximal supported sets under soft set theory. Finally, we visualize the maximal rules using three dimensional plots.

The rest of this paper is organized as follows. Section 2 describes soft maximal association rules. Section 3 describes association presentation and SMARViz framework. Section 4 describes Experimental result. Finally, the conclusion of this work is described in section 5.

2 Soft Maximal Association Rules

Soft set theory [20], proposed by Molodtsov in 1999, is a new general method for dealing with uncertain data.

2.1 Soft Set Theory

Definition 1. (See [20].) *A pair* (F,E) *is called a soft set over a universe U, where F is a mapping given by* $F : E \rightarrow P(U)$, *where* $P(U)$ *is the power set of U.*

In other words, a soft set over U is a parameterized family of subsets of the universe U. For $\varepsilon \in A$, $F(\varepsilon)$ may be considered as the set of ε-elements of the soft set (F, Λ) or as the set of ε-approximate elements of the soft set. Clearly, a soft set is not a (crisp) set. In Proposition 2, we present the relation between a "standard" soft set and Boolean-valued information system. The notion of an information system $S = (U, A, V, f)$ is refers to [8]. Note that, in an information system $S = (U, A, V, f)$, if $V_a = \{0,1\}$, for every $a \in A$, then S is called a *Boolean-valued information system*.

Proposition 2. *If* (F, E) *is a soft set over the universe U, then* (F, E) *is a binary-valued information system* $S = (U, A, V_{\{0,1\}}, f)$.

Proof. Let (F, E) be a soft set over the universe U, we define a mapping

$$F = \{f_1, f_2, \cdots, f_n\},$$

where

$$f_i : U \to V_i \quad \text{and} \quad f_i(x) = \begin{cases} 1, & x \in F(e_i) \\ 0, & x \notin F(e_i) \end{cases}, \quad \text{for } 1 \le i \le |A|.$$

Hence, if $A = E$, $V = \bigcup_{e_i \in A} V_{e_i}$, where $V_{e_i} = \{0,1\}$, then a soft set (F, E) can be considered as a binary-valued information system $S = (U, A, V_{\{0,1\}}, f)$. □

2.2 Transformation of a Transactional Data into a Soft Set

The process of a transformation, a transactional data need to be transformed into a Boolean-valued information system and since such information system is equivalent to a soft set, then we can present a transactional data as a soft set. The process is given as follows. Let $I = \{i_1, i_2, \cdots, i_{|A|}\}$ be a set of items and $D = \{t_1, t_2, \cdots, t_{|U|}\}$ be a transaction database. For a Boolean-valued information systems $S = (U, A, V_{\{0,1\}}, f)$, we have the following transformation

$$
\begin{array}{ll}
\begin{aligned}
i_1 &\to a_1 \\
i_2 &\to a_2 \\
\vdots \quad &\vdots \quad \vdots \\
i_{|A|} &\to a_{|A|}
\end{aligned}
\Leftrightarrow
\begin{aligned}
I &= \{i_1, i_2, \cdots, i_{|A|}\} \\
&\Downarrow \\
A &= \{a_1, a_2, \cdots, a_{|A|}\}
\end{aligned}
\quad \text{and} \quad
\begin{aligned}
t_1 &\to u_1 \\
t_2 &\to u_2 \\
\vdots \quad &\vdots \quad \vdots \\
t_{|U|} &\to u_{|U|}
\end{aligned}
\Leftrightarrow
\begin{aligned}
D &= \{t_1, t_2, \cdots, t_{|U|}\} \\
&\Downarrow \\
U &= \{u_1, u_2, \cdots, u_{|U|}\}
\end{aligned}
\end{array}
$$

For every $a \in A$ and $u \in U$, we define the map $f : U \times A \to \{0,1\}$ such that $f(u,a) = 1$ if a appears in t, otherwise $f(u,a) = 0$. Then, we have a binary-valued information system as a quadruple $S = (U, A, V_{\{0,1\}}, f)$. The information systems $S = (U, A, V_{\{0,1\}}, f)$ is referred to as a transformation of a transaction table into a Boolean-valued information system. Therefore, based on Proposition 2, a transactional data can be represented as a soft set.

2.3 Taxonomy and Categorization Using Soft Set Theory

Throughout this sub-section the pair (F, E) refers to the soft set over the universe U representing a Boolean-valued information system $S = (U, A, V_{\{0,1\}}, f)$ from the transactional database, $D = \{t_1, t_2, \cdots, t_{|U|}\}$. The starting point of maximal association rules mining is a categorizing the set of items based on a taxonomy. The notions of taxonomy and category are given as follows. Let (F, E) be a soft set over the universe U. A *taxonomy* T of E is a partition of E into disjoint subsets, i.e., $T = \{E_1, E_2, E_3, \cdots, E_n\}$. Each member of T is called a *category*. For an item i, we denote $T(i)$ the category that contain i. Similarly, if X is an itemset all of which are from a single category, then we denote this category by $T(X)$.

2.4 Soft Maximal Association Rules

Let (F, E) be a soft set over the universe U and $u \in U$. An *items co-occurrence* set in a transaction u can be defined as

$$\mathrm{Coo}(u) = \{e \in E : f(u, e) = 1\}.$$

Obviously, $\mathrm{Coo}(u) = \{e \in E : F(e) = 1\}$.

The *maximal support* of a set of parameters X, denoted by $\sup(X)$ is defined by the number of transactions U maximal supporting X, i.e.

$$M\sup(X) = |\{u : X = \mathrm{Coo}(u) \cap E_i\}|, \text{ where } |X| \text{ is the cardinality of } X.$$

Obviously, $M\sup(X) = |\{e : e \in X \wedge F(e) = 1\}|$.

A *maximal association rule* between X and Y, where two maximal itemsets $X, Y \subseteq E_i$ and $X \cap Y = \phi$ is an implication of the form $X \overset{max}{\Rightarrow} Y$. The itemsets X and Y are called maximal antecedent and maximal consequent, respectively. The *maximal support* of a maximal association rule $X \Rightarrow Y$, denoted by $M\sup\left(X \overset{max}{\Rightarrow} Y \right)$ is defined by

$$M\sup\left(X \overset{max}{\Rightarrow} Y \right) = M\sup(X \cup Y) = |\{u : X \cup Y = \mathrm{Coo}(u) \cap E_i\}|$$

The *maximal confidence* of a maximal association rule $X \overset{max}{\Rightarrow} Y$, denoted respectively by $M\mathrm{conf}\left(X \overset{max}{\Rightarrow} Y \right)$ and $\mathrm{conf}(X \Rightarrow Y)$ is defined by

$$M\mathrm{conf}\left(X \overset{max}{\Rightarrow} Y \right) = \frac{M\sup(X \cup Y)}{M\sup(X)} = \frac{|\{u : X \cup Y = \mathrm{Coo}(u) \cap E_i\}|}{|\{u : X = \mathrm{Coo}(u) \cap E_i\}|}.$$

3 SMARViz

3.1 Association Visualization

A visualization of association rules is a depiction of one-to-one or many-to-one mapping of information items. At least five parameters are involved in a visualization of association rules: sets of antecedent items, consequent items, associations between antecedent and consequent, rules' support, and confidence. The two prevailing approaches used today to visualize association rules are the two-dimensional matrix and directed graph [12]. For the further information of a classification of information visualization and visual data mining techniques can be found in [21].

3.2 SMARViz

The main goals or SMARViz are to discover and visualize maximal supported sets also capture and visualize a number of maximal association rules in a three dimensional (3D) display. The following figure is the framework of SMARViz.

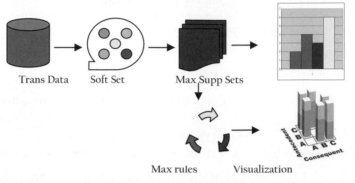

Fig. 1. The framework of SMARViz

In the proposed approach, to discover maximal supported sets, capture and visualize the maximal rules, we use programming of MATLAB® version 7.6.0.324 (R2008a). They are executed sequentially on a processor Intel Core 2 Duo CPUs. The total main memory is 1G and the operating system is Windows XP Professional SP3.

4   Experimental Results

We elaborate the proposed approach through three data sets derived from [1], [22] and [23].
a.   There is a database consisting of the 10 transactions [1];
     2 articles referring to "Canada, Iran, USA" and refers to "crude, ship";
     1 article referring to "USA" and refers to "earn'"
     2 articles referring to "USA" and refers to "jobs, cpi";
     1 article referring to "USA" and refers to "earn, cpi";
     1 article referring to "Canada" and refers to "sugar, tea";
     2 articles referring to "Canada, USA" and refers to "trade, acq" and
     1 article referring to "Canada, USA" and refers to "earn".
Based on the transaction data, we can create a taxonomy based which is contains two categories "countries" and "topics", i.e., $T = \{\text{countries}, \text{topics}\}$, where countries=\{Canada, Iran, USA\} and topics=\{crude, ship, earn, jobs, cpi, sugar, tea, trade, acq\}. The soft set representing the above transaction is given below.

$$(F,E) = \begin{cases} \text{Canada} = \{1,2,7,8,9,10\}, \text{Iran} = \{1,2\}, \text{USA} = \{1,2,3,4,5,6,8,9,10\}, \\ \text{crude} = \{1,2\}, \text{ship} = \{1,2\}, \text{earn} = \{3,10\}, \text{jobs} = \{4\}, \text{cpi} = \{3,10\}, \\ \text{tea} = \{7\}, \text{sugar} = \{7\}, \text{trade} = \{8,9\}, \text{acq} = \{8,9\} \end{cases}$$

Fig. 2. The soft set representing the transactional data

From Figure 2, we have the following supported sets.

$$\text{sup}\{\text{Canada}\}=\left|\{u_1,u_2,u_7,u_8,u_9,u_{10}\}\right|=6 \ , \ \ \text{sup}\{\text{USA}\}=\left|\{u_1,u_2,u_3,u_4,u_5,u_6,u_8,u_9,u_{10}\}\right|=9 \ , \ \ \text{sup}\{\text{Iran}\}=\left|\{u_1,u_2\}\right|=2 \ ,$$

$$\text{sup}\{\text{Canada, USA}\}=\left|\{u_1,u_2,u_8,u_9,u_{10}\}\right|=5 \ , \ \ \text{sup}\{\text{Canada, Iran}\}=\left|\{u_1,u_2\}\right|=2 \ , \ \ \text{sup}\{\text{Iran, USA}\}=\left|\{u_1,u_2\}\right|=2 \ ,$$

$$\text{sup}\{\text{Canada, Iran, USA}\}=\left|\{u_1,u_2\}\right|=2 \ , \ \ \text{sup}\{\text{crude}\}=\left|\{u_1,u_2\}\right|=2 \ , \ \ \text{sup}\{\text{ship}\}=\left|\{u_1,u_2\}\right|=2 \ , \ \ \text{sup}\{\text{earn}\}=\left|\{u_3,u_6,u_{10}\}\right|=3 \ ,$$

$$\text{sup}\{\text{jobs}\}=\left|\{u_4,u_5\}\right|=2 \ , \ \ \text{sup}\{\text{cpi}\}=\left|\{u_4,u_5,u_6\}\right|=3 \ , \ \ \text{sup}\{\text{sugar}\}=\left|\{u_7\}\right|=1 \ , \ \ \text{sup}\{\text{tea}\}=\left|\{u_7\}\right|=1 \ ,$$

$$\text{sup}\{\text{trade}\}=\left|\{u_8,u_9\}\right|=2 \ , \ \ \text{sup}\{\text{acq}\}=\left|\{u_8,u_9\}\right|=2 \ , \ \ \text{sup}\{\text{crude, ship}\}=\left|\{u_1,u_2\}\right|=2 \ , \ \ \text{sup}\{\text{jobs, cpi}\}=\left|\{u_4,u_5\}\right|=2 \ ,$$

$$\text{sup}\{\text{earn, cpi}\}=\left|\{u_6\}\right|=1 \ , \ \ \text{sup}\{\text{sugar, tea}\}=\left|\{u_7\}\right|=1 \ , \ \ \text{sup}\{\text{trade, acq}\}=\left|\{u_8,u_9\}\right|=2$$

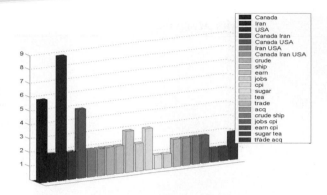

Fig. 3. The supported sets

From Figure 2, we have the following maximal supported sets.

$$M \, \text{sup}\{\text{Canada}\}=\left|\{u_7\}\right|=1 \ , \ \ M \, \text{sup}\{\text{USA}\}=\left|\{u_3,u_4,u_5,u_6\}\right|=4 \ , \ \ M \, \text{sup}\{\text{Canada, USA}\}=\left|\{u_8,u_9,u_{10}\}\right|=3 \ ,$$

$$M \, \text{sup}\{\text{Canada, Iran, USA}\}=\left|\{u_1,u_2\}\right|=2 \ , \ \ M \, \text{sup}\{\text{crude, ship}\}=\left|\{u_1,u_2\}\right|=2 \ , \ \ M \, \text{sup}\{\text{earn}\}=\left|\{u_3,u_{10}\}\right|=2$$

$$M \, \text{sup}\{\text{jobs, cpi}\}=\left|\{u_4,u_5\}\right|=2 \quad , \quad M \, \text{sup}\{\text{earn, cpi}\}=\left|\{u_6\}\right|=1 \quad , \quad M \{\text{sugar, tea}\}=\left|\{u_7\}\right|=1 \quad ,$$

$$M \{\text{trade, acq}\}=\left|\{u_8,u_9\}\right|=2$$

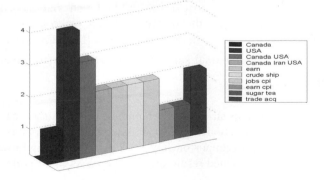

Fig. 4. The maximal supported sets

From Figure 4, the maximal association rules captured with $\min M \sup = 2$ and $\min M - \text{conf} = 0.5$ are given in the following figure.

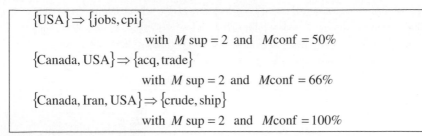

$\{\text{USA}\} \Rightarrow \{\text{jobs}, \text{cpi}\}$

with $M \sup = 2$ and $M\text{conf} = 50\%$

$\{\text{Canada}, \text{USA}\} \Rightarrow \{\text{acq}, \text{trade}\}$

with $M \sup = 2$ and $M\text{conf} = 66\%$

$\{\text{Canada}, \text{Iran}, \text{USA}\} \Rightarrow \{\text{crude}, \text{ship}\}$

with $M \sup = 2$ and $M\text{conf} = 100\%$

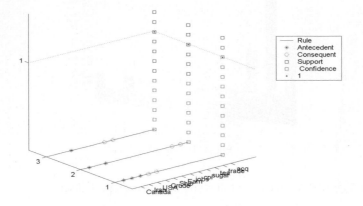

Fig. 5. The maximal rules captured from Figure 4

b.   A dataset derived from the widely used Reuters-21578 [22], a labeled document collection, i.e. a benchmark for text categorization, as follows. Assume that there are 10 articles regarding product corn which relate to the countries USA and Canada and 20 other articles concerning product fish and the countries USA, Canada and France. Based on the dataset, we can make taxonomy as follows $T = \{\text{countries}, \text{products}\}$, where countries $= \{\text{USA}, \text{Canada}, \text{France}\}$ and topics $= \{\text{corn}, \text{fish}\}$. The maximal supported sets and rules are given in Figures 6 and 7, respectively.

c.   We will further explain an example of mining maximal association rules using soft set theory from a transactional data set. It based on the observation of the air pollution data taken in Kuala Lumpur on July 2002 as presented and used in [23]. The association rules of the presented results are based on a set of air pollution data items,

USA Canada		10
USA	Canada	France
	20	
Corn		10
Fish		20

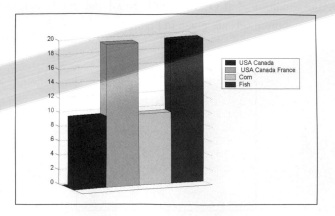

Fig. 6. The maximal supported sets

Antecedent	Consequent	Msup	Mconf
USACanada	Corn	10	100%
USACanadaFrance	Fish	20	100%

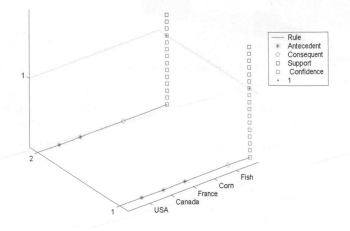

Fig. 7. The maximal association rules

i.e. $\{CO_2, O_3, PM_{10}, SO_2, NO_2\}$. The value of each item is with the unit of part per million (ppm) except PM_{10} is with the unit of micro-grams (μgm). The data were taken for every one-hour every day. The actual data is presented as the average amount of each data item per day. A taxonomy on the data set is given as follows $T = \{$ dangerous condition, good condition$\}$, where

   dangerous condition $= \{CO_2, PM_{10}, SO_2, NO_2\}$ and good condition $= \{O_3\}$.

The maximal supported sets are given in Figure 8.

```
CO2
        2
O3                      3
CO2  SO2                2
CO2  NO2                2
PM10 SO2                1
CO2          SO2        NO2
        4
CO2  PM10 SO2 NO2   13
```

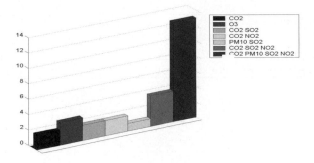

Fig. 8. The maximal supported sets

For capturing interesting maximal rules in the air pollution data set, we set the minimum Msupport and minimum Mconfidence as $\min M \sup = 2$ and $\min M\mathrm{conf} = 50\%$, respectively. And the rule discovered is given in Figure 9.

Antecedent	Consequent	Msup	Mconf
O3	CO2 PM10 SO2 NO2	3	100%

Fig. 9. Maximal association rules obtained

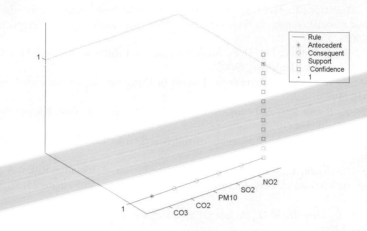

Fig. 9. (*Continued*)

5 Conclusion

The existing approach for visualizing association rules is still considering to the regular rules. In this paper, we have proposed *SMARViz* (*Soft Maximal Association Rules Visualization*), an approach for visualizing maximal association rules under soft set theory. We elaborate the proposed approach through three transactional data sets; a data set from [1], a benchmark data set for text categorization from Reuters and a data set of air pollution in Kuala Lumpur on July 2002. The results show that using three bar and three dimensional plots provide user friendly navigation to understand the maximal supported sets and rules captured, respectively. With this approach, we believe that our proposed approach can be used to capture interesting maximal rules in text mining.

Acknowledgement

This work was supported by the FRGS under the Grant No. Vote 0402, Ministry of Higher Education, Malaysia.

References

[1] Feldman, R., Aumann, Y., Amir, A., Zilberstein, A., Klosgen, W.: Maximal association rules: a new tool for mining for keywords cooccurrences in document collections. In: Proceedings of the KDD 1997, pp. 167–170 (1997)
[2] Agrawal, R., Imielinski, T., Swami, A.: Mining association rules between sets of items in large databases. In: Proceedings of the ACM SIGMOD International Conference on the Management of Data, pp. 207–216 (1993)
[3] Guan, J.W., Bell, D.A., Liu, D.Y.: The Rough Set Approach to Association Rule Mining. In: Proceedings of the Third IEEE ICDM 2003, pp. 529–532 (2003)

[4] Bi, Y., Anderson, T., McClean, S.: A rough set model with ontologies for discovering maximal association rules in document collections. Knowledge-Based Systems 16, 243–251 (2003)
[5] Guan, J.W., Bell, D.A., Liu, D.Y.: Mining Association Rules with Rough Sets. SCI, pp. 163–184. Springer, Heidelberg (2005)
[6] Pawlak, Z.: Rough sets. International Journal of Computer and Information Science 11, 341–356 (1982)
[7] Pawlak, Z.: Rough sets: A theoretical aspect of reasoning about data. Kluwer Academic Publisher, Dordrecht (1991)
[8] Pawlak, Z., Skowron, A.: Rudiments of rough sets. Information Sciences 177(1), 3–27 (2007)
[9] Amir, A., Aumann, Y., Feldman, R., Fresco, M.: Maximal Association Rules: A Tool for Mining Associations in Text. Journal of Intelligent Information Systems 25(3), 333–345 (2005)
[10] Herawan, T., Mustafa, M.D.: A soft set approach for maximal association rules mining (submitted 2009)
[11] Herawan, T., Mustafa, M.D.: A direct proof of every rough set is a soft set. In: Proceeding of International Conference AMS 2009 (2009)
[12] Wong, P.C., Whitney, P., Thomas, J.: Visualizing Association Rules for Text Mining. In: Proceeding of IEEE INFOVIS 1999, pp. 120–123 (1999)
[13] Bruzzese, D., Buono, P.: Combining Visual Techniques for Association Rules Exploration. In: Proceedings of the working conference on Advanced Visual Interfaces, AVI 2004, pp. 381–384. ACM Press, New York (2004)
[14] Ceglar, A., Roddick, J., Calder, P., Rainsford, C.: Visualising hierarchical associations. Knowledge and Information Systems 8, 257–275 (2005)
[15] Kopanakis, I., Pelekis, N., Karanikas, H., Mavroudkis, T.: Visual Techniques for the Interpretation of Data Mining Outcomes. In: Bozanis, P., Houstis, E.N. (eds.) PCI 2005. LNCS, vol. 3746, pp. 25–35. Springer, Heidelberg (2005)
[16] Lopes, A.A., Pinho, R., Paulovich, F.V., Minghim, R.: Visual text mining using association rules. Computers & Graphics 31, 316–326 (2007)
[17] Leung, C.K.S., Irani, P., Carmichael, C.L.: WiFIsViz: Effective Visualization of Frequent Itemsets. In: Proceeding of ICDM 2008, pp. 875–880. IEEE Press, Los Alamitos (2008)
[18] Leung, C.K.S., Irani, P., Carmichael, C.L.: FIsViz: A Frequent Itemset Visualizer. In: Washio, T., Suzuki, E., Ting, K.M., Inokuchi, A. (eds.) PAKDD 2008. LNCS (LNAI), vol. 5012, pp. 644–652. Springer, Heidelberg (2008)
[19] Leung, C.K.S., Carmichael, C.L.: FpViz: A Visualizer for Frequent Pattern Mining. In: Proceeding of VAKD 2009, pp. 30–49. ACM Press, New York (2009)
[20] Molodtsov, D.: Soft set theory-first results. Computers and Mathematics with Applications 37, 19–31 (1999)
[21] Keim, D.A.: Information Visualization and Visual Data Mining. IEEE transaction on visualization and computer graphics 7, 100–107 (2002)
[22] Reuters-21578 (2002),
     http://www.research.att.com/lewis/reuters21578.html
[23] Mustafa, M.D., Nabila, N.F., Evans, D.J., Saman, M.Y., Mamat, A.: Association rules on significant rare data using second support. International Journal of Computer Mathematics 83(1), 69–80 (2006)

Visualisation Enhancement of HoloCatT Matrix

Nor Azlin Rosli[1], Azlinah Mohamed[1], and Rahmattullah Khan[2]

[1] Faculty of Computer and Mathematical Sciences, Universiti Teknologi MARA Malaysia
[2] Department of Foundation of Education, Faculty of Cognitive Science & Human Development, Universiti Pendidikan Sultan Idris
4zlynn@gmail.com, azlinah@tmsk.uitm.edu.my

Abstract. Graphology and personality psychology are two different analyses approach perform by two different groups of people, but addresses the personality of the person that were analyzed. It is of interest to visualize a system that would aid personality identification given information visualization of these two domains. Therefore, a research in identifying the relationship between those two domains has been carried out by producing the HoloCatT Matrix, a combination of graphology features and a selected personality traits approach. The objectives of this research are to identify new features of the existing HoloCatT Matrix and validate the new version of matrix with two (2) related group of experts. A set of questionnaire has been distributed to a group of Personologist to identify the relationship and an interview has been done with a Graphologist in validating the matrix. Based on the analysis, 87.5% of the relation confirmed by both group of experts and subsequently the third (3rd) version of HoloCatT Matrix is obtained.

Keywords: Information Visualization, Graphology, Cattell's 16PF, Personality Traits, HoloCatT Matrix Graphology, Cattell's 16PF, Personality Traits, HoloCatT Matrix.

1 Introduction

Personality is one of the most interesting subjects, to know about and how it changes depends on certain factors that may contribute as a major cause of why and how personality change from time to time. As a matter of fact, one of the common factors that people do not realize is their own handwriting and signature. Handwriting and signature analyzing has been among the most famous subject nowadays which it is also known as Graphology [1]. A person who practices the art of graphology is called a graphologist. Graphologists use graphology mainly to assess personality traits, mental health, physical health, substance abuse and sexuality [1].

This research will cover new features that have been identified from graphology features in enhancing the current HoloCatT Matrix that has been constructed in previous study [5]. Several attempts in finding the relationship between graphology features and personality traits has been done by several researchers all over the world [2][3][4] as cited by [5]. In all of the previous studies, one (1) study that has been identified having the same intention with a current research by [5] where the

H. Badioze Zaman et al. (Eds.): IVIC 2009, LNCS 5857, pp. 675–685, 2009.

researcher examined the relationship between handwriting and personality by firstly testing 111 subjects aged between 16 and 30 with the Sixteen Personality Factor Questionnaire (16PF) of Cattell [1]. It is mentioned that there is some significant relationship between these two domains that are personality and handwrting. With respect to this finding, this research attempts to visualize the approach of both domains by extending the HoloCatT Matrix in adding two new graphology features into the HoloCatT Matrix. Next, was to validate the new constructed matrix with two (2) groups of experts, Personologist and Graphologist. The validated new matrix would be able to visualize the integration of two domains besides assisting both groups of experts in their daily routine by simplifying the process of analyzing handwriting and signatures.

In section 2, general information on selected personality recognition techniques are discussed. Section 3 discusses the research method of knowledge acquisition and abstraction followed by the research finding in section 4. Finally, the last section would conclude the research and its future work.

2   Related Works

There are several methods of recognizing people's personality that has been discovered by researchers all over the world. Some of the methods were through interviews, personality test, observer rating and situational test. Personologist normally used these methods, however it seems that identifying personality through handwriting and signature were widely used by Graphologist and has become more acceptable methods nowadays [5].

2.1   Graphology

Graphology is the study and systematic analysis of handwriting. Based on King [6], handwriting is an expression of personality. It is commonly accepted that people's emotions and motivations can be "read" from their body movements or "body language". In handwriting, signals from the brain guide the hand holding the pen, giving rise to the graphologists' saying that "handwriting is brainwriting" [6].

According to [1], graphology is a projective technique that allows graphologists to delve into the personality of an individual. The validity of graphology itself has been a debate by some researchers and based on [7], it mentioned that graphological judgement can be accepted as long as there are a fair number of studies that demonstrates the success of graphological judgments about people.

2.1.1   Graphology Features
The previous study on constructing the HoloCatT Matrix [5], five (5) features of graphology for signatures analysis have been identified and those features are caliber, proportion, space, baseline and slanting. In a study about graphology applied in signature verification by Luiz et al. [16], stated that besides those 5 features there are extra features that could be taken into consideration when analyzing signatures. These features are pressure and speed that would give more precise result. Therefore, the

enhanced HoloCatT matrix will have 7 signature features including the new proposed features that were identified and discussed in this research. The description of these features are as stated below.

Table 1. Description of Pressure and Speed in Signature

Pressure	:	It defines on the some signature that were signed in thick, spotty, and appeared heavy and dark. Or conversely, some signature might appear to be airy, light, and flighty.
Speed	:	In online system, speed of signatures will be captures based on the time while offline system, speed may only be read by the graphologist if the action was done in front of them.

The importance of these two (2) additional features in handwriting analysis was also mentioned in numerous researches [8][9][10].

2.2 Personality Traits

According to several researches [11][12], there are 6 personality approaches that were used to identify personality. These approaches are psychoanalytic approach, traits approach, biological approach, humanistic approach, behavioral/social learning approach and cognitive approach. Each approach represents different meanings however according to [12] most personality theories emphasizes on traits approach.

This is further supported by [13] where it is mentioned that the trait approach for personality is one of the major theoretical areas in the study of personality. Trait theory focuses on identifying and measuring individual personality characteristics. One of the theory commonly and widely used by psychologist in identifying the specific conflict that uses the traits approach is Raymond Cattell and the 16PF Application Trait Theory also known as Cattell 16PF [14]. Raymond Cattell and the 16PF consider personality as prediction of what a person in a given situation and he is convinced that an adequate theory of personality have to examine and explain the goal-directed motivations of individual [11]. Based on [14], in developing a common taxonomy of traits for the 16 Personality Factor model, Cattell relied heavily on the previous work of scientists in the field which focuses on a lexical approach to the dimensions of personality. Besides that, this theory is to be known commonly used among the psychologist and Personologist of Malaysia [5]. Furthermore, this theory was also used to establish the relationship between graphology and personality as conducted earlier in [1].

3   Materials and Methods

Referring to the approach used in constructing HoloCatT Matrix version 2 by [5], as described in figure 1 below, shows the integration of both domains in a relational table, where analysis were conducted and finally the establishment of the matrix.

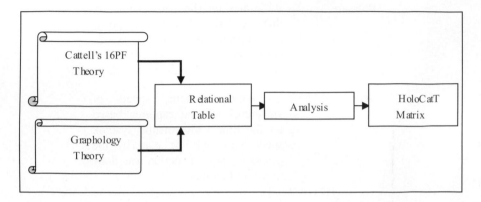

Fig. 1. HoloCatT Matrix Version 1 Approach (Source: Mohd, et al. (2007). Graphology and Cattell's 16PF Traits Matrix (HoloCatT Matrix)).

In line with their work, this research focuses on enhancing the existing HoloCatT Matrix as an information visualization of Personologist and Graphologist domain integration. Therefore in identifying and constructing the improved constructed matrix, an additional step has been added into the previous research approach as illustrated in Figure 2. Figure 2 shows the different approach where it involves two (2) group of experts which are the Graphologist and Personologist which could lead to a different interpretation especially during the knowledge acquisition, abstraction and even validation phase.

Four phases of research methodology has been designed throughout the studies together with activities and expected deliverables to fulfill the research objectives. The first phase of the research method was defining the research problem, and in this phase, a study on the existing data would be one of the important factor due to the purpose of this research is to enhance the existing matrix done by other researcher. Other than that, a literature survey on other related research was conducted in the first phase. Besides defining the research problem, this phase covers on identifying the possibility enhancement signature features and previous research limitations.

The second phase is knowledge acquisition and the method used in this phase is combined with the third phase, which is knowledge construction. In this phase, the major activity involved collecting and evaluating data. Since the research requires an expert in gaining and evaluating the collected data, Delphi method was used throughout the phase. The implementation of this phase is as described in the next subsection. The fourth phase is the knowledge representation. In this phase, once the new HoloCatT matrix is improved, a validation analysis is perform by doing a cross reference with verified information and interview.

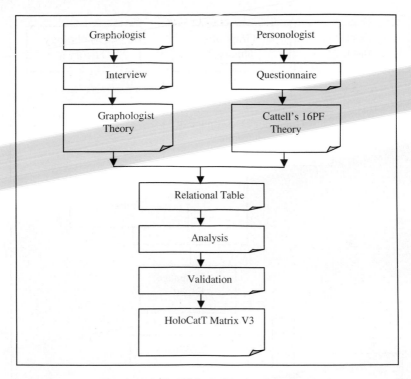

Fig. 2. HoloCatT Matrix Version 3 Approach

3.1 Interview

In gathering information on what and how does Graphologist perform the handwriting analysis, a closed and focused interview session with one of the two Malaysian Graphologists [10] was performed. The interview focuses on a set of questions corresponding to a number of signatures obtained from a local signature database used in [5].

3.2 Questionnaire

In obtaining information from the second group that is the Personologist, a set of questionnaire was designed. The purpose of the questionnaire is to evaluate and validate the relationship between graphology description (i.e pressure and speed). The questionnaire consists of six (6) questions referring to each classification of pressure and speed which are low pressure, medium pressure, heavy pressure, slow speed, medium speed and fast speed. These questions are developed based upon synonyms identified from theoretical information gathered and verified by a Personologist, Graphologist and a language expert. Figure 3 illustrated the questionnaire development process.

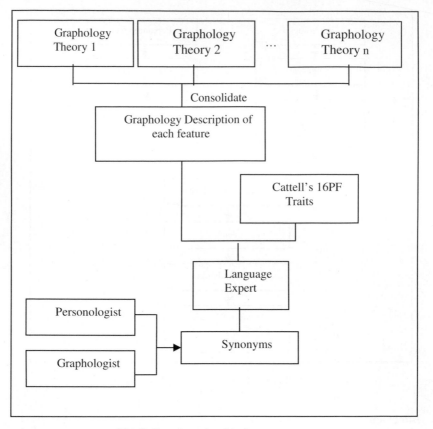

Fig. 3. Questionnaire development process

The developed questionnaire was distributed to a group of identified expert in personality study especially in Cattell's 16PF theory. A sample of the identified synonym is as shown in table 2. The situational questions given reflect the scenario addressed by the respondent of this questionnaire. In this sample, the words best describes Sensitivity and Vigilance in both domains are grouped together with the help of a language expert and being verified by a Personologist and Graphologist. Next, situational questions are designed to reflect the verified synonyms with the help of a language expert as illustrated in figure 4. The questionnaires were distributed to 25 selected respondents that administered Cattell 16PF in their psychology work. The selected respondents (psychologist) are among 3 universities, which are International Islamic University of Malaysia (IIUM), National University of Malaysia (UKM) and Sunway University College. All these respondents have more than 5 years of experiences in their field and had practice psychology before. A large portion of the distributions were by hand, however 10% were through email due to time and distance constraints. One respondent manage to answer the questionnaire on the spot and the rest require one week in answering the questionnaire due to some commitment. Some of the respondents refused to participate due to lack of interest, time constraint and mostly because they have limited knowledge on Cattell 16PF theory.

Table 2. Synonyms between graphology description and Cattell's 16PF

Situation	Definition in Graphology	Synonyms in Cattell 16PF
Alisya is (a) emotionally fragile. She (b) lacks of strength and (c) determination especially when she is put in a very demanding condition. She (d) hates noise and aggression. She is (e) caring and (f) forgives easily. She is (g) very responsive towards people and the environment surrounding her. But her views in (h) life are bound to what appears on the surface and she seldom figures out what lies within. Her emotional being may influence her to be (i) timid and (j) impractical at times.	Sensitive [1a, 2a, 3a, 4a, 5a, 6a], Fragile [1a] Lack of vitality [1a, 2a], Physically week [1a,4a, 6a] Week-willed [1a] Hates noise and aggression [5a] Tender [1a, 5a] Forgivable [1a, 6a] Empathy [2a, 5a] Skate over the surface of life without digging into it[3a, 5a] Timid [6a] Impractical [3a]	Sensitivity (+) Vigilance (-)

4   Results and Discussions

In this research, 2 groups of experts were identified to evaluate the outcome of the designed framework and questionnaire. The groups are the Graphologist (Experts in Handwriting Analysis) and Personologist (Experts in Personality Psychology). Different approach of collecting data were implemented for each group, as described previously, where an interview were used for the Graphologist, and a set of questionnaire were administered for the Personologist group. The goal of the analysis process is to validate the association of both graphology theory and selected personality theory which is the Cattell's 16PF traits.

4.1   Interview Analysis

Based on interviewed data, it shows that the additional two (2) features identified to be the new features in the current HoloCatT Matrix was namely to be among the most important features in performing the handwriting analysis. The graphologist was given the matrix and a set of 100 signatures with its analysis using the improved HoloCatT Matrix. The validation shows 100% acceptable response from the graphologist.

4.2   Questionnaire Analysis

Meanwhile, scoring technique is used in identifying the strength of the association in the questionnaire analysis. 10 answered questionnaires managed to be gathered and were used in this analysis. In identifying the strength of the relationship between both theories, the scoring will be given based on criteria which lead to either 0 or 1. In this technique, when the affirmation was totally agreed by the experts, the score will be 1 while 0 will be given when there is no or partial agreement between the two theories. Table 3 shows a sample of the relational table of question 1 in this research while table 4 represents the legend of table 3 in illustrating the data clearly.

Table 3. Score for question 1 (low pressure)

Respondent	Question Cattell's 16PF	Sensitivity		Vigilance	
		Tick	Score	Tick	Score
1		1;1	1	1;2	1
2		0;0	0	0;0	0
3		1;1	1	1;1	0
4		1;1	1	0;0	0
5		1;1	1	1;2	1
6		1;1	1	0;0	0
7		1;1	1	1;2	1
8		1;1	1	1;2	1
9		1;1	1	0;0	0
10		1;1	1	1;2	1
Total Score	:	9		5	
Average	:	0.9		0.5	
Percentage	:	90		50	

Table 4. Legend of scoring table

Legend		a;b			
High	1	a		b	
Low	2	Yes	1	High	1
		No	2	Low	2
Score					
Related		1			
Not Related		0			

Analysis from the questionnaire shows that additional personality factor has been identified and added to the initial matrix based on the experts review and the changes were made due to the level of trust to the expert knowledge.

From the questionnaire analysis, the association shows that 87.5% of the respondents agree to the association table of both Cattell's 16PF and graphology theory. The relationships are visualized in a form of improved matrix as shown in appendix A. Appendix A presents 11 out of 16 Catell 16 PF traits that contribute significantly to the two signature features identified in this research that are pressure and speed. The five traits that do not have any relationship in both domains for these features but have significant contribution to other features [5] are Reasoning, Social Boldness, Abstractedness, Privateness and Openness to Change. This shows that there is an increase number of agreement and trust on the improved HoloCatT Matrix known as HoloCatT Matrix Version 3 presented from 80.9% [5] in previous research to 87.5%.

5 Conclusions and Recommendations

This research was proposed with the aim to capture information from two domain experts and visualize this information in terms of a matrix with experts' validation from both domains. The results show that there exists a significant relationship between both theories and agreed upon by both domain experts. An enhanced HoloCatT Matrix was presented in visualizing the integration of both domains. It is hope that this integration would lead to a better understanding of both domains and establishment of a more precise measurement tools in defining people's personality based on their signature.

Acknowledgement

We would like to acknowledge Mr. Dawish Paramjit, Graphologist for his contribution in this research. We also acknowledge all Personologists and the language expert for their time and expertise. This study has been made possible under the support of the Ministry of Science and Technology Malaysia through the Science fund.

References

[1] Lowe, P.: An examination of the graphological indicators of sexual abuse Doctoral dissertation, University of Johannesburg (2005)
[2] Bushnell, I.W.R.: A Comparison of the Validity of Handwriting Analysis with that of the Cattell 16 PF. International Journal of Selection and Assessment 4, 12–17 (1996)
[3] Tett, R.P., Palmer, C.A.: The Validity of Handwriting Elements in Relation to Self-Report Personality Traits Measures. Personality and Individual Differences 22, 11–18 (1997)
[4] Furnham, A., Chamorro-Premuzic, T., Callahan: Does Graphology Predict Personality and Intelligence? Individual Difference Research 1, 78–94 (2003)
[5] Mohd, R.S., Ku, S.J., Zaidah, I., Rahmatullah, K.A.W.K., Azlinah, M.: Graphology and Cattell's 16PF Traits Matrix, HoloCatT Matrix (2007)
[6] King, S.: Graphology: Writing on the Wall. Management Development Review 7, 26–28 (2004)
[7] David, L.: The Psychological Basis of Handwriting Analysis. The Relationship of Handwriting to Personality and Psychotherapy (1981)
[8] Kumar, V.: All you wanted to know about graphology (1999)
[9] Wallechisky, D., Wallace, I.: The People's Almanac (1981)

[10] Paramjit (personal communications, August 25, 2008)

[11] Ryckman, R.M.: Theories of Personality, 8th edn. Wardsworth Thomson Learning, USA (2004)

[12] Matthews, G., Deary, I.J., Whiteman, M.C.: Personality Traits, 2nd edn. University Press, Cambridge (2003)

[13] Burger, J.M.: Personalities, 6th edn. Wardsworth Thomson Learning, USA (2004)

[14] Fehringer (2004)

[15] Simner, M.L., Goffin, R.D.: A Position Satement by the International Graphonomics Society on the Use of Graphology in Personal Selection Testing. International Journal Testing 3(4), 353–364 (2003)

[16] Luiz, S.O., Edson, J., Cinthia, F., Robert, S.: The Graphology Applied to Signature Verification. In: 12th Conference of the International Graphonomics Society, pp. 286–290 (2002)

Appendix A: The HoloCatT Matrix Version 3

Features		Warmth L	Warmth H	Emotional Stability L	Emotional Stability H	Dominance L	Dominance H	Liveliness L	Liveliness H	Rule-Consciousness L	Rule-Consciousness H	Sensitivity L	Sensitivity H	Vigilance L	Vigilance H	Apprehension L	Apprehension H	Self-Reliance L	Self-Reliance H	Perfectionism L	Perfectionism H	Tension L	Tension H
Upper Zone	small									■													
	medium									*	*												
	large										■												
Middle Zone	small	■				■										■							
	medium	*	*			*	*									*	*						
	large		■					■															
Lower Zone	small																			■			
	medium																	*	*				
	large																						
Caliber	small					■														■			
	medium						■							■									
	large							■												■			
Size	left	■				■									■								
	vertical											■		■						■	■		
	right		■	■						■		■						■					
Baseline	rising		■																				■
	straight				■																	*	
	falling		■	■					■														■
Space	narrow														■	■							
	well balance																						
	wide																		■				
Pressure	light												■		■								
	medium		■	■		■																■	
	heavy	■			■			■															
Speed	slow											■											
	medium					■																	
	fast															■				■			

* - The relation for this features has been removed due to its weight equal to 0.

Modeling of Electromagnetic Waves Using Statistical and Numerical Techniques

Hanita Daud[1,*], Vijanth Sagayan[1], Noorhana Yahya[1], and Wan Najwati[2]

[1] Fundamental and Applied Sciences Department
[2] Electrical and Electronics Engineering Department,
Universiti Teknologi PETRONAS,
Bandar Seri Iskandar, 31750 Tronoh, Perak, Malaysia
hanita_daud@petronas.com.my

Abstract. This paper presents a comparative study on the modeling of Electromagnetic (EM) waves using statistical and numerical techniques using MATLAB software. Authors focused only on amplitude modeling of EM waves at 0.25Hz frequency. The models using statistical and numerical techniques have been developed and sum square errors have been calculated and comparative studies have been made to find the best technique. First order and second order regressions were used for statistical models and polynomial curve fitting and spline interpolation were used for numerical technique. Results from these techniques were compared and we have found that spline interpolation gave the most fitted model to the EM wave amplitude.

Keywords: EM Waves, Regression, Spline Interpolation, Amplitude, Sum Square Error, Homogeneous.

1 Introduction

Electromagnetic wave (EM wave) is a self-propagating wave where its components, consists of electric field, $\overline{E}$ and magnetic field, $\overline{B}$ and they are orthogonal to each other and travel in a same direction [1]. Conventional analytical in electromagnetism do not use computation and visualization techniques [2] and due to this, it cannot solve many real and practical engineering problems. Therefore, computational EM wave is required to be modeled in order to solve real practical problems and improve engineering design using computer. To overcome such problems, modeling of EM wave using statistical and numerical techniques using MATLAB is proposed.

Finite Difference Time Domain (FDTD) has been the most popular numerical method to deal with the electromagnetic waves propagation. The solutions in the time domain method may cover wide frequency range with just a simulation run. The FDTD belongs to the general class of grid based differential time domain numerical modeling methods [7]. Here Maxwell's equations (in partial differential form) are modified to central-difference equations and the electric field is solved at a given instant of time followed by magnetic field at other instant of time. FDTD has emerged

* Corresponding author.

H. Badioze Zaman et al. (Eds.): IVIC 2009, LNCS 5857, pp. 686–695, 2009.
© Springer-Verlag Berlin Heidelberg 2009

as the primary means to model many scientific and engineering problems dealing with electromagnetic waves interactions with material structures [7].

Finite Integration Technique (FIT) is a spatial discretization scheme to solve electromagnetic field problems in time and frequency domain numerically. It preserves the basic topological properties of the continuous equations such as conservation of charge and energy. This method covers the full range of electromagnetism, from static up to high frequency and optic applications. Basic idea of this approach is to apply the Maxwell's equations in integral form to a set of staggered grids. This method stands out due to high flexibility in geometric modeling and boundary handling as well as incorporation of arbitrary material distributions and material properties such as anisotropy, non-linearity and dispersion. Furthermore, the use of a consistent dual orthogonal grid (e.g. Cartesian grid) in conjunction with an explicit time integration scheme leads to extremely high efficient algorithms referred to both computation time and memory requirements which are especially adapted for transient field analysis in Radio Frequency (RF) applications. Despite all the advantages highlighted here the limitation of this technique is that it needs high computing power to solve the given problem [8].

2 Methodology

The electromagnetic wave equation is a second-order partial differential equation that describes the propagation of electromagnetic waves through a medium or in a vacuum [3]. The homogeneous form of the equation, of EM wave equation can be written in terms of electric field $\mathbf{E}$ or magnetic field $\mathbf{B}$ [1], as shown in (1) and (2).

$$\nabla^2 E = \mu_0 \varepsilon_0 \frac{\partial^2 E}{\partial t^2} \tag{1}$$

$$\nabla^2 B = \mu_0 \varepsilon_0 \frac{\partial^2 B}{\partial t^2} \tag{2}$$

Where $\mathbf{B}$ = Magnetic field, $\mathbf{E}$ = Electric field, t = Time, $\mu_0 = 4\pi \times 10^{-7}$ H/m is the magnetic constant (vacuum permeability) and $\varepsilon_0 = 8.854187817 \times 10^{-12}$ F/m is the electric constant (vacuum permittivity).   If the wave's propagation is in vacuum, then the speed is

$$c = c_0 = \frac{1}{\sqrt{\mu_0 \varepsilon_0}} = 299{,}792{,}458 \text{m/s} \tag{3}$$

Otherwise if the wave's propagation is in other medium than vacuum, then the speed of light in a linear, isotropic and non-dispersive material is [1]

$$c = \frac{c_0}{n} = \frac{1}{\sqrt{\mu \varepsilon}}, \tag{4}$$

where n is the refractive index of the medium, μ is the magnetic permeability of the medium and ε is the electric permittivity of the medium. In the modern method, electromagnetic wave equation in a vacuum shall be obtained by 'Heaviside' form of Maxwell's equations. In the vacuum these equations are [1]

$$\nabla X B = \mu o \varepsilon o \frac{\partial E}{\partial t} \quad \text{and} \quad \nabla X E = -\frac{\partial B}{\partial t} \tag{5}$$

Taking the curl of the curl equations [1], gives us

$$\nabla X \nabla X E = -\frac{\partial}{\partial t} \nabla X B = -\mu o \varepsilon o \frac{\partial^2 E}{\partial t^2} \tag{6}$$

$$\nabla X \nabla X B = \mu o \varepsilon o \frac{\partial}{\partial t} \nabla X E = -\mu o \varepsilon o \frac{\partial^2 B}{\partial t^2} \tag{7}$$

Using vector identity of $\nabla X \left(\nabla X V \right) = \nabla \left(\nabla . V \right) - \nabla^2 V$, where V is any vector function of space, then it turns into wave equations [1]

$$\frac{\partial^2 E}{\partial t^2} - co^2 . \nabla^2 E = 0 \tag{8}$$

2.1 Regression Analysis

In statistics, regression analysis refers to techniques for modeling and analyzing several variables, when the focus is on the relationship between a dependent variable Y (response variable) and one or more independent variables X (predictors). The unknown parameters, *beta* and denoted as b is used to get the best fit of the model [11]. There are a few regression techniques available but we started our EM modeling using linear regression techniques to find the functions that illustrate the relationship among the variables because these functions are used to build mathematical models of the EM wave data set [5]. The general form of the multiple regression equation is shown in (9). Generally, more predictor (input, x) will yield a better and more accurate output, y [5].

$$y = a + b_1 x_1 + b_2 x_2 + b_3 x_3 + \ldots + b_n x_n \tag{9}$$

where,

y = The predicted output of Regression (estimated output)
ai , bi = Regression coefficient
X = inputs

2.2 Polynomial Curve Fitting

Polynomial curve fitting is the process of constructing a curve, or mathematical function that has the best fit to a series of data points, possibly subject to constraints. Curve fitting can involve either interpolation, where an exact fit to the data is required, or smoothing, in which a "smooth" function is constructed that approximately fits the data [12]. A related topic is regression analysis, which focuses more on questions of statistical inference such as how much uncertainty is present in a curve that is fit to data observed with random errors. Fitted curves can be used as an aid for data visualization, to infer values of a function where no data are available, and to summarize the relationships among two or more variables [4]. A first degree polynomial equation is $y = ax + b$, which is a line with slope a. As we know that a line connects two points, therefore a first degree polynomial equation is an exact fit through any two points. If we increase the order of the equation to second degree polynomial, then it may be written [5] as

$$y = ax^2 + bx + c ,\tag{10}$$

third degree as $\qquad\qquad y = ax^3 + bx^2 + cx + d .\tag{11}$

In general n degree polynomial may written as

$$y = ax^n + bx^{n-1} + cx^{n-2} + \ldots\ldots + k .\tag{12}$$

2.3 Spline Interpolation

Spline interpolation is a form of interpolation where the interpolant is a special type of piecewise polynomial called a spline. Spline interpolation is preferred over polynomial interpolation because the interpolation error can be made small even when using low degree polynomials. Thus, spline interpolation avoids the problem of Runge's phenomenon which occurs when using high degree polynomials [13]. The general form of spline interpolation for $n + 1$ distinct knot x_i such that $x_0 < x_1 < \ldots < x_{n-1} < x_n$ with $n + 1$ knot values y_i, we are finding a spline function of degree n in the form of

$$S(x) = \begin{cases} S_0(x) & x \in \left[x_0, x_1\right] \\ S_1(x) & x \in \left[x_1, x2\right] \\ \ldots\ldots & \ldots\ldots \\ S_{n-1}(x) & x \in \left[x_{n-1}, x_n\right] \end{cases}\tag{13}$$

where each $S_i(x)$ is a polynomial of degree k.

2.4 Data Acquisition

The Sea Bed Logging (SBL) method has been described in detail by Eidesmo and Kong [6]. It uses a horizontal electric dipole (HED) source, which generates ultra low frequency (~0.1-5Hz) EM signals which being towed approximately 30-40m above seabed. The EM signal is recorded by stationary seabed EM receivers. EM energy propagates through seawater, the seawater / air interface (air waves) and the subsurface layers as depicted from Figure 1. The transmitted energy rapidly attenuates in seawater and seafloor sediments saturated with conductive saline water. Therefore, the direct energy (primary field) transmitted through seawater dominates the recordings only at short source-receiver offsets. The air-wave (down-going field) dominance depends on the source frequency, sea water depth, sea water and the subsurface resistivity distribution, and source-receiver distances.

A set of data of EM waves that have been collected from three (3) receivers namely Rx1, Rx2 and Rx3 as in Fig.1are to be used to model the EM wave amplitude. Fig. 1 [6] shows how EM wave signals are being transmitted and captured by the three receivers (we concentrate only on first three receivers). The captured signals are being processed to extract the required information (how data being extracted is not to be discussed in this paper). The extracted data are given in the form of amplitudes, frequencies, phase differences and etc.

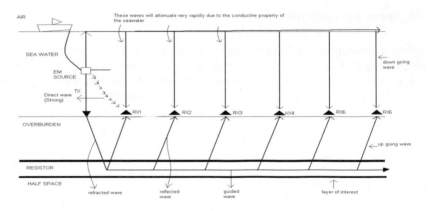

Fig. 1. EM waves are being transmitted and captured by the EM receivers

3 Results and Discussions

All the results discussed in this section are produced and calculated by using MAT-LAB software. Our data set contains 248 observations from the three receivers. We started our modeling using First Order Regression and Second Order Regression Analysis as in Fig. 2 (a) and Fig. 2 (b) respectively. All X-axis of the graphs represents the 248 data set and the Y axis represents their amplitudes in log scale. All the

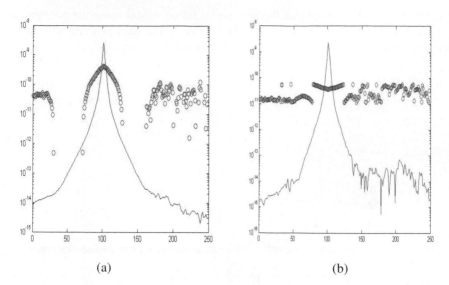

(a)   (b)

Fig. 2. (a) Estimated Model using First Order Regression (b) Estimated Model using Second Order Regression

graphs are using log on y axis because if we were to use the normal scale we can hardly see any different between the data because their differences are very small.

The smooth line represents the real data while the circles represent the estimated model from observed data. Fig. 2 (a) and (b) are compared, and we have concluded that First Order Regression gives better fitted curve. Therefore, in Fig. 3, we used first order regression as comparison to Polynomial Curve Fitting from order 4 to order 10.

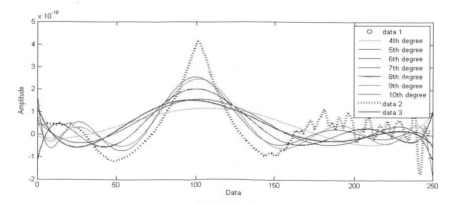

Fig. 3. Polynomial Curve Fitting vs First Order Regression

Again these plots showed that the new curve fitting model using the polynomials of order 4 to 10 are not approximating the real data. We then proceed with Spline Interpolation Technique to obtain the estimated model.

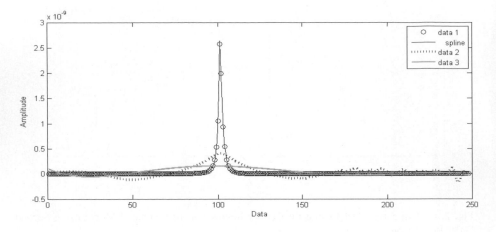

Fig. 4. Spline Interpolation Curves for Real Data and Observed Data

From Fig. 4 we may see that Spline Interpolation curves gives very good estimation for data from receiver 1, and acceptable estimation for data from receiver 2 and 3. Therefore, Spline Interpolation technique is used for further EM wave amplitude modeling and testing. This testing is done to observe whether the model fits well to the real data from the three receivers and errors will be calculated to see the variation between real and observed data. Fig 5. shows Spline Interpolation Model for real EM wave amplitude data.

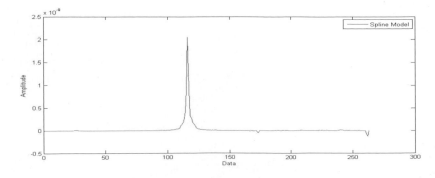

Fig. 5. Spline Interpolation for Real Data

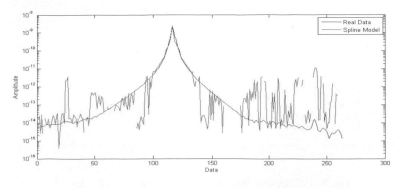

Fig. 6. Real Data vs Observed Data For Receiver 1

Fig. 6 shows the real model (smooth line) from Fig. 5 being compared to observe data from receiver 1 (spikes). Sum square error (SSE) is then calculated using MAT-LAB software which uses this formula **SSE = mean [(Model Amplitude – EM Wave Amplitude)]** and the error plot may be seen as in Fig. 7.

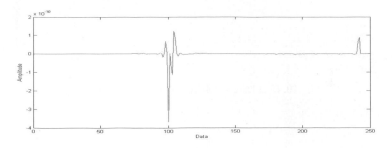

Fig. 7. SSE between Real and Observed Data from Receiver 1

SSE of Fig. 7 is very small, that is SSE = 7.798 x 10^{-22}. Remembering that this amplitude is in log scale, this error plot shows some error indication at reading 100. Fig. 8 shows the comparison of the real model with data from receiver 2 and again SSE is also calculated as in Fig 9. Fig. 10 shows the comparison of the real model with data from receiver 3 and again SSE is also calculated as in Fig 11.

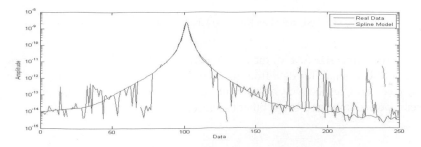

Fig. 8. Real Data vs Observed Data For Receiver 2

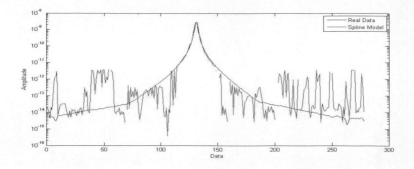

Fig. 9. SSE between Real and Observed Data from Receiver 2

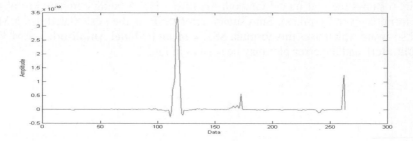

Fig. 10. Real Data vs Observed Data For Receiver 3

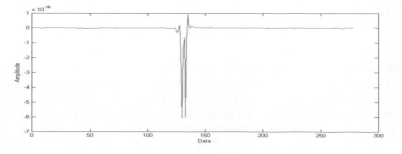

Fig. 11. SSE between Real and Observed Data from Receiver 3

We may summarize SSE of the three receivers in Table 1. From Table 1, it may be seen that SSE is small for data from receiver 1 but the error is increasing for receiver 2 and receiver 3 respectively. This indicates that Spline Interpolation represents receiver 1 well if compared to the other two receivers.

Table 1. SSE for the three Receivers

Receiver No	1	2	3
SSE (Sum Square Error)	7.798×10^{-022}	1.422×10^{-021}	2.870×10^{-021}

4 Conclusion

It has been shown that Spline Interpolation gives the best approximation model to all the three receivers especially receiver 1. The first and second order regressions techniques are not fitted for the data as they deviated so much. We shall extend our work in the future to take into considerations more receivers as well as any attenuation that affect the EM waves.

References

1. Hasnadar, Z., Stih, Z.: Electromagnetic Fields, Waves and Numerical Methods. IOS Press, Ohmsha (2000)
2. Lavergnat, J., Sylvain, M.: Radio Waves Propagation: Principles and Techniques. John Wiley & Sons, Chichester (2000)
3. Zahn, M.: Electromagnetic Field Theory: A Problem Solving Approach. John Wiley & Sons, Chichester (1997)
4. Mosteller, F., Tukey, J.: Data Analysis and Regression. Addison-Wesley, Reading (1997)
5. Chatterjee, S., Hadi, A.S.: Influential Observations, High Leverage Points and Outliers in Linear Regression. Statistical Science (1986)
6. Eidesmo, T., Ellingsrud, S., MacGregor, L.M., Constable, S., Sinha, M.C., Johansen, S., Kong, F.N., Westerdahl, H.: Sea Bed Logging (SBL), a new method for remote and direct identification of hydrocarbon filled layers in deepwater areas (2002)
7. Warnick, K.F.: An Intuitive Error Analysis for FDTD and Comparison to MoM. IEEE Antennas and Propagation Magazine 47(6), 111–115 (2005)
8. Weiland, T.: A Discretization Method for the Solution of Maxwell's Equations for Six-Component Fields. Electronics and Communications AEUE 31 (1977)
9. MATLAB - The Language of Technical Computing,
   http://www.mathworks.com/products/matlab/
10. IEEE Xplore, http://ieeexplore.ieee.org/
11. Tibshirani, R.: Regression Shrinkage and Selection via the Lasso. Journal of the Royal Statistical Society. Series B (Methodological) 58(1), 267–288 (1996),
    http://www.jstor.org/stable/2346178
12. From Wikipedia, the free encyclopedia,
    http://en.wikipedia.org/wiki/Curve_fitting#cite_ref-0
13. From Wikipedia, the free encyclopedia,
    http://en.wikipedia.org/wiki/Spline_interpolation

Visual Language Framework for Plant Modeling Using L-System

Bee Hwa Siew and Abdullah Zawawi Talib

School of Computer Sciences, Universiti Sains Malaysia, 11800 USM Penang, Malaysia
sbh.com08@student.usm.my, azht@cs.usm.my

Abstract. The L-system algorithm can be very useful in modeling realistic plants for virtual environment modeling and also in graphics applications besides as a tool for biological plant simulation. However, there are hardly any L-system applications which cater for people who do not have prior knowledge in L-systems nor programming skills. This paper describes how we design and develop a visual language framework for L-system plant modeling to cater to this group of people as well as experts in L-system modeling. The purpose of this research is to design a visual language framework for L-system and to study the usefulness and effectiveness of visual language in L-system plant modeling. The visual language framework covers the L-system attributes and grammar in the form of icon-based visual language.

Keywords: Visual programming Language, L-systems, Plant Modeling.

1 Introduction

Shu [1] defines visual programming as the use of meaningful graphic representations in the process of programming. From Boshernitsan and Downes [2], visual programming language (VPL) is defined as a set of graphical icons in which each icon is a pair of image representation and a programming operation or an object in the program. Combinations of these graphical icons in a predefined syntax generate different semantics and instructions to perform tasks just as any textual programming language would. VPL has the advantage over textual language in terms of human cognition because a single image can be used for conveying the same meaning to people who understand different languages.

The Lindenmayer System (L-system) is a mathematical modeling system on the development processes and structures of plants proposed by biologist Aristid Lindenmayer in 1968 [3]. It began with simple multi-cellular organism modeling and subsequently progressed to complex plant developments. The interest in L-system research is more on improving the L-system algorithms to resemble the real biological plant development process. However tools available for L-system modeling are more biased towards L-system research and therefore lacking in usability for non-researchers in this area and non-programmers. Besides biological growth simulation of plants, realistic tree modeling can also be applied in other applications such as virtual environment modeling and graphics application that can be used by non

H. Badioze Zaman et al. (Eds.): IVIC 2009, LNCS 5857, pp. 696–707, 2009.

L-system experts. Our research aims to propose a simpler icon-based VPL dictionary for L-system tree modeling which caters mainly for non L-system experts. The rest of the paper describes the related work of this research, the proposed framework and its implementation, evaluation, and analysis and discussion. In the final section of this paper we conclude our work and suggest possible future work.

2 Related Work

Several tools exist that mainly cater for the needs of L-system plant modeling research community. Table 1 summarizes the advantages and disadvantages of these plant modeling tools. All these L-system visual interfaces lack in catering to non L-system researchers and their tree modeling process can be as tedious as conventional graphical tools. There is a need for a simplistic tree modeling application catering the needs of non L-system experts which appeals to non-programmers and non L-system researchers alike.

Table 1. Advantages and disadvantages of exiting plant modeling systems

Software	Advantages	Disadvantages
JFLAP[4]	• Comes with extensive editor and user control package for L-system modeling • Easy to use for classroom teaching for formal language	• Not for complicated L-system modeling and simulation • Not for users with out knowledge on formal language
GROWTH[5]	• Able to generate an actual 3D L-System plant model • Comes with basic L-system parameters and can be extended for newer L-System and other tools	• Requires costly 3D printer materials and requires supervision
L-Studio[6]	• Provides extensive tools that cover L-system editors, color map, modeling languages and environmental simulation function	• User needs prior knowledge of L-System and C++ language in order to use the L-studio modeling languages
Sketch L-System [7]	• Needs single stroke to generate an L-system tree and to modify the L-System rules.	• Lacks of extensive controls on changing L-system attributes • Only supports changing rules at the axiom
OpenAlea [8]	• Allows fast integration of different L-system modeling from different research group	• Targeted only towards the plant modeling research community

Menzies [9] provides an interesting view on the benefit claims made by researchers on VPL. The work reveals that there is still lack of proper evaluation behind these claims and also the lack of evidence to back these benefits. However, it does agree that VPL is indeed beneficial for beginners in learning something new. Bergin et al. [10] give a comprehensive view on the advantages of VPL. The factors mentioned in the paper that contribute to good visual programming norm also serve as an important guideline for this research.

Peter Deutsch [11] commented on a limitation of visual programming languages that is there cannot be more than 50 visual primitives on the screen at the same time. This is due to problem that may arise when writing large programs since there will be some difficulties in reading and writing the program. This limitation is known as the "Deutsch Limit". While this may be true, we believe that applying 3-dimensional visualization can help in reducing the difficulty by providing rotational viewpoint on the system. Furthermore, textual programming with more than 50 primitives may be facing the same limit as well, which is why good programming practices are always strongly recommended for program readability.

3   Proposed Visual Language Framework

The proposed visual language framework consists of three parts: the L-system visual language, its syntax and its semantics. The type of visual language used in this research is the icon-based visual language. The visual language consists of elementary object icons, composite object icons, and process icons. The L-system attributes such as Step Size and Angle are the elementary object icons. The axiom and production rule are composite object icon because they contain multiple L-system attributes. The process icons are the L-system attributes such as Move Forward, '+' (plus sign), '-' (minus sign), and the '[' and ']' attributes in the bracketed OL-system class. All these attributes are assigned with an icon representation and a function in the implementation as shown in Table 2.

Table 2. L-system class attributes and their icon representations

Attribute	Icon	Attribute	Icon
Axiom/Step Size		Step Forward	
Angle		Push Current State	save
Turn Left		Pop Current State	load
Turn Right			

The syntax part of the visual language framework is the arrangement of these icons. Basically our framework syntax follows the L-system syntax, and a line of visual language sentence in the framework is interpreted from left to right. For example, when user wants to draw a branch that turns left, user must put the `Turn Left` icon before the `Step Forward` icon to make the branch turns to its left before moving the branch forward. If user puts the `Turn Left` icon after the `Move Forward` icon, the resulting branch will become a straight branch instead.

The semantic part of this framework is the meaning behind a group of composite icons. It is determined by the syntax of the framework and also the functions behind each icon. The semantics may be as simple as doing a single function, or it may be many complicated functions to model a complex tree model with many branches and turning points. Just like the framework syntax, the framework semantics follows the L-system semantics as well.

4 Implementation

The proposed visual language framework is implemented as a plant modeling L-system application. The L-system code is taken from a functioning Java L-system application available for public use. For the software architecture, the model-view-controller (MVC) model is being used to separate front end and the back end logic, and also for easy modification purpose so that the front end modification will not affect the back end. The programming language used here is Java, as it is the language commonly used in L-system application. The development toolkit used is `Eclipse` IDE.

The system is divided into three layers as in the MVC framework: `Model`, `View`, and `Controller` as shown in Figure 1. Each layer contains a number of classes. Our visual language framework is implemented in the classes under both `View` and `Controller` layer. The classes under the `Model` layer are sourced and modified from an existing L-system application called the Java 3D L-System Interpreter project which is used for generating L-system plant models [12]. The details of the `View` layer and the `Controller` layer are described next.

4.1 View Layer

Basically all the classes under the presentation layer are implemented using the Java Swing API, which is the GUI library for Java. Figure 2 shows the `GrowInterface` GUI. The labels in bold are the sub GUIs under this GUI: (A) the `Samples` menu; (B) the `Help` menu; (C) the `Toolbar`; (D) the `Rules Window`; and (E) the `Welcome Dialog`.

The `MenuInterface` contains the `Samples` menu and the `Help` menu. The `Samples` menu is mainly to provide tree samples that can be modeled under the system. Four tree samples are provided as shown in Figure 3. By selecting a sample tree under the sample menu, a new window will pop up to display the tree model and another window will display the L-system rules behind the tree model. All these samples are modeled based on the predefined rules in the sample folder files. The `Help` menu provides some brief explanations on the L-system attributes and rules.

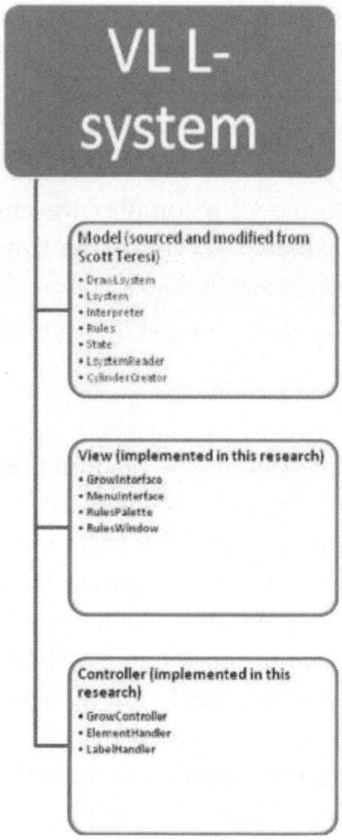

Fig. 1. The overall architecture of the implementation

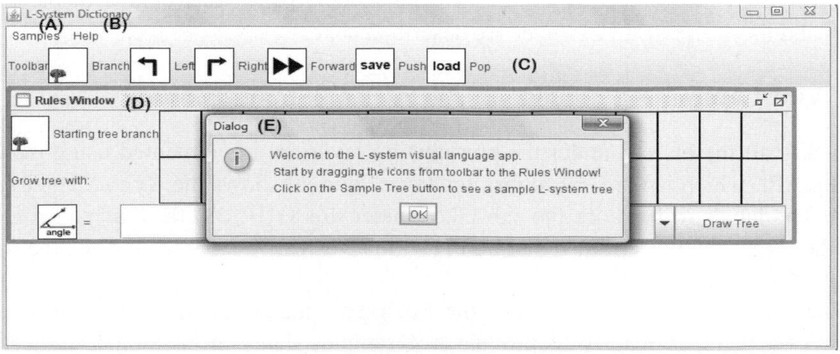

Fig. 2. GrowInterface GUI

Fig. 3. Four sample trees: (A) basic tree, (B) willow tree, (C) pine tree, (D) tropical tree

The `RulesPalette` class creates all the L-system attributes and puts them into a `JToolbar` object as shown in the encircled area in Figure 4. The main constructor in `this` class creates each L-system attribute as a `JLabel` object with its own pair of image icon and function name. The image icon is the icon representation of the attribute, and the name defines the function of the attribute. Each `JLabel` object is then incorporated with the `setElementFunction()` method from the `GrowController` class for user input handling purposes.

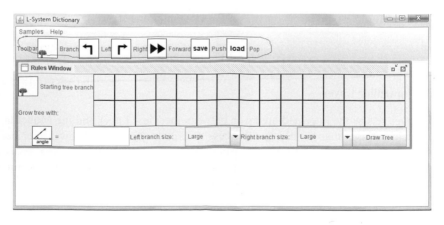

Fig. 4. The toolbar for visual language icons

The `RulesWindow` allows user to model their own L-system plant by dragging the icons from the `RulesPalette` and consists of the following six components as shown in Figure 5. Both root and the replacement rule have 15 empty boxes. The empty boxes are JLabel arrays that are incorporated with the `setLabelFunction()` method in the `GrowController` class. To model an L-system plant, users need to drag the icons from the `RulesPalette` and drop them into the empty boxes. The "Starting tree branch" (Label (A) - the root from the ground) is the L-system axiom and the "Grow tree with" (Label (B) - the replacement rule for the root) is the L-system production rule. The angle (Label (C)) accepts any number including decimal point numbers. To generate plants with different sizes, users can adjust the size for left and right sides of the tree branch (Labels (D) and (E) respectively). User needs to click on the "Draw Tree" button (Label (F)) to generate the L-system model. The JLabel arrays for axiom and replacement rules are passed down to `getRules()` method in `GrowController` class. This method will translate the user input icons into a string of axiom and rules for back end processing. Figure 6 shows a set of user-defined L-system parameters using our visual language framework and the actual L-system grammar behind it.

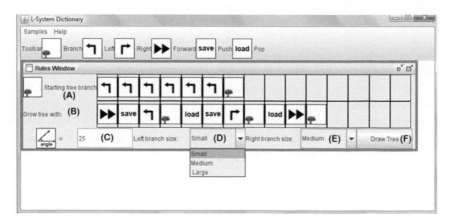

Fig. 5. Rules Window

4.2 Controller Layer

This layer acts as the intermediate layer between the View Layer and the Model layer. It contains classes that handle and process user inputs from the View Layer before sending them to the Model layer for plant modeling generation, and also sends the generated results from the Model Layer back to the View Layer for display. There are three classes under this layer namely the `GrowController`, the `ElementHandler` and the `LabelHandler`.

Fig. 6. An example of user-defined L-system parameters using the visual language framework and the actual L-system axiom, rules and angle

The `GrowController` class is the main class that interprets incoming user inputs and assigns them to the respective classes. This class also performs some preprocessing on the user inputs, such as translating the axiom and the production rule into icon format that come from the `RulesWindow` GUI. There are three fundamental methods inside this class: `getRules()`, `getAxiom()` and `translateString()` methods. Both the `getRules()` method and the `getAxiom()` method receive a JLabel array that contains function names of the icons. The JLabel arrays are the rows of empty boxes in `RulesWindow`. These two methods will change the function names into meaningful L-system axiom and production rules. The `translateString()` method will accept the function name of these icons and return back the correct L-system attributes that are associated with these function names.

The `ElementHandler` class handles the drag and drop mechanism for `RulesPalette`, which is the toolbar GUI. There are two types of data supported: image and string. The image is the iconic visual language in the toolbar, and the string is the function name behind the icon. This class allows the icons on the `RulesPalette` to be copied onto clipboard by dragging, and then the icons can be dropped off at another drop-enabled location in the GUI. However the drop mechanism is not enabled for the toolbar because we do not want the icons to be replaced.

The `LabelHandler` class handles the drag and drop mechanisms for the axiom and replacement rules in `RulesWindow`. As for the `ElementHandler` class, there are two types of data supported: image and string. The image is the iconic visual language that comes from the toolbar, and the string is the function name behind the icon. This class allows user to drop off the icons from the `RulesPalette` in the `RulesWindow`. Also, it allows user to move icons that are already dropped off in the empty boxes inside the `RulesWindow`. These empty boxes are blank JLabel arrays that accept new image icons and function names from both the `RulesPalette` and the `RulesWindow`.

5   Evaluation

A lab experiment is conducted for the two L-system plant modeling systems: JFLAP system, an existing textual based system and our Visual Language plant modeling system (VL L-systems). The respondents consist of Computer Science students of Universiti Sains Malaysia and also people who are currently working as programmers. They do not have prior knowledge in L-system concepts and they have not come across any L-system applications previously. The aim is to compare the users' preferences between conventional plant modeling system (where user needs to be able to write L-System rules in mathematical-like notations) and our plant modeling system (where user needs to arrange the iconic visual language representations of L-System to generate the plant models). This evaluation also attempts to find out how our framework can help the respondents to understand the L-system concepts compared to the JFLAP system.

The respondents need to fill out a questionnaire after carrying out some testing in order for us to gather feedbacks on both systems. The questionnaire is divided into two types: (i) whether the system achieves the purpose of this research, and also (ii) the effectiveness of the visualization used. The questions are formulated based on the factors that contribute to effective visualization as stated by Bergin et al. [10] and the purpose of this research. The respondents need to provide feedback on the followings:

- User friendliness of the interface, such as navigation, samples, tutorial, help menu and so on.
- Usefulness of the system in helping user to understand L-system concepts.
- Effectiveness of user controls in the system.
- Ease of use of the system.

The respondents need to rate both systems according to the questions asked. At the end of the survey, they are required to provide comments on the visual language framework in order to identify what the system is lacking from users' point of view and to identify the future work for this research.

6   Analysis and Discussion

The evaluation results are generated from the questionnaire feedbacks and subsequently summarized. Firstly, we would like to know whether both systems are able to help users to do L-system plant modeling although they do not have any knowledge in L-system concepts previously. As shown in Figure 7, all respondents are able to draw a tree model using the VL L-system as compared to only one third of respondents that are able to draw a tree using the JFLAP system.

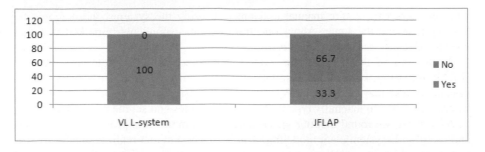

Fig. 7. The percentage of users that can draw a tree using both systems

In Figure 8, the VL L-system has a generally higher rating as compared to JFLAP. In terms of user interface navigation, the VL L-system gain a rating of 3.7 as compared to JFLAP's rating of 1.3. A significant gap is also found when comparing the ease of use of the user controls for the systems. Therefore in terms of user interface effectiveness, the VL L-system is preferred by respondents compared to JFLAP. This figure also shows the rating of the respondents for the Help Menu and the Samples Menu of both systems. In general, the respondents preferred the help menu and samples provided by the VL L-system compared to JFLAP.

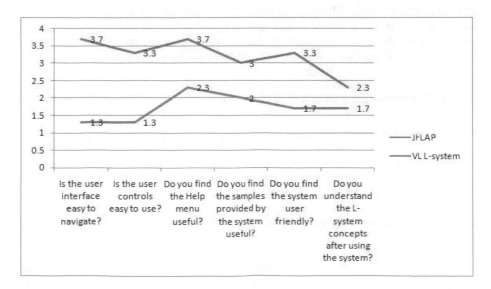

Fig. 8. Ratings of the systems

The rating for user friendliness of VL L-system is much higher than the JFLAP system. This proves that the VL L-system is more user friendly compared to JFLAP. In terms of helping users to understand the L-system concepts, there is only a slight difference in the rating between VL L-system and JFLAP. When trying to find out whether users will require manual assistance in using the systems, the outcome for both systems are the same. About one third of the respondents remarked that they need to ask us for assistance when using the system.

At the end of the survey, respondents are asked for their preference between JFLAP and VL L-system. All respondents show that they prefer to use the VL L-system because they find that the VL L-system is easier to use, as opposed to JFLAP where users have to manually type in the L-system rules and set the parameters.

As a result, we found that our visual language framework is proven to be efficient and useful in L-system plant modeling. The VL L-system that realizes our framework has managed to get a higher rating in individual comparisons as well as the overall ratings against the JFLAP system. The respondents also gave their comments on how the VL L-system interface can be further improved so that it can be more useful to the users.

We have successfully come up with an icon-based visual language framework and realized the framework as an L-system modeling application (VL L-system). The framework is modeled according to the L-system concepts. The evaluation of the efficiency of the framework is carried out by doing user evaluation of our framework with another existing L-system plant modeling application, JFLAP. The JFLAP is a formal language automata application that requires prior understanding of the subject matter in order to use it. The main reason for comparing our VL L-system with JFLAP is that this system and ours require users to specify L-system rules and parameters, with the only difference in that visual language is used to model a tree in our systems instead of textual language used in JFLAP. This is very important in order to prove that our visual language framework is more effective than the conventional textual language used in all other L-system modeling applications.

7   Conclusion and Future Work

From the lab experiment, our visual language framework is proven to be efficient and effective in aiding users that are not from the plant modeling research community to draw trees according to the L-system rules. It is found that the users prefer icon representations of the L-system attributes instead of the textual L-system attributes because it is easier to understand. Also, this framework is able to present a clearer concept on L-system to help users to understand more effectively on the subject. By considering the factors that make up a good visual language, this visual language framework is proven to be effective in visualizing the L-system concepts which cannot be achieved through textual language.

There are quite a number of potential extensions that can be done on our framework. First of all, the visual language framework can be expanded to include more L-system classes as there are many types of L-system classes available, not to mention the ever growing research on various L-system variations. Furthermore, the framework should include extra attributes especially for production rules, because L-system with more production rules is able to generate a more realistic tree.

Moreover, we would like to propose that the back end L-system modeling program should be modeled in 2D instead of 3D. This is due to the fact that 3D modeling takes up extensive memory of the PC and thus the iterative steps of each plant model has to be restricted to six iterations only. In actual L-system plant modeling, the number of iterations should be decided by the users instead.

References

1. Shu, N.C.: Visual Programming. John Wiley & Sons, Inc., Chichester (1992)
2. Boshernitsan, M., Downes, M.: Visual Programming Language: A Survey (2004), http://www.cs.berkeley.edu/~maratb/cs263/paper.pdf (accessed December 15, 2008)
3. Prusinkiewicz, P., Lindenmayer, A.: The Algorithmic Beauty of Plants. Springer-Verlag New York Inc., Heidelberg (1990)
4. Cavalcante, R., Finley, T., Rodger, S.H.: A Visual and Interactive Theory Course with JFLAP 4.0. In: Proceedings of the SIGCSE Technical Symposium on Computer Science Education, pp. 140–144 (2004)
5. Anderson, D., Bennett, c., Hunyh, P., Rassbach, L.: Printing out Trees: Towards the Design of Tangible Objects for Education. In: Proceedings of the IASTED International Conference on Education and Technology, pp. 61–66 (2005)
6. Karwowski, R., Prusinkiewicz, P.: The L-system-based plant-modeling environment L-studio 4.0. In: Proceedings of The 4th International Workshop on Functional-Structural Plant Models, pp. 403–405 (2004)
7. Ijiri, T., Owada, S., Igarashi, T.: The Sketch L-System: Global Control of Tree Modeling Using Free-form Strokes. In: Butz, A., Fisher, B., Krüger, A., Olivier, P. (eds.) SG 2006. LNCS, vol. 4073, pp. 138–146. Springer, Heidelberg (2006)
8. Pradal, C., Dufour-Kowalski, S., Boudon, F., Fournier, C., Godin, C.: OpenAlea: a visual programming and component-based software platform for plant modeling. Functional Plant Biology 35(10), 751–760 (2008)
9. Menzies, T.: Evaluation issues for Visual Programming Language: Handbook of Software Engineering and Knowledge Engineering, vol. 2, pp. 93–101 (2000)
10. Bergin, J., Brodlie, K., Goldweber, M., Jimenez-Peris, R., Khuri, S., Patino-Martinez, M., McNally, M., Naps, T., Rodger, S., Wilson, J.: An overview of visualization: its use and design, report of the working group on visualization. In: Proceedings of the 1st conference on Integrating technology into computer science education, pp. 192–200 (1996)
11. Deutsch, P.: Deutsch Limit, http://en.allexperts.com/e/d/de/deutsch_limit.htm
12. Teresi, S.: Programming Projects, http://teresi.us/html/main/programming.html

Inclusion of Property Profile in the Production Rule Pattern for Visualization Software Design

Sim Hui Tee

Faculty of Creative Multimedia
Multimedia University
Cyberjaya, Selangor,
Malaysia
shtee@mmu.edu.my

Abstract. The rapid development of information visualization in recent years has prompted new domain of problems in visual software engineering. Different design patterns have been proposed by the researchers with the purpose to guide the development of visualization software. The production rule pattern, as one of the important design patterns, uses a chain of if-then-else rules to dynamically determine the visual properties. It is a rather general pattern which does not provide much specific guideline on how the returned properties being determined. This paper improves the production rule pattern by developing a property profile for visualization software design. Property profile provides a convenient way to set the customized values. The use of property profile enhances the generality of the production rule pattern to cater for a wide range of visualization software applications.

Keywords: Property profile, production rule pattern, visualization software design, overridden methods, information visualization.

1 Introduction

Information visualization can be broadly defined as visual representation of the semantics of information [1]. Although there is a variety of software design framework supporting information visualization, it is always difficult to evaluate and re-apply the design solutions within these frameworks [2]. Visual information cannot be represented satisfactorily by the existing software design frameworks which are aimed to cater for the non visual application. New design patterns are needed in order to represent the visual information for the visual software design.

Heer and Agrawala have proposed a set of twelve design patterns for information visualization software [2]. Their design patterns are developed according to the context of usage. The production rule pattern, being one of the design patterns, was proposed with the objective to dynamically determine visual properties using rule-based assignment or delegation [2]. A chain of if-then-else rules uses predicate objects to encapsulate the rule condition [2]. However, Heer and Agrawala do not specify how to return the requested properties to the invoking object. This unattended issue leads

H. Badioze Zaman et al. (Eds.): IVIC 2009, LNCS 5857, pp. 708–714, 2009.
© Springer-Verlag Berlin Heidelberg 2009

to the ineffectiveness of value customization. This paper improves the production rule pattern by developing a property profile to tackle the aforementioned issue. This paper demonstrates that property profile is a convenient and efficient approach in developing visualization software.

2 Related Work

Heer and Agrawala depict the production rule pattern by a structural diagram. It is an object-oriented based pattern which depicts the classes and the relations between them [2], as shown in Fig 1 below. There is an abstract class which serves as a superclass that defines the general property value. The property value in the abstract class is a visual property in general. The general property value of the abstract class is inherited by a concrete class. In the concrete class, the property is initialized to a specific value of a type, such as color, texture and so on.

The concrete class has an accessor method that returns the property value to the invoking object. The invoking object references to a predicate object which encapsulates the rule conditions. Based on the rule conditions, a specific production rule will be carried out corresponding to the user interaction with the software.

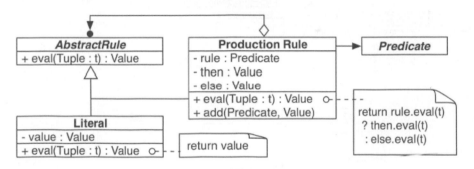

Fig. 1. The production rule pattern [2]

The main advantage of the production rule pattern is that it provides a guideline for the developers of visualization software to implement the value overriding in special cases [2]. The production rule pattern specifies how the customized classes use the production rule to override the default value specified in the *AbstractRule* superclass, as shown in Fig. 1. The customized classes are free from handling the implementation of the specific rule [2]. This practice of separating customized classes from the production rule mechanism would reduce the class definition in visualization software [2]. As the result, it reduces the software maintenance time and cost.

However, the production rule pattern does not specify a feasible way to override the default value in accordance to the type requested by the invoking object. This limitation leads to the raise of information access issue. Information access needs to be coordinated to ensure data integrity [5]. The existing production rule pattern is unable to determine the returned values effectively according to the rule condition. It is because the returned value in Fig. 1 is too general to cater for a wide range of divergent value types.

3 Using Property Profile in the Production Rule Pattern

This research proposes to use a property profile that returns the specific value according to the invoking object. Overloaded methods are proposed to be used in the property profile to overcome the limitation of the existing production rule pattern.

To visualize the implementation of the production rule, a dependency relation is depicted between the production rules and customized classes. Fig. 2 exhibits the separation of customized classes from implementing the specific rules.

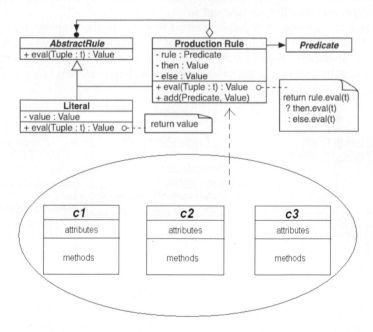

Fig. 2. Separation of customized classes from implementing the specific rules.

As shown in Fig.2, the production rule is invoked by any customized classes (c1, c2, c3). The class which implements the production rule evaluates the passing values from the customized classes and returns a value according to the rule condition. In order to return a specific value according to a specific requested value type, a property profile needs to be included in the production rule pattern, as shown in Fig. 3.

The property profile defines the values of all value types. Overloaded methods are used in the property profile in order to set the appropriate values according to the requested value type. In Fig.3, *ValueM* and *ValueN* depict the different value type;

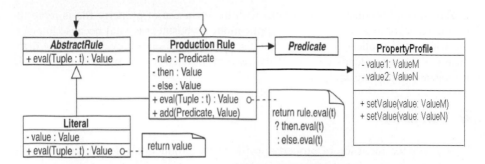

Fig. 3. Inclusion of a property profile in the production rule pattern

whereas *setValue( )* depicts a range of overloaded methods. With the inclusion of property file, specific value customization is possible according to the type specified by the client classes. The customized values are then implemented by the production rule in the expected way, according to the invoking object.

The primary advantage of using overloaded methods in the property profile is that it reduces the complexity of the application. The methods that return a specific value share the same method name with different parameters [3]. In the runtime, the object type will determine which method is invoked.

The second advantage of using overloaded methods in the property profile is that the specific behaviors are provided. This feature makes the production rule pattern more universal to the visualization software development.

The third advantage of using overloaded methods in the property profile is that it provides a convenient way for mapping the data onto visual parameters. Mapping data values onto visual parameters is a way of information representation. Abstract data is mapped to a representation through a process called filtering [4]. Overloaded methods serve as filters that manage and handle visual properties.

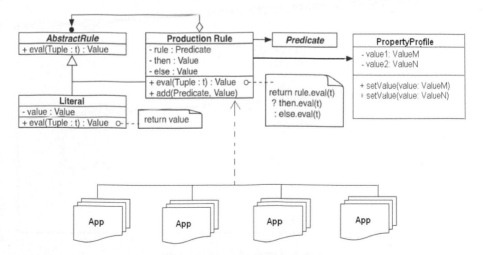

Fig. 4. Compatibility of the revised production rule pattern with different applications

The revised production rule pattern with the inclusion of property file is more robust to cater for any visual software application. Robustness is vital because interacting with visual application is more than discrete information retrieval [1]. Fig.4 demonstrates the dependency context of the revised production rule pattern and multiple visualization software applications.

4   Validation

To validate the inclusion of property profile in the production rule pattern, a sample class that contains a list of properties is created, as shown in Fig. 5.

```
public class Properties{

 private FontSize fsize;
 private FontColor fcolor;
 private FontStyle fstyle;
 private FontEffect feffect;
 private Alignment align;
 private Indentation indent;

 public void setFont(FontSize fsize){
   ... //implementation
 }

 public void setFont(FontColor fcolor){
   ... //implementation
 }

 public void setFont(FontStyle fstyle){
   ... //implementation
 }

 public void setFont(FontEffect feffect){
   ... //implementation
 }

 public void setParagraph (Alignment align){
   ... //implementation
 }

 public void setParagraph (Indentation indent){
   ... //implementation
 }

}
```

Fig. 5. Sample of *Properties* class

In Fig.5, the class *Properties* which represents a property profile defines six types of value. These value types can be categorized into Font category (*FontSize*, *FontColor*, *FontStyle*, *FontEffect*) and Paragraph category (*Alignment*, *Indentation*). Two categories of overloaded methods are defined accordingly (*setFont* and *setParagraph*). The specific value of the requested type will be returned accordingly to the invoking object.

5 Experiment

An experiment had been carried out to test the inclusion of property profile. Four client classes were written in Java Programming to perform different tasks, as shown in Table 1. Each task requires the return of appropriate values from the *Properties* class.

Table 1. Different tasks of client classes

Client classes	Task	Requested returned values
FontMaster	Font setting	Font size, font color, font style, font effect
ParagraphMaster	Paragraph setting	Alignment, indentation, spacing
PageMaster	Page setting	Orientation, margin, background color, layout
ImageMaster	Image setting	Orientation, opacity, border style

Each client classes were tested by invoking the relevant overloaded methods of the *Properties* class (which represents the property profile). The results showed that the invocation is error-free. Each client classes obtained the appropriate specific values that returned from the *Properties* class. This implies three things. First, the inclusion of property profile is successfully integrated with the production rule. Second, property profile facilitates the return of specific values. Third, the inclusion of property profile does not reduce the cohesiveness of the class which implements the production rule.

With the same set of client classes as shown in Table 1, another experiment was carried out to test the production rule without the inclusion of property profile (*Properties* class). It was found that the class which implements the production rule needs to be customized in order to return the requested values to the client classes. The customization decreases the cohesiveness of the class which implements the production rule. This phenomenon is inevitable because the rule of single functionality of class is not adhered to. It is expected that as the number of client classes grow, the class complexity will be introduced into the application. Moreover, without inclusion of property profile, the class that implements the production rule is defined according to the specific request of client classes. It will be more specific and less universal to be used as a superclass at the application-wise level.

6 Conclusion

The inclusion of property profile in the production rule pattern provides a revised pattern to return the specific values of a requested type using overloaded methods. The property profile increases the runtime efficiency as the class complexity is reduced with the use of overloaded methods. Greater class cohesiveness is achieved as the methods are functionally related. In addition, the property profile enhances the generality of the production rule pattern to cater for a wide range of visualization software applications.

References

1. Chen, C.: Top 10 Unsolved Information Visualization Problems. IEEE Computer Graphics and Applications 25(4), 12–16 (2005)
2. Heer, J., Agrawala, M.: Software Design Patterns for Information Visualization. IEEE Transactions on Visualization and Computer Graphics 12(5), 853–860 (2006)
3. Sierra, K., Bates, B.: Sun Certified Programmer & Developer for Java 2 Study Guide. McGraw-Hill/Osborne, USA (2003)
4. Heer, J., Card, S., Landay, J.: Prefuse: A Toolkit for Interactive Information Visualization. ACM Human Factors in Computing Systems (2005)
5. Isenberg, P., Carpendale, S.: Interactive Tree Comparison for Co-located Collaborative Information Visualization. IEEE Transactions on Visualization and Computer Graphics 13(6), 1232–1239 (2007)

Low Memory Implementation of Saliency Map Using Strip-Based Method

Christopher Wing Hong Ngau, Li-Minn Ang, and Kah Phooi Seng

School of Electrical and Electronic Engineering
The University of Nottingham Malaysia Campus
Jalan Broga, 43500 Semenyih, Selangor Darul Ehsan, Malaysia
phone: +603 8924 8000; fax: +603 8924 8002
{keyx8nwh,kezklma,kezkps}@nottingham.edu.my

Abstract. Works in the area of visual saliency are expanding rapidly where visual salience is beginning to find importance in many multimedia and object detection applications. The core of the visual saliency models is the saliency map where information from various features such as intensity, colour, and orientation are encoded onto a single master map. However, the required amount of memory to hold the related maps in the computation of the saliency map is large. This could be seen as a potential complication in hardware constrained environment. In this paper, a low memory implementation of a saliency map using strip-based method is proposed. Simulation results showed that the strip-based method is able to provide a reasonable saliency map while keeping the memory requirements low.

Keywords: Visual saliency, saliency map, low memory, strip-based method, hierarchical wavelet decomposition, Le Gall 5/3.

1 Introduction

In the human visual system (HVS), the brain filters out irrelevant information and then redirects attention to the important objects in the search field [1]. This capability to reject unimportant information reduces the number of information to be processed by the brain and therefore, is significantly crucial when the number of incoming information is large. Moreover, the system is able to detect important objects based on low-level features such as colour, intensity, and orientation alone. The ability of the HVS to filter out unnecessary information and detect object based on basic features is seen as a solution to object detection in computer vision. Motivated by this phenomenon, many research works are conducted to model the HVS [2-5].

Among the many visual saliency models available, the works of Itti and Koch [5] is used in many variations of saliency models. The Itti and Koch model deals with static colour images, using intensity, colour, and orientation as features. The input image is repeatedly sub-sampled and decimated by factor of two to obtain the image pyramid of nine scales where the original image is located at scale zero. Then, topographical feature maps of intensity, colour, and orientation are computed. A center-surround process is applied for the different spatial locations to compete for saliency

H. Badioze Zaman et al. (Eds.): IVIC 2009, LNCS 5857, pp. 715–726, 2009.

within each map. Resulting center-surround maps are summed and normalized to form the conspicuity maps for each feature. Summation of the conspicuity maps gives the final saliency map.

Although the Itti and Koch model is able to detect most salient objects in a given static image, the saliency map of the model is low in resolution due to computations at a down-sampled image size. Regions surrounding the highlighted salient objects are irregular with random boundary enclosing. The detection of the salient objects is done by circling the highlighted region. A more accurate segmentation of the salient objects is difficult to perform due to the irregularity and the incompleteness of the highlighted regions. Recently, Achanta et al. [6] proposed a high resolution saliency map to overcome the low resolution problem of Itti and Koch's model. The model in [6] operates based on feature contrast whereby three different sized filters are used instead of resizing the image.

While Achanta et al.'s model provides high resolution saliency maps; the model does not consider the mechanics of the HVS. Their model mainly detects the difference between neighbouring contrast and this method does not work well with images of low contrast between objects. The orientation feature is also not available in their model. To model a HVS which provides a good resolution saliency map usually require more hardware resources since many features are considered. Implementing the saliency model in hardware constraint environment could be a complication if memory requirements are not considered. We proposed to use the wavelet-based attention model of Tsapatsoulis and Rapantzikos [7] with some modifications and extending the algorithm to the strip-based method to conserve memory resources. The model in [7] provides a good resolution saliency map; however, comes with the tradeoff of high memory requirements.

2   Visual Saliency Model

The visual saliency model used in this paper adopts the method from the wavelet–based visual attention model of [7] with some modifications to the computation of the conspicuity maps, normalization, and the generation of the saliency map. Instead of using the dyadic Gaussian pyramid used in many saliency models, a hierarchical wavelet decomposition of Mallet [8] is used. By using the wavelet decomposition method, a lower resolution approximation of the image at the previous level can be obtained along with the orientation sub-bands. From there, the orientation feature can be directly used from the orientation sub-bands instead of using the Gabor filters to obtain the orientation features.

In the visual saliency algorithm, the Discrete Wavelet Transform (DWT) is used to construct the image pyramid. There are two approaches to perform the DWT. The first approach uses the convolution based filter bank method [9-11] and the second approach uses the lifting-based filtering method [12]. The lifting based DWT method is preferred over the conventional convolution based DWT due to computational efficiency and memory savings [13]. The overview of visual saliency model is shown in Fig. 1.

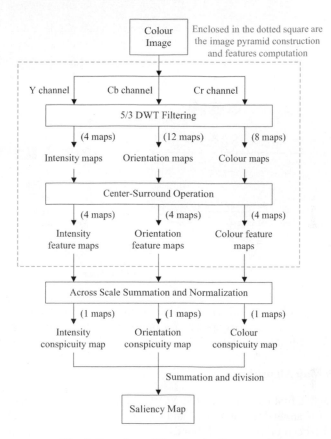

Fig. 1. Overview of the visual saliency model

2.1   Lifting-Based 5/3 DWT

In our visual saliency algorithm, the reversible Le Gall 5/3 [13] filter is used. Eq. 1 and Eq. 2 show the lifting implementation of the 5/3 DWT filter used in the JPEG2000 standard.

$$H = Y[2n+1] = X[2n+1] - \left\lfloor \frac{X[2n] + X[2n+2]}{2} \right\rfloor. \tag{1}$$

$$L = Y[2n] = X[2n] + \left\lfloor \frac{Y[2n-1] + Y[2n+1] + 2}{4} \right\rfloor. \tag{2}$$

The outputs of the lifting-based 5/3 DWT are indexed by either odd or even terms. The odd terms are the high pass output (Eq. 1) and the even terms are the low pass output (Eq. 2). Fig. 2 shows the one level decomposition of the lifting-based method. The lifting-based implementation consists of three steps: 1) split; 2) predict; and 3) update. The split step splits the input $X[n]$ into odd and even components. In the predict step, a high pass filter is applied to the input signal resulting in the coefficient H.

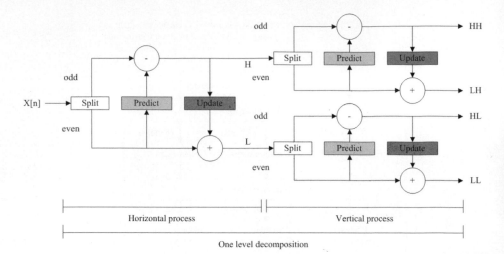

Fig. 2. Lifting-based 5/3 DWT filter

In the update step, a low pass filter is applied to the input signal to obtain the coefficient L. These two steps are first applied for horizontal filtering and then vertically to obtain the four sub-bands: LL, HL, LH, and HH.

2.2 Saliency Map Algorithm

The input image is first converted to the YCbCr colour space. Then, the lifting-based 5/3 DWT filter is applied to the Y, Cb, and Cr channels. For one level of decomposition, there will be four output sub-bands. Each sub-band will have a size down-sampled by a factor of two of the input image size. The LL (approximate coefficients, A) band is a coarser representation of the input image. The LL band of the Y channel is used to compute the intensity feature. Both the LL band of Cb and Cr channels are used to compute the colour feature. The other three sub-bands: HL (vertical detail, V), LH (horizontal detail, H), and HH (diagonal detail, D) will be used in the computation of the orientation feature. The LL band for the Y, Cb, and Cr channels is further decomposed three times to obtain a four level image pyramid. The HL, LH, and HH sub-bands of the Y channel are kept where else for the Cb and Cr channels, the bands are discarded. After the wavelet decomposition process, there will be four intensity maps, eight colour maps and 12 orientation maps at scale $j = 1$ to 4.

Having obtained the maps, the center surround difference is applied to the maps at each scale, from $j = 1$ to 4. The center-surround process is important to enhance regions that locally stand-out from the surround [7]. Finer details stand out at lower scales while large coarser details stand out at higher scales. From observation, it is found that having up to scale four for the decomposition is sufficient to detect most of the salient parts in images. Having more than four scales did not affect the saliency map to such an extent that they are considered as important. By having just enough levels of composition to construct a reasonable saliency map is justifiable in terms of resources saved.

The center-surround at a particular scale is computed using morphological close minus open (CMO) operation. The CMO operation is applied to the intensity and colour maps as shown in Eq. 3 to Eq. 6.

$$I^{-j}(m,n) = Y_A^{-j}(m,n) \bullet se - Y_A^{-j}(m,n) \circ se . \tag{3}$$

$$Cb^{-j}(m,n) = Cb_A^{-j}(m,n) \bullet se - Cb_A^{-j}(m,n) \circ se . \tag{4}$$

$$Cr^{-j}(m,n) = Cr_A^{-j}(m,n) \bullet se - Cr_A^{-j}(m,n) \circ se . \tag{5}$$

$$C^{-j}(m,n) = Cb^{-j}(m,n) + Cr^{-j}(m,n) . \tag{6}$$

For the orientation features, the center-surround is computed as shown in Eq. 7.

$$O^{-j}(m,n) = \left|Y_D^{-j}(m,n) - Y_H^{-j}(m,n)\right| + \left|Y_D^{-j}(m,n) - Y_V^{-j}(m,n)\right| + \left|Y_V^{-j}(m,n) - Y_H^{-j}(m,n)\right| . \tag{7}$$

In Eq. 3 to Eq. 7, I^{-j}, C^{-j}, and O^{-j} each represents the intensity, colour, and orientation feature map at scale j respectively. The symbol $\bullet$ denotes morphological closing and the symbol $\circ$ denotes morphological opening. The structuring element se is a disk of radius $r = 4$.

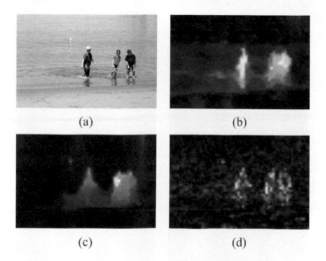

(a)

(b)

(c)

(d)

Fig. 3. (a) Original image; (b) – (d) stand-out regions in the intensity, colour, and orientation feature maps respectively

Fig. 3 shows (a) the original image; (b) – (d) the intensity, colour, and orientation feature maps at scale 3 respectively. Notice that the white object in the water does not stand out clearly in the intensity feature, but does in both the colour and orientation features. The girl with the pink blouse has the most noticeable colour compared to the other two kids and therefore, stands out the clearest in the colour feature map.

To compute the conspicuity maps for the intensity, colour, and orientation features, the 12 feature maps at scale $j = 1$ to 4 are up-sampled to the image original size using bilinear interpolation. The up-sampled feature maps are then normalized by maximal dynamic range so that the feature values will be clamped to the range of 0 and 1. The conspicuity map is computed using Eq. 8 and then is normalized once more. Eq. 8 describes the computation of the conspicuity map for the intensity feature. The same process applies to the colour and orientation features.

$$CM_I(m,n) = N(I^{-1} + I^{-2} + I^{-3} + I^{-4}) . \tag{8}$$

The notation I^{-j} where $j = 1,2,3,4$ are the intensity feature maps at scale 1 to 4 and $N(\cdot)$ is the normalization operator.

The saliency map $S(m,n)$ is computed by summing all three conspicuity maps and then divided by three as shown in Eq. 9.

$$S(m,n) = (CM_I(m,n) + CM_C(m,n) + CM_O(m,n))/3 . \tag{9}$$

where $CM_I(m,n)$, $CM_C(m,n)$, and $CM_O(m,n)$ are the conspicuity maps for intensity, colour and orientation respectively.

Fig. 4 shows the three conspicuity maps and the final saliency map.

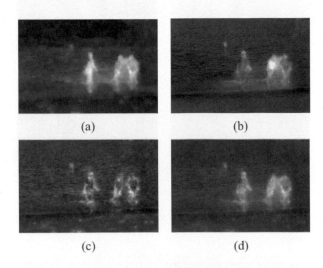

(a)   (b)

(c)   (d)

Fig. 4. (a) – (c) Conspicuity maps for intensity, colour, and orientation respectively. (d) final saliency map.

3   Extension to Strip-Based Method

A low memory implementation of the visual saliency model in Section 2 is proposed in this paper by extending the model to the strip-based method. By using the strip-based method, the number of memory required to store the maps in each step of computation can be reduced. The idea of this method is to divide the input colour image into strips and then process the strips individually before recombining them at a later stage.

In the image pyramid construction and the features computation part shown in Fig. 1 (dotted square), the values required for computation are available locally. This means that at this particular part, computation within maps only requires values at the same pixel coordinate. Because of this, the conspicuity map value at any point can be computed without requiring the value of other points on the map. However, in order to normalize the conspicuity maps, the strips are required to recombine at the conspicuity level. This is due to the fact that dynamic normalization requires the maximum and minimum values of the entire map to properly rescale the values to the range between 0 and 1.

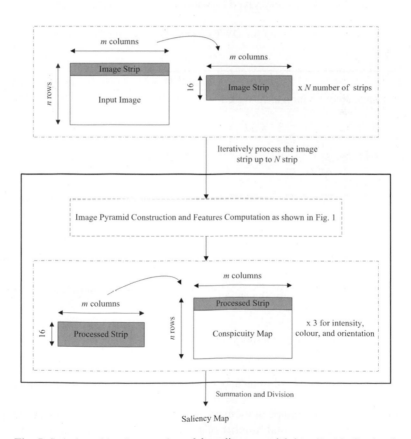

Fig. 5. Strip-based implementation of the saliency model described in Section 2

Although the conspicuity values can be calculated locally, the minimum number of lines required in the DWT filtering process has to be taken into consideration. For a four level decomposition, each with a down-sampling by factor of two, the minimum number of lines required is 16. Therefore, the input image is separated into N numbers of strips, each with 16 lines row-wise. An overview of the strip-based implementation of the visual saliency model is shown in Fig. 5.

A single image strip is processed at a time, going through the image pyramid construction and features computation similar to the one in Section 2. After the center-surround process, the strips (4 each for intensity, colour, and orientation) are up-sampled to size $16 \times m$ and summed linearly. The resulting strips are then added to three empty conspicuity maps (each of size $n \times m$) according to the feature type and original strip location to gradually construct the conspicuity map. The process is repeated until all N strips are processed. Then, the three conspicuity maps are normalized, summed and divided by three to obtain the final saliency map.

Consider the memory consists of many blocks where a single block holds a single value at a certain coordinate. Table 1 shows the memory buffer size required for DWT computation of the input image with and without the strip-based method, and the percentage of block memory saved by using the strip-based method.

Table 1. Memory buffer size used for DWT computation for non strip-based and strip-based methods

Image size	Required memory buffer size		Memory saved using strip-based
	Non strip-based	Strip-based	
32 x 32	32 x 32	16 x 32	50%
64 x 64	64 x 64	16 x 64	75%
128 x128	128 x128	16 x 128	87.5%
256 x 256	256 x 256	16 x 256	93.8%
512 x 512	512 x 512	16 x 512	96.9%

The block memory savings for the strip-based method is given by Eq. 10.

$$\text{Percentage of memory saved} = \left(1 - \left(\frac{16 \times m}{n \times m}\right)\right) \times 100\% \qquad (10)$$

where m is the number of columns and n is the number of rows (n must be multiples of 16).

In terms of storing the maps in memory, Table 2 shows the breakdown of maps according to feature and the total number of memory blocks consumed of an input image of size 256×256. The breakdown excludes the temporary memory/buffer used in

Table 2. Breakdown of memory consumption according to saliency model

Image Size	Itti and Koch Model						Modified Model of [7]						Strip-based Model					
	Image Pyramid			Feature maps			Image Pyramid			Feature maps			Image Pyramid			Feature maps		
	I	C	O	I	C	O	I	C	O	I	C	O	I	C	O	I	C	O
1 x 1	1	2	4	0	0	0	-	-	-	-	-	-	-	-	-	-	-	-
2 x 2	1	2	4	0	0	0	-	-	-	-	-	-	-	-	-	-	-	-
4 x 4	1	2	4	0	0	0	-	-	-	-	-	-	-	-	-	-	-	-
8 x 8	1	2	4	6	12	24	-	-	-	-	-	-	-	-	-	-	-	-
16 x 16	1	2	4	0	0	0	1	2	3	0	0	0	1	2	3	0	0	0
16 x 32	-	-	-	-	-	-	-	-	-	-	-	-	1	2	3	0	0	0
16 x 64	-	-	-	-	-	-	-	-	-	-	-	-	1	2	3	0	0	0
16 x 128	-	-	-	-	-	-	-	-	-	-	-	-	1	2	3	0	0	0
16 x 256	-	-	-	-	-	-	-	-	-	-	-	-	0	0	0	4	4	4
32 x 32	1	2	4	0	0	0	1	2	3	0	0	0	-	-	-	-	-	-
64 x 64	1	2	4	0	0	0	1	2	3	0	0	0	-	-	-	-	-	-
128 x 128	1	2	4	0	0	0	1	2	3	0	0	0	-	-	-	-	-	-
256 x 256	0	0	0	0	0	0	0	0	0	4	4	4	-	-	-	-	-	-

Saliency Model	Memory Blocks Consumed
Itti and Koch Model	155,603
Modified Model of [7]	916,992
Modified Model of [7] with Strip-based Method	72,192

Notations:
I - Intensity
C - Colour
O - Orientation

computations. Only the maps that are stored to be used in computing the features and conspicuity maps are considered.

It can be seen from Table 2 that our modified model uses 761,389 memory blocks more than the Itti and Koch's model for an image size of 256×256. The high consumption is due to the interpolation of the feature maps to the actual image size before computing the conspicuity map. In Itti and Koch model, the maps are resized to the size of the image at scale 5 before the center-surround process takes place. Because of this, the resolution of the maps is rather low but has an advantage in terms of memory savings.

By using the strip-based method, only 72,192 memory blocks are used. This is accounted for only 7.873% of the memory blocks consumed by the non strip-based method at the image pyramid and features computation stages. By using the strip-based method, a saving of 92.127% can be achieved for image size 256×256.

4   Simulation Results and Discussion

Simulations are performed on random test images from the Berkeley image database [14] and Flickr [15] using three different visual saliency models: 1) Itti and Koch biologically plausible visual saliency model (approximated using Saliency Toolbox [16]; 2) our visual saliency model modified from [7]; 3) our visual saliency model with strip-based method. The simulation results are shown in Fig. 6.

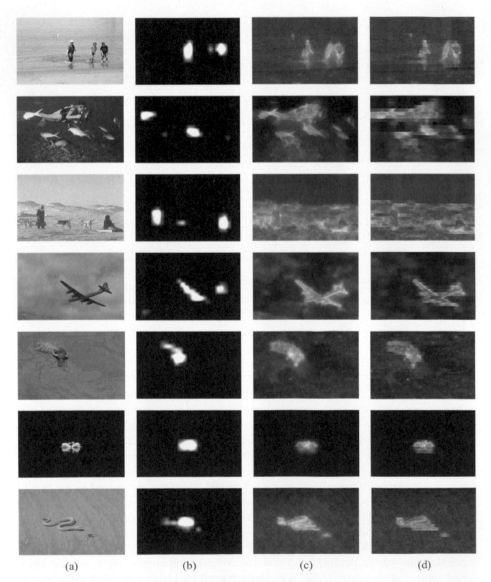

Fig. 6. (a) Original image; (b) saliency map of Itti and Koch's model; (c) saliency map of our model; (d) saliency map of our model using strip-based method

From Fig. 6, it can be seen that our model modified from [7] performs better than Itti and Koch's model. In images where multiple salient objects are present, Itti and Koch's model failed to detect almost all the objects where as in our approach, almost all salient objects are captured on the saliency map. Furthermore, the resolution of the saliency map in our approach is consider good in a way that the objects' boundaries are recognizable. Considering column (d) of Fig. 6, the strip-based approach detects the salient objects as well as the non strip-based method. One drawback of the strip-based approach is that horizontal artifacts appear on the saliency map. This is due to the insufficient data of the row above and below the processed image strip during the up-sampling process. However, even with the presence of the artifacts, the salient objects' boundaries can be roughly estimated.

In order to investigate the effect of repeated iterations of the strip-based method on the processing time, Fig. 3(a) is resized to different scales for comparison between non strip-based method and strip-based method discussed in Section 2 and 3. Table 3 shows the comparison between the two methods simulated on a laptop with 2.2 GHz Intel Centrino Duo and 2 GB RAM.

Table 3. Comparison between non strip-based and strip-based methods in terms of processing time and memory consumption using the image in Fig. 3(a)

Image size	Non-strip based method		Strip based method		Savings using strip-based method
	Memory consumption (blocks)	Time taken (sec)	Memory consumption (blocks)	Time taken (sec)	
160 x 240	537,300	2.75	67,680	4.72	87.40%
320 x 480	2,149,200	3.96	135,360	6.56	93.70%
640 x 960	8,596,800	15.41	270,720	22.22	96.85%
1280 x 1920	34,387,200	63.30	541,440	89.86	98.43%

From Table 3, it can be seen that the non-strip based method is approximately two times faster that the strip-based method. In terms of memory consumption, the strip-based method saves more than 87% of the memory resources in the computing the saliency of the images simulated.

5   Conclusion

In conclusion, a modified saliency model of Tsapatsoulis and Rapantzikos is presented and discussed. The modified model is extended to the strip-based method which significantly reduces the memory requirements to hold the computed maps. The resolution of the methods proposed is high enough for object boundary reorganization while providing good detection results. In the strip-based method, although the resolution is degraded compared to the non-strip based method, the detected salient objects are still recognizable. Memory requirement wise, the strip-based method only uses a small amount. This method is suitable for visual saliency application in hardware constraint environments.

References

1. Wolfe, J.M.: Visual Search. In: Pashler, H. (ed.) Attention. University College London Press, London (1996)
2. Burt, P.: Attention Mechanisms for Vision in a Dynamic World. In: Proc. 9th International Conference on Pattern Recognition (1988)
3. Sandon, P.: Simulating Visual Attention. J. Cognitive Neuroscience 2, 213–231 (1990)
4. Tsotsos, J.K., Culhane, S., Wai, W., Lai, Y., Davis, N., Nuflo, F.: Modelling Visual Attention Via Selective Tuning. Artificial Intelligence 78(1-2), 507–547 (1995)
5. Itti, L., Koch, C.: Computational Modelling of Visual Attention. Nat. Rev. Neuroscience 2, 194–203 (2001)
6. Achanta, R., Estrada, F., Wils, P., Susstrunk, S.: Salient Region Detection and Segmentation. In: Computer Vision Systems, pp. 66–75. Springer, Heidelberg (2008)
7. Tsapatsoulis, N., Rapantzikos, K.: Wavelet Based Estimation of Saliency Maps in Visual Attention Algorithms. In: Kollias, S.D., Stafylopatis, A., Duch, W., Oja, E. (eds.) ICANN 2006. LNCS, vol. 4132, pp. 538–547. Springer, Heidelberg (2006)
8. Mallat, S.: A Theory for MultiResolution Signal Decomposition: The Wavelet Representation. IEEE Transaction on Pattern Analysis and Machine Intelligence 11, 674–693 (1989)
9. Jensen, A., Cour-Harbo, I.: Ripples in Mathematics: The Discrete Wavelet Transform. Springer, Heidelberg (2000)
10. Weeks, M.: Digital Signal Processing Using Matlab and Wavelets. Infinity Science Press LLC (2007)
11. Strang, G., Nguyen, T.: Wavelets and Filter Banks, 2nd edn. Wellesley-Cambridge (1996)
12. Sweldens, W.: The Lifting Scheme: A Custom-Design Construction of Biorthogonal Wavelets. Applied and Computational Harmonic Analysis 3(2), 186–200 (1996)
13. Archarya, T., Tsai, P.-s.: JPEG2000 Standards for Image Compression: Concepts, Algorithms and VLSI Architectures. Wiley-Interscience, Hoboken (2004)
14. Bekerley Image Database: http://www.cs.berkeley.edu/
15. Flickr: http://www.flickr.com/
16. Saliency Toolbox: http://www.saliencytoolbox.net/

Baseline Image Classification Approach Using Local Minima Selection

Mohd. Razif Shamsuddin and Azlinah Mohamed

Faculty of Computer & Mathematical Sciences, Universiti Teknologi MARA
{razif,azlinah}@tmsk.uitm.edu.my

Abstract. This paper covers the area of baseline identification, which leads to signature recognition. It addresses the usage of a proposed algorithm, which identifies the minima points of a signature to be applied in signature baseline recognition. Signature baseline is vaguely identifiable and hard to determine for its baseline form. In this study, the aim is to determine the baseline form and categorizing it into ascending, descending and normal baseline. An algorithm using local minima selection technique is proposed in solving this problem. The total of 100 acquired signatures is used to determine the baseline classification range. Identifiable minima point values are extracted using an identification algorithm to yield a distribution of data that would represent the signature baseline. Then, a linear regression formula is applied to identify the direction of the baseline. The result is then tested for its accuracy with an available 100 sample of expert verified signatures. The result shows a favorable accuracy of 76% correct baseline identification. It is hoped that the implementation of this technique would be able to give some degree of contribution in the area of signature or handwriting baseline recognition.

Keywords: Baseline, Signature Baseline, Online Signature, Baseline Extraction.

1 Introduction

Advances in pattern recognition, document analysis, signature recognition and handwriting recognition have led many researches on baseline identification. There is such research that focuses on identifying Arabic letter baseline [2]. Some other researches focus on baseline detection and segmentation [8][9][10] and a few researches focuses on correcting baseline skew [3]. Oliveira [4] asserts that baseline is a generic feature of a signature. This means, that every signature or handwriting must have a baseline. According to [1], baseline is a hidden straight line at the bottom of middle zone.

A signature consists of many features namely size, proportion, spacing, alignment to baseline, progression, form and slant. The first four of these features are categorized as static features while the last three is categorized as pseudo dynamic features [4]. Oliveira asserts that, pseudo dynamic features contain rich element of signature feature as it is directly related to the signature strokes. In order to identify a baseline of handwriting, graphologist searches for an invisible line under the middle zone and at the upper lower zones of the handwriting. These techniques can also be applied for

H. Badioze Zaman et al. (Eds.): IVIC 2009, LNCS 5857, pp. 727–737, 2009.

Fig. 1. Example of signature baseline

a signature. The example of signature baseline can be referred to Figure 1. The calculated angle for a baseline is based on a vertical line that crosses over the baseline.

[11] proposed accuracy improvement technique of slant estimation for handwritten words. A chain code method for slant estimation is introduced in order to solve the problem. The chain code method repeats the slant estimation and the correction until the slant angle reduces to a fairly small size. [12] has also proposed a slant correction based on radon transform. Radon transform is used to estimate the long strokes of a slant. Then global measure is defined to transform the image and gradient to its estimated slope. Other study regarding baseline skew correction is proposed by [3] in order to correct the baseline of handwritten word skew in bank check dates. Morita uses weighted least squares in order to correct the baseline skew. Similar to this problem, [13] uses a pseudo convex hull to correct a baseline skew in bank check dates. [14] has introduced an extended-shadow-code based approach for off-line signature verification. In this approach global feature vector is used for the verification process.

Section 2 discusses the research method of the algorithm construction followed by the research finding in section 3. Finally, the last section would conclude the research and its future work.

2   Formulas and Methods

Figure 2 shows the overall steps involved in the constructed algorithm. The arrows indicate the step-by-step process. The process of baseline identification algorithm is broken into several steps in order to ease the development process of the baseline identification algorithm. In order to extract the baseline features contained in the signature, the captured raw signature data will be analyzed for its y values.

Next, the analyzed data will be filtered to acquire the minima values of the signature baseline. After acquiring all the minima values, the baseline linear equation is calculated by using linear regression function. After acquiring the linear equation of the signature baseline, the baseline angle and degree is calculated and classified into its category.

2.1   Data Acquisition

Since the raw data of the signature is captured in x and y values, baseline identification will be using this representation as well. All signatures have a unique baseline representation. This can be perceived easily by looking at the bottom of the middle zone of a signature.

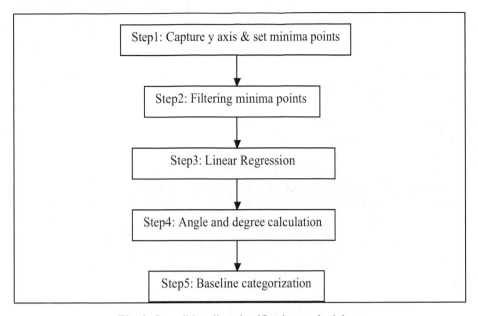

Fig. 2. Overall baseline classification methodology

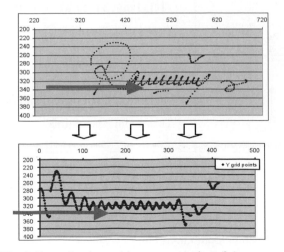

Fig. 3. Example of y-position representation of signature

The baseline is created from the up stroke and down stroke of handwriting. In baseline identification algorithm, the pattern of up and down strokes of a signature or handwriting can be represented by the y values in the signature grid. As shown in Figure 3 when the entire y position of a signature is extracted and mapped to a grid according to its series. The local minima of the generated scatter plot usually represent the baseline of the signature. Nonetheless, the identification process of the local minima point is needed to perform. In order to select the lower points of the y values, a minima selection rules is created and explained in the next subsection.

2.2   Minima Selection Rules

In the data capturing phase, it is noted that the y values of the captured data will increase when the stroke moves downward [5][6][7]. From this information, it is agreed that the minimum value is supposedly to be a high y position. In order to evaluate the rules, three temporary points is assigned to identify the changing values of y position. The first, second and third point of the signature will be assigned to temporary point 3, point 2 and point 1 consecutively. Then, the minima selection rules as shown in Table 1 will be executed.

Table 1. Minima selection rules

Direction of Point	Rules
	IF Point 1 is Lower than Point 2 AND Point 3 is Lower than Point 2 Then Point 2 is minima
	IF Point 1 is -1 AND Point 3 is Lower than Point 2 Then Point 2 is minima
	IF Point 3 is -1 AND Point 1 is Lower than Point 2 Then Point 2 is minima
	IF Point 3 is equal to Point 2 AND Point 1 is Lower than Point 2 Then Point 2 is minima

* Downward position represents a higher y value.

Identified minima points are stored in a minima list. Subsequently, it proceeds to the next point where the previous point in temporary point 1 is moved to temporary point 2. Similarly, the same process would be iterated for temporary point 2 and 3. This process will be repeated until the last point of the signature.

Once the processes are completed, a minima list is acquired. However, the minima list needs to be filtered to discard outliers. The outliers are required to be discarded in order to represent the actual baseline of the signature. A filtering technique is done to accommodate this setback. The filtering technique will be explained in the next subsection. The process involved in data acquisition is as illustrated in Figure 4.

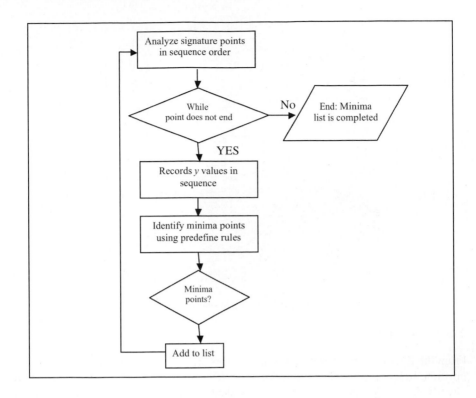

Fig. 4. Data acquisition process flow

2.3 Data Filtering

A filtering technique is imposed to discard the unwanted outliers that may affect the calculation of the baseline degree. To discard the outliers, firstly an average difference between two consecutive minima is calculated between all the minima points that have been identified and are defined as follows,

$$\text{Average} \quad = \quad \frac{\sum_{a=1}^{n} |y_a - y_{a+1}|}{n} \tag{1}$$

Where n is the total minima points.

The calculated average minima will be used as a benchmark boundary between two minima points. Next, the difference between each consecutive minimum is calculated again in the minima list and compared with the calculated average value in Equation (1). If the difference value is higher than the calculated average value, the current minima point will be identified as outliers and will be discarded from the minima list. Figure 5 shows an example of filtered minima points in a signature. The triangle points in the figure indicate end result of filtered minima.

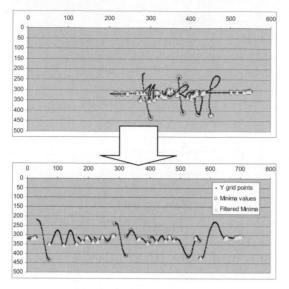

Fig. 5. Filtering stroke points

2.4   Feature Extraction

From the filtering steps, baseline minima points are extracted from the accumulated *y* position. Before the baseline features can be determined, two things are required to be identified. The first thing that needs to be identified is the signature baseline and the second one is the angle of the baseline. The line of the baseline can be extracted from the acquired minima values, which have been filtered earlier. A linear regression technique is used to acquire the linear equation of the baseline. Fundamentally, the equation is denoted as follows:

$$y = mx + c \qquad (2)$$

The baseline of a signature is represented in a linear equation (2). From the linear equation, the gradient (*m*) and the intercept *y*-intercept (*c*) are required to construct the baseline. The calculation of the gradient value (*m*) for linear regression technique is given by equation (3) as follows.

$$m = \frac{n(\sum xy) - (\sum x)(\sum y)}{n(\sum x^2) - (\sum x)^2} \qquad (3)$$

Where *m* is the gradient, n is the number of data points. The *y*-intercept is calculated using equation (2).

   After the linear regression technique is performed, the angle of the baseline is determined by a mathematical function based on the value of first and last point of the extracted baseline using Equation (4). The angle will determine whether the baseline attributes is raising baseline, falling baseline or straight baseline. From the angle, the degree can be determined using equation (5), (6) and (7). Next, the baseline will then be categorized for its attributes.

$$c = \frac{\sum y - m(\sum x)}{n} \tag{4}$$

$$\text{Ascending, } , \theta = \theta \text{ where } dy < 0, dx > 0 \tag{5}$$

$$\text{Descending, } \theta = 360 - \theta \text{ where } dy > 0, dx > 0 \tag{6}$$

$$\text{Straight, degree, } \theta = 0° \text{ where } dy = 0, dx > 0 \tag{7}$$

According to [15], there are three possible positions that can be used to categorize the three types of a baseline. These three positions are as shown in Figure 6. The equation to acquire the degree of baseline uses the same equation in slant degree identification [6]. Nevertheless, using the same equation, the two points in baseline are based on the starting and end points of the acquired linear equation in (2).

The linear equation is produced by the linear regression technique explained earlier. In this equation [6], xa and xa-1 refers to the end of the baseline point and the start

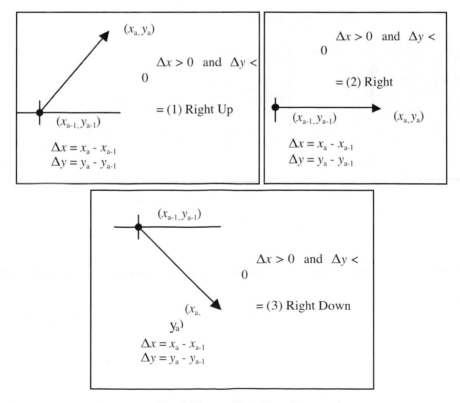

Fig. 6. Three angles of baseline

of baseline point of *x*-axis consecutively. Meanwhile y_a and y_{a-1} refers to the end of baseline point and starting point of *y*-axis. In the created algorithm, the degrees for baseline for each signature may only have three possible options since baseline angle is only calculated from the left to the right of the signature. The three possible degrees, θ are denoted as in equation 5 to 7 above.

After the linear regression calculation is completed, the angle and degree of the baseline is calculated. Finally, the classification of the baseline is executed. Strictly determined classification of baseline in terms of category such as ascending, descending and straight does not exist due to the variation of handwriting. In addition, predetermination of baseline angle measurement is hard, very time consuming and prone to subjectivity. For the purpose of this study, an objective measure of baseline will be categorized as following based on the distribution of signature data, and the range of ascending, descending and straight baseline is denoted as:

Degree, θ ∈ {0° - 360°}:
$$90° > θ > 7°$$ } Degree, θ = Ascending baseline.
$$6° > θ \text{ or } θ > 354°$$ } Degree, θ = Straight baseline.
$$270° < θ < 353°$$ } Degree, θ = Descending baseline.

An example of baseline categorization range is as shown in Figure 7.

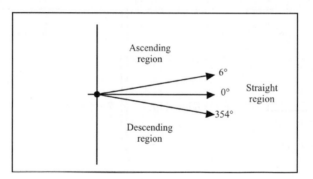

Fig. 7. Calculation of angle of degree of baseline

3   Results and Findings

The completed architecture design of the algorithm is coded in c++ and tested for its accuracy. 100 proofed signatures are analyzed using the algorithm and the results are as stated in figure 8.

From the analysis, it shows that the algorithm is able to identify signature baseline with a favourable accuracy of 76% as compared to the expert result. Only 24 out of 100 signatures analyzed from the algorithm gave different result from the expert evaluation. This proves that the algorithm is able to identify baseline in signatures.

One sample of a non identical result is extracted from the data and analyzed as shown in table 2. It is shown that the result of the algorithm is able to identify hidden pattern embedded inside the signature. Referreng to figure 9, if the signature is analyzed from the expert point of view, the signature is classified as a straight signature. This is due to the alignment of the signature that looks straight if percieved by the naked eye.

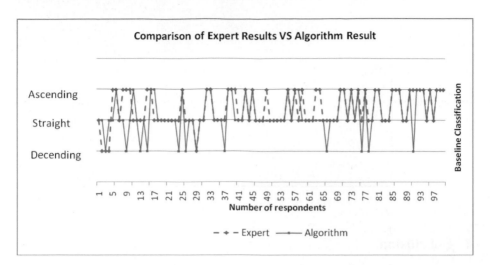

Fig. 8. Calculation of angle of degree of baseline

Table 2. Comparison Result from Analysis for signature sample 26

No.	ID	Expert Evaluation	Algorithm Results	Indicatior
26	D056	Straight	Descending	Non Identical

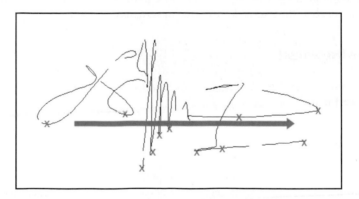

Fig. 9. Expert evaluated baseline

Meanwhile, the results of the algorithm indicated otherwise. By eliminating the unwanted minimal points or the outliers, the algorithm is able to detect the alignment of the whole signature. This can be viewed from the generated baseline in figure 10. Nevertheless, the results indicated by this algorithm can still be enhanced using other techniques or adding up new formulas. The results of this finding are still open for discussions.

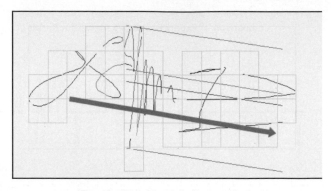

Fig. 10. Algorithm baseline result

4 Conclusion

This paper has contributed a way to identify signature baseline using the local minima identification technique. The algorithm was successfully tested by a developed proto-type. The prototype is able to extract the minima points and classify its baseline from a sample of signatures. Although the result shows that it has potential, the prototype need to be calibrated for better results. The most appropriate range and points to be considered are yet to be determined. Many new techniques can be applied in order to enhance this flaw such as fuzzy clustering technique or implementing hybrid tech-nique by incorporating a neural network to classify the baseline. It is highly hoped this paper can contribute some knowledge in signature recognition.

Acknowledgement

This research is funded by the Ministry of Science and Technology Malaysia through the Science Fund.

References

[1] Amend, K.: Handwriting Analysis. The complete basic book (1980)
[2] Pechwitz, M., Margner, V.: Baseline Estimation For Arabic Handwritten Words. In: Pro-ceedings of the Eighth International Workshop on Frontiers in Handwriting Recognition (IWFHR 2002), pp. 78–84 (2002)
[3] Morita, M.E., Facon, J., Bortolozzi, F.: Mathematical Morphology and Weighted Least Squares to Correct Handwriting Baseline Skew, Document Analysis and Recognition 1999. In: ICDAR apos;1999. Proceedings of the Fifth International Conference on Vol-ume, pp. 430–433 (1999)
[4] Oliveira, L.S., Justino, E., Freitas, C., Sabourin, R.: The Graphology Applied to Signature Verification. In: 12th Conference of the International Graphonomics Society (IGS 2005), pp. 286–290 (2005)

[5] Mohd Razif, S., Azlinah, M.: Online Slant Identification Algorithm for Curved Stroke. In: 7th International Conference Advances on Software Engineering, Parallel and Distributed System, pp. 13–18. WSEAS Press, Cambridge (2008)

[6] Mohd Razif, S., Azlinah, M.: Online Signature Slant Feature Identification Algorithm. Wseas Transactions on Computer Research, 21–30, Manuscript received October 3, 2007; revised February 25, 2008 (2008)

[7] Mohd Razif, S., Azlinah, M.: Slant Classification Using FuzzySIS. In: Third International Conference on Convergence and Hybrid Information Technology, vol. 1, pp. 1080–1085 (2008 iccit)

[8] Feldbach, M., Tonnies, K.D.: Line Detection and Segmentation in Historical Church Registers. In: Sixth International Conference on Document Analysis and Recognition, pp. 743–745 (2001)

[9] Feldbach, M., Tonnies, K.D.: Segmentation of the Date in Entries of Historical Church Registers. Lecture Notes in Computer Sciences, pp. 403–410 (2002)

[10] Feldbach, M., Tonnies, K.D.: Word Segmentation of Handwritten Dates in Historical Documents by Combining Semantic A-Priori Knowledge with Local Features. In: Proceedings of the Seventh International Conference on Document Analysis and Recognition, vol. 1, pp. 333–337 (2003)

[11] Ding, Y., Kimura, F., Miyake, Y., Shridar, M.: Accuracy Improvement of Slant Estimation for Handwritten Words. In: Proceeding of the 15th International Conference on Pattern Recognition, pp. 527–530 (2000)

[12] Dong, J.X., Dominique, P., Kryzyzak, A., Suen, Y.: Cursive word skew/slant corrections base on Radon transform. In: Proceedings of the 2005 Eight International Conference on Documrnt Analysis and Recognition. The Euro Working Group Transportation (EWGT), Rome, Italy, pp. 478–483 (2005)

[13] Rocha, A., Facon, J.: Mathematical morphology and weighted least squares to correcthandwriting baseline skew. In: Proceedings of the Fifth International Conference on Document Analysis and Recognition, pp. 430–433 (1999)

[14] Sabourin, R., Cheriet, M., Ginette, G.: An Extended-Shadow-Code Based Approach for Off-Line Signature Verification. In: Proceedings of the Second International Conference on Document Analysis and Recognition, pp. 1–5 (1993)

[15] Rohayu, Y.: Slant And Baseline Algorithm For Online Signature Identification. Universiti Teknologi MARA MSc Thesis, pp. 1 78 (2007)

Orientation Features-Based Face Detection by Using Local Orientation Histogram Framework

Somaya Majed [1], Hamzah Arof [1], and Zafar Hashmi[2]

[1] Department of Electrical engineering, University Malaya, Malaysia
nawalm2001@yahoo.com, ahamzah@um.edu.my
[2] Center of Health Informatics, University New South Wales, Australia
zafarh@cse.unsw.edu.au

Abstract. Detecting faces in an image is a challenging problem owing to the variations in pose, appearance, illumination, background clutter and is well known pattern recognition problem to date. In this paper we present our simple yet effective approach with LOH face detection framework to detect faces. In our approach we use, local orientation histogram and back propagation neural network classifier. We present the functional flow of LOH face detection framework and discuss experiments and results of face detection performance.

Keywords: face detection, image processing, orientation histogram, face recognition.

1 Introduction

We have seen rapid expanding in research in face processing, computer vision system, face recognition systems due to emerging applications in human-computer interface, surveillance systems, secure access control, financial transaction systems, forensic applications, and so on.

Face detection is regarded one of the important step of some of such systems and applications. However face detection is well known pattern recognition problem. Many methods and approaches have been proposed over the years but it is still a very challenging problem today. It is a challenging task because of variability in scale, location, orientation, and pose. Facial expression, occlusion, and lighting conditions also change the overall appearance of faces [1].

Some of the techniques proposed recently are given as follows: Lam and Yan [2] have used snake model for detecting face boundary, Yang et al.[3] proposed three-level hierarchical knowledge-based approach for detecting human face region. Wang et el [4] have employed genetic algorithm to detect human faces by calculating the projection of each face candidate onto the eigen faces space. Rowley et al [5] have improved a frontal face detection system based on neural network. Most of the face detection methods are feature based [9][10]. In such methods face is detected by detecting distinct features of human face and then measuring the geometric relations of human face. The drawback of such methods is that the complexity and difficulty in translating human knowledge about the face to computer representation.

H. Badioze Zaman et al. (Eds.): IVIC 2009, LNCS 5857, pp. 738–747, 2009.

In this paper we present Local orientation histogram face detection framework to detect face in an image. LOH functionalities are derived from our method and algorithm of histograms of local orientation and back propagation neural network. Histograms of local orientations of images are simple and fast to compute, yet effective. These orientation histograms are then used as input feature vectors for a neural network classifier.

Paper is organized as follow. Section two describes image preprocessing and dataset, section three puts forward the functional workflow of LOH face detection framework along with the functionalities of all its modules. Our algorithm and methods for this approach are described within the functionality of relevant module. Experiments and results are discussed in section four and paper is concluded in section 5.

2   Image Preprocessing and Dataset

Training Images repository was derived from our images database. Image database was obtained from university of Bern Switzerland that contains 450 images of different subjects and objects. In training images subjects have different poses for each faces. During pre-processing, the input image is first converted into gray-level image. We resize all images to [150 *140].

3   Functional Flow of LOH Face Detection Framework

Orientation histogram has been introduced by Roth and Freeman in their work for hand gesture recognition [6]. LOH uses the orientation histogram as a feature vector for face detection. This is simple and fast to calculate, and has advantage against illumination changes. Additionally, because of using angle information, a feature vector is invariant and the result will not be affected by any change in face location. Fig. 1 shows the architecture and workflow of LOH face detection framework. It consists of four modules: (i) Orientation space processor, (ii) Edge detector, (iii) Gradient orientation processor, and (iv) Face detector module. Our developed methods and algorithm will be described within the functionalities of relevant modules.

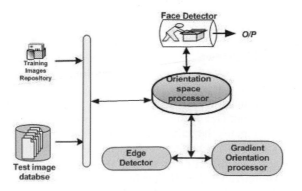

Fig. 1. LOH face diction framework architecture

LOH does not use the original image space value; instead it applies the orientation histogram which uses the local structure. This algorithm has advantages that can decrease illumination sensitivity. Orientation Histogram is a technique which operates on the orientation map of an image rather than on the image itself. The orientation map for an image is an array of two dimensional vectors which indicates the angles and magnitude of the dominant orientations that are present locally throughout the image. To get the orientation map, it is necessary to get the angles and magnitudes from the procedure of edge detection.

3.1 Orientation Space Processor

To compute the orientation histogram for each image $I(x, y)$ in the dataset, orientation space processor carries out the following steps:

- Choose simple filter T to apply transformation on an image I.
- Apply convolution between the selected filters and image I.
- Calculate the gradient for each point in the image I by using the result after convolution operation on filter and an image.
- Calculate the number of angles falling into the respective bin.
- Compute the running Sum of each bin separately.
- Accumulate the sum in one vector S.
- In final step at this stage it normalizes the vector S to get normalized vector V that has values in the range of [0 1].

Orientation space processor works with two modules (i) Edge detector, (ii) Gradient orientation processor to carry out its defined tasks.

3.2 Edge Detector

In order to work on orientation histogram space, edge detector carries out transformation T on the image space. It applies the simplest possible transformation T that helps achieve the objective. To do so, two filters 1x3 are used for the x and y directions to find the edges. After doing the simple transformation it carries out convolution operation to get the new values of x and y in an image.

3.3 Gradient Orientation Processor

As described in edge detector functionality that applying convolution on an image space, new values D_x in x-direction and D_y in y-direction are obtained. Gradient orientation processor divides the two resulting matrices D_x and D_y element by element and then gets the value of α (x,y) by taking the arctan $(\tan^{-1})$ that generates the gradient orientation values.

After doing some quantitative calculation and experiments, we have chosen the number of histograms bin size as m=10. Gradient orientation processor uses number of bins m =10 and computes the values of angle that fall under the same histogram bin and then running sum of each bin is calculated separately. In order to reduce the effect of noise, the contribution of each point in α (x,y) to the corresponding bin is weighted by its magnitude $C(x,y)$. The angle information is divided into 18 equal size bins (from 0-π).

3.4 LOH Algorithm

In this section we describe the functionalities of above described three modules in somewhat formal algorithm representation with detailed information using equations.

For each image I(x,y) the orientation histogram of N different directions (range from 0-π) is calculated, we divide orientation into 18 equal size bins (N/m), where the size of each bin m=10. The orientation histograms of all directions are concatenated into feature vector S, which will be the input to neural network classifier.

Two 1X 3 filter are used here T_x and T_y for horizontal and vertical filtering respectively, and are convolved with the image I(x,y) to generate two gradient images D_x (x,y) and D_y(x,y) defined in "(1)" and "(2)".

$$D_x \ (x,y) = T_x \ast I(x,y) \tag{1}$$

$$D_y \ (x,y) = T_y \ast I(x,y) \tag{2}$$

(Where $\ast$ denotes the convolution operation)

The magnitude C(x,y) is calculated using "(3)".

$$C(x, y) = \sqrt{D_x(x, y)^2 + D_y(x, y)^2} \tag{3}$$

Then the gradient G(x,y) is calculated using "(4)".

$$G(x,y) = D_y \ (x,y)/ D_x \ (x,y) \tag{4}$$

The gradient directions α (x,y) are calculated with respect to x-axis using "(5)".

$$\alpha \ (x,y) = \arctan (G(x,y)). \tag{5}$$

Summation M(x,y) of α (x,y) for each bin (m=10) is calculated using "(6)".

$$M(x,y) = \sum_{m=0}^{m=10} \alpha \ (x, y) \tag{6}$$

Once we get M(x,y) for each bin we accumulate those values in one Vector S.

The histogram values are calculated by counting the number of angles falling into the respective bin. Histogram are normalized to the values falling between [0 1]

This vector are normalized to the value between [0 1] which is defined in "(7)".

$$V = S/\max(S) \tag{7}$$

3.5 Face Detector

Face detector module uses back propagation neural network as a classifier to detect the face or non-face by classification based on the futures vector V received from orientation space processor which is defined in "(7)". The output of this module tells whether the image is a face image or any other object.

4 Experiments and Results

LOH face detection system consists of two phases (i) training phase and (ii) testing and face detection phase.

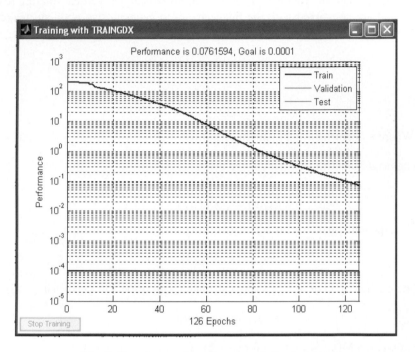

Fig. 2. Neural network performance during training

4.1 The Training Phase

In training phase we use set of training face images and choose (histogram of N different directions)$N = 0\text{-}180^\circ$ and m=10 bins so we get 18 values (divided N/m) of orientation histogram for each face image and we have 300 different faces for training images.

We accumulate these values for each image in a vector and at the same time the output is fed to neural network for training. We set our target output for each training set of neural network. Fig. 2 shows the neural network performance during the training time. Fig. 3 and Fig. 4 show the results of orientation histogram for some of faces from training set. Fig. 5 shows the neural network output versus the targets. Fig. 6 explains the neural network performance after finishing training.

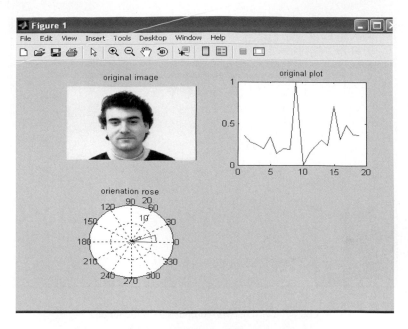

Fig. 3. Analysis of the results of orientation histogram

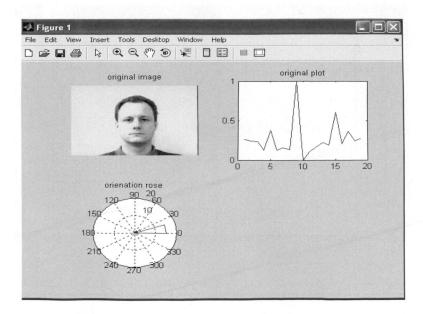

Fig. 4. Analysis of the results of orientation histogram

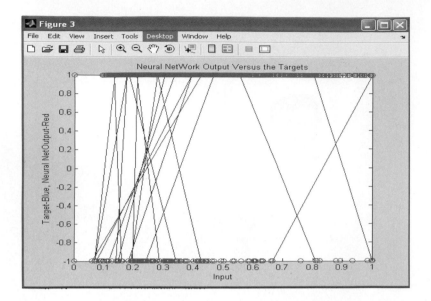

Fig. 5. Neural network output versus the targets

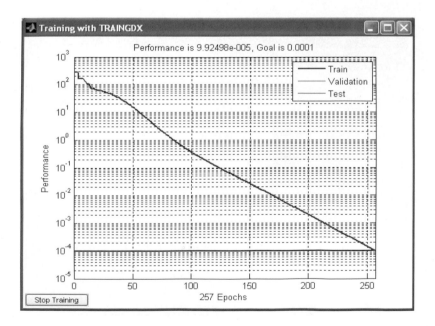

Fig. 6. Neural network performance after finishing training

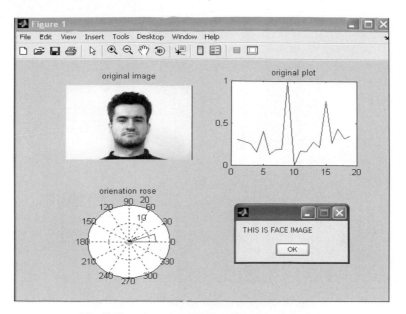

Fig. 7. Face detection result and histogram analysis

4.2   Testing and Face Detection Phase

In this phase test image is fed to LOH system chosen randomly for any face or object without any target output. LOH detects whether it is face or object. Fig. 7, Fig. 8 and Fig. 9 show LOH face detection results and also show the difference between orientation histogram for face and object images. Both face and object have totally different histograms.

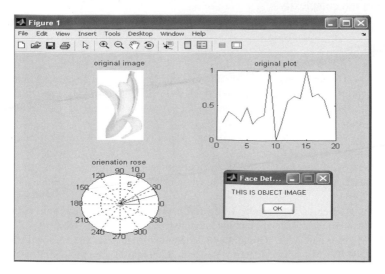

Fig. 8. Object detection and histogram analysis

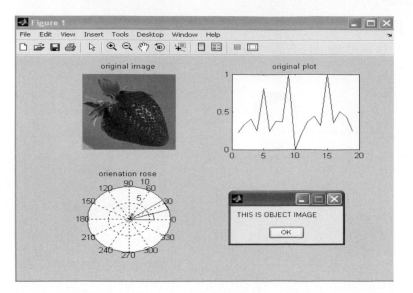

Fig. 9. Object detection and histogram analysis

5   Conclusion

We conducted more experiments with all test images set and found very promising results with 98% correct detection rate. We compared our method and algorithm for face detection using local orientation histogram with our work of different face detection method in [11] and found that this technique not only gives high detection rate for same dataset of images but also provides simple and easy approach in term of computing and complexity.

References

1. Yang, M.-H., Kriegman, D.J., Ahuja, N.: Detecting Faces in Images: A Survey. IEEE Transactions on Pattern Analysis And Machine Intelligence 24(1) (January 2002)
2. Lam, K.-M., Hong, Y.: Locating and extracting the eye in human face images. Pattern Recognition 29(5), 771–779 (1996)
3. Yang, G., Huang, T.: Human face detection in a complex background. Pattern Recogniton 27(1), 53–63 (1994)
4. Wang, K.-W., Lam, K.-M., Siu, W.-C.: An efficient algorithm for human face detection and facial feature extraction under different conditions. Pattern Recognition 34(10), 1993–2004 (2001)
5. Rowley, H., Baluja, S., Kanade, T.: Neural network-based face detection. IEEE Transaction on Pattern Analysis and Machine Intelligence 20(1), 23–37 (1998)
6. Roth, M., Freeman, W.T.: Orientation histograms for hand gesture recognition. Technical Report 94-03, Mitsubishi Electric Research Laboratorys, Cambridge Research Center (1995)

7. Schwenker, F., Sachs, A., Palm, G., Kestler, H.A.: Orientation histograms for face recognition. In: Schwenker, F., Marinai, S. (eds.) ANNPR 2006. LNCS (LNAI), vol. 4087, pp. 253–259. Springer, Heidelberg (2006)
8. McConnell, R.K.: Method of and q,yaratus,for- pnttern recognition. U. S. Patent No. 4,567,610 (January 1986)
9. Turk, M., Pentland, A.: Eigen Faces for Recognition (1991); McConnell, R.K.: Method of and q,yaratus,for- pnttern recognition. U. S. Patent No. 4, 567, 610 (January 1986); Rowley, H., Baluja, S., Kanade, T.: Neural Network-Based Face Detection. IEEE Transaction on Pattern Analysis and Machine Intelligence 20(1), 23–38 (1998)
10. Adwan, S.M., Arof, H.: Pattern Correlation Approach Towards face Detection System Framework. In: International Symposium on Information Technology 2008, ITSIM 2008, Malaysia, August 26-29 (2008)

Estimating Extremal Planes to Extract Crest Lines from Volumetric Data

Ding Choo Sheong and Bahari Belaton

School of Computer Sciences, Universiti Sains Malaysia, 11800 USM, Penang, Malaysia
choosheong@yahoo.com, bahari@cs.usm.my

Abstract. The aim of this research is to study and investigate crest points extraction technique from 3D volumetric data. Our goal is to propose an enhancement to extremal planes estimation technique for crest lines extraction and to test the method for medical purpose. Differential geometry approach is applied to the 3D surfaces based on 3rd order derivatives computation of principal curvatures and principal directions to estimate extremal planes for crest lines extraction. Gaussian smoothing is applied into the proposed method with various scales to filter the noise from volumetric data. These techniques are incorporated into marching tetrahedra algorithm to trace and extract the crest lines. We present and evaluate the results of the extracted crest lines using 3D visualization with several sample volumetric data.

Keywords: crest lines, differential geometry, extremal planes, marching tetrahedral.

1 Introduction

Landmarks are standard reference points or extremal points on craniofacial of 3D images. Landmarks identification is an important process before a craniofacial surgery. Craniofacial surgeons depend on landmarks to plan and analyse the physical measurements of patient skull where the positions of the anatomical landmarks need to be precise for craniofacial reconstructive surgery.

Crest lines are intuitively the loci of a perceptually salient ridge points on the surface where the magnitude is the largest [1, 2]. Automatic crest lines extraction is done in two steps where the first step is to estimate the extremal planes based on 3rd order derivatives of principal curvatures and principal directions and second step is to trace the crest lines of the volumetric data using marching tetrahedra algorithm. Practical computation of crest lines and curvature extremal points is a complex and difficult task which require high assessment of curvature tensor and curvatures derivatives [3].

The aim of this research is to propose an enhancement to the extremal plane estimation technique by incorporating the technique into marching tetrahedra algorithm and extract crest lines from volumetric data. There are two kind of extremal plane which is the maxima and minima extremal planes based on the value of the principal curvatures and principal directions. Crest lines is also known as zero-crossing because the gradient is the maximum when the value of the extremality is equal to zero on the surfaces of the images.

H. Badioze Zaman et al. (Eds.): IVIC 2009, LNCS 5857, pp. 748–758, 2009.

We aspect to get a reliable and accurate crest lines using our proposed technique from volumetric data. Gaussian smoothing operator is used to filter the noise of the volumetric data and marching tetrahedra algorithm is used to trace to crest lines to avoid the ambiguous case for extracting the crest lines.

2 Proposed Method

The proposed methodology for this research is described in a few sections according to the overall research method design. First, we need to filter the noise of our data using Gaussian smoothing operator. After that, we used the data to compute the principal curvatures and principal directions to get the extremal planes. We can get the crest lines by evaluating the intersection point between the extremal planes and iso-surface. Figure 1 below show the overall methodology design:

Fig. 1. Overall proposed method design

2.1 Gaussian Smoothing for Volumetric Data

Gaussian smoothing is an operator used to filter detail or noise from volumetric data. In partial derivatives computation process, instability problems may arise because of the noise from the complex volume data [5]. Therefore, filtering the noise is important to get reliable results. In our proposed method, 1D Gaussian smoothing operator is applied to the image intensity value in the x, y and z vector directions.

We filter the noise of the volumetric data by convolving the Gaussian kernel we computed with the images which is $f(x) = f \times g(x)$, where f is image value and g is Gaussian kernel value. We compute 9 Gaussian kernels based on the directions and derivatives of the kernels and convolve the 9 Gaussian kernels with the volumetric data to get the first order and second order derivatives of the image value in x, y and z directions. The first order and second order derivatives value is used to compute the principal curvatures and principal directions to get the extremality value. The degree of smoothing is determined by the standard deviation value of the Gaussian operator and we discovered that the value of standard deviation varies according to the types of data.

2.2 Estimating Extremal Planes

We need to estimate the extremal planes to extract the crest lines from the volumetric data. Crest lines is the intersection points between the iso-surface of the data with the extremal planes [3]. An extremal plane is the product of the principal curvature and a principal direction which is defined from average curvature and Gaussian curvature. There are two types of extremal planes which can be defined for each point on the surface corresponding on two principal curvatures, maxima and minima curvatures $e_1 = \nabla k_1 \cdot t_1$ where $k_1 > 0$ and $\nabla e_1 \cdot t_1 < 0$ and $e_2 = \nabla k_2 \cdot t_2$ where $k_2 < 0$ and $\nabla e_2 \cdot t_2 > 0$. Maxima curvatures are more stable than minima curvatures because minima curvatures are sensitive to small perturbations on the data [4].

We can get the largest curvatures point on the surface of the images of the intersection point of three implicit surfaces which is the iso-surface of the data, maxima extremal plane and minima extremal plane. The computation of the extremal planes is based on the implicit function theorem of the iso-surface where the principal curvatures and principal directions of the surfaces can be calculated as the Eigen values and Eigenvectors of matrix for the Weingarten maps [4]. We estimate the extremal planes e based on the summation of the principal curvature k and principal direction t value in the x, y and z directions.

$$e = k_x \cdot t_x + k_y \cdot t_y + k_z \cdot t_z \tag{1}$$

2.3 Concept of Marching Tetrahedra Algorithm

Marching tetrahedra algorithm is computer graphic method to extract polygonal mesh of iso-surface from implicit functions or discrete volumetric data. Marching tetrahedra is used instead of marching cubes or marching lines algorithm because it can solve the topological inconsistent problem which is shown in Figure 2 and search the volumetric data exhaustively without losing any crucial data [6,7]. Marching tetrahedra algorithm can be used to overcome the topological problem by decomposition of each 8-cell correlated with the vertex of the cube into five tetrahedra as shown Figure 3. We modified the marching tetrahedra algorithm which is used to trace and evaluate the extremality value of every tetrahedron to determine the largest curvature to extract the crest lines.

Fig. 2. Topological inconsistent case (left) and topological consistent case (right)

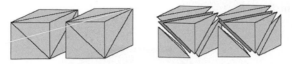

Fig. 3. Decomposition of cube into 5 tetrahedra

2.4 Extraction of Extremal Points

Extraction of extremal points involves the intersection points of three implicit surfaces which is the iso-surface, maxima extremal plane and minima extremal plane [8]. Linear interpolation or tri-linear interpolation approach can be applied to every vertex of the tetrahedral to find the intersection points for the extremal planes. We divide the extremal point's process into three stages where the first stage is to estimate the iso-surface, second stage is to estimate the extremal plane and third stage is to estimate the extremal point. The iso-surface can be estimated based on the predefined iso-value by linear interpolating the edge of every tetrahedron while the extremal planes can be estimated by interpolating the edge of every tetrahedron with the maxima extermality value on every vertex and find the intersection point between the iso-surface with the maxima extremal planes. Crest lines are the lines connecting two intersection points between the extremal planes with the iso-surface in a triangle and this process can be known as zero-crossing [9,10]. The extremal points on the surface can be estimated by interpolating edge of every tetrahedron with minima extremality value and find the intersection point between the iso-surface, maxima extremal plane and minima extremal plane. Marching tetrahedra algorithm is used to trace the existence of zero-crossing from tetrahedra to tetrahedra and output the coordinate of the crest lines to be visualized.

3 Applications and Results

3.1 Experiment Datasets

In the experiment we use three different datasets which are, the control dataset based on an implicit function $z = x^4 + y^4$, temperature dataset and the skull dataset. The first dataset choice is for pragmatic reason, we need a control dataset for which we know the salient features like ridges and valleys (equivalent to crest-lines), to test and evaluate our proposed technique. We evaluated the implicit function over $20 \times 20 \times 20$ grids to get the scalar data.

The temperature dataset is the result of simulation of temperature distributions over a double's glazing window to visualize the shape of the distributed temperature. The simulation has been run over the grid size of $18 \times 18 \times 10$ in x, y and z direction respectively. The skull dataset comes from a CT scan image we gathered from the visualization package we have in our lab. This data is originally in DICOM[1] format, and we have converted it into text format in order to use with our proposed technique. We noted that this conversion may introduce errors in the process; unfortunately it is unavoidable as our technique (at this moment) works only with text input data. The size of the skull datasets is $64 \times 64 \times 93$.

---

[1] **D**igital **I**maging and **Com**munications in **M**edicine (**DICOM**) is a standard for handling, storing, printing, and transmitting information in medical imaging [source : Wikipedia].

3.2 Experiment Results

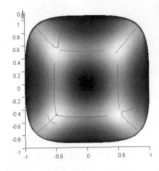

Fig. 4. Ground truth of crest lines over control dataset

3.2.1 Case Study 1

The data used for case study 1 is generated from the formula $z = x^4 + y^4$. This data is computed over the range from -1 to 1 with the grid size of $20 \times 20 \times 20$ in x, y, and z directions. First, crest lines are extracted from the iso-surface using analytical method. Since the function is known, and differentiable up to 3rd order, we can easily derived first, second and third derivatives. The values of the first and second order derivatives are obtained using partial differential equation. These will form the values we can assign to the parameters likes $f_x, f_y, f_z, f_{xx}, f_{xy}, f_{xz}$, etc. We then applied these values to estimate extremal planes and then subsequently used them to extract crest lines (using marching tetrahedra) from the iso-surface.

3.2.2 Case Study 2

The data used in case study 2 is the data for the formula $z = x^4 + y^4$. In this case study, we are going to implement different type of finite difference methods – a class of method used to estimate gradient from dataset -- into our proposed method. The finite

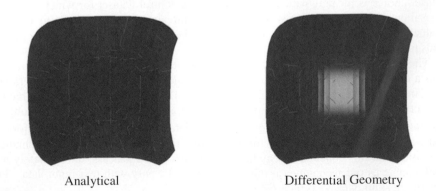

Analytical   Differential Geometry

Fig. 5. Crest lines of $z = x^4 + y^4$ extracted using analytical and differential geometry method

difference methods used are the central differential equation (CDE), forward differential equation (FDE) and the backward differential equation (BDE). Finite difference is used to approximate the derivatives of the data used to estimate the extremal planes. Figures 7 to Figure 9 show the set of outputs we get when applying different derivative estimation methods.

Fig. 6. Superimposed of crest lines extracted from differential geometry method(blue) with crest lines of control data(red) with iso-surface (left) and without iso-surface (right)

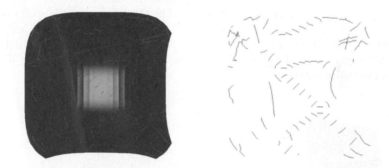

Fig. 7. Crest lines of control data extracted using Central Differential Equation

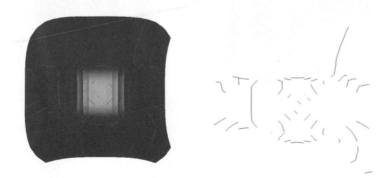

Fig. 8. Crest lines of control data extracted using Forward Differential Equation

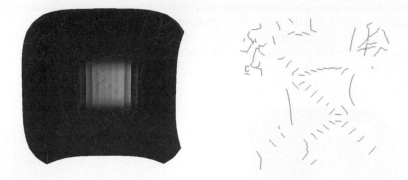

Fig. 9. Crest lines of control data extracted using Forward Differential Equation

3.2.3 Case Study 3

Case study 3 uses temperature data with the size of $18 \times 18 \times 10$ and with the iso-value of 0.5. Temperature data is used in order to test the proposed method using simple and small size data. In this case study, we are going to test the result using the differential geometry method with and without the Gaussian smoothing operator. The result obtain is evaluated by means of visual comparison. Gaussian smoothing operator is used to filter the noise of the data before we estimate the extremal planes for the crest lines extraction. The Gaussian operator scales or standard deviations used in the experiment are 3 (to represent low scale) and 15 (to represent high scale). The range for the scale depends on the value of the data used. Figure 10, Figure 11 and Figure 12 show the crest lines extracted using different gradient estimation methods.

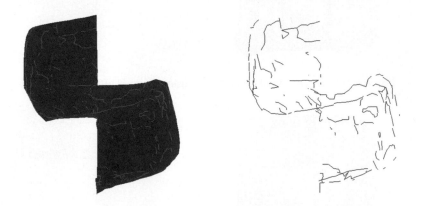

Fig. 10. Crest lines of temperature data extracted using differential geometry method with and without iso-surface

In Case Study 3, we can see from figure 10 that the extracted crest lines exhibit a good depiction feature lines in the location where we expected to find them – for instance near edges, corners, or even in areas with abrupt changes. However, some of these lines appear in the area where we least expecting them to be, for instance around the flat area which may be cause by noise. Figure11 and figure 12 show the results of crest lines extracted with Gaussian smoothing to filter the noise. The results produced seems better compare to results produced without filtering the noise. We can see that the amount of short lines in figure 11 is more than figure 12; this show that the lower scale produces a smoother and better results.

In Case Study 4, we can see from the result that the crest lines extracted are too many, short and they do resembles some important anatomical landmarks of a human's skull. This may be due to the noise in the data. The result in Figure 13 shows a lot of unconnected short lines but we are able to extract the crest lines on the surface of the skull and the shape extracted is acceptable. From figure 14 and figure 15 we can see that the crest lines extracted with Gaussian smoothing filtering the noise of the data also produced not encouraging results. The result shows a lot of short unconnected crest lines but we are able to extract the crest lines on the surface of the skull with acceptable shape. This can be due to the nature of the data because this problem does not occur in Case Study 3. Marching tetrahedra algorithm is maybe the cause of the short crest lines because it produces 5 short crest lines in a cube instead of 1 long crest line. A closer inspection on the crest lines outputs, we noticed that sometimes there are two lines connecting on the same edge of the triangle, and worse they are not joining at the same location, this can be due to numerical errors in our implementation.

4 Conclusions

From the evaluation of the case study, we can conclude that the extraction of crest lines was successfully performed. Crest lines extracted using differential geometry approach is acceptable for small size data but it is not acceptable for large size data due to some factors such as the nature of the data and marching tetrahedra algorithm.

The problem of large data can be improved because this problem was encountered before by others researcher who used triangular meshes to extract crest lines. The crest lines extracted using the proposed method from the data filtered by Gaussian smoothing gives a better result compares to the result of crest lines extracted without smoothing the data. This also concludes that pre-process and post-process procedure for crest lines extraction is important in order to get good and acceptable results.

References

[1] Pennec, X., Ayache, N., Thirion, J.P.: Landmark-based registration using features identified through differential geometry. In: Handbook of Medical Imaging, pp. 499–513 (2000)

[2] Thirion, J.P.: The extremal mesh and the understanding of 3D surfaces. International Journal of Computer Vision 19, 115–128 (1996)

[3] Stylianou, G., Farin, G.: Crest lines extraction from 3D triangulated meshes. Hierarchical and Geometrical Methods in Scientific Visualization, 269–281 (2003)

[4] Thirion, J.P., Gourdon, A.: The 3D marching lines algorithm and its application to crest line extraction, Technical Report, INRIA Sophia-Antipolis, France (1992)

[5] Monga, O., Lengagne, R., Deriche, R.: Crest lines extraction in volume 3D medical images: A multi-scale approach. In: Proc. of the 12th IAPR International Conference on Computer Vision & Image Processing, Jerusalem, Israel, pp. 553–555 (1994)

[6] Treece, G.M., Prager, R.W., Gee, A.H.: Regularised marching tetrahedra: Improved isosurface extraction. Cambridge University Engineering Department Technical Report, Cambridge University, Cambridge, UK

[7] Gueziec, A., Hummel, R.: Exploiting triangulated surface extraction using tetrahedra decomposition. IEEE Transactions on Visualization and Computer Graphics 1, 328–342 (1995)

[8] Stylianou, G., Farin, G.: Crest lines for surface segmentation and flattening. IEEE Transactions on Visualization and Computer Graphics 10, 536–544 (2004)

[9] Yoshizawa, S., Belyaev, A., Seidel, H.P.: Fast and robust detection of crest lines on meshes. In: ACM Symposium on Solid Modelling and Applications, Cambridge, Massachusetts, USA, pp. 227–232 (2005)

[10] Yoshizawa, S., Belyaev, A., Yokota, H., Seidel, H.P.: Fast and faithful geometric algorithm for detecting crest lines on meshes. In: Proceedings - Pacific Conference on Computer Graphics and Applications, Maui, Hawaii, pp. 231–237 (2007)

Designing of Roaming Protocol for Bluetooth Equipped Multi Agent Systems

Fazli Subhan and Halabi B. Hasbullah

Department of Computer and Information Sciences
Universiti Teknologi PETRONAS
Bandar Seri Iskandar, 31750 Tronoh,
Perak, Malaysia
fazlisu@gmail.com,
halabi@petronas.com.my

Abstract. Bluetooth is an established standard for low cost, low power, wireless personal area network. Currently, Bluetooth does not support any roaming protocol in which handoff occurs dynamically when a Bluetooth device is moving out of the piconet. If a device is losing its connection to the master device, no provision is made to transfer it to another master. Handoff is not possible in a piconet, as in order to stay within the network, a slave would have to keep the same master. So, by definition intra-handoff is not possible within a piconet. This research mainly focuses on Bluetooth technology and designing a roaming protocol for Bluetooth equipped multi agent systems. A mathematical model is derived for an agent. The idea behind the mathematical model is to know when to initiate the roaming process for an agent. A desired trajectory for the agent is calculated using its x and y coordinates system, and is simulated in SIMU-LINK. Various roaming techniques are also studied and discussed. The advantage of designing a roaming protocol is to ensure the Bluetooth enabled roaming devices can freely move inside the network coverage without losing its connection or break of service in case of changing the base stations.

Keywords: Keywords-component; Bluetooth; Roaming; Handoff; Multi Agent Systems; Simulink.

1 Introduction

Bluetooth is a short range wireless radio technology that enables Bluetooth enabled electrical devices to wirelessly communicate in the 2.45 GHz ISM (license free) frequency band [1]. The communication changes the transmitting and receiving frequency 1600 times per second, using 79 different frequencies. The range of Bluetooth network can be 0 to 100 meters. It is used to transmit both synchronous as well as asynchronous data. The bandwidth of the Bluetooth network at physical layer is 2.1 mb/s [2].

The basic unit of networking in Bluetooth is a PAN or piconet, consisting of a master and one to seven slaves. In a piconet, the devices share the same frequency hopping spread spectrum (FHHS) channel, which is a transmission technology used in

H. Badioze Zaman et al. (Eds.): IVIC 2009, LNCS 5857, pp. 759–769, 2009.
© Springer-Verlag Berlin Heidelberg 2009

local area wireless network (LAWN) [3]. Two or more than two piconets form one scatternet. So, a scatternet is collection of piconets and the connection node which links the two piconets is the member of the both piconets. This node can be simultaneously a slave of multiple piconets, but can be a master in only one piconet. Fig.1 shows the basic structure of a piconet, in which six salve devices are connected with master. In Figure 2, two piconets are combined with the help of a bridge node which acts as a slave in both piconets at the same time.

A multi agent refers to an entity that functions continuously and autonomously in an environment in which other processes take place and other agents exist [4]. It can be a physical or software entity. When many agents combine, it is called multi agents. Multi agent systems involve a team of intelligent agents working together to accomplish a given task. The accomplishment of a task depends on the coordination of actions and behavior of the agents [4]. To achieve coordination between agents, communication can be used. Usually, multi agents work in a close proximity; hence Bluetooth technology can be employed for communication among agents. Multi agents can be of any handheld device, which have the functionality of data collection and transferring it to the central device, using Bluetooth. The data that can be collected using multi agents or any handheld device may be temperature, pressure or any physical parameter.

Roaming in Bluetooth networks can be defined when the Bluetooth equipped multi agent moves freely without its connection being terminated. The service should be continued when it is going out of the range of one master transferred to another. Currently Bluetooth network does not support any roaming protocol in which handoff occurs dynamically. Figure 1 shows a scenario of multi agent systems.

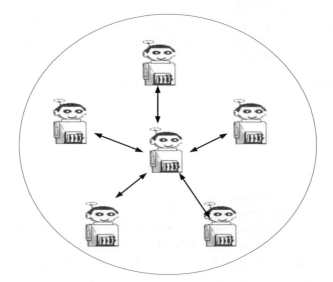

Fig. 1. Structure of piconet with five agents and one Master agent

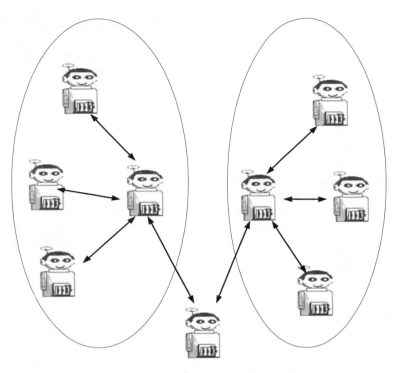

Fig. 2. Structure of scatternet with two piconets

The advantage of designing a roaming protocol is to ensure the Bluetooth enabled roaming device can freely move within the network coverage without losing its connection or break of service in case of changing from master device to another. In [5], the handover is categorized as hard and soft handoff. In case, when a mobile device is connected simultaneously with more than one APs then it is considered as soft handoff, while when it is connected to only one AP, then it is called hard handoff. Soft handoff is made before break; while hard handoff is break before make approach. In soft handoff, service does not break, and is considered as continuous during the AP switching. The main objective of this research is to present Bluetooth technology, its applications and to identify the roaming issue. The main focus of this paper is to define the roaming boundary. Furthermore to propose the solution for roaming issue and to verify the proposed trajectory for an object using Matlab and Simulink.

There are various localization techniques proposed by various researchers [7],[8],[9]. These techniques are used to locate the position of the incoming signal. On the basis of these techniques a roaming protocol for Bluetooth equipped multi agent system (MAS) will be designed. One of the ways of localization is Global Positioning System (GPS) usually used for navigation system. Two main requirements in this system are the transmitter and receiver. A transmitter is usually a satellite and the receiver is built in the device. GPS system is not feasible for indoor applications and also it is costly as compared. Hence, for low cost multi agent systems and indoor operating multi agent system, it is not feasible to employ GPS to implement roaming.

Broadly, localization techniques are categorized in to three categories. Angel of Arriva 1 (AOA)measurement, Distance based, and Received signal strength (RSS) based. In [13], AOA is discussed which is used to determine the direction of a signal which is received by the antenna. So, finding the angle between propagation direction and reference direction gives us AOA. The incident angel is determined. This technique requires array of antennas in some specific direction. The number antennas lead to the accuracy of the incident angel. The angle-of-arrival technique can be categorized into two subcategories [original] those making use of the receiver antenna's amplitude response and those making use of the receiver antenna's phase response.

Distance related localization techniques include propagation time based measurements, i.e., one-way propagation time measurements, roundtrip propagation time measurements and time difference-of-arrival (TDOA) measurements, and Received Signal Strength (RSS) measurements [13]. Another technique measuring distance is the lighthouse approach discussed in [10], which derives the distance between an optical receiver and a transmitter of a parallel rotating optical beam by measuring the time duration that the receiver dwells in the beam. One-way propagation time and roundtrip propagation time measurements are also known as time-of-arrival measurements. Distances between neighboring sensors can be estimated from these propagation time measurements.

One-way propagation time technique measures the difference between the sending time of a signal at the transmitter and the receiving time of the signal at the receiver. It requires the local time at the transmitter and the local time at the receiver to be accurately synchronized [13]. The TDOA method is based on measuring the time difference of arrival of incoming signals at two or more than two receivers. The TDOA method requires at least three properly distributed sensors for two-dimensional (2-D) location but it may cause location ambiguity if the TDOA measurements are performed on different pulses of a pulse train [13].

The RSS profiling-based localization techniques [13], based on constructing a form of map of the signal strength behavior in the network coverage area. The map is obtained either offline by a priori measurements or online using sniffing devices [12] deployed at known locations. These methods have been mainly used for location estimation in WLANs, but they would appear to be attractive also for wireless sensor networks. The main focus of this paper is to design a roaming protocol for Bluetooth equipped MAS. This process is carried out in two steps. First is to define when to start the roaming and how to design. For this process a mathematical model is derived for an object which is going out of the range of one master and the roaming boundary is defined according to standard piconet profile specification.

The remainder of this paper is structured as follows. Section II, discusses methodology. Section III discusses Mathematical modeling, section IV discusses simulation and results and finally conclusion and future work discussed in section V.

2 Methodology

The design process of a roaming protocol for Bluetooth equipped MAS, will be carried out in two steps. First step is to define roaming when it should occur, for example when an object will know that it is going out of the range. And the second step is how to design a roaming protocol. For step first the value of RSSI will be checked if it is equal to acceptable level then it means that the roaming object is within the range of the network coverage. If the RSSI value of the moving object is less than the acceptable level then it means that the object is going out of range of the network coverage and that is the point the where the object will start roaming for finding the value of RSSI there is a command used in HCL layer of the Bluetooth protocol stack get_link_quality [14].This command gives us the quality of RSSI, on the basis of this RSSI, roaming will occur. This paper focuses on the point where an object will start roaming. so In this paper step first is defined and a mathematical model for an object which is going out of range is derived. For step two how to design a roaming protocol for the Bluetooth equipped MAS. The standard inquiry and paging procedure will be used. The mathematical model for MAS using Bluetooth for communication purpose will be derived. Various localization techniques exist in order to find out the exact position of the incoming signal. All the three localization techniques will be compared and the best one with maximum accuracy will be selected for the design process. The whole process will be simulated in MATALB Simulink.

3 Mathematical Modeling

Consider an object using Bluetooth technology for communication wants to move in x-y coordinate system. The position of the object with reference to x, y is V(x, y).

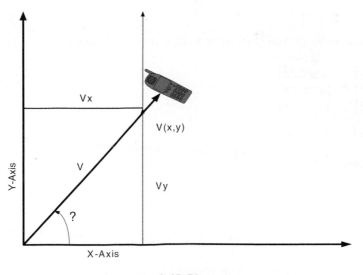

Fig. 3. 2D Plane

  (1)

After resolving the vector V into its rectangular components, the horizontal and vertical components becomes as:

$$Vx = V\cos\theta \qquad (2)$$
$$Vy = V\sin\theta \qquad (3)$$
$$V = \sqrt{Vx^2 + Vy^2} \qquad (4)$$

To find out the magnitude of vector V, standard pathagorous theorem is used:

The position of the object with respect to X and Y coordinate system

$$\tan\theta = {Vy}/{Vx} \qquad (5)$$

$$\theta = \tan^{-1} {y}/{x} \qquad (6)$$

Velocity can be defined as:

$$velocity = displacement / time \quad (taking\ derivative\ with\ respect\ to\ time)$$

$$v = {dx}/{dt} = \dot{x} \qquad (7)$$

Equations II, III and IV becomes

$$\dot{x} = V\cos\theta \qquad (8)$$
$$\dot{y} = V\sin\theta \qquad (9)$$
$$\theta = \tan^{-1} \dot{y}/\dot{x} \qquad (10)$$

$$acceleration = \frac{velocity}{time} \quad (taking\ derivative\ with\ respect\ to\ time)$$

$$\omega = \dot{\theta}$$

The equations (8), (9) and (10) can be written in matrix form as:

$$\begin{bmatrix} \dot{x} \\ \dot{y} \\ \dot{\theta} \end{bmatrix} = \begin{bmatrix} v\cos\theta \\ v\sin\theta \\ \omega \end{bmatrix}$$

$$\begin{bmatrix} \dot{x} \\ \dot{y} \\ \dot{\theta} \end{bmatrix} = \begin{bmatrix} v\cos\theta \\ v\sin\theta \\ 0 \end{bmatrix} \begin{bmatrix} 0 \\ 0 \\ \omega \end{bmatrix}$$

$$\begin{bmatrix} \dot{x} \\ \dot{y} \\ \dot{\theta} \end{bmatrix} = \begin{bmatrix} \cos\theta \\ \sin\theta \\ 0 \end{bmatrix} v \begin{bmatrix} 0 \\ 0 \\ 1 \end{bmatrix} \omega \qquad (11)$$

Differentiating equation (11) with respect to time, t. The equations for feed forward controller are obtained as follows:

$$\omega(t) = \frac{\ddot{y}(t)\,\dot{x}(t) - \ddot{x}(t)\,\dot{y}(t)}{\dot{x}^2(t) + \dot{y}^2(t)} \qquad (12)$$

$$v(t) = \pm\sqrt{\dot{x}^2(t) + \dot{y}^2} \qquad (13)$$

The equations (12) and (13) give us the standard model for the feed forward controller, which is used to obtain the desired output from the un understandable inputs.

4 Simulation and Results

In this paper, Mathematical model is derived for an object in X, Y coordinate system. Mathematical formulas are modeled in MATLAB SIMULINK which are the basic equations for feed forward controller. A desired circle trajectory is obtained for an object moving on the desired trajectory. The movement of the object is traced by feed forward. Mathematical model generates different trajectories, by changing the parameters in equations XII and XIII. Figure 4 shows the desired trajectory. The feed forward controller generated the inputs velocity 'v' and angular acceleration omega for the object to move on the desired trajectory.

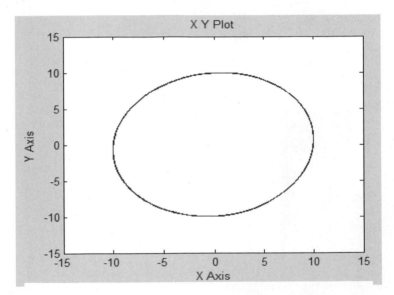

Fig. 4. Desired trajectory for feed forward controller

Figure 5 and 6 shows input velocity 'v' and acceleration 'omega'. Figure 7 shows the flow chart for desired circle shape trajectory and figure 8 shows the actual simulation environment for the feed forward. The amplitude of the circle shape trajectory is taken as 10 in this case. The RSSI value of the moving object will be checked periodically by Host controller in Bluetooth protocol stack. If the value of RSSI is zero or positive then its means the object is within the range of the network. If the value is negative then it means the object is going out of range. And that is the point where the moving object will start roaming. Standard inquiry and paging procedure will be used in order to connect to the next available master. Localization techniques also exist, which will be used to find out the position of the next master.

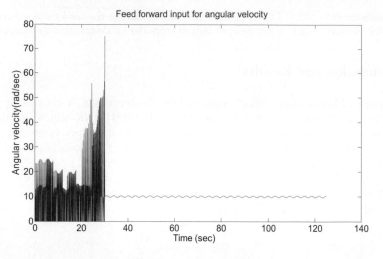

Fig. 5. Angular velocity

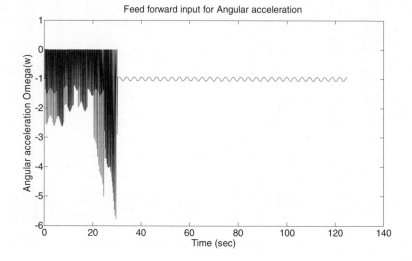

Fig. 6. Angular acceleration

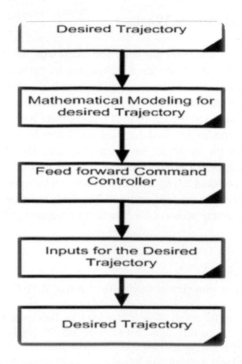

Fig. 7. Flow chart for desired trajectory

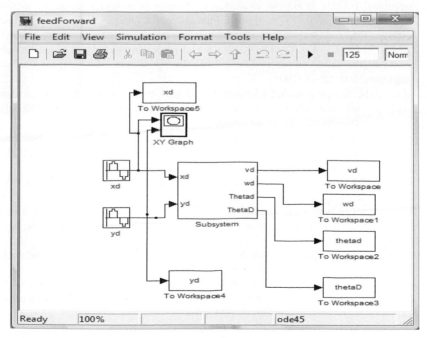

Fig. 8. Feed Forward Controller

5 Conclusion and Future Work

In this paper Bluetooth technology has been presented with the deficiency of roaming has been identified. Various localization techniques including GPS, AOA, Distance based and RSS based techniques been briefly discussed. A mathematical model for an object equipped with Bluetooth technology in XY coordinate has been derived. Simulation results for the proposed trajectory in XY coordinate has been modeled in Simulink. Mathematical formulas for feed forward controller have been proved. Desired circle shape trajectory for an object has been obtained. The point where an object starts roaming is identified. Further research will be needed to include the design process of roaming protocol using the localization techniques. Existing techniques needed to be compared and the best one with the high location accuracy will be selected to design the roaming protocol for Bluetooth equipped MAS.

References

[1] Leeper, D.G.: A long-term view of short-range wireless. IEEE Computer Magazine 34(6), 39–44 (2001)
[2] Specification of the Bluetooth System (version1.1), Bluetooth Special Interest Group, http://www.bluetooth.com (last accessed june 29, 2009)
[3] Wekipedia Computer Dictionary (last accessed November 21, 2008)
[4] Ferber, J.: Multi Agent Systems: An Introduction to Distributed Artificial Year of Publication (2001), ISBN:1-58113-326-X
[5] Sreenicas, H., Ali, H.H.: An evolutionary Bluetooth scaternet formation protocol. In: Proceedings of the 37th Hawaii International Conference on System Science (2004)
[6] Guolin, S., Jie, C., Wei, G., Liu, K.J.R.: Signal processing techniques in network-aided positioning: a survey of state-of-the-art positioning designs. IEEE Signal Processing Magazine 22(4), 12–23 (2005)
[7] Sayed, A.H., Tarighat, A., Khajehnouri, N.: Network-based wireless location: challenges faced in developing techniques for accurate wireless location information. IEEE Signal Processing Magazine 22(4), 24–40 (2005)
[8] Gustafsson, F., Gunnarsson, F.: Mobile positioning using wireless networks: possibilities and fundamental limitations based on available wireless network measurements. IEEE Signal Processing Magazine 22(4), 41–53 (2005)
[9] Koks, D.: Numerical calculations for passive geolocation scenarios. Tech. Rep. DSTO-RR-0000 (2005)
[10] Romer, K.: The lighthouse location system for smart dust. In: Proceedings of MobiSys 2003 ACM/USENIX Conference on Mobile Systems, Applications, and Services, pp. 15–30 (2003)
[11] Bahl, P., Padmanabhan, V.: RADAR: an in-building RF-based user location and tracking system. In: IEEE INFOCOM, vol. 2, pp. 775–784 (2000)
[12] Krishnan, P., Krishnakumar, A., Ju, W.H., Mallows, C., Gamt, S.: A system for LEASE: location estimation assisted by stationary emitters for indoor RF wireless networks. In: IEEE INFOCOM, vol. 2, pp. 1001–1011 (2004)

[13] Mao, G., Fidan, B., Anderson, D.O.: Wireless Sensor Network Localization Techniquest. International Journal of Computer and Telecommunication Networking 51, 2529–2553 (2007)

[14] Pals, H., Dai, Z.R., Grabowski, J.H.N.: UML-based modeling of roaming with Bluetooth devices. In: Proceedings of the First Hangzhou-Lübeck Workshop on Software Engineering. University of Hangzhou, China (2003)

Logical Heuristic Algorithm in Extracting 2D Structure Thinned Binary Image into Freeman Chain Code (FCC)

Haswadi Hasan, Habibollah Haron, Siti Zaiton Hashim, and Fakhrul Syakirin Omar

Faculty of Computer Science and Information System
Universiti Teknologi Malaysia
81310 UTM Skudai, Johor Bahru, Malaysia
{haswadi,habib,sitizaiton}@utm.my, fsyakirin2@siswa.utm.my

Abstract. In 2D structure with junctions, problem arise as which way first should be followed when junction is found while generating chain code. This paper presents new algorithm using special characters as the means of marking the junctions to ensure all paths have been crossed. The proposed chain code will be consisting of one long alphanumeric sequence with digit characters representing direction codes and alphabets for junction markers. The aim is to reduce the chain code's length to the minimum, as opposed to other chain code generation algorithms when facing with junction problem.

Keywords: feature extraction, Freeman chain code, 2D structure, logical heuristic, junction problem.

1 Introduction

Chain code is a type of image representation that has been commonly used in image processing fields such as feature extraction and image compression. One of the chain code schemes is Freeman chain code (FCC) [1], introduced by Freeman in 1961 which is used in this paper. Other schemes can be found in Lili and Habib [2].

Prerequisite in extracting the chain code is a thinned binary image, which is obtained from applying thinning algorithm to binary image. As there are various thinning algorithm already proposed for different purposes, converting image into binary is quite straightforward.

There are many techniques in extracting 2D and 3D structure thinned binary image such as Bribiesca [3,4] and Haron [5]. While chain code extraction process for junction-free structure is rather simple, structure containing junctions is making the extraction process difficult. Thus, this paper is proposing a logical heuristic algorithm to solve junction problem in 2D structure to extract the shortest chain code length possible.

This paper is organized as follows. Section 2 presents a literature review on thinned binary image, chain code and junction problem. Research methodology is described in Section 3 and the proposed algorithm is explained in detail in Section 4. In Section 5, experimental result using test images is brought out and discussed in the next section. Finally, conclusion and future work for the paper is put in Section 7.

H. Badioze Zaman et al. (Eds.): IVIC 2009, LNCS 5857, pp. 770–778, 2009.
© Springer-Verlag Berlin Heidelberg 2009

2 Literature Review

Binary images are defined as images that have only two color values for the pixel, commonly 0 and 1 which are black and white, respectively. The object's color (usually white) is referred to as the foreground color while the background color uses the black part. Thresholding a grayscale or color image in order to separate the object from the rest of the image is a quick way to produce the equivalent binary image. Before chain code extraction can be done, image must be thinned first to obtain the image's skeleton by removing external layers of object's border from the image until one pixel thick is left. Significant result that can be observed after thinning is memory space usage for storing image's fundamental structure information is reduced. Furthermore, it simplifies the image information needed when performing pattern analysis [6].

Current widespread use of chain code is due to its ability for information preservation and allows considerable data reduction when representing images. The initial attempt for representing digital images using chain code is due to Freeman in 1961, known as Freeman chain code (FCC). This code symbolize the counter-clockwise direction with a set of continuous sequence of integers and records the direction as one moves from current pixel to the next. The code can be implemented for 4–connected or 8–connected paths[1].

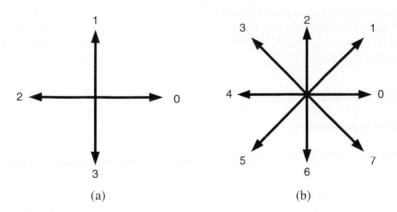

(a)   (b)

Fig. 1. Direction symbol of FCC for 4-connected and 8-connected path

In extracting the chain code for a structure, it is common to assume that the structure is junction-free or the algorithm itself is designed for those structures. To solve junction problem, special care must be taken to make sure the image has been presented completely or included at every branch. Some solutions for the problem are proposed by O'Gorman [7] and Bribiesca [8], but only a few of such algorithms are geared towards reduction of chain code's length. Therefore, this paper proposed a logical heuristic algorithm to extract the shortest Freeman chain code of 2D structure with junction thinned binary image.

3   Methodology

There are four stages in the research methodology namely the data definition, the thinning process, development of the extraction algorithm and followed by testing and validation.

In the first phase which is the data definition of test structure images, the data can be categorized into two-dimensional graphic, representing character and building block. Image dimension for every image is set to 32x32 pixels, free from noise and are selected based on complexity in terms of having many junctions and paths' connectivity to each other, which are crucial to test algorithm's ability to handle different kinds of structure. For this purpose, various wireframe structure designs are collected from Haron [5, 9, 10]. Also, handwritten characters from Special Database 19 (SD19), National Institute of Science and Technology (NIST) are used, particularly for digit '2' and '4'.

The raw images are then converted into binary images with black as the background and white for foreground, represented with 0 and 1 respectively, before being subjected to MATLAB thinning function to obtain its skeleton before being used in chain code extraction.

The algorithm is developed based on the logical flow in manual operation in extracting the FCC on a graph paper and is converted into rules and steps to be compiled as general algorithm which can cater generic structure. The algorithm is then converted into C program, compiled and debugged to produce a valid algorithm implementation.

Final stage which is algorithm testing is done by executing the routine to the test structure to obtain the chain code and checks whether that same structure can be reconstructed from the output chain code. Similar to testing, validation process is also involving cross-checking the structure from output chain code against the original one, plus comparing program generated chain code against the chain code obtained manually by hand.

4   The Extraction Algorithm

4.1   The Input Data

The dataset of the extraction algorithm is collected from NIST database and literature review of previous works by Haron [5, 9, 10]. Fig. 2 show the example of test images taken from NIST and Haron [9], respectively. The images were converted into binary images using MATLAB by image thresholding and then are inverted to get the correct

(a)   (b)

Fig. 2. Examples of original test structure images

representation value for foreground and background color. From here, the images' dimension are sized to 32x32 pixels using Microsoft Paint to meet data specification.

4.2 The MATLAB Thinning Function

In the next step, thinning process is implemented by using MATLAB function:

```
bwmorph(binaryImage,'thin',Inf)
```

which can be found in MATLAB Image Processing Toolbox. The function's underlying algorithm can be found in [11]. Fig. 3 shows example of the thinned binary image by the function.

(a)   (b)

Fig. 3. Examples of thinned test structure images

4.3 The Logical Heuristic Extraction Algorithm

Based closely to Freeman chain code standard, the algorithm aims to solve junction problem occurred in multiple connected path structure by introducing junction markers in the chain code. In this paper, alphabet character sequences are used to represent junction markers starting from 'A' to 'Z', 'AA' to 'AZ' and so on.

```
Starting from structure's lowest point at middle col-
umn, while moving along the path until all paths have
been crossed:

    If a junction is found, register junction if all
    checks are failed:

    Any 8-neighborhood members can reach all branches

    Junction has already been registered

    Any junction in its 8-neighborhood can reach all
    branches

    If reaches dead end, start back from last registered
    junction
```

Fig. 4. Algorithm pseudo code

Fig. 5. A junction problem. When 'A' is the initial point, it becomes the junction that connecting the other 4 branches. Applying the path choosing algorithm, the first path is with the '1' mark, '2' mark for the second and so on.

The algorithm starts with finding an initial point being the lowest point at the middle column. The aim is to keep the process simple since location of the starting point is unimportant in generating the chain code, though can be carefully chosen to lessen the chain code length. From there on, path choosing priority is based on Freeman direction; east being the first direction chosen and south-east for the last, when a junction is found.

A junction is defined as a point connecting multiple paths, with the problem for which path should be chosen first and how to return back to the junction to completely cover the structure map. When the junction is encountered during path journey, junction validation checks are performed to ensure chain code correctness and length to a minimum. Chain code correctness meaning only a single marker is used for a unique junction since there is possibility multiple markers will be used at the same junction when applying the junction concept. From the chain code correctness also the chain code's length can be keep short.

Junction validation checks are consisting of 3 independent levels which can be freely omitted when there is any asserted check level. First level searches, if present, any member of current point's 8-neighborhood that also can reach all the branches of the tested junction to make sure that only a unique junction is used to reach the multiple paths available. When the junction is confirmed to be the only one available to address all the paths, next level check which is checking whether the junction is already being registered is performed. The check is based on the location of the tested junction against the list of currently registered junction. Lastly, if all previous checks are failed, a search for any junction in the current point's 8-neighborhood that can reach all branches of the tested junction, slightly different from the first level check. The significance of this check is to avoid redundant junction as other junction is already available to act as the path connector.

During the path circling journey, when path's end is reached, the option is whether to return to the last registered junction if available or to end the trip. The junction list acts as a first in, last out (FILO) stack, making a depth-first trip to completely mark the structure.

4.4 Post-processing

To reduce the chain code length to the minimum, string parsing can be done to check the usage of orphan junction markers that only used once in the chain code, meaning that the junction is insignificant to the structure representation as other path can be used for a complete structure representation. While junction exclusion can be useful for chain code length reduction, doing so might be improper when presence of every junction in the structure is crucial.

4.5 Chain Code Interpretation

The correct way of reconstructing back the structure using the chain code is by following the direction in the chain code and when the particular junction marker is found for the first time, the current point location is marked and registered with the respective junction marker. The consequent previously registered marker encounter means to start back from the said junction and continue the parsing.

5 Experimental Result

Here are the examples of various test structures being encoded into chain code using the proposed extraction algorithm. The algorithm is implemented in C and executed on Windows x64 platform while the thinning algorithm is performed in MATLAB version 7.6.

6 Result Analysis and Discussion

From the presented image results in Fig. 6, the process can be tracked starting from point marked as junction 'A' as the lowest point for the structure at the middle column. Including the junction markers, the points constructing all the structures are marked with '#' characters to differentiate with the original binary images which are consisting of binary digits.

   The length of extracted chain code will be affected by junction count and amount of characters defining the structure. Increasing junction count will call for longer junction markers to address with thus producing longer chain code, while apparently also with the case for larger structure but with lesser impact on the chain code's length. Below is the table comparing the resulting chain code's length and its actual defining point count for each test structure in Fig. 6. Apparently increasing structure complexity will add up to longer chain code compared to actual points making up the structure.

A110B33C11222212223344555555C4444
545565667701111B7777010

(a)

A00B0B31211121221211A434332C2121
22C5554565A55655655

(b)

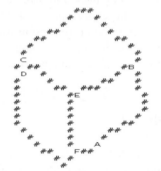

A1101011223223B1233433334455545 4556C57D10777070E1001011E56666667F00F
553343333222222

(c)

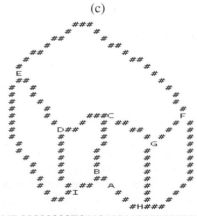

A33B22212221C4445544D33233233E21101101100777077077777676F5555G3343
4G566666665H0001111222222222H433E656666666767767677010I101I33222222

(d)

Fig. 6. Examples of various test structures with obtained chain code and junction locations:
(a) character '2'; (b) character '4'; (c) cube; (d) L-block; and (e) stair, respectively

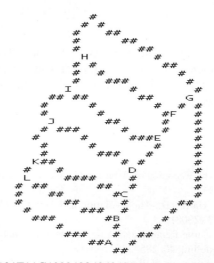

A122B122C122D1112E121F11G1333433434343343355667H5665I54567J55765K0077
000707K56L5667700770070L7070707007J700777007I7077707700H7770077077G
766666666666665455554554

(e)

Fig. 6. (*Continued*)

Table 1. Comparison of defining point count and resulting chain code length for test structures.

Test structure	Defining point count	Chain code length	Difference
Character '2'	52	56	4
Character '4'	45	51	6
Cube	76	83	7
L-block	120	132	12
Stair	138	155	17

7   Conclusion and Future Work

This paper has presented the algorithm of producing Freeman chain code for 2-D structure to solve the junction problem with junction marker. The marker will consist of sequence of alphabets in the chain code that will grow depending on the junction count. The result shows that the resulting chain code's length using the algorithm is directly proportional to structure size and complexity.

The algorithm is expected to be easily extended to represent 3-D structure with special measure is taken for chain code to address more directions involved, presumably 26 unique directions in 3x3x3 neighborhood.

Acknowledgement

The authors honorably appreciate Ministry of Science, Technology and Innovation (MOSTI) for the eScienceFund grant with VOT number 79369 and Research Management Center (RMC), Universiti Teknologi Malaysia (UTM) for the support in making this project success.

References

1. Freeman, H.: On The Encoding of Arbitrary Geometric Configurations. IRE Trans. EC-10 (2), 260–268 (1961)
2. Wulandhari, L.A., Haron, H.: The Evolution and Trend of Chain Code Scheme. ICGST-GVIP 8(III), 17–23 (2008)
3. Bribiesca, E.: 3D-Curve Representation by Means of a Binary Chain Code. Mathematical and Computer Modelling 40, 285–295 (2004)
4. Bribiesca, E.: Scanning-curves Representation for the Coverage of Surfaces Using Chain Code. Computer & Graphics 27(1), 123–132 (2003)
5. Haron, H., Shamsuddin, S.M., Mohamed, D.: Chain Code Algorithm In Deriving T-Junction And Region of A Freehand Sketch. Jurnal Teknologi 40(D), 25–36 (2004)
6. Hanmandlu, M.M.: Fuzzy model based recognition of handwritten numerals. Pattern Recognition 40(6), 1840–1854 (2007)
7. O'Gorman, L.: Primitives chain code. In: ICASSP 1988, International Conference on Acoustics, Speech, and Signal Processing, vol. 2, pp. 792–795 (1988)
8. Bribiesca, E.: Three-dimensional tree-object representation by means of a binary descriptor. Optical Engineering 47(12), 127002-1–127002–10 (2008)
9. Matondang, M.Z., Haron, H., Talib, M.S.: A New Framework in Interpreting Two-Dimensional Line Drawing. In: Proceedings of the International Conference on Electrical Engineering and Informatics, pp. 500–503. Institut Teknologi Bandung, Indonesia (2007)
10. Haron, H., Subri, S.H.: A New Framework in Extracting Features of Irregular Line Drawing. In: Proceedings of the International Conference on Computer Graphics, Imaging and Visualization, pp. 83–87. Universiti Sains Malaysia, Malaysia (2004)
11. Lam, L., Lee, S.-W., Suen, C.Y.: Thinning Methodologies-A Comprehensive Survey. IEEE Transactions on Pattern Analysis and Machine Intelligence 14(9), 879 (1992)

VisEL: Visualisation of Expertise Level in a Special Interest Group Knowledge Portal

Wan Muhammad Zulhafizsyam Wan Ahmad, Shahida Sulaiman,
and Umi Kalsom Yusof

School of Computer Sciences, Universiti Sains Malaysia,
11800 USM, Penang, Malaysia
zulhafizsyam.com08@student.usm.my,
{shahida,umiyusof}@cs.usm.my

Abstract. A variety of portals are available nowadays to support diverse purposes such as commercial, publishing, personal, affinity and corporate portals. Affinity portals promote electronic communities who share common interest such as a special interest group (SIG). Knowledge portal is an emerging trend that benefits the existing portal technology by designing such portals with proper representation of the members' shared knowledge. Besides textual representation for diverse expertise levels, graphical visualisation will be able to support the requirements in searching and representing expertise level among e-community. There is a number of existing SIG portals available. However, they do not visualise effectively and accurately the expertise level of members and make it difficult for users to search their targeted experts for instance searching the highest expertise level to have a discussion and to solve their problems related to a project. The goal of this paper is to propose a graphical visualisation of expertise level method (VisEL) using an interactive tag cloud technique that represents expertise level of each member based on their knowledge in a software engineering SIG portal.

Keywords: Expertise level, information visualisation, knowledge base, data visualisation, expert evaluation, visualisation technique.

1 Introduction

An electronic community or e-community portal becomes a medium for people such as a special interest group (SIG) to share their knowledge and expertise in respective fields. SIG can be described as a group of people with the same interests get together to become a community especially as an online community [1]. Users perhaps need to know who are the experts and their expertise level in a SIG e-community so that they can contact certain experts to discuss and share important topics among them. The portal must provide effective, interactive and user friendly pages for registered users to search targeted experts in a SIG easier and more accurate [2]. In providing such features, the detail information of experts must be collected and stored in a system. Then the evaluation of experts is performed to measure their expertise level such as in the work of Ismail et al. [1].

One of the current problems in such portals include registered members do not actively update their detail profiles such as the information on their research

H. Badioze Zaman et al. (Eds.): IVIC 2009, LNCS 5857, pp. 779–788, 2009.
© Springer-Verlag Berlin Heidelberg 2009

projects and publications. The information should be processed into knowledge that can further classify members' expertise levels. This is also the reason why such portals are also known as knowledge portals. In order to collect information of each member, we propose the use of Web data mining to extract valuable information such as publications and projects of each expert from other related portals or websites. There are only a few portals provide the methods to measure expertise level of members [3, 4]. Another problem in such portals involves the representation of expertise levels among the members. Most of the members' expertise is listed textually in such portals without any visual representation of the members. Textual methods and static visualisation will make the search of targeted experts to be less efficient.

Thus, we propose a method to visualise expertise level of a SIG using tag cloud that can improve the representation of members of e-community of SIG by their expertise levels. The classification of expertise is not the scope of the paper as it will adopt the existing classification [1].

Section 2 discusses the motivation of our work, followed by Section 3 on the proposed method called VisEL. We illustrate the example of implementation of VisEL method in Section 4. Section 5 describes the related work and finally we conclude the study in Section 6.

2   The Motivation

Collecting detail information of expert knowledge in e-community such as SIG is not an easy task. There are many factors that can determine members' performance and knowledge. This in turn will be processed to classify their expertise levels. Then the expertise levels should be represented to other members. A number of research find some limitations and problems in the process of evaluating experts [3][4][5]. Evaluation of experts' performance tends to face external influences mainly due to individual subjective judgement and discrimination on the result of expert selection [3].

For example, in National Science Foundation of China (NSFC) the method used to evaluate experts is not efficient because it is only based on subjective judgement from division manager which using word of mouth method when conducting the evaluation [4]. The method is incomplete, inefficient and unfair for other qualified experts. Besides, it is difficult for organization to predict the success of the project reviewed by experts [5]. Another problems faced by researchers are difficult to estimate level of knowledge of each expert, to show the creativity of experts and to display how experts working together in a group [6]. It is in fact very challenging to integrate classification of experts and visualise them accordingly in the design of e-community website such as SIG knowledge portal.

Besides it is also questionable whether the visualisation of expertise level will have an impact on accuracy and effectiveness in finding the target expert. Thus, this motivates us to propose a method to visualise expertise level of a SIG knowledge portal using graphical visualisation.

3   Visualisation of Expertise Level (VisEL) Method

We propose **Vis**ualisation of **E**xpertise **L**evel (VisEL) method to visualise the expertise level of each expert in a SIG using graphical representation. VisEL provides interactive technique that allows users to search their target expert. The variables involved in this study include visualisation of expertise level, text characteristic, experts in a SIG, portals that joined by the experts, and extracted experts' publications and projects. The attributes that can be considered include expertise level of members, quality of designed and developed method, font sizes and colour coded fonts.

The main research question is: How to visualise expertise level of a SIG using graphical visualisation for users to search target expert accurately and affectively?

The null hypothesis to be rejected is:

H_0: A visualisation expertise level method for experts in a SIG e-community does not significantly improve the accuracy and the effectiveness of searching the targeted experts by members.

As searching existing information of each member such as publications and projects are crucial; the proposed VisEL method is integrated with a data mining technique. Besides VisEL also integrates existing expertise classification method (PBaSE) [1] that has been developed and implemented in Malaysia Software Engineering Interest Group (MySEIG) portal [13].

The proposed VisEL method will use data mining technique to extract specific information which is publications and projects of each expert from several popular publication portals such as IEEE Explore [16], Scopus [17], ACM [18], and Science Direct [19]. This process will ensure the experts' profile is updated regularly and automatically without any action from the experts. PBaSE [1] method will classify members' expertise in a SIG portal based on members' interaction in the portal, members' rating and extracted members' publications and projects. The members here can be experts and users who join the portal. Integration between PBaSE method with extracted members' publications and projects will make visualisation of expertise level more accurate since more attributes are used to differentiate the expertise level of each expert.

Then the expertise level of each expert in a SIG will be visualised based on result from expertise classification. VisEL method deploys an enhanced tag cloud visualisation technique. The justification of using this technique is due to the interactive features it has and its ability to display certain information instantly [8]. That is one of the reasons why tag cloud technique becomes a ubiquitous interaction technique in the Web. This technique can better visualise the expertise level compare to other normal visualisation technique such as tree view which is not interactive, difficult to search target expert and not effective. Other important attribute of visualisation technique include diversity of font sizes and colour-coded fonts. Figure 1 illustrates the use of VisEL method in a SIG e-community called MySEIG [13] as the problem domain.

Effective visualisation technique must be able to attract users' attention and support ease of use particularly to identify targeted information. The enhanced tag cloud visualisation technique in VisEL method fulfils the criterion to differentiate expertise level of a SIG using different font sizes and colour-coded fonts. The various font sizes can illustrate different levels of experts. For example, the biggest font represents the

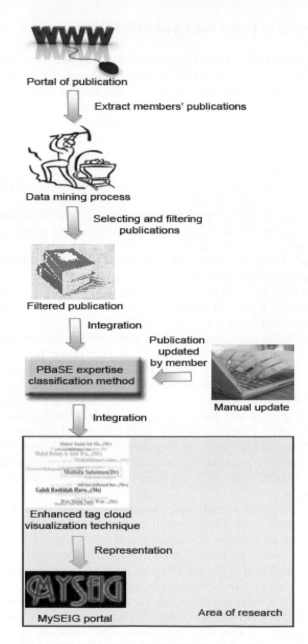

Portal of publication

Extract members' publications

Data mining process

Selecting and filtering
publications

Filtered publication

Integration

PBaSE expertise
classification method

Publication
updated
by member

Manual update

Integration

Enhanced tag cloud
visualization technique

Representation

MySEIG portal   Area of research

Fig. 1. VisEL method and its integration with PBaSE [1] to visualise expertise level of a SIG

highest expertise level and the smallest font represents the lowest expertise level in respective field. On the other hand, the colour-coded fonts can classify the members of a SIG for instance green for just joined members, blue for beginners, purple for intermediates and red for experts using existing PBaSE expertise classification method [1]. The use of different font sizes and colour-coded font in enhanced tag cloud visualisation technique will make searching for the target expert more accurate.

Another crucial attribute of visualisation technique is number of clicks and consumption of time. The number of clicks mentioned in this paper can be described as how many clicks user requires in reaching the target expert's profile. Consumption of time refers to the period needed for a user to reach the target expert's profile. The proposed VisEL method will save the time for searching the target expert by reducing the number of clicks to reach the target expert's profile and quickly search other experts in a specific field of interest. Compared to other visualisation methods for example alphabetical order and tree view used in Forums.sun.com [11] and Daniweb.com [12], users must have more clicks to reach the targeted expert's profile. This design will not provide ease of use among users or registered members of such e-community in general.

Thus VisEL method will be able to search the target expert effectively and accurately by using the enhanced tag cloud visualisation technique and existing PBaSE expertise classification. The data mining technique is currently not in the scope of this paper in order to extract experts' publications and projects. This research focuses on providing a method to visualise expertise level of a SIG using enhanced tag cloud visualisation technique.

There are two attributes included in the enhanced tag cloud visualisation technique, colour-coded font and font sizes.

3.1 Enhanced Tag Cloud Visualisation Technique

The algorithms to implement the enhanced tag cloud visualisation technique in VisEL method are shown in equations 1 to 4. Equation (1) shows how the technique applies colour-coded fonts to classify their members' categories either as just joined, beginners, intermediates or experts. Equation (2), (3) and (4) show how it sets font sizes to reflect different level of experts.

(a) Algorithm for colour-coded font:

$$S_i = \frac{f_{max} \cdot (t_i - t_{min})}{t_{max} - t_{min}} \tag{1}$$

1) Assign the minimum level of expertise t_{min}, the maximum level of expertise t_{max} and the maximum colour will be used f_{max}.

2) Assign the expertise level of each expert obtained from PBaSE [1] expertise classification final point t_i where i is the number of experts in a specific field available. The rule is t_i must be greater than t_{min} ($t_i > t_{min}$) else the colour of expert name is grey ($S_i = 0$).

3) Experts' expertise level t_i subtracts the minimum expertise level t_{min} then multiplies the maximum colour f_{max} available. This result generates a value.

4) The maximum level of expertise t_{max} subtracts the minimum expertise level of expertise t_{min}. This result generates b value.
5) Display the colour of each expert name S_i by dividing a with b ($S_i = a/b$).

(b) Font sizes:

$$F_i = \frac{k_{max} \cdot (m_i - m_{min})}{m_{max} - m_{min}} \qquad (2)$$

$$m_i = p_i + c_i \qquad (3)$$

$$G_i = F_i + R_i \qquad (4)$$

1) Assign the minimum value of experts' publications and projects m_{min}, the maximum value of experts' publications and projects m_{max}, the number of expert's publications p_i where i is number of experts in specific field available, the number of expert's projects c_i, and the maximum additional font size will be used k_{max}.
2) Assign the value of experts' publications and projects m_i by adding the number of expert's publications p_i and the number of expert's projects c_i ($m_i = p_i + c_i$). The value of m_i obtained by mapping of the number of expert's publications p_i and the number of expert's projects c_i to the value of experts' publications and projects m_i as: value 1 ($0 \leq p_i + c_i < 40$ publications and projects), value 2 ($40 \leq p_i + c_i < 80$ publications and projects), value 3 ($80 \leq p_i + c_i < 120$ publications and projects), value 4 ($120 \leq p_i + c_i <$ unlimited publications and projects). The rule is m_i must be greater than m_{min} ($m_i > m_{min}$) else the additional font size is 1px ($F_i = 1px$) the minimum additional font size.
3) The value of experts' publications and projects m_i subtract the minimum value of experts' publications and projects m_{min} then multiply the maximum additional font size k_{max}. This result generates c value.
4) The maximum value of experts' publications and projects m_{max} subtracts the minimum value of experts' publications and projects m_{min}. This result generates d value.
5) Obtain the additional font size of each expert F_i by dividing c with d ($F_i = c/d$).
6) Display the font size of each expert G_i by adding the additional font size F_i and the default or minimum font size in each members' categories R_i ($G_i = F_i + R_i$). The size of R_i is 7px.

4   Implementation of VisEL Method: An Example

This section will present an example of how VisEL method visualises the expertise level of each expert in MySEIG knowledge portal [13]. VisEL method consists of two parts: data mining part and visualisation. In this example, we will search the target expert named "Shahida Sulaiman" who has the highest expertise level in the searched field "Software Testing".

Before searching the target expert, the first part that involves data mining process plays a vital role in VisEL. Experts' publications and projects will be extracted from several publication portals to the system regularly as mentioned in Section 3. "Regularly" here means VisEL will perform extraction automatically in certain period for example once in a week as assigned by administrator. This process will ensure members' publications and projects always updated without any intervention from the members.

Then expertise classification will take place to classify the experts using existing PBaSE expertise classification method [1]. The result from this classification process will differentiate the members' expertise in four different colours as illustrated in Figure 2(a).

The second part in VisEL method will visualise expertise level using the enhanced tag cloud visualisation technique. Searching the targeted expert in this example "Shahida Sulaiman" using the proposed VisEL method requires minimum action from users. Users select field of interest for example "Software Testing" then all related experts will be displayed as shown in Figure 2(b). Users can see the highest expertise level which has red colour based on expertise classification mentioned above. The biggest font size displays "Shahida Sulaiman" that reflects the expert level (in red) and the most expert (biggest font size). The name can be clicked to go to her profile page. This design provides an interactive graphical representation.

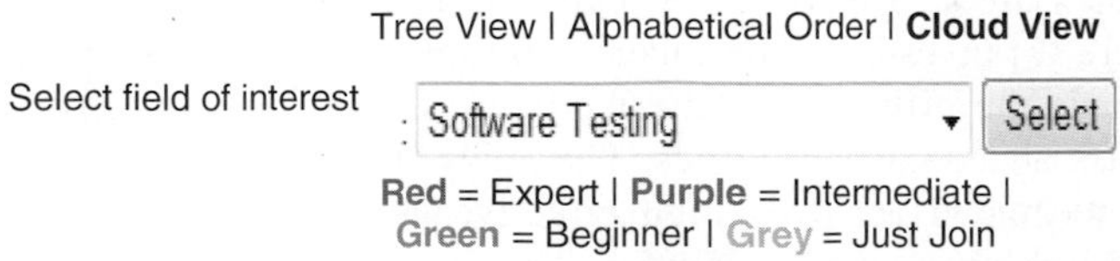

Tree View | Alphabetical Order | **Cloud View**

Select field of interest   : Software Testing   ▼   Select

Red = Expert | **Purple** = Intermediate |
Green = Beginner | Grey = Just Join

Fig. 2(a).

Shukor Sanim bin Mo...(Mr)

Mohd Helmy b Abd Wa...(Mr)

Mohd Ridzuan b Ahma...(Mr)

Shahida Sulaiman(Dr)

zaiyana mohamed hus...(Mrs)

Galoh Rashidah Haro...(Ms)

Wan Mohd Nasir Wan ...(Dr)

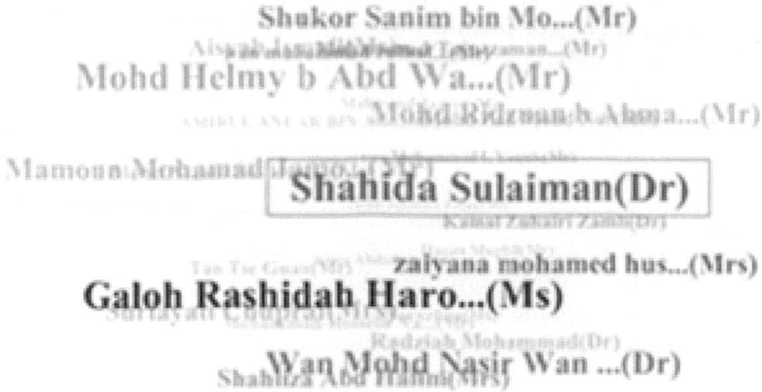

Fig. 2(b).

Fig. 2. Visualisation of expertise levels using VisEL method in the searched field

5   Related Work

Experts' evaluations are very important step to measure experts' performance and expertise level in their areas. Evaluation of experts is normally performed to select the best expert in certain area to become reviewer or evaluator in the project selection for fund or related activities. For instance this process can be found in large organization and government agencies to select the best project to be funded. Scientific method must be used to evaluate expert performance to keep justice, ensure technological project evaluation and prevent corrupted transaction during the process of project evaluation [3]. Hence, we anticipate that such factors should be considered in designing a knowledge portal that requires expertise levels such as MySEIG [13].

Experts involved in decision making process possess important roles as their opinions have great influence and potential on the result of project selection [4]. In addition experts with higher expertise level can be very useful to give professional judgement on the project to be selected [4]. Project selection is an important task that could involve complicated multi stage decision making process, which requires a group of experts or decision makers [5]. Since the experts have great influence and are able to give professional judgement, a group of experts with high level of knowledge can be formed to increase the quality on selected projects. The concept can be applied in a SIG portal in such a way the experts will be able to influence and attract other registered members to participate and share their knowledge. In our study we applied the proposed method in MySEIG [13].

Effects of aesthetic values on the usability of data visualisation play a significant role not only to catch users' eyes but to display the data effectively and accurately. Cawthon and Moere [7] investigate the relationship involving aesthetic in data visualisation and evaluate the efficiency and effectiveness, addition with erroneous response time and task abandonment metrics. The study shows that the most aesthetic data visualisation technique achieves high effectiveness, latency of erroneous response and rate of task abandonment metrics. Hence, in our research considers the effect of aesthetic as one of important elements in designing the graphical visualisation of expertise level in a SIG. We anticipate the relationship involving aesthetic in data visualisation and our study will achieve high effectiveness, latency of erroneous response time and rate of task abandonment metrics. In the nutshell, it will visualise the expertise level of a SIG effectively and accurately.

Tag clouds become popular as an interaction technique in the Web due to its ability to display certain information instantly. Schrammel et al. [8] assess the effects of semantic against alphabetical and random arrangement of tags in tag cloud technique via series of experiments. The study depicts that the semantic layout is suitable to be used when the quality of arrangement can be guaranteed. So, semantic layout may not be suitable to visualise expertise level of a SIG member. However random or alphabetic layouts are considered the best layout to be used in this research. Suitable layout of tag cloud technique will grab users' attention and make searching for targeted experts become faster which is similar with its ability to display certain information instantly.

In addition, Web data mining is crucial in gathering expert's information such as publications and projects by extracting the related information from related portals or websites. In the process, irrelevant information should be filtered out so that information extracted is not redundant. In solving this problem, Taibs *et al.* [9] attempts to eliminate redundant information for Web data mining by building a case model with a set of rules to represent abstraction knowledge of Web's structure. The study shows that the abstract case can improve classification with the aid of a suitable set of data and major approach of knowledge acquisition. This approach still can be enhanced to reduce the number of rules and increase the classification accuracy of section monitoring knowledge base. Therefore, filtering out the redundant information will increase the accuracy of information extracted that should be represented to reflect expertise level of each member mainly expert in a SIG.

6 Conclusion and Future Work

This paper has proposed VisEL, a method to visualise expertise level of members in a SIG knowledge portal. We tested the proposed method in a real problem domain of a SIG in Malaysia called MySEIG [13]. VisEL integrates with existing expertise classification method known as PBaSE [1]. Registered members of MySEIG [13] will be able to know the expert with the highest expertise level in respective field by searching their targeted experts effectively and accurately.

The proposed method focuses on a SIG who want to search their targeted experts for discussions and share important topics among specific members or other registered members. Therefore, we believe the integration of proposed method with expertise classification method like PBaSE [1] will be able to improve the effectiveness and accuracy in designing graphical representation of expertise levels among the problem domain of SIG.

In the future, we will further enhance VisEL to increase the information gathered into such knowledge portals to be classified and then visualise expertise level of a SIG e-community. Current study should be generic enough to be adopted in other types of e-community. Then we will evaluate the proposed method to reject the null hypothesis.

Acknowledgement

This research is supported by the Ministry of Sciences, Technology and Innovation (MOSTI) Malaysia: e-Science fund 305/PKOMP/613137. Acknowledgement also goes to School of Computer Sciences, Universiti Sains Malaysia for organizing the "Workshop on Writing for Proceedings" that provides the platform to produce this paper under APEX incentive grant.

References

1. Ismail, A., Sulaiman, S., Sabudin, M., Sulaiman, S.: A Point-Based Semi-Automatic Expertise Classification (PBaSE) Method for Knowledge Management of an Online Special Interest Group. In: International Symposium on Information Technology 2008 (ITSIM 2008), vol. 2, pp. 794–800. IEEE, Los Alamitos (2008)

2. Mitchell, S.: Create Your Own Website. Sams Publishing, United States of America (2005)
3. Yu, T., Zhou, J., Zhao, K., Wang, W., Wang, W.: Study on Project Experts' Evaluation Based on Analytic Hierarchy Process and Fuzzy Comprehensive Evaluation. In: 2008 International Conference Intelligent Computation Technology and Automation (ICICTA), vol. 1, pp. 941–945. IEEE, Los Alamitos (2008)
4. Sun, Y., Ma, J., Fan, Z., Wang, J.: A Group Decision Support Approach to Evaluate Experts for R&D Project Selection. IEEE Transactions Engineering Management 55(1), 158–170 (2008)
5. Tian, Q., Ma, J., Liang, J., Kwok, R.C.W., Liu, O.: An Organizational Decision Support System for Effective R&D Project Selection. Decision Support Systems 39(3), 403–413 (2005)
6. Stukach, O.V.: Teaching Computer Science Using Visualisation of the Evaluation Process. In: Computational Technologies in Electrical and Electronics Engineering, SIBIRCON 2008, pp. 82–84. IEEE, Los Alamitos (2008)
7. Cawthon, N., Moere, A.V.: The Effect of Aesthetic on the Usability of Data Visualisation. In: 11th International Conference Information Visualisation (IV 2007), pp. 637–648. IEEE Computer Society, Los Alamitos (2007)
8. Schrammel, J., Leitner, M., Tscheligi, M.: Semantically Structured Tag Clouds: An Empirical Evaluation of Clustered Presentation Approaches. In: 27th International Conference on Human Factors in Computing Systems, pp. 2037–2040. ACM, New York (2009)
9. Taib, S.M., Yeom, S., Kang, K.: Elimination of Redundant Information for Web Data Mining. In: Information Technology: Coding and Computing, pp. 200–205. IEEE Computer Society, Los Alamitos (2005)
10. Ghanbari, M.: Visualisation Overview. In: 39th South Eastern Symposium on System Theory, pp. 115–119. IEEE, Macon (2007)
11. Forums.sun.com, http://forums.sun.com/index.jspa
12. Daniweb.com, http://www.daniweb.com/
13. MySEIG Portal, http://www.myseig.org
14. Sekaran, U.: Research Methods for Business: A Skill Building Approach. John Wiley & Sons Inc., New York (2003)
15. Leedy, D.P., Ormrod, E.J.: Practical Research: Planning and Design. Pearson Merrill Prentice Hall, New Jersey (2005)
16. IEEE Explore, http://ieeexplore.ieee.org/Xplore/dynhome.jsp
17. Scopus, http://www.scopus.com/home.url
18. ACM, http://portal.acm.org/dl.cfm
19. Science Direct, http://www.sciencedirect.com/

genDMG: A Generic Graph Representation Layout to Visualize Existing Software Artifacts

Shahida Sulaiman[1] and Sarina Sulaiman[2]

[1] School of Computer Sciences, Universiti Sains Malaysia,
11800 USM, Penang, Malaysia
shahida@cs.usm.my
[2] Faculty of Computer Science and Information Technology, Universiti Teknologi Malaysia,
81310 UTM, Skudai, Johor, Malaysia
sarina@utm.my

Abstract. Examining software artifacts of an existing software system to understand their functionalities based on source codes can be a very daunting task. Many tools have emerged to assist software understanding or program comprehension, which normally consist of graph representations in a reverse engineering environment. These tools are known as reverse engineering or software visualization tools. This paper describes a document-like and modularized software visualization method called generic DocLike Modularized Graph (genDMG) that employs a graph drawing technique to represent software artifacts written either in structured or object-oriented. An example illustrates how the graph representations could assist software maintainers' program comprehension. A comparative study shows genDMG can improve what other methods could support in software visualization.

Keywords: Software maintenance, software visualization, program comprehension, graph representations.

1 Introduction

The objective of software visualization (SV) is to use graphics to enhance the understanding of a program that has already been written to at least to some degrees [1]. A research survey by Koschke [2] depicts that graph is the most often used kind of visualization because a graph represents a generic way to represent information, which is probably the reason why it is so popular and also chosen as the main element of our SV approach. The second in rank was Unified Modeling Language (UML) notation.

CASE (Computer-Aided Software Engineering) workbench in the class of maintenance and reverse engineering such as Rigi [3][4], CodeCrawler [5] and SNiFF+ [6] are normally incorporated with editor window in which the abstracted software artifacts will be visualized graphically besides their textual information. These kinds of tools are also called reverse engineering tools because they are integrated with reverse engineering technology to extract software artifacts. However in some studies these tools are also known as document generator tools because they also provide an alternative to automate or semi-automate production of documents. In other aspect both

H. Badioze Zaman et al. (Eds.): IVIC 2009, LNCS 5857, pp. 789–799, 2009.

reverse engineering and document generator tools are composed of various visualization methods such as graph representations, making them recognized as SV tools. In this paper we employ the term SV to refer to such CASE workbenches.

Since in practice software engineers are still confronted with out-dated or absence of documentation [7], SV in reverse engineering environment could be the best alternative to eliminate the problem related to understanding existing software systems without proper documentation. We will discuss how a graph drawing technique is utilized in the proposed generic DocLike Modularized Graph (genDMG) method via a software visualization tool called TubVis [8]. The proposed method is the improvement from our previous DMG method [9]. The method could improve the existing methods in the aspect of understanding a subject system or program comprehension using graph representations. It is generic enough to be used for both structured and object-oriented programming languages.

The following sections will discuss on the graph representations provided by the genDMG method, the example of a graph representation via TubVis, qualitative evaluation and finally the conclusion and future work.

2   Generic DocLike Modularized Graph Method

The generic, document-like, and modularized software visualization method named as genDMG method employs graphs to visualize software artifacts extracted from its own parser integrated with TubVis [8]. It is referred as "document-like" because the software artifacts are visualized in an explicit re-documentation environment. It is also called a "modularized" method because the visualization can only be generated after all components have been modularized.

Generally, a graph $G = (V, E)$ consists of a set of vertices V and a set of edges E, such that each edge in E is a connection between a pair of vertices in V [10]. A directed graph is described as directed edge $E_i = (v_i, v_j)$. A vertex in G can be of different types. TubVis prototype tool is based on generic language parser; hence it can be applied for both structured and object-oriented programming that are symbolized as module (M) or package, program (P) or class, procedure or function (F) or method and data (D). The genDMG method provides 5 types of graph representations that include DMG_1 or a system hierarchy view, DMG_2 or a hierarchy view for program or package level, DMG_3 or a call graph for function or method level, DMG_4 or a call graph for function (method) and inter-module (inter-package) level, and lastly DMG_5 or a data flow graph. The following sections will discuss the aspect of graph drawing in terms of aesthetic criteria or principles, grid layout algorithm employed in genDMG, and its graph representation layouts.

2.1   Graph Drawing

Graph drawing requires a graph layout algorithm. A study [11] outlines the objective properties for graph layout algorithms as follows:

(i) Easy to recognize and read individual objects for example having labeled nodes.
(ii) Avoid aliases including edge crossings, sharp bends and intersection of unrelated objects.

(iii) Reveal patterns by emphasizing symmetry, parallelism and regularity.

These properties are also recognized in other studies for example in [12] as the aesthetic criteria or principles.

In the genDMG method, graph is drawn using its own layout algorithm of a grid layout to accommodate the requirements of the SV method. The grid layout allows the maximum of four nodes in a row with unlimited number of rows. By having the maximum number of columns that is the number of nodes in a row, users are only required to scroll viewer vertically if the view cannot accommodate the rows of nodes to be drawn. The grid layout is currently the default layout utilized by the genDMG method.

Referring to the first aesthetic criterion discussed earlier, the five types of genDMG representations make the nodes and their dependencies can be recognized easily. Each node is colored according to its type for example a blue node represents a procedure; a red node represents a function i.e. a procedure that returns a value. Most SV tools have exploited this aesthetic criterion. In the genDMG method, if a node is searched, the node is filled with the color to set users' focus. Labeling of nodes is important for users to identify the required node promptly.

In addition, edges are drawn as arrows that show the direction of dependency of the two linked nodes. For example if node A calls node B, then the arrow should lead users' focus from node A to node B. Some SV tools like Rigi [4] just use straight lines. Thus it does not show the direction of the dependency.

For the second property or aesthetic criterion, the genDMG method attempts to reduce crossing of arcs by generating views module-by-module. Thus prior to generating views, modularization of software components is mandatory to be done. The five types of graph representations are also able to produce information abstraction at different level of information needs besides simplifying the views and preserving the mental maps of a subject system. In case crossing of arcs occurs, users can interactively move the concerned node to get a better graph view. Otherwise users can right-click the concerned node in order to view the textual information that lists the dependencies of the node with other nodes. A textual view is not actually perceived as part of SV if one does not consider a purely textual representation as a graphical representation [2]. Yet, the textual view can be a complementary aspect of SV. For instance, a function node is linked with its actual program by displaying source codes starting from the line where the function name is found in the source code window and also highlighting the function name.

In order to reveal patterns in the genDMG method, it draws nodes in a grid layout with the maximum four nodes in a row as the default layout for all the five types of DMG representations. However it allows users to re-arrange the layout in order to get a better view. Nodes are arranged according to the alphabetical order of the names or labels. For procedure or function (or method) nodes in a DMG representation, they are initially arranged according to the alphabetical order of the program or class names followed by the procedure or function (or method) names.

2.2   Grid Layout Algorithm for DMG

We use directed graph described as directed edge $E_i = (V_i, V_j)$. The genDMG method optimizes grid layout algorithm as the default graph layout. Firstly, the *width* w_1 and

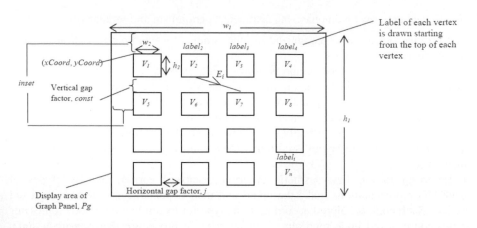

Fig. 1. Nodes or vertices are drawn in grid layout that can further re-arranged interactively

height h_1 of the Graph Panel that is currently opened should be determined (see Fig. 1). This area is called *display area* or *Pg*. Graph Panel has the minimum display area to ensure vertices of the graph are drawn with the most reasonable size. If users re-size the display area the value of w_1 and h_1 will be changed too. Based on the value of w_1 and h_1 the minimum of the two values should be indicated as *side s*. The value of s will be used to determine the width w_2 and height h_2 of each vertex to be drawn as shown in equation (1) and (2).

In equation (2), the value of w_2 is assigned to h_2 in order to draw a square of the same width and height to represent the node or *vertex V*. The value of *numberOf-Node, N_v* in equation (1) is the number of associated components derived from the repository based on the type of DMG representation to be displayed in the Graph Panel.

$$w_2 = s / N_v \qquad (1)$$
$$h_2 = w_2 \qquad (2)$$

Then the coordinate x and y for the first vertex V_1 to be drawn in the display area of the Graph Panel called as *xCoord* and *yCoord* respectively are indicated as in equations (3) and (4). The *inset* creates a barrier between the edges of the display area and the vertices drawn. The suggested minimum value of inset is $inset_{min}=10$.

$$xCoord = ((w_1 - s) / 2) / N_v + inset \qquad (3)$$

$$yCoord = ((h_1 - s) / 2) / N_v + inset \qquad (4)$$

For the following vertices to be drawn they are divided into two parts, which are the vertices in the first row and the vertices in the second and the following rows. In this grid layout algorithm only the maximum of four nodes can be drawn in each row for the first default layout generated on the display area. If the value of N_v is more than 4, the gap factor for two adjacent vertices in each row is as in equation (5) and if N_v less than or equal to 4, the gap factor is as in equation (6) to allow bigger nodes to be drawn. Hence the relative gap factor for the first vertex with the following vertices in the same row is determined by the value of k as in equation (7) where $i = 0,1,2... N_v$. Thus for the first vertex V_1 the value of k is equal to zero.

$$j = (s / 4) + (inset / 2) \tag{5}$$

$$j = s / N_v \tag{6}$$

$$k = 2 * j * i \tag{7}$$

Therefore the second and following vertices in the first row should be drawn at xCo-$ord + k$ and $yCoord$ is assigned with the value derived from equation (4). The vertices are drawn with the value of width w_2 and the height h_2. Then the label of each vertex in the first row is drawn at $xCoord + k$ and $yCoord + (inset - 2)$. The $inset$ value is reduced by 2 in order to draw the text label, $label_i$ starting from the top of each vertex (see Fig. 2).

For the first vertex of the following rows, the relative vertical gap factor is indicated by p as in equation (8) where $q = 0,1,2... N_v$ and $const$ is the constant value of the vertical gap factor that is assigned with the minimum value as $const_{min} = 80$. Hence the vertices of the second and the following rows should be drawn at $xCoord + k$ and $yCoord + j + p$, with the value of width w_2 and the height h_2.

$$p = q * const \tag{8}$$

2.3 Graph Representation Layout

In the genDMG method, the two lines that form an arrow is drawn at the middle of an arc not at the end of the arc as normally used by other graph layout (refer Fig. 2). The benefit of using this approach is that if a vertex has a lot of incoming arcs, the lines that form the arrows will not overlap with each other. Thus, the arcs drawn are simplified and indirectly, it makes the graph layout to be simplified too.

Hence the genDMG method optimizes the grid layout algorithm that is generic enough for both structured and object-oriented programs by the following approaches:

(i)   Each type of DMG representation is drawn in different sub-graph thus it can reduce the complexity of having one graph to represent the whole system.
(ii) Enforcing modularization prior to generating the graph, hence the value of *numberOfNode*, N_v can be determined. If value of N_v increases, the size of vertices to be drawn should be decreased. Therefore the display area can be better optimized when the number of vertices to be drawn is quite large.
(iii) The label of nodes should be drawn on each node and must be readable which is more important compared to the size of vertex to be drawn.
(iv) The arcs are represented as arrows in which the two lines that form the arrows are drawn in the middle of the arcs thus a vertex with a lot incoming arcs is simplified.
(v)   The default grid layout generated allows four nodes in a row only to avoid the scrolling of display area horizontally. Thus users need to scroll vertically only if display area is more than the size of the graph window or panel.

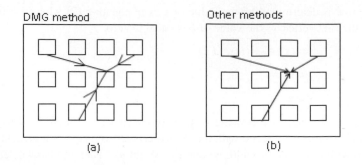

Fig. 2. DMG method in (a) shows how the arc drawn, while (b) shows arcs in other methods

(vi) Allow users to interactively re-arrange graph as they like and resize display area to have a bigger or a smaller graph.

(vii)Tag each graph layout with a particular section in the design document template provided to enable an explicit re-documentation of the subject system.

Rigi [3][4] is integrated with many layout algorithms including the Spring [13], Sugiyama [14] and SHriMP [15] layout. Both Spring and Sugiyama layouts manage to reduce crossing of arcs. However the approach used by RigiEdit that does not use arrow to show dependencies of two vertices and the long format for the label of vertices may disrupt the efficiency of the two layouts. Hence, a SV method must have effective ways to utilize any graph layouts integrated in its SV tool.

RigiEdit of Rigi [4] also provides the utility to scale the graph generated. However after a scaling is made towards the graph generated, the layout still looks quite complicated. This is because the size of each vertex is large and labels still overlap. DMG method attempts to eliminate this complexity by reducing the size of vertex to be drawn when the number of vertices of a graph is huge which is based on the display area of the graph. Logically, the size of vertex does not necessary to be so huge instead the size should be reasonable enough to represent the component that it stands for either by its color and more importantly by its label.

The nested graph of SHriMP [15] layout algorithm is capable to preserve mental map of users while studying and understanding and existing subject system. This is because the nodes are drawn in an overlaid layout in the same window. The outermost node represents the "root" followed by the inner node that represents the program or system. In the node, there are other collapsed nodes drawn and each node contains all the corresponding nodes such as files or programs, procedures and global variables. The SHriMP also employs fisheye view concept in which a concerned node can be enlarged to have a better view. It also provides the utility to filter the nodes and the arcs. By having this utility the complexity of the graph can be reduced by viewing the concerned components and relationships only. However, the SHriMP view has a tendency to be complicated if the subject system studied is quite large in size because all nodes are drawn in one overlaid window only. In addition, the SHriMP view does not allow re-arrangement of layout by users hence it hinders the

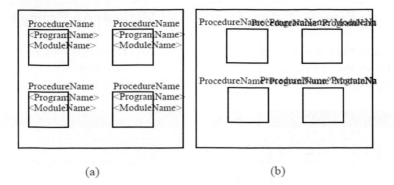

(a)   (b)

Fig. 3. genDMG method in (a) shows the labeling vertices as compared to other methods (b)

freedom of users to have their own preferred layout based on their own cognitive strategies to understand the subject system.

It is crucial to highlight that while employing graph layout algorithm to represent software components in a reverse engineering environment, the label is the most important element to be stressed compared to the size of vertex or color used. This is because a glance of a vertex without a label or readable label will not be as effective as that of with a readable label. For instance the method used in Rigi that provides a very long label format tends to cause overlapping of labels. Whereas in the SHriMP view, for smaller nodes it employs "tool tip" approach in which the label of a vertex is shown when the vertex is pointed. Imagine a user is studying a graph via the SHriMP view. After pointing and discovering the name of each vertex in a graph, users might forget the names of the vertices they previously pointed or observed.

Thus in the genDMG method the importance of labeling a vertex is stressed. To avoid overlapping of labels, the genDMG method creates the label for each vertex with at most three different lines depends on the type of DMG representations. Fig. 3 shows the label used in DMG_4 and DMG_5 of representations that need to indicate procedure (method) name, program (class) name and module (package) name. Therefore the genDMG method attempts to reduce the space required to draw a graph. In contrast, if a long label format is used; more space is required in order to make all the labels readable.

The graph representations proposed by the genDMG method can also be applied in the other three graph layouts of Spring [13], Sugiyama [14] and SHriMP [15]. However, for Spring layout all vertices in a graph must be connected. Thus for the DMG_2 and DMG_3 representations, the Spring layout cannot be utilized. This is because the DMG_2 representation displays all programs (class) in a particular module (package) thus some programs might have no link if there is no dependency with other programs in the module. Whilst the DMG_3 representation views all procedures or functions (methods) in a particular module (package) hence some of them might have no dependency with other functions within the module. Hence the graph representations in genDMG method can be applied to both structured and object-oriented programs.

3 Graph Representations by genDMG Method: An Example

This section illustrates an example of one of the DMG representations via our prototype tool called TubVis (see Fig. 4). It shows the representation derived from the
extracted artifacts of TubVis system itself. TubVis is written in Java.

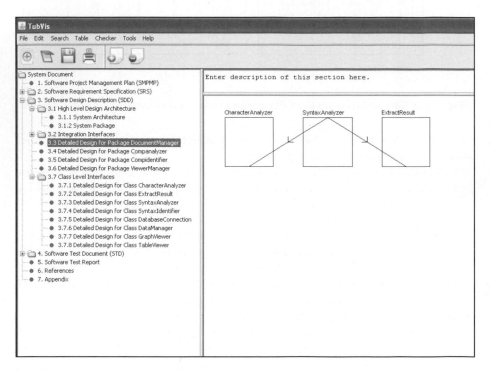

Fig. 4. A graph representation shows the relationships among the classes in a package

The example shows the DMG$_2$ representation in which a user has selected a section
of the tree view in the content panel. The associated graph for corresponding package
`DocumentGenerator` is generated in the graph panel that shows the dependencies
of class `SyntaxAnalyzer` with the other two classes in the same package that are
`CharacterAnalyzer` and `ExtractResult`. The textual description of the graph
requires users' intervention to explain the details of a particular view in the description panel. This example shows how graph representation may aid software maintainers' program comprehension.

4 Evaluation

This section describes the comparative study of TubVis using genDMG method with
other SV tools: Rigi [4], SHriMP [15], and Wind River Workbench [6] as listed in
Table 1.

Table 1. A comparison between TubVis applying genDMG method and other SV tools

Criteria	Tool			
	Rigi [4]	**SHriMP [15]**	**Wind River Workbench [6]**	**TubVis**
1. Method applied	Graph in multiple, individual window	Nested graph and fisheye view	Tree or tree-table view	genDMG
2. Modularization enforcement prior to generating views	No	No	No	Yes
3. Inter-module dependency views	No	Yes	No	Yes
4. Printing of information	No	No	No	Yes (graph and its textual description)
5. Local search of graph	Yes	No	Yes	Yes
6. Global search of graph	No	No	Yes	Yes
7. Link of node with source codes	Yes	Yes	No	Yes
8. Graph is interactive	Yes	No	Only tree view	Yes
9. Re-document explicitly	No	No	No	Yes
10. Parameter passing information	No	No	No	Yes
11. Graph complexity (assuming graphs are modularized)	Quite high (Children nodes in different windows)	Quite high (Nested graph is complicated)	Medium (Need more scrolling and windows navigation)	Low (Only need to scroll vertically)
12. Graph algorithm: vertex (See Fig. 1)	Not reduced if display area reduced	Outermost vertex is fixed	Text in the tree represents vertex	Reduce size if the display area reduced
13. Graph algorithm: arc (See Fig. 2a)	Straight line not arrow	Arrow at the end of line, optional straight line	Tree view can be expanded or shrunk.	Arrow in the middle of line
14. Vertex labeling (See Fig. 3a)	Long and overlapping	Shown by tool tip utility	Text in the tree represents label	Shown in different lines starting from top of vertex

5   Conclusion and Future Work

Current methods in SV tools tend to produce overloaded graph even if source codes parsed are not very large. Hence we proposed an enhanced method of SV called genDMG that provides five types of graph representations using graph drawing. The proposed genDMG is applied in TubVis tool. The graphical method is generic enough to represent software artifacts written in structured and object-oriented programming languages. The default graph layout employs grid layout algorithm. It improves the way to draw vertices, arcs and labels of the vertices. We also illustrated an example of how the genDMG method can aid program comprehension based on the graph representations. The comparative study shows the enhancement in genDMG as compared to other methods. Future work may include the extension of the genDMG method to accommodate more graph layout algorithms and the improvement of its aesthetic properties.

Acknowledgement

The main author would like to acknowledge School of Computer Sciences, Universiti Sains Malaysia for organizing the "Workshop on Writing for Proceedings" that provides the platform to produce this paper under APEX incentive grant.

References

1. Price, B.A., Baecker, R.M., Small, I.S.: A Principled Taxonomy of Software Visualization. Journal of Visual Languages and Computing 4, 211–266 (1993)
2. Koschke, R.: Software Visualization in Software Maintenance, Reverse Engineering and Re-engineering: a Research Survey. Journal of Software Maintenance and Evolution: Research and Practice 15, 87–109 (2003)
3. Muller, H.A., Wong, K., Tilley, S.R.: Understanding Software Systems Using Reverse Engineering Technology. In: Alagar, V.S., Missaoui, R. (eds.) Proceedings of 62nd Congress of L'Association Canadienne Francaise pour L'Avancement des Sciences (ACFAS), Object-oriented Technology for Database and Software Systems, pp. 240–252. World Scientific, Singapore (1994)
4. Rigi, http://www.rigi.csc.uvic.ca/
5. Lanza, M.: Lessons Learned in Building a Software Visualization Tool. In: Proceedings of the 7th European Conference on Software Maintenance and Reengineering (CSMR 2003), pp. 1–10. IEEE CS Press, USA (2003)
6. Wind River, http://www.windriver.com/products/development_tools/ide/sniff_plus/
7. Sulaiman, S., Sarkan, H., Azmi, A., Mahrin, N.: Visualizing Software Systems Using a Document-Like Software Visualization Method: a Case Study. In: International Conference on Computer Graphics, Imaging and Visualization (CGiV 2004), pp. 191–197. USM Press, Malaysia (2004)
8. Sulaiman, S., Idris, N.B., Sahibuddin, S.: Production and Maintenance of System Documentation: What, Why, When and How Tools Should Support the Practice. In: Proceedings of 9th Asia Pacific Software Engineering Conference (APSEC 2002), pp. 558–567. IEEE CS Press, USA (2002)
9. Sulaiman, S., Abdul Rashid, N., Abdullah, R., Sulaiman, S.: Supporting System Development by Novice Software Engineers Using a Tutor-Based Software Visualization (TubVis) Approach. In: Proceedings of International Symposium on Information Technology 2008 ITSIM 2008, vol. 4, pp. 2818–2825. IEEE, Los Alamitos (2008)
10. Shaffer, C.A.: A Practical Introduction to Data Structures and Algorithm Analysis. Prentice-Hall, New Jersey (1997)
11. Buchsbaum, A., Chen, Y.-F., Huang, H., Koutsofios, E., Mocenigo, J., Rogers, A., Jankowsky, M., Mancoridis, S.: Visualizing and Analyzing Software Infrastructures. IEEE Software, 62–70 (September/October 2001)
12. Gansner, E.R., Koutsofios, E., North, S.C., Vo, K.-P.: A Technique for Drawing Directed Graphs. IEEE Transactions on Software Engineering 19(3), 214–230 (1993)

13. Sugiyama, K., Misue, K.: A Simple and Unified Method for Drawing Graphs: Magnetic-Spring Algorithm. LNCS, vol. 894. Springer, Heidelberg (1995)
14. Sugiyama, K., Tagawa, S., Toda, M.: Methods for Visual Understanding of Hierarchical System Structures. IEEE Transaction on Systems, Man and Cybernetics 11(2), 109–125 (1981)
15. Storey, M.A.D., Fracchia, F.D., Muller, H.A.: Cognitive Design Elements to Support the Construction of a Mental Model During Software Exploration. Journal of Systems and Software 44, 171–185 (1999)
16. Sulaiman, S., Idris, N.B., Sahibuddin, S., Sulaiman, S.: Re-documenting, Visualizaing and Understanding Software Systems Using DocLike Viewer. In: Proceedings of 10th Asia Pacific Software Engineering Conference (APSEC 2003), pp. 154–163. IEEE CS Press, USA (2003)

An Automatic Optical Flow Based Method for the Detection and Restoration of Non-repetitive Damaged Zones in Image Sequences*

Roman Dudek, Carmelo Cuenca, and Francisca Quintana

Departamento de Informática y Sistemas,
Campus Universitario de Tafira, Las Palmas de Gran Canaria, Spain
roman@idecnet.com, {ccuenca,fquintana}@dis.ulpgc.es

Abstract. In this paper, we describe an automatic method for detecting and repairing non-repetitive damages in image sequences, caused by dust, fibers or local defects of the film emulsion. The method is a three frame window scheme based on the calculation of the optical flow (OF) relating adjacent frames and the first and the last frames of the sequence. The OF validity is checked in order to detect non-repetitive damage, and is later repaired using filtering and smooth blending of the damaged zones. The method works correctly for the set of tested image sequences providing perfect visual repairs of the damaged zones.

1   Introduction

There is a vast archive of celluloid film motion pictures documenting the modern history. With prolonged periods of storage in not always ideal conditions, they suffer from serious conservation problems. Neither the celluloid nor the chemical layer on it is stable over large periods of time. Most archive film motion pictures suffer from damages and need to be digitized and restored in order to preserve the invaluable cultural heritage they contain. Specially the older archive films can contain large amounts of film damage, like spots, dust, scratches, celluloid shrinking or unstable frame position. While for the news and documentary purposes digital video recording has gradually replaced the use of film negative, almost all existing feature film productions heve been shot using the traditional film technology, with only some of the latest features shot digitaly. The usage of traditional celluloid film technology inherently implies the presence of some drops, mostly caused by film emulsion defects and dust.

Among the different types of defects and damages there are the following:

- Processing liquids spots: This is a non-repetitive defect caused by the incorrect drying of the processing liquids, which can create spots on individual images of the sequence, like the spot shown in Figure 1(a).

---

* This work has been partially supported by The Spanish Ministry of Science and Innovation under contract TIN2007-60625 and by FEDER funds.

H. Badioze Zaman et al. (Eds.): IVIC 2009, LNCS 5857, pp. 800–810, 2009.

- Film emulsion drops: The film emulsion itself can contain defects. They usually appear as random dots or spots on individual frames. These dots are non-repetitive. We can see an example in Figure 1(b). If the defect is "hard" the emulsion can appear completely pealed off, as in Figure 2(b).
- Dust on film: It is normal that some dust particles get stuck on the film. The dust particles are fragments of fibers, hairs, plants, etc. Their amount can vary depending on the care taken during the film processing. A careful manipulation of the film can decrease these defects, but it will never make them disappear. The film dust will be seen as random fibers or dots on individual frames. They are not repetitive along multiple consecutive frames. In Figure 1(c) an example of a fiber stuck on the film can be seen.
- Mold: The photosensitive emulsion is hold on the celluloid by a common, animal based gelatine. The gelatine is prone to be attacked by mold in presence of humidity, thus creating non-repetitive spots on individual frames of the sequence.
- Dust on camera or film duplicating optics: If the dust is stuck in some part of the camera optics, in the path of the incoming light, then there will be a case like the above (dust on film), but in this case the dust will then be impressed on the same position along a sequence of frames.
- Film scratches: The film is mechanically threaded through the camera. If a hard dust particle is stuck in a point where the film slides along, a longitudinal scratch will be created along the film. These scratches will be visible as vertical lines in the film, provided that in typical cameras the film advances vertically. The scratches are usually visible in the same position along many consecutive frames of the sequence.

Some of the above defects can be physically cleansed in the laboratory, using special liquids and gasses. However, most archive materials are actually not the original film negatives. In the standard laboratory process, the negatives are optically transferred to distribution positives. The original negatives were frequently discarded or lost, so any dust present on the negative, or in the equipment, was permanently impressed on the positive, and in the copies made after these positives, thus propagating the effect.

Many works have been published regarding film restoring and dealing with various aspects of film repair [1] [2] [3] [4]. In the field of repairing localized defects we can distinguish methods aimed at repairing repetitive or non-repetitive damage. Non-repetitive damage appears only on individual frames, and generally can be repaired using information from adjacent undamaged frames. Repetitive damage is a damage which appear along a long sequence of frames, like a film scratch [5] or dust in optics. The information lost to such damage can not be easily patched using adjacent frames and need to be "guessed up" using much more advanced, complex assumptions about the scene depicted, like assuming that a scene consists basically from a static background with objects moving over, or that a walking person repeats over the same movements in each step of its walk [6]. Such advanced assumptions restrain the list of scenes that can treated, however they can be the only available solution in many cases.

(a) A processing liquid spot.　　(b) A dark spot.　　(c) A fiber.

Fig. 1. Examples of film damages

Our work concentrates on non-repetitive damage, like dust on film, emulsion defects, liquid drops and mold damage. We will concentrate on creating a simple to use, yet reliable automatic method to detect the damaged zones and integrate the repair as seamlessly as possible into the original footage.

The rest of the paper is structured as follows. Section 2 explains the automatic method based on the optical flow that detect and repairs non-repetitive damage. Section 3 presents the results obtained for different image sequences. Finally, section 4 depicts some conclusions.

2   Our Proposal

Our work deals with the film restoration of certain types of film damage using information from the adjacent frames in the film image sequence. Let suppose that in the present frame of the sequence there is a localized defect, like a spot, a fiber or a dot. Our solution is copying a similar but undamaged part of another image belonging to the same image sequence. We propose bringing the corresponding parts from the adjacent images in the image sequence to reconstruct the damaged part of the current image. Unfortunately, direct copying of pixels from the adjacent frame would only work on static image sequences. Using of the optical flow (OF) based movement interpolation extends the method usability to sequences with movement.

2.1   Optical Flow Based Image Interpolation

In our optical flow implementation, based on comparison studies by [7] [8] [9], we have chosen a variation of the Horn and Shunck [10] algorithm, extended by a multi-pyramidal scheme to account for large movements. We also added a modification into the calculation of the luminance gradient over time, using an image warping technique [11], thus improving the method's results and achieving really good results on real world image sequences.

Let suppose that we are repairing the image I_t, from the sequence of frames $I_1 \ldots I_n$. First, we will calculate the optical flow field $\mathbf{v} = (u,v)^T$ between the previous image I_{t-1} and the following image I_{t+1} of the sequence. We compute

$$\nabla I \cdot \mathbf{v} + I(u_x + v_y) = -\frac{\partial I}{\partial t} \tag{1}$$

Now, for each pixel of the I_t image that needs to be reconstructed, we will calculate its value bringing it from the following image:

$$I'_t(x,y) = I_{t+1}(x + \frac{u}{2}, y + \frac{v}{2}) \tag{2}$$

Notice that the optical field $\mathbf{v}$ describes movements along the interval of two frames. To interpolate the path along the interval of one frame (from I_t to I_{t+1}), we divide the vector size by 2. The coordinates of the pixel accessed in the I_{t+1} will usually be non integer values, so We use linear interpolation to access these pixel positions.

Although it could be thought that it would be a better solution to calculate the optical field between I_t and I_{t+1}, as it would lead to shorter movements to detect, with a better OF quality, this is not the case. Consider that the damaged spots are mostly of different luminance (black or white). In that case the presence of the spot in only one of the pair of the images used for the OF calculation will cause such OF field to be invalid just in the spot of the damage, exactly where we are actually going to use it. To avoid the interference of the damage in the calculation of the OF, we will use the previous and next frames of the sequence, but not the frame itself. If the damage is non-repetitive it is unlikely that the corresponding parts of the adjacent frames will be damaged too.

2.2 Optical Flow Based Process for Automatic Identification of the Damaged Zones

There is an obvious need for an automatic method that identify the damaged zones. While an operator could identify the damaged zones, such process is quite laborious, as the operator would need to review frame by frame the whole sequence, and mark the damaged zones using a pen-on-tablet repair brush interface. Even in case of treating current, correctly developed negative in a film production, which can contain less than one defect per frame for the operator to mark, a skilled operator can review and fix at most a few thousands of frames in a working day (1 minute of film = 24x60 frames = 1440 frames), making human assistance based process a reasonable proposition only for high budget productions. However, purely manual repair of damaged older film could require man-years of work.

For that reason, an automatic method for detecting and repairing damage is needed. However, as the ultimate criterion for film repairing is the visibility of the defects by a human, the operator could review the results and intervene only when it seems necessary, when noticed that the automatic identification did not work properly.

In order to identify the damaged spots we are concentrating on, we will use its non-repetitive nature. A non-repetitive damaged spot is present in the current frame, but it is not present in the previous or in the following frames of the sequence. To detect them, we will use the fact that the optical flow between a pair of images will be invalid or erroneous near an object that is present in only one of the images. This happens because the constant luminance assumption is broken by an object appearing in only one of the frames. We base the damage spot detection on the measure of the OF validity. We assume that where the OF is correct, the OF vectors will map the individual pixels of the source image onto pixels with similar luminance. We estimate the local validity of the OF field using this fact, defining an error measure for the OF error estimation as the square of the difference between the expected and the actual luminance of each pixel mapped by the OF,

$$E_{t-1,t+1}(x,y) = (I_{t+1}(x+u, y+v) - I_{t-1}(x,y))^2 \qquad (3)$$

However, damaged spots are only one of the possible phenomena creating OF errors. Many reasons for error in OF are valid phenomena in the scene, such as occlusions, transparencies or moving shadows. These cases would be false positives and therefore we do not have to repair them. To distinguish actual damage from false positives, we use that the damage is only present on an individual frame, not in the previous or in the following frames. Therefore, the OF between the previous and the following frames, but not using the damaged frame, will contain no error caused by the damaged spot. The reason is that an occlusion or moving shadow in progress, or in general any progressive change along the image sequence, will cause certain errors in the calculated OF. In general, these errors increase with the separation in time of the image pair we are using for the OF calculation. The larger the advance of the error-causing phenomena (a progressive occlusion, for example), the larger the OF error. In general, the OF error between a pair of frames separated by a long distance in the image sequence (a distance of two frames in our case), will be larger than the OF error between consecutive frames (a distance of one frame). Expressed as an equation,

$$E_{t,t+1}(x,y) < E_{t-1,t+1}(x,y) \qquad (4)$$

Now, consider the case of a non-repetitive damaged spot that is only present in the I_t frame, but not in I_{t-1} or I_{t+1} frames. The opposite of the above equation will be true: the OF error skipping the current frame with damage will be smaller than the OF error of the "shorter" OF relating the previous and the current frames. Using this property, we define the damage measure $D(x,y)$ for detecting zones of spot damage,

$$D(x,y) = E_{t,t+1}(x,y) - E_{t-1,t+1}(x,y) \qquad (5)$$

The damage measure D is a scalar value defined for each pixel of the current frame I_t.

Finally, based on the damage measure D, we can create a composition mask to combine the undamaged parts of the original image with reconstructed parts replacing the damaged zones of the current image. This is the mask the human would manually create in the simpler, human assisted method. The simplest way would be applying a threshold value to distinguish minor noise disturbances from actual film damage. However, the D measure will usually contain a large volume of noise as a consequence of the film grain noise [12] in the processed film sequence. To reduce this noise we used a simple Gaussian filtering, thus creating a filtered measure $D'(x, y)$,

$$D'(x, y) = (g \circ D)(x, y) \qquad (6)$$

Using a Gaussian filtering will reduce noise, but it will reduce the resolution of the measure mask. However, the resolution is not critical, as the OF is locally smooth and the detected errors tend to create clusters in the damaged zone.

Finally, we create the actual mask. To further improve the repair integration instead of a hard threshold we will use a linear clamped function to convert the damage measure $D'(x, y)$ into a composition mask,

$$p(x, y) = clamp((D' - c) * s) \qquad (7)$$

where c and s are user defined constants and $clamp()$ is a function limiting p to the range $[0, 1]$. Then, the final result is obtained by using a blending equation instead of using a threshold,

$$I_{result}(x, y) = p(x, y) * I'_t(x, y) + (1 - p(x, y)) * I_t(x, y) \qquad (8)$$

Adequate values for c and s are defined mostly by the image resolution in pixels and the level of noise in the processed film. As a consequence, usually the same values can be set only once and applied over many film sequences coming from the same origin (from the same day of shooting, for example).

Notice that the process we propose is symmetrical, that is, the OF could be calculated in the opposite direction, $(I_{t+1}$ to $I_{t-1})$, and then bring the corresponding pixels from the previous image. There seems to be no important advantage in doing so. One possible improvement to the method could be calculating the OF in both directions and then average the results to reduce the average method error. We tested this possible improvement but doing so produced a unwished side effect. In the reconstructed zones, the film grain noise inherently present in all film images, was reduced with the averaging. While noise reduction could be welcome, if applied only on some parts of the image it becomes visible and an unwished artifact on its own.

It is important to note that the proposed method will only work for non-repetitive damage, like emulsion defects, fibers and dust stuck on the film strip. The repetitive damage like film scratches is much more difficult to treat, as the part of the image covered by the defect can be completely lost along the whole image sequence, and would need to be guessed from scratch. Only some special cases, like an scene in constant, regular movement (pan over horizon) could be solved, as the damage is static relatively to the frame, although it is not static relatively to the depicted scene. If the number of frames affected by the defect is greater than one, but it does not include the whole of frames in the sequence, a more complex method could be designed, which included more than only three sequence frames.

3   Results

This section presents the results of our method on an example of three consecutive images, shown in Figure 2(a), 2(b) and 2(c) extracted from a longer film sequence. We are only showing a cutout of the complete frames so the results can be seen in more detail. The middle image, Figure 2(b), contains a large damage in form of white spots, probably caused by a pealed emulsion on the positive film print. The previous frame (Figure 2(a)) and the following frame (Figure 2(c)) contain no visible damage in the same zone, so if the damage is

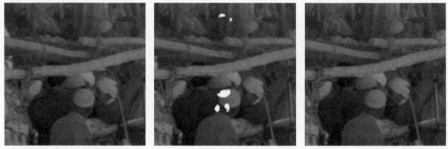

(a) First frame.   (b) Intermediate frame.   (c) Last Frame.

Fig. 2. A sequence of three consecutive frames. The intermediate frame contains white spots damage.

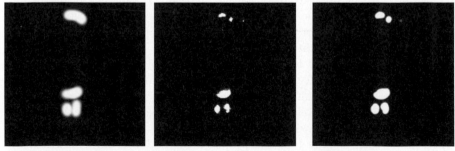

(a) A mask image as it would be created by a human operator if the process were manual. This mask image marks the damaged zone in the frame.

(b) The mask image created by our automated detection process, without Gaussian filtering.

(c) The mask image created by our automated detection process, with Gaussian filtered.

Fig. 3. Examples of mask images

(a) Simple repair example: Bringing the same zones from third frame of the sequence, using the mask created by our method.

(b) Optical Flow corrected repair example: Bringing the corresponding image zones from the third frame of the sequence and compensating the motion in the scene using the OF calculated between the first and third frames.

Fig. 4. Simple and OF corrected restorations

non-repetitive and the overall damage is not too extensive, it is unlikely they will contain damage exactly in the same zone.

First, in Figure 3(a) we present the mask image that would be created by a human operator, if the process was to be done manually. The human operator marked the damaged zone of the image we are repairing (Figure 2(b)). This mask can be created using a pen-on-tablet interface. In that case, only a few frames a minute can be treated if the damage is not extensive. Note that the outline of the mask is soft, allowing for smooth blending of the repaired zones with the original frame, thus making the repair less visible.

In Figure 3(b) we present the mask created by our automated detection process by simple thresholding of the damage measure D. No filtering is used on the damage measure, D, in this case. We can see that the mask outlines are quite hard and iregular, making the borders of the repair potentially visible. In order to avoid these borders, Figure 3(c) shows the mask obtained after Gaussian filtering the damage measure D. In D' the noise present in our initial D damage measure has been removed before extracting the mask. As a convenient side effect, the Gaussian filtering also widens the zone to repair, thus producing certain safety margin around the damaged spot, and it softens the spots outlines achieving better visual integration of the repaired zones.

We use the mask shown in Figure 3(c) to compose parts of the image following the damaged frame in the sequence (Figure 2(c)) over the image we are repairing (Figure 2(b)).

In Figure 4(a) we directly bring the same zones from the following image of the sequence using the mask created with our method. The damage is less obvious

(a) A processing liquid spot.   (b) A dark spot.   (c) A fiber.

Fig. 5. Examples of film corrected damages for images in Figure 1

(a) The automatic mask for liquid spot.   (b) The automatic mask dark spot.   (c) The automatic mask for the fiber spot.

Fig. 6. Examples of automatic image masks for images in Figure 1

now. However, a close examination reveals that the substituted zones do not fit well and the repaired spots look distorted. Finally, in Figure 4(b), we bring the corresponding image zones from the following image of the sequence also using the mask created with our method, while compensating the motion in the scene using the OF calculated between the previous and the following frames. We can see in that Figure a visually perfect repair of the damaged zones. The repair will be perfect with the condition that the following frame is not exactly damaged on the same spot.

We have also tested the method with different kinds of damages in image sequences, such as a processing liquid spot, a dark spot and a fiber spot. In Figure 5 we can see the same three frames as in the Figure 1 but in this case the damage has been properly corrected using optical flow. The images in Figure 6 correspond to the three automatically computed image masks. In all frames, white zones identify the damages in the frames and black zones identify parts of the images which are considered by the application of the method without spots.

4   Conclusions

There is a vast historical film archive that it is worthwile preserving and restoring as it is considered to be a cultural heritage. A large part of this historical footage, and to a lesser extent more recent or even current film documents, are affected by multiple kinds of film damage, ranging from old film shrinking to dust in camera. We concentrated our work on repairing irregular damage, like non-repetitive spots or drops in the images. We proposed and tested an automated method identifying this kind of damage, distinguishing it from other phenomena in the actual depicted scene. Our method is a three frame window scheme based on the calculation of the optical flow relating the adjacent frames and the first and last frames, skipping the central frame, comparing the OF validity for detecting non-repetitive damage. We use both filtering and smooth repair blending to achieve seamless repair of the detected damaged zones. We also use the same optical field relating the first and third frame of our window to create an interpolated frame to use as source for "patching" the damaged second frame of the window.

The automatic identification works correctly for most of the tested scenes. However some sequences containing special phenomena, difficult to distinguish from film damage, like scenes of snow, fire or a fly present in only one picture, can not be adjusted to prevent appearance of either false positives or false negatives. Some human assistance would be needed in order to identify correctly the damage. In these cases, the automatically cerated mask can be used as base to be corrected by the human operator, speeding up at least partially the process. Nevertheless, even in such difficult cases, once the operator points the defects, the system can still repair these automatically, with good visual results.

References

1. Van Roosmalen, P.: Restoration of Archived Film and Video, Delft University of Technology, Ph.D. Thesis (1999)
2. Joyeux, L., Boukir, S., Besserer, B., Buisson, O.: Reconstruction of Degraded Image Sequences. Application to Film Restoration. Image and Vision Computing 19(8), 503–516 (2001)
3. Harvey, N., Marshall, S.: Application of Non-Linear Image Processing: Digital Video Restoration. In: Int. Conf. on Image Processing, vol. 1, pp. 731–734 (1997)
4. Boulanger, J., Kervrann, C., Bouthemy, P.: Space-Time Adaptation for Patch-Based Image Sequence Restoration. IEEE Transactions on Pattern Analysis and Machine Intelligence 29(6), 1096–1102 (2007)
5. Joyeux, L., Buisson, O., Besserer, B., Boukir, S.: Detection and Removal of Line Scratches in Motion Picture Films. In: IEEE Int. Conf. on Computer Vision and Pattern Recognition, vol. 1, pp. 548–553 (1999)
6. Patwardhan, K., Sapiro, G., Bertalmío, M.: Video Inpainting Under Constrained Camera Motion. IEEE Transactions on Image Processing 16(2), 545–553 (2007)
7. Álvarez, L., Weickert, J., Sánchez, J.: Reliable Estimation of Dense Optical Flow Fields with Large Displacements. Int. Journal of Computer Vision 39(1), 41–56 (2000)

8. Beauchemin, S., Barron, J.: The Computation of Optical Flow. ACM Computing Surveys 27(3), 433–467 (1995)
9. McCane, B., Novins, K., Crannitch, D., Galvin, B.: On Benchmarking Optical Flow. Computer Vision and Image Understanding 84(1), 126–143 (2001)
10. Horn, B., Schunk, B.: Determining Optical Flow, AI Memo 572. Massachusetts Institute of Technology (1980)
11. Papenberg, N., Bruhn, A., Brox, T., Didas, S., Weickert, J.: Highly Accurate Optic Flow Computation with Theoretically Justified Warping. Int. Journal of Computer Vision 67(2), 141–158 (2006)
12. Minelly, S., Curley, A., Giaccone, P., Jones, G.: Reducing Chromatic Grain Noise in Film Sequences. In: IEEE Colloquium on Non-Linear Signal and Image Processing (Ref. No. 1998/284), vol. 5, pp. 1–5 (1998)

Are Visual Informatics Actually Useful in Practice: A Study in a Film Studies Context

Nazlena Mohamad Ali[1] and Alan F. Smeaton[2,1]

[1] Centre for Digital Video Processing and [2] CLARITY: Centre for Sensor Web Technologies
Dublin City University
Ireland
{nmohamadali,asmeaton}@computing.dcu.ie

Abstract. This paper describes our work in examining the question of whether providing a visual informatics application in an educational scenario, in particular, providing video content analysis, does actually yield real benefit in practice. We provide a new software tool in the domain of movie content analysis technologies for use by students of film studies students at Dublin City University, and we try to address the research question of measuring the 'benefit' from the use of these technologies to students. We examine their real practices in studying for the module using our advanced application as compared to using conventional DVD browsing of movie content. In carrying out this experiment, we found that students have better essay outcomes, higher satisfactions levels and the mean time spent on movie analyzing is longer with the new technologies.

Keywords: Video browsing, Film studies, usage study, educational technologies.

1 Introduction

With the increase in the current research agenda in visual informatics, teaching and learning is an application that can benefit from this. Numerous applications can be applied at school either in primary or secondary levels. In educational applications, the strategy of using add-on features and other visual informatics that incorporate technologies in particular video content analysis often strengthens the overall appeal of the video medium, and can provide richer interactions with very large data sets or archives for example in navigating and browsing a video sequence. People are now creating, editing, storing, indexing, searching, browsing and playing video directly and indirectly more easily then before. With the growth in management tools for digital video and its potential valuable usage as a learning tool, digital video can offer exciting ways for students to study better, especially in the context of film studies.

2 Emergence of Video Content Analysis Technologies

A video element describes sequences of moving pictures. At a logical level, a video document can be divided into a set of basic components such as episode, scene, shot, and frame. Video data can be retrieved using a number of approaches such as by

H. Badioze Zaman et al. (Eds.): IVIC 2009, LNCS 5857, pp. 811–821, 2009.

using metadata and browsing by keyframe, text transcript search, keyframe matching, semantic feature filtering, object matching and combinations of these techniques [3]. There is a complexity in video elements, which need proper organization as compared to when dealing with only text elements. In a huge video database, necessary indicators on the audio, visual and textual elements will help the video material to be more searchable and browsable [4].

In content analysis systems, video data is typically structured automatically into temporal shots, which represent basic access and retrieval units. This processing step is called shot boundary detection (SBD). In most approaches, SBD is based on a measure of similarity between two or more adjacent frames. Usually a shot change is indicated by large changes in the similarity value [2]. Colour histograms [7, 12, 2], edge detection [12, 2] and using macroblocks [2] are among the many features that can be used for similarity comparisons.

Among the possible video content analysis techniques is segmenting scenes into several event types such as *Exciting*, *Montage* and *Dialogue*, based on film grammar [5]. The key multimedia techniques used in this work are:

- Scene detection – automatically segment a movie into a number of scenes. Camera shot boundary detection is used first and segmented shots are clustered back together by considering their visual similarity and temporal distance;
- Scene classification – automatically classify the nature of a scene into *Action*, *Dialogue* and *Montage*. Within-scene shots are analyzed in terms of the amount of motion (in the case of Action), in terms of alternating shots (in the case of Dialogue), and in terms of motion speed and existence of music spanning multiple shots (in the case of Montage). Movie shooting and editing conventions are also used as heuristics for the classification.
- Keyframe extraction – automatically select a most representative still image from a sequence of video. For each scene and shot, the most average (common) visual frame is determined and selected as the keyframe.

These are among the active research areas in the field of multimedia at the moment and are steadily improving their accuracy and robustness. Taking advantage of these automatic content-based techniques, numerous possible application scenarios can be imagined and a large number of novel demonstration systems have been built. Our work incorporates these technologies into a system we called MOVIEBROWSER2.

Other work related to movie video browsing includes work at INRIA [14], and the *Virtual Screening Room* [17]. These tools provide novel movie content browsing and searching features. A project at the INRIA laboratory is related to the development of an integrated tool for watching, browsing and searching a movie, synchronized with its scripts. It was demonstrated with the movie "The Wizard of Oz". The *Virtual Screening Room* project is an informative browser for playing a movie with many useful features such as clip searching and various in-depth information representations. These projects are very useful and effective educational applications for students of Film Studies in understanding, appreciating, teaching and learning movies.

3   Film Studies Work Context

Our application domain area in this experiment is Film Studies. Film Studies is a study about film history, theory, and criticism. The typical tasks of Film Studies students are to read and analyze movies. Reading a movie in their context refers to the process of understanding and analyzing movie content closely, looking for different levels of meaning and critique from different elements like framing, depth of field, plot, shots, camera angle, lighting and so on. On a broader level it also involves an understanding of the generic conventions and narrative structure of individual movies [11].

The conventional approach for students to work is to get DVDs from the University library or rental shop. The restrictions of getting only a one-day loan and a lack of DVD resources (i.e. old production year, VHS format) contributes to the main problems in their studies.

Online technology enables movie content information to be accessed easily with the existence of the Internet, thus providing resourceful information such as the IMDB (imdb.com), the Internet Archive (www.archive.org), and other online web hosting video. Video material can be accessed by Film Studies students more easily than before.

4   Experiment Protocol

Our main experimental question to be explored is "Do students who use our newly-introduced technology (the software tool) get more 'benefit' compared to the conventional way of performing their work task?". We address this main question by dividing into sub-questions as the following:

- Q1. Do students make use of the alternative access features afforded by MOVIEBROWSER2 and spend less time in completing the essay-writing task?
- Q2. Given the same amount of time, is the 'outcome' for those using MOVIEBROWSER2 better or worse than those who use only a standard DVD media player interface for browsing movies?
- Q3. Do the students who use MOVIEBROWSER2 have a higher level of satisfaction than those using only a standard DVD media player?

We recruited all 7 students from CM524 *Film Theory and History* (Masters Class module). The task given is to 'read' small sequences of a film. Each student needs to produce a small piece of writing based on reading movie sequences and we will compare how students perform this task using MOVIEBROWSER2 versions and using only a standard movie DVD player as shown in Fig.1.

The first task was about reading and analysing a dinner conversation scene in the movie *American Beauty*, while the second task was comparing and contrasting a few related scenes from the same movie that had musical elements in them. Participants need to browse and analyse relevant scenes or sequences as described in the task by using the assigned interface systems as described below:

- Task 1 - Find the scene and perform some analysis of its content. Analyse the techniques used by the director to make the scene more tense between all the family members in the fighting dinner scene where *Lester* (the father) throws away the food plate onto the wall. [Hint: characters smiling to/at each other in the beginning and there are some recognizable changes in dress etc.]
- Task 2 - Find the scenes and perform some analysis. Analyse the director's use of music to express the characters' emotion more cinematically. [Hint: you could contrast these scenes — a scene where *Carolyn* (the mother) is driving and singing in the car on her way back home and a scene where *Lester* (the father) and *Angela* (*Jane's* friend) are together in the bath]

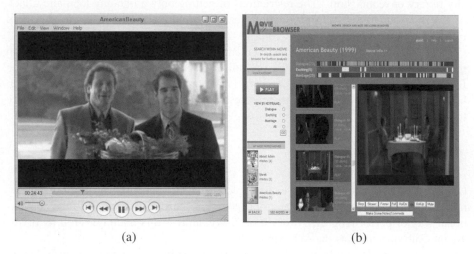

(a)   (b)

Fig. 1. (a): DVD player interface screenshot, (b) MOVIEBROWSER2 screenshot

We choose the movie, *American Beauty (1999)* and participants were brought to a 2-hour screening of the movie before the experiments were carried out. In order to reduce and control the learning effect during the task performance with a smaller number of participants, we choose a within-groups design [15, 1] approach.

For the MOVIEBROWSER2, the interaction logs were captured automatically by the system while for the DVD interface, they were observed by volunteer researchers from our research centre who took notes on what users clicked and their overall behaviour in accomplishing the task for example writing notes on paper then typing essay material into WORD. Some guidelines were given to colleague researchers before the session begin especially on what they need to observe such as the number of clicks participants do on the player interface (e.g. play, slider bar, pause, stop, etc.) and reporting overall user actions in accomplishing the tasks in a pre-designed form. Each task needs to be completed within 30 minutes. CCTVs were used (with participants' permission) to record the session and the CCTV footage was used to verify the observations made by colleague researchers.

5 Results

In answering Q1, we examined the user log data from both system variants (DVD and MOVIEBROWSER2 interface) on each task. Data were collected from MOVIE-BROWSER2 on the interaction clicks and from the observation sheets for the DVD interface where colleague researchers manually recorded the number of interaction clicks made and the button pressed (i.e. slider bar, stop and etc). The sessions were recorded (with student permission) using CCTV as part of the experimental protocol. CCTV content was then used for verification in this process and in determining participant activities during the session.

As shown in Table 1, highest interactions were found on the slider-bar when the tasks were carried out using the DVD interface. While interactions on MOVIE-BROWSER2 were no longer at the slider-bar but has been shifted into 'event-keyframe' that referred to playing the scene from the keyframe view and also from the respective timeline bar (either Dialogue or Montage).

Table 1. Interaction logs for a given tasks. Notes: Dialogue, Exciting and Montage referred to timeline bar; event-keyframe referred to play scene from keyframe view.

	TASK 1		TASK 2	
	DVD	MOVIEBROWSER2	DVD	MOVIEBROWSER2
Dialogue	0 (0%)	**8** (25%)	0 (0%)	2 (3%)
Exciting	0 (0%)	2 (6%)	0 (0%)	0 (0%)
Montage	0 (0%)	2 (6%)	0 (0%)	**24** (37%)
event-keyframe	0 (0%)	**14** (44%)	0 (0%)	27 (42%)
slider-bar	**52** (58%)	1 (3%)	59 (72%)	2 (3%)
pause button	16 (18%)	0 (0%)	11 (13%)	0 (0%)
play button	13 (15%)	0 (0%)	11 (13%)	2 (3%)
slow button	6 (7%)	0 (0%)	1 (1%)	1 (2%)
faster button	1 (1%)	0 (0%)	0 (0%)	2 (3%)
fullscreen button	1 (1%)	1 (3%)	0 (0%)	0 (0%)
stop button	0 (0%)	4 (13%)	0 (0%)	4 (6%)
volumn-up button	0 (0%)	0 (0%)	0 (0%)	1 (2%)
Total	89	32	82	65

We also determined participants' time completion for each task. The completion time when using MOVIEBROWSER2 is longer or almost to the maximum (30 minutes) for most of participants as compared to standard DVD player. Only one participant out of 7, finished the task with MOVIEBROWSER2 earlier, at 17 minutes.

These results only answer the research question in part. In a conventional DVD interface, usage on the slider bar seems higher and is used as the main interaction during navigation of movie content. This appears to be the 'only way' to accomplish the task, working with other support buttons such as pause/play/stop etc. This feature is useful for blind seeking of movie content. In the MOVIEBROWSER2 interface, participants make use of the alternative access features afforded by the technologies in completing their task. The process of navigating, and playing clips can be seen from the interaction log captured on the added features and not utilizing the standard buttons such as slider bar. For example, in looking for music background to appear in the scene, a montage timeline bar is used and further browsing is enhanced using the particular shot keyframe view instead of using a slider-bar. The time taken to accomplish the task when using the MOVIEBROWSER2 interface was relatively longer than when using the conventional standard player even though it was predicted to be faster initially.

In order to answer Q2, we performed a qualitative analysis and looked at the quality of the essay results from students who completed an assignment as part of this module. This resulting outcome was chosen for analysis mainly to provide a general overview of participants' performance as a result of having used either a DVD or MOVIEBROWSER2 interface. Participants' essays were marked based on a known, predefined answer scheme and were categorized into three quality groups, and these categories were formally approved by the module lecturer (i.e. 'Very Good', 'Good' and 'Basic').

Table 2. Essay quality remarks

	Standard Player	MovieBrowser2
U1	*Not much ... more to scene description.* Basic	*Solid enough but would like have liked a bit more detail [specific of lyrics and music...].* Good
U2	*Very good comparisons between the two scenes... would have liked a little more description of Lester's dream state as define by the 'off key' music.* Very Good	*Lots of good stuff from different perspective with excellent conclusion.* Very Good
U3	*Relatively basic scenarios description.* Basic	*Solid and good analysis [good on detail of music instrument and effect].* Good
U4	*Well done/describes.* Very Good	*Use of several techniques to express this [i.e. camera cut/editing pace]... solid description and compare other parts of the film.* Very Good
U5	*Describes the scene and lacking of explanation.* Basic	*Good re string instruments used to express sexual interest ... solid and good contrast of scenes.* Good
U6	*Lack of details.* Basic	*Basic description but use of camera techniques in the explanation such as shots mid/long and editing pace.* Basic
U7	*Good detail but not really well structured.* Good	*Good contrast and very good drawn conclusion – describes the music effect.* Very Good

Table 2 represents the results and remarks of the essay quality evaluation. Participants [i.e. U2, U4, U6] who used MOVIEBROWSER2, and then the standard DVD player stay with the same essay quality. Participants [i.e. U1, U3, U5, U7], who used the standard DVD player, followed by MOVIEBROWSER2 get a better essay outcome. This results shows there is some increased performance relatively either from 'Basic' to 'Good' or 'Good' to 'Very Good'. In order to provide more supporting evidence, we look further at the essay quality in a different way. The essay remarks also show interesting feedback given from the module lecturer. Most of the remarks given on essays after using MOVIEBROWSER2, from the lecturer's point of view show that participants' give more deep and critical essay analysis. In the essays, we are able to find these expressions or statements from a variety of analysis which makes the essay quality better as for example:

- Point of view: ("It might suggest/reflecting . . . /I think . . . /noted that . . . /The director succeeds in given . . . /tells us . . . ")
- Compare and contrast scene: ("Elsewhere in the film . . . /The scene is preceded by . . . /As the scene progress . . . /Directly contrast the earlier scene . . . .")
- Use of different techniques: ("The camera cut relatively fast . . . /Music helps to distinguish . . . /The pace of the scene is faster, hinting an explosion to come . . . /Non-descript colours (grey, brown etc) that complimented with music . . . ")

Participants who completed the task using MOVIEBROWSER2 generally have solid remarks that represent richness or variability in the written essay. On the other hand, when using the standard player, the remarks are basically only basic explanation details on sequences. An essay that was produced using the standard player generally has the basic type of description of scenes; the essay quality was limited in terms of variety of expressions, points of view and lack of detailed explanations. We are not comparing on each individual participant in this experiment, but referring to the individually produced outcomes from a given task.

By analyzing the essay outcome and the remarks given by the lecturer in a qualitative way, we answered the experimental question and reveal that the outcome (essay quality) of those using MOVIEBROWSER2 are better or at least stay at the same level (not worse) than participants' current performance. In relation to this as the findings found in the previous question, most participants who get better essay outcomes take a longer time to complete the task in MOVIEBROWSER2.

For Q3, we captured participants' responses to using both interfaces using semantic differentials and Likert point-scales of 1–7 (the higher values the better) for a variety of questions from post-task questionnaires. We used a paired sample t-test [8], for the statistically significant differences of means scores with $p <= 0.05$. However, in this explanation, we would not emphasize a significant difference due to the small number of sample users. We reported the means and standard deviations (SD) on each system variant. Participants perceived satisfaction levels on the system variants are more towards MOVIEBROWSER2 with generally higher mean scores in all aspects (Table 3).

In affirming the overall satisfaction results shown in Table 3, we asked participants how they felt about the task they performed in the experiment using both system variants. Responses from students favoured MOVIEBROWSER2, as can be seen from some extracts below:

"If you are looking for a particular scene (i.e. dialogue), you can narrow the search parameter by selecting a category, making it quicker to complete the search". [U2]

"MOVIEBROWSER2 is more useful because you could browse frames of the film together making it easier to contrast scenes. The DVD media player took longer to find scenes— it encouraged more random watching". [U4]

" MOVIEBROWSER2 is easier to use and (provides) more information".[U6]

Table 3. Post-task results. Note: A - DVD, B - MOVIEBROWSER2.

	System	$\bar{A}$	$\tilde{A}$	$\bar{B}$	$\tilde{B}$	p
Differential	easy to use	5.43	1.27	**6.29**	0.76	0.017
	easy to learn	6.00	1.15	**6.29**	0.95	-
	effective	5.14	1.68	**6.43**	0.53	0.049
	satisfying	5.14	1.57	**5.29**	1.50	-
	stimulating	5.14	1.57	**6.00**	1.15	-
	novel	4.57	1.72	**6.43**	0.53	-
	intuitive	5.00	1.41	**6.00**	0.82	-
	helpful	5.14	1.77	**6.29**	0.76	-
Likert	access movie content	4.14	1.77	**6.14**	0.69	-
	analyse movie efficiently	4.00	2.31	**6.29**	0.49	0.022
	explore movie scenes efficiently	4.00	2.24	**6.57**	0.53	0.019
	complete task quickly	4.71	2.06	**5.86**	0.69	-
	enhance reading ability	3.86	2.19	**5.71**	0.95	0.045
	better outcome/essay	4.57	1.27	**6.00**	0.82	0.008
	discover new ideas	3.71	2.36	**5.29**	1.38	0.042
	focus	3.71	2.50	**5.29**	1.38	0.033

Finally, we asked participants the question of which system they would prefer for their film reading task as part of their studies. All of the 7 participants chose MOVIEBROWSER2 as the favoured tool to be used. This question was asked mainly to gauge participants' future intentions.

6   Discussion

The findings from the essay outcome revealed that there are slightly improving or better results which is also supported by the remarks from the module lecturer that shows students have more variability (more opinions, expressions) in their written essay when using MOVIEBROWSER2. This is a better outcome from the lecturer's point of view. It would be better if this perception could be further explored to more detail on the improvement from the student's point of view particularly in their learning. We understand that in order to measure performance of a movie browser interface, many factors need to be considered. The link between 'cognitive' and 'pedagogic' learning and any measurement of the deepening of students' perceptions of the audio-visual stimulus, using technical or structured approaches, are of course difficult to prove in terms of any direct benefits. Any improvements also so much depend on the aptitude and linguistic dexterity of individual students and their motivation. These issues will give another interesting perspective and motivation for future work.

Our findings also show that satisfaction levels are higher after using the newly introduced tool with higher mean scores in all aspects of statements given as compared to when using a conventional standard player. User preferences and subjective opinions reflected from the comments favoured MOVIEBROWSER2. All 7 students intended to use the software application in their future learning. In discussing user perceived satisfaction in an experimental setup, especially from the perspective of student learning, we might have expected mixed satisfaction levels as the outcome does not always mean higher satisfaction when a new technology is introduced. In some cases, even though a new system with new technology is introduced, users still prefer their old ways as their tendency or practice does not change easily. Many factors influence such results. For example, previous studies in e-learning and work carried out in [9, 13] reported that students are less satisfied with the use of a technology in learning due to them already being accustomed to their traditional ways or experiencing frustration or worry during online learning. On the other hand, other studies as in [16, 6] found a higher level of subjective satisfaction from students with a new e-learning tool compared to the traditional classroom learning.

Besides expected findings from the lab setting experiment in terms of better performance in the essay outcome and students' perceived satisfaction levels, we also saw surprising findings that show the time taken to complete the task when using the newly-introduced software application is longer than the conventional way for the majority of students. The results of longer time taken to complete the tasks might indicate that students are engaged with the activity being performed using the newly introduced tool. From the learning perspective, the longer time spent represents the meaning of engagement (similarly to lecturer's feedback/remarks that show engagement, thus it was used as a 'measurement' in the essay outcome). Looking from this perspective, we cannot say that by having used the newly-introduced tool that afford extra features for navigating and browsing movie scenes in carrying essay analysis, the task can be completed faster than the conventional way. In this experiment, we interpret this phenomenon from another domain perspective, the sub-area of psychology, which is flow theory that reflects engagement in carrying out an activity. Flow Theory according to Csikszentmihalyi [10] is "The state in which people are so involved in the activity that nothing else seems to matter; the experience itself is so enjoyable that people will do it even at great cost, for the sheer sake of doing it".

We cannot claim from this finding yet that this phenomenon shows our design influenced the engagement or playing element which then brought into a sense of feeling intrinsic motivation in completing their assignment from this experiment. We reasoned that they are immersed with the tool from the feedback we collected either from written comments or verbally informal responses. Some students did request permission to use the tool after the experiment and are very interested to learn more. Our assumption here relates to the learning theory of engagement and flow as described in the psychology field. Having completed the task longer than the conventional way may look as a 'failure' in terms of scientific computing where it should be faster to complete, it does show interesting and good evidence from the perspective of the learning process for a newly-introduced educational technology.

We consider some limitation in this experiment, which is only 7 users, used in a pre-defined lab setting and limited time frame. 30 minutes duration might not be enough to evaluate essay performance. Future research should include more student cohorts and the experiment should be carried out over a longer time frame (i.e. a longitudinal study). Our interesting findings related to engagement factors were considered as surprising or unexpected, and we can suggest another research perspective of 'measuring' the flow or engagement level among students for example.

7 Conclusion

In conclusion, from carrying out this experiment, we found that students spent more time and use the alternative features afforded by new technologies based on visual analytics in completing their tasks, written essays resulted in various aspect of critical analysis and better outcome/remarks from the lecturer, positive quantitative and qualitative feedback with higher satisfaction levels in terms of interest and educational effectiveness.

We believe that, by implementing innovative technologies such as this need further work as consideration on issues in learning particularly in individual learning style, background and skill. The software application we developed could provide potential in learning for students developing the core skills of textual analysis, within the film studies domain, thus contribute in pushing the trend (i.e. starting to recognize the importance of user experience in multimedia) further to that direction. Integrating both knowledge from the technology on automatic movie content analysis, with the practice from the realistic contextual end-users, could provide a bridge to establish the Film Studies discipline and in the setting of Film Studies, it is shown to be useful.

Acknowledgements. The work was supported by the Ministry of Higher Education and University Kebangsaan Malaysia and by Science Foundation Ireland as part of the CLARITY CSET (07/CE/I1147).

References

1. Dix, A., Finlay, J., Abowd, G.D., Beale, R.: Human-Computer Interaction. Prentice Hall, Englewood Cliffs (2004)
2. Smeaton, A.F.: Indexing, Browsing, and Searching of Digital Video. Annual Review of Information Science and Technology 38, 371–410 (2004)
3. Smeaton, A.F.: Techniques Used and Open Challenges to the Analysis, Indexing and Retrieval of Digital Video. Information Systems, 32(4):545–559 (2007)
4. Haubold, A., Dutta, P., Kender, J.R.: Evaluation of Video Browser Features and User Interaction with VAST MM. In: MM 2008: Proceeding of the 16th ACM International Conference on Multimedia, Vancouver, British Columbia, Canada, pp. 449–458 (2008)
5. Lehane, B.: Automatic Indexing of Video Content via the Detection of Semantic Events. PhD Thesis, Centre for Digital Video Processing, Dublin City University (2006)
6. Amir, F., Iqbal, S.M., Yasin, M.: Effectiveness of Cyber-learning. In: Frontiers in Education Conference, 1999. FIE'99. 29th Annual, volume 2 (1999)
7. Mas, J., Fernandez, G.: Video Shot Boundary Detection Based on Color Histogram. In: Proceedings of the TRECVid Workshop, Gaithersburg, Maryland USA (2003)
8. Pallant, J.: A Step by Step Guide to Data Analysis using SPSS version 12, 2nd edn. Open University Press (2005)

9. Rivera, J.C., Rice, M.L.: A Comparison of Student Outcomes and Satisfaction Between Traditional and Web Based Course Offerings. Online Journal of Distance Learning Administration 5(3) (2002)
10. Csikszentmihalyi, M.: Flow: The Psychology of Optimal Experience. Harper Perennial, New York (1991)
11. Brereton, P.: How to write textual analysis of a film, CM135 Analyzing Media Content lecture notes. School of Communications, Dublin City University (2008)
12. Browne, P., Smeaton, A.F., Murphy, N., O'Connor, N.E., Marlow, S., Berrut, C.: Evaluating and Combining Digital Video Shot Boundary Detection Algorithms. In: Proc. Irish Machine Vision and Image Processing Conference, IMVI 2000 (2000)
13. Maki, R.H., Maki, W.S., Patterson, M., Whittaker, P.D.: Evaluation of a Web based Introductory Psychology Course: I. Learning and satisfaction in on-line versus lecture courses. Behavior Research Methods, Instruments and Computer 32(2), 230–239 (2000)
14. Ronfard, R.: Reading Movies: an Integrated DVD Player for Browsing Movies and Their Scripts. In: Proceedings of the 12th Annual ACM International Conference on Multimedia, pp. 740–741 (2004)
15. Smith-Atakan, S.: Human-computer Interaction. Thomson (2006)
16. Hiltz, S.R., Wellman, B.: Asynchronous Learning Networks as a Virtual Classroom. Communications ACM 40(9), 44–49 (1997)
17. MIT Center for Educational Computing Initiatives. The Virtual Screening Room, http://caes.mit.edu/projects/virtualscreeningroom/index.htm (Accessed 21 November 2008)

The Effect of Visual of a Courseware towards Pre-University Students' Learning in Literature

Mazyrah Masri, Wan Fatimah Wan Ahmad , Shahrina Md. Nordin,
and Suziah Sulaiman

Universiti Teknologi PETRONAS,
Bandar Sri Iskandar, 31750 Tronoh,
Perak, Malaysia
mazyrahmasri@gmail.com,
{fatimhd,shahrina_mnordin,suziah}@petronas.com.my

Abstract. This paper highlights the effect of visual of a multimedia courseware, Black Cat Courseware (BC-C), developed for learning literature at a pre-university level in University Teknologi PETRONAS (UTP). The contents of the courseware are based on a Black Cat story which is covered in an English course at the university. The objective of this paper is to evaluate the usability and effectiveness of BC-C. A total of sixty foundation students were involved in the study. Quasi-experimental design was employed, forming two groups: experimental and control groups. The experimental group had to interact with BC-C as part of the learning activities while the control group used the conventional learning methods. The results indicate that the experimental group achieved a statistically significant compared to the control group in understanding the Black Cat story. The study result also proves that the effect of visual increases the students' performances in literature learning at a pre-university level.

Keywords: Educational courseware, literature, effectiveness, usability, visual element.

1 Introduction

The development of the Multimedia Super Corridor (MSC) has paved the way to use multimedia in education. The use of computer technology and multimedia in the teaching has been frequently discussed as there are many advantages offered by their applications. The integration of different medium such as text, graphics, images, audio, video and the digital environment has proven that these elements can increase students' concentration during the teaching and learning processes; hence improving the students' overall learning performances [1]. With the development of computer and multimedia technology, many educators have chosen this technology as a tool to improve the students' learning performances.

Multimedia has become a preferred teaching aid by most teachers when conducting their classes. This is supported by a statement *"Most school systems in the developed world are including computer literacy or similarly named programs, into the curriculum"* [2]. The use of multimedia for classroom teaching has been widely spread

H. Badioze Zaman et al. (Eds.): IVIC 2009, LNCS 5857, pp. 822–831, 2009.
© Springer-Verlag Berlin Heidelberg 2009

including those in the developing countries. Malaysia has followed a similar trend by incorporating computer technology such as multimedia into its education system.

Computer Technology Research has reported that students can retain at about 80% of what they see, hear and do activities at the same time [3]. This learning capability should be exploited as it could be an influencing factor for students' acceptance towards a multimedia courseware. To suit the students' learning style, educational software developed tends to offer simultaneous activities that can be explored by the users. In most cases, the educational software has provided some visual and audio elements to increase students' potential in understanding a topic and quite sometimes a courseware is designed to solve specific problems in learning.

A number of studies have been conducted to investigate the students' attitudes towards the use of computer aided language learning. A study conducted by [1] reported a significant increase in the subjects' attitudes towards learning English language. [4] on the other hand investigated the effects of teaching using interactive multimedia on students' perception and understanding of chemical concepts in the Netherlands. While these studies focused on general attitudes and perceptions of students towards the use of multimedia in various subjects, not much is known on how specific media such as visual element affects the students' performances especially for language courses. Such a finding is necessary as it could inform system designers on a better way to exploit various media in relations to students' learning style. Incorporation of visual elements into a language course may pose a challenge as one needs to better illustrate the text-based information into visual representations in order to obtain a correct cognitive mapping.

This paper presents a study that involves designing and developing a multimedia courseware, Black Cat Courseware (BC-C), using a storytelling approach and exploiting the video elements. This courseware is developed for learning literature at a pre-university level in University Teknologi PETRONAS (UTP). BC-C is developed based on the Black Cat story. At present, this story is being taught in class using a conventional approach in which textbook is used as the main source of teaching aid. The developed BC-C is then evaluated in terms of its effectiveness and usability. This paper highlights the effect of visual on the literature learning through the Black Cat courseware implementation.

2 Visual in Education

Visual is defined as what has been received through the sight [5]. In the education perspective, learning through visual plays an important role as a medium for students during the class session. Some students are categorized as visual learners and others are classified as audio learners. Visual learner is one who achieves the learning content more through what they have seen, rather than learning through what they have heard. According to [5], the study has shown that percentage of information received by a learner depends on their receptors.

Based on Table 1, seeing process which is a visual process has gained the highest percentage of information received as compared to the learning through hearing, touching and feeling processes. The learning through visual can be presented via the image, graphic and video. Through these elements, students are easier to imagine the actual contents. Besides, the visual component can enhance the students' ability to

Table 1. Effectiveness of Multimedia Components for Memory Storage

Medium of Learning	Process	Percentage Gained
Graphic, video, images	seeing	75
Audio (Sound)	hearing	13
Integration of texts	touching	6
Digital environment	feeling	3

remember and understand the materials. However, the other mediums that have also influenced the students are the learning through audio, integrations of text and digital environment. The use of these kinds of multimedia elements would be able to enhance the quality of teaching and learning practice [6].

[7] conducted a study on collaborative story-based learning of Japanese characters by non-native speakers. The system was based on interactive use of visual media using Augmented Reality technologies. A collaborative pen-based handwriting interface had been used to create mnemonic stories. The effectiveness of such approach was investigated through experimental design by comparing learning behavior between experimental card-using conditions and the control group. The results indicate that that story-based Kanji learning can be realized as a collaborative, constructionist and computer-assisted language learning activity. Their study indicates advantages that can be obtained through story-based learning technologies that can be used in classroom scenarios which the current study is undertaking.

3   Adoptability of the Visual Elements

Prior survey has been conducted on 95 foundations second semester students to ascertain the problem in literature learning. As the medium of instruction at UTP is English, it is compulsory for students in the Foundation program to take English language subjects: English I and English II in two consecutive semesters. English literature is part of the syllabus. However, from the survey, three areas of difficulties in the literature learning have been identified: difficulty in imagining the story plot, unfamiliar words used and boredom phenomena in literature learning.

For second semester of Foundation study, students have to cover five literature short stories. However, according to the survey, more than 90 percents of Foundation students agreed that the story of the Black Cat is the most problematic story in the course syllabus.

Besides, according to the survey, it was indicated that about 66.67% of students agreed that they cannot understand the summative text of the Black Cat story on their own, in other words they need assistance. However, 85.3% of students wish to learn the Black Cat story through a movie presentation, which will simplify the story.

The findings are in line with some of the arguments posted in the literature. [8] for example mentioned that students are very often seen as passive learners and literature lessons are very often too teacher centered which make the lessons dull and less creative. As mentioned earlier, many studies have investigated the effectiveness of using computer and multimedia in the teaching and learning activities which are mostly in language classes. However, limited number of studies has been done in incorporating multimedia elements in the teaching of English literature which this study attempts to close the gap.

Teaching literature may cause a real challenge when teaching modern language students. Creative approach is thus essential to facilitate the teaching and learning activities. As there are many benefits offered by the multimedia elements, a courseware for literature learning of the Black Cat story has been developed. This courseware has used the storytelling approach that has been presented via the animated 2D cartoon video to help students learn the literature story. Hence, through the video application, it is aimed to ease students visualized the Black Cat story since this literature story is the longest and hardest story in the syllabus. The video in BC-C is developed to represent a summative scene from a conservative story book.

Additionally, there are also some images and animated graphics presented in BC-C. As stated in Table 1, the information received gained by the visual practice is about 75%, hence, graphics, image and video are created to solve the occurred problems during the literature learning of the Black Cat.

Fig. 1 shows the interface of the montage of BC-C. As stressed by [9] the initial key to build the cognitive theory for students is through the process of getting the students' attention. Therefore the purpose of having montage play as an opening page is to capture the attention among students because montage has the unexpected eye-catching movements of animation and attractive sound.

All scenes in the courseware are arranged according to the plots of the story which basically starts with the introduction, climax, solution and ending. Students have to understand the first scene before going on to the next although BC-C provides the option to navigate to any scene by clicking on the scene button in the sub-module. Fig. 2 and 3 show the interfaces of the modules in BC-C.

Fig. 1. Interface of Montage

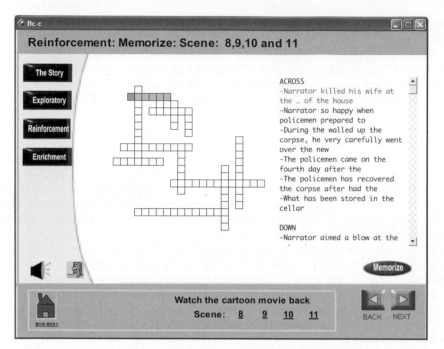

Fig. 2. Interface of Reinforcement Module

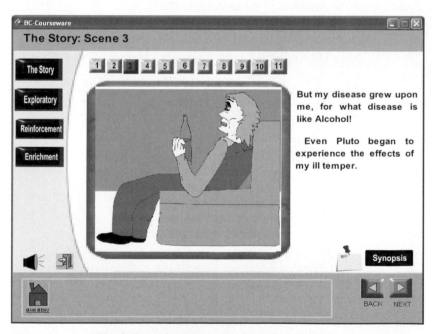

Fig. 3. Example of the interactive images in BC-C

Fig 4 presents the six main characters: the narrator, the wife, Pluto, second black cat, the crowd and the policeman. The students will be able to visualize the character through the characters shown which are not visible in the story in the text.

Fig. 4. Interface of characters in the story

4   Effectiveness and Usability Testing

An evaluation study was conducted to test the effect of multimedia (which involves mainly the visual elements) in BC-C. 60 Foundation students of UTP took part in the evaluation study. To perform this evaluation, two types of testing were carried out to examine the effectiveness and usability of BC-C.

By using the Quasi experimental design for the effectiveness evaluation, a pre-test and post-test have been carried out onto the control (X_1) and experimental (X_2) groups which involved 60 Foundation students of UTP. These pre and post-tests were based on the Black Cat comprehension questions. The results of these tests are compared to measure the students' performance before and after the treatment classes. Pre-test and post-test have been conducted onto both groups. The control group (X_1) is a treatment group consisting of students who learn the Black Cat using the conventional method while the experimental group (X_2) is a treatment group involving those students with the courseware learning.

For the usability evaluation, a set of questionnaires was distributed to the experimental groups after the students have learned the Black Cat story using BC-C. Four usability factors were used to evaluate the courseware i.e. learnability, satisfaction, efficiency and screen layout. These factors were also used to evaluate the usability of specific multimedia elements integrated into BC-C.

5 Results and Discussions

The findings from the evaluation could be analysed and presented into 3 parts: (i) the effectiveness of visual effect integrated into BC-C (ii) the usability of BC-C as a whole, and (iii) the usability of individual multimedia elements especially on the visual aspects.

5.1 Effectiveness of BC-C

Through the evaluation to examine the effectiveness of BC-C, the marks scored by both groups in pre-test and post-test were compared as depicted in Table 2.

Table 2. Pre and Post Test Results

	Pre-test	**Post-test**	**Increment**
Mean Marks	X_1= 42.96%	X_1= 61.67%	X_1= 18.70%
	X_2= 49.81%	X_2= 81.30%	X_2= 31.48%
Lowest Marks	X_1= 16.67%	X_1= 27.78%	
	X_2= 16.67%	X_2= 38.89%	
Highest Marks	X_1= 66.67%	X_1= 72.22%	
	X_2= 88.89%	X_2= 100%	

Based on Table 2, the mean marks of the pre-test and post-test for X_1 group are 42.96% and 61.67%, respectively. This shows an increment mean mark of 18.71%. However, X_2 group scored the mean marks of 49.81% for the pre-test while 81.30% for the post-test. Thus, the increment mean mark for X_2 group is 31.48% which is higher than the X_1 group.

The results shown in this study indicate that the visual elements (video, graphics and images) integrated into BC-C have improved students' performances in literature learning. Since visual learning contributes 75% of memory storage (Table 1), the effectiveness of the courseware indirectly indicates the users' acceptance towards the visual elements integrated into the system. This finding is parallel to those reported in [7] whereby the new learners of Japanese characters have shown an improved learning behaviour when visual media is introduced. In the case of BC-C, the visual elements such as those characters in the Black Cat story may have influenced the students to build a mental mapping from text-based description of the characters to their equivalent visual representations; hence, creating more interest in the learning process.

5.2 Usability of BC-C

The usability of BC-C based on the efficiency, learnability, satisfaction, and screen layout factors were evaluated using a set of questionnaires. The students responded to the questionnaire according to the Likert Scale: '5' indicates 'Strongly Agree', '4' signifies 'Agree', '3' means 'Neutral', '2' is for 'Disagree' and '1' is for 'Strongly Disagree'.

The results obtained were analysed using SPSS 11.5. The findings are presented in Fig. 5.

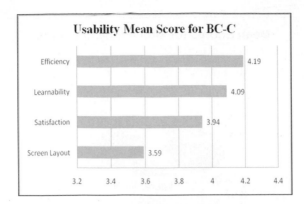

Fig. 5. The mean score for the usability factors in BC-C

From Fig. 5, the efficiency factor scored the highest mean value (4.19), followed by learnability (4.09), satisfaction (3.94) and screen layout (3.59). The average for the four usability factors is 3.95 which is more than the median scores (2.50). Overall, the usability of the courseware in a general is considered acceptable to the students.

The study findings as highlighted in Fig. 5 indicate that students agree on the efficiency of the courseware. This could be another reason students performed better when they learn English literature using BC-C as presented in Section 5.1. The high scores on the learnability factor also support this finding. Again, the visual effect may have influenced students' preferences towards BC-C as compared to the conventional method; hence, affecting their learnability pattern.

5.3 Multimedia Elements

A detailed analysis on the multimedia elements (i.e. interface, text, graphics, audio, video, animation and interactivity) incorporated into the courseware was conducted. A similar approach using questionnaires as described in Section 5.2 was used. The result of mean scores for each individual multimedia element is depicted in Fig. 6.

Fig. 6 indicates that most of the students agreed on the usefulness of interactivity in BC-C since this element scored the highest mean values. Interactivity in BC-C involves user actions interacting with the courseware in terms of dragging and dropping the images, typing, mouse movement and navigation. This finding is expected and in agreement with those reported in [2] which says, students can retain about 80% of what they see, hear, and do at the same time.

However, based on Fig. 6, out of the seven elements presented two of them could be classified under visual components i.e. graphics (and images) and video elements. In this case the total mean scores for visual components in BC-C are 7.29; thus, higher than scores for the interactivity element (3.95). The high scores for visual components indicate that students agreed on their accuracy and suitability in the courseware as the elements could assist them in visualising the story easier; thus, could have influenced their performance in the post-test.

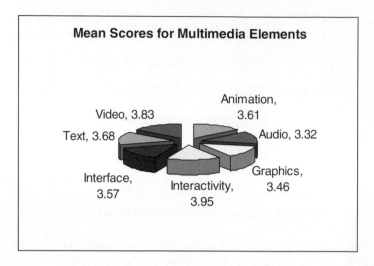

Fig. 6. The mean scores for multimedia elements in BC-C

The average mean of multimedia elements (3.63) in the evaluation is more than the median score (2.50). This finding signals that in general BC-C has successfully integrated the multimedia elements especially the visual component and interactivity element into the design. This has resulted in a more effective learning of literature story of the Black Cat.

6   Conclusion

This paper has described an evaluation on the effectiveness and usability of a multimedia courseware for English literature based on a Foundation syllabus in UTP. It addresses students' learning problem in English literature which is mainly taught using story books that heavily involves text-based description. The results of the evaluation study indicate that visuals developed in the Black Cat courseware have been beneficial and effective to the students during the literature English learning of the Black Cat story. It is shown in the evaluation study that visual elements play an important role in influencing students' performances in learning especially in literature learning at a pre-university level.

References

1. Ayres, R.: Learner attitudes towards the use of CALL. Computer Assisted Language Learning Journal 15(3), 241–249 (2002)
2. Multimedia Development Corporation,
   http://www.portalcentre.com/msc/topic/MSC+Malaysia+Milestones
   (Copyright 2008)
3. Hofsteter, F.T.: Multimedia Literacy. McGraw Hill, New York (1995)

4. Vrtacnik, M., Sajovec, M., Dolnicar, D., Pucko, C., Glazar, A., Brouwer, N.: An interactive multimedia tutorial teaching unit and its effects on student perception and understanding of chemical concepts. Westminster Studies in Education 23, 91–105 (2000)
5. Wehmeir, S., Ashby, M.: Oxford Advanced Learner's Dictionary, 6th edn. Oxford University Press, New York (2000)
6. Meng, E.A.: Pedagogi II Perlaksanaan Pengajaran. Penerbitan Fajar Bakti Sdn. Bhd. (1997)
7. Demetriadis, S., Triantafillou, E., Pombortsis, A.: A Phenomenographic Study of Students' Attitudes Toward the Use of Multiple Media for Learning. In: CM SIGCSE Bulletin, Proceeding of the 8th annual conference on Innovation and technology in computer science education ITiCSE 2003, vol. 35(3), pp. 183–187 (2003)
8. Lin, N., Kajita, S., Mase, K.: Collaborative story-based kanji learning using an augmented tabletop system, the jaltcall journal 5 (2009),
   http://www.jaltcall.org/journal/
9. Suriya Kumar, S.: A study of the motivational factors that influence the learning of literature among upper secondary school students in Negeri Sembilan. M.A. Practicum Report. Bangi: Universiti Kebangsaan Malaysia (2004)
10. Schneider, D.K.: Instructional Design Models and Methods. Slide. In: Online Learning in Diplomacy Workshop Geneva (May 30, 2006),
    http://tecfa.unige.ch/tecfa-people/schneider.html
    (December 16, 2008)

Visual Learning in Application of Integration

Afza Bt Shafie[1], Josefina Barnachea Janier[1], and Wan Fatimah Bt Wan Ahmad[2]

[1] Fundamental and Applied Sciences Department
[2] Computer & Information Sciences Department
Universiti Teknologi PETRONAS,
Bandar Sri Iskandar, 31750 Tronoh,
Perak, Malaysia
{afza,josefinajanier,fatimhd}@petronas.com.my

Abstract. Innovative use of technology can improve the way how Mathematics should be taught. It can enhance student's learning the concepts through visualization. Visualization in Mathematics refers to us of texts, pictures, graphs and animations to hold the attention of the learners in order to learn the concepts. This paper describes the use of a developed multimedia courseware as an effective tool for visual learning mathematics. The focus is on the application of integration which is a topic in Engineering Mathematics 2. The course is offered to the foundation students in the Universiti Teknologi of PETRONAS. Questionnaire has been distributed to get a feedback on the visual representation and students' attitudes towards using visual representation as a learning tool. The questionnaire consists of 3 sections: Courseware Design (Part A), courseware usability (Part B) and attitudes towards using the courseware (Part C). The results showed that students demonstrated the use of visual representation has benefited them in learning the topic.

Keywords: Educational courseware, literature, effectiveness, usability, visual element.

1 Introduction

With the advancement of multimedia technology, teaching and learning especially in mathematics can be more interesting and fun. The elements in multimedia such as text, graphics, sound, animation, and video help educators to create lessons that will interest and engage students during the learning process. Research has shown that using visuals in teaching has resulted in a greater degree of learning [1], [2]. The presence of visual elements in teaching and learning is increasing as the integration of images and visual presentations together with text in textbooks, instructional manuals, classroom presentations and computer interfaces broadens.

Visual learning is about acquiring and communicating information through illustrations, photos, diagrams, symbols, icon and other visual representative. Approaches in visual learning include visualization, colour cues, picture metaphors, concept maps, sketches, diagrams and graphic symbols [3]. Visual learning is not about just putting

H. Badioze Zaman et al. (Eds.): IVIC 2009, LNCS 5857, pp. 832–843, 2009.

related pictures on a page to illustrate text, instead, it is about well thought-out and carefully developed visual/verbal expression of content. Typically, it is about making sense of complex data using visual models.

According to Murphy [4], visual learning involves a specific set of skills. Observation allows a student to really see the object and examine its attributes, while recognition includes visual recall. Interpreting visual information leads to comprehension and understanding, perception deals with analysis and conjecture. Finally, sketching and image-making are ways for exploring ideas, communicating, and expressing creativity. These skills are useful in understanding abstract math concepts. For those students who are visual learners, these approaches provide opportunities for participating more fully in the learning process.

2 Visual in Education

Student engagement is critical to student motivation during the learning process. Mayer [5] in Elaine Huei-Lien Chen [6] suggested that active learning occurs when a learner engages in three cognitive processes:

1. Selection – the learner selects relevant words and relevant images for visual processing.
2. Organization – the learner organizes the information or the images in a meaningful way so that he/she can remember easily. The information can be arranged sequentially, hierarchically, or randomly according to the nature of information based on individual's knowledge and previous experience.
3. Integration – verbal and visual information can be linked and assist each other. The learner can process different modes of information all at once.

Active learning is also enhanced through the use of visuals. Visuals will also be able to promote a student's ability to organize and process information. Figure 1 shows how visual helps in the learning process.   Smith & Blankinship [8] highlighted

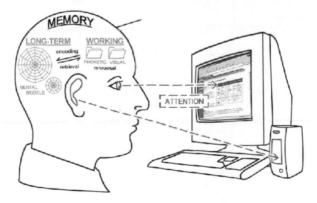

Fig. 1. How learning happens. Source: [7]

that visual can also be utilized to challenge students to think on levels that require higher order thinking skills. Mayer [9] also found that in nine different experiments, an average of 89% showed improvement in learning when relevant visual was presented. Serpil [10] observed that the visualization of mathematical objects plays a decisive role in learning as the visualization of abstract facts can be of vital contribution to a deeper understanding of mathematical concepts. By using visualization approach, many mathematical concepts can be concrete and clear for students to understand.

Allen [11] proposed that, in the context of mathematics, a student must have the ability to convert visual information into qualitative mathematical information and ultimately to quantitative information. He added that in order to gain the interest of students, it is important to create visual devices to convince students that mathematics has importance, value, and can be understood and went on to develop visual algebra. Visual algebra means the application of visual information and cues to generate and accumulate an understanding, meaning and belief in algebra where the emphasis is on identification of the right function at a given situation. It is an interactive tutorial through Web. The Visual Algebra process is shown below:

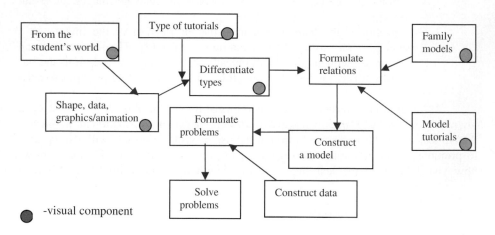

Fig. 2. The Visual Algebra process

Lambert and Carpenter [12] said, "Say it with words and you're lucky if they hear it or bother to read it. Tell your story with imagery, and it grabs attention, evokes emotion, and is more instantly processed. Sixty thousand times faster, say some researchers."

This paper presents how visual learning can be applied in teaching application of integration. A multimedia courseware has been developed for the foundation level engineering students in Universiti Teknologi PETRONAS [13]. It is based on the Engineering Mathematics II curriculum and has six modules which focused on the application of integration for area and volume. The courseware was developed using

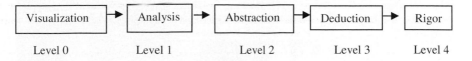

Fig. 3. Van Hiele's Thinking level

Macromedia Toolbook. The development of the courseware was guided by the Van Hiele's thinking model as depicted in Figure 3.

During visualization, the student will identify and draw the graph, while at the same time name and label it. In analysis, the student will identify and tests relationship between figures, by recalling appropriate properties in order to interpret and explain rules. Abstraction/integration where student will formulate and draw the required conclusions is carried out at level 2. The modules have been designed is such a way that the information is given in text form and some has animations. This means that students will be able to view on the screen text and the animations on the screen and has the option to listen to a narration. This is as inline with the research by [1] which has shown that visualization of the movement that are presented graphically allow for a deeper insights as well as heightened abilities to communicate data and concepts. Similarly, the developed multimedia courseware follows the visual process Algebra by Allen [11] where it includes the visual components and non-visual components shown in Figures 3, 4 and 5. The non-visual component parts are the identifying the conditions, formulation and solution of the problems while the visual parts are the graphs and animations.

3 Development of Modules

The courseware was developed with Macromedia Toolbook. It consists of five modules. The framework for each module is as follows: objectives, concept, examples, exercises and quizzes. The courseware is able to give prompts to the students' answers and feedback regarding scores obtained by them.

Each module starts with the definition of the concept; for example: Area of a plane region bounded by a curve and lines. Three different examples are given in each module. Upon clicking any of the three buttons, the student will be able to view a detailed example of each of the module. The students are able to see the graph, the area between the curves and the calculation of the bounded area. This interface helps students visualize the step by step solution to find the answer of a problem in area by integration. The presentation of this concept is shown in Figure 4(a), (b) and (c).

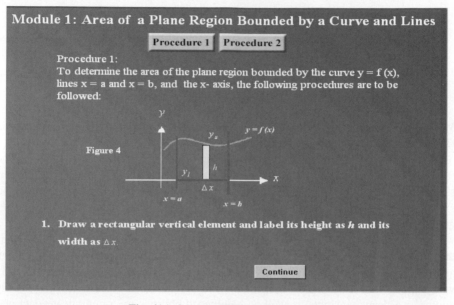

Fig. 4(a). Step 1 on Presentation on Area

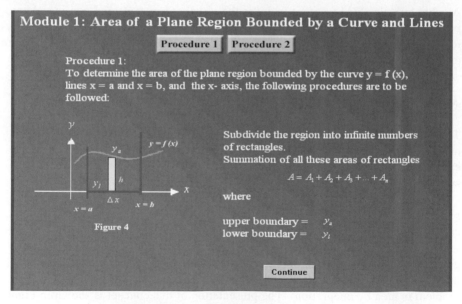

Fig. 4(b). Step 2 on Presentation on Area

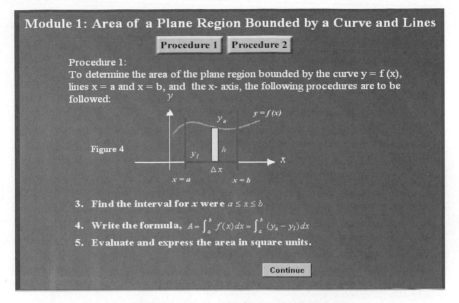

Fig. 4(c). Step 3 on Presentation on Area

This concept is further reinforced in the follow – up examples shown in Figure 5.

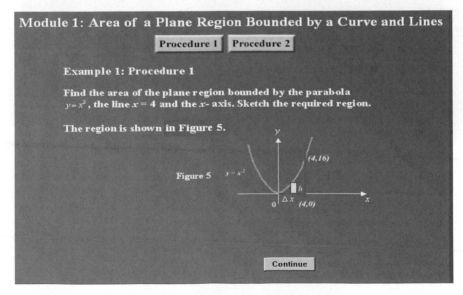

Fig. 5(a). Step 1 on Example in area by integration

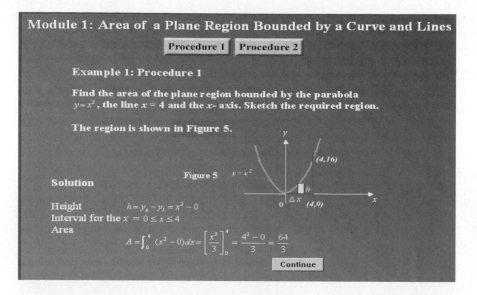

Fig. 5(b). Step 2 on Example in area by integration

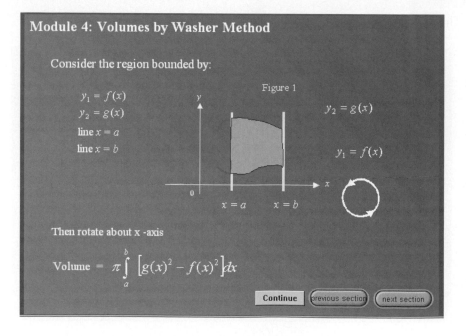

Fig. 6(a). Step 1 on Visual volume concept

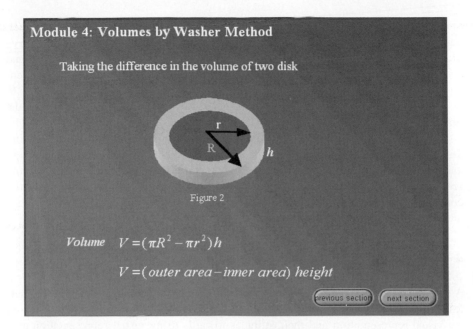

Figure 2

Fig. 6(b). Step 2 on Visual volume concept

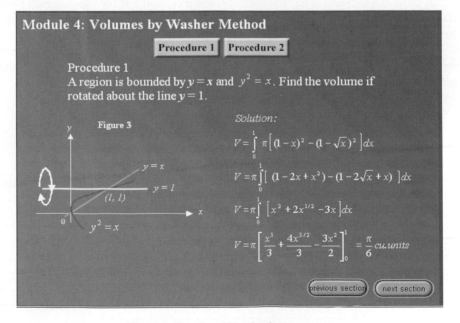

Fig. 6(c). Step 3 on Visual volume concept

These presentations can help students visualize the step by step solution to find the answer of a problem in area by integration. The presentation starts with the curve drawn, labeling its parts, then formula writing by recalling the principles learned and finally the answer. Using motion such as animation is one of the more powerful enhancements to almost any teaching functions because it shows or points to what is to be observed [11]. And once this concept is understood, the modules continue with the practice exercises and quiz.

Besides the area, there are also visual presentation on the concepts of finding volume using methods such as washer, cylindrical shell and disk method. Through animation the learners should be able to understand the concept of finding the volume using the washer method as shown in Figure 6. Immediately after the conceptual presentation, an example is shown as a follow –up for better understanding.

4   Results and Discussions

A survey was carried out to 30 students attending tutorials in Engineering Mathematics II for January 2008 semester. The objectives of the survey were to get feedback on the visual representation and their attitudes towards using visual representation as a learning tool. The questionnaire consists of 3 sections: Courseware Design (Part A), courseware usability (Part B) and attitudes towards using the courseware (Part C). A Likert scale of 1 to 5 was used: 1 is for 'most disagree' and 5 is for 'most agree'. Each respondent was given a hands-on on the courseware and after the completion of the final module; the respondent was given the survey form.

The survey showed that out of 30 students who used the courseware, 95% agree with the use of the courseware in visual learning the application of integration while only 5% strongly disagree to its usage, as shown in Figure 7.

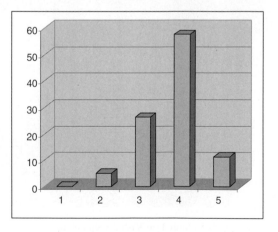

Fig. 7. Student's responses in %

Eighty eight percent (88%) of the students said they benefited in using the course-ware since it is more attractive and it helps in visualizing the concepts while only 12% said "No". These results are further supported by the mean score of 3.78 and 3.59 for Graphs and Texts, respectively, as shown in Table 1. The results also show that these components (courseware design) have played a role in learning as they can contribute to a better understanding in the topic as highlighted by Serpil [10]. In addition, 75% responded "YES" that the courseware is useful in visual learning the application of integration while 25% said "NO". This result is consistent with learnability being rated the highest (3.5) in courseware usability as shown in Table 1. These results imply that the respondents find visual representations have helped them in learning the topic.

Table 1. Survey results

Part A: Courseware Design	Mean Score
User Interface	2.95
Texts	3.59
Graphs	3.78
Interactivity	3.05
Suitability	3.19
Average	3.31
Part B: Courseware Usability	
Learnability	3.5
Performance Effectiveness	3.09
Screen Design	3.21
User Satisfaction	3.33
Average	3.28

Table 2 shows the results of the attitudes towards the courseware.

Table 2. Survey results

Questions (Part C)	Mean Score
1. I find math more interesting	4.0
2. I appreciate integration better with Courseware (CW)	3.87
3. It helps visualize concepts	3.75
4. I can analyze problems better now with use of CW	3.5
5. I am able to see relationship between the variables	3.5
6. It is easy to learn the topic by using CW	3.75
7. I learn better by CW than by book	3.85

Among the comments of the respondents are:
1.   It is able to help students to visualise the problems.
2.   It is easy to learn because the calculations shown are step by step.
3.   Its contents are good and systematic.
4.   It helps students to learn at their own pace.

On the whole, the average mean for Part A (Courseware design), Part B (Courseware usability) and Part C (attitudes) are 3.31, 3.28 and 3.71 respectively. This implies that the respondents are satisfied with the overall courseware as a learning tool. In addition, an evaluation to determine the effectiveness of the courseware as a tool for visual learning the application of integration was also done. The results of this study had been reported elsewhere [14].

5 Conclusion and Recommendation

Based on the above findings, the students have shown positive feedback towards the use of visual representation in learning the topic. Majority of them responded that they benefited because through visualization, it helped them to understand better the concepts in the application of integration. Further testing concluded that the courseware is an effective tool for visual learning the topics in area and volume by integration.

Since the experiment was only conducted for one semester and to a small group of students, it is recommended that the courseware be used for further investigation in order to ascertain the result. The contribution of this study is that the courseware could be used by the students for independent study and this will relieve instructors from the duty of conducting tutorial sessions.

Acknowledgment

The authors are grateful to the Universiti Teknologi PETRONAS with the financial support given to present the paper and our sincere thanks to Ms. Norbayah Mohd Suki for developing the courseware.

References

1. Stokes, S.: Visual Literacy in teaching and learning: A Literature perspective. Electronic Journal for the Integration of Technology in Education 1(1), 1–19 (2006)
2. Beeland, W.D.: Student Engagement, Visual Learning and Technology: Can Interactive Whiteboards Help (2002), http://www.editlib.org (June 2, 2009)
3. Armstrong, T.: Multiple Intelligence in the Classroom. Association for Supervision and Curriculum Development (1994)
4. Murphy, S.J.: Visual Learning in Elementary Mathematics, Research into Practice Mathematics. Pearson Education Inc. (2009), http://www.pearsonschool.com
5. Mayer, R.E.: The Cambridge Handbook of multimedia Learning. Cambridge University Press, New York (2005)
6. Chen, E.H.-L.: A Review of Learning Theories from Visual Literacy. Journal of Educational Computing, Design & Online Learning 5, 1–8 (Fall 2004)
7. Clark, R.: Leverage Multimedia for learning (2007), http://www.zdnetasia.com (June 20, 2009)

8. Smith, B.K., Blankinship, E.: Justifying imagery: multimedia support for learning through exploration. IBM Systems Journal 39(3/4), 749–768 (2000), http://www.galileo.peachnet.edu (retrieved June 20, 2008)

9. Mayer, R.E.: The Cambridge Handbook of multimedia Learning. New York (2005)

10. Serpil, K., Cihan, K., Sabri, I., Ahmet, I.: The role of visualization approach on student's conceptual learning (2005), http://www.clmt.plymouth.ac.uk/journal/konyalionglu.pdf (accessed date: September,2006)

11. Allen, Donald, G.: Visual Algebra with Technology, Texas, USA (2005), http://dallenmath.tamu.edu (accessed date: June 2009)

12. Lambert, M., Carpenter, M.: Visual Learning: Using images to focus Attention, evoke emotions, and enrich learning. MultiMedia & Internet@Schools 12(5), 20–24 (2005)

13. Ahmad, W.F.B.W., Shafie, A.B., Janier, J.B.: Development of a Multimedia Courseware for Visualization on Teaching and Learning: Area and Volume. Konvensyen Teknologi Pendidikan ke-19, 8–11 (2006)

14. Janier, J.B., Shafie, A.B., Wan Ahmad, W.F.B.: The Effectiveness of a Multimedia Courseware as an Alternative for Tutoring Application of Integration. Presented at 13th Asian Technology Conference in Mathematics (ATCM 2008), Suan Sunanda Rajabhat University Bangkok, Thailand (2008)

Learning Science Using AR Book: A Preliminary Study on Visual Needs of Deaf Learners

Norziha Megat Mohd. Zainuddin, Halimah Badioze Zaman, and Azlina Ahmad

Department of Information Science, Faculty of Information Science and Technology,
Universiti Kebangsaan Malaysia, 43600 Bangi, Selangor Malaysia
norzihamegt@gmail.com, hbz@ftsm.ukm.my, aa@ftsm.ukm.my

Abstract. Augmented Reality (AR) is a technology that is projected to have more significant role in teaching and learning, particularly in visualising abstract concepts in the learning process. AR is a technology is based on visually oriented technique. Thus, it is suitable for deaf learners since they are generally classified as visual learners. Realising the importance of visual learning style for deaf learners in learning Science, this paper reports on a preliminary study of on an ongoing research on problems faced by deaf learners in learning the topic on Microorganisms. Being visual learners, they have problems with current text books that are more text-based that graphic based. In this preliminary study, a qualitative approach using the ethnographic observational technique was used so that interaction with three deaf learners who are participants throughout this study (they are also involved actively in the design and development of the AR Book). An interview with their teacher and doctor were also conducted to identify their learning and medical problems respectively. Preliminary findings have confirmed the need to design and develop a special Augmented Reality Book called AR-Science for Deaf Learners (AR-SiD).

Keywords: Augmented reality, visual literacy, visual meaning, deaf learners.

1 Introduction

Augmented reality is also known as AR which allows users to view and manipulate vitural 3D objects in the real-world environment [1]. It also gives users additional information about the physical world which is not perceived by unaided human senses [2]. As shown in Fig. 1 a reality-virtuality continuum [3] describes the taxonomy that identifies how augmented reality and virtual reality are related.

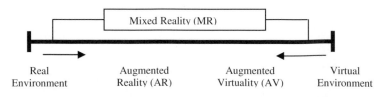

Fig. 1. Reality-Virtuality Continuum

H. Badioze Zaman et al. (Eds.): IVIC 2009, LNCS 5857, pp. 844–855, 2009.
© Springer-Verlag Berlin Heidelberg 2009

There are several advantages using AR. This is because the technology provides learners with a rich source of educational materials in a form that makes learning exciting and more realistic [4]. The educational experience offered by augmented reality is different compared to other learning materials for   reasons such as follows [5]:

i)   Support of seamless interaction between real and virtual environment.

ii)   Use of a tangible interface metaphor for object manipulation.

iii)   Ability to shift smoothly between real and virtual environment.

Besides that, augmented reality can also be easily implemented in the classroom environment. This is because it can be taught in the classroom in accordance with the teaching syllabus. At the same time, it can motivate learners, for self-learning and robust enough for personal users, using markers [6]. In addition, AR has the potential to make learning and teaching more meaningful by engaging learners in their experiential learning process.

Although augmented reality can be applied to various domain applications, the technology is projected to have more significant role in teaching and learning, particularly in learning and visualising abstract concepts in science education [7]; [8]. It is anticipated that learners can acquire knowledge better and are able to have deep impressions on the topics learned [4] through AR. Thus, the preliminary analysis conducted to acquire the software requirement specification (SRS) for the AR Book for learning Science to be developed suitable for deaf learners is highlighted in this paper.

1.1 Characteristics of Deaf Learners

Communication is an important element in every human being [9], and language is crucial in the communication process. However, this is not so for Deaf learners as deaf is a hidden disability. In most cases, deaf can only be realised when one tries to communicate with them [10],[11]. This is because they have similar physical characteristics as normal people but they communicates using sign language, lip reading, hand, body and from expressions in faces. Sign language is considered not an effective communication tool since it is exclusive to the deaf population who represents the minority in many societies. Sign language, is therefore not used extensively in many societies.

According to a genetic melecule expert for the deaf in Malaysia [12], deaf is caused by mutation or change in gen sequence, GJB2. GJB2 causes the production of protein called Connexin 26(CX26). The lack of this protein leads to deafness [13]. Hearing loss can occur in three stages: prenatal, natal and postnatal. Hearing loss can be categorised based on the decibels hearing level (dB HL) [14] as indicatedn in Table 1 .

Hearing loss can happen before or after having the adeptness speech. Fig. 2 shows when adeptness speech occurs on the left side, it is known as Prelingual. This means that, the hearing loss occurred before the adeptness speech. However, if the individual acquired adeptness speech after she or he can speak, this is called as Postlingual. This can happen as a result of an accident , which also affects the pronunciation and understanding [15].

Table 1. Deaf category and hearing loss

Deaf Category	Hearing Loss (dBHL)
Mild	26-40
Moderate	41-55
Moderate-severe	56-70
Severe	71-90
Profound	> 90

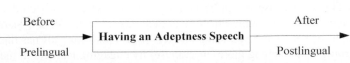

Fig. 2. Time frame to acquire a language

2 Preliminary Analysis of Study

There are 23 deaf schools in Malaysia. Based on the Department of Special Education, in 2007, there are 2,021 students in special education schools for the deaf in the country. Normally, many will perceive deaf learners to have problems in communicating. The typical consequences of this condition include significant delays in language development and academic achievement [16]. Besides that, these learners also show an obvious science visual literacy problems. This means that they do not make much accomplishment in learning science. This is illustrated in Table 2 which shows the results of *Ujian Pencapaian Sekolah Rendah* (UPSR) of science subject for the deaf students in 2007 and 2008. The number of students who failed (82.38%) is greater that the number who passed which is less than 17.63% in 2007. The same situation happens in 2008, which shows that the number of deaf students who failed is greater (84.77%) compared to those who passed (15.21%).

Table 2. UPSR result for the deaf in year 2007 and 2008

Year	Pass (%)			Fail (%)			Total Candidate
	A	**B**	**C**	**D**	**E**		
2007	2 (0.72)	9 (3.24)	38 (13.67)	41 (14.75)	188 (67.63)		278
2008	0 (0)	0 (0)	14 (15.21)	24 (26.08)	54 (58.69)		92

In Malaysia, deaf learners use the Malaysian Sign Language or known as *Bahasa Isyarat Malaysia* (BIM) to communicate. The BIM is almost the same as American Sign Language (ASL). In 1960, *Kod Tangan Bahasa Melayu* (KTBM) was introduced to special education teachers teaching the deaf by the Malaysian Education Department for the teaching of Malay. KTBM is equivalent to the Sign Exact English (SEE) used to learn English [11]. In 2003, the Malaysian Education Department introduced Science and Mathematics in English [17]. This means that, deaf students have to learn one more sign language called American Sign Language (ASL) for learning Science.

From the observation and interview conducted with teachers in deaf schools, it was found that teachers use the usual methods in teaching such as normal text books, whiteboard and computers. Besides that, teachers also use a courseware provided by the Curriculum Development Centre (CDC) in their teaching and learning. During the lessons teachers would use picture cards, posters and the like for the benefit of the deaf students. Teachers also stressed that students are also exposed to computers for experiential learning.

The trend of educational environment has changed with the advancement of learn-ingtechnologies. The shift in students' learning styles has also prompted the change from traditional methods to active construction of knowledge through mediated, im-mersion learning styles called "the neo-millennial students learning styles" [18]. One of the neo-millennial learning styles is based on Augmented Reality. The characteris-tics of the neo-millennial students' learning styles are that they show tendency for constructivist and experimental approach learning styles. They also show inclination towards social or collaborative learning. These approaches allow students to feel a sense in the virtual environment which permits them to be involved in a more blended approach of learning between the traditional teaching and new learning methods. The neo-millennial learning styles which propagates visual literacy is con-sidered suitable for deaf learners [6].

2.1 Visual Literacy

Previous study [19] indicate that there are no common definition for visual literacy. However it can be defined as the ability to recognize and understand ideas conveyed through visible action or images, as well as to be able to convey ideas or messages based on imaginary [20]. There are three categorization "sub-concepts" of visual lier-acy [20] based on the directionality of visual literacy components: visual learning, visual thinking and visual communication, which can be observed in Fig. 3.

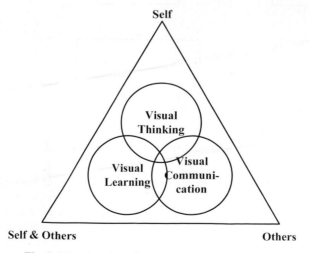

Fig. 3. Directionality of Visual Literacy Components

Due to the 'sub-concepts' of visual literacy, it is said that visual learning refers to visulisation of objects through images [21] whilst visual thinking refers to the acquisition and construction of knowledge as a result of interaction with a visual phenomena [21]. Visual communication is defined as using visual symbols such as pictures and graphics to express ideas and convey meaning. However, these visual learning concepts can be overlapped and can exist simultaneously. There are three theories related to visual literacy: information processing theory, dual-coding theory, and multimedia theory. These theories are basically related to cognitive processes that are frequently addressed in the field of visual literacy [22]. Visual literacy is a gradual process of gaining greater sophistication of perception, conception and visual and linguistic vocabulary. It is also known that visual literacy can be learned and practiced [23], [24]. Since deaf learners have been categorised as visual learners, it make sense that a visual literacy approach using AR would be a suitable approach to be adopted.

2.2 Scientific Acquisition in Science Process

Scientific acquisition is important in conducting activities which are based on science principles [25]. The scientific acquisition is divided into two: acquisition in science process and manipulative acquisition. The acquisition in science process is also divided in two components; basic and integrated. This can be seen in Fig. 4.

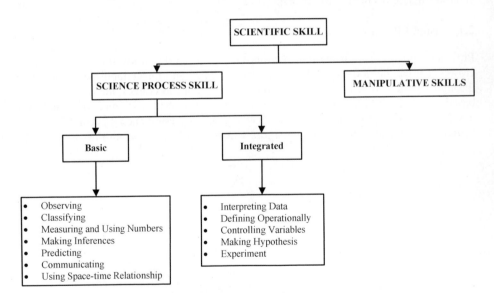

Fig. 4. Scientific acquisition in Science Curriculum

The basic acquisition process in science curriculum for level 5 are divided into five fields of study. There are universal life, physical life, material life, earth and universe, and lastly technological world. Microorganisms topic falls under 'universal life'. Based on this topic, the science process skills involved are observing and classifying. However, with deaf learners, the basic science process has to begin with 'observing and communicating', and this is what will be discussed in the findings section of this paper.

3 Research Methodology

The research methodology adopted in this study was the Iterative Triangulation Participatory Development methodology. This involved preliminary study to ascertain the SRS and then design the system (SDS) in order that development of the system after that can take place. As mentioned earlier this paper highlights this preliminary study. Firstly, it involved identifying the difficult topic for deaf learners at level 5. Microorganisms was found to be difficult to learn by these learners [26]. The ethnographic observational approach and interview technique were used to acquire the appropriate data.

3.1 Sample of Study

Three groups of respondents were involved and they were: education officers, teachers and deaf learners. The officers came from three departments which were related to education of deaf learners. They are officers from the Education Technology Department, Curriculum Development Centre and Special Education Department. The teachers too comprised of three groups: Science teachers teaching the deaf; teachers who coordinators Science subjects and the from the head teachers of deaf schools. The deaf learners comprised of three deaf students : 1 male and 2 females from the special education schools for the deaf in Kuala Lumpur. The deaf learners were selected with the help of the teachers. They are all 12 years old, and considered as achievers by their teachers. They are now in Year 5. The teachers consider their achievements as on par with one another.

3.2 Instruments

Three instruments were used in this study: two interview schedules namely i) *Skedul Temu Bual untuk Pegawai Pendidikan* (STBP) for the education officers; and the *Skedul Temu Bual untuk Guru* (STBG) for teachers and ii) is the observational checklist or *Senarai Semakan pelajar Pekak* (SSPP) for the deaf learners.

3.3 Research Procedure

The research procedure was conducted based on three phases as follows:

Phase1: obtain written permission from the Ministry of Education to work with the deaf learners who are the protected population from the selected deaf schools.

Phase 2: The education officers and teachers of the deaf learners were interviewed based on the instruments built: STBP and the STBG respectively.

Phase 3: Working with chosen deaf learners. A video was used to videotape the activities so that the researcher can make analysis of the learners learning behaviour. The tasks involved four aspects: i) identifying text, pictures, sign language and finger spelling. Words related to the difficult topic identified earlier (microorganisms) were used for them to identify; ii) using pictures, learners had to make the sign language and spell using finger spelling; write the word and choose the text given on the card;

iii) identify sign language and iv) identify finger spelling. All the activities conducted were related to the topic on microorganisms.

All the data collected were analysed qualitatively.

4   Results of Study

Findings of the interviews conducted with the education officers used the STBP. The officers came from three departments related to the education of deaf learners. Table 3 shows results of the interview.   ported that there were no current courseware in science that were developed particularly for the deaf students. Besides that, the deaf students used the same syllabus and courseware as normal children did in normal primary school. It can been seen in Table 3.

Table 3. Results based on   interview with education officers

Item	Problems
Material	• There are still no coursewares or televisyen programmes developed specifically for deaf students especially in Science. • Have to use the same materials as normal students do. • No expertise to develop this kind of courseware.
Curriculum	• Deaf students are using the same curriculum as normal students in primary school.

Findings of the interview conducted with several science teachers teaching   with the deaf students were able to portray problems faced by deaf learners as can been seen in Table 4.

Table 4. Main problem faced by the deaf students in learning science

Item	Problems	How teachers overcome this problem
Students	• Difficult to understand abstract words • Limited cognitive ability	• Using pictures because deaf students are visual learners. • Repeat the syllabus
Teaching Method	• Using the current traditional method	• Have to be creative in preparing the teaching materials
Material	• No specific courseware	• Have to use different sign languages to facilitate their teaching

From the interviews conducted, generally it can be said that the problems faced by the deaf learners are related to science literacy which are concerned with the ability to read, write, count and also skills in science process. These skills are divided into two; basic and integrated. One example of the problems faced by deaf learners wasthat they were not able to understand the scientific words such as habitat, photosynthesis, energy, alkaline and microorganism. These are abstractive and thus difficult for them to visualize. To overcome this, teachers used pictures to explain to them the meaning. However, it is not an effective method as the students have limited cognitive capability. To overcome this teachers have always to repeat the topics already taught. In addition, their language proficiency is also a barrier as they mostly speak their respective native language . Thus, they take longer time to read an instruction, sentence or paragraph [28]; [29];[15];[30]. In addition, they lack in critical and creative thinking which are crucial in learning science. To make it worst, there is no one sign language used to explain the concepts (be it the American Sign Language (ASL), *Kod Tangan Bahasa Melayu* (KTBM) or even the *Bahasa Isyarat Malaysia* (BIM).

Although teachers use multimedia coursewares in CD-ROM which is supplied by the Curriculum Development Centre, they still have to use sign languages to facilitate their teaching because the CD-ROM were all developed for the normal learners. Many teachers find the CDs interesting. However, previous research also shows that even the many coursewares available are not suitable for normal students [31],[32], what more the deaf. Initial work with the three samples (Student 1, 2 and 3) of the study can be seen in Table 5. The work involved i) visual thinking which required them to identify text and pictures; and ii) visual communication which involved them to use appropriate sign language, finger spelling and written text. Data was collected using the SSPP.

Table 5. Observation and interaction with three samples (student 1, 2 and 3) on Visual Literacy

Student 1

Observe	Visualization (%)		Visual Communication (%)		
	Chose Text	Picture	Sign language	Finger spelling	Written text
1. Text	-	75	100	100	100
2. Picture	100	-	75	75	75
3. Sign language	100	100	-	25	25
4. Finger spelling	100	100	100	-	75

Student 2

Observe	Visualization(%)		Visual Communication(%)		
	Chose Text	Picture	Sign language	Finger spelling	Written text
1. Text	-	75	100	100	100
2. Picture	100	-	75	75	75
3. Sign language	100	100	-	25	25
4. Finger spelling	100	100	50	-	50

Student 3

Observe	Visualization (%)		Visual Communication(%)		
	Chose Text	Picture	Sign language	Finger spelling	Written text
1. Text	-	75	100	75	75
2. Picture	100	-	100	75	75
3. Sign language	75	100	-	75	75
4. Finger spelling	100	100	100	-	75

From the table above, it can be observed that the three students share some similar characteristics as follows:

i.   Deaf students can visualize better compared to verbal communication.
ii.   They have a good ability in recognizing pictures and text but not in sign languages and finger spelling.
iii. They take longer time to recognize text compared to pictures.
iv.   They cannot understand abstract words related to living things and microorganisms.
v.   If they can spell the text by using finger spelling, they can also can write the text.
vi.   They can spell simple words by using finger spelling and write the words.
vii. They have problems with complex words.

Table 6 illustrates the mistakes done by the three samples (student 1, 2 and 3)

Table 6. Mistakes were made by three respondents

Item given	Mistakes
Text	Cocount tree
Picture	Microorganis, microormamis, *ketam* (crab)
Sign language	Melon water
Finger spelling	Micros, microorpe, grasshoper

5   Discussion and Recommendation

Below are the strategies for improving visual literacy among deaf learners and the proposed AR Book for deaf learners in learning science on the topic Microorganisms. Various strategies can be employed to improve the visual literacy for the deaf students as follows:

- Students need to learn in visual and teacher need to teach in visual
- Use colour graphics
- Young learners need to taught using simple graphics
- Use short texts
- Combine text with appropriate graphics
- Use sign language

In addition, if learners already have prior knowledge, visual literacy strategies can be more effective in the learning process. It would help if the deaf learners are exposed to many aspects in the environment by their parents to increase their prior knowledge.

5.1   Proposed AR Book in Science for Deaf Learners

An attempt to help deaf learners in visual literacy in acquiring science and science process skills, has prompted the researchers to develop as 'augmented reality book' based on a courseware to help deaf learners in understanding the topic on microorganisms. Thus, the 3D environment courseware called AR book for Deaf learners in Science (AR-SiD) will be developed. Based on previous works, AR books can be a good learning medium to support low ability learners [33]. AR book can also be enhanced by doing interactive visualization, animations, 3D graphics and simulations [34].Visual literacy for the deaf in the end, involves processes in visualsing: visual learning, visual thinking, and visual communication which they will respond by answering questions using sign language, fingger spelling or written text. It is anticipated that AR book with interactive 3D-visualisation applications can enhance better understanding of abstractive contents in science that can make them more active and engaging learners in acquiring the scientific skills required.

6 Conclusion

This research aims to develop an augmented reality AR book called AR-SiD for deaf learners in learning science, particularly on the topic Microorganisms. The book is useful for visualizing abstract concepts in learning science, especially deaf learners are visually oriented. The preliminary study conducted with the purpose of acquiring data for software requirement specification (SRS) was conducted using various instruments such as STBP, STBG and SSPP. Analysis carried out showed that deaf learners shared strong characteristics as visual learners and they have visual literacy problems particularly in learning science and in acquiring science process skills. It is expected that he 3D environment courseware called AR book for Deaf learners in Science (AR-SiD), specially designed and developed for deaf learners will help them acquire visual literacy for learning science and acquiring the appropriate science process skills.

References

1. Dunser, A., Hornecker, E.: Lesson from an AR book study. In: First international conference of tangible and embedded interaction (TEI 2007), Baton Rouge, Louisiana, USA (2007)
2. Sherman, R.W., Craig, A.B.: Understanding Virtual Reality. Morgan Kaufmann Publishers, San Francisco (2003)
3. Milgram, P., Kishino, F.: A Taxonomy of Mixed Reality Visual Displays. IEICE Transactions on Information Systems, E77-D(12) (1994)
4. Lui, W., et al.: Mixed Reality for fun learning in primary school. In: Lui, W., et al. (eds.) ACE 2006. ACM, Hollowood (2006)
5. Billinghurst, M.: Augmented Reality in Education (2002),
   http://www.newhorizons.org/strategies/technology/
   billinghurst.htm (cited, 2008 13 March)
6. Lui, W., et al.: Mixed reality classroom - learning form entertainment. In: DIMEA 2007. ACM Press, Perth (2007)
7. Awang Rambli, D.R., Sulaiman, S., Nayan, M.Y.: A Portable Augmented Reality Lab. In: 1st International Malaysian Educational Technology Convention (IMETC 2007). Meta, Skudai (2007)
8. Said, M.N.H.M., Ismail, N.B.: Overview of open source Augmented Reality Toolkit. In: 1 st International Malaysian Educational Technology Convention (IMETC 2007). Meta, Skudai Johor Malaysia (2007)

9. Budiman, H.B.: Semiotik dalam Bahasa Isyarat. In: Dewan Bahasa, pp. 18–20. Dewan Ba-
    hasa dan Pustaka, Kuala Lumpur (2008)
10. Yusoff, A., Mohamed, C.R.: Memartabatkan bahasa orang pekak: Konsep komunikasi, ba-
    hasa, pertuturan, isyarat dan perkaitannya dengan komunikasi orang pekak. In: Interan-
    tional Seminar on Sign Language Research. 2009: Faculty of language and lingustic, Uni-
    versity of Malaya (2009)
11. Jimadie, M.: Industri Pendidikan Bahasa Isyarat di Malaysia. In: Dewan Bahasa, Kuala
    Lumpur. pp. 16–17 (2008)
12. Ali Salim, M.: Mendengarkan Suara Tunakerna. In: Dewan Bahasa, p. 24. Dewan Bahasa
    dan Pustaka, Selangor (2008)
13. Zelante, L., et al.: Connexin26 mutations associated with the most common form of non-
    syndromic neurosensory autosomal recessive deafness (DFNB1) in Mediterraneans. Hu-
    man Molecular Genetics 6(9), 1605–1609 (1997)
14. Persekutuan Orang Pekak Malaysia, Bahasa Isyarat Malaysia. Persekutuan Orang Pekak
    Malaysia, Kuala Lumpur (2000)
15. Yusoff, A., Mohamed, C.R.: Proses Pendengaran dan Implikasi Kecacatan Pada Bahasa.
    In: Dewan Bahasa, pp. 54–59. Dewan Bahasa dan Pustaka, Kuala Lumpur (2002)
16. Yoshinaga-Itano, C., et al.: Language of Early and Later-identified Children with Hearing
    Loss. Pendiatrics Official Journal of the American Academy of Pendiatrics 102(5), 1161–
    1171 (2006)
17. San, G.S., Ahmad, R.B., Kim, W.T.: Persepsi Guru Tentang Pengajaran dan Pembelajaran
    Sains dan Matematik Dalam Bahasa Inggeris (PPSMI) Di Daerah Johor Baharu 2005. In:
    Seminar Pendidikan 2005. UTM, Skudai (2005)
18. Dede, C.: Planning for neomillennial learning styles. Journal of Educase Quartely 28(1),
    7–12 (2005)
19. Braden, A.R.: Visual Literacy. In: Jonassen, D.H. (ed.) The handbook of research for edu-
    cation communications and technology. AECT, Washington, DC (1996)
20. Aanstoos, J., Academy, C.: Visual Literacy: An Overview. In: 32nd Applied Imagery Pat-
    tern Recognition Workshop (AIPR 2003). IEEE Computer Society, Los Alamitos (2003)
21. Seels, B.: Visual Literacy: The Defination Problem. In: Moore, D.M., Dwyer, F.M. (eds.)
    Visual Literacy: A Spectrum of Visual Learning, pp. 97–112. Educational Technology
    Publications, Englewood Cliffs (1994)
22. Chen, E.H.-L.: A review of learning theories from visual literacy. Journal of Educational
    Computing, Design & Online Learning 5, 1–8 (Fall 2004)
23. Stokes, S.: Visual Literacy in Teaching and Learning: A Literature Perspective. Electronic
    Journal for the Integration of Technology in Education 1(1), 10–19 (2002)
24. Bamford, A.: The Visual Literacy White Paper (2003)
25. Hiang, P.S.: Pedagogi Sains 1 Kurikulum Sains, 2nd edn. Kumpulan budiman Sdn Bhd,
    Kuala Lumpur (2001)
26. Zainuddin, N.M., Zaman, H.B.: Augmented Reality in Science education for deaf students:
    Preliminary Analysis. In: Regional Conference on Special Needs Education 2009. Faculty
    of Education, University of Malaya (2009)
27. McLoughlin, C., Krakowski, K.: Technological tools for visual thinking: What does the re-
    search tell us? In: Apple University Consortium Academic and Developers Conference.
    James Cook University, Townsville (2001)
28. Adamo-Villani, N., Carpenter, E., Arns, L.: 3D Sign Language Mathematics In Immersive
    Environment. In: Proceedings of the 15th IASTED International Conference Applied
    Simulation and Modelling, Rhodes, Greece (2006)
29. Raugust, K.: Teaching the Deaf Through Animation. Animation World Magazine (2006)

30. Mohamed, J.K.A.: Pendidikan Khas Untuk Kanak-kanak Istimewa. PTS Professional Publishing, Kuala Lumpur (2007)
31. Ubaidullah, N.H.: Perisian kursus multimedia dalam literasi (D-Matematika) untuk pelajar disleksia. In: Fakulti Teknologi dan Sains Maklumat. Bangi, Universiti Kebangsaan Malaysia (2007)
32. Abd Kader, S.F., Ismail, M.: Comprehending a story among deaf children: Is it ICT or conventional? In: 2nd IMETC 2008. Malaysian Educational Technology Association (META), Ms Garden Kuantan (2008)
33. Dunser, A., Hornecker, E.: Lesson from an AR book study. In: 1st Interantional conference of Tangible and embedded interaction (TEI 2007). Baton Rouge, Louisiana (2007)
34. Shelton, E.B.: Augmented Reality and education, current projects and potential for classroom learning. In: New Horizons for Learning, New Horizons, US (2002)

Usage-Centered Design Approach in Design of Malaysia Sexuality Education (MSE) Courseware

Chan S.L. and Jaafar A.

Department of Information Science,
Faculty Technology and Information Science,
National University of Malaysia,
43600 UKM Bangi,
Selangor DE, Malaysia
leoprudencecsl@live.com, aj@ftsm.ukm.my

Abstract. The problems amongst juveniles increased every year, especially rape case of minor. Therefore, the government of Malaysia has introduced the National Sexuality Education Guideline on 2005. An early study related to the perception of teachers and students toward the sexuality education curriculum taught in secondary schools currently was carried out in 2008. The study showed that there are big gaps between the perception of the teachers and the students towards several issues of Malaysia sexuality education today. The Malaysia Sexuality Education (MSE) courseware was designed based on few learning theories approach. Then MSE was executed through a comprehensive methodology which the model ADDIE integrated with Usage-Centered Design to achieve high usability courseware. In conclusion, the effort of developing the MSE is hopefully will be a solution to the current problem that happens in Malaysia sexuality education now.

Keywords: Sexuality Education; Learning Theories; ADDIE; Usage-Centered Design; Usability.

1 Introduction

Sex education is education which increases the knowledge of the functional, structural, and behavioural aspects of human reproduction. However, sexuality education is not restricted to the narrow focus of the traditional definition of sex education. Sexuality education is lifelong process of acquiring information and forming attitudes, beliefs, and values about identities, relationships and intimacies. It addresses the biological, socio-cultural, psychological, and spiritual dimensions of sexuality from (i) the cognitive domain, (ii) the affective domain, (iii) the behavioural domain, including the skills to communicate effectively and make responsible decision [6].

Administrators, educators, parents and community leaders stated that a sexuality education program is needed to reduce sexually transmitted infection (STI), to stop pre-marital pregnancy, to control promiscuity, and to eliminate all other undesirable hanky-panky. However, there are at least three better reasons for sexuality education than those typically given: (i) sexuality education can treat sexuality in its proper

H. Badioze Zaman et al. (Eds.): IVIC 2009, LNCS 5857, pp. 856–867, 2009.
© Springer-Verlag Berlin Heidelberg 2009

perspective and sexual adjustment is part of total personality adjustment, (ii) sexuality education can place aspects of life in true perspective rather than people receiving a distorted view of life through the mass media, (iii) sexuality education can give factual information that will help reduce many misconceptions [1]. It is then possible for the learner to gain insight and understanding that will assist responsible decision-making. Furthermore, Vandemoortele and Delamonica described sex education as social vaccine to HIV/AIDS [16].

2 Sexuality Education in Malaysia

Sexuality topics are considered taboo and against the cultural and religious norms of Malaysia society. Hence, sexuality topics seldom been discussed among Malaysia citizen openly. Although sexuality education has been introduced indirectly to Malaysian Secondary School and Primary School in 1989 and 1994 consecutively, but the topic was absorbed in Science, Additional Science, Biology, Islam and Moral education subjects. This effort however does not appear to be good enough as sexual transmitted diseases such like Human Papilloma Virus (HPV) and HIV/AIDS seem increasing every years. It was reported in 2007 that 70 percent of cervix cancer cases that caused by HPV were transmitted through sexual activity. Furthermore, 64 percent of Malaysian women contracted HIV/AIDS through sexual transmission in 2002. Thus, unlike the case for Malaysian men, the main risk for Malaysian women is through unsafe sex, either from a regular sex partner, or from multiple partners [15].

Furthermore, the estimation of women been raped among 10,000 Malaysia women from 2000 to 2008 increases every year, as shown in Table 1 below. Situation getting worse when report showed 73.3 percent of the rape victims and 10 per cent of the rapists were below 18 years old. This happened possibly because of a lot of the Malaysian especially teenagers do not understand the concept of statutory rape. Rape means that a person who has sexual relationship with below sixteen years of age girl, although with or without her consent as showed in Section 375 (f) penalty law of Malaysia. The main reason of this crime type is lack of education.

Realizing the social problems amongst juveniles especially school children are increasing, the National Sexuality Education Guideline was outlined in 2005 by the

Table 1. Estimation of women been raped among 10,000 women 2000-2008

Year	Women been raped (Among 10,000 women)
2000	1.07
2001	1.15
2002	1.19
2003	1.21
2004	1.39
2005	1.51
2006	1.92
2007	2.38
2008	3.64

government of Malaysia. The aim is to provide knowledge and skills to cope with the physical and emotional changes they undergo as well as to maintain healthy relationships with family members and other members of the community. It is also to avoid the 4Ms; misinformation, misconception, misconduct and misguidance. However, it is not taught as an independent subject but absorbed in existing subjects such as Physical and Health Education, Science, Additional Science, Biology, Islamic Studies and Moral Studies. The guideline contains six components; (i) human development, (ii) relationship, (iii) marriage and family, (iv) interpersonal skills, (v) sexual health and behaviour, and (vi) society and culture. The targeted groups for the education are in five age categories; (i) four to six-year olds (pre-school), (ii) seven to nine-year olds (children), (iii) 10 to 12 year-olds (early teens), (iv) 13 to 18 year-olds (teenagers) and 19 year-olds and above (adults such as university students, parents and old folks).

3 Initial Study

An initial study was carried out on the target users on beginning of 2008. The users of the courseware are the students, and teachers. Randomly, 43 students (above 15 years of age) from 2 secondary schools were selected from various races, religions, cultures and backgrounds. At the same time, 28 teachers from Science, Biology, Islam Religion and Moral Education subjects were volunteered as respondents for the study also.

Surprisingly, the perceptions of both respondents, the teachers and the students, were very much diverse from each other. For example, 53.6 percent of the teachers thought that the knowledge prepared by the current curriculum is more than sufficient for student, but on the other hand 58.2 percent of students said that the sexual knowledge provided by the current sexual education curriculum is inadequate for them. The study also showed that 50 percent of the teachers have an inclination to state that most of the teenagers acquired the sexual knowledge through pornographic sources; however, only 14 percent of the students are of the same opinion. Furthermore, about 33 percent of the students said that they acquired most of the knowledge about sexual education from the (i) friends, (ii) mass media and (iii) teachers.

Most of the students point out that their parents are usually reluctant to discuss the related subject and wanted their children to acquire them from school. Obviously, this data is in tandem with the reason why the total of 42.8 percent teachers and 37.3 percent students quoted that the current Malaysia sexuality education is towards teacher-centered learning in school only. As a conclusion, the early study on respondents' perceptions, showed that Malaysian sexuality education in schools is very important and requires assistance from teaching and learning aids specifically interactive multimedia courseware. Therefore, MSE could play a main role in assisting the students and teachers in managing the weaknesses of the current style sexuality education and avoid misinformation, misconception, misconduct and misguidance among the students.

4 Methodology

Methodology is a set of tools, techniques, procedures and investigative methods, used to collect, store, analyze and present information. To create a comprehensive research

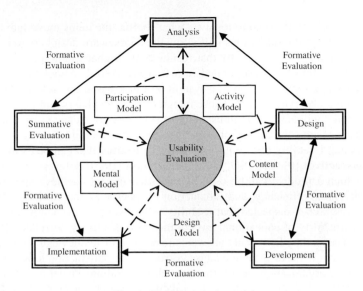

Fig. 1. Chan & Azizah model

methodology, the ADDIE model was integrated with a usage-centered design (USD) to achieve one goal, that is, high usability evaluation. The methodology model was given a name as Chan & Azizah model that contains several phases and models as shown in Figure 1.

The ADDIE (analysis, design, development, implementation, and evaluation) model is an instructional or prescriptive theories, which gave directions or guidelines for actions to be taken that would lead to a certain result [13]. The ADDIE model is an organized and systematic approach that allows the developer to save time, energy and cost [14]. However, there are seven common weaknesses of ADDIE [10]; (1) Comprehensive up-front analysis is often unrealistic, (2) Analysis often overlook essential success factors, such as who is in charge or what hidden goals are, (3) Specifications and even storyboards miscommunication, (4) Creativity becomes a nuisance to schedule, (5) Downstream insights identify "faults" that are squashed or lead to embroilment, (6) Performance outcomes are rarely measured, designs therefore focus on what is measured, and (7) Posttests are insensitive measures, but become outcome targets. Hence, to overcome the weaknesses of ADDIE, formative evaluation is carried out between each phase of ADDIE which are integrated with USD in Chan & Azizah model. Therefore, the last phase was named as summative evaluation in Chan & Azizah model.

USD is an approach to user interface design based on a focus on user task and usage pattern. USD is a systematic, model-driven approach to improve product usability. A few simple but powerful essential models of user roles, tasks, and interface content guide the user interface design towards a better fit with the real needs of users. Often, the result is also smaller, simpler systems that nevertheless fulfill all the genuine functional requirements [2]. Essential models are abstract, simplified, and generalized in comparison to concrete or physical models that represent designs literally [12]. Essential models such as participation model, activity model, content model, and design model are disposed to resolve "what" before the items move into the direction of "how". Such considerations will allow the courseware designers to understand their user's requirement profoundly that resulted in a higher usable product. Concurrently, a mental model is incorporated into Chan & Azizah model that enables the user establishing a representation of a system or a task based on previous and current experiences and observation [17]. Those integration of the phases and models in Chan & Aizzah model will ensure a high usability of sexuality courseware produced.

Usability measures the quality of a user's experience when interacting with a product or a system. Usability is a multi-dimensional construct that can be examined from various perspectives [9]. The ISO 9241-11 definition (1994) defines usability as "the extent to which a product can be used by specified users to achieve specified goals with effectiveness, efficiency, and satisfaction in specified context of use" [8]. However, other researcher suspected that usability (effectiveness, efficiency, and satisfaction) and learnability of educational environment are positively correlated [5]. Effectiveness is measured by how many answers are correct, efficiency can be measured by how much time it takes to complete a task correctly, and satisfaction looks at the areas of ease of use, organization of information, clear labelling, visual appearance, contents, and error corrections such as the Likert scale and questionnaires. However, learnability is measured by how quickly and pleasantly a new user can begin efficient and error-free interaction with the system [11].

4.1 Analysis Phase

In the analysis phase, the instructional problems were clarified. The goals and objective were established. The users of the MSE multimedia courseware are students and stakeholders (teachers and the Ministry of Education) of the lower secondary Science subject. The research purpose is to develop a highly usability research methodology and multimedia courseware. Furthermore, such participation model which involved user role and content map gives a quick overview of the content where the system takes place and provide deep understanding on users' characteristics and environment. User role is a model that abstractly represents a relationship between the users and the system, whereas, participation map represents the participants and their relationships with each other and with the various artifacts involved in the activity [2]. Based on the study carried out on the content, the characteristics and criteria of a teacher, the user role of MSE was obtained as shown in Table 2. MSE works as a tutorial courseware that involves storytelling approach of learning and testing modules as shown in Figure 2.

Table 2. User role MSE

Education and teacher role	
Context	Most education activities undertaken in the classroom, face-to-face with students and ending with performance testing.
Characteristics	Relatively complex task which requires professional training, perform learning activities and inculcate student for study. Performance improved with experience increased.
Criteria	Understand students' cognitive level, attractive presentation; ensure that every student gains new and more accurate knowledge than before.

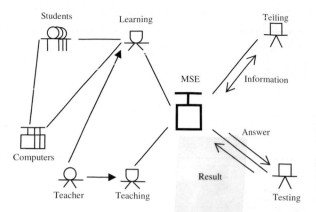

Fig. 2. Participation map MSE

4.2 Design Phase

In the design phase, the instructional strategies are used. The detailed strategies are shown with the activity model that contains task case and activity task map. A task case represents a single, discrete user intention in his interaction with a system in a complete and meaningful way to specify the user related role. Furthermore, an activity map represents relevant activity and interrelation among activities. During formative evaluation, iterative reviews on task case and activity task map of MSE fulfilled user role and participation map of MSE. Table 3 shows task case of MSE. Realizing the importance of the learning theories in MSE courseware, Conditions of Learning concept and Hermann Brain Dominance Instrument (HBDI) model were adapted in the activity map of MSE as actions and tasks as shown in Figure 3.

HBDI is a model claims to measure and describes thinking preferences in people. HDBI is a cognitive style module which shows process thinking happening in the human brain based on specific functions in four parts [7]. Herrmann identifies four different modes of thinking: (i) Analytical thinking, (ii) Sequential thinking, (iii) Interpersonal thinking, and (iv) Imaginative thinking. To fulfill and maximize the specific functions in the four parts for better learning process, a technique called Brain-Compatible Classrooms was described where learning should start with (i) the creation of a rich environment and an emotionally safe climate, (ii) the teaching of life skills and concepts from novice level to expert level, (iii) the construction of meaning with intense, active involvement of the learners, (iv) and the fostering application and transfer within metacognititive reflection [3]. In the mean time, the Conditions of Learning showed the nine instructional sequence of events will happen during learning, it comprises: (1) Gaining attention, (2) Informing learner about the objective, (3) Stimulating recall of prerequisite learning, (4) Presenting the stimulus material, (5) Providing learning guidance, (6) Eliciting the performance, (7) Providing feedback about performance, (8) Assessing performance, and (9) Enhancing retention and transfer [4].

Table 3. Task case MSE

User action	System responsibility
	1. Show all modules
2. Choose learning modules	
	3. Display learning modules
4. Choose exercise module	
	5. Display exercise module
6. Answer exercise module	
	7. Check answers
	8. Display wrong answered questions

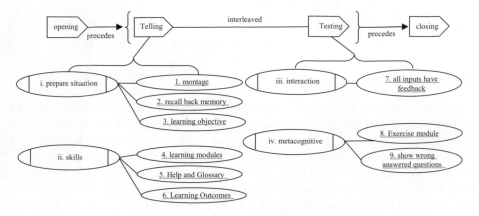

Fig. 3. Activity map of MSE

4.3 Development Phase

In the development phase, the content model is designed and developed. The content model comprises an abstract prototype and a navigation map. An abstract prototype is an overall organization and design architecture of software applications without any drawing component or detailing layout. Abstract prototypes consist of an interface content model describing the contents of the various contexts within which users interact with the system. In addition, a context navigation map shows how users move from one context to another in the course of enacting use cases. Figure 4 show the content model of MSE where abstract prototype in left side and navigation map in right side. Formative evaluation in this phase was to review and make sure the architecture design of MSE can perform as task case and activity map of MSE.

4.4 Implementation Phase

Implementation phase is a phase where the courseware is executed as it is planned in the early phases. All six multimedia elements such as text, graphic, animation, audio, video and navigation are put together to develop MSE prototype, namely design model. Software such as Adobe Illustrator for digital drawing, Adobe Audition for

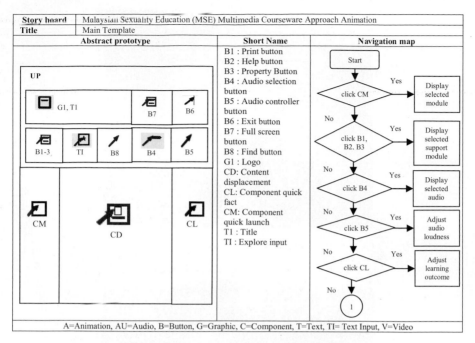

Fig. 4. Content model MSE

digital audio editing, Adobe Flash for animation, and object oriented programming Action Script are very important in this phase. Additionally, formative evaluation was conducted to ensure the prototype is free from errors and problems.

Figure 5 shows the main menu of MSE. It was one of the efforts to prepare environment where the students could start learning. A montage is also included. Description of all MSE modules and main navigation system are displayed and provided in the main menu MSE. This will ensure the users have the basic idea of the whole MSE design structure at very beginning. In addition, USD allows the users to choose retrieve and link to the module that they want quickly and concisely.

User interface metaphor is a process of representing the computer system with objects and events from a non-computer domain, which is a familiar process in the interactive educational multimedia. This technique is applied to the system and to enhance the easy to learn, use, remember, enjoyable and etc.

Every learning modules of MSE are divided into four steps, namely Introduction, Content, Activity, and Evaluation. Learning objective and learning outcome are shown in Introduction step, followed by Content step where students learn the skill of acquiring and expanding old and limited knowledge in their short-term memory. In Activity step, the students are provided with several small games. Drag and drop or exploring game and quizzes not just only ensures the users have active involvement and interaction with the system, but they also rehearse the knowledge at the same time. As result, the construction of meaning will be built profoundly. Finally, Evaluation step supports and monitors the correct, accurate acquisition of knowledge by the students and allow the knowledge to be transfered from short term memory to long term memory within metacognitive.

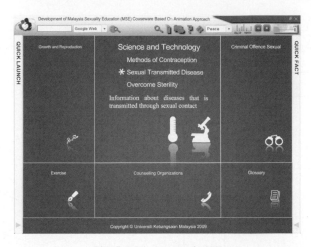

Fig. 5. Main menu of MSE

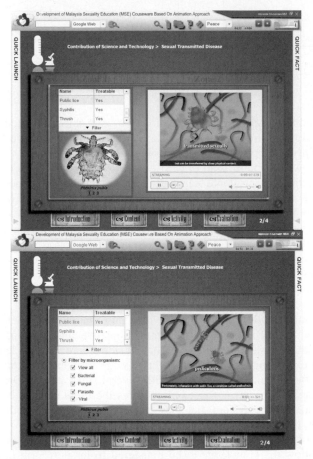

Fig. 6. Learning module of MSE

As to strengthen the structure of the interface design content, it is divided into three zones as show in figure 6. Zone 1 consists of data grid and filter system. The data grid will not only just conclude the learning content items, but also functions as buttons for zone 2 and 3. The filter system is a way to achieve the efficiency dimension of usability, where students can select and deselect categories of items. Data grid will hide the learning items that are not selected. Afterwards, options of students to be choose are reduced and students can chosen that what they want accurate and quickly. Zone 2 is a video player for animation and zone 3 is a location to display graphics that are related to selected learning items. Those are multisensory interactions handled. By these zones especially zone 2 will enhance the learning processing of the students through the virtual environment.

The final module is the Exercise module, it will make sure the students to transfer new knowledge from short-term memory into long-term memory within metacognitive. To evaluate the process, the exercise module divided into two sections, namely pre-test and practice. The system compares the scores and if students could not correctly answer 15 questions, they will be required to answer the practice section. These process are shown in Figure 7. At the end of implementation phase, a procedure of survey will be carried out to the appropriate teachers and students for the next phase.

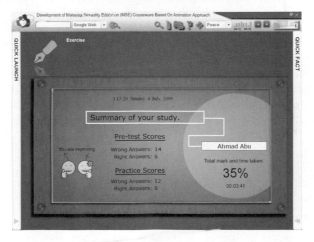

Fig. 7. Exercise module of MSE

4.5 Summative Evaluation Phase

The summative evaluation phase provides opportunities to determine the usability evaluation, study success or fail, strengths and weaknesses of study. The main factor in usability evaluation is user mental model. The representation of mental model will be stored inside user's memory, then will be compared and evaluated when user used a new system, as well as user's perception toward the MSE. Observation and data of questionnaires are collected and analyzed to determined the four main constructs of MSE usability evaluation, namely effectiveness, efficiency, satisfaction and learnability. Effectiveness in this research is measured through the number of questions answered correctly by the respondents in the Exercise module compare with conventional study. Whilst, efficiency is determined by the time used to accomplish Exercise module compare with conventional study. The learnability will determined the ease of use of MSE after incorporated with USD. Therefore, the satisfaction criteria will look into the areas of applicability of the Malaysia sexuality education courseware in user perspective. These perceptions mainly will be determined and measured using the Likert scale through questionnaires. Afterwards, some advices are suggested for future researcher.

5 Conclusion

The Malaysian education system including the curriculum of sexual education is slowly evolving corresponding to global change. Realizing the importance of sexual education knowledge to school children, specifically teenagers, the Malaysian government had constructed and outlined a national sexual education guideline for five age categories. Currently, sexuality education in Malaysia is not taught as an independent subject but integrated with other subjects such as Science, Additional Science, Biology, Islamic Education and Moral education. An initial study was carried out recently and it showed that most of the sexual knowledge acquired by the Malaysian secondary students was from the teachers rather than from their parents and media.

The MSE methodology is designed and developed with the integration of ADDIE, USD, and usability concepts to offer a comprehensive development cycle for a better quality product. Consequently, the sexuality education will soon be acceptable and effectively. In conclusion, the design and development of MSE has enormous potential to be a solution in teaching and enhancing the learning of sexuality education in Malaysia. As a result, the sexuality education and reproductive health issues are no more considered taboo and they will naturally accepted by the Malaysian society.

References

1. Bruess, C.E., Greenberg, J.S.: Sexuality Education Theory and Practice. Jones & Bartlett Publishers, US (2004)
2. Constantine, L.L.: Activity modeling: Toward a pragmatic integration of activity theory with usage centered design. In: The 2nd National Conference in Interacção Person-Machine (Interacção 2006), Keynote Presentation, Portugal (2006)
3. Fogarty, R.: Brain-Compatible Classrooms. Corwin Press, USA (2001)
4. Gagne, R.M.: The conditions of learning and Theory of Instruction. Wadsworth Publishing, US (1985)
5. Ghaoui, C.: In Usability evaluation of online learning programs. Information Science Publishing, USA (2003)
6. Haffer, D.W.: Sex education 2000: A call to action. In: Bruess, C.E., Greenberg, J.S. (eds.) Sexuality Education Theory and Practice. Jones and Bartlett Publishers, US (1990)
7. Herrmann, N.: The Creative Brain. Ned Herrmann Group, USA (1986)
8. International Organization for Standardization: ISO 9241-11: 1998 Usage in context. International Organization for Standardization, Geneva (1998)
9. Jeng, J.: Usability assessment of academic digital libraries: Effectiveness, efficiency, satisfaction, and learnability. Libri 55, 96–121 (2005)

10. Leaving the ADDIE Model Behind, http://www.alleninteractions.com/webinar-slides/Leaving_the_ADDIE_Model_Behind_ASTD_AllenInteractions_Webinar_Presentation_May2009.pdf
11. Linja-aho, M.: Creating a framework for improving the learnability of a complex system. Human Technol. 2, 202–224 (2006)
12. McMenamin, S.M., Palmer, J.F.: Essential Systems Analysis. Yourdon Press, Upper Saddle River (1984)
13. Smith, P.L., Ragan, T.: Instructional design. Wiley, John and Sons, New York (2004)
14. Soulier, J.S.: The design and development of computer based instruction. Allyn and Bacon, Inc., Massaachusetts (1988)
15. United Nations Development Program (UNDP): Malaysia Achieving the millennium development goals successes and challenges. United Nations Country Team, Malaysia (2005)
16. Vandemoortele, J., Delamonica, E.: Education 'Vaccine' against HIV/AIDS. In: Education and HIV/AIDS: A Window of Hope, The World Bank, Washington (2000)
17. Wilson, J.R., Rutherford, A.: Mental models: Theory and application in human factors. Human Fact. 3, 617–634 (1989)

V2S: Voice to Sign Language Translation System for Malaysian Deaf People

Oi Mean Foong, Tang Jung Low, and Wai Wan La

Computer & Information Sciences Department,
Universiti Teknologi PETRONAS,
Bandar Sri Iskandar, 31750 Tronoh, Malaysia
{foongoimean,lowtanjung}@petronas.com.my, lawai85@yahoo.com

Abstract. The process of learning and understand the sign language may be cumbersome to some, and therefore, this paper proposes a solution to this problem by providing a voice (English Language) to sign language translation system using Speech and Image processing technique. Speech processing which includes Speech Recognition is the study of recognizing the words being spoken, regardless of whom the speaker is. This project uses template-based recognition as the main approach in which the V2S system first needs to be trained with speech pattern based on some generic spectral parameter set. These spectral parameter set will then be stored as template in a database. The system will perform the recognition process through matching the parameter set of the input speech with the stored templates to finally display the sign language in video format. Empirical results show that the system has 80.3% recognition rate.

Keywords: image processing, sign language, speech recognition, spectral parameter.

1 Introduction

There are at least 70 million people around the globe who suffer from speech and hearing disabilities, either at birth or by accident [1]. It is somehow difficult for us to interact with them because of the unfamiliar communication means used. Sign Language (SL) is a common form of communication which is widely used by the speech and hearing impaired. Thus, probably the only way of easier communication/ interaction with them is by learning their language - the sign language [2].

We may have friends or family members who have hearing or speech disabilities. Such disabilities may be from birth, or by accident. Surely it is difficult for us to communicate with them if we do not know their language – the Sign Language. It is also difficult for them as well to communicate with us since they have such disability. One may be interested to learn up this language; however it may be costly to attend tuition classes to learn this language. Furthermore, tuition classes exhibits time constraint, where one does not have the flexibility in time on whether or not to attend the tutorial. He/she may prefer to have a self tutorial, however there is no such inexpensive software that can self-taught them. These may contribute to the negligence of the

H. Badioze Zaman et al. (Eds.): IVIC 2009, LNCS 5857, pp. 868–876, 2009.

public to learn the Sign Language to better communicate with those with hearing or speech impairment.

There are campaigns of speeches and talks given to the public. However, these talks usually are not able to reach those with hearing disabilities. So far, only the news on RTM 1 uses the Sign Language extensively to present the daily news to them. The cause of the lack of programs using this technique may be the reason for the extra cost incurred in hiring the translator to translate the speech. Furthermore, there are lack of trained personnel in Malaysia who are able to translate these speeches to Sign Language. These had caused those with hearing disabilities to know less on the ongoing news around them. The objectives of this research are three folds:

1. To ease the communication between normal people and the hearing/ speech disabled.
2. To eliminate the need of attending costly Sign Language classes – it can be done at home.
3. To be able to reach more audience (hearing impaired) during speeches and campaigns.

1.1 Research Motivation

According to The Star Online on the 20th December 2006, "Radio Television Malaysia (RTM 1) will be incorporating more Sign Language in their news segments and dramas for the benefits of the hearing-impaired" and on 22nd July 2007, "there is an acute shortage of Sign Language interpreters because at present there are only 10 qualified interpreters cater to 24,000 registered deaf people nationwide, according to the Malaysian Federation of Deaf".

This simply says that media agencies such as RTM is offering opportunities for more Sign Language interpreters to join its organization. But according to The Star report, the opportunity is not taken up due to the shortage of people with such qualification in this country.

The development of this V2S system shall be a solution to reduce the cost of employing special skilled employees for media agencies such as RTM. They may not need to hire workers as Sign Language interpreters to interpret their news segments or talk shows. Hiring extra interpreters is, for certain, will increase the cost of salary payout. Not only in reducing cost incurred in hiring SL interpreters, the media agencies are in fact directly providing community services to the less fortunate audiences.

V2S system can be taken as an alternative means to SL interpreter thus to replace the old fashion way (a real person doing interpretation) of translating Sign Language. The interpretation process is made available by taking the advantages of modern ICT technology via easily affordable gadgets such as computers, hand phones or PDA as a mediator (translator). In some ways this system may solves the problem of Sign Language interpreters shortage.

2 Related Works

Voice recognition can be generally classified into speaker recognition and speech recognition categories. Speaker recognition is a way of recognizing people from their voices. Such systems extract features from speeches, modeled them and use them to recognize the person from his/her voice. There is a difference between speaker recognition (recognizing who is speaking) and speech recognition (recognizing what is being said). Voice recognition is a synonym for speaker, and thus not speech recognition. Speaker recognition has a history dating back some four decades, where the output of several analog filters was averaged over time for matching. Speaker recognition uses the acoustic features of speech that was found to be different between individuals. These acoustic patterns reflect both anatomy (e.g., size and shape of the throat and mouth) and learned behavioral patterns (e.g., voice pitch, speaking style). This incorporation of learned patterns into the voice templates (the latter called "voiceprints") has earned speaker recognition its classification as a "behavioral biometric" [3].

The fundamental task of speech recognition is the deriving of a sequence of words from a stream of acoustic information. A more general task is automatic speech understanding, which includes the extraction of meaning (for instance, a query to a database) or producing actions in response to speech. For many applications, interaction between system components devoted to semantics, dialog generation, etc., and the speech recognition subsystem can be critical [4].

Feature extraction is a critical element in speech recognition since it is the first step of recognition process and generate the parameters on which the recognition is based. It is well known that Mel Frequency Cepstral Coefficients are the most widely used features parameters. One of the step of MFCC is Mel-scaled filter bank processing. This step may result in some loss of information from the original signal, but it is widely accepted that such step is helpful in extraction information component from the signals [5], [6].

A vector quantizer is a system for mapping a sequence of continuous or discrete vectors into a digital sequence suitable for communication over or storage in a digital channel. The goal of such a system is data compression to reduce the bit rate so as to minimize communication channel capacity or digital storage memory requirements while maintaining the necessary fidelity of the data. The mapping for each vector may or may not have memory depending on past actions of the coder, just as in well established scalar techniques such as PCM. Even though information theory implies that one can always obtain better performance by coding vectors instead of scalars, scalar quantizers have remained by far the common data compression systems because of their simplicity and good performance when the communication rate is sufficiently large. In addition, relatively few design techniques have existed for vector quantizers [7]. Even though there are other technique for pattern matching but Vector quantization is considered as one of the best approach for its flexibility in training as well as recognizing.

Sign Language is used primarily by deaf people throughout the world. Sign Language differs from spoken languages in that it is visual rather than auditory, and is composed of precise hand shapes and movement. This language has evolved in a completely different medium, using the hands and face rather than the vocal and is perceived by the eyes rather than the ears.

Sign Language is not a universal language shared by deaf people of the world because there are many sign languages that have evolved independently of each other. Just as spoken languages differ in grammatical structure, rules and historical relationships, sign languages also differ along these parameters.

An important property of human sign language is that the form of words is generally arbitrary, and there are no indigenous sign languages that are simply a transformation of a spoken language to the hands. Sign language is also equipped with the same expressive power that is inherent in spoken languages and it can express complicated, intricate concepts with the same degree of explicitness and eloquence as spoken language. Sign Language portrays the image, identity and culture of the country that the Deaf Community belongs to. In Malaysia, we have the Malaysian Sign Language (Bahasa Isyarat Malaysia—BIM).

BIM has many dialects, differing from state to state. American Sign Language (ASL) has had a strong influence on BIM, but the two are different enough to be considered separate languages. Other sign languages in use in Malaysia are Penang Sign Language (PSL), Selangor Sign Language (SSL or KLSL), and Kod Tangan Bahasa Malaysia (KTBM), and Chinese Sign Languages [8].

3 Proposed System

The proposed V2S system architecture is shown in Fig.1. As illustrated in the diagram, the main components are the sound recording component (with its supporting sound/voice training algorithm), digital signal processing component (with its supporting MFCC – Mel Frequency Cepstral Coefficients algorithm counterparts), and the vector quantization component (supported by its matching sub-component).

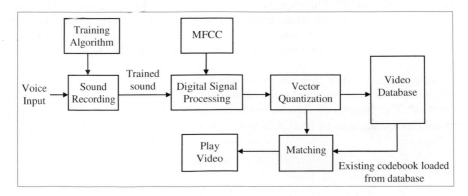

Fig. 1. The proposed V2S system architecture

3.1 Main System Components Description

A. Sound Recording – Sound recording process is responsible to capture and record the sound using microphone. Output of this process is the recorded sound which can be in *.wav* or *.midi* format. The quality of the recorded sound is highly dependent on the sound recording software used. However the quality of the recorded sound can be enhanced by applying proper noise filtering process. The sound training algorithm allows the user to "train" the system to capture the same sound/voice an appropriate number of times so as to produce a good quality recorded signal. The quality of the recorded sound/voice is an important factor in determining the accuracy of the system voice-to-signal translation.

B. Digital Signal Processing – The "trained" sound from the sound recording is then fed into the Digital Signal Processing(DSP) part. The DSP is the most important and a difficult process implemented in this S2V system. The main task of DSP is to convert the recorded sound from its time domain to the frequency domain. This is a necessary process for extracting the features (formant) of the recorded sound so that the system can recognize words spoken to it. MFCC (Mel Frequency Cepstral Coefficients) algorithm is used in formant extraction process.

C. Vector Quantization – Vector quantization is used to perform speech recognition. In fact vector quantization is one of the most effective matching techniques that is popularly used for speech recognition. The basic concept of vector quantization is to compress any vector of a speech/voice feature into one scalar vector. By compressing the feature vector a lot of space for feature storage can be saved and helps to increase the matching process efficiency since we just have to compare a new feature with one value instead of many. In vector quantization we need to train the system first. Then the trained sound will be stored in a codebook in the database. Each trained sound will have its own codebook. During the recognition stage, the new input signal will be used to compare with all the stored codebooks and the codebook which has the closest distance will be chosen as the recognized word.

In general the input (sound/voice) is compared with the existing codebooks in the database for video retrieval. The value of each codebook and the voice input are represented using matrices. The respective average value of each codebook and the voice input would be computed. Then, each codebook will be compared with the input voice (the trained recorded signal) value. The confirmation of which video to be played is based on the closest input voice value (distance) to the codebooks stored in the database.

Fig.2(a) and (b) show samples of sound/voice for single word matching process. That is, the matching of calculated codebook (from the input voice) with the stored codebook. The samples of these sound/voice matching were processed using one of the utilities available in the MatLab® application.

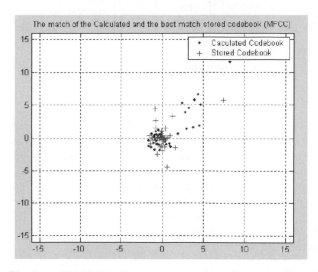

Fig. 2(a). Matching of the "me" voice with the stored codebook

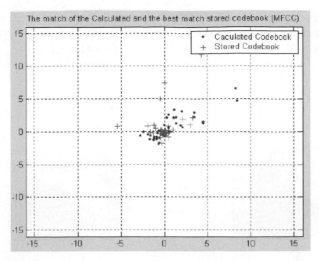

Fig. 2(b). Matching of the "us" voice with the stored codebook

4 Empirical Results and Findings

The interface of this project was designed to have few buttons and a display panel for simplicity purposes. By clicking on the "V2S" button on the screen the user is allowed to input raw voice i.e. recording of spoken voice into the system. There is a display panel to display the appropriate video output (Sign Language) which is the relevant translation of the spoken word(s).

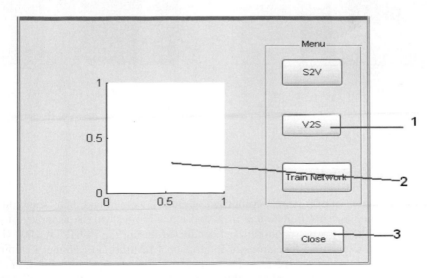

Fig. 3. The main user interface of the V2S system. (1) The V2S button – clicking it shall prompt the user for training the voice input. The system will then matches the voice to the corresponding video in the database. (2) The display panel – displays the relevant video for the translated voice. (3) Close button – exit the V2S system.

Fig.3 shows the main interface of the V2S prototype application. It is worth mentioning here that the prototype does include the S2V (Sign-to-Voice) system [9]. The S2V system was presented in WASET 2008 Congress in Singapore.

Fig.4(a) to (d) show some samples of the video output for the relevant translated words.

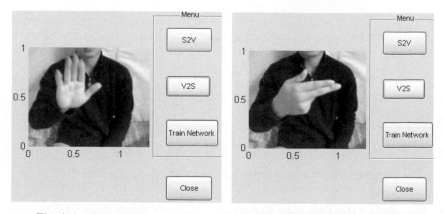

Fig. 4(a). Video for "come here"   **Fig. 4(b).** Video for "turn left"

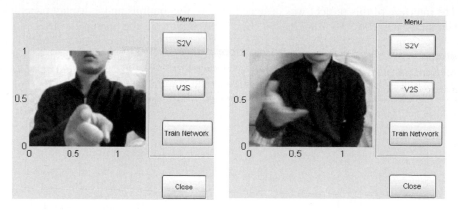

Fig. 4(c). Video for "you"   **Fig. 4(d).** Video for "us"

5 System Evaluation

We took a sample of 100 people comprised of elderly women and men, young male and female children, and middle age male and female to test on the accuracy of the V2S system. The test was monitored and conducted during the PECIPTA 2007 (Expositions of Research and Inventions of International Institution of Higher Learning) in Kuala Lumpur and CDC (Career Development Carnival) exhibitions in UTP. It was found that at least 80 out of the 100 people were able to callback the desired sign language video. That means the system is at least 80% accurate to display the correct sign language. It should be mentioned here that the words uttered by the test samples

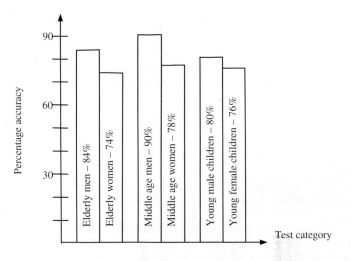

Fig. 5. Overall system accuracy test

were "you", "us", "come here", and "turn left". Fig.5 shows the overall statistic of the test conducted.

The graph shows the accuracy of each category by averaging the accuracy percentage of the 4 spoken words. The middle age man category shows the highest accuracy. This may be due to the training of the system via ONLY the middle age man. However, other categories do show high accurate responses. This implies that the more training the system gets for each word, the more accurate it would be.

6   Conclusion

Natural Language to SL translation is the main scope of this research. The fundamental idea of this system is to translate the human voice to SL. The system will match the captured voice with the pre-stored SL videos in the database to display the appropriate sign/gesture thus provide an alternative interactive way of communication between a normal person and a hearing impaired person.

The prototype allows translation of spoken English to SL in Malaysian context. The system accuracy depends on how much system training was conducted. With sufficient training, it will be able to recognize all the trained commands or words and execute the corresponding translation. Currently, the system has the accuracy of 80.3%. This system may be used by users who wish to learn SL and to help those who wish to communicate with the hearing disabled people more effectively. For future work, the system may be implemented in mobile devices with animated hand gestures [10] for deaf people.

References

1. The World Federation of the Deaf,
   http://www.hearinglossweb.com/res/hlorg/wfd.htm
2. Cornucopia of Disability Information: Disability Statistics,
   http://codi.buffalo.edu/graph_based/demographics/
   .statistics.htm
3. Zetterholm, E.: Voice Imitation. A Phonetic Study of Perceptual Illusions and Acoustic Success, PhD thesis, Lund University (2003)
4. Zue, V., Cole, R., Ward, W.: Speech Recognition. Cambridge University Press, New York (1997)
5. Hung, J.W.: Optimization of Filter-Bank to Improve Extraction of MFCC Features in Speech Recognition. IEEE Transactions on Intelligent Multimedia, Video and Speech Processing, 675–678 (2004)
6. Rashidul Hasan, M., Mustafa, J., Golam Rabbani, M., Saifur Rahman, M.: Speaker Recognition Using Mel Frequency Cepstral Coefficient. In: 3rd International Conference on Electrical and Computer Engineering, pp. 565–568 (2004)
7. Gray, R.M.: Vector Quantization. Morgan Kaufmann, San Francisco (1990)
8. Wikipedia, Malaysia Sign Language, http://en.wikipedia.org/wiki/
9. Foong, O.I., Low, T.J., Satrio, W.: Hand Gesture Recognition: Signs to Voice System (S2V). In: WASET conference proceedings, vol. 33, article 6, pp. 32–36 (2008) ISSN 2070-3740
10. Sequndo, R.S., Montero, J.M., Guarasa, J.M., Cordoba, R., Ferreiros, J., Pardo, J.M.: Proposing a Speech to Gesture Translation Architecture for Spanish Deaf People. Journal of Visual Languages and Computing 19, 523–538 (2008)

Real World Issues in Developing a Malaysian Forest Battlefield Environment for Small Unit Tactics Using 3D Graphics

Syed Nasir Alsagoff

Computer Science Lecturer, Faculty of Science and Defence Technology,
National Defence University of Malaysia

Abstract. In the military, training is essential as preparation for war. Small unit training involves training for platoon and section sized unit. The soldiers must train to maneuver, shoot and communicate. In order for the training to be successful, it must be as realistic as possible. Realistic training allows for the soldiers to be mentally and physically prepared for the battlefield. Unfortunately, there is a wide gap between training and the resources required to properly conduct the training [5]. Resources consist of suitable training location and material support such as ammunition, ration and fuel. Limitation on the resources means that training cannot be as realistic as possible. To ensure effective use of the limited training resources, training should be conducted in a simulated environment before migrating to a live environment. This paper will attempt to discuss the real world issues in developing a Malaysian Forest Battlefield Environment 3D Simulation for Small Unit Tactic using 3D Graphics.

Keywords: Simulation, 3D, Graphics, Image, Terrain, Training, Tactics, Move, Shoot, Communicate, Army, Sound, Weather.

1 Introduction

Battlefield environment simulation provides effective training and can provide many customized training scenarios. Simulation will be done using 3 dimensional (3D) graphics. 3D graphics is effective in simulating battlefield environment as it is flexible and can be modified to suit any requirements. Advancement and the widespread use of 3D video card allows for the simulation to be run on all modern PCs.

1.1 Background of Study

The study is related to simulation of a forest battlefield environment using 3D graphics. For the simulation to be effective, it must take into consideration all aspects of the environment to be simulated. The research will study the real world issues of simulating the Malaysian terrain, vegetation and small unit tactics.

1.2 Objective of Study

This study objective is to identify and discuss issues in developing a Malaysian Forest Battlefield Environment Simulation for Small Unit Tactics using 3D Graphics.

H. Badioze Zaman et al. (Eds.): IVIC 2009, LNCS 5857, pp. 877–885, 2009.

1.3 Scope of Study

This study will be for the Malaysian environment and will be for small unit tactics only. Only real world, and not technical, issues are discussed here. As Malaysia is diverse with many types of forest, this study will be on dipterocarp forest which is the biggest type in East Malaysia. Small units will only consist of 10 soldiers which is a squad or section. There are many types of military maneuvers but only the attack phase of the maneuver will be discussed here. The tools and software for developing the 3D simulation will not be discussed here.

1.4 Significance of the Study

Currently, there are no 3D simulators in Malaysia capable of simulating the forest environment to be used for training small units. All training is currently conducted in a live environment and this will use training resources. The 3D simulator will allow for more realistic training outside of live environment and also conserve training resources.

2 Literature Review

Some of the sources cited in this literature are from the US Army Field Manuals. All the information gathers from the field manuals are approved for public distribution. The concepts of training and small unit tactics are universal with all the armies of the world. In combat, the mission of a military unit will be to close in with the enemy by means of fire and maneuver and to destroy or capture the enemy. Despite all the technological advances of war, close combat is still necessary to win the battle. Small units can [3]:

- Attack over approaches that are not feasible for heavy forces.
- Make initial penetrations in difficult terrain.
- Retain existing obstacles and difficult terrain as pivots for operational and tactical maneuver.
- Seize or secure forested and built-up areas.
- Control restrictive routes for use by other forces.
- Operate primarily at night or during other periods of natural or induced limited visibility.
- Follow and support exploiting heavy forces when augmented with transportation.

Close combat means that the unit will be in direct contact of the enemy. The unit can see the enemy and at the same time the enemy can see the unit. If one side can see each other, then both sides can shoot at each other. Any mistakes in the maneuver can cause casualty and even wipe out the whole unit.

To close in with the enemy and engage them, a soldier will need to [3]:

- Maneuver towards the enemy in a battle formation to maximize the combat effectiveness.
- Shoot the enemy accurately without getting shot at.
- Communicate with each other fellow soldiers and his leader.

This maneuver will required close coordination among all the soldiers involved. Figure 1 show the steps involved in a squad movement to contact phase. This movement is used if contact is expected. The squad will break into two teams and one team moving forward with the other team covering the other team. The teams will alternate cover and movement until contact with the enemy is made.

Fig. 1. Squad Movement To Contact Phase [3]

To prepare for this, training is important. Training must be realistic and constant practice will make perfect [1].

3   Simulating Malaysian Forest Battlefield Environment

There are 3 major types of forest in Malaysia. The classifications are based on vegetation. The three main types are [6]:

- Dipterocarp forest,
- Peat swamp forest
- Mangrove forest

This paper's discussion will focus on the dipterocarp forest which is the biggest type in East Malaysia. The forest is catagorised as a dipterocarp forest as it populated by trees from the Dipterocarpaceae family. The dipterocarp forest occurs on dry land just above sea level to an altitude of about 900 metres [7]. The lower level of the forest is made up of small trees and vegetations. This lower level will play an important part during the discussion of this paper.

Fig. 2. Dipterocarp forest

As shown in Figure 2, the thickness of the vegetation might affect the maneuvering of the soldier. The ground and the lower vegetation will need to be accurately simulated. There are some areas that are clear and some areas that might pose as obstacles that a soldier might have to bypass or slowly move through.

Nature is also unique and random and not a single tree or vegetation is of the same size or height [9]. Different types of trees and vegetation have different type of density and flexibility that might or might not allow for a soldier to pass through.

3.1 Lighting and Weather

The time of the day and the weather are also random variables that need further study. The top canopy of the forest blocks the sunlight from reaching down. Different time of the day such as early morning, late morning, afternoon, evening, late evening and night will cause different lighting effect on the forest floor.

The random weather will also play an important factor in simulating the environment. Rain will cause the visibility range to be lower. Rain will also cause streams and small pool of water to form on the forest floor. As a result, the forest floor would be muddy and slippery and this might cause the soldier to slip and fall. A falling person will try to grab on anything available to stop their fall. Grabbing branches might cause sound that might alert the enemy. The muddy floor will slow down the movement of the soldier.

3.2 Maneuver

Small units will need to maneuver to close in on the enemy. To do so, they will have to do a fire and maneuver sequence. A unit will be split into two teams. There are the assault team and the suppressing fire team. The suppressing fire team will fire upon the enemy's location, either to defeat them or to ensure they cannot shoot back. During this time, the assault team will maneuver closer towards the enemy's position. Once reaching a designated area, the role of the teams will switch [2]. This will continue on until the enemy's position has been seized or the enemy has been totally defeated.

For this maneuver to be successful, the soldiers will need to maneuver parallel to each other towards the enemy's position. Moving in a parallel line will reduce the chances of casualty due to several soldiers getting shot by the enemy with the same bullet and also from friendly fire. A soldier in front of another soldier might get accidently shot.

Unfortunately, due to the thickness of the vegetation, soldiers might take the path of least resistance rather than stay in formation. The 3D simulation needs to be able to simulate the thickness of the vegetation. In addition to that, not all vegetation has the same thickness.

Some of the vegetation might allow for a soldier to maneuver while others might not. Some areas might have little or no vegetation and some areas might allow for a soldier to maneuver through but with some difficulty. This will cause the parallel line to be broken up and soldiers getting in front of the each other. The only way to overcome this problem is for the soldier to be aware of their surrounding and each other. If they know that they are in front or at the back of the line, the soldiers can either slow down or speed up to maintain the line.

As nature is random, the 3D simulation will need a random vegetation generator to simulate the randomness of the environment.

3.3 Shoot

Malaysian Army soldiers use the M4 Carbine 5.56 mm assault rifle. It has an effective range of 150 meters or less. The enemy might use a variety of weapons but the most common will be the Russian made AK-47 7.62 mm assault rifle with an effective range of 400 meters or less.

Fig. 3. M4 Carbine

Compared to the AK-47, why does the M4 have a lower effective range? This is because studies have shown most enemy engagement in previous conflict is 100 meters or less. Based on the experience of this writer, if the target is more than 100 meters away, it will be very hard to see. In a forest environment, the range will be even less. This is because soldiers will wear camouflage uniform. In order to be able to shoot the enemy, the soldier will need to see the enemy first. Firing blindly will be a waste of ammunition. Camouflage uniform will allow for the soldier to blend in with the terrain and vegetation and make them harder to see. As both side will be wearing camouflage uniform, the engagement range will be even less.

Fig. 4. Can you spot the soldier?

The camouflage uniform on a solder might make it harder for the enemy to see but it is still possible due to the movement of the soldier. If the soldier is still, he will be harder to spot but in an attack phase, the soldier is constantly moving towards the enemy's position.

The camouflage uniform might also affect the ability of other soldier to see their fellow soldiers. This will make it harder to maintain the parallel line.

Camouflage uniform cannot take into consideration all types of vegetation to blend in. For some areas, the camouflage system will work well but for some it might not. The random nature of vegetation can cause some soldiers and enemies to be seen but others to be well camouflaged.

The effective range of the M4 Carbine 5.56 mm assault rifle is 150 meters or less. This is if it is shooting in the open. In a forest environment, this will be even less as there are many obstacle for the bullet to travel through. For example, if the soldier sees the enemy behind vegetation and shoots the enemy, the vegetation might affect the trajectory of the small 5.56 mm bullet. This will also affect the enemy's line of fire.

To properly simulate the effect of vegetation on bullet trajectory, live firing on vegetation will need to be done to gather data. Older vegetation will also be thicker compared to younger ones. Some vegetation might allow for the bullet to pass through easily, some vegetation might slightly affect the trajectory, some might deflect the bullet and some might even stop the bullet. The distance from where the weapon is fired is also important as bullet fired from a shorter distance might not get affected as much compared to a bullet fired from a longer distance.

3.4 Communicate

Small unit will communicate verbally or visually. Before engaging the enemy, soldiers will communicate visually as not to alert the enemy. All visual signal of the soldier will need to be incorporated into simulating the soldier.

The vegetation which might affect the sighting of fellow soldiers and enemies might also affect the visual signal. The longer the distance, the less likely the soldier is able to see the visual signal. Studies must be conducted on the type of vegetations available on the forest ground and their effects of visual signal.

Hold the rifle in the ready position at shoulder level. Point the rifle in the direction of the enemy.

Figure 2-35. ENEMY IN SIGHT.

Fig. 5. Visual signal for "enemy in sight" [10]

Once the enemy is engaged, all signals will be verbal. Orders will be shouted for both sides. Shooting might cause for some of these orders to be lost due to the noise and confusion. The sound from a rifle being fired is very deafening. Sounds above 85 decibels will cause ear damage while 5.56 rifle being fired will generate 150+ decibels sound [8]. All this factors will need to be taken into consideration when simulating the environment.

The dense vegetation might also affect the communication as it will be disorientating to be able to hear orders and command and not know where the command is coming. This is why the battlefield is very confusing. Proper training will go a long way in alleviating these issues.

3.5 Sound

There are many ways that sound can effect a simulation. The first will be during maneuvering in the forest. To move in close enough to destroy the enemy, soldiers will have to move stealthily. There are many obstacles in the forest that can break the silence. Branches that have fallen on the ground will generate sound when stepped on. Trying to maneuver through dense vegetation will cause sound of broken branches. Leaves will rustle when one brush against dense vegetation.

Depending on the weather, wind will cause the branches to move and drown out any sound that soldiers might make. The same goes for rain that can drown out any sound.

Sounds cannot travel far due to air absorption. Studies should be made on how far sounds that a soldier might make in a forest can travel.

Sound will be absorbed by the dense vegetation causing it to travel even less. The study of how sound travel through object is call object occlusion [11]. Different trees and vegetations have different occlusion factor. Studies should be made on how trees and vegetations in Malaysia affect travelling sound.

4 Findings

A battlefield is always fluid, random and confusing. There are many variables and issues that need to be taken into consideration in order to simulate a battlefield. The finding of this paper is just a touch of the surface of enormous undertaking of simulating Malaysian Forest Battlefield Environment for Small Unit Tactics. Due to the randomness of nature and of live battlefield, there are some items that cannot be simulated. This same issue can also apply for live training. Only live combat can provide for this, and fortunately Malaysia is at peace.

In addition, this paper only discusses the attack phase of a maneuver. There are other phase that needs to be taken into consideration such as ambush, patrol, defence and many more. Due to the enormous scope of types of military maneuvers, only the attack phase is discussed here.

5   Conclusion

Some might say that all the items being simulated i.e. obstacles for soldiers to move through the forest might make it a chore and not fun for them to participate in the training. Training is serious, and unrealistic training will cause the soldiers to be complacent of their skills and abilities. This is not a video game where soldiers that get shot can be immediately healed.

All the issues and many more will need to be taken into consideration before a proper simulation can be developed. New 3D engine capable of simulating the terrain, weather, trees, vegetation and sound will need to be develop that can take all simulation factors into account. Hopefully, this paper will be the starting point of developing a Malaysian Forest Battlefield Environment Simulation for Small Unit Tactics using 3D Graphics.

6   Future Work

Once the Malaysian Forest Battlefield Environment can be simulated for Small Unit Tactics, it can be upgraded for a larger unit such as platoon, company, battalion, and brigade level. Other elements of forest combat such as mechanized support, artillery support and air support can be included. More ambitious simulation involving virtual reality (VR) will also be considered to make the training more realistic.

References

1. Headquarters, Department of the Army. US Army Field Manual 25-04 - How to Conduct Training Exercises, September 10 (1984)
2. Headquarters, Department of The Army. US Army Field Manual 90-05 –Jungle Operation, August 10 (1982)
3. Headquarters, Department of The Army. US Army Field Manual 7-8 – Infantry Rifle Platoon and Squad. US Army Field Manual, March 1 (2001)
4. Polack, T.: Focus on 3D Terrain Programming. Premier Press (2003)
5. Briggs: LTC Ralph and White, COL (Ret) Bob. Knowledge Acquisition Process for Close Combat Tactical Trainer (CCTT). In: Proceedings of Simtect 1997 (1997)

6. Mohd Hasmadi, I., Alias Mohd, S., Norizah, K.: Reclassifying forest type to a new forest class based on vegetation and lithology characteristics using geographic information system at southern Johore, Malaysia. International Journal of Energy and Environment 2(4) (2008)
7. WWF Malaysia. The Malaysian Rainforest,
   http://www.wwf.org.my/about_wwf/what_we_do/forests_main/
   the_malaysian_rainforest/
8. Anderson, D.: American Cop - Silence is Golden,
   http://www.americancopmagazine.com/articles/silenceIsGolden/
   index.html
9. Snook, G.: Real-Time 3D Terrain Engines Using C++ and DirectX 9. Charles River Media (June 2003)
10. Headquarters, Department of The Army. US Army Field Manual 21-60 –Visual Signal. US Army Field Manual, September 30 (1987)
11. Gardner, W.G.: 3D Audio and Acoustic Environment Modeling,
    http://www.wavearts.com

Students Perception towards the Implementation of Computer Graphics Technology in Class via Unified Theory of Acceptance and Use of Technology (UTAUT) Model

Norsila binti Shamsuddin

Faculty of Social Sciences & Industrial Studies, Universiti Industri Selangor

Abstract. Technology advancement and development in a higher learning institution is a chance for students to be motivated to learn in depth in the information technology areas. Students should take hold of the opportunity to blend their skills towards these technologies as preparation for them when graduating. The curriculum itself can rise up the students' interest and persuade them to be directly involved in the evolvement of the technology. The aim of this study is to see how deep is the students' involvement as well as their acceptance towards the adoption of the technology used in Computer Graphics and Image Processing subjects. The study will be towards the Bachelor students in Faculty of Industrial Information Technology (FIIT), Universiti Industri Selangor (UNISEL); Bac. In Multimedia Industry, BSc. Computer Science and BSc. Computer Science (Software Engineering). This study utilizes the new Unified Theory of Acceptance and Use of Technology (UTAUT) to further validate the model and enhance our understanding of the adoption of Computer Graphics and Image Processing Technologies. Four (4) out of eight (8) independent factors in UTAUT will be studied towards the dependent factor.

Keywords: Information Technology, Computer Graphics, UTAUT, technology adoption, Multimedia, Computer Science, Software Engineering, Technology Acceptance Model.

1 Introduction

Study shows that varieties of new technologies are able to improve the quality of learning computer graphics and image processing subjects. The result does not tally to the first impression towards the subject matter for students at the Faculty of Industrial Information Technology (FIIT). At the beginning of the semester students say that it is complicated and hard to learn when it came to programming. These are just a perception, thoughts that they have when they first sign up for the class. Due to the lack of information and student ignorant towards new technology, a small study took place. The aim of this study is to see how deep is the students' involvement as well as their acceptance towards the adoption of the technology used in Computer Graphics and Image Processing subjects. The study also will show whether there is a change in the students' perception towards the subjects.

H. Badioze Zaman et al. (Eds.): IVIC 2009, LNCS 5857, pp. 886–893, 2009.

Venkatesh et al.'s [1] [2003] UTAUT model draws upon and integrates eight previously developed models and/or theories that relate to technology acceptance and use. The eight factors are Performance Expectancy, Effort Expectancy, Social Influence, Facilitating Conditions, Gender, Age, Experience and Voluntaries of Use. These factors are independent factors, which will affect the dependent factor; Behavioral Intention and Usage Behavior.

Performance expectancy defines as the degree to which an individual believes that using the system will help him or her to attain gains in job performance [1]. **Effort expectancy** defines as the degree of ease associated with the use of the system [1]. **Social influence** define as the degree to which an individual perceives that the important others believe he or she should use the new system [1]. **Facilitating conditions** are the variables asserted to have a direct impact on system usage. They define as the degree to which an individual believes that an organizational and technical infrastructure exists to support use of the system [1]. **Behavioral Intention** defines as a measure of the strength of one's intention to perform a specified behavior [2].

2 Literature Review

2.1 TAM Model

Based on the Theory of Reasoned Action (TRA) by Fishbein and Ajzen [1975], one of the first and most widely used and accepted models is the Technology Acceptance Model (TAM) by Davis [3]. TAM has been used many times to assess user acceptance of traditional web applications such as e-mail, online shopping or online banking. Research in this area has generated adoption metrics that can be used to determine the probability of successful implementation of information system initiatives.

2.2 UTAUT Model

Venkatesh et al. [2003] reviewed user acceptance literature in their seminal work about their unified theory of user acceptance, and discussed and compared empirically eight different factors to explain user acceptance. They originated the Unified Theory of Acceptance and Use of Technology (UTAUT), which incorporates acceptance determinants across several competing. According to UTAUT, the intention to use information technology can be determined by three predecessors: performance expectancy, effort

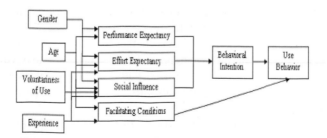

Fig. 1. Unified Theory of Acceptance and Use of Technology Modeled by Ventakesh et al.

expectancy and social influence. Hence, intention to use is to apply influence on actual behavior toward information technology adoption with facilitating conditions.

2.3 Related Works

A study on "College Students' Acceptance of Tablet PCs : An Application of UTAUT Model" is done by Omar F. El-Gayar and Mark [2006]. The study contributes both theoretical and practical. The author believes that the increasing technology-based initiates in education, the need of study towards the adoption of such technology is important. It is useful to evaluate students' learning and teaching effectiveness. Based on the findings of the study, the author identified factors that induce students to adopt such initiatives. From a theoretical point of view, the study will add to mandatory adoption of technical innovations. It also contributes to the study of the theoretical validity and empirical applicability of the relatively proposed UTAUT model.[8.]

3 Background of Study

The acceptance of the Computer Graphics Technology was evaluated by using a modified UTAUT model that was creatively proposed by Venkatesh et al.'s [2003]. This study will focus on performance expectancy, effort expectancy, social influence and gender. Additional one factor are added, that is students' course/programme. The facilitating conditions are not included in this study due to a specific research that will be done after the second groups of students finish their courses. This is to focus just on the technical infrastructure available at the faculty.

This study is focusing on the students from the Faculty of Industrial Information Technology undertake the programme of Bachelor of Multimedia, BSc. of Computer Science and BSc. of Computer Science (Software Engneering). The behavior of the students aged between 19 – 23 years old is extremely excited towards the new technologies that they can learn in class. It shows a positive impact from one month of class observation when the lecturer introduced new software to them. Three classes were involved and observed by the same person during their hands-on period. The software taught in class is Maya for Bachelor of Multimedia students and OpenGL Programming for BSc. of Computer Science and BSc. of Computer Science (Software Engneering) students. Although they found it is difficult to learn the new software but they managed to adapt it after three hands-on period.

The objective of the study is to find out whether there is a difference between genders towards the independent factors mention earlier. The study also will seek knowledge on the acceptance of the software used within the three different programmes, the strength between the underlying relationship between the factors as well as to seek the best model.

Forty-six (46) students out of sixty-six (66) responded to the questionnaire distributed after the students register for next semester. It is about 70% rate of response.

4 Methodology

The study was conducted through observation as well as answering questionnaire. A stratified random sampling method is used to determine the number of respondents to be selected in the survey.

4.1 Observation

The observation is done for the first month of the beginning semester to evaluate the behavior of the students' towards the introduction to the new software. The students used the software to create their own projects for final evaluation after three months of implementation of the particular software.

4.2 Survey Instrument

A set of questionnaire are distributed to the same students who are taking Computer Graphics subject in their past semester after they received the final results. The questions are based on profile demographics, factors such as Intention and Usage Behavior, Performance Expectancy, Effort Expectancy and Social Influences.

Intention and Usage Behavior is tested on the students' intentional of using the software as well as their usage behavior to seek how long they have use the software and whether they would use the software in future.

Performance Expectancy study on their expected result towards their class performance as well as their final project outcomes. It also studies on the students' competency of applying the new software implemented during class.

Effort expectancy is to inquire about the students' effort on using the software as well as their willingness to learn or explore more on the software on their own.

Social Influence factor studies on the students' usage behavior towards the software are influence by surroundings. It also studies whether the students' perceptions of the new software are influence by their surroundings.

The scaling for all the factors under studied is based on FIVE (5) Likert Scaling.

4.3 Data Analysis

The researchers used SPSS to analyze and evaluate the data. It is used to estimates the relationships among the factors as well as the strength of the underlying relationship. The Analysis of Variance (ANOVA) also being studied to determine the difference among the three Programmes.

5 Findings

5.1 Basic Analysis

The results are based on the completed questionnaire by 46 students out of 66 which is 70% of response rate from three different programmes. These students were enrolled in courses indicative of new software use of between one month and three months. The basic analysis of the sample is shown in Table 1 through Table 4 as follows:

Table 1. Frequency Table by Gender and Programme

Item	Frequency (%)			Mean
Gender	Male 21 (45.7)	Female 25 (54.3)		1.54
Programme	BCS 10 (21.7)	BCSSE 5 (10.9)	BMM 31 (67.4)	2.46

As in Table 1, the respondents are 45.7% males and 54.3% females. They came from 21.7% students from BSc. of Computer Science, 10.9% BSc. of Computer Science (Software Engineering) students and 67.4% students from Bac. of Multimedia. The number of students sampled is based on the actual proportion of class size.

Table 2. Frequency Table of Usage Behavior

Scale	Frequency (%)	Mean
Intent	1 (2.2)	
Somewhat	27 (58.7)	3.37
Not Intentional	18 (39.1)	

Table 2 shows that 60.9% of the student intent to use the software and another 39.1% did not have any intention to use the software for future projects.

Table 3. Frequency Table of Performance Expectancy

Scale	Frequency (%)	Mean
Somewhat	32 (69.6)	3.30
Bad	14 (30.4)	

Table 3 tells that 69.6% performed very well and another 30.4% of the student performed badly in class.

Table 4. Frequency Table of Effort Expectancy

Scale	Frequency (%)	Mean
Good	2 (4.3)	
Somewhat	23 (50.0)	3.43
Bad	20 (43.5)	
Worst	1 (2.2)	

Table 4 tells that 54.3% put an effort to learn and use the software and another 45.7% of the student did not.

Table 5. Frequency Table of Social Influence

Scale	Frequency (%)	Mean
Influent	1 (2.2)	
Somewhat	35 (76.1)	3.20
Not Influent	10 (21.7)	

Table 4 shows that 78.3% are influence to learn and use the software and another 21.7% of the student did not.

5.2 T-Test Analysis

T-Test analysis is chose to test the hypothesis whether there is a significant different between gender and the four factors. The result of T-test between gender and among other factors shows that there is no significant different between male and female towards the acceptance of the software at 5% level of significance.

5.3 Analysis of Variance

Analysis of Variance (ANOVA) test show there is a significant different between programmes for intentional and usage behavior ($\alpha=0.009$), effort expectancy ($\alpha=0.004$), and performance expectancy ($\alpha=0.036$) at 5% level of significance, whereas the social influence did not differ from any of the programmes ($\alpha=0.211$).

Further analysis has been done to seek which group is different among others by using Tukey's comparison and the result show that the perception of students from Bac. of Multimedia ($\alpha=0.006$) is different from BSc. of Computer Science students. It is supported by the LSD test as well, agreeing with the first test run with $\alpha=0.002$.

5.4 Correlation

There is a negative correlation between Usage Behavior and Effort Expectancy (-0.296) and between Usage Behavior and Programme (-0.483). The Pearson correlation shows that there is a positive correlation between Performance Expectancy and Programmes (0.378) and between Effort Expectancy and Programmes (0.466).

5.5 Regression Analysis

The model summary from regression analysis concluded that 40.3% of the relationship is explained by Programme; 13% of the relationship is explained by gender and 13.2% of the relationship is explained by the factor of Usage Behavior. Only programme show significant different for the factors analyzed ($\alpha=0.00$) at 5% level of significant. The following are the best model referring to the three factors mentioned above:

$$Y=0.992 + 0.53X_1+0.44X_2-0.006X_3-0.47X_4 \tag{1}$$

$$Y=2.5 + 0.0007X_1-0.27X_2+0.13X_3-0.21X_4 \tag{2}$$

Where $Y(1)$ = programme, $Y(2)$ = gender
 X_1 = performance expectancy
 X_2 = effort expectancy
 X_3 = social influence
 X_4 = usage behavior

$$Y=3.56 -0.005X_1-0.22X_2+0.24X_3 \tag{3}$$

Where Y = usage behavior
 X_1 = performance expectancy
 X_2 = effort expectancy
 X_3 = social influence.

6 Conclusions

As a conclusion, these studies are based on the students' responds after they get their final results the following semester. We can conclude that the respondents are 45.7% males and 54.3% females. They came from 21.7% students from BSc. of Computer Science, 10.9% BSc. of Computer Science (Software Engineering) students and 67.4% students from Bac. of Multimedia.

As for the Intentional and Usage Behavior factor we can conclude that 60.9% of the student intent to use the software and another 39.1% did not have any intention to use the software for future projects with the factor mean score of 3.37.

The students' Performance Expectancy towards using the software measures 69.6% performed very well in class and as for another 30.4% of the student performed badly in class with the factor mean score of 3.30.

As for their Effort Expectancy, 54.3% put an effort to learn and use the software and another 45.7% of the student did not with the factor mean score of 3.43.

The Social Influence factor shows 78.3% are influence to learn and use the software that are taught in class and another 21.7% of the student did not with the factor mean score of 3.20.

This study failed to reject the null hypothesis and we can conclude that there is no significant different between male and female towards the acceptance of the software at 5% level of significance.

The Analysis of Variance (ANOVA) test show that there is a significant different between programmes for intentional and usage behavior ($\alpha=0.009$), effort expectancy ($\alpha=0.004$), and performance expectancy ($\alpha=0.036$) at 5% level of significance, whereas the social influence did not differ from any of the programmes.

There is a negative relationship between Usage Behavior and Effort Expectancy and between Usage Behavior and Programme but positive correlation between Performance Expectancy and Programmes and between Effort Expectancy and Programmes. Regression analysis show that only Programme has significant different among the factors analyzed.

7 Future Works

This studies only discussed on four (4) out of eight (8) factors suggested by Ventakesh et. Al in Unified Theory of Acceptance and Use of Technology (UTAUT). There are a few constraint to study all the eight factors. They are due to time and cost constraint, the volume of batch of students' who are taking the subject, and the facility provided due to new programme developed.

For future development as well as the upbringing of the said programmes, research on the other four factors such as Facilitating Conditions, Age, Voluntariness of Use and Experience of using the software will be considered.

Further analysis will be done on the first four factors analyzed in this paper especially on Intentional and Usage Behavior and Effort Expectancy factors due to the lower percentages compared to the other two.

References

1. Venkatesh, V., Morris, M., Davis, G., Davis, F.D.: User Acceptance of Information Technology: Toward a Unified View. MIS Quarterly 27(3), 425–478 (2003)
2. Davis, F.D., Bagozzi, R.P., Warshaw, P.R.: User Acceptance of Computer Technology: a Comparison of Two Theoretical Models. Management Science 35(8), 982–1003 (1989)
3. Davis, F.D.: Perceived Usefulness, Ease of Use and User Acceptance of IT. MIS Quarterly 13(3), 319–340 (1989)
4. Fishbein, M., Ajzen, I.: Belief, Attitude, Intention and Behavior: An Introduction to Theory and Research. Addison-Wesey, Reading (1975)
5. Lederer, A.L., Maupin, D.J., Sena, M.P., Zhuang, Y.: The Technology Acceptance Model and the World Wide Web. Decision Support Systems 29(3), 269–282 (2000)
6. Manly, B.F.J.: Factor Analysis. In: Manly, B.F.J. (ed.) Multivariate Statistical Methods. Chapman & Hall, London (1994)
7. Surry, D., Land, S.M.: Strategies For Motivating Higher Education Faculty To Use Technology. Innovations in Education and Training International 1(37), 1–9 (2000)
8. El-Gayar, O.F., Mark: College Students Acceptance of Tablet PCs: An Application of UTAUT Model (2006)

Information System Development Model: Theories Analysis and Guidelines

Norshita Mat Nayan and Halimah Badioze Zaman

Department of Information System, National University of Malaysia,
Malaysia
norshita_nayan@yahoo.com,
hbz@ftsm.ukm.edu.my

Abstract. Development of information system project is one of the IT projects which have been developed to offer the best facilities for publics. Process of system development will go through its own life cycle and every process must be refined in order to fulfill aims and objectives. Eventhough information system development is always correlate with failure but a few key factors will help the systems to succeed. There are multiple success factors being discussed by other researches in the information system development but failure figure still at the higher side. The main purpose of this research is to discuss processes involved in the development of information system which positively contribute towards its success. Model of information system development which has been developed (PADM Model) consists of four fundamental processes; planning, requirement analysis, design and maintenance. All processes will be monitored by a main process namely quality as the key performance indicator. Quality plays a vital role in assessing the ability of information system developed in order to fulfill users' expectations. Analysis of theory can be used as a guideline and measurement base towards the system with hope that percentage of failure will reduce subsequently.

Keywords: Analysis, design, life cycle, maintenance, model, planning, quality.

1 Introduction

The growth of information technology projects plays an important role to the development of a country. Most companies realized the advantages of Information Technology therefore they are ready to put in huge investment to further improve the completion of daily tasks. One of the IT projects is development of information system which can help to simplify many things. Information system is defined in various ways such as IS are socio-technical system [1]. Information system technically as a set of interrelated components that collect or retrieve, process, store and distribute information to support decision making, coordination, control, analysis and visualization in an organization [2].

There is always an inter-relation between the development of information technology and failure. A research which had been carried out by Standish Group International [3] reported that 31.1% of IT projects were cancel before completion, 52.7%

dioze Zaman et al. (Eds.): IVIC 2009, LNCS 5857, pp. 894–904, 2009.

over budget and over time whilst only 16.2% of the projects are succeed. Percentage recorded were representing world records as a whole. Since 1990s, failure of these information technology projects have been discussed widely resulting to the discovery of methods that can be used to the success of the projects. However, Dahlberg and Jarvinen [4] reported that none of the methods seems to be workable. Despite, a number of models have been developed as the guidelines on how to reduce the projects failure. According to Von Hallens[5] important to IS developers to recognize that they are primarily engaged in a service oriented business, rather than being in the business of producing high quality software. To discuss more about this research, the next part will focus on literature review of the research. Chapter 3 will cover on data generating through appropriate research methodology. Proposed model (PADM Model) will be thoroughly discussed in Chapter 4. Features of the model and its importance will be elaborated in Chapter 5. Summary in the final part is to disclose the importance and the enhancement works that can be done to improve the quality of this research.

2 Background

2.1 Definition

Information system is a combination of tools, communication technology and software used to manage information related to business[6]. Information system also defined as a system consists of software, tools, communication system and human. It helps to improve business with the integration of process and structure of the organization[7]. Ozkan [8] defined information system as a development of organization framework using specific software. Information system is the main stream of any businesses[6]. It's integrates every aspect of the business towards excellent execution. Information system came to existence in order to combine information technology, procedures, model, basic knowledge as well as data server[6]. Symbolic of relationship between information system and information technology helps the businesses to smoothen its processes [7].

   Therefore, information system gives a very positive definition and advantages to the users. However, research statistics showed that overall percentage of information system failure is still at the higher side.

2.2 Failure Factors

Many factors contribute to the projects failure. Definition of failure itself brings a negative meaning as in many dictionary stated failure as something failed to fulfill its purposes. Failure is a feature that hardly to expect[9]. Many researchers classified failure of information system as unfulfillment to its objectives and incompletion system within the specific time and cost [7[,[10], [11]. Information system failure also classified as a system which is unable to be used completely even before its completion [12] and the projects do not reach users' expectations[13]. According to the discussions amongst researchers, projects failure can be divided into 4 categories i.e. failure to accomplish desired design, exceeding due and amount limits, users do not apply the system due to failure to satisfy their needs and wants [6], [14], [15].

   In addition, a research carried out by Gen Lally [7] resulted to the classification of three (3) different stages of failure i.e. low, high and critical. Standish Group [3], in the Chaos report allotted information systems projects into three (3) categories. First category contained projects which have been completed within the timeframe and cost supported by well-execution. Second category consisted of completed projects and well functioning but exceeding due and amount limits. The last category covered on the discontinued and completely failed projects before reaching completion date. Based on previous research, it has been identified that greater extension in due and cost were to be the main factors for the failure information system projects. Other than that, it was subsequently contributed by poor management, scarcity of sources (capital, time and human capital), unleaded vision and mission, less support from the top management, users needs were mistakenly identified and changes happened so rapidly [3], [7], [10], [11], [16], [17].

The implementation of open tender has created another set of problems. The main problem is poor distribution of tender [18] followed by conflict in management, top management, system developer and users [19].

2.3 Success Factors

Researches, analysis and discussions on the success factors of IT projects have been done tremendously. The researchers analyzed the successful projects and explained the success factors based on individual project. Kamus Dewan (Third Edition) [20] defined success as win and something leads to good in return. Even tough the main focus of this article discuss about process in information system development model, a failure factors of information system must be also taken into account as a great help to come out with a precision and confidence research analysis.

The success of an IT project is very much depending on its capability and strategies thus the project is able to complete according to plan, estimated cost and successfully implemented. Researchers considered this factor as the fundamental factor towards the success of IT projects. This factor must be closely monitored to avoid unforeseen problems disturbed the projects to run smoothly. Apparently, success factors of a project is begun with the ability to control cost and timeline. The project is not supposed to be overspent. Due to that, timeframe must be taken care off because this is the major factor contributes to cost surplus.

A project remains stagnant if users do not realize of its existence. Inputs (either positive or negative) from users are needed for continuous improvement to take place, therefore, close relationship with users must be developed and maintained constantly. Scopes and objectives of a project must be made clear to all parties to ensure every party receive the same message. Besides that, there are few other success factors for example good support from the top management. This includes motivation, high tolerance coupled with attractive incentives will definitely boost up the employees to accomplish all tasks assigned to them with good faith.

Furthermore, users needs and wants must be correctly identified. System developers must be able to understand and sensitive to users' current needs and wants. Any changes made must be agreeable to both parties; users and system developers. This is due to the fact that success or failure of a project is very much depending on users' satisfaction. Proper planning and realistic deadline are also part of success factors. Good teamwork and communication skills among the developers' team members as well as users and top management subsequently bring the added values to the success of IT projects.

Based on research done by Glen Lally [7] on four information system models concluded that technical aspects is one of the most critical areas used to determine the level of success of IT projects. Technical issues are the social manifestation to individuals, groups and organizations that possess their own functions and interactions [14]. Research that has done by Glen Lally [7], involved four information systems which had been developed and widely used in United States. Based on that research, discovered that high self-belonging among users especially the top management and system developers managed to transform a plan into reality. This is well supported by high motivation, focus and dedication of human capital thus time and cost estimated are well obliged.

Subsequently, user involvement and commitment and also support from management contribute to all four models succeeded through that elements. Standish Group [3] in its report listed down the success factors of IT projects. There were; involvement of users, supported by top management, users needs and wants were well recognized and possession of high dedicated employees hold the highest percentage of all. No doubt that proper planning, realistic time estimation, lucid indicators, complete timetable, understand vision and mission plus high self-belonging became part of the success factors.

3   Methodology

Researches must use various methods instead of single method in the process to produce a solid and well accepted research. This research methodology concentrates on literature review to obtain as much information as possible from previous researches. Along the way, few models have been used in the process of developing information system. Features of the models used are shown in the table below:

Table 1. Features of Information System Models

CIRI	ITIL	COBIT	ISO /IEC 27002	TRIPL E–S	LEARNI NG CYCLE FOR IS PROJECT	IT PROJECT MODULE
Implementation planning	√			√	√	√
Cost planning						√
Risk planning						√
Architecture planning	√					
Changers planning	√					
Maintenance planning	√					√
Management quality		√				
Implementation quality		√				
Delivery and support		√		√	√	
Monitor and evaluate		√		√		
Security			√			
Lack assessment					√	√
Review					√	√
System ability assessment						√
User training						√

From the above table, we can see that every model has different characteristics. However, every model has its own strength and weaknesses. For example, ITIL [21] model is only focus on planning processes, COBIT [21] focus on management, evaluation and delivery whilst ISO/IEC 27002 [21] only focus on security. Whereas TRIPLE-S [6] put more attention on planning, delivery and evaluation as to compare with Learning Cycle for IS Project [12] which is to focus on planning, delivery and maintenance.

Based on   past research shown in Table 1 , only one information system model recognized to have most of the characteristics namely IT Project Schedule. Although it does not contain every required features but the said model seems to be the best model as it widely focus on budget, risk and maintenance planning. The model also emphasize on system review, evaluation process and user training. Eventough there are still other aspects to consider but IT Project Schedule obviously won the highest votes.

Hence, PADM model will take into account of all features as well as other available features which are able to contribute to the success of information system development and to enhance interrelation of the model. All processes and criterias in the PADM model are the outcome from literature review and previous researches' results.

4   Information System Development Model – PADM MODEL

PADM model is a theory model which is developed for the purpose of being as the guidelines in the development of information system. There are four main processes in PADM Model; planning, requirement analysis, design and maintenance. Every process has its own tasks specification where it can be used as a guideline as well as checklists to the project stakeholder (user, management, developer) and specifically for the system developers.

Four processes in PADM model is controlled by main process which is quality to ensure this model works effectively. Quality is the fundamental key in every aspect of life not only restrict in the information system development. Thus, good result always begins with excellent quality management [4].

Based in the finding of Von Hellens [5], organization using IS should be aware that the artifacts that they are using are not only software but a service, and they should be treated as services. Difficulties of developing a comprehensive model of IS quality arise from an incapability and inability to settle the varied perspectives taken by the IS stakeholders (management, user, developer) each with their own idea of quality [5].

PADM model is designed to have specific assessment incriminate of cost, time and stakeholders including management team, system developer and system users. Table 1 illustrates the PADM model consists of four main processes with close monitoring by quality processes.

Four main processes in PADM model as in above table have close relationship with quality processes. This is shown that every task in the PADM model processes must go through quality assessment procedures which comply to cost and timelines with the consent from stakeholders. Every task in the four processes must get approval from stakeholder for the assurance of quality and efficient processes.

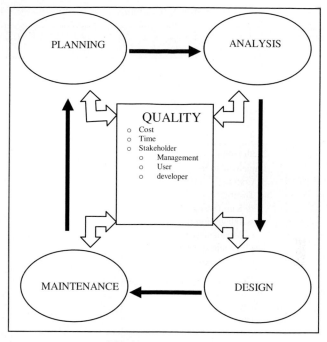

Fig. 1. PADM Model

5 Features of PADM Model

PADM model outlined its four main processes as planning, analysis, design and maintenance. All processes are monitored by main process i.e. quality to ensure every task is well executed. The most crucial goal in PADM model is to make it as a guideline and checklist to users, management team and system developers in the development of information system.

Each task in PADM model carries an important role that need special emphasize to avoid failure in the development of information system. Quality control is the main criteria in PADM Model especially on the main resources i.e. time and cost. Table 2 shows all features of PADM Model:

Table 2. Features of PADM Model

PROCESS	TASK	QUALITY
Planning	1. Goal and objective 2. User requirement 3. Scope 4. Cost 5. Time 6. Resources 7. Risk	QUALITY MEASUREMENT BASED ON: o COST o TIME o STAKEHOLDER (management, developer and user)

Table 2. (*Continued*)

PROCESS	TASK	QUALITY
Analysis	1. Project goal 2. User requirement 3. Scope 4. Work Breakdown Structure 5. Risk and problem	

Design	1. Methodology
	2. Implementation
	  o Coding
	  o Testing
	    o Unit testing
	    o Integration testing
	    o Module testing
	    o System testing
	    o User testing	

Maintenance	1. Support 2. Changes 3. Enhance 4. Update	

5.1 Planning

There are seven major tasks in the planning process that requires conscientious plans. Vission and mission must be identified at the earliest stage of the projects. Next step is to make stakeholders understand the vision and mission thus every step taken fits the common purpose. According to Gary [23], Taylor [24], Neimat [10], Glen Lally [7], Yeo [6], Bruce [9], Goulielmos [14], [11], Munn and B.F Bjeirmi [26] and Lytinen [15] in their researches considered a project as unsuccessful whenever the project failed to fulfill the objectives or objectives project not achieved.

Analysis and early planning of users needs must be prioritized in the planning process. Forbid to obey users needs will cause failure to the information system projects as no one will use the system offered to them [3], [6], [7], [9], [10], [11], [13], [14], [15], [25], [27], [28]. Clear identification and equal deliberation of projects development scope are very important. Scope must be in line with cost and time allotted coupled with sources and employees management in developing the system. Those need an efficient supervision otherwise the projects will not be able to complete within the stipulated time and cost [3], [6], [7], [9], [10], [11], [14], [15], [25], [26], [27].

Sufficient sources especially human capital is important to ensure the development process runs smoothly. This is supported by wise planning and strategy by the management group in the development and implementation stages of the information system. Life and risk are two things that is very well-connected to each other. Risk avoidance will just lead to nowhere therefore mastering the risks taking techniques will help to properly identify and manage risks [29]. Three other processes under risk management [29] will be discussed in the second process of PADM Model, analysis [29].

5.2 Analysis Process

Analysis phases consists of five (5) major tasks:

1.   Project goal
2.   User requirement
3.   Scope
4.   Work Breakdown Structure
5.   Risk and problem

Projects' aims must be analyzed to ensure it is aligned with project objectives. Thorough analysis based on research outcomes to identify what kind of systems required by users must be done first before it can be arrange according to functions and scope of projects. Scope, work breakdown structure and user requirements are the elements interconnected to each other. Risks and problems analysis in the analysis process are more focus on qualitative and quantitative risk analysis, risk planning, controlling and monitoring [29].

5.3 Design Process

The two main tasks in design process are methodology and implementation. Methodology which will be used in the system development must be designed first. The design must contain clear and unmistakable process so that stakeholder shares the same mission as the rest. A wide range of system development methods are available to choose according to goal and objectives of the projects. To name a few are prototyping, Joint Application Design (JAD), Rapid Application Development (RAD), Extreme Programming (EX) etc [30]. Implementation task is another important part in the design process. System will be developed and incriminate few other sub tasks like coding and testing. Coding involves programming so software used must be predetermined. Normally software chosen will suit the future system features by considering software support power. Users' requirements need to be considered because they tend to choose new software similarly to what they are using presently [31]. Although coding is the main task in implementation process, testing also plays an important role to ensure systems developed are completely utilized. Testing involves sub task as follows:

1.   Unit testing
2.   Module testing
3.   Integration testing
4.   System testing
5.   User testing

Testing unit will undergo trial run to prove that it can be operated as actual unit [32]. Module testing is an integration testing process of integrated module units. System testing is a testing done on the sub system integration. User testing is the final process before users can fully utilize the system. User testing is done to ensure it is well accepted by users.

5.4 Maintenance Process

The fourth process in PADM model is maintenance. Maintenance is compulsory when any changes are required by the system. Instead of system changes, process system enhancement and updating system will be carried out in maintenance process. Support system will be put in place as precaution if any problem arise during its operation. Support system normally useful in system application aspect and software used in the system implementation.

5.5 Quality Process

Quality process is the strongest point of PADM model where the process main function is to monitor processes of systems which have been implemented. Quality process plays the following roles:

1.   Control tasks as in planning, analysis, design and maintenance
2.   Monitor sub tasks to comply to pre-determined measurement
3.   Evaluate sub tasks implemented in the four processes

There are three important elements in quality process i.e. cost, time and stakeholder (user, management and developer). Every sub task implemented must comply with quality assessment process so that everything runs smoothly and mistakes will be easily detected. Changes must go through quality process assessment before getting approval from stakeholder who involved in the project. Implementation of quality process in developing information system will reduce failure of information system projects.

6 Conclusion

This research is done basicly to know what is the best model used to develop a system especially information system. From the previous researches, there were plenty models used in the development of information system. However, the models posses very limited features and categorized as incomplete models. Methods applied did not cover the whole aspects of system development processes.

Hence, this research brings the intention to create an information system model which embrace every aspect required in the development of information system. Research is done on used and modified models as well as enhancement works done in PADM Model. PADM Model includes four main processes and monitored by a main process that works as the monitoring element to sub tasks in each processes.

PADM model is developed to eliminate weaknesses in the previous information system models. However, this research can be further enhanced by testing the proposed models. Case study can be used to prove that this model is workable. Besides that, validation process is another option to strengthen this research by getting views from specialist on the particular model. A number of techniques available to be used in validation and verification processes namely Delphi Techniques, brainstorming, interview etc [29].

Acknowledgment

The authors wish to thank all the UKM siswazah multimedia group members for the moral support and guidline.

References

1. Munford, E., Hirschheim, R., Fitzgerald, G., Wood Harper, T.: Research method in Information System. In: Proc. IFIP WG 8.2 Colloquium (1984)
2. Laudon, K.C.: Management Information System. Prentice-Hall, Englewood Cliffs (2001)
3. Standish Group Report, Failure record (1995),
   http://www.cs.nmt.edu/~cs328/reading/Standish
4. Dahlberg, T., Jarvinen, J.: Challenges to Information System Qulity. Information and Software Technology 39, 808–818
5. Von Hellens, L.A.: Information Quality vs software quality: a discussion from a managerial, an organizational and engineering view point. Information and software Technology 39, 801–808
6. Yeo, K.T.: Critical failure factors in information system projects. International Journal of Project Management 20, 241–246 (2002)
7. Glen, L.: Understanding information technology system project failure. Dublin Institute of Technology (2004)
8. Ozkan, S.: Process Based Information System Success Model. In: European Conference on Information System, Spin (2006)
9. Bruce, R.: Goverment information system problems and failure: a preliminary review (1997), http://www.pamij.com/roche.html
10. Al Neimat Taimour, T.: Why IT project Fail. The project prefect white paper collection (2005)
11. Coley Consulting. Reducing your acceptance testing risk: Why project fail (2005),
    http://www.coleyconsulting.co.uk/failure.htm
12. Kwenku, E.M.: Critical issues in abandoned information systems development projects. Communication of the ACM 40(9) (1997)
13. Sauer, C.: Why information system fail: a case study approach. Information system series. UK (1993)
14. Goulielmos, M.: Outlining organisatinal failure in information system development. Disaster Development and Management Journal 12(4), 319–327 (2002)
15. Lyytinen, K., Hirschheim, R.: Information failure- a survey and classification of the empirical literature. Oxford survey in Information Technology, 257–309 (1997)
16. Lemon, F.W.: Information system project failure: a comparative study of two countries. Journal of Global Information Management (2002)
17. Robert, F.: Project success and failure: what is success, what is failure and how can you improve your odds for success? (2003),
    http://www.umsl.edu/~sauterv/analysis/6840_f03_papers/frese
18. Martin, B.: The Brampton factor: Why big government IT projects fail (2008),
    http://www.silicon.com/publicsector/
    0,3800010403,39169765,00.htm

19. Warne, L.: Conflict as a factor in Information System failure. In: The 8th Australasian Conference on Information System, ACIS 1997 (1997); Warne, L.: Conflict and politics of information system failure: a challenge of information system professionals and researchers. In: Defense Science and Technology Organization, pp. 104–134 (1997)
20. Dewan, K.: Dewan Bahasa dan Pustaka (2005)
21. Shamsul, S., Mohammad, S., Masarat, A.: Combining ITIL, COBIT and ISO/IEC 27002 in order to design a comprehensive IT framework in organization. In: Second Asia International Conference on Modelling & Simulation (2008)
22. Rodney, A.S.: A framework for the life cycle management of information technology projects: Project IT. International Journal of Information Management 26, 203–212 (2008)
23. Gary, P., Shan, L.P.: Examining the coalition dynamics affecting IS project abandoment decision-making. Decision Support System 42, 639–655 (2006)
24. Gary, P., Ray, H., Shan, L.P.: Information system implementation failure: Insight from prism. International Journal of Information Management 28, 259–269 (2008)
25. Taylor, J.: Managing Information Technology Projects: Applying Project Management Strategies to Software, Hardware and Integration Initiatives. American Management Association, New York (2003)
26. Sheila, W.: Failed IT project (The human factor). Degree dissertation, University of Maryland Bowie State University (1998)
27. Munns, A.K., Bjeirmi, B.F.: The role of project management in achieving project success. International journal of project management 12(2), 81–87 (1996)
28. Lynn, C., Julien, P.: Hard and soft project: a framework for analysis. International Journal of Project Management 22, 645–653 (2004)
29. Rowe, G., Wright, G.: The impact of task characteristics on the performance of structured group forecasting techniques. International Journal of Forecasting (12), 73–89 (1999)
30. Futrell, R.T., Shafer, D.F., Shafer, L.I.: Quality Software Project Management. Prentice Hall, Englewood Cliffs (2002)
31. Barry, W.: A spiral model software development and enhancement. TRW Defence System Groups, 001162/X8/0500-0061-88 IEEE (1988)
32. Dominik, V., Mladen, V.: Bad practice in complex IT project. In: Proceeding of the IT 30th International Conference of IT Interface (2008)
33. Ram, C.: Software testing best practices. Technical Report RC 21457 Log 968564/26/99, Center os software enginnering, IBM (1999)
34. Drucker, P.F.: Management: Tasks, Responsibilities, Practices, The Best of Business Books, The World Executive's Digest Library, p. 13 (1989)
35. Kerlinger, F.N.: Foundation of behaviour research, UK (1986)
36. Maria, Esperanza: Approach to the integration on qilitative and quantitative method in software engineering. Philisophiocal Foundations on Information Systems Engineering (2006)
37. Nitin, A., Urvashi, R.: Defining success for software projects: An exploratory revelation. International Journal of Project Management 24, 358–370 (2006)
38. Wateridge, J.: IT project: A basic for success. International Journal of Project Management 13(3), 169–172 (1993)
39. Whittaker, B.: What went wrong? Unsuccessful information technology project. Information Management & Computer Security 7(1), 23–29 (1999)
40. Gore, V.: Failure rate: Statistics over IT project failure rate (2005), http://www.it-cortex.com/Stat_Failure_Rate.htm

Assistive Courseware for Visually-Impaired

Nurulnadwan Aziz[1], Nur Hazwani Mohamad Roseli[1], and Ariffin Abdul Mutalib[2]

[1] Universiti Teknologi MARA Terengganu, Kampus Dungun,
23000 Dungun Terengganu, Malaysia
[2] Universiti Utara Malaysia
06010 Sintok Kedah, Malaysia
nuruln746@tganu.uitm.edu.my, nurha5338@tganu.uitm.edu.my,
am.ariffin@uum.edu.my

Abstract. Research in aiding disabled people with electronic applications should be one of the focuses in the area of human-computer interaction. The population of disabled is big and increasing, so they should be entertained well so that they will be potential resources to the nation. This paper discusses the Assistive Courseware (AC) in terms of how visually-impaired (VI) can make full use of them. It aims to propose guidelines for developing AC for VI people. In the introduction part, current issues regarding disabilities and the population is discussed. It also outlines the objectives of the paper. Next, the research methodology is outlined. There are three phases in which AC development is in the second phase which adapts the IntView courseware development methodology. The final part of the paper contains results of the test, which proposes basic guidelines for developing AC for VI.

Keywords: Assistive courseware, visually impaired, edutainment courseware.

1 Introduction

The increasing number of people with disabilities in Malaysia attracts the concerns of researchers to cooperate with the IT expertise to develop various technologies inclusive of hardware and software, hoping that these technologies can assist the population in carrying out their tasks in everyday life. The examples are accessing information and services (such as learning), and improving their quality of life. This type of technology is known as assistive technology (AT). Unluckily, most of the ATs available in the market are very expensive, whereby disabled people have to spend a big amount of money to afford for the AT. It is also observable that the availability of AT in Malaysia for this population is still lacking. AT can be designed in terms of hardware (such as a wheelchair) and software (such as courseware) [1]. This paper focuses on designing a software-based AT, particularly on the design of the interface for assistive courseware (AC) for education. The development will be tailored for visually-impaired (VI) people. In designing the interface of AC for VI, guidelines are needed to ensure users' requirements are adapted in the AC [2]. It is a hope that the guidelines help developers in developing the AC and that the AC can help VI students in their learning process.

H. Badioze Zaman et al. (Eds.): IVIC 2009, LNCS 5857, pp. 905–915, 2009.
© Springer-Verlag Berlin Heidelberg 2009

Visual impairment is the functional loss of vision [5]. According to [8] visual impairment consists of (i) totallyz blind; (ii) low vision; and (iii) color blindness.

i. Totally blind- Blindness involves a substantial, uncorrectable loss of vision in both eyes.

ii. Low vision- There are many types of low vision (also known as "partially sighted" in parts of Europe), for instance poor acuity (vision that is not sharp), tunnel vision (seeing only the middle of the visual field), central field loss (seeing only the edges of the visual field), and clouded vision.

iii. Color Blindness- Color blindness is a lack of sensitivity to certain colors. Common forms of color blindness include difficulty distinguishing between red and green, or between yellow and red. Sometimes color blindness results in the inability to perceive any color.

In Malaysia, the National Eye Survey in 1996 indicates that 2.73% of the populations are visually impaired, of whom 2.44% have low vision, and 0.29% is blind. This would put the present number of Malaysians who are visually impaired at close to 700,000; with 74,000 of them blind. In 1996 a Malaysian Ministry of Health survey found among Malaysia's in its population of 24 million people an estimated 5,000 children are blind and a further 50,000 are visually impaired and at risk of losing their sight, 60,000 blind adults, and 450,000 adults with visual impairment [6].

An initial interview recommends that students with VI disabilities should be helped with electronic application to help them learning on their own. In St. Nicholas Home, VI students learn softwares such as JAWs (Screen reader), Microsoft Words, Microsoft Excel, Microsoft Power Point, Email, HTML Development, and Web Accessibility. Their objectives are to expose and introduce IT to the blind and VI persons, and to ensure that all trainees can effectively utilize the learned skills [7]. This paper extends a doubt that not only software which are usable in schools are considered, but also in the forms of AC which they could bring along with them to access at anytime no matter where the location is. More importantly, the AC contains learning contents. The AC should be designed following certain guidelines. However, there is no standard guideline to design and develop an AC for VI people found in literature.

Based on discussions in the previous paragraphs, this paper aims to propose guidelines for developing AC for VI people. To achieve that, the objectives are set as follow:

i.   To identify characteristics of AC for VI
ii. To develop a prototype of AC for VI
iii. To measure level of user acceptance of the developed prototype

2   Methodology

To achieve the listed objectives, a research methodology called Iterative Triangulation Methodology was followed, adapted from [4]. The methodology suggests that data sources, methods, theoretical, and data analysis are composed of different ways (Figure 1). Figure 1 describes that there is a third party between development and empirical testing, which is the theoretical aspect. Data regarding theoretical could be obtained from document review or interviews.

The activities of the research are outlined in Figure 2, which is divided into three phases. The first phase is to gather characteristics of AC for VI. Documents were reviewed, and interviews with teachers of VI people were carried out. The characteristics

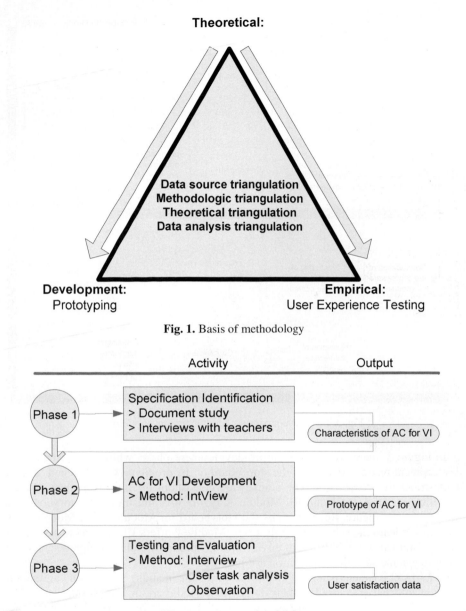

Fig. 1. Basis of methodology

Fig. 2. Summary of activities

of AC for VI were gathered from this phase, which is utilized and applied in the proto-type developed in phase 2. The development of the prototype is based on IntView methodology. [3] proposed the IntView methodology for developing small scaled courseware. Figure 3 illustrates the steps in IntView adapted in this study. There are two major phases in IntView v1, which separate the tasks into pre-development phase and development phase.

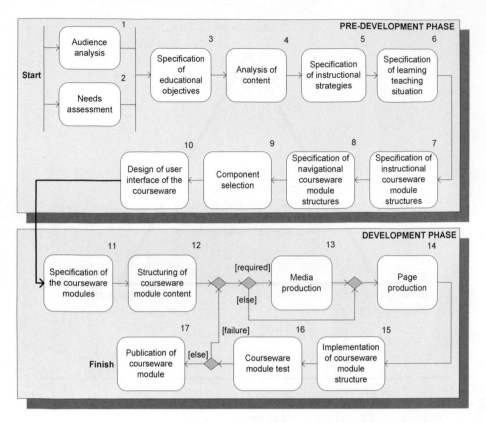

Fig. 3. IntView courseware development methodology

In Figure 3, there are 10 steps in pre-development phase, while seven steps in the development phase. At step 10, the storyboard of the prototype was sketched. Figure 4 illustrates the storyboard. The courseware consists of three main modules. Figure 4(a) illustrates the storyboard for Module 1, Figure 4(b) illustrates the storyboard for Module 2, and Figure 4(c) illustrates the storyboard for Module 3. In Module 1 the VI students learn the subject through songs. Module 2 offers VI students to learn three types of animal in three different environments, and in Module 3 simple exercises in order to test the students' interaction are provided.

In terms of characteristics, AC for VI should contain audio, graphic and animation, and contents that are closed to their daily lives. Audio are in .mp3 format, and all of the graphics and animations are in .gif format. The basic background color for each module is green. In Modules 1 and 2 background images are utilized and green is basic background color. Comic Sans between 30 and 90-point sized is utilized. Premier colours and secondary colours have been chosen as colours for texts. Two songs are utilized i.e. "Baa, Baa, Black Sheep" and "Old Mac Donald" because they are popular. Animation graphics for this module were black sheep, white sheep, cow, duck, and horse. At the end of the process, a working prototype was obtained. Samples of snapshots are shown in Figure 5.

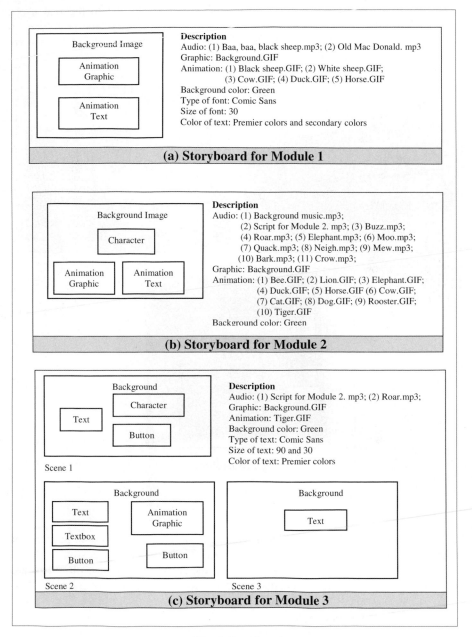

Fig. 4. Storyboard

The prototype is used to convey the guidelines of AC for VI to the real users. Phase 3 of the study is to measure the levels of user acceptance of the prototype. It involved testing procedures including user task and interview. Results of the test are discussed in the next section.

Fig. 5. Snapshots

3   Results

17 VI students of Sekolah Kebangsaan Kubang Ikan, Kuala Terengganu participated in the test. They are between 7 and 12 years old. The results are discussed according to user tasks and interview. During user task, the students were also observed, and findings of the observation are also discussed.

3.1   Results from Observation

Results of the observation are classified based-on the modules. Two modules involved which were learning through songs, and learn types of animals. In the second module, learning wild animals, learning domestic animals, and learning pets were experienced by the learners. For the learning through songs module two songs i.e. "Baa Baa Black Sheep" and Old Mac Donald" were provided.

Module 1: Learning through songs

Both songs were played twice. For the first round for "Baa Baa Black Sheep" song, it was found that all the participants did not sing similarly with the song, but 100% of them tried to capture the song. For the second round it was found that some of the participants tried to enjoy the song and sang similarly with the song especially at the chorus part. 82.3% of the participants gave good responds and 17.6% of them were still passive. For the "Old Mac Donald" song, in the first round it was found that 94.1% of the participants gave good responds in which they sang together and clapped their hand with the songs. In the second round it was found that 100% of the participants gave very good responds.

Module 2: Learning wild animal, domestic animal, and pets

For the learning wild animal module, it was noted that 82.2% of the participants which was low vision and totally blind students gave good responds. They tried to guess the animals when they hear the animal's sounds and spell together with the AC. Other 17.8% of the participants which were totally blind students behaved passive. In learning domestic animals module, the study found that 94.1% of the participants gave good responds. The participants were interested to learn and participate except for one of the totally blind that is still passive. In the learning pets module, the study noted that 58.8% of the participants gave very good responds, while other 36.8% gave good responds, and 5.8% were still passive.

3.2 Results of Interview

Results of the interview are categorized based on the elements provided by the AC. Six or 35.3% of the participants reported that they use PC sometimes at home and 17 or 100% of them never use any type of courseware either at school or at home.

3.2.1 Audio

Question 1: Do you depend on the audio to understand everything on the screen?
100% of the participants reported that they really depend on the audio to understand everything that appears on the screen.

Question 2: Do you hear the sound clearly?
The participants reported that 76.5% of them hear the sound clearly, 5.9% of them reported that the sound can be categorized as barely acceptable, and 17.6% of them reported that the sound were not heard clearly.

Question 3: Can the background music assist you in the learning process?
100% of the participants reported that background music could not assist them in the learning process. All of them reported that background music will make them feel confused with the learning process.

Question 4: Can the sound effect enhance your interaction with the AC?
82.4% of the participants reported that the sound effect can enhance their interaction with the AC, while 17.6% of them reported that the sound effect of the AC can be categorized as good.

Based on the findings, audio is the most important element for visually impaired people. Even though there are some graphics and text shown in the AC (for low vision people), they still depend on the audio to recognize these graphics and text. Furthermore, sound effect can enhance students' interaction with the AC. However, the background music should be avoided because it disturbs VI students' focus; moreover, they are not able to differentiate the music with desired information.

3.2.2 Formatting Style and Text
Question 1: Is the font size large enough?
41.2% of the participants agreed that font sizes between 30 and 90 as good, while 11.8% of the participants reported that the font size was good, 5.9% reported that the font size was barely acceptable and 41.2% reported that the font size was very poor.

Question 2: Is the font type easy to understand?
41.2% of the participants reported that the Comic Sans was very good, while 11.8% of them reported that the font type was good, 5.9% reported that the font type was barely acceptable and 41.2% reported that the font type was very poor.

Question 3: Is the font face easy to understand?
41.2% of the participants agreed that Comic Sans is easy to understand, while 11.8% agreed that the font face was barely acceptable, 5.9% agreed that the font face was poor, and 41.2% agreed that the font face was very poor.

Question 4: Does the font color contrast with the background color?
52.9% of the participants reported that contrasts color between font and background was very good, 5.9% of them reported barely acceptable, and 41.2% of them reported very poor.

Question 5: Does the animated text acceptable?
35.3% of the participants reported that the animation text was barely acceptable, while 23.5% of them reported that the animation text was poor, and 41.2% of the participants reported that the animation text was very poor.

For the formatting style and text, it was found that the best font size for visually impaired people is 18 and above and must use standard font face. Otherwise, visually impaired people (except for totally blind people) will face difficulties in reading the text. Moreover, font color must contrast with the background color and the text must be outlined. Other than that, participants commented that the animated text should be avoided so that they can focus on the text.

3.2.3 Graphic and Animation
Question 1: Are the graphics and animations shown on screen meaningful?
41.2% of the participants reported that the meaningfulness of graphic and animation shown on screen was good, 17.6% of them reported barely acceptable, and 41.2% reported very poor

Question 2: Are the graphics and animations shown on screen understandable?
41.2% of the participants responded positively, 17.6% of them reported agreed that it is acceptable, and 41.2% reported that the graphic and animation are very poor.

Question 3: Are the size of important attributes large enough?
41.2% of the participants reported that the size of attributes is very good, 5.9% of them reported good, 5.9% of them reported barely acceptable, 5.9% reported poor, and 41.2% reported very poor.

Question 4: Does the foreground of attributes contrast with the background color?
47.1% of them reported that the contrast color between foreground of attributes and background color was very good, 11.8% of them reported good, and 41.2% reported very poor.

Question 5: Is the graphic and animation clearly identified?
52.9% of the participants reported very good, 5.9% reported good, and 41.2% reported very poor.

Question 6: Is the number of graphic and animation minimal in one scene?
58.8% of the participants reported the number of graphic and animation in one scene was barely acceptable, and 41.2% of them reported very poor.

Based on the results, AC should avoid collecting too much information in terms of graphics and animation on one screen. VI people will confuse, when they have to focus on many things, especially if they are animated. Size is another matter. VI people will give more attention to attribute with bigger sized over the other. This suggests that the most desired attribute should be emphasized in terms of size.

3.2.4   General Interaction
Question 1: Do you satisfy with the keyboard used in this courseware?
29.4% of the participants reported that the keyboard usage provided by the courseware was good, 29.4% of them reported barely acceptable, and 41.2% of them reported very poor.

Question 2: Does the directions and instructions in the courseware explicit?
35.3% of the participants reported that the directions and instructions that provided by the courseware was barely acceptable, 23.5% of them reported poor, and 41.2% reported very poor.

From the findings, the best method for visually impaired people to interact with the courseware is by using 100% keyboard. According to the comments from the participants, the usage of the mouse was not practical for them. Furthermore, instructions given in the courseware were not very clear. Hence, students could not depend on the keyboard only to do the exercises and they need assistance from the instructors.

3.3   Practical Testing

For the practical testing the results show that 35.3% of the participants showed good performance in doing exercise; all these participants were low vision students. During the practical testing these participants just need the help from instructors when they wanted to click on the button. Another 41.2% which is seven participants need the instructors to facilitate them all of the time, and 23.5% of the remaining participants cannot do the exercise at all.

4 Conclusion

From the observation, it was found that the VI learners enjoyed learning with the prototype. This could be deduced that AC can be a good tool to locate learning contents for the VI people, providing that the AC is developed appropriate to their requirements. Based on the results obtained from the test, there are several basic guidelines to apply in developing the AC for VI. The guidelines are listed below:

- Use of audio is very important – the audio should be clear to the user, and differentiated clearly from the background music. If possible, omit the background music.
- Sound effect is important to enhance users' alert – supply sound effect to the interaction so that users understand whether computer has accepted their input and whether they have made correct action or vice versa.
- Fonts must be big enough for the VI people – at least use generally 20-point and above
- The fonts must be standard face – VI people face difficulties to read if otherwise.
- Font color and background color must be highly contrast – VI people are different that normal people in color perception. They are not able to differentiate blue and green because the colors are less contrast. Combination of yellow and green is an example of good pair for them.
- Animated should be avoided – VI people are not familiar with animated text, moreover the animated text will make them confused.
- Lessen overload information on a screen – VI people are not able to absorb information like normal people. They pay attention to information they are attended to. Use of graphic should be minimized.
- Important information should be bigger – VI people are attended to biggest element on screen first, followed with smaller. So, the most important information should be made appeared biggest.
- Avoid mouse-based interaction – VI people are not able to use the mouse, so AC for VI must only utilize the keyboard.

This study tested only several elements as guidelines. It is believed that there are many more guidelines to be standardized, which requires fund to carry the extended study.

References

1. Dawe, M.: Desperately seeking simplicity: how young adults with cognitive disabilities and their families adopt assistive technologies. In: Proc. SIGCHI 2006, CHI 2006, pp. 1143–1152. ACM, New York (2006)
2. Dawe, M.: Let me show you what I want: engaging individuals with cognitive disabilities and their families in design. In: Proc. CHI 2007, pp. 2177–2182. ACM, New York (2007)

3. Grützner, I., Angkasaputra, N., Pfahl, D.: A systematic approach to produce small course-ware modules for combined learning and knowledge management environments. In: Proceedings of the 14th International Conference on Software Engineering and Knowledge Engineering (SEKE), Italy (2002)
4. Marianne, L.W.: Iterative triangulation: A theory development process using existing case studies. Journal of Operations Management 16, 455–469 (1998)
5. National Dissemination Center for Children with Disabilities,
   http://www.nichcy.org
6. ORBIS, http://www.orbis.org
7. Rosidah, W.: Visually Impaired (Recorded by AIWA Cassette Recorder) (Cassette). St. Nicolas Home, Penang (2006)
8. W3C, Web Accessibility Initiative, http://www.w3.org/wai

Author Index

came at me to change my mind about wanting to take the pheasant away. Whenever Simba lunged toward me, Shane would step in and fend him off. This action would turn the assault toward him. Then I would step in and lure Simba away from Shane and turn the assault toward me. This went on over and over and over again until Simba became tired of the back-and-forth and ran back to his kennel, leaving the pheasant behind. Not an easy way to make a living and definitely not the safest way. We were young rookies in the animal world, we enjoyed the adrenaline rush, and even though it was very unethical and cruel in retrospect, I learned a lot from those days about animal behavior and the do's and don'ts of working with wildlife, namely respecting an animal for what it *is*. Engaging with wild animals without understanding their behavior can be dangerous.

I have a deep scar in the meat of my right hand, just below my pinky, from Simba. Back at the farm, in our daily feeding regimen, Simba had a 1-foot-by-1-foot hole cut in the front of the door to his kennel just big enough to throw whole plucked chickens through. Simba was very much a food-focused animal, so the chickens would rarely hit the ground. He would snatch them out of the air the way he did the pheasant. Day after day, I would get familiar with each animal's feeding habits, and I developed my own patterns for feeding them. As I walked toward Simba, he would usually be in his shelter box and would focus on me as I walked up, knowing he was about to be fed. That day, I grabbed the first chicken and threw it through the hole, knowing that he was going to grab it as usual and start eating it immediately. As I lackadaisically threw the first chicken through, I left my right hand dangling through the hole in the door as I reached with my left hand to grab the next chicken in the bucket. Somehow Simba missed the first chicken and in his mind, the second chicken was hanging there for him through the hole in the door, dripping in chicken blood and grease. I remember the sharp pain when he leapt up and sank one of his claws deep into my hand, pulling it toward his mouth to take a bite. I pulled as hard as I could to avoid the canines popping through my hand. I was arm wrestling with a 110-pound mountain lion, and he had the upper hand, literally. As I attempted to pull my hand from inside the cage, I felt the muscle tear as he pulled in the opposite direction. Finally, with a quick snap, Simba released my hand with a growl, wanting his chicken back. I dropped the bucket and rushed inside with blood gushing out of my hand. Cat claws and mouths are laden with dangerous bacteria, so I knew that I needed to clean it immediately. You can't imagine how excruciating it was to take hydrogen peroxide and a toothbrush and scrub deeply into the deep tear in my hand, already sensitive and throbbing. I scrubbed it clean, stitched myself up, and topped the stitches off with my favorite fixative material, SuperGlue. Compared to all the professional wound mending I have had over the years, I have to say this home job healed up pretty nicely.

So after all these incidents with Simba, you would've thought he'd be the last cat on earth that I would've suggested using to help out my friend Ken. But I had tunnel vision, and Grizzly Encounter needed money. So it was a risk worth taking, and one that I was excited about just because I wanted to be reunited with Simba, who still fascinated me.

So after talking to John and Troy and making arrangements, I called Ken back and said we would gladly make his promotional video in Montana. We scheduled a date, arranged a meeting, and we all drove to a rocky cliff area that was a perfect mountain lion habitat. It was a beautiful morning and everybody was excited to work with Simba. Simba paced anxiously in his trailer as I sat everybody down in the sun and gave them a safety briefing about our photo shoot that day. I knew Simba's history, and I knew mountain lions well, and they are not the most predictable creatures. That morning, my lecture was very detailed and matter-of-fact. Everybody listened attentively, and I could tell that they were a bit nervous.

But once upon the cliff edge, it was just like old times. I could tell that Simba remembered me, and we instantly started to play as if we had never missed a day. I scratched his neck and behind his ears and he purred loudly. Simba lay on the sandstone boulders and posed for photos, and then Ken sculpted in clay as Simba sat proudly like the king of the mountain. Next up were some action shots. I let Simba off his leash and ran up the hill calling to him, and he chased me around the sagebrush. It was a great workout for both of us. The day was going perfectly and the two-hour film session was now coming to an end. I could sense everybody letting their guard down a bit, as if Simba had gone from being a dangerous mountain lion to a big pussycat. Even I had let my guard down a little and was standing there laughing, rubbing Simba on the head and having a conversation with John as he stood behind the camera. I don't know what alerted me, some sort of sixth sense, but I looked down at Simba as his purring abruptly came to an end. A very familiar sight awaited me: dilated eyes and ears pinned down flat. This was not a good situation at all. At that moment, Simba leapt for my throat. In a fraction of a second, I had grabbed him by his throat to fend off the death bite. With my hands around his neck, he dug his claws into my torso and began to pull and move his jaws in closer to my throat. As in any moment of crisis, time slowed to a virtual stop, and for that moment there was only Simba and me.

At the edge of a cliff we now danced the dance of death, looking into each others eyes, as Simba dug his claws deeper into my flesh, pulling himself closer and closer to my neck. I pushed and resisted as hard as I could. And I was not winning. Most would have panicked, but with my years of facing attacks, I knew that the only thing that would save me was focus and decisive action. I knew I was losing and that soon he would sink his canines into my carotid artery and jugular vein, killing me in minutes. I was fighting for my life.

Simba then went to his next killer strategy, picking his hind legs off the ground in a effort to rake his rear claws simultaneously through my stomach wall. Once his feet left the ground, he lost leverage and our dance turned into a spiraling collapse toward the rocky ground. As I continued to look him in the eyes and push him away, we came down to the earth with a giant thud. With the impact, I saw a change in his eyes. Now I had the edge and it was time to take advantage of it. Simba's mind-set went from thoughts of killing to confusion. Luckily, his leash was lying in the dirt next to our bodies. I quickly grabbed the leash, fastened it to his collar, and started to walk him as if nothing had happened. My intention was to reassert control and keep his mind away from attacking me again. I had to walk him a quarter of a mile down to his trailer, and I kept my pace and my control until I loaded him into the trailer. Once the trailer door was latched, I suddenly felt the pain. I knew that during the attack on the hill, he was inflicting damage, but when you're in that kind of situation you never feel it. Now I felt it. I walked back up the hill to help carry the remaining camera gear down, and I was met halfway by Ami and the rest of the crew, who looked like they had just seen a ghost. Ami asked how I was doing, and we pulled up my sleeves to see the damage. It didn't take me long to realize I needed to go to the hospital. We loaded up the gear and I instructed Ami to drive Simba back to the ranch and leave him in the trailer until I got back. John and I jumped in another truck and headed to the nearest hospital, which was forty-five minutes away. I remember telling John to slow down as we were sliding around corners on the dirt road, and telling him that I would not die from the wounds but that I would certainly die from his crazy driving.

We reached the hospital in Livingston, and in typical documentary filmmaking fashion I posed for some pre-stitch photos in the parking lot before we went inside. I told the triage nurse I'd been attacked by a barn cat, knowing that the truth would provoke newspaper and television interviews that I had no interest in giving. She didn't like my explanation but seemed to go along with it. The doctor who examined me thought I had driven a motorcycle through a barbed-wire fence. Deeply concerned about possible infection from the bacteria of Simba's claws, I admitted that I had been attacked by a mountain lion but asked that it be kept quiet, and they agreed. After being stitched up, I headed back to the game farm to face my attacker and unload him from the trailer to his kennel. I spent some time with him, scratching his neck and making him purr. I patted him on the head and left him behind for the very last time. Now it was time to find anything useful from the attack that I could. I wanted to sit down with my crew and go over what had happened and how we could've avoided it, and analyze how we had handled an emergency situation.

I had no idea what anybody else did or didn't do during the attack, so I let them tell me, one by one, their side of the story. I remember in the middle of the attack saying the words "Spray him" in a very low-key way. Part of our emergency plan was the use of bear pepper spray on a attacking animal, and I knew that no spray had been deployed even when I asked for it. I found that most of my crew had been confused or frozen, or made bad decisions. I also learned that Ken, who wasn't supposed to do anything, had tried to reach between Simba and me to grab my bear spray, but was unsuccessful. It was a great learning moment for all of us, one from which I wear the scars proudly, because I know that my crew will react differently next time. There's no better way to learn than from an experience of such intensity. Sometimes it takes an actual emergency to know exactly how you will react.

That evening we finished off the film shoot with Brutus and a little baby mountain lion cub that was the exact same size as Simba when I first met him. I remember Brutus sniffing my bandages and wondering what had happened to me. He sympathized with me and was very gentle, never tearing at my bandages or being extra pushy. He knew that his friend was hurt and gave me the compassion that I deserved. I could tell by his actions and body language that he could feel that I was in pain and that something was wrong. He moved around me slowly, and poked his nose gently at me in sympathy, looking at me with his loving brown eyes.

When you sign up for your animal body language class, it comes with its share of "learning things the hard way" assignments. Animals never lie; they will lay it all out there for you. With Simba, I had created a cat-and-mouse situation, and he held up his end of the bargain. I should have been smarter than that, but when we make mistakes, we usually pay the price. Whether the moment is violent or gentle, an animal's honesty is constant. This is what makes it easier to understand the actions of animals than those of people. Humans possess the capacity to deceive, which makes us unpredictable.

Simba taught me the power of wild emotion and passion, and it helped me understand the unconditional love Brutus has in his heart. He appreciates every moment I spend with him because he lives only in that moment. I have the responsibility to make sure that Brutus's life is full and happy, to understand his wants and needs, and to make sure that he isn't pushed to the point of having to defend himself. Wild animals are just that—wild. Forgetting that can leave a deep wound or even cost you your life. I reflect every day on my scars and how I got them. That reflection fuels the reverence and respect I hold for Brutus.

CHAPTER **18**

BEARANOIA

W E HAVE TURNED THE GRIZZLY BEAR, WHO WANDERS THE mountains alone, into an outlaw. We fear him in the valleys below. When he comes to town it almost certainly means trouble. The WANTED posters make headlines, and so he vanishes into the forest again, yet still we fear him. He's a solitary soul and means no harm. But when we make mistakes, he seizes the opportunity. He's wanted dead or alive, but he is tough to catch. He is the last of the wild west.

We have been trained to fear the grizzly bear. Every time you hear about a grizzly bear it's because it has done something wrong. One of the grizzly bear's biggest enemies is its reputation. When you read about a grizzly in the newspaper, it's because it has broken into a family's cabin looking for food, or a female protects her cubs, as a good mother should, and leaves some poor guy with a couple of hundred stitches. When you see a grizzly in a movie, it is always part of some bloodthirsty nightmare, which is good for Hollywood but far from the truth about bears. Unfortunately, most people make their judgments base on this representation. They believe that grizzly bears want to kill and eat people. And every once in a while it happens, but people are vastly more likely to be struck by lightning, or hit in the head by a falling coconut. When most people go into grizzly country, they go with fear. Growing up in Montana, I found that the majority of the locals feel the same way or even though most of them have only seen a grizzly from a mile away or through a spotting scope, or else they have seen a brown-colored black bear that has been embellished into a bigger-than-life grizzly. There is a remnant fear passed on from the oldtimers. Most of Montana was settled by cattle ranchers and men looking for gold at the turn of the last century. When the gold ran out, ranching was the only way to make money. Predators were no longer welcome. To lose a cow to a wolf or a bear was devastating in those days. It could be the difference between feeding your family or not. If there was even a small chance that a bear would chow down on some farmer's cow, it wasn't a risk worth taking. Complete eradication was the only way to make sure nothing would happen. And people did their best. Hunting, trapping, poisoning, and setting bounties on all predators was the answer. Most of the wolves and grizzly in Montana were killed off in this fashion. As generations passed, the bears' reputation as a cattle and man killing

machine was handed down through stories and ideals. Eve
today, some of my most savvy Montana mountain m
friends are terrified of the grizzly. They say things like "
got that close to me, I would have shot it," or "I'm not hiking
up there, grizzlies are all over that place."

Every year one or more bears die just because of this mentality. I read the stories in the paper, and I listen to the
accounts of the mauling victims on the local news, and I recognize over and over again that either the attack could have
been avoided completely or that something could have been
done to prevent the loss of the bear's life. One example is the
use of firearms in self-defense of a bear attack, or should I
say bear encounter. Over and over again, regardless of what
the statistics show, people feel safe behind their guns when
they go into the wilderness. But over and over again, you read
about a wounded or dead bear, and a guy with his face torn
off. The fact is that in most of those cases, the face was torn
off *after* the bear had been shot. Doesn't seem too effective
to me. They just don't want to eat us. It has happened very
few times in very unique situations, usually a starving and
desperate bear combined with an injured or ill-prepared
human.

This morning I read the latest grizzly bear news on
Google. A man hunting pheasant north of Choteau, Montana, was walking through some thick brush. The area had
a lot of buffaloberry and the grizzly bears usually gorge
themselves there in the fall to fatten up for the winter. In
the interview the hunter gave, it was quite apparent that the
presence of a grizzly bear in the area was a surprise to him.
If he had done his homework, he would have known that

the area was frequented by grizzlies. Unfortunately, he shot and killed a female bear and left her three little cubs to die. The loss of four grizzly bears of this ecosystem and population is fatal. Whenever I read stories like this in the newspaper, it reinforces the need for public education about grizzly bears. These bears died as a result of ignorance. If the hunter had been carrying bear spray in addition to a shotgun, all four bears would still be alive. But he went into the area without taking the proper precautions, which include learning about the animals that live in the area as well as being prepared for a possible encounter. He is still alive, and we're all thankful for that, but unfortunately the protective mother bear and her defenseless cubs lost their lives. I have read the exact same story countless times. "The bear was going to eat him" is a common phrase, and one that's far from the truth. But this is what the public believes, and you cannot blame them because they've all been Hollywoodized. All the sensationalized films about the bloodthirsty grizzly bear who stalks people through the woods feed the frenzy. As children we snuggle with teddy bears, but at the same time we watch TV and films that show bears destroying humans with their claws and teeth. The result is people walking through grizzly country who are confused about the creature that they share the area with.

The Boy Scout motto Be Prepared is about much more than bringing the right equipment into the woods. It also means having accurate knowledge and awareness of the animals that share them with you. You don't need to be a grizzly bear behavior expert to be safe in a grizzly bear habitat. We are the adaptive species. We can carry bear spray, put up electric fences, or carry our food in bear-proof containers. There is literature all over the Internet teaching you what to do and what not to do while you are in bear country. Four dead bears is four too many. With the increasing effects of climate change, urban sprawl, and other factors that the bears are already facing, the introduction of ignorant humans into their habitat is very detrimental. It's wonderful that grizzly bears are in our wilderness, and we need to ensure their continued survival in these areas.

CHAPTER 19

THE HUMAN SKUNK

THERE IS A WAY TO DEFLECT A BEAR AWAY FROM YOU IN any situation, and that is bear pepper spray. I have yet to read about someone who has used bear spray during an attack and has been killed, and the injuries of those who were mauled are less extensive, and once the spray was deployed, the bear disappeared immediately. If it is a sow, she will pass the spray experience along to future bear generations. A dead bear does not have this opportunity. I like to make the analogy with a skunk when I am explaining it to children, but it works for adults, too. When you see a skunk, you avoid it at all costs because you have been sprayed or someone has told you about the results of being sprayed.

Being sprayed by a skunk or by bear pepper spray is a miserable experience. Grizzlies are smart creatures and they will come to the same conclusion. The next time they see humans, they will avoid us at all costs, the way we do when we see a skunk. And so goes the game of coexistence. We are the adaptive species, so we have to make the adjustments. These are the adaptations that will save our wild places and, in turn, that will save us.

People kill bears with rifles all the time despite the overwhelming evidence that it is not a good idea. Big bears are hunted every year in Alaska and killed with one shot, but these bears are usually unaware of their hunter, eating on a hillside or walking over the tundra. When you have a bear charging you at 35 miles per hour, and you have to make a kill shot, you have to be Jesse James, the famous gunslinger, known for his accuracy and swift hand. But every year, firearms are carried into grizzly country. This deadly combination of ignorance and power results in lost lives. What happens in most cases is that the bear is wounded and not killed. This causes the bear to increase its fight response. So instead of the warning slap that you were about to receive, you get a barrage of claws, consequences of the bear's painful anger. I like to use another analogy when putting the two choices, bear spray and bullets, next to one another.

A police officer is called to the scene of a bank robbery. As he approaches the building, his adrenaline runs high and he is on edge. Suddenly, an intense firefight breaks out between the robbers and the police. He fires back, takes cover, and fights for his life. The moment is so intense and all of his body's defense mechanisms are operating at such a heightened level that when the battle is over, he doesn't realize that he has been shot in the arm. Now do you think a grizzly bear, reacting to a threat, hopped up on the same personal defense chemicals pumping through its blood, will notice when it's been shot? In fact, unless you can place that bullet in a very small vital area, the bear won't even flinch. The same thing happens when police use pepper spray on crazed men high on methamphetamine. But modern society refuses to give up guns and continues to wound bears. Men get themselves mauled, and it's the bears who get blamed.

The battle to get the grizzly bear off the endangered species list is going to have to be fought on all fronts. It is going to take the effort of fish and game departments, environmental groups, and especially the public.

Recently, there was an educational project that needed some funding and support. The project was an educational kiosk that would be placed along the highway near the east entrance of Yellowstone. This is a highway that sees a lot of visitors, most of them people who live or are traveling in grizzly country. The importance of educating these people in the do's and don'ts of being in bear country is absolutely essential to the bears' survival. The kiosk's producers went to many sources to drum up minimal finances to make this a reality. Even more important, they wanted to get it done by summer so it would have the greatest impact due to the high volume of vacation traffic. Unfortunately, they ran into some major speed bumps. But not speed bumps of logic, as you might think, but more of the kind you might find on the kindergarten playground. One agency would not allow the show to go on because they found out that an environmental group had contributed money to the cause. This project had no environmental twists or agency rhetoric, it was just a factual infomercial of sorts that would save both grizzly bear and human lives. It was put to a halt because of the "I won't be your friend if you are friends with them" political mentality. Some things never change, and ladies and gentlemen, these are your tax dollars at work. That year eighty grizzly bears died in the Yellowstone region.

THE SOUL OF A BEAR

I T WAS NOT TOO LONG AGO THAT HUMANS WERE PLAGUED by some very irrational thoughts and ideals. Females and people of certain colors were not considered the equal of others. Over time, these prejudices have abated to an extent and their ridiculous nature has become more apparent. All of the universe is made of the same protoplasm. We are all a collective universe of individual energies. Pain is felt in the same way from one being to the next. Emotion is not exclusively ours. It runs deep in the lives of all living things, but in these times, many of us choose to ignore this immutable truth. We must respect these characteristics that all beings possess. As we dig deeper into the makeup of their souls, we find that we are not all that different, and that the basic foundation is the same. Love is love.

I held Brutus in my arms when he was about the size of a loaf of bread. He looked up at me and stared into my eyes as I bottle-fed him. We were the same, just two beings in this universe, experiencing mutual love. Sharing the moment, breathing the same air, we were both filled with an overwhelming feeling of elation. Then all of a sudden, tears formed in his little brown eyes as he continued to look at me. Simultaneously, my eyes began to flood with evidence of a mutual emotion. Several years later, Brutus was lying in a large hole that he had dug in the shade at the sanctuary. I could tell he wasn't feeling well. He was lethargic and lay on his side almost motionless. I walked over to my buddy and soothed him with soft baby talk, saying, "You will be okay, Brutie." He gave me a small glance and laid his head down with a big sigh. I sat next to him and gently rubbed his belly. He hugged me with one of his massive paws and pulled me closer. There we sat. I was now in his powerful arms, rubbing his belly. He had a terrible tummyache and needed a friend and some comfort. We locked eyes and began to cry together. This struck me so deeply that in that moment the whole world changed. If this giant grizzly bear can feel this way, then why not every other being in the world? From that moment on, I never looked at anything on earth the same way. It was the greatest gift I have ever received, and it came from my friend Brutus.

We have been hiding behind the flames of our campfires for centuries afraid of the unknown that lurked in the darkness outside of the firelight. There we sat safely and told embellished stories of the horrific monsters and beasts that waited for us in the shadows. Fear of the unknown seems foolish. Some of us are pioneers and explorers, seeking to understand the unknown. Others cower from the obscure world. Like outer space, the grizzly bear's soul is an undiscovered wilderness that we gaze at in awe and in fear. We guess and contemplate what it might hold and are afraid of the possibilities. But until someone reaches deep into the vast unknown and learns what lies there, it is only theory and speculation. We have climbed the highest peaks and explored the bottoms of the oceans, but there is one frontier on earth left to explore. It is the souls of the beings that we share this planet with. We cannot understand and protect something we are afraid of, and a grizzly bear is one of the most misunderstood animals on earth. Through my experiences with Brutus, it is my hope that everyone will see the grizzly bear in a different light, and fall in love with all life, inspiring people to care for and protect the planet. The only grizzly bear expert on earth is the grizzly bear, and still I explore the grizzly and hope it continues to give me the gift of glimpses into its soul and its very existence.